THE BUILDINGS OF ENGLAND

FOUNDING EDITOR: NIKOLAUS PEVSNER

BEDFORDSHIRE, HUNTINGDONSHIRE AND PETERBOROUGH

CHARLES O'BRIEN
and
NIKOLAUS PEVSNER

Bedfordshire

Boundary of Bedfordshire — Motorways — Railways

Area covered by Luton entry — 'Trunk' roads

0 ——— 5 ——— 10 ——— 15 miles

0 ——— 10 ——— 20 km

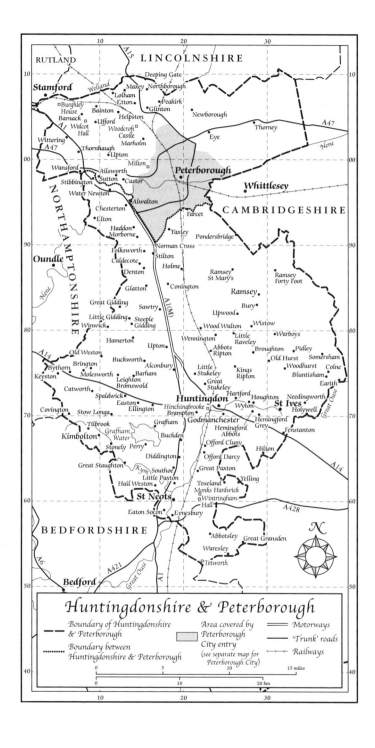

Huntingdonshire & Peterborough

Boundary of Huntingdonshire
& Peterborough

Boundary between
Huntingdonshire & Peterborough

Area covered by
Peterborough
City entry
(see separate map for
Peterborough City)

Motorways

'Trunk' roads

Railways

0   5   10   15 miles

0   10   20 km

Bedfordshire, Huntingdonshire and Peterborough

BY

CHARLES O'BRIEN

and

NIKOLAUS PEVSNER

WITH CONTRIBUTIONS FROM

BETH DAVIS

and

STEPHEN G. UPEX

THE BUILDINGS OF ENGLAND

YALE UNIVERSITY PRESS
NEW HAVEN AND LONDON

YALE UNIVERSITY PRESS
NEW HAVEN AND LONDON

302 Temple Street, New Haven CT 06511
47 Bedford Square, London WC1B 3DP
www.pevsner.co.uk
www.lookingatbuildings.org.uk
www.yalebooks.co.uk
www.yalebooks.com

Published by Yale University Press 2014
2 4 6 8 10 9 7 5 3 1

ISBN 978 0 300 20821 4

Printed in China
through World Print
Set in Monotype Plantin

CONTENTS

LIST OF TEXT FIGURES AND MAPS

BEDFORDSHIRE

MAPS

HUNTINGDONSHIRE AND PETERBOROUGH

MAPS

PHOTOGRAPHIC ACKNOWLEDGEMENTS

MAP REFERENCES

The numbers printed in italic type in the margin against the place names in the gazetteer of the book indicate the position of the place in question on the index maps (pp. ii-iii), which are divided into sections by the 10-km. reference lines of the National Grid. The reference given here omits the two initial letters which in a full grid reference refer to the 100-km. squares into which counties are divided. The first two numbers indicate the *western* boundary, and the last two the *southern* boundary, of the 10-km. square in which the place in question is situated. For example, in the Bedfordshire map Cranfield (reference 9040) will be found in the 10-km. square bounded by grid lines 90 (on the *west*) and 00, and 40 (on the *south*) and 50; in the Huntingdonshire and Peterborough map Yelling (reference 2060) will be found in the square bounded by the grid lines 20 (on the *west*) and 30, and 60 (on the *south*) and 70.

The maps contain all those places, whether towns, villages, or isolated buildings, which are the subject of separate entries in the text.

FOREWORD AND ACKNOWLEDGEMENTS

The first edition of this volume was published in 1968 as *Bedfordshire and the County of Huntingdon and Peterborough*. Research for it was commenced in 1964 but Nikolaus Pevsner's researcher abandoned work within a fortnight. The original intention was a volume for Bedfordshire and Huntingdonshire but in 1965 the County of Huntingdon and Peterborough was formed and the entries for the Soke of Peterborough, which had been written by Pevsner for his Northamptonshire volume in 1961, were reprinted in the new guide, along with the entry for Thorney which had been part of the Isle of Ely and had therefore been included in the Cambridgeshire volume in 1954. An effort was made to correct what mistakes it contained and to eliminate what had since disappeared and add what had since been built. An error, however, in the offices at Penguin, then the publisher of the series, unfortunately led to the omission of Thornhaugh, Newborough and Oxney from the new volume and since the Northamptonshire volume was updated in 1973, minus the entries for the Soke, these places have been omitted from the series altogether. So the first task in producing a new edition has been to restore these to their rightful place in the gazetteer.

The title of this new volume, *Bedfordshire, Huntingdonshire and Peterborough*, is unwieldy. The change from the title of its predecessor is subtle but correct, for the County of Huntingdon and Peterborough was abolished in 1974 when Huntingdonshire became a district of a newly enlarged Cambridgeshire and Peterborough became an independent unitary authority (with its own administration but for ceremonial purposes also under Cambridgeshire). In spite of these changes, the boundaries of the area remain as they were, and it was decided for the new edition of this guide that in the Buildings of England, if nowhere else, Huntingdonshire and Peterborough should remain together and so an integrated gazetteer is provided once more with a separate gazetteer for Bedfordshire, and each gazetteer with its own introduction. For the new edition it has also been decided that the photos should more genuinely display the different characters of the buildings in the gazetteers and accordingly the inset is divided.

The East Midlands is not a region of England which held much appeal for Pevsner, whose declared preferences were for the counties of the West and North. The first edition of this guide was also written in the busiest period of his career with inevitable results that much had to be seen in a hurry. This new edition has been prepared with a much more generous timescale for visiting, research and detailed checking that only further emphasizes Pevsner's remarkable achievement in covering the same ground in a matter of weeks. In general terms the principal task has been to check, correct and where necessary supplement Pevsner's gazetteer entries. The principles on which the gazetteer is founded are unchanged. I have myself seen everything that I describe. Where this is not the case the information obtained by other means is placed in brackets. Much of Pevsner's writing remains but deeper research has sometimes rendered his interpretation and understanding of buildings redundant, in which case a new description has been required. Information ought to be as complete as the space of the volume permits for churches prior to 1945 and is only a little more selective for the period thereafter. Many more secular buildings of every period are now included for the towns and villages and consideration is given to the most significant developments since the 1960s. Nevertheless, what appears in this edition is once more only a selection of the totality of buildings in Bedfordshire, Huntingdonshire and Peterborough. While much more will be found for example on nineteenth- and twentieth-century buildings, on stained glass and furnishings in churches and chapels and on the industrial and vernacular architecture of the area, no attempt has been made to be comprehensive. Judgements on architectural interest and quality remain in many places subjective and personal, if not occasionally prejudiced by the conditions in which the buildings were seen. Pevsner's dedication of the first edition, reprinted here, suggests that his fieldwork was undertaken in sunny weather.* Mostly this has also been true for the second edition but the protracted winter of 2012–13 may explain some ungenerous assessments of some places in Bedfordshire. All told, however, the work of updating has been a considerable pleasure.

For this edition it has been possible to take in not only a vast quantity of research published since 1968 but also to make use of primary sources. So my first acknowledgement should be to the staffs of the Huntingdon Library and Archives, the Bedford and Luton Archives and Record Service, the Bedford Local Studies Library, Wardown Museum, Luton, the Northamptonshire Record Office and the Peterborough Local Studies Library. I am in particular exceedingly grateful to Richard Hillier at Peterborough who not only guided my research for buildings in the city and surrounding villages but also continued to supply numerous pieces of valuable information over the period it took to complete the work for Huntingdonshire and Bedfordshire. In Huntingdonshire I was given access to the remarkable collection of notes on the county compiled by Sidney Inskip Ladds which are held at the Norris Museum, St Ives, and much assistance was given there by Bob Burn Murdoch. I have also depended heavily on Beth Davis for her intimate knowledge of the county's

---

*The 'invention' of the iced lolly is now credited to Frank Epperson, a Canadian, in 1923 (information supplied to the Pevsner Architectural Guides office in 1991 by Elsie Pope).

buildings, partly derived from her work on the re-Listing survey for the Department of the Environment and her own investigations of the vernacular buildings of Huntingdonshire. I am doubly grateful to her for having agreed to write the appropriate section of the Introduction. Further information supplied by her is marked BD in the gazetteer. Stephen Upex willingly agreed to introduce the complex history of the Prehistoric and Roman monuments in Peterborough and Huntingdonshire, a subject little understood forty years ago. Bruce Bailey has shared his research on buildings in the Soke and has been an invaluable help in drawing my attention to comparisons with buildings in Northamptonshire with which Huntingdonshire and Peterborough's architecture has so much in common. He also took on the task of accompanying me on several visits and furthermore volunteered to read the entire draft of this guide as well as supplying information extracted from nineteenth-century newspapers. At Peterborough, Jackie Hall, the Cathedral archaeologist, provided me with a wealth of information on the church and the results of detailed investigations of all the buildings in the precinct as well as arranging access to many private properties. Tim Skelton illuminated the story of Peterborough New Town and the complexities of its planning as well as drawing my attention to buildings of special interest from the period after 1970. Paul Sharpling made available his research on stained glass in Peterborough and the surrounding villages and Michael Kerney did his best to furnish me with all the documented references to Huntingdonshire stained glass from the periodicals. Finally I am grateful to Jim Daley at Peterborough City Council, to Ben Robinson, formerly of the Peterborough Museum, and to Louise Brown and colleagues on the Conservation team at Huntingdonshire District Council, who made the re-surveys of the Listings for the towns by Michael Eaton available to me.

In Bedfordshire, my first thanks should be to Chris Pickford, who in advance of work commencing donated his substantial body of research, undertaken while County Archivist, on churches, Nonconformist chapels, stained glass and parsonages among other subjects. He also handed over his collection of church guides and it is impossible to say how much longer the work on preparing the gazetteer would have taken without his generous gift. Furthermore, he had already compiled a set of corrections and other notes on buildings expressly for the purpose of informing a new edition of this volume. That work was continued by Alan Cox and has been a most valuable asset through the period of revision. Alan very kindly also agreed to read the complete drafts of the Bedfordshire gazetteer and I am deeply grateful for his observations and corrections. The same task was also performed by James Collett-White who provided essential advice on the collections in the Bedford and Luton Archives and Records and was my guide at Southill Park. The revision of the entry for Bedford could not have been done without the assistance of Richard Wildman, who has the distinction of also having written in with information about the town's buildings for the

1968 edition. At Central Bedfordshire Council I have had much help from Stephen Coleman, who gave me access to the Historic Environment Record and guided me in the revision of the chapter on Prehistoric and Roman archaeology for the county. David Baker has also been generous in his comments on the drafts and in particular on the most important medieval sites as well as supplying the plan of Elstow Abbey. Geoff Saunders provided access to material in the Bedford Borough Historic Environment Record and Gemma Pike, Conservation Officer at Luton, gave me access to the Town Hall.

Others have given me their time and the benefit of their knowledge and research and I am very grateful to Katie Carmichael of English Heritage for revealing the interest and significance of Luton's industrial buildings. I would also like to thank Claire Gapper for sharing her expertise on plasterwork and Andrea Kirkham on domestic wall paintings.

There are many others who have helped by sending in corrections since 1968. I am particularly indebted to Geoff Brandwood for his notes on churches and for his willing investigations into the files of the Incorporated Church Building Society. Geoffrey Fisher has once more supplied in advance notes on seventeenth- and early eighteenth-century monuments and their possible sculptors and has continued to answer my questions on this subject during the course of revision. His attributions are denoted (GF) in the gazetteer. Michael Kerney, indicated (MK) in the gazetteer, and Peter Cormack have helped identify the makers of other significant windows in the area. Lists of various corrections have been gratefully received from Peter Howell, G. Hooper and P. C. Edwards and there is a longer list of others who wrote in with corrections after publication of the first edition, or have supplied answers to my queries during the period of revision or permitted me to make use of their unpublished research. In particular I would like to acknowledge: W. J. Adnitt (Peterborough and locality); Justin Ayton (Thorney Abbey House); Rev. Alan Betteridge; Timothy Brittain-Catlin (Lloyds Bank architects); Michael Brook (Aspley Heath and Little Gidding); J. T. Cliffe (Willington); Nicholas Cooper (Willington); M. T. Davis (Conington); Andrew Duerden (Vauxhall, Luton); Dennis Farr (Luton); Richard Garnier (Sir Robert Taylor); Keith Garrett (Castor, etc.); R. N. Hadcock (religious houses); Richard Hewlings (Huntingdon Town Hall and Kimbolton Castle); Mrs K. Houfe (Sir Albert Richardson and Woburn Abbey); Rodney Hubbuck (stained glass); David Hufford (Robert Hutchinson); Jill Husselby (Burghley House); Alison Kelly (Melchbourne); David H. Kennett (Luton); Moira Knight (Biddenham); W. H. Kuhlicke; Sarah Markham (Renhold); George McHardy; Eric G. Meadows (Dunstable, Stevington, Luton); Peter Meadows (Ely Diocesan Records); Mervyn Miller; Rev. D. H. Palmer (Peterborough); Canon Peter Pavey (Clifton); The Rt Hon. J. Enoch Powell; Caroline Stanford; J. T. Smith (Ampthill); David Parsons; Avril Lumley-Prior; David Soskin (Hockliffe Grange); Rev. P. S.

Thomas (Marholm and Leighton Bromswold); Alan Teulon (S. S. Teulon): and Peter Waszak.

It is impossible to thank all those who have given me access to buildings in their possession or care, often without any prior appointment, but the following gave considerable time to me and shared their knowledge: Julie Benson (Chicksands Priory); Nora Butler (Kimbolton); Will Clayton; Sir Timothy and Lady Clifford (Park House, Ampthill); William Craven (Milton); Mr and Mrs Dennis (Walcot Hall); Amanda Done (Old Warden Park); Chris Gravett (Woburn Abbey); Barry Groom (Sandy); Dorothy Halfhide (Thorney); Andrew Hann (Wrest Park); Robert Hart (Bedford Modern School); Simon Houfe; Peter Inskip; Oonagh Kennedy and Zena Dickinson (Luton Hoo); Sir William and Lady Proby (Elton Hall); Lord de Ramsey (Abbots Ripton); Mr and Mrs Trevor (Northborough); Christopher Vane Percy (Godmanchester); Charles Turner (Great Gransden); Tom Wheeley (Hinchingbrooke). At Burghley House exceptional freedom was obtained to visit many parts of the house that are private and I am very grateful to Mr and Mrs Orlando Rock for making this possible and to Jon Culverhouse and Carolyn Crook-all for all their time and help and to Carolyn for playing host on so many occasions while I was exploring Huntingdonshire and Peterborough.

In my office at Yale, I owe a great debt to my colleagues and firstly Simon Bradley, who while revising Cambridgeshire for the series has exchanged useful comparisons from the other side of the border and offered general advice and comment from the other side of the desk. Phoebe Lowndes and Catherine Bankhurst have steered the manuscript into the hands of my copy-editor, proof-reader and printer and assembled the photographs provided by Steve Cole and John Roan into beautiful layouts. Alice Winborn searched for and found all the text illustrations and arranged all the redrawing of maps and plans by Martin Brown. I am sincerely grateful to them all and to Sally Salvesen, who looks after the interests of our series. Funding of the research and fieldwork so essential to these books was supervised for many years by Gavin Watson of the Buildings Books Trust and continues under the Paul Mellon Centre. Only their support makes the continuation of this endeavour possible.

The research notes compiled for this edition and its predecessor will be deposited with the English Heritage Archive, Swindon, and may be freely consulted by prior arrangement with the public search room.

Finally, the entreaty usual to the series for users of this book to advise me of serious omissions and to draw my attention to errors.

Charles O'Brien, 2014

BEDFORDSHIRE

INTRODUCTION

BEDFORDSHIRE is one of the least appreciated counties. A county of pleasant, not of exciting landscape, which too many will travel through rather than to. The impression given of the county from the routes N and S along the M1 in the W, or the A1 to the E, or across its waist along the Bedford bypass is, however, misleading, and off these well-trodden tracks there is much to see. Variety is greater in architecture than in scenery indeed and the variety is well-spread across the centuries. While it has perhaps only one monument of national significance – Woburn Abbey – and no major ecclesiastical building, its strengths lie instead in the ability to surprise. In architectural terms there remains the sense that Bedfordshire is still *terra incognita*. Partly this is a consequence of its position precisely between counties that are readily recognized and accepted as the Midlands or the Home Counties or East Anglia. Bedfordshire is all but none of these and its buildings are eloquent of that fact. Across this small county – in size it comes thirty-ninth in England and with a population of about 616,000* – there are five distinct zones in the LANDSCAPE, from the stone area of the Great Ouse valley in the NW and the pretty but dispersed settlements of the agricultural country of the N and NE up to the Huntingdonshire border, to the broad flat Marston Vale running S of Bedford up to the escarpment of the still heavily wooded Greensand Ridge crossing the county from SW to NE, then a second valley to the S of the ridge up to the commencement of the Chilterns at Dunstable. In total only a few miles of these hills lie in Bedfordshire but they reach over 800 ft (243 metres) at the highest point, and from the vantage points of Totternhoe Knolls, or the National Trust visitor centre above Dunstable, or the Zoo at Whipsnade they offer panoramic views of real beauty. The same can be said of the top of the Greensand Ridge near Houghton House above Ampthill,

*This is the combined total for the unitary local authorities of Bedford, Central Bedfordshire and Luton into which the historic county has been divided since the abolition of Bedfordshire County Council in 2009.

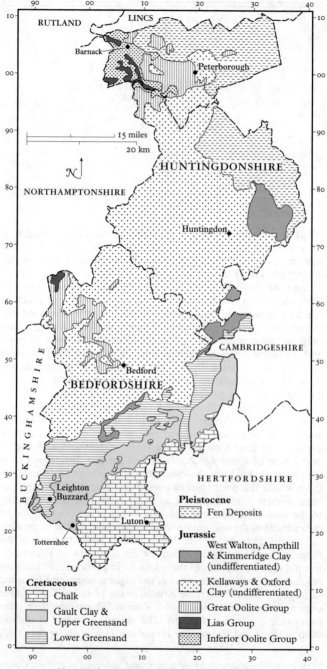

Simplified solid geology map of Bedfordshire,
Huntingdonshire and Peterborough.

where the four fingers of the chimneys at Stewartby make a sublime assault on the rural scene, or further E on the ridge above Sandy which provided the commanding *point-de-vue* needed by Iron Age, Roman and Romano-British people to supervise the main road N along the valley of the Ivel which breaks the ridge here.

Before an architectural introduction can be made to the gazetteer, it is necessary to describe first the GEOLOGY not only of Bedfordshire but also of Huntingdonshire and Peterborough, since so much of the underlying structure of the landscape is held in common.* What concerns readers of the *Buildings of England* are the implications of the geology for BUILDING MATERIALS. The area covered by the two gazetteers in this volume occupy a roughly oblong fifty-by-twenty-mile strip slightly across the geological grain of the East Midlands, which in South Bedfordshire has a SW–NE orientation swinging to N–S through Huntingdonshire, where it is almost entirely concealed under the fens. The main features dominate the physiography: the escarpments of the Cretaceous Lower Greensand and Chalk in S Bedfordshire; the wide, flat valley of the Great Ouse running through both Bedfordshire and Huntingdonshire like a recumbent reversed S; the fenland of East Huntingdonshire and E and NE of Peterborough city; the Nene valley dividing Huntingdonshire from the former Soke of Peterborough, and the Welland valley dividing Peterborough from Lincolnshire and draining into the Wash. The first of these is the only considerable tract of relatively high and well-drained ground, over 800 ft (243 metres) at the top of the Dunstable Downs. For the rest, Bedfordshire and Huntingdonshire spread over a variety of Upper Jurassic clays – Oxford Clay, Ampthill Clay and Kimmeridge Clay – together with a narrow strip of Lower Cretaceous Gault Clay running from the SW to E of Bedfordshire. Unless one is a palaeontologist, or an amateur of the minutiae of Jurassic and Cretaceous stratigraphy, the geology is rather a dull affair.

In the Great Ouse valley above Bedford, in the extreme N of Huntingdonshire, and between the Nene and Welland rivers in the W edge of the former Soke of Peterborough, older, harder Jurassic LIMESTONES emerge from beneath the dominant clays and in both areas they share a similar shelly character and pale grey appearance that weathers to the familiar yellow. These, the Lincolnshire and Great Oolite Limestones, create the gently rolling landscape in the Peterborough area N of the Nene towards Stamford (Lincolnshire). The most famous quarry of Upper Lincolnshire limestone for building was at Barnack, where the remarkable deeply pitted landscape produced by the quarrying, justifiably known as Hills and Holes, remains protected on the edge of the village. It is of the same formation as the Weldon, Glendon and Kings Cliffe quarries in Northamptonshire. The Barnack quarries were worked from the Roman period and from

p. 2

*The following section has been revised from the first edition of this guide by Terence Miller.

them stone was sent in Saxon times down the river to Peterborough (whose abbey owned Barnack), later to Crowland, Thorney, Ely, Bury and Cambridge, and to almost every church or abbey in East Anglia. Its distribution was aided by the ability to transport it along the Nene from Milton, a short distance SE of Barnack. There were other smaller quarries in the Soke and on the other side of the river in Huntingdonshire around Wansford, Stibbington, Water Newton and Alwalton, conveniently close to the river and the Great North Road. The Alwalton 'marble' can be seen in a few small pillars in Peterborough Cathedral. It is not of course a true marble but a hard, compact limestone, often mistaken for Purbeck, which will take a polish, as demonstrated by the series of monuments to the abbots of Peterborough in the cathedral. Raunds in Northamptonshire produces a similar 'marble', and one occasionally encounters this in the border areas of Bedfordshire, e.g. a fireplace at Hinwick House. Quarrying of Oolitic limestone in the Great Ouse valley in Bedfordshire NW of Bedford took place in several places, e.g. Harrold, Pavenham, Oakley etc., and distinguishes the majority of the villages in this area from the rest of the county. Stone from Pavenham was used to build St Mary's, Bedford, in the C11. Again the river was the means for transporting it from the pits and quarries over a wider area. Of course much limestone was also quarried for lime, and in addition to building it is widely seen in the stone areas and neighbouring areas for gravestones, permitting a greater opportunity for carving in the enjoyably rustic C18 styles.

Typical of an area with limited sources of building stones of its own and with geologically richer areas as its neighbours, a fair quantity of limestone employed in Bedfordshire, Huntingdonshire and Peterborough comes from outside the area, so that for example Burghley House is constructed primarily of limestone from Lord Burghley's quarries at Cliffe Park, Northamptonshire; and in the mid C18 the S front of Milton was built of stone from Ketton in Rutland; Woburn Abbey too in the 1750s employed Ketton stone, and in other places stone was brought from Weldon (e.g. for Willington church, Beds.). In Podington, at the very border with Northamptonshire, it is not surprising to find that county's distinctive orangey ferruginous sandstone being employed together with the local limestone. Roofs in the former Soke of Peterborough and parts of Huntingdonshire are usually the distinctive so-called slates from Collyweston, just W in Northamptonshire (in fact friable limestone from the Lower Lincolnshire formation). Other imported stone seen here and there is true slate from Leicestershire, employed for C18 headstones. A very good example is at Folksworth in Huntingdonshire.

No 'solid' rocks are seen in the deep fenland, except where a temporary clay-pit is opened to provide material for the dyke walls, or an 'island' like Eye, Thorney or Ramsey sticks up above the silt and peat. Along the fen margin, however, particularly round Peterborough and Fletton, huge pits were excavated in the CLAY, to provide the raw material for the major British brickmaking industry, which lasted into the later C20, and on which *see* p. 8. The Oxford clay country covers almost the whole area of Bedfordshire N of the Greensand Ridge and all of Huntingdonshire up to the fen edge and the s bank of the Nene river. Many pits survive in the post-industrial landscape of the southern fringe of the City of Peterborough and over a wide area of Marston Vale in Bedfordshire as lakes. On a smaller scale such pits, opened in clays of various ages, can be seen through the two counties as far s as the Lower Greensand scarp, and even beyond this in the Gault vale which runs from Billington (s of Leighton Buzzard) to the upper tributaries of the Cam E of Biggleswade. The clay country is without distinctive form. Low, rounded elevations – hardly worthy to be called hills – separate the stream courses. Only between the Ouse and the Nene valley in the former Soke of Peterborough does the land rise slightly towards the margin of a limestone ridge. Most of the countryside is in addition plastered with a blanket of glacial boulder clay, silt or sand, with an abundant scatter of stones and boulders of all sorts and sizes.

In s Bedfordshire, however, a more positive scenery is found. Here, from Leighton Buzzard to (appropriately) Sandy, and just into Huntingdonshire, the LOWER GREENSAND produces a strong, well-wooded ridge overlooking Bedford and the Great Ouse valley. The ridge is continuous except for the wide cross-valley of the Ivel around Biggleswade, where the bedrock is again covered by thick sheets of glacial and river-spread sands, gravels and clays. The Greensand is somewhat misnamed, as it is usually a fine golden-brown, with sweeping lines of oblique stratification. The layers of the Lower Greensand are well seen in the still active quarries at Heath and Reach or exposed in the quarries near Sandy Lodge. There are interesting varieties in the Greensand. Around Leighton Buzzard and Linslade is an extremely pure 'silver sand', in the sense of having a very high silica content, and is extracted for glass-making as well as casting. A very rare layer of red sands above this also occurs around Billington. These loose sands have been useful to the construction industry but only where the sand is well-cemented by quartz or iron oxide compounds can it serve very well as SANDSTONE for building. It appears in all the churches along the Greensand Ridge as a hard, dark brown gritty rock like coarse gingerbread. E along the outcrop, near Silsoe, the Greensand has an abnormal proportion of iron oxide (so the term 'ironstone' is frequently used), making it very dark. About the greenest of all Greensand stones is at Husborne Crawley, produced by an excess of glauconite in the UPPER GREENSAND; sources of this stone are very limited hence its rare appearance here. The best of the sandstone can be cut and dressed and it is quite usual to find it neatly coursed in many buildings from the medieval period to the C19. Dressings and tracery in the churches are, however, necessarily made up from harder limestone. Elsewhere weaker cementation means that the Greensand is only suitable as rubble, and at its weakest it breaks into thin, tabular pieces (in that form sometimes known as 'carstone' slips), just as one finds it in N Norfolk. In this form it turns up in isolated places, e.g. in Huntingdonshire in houses at Fenstanton and Brampton, and in Bedfordshire in the former Congregational Chapel at Potton. At Shenley Hill, E of Heath and Reach, isolated compact masses of a pinkish-yellow pebbly or sandy limestone occur in the top layer of silty sands. These, if one is lucky enough to find one, are crammed with a fascinating collection of small fossils – sea shells, fish teeth, crab claws, sea urchins, barnacles, and many others.

SE of the Greensand Ridge, the next higher formation, the GAULT CLAY, forms a wide vale from S of Leighton Buzzard, continuing NE across Bedfordshire but only just into Huntingdonshire S of St Neots – its nature suggested by place names like Barton-le-Clay. SE of the gault clay there follows the main scarp of the CHALK. This high ground – reaching 600 ft (182 metres) around Whipsnade, Dunstable (where the steep scarp front makes conditions ideal for gliding) and Luton – is an extension of the Chiltern ridge-line. Its basal Chalk layers were once quite extensively mined for the phosphatic nodules contained in them, formerly used for fertilizer. The main mass of the Chalk is too soft for building. Here and there, however, thin, heavily cemented layers occur in the Lower Chalk, known as CLUNCH, which can be worked as a freestone. It does not weather well (see e.g. the S porch of Toddington church and the sculpture of its N aisle), but it could be well applied to interior work and is the predominant material for arcade piers, arches, tombs, figure sculpture etc. throughout the medieval period; see for example the carved work at Eaton Bray. It is of course much less in evidence in the area around Peterborough, where high-quality limestone was available, but there are instances of its use, e.g. the tomb of *c.* 1400 at

Totternhoe Quarry.
Watercolour by G. Shepherd, 1813

Marholm, and it also appears in the southernmost tail of Huntingdonshire, e.g. at Great Gransden. In Bedfordshire its use was widespread in the form of the TOTTERNHOE STONE, which is a darker grey than most Chalk, slightly gritty, and with a distinctive 'curly grain'. The quarries at Totternhoe were used by the Romans (a carved stone was recovered from the site of the Roman villa at Totternhoe) and were active from at least the C12 until the C15 for in 1131 the Crown passed control of the quarries to Dunstable Priory and stone from Totternhoe appears in later medieval Royal accounts e.g. for Windsor Castle. Its use seems to have declined in buildings in the C16 and C17, though it was still employed for dressings and carved work at Houghton Hall and Hillersdon Mansion, Elstow, in the early C17, and still favoured for interior work, e.g. an early C17 fireplace at Wrest Park (now in the Orangery) and late C16 monuments at Turvey and Tilsworth. Perhaps the best demonstration of its qualities, however, is in the exquisite flower work of the 1750s chimneypieces in the W entrance hall at Woburn Abbey. Its use was much revived in the mid–later C18 with the classical phase in architecture, where the blocks could be dressed and coursed to emulate ashlar. It may also be significant that the quarries were taken over at this time by John Wing, the Bedford architect. No doubt he heavily encouraged his clients to use his wares, however ill-suited, and so it is found in the Swan Hotel, Bedford, at Woburn Abbey, at Southill, and in Wing's own house in Cardington Road, Bedford. All have required much patching, and repairs for Woburn saw resumption of opencast quarrying from *c.* 1972. Otherwise the Totternhoe stone fell out of use for building in the C19 as brick took over. Still on the quarry site is a lime works, opened in 1869.

Associated with the chalk are of course FLINTS, which either form in bands in the chalk or are recovered from the layer of 'clay-with-flints' close to the chalk's surface. In S Bedfordshire churches one may find clunch and flint used together in a chequerboard pattern, in particular in the W tower of St Mary's, Luton, but also at Dunstable, Houghton Regis and Totternhoe. A good deal of knapped flint is also used as a facing for the walls of St Mary's, Luton. Finally, the common brown COBBLES deposited by the glaciers in the clay and rivers. They are found in churches employed as random rubble and predominate in the eastern side of Bedfordshire from Little Staughton down to Langford and in the corresponding area of SW Huntingdonshire, e.g. around Grafham, Perry etc. It is rare to find them used exclusively. Much more common is to see them mixed up with flints and other materials.

The clay country has been referred to in passing. Within N Bedfordshire some uses of clay itself for building have been identified, notably in a row of cottages (The Street) at Melchbourne which are made of COB, and buildings of CLAY LUMP have also been recorded in Riseley, e.g. a barn at No. 135 High Street. So far no examples of this type of construction have been found in Huntingdonshire. THATCH is the traditional roofing material in the river areas and on the fens, and of course was

much favoured in the Picturesque phase of building in the late
C18 and early C19 but much of it was done away with once slates
and tiles became widely available in the C19 and C20. It is interesting to note here the attempt made at Hemingford Abbots,
Huntingdonshire, to design council housing in the 1940s with
thatched roofs.

Clay's principal use is of course its exploitation for the making
of BRICKS, which was a major industry in Bedfordshire and
around Peterborough until the late C20. It demands a section of
its own. In basic terms there is little evidence of medieval brickmaking, with the one-off exceptions of Someries Castle, Bedfordshire (1448), and the Bishop's Palace, Buckden, Huntingdonshire
(*c.* 1472–94), and only relatively little of it in the C16 (Warden
Abbey, the round tower at Toddington Manor, and church towers
at Whipsnade (Beds.) and Diddington (Hunts.), when the first
documented works were in operation in Bedfordshire, and more
in the Jacobean period at Houghton House, Ampthill; in Huntingdonshire the tower of Morborne church). Clearly the continued
availability of timber for building in Bedfordshire (*see* p. 24) and
Huntingdonshire (*see* p. 378) and of stone in the Soke of Peterborough (*see* above) held back the demand for brick until the
mid- to late C17. Only in the C18 is there a comprehensive switch
to it in a wide variety of buildings, though again it is much less
pronounced in the stone areas of NW Bedfordshire and the Soke
of Peterborough until the C19. All the early uses are soft red brick
for the best houses.

In the pre-industrial phase there were much-favoured brickworks at Wootton SW of Bedford (active at least from the mid-
C17) but otherwise bricks were supplied from the immediate
locality. The methods of firing may be the reason for the prepon-
derance of glazed grey/blue brick in much of the lime-rich clay
area around Leighton Buzzard in the first half of the C18. That
changed dramatically with the introduction in the C19 of coal-
firing, which brought out the varied colours inherent in local
clays, generally producing bricks of predominantly red and yellow
in the N and central area of the Oxford Clay, where the surface
clays were used, to yellow or near-white from the gault vale in
the SE (see for example the former asylum at Stotfold, of local
Arlesey brick) and, in the very S around Luton, the distinctive
plum-coloured variety (a.k.a. Luton 'greys') that is the result of
iron oxides in the local brick-earth. Caddington was a major
centre for producing many of the gault bricks seen locally. Bricks
from Huntingdonshire follow a similar pattern according to the
clay deposits and unfortunately it must be said that in Huntingdonshire's C19 buildings there is a predominance of a rather hard
characterless yellow brick.

After 1850 the industry was liberated from taxation and grew
prodigiously with mechanization and the development of the
railway systems, especially concentrated around expanding urban
centres (e.g. Bedford, Luton and Peterborough) or to meet the
demands of specific projects, e.g. the Duke of Bedford's estate
development at Thorney in the 1840s and 1850s, where the

cottages are made of unusually large bricks, known locally as the 'Thorney Lump' but not probably used exclusively there. Indeed the Duke maintained an impressively large estate brickworks – the Crawley Kiln - at Husborne Crawley to build the numerous red brick model cottages and farmsteads of his Bedfordshire estates.

The first major commercial development in the Bedfordshire industry was in the gault clay area in the S E of the county, where the arrival of the Great Northern Railway in 1850 was followed by construction of the Arlesey brickworks with connections to the line. Its founder, Robert Beart, had started with brickworks at Huntingdon, and the results are a distinctive light-coloured brick with perforations along the top. Richard Hillier dates the establishment of the commercial industry at Peterborough to 1877 and the sale of the estate of Fletton Lodge, s of the Nene, which led to the first experiments in digging in the Lower Oxford Clay itself rather than in the surface deposits. What transformed the industry and massively reduced its production costs was the discovery that the clay was easily processed, naturally dry, and self-firing; i.e. once the right heat was achieved in the kilns, the high levels of carbon in the clay would burn and do the rest. The contemporary development of the railways enabled these low-cost Fletton bricks to be sent in considerable numbers to assuage the thirst of Victorian and Edwardian London's builders. One of those builders, J. C. Hill, then bought into the Fletton brickworks and set up the London Brick Company, which became the dominant name in Peterborough, absorbing the smaller businesses of its neighbours. Its successor (Hanson) still operates at Whittlesey in Cambridgeshire, the last of the major brickworks on the Oxford Clay.

The achievements at Fletton soon spread to the Oxford Clay area in Marston Vale, Bedfordshire, where again proximity to the Midland Railway through Bedford and the Bedford–Bletchley line was decisive in the location of new works. The firm of B. J. H. Forder & Son were operating lime works in Bedfordshire from *c.* 1890 but expanded into the brick industry by acquisition of works at Westoning on the gault clay in 1894 and Wootton Pillinge (what is now Stewartby) and Elstow on the Oxford Clay in 1897 and quickly formed partnerships with competitors in Peterborough. As the bricks in Marston Vale were dug from the Oxford Clay, they too are known by the generic term Flettons. Forders and the London Brick Company combined in 1924 and gobbled up their rivals. Their headquarters at Stewartby (named after the Stewarts, successive company chairmen) became the largest brickworks in the world. The firm supplied much of the brick for the interwar and postwar housing programmes and in time they absorbed the Arlesey brickworks too. Fletton bricks are naturally a pale mottled red and yellow but by the application of other finishes a variety of colours can be produced. A popular finish in the interwar and postwar period was the so-called Rustic, a red brick with a zigzag surface pattern extensively employed by the London Brick Company in the buildings of its

model village at Stewartby in the 1930s. The industry was subject
to chronic cycles of boom and bust according to the fortunes of
the building industry, and some works closed by the mid C20:
production of Luton grey brick, for example, had more or less
ceased by 1939. The highwater mark for the London Brick
Company was reached in 1973, but by this time the use of brick
was being overtaken by system building and many of the major
Bedfordshire works began to close. Plans for redevelopment for
a new generation of works at Ridgmont (Brogborough) were
halted amid growing awareness of the environmental impact of
the industry, leaving Stewartby to continue alone until the early
C21. In Peterborough the same pattern occurred at the works at
Fletton, whose tall chimneys were memorably described in the
first edition of this volume as 'almost a palisade' along the s side
of the town. The brickworks closed throughout the 1980s and
1990s leaving not a trace other than the flooded brick pits of their
former existence.

TILES are a related industry. Alan Cox has noted a reference
to 'Simon le Tylere' at Dunstable in 1269, and the early C14 tiles
discovered at Warden Abbey indicate the sophistication of decorative tilemaking by then (the patterns inspired the C19 scheme
at Willington); there are good groups of tiles also at Barton-le-
Clay and Cranfield. They vary from the simplest clay tiles to
pantiles, an East Anglian roofing tradition once quite common
on houses close to the fen edge in Huntingdonshire; see e.g.
Manor House Farmhouse, Sawtry. The more elaborate fishscale
patterns were popular in the C19, and taking us up to the present
is the concrete tile, still made by Redland (Van Dyke Works) from
the sands at Leighton Buzzard, where Marley tiles were also
produced.

PREHISTORIC AND ROMAN BEDFORDSHIRE*

Development-related investigations of the last half-century have
placed their own bias on the archaeological record of Bedfordshire, but their justifications in terms of research objectives, especially for larger long-term projects, have advanced knowledge on
a broad front. An important precursor of 'rescue archaeology'
was the manual digging for gravel and brick-earth in the county
in the late C19 and early C20 that led to some of the earliest
English discoveries of PALAEOLITHIC tools. Large numbers of
hand axes of Acheulean (Lower Palaeolithic) type have come
from deposits in the clay at Caddington, Whipsnade and Round
Green, Luton, and in gravel deposits on the highest terrace of
the Great Ouse valley at Kempston and Biddenham near Bedford,

*The account of Prehistoric Bedfordshire is revised from the text of the first edition
by Derek Simpson, with advice from Stephen Coleman.

together with numerous cores and waste flakes produced in the manufacture of finished tools.

With the retreat of the ice from southern Britain about 10,000 years ago the climate gradually changed, populating the landscape with birch and pine woodland followed by oak and elm. Evidence for MESOLITHIC activity is limited and primarily restricted to flint scatters. Some assemblages are considerable: e.g over 500 flints were found on the site later used by the priory of La Grava near Leighton Buzzard, close to the Ouzel. Mesolithic sites have been found above rivers e.g. in the loop of the Great Ouse at Biddenham, on the Lea near Luton and the Flit in mid-Bedfordshire. Others favoured elevated sites on e.g. the Greensand Ridge (Leighton Buzzard and Sandy Lodge) or on the Downs in the S of the county.

The EARLY NEOLITHIC (c. 4000 B.C.–c. 2500 B.C.) is regarded as the period of a change from Mesolithic nomadic hunter-gathering to a more sedentary existence based on agriculture and the clearance of woodland to enable cultivation of cereals. As in the earlier periods the evidence of these people is from chance finds of flint axes and some pottery. The nature of settlement during this period is uncertain, though it appears again to have been concentrated on the chalk of the S and above the floodplain of the Great Ouse valley. The earliest surviving FUNERARY MONUMENTS belong to this time. Although many are known by cropmarks and aerial survey in the Ouse valley, e.g. at Biddenham and at Cardington, Cople and Willington and Roxton, showing that these monuments once existed in complexes, there are only very small numbers of visible earthworks. The most numerous are the LONG BARROWS beneath which the dead were buried. Five examples have been recorded in Bedfordshire, all occupying prominent positions within the landscape on the chalk in the S of the county. One survives as an earthwork at Knocking Knoll, Pegsdon (Shillington). Within the complex of monuments at Cardington, Cople and Willington have been identified SQUARE BARROWS. One was accompanied by an antler as a grave good. Other probable square barrows have been located at Barton-le-Clay, Harrold and Staploe. Also within the Cardington complex are three LONG MORTUARY ENCLOSURES. Intimately associated with long barrows elsewhere in Britain, these were intended as structures in which corpses might accumulate until their numbers warranted the construction of a long barrow. A CURSUS is a third category of ritual or ceremonial monument, again associated with long barrows and long mortuary enclosures elsewhere but of uncommon length. One has been discovered at Biggleswade, which even in its incomplete state is some 700 metres (2296 ft) long. Another is thought to have existed at Cardington within the large ceremonial complex there and may have been of comparable length. At Kempston is another possible site, and others have been proposed at Felmersham. All except that at Biggleswade may, however, be further examples of long mortuary enclosures.

A mixed farming economy appears to have been practised, grain-growing being indicated by cereal impressions on pottery (among other evidence) and stock-raising by animal bones found in the pits of settlement sites and ditches of monuments, including CAUSEWAYED ENCLOSURES. Maiden Bower, Dunstable, has long been regarded as an example of this category of hill-top enclosure. The function may have included gatherings for ceremony, feasting or markets and fairs but remains unclear. The enclosure is overlaid by Iron Age development and the evidence provided by the surviving ditch is disputed. More certain are the cropmarks of another such enclosure at Cardington which show three concentric circular rings of ditches interrupted by the causeways. From the ditch at Maiden Bower came sherds of typical, well-fired, round-based Western Neolithic wares, sherds of which have also been found on Barton Hill (Streatley) and in a barrow in the Five Knolls cemetery, Dunstable. Another site to produce finds of Neolithic ware but whose purpose is somewhat enigmatic is Waulud's Bank, Luton, a D-shaped earthwork formed around the source of the River Lea at Leagrave, now engulfed within the built-up area of Luton.

Even light forests must have presented a formidable obstacle to these primitive agriculturists, and to clear tracts of land for cultivation and grazing both flint and stone axes were employed. There is a considerable body of evidence for the working of suitable stone outcrops in Britain and for the distribution of the products of these axe factories. Stray finds of flint and stone axes are known from the county, but only one of the stone axes, from Great Barford, has been examined petrologically. It was shown to be a product of one of the Cornish axe factories. Among the other finds of this period one may mention leaf-shaped flint arrowheads from various localities and an antler comb, used in skin dressing, from Maiden Bower.

For the LATER NEOLITHIC (from c. 2000 B.C.) there is as yet insufficient material from the county to build up a detailed picture. Two main elements appear to be represented: on the one hand, the continuing and evolving material traditions of the descendants of the first Neolithic colonists, best expressed in pottery, such as that represented at Kempston and Barton Hill, Streatley, which is less well fired and more profusely ornamented than the wares of the preceding period but whose decoration and form betray its ancestry in earlier ceramic traditions; on the other hand, the adoption of new material forms, perhaps due to migration, represented by drinking cups or Beakers placed in graves with the dead. Finds of Beaker material in Bedfordshire are concentrated along the banks of the Ouse and in the Chilterns. The evidence for settlement is represented entirely by graves – either flat graves, as at Clifton, or covered by a round barrow (Dunstable Downs, Five Knolls Group) – or by stray finds such as the archer's wrist-guard from Sandy and the fine flint daggers from Kempston and Jackdaw Hill, Linslade.

In the EARLY BRONZE AGE (c. 1650 B.C.) the evidence is again largely provided by burial monuments. Large numbers of ring ditches, associated either with round barrow or other ceremonial activities, have been identified within the Great Ouse and Ivel valleys and a smaller number on the chalk upland and on the Greensand Ridge, especially around Potton. Some of these ring ditches may have been henge monuments but these are often hard to distinguish. While the bowl barrow, as excavated at Goldington, continued to be constructed, new forms appear at this time – notably the bell barrow. The barrow cemetery at Five Knolls, Dunstable, belongs to this period and includes three large bell barrows surrounded by a common ditch. It contains Late Neolithic inhumations but one of the barrows in this group produced a cremation burial in a collared urn, a form of pottery which develops from Neolithic ceramic traditions. Other urn burials have been found at Barton Hill (Streatley), Foulkes Pit, Kempston and Elstow. Two barrows, The Knolls, survive at Leighton Buzzard. The barrows that have been excavated are generally poorly furnished with grave goods other than pottery, but a jet and amber necklace and a bronze awl were found in excavation of a ring ditch at Radwell, near Felmersham.

For the MIDDLE AND LATE BRONZE AGE the evidence of settlement is even more scanty. Sherds of coarse, badly fired bucket urns have been found at Toddington and Dray's Ditches (Streatley). The greater quantity of metalwork in circulation at this period is reflected in the increasing number of stray bronzes. The majority of these finds are of isolated socketed axes, but one large metalsmith's hoard of sixty socketed axes was found at Wymington, and further hoards of scrap bronze and ingots at Park Close and Fancott (Toddington) and Ickwell Bury.

The introduction of the knowledge of iron-working by settlers from the Continent in the C6 B.C. does not in fact appear to have markedly changed the economic pattern as established in the Middle and Late Bronze Age. The normal economic unit appears to have been the small isolated farmstead with its associated group of fields. The finds from Totternhoe indicate just such a settlement, marked by an enclosure ditch and storage pits; the adjacent group of fields is probably to be related to it.

There is growing evidence of settlement in the transition to the IRON AGE, and this also coincides with the appearance of the first univallate HILLFORTS (e.g. Maiden Bower, Dunstable, and possibly Waulud's Bank, Luton). Further forts were built in the middle and late Iron Age, e.g. Sharpenhoe Clappers (Streatley), two at Sandy Lodge, all of which appear to have been promontory forts, a third fort at Sandy called Caesar's Camp and others at Billington and Mowsbury (Ravenstone). Such forts indicate the corporate activity of large numbers of individuals and the existence of larger political and social units. The multiple banks and ditches of Dray's Ditches (Streatley), which cut across Icknield Way, are the westernmost of a series of such dykes and probably related to a tribal territorial area, part of a wider process in the Iron Age of defining boundaries and defending them. Similar features at right angles to the Icknield Way have been recorded at Arlesey and Stotfold and a similarly aligned earthwork at Pegsdon (Shillington) marks the county boundary. Triple ditches at right angles to the Ouse have been identified at Eastcote and Willington. In this period settlement spread to the previously unoccupied heavier clay lands of the northern county and between the greensand and the chalk escarpment. Of settlements on farmsteads, the characteristic forms of post-built structures and round houses have been found in excavations at Biddenham, Broom and Salford, and some of these settlements grew considerably in size and density through the Iron Age.

In 54 B.C. Julius Caesar defeated Cassivellaunus, who held a large territory that certainly included most of Hertfordshire and probably part of southern Bedfordshire. This belonged to the Catuvellauni, the most powerful of the tribes of Britain, and their king Tasciovanus († c. A.D. 5–10) probably established their capital at Verulamium (St Albans). Under his successor Cunobelinus, who may have come from the neighbouring tribe of the Trinovantes, the whole of Bedfordshire, together with neighbouring counties to the N and E, was united into a single kingdom; and under his sons c. A.D. 40 suzerainty was established over the whole of SE England. The greater political complexity of this last hundred years of prehistory in the area is matched by increasing technological sophistication, the most marked developments being the introduction of wheel-turned pottery produced on an industrial scale – and in a Gallo-Belgic style dramatically different from Iron Age ceramics – and by an established coinage. Gallo-Belgic coins appear in the period c. 150–100 B.C. but their forms of the late CI B.C. show the effect of contact with Rome and bear the names of Catuvellaunian kings or of their war god Camulos. In Bedfordshire there is a marked concentration of these coins at Limbury (Luton), many bearing the name of Cunobelin or of Tasciovanus, but the occurrence of these coins in the N of the county shows how far their rule had spread by the early CI A.D. Sites of new settlement in this period almost always favour the best, well-drained soils of the river valleys. A farmstead at Odell newly built at the end of the CI B.C. was completely excavated in 1974–8 and shows a common pattern of round houses within an enclosure surrounded by fields for crops and pasture for livestock. There were large numbers of such farmsteads by the time of the Roman invasion. A feature of the archaeology of Catuvellaunian territory is the series of princely burial vaults, richly furnished with fine metalwork, amphorae containing wine, and other imported luxury goods from the classical world. There are a number of sites of cremation burials, especially in the Ivel Valley, that are of an aristocratic class. An early CI9 find at Stanfordbury (Southill) included Roman goods such as bronze vessels, amphorae and games for the afterlife, and a finely ornamented bronze mirror and shale vessels were found at Old Warden. The pair of bronze bowls, ceremonial bucket, and fish-head spout from Felmersham could certainly all have graced the table of a Belgic prince. The discovery at Shefford and

Biggleswade of well-furnished graves dating from after the Conquest confirms that aristocratic life was unthreatened by the invaders, and no doubt those at the top of society found new roles as administrators under the new rulers.

The transition to the ROMAN* occupation was probably undramatic for many in rural Bedfordshire. The evidence is that many of the established settlements and practices continued under the Romans and developed rather than being set down afresh. The principal change in the landscape was the introduction, very early after the invasion of A.D. 43, of ROADS to supplement the existing system of track-ways and improve supply routes and communications across the country. Their lines in Bedfordshire are recognizable still: Watling Street through part of the W of the county, which lies below the A5, and the branch of Ermine Street via Baldock to Sandy, partly underlying the A1, which then rejoined the main road N at Godmanchester in Huntingdonshire. Both roads clearly follow the direction of advance of the Roman legions striking N and NW from Camulodunum (Colchester). Doubt has been cast over a network of lesser roads proposed by the Viatores in 1964 (*Roman Roads in the South-East Midlands*).

While there are no major Roman TOWNS in Bedfordshire the roads provided the impetus for development of two large settlements and in particular at Dunstable, which is the site of *Durocobrivae* on Watling Street at its intersection with the older Icknield Way. It lay between *Verulamium* (St Albans) and a fort at *Magiovinium* in Buckinghamshire and probably came into being for military use during the Conquest itself before evolving into a more substantial market town for the locality. Sandy, on the E bank of the River Ivel where it cuts through the Greensand Ridge, has already been noted as a site of probable Iron Age settlement in the purview of the hillforts there, and the Romans, recognising its important strategic location, probably established it as a military post by the river crossing. At its fullest extent in the C3 the town at Sandy occupied 10 hectares (25 acres), and evidence has been found not only of its buildings but also industrial zones and two cemeteries, one of which has demonstrated the change in burial practice from cremation to inhumation, including coffin burials; such burials also occurred at Dunstable and there have been found several graves with offerings accompanying skeletons, a practice which declined with the spread of Christianity. Aside from these settlements, there appears to have been another of considerable size along part of the Icknield Way at Limbury, now a northern suburb of Luton.

Within the hinterland of the towns and in the countryside were VILLAS, i.e. higher-status houses. The identification of their sites remains patchy, but there is clear evidence of their distribution at intervals along the Ouse from Tempsford to Odell and another

*This account relies heavily on A. Simco, *Survey of Bedfordshire: The Roman Period* (1984).

band across the SE side of the county on the lighter soils from
Eyeworth to Totternhoe, where a villa of the C1 A.D. has been
investigated; it was in occupation until at the least the C4. It was
of the familiar type with three wings around a courtyard and
contained mosaic and tessellated floors. It also had a bath house,
an amenity also found in excavations at Newnham (Bedford).
Other villa sites have revealed much less to indicate the standards
of living enjoyed by their occupants, but decorative marble wall-
facing has been retrieved from a villa site at Tempsford. The lesser
farmsteads appear to have been altered by Roman influence only
gradually in the introduction of new building techniques such as
stone construction and tile roofs. By the C5 there is evidence of
the decline of standards of living and abandonment of sites as
the Roman empire retreated and the transition to the Saxon era
began.

MEDIEVAL ARCHITECTURE

The first Saxon cemetery in Bedfordshire to be discovered was
in the C19 at Kempston and contained large numbers of C5 and
C6 pagan burials as well as Christian burials of the C7. The cemetery discovered at Leighton Buzzard produced an exceptionally
rich collection of grave offerings. In architecture, however, there
is nothing ANGLO-SAXON in Bedfordshire to compare with
Huntingdon and Peterborough. Bedfordshire was part of Mercia
and on the edge of the Danelaw, with Bedford as a frontier town.
It is the only town in Bedfordshire to show evidence, from excavation, of Saxon urban settlement and two of its churches, St
Peter de Merton, N of the river, and St Mary to the S, have late
Anglo-Saxon remains. St Peter has a W tower which is now the
crossing tower, St Mary a crossing tower and S transept. St Paul's
church, rebuilt after the siege of Bedford Castle in 1224, is
thought to have originated as the principal church of an ecclesiastical centre at Bedford. The other churches with Saxon evidence are also concentrated overwhelmingly in the stone area of
the Ouse valley NW of Bedford. Stevington has a tower with
openings into a former *porticus*, i.e. side chamber. Turvey also
appears to have a Saxon tower and nave. The nave had double-
splayed windows, a late Saxon type which indeed occurs in the
towers at Clapham and Stevington and appears to be found in
the chancels of Carlton and Kempston too. Thin walls are a supporting indication of Saxon building, so the nave of Shelton may
belong to this period; also characteristic of the time is the use of
roughly coursed rubble not only for the walls but also for the
quoins and dressings. Sometimes it is laid in herringbone patterns, as one finds in the walls of the transept at St Mary,
Bedford, and the chancel at Carlton. It occurs away from this
area at Kensworth, which may be Norman, however. Clapham's
impressively tall W tower shows Saxon constructional techniques,
but with volutes to the bell-openings of distinctively post-

Conquest type, and appears to be entirely late CII. Of Anglo-Saxon SCULPTURE there is very little to see. From the earlier period there is a large section of a cross-shaft which was found built into the (1580s) E wall of the church at Elstow and is now displayed in the Moot Hall. It has two confronted animals whose feet turn into interlace, a motif of the late C8 and a smaller but stylistically very similar fragment is built into an opening of the tower at St Peter de Merton, Bedford. From the late C10 or early CII are two grave covers at Cardington and Milton Bryan, with crosses and interlace in the style found elsewhere in the East Midlands and cf. Peterborough Cathedral. All of these pieces are carved from Barnack limestone.

NORMAN ECCLESIASTICAL ARCHITECTURE is not abundant either. St Mary, Luton, had a C12 crossing tower but it collapsed in the early C14. Meppershall's crossing tower remains, but the date is only made obvious inside by the roll moulding on the chancel arch. Thurleigh's tower has the long-and-short quoins of Saxo-Norman overlap and windows with single splays. The Normans made alterations to the tops of the towers of the churches of St Mary and St Peter de Merton, both at Bedford. But there is one major building: Dunstable Priory church, of which most of the nave survives, below c. 1150–60, on the gallery level c. 1180–90, in the façade from c. 1180 to the dedication in 1213 and after, i.e. into the full-blown E.E. The church at its fullest extent was probably cruciform and had not only a crossing tower but also two W towers that collapsed in 1222. The façade is confused, the nave interior unified and powerful.

Dunstable was the most important monastic foundation in the county, founded by 1125 for the Augustinians. The only other foundation of which any remains can be seen is Elstow Abbey, a house of Benedictine nuns founded c. 1078, probably on the site of an earlier Saxon church. The evidence is that the late CII church had an extensive presbytery with an apsidal end and transepts. Five bays of the nave only survive, of which three are early C12. There were of course several other MONASTIC FOUNDATIONS. Besides Dunstable there were Augustinian priories at Bushmead (founded c. 1195), Cauldwell (Bedford, 1154) and Newnham (Bedford, c. 1165), the last two both gone all but entirely. Apart from Elstow, Benedictine also were Millbrook (1097, later at Beadlow, founded c. 1145) and Grove Priory (Leighton Buzzard, later C12), a cell of Fontevrault, both again no longer surviving even in parts. Warden Abbey (Old Warden) and Woburn Abbey were Cistercian, the former founded from Rievaulx in 1135, the latter about ten years later. There was also a cell of Woburn at Linslade. Chicksands was one of the much rarer Gilbertine houses, founded c. 1150. Of Friars' establishments there were only two: Blackfriars at Dunstable and Greyfriars at Bedford. Harrold had a house of Augustinian canonesses. Again, nothing survives of these friaries. Several of the establishments listed above have been excavated, but of those where remains are preserved there is nothing earlier than the C13 and they are described below.

Among the parish CHURCHES there are about thirty in the following gazetteer with Norman remains, but these are often very fragmentary. The ruins of Segenhoe suggest it began as a two-cell church. Just conceivably it is Late Saxon but the windows of its chancel are single-splayed with a single stone as the head of the window, features which tend to suggest a post-Conquest date. It has a more obviously Norman chancel arch and what appears to be the remains of a second arch inside the chancel. This might indicate an apse arch, and clearer evidence of such an arrangement appears to occur at Milton Bryan. Knotting is a puzzle: it has an extraordinarily rough arch between the Norman tower and nave. Scallop capitals, chevron, dogtooth, saltire and beakhead mouldings can be found in several churches on doors and chancel arches, e.g. Bedford St Peter, Caddington, Flitwick, Knotting, Little Barford, Meppershall (St Thomas). There are of course arcades where aisles were added to older churches. They

Thurleigh, St Peter, south door and tympanum.
Drawing by Sir Henry E. L. Dryden, 1843

mostly have round piers with square capitals and abaci. In Bedfordshire the square abacus seems to have been used right to the
end of the century (see e.g. Shelton).

Besides these standard C12 motifs, a few precious pieces of
NORMAN SCULPTURE survive on the capitals of the façade and
N door of Dunstable, which have hunting scenes and animals.
Some figure capitals also to the s door of Kensworth, not far
away. The tympanum of Elstow's N door is a small sculptured
panel of *c.* 1140 with Christ seated and two saints, very French.
There is very little other sculpture. At Cranfield is another
seated figure, very defaced, and Thurleigh has a primitive tympanum with Adam and Eve, the tree and the serpent. The
tympanum at Ravensden has just chequerboard decoration. A
pillar piscina at Henlow also has a finely carved capital. Fonts
are quite frequent, but only those at Houghton Regis and Dunstable need mention here because they belong to the late C12
so-called Aylesbury Group with an inverted base, fluted bowls
and carved frieze around the rim. The font at Linslade is a relative of this group, with beasts in the chain around the bowl; a
rather similar font is in the same area, at Studham, although
this appears to be E.E.

So we move to EARLY ENGLISH ARCHITECTURE, only to find
that here also major monuments are rare, and only one is of the
highest beauty: Felmersham of *c.* 1220–40, with its reposeful w
front, its grand crossing, and the fine balance achieved in the
nave by arcade piers alternating between round and octagonal
not only along the arcade but also across the nave. What is of
unusual wealth in the county, but not at Felmersham, is stiff-leaf
capitals, from the early ones of before 1200, with small leaves
keeping closely to a bell left exposed for most of its height (e.g.
Caddington), to the bigger leaves still close to the bell, and in
the end to the rich, mature 'wind-swept' leaves. Of special interest
are the approximately datable specimens at Chalgrave, consecrated in 1219, Studham, consecrated in 1220, and the w bays of
Elstow, also of *c.* 1220, and the Eaton Bray capitals, where *c.* 1220
can be compared with superb *c.* 1240. Eaton Bray also has a font
with stiff-leaf of *c.* 1240. More generally the development from
Norman into E.E. can be followed in arcades by steps in various
directions: round arch to pointed, unmoulded arch to slight
chamfers and full chamfers, square to round abaci, and so on.
The Transitional phase from Norman to Early English is well-
represented by the w door at Blunham, still with a round arch,
to the s door of Farndish with its pointed arch and stiff-leaf
capitals. The outer parlour (now the vestry) at Elstow Abbey is
a particularly good example of the increasingly complex forms
of rib-vaulting in the C13.

Architecturally as against decoratively one more building must
be referred to: the proud crossing tower of Leighton Buzzard.
Thomas of Leighton made the iron railings round Queen Eleanor's
monument in Westminster Abbey. That was in 1293–4, and as the
county has some beautiful IRONWORK of the late C13, this has
been ascribed to him. Where Thomas obtained his training is

uncertain, but Jane Geddes suggests he may have emerged from a workshop at Dunstable Priory, which had a renowned and very early mechanical clock for which an expert smith would have been required. It is also an odd fact that there is no good local source of iron in the county (despite the erroneous term 'ironstone' applied to the dark local sandstone). The wonderful door scrolls of the hinges of the w door and vestry at Leighton Buzzard are no doubt by the same hand that stamped and wrought the Eleanor grille, for the patterns are identical. Indeed many of the same motifs are to be found on the even more elaborate hinges of the door at Turvey, which Jane Geddes believes to have come before Leighton Buzzard in Thomas's career. The door at Eaton Bray is commonly also ascribed to Thomas, but in its details, e.g. tighter scrolls and a thicker profile to the castings, it indicates either a workshop from which Thomas emerged or a continuation of his tradition. There is another work to consider, though it is early C14 and hitherto unknown: the chancel door at Hulcote. This has generous serpentine scrolls without the foliage stamps of the late C13 style. It is a remarkable survival in a church very significantly rebuilt in the C16.

At Linslade, also of the C13, is a stone SEAT – and that is a rare thing (but cf. Farcet in Huntingdonshire). Of other stone fitments the DOUBLE PISCINA at Toddington deserves notice. It is of the type with two pointed arches under one round arch. There is another at Felmersham. This is also the time when in Bedfordshire effigies begin to appear on FUNERARY MONUMENTS. There is a knight at Salford, ladies at Goldington and Oakley, a civilian holding his heart at Yelden, and so on to the late C14 knight at Houghton Regis. Typical of the C13 are coffin lids with foliated crosses. Most of these are not listed in this book, but there are two specially interesting ones at Pavenham and Oakley, where the cross grows out of a beast (cf. St Neots, Huntingdonshire). The motif occurs in other places as well. By then new materials such as brass and alabaster had come into use, but Bedfordshire has no early examples.

DECORATED ARCHITECTURE, if one wishes to see fairly complete examples, will be found at Dean, Sundon, Langford, and at Swineshead (where the tower has a curious shallow w porch). Marston Moretaine has a detached tower. It also has a vaulted vestry, as has St Mary at Luton. Dates are rare but not wholly absent. At Shillington in 1333 the Bishop of Lincoln admonished the parishioners to repair their nave. So the nave will be after that, and the chancel was probably done just before. At Lower Gravenhurst the man 'qe fiet faire' the new church died c. 1360, and at Wymington John Curteys, who, according to the inscription on his brass, also built the church, died as late as 1391, and yet it is still Dec in style. There is no record of when Perp first appeared. The octagonal pier carrying a double-chamfered arch was common already in the C13 and remained common to the end of the Middle Ages. The two together in the following gazetteer are simply referred to as 'standard elements'. The C13 had also known quatrefoil piers, true ones and those which are really a square with four semicircular projections. Big versions of this style are the crossing piers of St Mary, Luton. What the Dec seems to have introduced and liked is the quatrefoil enriched by four slim shafts in the diagonals, and there are numerous examples of this across the county.

DECORATED CHURCH FURNISHINGS are naturally more plentiful than Norman or E.E. and the theme of the C14 is an enrichment with furnishings and fittings, concomitant with a greater elaboration of liturgy and ritual that continues up to the end of the medieval period, and expenditure on which is sometimes recorded in legacies given in wills. The most spectacular piece is the stone font enclosure of Luton, probably contemporary with early C14 rebuilding after the collapse of the church tower. It is a piece unique in England. Some good tomb recesses must be quoted, all in the N of the county, especially Dean, Milton Ernest, Swineshead and Yelden, with crocketed arches over the tomb-chests. There is an exquisite early C14 WALL PAINTING of the Crucifixion at Turvey, and Chalgrave has extensive wall paintings of about the same date. The refectory at Bushmead Priory had a cycle of paintings on the theme of the Creation, and significant elements of this survive. An interesting though faded wall painting is at Swineshead where the decoration of censing angels flanks a niche for a devotional image. In St Mary, Bedford, the painting depicts a walled city. C15 wall painting favours large figures of St Christopher and there are a few larger Doom paintings over chancel arches, e.g. at Marston Moretaine, dated to *c.* 1505, and C15 at Wymington. Extensive schemes comprising a variety of subjects but now hard to read include Toddington.

Also early C14 is the STAINED GLASS of saints at Cockayne Hatley, but it has come from elsewhere (like the furnishings of that church), and no comparable windows native to Bedfordshire survived intact the changes of the C16 and C17. Among what remains of the smaller fragments there is much that is worthwhile, such as the reassembled early C14 pieces at Potsgrove, the mid-C14 figures of saints at Edworth, and especially the whole window at Old Warden given in 1381–2 by Walter Clifton, abbot of Warden, and depicting him in the usual kneeling position of the donor. There is also a figure of a priest in a window at Dean. The Old Warden window is in the more refined style of the period more commonly found after 1400, for which see also the fragments of glass at Odell. Dec SCREENS survive at Campton and Potsgrove but are of no special merit, and net-traceried C14 doors survive at Luton and Swineshead, which can be compared with the traceried front of a chest at Sundon. The details are as characteristically different from the C15 tracery of the door at Biggleswade as are the details of the Campton and Potsgrove screens from the many Perp screens all over the county. The best Early Perp one is at Clifton, dated to *c.* 1390, its brilliant colours and the figures of prophets its dado revealed by cleaning. There is a fragment of a dado with prophets at Marston Moretaine and a complete dado at Roxton. The later Perp screens with lofts are

at Felmersham, delightfully detailed, and Oakley. Stagsden has a
Late Perp screen but no loft. After the screens the STALLS, and
especially the misericords. The origin of those of Leighton
Buzzard is uncertain, but the date is early C15 and they share
motifs found in the stalls at Lincoln Cathedral; more are in St
Paul at Bedford. There are also good stalls with poppyheads at
Northill, a church which became collegiate in 1404. After the
stalls the BENCHES. The majority of the ends are just straight-
topped with thin buttresses, but there are poppyheads at Houghton Conquest and Stevington and some of these are in the form
of beasts, as found also at e.g. Edworth. Four Perp PULPITS
remain – at Dean, Tempsford and Yelden. A fourth, from Elstow,
is now in the Moot Hall. Also some stone REREDOSES; those
which survive are mostly found in side chapels. By far the best
must have been the one of which parts now make up the pulpit
of St Paul at Bedford. The Nottingham alabaster panels at Sandy
and (in fragments) at Blunham also belonged originally to
reredoses.

But we have not so far examined PERPENDICULAR ARCHI-
TECTURE. A few words first on towers and steeples, because they
refer not only to Perp but also to earlier evidence. The earliest
spire is at Souldrop (late C13). In the s of the county there are
no spires, and the towers have often higher stair-turrets; all along
the Greensand Ridge this is the standard type, almost always of
the dark sandstone, in the area further s a mixture of clunch, flint
etc. Very occasionally, as at Houghton Conquest it is possible to
attach a date for building. The C16 tower of Whipsnade is unusual
in the use of brick. In the N, spires are quite frequent, and in
some places such as Colmworth they have much in common with
the more famous spires of Huntingdonshire. Good examples are
Dean, Swineshead and Yelden. St Paul at Bedford has a recessed
spire, and at least five others exist, plus two whose spires are
connected by delicate flying buttresses with the pinnacles on the
corners of the tower (Harrold, Sharnbrook). Broach spires are
about equally represented: five, and one (Podington) which is
recessed as well. At Wymington the lucarnes at the foot of the
spire are so high and so broad that they form an octagon as the
preparatory stage of the spire. Most unusual are the detached
bell-towers at Marston Moretaine (Dec) and Elstow (Perp). The
latter is partly explained by the tradition of such bell-towers in
monastic establishments but the decision to build in this way at
Marston is a puzzle.

Many churches exhibit evidence of Perp remodellings and
additions of aisles, chapels etc. There are also good roofs at Dean
and Leighton Buzzard, both of the angel type. As for whole Perp
churches, five deserve to be singled out: St Paul at Bedford, a
hall church with wide aisles; Toddington, large and good; Totternhoe with some fine features; Flitton probably of *c.* 1440–89
with piers of the most typical section (four shafts and four
diagonal hollows – in the gazetteer to be called 'standard moulded
section'); and Willington, built by Sir John Gostwick, Master of
the Horse to Cardinal Wolsey and Treasurer of the First Fruits

under Henry VIII. He began the church *c*. 1530, and it is char- ²¹
acteristic of the late date that the porch is placed symmetrically
between two large transomed windows. There is a Renaissance
feeling in this. Sir John died in 1545, and his monument in the
church is completely plain.

It is high time to catch up with MONUMENTS, for there are
fine ones in Bedfordshire. John Curteys at Wymington died in
1391. He has a monument with brasses and a big ogee arch. Of
almost exactly the same date is the monument to William Wenlock
in Luton parish church between chancel and N chapel. He is
shown in effigy and the date of death here is 1392. Its setting
however is the lavish screen of *c*. 1460 with its splendidly high ¹⁹
and richly panelled arch encompassing two pointed arches over
the tombs. Opposite is the charming little chantry chapel of
Richard Barnard †1492, with its miniature vault. The creation of
chantry chapels, sometimes accompanied by a residence for a
priest to say prayers, is also to be noted elsewhere at this period
at Blunham (1467), Northill (1489) and Turvey (1504). At Clifton
is the only alabaster monument of the complete type with tomb- ²⁰
chest with angels holding shields and two recumbent effigies. It
is early C16, is identified as Sir Thomas Lucy †1525. Cardington
has two tombs between chancel and chapels, again with very
elaborate architectural surrounds; one has the tomb-chest of Sir
William Gascoigne †1540. The effigy is a brass. But the best
BRASSES in the county are earlier: one at Elstow who died in
1427, Thomas Wideville and his two wives at Bromham, †1435,
William Hicchecok at Ampthill †1450, the Rotherham brass at
Luton *c*. 1490, and Isabel Conquest at Houghton Conquest
†1493, with husband and son. The Wideville brass is an interesting case of post-Reformation appropriation, having been taken
from St James' monastery in Northampton for reuse in the monument to Sir John Dyve †1535. Most of the brasses conform to
the styles identified with the London workshops and to a lesser
extent Cambridge. John Acworth †1513 at Luton is interesting
for it depicts, instead of the usual kneeling children, members of
his Fraternity of Holy Trinity. This Guild was founded in 1475,
one of a number sponsored by Bishop Rotherham, and had
its own chapel in the S transept at St Mary, Luton. The early
to mid-C16 brasses are often to those who prospered at the
Tudor court. At Cardington, Sir William Gascoigne, mentioned
above, was of Wolsey's household, and is shown splendidly
attired in heraldic costume. Overall the best collections of C15–
C16 brasses are at Dunstable and Cople. At the latter, Sir Walter
Luke, a Justice of the King's Bench, †1544 has the brass in a
classical arch. One of very similar character at Haynes is for
Anthony Newdegate †1568, who had been one of the commissioners for the sales of the abbeys. This is a rare instance in
Bedfordshire monuments where one can see the transition from
Gothic to Renaissance motifs. Only that to Sir John Mordaunt
†1504 at Turvey exhibits both forms side by side, and only to
the extent of spiral carved colonnettes at the angles of the
tomb-chest.

Secular Buildings

After this complete survey of churches up to the beginning of the C16, the way is now clear for starting on SECULAR BUILDINGS. Bedfordshire has not a single castle, except for the early MOTTE-AND-BAILEY CASTLES, i.e. Norman earthworks. There are about fifteen of these surviving in one form or another, mostly on river edges. The most basic is the motte alone (e.g. Risinghoe (Goldington) on the Ouse E of Bedford) but there are a number of more fully developed types, of which the most important are Bedford, Cainhoe (Clophill), Totternhoe and Yelden. Others, such as those at Luton, have entirely vanished. The most important castle was at Ampthill, built by Sir John Cornwall in the early C15, improved for Henry VIII after 1524 but demolished by the C17. As in Huntingdonshire there are many MOATED SITES to indicate building or rebuilding of manor houses in the C13 and C14. They occur most often in the N and centre district, though they are not mentioned in the following gazetteer unless a house continues to occupy the site, e.g. Basmead (Staploe), Tilsworth Manor, or Eaton Bray Castle. But for standing medieval buildings there is hardly anything to draw attention to until the dawn of the Tudor period. One is the minor remains of a major house – the derelict fragment of Someries Castle built for John, Lord Wenlock, outside Luton. It dates from *c.* 1447–8 and represents not only the first use of brick in the county but is, along with the Rye House gatehouse in nearby Hertfordshire and Fulkbourne in Essex, among the earliest complete or partially complete buildings to do so in England. The motifs of moulded and cut brickwork are common to all of these examples, and it may be that they are the work of the same, probably Flemish or German, craftsmen. Someries is also an important first occurrence of decorative brickwork, e.g. diaper patterns and moulded corbels, that would become a motif of the Tudor years (e.g. Warden Abbey).

Someries was a house at the aristocratic level. The subject of SMALLER DOMESTIC BUILDINGS for the medieval period is difficult to sum up from the standing evidence owing to the exceptional rarity of buildings earlier than the C16. As in Huntingdonshire the evidence is affected by the concealment of early houses in later remodelling and the rate of destruction in the C20, at which time the early origins of some houses was realized too late. Except in the stone villages of the NW, the smaller Bedfordshire house was TIMBER-FRAMED. Good stands of oak grew on the heavy soils of the clay district and along the Greensand Ridge, and even in the southern chalklands there is no lack of timber houses. Elm and Baltic pine are more common in later houses, as supplies of oak declined. Dating of these buildings by dendrochronology (tree-ring analysis) has not been widely practised in Bedfordshire and it is generally assumed that most are post-medieval.

Most houses, whether stone or timber, follow traditional types of PLAN with an open hall. The earliest and most basic type is a single room with an open hearth, e.g. No. 135 High Street,

Riseley, where smoke from the fire was vented through the roof or other openings. The more common plan is for the hall to be flanked by a two-storey service end and a parlour with chamber over. In many houses a cross-passage separated the hall from the low end. A small but significant number of high-status houses in the N of the county have been revealed (by the late John Bailey) to have begun as AISLED HALLS, notably Bromham Hall; Blackburn Hall, Thurleigh; The Old House, Ickwell; No.8 High Street, Elstow, and the building which is now a barn at The Barns Hotel, Bedford. In every case, the aisles have been removed in later remodelling. The likely date for all of these buildings is early C13 to early C14. A typical Bedfordshire plan for larger houses is the T-plan with a single cross-wing at the upper end. It developed at the highest level into the familiar H-plan of two wings. Internally a refinement to the open hearth was the addition of a smoke bay at the end of hall, e.g. Nos. 2–3 Old Way, Bletsoe, dated to 1459–60. Proper chimneys were often added in the C16 and C17, and concurrent with this is not only the introduction of the lobby entry against the side of the chimney but also the practice of inserting a floor in the hall or, if building new, to construct the house with a single-storey hall and chamber over.

A number of CRUCK-FRAMED HOUSES have been identified in Bedfordshire, though the surviving examples are few and concentrated in the W, where they may be evidence of overspill of this technique from Buckinghamshire where it is widely recorded. The best example, and uniquely grand for Bedfordshire, is Moretyne Manor at Marston Moretaine for which a C14 date is given. Its frame shows it had a two-bay hall open to the roof with a moulded tie-beam to the main hall truss and a spere truss separating the hall from the cross-passage. There is another at Husborne Crawley (Henry VI Cottage) with four cruck-trusses remaining. An odd feature is that the hall truss in both examples seems to be emphasized externally by the attachment of a post. A variant is the raised cruck, i.e. raised on the walls of the house rather than starting from the ground. This is found in a stone cottage in the High Street, Sharnbrook. BOX-FRAMING is the standard form of construction in Bedfordshire. Straight posts and rails form the walls and are joined together across the frame by tie-beams which carry the roof trusses. The wall panels are typically infilled with wattle-and-daub and later on by brick or plaster, and although widespread in use across the county it is often the case that the framing is wholly concealed by plastering or refacing in brick. The frames of earlier buildings tend to have large panels but in C15 and C16 buildings the posts of the frame move closer together, known as close-studding, often indicating higher-status houses. Good examples of this are Tyrells End, Eversholt; Lancotbury, Totternhoe; and Manor House, Husborne Crawley. Early timber-framed buildings include the range of buildings along the High Street at Elstow, where the pattern of vertical studs is supplemented by remarkable repeated use of ogival tension braces, dated by John Bailey to c. 1300. The buildings at Elstow also have JETTIES, and the C16 is the probable date of this feature first appearing in timber-framed houses. The

22

types vary from a jetty at one end or on the front of a cross-wing, e.g. Sun House, Potton, and The Porch, Shefford, to double jetties on the grander houses, e.g. Moretyne Manor, Marston Moretaine, or long jetties running for the length of a house front, e.g. Lancotbury, Totternhoe, which coincides with the phase in which open halls were disappearing from houses in favour of a single-storey hall with chamber over.

WEALDEN HOUSES have jettied upper storeys to the bays either side of a central hall and a pitched roof overall, giving the appearance of a recessed centre. In spite of the name, the type is not confined to the Weald of SE England, and a number have been identified in Bedfordshire. One, known as Poet Rowe's House at Little Barford, is now at Glatton, Huntingdonshire, but another can be seen in Orchard Lane, Harrold. A third, at No. 17 Elstow High Street, is disguised by later alterations. The most impressive kind of jetty is that which encompasses all four sides of a building. Although this is not generally seen in houses, it is used for the Moot Hall at Elstow of *c.* 1500, where the jetties require diagonal dragon beams to support them at the angles. A dragon beam also survives in a former house in Church Street, Dunstable, but the front jetty has been removed. The Moot Hall has, instead of the usual open ground floor, partition walls creating six individual SHOPS, each with its own entrance. No. 20 High Street, Elstow, is a good example, albeit altered, of an urban plan type with the merchant's house and shop in one. It is unusual in adopting a side-by-side arrangement. Much more common in late medieval towns was to turn the house at right angles so that it is only one bay wide and extends over the narrow plot behind with a shop to the street and accommodation over. Such houses survived in Dunstable until the 1970s and investigation at the time of their demolition showed one group of four to have had shops below two jettied storeys on each end so that they were shops on two streets.

ROOFS of earlier medieval houses are usually of the crown-post type, of which Bushmead Priory is an early and exceptionally elaborate example of late C13 date. After the early C15 roofs are commonly side purlin roofs, with the purlins either clasped by the principal rafters or tenoned directly into the rafters; or for stability windbraces were added vertically between tie-beam and rafter or laterally between principal rafter and purlin. The late medieval roof at St John House, Bedford, is a good example, as is the barn at Old Warden. A unique survival is the queenpost roof at Sewell Manor, probably late C15, with tracery carved on the spandrels.

Timber houses with DECORATION in the façade appear to be pretty rare in Bedfordshire, but it should be said that the recorded examples have usually come to light only with the removal of later casings of plaster or brick as at Francis House, Dean, which has decorative patterns of circles with fleur-de-lis spurs in its gables, and Meppershall Manor also has similar decoration of the kind which one associates with Elizabethan timber-framing. What is completely unknown are the overall patterns of lozenges and quatrefoils etc., but they did exist in a demolished house at Calcutt Farm, near Houghton Regis. To date no other examples have come to light. More typically one finds timber frames infilled with brick in straight courses as at the Elstow Moot Hall or herringbone patterns as at Lancotbury, Totternhoe.

In terms of INTERIOR DECORATION, Basmead Manor, Staploe, began as a late medieval two-unit plan of hall and two-storey chamber block and has the rare survival of a screen or window from the chamber into the hall. It was then improved in the early C16 by the addition of a cross-wing, and this contains moulded beams and carved decoration of a quality hardly known elsewhere in the county. Campton Manor, dated *c.* 1591, has inside a remarkable screen with Jacobean cresting. In sharp contrast to Huntingdonshire the survival of C16 or early C17 STAIR-CASES in smaller houses is limited. Bromham Hall, the house of Sir Lewis Dyve, has a good example of an Elizabethan staircase of massive oak treads around a square newel, and there is some Jacobean woodwork at Heath Manor, Heath and Reach. Interior decoration, in the form of WALL PAINTING, rarely survives. It was often not elaborate and may have been confined to painting of exposed timbers, but where traces of red or green are found it is an indication of wealth. Survivals in Bedfordshire are rare but in The Priory Heritage Centre, Dunstable, there are early C17 *ex-situ* paintings of a more ambitious kind painted onto the plaster panels which infilled the frame; in its complete state this would have been an all-over pattern. Even more important is the scheme showing bull baiting in Box End House, Kempston (Rural), which is painted in grisaille with red tongues for the animals – another clear indicator of expense. At Little Park Farm, Ampthill, a decorative ceiling of octagonal patterns shows the influence of Serlio by the C17.

A handful of houses in the NE of the county have early C17 PLASTERWORK. The decoration is clearly by the same workshop and appears at its most elaborate in a ribbed ceiling dated by heraldry to before 1612 at Manor Farm, Cotton End, with a central scene of Adam and Eve. Several of the patterns then reappear in two rooms at Low Farm, Colmworth, one of them containing an impressive overmantel of the Stuart royal arms. The arms, from the very same moulds, appear once more at Church Farm, Roxton. Dr Claire Gapper associates some of the motifs of this group with plasterwork found in Hardwick House, Oxfordshire, Dorton House, Buckinghamshire (1626) and Canons Ashby, Northamptonshire, indicating the activity of the same plasterer or his influence across the East Midlands.

TUDOR AND STUART BEDFORDSHIRE

The discussion of churches and smaller houses above has taken us beyond other aspects of TUDOR, ELIZABETHAN AND

JACOBEAN ARCHITECTURE. It can start with the MANSIONS but as we will come to see in the discussion of large houses generally in Bedfordshire, the picture is clouded by destruction in the following centuries. Of the houses associated with families established in Bedfordshire in the medieval period only Bromham Hall, which belonged to the Dyves, remains substantially intact and externally showing evidence of its remodelling in the late C16. The largest houses were Wrest and Haynes (or Hawnes), but both were replaced in the C18 and early C19. Among those on the rise in this period, Sir John Gostwick stands out. His family came from Willington and he entered court circles through service in Wolsey's household, and this put him in a position to buy Willington manor from the Duke of Norfolk in 1529. The house he raised on his new property has vanished except for a few fragments incorporated in the present manor house, but the stables and dovecote offer clear confirmation of his status. The latter in particular is on a stupendous scale, in fact two independent dovecotes joined together. Both stables and dovecote have stepped gables and nothing of the Renaissance. Through connections with Thomas Cromwell, Gostwick after 1537 obtained the lands of Warden Abbey, Old Warden, and, like Richard Williams in Huntingdonshire, he continued in favour even after Cromwell's fall. At Warden his son Sir William remodelled the buildings *c.* 1552 into a large brick house. Of it too only a picturesque fragment remains, but it is enough to indicate changes in style and materials by this period – brick and terracotta.

Other religious foundations which were turned over to domestic use by their new owners and remain so in whole or part were Bushmead Priory (the Gerys), Chicksands Priory (the Osborns) and, most famously, Woburn Abbey (the Russells), of which more below. Chicksands in particular is of significance because in its post-Dissolution remodelling it was almost certainly given the panelled room (the so-called Haynes Grange Room, now in the Victoria and Albert Museum) which shows at an early date the spreading influence of classicism learned from Serlio's publications. Toddington Manor was a magnificent courtyard house built for Sir Henry Cheyne *c.* 1570–80, but it was mostly pulled down in the early C18, and only one corner remains *in situ*, much remodelled in the mid C19. A few sad pieces of wood carving from Toddington fixed to the former White Horse Inn in Hockliffe are the evidence for what must have been the mansion's impressive interior.

There is only one major Jacobean house and it has been in ruins for well over a hundred and fifty years: Houghton House, Ampthill, of *c.* 1615–21, built for the Countess of Pembroke. It is on an H-plan with four angle turrets, and pedimented cross-windows. In two ways it was very progressive for its date. The centre of the house is two rooms deep, and the hall was entered not close to one end, as was the custom, but in its middle, as John Thorpe just at that time proposed in some of his drawings, and as was indeed done at Aston Hall near Birmingham in 1618 etc. The most remarkable aspect, though now hard to appreciate, are the centrepieces of its show fronts, which seem more advanced than the rest and yet must at the most have been built within just a few years of the first parts. They are the first reflection of the revolution in English architecture brought about by Inigo Jones. The one frontispiece, with two arched loggias one on top of the other, attached columns in three orders, and a top pediment, is reminiscent of the W front of St Paul's as redesigned by Inigo himself and in its details recalls a loggia for the queen at Byfleet, Surrey. The other, with loggias screened by three orders of columns with straight entablatures and again a top pediment, has no parallel but also presupposes a frame of mind which, at that early moment, few others can have been in. In Bedfordshire anyway nothing can be compared with these two frontispieces, and indeed no architectural events can be reported for a whole generation or more after. Nevertheless there were other houses of this period whose existence needs recording. The Russells were granted the remains of Woburn Abbey in 1547 but it only became the chief residence after the accession of Francis Russell to the Earldom in 1626. The appearance of the house he created from the claustral buildings at Woburn Abbey is known from mid-C18 surveys made before Flitcroft's recasting of the house, and a fragment of this period remains on the N front which can be attributed to *Nicholas Stone*, with a remarkable grotto within, probably designed by *Isaac de Caus*. A rusticated open loggia of the same period on the S front disappeared in the late C18 remodellings. After these the other houses are minor; they include Hillersdon Mansion, built in 1616 on the E-plan into the ruins of Elstow Nunnery. Harrold Hall, built on the site of the priory in 1608–10 by Francis Farrar, was also an E-plan house. Its staircase is now in St John House, Bedford. Bletsoe Castle, the seat of the St Johns, has a flat front with mullioned and transomed windows and originally shaped gables to the attic. There was a second mansion for the family at Melchbourne but only the general H-plan form can be discerned in the remodelling of the C18, when it succeeded Bletsoe as the principal seat.

In contrast to the houses, ELIZABETHAN AND JACOBEAN MONUMENTS make a considerable series in Bedfordshire. The St John monument †1559 at Bletsoe already has the figures kneeling towards one another across a prayer-desk, one of the favourite compositional schemes of the age. It repeats shortly after at Elstow (†1566), Great Barford (†1591) and still at Biddenham (*c.* 1621), Cockayne Hatley (†1627) and Willington (†1630). There is nothing Gothic left in any of these.

Pure Early Elizabethan at its national best is the monument at Turvey to the 1st Lord Mordaunt. He died in 1562. The monument has recumbent effigies and chest of alabaster, but the rest is clunch with an arch between pairs of Roman Doric columns, caryatids above, and a solemn top pediment all across. Both in materials and style it appears, as Jon Bayliss and Jonathan Edis have shown, to be one of a related group of monuments by a single workshop active *c.* 1560–80 in Buckinghamshire (e.g. Chicheley) and Northamptonshire. Another monument in

27 Bedfordshire possibly of this group is at Tilsworth (†1582). It is of the type, specially characteristic of the early Elizabethan decades and specially well represented in Northamptonshire (e.g. Stanford, Fotheringhay), with no effigies and indeed no figures at all. A second group of late Elizabethan monuments also appears to begin with one of the Mordaunt monuments at Turvey. That to the 2nd Lord, who died in 1571, is entirely of alabaster and is an eight-poster with three recumbent effigies on a chest whose motifs are drawn from Hieronymus Cock's *Pictores, Statuarii, Architecti, Latomi* . . . That is the most ambitious Elizabethan type but odd in that the eight posts stand on pedestals around the tomb-chest rather than rising from it, which is the more conventional design and one represented by the closely related set of alabaster monuments at Husborne Crawley (John Thompson, 'one of the auditors of the Council of the Treasury of her Royal Majesty', †1597), Marston Moretaine (Thomas Snagge, Speaker of the House of Commons and Queen's Sergeant, †1593) and Bromham (Sir Lewis Dyve †1592).

The turn of the century brings a few changes. Between 1600 and 1625 the main Elizabethan types continue and alabaster remains a preferred material. John Burgoyne †1604 at Sutton has the recumbent effigy, the two columns and strapwork and an arch over the effigy as the one innovation for the age; Sir Edmund Anderson †1605 at Eyeworth has the same elements, and so does the monument at Blunham for the daughter of the 7th Earl of Kent †1620. The 6th Earl of Kent †1614 at Flitton has just a tomb-chest with effigies and a back panel and columns but no canopy. Sir William Gostwick †1615 at Willington continues the tradition of an effigy with its head on a half-rolled-up mat. There is not much difference when we move on to the early forties with

28 the Dyer monument at Colmworth, but it has below particularly noble caryatids, and a novelty is the way in which the figures of the children turn outwards to the viewer. A great exception, and as inventive as anything of those years at court and in Westminster Abbey, is the monument at Turvey to the 3rd Lord Mordaunt, who died in 1601. This is a tomb-chest with a black-marble cloth draped over it and a white inscription plate on the black. With this we move out of the world of Queen Elizabeth I and James I, and so a temporary stop is necessary; for the monuments ought not to be taken out of the context of the churches and their other furnishings.

ELIZABETHAN AND JACOBEAN CHURCHES are of course rare. The Middle Ages had left enough. At Elstow, work of 1580 on the former nunnery church is entirely in the Perp tradition. The W tower of Blunham is largely of 1583. At Hulcote about 1590 the general tenor remains Perp, but the windows have mullion-and-transom crosses. The W tower of Knotting is of 1615, and that is all one can say about it, and at Campton as late as 1649 the N arcade and the N chapel are again Perp in intention. No doubt many churches experienced repairs and occasionally one finds this inscribed, e.g. the S transept window of 1608 at Eaton Bray, or again at Knotting a roof beam dated 1669.

It is different with the CHURCH FURNISHINGS. Here the Elizabethan and Jacobean style was quite different from the Perp, and there was no question which to use. Of dated items there are the pulpits at Sutton (1628) and Leighton Buzzard (given 1638), the screens at Odell (1637) and Campton (c. 1649) with closely set balusters, and the chancel gates at Knotting (1637), installed after cock-fighting had been staged in the chancel.

Surviving evidence of the interesting provincial developments of the COMMONWEALTH AND RESTORATION, i.e. the fifties to seventies, which we get in Huntingdonshire and Peterborough are absent. In Ampthill (behind No. 35 Church Street) there is a small piece of evidence for the post-Restoration motif in brick houses of windows with raised brick frames (cf. Tyttenhanger, Herts.). Huntingdonshire has a number of examples, Bedfordshire only this one. Drawings show that Odell Castle was given a more regular classical appearance by Sir Thomas Alston, and during the mid C17 new money made in the City enabled Henry Brandreth to buy Houghton Regis manor and build anew (but his house has been demolished) and Humphrey Monoux to do the same at Wootton after he had been raised to the baronetcy.

In Bedfordshire COUNTRY HOUSES, the period after 1660 and up to 1714 is indeed distinguished by changing names and fortune among the gentry. The major event of the 1670s is the remodelling of Wrest Park for the 11th Earl of Kent; the construction of its entirely new two-storey N front, known through Kip and Rocque's engravings, shows clearly the influence of Pratt and others in the development of post-Restoration classicism, resulting in a façade of 2–8–3–8–2 bays with short wings and a pedimented centre and a central belvedere. At about the same time it is evident from building accounts of 1682–4 that the 1st Earl of Ailesbury (†1685) was making improvements to Houghton House. Of this period is the staircase from Houghton now in the Swan Hotel at Bedford, and this has the characteristic twisted balusters and closed string of its time. Shortly afterwards the Dowager Countess of Ailesbury initiated the building of Park House, Ampthill (a.k.a. Ampthill Park), though it was not completed before her death in 1689. This is the period of mature Wren and the mason was *Robert Grumbold*, who worked with Wren in Cambridge. Two rooms of the house have excellent carved work to the doors and may be due to *Alexander Fort*, who carved the Ashburnham pew in Ampthill church in 1696. Ickwell Bury was also remodelled after 1680, for John Harvey, a lawyer of the Inner Temple. Just outside Ampthill is the Oxford Hospital (for former college servants), built in 1697, which, though otherwise entirely in the so-called Wren style – cf. e.g. Morden College in London of 1695 – still has wooden mullion-and-transom cross-windows. In this respect Aspley House, Aspley Guise, is an up-to-the-minute gentry house for an incomer with considerable wealth. It is said to have been built in 1695 and certainly for William Norcliffe, a Yorkshireman, who married into the Snagge family of Marston. It has a front of chequered brick (i.e. Flemish

Bond brickwork, in which the headers are coloured differently from the rest), a heavy modillion cornice, a pediment and a door with curly brackets. Houghton Hall, Houghton Regis, seems to have had a very similar appearance when it was erected c. 1700–10 for Alice Milard, daughter of Henry Brandreth (see above). A third house at the forefront of fashion is Eggington House, for here are the segment-headed windows and the panelled parapet which were favourite motifs under Queen Anne and indeed George I. It is dated to 1696 and believed to have been for John Reynal, a London Huguenot. The date, it must be said, is slightly uncertain and the style might lead one to believe it to belong to a date closer to 1710.

There are no church buildings to report between Campton in 1649 and the later C18, and no CHURCH FURNISHINGS for the period before 1710, except the gorgeous heraldic glass of 1664 at Northill. We can only look for parallels with the Houghton to Eggington development amongst MONUMENTS, and in that field much was in fact done. The search for new types had been initiated early. The frontal demi-figure, used chiefly for divines and academics, appears at Everton (†1624), at Houghton Conquest in 1629, at St Paul in Bedford (†1633), and still for a vicar of Meppershall who died in 1672. A relative of this type is the superb wall monument at Eyeworth †1638 with two demi-figures side by side, holding a heart, and the bust of their little girl in a circular recess below. It is attributed to *Edward Marshall*, one of the London tomb sculptors whose workshops increasingly dominate C17 monumental sculpture. Marshall was paid for the Gostwick monument †1630 at Willington, and another work attributed to him is at Leighton Buzzard (†1645), again with a demi-figure. The Wentworth Monument of †1632/3 at Toddington is another novelty, with a frontal seated figure under a baldacchino. In the 1650s and 1660s, as it happened, particularly much was done, from so rare a type as that of the Countess of Elgin at Maulden in 1656, showing her rising in her shroud out of a kind of oblong basin – a conceit favoured by the age of Donne – to cartouches without effigy but with characteristic gristly or fleshy ornament. Two other monuments at Maulden (†1663) have good portrait busts. A bust in an oval recess is at Pulloxhill (†1653), and there appears here already the open scrolly pediment; earlier still it crowns a mid-C17 wall monument at Battlesden and one at Tilsworth (†1666). Specially rich in work of these years is Flitton. The monument to the 10th Earl of Kent of 1658 still has the traditional marble tomb-chest with effigies, but also two typically Mannerist allegorical figures which appear to have been added. By Nicholas's son *John Stone* is the Osborn monument of 1655 at Campton. This has the gristly ornament, but otherwise is already quite classical. At Flitton a monument of the year 1653 has a reredos, as it were, and no figures, and this again is unhesitatingly classical. A monument, again at Flitton, of 1673 on the other hand shows Lady Jane Hart reclining. Two other monuments must be added to finish the series, one at Higham Gobion (†1684/5), because the man recorded was Professor of Arabic at

Cambridge and hence the end of the inscription is in Arabic, the other, at Sutton (†1677), because it is the first documented monument by *Grinling Gibbons* himself, better known for his wood-carved leaf, flower and fruit – such as the work from Cassiobury in Hertfordshire now at Luton Hoo – than for work in stone. The monument at Sutton has an urn and cherubs. Minor late C17 and early cartouches and tablets abound and are, with their curtains, garlands and putto heads, often very good indeed and again often London work. There are worthwhile collections in Bedford, St Paul; Elstow Abbey; and the churches at Sandy and Leighton Buzzard in particular. The sculptors to look out for are the three generations of the *Stantons*, and *William Woodman* and others listed in the index. The monument by *Thomas Green* of Camberwell at Dunstable (†1712) is a much larger piece and still stylistically pre-Georgian.

GEORGIAN BEDFORDSHIRE

The early C18 is the beginning of a change in the interest and significance of the county's buildings. From now on it can hold its own in the general story of English architecture in all areas. That said, among CHURCHES Whipsnade (1719), Shillington (1750) and Melchbourne (1779) are a meagre harvest and at Whipsnade it is only the nave which is new in any case, and at Shillington only the rebuilding of the w tower. Melchbourne is more truly of its time with arched windows and, inside, arcades of Tuscan columns and plaster coved ceilings. This may be due to the influence of Samuel Whitbread I over the rebuilding, for he seems to have had aspects of Cardington church remodelled in a similar way. The evidence there, however, was erased by C19 restoration and that of course was the fate of other church interiors where remodelling had been carried out in the C18 to equip them with galleries etc. more suited to preaching. St Mary, Luton, was given a large round-arched E window in the C18 but that did not survive *Street* in the 1860s. A triple-decker pulpit made for Everton in 1729 has been destroyed except for its sounding-board which is now at Sutton. Astwick has box pews, a screen and two-decker pulpit amazingly as late as the mid-1820s, and Milton Bryan and Farndish also retain box pews at the cusp of the Victorian age. Towards the end of the Georgian period there are a few rebuildings along very basic lines, e.g. Heath and Reach by *R. F. Nixon* of Woburn; but the best Regency work is at Southill (which was extensively repaired in brick), in the form of a commodious family pew at one end in Gothick style. It also has tablets for the Creed and Commandments, a feature of the C18 and early C19 once more widespread. That at Yelden is a very odd example, the Commandments painted onto the N wall rather than beside the altar, as was more usual.

There are just a few C18 FURNISHINGS, but some are notable, including the brass chandelier of 1728 at Milton Ernest, and the charming and very exceptional bread cupboard of 1729 in the same church (three tiers of four arched pigeon-holes and a steep pediment). But foremost among them is the black-basalt *Wedgwood* font at Cardington given in 1783, which belongs with a set given by female Whitbreads to Essendon (Herts.) and to Melchbourne.

The Earl of Harrold at Flitton of 1726 is the first of truly GEORGIAN MONUMENTS. It has the earl reclining in the way it had been done for fifty years (*see* above), but he is now in Roman dress, white on a black sarcophagus. The sculptor is one *Dowyer*, otherwise totally unknown, and it is a very unsophisticated work, trying for an effect only successfully achieved a little later. Also reclining and also in Roman dress is the Duke of Kent †1740 and his first Duchess †1728, attributed to *Rysbrack*, the finest funerary monument in the county. The attribution rests on regular payments to Rysbrack from 1727 until 1731, but it should be remembered that the Duke of Kent was rebuilding his London house at this time and there are payments *inter alia* to Peter Scheemakers too; indeed the reclining figures are markedly similar to Scheemakers' monument for the Duke of Buckingham in Westminster Abbey. The architectural parts were designed by *E. Shepherd*. Again in Roman dress and standing assertively like a Roman Emperor is Sir Samuel Ongley †1726 at Old Warden by *Peter Scheemakers* and *Laurent Delvaux*. By Scheemakers is one more monument, the first of the Whitbread monuments at Cardington. It probably dates from after 1750 and has two busts not of special merit. That leaves only two more of before 1770, and then there is another gap. They are by *Benjamin Palmer*, but only one of them is a monument (to Sir William and Dame Alice Harpur in St Paul Bedford, 1768). The other is the statue of Sir William on Harpur's little school building (now Old Town Hall) of 1767 just w of St Paul's. There are many other worthwhile church monuments of the mid to later C18, of which that to Anne Edwards at Arlesey has been attributed to *Henry Cheere, c.* 1738. The largest group of monuments associated with an individual sculptor are those by *Sir Robert Taylor* in Dunstable church which stand testament to a town dominated by a small group of related families.

MAUSOLEA are something of a central Bedfordshire speciality; the following make an interesting group over the course of a century: Maulden is the first, designed to hold the monument for the Countess of Elgin referred to above. It appears to have been the intention that busts of her husband, son and descendants should surround and face her in tribute. The mausoleum stands over a crypt and was originally connected to the church, but was detached in the C19. Then in order of date comes Flitton, again accessed from within the church and developed in the early C18 from the normal kind of chancel chapel into a cruciform-plan storehouse for the de Grey monuments from the C17 to the mid C19. The later examples are structures to cover burial vaults. Campton, to hold the Osborns of Chicksands from *c.* 1743, is small and pedimented with panels of knobbly rustication; Old

Warden, for the 1st Lord Ongley †1787, is Gothick in parts, classical in others; Blunham, for the Thorntons of Moggerhanger, 1805–6, is wholly but unelaborately Gothick. The last, after an interval, is Turvey, for the Higgins family after 1825. It is the most peculiar, with a pious inscription in place of a balustrade and what appears to be an old fireplace set into the front.

Time then to catch up the final phase of funerary monuments. The roll-call after 1770 is not long. There is a white mourning woman seated on the ground in *Thomas Banks*'s monument at Flitton (†1790); the *Bacon* monument of 1799 at Cardington to Samuel Whitbread, more moving than Bacon usually is; two or more *Bacon Juniors* at Blunham (†1805) and Odell (†1807); a *Flaxman* (†1815) at Sharnbrook; and a *Chantrey* of 1832 at Milton Bryan with a white recumbent effigy of Sir Hugh Inglis, whose son paid for much of the church. The best comes near the end with *Sir Richard Westmacott* at Millbrook, the conception of which dates from 1819, since it is really a monument to the beloved daughter of Lord and Lady Holland of Ampthill Park, with the parents attending her to each side.

Before going further, a word needs to be said about NONCONFORMIST CHAPELS, which have not been described yet. That is because although Bunyan was born at Elstow and formally established an independent chapel in a barn in Mill Street in 1672, there are no standing buildings to attest to the strength of Nonconformity until the c18, and the lion's share are much later. There are early to mid-c18 examples, all brick built, at Blunham, Stevington, Carlton and Keysoe (Brook End), of which the last two have been converted to houses. Indeed, their architectural character is very domestic, with windows on two storeys, the upper ones on front and sides lighting galleries within, and usually one or two windows in the rear behind the pulpit. Southill Chapel, although of 1805, is equally difficult to distinguish from the village cottages. Two charming examples from the early years of the c19 are in the county: the Congregational Chapel at Roxton, in *cottage orné* style, of 1808, and the barn converted at Keysoe Row for the Baptists in 1808. These also have original fittings. A rather lavishly fronted Baptist chapel at Ridgmont, dated 1811, is a good introduction to the pedimented Italianate style that dominates chapel architecture for most of the c19.

Other GEORGIAN ARCHITECTURE is more fully represented than anything we have had to summarize so far. This applies particularly to HOUSES, and here the coverage is even, from the years just before George I to the end of the dynasty. In the phase of work to complete Park House, Ampthill, *c.* 1704–7 for Lord Ashburnham, the surveyor was *John Lumley* of Northampton, who worked at Burley-on-the-Hill, Rutland, and with Francis Smith of Warwick at Cottesbrooke Hall, Northamptonshire. Here we find the top pediment, the doorway with columns set against rustication, and the open curly pediment. The hipped roof does not, however, appear to have been the original form and in the roof there was a cupola. With mention of Lumley and Smith we may as well carry on up to the typical Queen Anne style, of which Hinwick House of 1708–14 for the Orlebars is the finest representative. It is a house sometimes attributed to *Smith*, and there are the giant Corinthian pilasters, the window with moulded surrounds, the doorways with open curly pediments typical of his style. But other aspects of the house seem less sophisticated, and as Bruce Bailey has noted in his introduction to the guide to *Northamptonshire* in this series, it may be significant that sculptural pediment is signed by *John Hunt* of Northampton, who is not known to have had any association with the Smiths. Might *Lumley* have been the mason-architect here too? Some of the motifs at Hinwick House occur in the alterations to Hinwick Hall of about the same years, but it is a little more naive than the House, especially the porch tower with its clock turret. Haynes, with a thirteen-window front, is of the same type with giant angle pilasters, but about ten years later, and contains an exemplary staircase of the period with parquetry. Colworth House, near Sharnbrook, was begun in 1715 on the site of a house of the Montagus after their steward Mark Antonie acquired the estate. No architect is known but the mason was *Richard Knight*, who had worked at Hinwick with *John Sumpter* of Higham Ferrers. Again, as first built it had giant pilasters, rusticated, to its three-bay front and a pediment in the centre.

One level down from these houses are some distinguished smaller examples of *c.* 1700–25, such as the Old Rectory at Houghton Conquest; Guise House, Aspley Guise; Segenhoe Manor, Ridgmont; Henlow Grange; and The Hyde, East Hyde. The last three have or had a central block with lower wings attached, and the last two demonstrate the change from hipped roofs to houses with parapets or an attic above the eaves.

Palladianism first appeared probably *c.* 1730 with the new house built at Southill Park by the 1st Lord Torrington. It had not only lower flanking wings attached to the main block but also colonnade links to distinct pavilions with Venetian windows. It was demolished by the Whitbreads at the end of the century. But Palladianism at its grandest is in *Flitcroft*'s w front of Woburn Abbey of 1747 etc. Flitcroft also built the enormous stables, two large quadrangles. His interiors at Woburn are splendid too. He was followed first by *Chambers* and then by *Henry Holland*, who from 1787 onwards worked on the s range and furnished it in his exquisitely restrained taste. Holland also built the majestic Sculpture Gallery (as a conservatory) and meanwhile remodelled Oakley House for the duke's heir. While this was done for the 5th Duke of Bedford, Southill, Holland's most perfect ensemble, was done for Samuel Whitbread, the brewer. Here is a sociologically eminently telling fact, and just as telling in its own way is that the Duke of Bedford commissioned Holland to design an hotel, i.e. an inn, for Bedford. The Swan Hotel is indeed the noblest English hotel of the age, very severe and classical with its dressed Totternhoe masonry and pediment.

Ornamental GARDEN BUILDINGS are altogether plentiful in Bedfordshire. At Wrest is one of the greatest formal gardens in England, begun in the 1680s concurrent with the remodelling of the house and continued by the Duke of Kent in the early C18. To this second phase belongs one exceptional building: *Thomas Archer*'s Pavilion of 1726, an essay in the Borrominesque in its plan with interlocking triangles, one expressed in apsidal ends, the other in oblong ends, like chapels round a perfectly circular domed room. The details, especially the doorway, have all Archer's interesting mannerisms. The Bowling Green House in the garden at Wrest of *c.* 1720 has an interior firmly in the Kent style. In the third major phase of work there, a bath was added in 1769–70 by *Edward Stevens* and there are numerous other incidents in the gardens. There is also a remarkably original summerhouse at Old Warden in Shuttleworth Park, first noted in 1736. At Chicksands, where *Isaac Ware* was engaged in the 1740s to tidy up the priory remains into an evenly arranged series of Gothick façades, Sir George Osborn populated his grounds with several follies and inside the house built an equivalently Romantic Gothic bedchamber. At Woburn Abbey are *Holland*'s Chinese Dairy by the lake, several temples, and the thatched Thornery with tree-trunk veranda; at Southill, by another lake, a Fishing Temple with porticoes was put up. The grounds at Wrest and Southill were both worked on by *Capability Brown*, who is commemorated by a column in the park at Wrest and who did the superb grounds of Luton Hoo from 1764 onwards.

So back to the houses. The mansion at Luton Hoo for Lord Bute was by *Robert Adam*, but little of that can be recognized now, and his most ambitious plans were not even considered for execution. The large bow-window on the E side survives, but it was originally surrounded by a giant portico. One ceiling inside is in his style but the changes in the C19 and early C20 make its authenticity uncertain. The new S façade at Haynes, attributed to *James Lewis*, is the best work of the late C18 – otherwise a period of relative quiet in Bedfordshire houses – with two-storey bows and fine Neoclassical interiors, including groin-vaulted corridors. Lewis also worked at Sutton Park *c.* 1786 but that house is now mid-C19. The most important house however is Moggerhanger Park, built by *John Soane* for the Thorntons – again new arrivals in the county – and for which the final design evolved over a long period, 1790 to 1812. The chief interest lies in the façade and the rooms with apsidal ends on the first floor. At about the same time Soane remodelled Everton House for the Astells, but nothing more than service buildings survive. Turvey House dates from 1794, yet the façade is of some time later, on the strength of its freely used Grecian motifs. *Sir Robert Smirke*'s sweeping remodelling of Robert Adam's Luton Hoo *c.* 1827 etc. is in a more correct and competent Grecian. The hexastyle portico is excellent, even if not moving. Altogether the anticlassical revivals were thriving by then. Their chief representatives in Bedfordshire are *James Wyatt*'s Neo-Gothic of Chicksands Priory (1814) and the whole-hog Picturesque and orné of *Humphry & J. Adey Repton*'s Henry VII Lodge at Woburn Sands. This dates from 1810–11 and displays timber-framing with closely set vertical studs, brick-nogging, and highly ornamented

Leighton Buzzard, Market Place.
Lithograph by J. Sunman Austin, 1853

terracotta chimneys. Humphry Repton was active elsewhere in Bedfordshire, in the park at Hazells Hall, Everton, then at Moggerhanger, and was consulted at Sutton Park *c.* 1792.

The Georgian period is quite well represented in the TOWNS. Potton is predominantly C18 at its centre despite a fire in 1783. There were fires at Leighton Buzzard too and it has a strong showing of early to mid-C18 brick houses. Most display the trend specific to that area of SW Bedfordshire of blue bricks, very often glazed in the firing, combined with rubbed red bricks. They frequently have the motif of red brick lacing, which appears also on Guise House, Aspley Guise, and the rear façade of Aspley House in the same village. For this period header bond is much favoured, with reds providing only the trim (cf. e.g. the White Horse Inn at Hockliffe) or chequered brick with headers of a different colour to the stretchers. Woburn has the finest ensemble of C18 architecture in the county, including one house with a façade of Batty Langley style Gothick windows. Several specially good shopfronts are also preserved, and the same is true at Ampthill. In both places occurs a curious doorcase type with pilasters that curve forwards at the top like a shepherd's crook as a support for a flat canopy. There are examples also in Clophill, Ridgmont, and Bedford, and even in St Neots across the Huntingdonshire border; but where and when they first begin is uncertain. The Late Georgian phase is best appreciated in Bedford in the area around Bromham Road, with houses in a mixture of classical and Gothic styles, e.g. Adelaide Square.

The only early to mid-Georgian PUBLIC BUILDINGS of interest in Bedfordshire are the Chew Grammar School of 1715, a very sweet design that goes with the neighbouring almshouses at

Dunstable, and the former Grammar School at Bedford of 1767. It is a remarkably thin showing for any county. Towards the end of the century and into the next, however, the focus is on Bedford and so comes the former House of Industry of 1794–6 (by *John Wing*), the Gaol of 1801 (by *John Wing*, of double significance for the influence locally of John Howard, the penal reformer, who lived at Cardington), the ponderously Grecian Doric façade of the former Assembly Rooms (Harpur Suite) at Bedford of 1834 (by *T. G. Elger*); and finally the large former Bedford Modern School in Harpur Street by *Blore*, 1830–3. The last of these is Tudor. It will be noticed that for the later public buildings the names of architects are recorded. The Wings went through several generations. The first *John Wing Sen.*, born in 1728, came from a family of masons in North Luffenham, Rutland, but moved to Leicestershire (his father, also John, built the remarkable church of Galby in 1741). He bought a lease on the Totternhoe quarries, built Girtford Bridge, Sandy, in 1781, and died in Bedford in 1794, by which time his son, again *John Wing*, had established himself in the town and was as much an architect as a mason. He did the buildings here mentioned, but also designed the superb Town Bridge, was Holland's clerk of works at the Swan Hotel and worked with him also at Woburn and Southill, as well as at Colworth House (Sharnbrook). He continued to supply good stone and marble church monuments before he died in 1826. Finally there is his son, *James Tacy Wing*, whom we can follow into the 1840s.

VICTORIAN AND EDWARDIAN

CHURCHES form the most important subject for Victorian architecture in Bedfordshire. The Neo-Norman fashion characterizes the 1840s, as in all other counties. Examples are East Hyde by *Ferrey* of 1840–1 and St Cuthbert at Bedford by *Woodroffe* of 1844–7. But Gothic of course was the standard. However, Gothic can mean many things. The somewhat lean Commissioners' type with long lancet windows is represented in Holy Trinity, Bedford, by *Brown* of Norwich (1839–41), the first new church for the town's expanding late Georgian suburbs. *Blore* in his remodelling of the tower of the old church at Woburn in 1829 gave it a memorable Gothic flourish, a reminder of the architect's gifts as an observer of medieval detail. An amazingly early case of archaeologically knowledgeable imitation of Perp is Silsoe of 1829–31 by *Thomas Smith* of Hertford for (and undoubtedly under the influence of) Earl de Grey at Wrest. Smith reappears at Clophill in 1848–9, and again the result is convincingly medieval. Then comes the revolution of the Ecclesiologists. *G. G. Scott*'s Ridgmont of 1854–5 on the Woburn estate is High Victorian 'Middle Pointed', i.e. late C13 to early C14 in style, and handled both competently and confidently on a big scale. *William Slater* at Moggerhanger in 1859–61 is just as competent, but more personal and of an austerity inherited by him from his erstwhile partner Carpenter. *Henry Clutton* is quite a different case. His churches in Bedfordshire are amazingly original and of a breadth and unfussy, unostentatious boldness entirely his own. This applies to the large parish church of Woburn (1865–8), with its wide hall-church space and its French Early Gothic arcade columns set two-deep, and to St Michael, Aspley Heath (Woburn Sands, 1868), with its straight-headed windows, its German 'stump' tracery, and its totally original rose window. Souldrop is a much smaller work of 1860–1 but concentrates the richness with spectacular effect, almost a trial run for the set-piece of Woburn. To a lesser extent also Steppingley (1858–60) has some of his quirks. All of the aforementioned were churches for the Duke of Bedford, for whom Clutton was his preferred architect (see also schools, p. 46). Rose windows with unexpected tracery patterns also occur in *Woodyer*'s Haynes in 1850 and Northill in 1862; bar tracery is used to excellent effect in the mighty N aisle added to Clifton by *Edward Haycock* in 1862. Bedford and Luton were expanding in the mid to later C19 and both boast the cavernous churches familiar to Victorian towns. Luton in particular has two mighty High Church plantations in the working-class suburbs of High Town and New Town: St Matthew (1875–6, essentially E.E.) and St Saviour (1897–8 and 1905, but never fully completed, by *Micklethwaite & Somers Clarke* in a Late Perp manner). The equivalent in Bedford is St Martin by *Chatwin* of Birmingham, a barn of a church of 1888–9. In all three, bare brick defines the character inside and out. But the best church of this period is the Catholic church at Shefford of 1882–4 by *S. J. Nicholl*, with rich Perp fittings, which is integrated into the façades of the High Street and is part of a larger group of orphanage, presbytery etc.

RESTORATIONS are the norm for the majority of parish churches. The state of church buildings in Bedfordshire is well recorded by Thomas Fisher and George Shepherd in the early C19 and in several written surveys (which are quoted in Chris Pickford's four volumes on *Bedfordshire Churches in the Nineteenth Century*) that attest to significant decay by 1840. An early restoration of note is Aspley Guise, of 1845 by *J. T. Wing*, who also rebuilt Pulloxhill and restored Ampthill. Indeed most of the restoration work in the county was charged to local men, notably *T. J. Jackson* who undertook the extremely far-reaching restoration of Elstow in 1880–2, *James Horsford* of Bedford, *John Day*, *George Highton*, who went too far at Cardington in the 1890s, and *J. R. Brown & Son* in Luton. Names with a reputation beyond the county begin with *Scott*, already mentioned at Ridgmont; he also undertook restorations from the 1850s to the 1870s at Turvey, Clapham, Eversholt, Houghton Conquest, Marston Moretaine and the addition of the Thynne Chapel at Haynes. Turvey is his outstanding contribution here.

The only other famous church architects represented in Bedfordshire are *William Butterfield* at Biggleswade, Bromham, Flitwick,

Marston Moretaine, Millbrook and Milton Ernest, and *Street* at St Mary, Luton. His chapel at Luton Hoo is, or rather was, Byzantine and not Gothic. It was built into the house in 1875. Of the next rank, *A. W. Blomfield* is the most familiar name and with plenty of work to attach to it at Henlow, Little Barford and Wilstead. Other architects appear once only, e.g. *J. D. Sedding* at Potsgrove.

Among CHURCH FURNISHINGS, the restorations at Turvey and Haynes are accompanied by good new work for pews, stalls, pulpits etc. Not much else needs singling out over the century but the Arts and Crafts movement produced one outstanding item: the lectern at Biddenham, 1901, by *Charles Mallows*, who 56 lived in the village. It is an exquisite piece. WOODWORK is a subject of special interest in Bedfordshire, which has three churches filled by magpie-squires with woodwork picked up on the Continent, mostly in the Netherlands, and supplemented by English Tudor and Stuart and indeed Late Georgian and Early Victorian bits. The churches in question are Cockayne Hatley, where the collecting was done in the 1820s, and Old Warden and 49 Pavenham, where it was done in the late 1830s. In a minor way it is also found in the pulpit at Aspley Guise.

Victorian STAINED GLASS has been thoroughly researched in Bedfordshire and the gazetteer identifies the majority of windows and their makers; mostly it was in the hands of the principal London firms: *Clayton & Bell*, *Hardman*, *Lavers & Barraud* and *Heaton, Butler & Bayne*. They are often found together in the principal churches at Bedford and Luton. So for this introduction only a selection is needed of the best examples. Early glass is essentially pictorial and often unrelated to the tracery of the windows into which it is inserted. Emblematic of this is *Willement* at Cockayne Hatley in 1829, then the late 1840s work by *W. J. Bolton* at Tingrith and the windows by *Baillie* and *Mayer* and *O'Connor* at Aspley Guise of the 1850s, with their reverence for C13 styles. Of the next period, once a more scholarly approach was in place, the w window at Clifton by *Hardman*, 1863, is a major piece. *Morris* glass is represented by one early window at Linslade, 1865; but otherwise only one of 1901 at Marston Moretaine, reusing *Burne-Jones* designs. *C. E. Kempe* and his successor firm *Kempe & Co.* are well represented, and nowhere better than at Leighton Buzzard, where they account for almost all the windows. Sandy has a good complement of windows from the 1890s to the early years of the C20. Of the early C20 glass a fine design is the w window at Moggerhanger by *Powells*, 1909–13, and also the windows by *Carl Almquist* for *Shrigley & Hunt* at St Mary Luton, 1914. In some churches, however, the absence of stained glass is what one remembers, e.g. Colmworth.

PAINTED DECORATION is the complement to some High Victorian restorations, and the best is found at Haynes in the 1850s and 1860s. The enthusiasm for enrichment was evident originally in the chancel of St Mary Luton but alas watered down in the C20. But at Eversholt is a complete scheme of painting by the local artist *Edward Aveling Green*, begun in 1910.

CHAPELS grew in size and architectural confidence during the Victorian age. Of the Neo-Grecian phase the Union Chapel, Luton, 1837, is the outstanding representative. The first significant new chapel at Bedford was the Howard Meeting in Mill Street, but it has only its stuccoed façade of 1849 now. Much better is the Bunyan Meeting rebuilt on the site of the first church in Mill Street in a Baroque style unexpected for 1850. The customary Italianate with a big pediment over the centre goes on *ad infinitum* to the end of the century, e.g. High Town Methodist Church, Luton, of 1897 but after the mid C19 there is a diversification into varied forms of Gothic, mostly of a superficial kind. With the turn into the C20 the Free Perp style found in some Anglican churches is successfully applied to a series of Methodist and Baptist churches by *G. & R. P. Baines*. The largest example is the church at Bury Park, Luton, but a nice smaller version of their style can be seen at Shefford, and the Methodist church, Dunstable, of 1909 by *Withers & Meredith* is also very fine. The Bunyan Meeting in Bedford was given in 1876 a distinguished set of doors by *Frederick Thrupp* with scenes from Bunyan's writings. From around this date Bunyan achieved a sort of cult status beyond the Nonconformists, with a statue on St Peter's Green, Bedford, by *Boehm*, 1874; two large windows of 1883 and 1885 in the church at Elstow; and another large stained-glass window illustrating scenes from *The Pilgrim's Progress* at the Bunyan Memorial Hall, also in Elstow, in 1908.

This brings us to other Victorian MONUMENTS. Many, once 1830 is passed, settle into routine white marble tablets on a black ground for the local gentry by London makers such as *Gaffin*, *Denman* or *M. W. Johnson* or more local practitioners like *Tomson* of Cambridge. Sometimes these are very good and readers will find the best included in the gazetteer. Of the more elaborate works there is a Neo-Norman monument at St Peter de Merton, Bedford, by *Blore*, 1832. *H. Weekes* in his Whitbread monument at Cardington of 1849 is still Grecian. Classical also still the little-known *Terence Farrell* in his monument at Flitton of 1853 with the compassionately carved mourning family of the Countess de Grey, who ascends to heaven (cf. Eva Trevor at Bromham †1842). The last of these are in their sentimentality and heightened emotion more obviously Victorian. The effigy of the Earl de Grey †1859 in the same room at Flitton, by *Matthew Noble*, is a quintessential high Victorian type, but even better is Lady Anna Thynne at Haynes, by *H. H. Armstead*, 1868, in a tomb recess designed by *Scott*.

Standing slightly outside the mainstream of church monuments and more redolent of public monumental sculpture is the statue at Sandy, by *William Theed* to Captain Sir William Peel V.C. †1858, shown ready for battle. Also slightly unconventional but later is the bust of the Rev. J. W. Coventry Campion †1872 at Westoning, signed by *Adams-Acton*. It is unusual to find such domestic work in an ecclesiastical setting. Completely independent of any other strain in Victorian funerary art are the Magniac Mausoleum and the corresponding wall tablet inside the church at Sharnbrook, both designed by *Burges* in a riotous and unexpected Renaissance-cum-Baroque, the mausoleum now sadly in bad condition. It is a mad jump from there to the only other memorable church monument in the county: Caroline Jane Shuttleworth †1899 at Old Warden, signed by *C. H. Mabey*. This is in an unbridled Baroque – like a Magdalen in a Belgian church. Also worthwhile at Old Warden is Colonel Frank Shuttleworth †1913, with a portrait of the commemorated, by *W. Goscombe John*, and there are others of a similar type at Cardington (General Charles Conway Mills †1894, unsigned) and St Mary, Luton (Rev. J. O'Neill by *F. W. Pomeroy*, 1898). To complete the period, the monument to W. E. Henley's daughter at Cockayne Hatley by *Onslow Ford* exhibits the freer tendency in memorial sculpture by the early C20. More conservative but impressively lavish is the superb Dec reliquary for Sir Julius Wernher †1912 at East Hyde, perhaps by *W. H. Romaine Walker*, whose refurbishment of the Someries Chapel at St Mary Luton in the same period (as a memorial to Wernher, and shortly afterwards to his son killed in the First World War) shows the same good eye for Gothic sculpture. There is only one major piece of public sculpture in the whole county: John Howard by *Alfred Gilbert* in St Paul's Square, Bedford, 1894.

Of COUNTRY HOUSES there is astonishingly little to say for the whole period from 1840 to the First World War, and this is not the consequence of demolition in the C20, as may be found in other counties. The major older houses did not even bother making additions or updating their interiors much, so Woburn is still essentially a house of before 1800, and the same is true of Southill, though there is an under-used entrance hall tacked onto Holland's mansion. At Haynes, *Cubitt's* added one wing. Elsewhere, e.g. Melchbourne, the changes are so modest as to make little or no difference.

Only a few houses are completely new in the C19. They are heralded by the fanfare of Wrest Park. This, considering its date, 48 1834–6, is a building unique in England in its consistency of style. It is done in a French Dixhuitième throughout, externally and internally, and the interiors are very lavish indeed. The French Baroque and Rococo had in fact been revived in England by Benjamin Wyatt already occasionally in the 1820s, but never with so much conviction and panache. The architect was the *Earl de Grey* himself, and in his attention to detail he was in the vanguard of a fashion that only really asserted itself in the 1870s and again in the *belle époque* pre-1914. After Wrest, the door was wide open to historicism in all its stylistic aspects. Howbury Hall, Renhold, just outside Bedford, had to be rebuilt in 1849, but the feel is still the transition from Regency to Early Victorian, with a screen of Ionic columns inside the central entrance hall; this is perhaps the consequence of it being the first known work of *J. Horsford* of Bedford. Sutton Park was rebuilt for the Burgoynes in 1858 in a quasi-Jacobean style, by whom it is not clear. But the other new houses were all designed for incomers with money. Milton Ernest 52 Hall, 1853–8 for Benjamin Starey, whose fortune came from linen

bleaching, is the only country house by *Butterfield* and so makes up for the lack of Victorian houses elsewhere in the county. It displays all his characteristic structural polychromy and expresses in its asymmetrical façades the disposition of rooms inside, a quintessentially Victorian Gothic trope. Two others are both by *Clutton*. One is the Tudor-ish Sandy Lodge, 1869–72 for Viscount Peel, the other is the much larger and more impressive Jacobean Revival of Old Warden Park, for Joseph Shuttleworth, a Lincolnshire industrialist, 1875–8. Clutton had plenty more to do in the county for the Duke of Bedford (for which *see* below). There are some oddities, in particular Clapham Park, a mixed Gothic mansion of 1870–3 for James Howard, the Bedford industrialist. It is by *John Usher*, an eccentric local architect who was born at Blunham and designed the rectory there as well as adding a curious tower to Barford House, Great Barford, in the 1850s and some villas of individual character in Bedford itself. Another one-off was Battlesden Park, a house in a grand François Premier style by *G. H. Stokes*, Joseph Paxton's son-in-law, built for the Page-Turner family in 1860–4 but never lived in by them and demolished within a few years. But then right at the end of the period comes Luton Hoo, which received its almost total internal remodelling for Sir Julius Wernher, the South African captain of industry, at the hands of the Paris-trained and Paris- and London-based *Mewès & Davis*. They are known as the architects of the Ritz, the Carlton and the Waldorf, and that shows at once to anybody who knows or knew these hotels with what panache they could handle the materials of the French C18. Luton Hoo
58 is their *chef d'œuvre*, especially the palatial white staircase hall, but also the other large apartments with their marble-faced walls or *boiseries* and their large mirrors, carried out in co-operation with the Parisian decorator *Georges Hoentschel*.

In some ways the history of ESTATE HOUSING is a much more interesting story in C19 Bedfordshire than the houses of their landlords. The impulse to provide improved dwellings is evident even before the Victorian period and early examples are the late C18 thatched cottages for the Whitbreads at Southill, the sweet group of *c.* 1815 in Woburn Street, Ampthill, provided by the Earl of Upper Ossory, and the much more extensive and even more consciously Picturesque buildings throughout Old Warden village, erected at about the same time for the 3rd Lord Ongley.* No architects can be attached to these and in all probability their designs were at the hands of nameless estate surveyors following principles set down, for example, in the publications of Robert Lugar, J. C. Loudon and particularly P. F. Robinson, who published *Rural Architecture or a Series of Designs for Ornamental Gardens* in 1823. Much the most interesting experiments were conducted on the Bedford estate, beginning with the unusual

---

* It is worth noting here how many interesting buildings were commissioned by the Ongleys in the C18, e.g. Queen Anne's Summerhouse at Shuttleworth (Old Warden), the mausoleum at Old Warden church, the Swiss Gardens at Shuttleworth and the estate housing, and yet nothing is known about their designers.

ELEVATION OF THE FRONT.

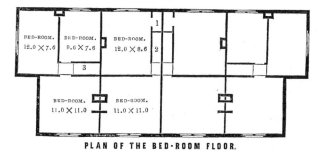

PLAN OF THE BED-ROOM FLOOR.

1. CLOSET   2. STAIRS   3. STAIRS

Bedford estate housing.
Elevation and plan, 1849

group of octagonal farmhouses (at Cople, Staploe and Willing-ton) designed *c.* 1800 by *Robert Salmon* for the 5th Duke of Bedford. Salmon had come to Woburn with Henry Holland and began with the Duke's model farm at Woburn in 1795–8 as the setting for the annual sheep-shearing shows. In new cottages and farmhouses Salmon experimented with *pisé* walls as an economi-cal form of construction, though no examples appear to survive. The concerted campaign of model housing for tenants on the Bedford estate begins with the accession of the 7th Duke in 1839. The effect is apparent within a decade in Woburn in particular but also generally in the nearby villages such as Husborne Crawley, Ridgmont, Steppingley, and across the county wherever the estate held land (cf. Thorney, Thornhaugh and Wansford in Huntingdonshire and Peterborough). They are easily identified by the 'B' monogram and date. The variations of model types for gabled double cottages or terraces with outhouses in a row behind were published in the *Royal Agricultural Journal* in 1849 and repeated for many years. There are variations in the designs in the later C19 and again *c.* 1900 when *H. Percy Adams*, or rather his chief designer *Charles Holden*, produced a series of attractive Arts and Crafts designs for the estate at Woburn, as well as the charming former Cottage Hospital (Maryland) there and servicemen's homes at Oakley and the extension to Bedford Shire Hall in 1910.

Concurrently with improvement in the living standards of their workers the Bedford estate also provided SCHOOLS. The 6th Duke of Bedford was interested in educational reform, adopting the Lancasterian (monitorial) system for the village school at Woburn, which was remodelled by *Blore c.* 1830, and providing new buildings, for example, at Oakley. But the best new designs are a little later and all by *Clutton*, who became the Duke's architect after Blore's death, at Steppingley and Husborne Crawley. At about the same time Clutton also built two farmhouses, at Stevington and Milton Bryan, as well as the school at Old Warden for the Shuttleworth estate. The Whitbreads too continued to provide model housing on their estates right up to the early C20. Southill and its hamlet, Broom, give a complete picture of the evolving style.

What then of private HOUSING of the smaller type in the towns and villages? There are some pleasant suburban developments in Bedford, e.g. some stylistically varied stucco villas in Kimbolton Road of *c.* 1840, but from the beginning of the Victorian phase the most interesting development is at Leighton Buzzard, with a terrace close to the church in an up-to-date Italianate of the Bayswater type, evidently a response to the arrival of the railway. The area along Heath Road and Plantation Road in Leighton Buzzard was a sylvan setting for individual large houses in the later C19, but is now completely swamped by infill. Here is The Knolls by *Richard Norman Shaw*, but it is minor Shaw. The Queen Anne style that he popularized at Bedford Park, West London, in the 1880s finds expression in large villas in the late C19 suburban developments at Bedford by local architects such as *John Day* and *Usher & Anthony*, but there is nothing of really first-rate quality until the very end of the century, when the influence of Shaw, William Morris and Philip Webb on a younger generation becomes apparent. At Bedford is a house, No. 56 De Parys Avenue, by *A. N. Prentice*, 1900, explicitly under Shaw's influence, with Ipswich windows and attic storey on a deep cove. The allegedly healthy air and climate of the sandy, wooded ground around Aspley Heath at Woburn Sands also produced some sanatoria and individual houses, notably Silverbirches by *Brewill & Baily* of Nottingham, 1898. Just a few years later at Biddenham, W of Bedford, are some interesting Arts and Crafts cottages designed by *Charles Mallows* of *Mallows & Grocock*. The best is his own house, Three Gables, but in the same village are two houses by *M. H. Baillie Scott*, who moved to Fenlake, SE of Bedford, in 1901 and had his office in the town. It was an ill-fated period in his life, concluding with the destruction of his home (and papers) in 1911. He left Bedfordshire for London in 1913. Little work seems to have been obtained by him during this period, so the Biddenham cottages are the only evidence. Here it should also be noted that Mallows and Baillie Scott developed a relationship with *John P. White*, owner of the *Pyghtle Works* in Bedford, who produced furniture and fittings for their houses. White started as a builder in the town in 1884 and published a catalogue of domestic furniture designed by Baillie Scott in 1901 before establishing *J. P. White & Sons* as a major supplier of joinery (producing for example the fittings for the Edward VII Galleries at the British Museum as well as Vauxhall's offices at Luton). The business continued well after the Second World War but the end came in 1960 and the works are now demolished.

New PUBLIC BUILDINGS are no less apparent in Victorian Bedfordshire than elsewhere, but C20 replacement has slightly obscured the evidence of the provision. Biggleswade Town Hall (by *J. T. Wing*) of 1844 has a fine classical front, and one can compare with it the Ionic temple front of the former Institute (or temperance hall, now Lecton House), in Lake Street, Leighton Buzzard, built in 1845 by the Bassetts, bankers in the town. Luton's town hall of 1847 was also of this familiar classical type, stuccoed with a pediment, but famously was burned to the ground by rioters in 1919. Bedford's town hall was simply adapted from the C18 Grammar School but towards the end of the century the county town required major civic buildings, which it got with the Shire Hall by *Waterhouse*, 1878–83, incorporating the assizes and subsequently the county council offices under one roof. Waterhouse incidentally had connections with a number of Quaker families, and at Leighton Buzzard he not only designed the fine Gothic bank (1865–7) for his friends the Bassetts but also a house for them (now dem.). The C20 replaced a number of other Victorian public buildings, notably libraries, of which sadly there are now no good C19 examples. Market halls tended to be upgraded for civic use, as occurs at Ampthill, Woburn, Leighton Buzzard etc. CORN EXCHANGES were a feature of market towns in Bedfordshire but became redundant with the agricultural collapse of the 1870s. Only that at Bedford survives; the buildings at Leighton Buzzard, Luton and Biggleswade having fallen to the wrecker's ball in the second half of the C20.

SCHOOLS of the period after the Education Act of 1870 make an interesting collection. Bedford takes precedence over all others, for its schools were provided by the Harpur Trust and to a high architectural standard. While Bedford School's new building of 1889–92 is of impressive scale it is of a somewhat routine Neo-Tudor character. Much more lively is *Basil Champneys'* design for the Girls' High School (1878–82, now Bedford Sixth Form College) and his addition to the Girls' Modern School (Cowper Building, now offices) in St Paul's Square, 1884–6. Of the smaller establishments, Dunstable's former Grammar School is the most impressive, designed by *E. R. Robson*, 1887–94, with the suggestion of a Tudor great hall as its schoolroom, quite unlike Robson's work for London's School Board at this time. There was no School Board at Bedford at first, but the Harpur Trust gave the design of its public elementary schools to *Henry Young*, a competent local architect, and the results are good, especially e.g. Castle Lower School. The same role was fulfilled at Luton by *J. R.*

Brown, a local architect who also undertook church work, industrial buildings etc. At Sandy and Dunstable are buildings by *Gotch & Saunders*, who had established a reputation for school design in their native Kettering (Northants). They are often identifiable by the rather funny emphasis given to the chimneys. One of the best Board Schools, however, is at Biggleswade, where for once a national competition was held, won by *Thomas Elworthy*, the Hastings architect. The village schools provided by the Bedford estate have already been mentioned; there are other good early examples, e.g. at Bromham of 1861 and Cranfield of similar date.

WORKHOUSES were a new purpose-built type after the 1834 Act. The best example in Bedfordshire is Ampthill, now successfully converted for housing, of 1835–6 by *James Clephan*, who worked for Earl de Grey at Wrest. There were others, e.g. Leighton Buzzard and Eaton Socon (now Hunts.) but those at Biggleswade and Woburn have been demolished and that at Luton much-reduced. Bedford can also boast a well-preserved prison, one part dating from the late 1840s, a period of reform in prison design. It is astonishing to come across it in the heart of the town, rubbing shoulders with the Girls' High School. Bedford's Victorian County Hospital, 1878–9 by *H. Percy Adams*, has been preserved only in part, but almost entirely complete is the gargantuan former Three Counties ASYLUM, called Fairfield Hall, at Stotfold, built in a Neo-Elizabethan style from the dazzling white bricks made at Arlesey. Such large establishments formed self-contained communities in their own right with their own church and railway branch. Conversion to apartments in the early C21 has been achieved with ease.

Some discussion of INDUSTRIAL BUILDINGS is now overdue. It goes without saying that until the C19 Bedfordshire was a primarily agricultural county and its industries were those common to rural economies. There are still good examples of WIND MILLS to be seen, notably in a complete state at Stevington or converted to dwellings as at Dean and Thurleigh. Doolittle Mill near Totternhoe combined water and wind power in a single structure. Of the more advanced type of large WATERMILLS the building at Stotfold is notable, of the traditional type with weatherboarded cladding, while the brick-built Jordans mill at Holme (Biggleswade), familiar from the cereal packets, was innovative in introducing the use of rollers instead of stones for grinding. In architectural terms the mill of 1857 at Milton Ernest by *Butterfield* is the best.

LEATHERMAKING went on at Harrold and Odell, supplying the Northamptonshire boot and shoe factories, but there is nothing by way of built evidence left for it, nor for LACEMAKING which was an active industry from the C17 to the C19. Some rural industries were developed in the C19 to serve a wider demand. The first of these were STRAW MATTING, at Pavenham on the Ouse from river reeds (see examples in the church), and the cottage industry of STRAW-PLAITING for hatmaking, which was well-established by the late C17 in Bedfordshire,

Buckinghamshire and Hertfordshire and grew as an industry once supplies of Italian plait were closed off by the Napoleonic Wars. The silica-rich soil of s Bedfordshire is credited with the superior quality of straws for plaiting. Dunstable and neighbourhood was the centre and it then became *the* industry of early to mid-C19 Luton. The peak was 1871, by which time large purposebuilt Plait Halls for display and sale had been erected in Luton and Dunstable. Machines for sewing plait for straw hats were introduced in the same decade. As plaiting itself declined as an industry, HATMAKING boomed as Luton turned from straw to machine-sewn and hand-finished felt hats. From the 1880s Luton developed numerous purpose-built hat factories and warehouses, many in a Free Renaissance style, especially in the area closest to the station on the Midland Railway to London. A good number survive, though less than at the industry's early C20 height. Like plaiting, a significant proportion of manufacturing and finishing hats was a domestic activity with workshops in the home; what is surprising is to discover the extent to which houses were built rather than simply adapted to accommodate this use (just as weavers' cottages in the textile areas began as adapted dwellings and eventually demanded a purpose-built variety). The development of the BRICK INDUSTRY has been outlined above (p. 8) and sadly there is precious little to see of it other than at Stewartby, where two enormous 'Hoffman' kilns (a type introduced in the C19 to allow the continuous manufacture of thousands of bricks a day and developed after 1870 into a version with two kilns in parallel, known as English kilns) and their four chimneys, give a small but powerful impression of how the industrial landscape of Marston Vale looked before *c.* 1980.

What really made the difference to hatmaking and brickmaking was the revolution in TRANSPORT. Bedfordshire had the Grand Junction CANAL at Leighton Buzzard from 1805, but it was the coming of the RAILWAYS that fostered major industry. The first event is the opening of the branch line from Bedford to Bletchley by the London & Birmingham Railway in 1846, with stations and halts at Woburn Sands, Aspley Guise, Ridgmont, Lidlington and Millbrook. The designs of the stations appear to have been influenced by the 7th Duke of Bedford and are consequently highly picturesque. The L&B railway also opened the line through Leighton Buzzard in 1838. The Great Northern Railway between London and Peterborough was opened in 1850 and had stations at Arlesey, Biggleswade and Sandy (as the place on the line nearest to Bedford) and branches to Luton and Dunstable by 1860, with significant effect on the industrial enterprises of both towns. The Midland Railway reached Bedford in 1859 on the route between Leicester and Hitchin, but the main line from St Pancras was only completed in 1868 with a station at Luton and Leagrave and later at Harlington and Flitwick.

The effect of the Midland and the Great Northern on brickmaking in Marston Vale and at Arlesey has been noted (*see* p. 8). The other impact was on MARKET GARDENING, which was carried on in a large way on the land around Sandy. Once the

Bedford, Britannia Works, Kempston Road.
Bird's eye view, 1860s

GNR station opened at Sandy, Captain William Peel lobbied for
a branch line to Potton, which he constructed over his own estate
and at his own expense in 1857. It was for goods only and in
particular fruit and vegetables intended for the London market.
There is still an engine shed at Potton of this period, but the
former station there dates from its incorporation into the line
from Bedford to Cambridge. The most recognizable structure
associated with market gardens are the once ubiquitous timber-
framed and weatherboarded onion sheds; a good example can be
seen at Manor Farm, Caldecote.

ENGINEERING in Bedford begins with the manufacture of
agricultural implements. The sole monument to it is the florid
gateway of 1856 for the Howards' Britannia Ironworks by *Robert
Palgrave*. It spread to Luton and CAR MAKING, in part at least
to deal with an under-employed male workforce in a town
devoted to the largely female-dominated hatmaking industry.
Vauxhall was the dominant force in this industry from 1907, the
date of its agreeable office buildings (now in other use), and still
continues. A related industry at Luton was BALL BEARINGS
produced by SKF, a Swedish firm. Their original offices remain
in Leagrave Road, a grand Beaux Arts style façade by *Percy Blow*,
the St Albans architect. Dunstable's notable industrial buildings
have all gone. A coda one might add is that two of the most
attractive industrial buildings in Bedfordshire are associated with
57 WATER SUPPLY: the beautiful water tower at Luton by *Henry T.
Hare*, 1898, and the highly characterful pumping station for the
Biggleswade Water Board by *George F. Deacon*, engineer, of 1906,
both in a free Arts and Crafts style.

BEDFORDSHIRE SINCE 1914

The years up to 1914 have been dealt with. The First World War
left a significant impression on Bedfordshire in the never-to-be-
59 forgotten monuments of the AIRSHIP HANGARS at Shortstown.
This was the initiative of the Admiralty (for these were air*ships*)

and were built up from 1917, initially for war use, but continued after 1918 to pursue the civil programme which led to the production of the R101. Such purpose-built works required homes for their workers and the military were in the vanguard in providing good-quality housing of garden suburb type, following the principles set down by Raymond Unwin and which would prove so influential after the War. Also prompted into existence by the First World War is RAF Henlow, established as a repair depot and still with some early service sheds of 1917–18. It was enlarged in the 1930s along with the general expansion which also saw establishment of airfields at Cranfield, Thurleigh etc. Both Henlow and Cranfield retain housing of the type found in the large new cottage estates of this period in England's towns and cities. The best group of model housing on this pattern is the London Brick Company's estate at Stewartby, developed from the 1920s and with a fine group of social and recreational buildings by *E. Vincent Harris*.

The R101 disaster of 1930 is commemorated by a chest tomb in the churchyard at Cardington, designed by *Albert Richardson*, who had moved to Avenue House, Ampthill, in 1919 and remained there until his death in 1964. Here a short diversion is deserved to survey his contribution to the county's architecture, for he is the one architect of national significance to have lived and worked in Bedfordshire after 1914. He began with a series of small works, not surprisingly mostly in Ampthill, including a house for a neighbour and the town's two war memorials. Then there are a number of additions to houses, all quite modest but sensitively done, at Salford, Flitwick and Harlington. In some ways his greatest testament is the works where it is almost impossible to detect his hand, and this is particularly true of his church work, much of which resulted from the efforts made by Archdeacon Parnell to attend to the essential repair of over twenty-six churches in St Albans Diocese. In some cases, e.g. Streatley, this meant returning to use a church that had been abandoned for worship altogether. At Knotting, Shelton and Millbrook, it is often hard to know what Richardson did, so brilliantly is the unrestored atmosphere preserved. However, given Richardson's connections with the county there are surprisingly few new buildings by him until after 1945, even if one includes his well-handled attempt to restore some dignity to Woburn Abbey after the catastrophic amputations by the 12th Duke. Before the First World War Richardson (in partnership with *C. Lovett Gill*)* had been architect to the Duchy of Cornwall. The experience of providing the Duchy estate with model housing etc. seems to have paid off years later in the design of council housing at Ampthill (Chiltern Close), in the late 1940s, a charmingly composed group at Old Warden, and in particular the large group of single-storey cottages at the London Brick Company's estate at Stewartby which has as its anchor a community hall in a light-hearted Regency 61

---

*The partnership of *Richardson & Gill* was not formally dissolved until 1939. In the gazetteer works credited to the partnership were published under that name.

manner. By this time the firm was *Richardson & Houfe* and it eventually became *Sir Albert Richardson, Houfe & Partners*, for the swansong of the Ampthill former Rural District Council Offices, 1961–5. It should be noted that Ampthill is in three directions around its centre surrounded by large tracts of open land that make a decisive contribution to its special character. This was Richardson's doing, through the purchase of the extensive grounds behind his own home, through lobbying for the position of his war memorial on the high ground to the sw, and finally by convincing the town to acquire Ampthill Park for its own recreation.

Richardson, as his designs make clear, was a traditionalist. So it is an irony that Bedfordshire is also a surprisingly good place to see a small number of significant representatives of the International Modern of the 1930s. Even more remarkably, most are still serving the purpose for which they were designed. First in order of date comes the work of *Berthold Lubetkin & Tecton* after 1934 at Whipsnade Zoo, where the success of the firm's designs for London Zoo secured the commission for animal shelters, tea room etc., and in the immediate hinterland also two striking villas, one for Lubetkin himself. Below the same ridge of the Downs is *Christopher Nicholson*'s Gliding Club, at Dunstable, of 1935–6, an integrated design of hangar, clubroom and originally some accommodation, in a low horizontal and appropriately streamlined envelope. The traditionalists were not immune to exploring new directions and at Bedford the effect of the new style on *Oswald P. Milne*'s Girls' Modern School (now Bedford Girls' School), 1938, is very apparent in the streamlined curves of its entrance tower and cloakroom wing. Milne trained in Edwin Lutyens' office and was by instinct happiest with C17 and C18 styles, which is much in evidence in his multiple additions to Bedford School between the wars. His contribution to the competition for a new Shire Hall at Bedford in 1939 shows him embracing the manner of Stockholm Town Hall (much disliked by Richardson, who proposed a grand palazzo). More popular forms of interwar modern styles are represented by Art Deco cinemas. There are good examples at Dunstable and Luton with interiors intact but Bedford has lost its cinema, which had an 'atmospheric' interior by Theodore Komisarjevsky. Luton is, or rather should be, the best place to admire the period 1918–39 in Bedfordshire. It was a rich town on the back of its engineering works and in George Street there are several admirable, if neglected, commercial buildings of the time to complement the Town Hall by *Bradshaw, Gass & Hope*, 1934–6; a distinguished conclusion to the interwar classical revival. Luton has also one of the best churches: *Giles Gilbert Scott*'s dark brick St Andrew, 1931–2; still Gothic but reduced to its essentials and in its setting as powerful as Albi.

Finally, the PERIOD SINCE 1939. Bedfordshire's flat terrain was well suited to the establishment of temporary airfields for the RAF and USAAAF, of which runways at least remain, and expansion of existing establishments at Henlow and Cranfield.

The propaganda war has left a memento in the form of the radio station at Milton Bryan. There was hardly any war damage in the county by enemy action, but most of the COUNTRY HOUSES were taken into military use. Chicksands Priory remains in that state. Elsewhere houses returned shopworn to their owners. The choices for some were stark: repair or abandon. At Woburn Abbey the incoming (13th) duke in 1952 was faced with a complicated inheritance, death duties and a house literally cut by a third by his predecessor. His response, to make the house and park into a huge commercial enterprise, was a novelty and set the pattern for many other great houses to follow to this day. At Luton Hoo, the Wernhers returned home and *Philip Tilden* was engaged to remodel the mansion into a house-cum-museum, a role which it continued to perform until the 1990s. Tilden was also employed before the war at Woodbury Hall, Everton, but as the army vacated the house it was nearly destroyed by a fire; it was put into its present Neo-Georgian shape by *Basil Spence* in 1952–3, a reminder of his style before Coventry. Elsewhere the St Johns quit Melchbourne and the Pyms opted for a new house in the grounds of Hazells Hall (Everton), but the house survived to be converted decades later into apartments. A new Georgian house for the Lukes replaced Odell Castle in 1962; *Richardson* had submitted designs for rebuilding before the War. Haynes was already in school use, Old Warden Park passed into educational use after the death of its heir in an aircraft crash in 1940, and Moggerhanger became a military and then civilian hospital. Only when it fell out of the latter use in 1987 was the significance of the house in *Soane*'s œuvre properly recognized and its exemplary restoration embarked upon. Wrest Park had been sold after the First World War and it too fell into institutional use, although again fortunately paving the way for its eventual restoration and opening to the public by the state. Only the Whitbreads at South-ill Park showed no sign of change.

In the towns, there was need for housing and industrial expansion and this has continued right up to the present day. At Luton the housing shortage was particularly acute, resulting in much activity immediately after 1945, e.g. prefabricated steel-framed housing in and near Burnham Road, Luton. Bedford embarked on replanning its centre in 1952 with some unfortunate results, especially s of the river, where traffic planning has led to a singularly incoherent townscape. Of this same period the new County (now Borough) Hall, 1965–70, in fact a rather impressive if challenging design by the *County Architect's Department*. The postwar churches at Luton are intriguingly varied, from the traditional, albeit quirky, contributions of *Seely & Paget* at Leagrave and *Richardson & Houfe* at St Christopher, Round Green, to the entirely ahistoric St Francis, with its remarkable mural by *Mary Adshead*. A number of postwar schools by the *County Architects' Dept.* are worthwhile, as a rule the earlier the better (e.g. Totternhoe, 1948–50).

There is a very great deal of much less interesting 1950s, 1960s and 1970s housing in the major towns, and in many villages the pressures common to the whole of the SE of England mean a historic core surrounded by acres of houses of unvaried design. A notorious example of sprawl in the rural area was Barton-le-Clay, but it did much to determine the efforts of the County Council towards a policy of CONSERVATION. The county had already shown interest in this direction as part of its contribution to the Festival of Britain, 1951, overseeing the restoration of the Moot Hall at Elstow and the windmill at Stevington but also commissioning the distinctive VILLAGE SIGNS which still survive in many places, sporting the *Abram Games* logo of the Festival and the county arms. The logo appears again on The Exhibition pub sign at Upper Shelton near Marston Moretaine. A more concerted effort to preserve historic buildings followed from the 1975 Architectural Heritage Year, and it is encouraging to see how many of the buildings noted as in a perilous condition at that time have been repaired and returned to use. One of the signal achievements of the county was to restore the Swiss Gardens at Old Warden. It has taken longer – too long in some cases – for the qualities of the buildings of the hatting industry at Luton to be recognized, and the nature of the rebuilding in the town centre in the late 1960s is to be deeply regretted. Otherwise the only significant demolition since the previous edition of this book, and one which belonged to the Space Age, is the modestly termed Antenna built by the Americans at Chicksands – nearly a quarter-mile in circumference – which was lost in the 1990s. Significant NEW BUILDINGS since 1970 are not numerous and what there is is mostly restricted to the sphere of educational buildings in the 1990s, notably on the campus for Cranfield University with the Library by *Foster & Partners*, 1989–92, two buildings at Bedford School by *Eric Parry Architects*, 2002–3 and 2005, and the Centre for Carnival Arts at Luton by *Ash Sakula Architects*, 2009.

FURTHER READING

The *Victoria County History* (VCH) has covered Bedfordshire completely in three volumes plus an index, though a long time ago (1904–14), and is not as strong on the buildings of the county as compared with Huntingdonshire. Remarkably, given the modest size of the county, no inventory was made by the Royal Commission on Historic Monuments. Accordingly, for the first edition of this volume (1968) there was rather slender material from which to produce the gazetteer descriptions. Since then the Listed buildings descriptions have become available (now the *National Heritage List for England*) and the literature on the county has expanded prodigiously. Joyce Godber's *History of Bedfordshire 1066–1888* (1969) remains the most comprehensive work. The same author, formerly the County Archivist, applied her extensive knowledge to the Bedfordshire gazetteer in *Bedford-shire and Huntingdonshire* in the *King's England* series (rev. edn

1973). Otherwise for general surveys, the best is Peter Bigmore's *The Bedfordshire and Huntingdonshire Landscape* (1979). Simon Houfe's *Bedfordshire* (1995) is a more personal and lively appreciation of the county, strongly slanted towards its buildings. From its inception in 1947 to its final issue in 1999 the *Bedfordshire Magazine* (*BM*) was a model of local history publishing, with numerous scholarly articles on its buildings among many other subjects. Since 1912 the *Bedfordshire Historical Record Society* (BHRS) has published volumes on various aspects of the county's history drawn from documents. Those relevant to its buildings are noted below. The Society has also produced its own *Bedfordshire Bibliography* (1962 with supplements 1967, 1971, 1978).

For EARLY HISTORIES, W. M. Harvey, *History and Antiquities of the Hundred of Willey* (1872–8) is very useful. The copy held by the Bedfordshire Library and Archives Service is supplemented by many excellent early nineteenth-century drawings and watercolours by Thomas Fisher. *Magna Britannia*, the topographical survey of the county by Daniel and Samuel Lysons, 1806, also remains valuable.

On ARCHAEOLOGY the *Bedfordshire Archaeological Journal* (called *Bedfordshire Archaeology* since vol. 16, 1983) has been published annually since 1962. Its index of articles is published online (*www.baalhs.org.uk*), and, while primarily concerned with archaeology, the journal has from the earliest issues devoted space to architecture, e.g. Anglo-Saxon work in the churches (vol. 6, 1970) as well as reports on excavations of medieval sites such as Elstow Abbey. There is a related series of occasional monographs detailing the results of major excavations, but for the general reader vol. 9, *Bedfordshire Archaeology: Research Agenda and Strategy* (2007), is the most useful for its summary statements on the county's archaeological record, and comprehensive bibliographies. A. Simco, *The Roman Period* (1983, in the *Survey of Bedfordshire* series) is the most readable account of that period. By the same author, with Peter McKeague, is *Bridges of Bedfordshire* (Bedfordshire Archaeology Monograph vol. 2, 1997). The *Archaeological Journal*, 139 (1982), includes the proceedings of the Royal Archaeological Institute's tour of the county and has a very useful summary introduction not only to the archaeology but also short studies of numerous sites and buildings and a useful bibliography of its own. Of most recent date E. Baker, *La Grava: The Archaeology and History of a Royal Manor and Alien Priory of Fontevrault* (2013), is the result of over a decade of excavation of Grove Priory, Leighton Buzzard, prior to quarrying on the site.

For CHURCHES there is one essential source: *Bedfordshire Churches in the Nineteenth Century*, edited by Chris Pickford (BHRS, 4 vols, 1994–2001) which draws together written accounts of the county's churches *c.* 1822–70. The title is misleading, however, for it also summarizes the architectural history of each church from medieval to the C20, with notes on furnishings and stained glass and their makers. It incorporates research on church

restorations derived from the records of the Incorporated Church
Building Society (online at *www.churchplansonline.org*). In addition, publications by Richard Marks on the medieval period are
essential. *Image and Devotion in Late Medieval England* (2004)
draws many of its examples from Bedfordshire. See also his two
articles on 'Medieval Stained Glass in Bedfordshire', in *BM*,
vol. 15 (Summer/Autumn 1976). Victorian and post-Victorian
STAINED GLASS is a subject covered comprehensively for the
county through the publication of Chris Pickford's research on
the Stained Glass Records website (*www.stainedglassrecords.org*).
Selected chapels are described in C. Stell, *Nonconformist Chapels
and Meeting-Houses in Eastern England* (2002). Also essential is
The Monumental Brasses of Bedfordshire by W. Lack, H. Martin
Stuchfield and Philip Whittemore, 1992. On the important
subject of ironwork, J. Geddes, *Medieval Decorative Ironwork in
England* (1999). For wall paintings see *BM*, vol. 12 (Winter 1970).
For sources for tomb sculptors see the Huntingdonshire and
Peterborough Further Reading (p. 405). Of special interest for
Bedfordshire, however, is J. Edis, 'Beyond Thomas Kirby: Monu-
ments of the Mordaunt Family and their Circle, 1567–1618' in
Church Monuments vol. 16 (2001), which derives from his unpub-
lished PhD thesis on *The Totternhoe School of Masons* (De Mont-
fort University, 2000).

On COUNTRY HOUSES, J. Collett-White, *Inventories of Bedfordshire Country Houses 1714–1830* (BHRS, vol. 74, 1995), gives an
excellent general introduction to the subject followed by summary
architectural histories of sixteen houses for which inventories
survive in the Bedfordshire Library and Archives. For studies of
individual houses the best source, as always, is *Country Life*. The
larger houses have been the subject of articles along with a
number of the smaller Georgian houses, which are usually found
in the Supplements published by the magazine but not recorded
in the main Cumulative Index. Albert Richardson's *Southill: A
Regency House* (1951) is still the best single account, but see also
Country Life and J. Collett-White, above. P. Pugh, *Luton Hoo*
(2012), is a sumptuously illustrated history. The Adam period of
the house is covered by E. Harris, *The Genius of Robert Adam: His
Interiors* (2001), and the Edwardian refashioning by U. Leben,
'Interiors by Georges Hoentschel', in *Salvaging the Past: Georges
Hoentschel and French Decorative Arts* (2013). On the Wernhers
more generally see R. Trevelyan, *Grand Dukes and Diamonds*
(1991). On Woburn Abbey there has been a great deal of writing.
The scholarly publications on the architectural history of the
house are mostly in articles: D. Duggan, 'Woburn Abbey: The
First Episode of a Great Country House', *Architectural History*,
No. 26 (2003), and 'Isaac de Caus, Nicholas Stone, and the
Woburn Abbey grotto', *Apollo*, August 2003; M. Draper, 'Houses
of the Russell Family', *Apollo*, June 1988, and in the same issue
an article on 'The Interior Design and Furnishings at Woburn
Abbey' by G. Beard and H. Hayward. More on the interior work
will be found in *William and John Linnell* by H. Hayward and
P. Kirkham (1980). Repton's work on the garden and park is

covered by S. Daniels, *Humphry Repton* (1999), and the design of the Temple of Liberty by John Kenworthy-Browne in *Apollo*, July 1989. On estate improvements and estate buildings see T. Batchelor, *General View of the Agriculture of* Bedfordshire (1808) and on the development of estate housing *Journal of the Royal Agricultural Society* vol. 10, 1849. For the buildings at Woburn, see J. Martin Robinson, 'Farming on a Princely Scale', in *Architectural Review*, November 1976, and for the general context the same author's *Georgian Model Farms* (1992) and S. Wade Martins, *The English Model Farm* (2002). Wrest Park has a very well-researched guidebook, but see also articles by J. Collett-White in *BM*, vols 22 and 23 (1991), for the history of the earlier house, and L. C. Halpern on 'The Duke of Kent's Garden at Wrest Park', in *The Journal of Garden History*, vol. 15, 1995. Ampthill Park is the subject of five articles by S. Houfe in *BM*, vol. 13 (1972).

The focus of study for VERNACULAR BUILDINGS has been primarily on the timber-framed buildings of the county. The best general surveys are John Bailey, *Timber Framed Buildings: A study of medieval timber buildings in Bedfordshire and adjoining counties* (1979), which covers all the relevant details and has many useful illustrations and the same author's article on 'The development of carpentry in Bedfordshire 1200–1550' (1994, reprinted in *Bedfordshire Archaeology*, 26, 2010) and T. P. Smith, 'Bedfordshire Timber-framed Buildings', covered in three articles in *BM*, vol. 17. There are several articles in the *BAJ* (see for example N. Alcock, vol. 4, 1969, on buildings in the north of the county, and N. Alcock and P. J. Woodward in vol. 11, 1976, for 'Cruck Frame Buildings of Bedfordshire', and J. Bailey in vol. 12, 1977, for the distribution of Wealden houses, as well as articles on individual houses also by J. Bailey in vols. 10, 12 and 14). On other MATERIALS, for brick and the brick industry in Bedfordshire and Peterborough, A. Cox, *Brickmaking: A History and Gazetteer* (*Survey of Bedfordshire*, 1979), and R. Hillier, *Clay That Burns: A History of the Fletton Brick Industry* (1981), are absolutely indispensable. D. J. Tilbury, *Brick and Tilemaking in Huntingdonshire*, unpublished thesis, 1985 in the Huntingdon Archives fills in the gap between the published works. Stone building is less of a subject for written studies but the *Strategic Stone Building Study* produced by English Heritage is a good clear survey. J. Curran, *The Story of the Totternhoe Quarries* (2005), is also useful, and three articles by B. West in *BM*, vol. 20, 1985, set out the geology of the county and its relevance for sources of building stone. A more recent study is *The Building Stones of Bedfordshire* by J. Eyers and the Bedfordshire and Luton RIGS Group (available online at www.bedfordshiregeologygroup.org.uk). In addition, the *Geology of Peterborough*, A. Horton et al. (HMSO, 1974). INDUSTRIAL ARCHAEOLOGY is covered in *Bedfordshire Archaeology*, Monograph vol. 9. Also useful, however, is H. Howes, *The Windmills and Watermills of Bedfordshire* (2009).

For TOWNS AND VILLAGES there is a considerable literature and Bedford Central Library holds a comprehensive collection, but only a minority give significant attention to architectural matters. The Parish Surveys written by Stephen Coleman of Bedfordshire County Council in the 1980s are particularly useful. The best publications for Bedford are by Richard Wildman (e.g. *Bedford Then and Now*, 2011); his pioneering article on John Usher, 'The Houses of Usher', in *AA Quarterly*, vol. 2, No. 1 (1970) should also be noted. For Luton, the best general history is J. Dyer, F. Stygall & J. Dony, *The Story of Luton* (1964). S. Bunker, *Strawopolis Luton Transformed 1840–1876* (BHRS, vol. 78, 1992), covers the period of greatest change in the town. T. G. Hobbs, *Luton and Neighbourhood Illustrated* (1908) is a precious record of many buildings now lost. There are a number of other general histories and the history of the hatmaking industry is now covered in K. Carmichael, D. McOmish, D. Grech, *The Hat Industry of Luton* (2013). Books on the automobile industry are as a rule more interested in models of cars than in the buildings in which they were manufactured. Andrew Underwood's publications on Ampthill are the best for that town: *Home Rule for Ampthill* (1974) and *Ampthill: A Goodly Heritage* (1976). For the region round Woburn, the Aspley Heath Historical Society's *A History of our District* (rev. ed. by W. F. Cooper, 1962) is rather out of date but the Woburn Sands & District Society's website fills a gap (*www.woburnsandsanddistrictsociety.org*). For the Arts and Crafts houses in Biddenham, M. Knight's Building Conservation Diploma Thesis (Architectural Association, 2010, unpublished) is essential reading. Some older books are still worthwhile, e.g. F. A. Fowler, *Dunstable Priory* (1962), and R. Richmond, *Leighton Buzzard and its Hamlets* (1928) and more will be found on *www.leighton-lindslade.com*, which also publishes entries from trade directories. *Kelly's Directories* remain helpful for information on Victorian churches and public buildings, as in the same way are the Official Handbooks produced for larger towns like Luton, Dunstable and Bedford in the decades after the war. Websites now play an increasingly important role in publishing local history research. The Community Archives section of *www.bedfordshire.gov.uk* is extremely valuable since it draws its content from the holdings of the Bedford and Luton Archives and Records Service.

A number of major ARCHITECTS were active in Bedfordshire and so the following monographs should be noted: D. Stroud, *Henry Holland* (1966); J. Harris, *Sir William Chambers* (1970); C. Cunningham, *Alfred Waterhouse 1830–1905* (1992); J. D. Kornwolf, *M. H. Baillie Scott and the Arts and Crafts Movement* (1972); S. Houfe, 'The Architectural Work of Sir Albert Richardson in Bedfordshire', *BM*, vol. 13, no. 100 (1972); *Sir Albert Richardson: The Professor* (1980), and S. Houfe, A. Powers and J. Wilton-Ely, *Sir Albert Richardson, 1880–1964* (1999); J. Allan, *Berthold Lubetkin: Architecture and the Tradition of Progress* (new edn, 2011); E. Karol, *Charles Holden* (2007); and P. Dean, *Sir John Soane and the Country Estate* (1999). A good summary biography of local Victorian architects is provided in the introduction to *Bedford Churches in the Nineteenth Century*, vol. 1 (1993) and *Bedfordshire*

Magazine, vol. 23 (Summer 1992). The work of the Bedfordshire County Architect's Department 1960–1977 is described in D. J. Chalk, *Architecture of the Sixties and Seventies: Meeting Local Needs in Bedfordshire* (1990), which includes a comprehensive list of works. For architects active before 1840 the chief source is of course H. M. Colvin, *A Biographical Dictionary of British Architects, 1600–1840* (4th edn, 2008).

Finally PRIMARY SOURCES. These are mostly to be found in the collections of the Bedford and Luton Archives and Record Service at Bedford. Their catalogues are partly online via *www.bedfordshire.gov.uk*. Also online now are an increasing number of C19 newspapers via the British Newspaper Archive website (*www.britishnewspaperarchive.co.uk*). This has yielded much in the way of names of architects for numerous Victorian buildings in the county.

BEDFORDSHIRE

AMPTHILL

After Woburn, the most attractive little town in Bedfordshire, not least for the quality of its setting on the s slope of the Greensand Ridge.

ST ANDREW. The church, of ironstone, like all the churches in this part of Bedfordshire, stands close to the E end of the little town and still enjoys an almost unimpeded view into the rolling country around. W tower with higher stair-turret, nave and aisles, a two-storey s porch (with fireplace inside the upper room), and a chancel. It is all Perp outside – though over-restored in 1847 by *J. T. Wing*, and in 1872–3. The N vestry, of 1847, was doubled in size by *J. P. St Aubyn* in 1877 and further remodelled when the organ chamber was added to the chancel during its restoration by *W. M. Fawcett* in 1889–91; the chancel N arches are of this date. But the four-bay nave arcades are of tall early C14 quatrefoil piers with four thin shafts in the diagonals. The arch mouldings are typically early C14 too. So is the chancel arch. The 1840s galleries were removed only in the 1940s.* The nave roof is Perp but largely remade in 1967–71 with a few original angels, heraldic shields for bosses, and a ceilure above the former rood. In the N aisle NE corner, an image niche with some original gilding, for which monies were left in 1524. The canopy is by *Victor Farrar*, *c.* 1985. – PULPIT. 1891 by *Fawcett*. Stone with ogee arch over the entrance from the former rood stair. – FONT. Also 1891, replacing a C14 font. – CREDENCE TABLE (s aisle E), made up of fragments, including the head of a lantern cross. – ROYAL ARMS. Cast-iron, supplied by *John Howard & Sons* of Bedford in 1848 but evidently from old stock for it shows the Hanoverian arms of 1816–37. – STAINED GLASS. In one N aisle window a panel of old bits. – E window (Ascension) by *Heaton, Butler & Bayne*,

---

*Until 1847 there existed a private pew in the chancel for Lord Ashburnham, designed by *Wren* with *Hawksmoor*'s assistance and made by *Alexander Fort*, the King's joiner (cf. Park House).

1891; by them too the chancel S window, 1901. – The rest are by *Christine Boyce*, best when abstract,* e.g. S aisle E of 1998. – MONUMENTS. On the w wall of the nave, brasses to William Hicchecok, a 'wolman' and merchant of the Staple of Calais, †1450 and his wife (35½-in. (90 cm) figures), to the wife of John Lodyngton †1485 (15 in. (38 cm)), and to John Bernard †1506 and his wife (17½ in. (44 cm)). In the N aisle E wall, brass to Sir Nicholas Harvey †1532 (24 in. (61 cm)), who died while attending the King at Ampthill. – Anne Urlin †1681. A stiff curtain tablet with scrolly achievement and death's head. – Very fine standing monument without any figures to Richard Nicolls †1672 at Sole Bay. The cannonball which killed him is in the steep pediment. This crowns a centre piece between the two sides of a broken pediment. Attributed to *Joshua Marshall*. The Union flag and Stars and Stripes adorning it acknowledge Nicholls's role in the capture of New Amsterdam in 1664. – 2nd Earl of Upper Ossory †1818. A slender column with an elegant pitcher – that is all. The Earl is buried at Grafton Underwood, Northants.

In the churchyard, the WAR MEMORIAL of 1921 by *Albert Richardson*, copied from the C14 White Cross at Hereford. – CHAPTER HOUSE, 1976 by *Roger Forrester*. – LYCHGATE. 1903 by *W. M. Fawcett*.

Two CHAPELS in Dunstable Street tell a story of Nonconformity. The BAPTISTS at the Union Chapel in 1870 still did the traditional, anti-churchy Italianate job, and did it poorly – yellow brick, three bays, big pediment, arched windows. They repeated it for the Sunday School in 1893. But the METHODISTS in 1884 built in the E.E. style, using purplish Luton-grey brick with red dressings, and to a much larger scale, with a tall nave and transeptal stair-towers. Even they, however, still refrained from a steeple. Their architect was *Charles Bell* of London (P. C. Edwards).

COURT HOUSE, Woburn Road. Pleasant and unmonumental, of 1961–3 by *J. C. Barker*, the County Architect, and next to this the unassertive POLICE STATION of 1958.

DRILL HALL, Woburn Road. 1937. Good Neo-Georgian by *Ivan Daughtry*.

PERAMBULATION

Ampthill is essentially a cross of streets at the former market place. At the meeting point is the MOOT HALL rebuilt by *Edward Blore* for the Duke of Bedford in 1852 and very much in the estate style: brick, diamond-pattern glazing and shaped gables. The cupola is from its predecessor and appears to have come from Park House (*see* below) as a discard during the 1760s remodelling. Also at the meeting point the OBELISK PUMP, provided by the 2nd Earl of Upper Ossory in 1784 to

*One window copies the recorded design of C15 glass in the N aisle E window depicting Sir John Cornwall and Princess Elizabeth of Lancaster.

Sir William Chambers's design. Rusticated base and originally a lamp (replaced) on top. Engraved directions and distances to four places as well.

CHURCH STREET is the best street in Ampthill and begins in the market place (s side) with the former King's Arms. Four bays, of mid-C18 painted brick and to the street a pair of bowed shopfronts, just one pair among many late C18 or early C19 examples one finds in the town. In the long yard behind, an interesting range on the w side with plaster decoration dated 1677 with crown, shields and initials W.H. Then another superior Late Georgian shopfront at No. 11 (Buckles & Bows) and, across the street, one (No. 12) with a strange variation of a local motif in which flat fluted pilasters continue up to curve outwards to support the canopy on volutes (*see* Brandreth House, below).

But the finest house is AVENUE HOUSE, where Sir Albert Richardson lived from 1919 to 1964.* It was built in 1795 for John Morris, the Ampthill brewer, and enlarged on the r. for his son in 1819–21. This work is attributed by Simon Houfe to *John Wing*, who was earlier employed on the stable wing. It was before then quite a modest red terrace house of five bays, and only the very elegant Doric porch is a later addition. The extension is also brick but of four spacious bays with an emphatic stone cornice. The rooms are small, except for the one large room in the extension, which is so lofty that the bedrooms above are set at a higher level than those of the first part. Inside, good fireplaces of both periods and in the large room especially finely detailed plaster cornices with patterns similar to the delicate mouldings at Southill (q.v.). The entrance to this room is by a passage, with austere round arches, which opens onto an elegant garden veranda, cast-iron with a tent roof. As well as faithfully preserving the Georgian atmosphere of the house, and enhancing it with his own miscellaneous collections, *Richardson* replaced the Victorian staircase with one of convincingly late C18 character. At the back is a long brick service wing and parallel with it the former stables. The great surprise, however, is the GARDEN, which is as large and informal as though the house were in the country, rambling over the rising ground behind. Below to the w was the Morris Brewery, and the grounds were even more extensive in the C18, continuing up to Bedford Street. At that time, however, they belonged to Dynevor House (*see* below); orientated on an axis with it at the end of a lime avenue is a mid-C18 SUMMERHOUSE (or Temple). It is of wood and rather heavy, with the pilasters and triglyph frieze of the doorway. The glazing bars of the rear window are skewed to receive a particular view into the NW corner of the property (separate since the early C20;

---

*The house contained his miscellaneous collections until 2013, when they were sold. Efforts to preserve the house for the nation alas came to naught, but see *Country Life*, Dec. 11, 2013 for photographs of the furnished interiors before their dispersal.

see Warren House, below).* In the grounds also a gardener's cottage adapted by Richardson as a retreat.

A few houses further on from Avenue House in CHURCH STREET are wrought-iron GATES and piers with vases. A very fine c18 piece, which may have come from Houghton or Park House,[†] but set up here when the house (No. 28), lying back, was erected in the late c18. It is of three bays, with a good doorway. On the other side of Church Street, the old COUNTY COURT, tall, brick, Italianate; 1864 by *John Taylor*, Assistant Surveyor in the Office of Works. Next, Nos. 31–35, which has to the r. end a timber-framed and jettied wing with a gable, one of the rare instances in the town where buildings with fronts earlier than the c18 can be found. The rest has been remodelled but at right angles behind No. 35 is a brick wing with raised window architraves typical of *c.* 1660. Then No. 37 (WINGFIELD CLUB), early c18, five bays and three storeys with stone quoins and a square middle projection, making the open Ionic porch on the ground floor. Nice staircase.

At the corner of the approach to the church is DYNEVOR HOUSE, dated 1725 on the E front, with the initials of Sir Simon Urlin, Recorder of the City of London and attorney to the Earls of Ailesbury. This is a seven-bay chequer-brick house of two and a half storeys with parapet. Doorway with fluted pilasters and a triglyph frieze. The first-floor and attic windows have frilly lintel bricks. Cut brick dentilled cornice. Inside, the finest staircase in Ampthill, with moulded treads and carved ends. Superb, double-height first-floor saloon with coved ceiling, created after *c.* 1750. Opposite, BRANDRETH HOUSE, probably early c19 and a neat red brick rectangle with a hipped roof behind its parapet. It has the most curious corbels to its door-hood, a motif once occurring in other doorways in this part of Bedfordshire (cf. Woburn). The flanking pilasters bend forward without any capital and curl over to be brackets for the hood. On the l. of this the FEOFFEE ALMSHOUSES with a c16 timber-framed front part and, to the l., a jettied cross-wing with dragon beam. It originally contained an open hall, but was altered after it was converted to its present use in the c17 or c18. Elaborate door to the entrance with leaf foliage in the spandrels. At the rear a single-storey L-shaped wing, purpose-built for tenements, possibly of *c.* 1816. Beyond the church, DYNEVOR COTTAGE by *Richardson & Houfe*, 1952, its symmetrical front incorporating l. an c18 outbuilding of Dynevor House and copying it to the r., with an octagonal-plan rear wing.

Back to the Moot Hall, and just before the start of DUN-STABLE STREET another door (No. 3 Church Street) with the

---

* It was suggested by Richardson that the summerhouse was acquired from Houghton House when it was dismantled in 1794, but improvements are known to have been made to the grounds here *c.* 1746.
[†] If the gates are from Park House then they may well be those made for the court of the house by *Thomas Grimes* in 1707.

same brackets as Brandreth House. Then at once the WHITE HART, early C18 front of seven bays and three storeys, brick, with later stuccoed mouldings and pilasters. Doorway with broken pediment. Its structure is earlier, timber-framed; inside, a wall painting of Prince of Wales feathers dated 1646 was uncovered in 1975. Further down, No. 119 (Earl's Restaurant) with exposed framing in the gable end with herringbone brick-nogging, and then a number of good late C17 and C18 fronts, many no doubt concealing earlier structures. Among them No. 103 has a doorway with hood on scrolly brackets. More fine doorcases to come at No. 99, with a smart late C18 pedimented surround in the middle of its three l. bays, and No. 97, of comparable date and features with excellent railings of inter-lacing double curves. Opposite, No. 86 is an Early Georgian brick GAZEBO, triangular with a pyramid roof, originally in the garden of a house now demolished. Further s, the Methodist church (*see* above). Then a long gap until on the w side, THE LIMES, formerly the Rural District Council Offices, 1961–5 by *Sir Albert Richardson, Houfe & Partners*. Quite unbelievable for their date when public buildings rarely deviated from Modern-ist principles – still symmetrical simplified Neo-Georgian, yellow brick, with clock turret. Three storeys, with plain astylar concrete porch *in antis* in the three-bay centre below a balcony, the wings either side with subtly canted fronts (cf. Richard-son's Jockey Club, Newmarket, of 1933–6). At the rear, a 1990s extension revamped as flats in 2012 by *Hinton Cook*.

Where the road becomes FLITWICK ROAD, the LIBRARY, built 1902 by *Gotch & Saunders*, as the Board Room for the Poor Law Guardians who controlled the former WORKHOUSE (now THE CEDARS), which stands behind, of 1835–6 by *James Clephan* (cf. Wrest Park). Red brick, large, of the standard cross plan with octagonal centre and three-storey pavilions at the ends of the wings. The windows are still arches. No Victorian signs yet. A little s of this, off Flitwick Road in THE AVENUE, MULBERRY HOUSE (originally Hill Crest), of *c.* 1900, designed by and for *Edwin Tutt*, the Morris Brewery's architect (*see* Bedford Street). Tall with tile-hung gable. In CHILTERN CLOSE, off Saunders Piece, E of Dunstable Road, some COUNCIL HOUSING of 1945–9 by *Richardson*. Almost all the town's postwar housing is concentrated in this area, laid out over the grounds of AMPTHILL HOUSE (dem. 1953–4), built *c.* 1830 for a member of the Morris family.

Back to the Moot Hall again and out w along WOBURN STREET. Again, the same pleasant C18 and C19 mix as Dun-stable Street but in a more minor key. The street climbs quickly uphill and then down again. On the N side a group of four pairs of picturesque *cottages ornés*, thickly thatched and of timber frames with brick infill. They are dated 1812, 1815, and 1816 and bear the Earl of Upper Ossory's badge. Their entrances were in the ends and provided one room and a scul-lery. Opposite, the plain brick former WESLEYAN SCHOOL of 1844, now a restaurant. This stands by the entrance to THE

ALAMEDA, a lime walk planted by Lord and Lady Holland of Park House in 1821–7. Its iron GATES are by *Albert Richardson*, 1921, to succeed the originals presented to Bedford School in 1897 (*see* p. 95). Brick piers with *Coade* stone urns of 1795. ¼ m. SW, at the end of the avenue on Coopers Hill, *Richardson & Gill's* town WAR MEMORIAL, 1921, a classical cenotaph with fluted pilasters at the chamfered corners, carved by *Farmer & Brindley*.

Back on the main street, now WOBURN ROAD, the police station and Court House (*see* above) on the S side, but opposite only the wooded fringe of AMPTHILL PARK, i.e. the former park of Park House (*see* below), which was acquired for public use in 1947. It was landscaped by *Capability Brown* in 1771–3, including the creation of a lake and the mix of wooded and open areas. Above the parking area on the flat top of the Greensand Ridge is KATHERINE'S CROSS, which commemorates Ampthill Castle and Katherine of Aragon, who lived there during her divorce proceedings. It was erected in 1773 by the 2nd Earl of Upper Ossory and designed by *James Essex*; the inscription is by Horace Walpole. On a stepped octagon, the foot has close and dainty tracery, the cross itself has arms whose ends are little transversely set crosses of foliage. 100 yds away, a second MEMORIAL CROSS of matching character, erected by the 11th Duke of Bedford to commemorate the fallen of the Bedfordshire Regiment who trained at his camp in the park 1914–18. ¼ m. E, along a footpath, one reaches RUSSETT'S LODGE, a very curious pavilion added to a C17 cottage as a lodge to Park House (*see* below). It is of three bays, one storey, blue brick headers, and has heavily (but smoothly) rusticated window surrounds. Doorway with bulgy Doric pilasters and a frieze. Top pediment (of brick slag) with shaped modillions and a lunette. Stone quoins.

Back again to the centre and N into BEDFORD STREET. Little to report, but a house on the E side, with a curved corner to the square, has again frilly lintels. Opposite, the former FIRE STATION of 1902 by *Edwin Tutt*, architect to the Morris Brewery, which stood opposite (dem. 1940). Further up on the W side, some typical mid-C19 BEDFORD ESTATE COTTAGES, dated 1847 and 1849. On the hill opposite, WARREN HOUSE, the earliest work by *Richardson* in the town, of 1921–2 for a Mrs Ridgeway. Stuccoed with slate roof and porch with columns.

From the road to Bedford a turn to the l. took one to Park House along a lime avenue which Capability Brown in his re-landscaping of the park left in place. Uphill, a turn to the r. leads to the ruins of Houghton House (*see* below). The present entrance to Park House is further on.

Former OXFORD HOSPITAL, W of the A507 bypass. This is an exceptionally stately almshouse, founded by John Crosse of Oxford University in 1697 for college servants. Chequer brick, five-bay centre with one-bay wooden pediment and lantern and one-bay wings. Two storeys plus dormers, hipped roof, wooden cross-windows. From the sides, the group is simply a three-bay doll's house. There was originally a small chapel in the middle below the pediment. Converted into three houses in 2010. (Near to it, LITTLE PARK FARM. Inside one room are WALL PAINTINGS, black-and-white based on a Serlio design of interlocking octagons, each compartment containing scrolls and floral motify in the central square. The top border contains antiquework and putti supporting a text panel. Andrea Kirkham.)

OAKLANDS, Maulden Road. 1883–5 by *Usher & Anthony* for George Claridge, the town's grocer. Quite conservative, brick with a shallow roof, of four bays on the main front with a cast-iron veranda. Fine small glasshouse with stepped roof on the N side.

WOODEN HOUSE, Oliver Street/Willow Way. An intriguing two-storey cube, entirely weatherboarded, with a pyramid roof and central chimney. Possibly C18. Originally it must have stood entirely isolated in the country.

The manorial history of Ampthill is complicated. The CASTLE (*see* Introduction p. 24) and park belonged to the Crown from 1524, Katherine of Aragon was sent here in 1531, but the castle was 'sore decayed' in 1552. Probably *c.* 1525–5 the house called the Great Lodge had been built for the King's steward. It was a popular hunting resort; additions were proposed in 1567 and plans were laid by the Royal Works in 1605 for a new building on a palatial scale, but in 1615 James I gave most of the park to Mary Countess of Pembroke, sister of Sir Philip Sidney. This is the land on which Houghton House stands, N of the town.

HOUGHTON HOUSE is a mysterious building, and the last word has certainly not yet been said about its date or dates and its architectural history, though James Collett-White has collated as much as is known or has been conjectured.[*] It must have been begun about 1615 for Mary Countess of Pembroke, after the grant of the park to her and may have been complete when she died, in 1621. It reverted to the King but by 1624 it was occupied by Thomas Bruce, whom Charles I made 1st Earl of Elgin (*see* Maulden). His son Robert, who became the 1st Earl of Ailesbury, leased the rest of Ampthill manor from the Crown in 1677 and died at Houghton in 1685. In the former year he spent over £4,000 on the buildings, and large quantities of bricks were being supplied in 1682. In 1738 the Duke of Bedford bought Houghton, and his son, the Marquess of Tavistock, lived there from his marriage to Elizabeth Keppel in 1764 till he was killed in a hunting accident in 1767; she died a year later. In that short time the house had been substantially redecorated and it is quite probable that the architect was *Chambers*, who was at Wrest and Woburn around this time. *Nathaniel Bayliss*, the carver who supplied chimneypieces, was

[*] *See* J. Collett-White, *Inventories of Bedfordshire Country Houses 1714–1830*, BHRS, v. 74, 1995.

also at Woburn in the 1760s. Thereafter the house was let to
the Earl of Upper Ossory, while Chambers renovated Ampthill
Park for him (*see* Park House below), but it was finally dismantled by the Duke of Bedford in 1793–4, quarried of its
materials and some fittings (including the fine 1680s staircase)
to make the Duke's new Swan Inn in Bedford (q.v.). More was
taken down in 1877; the property was sold by the Bedford
estate in 1918 and the final act was its acquisition for the public
in 1931, after a campaign by Albert Richardson, and the consolidation of its ruins by the *Ministry of Works* from 1936. It is
now in the care of English Heritage.

Houghton House is of brick with some diaper patterns, and
clunch dressings and quoins, now of course heavily weathered,
but in the inner walls there also occurs a good deal of ironstone
rubble. Basically it belongs to a normal Jacobean type. The
plan is H-shaped with two square projections in the two re-
entrant angles of the s façade. The windows are upright, mul-
lioned-and-double-transomed and pedimented at the first
floor but to the ground floor there are just brick panels over.
There are two storeys, and originally an attic, but owing to the
fall of the land to the E there is here a high basement and on
this side was also formerly an extensive service wing. The N
front has, or had, two canted bay windows in the projecting
wings. A little less normal, but far from unique, are the four
square angle turrets for staircases. They had, at least according
to drawings by Kimpton of 1788, concave-sided pyramid roofs.
There were then also plenty of shaped gables. So far there is
nothing worth special architectural comment. But the house is
two rooms deep, and has its hall in the middle of the s front,
entered in its middle and towards the room behind also by its
middle, and this abandoning of the traditional hall position
and arrangement, i.e. of the screens passage etc., would be very
early indeed for 1615 (but cf. Aston Hall, Birmingham, 1618,
and several of John Thorpe's designs). The hall had two fireplaces. Nor is this all: the s, N, and w fronts all have prominent
decorative features in their middle. The s porch tower is
unquestionably an addition, but one made possibly only a little
later. The porch is again brick but different from the purplish
colour of the rest and clearly cuts across the base course of the
s wall. It has concave corners instead of quoins and very odd
details in the doorway and the window above it. The big keystones cannot be overlooked. Those of the doorway carry a
segmental pediment, those of the window above are formed
into a depressed arch with larger keystone, also originally supporting an open segmental pediment. A late C18 drawing
clearly shows IR inscribed above this window, so it must have
been here by 1625. Above the inner doorway is a horizontally
placed oval. Much more spectacular are the centre pieces or
frontispieces of the N and w sides. To the N it is a three-bay
arcaded element with clunch Doric columns and entablature
with a triglyph frieze. One surviving metope is decorated with
a drooping flower, an emblem of the countess. There were two

Ampthill, north front of Houghton House.
Drawing by W. Kimpton, 1785

storeys of this, plus a third with an arched window and two arched niches plus a one-bay attic with volutes l. and r. and a pediment. This is highly progressive for 1615–21, and the form of the arcading has been related by Giles Worsley to sketches by *Inigo Jones* of the loggia at the Villa Thiene and the similar pedimented centrepiece, attributed to Jones, that was added for the queen to Byfleet House, Surrey, in 1617. Yet the piers of the arcading are of gauged orangey-red brick, quite different from the rest. If it is early C17 then it is about the earliest use of gauged brick in England. Or have these piers been refaced, perhaps because of the instability which has caused this frontispiece to separate from the N wall? The W frontispiece was in its original, complete form of three loggias one on top of the other, with columns carrying straight entablatures and balustrades. The two lower loggias were of five bays, the top one of three and crowned by a pediment. The ground-floor columns survive. They are stone, Doric with a frieze of triglyphs and decorated metopes whose surviving heraldry is of the Dudley and Sidney family and thus also confirms its construction before 1621 (cf. Hambleton Old Hall, Rutland, *c.* 1620). Inside there is another horizontally placed oval opening in the brickwork but here it is blocked by the pediment of a later doorcase. There are or were other horizontal ovals in the NW and SW stair-turrets and in the windows of the N front, motifs entirely acceptable for *c.* 1615–20. The decoration of the interior can only be guessed at but in the space left by the principal staircase there are niches in each wall and traces of rusticated plaster. This may have been the location of the stair now at the Swan Hotel in Bedford (q.v.).

To the E of Houghton House is a C17 six-bay HOUSE with a hipped roof. Doorway with big corbels.

PARK HOUSE. In 1661, Charles II handed the Great Park portion of the manor to John Ashburnham. This was the portion that contained the C16 Great Lodge, and was immediately leased by the Bruces of Houghton. It was the Lodge to which the widowed Countess of Ailesbury moved in 1685 from Houghton House. Extensive rebuilding of 'Great Park House' was done from 1686 for which the mason *Robert Grumbold* and a *Mr Drinkwater* were paid, but the countess died in 1689 and the property was returned to Lord Ashburnham. He finished off what was begun of the gardens around the house and a new court on the N side. *Alexander Fort*, the king's joiner and surveyor, was asked to 'send . . . back draftes of the building designed here at Ampthill House' in 1696 and fittings for the interior were being made in 1699. Hawksmoor was consulted but his plans for a new house were not proceeded with, and instead all we know is that *John Lumley* of Northampton was engaged in 1704–5 and supervised extensive remodelling up to 1707. *Capt. William Winde*, the architect of Buckingham House, certainly advised in 1706 on interior matters including proposed painting by *Laguerre* and the provision of ironwork by *Tijou*. Payment was indeed finally made to the wife of the latter in 1712 for a staircase balustrade.

35   On the N front, from where the land falls steeply away, the house is eleven bays wide and of basement and two storeys. It is of blue brick with red dressings, a characteristically early C18 mix, and has a three-bay projection with spacious doorway with unfluted Ionic columns in front of rustication and a wide open curly pediment and a coronet on the keystone. This door was installed by *Lumley* in 1707. A wide curving open staircase in two flights with wrought-iron handrail leads up to it; the style however seems too late for the ironwork supplied by Tijou. Above, a three-bay pediment with late C18 rinceau decoration and the coat of arms of the 2nd Earl and Countess of Upper Ossory, for whom the house was altered and redecorated in 1769–72 under *Chambers*, no doubt recommended by the earl's great uncle and guardian, the Duke of Bedford. The hipped roof was also added to the main block, previously the house had the cupola which adorns the Moot Hall (*see* p. 62). The garden side is similar to the N front but there is no basement. It too has a three-bay centre projecting, again of blue brick with red dressings, and a doorway with Doric pilasters and a big broken segmental pediment, supporting a griffon in the taste of Piranesi, added *c.* 1769. In the top pediment there is an allegorical medallion of the 'conquered province' copied by Chambers from the Capitoline Palace,⋆ the decoration

---

⋆I am grateful to Sir Timothy Clifford for identifying this. The drawing of this is in Chambers' Italian sketchbook at the Victoria and Albert Museum. This unusual subject might be a tribute to the loss of the Earl's friend and cousin, the Marquess of Tavistock (†1768), designed to be seen in the view from the Marquess's home, Houghton House.

in both pediments probably by *Joseph Rose*. The four bays l. and r. and the walls of the E and W fronts are red brick only and the platband is set lower than the centre. Is this the house as begun in the 1680s? The two rooms behind the E bays have indeed late C17 door surrounds with bolection mouldings very richly carved with acanthus, pilasters with fruit and foliage and overdoors of laurel, oak etc. below broken segmental pediments. Also one good veined marble fireplace. The upper rooms and the rooms W of the centre also have minor bolection-moulded panelling. In only one room on the ground floor (NE corner) is panelling and decoration of *c.* 1705, though this may not be *in situ*. The Entrance Hall has early C18 paving, a pretty carved wooden chimneypiece almost certainly by *Sefferin Alken* for Chambers, and a coved ceiling above a cornice with a dainty plaster ceiling. The same is true of the former Dining Room E of this but it has a typical Chambers plasterwork of guilloche bands in geometric frames. It also has an excellent fireplace, rosso antico with white marble bucrania and patera frieze. The best stucco is in the Drawing Room in the centre of the S front, a circular pattern of guilloche and rinceau supporting sphinx and full female figures holding looping floral garlands around a central oval of delicate foliage sprouting from urns. This is the work of *Joseph Rose*. In the same room, a good marble fireplace, probably by *Joseph Wilton*. The ceiling heights in these rooms account for the raising of the floors of bedrooms above and the blocking of the windows. The Staircase is C18 but at the top has a gallery behind arches and an oval top light carried on small pendentives that must be a refinement by Lord and Lady Holland, who inherited from the 2nd Earl in 1818. A second stair, in a corresponding position at the E end of the house, has been altered. (Part of a late C17 staircase survives in the W wing.) The placing of the stairs at the ends of the house is a little unusual, but Bruce Bailey notes it is found also *c.* 1700 at Winslow Hall, Bucks., attributed to Wren; Grumbold of course had worked with Wren at Trinity College, Cambridge, 1676–84. Below the entrance hall, a vaulted room of two by two bays with square piers in the centre and a large fireplace.

The WINGS are again of blue brick, but headers only, and contained kitchens (W) and a private suite of apartments (E). E wing remodelled by Chambers and given a broad canted bay. It contained a library and gallery on the upper floor, again with fine stucco ceilings. The links between them and the house are two-storey, the upper storey with aproned windows and pilasters probably added *c.* 1725 by Lord Fitzwilliam. On its parapet are reset stone urns.

In front of the entrance court a SCULPTURE, the so-called 'Farnese Dog', on an C18 pedestal. For the Park, *see* p. 66.

ARLESEY

An elongated village running N–S, originally in two parts but
joined up by considerable C19 and C20 development, with the
Great Northern Railway station (opened 1850, closed 1960,
reopened 1988) at Church End. It was the railway which made
it possible for the establishment of large brickworks (principally
those of Robert Beart who moved from Godmanchester) to
produce industrial quantities of the distinctive white gault bricks
to which Arlesey gave its name.

St Peter. A complicated history. It starts with the chancel
added to the preceding church. This is clunch and has lancet
windows, mostly renewed, but a small Dec E window with
reticulated tracery. At about the same time the nave received
a one-bay NE chapel which, very soon afterwards (see the
matching bases of the piers), was lengthened W by a further
bay. A length of wall and a wider span to the W arch mark this
second stage. A still longer length of wall further W marks
where the original W wall of the nave was. Only a little later
the S arcade was built. It was of five bays, the Perp tower
encroaching on the W bay. So by then a considerable W extension had been decided on, and another two bays were added
to the N aisle in the early C14, see the aisle's Dec W window.
The arcade elements are standard throughout. The S doorway
with continuous mouldings corresponds to the S arcade. Externally there is less of interest. The W tower is of 1877 by *A. W.
Blomfield*, of mixed stones; the C15 tower collapsed in 1665 and
from the early C18 there was only a wooden belfry. The N and
S aisle windows are Perp; the N aisle E window with crenellated
transom inside is especially good. The chancel arch is Perp too,
and so are the roofs of nave and aisles with angel corbels and
figures with shields. Also Perp, two niches in the N aisle, one
of them very pretty, with shafts ending in crocketed pinnacles.
The other appears to relate to the very plain tomb recess below.
There was also a Perp chantry chapel S of the chancel until
John Norton's restoration of 1855–7 when the vestry was built.
So his are the chancel S lancets. An unusual feature are the two
rectangular squints in the N aisle W wall, the r. one aligned on
the N chapel altar, the l. one on the high altar. – FONT. An
elaborate Perp piece, unfortunately much mutilated. Statuettes
against the shaft, in the East Anglian way. Bowl with scenes
from Genesis and the Crucifixion, also in the East Anglian way.
– FAMILY PEW (S aisle E end). Mid-Elizabethan, with thin
columns and a broad, bold dolphin frieze. – ROOD SCREEN.
Tall, Perp, with two-light divisions; above this a grand ORGAN
LOFT of 1908–9 by *Geoffrey T. Lucas* of Hitchin. – STAINED
GLASS. E window, 1951 by *Francis W. Skeat*. – W window by
F. R. Leach of Cambridge, 1885. – N aisle E, by *J. Powell & Sons*,
1915. – MONUMENTS. In the N aisle W bay a C14 tomb recess.
For the Perp recess, *see* above. – Anne Edwards †1733 and her

husband Vigerus †1760. He erected the good standing monument with a grey obelisk on ball feet and on it two well-done oval portrait medallions; finely carved urns l. and r. Attributed to *Henry Cheere* c. 1738, cf. Arthur Barnardiston's monument at Brightwell, Suffolk, †1737 (GF). – William Edwards †1800, by *C. Drew* of Bedford. Nicely lettered.

Former St Andrew's Mission Church, Hitchin Road, 1¼ m. s. 1900–1 by *A. H. R. Tenison*. Domestic Gothic. Now a house.

Dove Lake House, Etonbury, N of the bypass, beside a lake created from a former brick pit. A Self Build house completed in 2009 by *Graham Applin* of *Applin Design* with *Tim Drewitt*. Frank Lloyd Wright's Fallingwater is an inspiration. Four storeys, stacking up in a series of white boxes, with a liftshaft/stair-tower rising higher in the centre. Pilotis carry the living room over the lake.

ASPLEY GUISE

St Botolph. Of ironstone, externally almost entirely Victorian. The w tower e.g. is Perp, but the w window is Victorian. There is in fact a date, 1855, on the tower but much else was done before then, by *J. T. Wing*, beginning in 1844 with rebuildings of nave, chancel, N aisle, and probably the addition of the s aisle. The rose w window of the N aisle with cusped tracery is very typical of its time and the arch from tower to nave is very fanciful – not a bit archaeologically faithful – with a cusped and subcusped arch to the nave. The N arcade is partly genuine, typical octagonal C14 piers, but redone. The present chancel is a rebuilding by *C. Hodgson Fowler* in 1890–1; contemporary with it the s chapel and the vestries, and of a little later the reredos, organ etc. – FONT. Drum-shaped, with four shafts. Is it late C13? – SCREEN (N aisle). Perp. Of one-light divisions. – PULPIT. With Netherlandish C17 panels and English late C17 decoration, presumably made up in the 1840s. – STAINED GLASS. The majority by *T. Baillie & Co.* of 1849 and after, with the bright colours of early Victorian glass. s aisle w window signed by *E. Baillie* and *G. Mayer*, 1854. The Ascension, completely pictorial. The s chapel E window looks earlier still, in spite of the death date of 1852. It is by *O'Connor*. The Gothic MEMORIALS which flank it also seem 1840s: Mrs J. P. Moore †1820 to the r., and to the l. her son, the Rev. John Vaux Moore †1864. – The s chapel s window is by *Kempe*, 1894, and following firmly in his style the chancel E window of 1910 is by his pupil, *Herbert W. Bryans*. – N aisle window †1918, signed by *T. F. Curtis, Ward & Hughes*. – MONUMENTS. Defaced late C14 knight, identified as Sir William de Tyrington †c. 1400, on a tomb-chest with quatrefoils as well as gabled niches. All of clunch. – Brass to a priest, c. 1410 (18-in. (46 cm) figure). He kneels, and to his r. is St John the Baptist. It probably once belonged to a foliated cross. – Brass to a knight, with heraldic shields, probably Sir John Guise †1501 (23-in. (58 cm) figure). Both in the N aisle floor. – Norcliffe family, erected *c.* 1724. Marble wall tablet with strange broken cornice to accommodate their crest. – William Wright †1807. Large, good, tapered wall tablet, signed by *John Wing*.

The village has an unusually large number of very fine houses. First, s of the church in The Avenue, the OLD HOUSE, thought to have been built *c.* 1575 for Edmund Harding. H-plan, exposed timber frame, with brick infilling and gables to the wings with small lunettes. Fisher shows it in the early C19 with a parapet and hipped roof. Only the sash windows of that time survive, its present appearance due instead to a restoration of 1906–7 and 1911 by *W. H. Cowlishaw* for Dr George Herbert Fowler, professor of Zoology at University College, London, who established the collections of the County Record Office. The gabled three-storey porch with weatherboarded upper storeys and a hoist, redolent of mill architecture, is an imaginative recasing of a late C19 porch. At the rear – originally the main front – smaller gabled projections (l. for the stair) in the angle with the wings. In the centre a room with canted façade, added in the C19 but refaced in red brick in 1906–7. In the room over the hall, a wagon ceiling with bold early or mid-C17 strapwork, bands as broad as metal bands and with studs. In the middle a panel with Cupid. The ceiling was carefully removed and repaired in 1921 by *Herbert Read* of *Read & Macdonald*. Some plasterwork also on beams in a ground-floor room.

ASPLEY HOUSE, s of the church, facing the Bedford road. The E front is a perfect specimen of its claimed date: 1695. The front part appears to have been built for William Norcliffe, a Yorkshireman who married into the Snagge family of Marston *c.* 1690. Seven bays, two storeys of chequer brick on an ironstone basement, with a three-bay pediment. The bricks were made on site. Porch doorway with broken pediment on corbels with cherubs' heads. The garden side was 'new' in 1749, when Walter Scott, 'a merchant in the Maderas', took up residence. Also seven-bay but of blue headers and red dressings, including the mid-C18 motif of lacing. The middle bay projects and has two storeys of Venetian windows and a steep broken pediment cut into by a chimney. At the base a large arch and l. and r. two doorways with Doric pilasters and triglyph frieze. Four-bay flanks; a l. extension of 1902 by *Reginald Blomfield* was pulled down and the house repaired in 1956–61. (Good openstring staircase with two twisted balusters to the tread. The arches between it and the entrance hall have been moved to another room. In this room also a fine late C18 chimneypiece.) Stables rebuilt in the 1950s. At the back a substantial garden wall sweeping up to a brick gateway to Church Street, of a major and two minor arches.

s of the garden is GUISE HOUSE, which must date from before 1715, when the Aspley Academy was established here. Handsome E front of blue brick headers with bright red dressings. Five bays with a three-bay centre, its middle window arched under a broken pediment. The other main windows with aprons. Doorway with hood on carved brackets. C19 extensions. The pleasant centre of the village is a stone OBELISK lamp, erected *c.* 1868, later enclothed with a tiled roof.

S of this, MOORE PLACE (now an hotel) of *c.* 1786, three storeys with three Venetian windows and a Diocletian in the centre and a similar pattern at the rear. In Woburn Lane, uphill from the centre, an Arts and Crafts-style PARISH HALL of 1901–2 by *F. Selby* of London, nephew of one of the donors. Roughcast with a weatherboarded upper storey to the wing and quirky chimneys. Fireplace inside nicely detailed with Art Nouveau roundels of beaten copper. Uphill also the former NATIONAL SCHOOL, a robust Neo-Tudor design of 1847–50 by *Richard Sheppard* of Newport Pagnell, in the local sandstone. Towards Woburn Sands (q.v.) on West Hill, RADLETT HOUSE (formerly The Hoo), red-and-white Norman Shaw-style of *c.* 1890.

ASPLEY HEATH *see* WOBURN SANDS

ASTWICK

2030

A remarkably quiet and rural group, despite its closeness to the A1 Great North Road.

ST GUTHLAC. The church has a short W tower, its base of clunch, the upper parts brown cobbles. It is literally surrounded by mystery; for off it to the S is a tall blocked arch, triple-chamfered with a shaft between the chamfers below the capitals; a C15 style (VCH), that is much too big to belong to a porch. Was the tower then a crossing tower before the present nave and chancel were built? Hardly; for there is no indication of an arch to a nave W of the tower, and instead of a N transept arch there is just a small arch with timber lintel as of a doorway but with remarkably big quoin stones. Furthermore the arch to the present nave is no more than a door with continuous hollow chamfers. The tower now has a Perp window to the W. Perp nave windows of three lights, though in their present form possibly early C19, for they are shown by Fisher with more elaborate panel tracery in the heads. Perp chancel arch. In the chancel E wall two brackets, one with a head. The E window now has a brick segmental arch and timber mullions. – BENCHES. The plain buttressed type of the county. – BOX PEWS and a TWO-DECKER PULPIT and a SCREEN, all apparently of 1823–6, the latter furnishing very unexpected for the date.

OLD RECTORY, N of the church. Dated 1720. Five bays, blue brick with red dressings, pitched roof, still wooden cross-windows.

BOWMAN'S MILL, ¼ m. ESE on the Ivel. Dated 1847. Yellow
brick, with recessed arches on the façade. It used both water
and steam power. The cast-iron overshot wheel survives.
(Octagonal cast-iron hurst frame, classically detailed.)

BARFORD HOUSE *see* GREAT BARFORD

BARTON-LE-CLAY

0030

A sprawling village E and w of the Bedford Road, mostly of the
1960s, but the church, off to the SE corner, still has its own separate character.

ST NICHOLAS. Impressive Perp w tower with battlements and
slightly higher stair-turret. Tierceron-star vault inside and in
the tower a fireplace. This suggests a dwelling. There is an outer
doorway higher up the tower but this is a bell-hole. Externally
a nice variety of materials, the tower itself of knapped flint and
stone chequer. Inside, however, the church has E.E. arcades,
more elaborate on the s side, standard on the N side. The sw
and SE responds are of three detached shafts with shaft-rings
and have capitals with close stiff-leaf. The piers are circular, as
are those of the N arcade, with plain, bold moulded capitals.
Double-chamfered arches, the first on the s side with broach
stops above the capital. So the s arcade must have begun as
three bays, the four-bay N arcade following soon after along
with the added w bay of the s aisle. The N aisle w window is
a lancet. Chancel arch of the same time, and see also the late
C13 SEDILIA, PISCINA and EASTER SEPULCHRE, although
the chancel itself was substantially rebuilt in 1879 by *W. O.
Milne* for the Rev. Arthur Blomfield, cousin of Milne's former
master, A. W. Blomfield. A N vestry was dem. at this date. High
Perp arch to the tower. Good low-pitched roof with moulded
beams, carved bosses, angels with Instruments of the Passion,
and the Apostles supporting the beams with eagles at their feet
and stone corbels with C14 faces. Over the former rood a
ceilure with cusped tracery in panels. – FONT. Originally
Norman, see the rope moulding, but re-carved Perp, octagonal
with quatrefoils, and further restored in the C19. – BENCHES.
With buttresses and linenfold. – TILES. C13? Relaid in the
chancel but with some complete patterns of flowers in linked
circles and others with grapevines in quatrefoils. Red and
yellow. – PAINTING. A panel, presumably from a triptych, with
on one side St Nicholas, 4 ft 8 in. (1.4 metres), early C16 and
very good. On the reverse, three figures, with bow and cross-
bow (possibly a martyrdom of St Stephen). Is it South German?
– STAINED GLASS. Many small bits in the aisle windows, some
of high quality, e.g. the Adoration in the N aisle E window. –
Chancel E by *Mayer & Co.* 1888. Two by *Clayton & Bell*, in the

war memorial (s) chapel, 1919 and 1921. Good w tower window by *Edward Smith* of Spalding, 1904. – BRASSES. Richard Brey †1396, priest; demi-figure 12 in. (30.5 cm) long. – Bearded civilian, 13 in. (33 cm), *c.* 1400.

CHURCH HALL, SE. 1995 by *Michael Dales* of the *John Manning Partnership*. Large and well-designed in brick with flint frieze below the eaves of a big tile roof. Gabled porch with an arch of tile creasing. Inside, a splendid LAMP, also 1995 but with panels of *c.* 1800 heraldic stained glass.

OLD RECTORY, s of the church. Probably Elizabethan but with a petite Victorian porch with half-timbered upper storey. Three gables on the garden side and an C18 doorcase.

BASMEAD *see* STAPLOE

BATTLESDEN   9020

ST PETER. Small and much repaired, as the ragbag of materials shows. Restored in 1897–8 by *J. T. Lawrence*, who also added the brick crenellation to the aisleless nave.* In the w tower's s wall, late C13 window with bar tracery, proving that the tower was put into the existing nave later. In the nave N wall a big three-light early C16 window. Dec chancel arch. Two image brackets l. and r. of the E window. The putti on them may be re-cut Perp angels. – FONT. Norman, drum-shaped, with a few sparse decorative motifs. – STAINED GLASS. E window, 1875 by *Lavers & Westlake*; *Lavers, Barraud & Westlake* sign the N window of 1879. – MONUMENTS. William Duncombe †1603, bearing his arms and those of his wife Ellen Saunders. Alabaster. It must have been erected after the death of their son, Sir Edward Duncombe †1638, see the open scrolly pediment and cherubs, and probably erected by Sir Sanders Duncombe, who introduced the sedan chair to England. – Elizabeth Duncombe †1688 and John, her husband, †1687. Inspired at several removes from Italian later C16 Mannerism. Big cartouche with fleshy, gristly surround. Attributed to *John Bushnell*.

The church stands in the former grounds of BATTLESDEN PARK, a house of 1860–4, built by the Page-Turner family in a François Premier style but never occupied by them. *Joseph Paxton*, who had been a garden boy at Battlesden, advised his son-in-law *G. H. Stokes* on the rebuilding and remodelled the grounds for the son of his erstwhile employer. The mansion was demolished by the Duke of Bedford *c.* 1886, and the present house is the Italianate former STABLES. The GARDEN

---

*The church was closed 1928–49; even in the mid 1960s Pevsner was moved to ask 'But how can it be maintained now, with so small a congregation?'

HOUSE remains s of the church. Originally a little more picturesque, for it had a veranda to its gabled and half-timbered s front. The l. wing has a half-hipped roof over a gallery, Swiss Cottage style. The r. wing and back range added. On the London Road and Watling Street, LODGES and gates survive.

BEDFORD

INTRODUCTION

Bedford was a trading place already in the C10 and two of its churches show Saxon traces. Indeed the main N–S road crossing the Great Ouse was very probably established by the C9 (suggested by discovery of a house on St John's Street). The town lies on both sides of the river and the area to its s was enclosed c. 910 by the so-called King's Ditch, of which parts remain visible near Rope Walk and Cardington Road and running under Bedford Girls' School. Houses have been discovered through excavation. Shortly after the Conquest a castle (see below) was built. In the Middle Ages Bedford had two Augustinian priories. NEWNHAM PRIORY, founded c. 1165 by Simon de Beauchamp, formed out of the Canons of St Paul's, the principal parish church. The establishment of the priory on a new site E of the centre was at least in part because the Beauchamps wished to develop the centre of Bedford as a market (its earliest charter is confirmed c. 1166). Two lengths of wall, N of the Ouse, one in Barker's Lane and the other in Priory Marina, belonged either to Newnham Priory or a C16 successor house and the extent of its buildings is known from excavation. CAULDWELL PRIORY (founded c. 1154) also stood on the edge of the town in Kempston Road s of the Ouse. The site was later occupied by the Britannia Ironworks and the remains of the priory entirely lost to view. There was also a GREYFRIARS house in Priory Street (founded by 1238). Of this again there are no remains, nor of medieval secular buildings, but the late Saxon planned street pattern is still quite clear in the centre of the town, and much as it is depicted in John Speed's map of 1610. In the C18, largely thanks to the Ouse which was navigable then, Bedford was prosperous in a moderate way. Defoe c. 1725 called it a 'large, populous, well-built and thriving town', Torrington in 1793 'vile, unimproved and without trade' – but that may tell more of the characters of the writers than of the condition of Bedford. It was also by then a centre for Nonconformity. An Improvement Act in 1803 cleared some of the medieval buildings. Suburban expansion in the C19 was in no small part due to the growing reputation of the schools managed by the Trustees of the Bedford Charity (the Harpur Trust) established by Sir William Harpur in the C16: one phase of new housing is apparent *c.* 1820–30 and a second, much more extensive, phase around 1880–90 when the town became very popular with returning Anglo-Indian officers and administrators. By now Bedford's inhabitants could also take advantage of the railway to and from London. The growth of the architectural profession in the town over the course of the C19 is reflected in the names to be attached to the new churches, public buildings and houses of the town, notably *J. T. Wing*, *John Usher* (later on in partnership with *A. E. Anthony*), *James Horsford*, *T. J. Jackson* and *G. P. Allen* who also account for many of the new buildings in the wider county during this period. Industry began to expand in the W of the town in the mid C19, first with the Britannia Ironworks and later with W. H. Allen's Queen's Engineering works, adding suburbs of working-class houses close to their premises. By 1911 the population was about 40,000, four times that of the early C19 town, with a large Corporation housing estate of 1,000 houses, completed 1938, S of the river at Fenlake. But the rate of growth accelerated greatly after the Second World War and towards Goldington. A report by *Max Lock & Partners* in 1952 (*Bedford: By The River*) envisaged much redevelopment in the lightweight Festival of Britain manner, but little was acted upon other than clearance in the W of the centre and redevelopment of a new commercial district and residential flats, with questionable results. New outer suburbs of housing emerged to the N at Brickhill and Putnoe and surrounding Goldington (q.v.), bringing the population to some 70,000.

RELIGIOUS BUILDINGS

The medieval churches are described first:

ST PAUL, St Paul's Square. The major church of Bedford. It is a *p. 80* large town church, and over-restored, but, inside, an exemplary Anglo-Catholic ensemble. The total length is 167 ft (50.9 metres). Externally there is little of genuine untampered-with detail. The church has a crossing tower with a recessed spire. Three sets of lucarnes in alternating directions. The earliest feature of the exterior is the E.E. w doorway, which agrees with the date of new construction after the destruction of Bedford Castle (*see* below) in 1224 (the construction of the castle having led to the demolition of the previous church here). Heavily restored in 1936, with image niches and a canopy of ribwork. The rest all appears C14 and C15, e.g. earliest the Dec chancel windows; reticulated (s) and intersecting with cusped

Bedford, St Paul.
Lithograph by J. Sunman Austin, 1850

units (N). Aisles and clerestory are embattled. Two-storey S
porch with quatrefoil base-frieze and foliage spandrels. Statue
niches on the upper floor (the statues inside, see below). Four-
bay S chapel, called newly built in 1416 for the Guilds of the
Trinity and Corpus Christi; see e.g. the ANGLE PISCINA
inside. It later became the Archdeacon's Court. One-storey NE
vestry. The one-storey N porch is Perp but entirely rebuilt when
the N aisle was added in 1884 by *G. G. Scott Jun*. The consequence of this, and the most interesting feature of the interior,
is that it is a 'hall', i.e. the five-bay aisles are of the same height
as the nave. For that reason they have clerestory windows. The
aisles are about as wide as the nave, adding to the sense of
spaciousness. Good C15 roofs in nave and S aisle. The interior
is almost as totally redone as the exterior. Only the S aisle
arcade is partly original. Its date must be early C14. Quatrefoil
piers, double-chamfered arches; the design followed faithfully
by Scott for the N arcade. The crossing arches belong to about
the same years as the S arcade, but are again a rebuilding of
1865–8 that included the N transept. This was done by *R. Palgrave*, with advice from *Street*. The chancel chapel arcades are
entirely of 1878–80, again by *Scott Jun.*, whose comprehensive

refurbishment of the E end also provided the chancel roof, clerestory, E window, new vestry and organ chamber. The present vestry is of 1898–9 by *Bodley*; the annex to the N transept of 1924. – FONT. Dec. Base with a little ballflower and fleuron decoration. The top Victorian, the pinnacle cover C20 by *J. P. White* (*Pyghtle Works*). – PULPIT. Made of clunch. This is really part of the early C16 canopy of the former reredos, very ornately done, with the miniature rib-vault inside the top part of a niche. In its present form it is a very intelligent adaptation of 1680. Restored to this position in 1929, the date of the good iron stair. The PULPIT of 1871 by *John Day* is now in the S aisle. – SCREENS. S chapel screen, Perp with one-light division. Formerly the chancel screen. The rood screen is by *Bodley*, 1905, very delicate cusped tracery and fine scrolly wrought-iron gates. Painted by *F. C. Eden*, 1938; the painting of the chancel roof of about the same time. – STALLS. In the chancel. Of *Bodley*'s reordering, 1898–9, but incorporating medieval carved arms and much defaced MISERICORDS of *c.* 1400. One shows a barbican-like abbreviation of a castle with a crossbowman and a figure running away, probably representing the siege of Bedford Castle in 1224. S stall screen altered 1939 for the ORGAN LOFT, which has its stair in an open frame. Probably by *Albert Richardson* (cf. Eaton Socon, Hunts.). – MAYOR'S STALL, S transept. 1872 by *J. T. Wing*. – WEST GALLERY, 1982 by *Victor Farrar*, the DOORS below engraved by *David Peace* and *Meinrad Carighead*. – HANGING LIGHTS. 1920s, by *W. A. Forsyth*. – SCULPTURE. S porch. C15 (?) statues of St Peter and St John. From the niches on the porch.

STAINED GLASS. A large collection but the best individual window is in the N aisle by *Shrigley & Hunt*, with typical Walter Crane-ish foliage and figures influenced by the Pre-Raphaelites. Date recorded: 1885. Otherwise, works by *Clayton & Bell* (chancel S, 1889, and two in the S aisle, 1872), *Hardman* (the good E windows of chancel, 1883, and the S chapel, 1889), *Burlison & Grylls* (three in the S chapel, one of 1902 designed by *Bodley*, but also the N transept N (Beds Regiment Memorial), 1910, and mighty Te Deum W window, 1930). – In the N aisle also one window by *A. E. Tombleson* for *C. E. Kempe*, 1892, and in the S chapel a creepy Arts and Crafts one by *Paul Woodroffe*, 1908. – Harpur Trust window, N aisle, 1976 by *Brian Thomas*. MONUMENTS. S of the altar, the indent of a brass, traditionally to Simon de Beauchamp †1208. It is said that if the brass were preserved, it would be by far the earliest in England. – In the S chapel, brass to Sir William Harpur, Lord Mayor of London and founder of the Grammar School, †1573, and his second wife, Dame Margaret. He is in armour, but also wears his alderman's gown. 20-in. (51 cm) figures. Near to it, again for Sir William and for his first wife, Dame Alice, a magnificent hanging monument signed by *Benjamin Palmer*, 1768, paid for by the trustees of the Bedford Charity. Obelisk with an oval medallion with the Harpurs' portraits in profile. Sarcophagus below on Rococo feet and big square chest. – In the

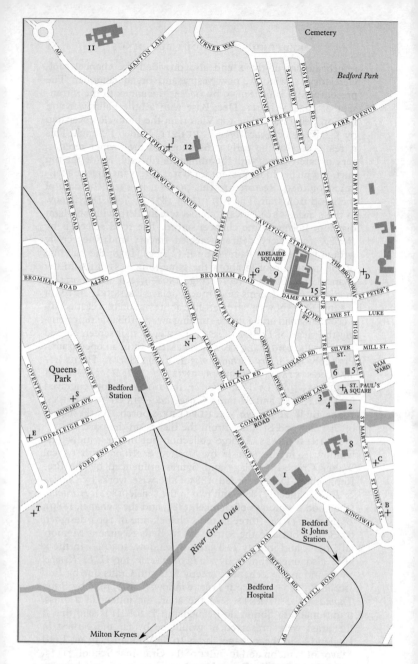

A	St Paul	L	Holy Child & St Joseph (R.C.)
B	St John the Baptist	M	Sacred Heart of Jesus and St Cuthbert
C	St Mary	N	St Francesca Cabrini (R.C.)
D	St Peter de Merton	O	Bunyan Meeting
E	All Saints	P	Moravian Chapel (former)
F	Christ Church	Q	Providence Baptist Church
G	Holy Trinity (former)	R	Priory Methodist Church
H	St Andrew	S	Moravian Church
J	St Martin	T	Guru Nanak Gurdwara
K	St Michael & All Angels		

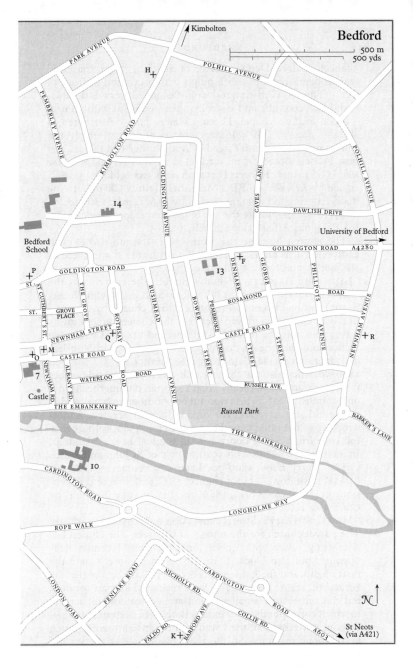

Bedford

Kimbolton

500 m
500 yds

PARK AVENUE

POLHILL AVENUE

H

PEMBERLEY AVENUE

KIMBOLTON ROAD

CAVES LANE

POLHILL AVENUE

GOLDINGTON AEVNUE

DAWLISH DRIVE

14

University of Bedford

Bedford School

GOLDINGTON ROAD A4280

P

GOLDINGTON ROAD

DENMARK ST.

F

GEORGE

ST. CUTHBERT'S ST.

13

PHILLPOTS ROAD

BUSHMEAD

ROSAMOND

NEWNHAM AVENUE

THE GROVE

BOWER STREET

PEMBROKE STREET

CASTLE ROAD

STREET

STREET

GROVE PLACE

ROTHSAY

NEWNHAM STREET

Q

R

M

CASTLE ROAD

O

RUSSELL AVE.

ALBANY RD.

WATERLOO ROAD

AVENUE

ROAD

7

Castle

NEWNHAM RD.

THE EMBANKMENT

Russell Park

BARKER'S LANE

THE EMBANKMENT

10

CARDINGTON ROAD

LONGHOLME WAY

ROPE WALK

LONDON ROAD

FENLAKE ROAD

NICHOLLS RD.

CARDINGTON ROAD

FALDO RD.

K

BARFORD AVE.

COLLIE RD.

ROAD A603

St Neots (via A421)

N

chancel, Andrew Dennys, rector of St John, †1633; the usual frontal demi-figure but in a pulpit with a cushion in front of him. – Thomas Christie †1697; old-fashioned, very dark tablet with black columns and a scrolly open pediment with an urn. – Again in the s chapel, Thomas Hawes †1689. Attributed to *William Stanton* (GF). Ionic columns and very crisply cut achievement and death's head. – Many other C18 tablets, the best Francis Brace †1713, attributed to *William Woodman the elder* (GF), and Robert Battisson and his widow (†1788), signed by *John Wing*. – BBC Memorial (Trinity Chapel). In the floor, lettering in radiating circles, by *Lida Cardozo Kindersley*, 2009, to commemorate the use of the chapel for broadcasts by the Religious Affairs Department, 1941–5.

The church has fine C18 iron RAILINGS and GATES with gadrooned urns on the gatepiers. The ironwork is attributed to *William Stewardson* of Bedford, *c.* 1730.

ST JOHN THE BAPTIST, St John's Street. The church was the chapel of the Hospital of St John (for which *see* St John House, p. 102) but had become a separate parish church by the early C14. The chancel is indeed Dec, see the chancel arch with its wave moulding, the renewed SEDILIA and PISCINA with ogee arches, and the priest's doorway. The E lancets, with stiff-leaf and dogtooth inside, date from a restoration by *J. T. Wing* in 1869–70, when also the chancel arch was rebuilt, its side arches were made and the typically High Victorian hammerbeam roof on naturalistic leaf corbels was put on. Another arch was added to the aisleless nave and the organ chamber erected. Lancet windows of the same date. Perp w tower, *c.* 1500, with quatrefoil base frieze and a doorway with big leaf in the spandrels. In its front are niches with SCULPTURE of St John and Agnus Dei by *Harry Hems*, 1869–70. Later C19 vestries. – STAINED GLASS. E window, *c.* 1870; chancel s (Crucifixion and Ascension) by *J. Powell & Sons*, 1886; another of 1913 (St John) by *Clayton & Bell*.

ST MARY, St Mary's Street. Now Albion Archaeology offices. The parish church for the town s of the river. The church has a crossing tower with quoins and big twin Norman bell-openings but also blocked late Saxon ones above, where the belfry lights and the battlements are Perp. Late Saxon also the s transept, whose E wall has a large blocked Norman window, but this cuts into a smaller round-arched window higher up, to which corresponds a w window. Both have deep single splays without any rebate. In the s wall of the transept there is much herringbone masonry. So the most likely date is the second half of the C11. The chancel is Dec, see the reticulated tracery and the cusped intersected tracery, both drastically renewed. Contemporary N chapel, the date confirmed by the discovery of floor tiles, but in its present form of 1882 by *Henry Young*. The N aisle windows have uncusped, i.e. C16, lights and straight tops. A date of 1545 is assumed, following the demolition of St Peter de Dunstable, which stood directly opposite. Nave w window tracery redone in the 1830s. In 1853 *T. J. Jackson* of

Bedford added the S aisle, N porch and NE vestry (enlarged 1908 by *G. H. Grocock*). The E window is also Jackson's but *c*. 1874. Inside, the four tower arches are all redone. The W arch has a Victorian hoodmould of dogtooth but above this another late Saxon window. The nave has Perp arcades, the N one rebuilt in 1842 by *J. T. Wing*, the S one of 1853. The piers are thin and of the standard moulded section. Thin arches too. – SCULPTURE. One good Norman head from a corbel table. – WALL PAINTING. In the blocked Norman window in the S transept. C14. Much architecture of a walled city. – STAINED GLASS. E window and chancel S by *Clayton & Bell*, 1874 and 1895. – W window signed by *H. Hughes* (*Ward & Hughes*), 1874. – MONUMENTS. Bridget Barbor †1660 and Mary Lysons †1682 (N chapel); a nice contrast of Baroque styles. – Major William Mills †1838 (chancel). By *J. Loft* of 92 Dean Street, Soho. Mourning young people by a pedestal. A palm tree behind. Quite good.

ST PETER DE MERTON. The archaeological thrill of the church is the Anglo-Saxon evidence. The church appears now to have a Norman central tower but the twin bell-openings were only introduced in 1850 and are copied of course from St Mary; and the very top is of course not genuine but an alteration of 1827–8. In fact the Anglo-Saxon church originally had a W tower, and the present chancel was the nave belonging to it. This is evident from the fact that the chancel is just that little wider than the tower. The tower has long-and-short quoins, visible on the W face inside. On the N as on the S, one exceptionally huge upright stone. Also in the tower are traces, visible outside, of blocked upper windows, and there is, visible again inside, one of those fairly frequent doorways in the E face which may have led on to a wooden balcony. In the bell chamber, built in to the N jamb of the E aperture of the tower is part of a late C8 cross-shaft, with confronted animals developing into interlace, and a band of interlace along the side (cf. Elstow). Of the present chancel the long-and-short W quoins are equally plain to see, S outside, N inside the vestry. Norman, but moved from St Peter de Dunstable *c*. 1545, the S doorway, a fine piece with two orders of shafts, carrying decorated scallop capitals, with saltire crosses in the abacus, and roll mouldings, one of them with a spiral beaded band. The C13 is represented by the E arch of the tower (triple-chamfered) and two N lancets, one being blocked. The nave arcades of six bays look convincingly C14, but are Victorian, the N created in 1845 by *J. T. Wing*, originally three bays but then extended W in 1851, by *J. Woodroffe*, at the same time as the addition of the four-bay S aisle. The whole nave was brought to its present extent by *J. P. St Aubyn* in 1881 and 1885, the W porch then added. S porch of 1902, to protect the Norman door, by St Aubyn's former assistant *H. J. Wadling*. – CHAPTER HOUSE. 1982 by *Victor Farrar*. – FONT. Big, octagonal, Perp, with quatrefoils, tracery motifs, and other motifs. – CHANCEL GATES. Brass. Gothic. 1907. – ROOD SCREEN. 1920. – STAINED GLASS. In the chancel lancet medieval fragments not originally in the church; partly foreign. Assembled *c.* 1820. – E window by *Burlison & Grylls*, 1876; chancel windows by *Clayton & Bell, c.* 1865 (SE), and *Preedy*, 1870 (SW), tower S signed by *O'Connor*, 1872, with beautifully detailed landscape. – W window by *A. L. Moore & Co.*, 1885; to Col. F. G. Burnaby (a classic Victorian adventurer, best known from his portrait by Tissot), killed at Abu Klea in the Sudan Campaign. A big, richly coloured scene of beating swords into ploughshares. – MONUMENTS. Sarah Anne Jones †1894. Arts and Crafts beaten copper plaque with enamelled drops in a tree. – Dr Joseph Thackeray, physician at Bedford Infirmary †1832. Neo-Norman reliquary chest on a plinth. By *Blore*.

*Post-medieval Anglican**

ALL SAINTS, Westbourne Road. 1909–10 by *A. W. Blomfield & Sons* with their pupil, *G. P. Allen*, whose father founded the Queen's Engineering Works in 1894. The development of Queen's Park followed. Red brick and stone, only partly completed to the original design, which anticipated a longer nave, NW tower, baptistery and Lady Chapel. Goodhart-Rendel writes: 'Good taste, after Bodley'.[†] The W front is by *Felix & Sean Lander*, 1961–3. Arcades with dying mouldings, broad aisles and hammerbeam roof with scissor bracing. – FONT. Norman? Curious oval-shaped recesses on each side. Originally at St Paul's, later in use as a horse trough. Base by *Albert Richardson*, 1949. – ALTAR RAILS, 1959 by *Felix Lander*, wrought iron with grapes and wheatsheaves; his also the LAMPS to the choir stalls with musical note motif. – REREDOS (N aisle). Triptych by *Bodley & Hare*, 1903. From the chapel at St Etheldreda's Children's Home (*see* p. 105). Paintings after Raphael and Perugino. – STAINED GLASS. E window (war memorial), designed by Allen, made by *Clayton & Bell*, 1920. – N aisle window, 1947, signed by *A. L. Wilkinson*. – WAR MEMORIAL. A Calvary cross by *J. P. White & Sons*, 1916.

SUNDAY SCHOOL (Community Centre), Marlborough Road. By *Mallows & Grocock*, 1902–3.

CHRIST CHURCH, Goldington Road. By *N. F. Cachemaille-Day*, 1956–8. Yellow brick, with tall, oblong windows and a square bell-tower. Red brick square piers for the arcades.

HOLY TRINITY, Bromham Road. Now part of Bedford Sixth Form College. 1839–41 by *John Brown* of Norwich, who signs one of three large bosses in the nave roof. Largely paid for by Lord Carteret of Haynes. The Commissioners' type. Pairs of lancets along the sides. Lancets also in the W tower (pinnacles

---

*Of the Victorian and Edwardian churches, ST LEONARD, Victoria Road, of 1911–12 by *G. P. Allen*, was demolished 1990.

[†]*Bodley & Garner* were approached for a design in 1895 but an iron church was erected instead.

removed *c.* 1928). Trefoil parapet. The chancel was added with transepts by *F. C. Penrose* in 1865–6. Interior converted 1980, originally for the Girls' High School. – MONUMENT. Joseph Browne †1850 (tower). A mourning female draped across a broken column. Signed by *S. Manning.*

ST ANDREW, Kimbolton Road. By *G. P. Allen* and built in stages 1921–30, all in rock-faced Northamptonshire ironstone; brick chancel and impressively austere crossing tower added in 1962–3 by *Cecil Brown.* – STAINED GLASS. Mostly by *Arthur Savell,* 1922 and 1925. – One S aisle window by *Heaton, Butler & Bayne,* 1892, from Bedford Hospital chapel. – N aisle window by *Marion Grant,* 1958. – Circular E window, Christ seated in glory, 1963, designed by *Brown.* – PARISH CENTRE, 2004 by *Bruce Deacon.*

ST CUTHBERT. *See* Sacred Heart of Jesus (R.C.), below.

ST MARK, Calder Rise, North Brickhill. 1984 by *David Sutcliffe.* Shared with the Methodists (cf. Putnoe Heights Church, p. 89). – STAINED GLASS. By *Joseph Nuttgens,* 1983, 1997 and 2001.

ST MARTIN, Clapham Road. 1888–9 by *J. A. Chatwin* of Birmingham. Unexciting externally, much more convincing inside. Buff brick with thin red brick bands and a little stone dressing. E.E. style. No tower, though one was intended at the SW. Double transepts with double gables to N and S corresponding to two bays of the arcades inside. Polygonal apse. Vestry, NE, by *Mallows & Grocock,* 1902. Inside, exposed yellow and red brick – a muscular character. – REREDOS. 1908 by *Jones & Willis.* – ALTAR RAILS. 1914 from the *Pyghtle Works (J. P. White & Sons).* – SCREENS (All Souls' Chapel). By *Richardson & Houfe,* 1959. Thin classical columns. – HANGING ROOD. 1962 by *J. N. Lawson,* the rather futuristic styling of the figures gives the date. – STAINED GLASS. Mostly by *Clayton & Bell,* notably good the E window, 1902. – S aisle, 1898, by *Jones & Willis,* who supplied others.

ST MICHAEL AND ALL ANGELS, Faldo Road. 1965–6 by *Martin B. Caroe (Caroe & Partners).* Plain brick walls, shallow seamed copper roofs, tall windows in the front gable and a cross at the apex.

Roman Catholic

HOLY CHILD AND ST JOSEPH, Midland Road. By *G. R. Blount.* Rock-faced stone, the (liturgucal) E end erected 1872–4, the rest by 1911 by *A. E. Purdie.* SW tower never built. Polygonal apse. Geometrical tracery. There is much to recommend in the interior, especially the rib-vaulted sanctuary and side chapels. The wall-shafts of the sanctuary arch end in figure sculptures of St Cecilia and Pope Gregory. – TABERNACLE and ALTAR (remade from pieces of the communion rail during reordering) have mosaics by *Salviati.* – REREDOS. In the sanctuary and chapels; stone, with figures under canopies, by *Farmer & Brindley.* – ENGRAVED GLASS (Reconciliation Chapel). By

Alfred Fisher, 1986. – STAINED GLASS. E window, 1876 by *Campbell & Smith*, who supplied the furnishings. Otherwise much by *Jones & Willis*, e.g. the two apse windows (1916) and major W window, 1919 (all war memorials), and *Hardman*, 1920s.

Adjacent is the PRESBYTERY AND GUILD ROOM (the first church of 1869), also by *Blount*.

CHRIST THE KING, Harrowden Road. 1959–60 by *J. S. Comper*. Spare Romanesque. Nave and aisles under one roof, a narthex, wheel window and a bellcote in the peak of the gable. Polygonal apse. Inside, striking use of brick arches to span the nave, pierced at the top by double arches.

SACRED HEART OF JESUS AND ST CUTHBERT (Polish Church), Mill Street. Originally St Cuthbert, built for the Anglicans in 1844–7 by *J. Woodroffe*. Neo-Norman with a crossing tower. The aisles by *F. C. Penrose*, 1864–5, the N one ending in an apse (baptistery) with flat pilaster buttresses. Enlarged by *J. Horsford*, 1877, with W porch and N organ chamber which was converted to the vestry in 1886, when *Henry Young* added the S organ chamber. N porch by *G. H. Grocock*, 1907. Vestry enlarged in 1925 by *G. P. Allen*; since 1980 the priest's house. (The details round the crossing quite ornate with chevron mouldings etc. Under the E window, five round arched openings. – FONT. With four shafts in the corners of the rounded bowl. Probably early C14. Given to Great Woolston in the C19, returned in 1925. – STAINED GLASS. The E window with medallions and W window with royal arms by *Baillie*, 1847. – N aisle W (baptistery), by *A. Gibbs*, 1882.)

ST FRANCESCA CABRINI (Italian Church), Woburn Road. 1963–5 by *Peter Dunham, Widdup & Harrison* for the Scalabrinian Missionaries, serving the large southern Italian population established in the town after 1945. Rather startling concrete front of thin triangular columns to a canopy and a screen of faceted blocks with slips of *dalle de verre*. The first Italian parish church in England since the Italian Church, London, in 1863. Plain interior, top-lit sanctuary.

Other denominations

BUNYAN MEETING (Baptist), Mill Street. 1849–50 by *Wing & Jackson*, succeeding the meeting house of 1707. The congregation was established in 1650. Red brick and very handsome with a big pediment across the front with a cartouche, and round arched windows in Gibbs surrounds, and a lower tier along the pilastered sides with segmental heads. The impressive doors have scenes from *The Pilgrim's Progress* in bronze reliefs by *Frederick Thrupp*, 1868, given by the Duke of Bedford in 1876. The model of course is Ghiberti at the Baptistery in Florence. Of lesser connoisseurship, the contemporary Italianate porch. Classical interior, the gallery continuous around four sides and with the ORGAN CASE in a recess at the S end.

Rostrum pulpit below. (ALTAR TABLE. Part of the original of 1650?) – STAINED GLASS. All the subjects are drawn from Bunyan's life and writing. First in date, 'Faithful Helping Christian' (w wall) signed by *A. L. & C. E. Moore*, 1927. Others 1950–2000, several by *Goddard & Gibbs*. – SCHOOLS, S, by *John Usher*, 1866–7, following the style of the chapel. OFFICES and former MUSEUM, by *Usher & Anthony*, 1891, with shaped gables. New museum, 1990.

Former HOWARD CONGREGATIONAL CHAPEL, Mill Street. Now a nightclub. It was of 1774 by *Daniel Millard*, joiner, for a congregation who split from the Bunyan Meeting. After a fire in the 1990s all that remains is its Italianate rendered façade of 1849, with slightly projecting outer bays with raised quoins and block pediments. Porch of columns *in antis* in the centre. An early work by *John Usher*. – SCHOOLS by *Usher*, 1862, in Ram Yard, behind.

Former MORAVIAN CHAPEL (St Luke's), St Peter's Street. *See* Bedford School, St Luke's Theatre.

Of the other later NONCONFORMIST CHAPELS of Bedford, quite a number are, or were, also of the vaguely Italianate mid-C19 type with a big pediment across the front and round arches, e.g. the PROVIDENCE BAPTIST CHURCH, Rothsay Road, of 1894 by *Usher & Anthony*, its tripartite façade divided by rusticated brick pilasters and the central windows under a single round arch, of stone and rubbed red brick, rising into the pediment. The exception is SOUTHEND METHODIST CHURCH, Ampthill Road/Offa Road, of 1873 (foundation stone) of ragstone, with Gothic plate tracery, a gabled nave and a little spire. RUSSELL PARK BAPTIST CHURCH, Denmark Street, exhibits the fashion by 1912 for the free Gothic in brick and stone and is the unmistakable work of *G. & R. P. Baines*.

PRIORY METHODIST CHURCH, Newnham Avenue. A church of 1953, completely remodelled in 1968–9 by *M. Edmonds* of *Edward D. Mills & Partners*, its roof stepping up to a tall E clerestory. Low brick ancillary rooms. Some minor alterations since, e.g the gable porch. – STAINED GLASS, filling the wall of the chapel. The Creation, by *Gillian Rees Thomas*, 1969.

PUTNOE HEIGHTS CHURCH. Originally Methodist, now shared with the Anglicans. 1972–3 by *Building Design Group (Bedford)*, its roof rising over the worship area into an unequal pitch with glass panels lighting the E end. Lower aisle and later meeting room with curved wall. – STAINED GLASS. Aisle E end. Garden of Eden by *Joseph Nuttgens*. – The HALL is the previous church of 1956–7 by *A. J. May*. Angular lancets and saddleback-roofed tower.

MORAVIAN CHURCH, Howard Avenue. A mission room for Queen's Park, by *Henry Young*, 1895, survives as the hall. Gable swept up to a bellcote. Church, with transepts and SE tower added 1911–12. Purplish brick with pale buff terracotta dressings and Gothic tracery. By *A. E. Allen* of Banbury. Nicely preserved interior, with a gallery.

GURU NANAK GURDWARA, Ford End Road. By *Calford Seaden*, 1999–2007. A substantial complex in traditional Sikh style, built by Indian masons using Indian pink and grey granite and white marble. Three-storey, with octagonal towers at the corners. Projecting eaves at each floor and towers of loggias in the centre of the sides above the entrances, all with ribbed ogee domes and scalloped arches. Rising above the shrine a two-stage tower, with larger dome. On the wallheads smaller domed chattris.

The SRI GURU RAVIDASS TEMPLE, Ashburnham Road, Former Drill Hall, 1922 by *J. H. Fenning*. Good Neo-Georgian with a modillion pediment, segmental pedimented doorcase and brick quoins.

CEMETERY, Foster Hill Road. LODGE and CHAPEL, 1855 by *T. J. Jackson*, the former red brick Tudor, the latter Gothic, stone with a porch tower under a pyramid roof.

CEMETERY, Norse Road. CHAPEL OF REMEMBRANCE and offices, 1988 by *North Bedfordshire Borough Council* (chief architect, *Terry Hinchcliffe*). Curved plan, the roof embracing a tiled spire. CREMATORIUM, 1995–6 by *Jim Burnett*, Chief Architect, Bedford Borough Council. Brick with big pitched and pyramidal tiled roofs, and a square chimney making a nicely varied silhouette, indebted to Frank Lloyd Wright. Fittings by *Toby Winteringham*.

PUBLIC BUILDINGS

BOROUGH HALL, Prebend Street/Cauldwell Street. Formerly County Hall. 1965–70 by the *Bedfordshire County Architect's Dept (J. C. Barker*, County Architect; project architect, *D. J. Chalk*).* There are three elements – Council suite, County Hall offices, Record Office and Library – drawn together in a single megastructure by means of a deck-cum-covered walkway at first floor, all very characteristic of its date. Equally characteristic are the materials and Brutalist aesthetic: reinforced concrete frame and floor slabs, clad with panels whose ribbed surfaces were cast *in situ*. Limestone aggregate bestows the piercing white finish. The offices take precedence, a curved plan eight storeys high with an open top storey (originally to have been filled in) and façades divided into a grid of recessed rectangles by the exposed frame. Emphasis is given here and there by windows in projecting boxes (originally to signify the offices of senior staff). The Council suite is a mere single storey, the Council chamber with a shallow pyramid roof. In a subsidiary wing, the former COUNTY LIBRARY (present RECORD OFFICE), a tough box with nicely varied patterning on the lakeside elevation and castle-like slots to the road. Like all the postwar buildings along the S bank of the Ouse, it is the failure to relate to the river that disappoints. Landscaping by *Sylvia Crowe*, 1969, poorly maintained. Since 2009 the headquarters of Bedford Borough Council.

---

*A competition for buildings to replace the Shire Hall was held in 1939 and won by *Oswald P. Milne* and *Harvey & Wicks* but remained unexecuted.

SHIRE HALL (MAGISTRATES' COURT/COUNTY COURT), St Paul's Square. On the site of the Sessions House of 1753. Of two phases, 1878–81 to the river, the rest 1881–3, all by *Waterhouse*, for the County and Assize Courts. Unmistakably by the hand that designed the Prudential in London. Red Suffolk brick with red Ruabon terracotta. Gothic porch, Elizabethan windows, pavilion roofs. Ironwork railings by *Hart, Son & Peard*. Inside, a great hall with hammerbeam roof. Tiles by *Craven Dunnill* and *Godwin*. Courtrooms with ceiled hammerbeam roofs and original fittings. It became the Shire Hall and was extended E in 1910 for the County Council Offices by *Charles Holden* (*Adams & Holden*) with *W. H. Leete*, the County Surveyor. Holden may have contributed to the design, see e.g. the chequerboard patterning. The riverside E extension (originally Treasurer's Dept), dated 1929, by *S. C. Jury*, County Surveyor, is, remarkably for its date, in keeping with Waterhouse. Former Council Chamber (now Court No. 3), 1938, in courtyard to the E.

OLD TOWN HALL (Tourist Information Centre). Originally Bedford Grammar School. The building consists of two parts, the l. being Sir William Harpur's school house as refronted in 1767 by *Isaac Clayson* for the Bedford Charity (Harpur Trust). Ashlar-faced, of four bays with two-light windows (very old-fashioned for 1767) and in the middle Harpur's statue in Georgian costume by *Benjamin Palmer* (cf. his monument in St Paul's). Doorway with pediment and top pediment over the two middle bays. The r. part is of 1859–61, low and irregular, with a turret, and quite picturesque. The architect was *J. Horsford*. Facing Horne Lane, the tall former Assembly Hall. Slightly extended in 1880, but the school moved to its new site in 1892 (*see* Bedford School) and the hall was converted into the Council Chamber in 1900. Civic Theatre from 1947 to 2012, now offices. (– MAYOR'S STALL. Formerly in St Paul's. It has fluted Corinthian pilasters and a high pedimented canopy.) – The COWPER BUILDING, on the S side of St Paul's Square, was originally an extension to the Grammar School but is also now in council use. By *Basil Champneys*, 1884–6. A very handsome ashlar-faced building. The façade is quite narrow (two plus two bays) with cross-windows crowned by a steep pediment, swags and a cartouche, a free interpretation of, say, 1660. On the top an elegantly shaped cupola, a little sister to those of the Girls' High School (*see* Bedford Sixth Form College, below). Longer and plainer W front, with curiously unemphasized entrance on the E side. Facing the river, red brick additions by *Henry Young* 1899, by when this was the Girls' Modern School.

CORN EXCHANGE, St Paul's Square. By *Ladds & Powell*, 1871–4. Stone, of three bays with very big segment-arched first-floor windows and an attic with four big chimneys like pinnacles. Strange frieze of terracotta paterae with knobbly projections. Lower one-bay entrance wings. The interior of the hall is two-storey with arches, originally windows, on the W side, and shallow central dome. Refurbished in 1992 as a concert hall etc. by *Lees Associates*. – SCULPTURE. Bust of Glenn Miller in the front by *Patricia Finch*, 1994. Miller played his last concert here before his disappearance in 1944.

Former COUNTY POLICE STATION, Nos. 21–23 Gadsby Street. By *J. Horsford*, 1872. Symmetrical, gault brick, with a pediment over the centre. Small yard behind.

Former ASSEMBLY ROOMS (Harpur Suite), Harpur Street. A noble, though only rendered, Greek Doric temple front with low one-bay wings. 1834 by the local architect *T. G. Elger*. One good large Neoclassical room inside, with apsidal ends, a gallery over one end and statues in niches at the other. Two tiers of windows with flat cornices on console brackets. Elegant plain stair to the upper floor. Stained glass E window by *Willement*, 1835.

BEDFORD CENTRAL LIBRARY, next door to the old Assembly Rooms. 1969–72 by *E. B. Heath*, the Borough Architect. Modest attempt at harmonizing with its stone-fronted neighbours. Good practical interior.*

THE HIGGINS (Museum & Art Gallery), Castle Lane. Charles Higgins, landlord of the Swan Inn, built his brewery in the grounds of the castle in 1838. The surviving parts are brick, three storey, with windows in giant arches l. on the S front and a central lucam. Small square kiln to the r. Inner courtyard. The house, Castle Close, was built alongside *c.* 1846 for his son and is a modest villa of two storeys and three bays with single-storey canted bays on the S front. The collection of fine and decorative arts was assembled by Cecil Higgins after he sold the brewery in 1927 to Wells & Winch of Biggleswade, given to the town at his death and the house converted for its display in 1949. The brewery buildings were adapted as the Bedford Museum in 1981. Between house and brewery a wing of *c.* 1976, brick with short vertical concrete openings. Incorporated at the rear is the hexagonal former MILITIA BUILDING of *c.* 1805, perhaps by *John Wing*, and the former WHIG CLUB (1841, now Bedford Gallery), which were restored by *Peter Inskip*, 2009. Further refurbishment, with new entrance in the courtyard, in 2012–13 by *Buttress Fuller Alsop Williams*. The collection is beyond the scope of this guide, but its furniture includes works by *Waterhouse*, *Voysey*, *Frank Lloyd Wright* and especially *William Burges*, including pieces from Tower House, Holland Park (acquired with the Handley-Read collection in 1972). But nothing by *Baillie Scott* who lived and worked in Bedford 1901–11.

UNIVERSITY OF BEDFORDSHIRE, Polhill Avenue. Formerly the Bedford College of Education of 1967–8 by *Bedfordshire County Architect's Dept* (job architects *Norman Browning* and *David Carter*). The buildings of that period are yellow brick,

---

*On the site of ST PAUL'S METHODIST CHURCH of 1831–4, closed in 1968 (*see* Priory Methodist Church).

flat-roofed and low, except for a daringly tall accent of a tower with corner windows. Developed from 1992 as the Bedford Campus of De Montfort University, Leicester.* The LIBRARY is by *Van Heyningen & Haward*, 2001. A graceful four-storey cube, concrete-framed with an outer skin of steel and glass sheltered by an attached screen of horizontal timber louvres. Internal atrium with galleries to each of the floors and a glass lantern at the top and drum-shaped vents at each corner. N of this the CAMPUS CENTRE by *Short & Associates*, 2006–7, white-walled with on the front a ground floor recessed behind piers and windows shaded by reversed-F shape aerofoils. Also STUDENT RESIDENCES, 2005–7 by *O'Connell East Architects*.

BEDFORD COLLEGE, Cauldwell Street. Formerly Mander College of Further Education. By the *Bedfordshire County Architect's Dept* (*S. V. Goodman*, County Architect; job architect *J. H. Branwell*). An eight-storey tower, curtain-walled with blue panels. This is of 1958; the rest of the college was added by 1965 and much rebuilt quite recently.

SCHOOLS in Bedford are of significant interest, largely thanks to the contribution of the Harpur Trust (Bedford Charity), whose buildings should be described first:

BEDFORD SCHOOL, De Parys Avenue. After the school run by Newnham Priory was dissolved *c.* 1540, a grammar school was opened *c.* 1548 and authorized by letters patent of 1552. Sir William Harpur, Merchant Taylor and Lord Mayor of London in 1561, endowed the school liberally. Its small premises in St Paul's Square have already been mentioned (*see* Old Town Hall above). Between 1769 and 1868 the school grew from ten to 216 boys. New premises were needed for the Writing School, so in 1834 a remarkably large building was occupied in Harpur Street, for which *see* Harpur Centre, p. 99, below. In time further additions were made to the premises in St Paul's Square (*see* Cowper Building, above). Finally the present site, N of St Peter's church, was acquired and the Grammar School given entirely new buildings.

The school of 1889–92 is by *E. C. Robins*, commissioned on the advice of E. R. Robson, the London School Board Architect. Red brick with stone dressings. Symmetrical, Gothic, with a central turret and spirelet over the Great Hall, which has tall Perp windows, a stair-tower over the porch and an open ambulatory at ground floor with Tudor arches. Gabled wings l. and r. for classrooms and stairs with mullioned and transomed windows. Heavily damaged by fire in 1979, but reconstructed internally in 1981 by *Philip Dowson* of *Arup Associates*, who inserted a floor at the level of the hall's former first-floor gallery. In place of the hall's original hammerbeam roof is a

63

---

* The University succeeded, among other institutions, the COLLEGE OF PHYSICAL EDUCATION. Its buildings in Warwick Avenue, including the GYMNASIUM by *S. Vincent Goodman*, 1955–6, described in 1968 as 'a very pleasant job', have gone.

tour-de-force of timber rib-vaulting springing from the original wall-shafts into diamond patterns of complex geometry along the flat centre.

The separate CHAPEL, NW, is of 1907–9, designed by *Bodley* in 1905 but completed after his death by his partner, *C. G. Hare*. It is very nearly Bodley's last work and a strapping junior sibling to his chapels at Queens' College, Cambridge, and Marlborough College, Wilts. Red brick, with the barest stone dressings, very erect with buttressed sides and a flat entrance tower above steps on the front which have elegant swooping side walls. Collegiate seating inside, hence the high placing of the windows. Segmental barrel-vault ceiling, with curved ribs and tie-beams with brattishing, all beautifully stencilled (reinstated *c.* 1990). The STALLS, with canopied rear stalls, are carved by the *Pyghtle Works (J. P. White & Sons)*. – REREDOS. A First World War Memorial (by *Hare?*), filling the narrow chancel. A tryptych with lavish Gothic details. Crucifixion in the centre, and small figures in niches and paintings in the doors of Pre-Raphaelite style. Bodley intended a taller reredos and no E window but his plans were frustrated by Old Bedfordians who favoured a Boer War Memorial with STAINED GLASS of *c.* 1909, attributed to *Gamon & Humphrey* (P. Cormack). In the side aisles, one (†1909) is Kempe-ish in style, by *Burlison & Grylls*. The other is by *Alfred R. Fisher (Chapel Studio)*, 1991. Several brick additions date from between the wars. All of the following are by *Oswald P. Milne*:

MEMORIAL HALL (and former Library, now Common Room) of 1925–6, designed with *Paul Phipps*. Restrained Neo-Elizabethan with a bronze statue of St George by *H. W. Palliser*, 1928, in a classical stone aedicule on the front. Two tiers of recessed cross-windows. (Segmental barrel vault inside; war memorial with pedimented frame.) Good ironwork screen for the cloister link to the main school building.

GATES to Burnaby Road. Wrought-iron, C18 style, but 1930.

SCIENCE BLOCK. 1932–3, absolutely plain, of brick, with cross-windows, a big hipped roof and two shallow wings with fine cast-iron clock and sundial. Charming bronze oil lamp finials to bootscrapers by the door. Extended by *Bernard Feilden*, 1974–5.

SPORTS PAVILION, 1935. A nice design, raised above steps. Essentially Neo-Georgian, with a tiled roof and cupola, but streamlined side wings flanking the steps and nautical railings. Slightly over-scaled addition of 2012 by *mk40 Architects*. Of later additions the following are notable.

DINING HALLS. Admirable single-storey, the shell concrete roofs making a wave; by *Deacon & Laing* of Bedford, 1965–6. – LIBRARY. By *Eric Parry Architects*, 2002–3, a closed façade of windowless brick upper storey, subtly curved at the corners. The main part is two-storey under a curved roof pierced by openings. On the garden elevation the arch of the roof set between plain brick walls recalls Spence at Sussex. – MUSIC SCHOOL. 2005, again by *Eric Parry Architects*. A tougher proposition than the Library, especially in this location beside the chapel. Walls faced in dark brick ranging in tone from red to silver. To the fore a recital room under a curved roof, its walls of full-height glazing between vertical stainless steel panels. Rehearsal rooms in a longer wing, connected by a glazed link.

S Luke's heatre, St Peter's Street. The former Moravian chapel of 1864–5 by *J. Horsford*, succeeding a chapel established in 1745. Brick with stone quoins and Lombardic windows, with a transom denoting the gallery level inside. Separate entrances for men and women. The impressive interior is focused on the organ in the domical apse extension of 1888 by *John Day*. The ORGAN CASE, made in 1715 by *Gerard Schmidt* for St Paul's church, was given to the Moravians in 1832. Although altered in 1858 and 1888, it is a recognizable early C18 type with pipes in towers and a scooped centre and sides. The chapel closed 2008; converted and extended by *Foster Wilson Architects*, 2014.

PREPARATORY SCHOOL, on St Peter's Green/De Parys Avenue. By *Henry Young*, 1898, on the site of St Peter's rectory. Neo-Elizabethan with a wing by *Milne*, 1932. The GATES onto St Peter's Green are from the Alameda at Ampthill (*see* p. 66), erected here 1897.

BEDFORD SIXTH FORM COLLEGE, Bromham Road. The former BEDFORD HIGH SCHOOL FOR GIRLS of 1878–82 by *Basil Champneys*. The best of the Bedford school buildings erected by the Harpur Trust. It was originally shared premises for the Girls' High School and Girls' Modern School but the latter moved to the former Grammar School in St Paul's Square in 1892 (*see* Cowper Building, p. 91). In 2012 the High School abandoned its home for Bedford Girls' School in Cardington Road (*see* below). In a free Tudor-Jacobean. Symmetrical front, of wings with shaped gables and a centre (for the hall shared by the two schools) with giant stone pilasters topped by scrolls, very large two-transomed windows, and a cupola. In the links with the wings, square towers also with cupola. Round the corners some extremely pretty half-domed bow-windows with gadroon moulded tops. The centre wing is an addition of 1896–8 by *Henry Young*, seamlessly copying Champneys and reusing his porch. Undeniably a feminine job, compared with the Bedford School and the former Bedford Modern School. In fact Champneys was commissioned on the strength of his Newnham College, Cambridge.[*] The hall is stupendous, T-plan, with Jacobean panelling and galleries E and W, one containing the organ. Strapwork ceiling decoration. Library, converted from the gym in 1932. Fittings by the *Pyghtle Works* (*J. P. White*). There are later additions: the JUNIOR SCHOOL, again by *Young*, in an economical version of Champneys' style, a plain SCIENCE BLOCK (1927) and GYM

55

---

[*] It is said that he fell out with the Headmistress-elect, Ada McDowall, so was not invited to submit designs for Bedford School.

(1931) by *G. P.Allen,* and the SUSAN COLLIEWING by *Oswald P.Milne,* 1934–5. See also Churches, former Holy Trinity above.

BEDFORD GIRLS' SCHOOL (formerly Dame Alice Harpur School), Cardington Road. 1938 by *Oswald P. Milne* for the Bedford Girls' Modern School, which began in Bromham Road (*see* the former High School for Girls above) and was then in St Paul's Square (*see* Cowper Building, above). Red brick with stone dressings, two storeys, flat-roofed. On the front a dominant clocktower and a bowed porch to its l., and a long low curved cloakroom wing, i.e. streamlined modern but with conservative instincts. Sympathetic additions by *E. H. C. Inskip & Son,* 1970s onwards.

BEDFORD MODERN SCHOOL, Manton Lane. Red brick buildings of 1972–4 by *Greenwood & Abercrombie* to succeed the school in Harpur Street (*see* Harpur Centre, p. 99, below). Flat-roofed with tile-hung upper storeys. Inside, STAINED GLASS by *Hugh Easton,* 1959. Figure of Sir William Harpur, taken from the brass in St Paul's church. – RUTHERFORD BUILDING. 2006 by *The Inskip Partnership.* Butterfly plan with two-storey wings and a drum at the hinge and sloping glass-roofed dining room between.

PILGRIMS PRE-PREP SCHOOL, Brickhill Drive. 1998–2000 for the Bedford Charity (Harpur Trust) by the *Hampshire County Architect's Dept,* under *Sir Colin Stansfield Smith;* their first school design outside their own county. The principal feature is a glass polygonal drum in the centre, serving as a winter garden to the two ranges of monopitch-roofed brick buildings around it. The predecessor Pilgrims School of 1961–2 by the *Bedfordshire County Architect's Dept* (*J. C. Barker,* County Architect; job architects *D. J. Chalk* and *R. D. Walshaw*) is alongside; its campus-style planning, on the edge of Bedford Park, was something quite new. Now offices.

The town's OTHER SCHOOLS are worth taking in order of date. There was no School Board until 1898, instead provision after the 1870 Act was in the hands of the Bedford Charity. All their schools were designed by their surveyor, *Henry Young:*

First is the former AMPTHILL ROAD SCHOOLS (now Raleigh and Southway Centre), 1875–6, with infants' school added 1880. Two-storey main part with lancet windows and plate tracery, indicative of the period before state elementary schools developed their own secular style. Of that later type, and single-storey, is LIVINGSTONE LOWER, Clapham Road, 1893–4, with straight gables and still some pointed windows, but Queen Anne-style glazing. Some nice terracotta details. CASTLE LOWER, Goldington Road, 1899–1900, again by Young, has shaped Flemish gables and hammer-beam roofs inside. The grander style of the Northamptonshire Board Schools, e.g. Kettering, provided the inspiration but Champneys' High School must have been a local influence.

In the suburban areas, fewer schools of note, but HAR-ROWDEN MIDDLE SCHOOL (formerly Kingsbrook School) is a good example of the postwar style: 1951 by the *Bedfordshire*

County Architect's Dept (*S. V. Goodman*, County Architect; job architect *Ted Collins*), with low flat-roofed brick classrooms and an emphatic square tower at the entrance. The Infant School of 1957 (also by *Collins*) has a hall with parabolic roof.

BEDFORD HOSPITAL, Britannia Road/Ampthill Road. The County Hospital of 1897–9 by *H. Percy Adams*. The principal block survives, red brick and terracotta with tall canted bays, shaped gables and pavilion roofs on the front. Over the door, a SCULPTURE signed by *S. W. Elmes & Sons*. In the former children's ward (VICTORIA WARD), complete and excellent tile panels of nursery rhymes by *P. H. Newman* for *W. B. Simpson & Son*, the other tiles by *Maw & Co*. Everything else is much later, of many phases and incoherent.

BEDFORD HEALTH VILLAGE, Kimbolton Road. This incorporates the red brick former HOUSE OF INDUSTRY, 1794–6 by *John Wing*, which succeeded five smaller workhouses in surrounding parishes. An eleven-bay front, the seven middle bays being recessed. Two and a half storeys; hipped roof. Stone doorcase. The placing on a slight rise must have made it a visible and cautionary presence above the Georgian town. It was expanded after 1834 as the Bedford Union Workhouse and in the C20 as a hospital. Now disused.

H.M. PRISON, Dame Alice Street. 1798–1801 by *John Wing*, originally as the County Gaol, succeeding the gaol in Silver Street which inspired John Howard's reforms of the system and where Bunyan was imprisoned. Cross-shaped, with wings opening off a central vestibule and gaoler's house in the S wing; quite an unusual plan for its date, when separate blocks were the norm. E wing extended 1834. An extension to the N of this, the House of Correction, 1819 by *James Elmes*, stands no longer. The front is of 1848–9 by *Thomas Smith*, County Surveyor. Red brick. Three pavilions, the middle one with the archway. This pavilion has some chippy rustication. The side pavilions of three bays and two storeys were built as living houses for the governor and the chief warder. Also of 1848–9, the large T-plan cell block (A–C Wing) with a pitched roof over the octagonal crossing ending in a chimney and tripartite windows in the gables of the wings lighting the central corridors. The present entrance in the extension to the E, by *Architects Co-partnership*, 1985–92, is on a much grander scale, sheer walls of yellow and red brick and part of the upper storey jettied. Windows only at ground and top floor. Cell blocks of the same date and style behind.

BEDFORD STATION, Ashburnham Road. The Victorian building (1857 by *C. H. Driver*; dem. 1980) stood a little S of its replacement, a modest but commendable design of 1978 by *J. S. Wyatt*, regional architect for BR London Midland. Sleek glass envelope of lightly gridded elevations around a painted steel frame and lightweight tubular roof trusses.

BEDFORD PARK. A good rising site between the town and cemetery. Laid out 1883–5 (landscaping by *W. Barron & Sons* of Derby) after the sale of the St John's Hospital estate. The

SOUTH GATES are ornate Carolean-style work of 1888 designed by *Starkie Gardner & Co.* of Lambeth and made by *Bacchus & Ison* of Bedford. Brick and stone piers by *Joseph Miller*. The Domestic Revival-style LODGES and CAFÉ PAVILION are by *J. Lund*, Borough Surveyor. – BANDSTAND, 1892, and CRICKET PAVILION, 1894, with much half-timbering.

OASIS BEACH POOL, Cardington Road. By the *Yates Owen Partnership*, 1991. The enclosure is a 35-metre (115 ft) -high pyramid, with a split along the middle for a vertical seam of glazing. Profiled sheet metal roofs and tiled base. A smaller pyramid for services alongside, and a moat in front.

BEDFORD CASTLE
Castle Close

Shortly after the Conquest a castle was built of which nothing now remains but the lower part of the motte or mound, 160 ft (48.8 metres) in diameter. The castle lay E of the High Street and extended as far as Newnham Road. The motte is just W of the latter and N of The Embankment. The baileys were to the W, the inner bailey to its SW, over much of the site towards the Swan Hotel, where the footings of the Great Hall, buttery (E) and solar (W) were revealed by excavations in 1970–2 and 2007. The outer bailey was NW of the mound, with its N boundary at Ram Yard. The castle was refortified in the early C13 by Falkes de Breaute and then subjected to a well-documented siege by Henry III in 1224, after which it was slighted. Its surroundings were landscaped in 2001–2. C13 LIME KILN in Castle Lane, now on show beneath the Castle Quay flats.

PERAMBULATIONS

1. Town centre

The best thing visually about Bedford is the way the town has treated its river. Few English towns can be compared. The Embankment is a handsome street, and otherwise there are public gardens on both sides. The centre of the centre is ST PAUL'S SQUARE, though as a square it only dates from 1803 and demolition of two rows of houses between the church and High Street. Here is a STATUE of John Howard by *Alfred Gilbert*, 1894, and one savours the contradiction between the realism of the stout figure, pensive, moral and upright, and the melting sensuality of the bronze ornaments of the shapely plinth with weird babes peering through grotesque masks. Besides the public buildings of the square (for which *see* above), No. 1 is a five-bay house rendered as ashlar, with a nice early C19 doorway, the house itself originally two-storey, perhaps C15, and timber-framed. It belonged to the Barnards, bankers in the town, in the C18. No. 4, white brick of 1849, was the vicarage of St Paul's church. All are in bad condition. On the

N side the former Corn Exchange (*see* Public Buildings above) tries to dominate the scene.

HIGH STREET runs N from the square's E side with painted brick and stucco fronts. It starts grandly with Nos. 19–21, of five bays with attached giant Corinthian columns and pilasters in two storeys, a full entablature and attic and windows under swept pediments at first floor. Attributed to *Robert Palgrave*, *c.* 1850, as premises and a residence for his chemist uncle who owned the site. It goes without saying that the street's shop-fronts have been sacrificed to mediocrity. No. 49 (originally for John Bull, jeweller) is by *John Day*, 1878, in Queen Anne style with fancy clock of 1884 with a golden bull (now a replica). The niche above held a figure of Father Time. Then the former RED LION HOTEL, or rather its façade, probably of *c.* 1830, seven bays, stuccoed, with giant pilasters all along and cast-iron first-floor balconies with anthemion leaves. Next a lively Venetian Gothic front (No. 57) by *John Usher*, 1871, for Henry Adkin, gunsmith. Gun dogs on the pinnacles of the crocketed gable, by *Harry Hems*. Further up (Nos. 77 and 79), another stuccoed front, built as the Post Office, 1855, with Composite columns in the upper floor, unfluted Greek Doric below. Next to it, NATWEST, 1881 by *Usher & Anthony*, red brick with pedimented dormers, the two N bays duplicated in 1921. Then a consistent terrace (Nos. 95–105) of the 1860s by the local builder *George Handscombe Miller*, originally with Ionic columned shopfronts. Finally, BARCLAYS (E side), a good example of a banker's palazzo in ashlar, 1929 by *Stonebridge & Harris*, quite late for the Italianate style.

On the other side of the street from the square, LLOYDS BANK, 1936 by *W.B. Stonebridge*, originally for Dudeney & Johnston, grocers. Adam-revival, with a Venetian-type window with fan pattern in a superarch in the centre *à la* Boodles. At Silver Street, DEBENHAMS (formerly E. P. Rose & Son, drapers), 1937 by *Usher & Anthony*, is red brick with a landmark Art Deco stone tower at the corner. The rest of SILVER STREET also has customary interwar commercial frontages. At the beginning a SCULPTURE of two disproportionately large profile heads by *Rick Kirby*, 2009. Further down, a good BUST of Trevor Huddleston by *Ian Walters*, 1999; dedicated by Nelson Mandela, 2000.

In HARPUR STREET, immediately N of St Paul's Square, the HARPUR CENTRE shopping mall by *Frederick Gibberd & Partners* (job architect *Jack Forrest*), 1976, behind the retained stone façade of the former BEDFORD MODERN SCHOOL. This is by *Blore*, 1830–3 for (from N to S) the Harpur Trust's English School, orphanage, boardroom, Clerk's House and Elementary School. The building is symmetrical, ashlar-faced, in the collegiate Tudor style, as required under the terms of the original competition (which had in fact been won by *J. T. Wing*, but his plans were discarded). High projecting open entrance hall with tierceron vault under a tower. The school stayed here till 1974. Some other good items in Harpur Street, notably

Association Buildings at the corner with Silver Street, Free Style of 1899 by *Mallows & Grocock*, though the loss of a shapely domed roof at the corner and overpainting has dulled its qualities. Also the former BOOTS store, 1896 by their architect *A. N. Bromley*, on the opposite corner, with very good terracotta dressings and scrolly Flemish gables. N of this THE ARCADE, 1905 by *Usher & Anthony*, a glass-covered passage with two-storey fronts for shops and rooms above. Half-timbered. Nicely kept; some original shopfronts survive. Further up, the former TELEPHONE EXCHANGE, by *H.M. Office of Works*, 1939–40, streamlined around the corner with St Loyes Street.

To the E of Harpur Street is DAME ALICE STREET, with one long range of Harpur Trust ALMSHOUSES, 1801–6, low, of dark red brick, with paired steep dormers and Tudor details. They were erected by *John Wing* as cottages for rent by inhabitants of the neighbourhood who had lost their houses to a fire in 1802. But they were then quite plain, their present guise adopted in *Henry Young*'s remodelling, 1882–95. A W range extended up to the prison (dem. 1969). Opposite, a good but neglected former POST OFFICE (Central Club), Free Jacobean style by *Henry Tanner* of *H.M. Office of Works*, dated 1898; the W part is a duplication in 1924.

Back E, at the top of High Street, ARDOR HOUSE, the former Bedford District Gas Co. offices of 1930 by *Ivan Daughtry*, Queen Anne style. On ST PETER'S GREEN, a STATUE of Bunyan by *Sir J. E. Boehm*, 1874. Bronze panels in the plinth of scenes from *The Pilgrim's Progress*. In ST PETER'S STREET the former PROVIDENT DISPENSARY (now Probation Service) by *Usher & Anthony*, 1887, one large gable over the façade. Nearby, Nos. 11–13 (Baker Bros), timber-framed. Stuccoed early C19 frontages (No. 13 has its gable end to the street), but C16 in origin and a rare survival now. Then the former ST PETER'S CHURCH HALL, Edwardian Baroque by *Kensington Gammell*, 1910. Further up on the N side, the 1860s former MORAVIAN CHAPEL (now Bedford School, *see* p. 95) for the settlement established in Bedford in 1745, the first outside London. It is flanked by houses of 1757 for the Sisters (l.) and Minister (r.). Of red brick chequered with blue headers, they have steep pitched roofs, allowing for two full attic storeys. In the gable end of the l. house a Venetian window and a semicircular window above it. Next to this group a smaller terrace, early C19, with a pediment over the centre and consoles with pendants along the eaves. The former Brethren's House is behind (now the Howard Building of Bedford School), seven bays in all and three storeys.

Round the corner, the beginning of KIMBOLTON ROAD with stuccoed houses of *c.* 1838–41 exhibiting a variety of styles at Nos. 10–12 (bows and Ionic porches), No. 14 (Gothic), Nos. 16–18 (porches paired in the centre), Nos. 20–22 (giant pilasters, a pediment across the top and recessed porches with consoles). All are attributed to *James Woodroffe*, who bought the land in 1836. Opposite, KIMBOLTON LODGE, a yellow brick Italianate villa. Evidently this was once a select suburb, now thoroughly spoiled by the road planners.

Now back s down ST CUTHBERT'S STREET where there is CROFTON HOUSE (No. 27 E side), early C18, low, of five bays, red brick, with a pedimented one-bay projection. Further down a few other buildings that look C18, but probably conceal earlier origins, e.g. No. 9, which appears to have its staircase in the bay to the r. (i.e. behind the chimneystack). The SHIP INN is C17 with two hipped bays and some internal timber-framing. To the E in NEWNHAM STREET, Nos. 12–16, red brick cottages of 1798.

At the s end, St Cuthbert's church (*see* above), and in MILL STREET, heading w back to High Street, the Bunyan Meeting and Howard Chapel on the s side (*see* above), and on the N side a house, No. 38 dated 1760, three bays plus one to the l., in red brick with a modillion cornice and a tiled attic mansard behind the parapet. Also the former FIRE STATION, a narrow front under a gable all in rock-faced Lum's Hill (Derbyshire) stone. 1888 by *Usher & Anthony*. No. 30 was John Usher's own house, probably built *c.* 1854 soon after he arrived in Bedford. Fine rusticated doorcase with a pediment.

Parallel with Mill Street to the s is CASTLE LANE and s of that The Higgins museum (*see* Public Buildings) and CASTLE QUAY, large blocks of flats by *Burrell Foley Fischer* and *Ash Sakula Architects*, 2009.

2. The riverside and south

s of the High Street and St Paul's Square one reaches the river, and here in the bridgehead position is that remarkable monument, the SWAN HOTEL, built by *Holland* for the 5th Duke of Bedford in 1794–6, with *John Wing* as the mason. It is an uncompromisingly oblong block of three wide bays by five with a pediment across the front, faced in Totternhoe clunch, from Wing's own quarries. Porch of two pairs of unfluted Ionic columns, flanked by tripartite windows. The three first-floor windows are under blank segmental arches. In the pediment is a lunette. On the low-pitched temple roof four unrelieved oblong chimney blocks. There were formerly flat archways N and s at the ground floor, the N one preserved. To the river, bows at first floor and fine cast-iron railings. The back is similar to the front but of undressed rubble. Inside, the staircase of Houghton House, Ampthill (q.v.), was re-erected after that house had been abandoned in 1794. The staircase has twisted balusters and still a string. It dates from 1688. Paving and chimneypieces were also imported from Houghton House, but the hotel interior has been extensively refurbished. Abutting Holland's building, an L-shaped wing extending N, three-storey with a pediment facing the river. It is of 1906–8, by *Thomas Thurlow* of High Wycombe and remarkably tactful. Less so the other C20 additions to the E. In front, a small square formed by an unworthy postwar building. Here is the BOER WAR MEMORIAL, 1904, by the French sculptor *L. F. Chavalliaud*, cast by *Farmer & Brindley*. The TOWN BRIDGE is of 1811–13, with its five segmental arches and stone balustrades still entirely in the Georgian tradition. It was designed by *John Wing*. Widened sensitively on the upstream side 1938–40, when an impressive range of mid-C19 buildings on High Street facing the Swan was taken down.

In ST MARY'S STREET at the very bridgehead opposite the Swan, the PARK INN, a tower block on a low podium by *Ronald Salmon & Partners*, c. 1968. It was the first such intrusion into the townscape along the river, and the scale is a blow to the immediate surroundings, though since then those surroundings have also grown up to meet it, in particular the Borough Hall (*see* above). s of the hotel, one tall commercial frontage with four shaped gables, of shops with dwellings above, dated 1866, by *J. T. Wing* for the Rev. J. W. Coventry Campion (*see* Westoning).

ST MARY'S SQUARE, at the s end of St Mary's Street, is the site of St Peter de Dunstable (dem. 1545; for its door *see* Religious Buildings: St Peter de Merton above). Now hardly a square, but on the N side a brick house, COLLEGE HOUSE, built in 1694, its windows with frilly lintels distinctive of the years *c.* 1700.

On s to the end of ST JOHN'S STREET, and here, N of the church, ST JOHN HOUSE, the range which was the Hospital of St John. The Masters of the Hospital were the rectors of the church and the hospital was later the rectory. Its appearance,

Bedford, remains of St John's Hospital.
Watercolour by T. Fisher, *c.* 1815

restored in 1968–70 by *John V. Gedge*, is an engaging mix. The core is said to be of before *c.* 1216, and of that date probably much of the stone walling. The wing to the street extended further N, where there is now the enclosing wall. On the street front are revealed inserted brick ogee window arches, presumably C18. The main range extended E and had a N porch, but in 1850 all this was cut back and the E cross-wing added by *J. T. Wing*. This part has two-light windows under hoodmoulds; others were removed from the older part in 1970. Inside the middle range the E end is open to the roof as a hall and some blocked openings in the N wall may be C13. The W end is separated from the hall and its arch-braced roof is C15 with two tiers of windbraces and a castel-lated wall-plate. It is of two bays and a half (smoke) bay behind a low truss. On the ground floor below this and in the W cross-wing are two rooms with ceiling decoration of ostrich feathers and roses, early C16. Also traces of wall paintings here and in the hall. The N front of the W wing, containing the entrance, was remodelled in 1970; red brick with two gables. The early C17 staircase with classical columns above the newels carrying arches with guilloche patterns is from Harrold Hall (*see* Harrold).

Returning N from St John House, turn into CARDINGTON ROAD, the finest residential street of the town S of the river, though many of its old houses are now occupied by Bedford Girls' School. TRINITY HOUSE (formerly St Mary's House) is described as 'newly erected' in 1771–2 for the Rev. Thomas Birt, rector of St Mary's. (The 1707 datestone is said to come from the Old Meeting, Mill Street, dem. 1849.) Six bays and two and a half storeys, red brick, with a steep two-bay pedi-ment above a modillion cornice with an oculus window. Nice doorcase with an open pediment. Extensions for the Girls' School behind. Opposite, No. 26 has a door-hood on curious forward-curving brackets developed direct out of the framing shafts (cf. Brandreth House, Ampthill), but in its present form is a 1980s copy. A Doric porch at No. 46 (WING HOUSE) which *John Wing* built in 1807 for himself, the stone almost certainly from the Totternhoe quarries that he took over in the late C18. Tripartite windows and slender doorcase with a pedi-ment. Close to the entrance to the Girls' School and occupied by it, No. 50 (DAME ALICE HOUSE), also built by Wing *c.* 1817, has a fine three-bay ashlar front with a pedimented porch on Roman Doric columns and wreaths in the frieze. Windows in lugged architraves. There is an C18 brick wing behind, extended for the school in 1984 in matching style by *E. H. C. Inskip & Son*. Opposite, No. 19 is a Picturesque Tudor cottage said to have been designed by *J. T. Wing* for his brother Samuel *c.* 1847. Its much larger neighbour, the Neo-Elizabe-than HOWARD HOUSE (Prep School), is certainly by *J. T. Wing*, built for Frederick Howard *c.* 1870 and a real industrial-ist's mansion. Neo-Jacobean, H-plan, in rock-faced limestone blocks. Canted bays on the front and an arcaded porch between. Lavishly decorated trabeated ceiling over the former entrance hall (now subdivided), its coving painted with scenes from the Parables. After that no more in this direction, and much less in others.

THE BARNS HOTEL, Cardington Road, 1 m. E by the river. Originally a grange of Newnham Priory. Staggered front, the l. wing dated 1630, and 1760 on one of several dormers with turned timber finials. The r. wing, set forward, was probably the kitchen. Garden Suburb-style porches of low semicircular brick arches; attributed to *M. H. Baillie Scott*, who took refuge here in 1911 with Lt-Col. Duberly after his own house, Fenlake Manor, was destroyed by fire. Mid-C18 staircase. Impressively long range of BARNS in two parts, timber-framed with red brick infill. The S barn is very tall and John Bailey identified this as originating not as a barn but as a two-bay early C13 aisled hall, divided into four bays in the late C13, with hipped roofs supported on end crucks, a rare use. The N cruck-blade survives. Moulded capital to the central arcade post. The aisle posts were later removed. Parallel rafter roof.

3. East and north-east of the centre

The EMBANKMENT beyond The Swan was laid out from *c.* 1860 and is open to the river and to the castle grounds. Public gardens on both sides of the river and BOATHOUSES, including one for the Bedford Schools by *G. P. Allen*, 1922. On the N bank, also by Allen, the Borough WAR MEMORIAL, 1921, the sculpture by *C. S. Jagger*, in white stone. An unconventional depiction of Justice Armed, as a female Crusader knight crushing a dragon. Further down, crossing the river to the Mill Meadows, which were purchased in 1885, a SUSPENSION BRIDGE built in 1888 by *John J. Webster** and restored 1983–4. For pedestrians only. A charming design of a bowed lattice girder, carrying a less steeply arched deck. The way the two pieces intersect at the ends is delightful. Downstream the 'BUTTERFLY' BRIDGE of 1996–8 by *Chris Wilkinson Architects* (*Jan Bobrowski & Partners*, engineers), its two arches sloping outward like wings from the spine of the deck.

On the EMBANKMENT, large villas predominantly of *c.* 1880–90. Here, next to the Swan, was the TOWN AND COUNTY CLUB of 1885 by *Henry A. Cheers*, demolished in 1971; noted by Pevsner as 'Tall with two half-timbered gables, the rest brick, with a very Gothic centre'. Of comparable scale and style is the EMBANKMENT HOTEL, of 1891 for the Higgins Brewery, big black-and-white Tudor Revival with one very large jettied gable and two smaller ones. In NEWNHAM ROAD, facing Castle Close, the THOMAS CHRISTIE ALMSHOUSES by *Trenwith Wills & Wills*, 1965–8, successors to a 1697 foundation. Very good, red brick Wrennaissance with a tower in the centre and flanking ranges swept back into curves at the ends.

---

*The cast-iron PREBEND STREET BRIDGE was also by *Webster*, 1883, but was replaced by COUNTY BRIDGE, 1992.

At the corners elegant curved porches, containing stairs to the upper rooms. ROTHSAY ROAD is the principal street of this Late Victorian villa-land and is punctuated by a circus at its junction with Castle Road. The houses are big, good but ordinary. Close to the street's N end, the Providence Baptist Church (*see* Religious buildings above). The street then opens into an elongated garden square, ROTHSAY GARDENS, with earlier houses, e.g. No. 9, a villa of 1873 by *A. E. Anthony*, Italianate with fine rusticated doorpiece, and No. 4, Gothic, by *J. Horsford*, 1870. THE GROVE, W of Rothsay Gardens, has modest two-storey Tudor Gothic houses of *c.* 1841 at its S end but also HOLLY LODGE (E side), a large wilder Gothic villa, with a carved bargeboard to the gable and eccentric stone details with strong-orange brick polychromy tracing their outlines: the architect can only have been *John Usher*, the date 1869. ONSLOW VILLAS, next door, exhibiting some of the same rather exaggerated colouring, is his too. Usher's most important design was his own house, called Hiawatha, on GOLDINGTON ROAD but it alas has been demolished. Still on Goldington Road, No. 55 of 1889–90 by *R. Lund*, a villa on a massive scale. Three storeys with stone bays and a pyramid-roofed tower. It later became the County Police Headquarters.

4. North-west and west of the centre

Genteel Bedford moved to BROMHAM ROAD early in the C19. PRIORY TERRACE (Nos. 22–48, opposite the former High School) is of 1832 by *Thomas & George Bryant*. Nos. 30–32 has one combined Greek Doric porch with pediment, Nos. 38–48 one long first-floor cast-iron balcony. Refurbished and very intelligently extended as flats by *Victor J. Farrar Associates* in 1973–5, after its demolition was opposed by the Bedford Society. Nearly opposite and set back, Nos. 9–10, a ten-bay pair of ashlar-faced houses, again with Greek Doric porches. At their r. end a red brick former refectory-cum-oratory chapel, added for the St Etheldreda's Children's Home in 1890 by *Carpenter & Ingelow*, the STAINED GLASS by *Clayton & Bell c.* 1904–6.

Further W along Bromham Road, on the S side is ST BEDE'S, 1886–9 by *John Day* as Crescent House Ladies College (now flats). A little further on, two very wayward designs: CLOCK HOUSE (No. 122, a.k.a. The Den, now flats), originally a highly Picturesque Gothic *cottage orné* of 1852 for Charles Trapp, a Moravian businessman, but extended in red brick in the 1870s for Mark Whyley, the county coroner, an horologist (hence the tower); and cottages (Nos. 126 and 128) with the same appearance. Opposite, at the corner with Shakespeare Road, HEATHFIELD, dated 1884, an exceptionally large red brick villa, with lively roofscape, half-timbered black-and-white gables and some incised plaster decoration. It was built for *Thomas Spenser*, a local contractor who also signs the plans. But he often worked for *John Usher*, so the latter may have influenced the design. Many more houses like this in the streets to the N.

Bromham Road continues out of town across the railway and becomes progressively more early C20 suburban. In this part, set back from the road, a Neo-Georgian house (No. 93) for James N. White by *Richardson & Houfe*, 1953–4. Five-bay front; the deep ground-floor windows light a single sitting room and the staircase; small bow at the side for the dining room. No. 95 is a Neo-William-and-Mary job with projecting wings and a hipped roof. It is by *James Cooper* of Bishops Stortford and dates from 1893. Shallow bows on the ground floor in the fronts of the wings. Plastic windows now, alas.

Otherwise, turn N along UNION STREET for ALBERT TERRACE (Nos. 1–11) of 1850 by *Thomas Bryant* on the E side, a smart three-storey group with Ionic column porches in pairs, a rhythm of pedimented and straight-headed windows along the ground and first floors with Grecian cast-iron balconies and a fine stone parapet with carved scrolls and acroteria. Parallel to the E, THE CRESCENT has three pairs of red brick houses erected by *John Austin*, carpenter and joiner. The centre one, dated 1825, has a pediment. All three have nice cast-iron Gothic balconies and latticework porches. At the top, at the W corner with Tavistock Street, No. 14, the former BEDFORD TRAINING COLLEGE AND KINDERGARTEN SCHOOL of 1904–8, an early work by *Oswald P. Milne*, soon after he left Lutyens' office. Neo-Early Georgian with tall sashes but with a contrastingly Surrey-style porch under a tile-hung gable, clearly showing the influence of his former master. Extended by Milne, 1925–7. Now flats.

Nearby, on the N side of TAVISTOCK STREET is PLEASANT PLACE (Nos. 121–123), more good demure early C19. The street is otherwise very ragged, so returning E a brief detour instead into ADELAIDE SQUARE, conceived *c.* 1830 as a garden square but later filled in. Small group of three fine stuccoed Gothick cottages on the W side (Nos. 52–54, 56–58, 60–62), all slightly different. They were erected by 1848. Nos. 52–54 share a fine fretwork porch.

N of St Peter's Green is tree-lined DE PARYS AVENUE, a set-piece development of *c.* 1880 with lots of big brick villas of the years immediately following. The BEDFORD CLUB (No. 11) by *A. E. Anthony* and *Henry Young*, 1885, is a good example of the type: two storeys with canted bays and sharp gables fronting the attics. But the best house, indeed the best in the whole town, is not in this vein at all: No. 56, designed in 1900 by *A. N. Prentice* for Susan Collie, the principal of the Girls' High School. Shavian style, of red brick, red tile and white render, with two storeys of Ipswich windows cutting into a deep cove below the big roof and the entrance discreetly placed at the side. Panelling etc. by Prentice; his builder was *J. P. White*, whose firm no doubt made the fittings. At the top, facing PARK AVENUE, No. 14 by *Albert Prosser* for himself, 1925; the single-storey part was his office.

p. 107

Bedford, No. 56 De Parys Avenue.
By A.N. Prentice, 1900

PEMBERLEY AVENUE, E of the Bedford School grounds, was developed before the First World War. PEMBERLEY HOUSE was purpose-built as a school boarding house in 1908 by Bodley's former partner *C. G. Hare*. Deep roofs, on the front a half-hip with pebbledash above brick and two-storey square bay windows. N of this a few good minor Arts and Crafts houses exhibiting early Neo-Georgian features, all very homely, e.g. Nos. 25 and 27 (by *H. H. Dunstall*), roughcast with buttresses and bracketed eaves, No. 20 (by *Albert Prosser*) with shallow segmental bows, and No. 39, dated 1913, with deep single-storey bows and leaded windows.

There is much less in the area W and SW of the centre where the shopping area was extensively replanned after the Second World War. Even by contemporary standards it lacks personality. In MIDLAND ROAD at the corner with River Street, TESCO, formerly the Co-Op Centre, of 1973 by *E. H. C. Inskip & Son*, stands out for its curious upper storey of vertical white concave projections emblematic of wheatsheaves. The earlier rebuilding here includes the precinct to the N and, in view N along River Street, three ungainly tower blocks by *F. W. Dawkes*, 1958, after clearance of the Greyfriars district of C19 streets. Between Midland Road and Commercial Road is the KIRK-PATRICK estate of artisan-class housing laid out by *John Elger* c. 1860 after the arrival of the railway. In ASHBURNHAM ROAD is ASHBURNHAM COURT, opposite the station, by *Max Lock & Partners*, 1954–5, the earliest of the postwar flats at Bedford, designed for couples and single people. Cranked plan for the six-storey front block and raised on pilotis. Yellow brick facings in a concrete frame. Taller block to the rear and a link between. W of the railway and N of Ford End Road, the industrial suburb of QUEEN'S PARK, developed in the 1890s around Allen's engineering works (now demolished). The former ALLEN INSTITUTE in Hurst Grove is by *G. P. Allen*, son of W. H. Allen, proprietor of the works, 1907. Windows replaced.

s of the river, KEMPSTON ROAD skirts the site of the Britannia
Ironworks, started here in 1856 by James and Frederick
Howard. The original buildings, including the fanciful 'mixed
Renaissance' GATEWAY on Kempston Road, were by *Robert
Palgrave* of London. The *Illustrated London News* called his
building 'a handsome pile' done with 'taste and skill in appro-
priate embellishment'. Another journal speaks of the gateway
as of 'some Sybaritic Castle of Indolence or some luxurious
palace of learning'. It is all that remains in the BRITANNIA
WHARF housing development. This was also the site of
Cauldwell Priory (*see* Bedford Introduction, above).

In the suburbs to the NW, across Clapham Road and up MANTON
LANE is BEDFORD HEIGHTS BUSINESS CENTRE, formerly
the factory premises of TEXAS INSTRUMENTS by *O'Neil, Ford
& Colley*, 1960. Two-storey with a series of hyperbolic paraboloid concrete shell roofs like inverted umbrellas in units 48 ft
square, following the design of the head factory in Dallas,
Texas, of 1957. The walls are curtain-walled on a frame with
brick towers attached at intervals.

BIDDENHAM

On the w edge of Bedford but unspoiled and thankfully bypassed.

ST JAMES. Externally Perp but heavily restored in 1861–2 by
J. Horsford. Norman, however, the unmoulded chancel arch
and one blocked s window and probably the nave SE quoin of
rubble (i.e. of the Saxon style of construction before the use
of dressed stones); E.E. the tower with one blocked s lancet
visible inside (but the top and the recessed lead spirelet are of
course later); Dec the tower arch (half octagonal responds);
Perp the wide opening into the one-bay s chapel and the
two-bay N arcade with a pier of standard moulded section and
moulded four-centred arches. Dragon stops for the w and E
imposts. The work was done in 1522 by *John Laverok* of St
Albans for Sir William Boteler; see his arms between the
arches. Specially nicely detailed Late Perp N aisle windows. –
FONT. Octagonal, Perp, with tracery patterns. – LECTERN. An
outstanding Arts and Crafts piece of 1901 by *C. E. Mallows*,
who lived at Biddenham. Brass, copper and iron. The support
is a cross against a tree bearing solid fruit. Other fittings also
by him, e.g. the reading desk and rood cross with finely carved
detail. – SCREEN (s chapel). The dado and cresting Early
Renaissance, the thin varying tracery still Gothic. It was the
screen for the Boteler Pew in the N aisle, so no doubt also
c. 1522, but reset here in 1939 by *Albert Richardson*. Of the same
date the chapel stall screening a stair to the room over the
porch. (TAPESTRY. Signed by *Rolof Vos*, Flemish, 1549, with a
trellis grid and small ornamental motifs.) – STAINED GLASS.

The E window by *C. E. Kempe*, 1897. Chancel window (St John and St James) by *Alfred R. Fisher (J. Powell & Sons)*, 1969. Others of 1949 (by *A. L. Wilkinson*) and 1990 (N aisle E) by *Alfred R. Fisher (Chapel Studio)* in memory of the civil engineer Sir John Howard (†1986). A distinguished, multi-layered design including natural and industrial scenes, e.g. the Humber Bridge etc. – MONUMENTS. Brasses in the N aisle: a husband, wife and son (18 in. (45 cm) and 13 in. (33 cm)) and two women in shrouds (18–19 in. (45–48 cm), late C15 and early C16. – In the chancel, William Boteler †1601 and his wife †1621. Erected according to her will by their son, Richard Taylor. Kneeling couple in the usual position between two columns, but the kneeling children slightly below in the round, not in relief, and one turning outward to the viewer. Strapwork and arms on the top. Attributed to *William Wright* (GF). – Alice Osborne †1615. Small tablet with pretty surround. Helen Boteler †1639. Stone-framed brass portrait (N aisle). – E of the chancel, a CROSS with open-ringed head for Edith Guigan †1912, by *Mallows* and at the end of the same row a similar cross for C. E. Mallows †1915, by his former apprentice *F. L. Griggs*. Both nicely lettered.

The VILLAGE stretches from the church to the edge of Bedford. At the centre a long straight green flanking the village street and many good stone and thatched houses (e.g. Nos. 20–28 Main Road and Grove Farm, with Gothic windows). On the green the WAR MEMORIAL cross by *F. L. Griggs*, 1922. In the village are several houses of *c.* 1900 and the following years by *C. E. Mallows* (then of *Mallows & Grocock*), whose family were bootmakers in Bedford. They are in the Voysey style and very handsome. First was KINGS CORNER, No. 9 Main Road, built 1898–9 for J. P. White, owner of the Pyghtle Works in Bedford. The company built the house and no doubt supplied the fittings for this and the other houses. Brick and roughcast walls, originally with a single asymmetrical gable on the front ending in a catslide. Strips of square and vertical flush windows. The porch is hooded with small brackets for flower pots l. and r. Drawing room with a large inglenook topped by short columns with Art Nouveau foliage. Doorcases of tapered profile with cornices and a staircase behind a panelled screen. Sympathetically enlarged in 1992 by *Peter Lloyd*. Further E, THREE GABLES, No. 17 Biddenham Turn, was built for Mallows's father-in-law, H. J. Peacock, in 1900, but the architect also lived here 1905–15. Exquisitely homely in brick with the gables to the front and canted bays l. and r. of a ground-floor recess. The eaves carry over the sides as verandas. At the back a canted oriel for the stair. Beautifully crafted metalwork and in the drawing room, panelled in Canary whitewood, a fine inglenook with seats and benches in a window recess. Designs for the garden, in the Jekyll style, were not carried out. WHITE COTTAGE, No. 34 Days Lane, was built for Mallows's brother, Ernest, in 1908. Of a more conventional Arts and Crafts style, white roughcast all over, with a flat front and

p. 110

Biddenham, Three Gables.
Engraving by F. L. Griggs, 1902

gabled two-storey stair-tower abutting the porch. W of King's
Corner is KING'S CLOSE (No. 11 Main Road), designed 1909
for a Miss Steele by *M. H. Baillie Scott* while resident in
Bedford. It repeats his design for Tanglewood, Letchworth,
Herts., with gables l. and r., one with a catslide and a chimney
piercing the apex. Timber-framed centre. Paired gables to the
garden side. Compact plan of two main rooms on the ground
floor, divided by a moveable screen, and an entrance lobby set
into it. Impish figure on the stair newel. *Baillie Scott* also did
WHITE COTTAGE (No. 17 Church End) in 1910 for a Miss
Street (CS in the datestone). White roughcast and red tiles but
also some timber boarding. Asymmetrical front of gabled
porch and one large gable to the r. with the roof descending
low in the space between over a window lighting a settle inside.
Three gables at the rear.

1040

BIGGLESWADE

Biggleswade stands close to where the Great North Road crossed
the River Ivel, serving as a stop on the coaching roads and further
benefiting from the 1757 Act to make the river navigable, granting
access to goods being imported along the Ouse from King's
Lynn. Gardening for the London market was the principal activity in the C19, especially after the railway arrived in 1850. A
destructive fire in 1785 removed much evidence of the town
before that date and in the centre there is alas too much of the
lacklustre later C20.

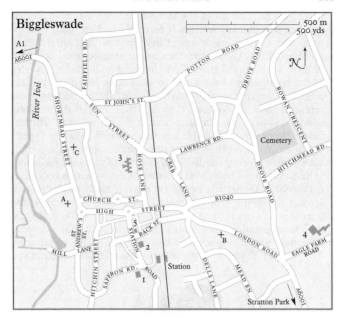

A   St Andrew
B   Baptist Church
C   Wesleyan Chapel
    (Trinity Methodist Church)

1   Town Hall
2   Police Station
3   Board School (former)
4   Stratton Upper School
5   Regal Cinema (former)

CHURCHES*

ST ANDREW. A large church and, like so many in Bedfordshire,
nearly all Perp, but all external detail new following restoration
in 1870 by *Habershon & Pite* (cf. Sandy). The 'nearly all Perp'
excepts most prominently the w tower, which, except for the
stair-turret and its base, is of 1720: grey ashlar, with round-
arched bell-openings. The rest is ironstone. The high tower
arch towards the nave is early C14, and so is the s doorway with
two continuous chamfers. Long chancel, the rebuilding of
which is credited to John Rudying, prebendary of Lincoln,
c. 1467–81. Seven-light E window. The N aisle and the clerestory
have large windows. Contemporary with the chancel, the Late
Perp two-storey s porch – blocking a window in the s aisle –
with a tierceron-star vault and a bold ogee-arched entrance.
The cusping is blank, each cusp with two little blank quatrefoils. At the top of the arch a weathered sculpture, probably of
the Trinity. The upper floor contained a Guild chapel founded

*ST JOHN, by *A. W. Blomfield*, 1883, has been demolished since the first edition of
this guide.

in 1475. The S DOOR of the same time with a fully traceried head of curvilinear patterns. It formerly had an *orate* inscription. The arcades inside are of four bays with standard Perp pier mouldings. Good Perp S aisle roof with bosses. Nave roof of 1870 with braced trusses on clustered wall-shafts. N vestry of the restoration of the E end in 1885–8 by *Butterfield* but his adjoining organ chamber was destroyed by fire in 1953 and replaced by a single-storey link by *M. J. Tapper*; the chancel window above was reconstructed at the same time. Butterfield's chancel roof was also lost but restored. Also by Tapper the fine ORGAN CASE in the W tower arch. – FONT. Perp shaft with simple tracery motifs. – REREDOS. 1877 by *R. J. Withers*, with *Salviati* mosaic of 1881. – SCREEN. 1919 with a rood loft. CURIOSUM. Donations board (W tower). Early C19? Painted. It uses the motif of a column to show the yearly sums disbursed. – STAINED GLASS. E window, 1877 by *Barnett* of York, the Transfiguration with saints in the upper lights. One chancel S window a Last Supper by *Clayton & Bell*, 1889; another by *Kempe*, 1895. Tower window, sadly obscured by the organ, 1870

Biggleswade, St Andrew.
Brass to John Rudying †1481, detail

by *Lavers, Barraud & Westlake* (Michael Kerney). – Two windows by *Lawrence Lee*, 1953 (S aisle) and 1954 (Lady Chapel, with *C. R. Wallis*). – BRASSES. William Halsted †1449 and his wife, labelled Alicia. 18-in. (45 cm) figures. – John Rudying †1481. In the floor of the chancel that he built. A few remarkable fragments of a remarkable design, reassembled when the chancel was repaired in 1955. On one side Death with a cluster of spears above a long inscription. The figure of Rudying knelt opposite and above were figures of St John the Baptist, St Anne, St Elizabeth and Mary of Egypt.

BAPTIST CHURCH, London Road. By *C. M. Lock & Partners*, 1969. Yellow brick periphery with a startling peaked roof shape over the worship space.

WESLEYAN CHAPEL (Trinity Methodist Church), Shortmead Street. Good sober brick front of 1834 with a pediment, stucco pilasters and three arched windows. Refurbished by *Potts, Sulman & Hennings*, 1889, the date of the porch and galleries. Equally large SUNDAY SCHOOL of 1905 behind.

Former PRIMITIVE METHODIST CHAPEL, Shortmead Street. 1873. Primitive Gothic. Now a house.

CEMETERY, Drove Road. 1869, won in competition by *John Ladds & J. M. Hooker*. Chapels in C14 style with a central tower over an arch and carrying a slated pyramidal spire. Hard Butterfieldian character with sparing polychromy.

PUBLIC BUILDINGS*

Former TOWN HALL, Market Place. *See* Perambulation below.

TOWN HALL, Saffron Road. Charming Neo-Georgian box, a single-storey originally for the Court House, of 1927 by *S. C. Jury*, architectural assistant to the County Surveyor.

Former COUNTY COURT, High Street. 1861. Now a house. Italianate, single-storey with four round arches. All in brick, the ends with channelled rustication and a bracketed cornice along the top.

POLICE STATION, Station Road. Neo-Georgian of 1939 by the County Surveyor, with an archway in the centre and offices in the court behind. The police station of 1855 is opposite, the style entirely domestic.

Former BOARD SCHOOL, Rose Lane. 1874–5 by *Thomas Elworthy*. Very long and low with gable-fronted classrooms spreading l. and r. of the taller central hall with a bellcote. Windows of 'Venetian' type but Gothic with intersecting cast-iron tracery. Now housing.

STRATTON UPPER SCHOOL, Eagle Farm Road. The Grammar Technical School of 1950 by *S. V. Goodman*, County Architect. The style is still prewar modern with a monolithic clocktower to the fore, but an asymmetrical layout and a sparing austerity in the long and low elevations.

*The former WORKHOUSE in London Road, 1835–6 by *T. G. Elger* of Bedford, noted by Pevsner, was demolished in 1972.

Former REGAL CINEMA, Back Street. 1936 by *Arthur Singleton*. Economic Art Deco. Angled corner with brick flanks.

BRIDGES, over the Ivel. Three pointed arches; C14.

PUMPING STATION, London Road, SW. 1906 by *George F. Deacon* of Westminster, engineer, for the Biggleswade Water Board. A striking building in ironstone with arched entrance between square buttress towers. Superintendent's house linked to the l. with a recessed porch and a pyramidal red-tiled roof between corner bartizans. The appearance and massing recalls the contemporary Glasgow Style.

PERAMBULATION

The centre of Biggleswade is the Market Place, a disappointing centre in a visually disappointing little town. The former TOWN HALL is the only building of note. Five-bay stuccoed front with two giant Roman Doric columns *in antis*. 1844 by *J. T. Wing*. Next to the town hall on the S side of the square, another timber-framed building, the WHITE HART, a C16 hall-house, but also largely re-done with false timbers. Otherwise, in or near the Market Place, the former MARKET HOUSE, timber-framed and externally not ancient at all, rebuilt in 1937, but with C16 timber roof. E of the square, GEORGE'S HALL, (Liberal Club) in red brick and stamped terracotta is pretty old-fashioned for the date: 1912, by *W. C. Owen-Jones*. Large hall on the first floor above shops. In HIGH STREET, visible from the Market Place, the CROWN HOTEL, late C18, with enjoyable Art Nouveau lettering to the doors. Also NATWEST, Bankers' Georgian of 1927. Opposite, some shops, flats and offices of 1976 by *Marshman, Warren & Taylor*, on the site of the Swan Hotel. Closing the view E, i.e. along St Andrew's Street, some gabled and jettied fronts, the timbering again applied. In CHURCH STREET, behind, the C18 OLD MALTINGS, close to the site of the brewery (for Wells & Winch by *George Adlam & Sons*, 1901, but cleared after 1997).

To the W, in ST ANDREW'S STREET, the CONSERVATIVE CLUB, an imposing merchant's house of *c.* 1800, in gault brick with a panelled parapet. Five bays wide, the centre one slightly recessed but the entrance in it curiously underplayed. N of the church, BEAUMONT PARK, dated 1840, Neo-Jacobean with straight and shaped gables. Opposite, in SHORTMEAD STREET, one notable early to mid-C18 frontage (ELPHICK COURT) with a slightly projecting centre and stucco classical embellishments of *c.* 1834 for Mead House School; inscribed 'An Establishment for Young Gentlemen'. Just before the Baptist church, two nicely restored late C18 cottages (Nos. 66–68); they are a pair, but very oddly the doors do not align.

Away from the centre to the E, in LONDON ROAD, Mead Road and Dells Lane, some flat-roofed modernistic pairs of 1937. N, in DROVE ROAD, some early COUNCIL HOUSING of 1913 in three rows, the walls of the local Arlesey white brick.

SHORTMEAD HOUSE, Fairfield Road. Yellow brick with a small stone cornice below the parapet. Five bays by three, with a big porch with Tower of the Winds-type capitals, door with broad arched fanlight and a tripartite window over. Late C18. Arched stair window at the rear, where the walls are red brick.

STRATTON PARK, out to the SE along London Road. The house was pulled down in the 1950s. It belonged to Sir Thomas Cotton from 1639 and contained a marvellous late C17 staircase with openwork acanthus panels. One panel is preserved in the small successor house, built from the materials and with a few other fragments preserved from the remodelling of the house by *John Usher* for Lucy Jane Barnett in 1878; LODGE of the same period.

BIGGLESWADE MILL, Mill Lane. C19. Now flats. Windows in three-storey arches. Beside it is IVEL HOUSE, built in 1898 for Henry Franklin, who became the miller in 1883.

JORDANS MILL, Holme, 1 m. S on the Ivel. The Jordans first leased and then bought the mill in 1893, rebuilding it in 1894 after a fire, installing roller grinders for the production of pure (i.e. branless) white flour. The buildings will be familiar to muesli-chewers worldwide and only ceased operation in the 1990s; the machinery is preserved for display.

BILLINGTON

ST MICHAEL, and indeed, like many St Michaels, overlooking a valley from a steep escarpment; the site of an Iron Age hillfort. A small church, originally quite low but heightened in 1852 by *E.C. Hakewill*. Polygonal stone bell-turret over the W end on two big buttresses. The turret is 1840s and came from St Barnabas, Linslade (q.v.) when that church got its tower in 1869. But the blank window inside the W wall is real C13 work, probably reset. – STAINED GLASS. E window by *Lavers, Barraud & Westlake*, 1884. Two others by *Mayer & Co.*, 1885 (w window) and 1909 (chancel N, signed).

Former RECTORY, E of the church. By *S. S. Teulon*, 1859. Big, gloomy brick job with some polychrome patterns.

BILLINGTON MANOR, 1/8 m. SSE. Neo-Elizabethan, built by Arthur Macnamara who acquired the manor in the 1880s. Several estate cottages in the village bear his initials.

BISCOT *see* LUTON

BLETSOE

A St John estate village from the C16 to the 1950s, with a compact plan, possibly of Norman origins, below manor and church, around what is called the 'Great Green' in the 1620s.

ST MARY. Mostly Dec, but extensively renewed in its details in
1857–66, seemingly by *S. S. Teulon*.* Since the 1970s the
chancel has been separated from the nave and disused. The s
doorway C13, and perhaps the crossing tower in its bones too,
if not earlier (cf. Thurleigh). There is a lancet giving onto the
chancel. The arches for the tower on the other hand are Dec,
w and E higher than N and s. The nave has reticulated tracery
in the w window and flowing tracery in N and s windows.
Flowing tracery also in the N transept. The chancel has Dec
recesses: with crocketed gable in the N wall, with rather bleak
cusping in the s wall. The N transept (originally a chantry
chapel founded by John de Patishull after 1279, dedicated to
St Edmund by the C16 when it became the St John Chapel,
and substantially remodelled in the mid C19) has a double
PISCINA and an excellent roof, a barrel vault with ribs forming
diamond patterns and bosses in the spandrels. Harvey calls the
ceiling 'modern' in 1872 so this too may be of the restoration,
along with the balustrade of quatrefoils with shields to the
raised burial vault. The High Victorian treatment of the nave
E wall belongs to 1883, with trefoil-headed arcading for memorial panels. – FONT. Perp, octagonal, with arched panels.
– REREDOS (former chancel). 1882 by *R. L. Boulton* of Cheltenham. – STAINED GLASS. Chancel E and s window by *Mayer
& Co.*, 1885 and 1888. w window by *H. Warren Wilson*, 1939, in
memory of Harry Cheetham, craft printer and founder of the
Broadwater Press, Welwyn, with appropriate iconography. –
MONUMENTS. In the nave, but formerly in the N transept, Sir
John St John †1559 and family. Large standing alabaster monument. He and the sons kneeling to the w, she and the daughters
to the E. Two columns and a straight top. Latin inscription in
hexameters. It is not an over-elaborate piece. Still in the N
chapel, Frances Countess Bolingbroke †1678, wife of Oliver St
John, the 2nd Earl. Large tablet with two urns, a broken pediment and an arched top. Fine workmanship. Attributed to
Abraham Storey (GF), no doubt the same hand as the Alston
Monument at Odell (q.v.). LYCHGATE. An impressively solid
piece of timber-framing of 1912.

BLETSOE CASTLE. There is no surviving evidence for anything
resembling a Norman fortification that might have been occupied by Osbert de Broilg in the late C11. John de Patishull
received his licence to crenellate in 1327. It passed to the
Beauchamps and then by marriage to the St Johns. The Lady
Margaret, Henry VII's mother, was born here, and Queen
Elizabeth I and King James I visited. Oliver St John became
Baron St John of Bletso in 1558. Nothing medieval is visible in
the present house but nearby are the remains of a substantial
moat, 55 ft (16.7 metres) wide and about 15 ft (4.5 metres) deep,
crossed by a C16 BRIDGE of two arches. The moat is probably
manorial and post-Norman, expanded in C16 and C17 land-

---

*The work appears to have been superintended first by *Edward Browning* of Stamford and then by *J. T. Wing*.

scaping of which other garden earthworks survive to the N and E. A written survey of 1623–8 shows that the house and inner court lay within the moat, and to the S was a base court for stables etc. Only the house remains. Long, flat front. Eight bays, two storeys, hipped roof, substantial chimneys and gabled projections at the rear. It had a third storey topped by shaped gables. Three- and four-light transomed windows, some with mullions. Jacobean staircase. It was abandoned by the St Johns for Melchbourne in the C18 and then reduced to a farmhouse.

Nos. 2–3 OLD WAY. The house contains a two-bay open hall with a smoke bay, tree-ring felling dates give a date for construction of 1459–60 and for insertion of a ceiling 1642. The half bay extension of *c.* 1700 has Northamptonshire-style ironstone quoins, the furthest SE example in Bedfordshire.

BLETSOE PARK FARM, 1.5 m. NNE. Early C17. Unusual cruciform plan of four rooms on each floor around a central chimney.

BLUNHAM

1050

ST JAMES AND ST EDMUND. The most interesting feature of the church, speaking from an architectural point of view, is the W tower. It is of ironstone and has several strange motifs, such as clasping buttresses with shallow set-offs, and eight pinnacles, four of them on decidedly post-medieval-looking gablets. There is indeed a date 1583 inscribed, and with this date the Latest-Perp-looking W windows harmonize, though they are completely restored. Buttresses show inside the aisles. Yet the tower is structurally much older, for it has a Norman arch towards the nave, with a strong roll and the outer voussoirs of alternating limestone and ironstone polychromy. The W doorway also has a Norman, or rather a Transitional, arch with several rolls and also the alternation of colour of the voussoirs. Visible only inside the tower is one Norman window and the blocked arch of another. The chancel is structurally C13 – see the SEDILIA and PISCINA and the sill course with its complex moulding and leaf stops – but the windows (except of course those of the Perp clerestory) are Dec. One in the N wall is blocked and there is also a blocked door, possibly to a former vestry. Also Dec the cusped and subcusped tomb recess in this wall with a spreading ogee arch and crockets on it. Leaf spandrels. Quatrefoil frieze to the chest. In the S aisle two Dec windows and one Perp. The three-bay arcades are Perp (standard moulded section of the thin piers) but have arches still with the Dec sunk quadrants. The responds are of ironstone. The chancel arch is similar to the arcades. The chancel roof has interesting bosses – angels, heads, an animal, griffins(?), and also a kneeling cleric. The N and S chapels are again both Perp; the S chapel has an impressive Late Perp stone SCREEN between it and the chancel, with a doorway and a straight top with panel tracery under. It may have belonged to a chantry chapel associated with the fraternity of the Holy Trinity, established after 1467 by Edmund de Grey, Earl of Kent. The chapel had a door to a stair to a possible priest's room over the intriguing s porch. This extends up to the s boundary wall and has arches E and W to permit processions around the church. Perp s door with shields and foliage in the spandrels. – PULPIT. Elizabethan, with two tiers of the frequent blank arches. TOWER SCREEN. C17? Splat balusters. (– SCULPTURE. Four fragments of Nottingham alabaster, three C15, but the exquisite though headless Virgin undoubtedly still C14. The fragments retain quite a bit of their original painting. Discovered built into the E wall in 1862 when the church was restored.) – STAINED GLASS. E window by *Ward & Hughes*, 1864. Chancel SE by *Clayton & Bell*, 1911. – MONUMENTS. Brasses to Richard Maulaye, mercer, †1506, and wife, 18-in. (45 cm) figures. – Susan Lady Longueville, daughter of the 7th Earl of Kent,★ †1620. This is a very good standing alabaster monument. Recumbent effigy on a tomb-chest with two floral wreaths, shallow coffered arch. Small kneeling figures on the back wall. Attributed to *William Cure II* (GF). – Godfrey Thornton, Soane's client at Moggerhanger, †1805, by *Bacon Jun*. Shallow relief tablet with urn before obelisk and finely carved reliefs of maritime and agricultural motifs. – Mrs Thornton †1862 by *Samuel Manning Jun*. Elegant group of a kneeling woman by a pedestal with an urn. Two other good tablets by *Manning Sen.*, jointly with *Bacon*: R. P. Beachcroft, erected 1833, and Sarah Beachcroft †1834. – MAUSOLEUM, s of the chancel. For the Thorntons of Moggerhanger. Erected by Stephen Thornton, 1805–6. Gothick, quatrefoil openings in circles and an armorial panel over the door.

BAPTIST CHAPEL, High Street. Very domestic design in red brick, dated 1751, much rebuilt in yellow in 1832. Two entrances l. and r. and round-arched windows at the back.

OLD RECTORY. 1873–4 by *John Usher*, who was born at Blunham. A huge and grim building of yellow brick with half-hipped roofs and plenty of chimneystacks. Mostly three-storey but on one side a tall window, two-light with transoms, in an arched recess. Nearby, BLUNHAM HOUSE (now subdivided), its earliest part probably built *c*. 1727 for Thomas Bromsall II. This shows only on the W front, and is of three bays in red brick with rubbed dressings, a moulded string and cornice. The rest appears to have assumed its present appearance in the early C19. Principal front with a Venetian window above a Doric porch. Yet behind this is a fine staircase with twisted balusters and ramped handrail which must be 1720s. There are undated plans for alterations by *Usher & Anthony* for Sir Salusbury Payne, probably to the service side.

★The 7th Earl appointed John Donne as rector in 1621.

BOLNHURST

St Dunstan. A substantial church, quite on its own. Big Perp W tower with pairs of two-light bell-openings. It had a short spire until 1806. In the nave on the s side mixed windows, one Dec and two Early Perp with straight-sided hexagons above the main lights and a transom; one with cusping. On the N side two large, transomed Late Perp windows and a blocked N door. Horribly scraped interior. – C13 DOUBLE PISCINA in the chancel with trefoil heads. On the s side, between the middle and E window, a curious stub of walling with a roll-moulding on the E face, apparently associated with the former Francklin Pew. The pew RAILING and marble flooring are early C18. – BENCHES, C16, of the usual buttressed design. – PULPIT. Jacobean, with plain panels. Chancel fittings of a restoration of 1850–4 by J. T. Wing, who added the vestry. The STALLS return against a SCREEN of two-light divisions; not much of it old. – ORGAN CASE. A Gothic design by F. H. Sutton, the organ made by Bryceson Bros & Morten in 1873, originally for Keysoe.* The decoration outside has sadly deteriorated, but the bold pattern inside is quite fresh. – WALL PAINTING. Large St Christopher over the N doorway. – STAINED GLASS. In a nave N window, demi-figure of the Virgin; C15. – The nave s window (Francklin Pew) has the Francklin arms, early C18. – E window initialled by W. Holland of Warwick. It is of 1853; the other two chancel windows also by him. – W window by Hardman, 1883. – MONUMENTS. John Francklin, Master in Ordinary of the High Court of Chancery, †1707. By Edward Stanton. White marble, quite lavish, with two columns, an open segmental pediment, two putti on it, and between them an urn. – Dame Dorothy Francklin †1727. Cartouche with putto heads; very pretty. Attributed to Stanton & Horsnaile (GF).

BRICKHILL see BEDFORD

BROGBOROUGH

The village was built by the Marston Valley Brick Co. for its workers. It has no church, and the brickworks (opened 1935), with their more than twenty chimneys which once made it a prominent object in the landscape, have gone. On their site the MARSTON GATE DISTRIBUTION PARK, including the AMAZON WAREHOUSE, the company's first permanent UK distribution centre. It covers 500,000 sq. ft with five linked units with shallow curved roofs. By UMC Architects, 2012.

---

*Correspondence in the Keysoe parish records disproves an earlier attribution to Pugin (see British Institute of Organ Studies Reporter, April 2002, v. 26, no. 2).

BROGBOROUGH PARK FARM, ½ m. N of the brickworks site, is the ruin following a fire in 1993 of a small square brick country house of the mid-C17 doll's-house type. It was called the 'Round House' for its internal circulation, having a big hipped roof and a central chimneystack. It was in fact the cross-wing only of the house built for Colonel John Okey, the Regicide, the rest of which was demolished sometime between 1728 and 1820.

RIDGMONT STATION, ½ m. S, on the Bedford–Bletchley Line. 1846. In the Picturesque half-timbered style demanded by the Duke of Bedford (cf. Millbrook and Woburn Sands).

0050

BROMHAM

ST OWEN. The church stands in the park of the Hall, all on its own. The earliest part is the three-bay N arcade, with quatrefoil piers and arches of one step and one chamfer. This work is probably of *c.* 1300. The dainty minor S doorway would go with it. The chancel looks Dec, and the ANGLE PISCINA is, but otherwise it was rebuilt in 1868–9 by *William Butterfield*, who added the Dynevor* Chapel (N). The adjoining organ chamber is by *G. P. Allen*, 1907–8. The rest of the church is Perp. W tower with higher stair-turret, S aisle with two windows l. and r. of the two-storey S porch. External stair to the upper floor which contained a library given by the 2nd Lord Trevor in 1740: 'No Book to be Let Out Without Leave of the Minister or Lord of the Manor'. The N porch, also two-storey, has some old timber. – FONT. Octagonal, Perp, with pointed quatrefoils etc. and tracery. – READING DESK. With two bearded heads as poppy-heads, copied by Butterfield for his STALLS. – HOURGLASS STAND. Plain. – STAINED GLASS. Old bits in a chancel S window, reset in 1869 by *Lavers & Barraud*, who executed the Dynevor Chapel window in 1870. Two windows (2003 and 2004) by *Michael Stokes*. – MONUMENTS. Brass to Thomas Wideville and two wives †1435, excellent figures, 4 ft (1.2 metres) long, under ogee gables. The monument was originally at St James' monastery, Northampton, but was appropriated by Sir John Dyve †1535 and given his heraldry etc. – Sir Lewis Dyve †1592. Completely of alabaster. Five-poster with recumbent effigy on a half-rolled-up mat. He wears a long beard. Strapwork achievement on the top. Erected 1603. It is clearly from the same workshop as the 2nd Lord Mordaunt's monument at Turvey, the Snagge monument at Marston Moretaine, and the Thompson monument at Husborne Crawley (qq.v.). – 1st Lord Trevor †1730. Standing wall monument with two putti l. and r. of a

---

*Seemingly a conflation of the names of the successive lords of the manor, the Dyves and Trevors.

black sarcophagus and obelisk. *Richard van Spangen* of Camberwell was paid £250 for it. – 3rd Lord Trevor †1764. By *Prince Hoare*. Tablet in several marbles. Woman seated on a black sarcophagus by a black urn. – Eva Trevor †1842, twelve years old. She is seen floating to heaven. Gothic surround. – GATE. Also by *Butterfield*, recognizably no-nonsense.

BROMHAM HALL, ¼ m. E. A rambling house, awkward to unpick from the external evidence. John Bailey discovered that the earliest part is an aisled hall, probably early C14, of which the stone entrance doorway to the cross-passage S of the two-bay hall is still *in situ*. The crown-post roof survives over the hall, cross-passage and one S bay. Curved braces between the post and tie-beam. Externally however nothing seems earlier than the late C16, when the hall belonged to Sir Lewis Dyve (†1592). On the front, a large gabled cross-wing to the N of the former hall and to the S a range under three gables and incorporating the porch. All the gables have kneelers of orange Northamptonshire ironstone; the dressings of mutilated mullioned windows are the same. Inside the cross-wing a robust stair rising around a solid core. Crown-post roof above the former hall and a scarf joint. Arch-braced roofs with windbraces in the southern part. There is a SE wing, apparently early, projecting at the rear with chimneystack and another part with heavy buttresses to its S. The hall was extensively reworked and extended on this side in the C18, after Sir Thomas Trevor (later 1st Lord Trevor), Chief Justice of the Common Pleas, acquired the manor in 1708. The SW wing, curiously splayed at an angle, contains a suite of good Early Georgian panelled upper rooms. Some further remodelling in 1924 by *A. S. G. Butler*. – ORANGERY. Handsome C18 red brick with oval windows and glazed front. – Gothick LODGE at the park entrance.

SCHOOL, Village Road, 1861 by *W. Tucker* of London. Memorable for the blackletter inscription along the bargeboards and diaper-pattern roof tiles.

BROMHAM HOUSE (now Parklands), 1¼ m. W. 1897–8 by *G. P. Allen* for his father, who owned the Queen's Park Engineering Works at Bedford. Allen's master, *A. W. Blomfield*, probably had a guiding hand in the design. Neo-Jacobean. (Galleried hall. Library added 1913, again by *Allen*.)

BRIDGE and CAUSEWAY over the Ouse, ⅜ m. SSW. With many cutwaters. There are altogether twenty-six arches. The oldest go back to 1224. There was a chantry chapel at the W end from 1295. Extensive repairs in the late C15 and much rebuilding in 1813–14 by *Robert Salmon*, the Duke of Bedford's surveyor. The principal S arches over the river are of 1902.

N of the Bridge, BROMHAM MILL (Arts Centre). Red brick with some timber-framing in the upper storey (dated 1695 and 1722) and a stone extension of 1858. Of two wheels, an iron breastshot type of 1908 survives (makers, *Anstee* of Kempston). Restored after 1974.

BROOM
2½ m. ENE of Southill

A hamlet with much Whitbread estate housing. One very good tall terrace of 1881 in Southill Road has projections under half-hipped roofs and porches in the angles.

BROOM HALL, N of this, is Late Georgian. Three-storeys with parapet. Semicircular porch with thin Doric columns and Adamish plaster ceiling. Tripartite upper windows in the centre. At the rear a Gothick addition with three large ogee-headed windows. A fine cedar-tree on the l. of the front. Now flats.

On High Street, FORDHAM ALMSHOUSES, 1913–14 probably designed by *Rupert O. Fordham,* an amateur architect, of Broom Hall. Decidedly odd façade of crazy-paving and eyebrow dormers.

BUSHMEAD PRIORY
1½ m. NNE of Colmworth

The priory was founded *c.* 1195 for Augustinian Canons. It was already much reduced before its Dissolution in 1536. All that remains of it now is the REFECTORY range, originally N of the cloister. It has a tall W window (tracery of 1980), angle buttresses and in the S wall a large resourcefully trefoiled arch for the LAVA-TORIUM, probably *c.* 1250. Magnificent late C13 ROOF, of five bays (and originally a sixth to the E), which combines crown-post construction with an older tradition of parallel rafters scissored at the apex. Two sets of braces between the crown-post and collar and rafters. On the W wall, significant traces of WALL PAINTING: fictive masonry, flower trails, capitals on the window jambs and a bird. It included a scene of Creation. The date is *c.* 1310. In the N wall, E end, a window shafted inside and with a depressed arch starting with a short vertical piece. Inside the S wall, remains of the stair to the pulpit. Behind the range, the KITCHEN fireplace. The whole range was apparently divided into two floors before the Dissolution. Straight-headed, typically Late Perp windows were put in on the upper floor.* SCREEN on the first floor. The W end was returned to full height in the C18 and used as stables. Fragments of C18 STAINED GLASS in the N window. – SCULP-TURE. An alabaster fragment of a canon. *c.* 1400.

The E bay of the range and the chapter house were incorpor-ated into a new HOUSE *c.* 1620 for the Gerys (later Wade-Gerys); the church was taken down at about that time. Again rebuilt in

---

*The Bucks, *c.* 1730, illustrate the remains but confusingly show a series of Dec windows in the upper storey.

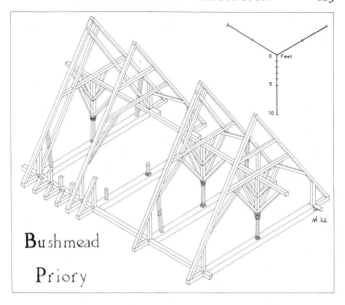

Bushmead Priory.
Axonometric of roof trusses

the C18 but reduced to its present extent and remodelled in Neo-Georgian style in 1965.

About 350 yds s a SUMMERHOUSE, C18 probably, square, of brick and tower-like, with a pyramid roof, small corner turrets and at the back (now enclosed) the back wall of a former grotto. Later stair abutting.

CADDINGTON

0010

The village was until the C20 the source for many of the so-called 'Luton grey' bricks widely found in the southernmost part of the county.

ALL SAINTS. The church has been restored all round, in particular by *Ewan Christian* in 1875–6, when e.g. the chancel was rebuilt with its N vestry. Peculiar to Caddington is a tradition of commemorating alterations by chronograms inscribed in the window sills inside. The story begins, however, with the w quoins of an aisleless nave. They look Anglo-Saxon and may be of the C11. Then follows the (reset) Norman s doorway. Its arch has chevron, including that type which operates at right angles to the wall face, but the colonnettes have early stiff-leaf capitals, i.e. keeping close to the bell. So this must be *c.* 1190–1200; indeed it should be noted that the Canons of St Paul's, Bedford, held the church from at least the 1180s (cf. Kensworth). The chancel arch is a little later. The responds include keeled shafts, and the capitals also have close stiff-leaf. The arch itself must have been renewed in the early C14 (see the mouldings), and the CREDENCE TABLE on a short shaft in the chancel N wall is contemporary with it. Later in the C13 the chancel SEDILIA and PISCINA were made (cusped pointed arches). The early C14 extension is the feature of the highest quality. It is a two-bay N chapel or short N aisle added to the then existing nave. The pier and responds have fleurons in the capitals – the N aisle W respond must be the reset W respond of this N extension. And the E window, now opening into the vestry, is a delightful oculus with an inset concave-sided lozenge, all nicely cusped. The aisles are otherwise Perp. They have standard elements, but differ in proportion and the S aisle has no E respond. The finest part of the exterior is the W tower, complete by 1458, much repaired in the C18, C19 and C20, but with picturesque results: flint, squared stone, and brick and tile, quite irregular. Higher stair-turret. Stately Perp W doorway. – FONT. Big, octagonal, Perp, but inside a small circular basin with inscribed rim (C18?). – PULPIT. About 1650, with typical panels and the exclamation-mark-like vertical motifs. – BENCHES (nave, W end). Early C16, buttressed with linenfold on the ends. – HELM. On the chancel S wall, with cockerel crest; for one of the Coppins of Markyate Cell (Herts.). – ORGAN. Very large case, filling the W end and raised on columns. By *J. J. Binns*, 1912. – STAINED GLASS. E window by *W. F. Dixon* in memory of Annie Macnamara †1877, who contributed to the chancel rebuilding. Subtly coloured against grisaille. Two others of 1913 (S aisle) and 1922 (N aisle) by *A. L. Moore.* – BRASSES. – John Hawtt, dated 1505, with wife and children. Edward Dormer (N aisle) †1518. Two wives and children. – MONUMENTS. – John Pedley of Caddington Hall †1838. Well done; without figures. By *Sanders* of New Road, Marylebone. – CURIOSUM (in store). A CONSTABLE'S TRUNCHEON of 1832.

CAINHOE CASTLE *see* CLOPHILL

1040

CALDECOTE
1½ m. SE of Northill

ALL SAINTS, Upper Caldecote. A chapel of ease to Northill. 1867–8 by *A. W. Blomfield.* Yellow brick with red bands and trim. Double bellcote on the chancel W gable. Round-arched windows, but Early Gothic roses in the E, W and S transept S walls. Straight chancel end, and the novel feature of a low apsed W baptistery. The principal capitals are of the French Early Gothic foliage type, and the chancel chapels have pointed arches with dogtooth to the piers. What style then is intended? – REREDOS. Charming painting of censing angels and the Evangelists symbols, by *Heaton, Butler & Bayne*; the baptistery STAINED GLASS by the same. – PULPIT. 1960s, but traditional, with the badge of the Grocers' Company, the patrons of the living (cf. Northill).

VICARAGE, W of the church, again by *Blomfield*. English Domestic Revival, of brick with tile-hung upper storeys and a sgraffito panel in one gable with the date, 1873. NE of the church, brick ALMSHOUSES built by the Harveys of Ickwell (q.v.), 1876. S of the church, CALDECOTE HOUSE, early C19 with arched centre windows and bows l. and r. of a fine Gothick iron porch and door with a nice Late Georgian fanlight.

MANOR FARM, Lower Caldecote, 1 m. ENE. Well-preserved timber-framed ONION SHED, once a common feature of the locality. Three storeys above an open ground floor with weatherboarding and hinged flaps at each stage.

CAMPTON

ALL SAINTS. Ironstone. Externally predominantly of the restoration by *A. W. Soames*, 1892–6, which included the rebuilding of the Perp W tower. But of the late C13 or *c.* 1300 the S doorway and the S arcade of four bays with short quatrefoil piers. The taller N arcade Perp: yet in actual fact it is of 1649, when the Osborn Chapel with its Late-Perp-looking E window was also built. Unfortunately the outer wall is all of 1896 and so too the Perp-style reredos in the N aisle. The chancel, though over-restored too, is early C14, see the PISCINA and the niches l. and r. of the E window. Attached to the Osborn Chapel's N side is an C18 mausoleum of blue and red brick, with a pediment and panels of knobbly rustication. Probably built by Sir Danvers Osborn for the internment of Lady Mary †1743. – FONT. C18. Small oval grey marble bowl on square baluster. Much less appealing late C19 Gothic font. – SCREENS. Very interesting tower screen with unusual Dec(?) motifs in two-light divisions. Fragments of another screen used in the PULPIT. They are specially good and certainly C14 Dec. – A third screen between chancel and Osborn Chapel. Two tiers, the lower of closely set balusters, the upper of columns carrying arches. The date is no doubt *c.* 1649. – COMMUNION RAIL. C18. Slender balusters.* – ARCHITECTURAL FRAGMENTS. C13 and C14, e.g. stiff-leaf capitals, perhaps from Chicksands. –

---

*The BENCHES, some with buttressed ends, noted in the first edition have been removed.

STAINED GLASS. All by *Heaton, Butler & Bayne*, 1888–1914, to the Osborns. – MONUMENTS. Brasses to Richard Carlyll †1489 and wife, 12-in. (30 cm) figures. – Sir Peter and Sir John Osborn, erected in 1655 and highly memorable. By *John Stone*. Two big white altars and two big white reredoses with volutes l. and r. and segmental tops. Between are cartouches with swags. The fleshy, gristly forms are typical of 1650, but the general tenor is far more classical than one would expect. – Outside, John Fuller †1819, a fine large tapered stone sarcophagus on claw feet and topped by acroteria.

MANOR HOUSE, w of the church. Built *c.* 1591 for the Ventris family. Timber-framed, with a long symmetrical E front with five gables, two large and three small, including that of the central porch. But the entrance was before the C18 in the bay to the l. and the close-studded timber-framing appears to be completely C20; the VCH in 1912 refers to it 'now after a period of neglect being put into a state of repair'. The back is brick, early C18 with a canted bay. (Inside the hall has a central fireplace and SCREEN at the s end with strapwork cresting. In the N wing a room with panelling, beams carved with late Elizabethan square and circle motifs and a chimneypiece of two arches and pilasters. The former chamber over the hall has a barrel vault.)

OLD RECTORY, opposite the manor house. C18, five bays, red brick, with recessed hipped roof. Very plain. Altered 1839 by *John Woolfe Jun.* (NHLE).

CARDINGTON

Despite its proximity to Bedford, remarkably rural and undeveloped, the consequence of its ownership since the late C18 by the Whitbread estate.

ST MARY. Large, and unfortunately mostly of 1897–1901 by *George Highton* of Bedford in an unwarrantedly extensive reworking for Samuel Whitbread III in rockfaced and coursed sandstone. The C12 tower was between nave and chancel but is now at the w end, and its round arch inside has a single step with some retooled Norman voussoir stones. Most of the rest – chancel, nave, s aisle and chancel chapels with crenellations – though over-restored, is Late Perp, see the s doorways of the nave (the w door reset) and s chapel and the N chapel windows with panel tracery. Inside, the two-bay arcades to the chapels have slender piers with standard moulded section, and four-centred arches. The nave arcades of quatrefoil piers and moulded arches are all by Highton, except for the capitals of the SW respond and the first s pier from the w, which are genuine work of *c.* 1300. There was formerly no N aisle and a fine classical arch divided the nave from the crossing, one of

the adjustments made by Samuel Whitbread I *c.* 1760–83. A W
adjunct to the N chapel provided a family chapel for the Whitbreads; Highton opened this to the N aisle as an effective *coup
de théâtre* for their memorials (*see* below). It contains the *Wedgwood* black basalt FONT given in 1783 by Harriot Whitbread,
whose sister Mary gave the identical font to Essendon in Hertfordshire. It stands on a tapering square fluted pillar and inside
the bowl is a small circular stand for a christening cup.* –
ROYAL ARMS. 1779. An unusual kind, of carpet work.† –
STAINED GLASS. Three windows by *Clayton & Bell*, the E
window of 1872 and two in the S aisle, both designs by *George
Daniels*. – MONUMENTS. One of the richest assemblies in the
county. – The earliest memorials are a series of grave covers in
the S chapel from the C10–C11 (cross and interlace; cf. Milton
Bryan) to the C13 (double omega etc.). – Then follow the pair
of splendid earlier C16 monuments between chancel and N and
S chapels. They both have a small doorway with four-centred
head on the W and then the tomb-chest with a large traceried
canopy over the whole. Vine trail friezes and elaborate cresting.
The tomb-chests have equally elaborately cusped quatrefoils
and shields. The N monument was originally railed at the back
and on the tomb-chest are BRASSES of Sir William Gascoigne
†1540 and two wives, 3 ft 1 in. (94 cm) figures. He was comp-
troller of the Household of Cardinal Wolsey, and the figures
are in heraldic attire. – On the other tomb-chest BRASSES to
Sir Jarrate Harvye †1638 and wife (26 in.; 66 cm) with children
kneeling below. The monument was appropriated for him and
altered. To the C17 belong the Doric pilasters and the coffered
ceiling. His effigy in armour on the other hand is a piece of
delicate archaism. – The S chapel tomb enclosure has plain C18
RAILINGS. So has the small ledger-stone for Henry Whitbread
†1727. – In the N transept on the W wall, a large monument
signed by *Peter Scheemakers*, erected by Ive Whitbread, with a
grey obelisk and high inscription base relating the beginnings
of his ancestors and the names of those living in 1750, the
probable date of erection. Supplementary inscription for Ive
and his wife (†1765/6), whose well-done busts are on top. –
Samuel Whitbread I †1796. By *John Bacon*, 1799. Large white
relief with a pointed surround hung with curtains. He lies half-
draped on a Grecian couch. By his head, Faith points to
Heaven; a mourning woman kneels by his feet. The Pelican
beside her is a familiar Bacon motif but this is a work more
moving than Bacon usually tries to be and was his last major
work, completed by his son. – Samuel Whitbread II (†1815)
and his wife Elizabeth (†1846). By *H. Weekes*, 1849. Grecian
background. Husband and wife kneel in prayer; her gesture is

40

40

40

---

*A third such font given to Melchbourne (q.v.) by Emma (Whitbread) St John is
now in the Birmingham Art Museum, Alabama. A slightly smaller version made for
Moreton Say, Shropshire, is in the Lady Lever Art Gallery, Port Sunlight.
†LECTERN (in store). By *Sir Albert Richardson* and carved by *Frank Dobson*, 1955.
An impressively stylized eagle.

intensely affecting. One of Weekes's best works. – In the chancel Harriot Whitbread, first wife of Sam Whitbread I, †1764. Signed by *Richard Hayward*. Urn on top, here three children below. Also Lady Mary Whitbread, the second wife, †1770, attributed to *Hayward* (GF). – In the s chapel, William Charles Whitbread †1791 as a small child. Simple tablet with a very pretty wreath. – Dorothy Wagstaff †1752. Good cartouche with lively Rococo surround for Gen. Charles Conway Mills †1894. Bewhiskered bust in classical dress against an arched niche.

In the churchyard extension, to the NW, monument in the form of a large chest tomb with reeded pilasters and the RAF arms, to those killed in the R101 airship disaster of 1930 (*see* Shortstown). By *Albert Richardson*, 1931. Opposite this is the VICARAGE *c.* 1966 by *Richardson, Houfe & Partners* (i.e. by *E. A. S. Houfe*).

The GREEN at Cardington is made specially attractive by extending not only s of the church but also round it. JOHN HOWARD'S HOUSE, a three-bay C18 house (in spite of the 1642 datestone), is N of the church. John Howard, the philanthropist and social reformer, lived at Cardington most of his life and left the house to his cousins, the Whitbreads, in 1790. In the garden, VASE on pedestal: 1812, erected by Sam Whitbread II with his tribute to the plantings by Howard and his gardener *Joshua Crockford*. There were major additions in the mid to later C19 but these were reduced to two unobtrusive wings in the 1930s (library fittings by *Gerald Wellesley* and a fireplace copied from one by Holland at Southill, q.v.). SE and W of the house, and originally belonging with it, COTTAGES, 1762, eloquent of Howard's improvements to his estate.

The best house is W of the church, MALTING FARM (originally Cardington House): early to mid-C18, red brick, five bays, the three middle ones recessed between square wings. Asymmetrically set doorway, perhaps originally in the centre,* with hood on carved brackets. To the N a big bow. Geometric glazing patterns must be mid-C19. Staircase with twisted balusters and one large room on the first floor with pedimented doorcases and fielded panels.

The third house of consequence, E of the church, is the OLD VICARAGE, built in 1781 at the behest of Sam Whitbread I, and very probably by *John Carter*, whose drawings survive. Two storeys above a basement, with a hipped roof. Spacious four-bay front, its centre projecting and with a plain porch. To the garden a two-storey bow and at the back a recessed centre. The sash windows have Gothic glazing. Inside, an elegant plain stair, tightly curved, and in an upstairs passage a series of mini groin vaults rising from pilasters.

Also along the Green, several ESTATE COTTAGES built by John Howard (dated 1763, 1764) and even more by the Whitbreads up to the early C20, e.g in Harrowden Lane. Each has

---

*It is shown thus in a plan and elevation of 1771.

its estate number, hence the high count. S of the Green, the HOWARD READING ROOM, 1893, Neo-Tudor with a cupola. Nice bas-relief portrait roundel inside. The SCHOOL of 1848 has a gable, bellcote and roof tiles like fishscales. Opposite, a former Industrial School (now PARISH COTTAGE), in the tough Gothic idiom of the 1860s.

E towards Cople, the HOWARD MEMORIAL CHAPEL, Gothic, of 1908 by *E. H. C. Inskip & Son*, and the METHODIST CHAPEL, 1823, a simple brick box with pedimental gables and arched windows.

CARDINGTON BRIDGE, N of the village. By *John Smeaton* for Samuel Whitbread, 1778. Five simple brick arches.

CARDINGTON CROSS, N of the bridge by the A603. Stone with little volutes under the arms. Erected in 1837 by W. H. Whitbread, said to have been designed by *Francis Chantrey*, a friend of the family (Alan Cox).

For the airship hangars *see* Shortstown.

CARLTON

ST MARY. On its own amid pine trees planted to surround it. The earliest fabric is probably the thin, rubble-built walls of the chancel, providing evidence of a late Saxon two-cell church. The chancel's original extent is marked on the N side by herringbone masonry and a blocked arched window, described as double-splayed by the VCH, with rubble jambs and head of a recognizably Saxon style. The W tower is a little later, possibly post-Conquest but also predominantly late Saxon in style of construction, with single-splayed windows N and S, their jambs rubble but with heads formed of a single arched stone. Dec tower arch, Perp top, buttresses and stair. The small straight-headed W door must be C17. S aisle of *c.* 1300. One window has three stepped lancet lights, cusped. The three-bay arcade has octagonal piers and arches with one chamfer and two fine hollow chamfers on broaches. The N arcade has taller quatrefoil piers, and the two hollow chamfers are replaced by one wider one. The date is probably a little later. The windows are Dec too, except the deeply splayed lancet at the W end. At the E end of the N arcade is a Perp half-arch. Was it a squint? Lengthening of the chancel took place in the early C14, see the ogee-headed PISCINA, the reticulated tracery of the E window, and the tracery of the other windows. A one-bay S chapel, contemporary with the chancel lengthening, was at some time demolished. In this position now a mid-C19(?) window in the style of *c.* 1300. Other windows seem to have been renewed and the porch rebuilt before 1875. At the W end of the S aisle a large chimney, C14, evidence of a priest's house with living room on the first floor. In this position now, toilets etc. by *Bruce Deacon*, *c.* 2000. –

FONT. Norman, round, but *c.* 1300 made sexfoil at the bottom. Loose scrolls and straps and beaded bands, masks, two blind arches and a top rope moulding. – PULPIT. With Jacobean panels. – LECTERN. Also reusing Perp woodwork. – SCREEN. Perp, with two-light divisions. The coving has gone. – BENCHES. With the usual buttressed ends. – STAINED GLASS. E window signed by *F. X. Zettler*, Munich. †1904. S aisle window, 2000 by *Goddard & Gibbs*.

In The Causeway, the former BAPTIST CHAPEL of 1760, also stone with a hipped roof and gables at the rear. Large multi-paned windows. Later yellow brick porches and manse. Converted as a house by *Lloyd Thomas Architects*, but preserving pews, font and gallery. Many good C17 and C18 stone houses along High Street and Bridgend but also plenty of infilling.

CHALGRAVE

The church stands alone; its villages are at Tebworth and Wingfield.*

ALL SAINTS. The church looks curious because in 1889 the upper part of the clunch and flint chequerwork tower collapsed and has never been rebuilt. It was only finished off short by *J. P. Seddon*, 1901–5. Inside, the church is gratifyingly unrestored; indeed it was largely left alone until 1931 and still has its open crown-post roof and Victorian oil lamps and candelabra to the pews. The importance of the church is the E.E. work, which corresponds to a consecration in 1219. Five-bay N arcade with octagonal piers and double-hollow-chamfered arches. Fine stiff-leaf capitals, the leaves big but only high up the bell (cf. Eaton Bray). The S arcade is Dec and also impressive. Big quatrefoil piers with thin diagonal shafts in the angles, typical moulded capitals, typical arches with two sunk quadrant mouldings. The S doorway is earlier than this but later than the N arcade, say of *c.* 1250. It is pointed-trefoiled with an odd continuous moulding with a fillet and in addition one order of columns with stiff-leaf capitals. The chancel arch goes with the S arcade and see also the priest's doorway of *c.* 1300. The very pretty PISCINA is Dec again (ballflower and fleurons in an ogee arch). The tower is probably late C14; see the tower arch with double chamfered responds. The infilling of the arch for rooms behind was done in 1994. – WALL PAINTINGS. An exceptional wealth, uncovered in 1933–4 by E. Clive Rouse and largely reconserved in the 1980s by the *Perry Lithgow Partnership*. At the W end of the aisles, the twelve Apostles in pointed niches with trefoiled gables. On the S wall a large figure of an archbishop in a niche. On the N wall, traces of an angel and other

---

*The low oval motte of the CASTLE and its small bailey which stood SE of the church have been ploughed flat.

figures and, near the N doorway, a much more sumptuous niche with a large figure of St James and to its E a similar figure, probably St Thomas of Canterbury. On the N aisle E wall, the Annunciation. They are of 1290–1300. Also on the nave walls and the inner aisle walls in the spandrels of the arcades, scrolling foliage and shields suspended by painted loops from a band of geometric pattern, almost completely preserved. A second band of foliage at the top of the wall. These are datable to c. 1352–82 and heraldically interesting, referring to families connected with the Lorings who held the advowson from 1185. Superimposed C18 texts above. Over the N door was a large St Christopher of c. 1400, now very faded. Over the S door, painted over the earlier work, St Martin of Tours on his horse, with billowing long cloak. – BENCH ENDS. Two with tracery. – STAINED GLASS. In the chancel only. One of 1866 by *J. Powell & Sons*, the other 1999 by *Alfred R. Fisher*. – MONUMENTS. In the S aisle, knight of c. 1360–70, his feet against a lion. Tomb-chest with shields on loops. – In the N aisle, knight of c. 1380–90, his feet against a dog. Identified as Sir Nigel Loring †1386 (hero of Conan Doyle's *Sir Nigel* and *The White Company*). Tomb-chest with shields in quatrefoils alternating with blind tracery. – In the churchyard, E of the church, a good tapered headstone to Enoch Bennett †1902, father of the novelist Arnold Bennett, by *Edwin Rickards*.

OLD VICARAGE, Tebworth, 1 m. W. 1862 by *George Halton* of Luton. Gothic, very red, with bands of hard blue brick. Nearby an impressivly tall Tudor-Gothic former METHODIST CHAPEL of 1842 with lattice windows, pinnacled buttresses and castellated parapet.

CHELLINGTON

9050

ST NICHOLAS (The Chellington Centre). To be reached across a field. Dec W tower with spire. Low broaches and two tiers of lucarnes (cf. Pavenham). Niche below the W window and also on the N and S walls. E.E. N aisle with W and E lancets and a doorway with shafts and a little dogtooth. S aisle also C13, see the W lancet, but with flowing tracery in the later windows occurring here and in the chancel; however, its E window tracery shows, by its two mullions reaching right into the arch, and in spite of the use of reticulation, that the Perp style is on the doorstep. Perp clerestory. Inside, the tower arch dies into the imposts, the N arcade has quatrefoil piers with one chamfer and one hollow chamfer, and the S arcade has standard c. 1300 elements. The details of all of them go with the dates assumed from the exterior. The chancel arch, however, has typically early to mid-C13 mouldings dying just before the capitals of the shafts, i.e. earlier than the windows suggest. Well-judged extension of 2005 by *Bruce Deacon*, with a bowed meeting room overlooking the Ouse valley towards Harrold and Odell. The nave aisles were converted to bedrooms, much like a medieval hospitium. – STAINED GLASS. Fragments in the E window, mostly C17. – MONUMENT. In the churchyard, to Sir Robert Darling †1770. Large structure, originally with a big urn on top.

1030

CHICKSANDS PRIORY

Chicksands Priory was founded for Gilbertines *c.* 1150. The Gilbertines are the only monastic order created in Britain and confined to Britain. It was an order whose houses were for both nuns and brothers. Chicksands was for 120 nuns and 55 canons. The Priory followed the distinctive Gilbertine plan of cloisters for nuns and canons separated by the church. What remains is the canons' cloister S of the church. The felling dates for the timbers of the roofs of the S and E ranges are 1468–9, the N range 1504 and 1524–39, and the W range 1540–1 (i.e. after the Dissolution of the house in 1538). The premises were purchased in 1576 by Sir Peter Osborn and his son John Osborn, the amateur designer, although they did not take full possession until 1587. Nothing of their period survives but a panelled room now at the Victoria and Albert Museum, exhibiting a precociously early display of classicism learned from Serlio, is believed by Mark Girouard to have been designed by the younger Osborn and to have come from Chicksands.★

THE SOUTH-EAST VIEW OF CHICKSAND-PRIORY, IN THE COUNTY OF BEDFORD.

THIS Priory was founded in the Reign of K. H. I by Rose Wife of Paganus de Beauchamp Baron of Bedford, for Nuns of the Order of S.t Gilbert of Sempringham, & dedicated to the Blessed Virgin. This Paganus & his Wife gave divers Lands & Privileges to this House, which were confirm'd by K. S. II who in the 10 Year of his Reign granted Licence to John Blundel to settle y.e Manor of Chicksand w.th all its Appurtenances on this Convent. _____ The present Owner is S.r Danvers Osburn Bar.t

Chicksands Priory.
Engraving by S. and N. Buck, 1730

★The panelling was later removed to Haynes Grange (*see* p. 180), perhaps in the early C18, and taken from there *c.* 1904. It is always thus known as the HAYNES GRANGE ROOM.

As one approaches the house now from the E, one is faced with a rendered block, a brick range to its r., and older brick-work further r. The C18 and early C19 are what gives the whole building its character. The Bucks' view of *c.* 1730 shows the claustral buildings domesticated but little altered from their medieval state. However, *Isaac Ware* was brought in by Sir Danvers Osborn in the 1740s and he transformed the S and E ranges into symmetrical façades with Gothic windows on two storeys and added the canted bay for a porch on the S front. Then in 1814 Sir George Osborn employed *James Wyatt* to remake the E front into a symmetrical seven bays with a one-storey porch with crocketed pinnacles. His windows are Gothic, of two lights, and there is a pretty quatrefoil frieze below the eaves which also continues along the S front. The other sides are less regular. The angle buttresses with their big pinnacles existed before the C18 changes but in the two principal façades there is one small feature only which makes one suspect a more ancient history: the canted oriel l. of the l. bay in the E front. This is indeed of the C15. What can the oriel have belonged to? Possibly the abbot's lodging? On the Bucks' view it is shown close to an entrance apparently in the space between the angle buttresses and with a staircase to the garden.

As one enters by the E porch one is in Wyatt's Entrance Hall, long, low and impressively rib-vaulted in plaster, with the vaulting continuing into the S passage. Behind the Entrance Hall is the Grand Staircase, also vaulted; the plasterwork is by *Francis Bernasconi*. It rises within a square well decorated with niches and pointed arches opening into lobbies at first floor, a small-scale echo of Wyatt's stair at Ashridge, Herts. The stair projects into the square courtyard, and this was the original CLOISTER, in its present form Perp, as the two surviving broad four-light windows of the S range prove. Otherwise what remains of the priory is one fine C13 doorway which led from the cloister N into the church, and the whole undercroft of the W range, i.e. the storerooms, of the familiar type with piers along the middle. Seven bays, octagonal piers. The arches are single-chamfered, except oddly in one section where they are moulded. There is also a big Perp doorway. The undercroft has long been subdivided. The S room even appears to have had its vaulting extended E by one bay in the C18.

Above the entrance hall in the E range is the big former SALOON, in form probably mid-C18, with coved ceiling (as in the adjoining room to its N), but with a screen of columns at one end and painted decoration à la Gotzenberger of the mid-C19, a remarkable Neo-Raphael scheme. The rooms of the S range are a suite of three. The first, known as the Music Room, has the oriel window. In it STAINED GLASS fragments, C15 and later, probably collected by Sir George Osborn, who inherited in 1763, and including an interesting glass sundial, *c.* 1700. More stained glass was removed from the house in the mid C20 and is now at Audley End, Essex. The decoration of these rooms is again essentially mid-C18; in the furthest one a good

45

Kentian chimneypiece, perhaps by *Ware*. Projecting into the site of the church an C18 brick octagon. The upper floor inside, the so-called KING JAMES ROOM, has a thin star vault on slender Gothic shafts *à la* York Minster Chapter House and a four-light w window with very ornate tracery and *memento mori* in the glass that looks very Strawberry Hill-ish. It must belong to Sir George's time and seems to have been designed to hold the state bed in which Mary of Modena was purported to have borne the Old Pretender. Certainly the bed was here by 1789, when Lord Torrington mentions it, and is now in Kensington Palace.* – MONUMENT. In the w range. Thomas of Cotgrave, abbot of Pipewell, a Cistercian abbey in Northamptonshire. Large, flatly carved effigy with angels at his shoulders and border of foliage scroll. Lombardic inscription. The date is †1279 or †1320 or †*c*. 1335 (all these dates refer to abbots called Thomas). It was brought to Chicksands in the late C18.

NE of the house, the ORANGERY. Five bays with slim Gothick shafts and glazing between. Formerly with a Latin inscription in the entablature. Probably one of the garden buildings whose construction is noted by Lord Torrington in 1789. In front of the E range on the lawn is an OBELISK, not in its original position, erected in 1815 to commemorate peace after the Napoleonic Wars, and reinscribed for the ends of the Crimean War and Second World War and the Bicentenary of the American War of Independence. Another OBELISK, *c.* 500 yds SW of Appley Corner, was put up to commemorate the second Earl of Halifax †1771, a brother-in-law of Sir George Osborn.

Chicksands was taken over by the RAF in 1941 as a listening centre and postwar was handed to the USAAF for interception of Soviet communications.† It has been a training establishment since the 1990s. Since 1975 the house has been cared for and repaired by the Friends of the Priory. – CHAPEL. Brick with a copper roof bucking up into a clerestory over the centre. By *Zbigniew Gasidwicz* of the *Property Services Agency*, 1978.

Close to the s entrance on the Shefford-Clophill road, a late C19 LODGE and PRIORY HOUSE of 2006 by *Hamiltons Architects*, built as the headquarters of Mid-Bedfordshire Council (now Central Bedfordshire Council). Brick, flat roof, and at the w end the circular council chamber with full-height glass outer wall. Long office fingers to the N.

---

* I am grateful to Olivia Fryman of Historic Royal Palaces for supplying information on this bed.

† In the grounds was a remarkable ANTENNA (dem. in the 1990s) that Pevsner described as 'a vast circle of steel uprights, 120 ft high and nearly a quarter of a mile in circumference, with an inner, more complicated circle in the middle. It looks like a C20 super-Stonehenge, or like the elegant steel skeleton for the biggest bull-fighting arena ever.' It was also technically a piece of great importance, the circular form allowing receipt of signals from all directions and pinpointing of their source, a type of structure pioneered by the Germans during the Second World War.

CLAPHAM

St Thomas of Canterbury. The rubble-built w tower is not   6
easily forgotten. It is a Saxo-Norman tower, strong and high
with twin bell-openings in the top piece. These have capitals
with volutes, indicating a late CII date. Simple single-
chamfered tower arch and double-splayed windows. Norman
chancel arch, unmoulded, taken down and re-erected when the
chancel was rebuilt in 1861–3 by *G. G. Scott*. He lengthened
the nave, so the third bay of the s and N arcades is Scott's, the
other two bays are E.E., s just a little later and heavier than N.
The elements are standard. High up at the w end an organ
loft, on a cove, added by Scott and using a flat-headed doorway
from the first floor of the tower. – BENCHES. Three old ends
in the N aisle, the details as usual. – LADDER with Jacobean
balusters, to the ringing floor of the tower. – STAINED GLASS.
s aisle. Contemporary with Scott's restoration, one by *Clayton
& Bell*, two by *J. Powell & Sons*. – MONUMENT. Thomas Taylor
†1689. Standing monument, attributed to *William Stanton*
(GF; cf. the Warton monuments in Beverley Minster). Inscription with drapery between fat volutes. Urn at the top. The
inscription makes good reading. On the base two mourning
putti, one with tears of great realism, but these may be later,
supplied by the Stanton workshop along with the pedestal and
lower inscription to Taylor's widow, Ursula †1703/4 (the text
was supplied by *Edward Stanton*).

Methodist church, High Street. Gothic, 1876 by *Charles
Day* of Bedford. Northamptonshire ironstone.

Clapham Park. The house was built in 1870–3 for James
Howard, founder of the Britannia Ironworks at Bedford.
Fareham red brick and Harehill stone dressings. Gabled, in a
dour Gothic, it is not of much architectural merit but nevertheless a *magnum opus* of the highly idiosyncratic style of its
architect, *John Usher*. On the garden front a big canted bay
abutting a balcony recessed below a turret with steeply pointed
spire. The entrance side is similarly eclectic with a rib-vaulted
porte cochère and to the l. in the upper floors a Burgesian
stair-turret with stepped windows. In the porch, tiles by *J. K.
Cooper* of Maidenhead. (Inside, a top-lit staircase hall, of blind
shouldered arches to the walls and doors and an upper arcade
inset with scrolly wrought-iron. The carving is by *Harry Hems*.)
Former LODGES, on Kimbolton Road in Bedford's N suburbs
and another in Hawk Drive, are unmistakably Usher's design.

CLIFTON

All Saints. Entirely of ironstone. Dec nave and chancel, the
top of the w tower with its higher stair-turret Perp, and an
impressive N aisle of 1862–3 by *Edward Haycock* of Shrewsbury,

whose brother-in-law was the rector. He enlarged the N vestry with its steeply pitched roof and iron cresting in 1874. Instead of a lean-to roof, Haycock gave his aisle a high-pitched roof, and thus raised the aisle in prominence. The windows have bar tracery, except for the W window, which has plate tracery. A mid-buttress runs up to that window. The steep pitch of the nave roof and the two-tone tiling is of the same time. In the nave a large S window with reticulated tracery and a small blocked C15 one to give light to a nave altar. In the chancel, a S window with a lowside below a transom and visible inside one unrestored Dec N window. The tower arch is a standard type of *c.* 1300, half-quatrefoil responds with shafts and ogee stops (cf. Stotfold). The chancel arch is however very puzzling. The responds are again clearly of the early C14 and again of a frequent type (half-quatrefoil, with fillets), but they start high up, and below them are recesses for small altars. Moreover, behind the responds vertical mouldings run straight up, and the arch to the chancel itself grows out of them and the responds together. It is most irregular. The arch to the N chapel is much more conventional. Fine three-bay Perp N arcade, the tall piers of four shafts and four thin filleted shafts in the diagonals. The C19 arch from Haycock's aisle to the organ chamber has naturalistic brackets. – FONT. C13, of the octagonal Purbeck type with two flat arches each side. – SEDILIA and DOUBLE PISCINA. The display of lily is of course Victorian; Fisher *c.* 1815 shows it with crockets. *Thomas Earp* carved the REREDOS and blind arcading l. and r. in 1874. – SCREEN. Under the tower. Reassembled in 1972 from two panels of the fomer rood screen, with sixteen painted figures and prophets. Dated *c.* 1390. Cleaned in 1988–92 by *Anna Hulbert* and *Dianne Britton*, the figures revealed in all their individual excellence. – PULPIT. Alabaster and marble, 1863. – TILES, in the choir, by *Minton*, 1863. – Above the chancel arch, a MOSAIC roundel of Christ in Majesty of 1874 by *Maw & Co.*, who provided the mosaic pavement in the sanctuary. – STAINED GLASS. W window, The Last Judgement, an outstanding design by *Hardman*, 1863, in hard-boiled colours. Restored 1992 by the *Chapel Studio*. Other smaller windows by Hardman in the lowside window of the chancel. The E window, and the figures of St Nicholas and Dean Colet (chancel S) are by *M. C. Farrar Bell* (*Clayton & Bell*), 1951. – MONUMENTS. Large alabaster monument with recumbent effigies; identified as Sir Thomas Lucy, server of Henry VIII †1525. The tomb-chest with frontal angels under arches on three sides (the fourth side now reset as a back panel). They hold shields. It is a familiar type. The effigy of his wife had angels at her head. – Brass to John Fisher †1528 and wife; 28-in. (71 cm) figures.

In the village, S of the church, the Picturesque, debased and thoroughly delightful VILLAGE PUMP of 1881. Adapted in 1922 as the war memorial.

STRICT BAPTIST CHAPEL, Broad Street. Three-bay front with arched windows. 1853. Nearby, where Shefford Road begins, the ALMS COTTAGES (Gleaner & Sower Widows Homes) of 1871 for Septimus Sears, the chapel's minister. A tiny single-storey pair now made into one house. Square plan with central chimney.

CLIFTON GRANGE, ¼ m. SW of the church. C16 and C17, timber-framed with large brick stacks, but worked over in the C20. In the garden wall a fine brick arch, with moulded keystone, presumably mid-C17.

WREN PARK, I m. SW, on Hitchin Road. A slight and eccentric design of c. 1868 built for and probably designed by *William Watson*, Bedfordshire County Surveyor. Red and yellow brick, with gables, and a square glazed belvedere on top for a panoramic view of his jurisdiction.

CLOPHILL

0030

ST MARY. 1848–9 by *Thomas Smith* of Hertford, and, like his earlier work at Silsoe (q.v.), an archaeologically convincing job, i.e. a church which the casual visitor might regard as genuine. Only the chancel is short, still in the pre-ecclesiological tradition. Ironstone, W tower with higher stair-turret, S aisle. There was a clerestory until 1966–7. Mostly two-light windows. The fenestration on the N side, 3–2–2–3 lights, also betrays a still Georgian wish for symmetry. The patent terracotta ornament, e.g. the hoodmould of the door, is by *James & Obadiah Pulham*, who often worked with Smith. The E window is probably of the restoration of 1879 by *John Day* of Bedford. – SCREEN, enclosing the S chapel. Made up in 1958 from Elizabethan timber from Old St Mary, with plain muntins and a length of leaf frieze from a former roof truss. Meeting rooms etc. at W end by *Bruce Deacon*, 2002–3. – STAINED GLASS. E window. 2005 by *Michael G. Stokes*.

OLD ST MARY, ½ m. NE, on the top of the Greensand Ridge. Perp, with a W tower with higher stair-turret. Deprived of its chancel in 1849 and converted as a mortuary chapel; unroofed in 1956 and the interior stripped. It has in the nave just one large five-light S and one large five-light N window and no others. The chancel E window was reset in the E wall of the nave. Ruins repaired by *Caroe & Partners* for the Clophill Heritage Trust 2013–14, for community use; immediately W built into the slope of the ridge the ECO LODGE, a crescent of timber-clad bothies and meeting room by *Nicholas Tye Architects*.

In the main street, the METHODIST CHURCH of 1936 by *Arthur Brocklehurst* of Manchester, with Art Deco window. Nearby, CLOPHILL HOUSE, a five-bay brick house with segmental-headed windows and blind parapet with urns. Of more than one phase, the earliest part dated to 1719. Handsome wrought-iron railings, gates and piers. Diagonally on the opposite side,

IVY HOUSE (No. 52) with the same very odd brackets to support the door-hood as at Brandreth House, Ampthill, and houses in Woburn. There is another at OAKLEY HOUSE further W. At THE GREEN, a nicely restored C19 LOCK UP and POUND.

CAINHOE CASTLE, ¾ m. SE by the A507. The well-preserved earthwork of a motte-and-bailey castle, held by Nigel D'Albini at Domesday. Cone-shaped motte about 60 metres diameter at the base. The W bailey is the earliest; the other two, to S and E, are later but contemporary with each other, the S bailey with a 20-metre ditch. Traces also to the SW of a later manorial site, including fishponds to the N.

COCKAYNE HATLEY

ST JOHN THE BAPTIST. Of brown cobbles. Good E.E. four-bay N arcade with round piers, strong and simple capitals, and arches of two hollow chamfers. The S arcade is Dec. It is of four bays too and has octagonal piers and arches with two sunk waves. Very tall Perp tower arch. The tower itself is of four stages, the bell-openings a pair of very long two-light windows on each side with ogee mouldings. The W door and W window also with ogee arches. The aisle windows are Dec, straight-headed, with reticulation units (cf. Wrestlingworth). The N doorway is Dec too. Finely detailed Perp S aisle E window.

What makes the church unique in the county is its Baroque WOODWORK, brought, from Belgium, by the squarson, the Hon. and Rev. Henry Cockayne Cust, son of Lord Brownlow of Hatley Park across the Cambridgeshire border, who was the incumbent 1806–61. His agent in securing these imports was the connoisseur Col. Robert Rushbrooke. Cust first rebuilt the chancel, a restoration that also included the tower pinnacles and nave roof in 1820. Introduction of the woodwork was completed in 1830, followed by further embellishments of ecclesiologically correct type. Under the tower large SCREEN from Louvain. The RAILS above are from Mechelen (cf. communion rail below). They display musical instruments and trophies. ORGAN CASE (but no organ) with pretty Rococo carving and painted pipes. – The splendid STALLS and STALL BACKS, dated 1689 and 1692, came first, installed in 1826, and are from the Augustinian Priory at Oignies. The stalls, which continue into the nave, have inlay and putto heads between them. The backs abound with Catholic saints, looking very Catholic indeed. Between them putti holding Instruments of the Passion. Thirty years later no one would have dared to introduce such a display into an Anglican church. The saints are in oval foliage surrounds with scallop-shell tops. The front of the stalls to the W has splendid acanthus foliage. – The COMMUNION RAIL again comes from Mechelen and has lively scenes of putti: Corn Harvest, Vine Harvest, Drinking Water, Gathering Manna. – The READING DESKS have all sorts of collected bits. – More in the FAMILY PEW in the N aisle. The screen comes from St Bavon at Ghent and is a mixture of parts from *c.* 1540 into the C17.*The angels on the nave roof include four (on the tie-beams) from Biggleswade church, which was rebuilding in 1827–9. – CREED AND COMMANDMENTS BOARDS. In complementing Flemish style. – ROYAL ARMS. Painted and gilded. C17. Unusually in the form of a medallion with a fruit garland.

The STAINED GLASS in the N aisle E window is among the finest in Bedfordshire. It comes from Yorkshire. SS Sebaldus, Dunstan, Oswald, king of Northumbria, and Edward the Confessor, under canopies, early C14, the characteristic yellow and green, but also still the deep red and blue of the C13. In the head also C15 angel figures. – The E window of Scenes from the Life of Christ is by *Willement*, 1829, still entirely pictorial, but not in the C18 way. The inspiration is Netherlandish early C16 glass, the figure groups set against an intense blue. – Much more staid and conventional Willement's armorial S and N windows of 1839, the same date as his W window of St Peter, which incorporates some English medieval fragments collected by Cust.

MONUMENTS. Brasses to a knight of 1430 (38 in.; 96.5 cm) and on the same slab a lady of *c.* 1490 (25 in.; 63.5 cm); to Edmond Cokayn †1515 and wife (28 in.; 71 cm), with children below; and to William Cokyn †1527 and two wives (28 in.; 71 cm). The last is an excellent example of the Cambridge style of brass engraving. – Sir Patrick Hume †1627. Alabaster wall monument. The usual type with two kneelers facing one another across a prayer-desk. – Henry Cockayne Cust †1861. Renaissance tablet. By *Burke & Co.* – Maria Adelaide Cust †1864. Scrolly tablet with wilting rose in relief. Signed by *M. Noble.*

In the churchyard a gravestone to Margaret Emma Henley †1894, J. M. Barrie's inspiration for Wendy in *Peter Pan,* and her father, W. E. Henley, writer, †1903. *Onslow Ford* did the marble gravestone with three bronze plaques to Margaret first; *J. W. Simpson* designed the larger classical monument to her father which embraces it.

In the village to the SE, the OLD RECTORY by *W. M. Teulon,* 1859.

COLMWORTH

St DENIS. All Perp and all limestone except the cobbled chancel walls which may be earlier. It was ready for consecration in 1396. W tower with recessed spire and three tiers of lucarnes in the same direction. Pairs of two-light bell-openings. Very large N and S windows, and buttresses between them. The large

---

*There was also a PULPIT from St Andrew's, Antwerp, but it was sold to Carlisle Cathedral in 1963.

windows create a beautifully airy interior to the aisleless nave. High, embattled porch, with springers for a vault. There was a room above. Inside, W gallery of 1988. – FONT. Perp; on the underside small motifs. – ROOF. Carved figures on the wall-posts, angels against the rafters. – STAINED GLASS. Fragments, including a whole C15 angel, in the N windows. – Chancel windows, three of 1893 by *Heaton, Butler & Bayne*. – MONU-MENT. Excellent large alabaster monument to Sir William Dyer †1621 and family, erected in 1641 by his widow, Lady Katharine, who also composed the double poem of the back panel, including the epitaph:

> My dearest dust, could not thy hasty day
> Afford thy drowsy patience leave to stay
> One hour longer, so that we might either
> Have sat up or gone to bed together?

Two reclining effigies propped up on their elbows, he behind and above her: they 'multiplied themselves with seven children'. Three front Composite columns, three back pilasters, coffering with angels' heads and a strange cresting of two bald volutes and a central square with a rounded top to hold the coat of arms. Against the base three noble caryatids (Faith, Hope and Charity) and the standing adult children. A baby grandson (†1637) stands at her feet. Attributed to *William Wright*.

OLD RECTORY. 1837–9 by *William Clark* of St Neots. Three bays square, low hipped roof, in yellow brick. Porch with a balustrade and some Gothic heads to the sash windows.

MANOR FARM, SW on a formerly moated platform. (A beam is inscribed '*Edmund Ibbot*, Architect, 1609,' who erected the house at the expense of Katharine Dyer.)

MEADOWVIEW, ½ m. N. 2007–8 by *Platform 5 Architects*. Two-storey, flat-roofed and horizontal. White rendered walls and a jettied upper storey clad in chestnut strips.

LOW FARMHOUSE, 1¼ m. SSW. H-plan, probably *c.* 1630 on the evidence of some excellent PLASTERWORK in the W cross-wing. In one room a beam moulded with foliage and a nearly complete frieze of grapevine, birds and naked figures (cf. Manor Farm, Cotton End, q.v.). In the room above, a fireplace with handsome plaster overmantel of the Stuart ROYAL ARMS, flanked by curtains, thistles and caryatids (cf. the identical overmantel at Church Farmhouse, Roxton).

COLWORTH HOUSE *see* SHARNBROOK

COPLE

ALL SAINTS. Of buff and brown stone. A Perp church, except for the W tower (with higher stair-turret), which is probably earlier – see the ironstone lower stages, the arch towards the nave and the buttresses inside – and all carefully conserved during the restorations begun by *G. G. Scott Jun.* in 1877–9 (chancel) and carried on by *Temple Moore*, 1880–1902. High C15 S doorway with big leaf spandrels. Tall three-bay C15 arcades, the piers with four polygonal projections and four thin diagonal shafts. Moulded, two-centred arches. The chancel arch is of the same type. The later chapels of two bays, however, have the standard moulded section and four-centred arches. They probably date from the C16. The S chapel was provided for in the will of Thomas Grey †1506. All responds here are angel brackets, those on the S side recarved. In the S chapel SE corner yet another, very good, angel bracket. – SCREEN. With one-light divisions, and delicate detail, clearly repaired by Moore. His STALLS incorporate Perp poppyheads. – BENCHES. Some ends of frame and panel construction, i.e. probably later C16. – STAINED GLASS. E window and clerestory by *Burlison & Grylls*, 1890 and 1900. – MONUMENTS. The largest collection of BRASSES in Bedfordshire. – Nicholas Rolond, *c.* 1410, and wife, 36-in. (91 cm) figures, and John Launceleyn †1435 and wife, 25-in. (63 cm) figures. The latter pair remade from a brass of a cross-legged knight of *c.* 1320 (both chancel floor, now covered up). – Walter Roland, *c.* 1415. He is in armour, the figure 36 in. (91 cm) long (N chapel N). – Tomb-chest of the early C16 with the brasses of Thomas Grey (†1507), wife and children (18-in.; 45 cm) figures; chancel S). – Tomb-chest with back panel in a classical frame with the kneeling brass figures of Sir Walter Luke †1544 and wife (chancel N). – A similar tomb-chest back panel with the kneeling figures of Nicholas Luke †1563 and wife (N chapel N) and family. – Brass plate with big coat of arms and the kneeling figures of Robert Bulkeley †1556 and family (S chapel).

Pretty BIER HOUSE (late C19) facing the street NE of churchyard.

OCTAGON FARM HOUSE, ¾ m. N. Best-preserved of the eight-sided farmhouses erected *c.* 1800 by *Robert Salmon*, surveyor to the 5th Duke of Bedford (cf. Willington and Staploe). Red brick, two-storey with rooms quartered around a central top-lit stair, cellars under and a brewhouse wing. Nice timber-covered porch like a sentry box. W wing of 1919 by *W. B. Stonebridge*.

COTTON END

0040

Eastcotts

BAPTIST CHURCH. 1836. Yellow brick, three bays, two-storey fenestration. Arched windows. Big pediment. Horseshoe gallery on fluted cast-iron columns.

MANOR FARM. A late C16 brick house, with stone mullion and transomed windows, of two storeys and attics in the gabled N cross-wing; the corresponding s wing has gone. (In the principal upper chamber of the main range (now subdivided), a fine plaster ceiling of geometric ribs patterned with vines forming quatrefoils etc. and a variety of standard elements and cast motifs including Adam and Eve in the Garden of Eden, pastoral scenes and a frieze of male and femal figures (of identical pattern to Low Farmhouse, Colmworth, q.v.). The coats of arms are for the Colby family, who held the manor 1566–1612.)

HERRING'S FARM, Herring's Green, ½ m. s. A handsome early to mid-C18 farmhouse, slightly remodelled *c.* 1960 when its pediment with blind oculus was reset in the first floor. The shaped gable ends are uncommon in Bedfordshire.

MOTTE, in Exeter Wood, 1 m. SE. Of a late C11 or C12 castle. Badly overgrown. Low, about 65 ft (20 metres) in diameter and approximately 6 ft (1.8 metres) tall with a ditch surrounding. It was a property of the de Beauchamps who held Cardington manor.

CRANFIELD

ST PETER AND ST PAUL. Norman N doorway in a bad state. Scalloped capitals. Also Norman a SCULPTURE W of the s doorway of a figure in relief, seated, alas defaced. Late C13 four-bay arcades. Quatrefoil piers, double-chamfered arches, with curled broaches on the s side. The chancel arch belongs to the same build. Occasional bits of nailhead in the abaci (cf. Salford below). Also C13 or early C14 the tower arch, dying into the imposts. The formidable two-storey NE vestry seems to be contemporary. The lower E window is Victorian; the upper slit windows are genuine. The rest is Perp, the upper parts of the tower with interesting blank four-centred arches high up, and pairs of two-light bell-openings, above these arches; the bell-frame is dated by its timbers to 1479–1519.* Perp battlements on both sides of the church to aisle and clerestory, their roofs good, with carved bosses and angels. Restored in 1846 for the squarson, the Rev. George Gardner Harter: the DECALOGUE in stone Dec frames, the SEDILIA and PISCINA clearly of that time. W gallery, 2010 by *Acanthus Clews.* – FONTS. One is early C14, a chamfered square with eight shafts, but the panels carved in the C15 with blank Perp windows. The other, 1891, in stone and marble like the PULPIT of 1882; both were Harter family gifts. – PEWS. 1840s with poppyheads; under the gallery, tiered BENCHES for servants. – TILES. Medieval encaustic tiles at the nave's E end; C19 in the chancel. – STAINED GLASS. E window by *Willement,* 1851, but the figures reset in crazy-pattern clear glazing after war damage; also by Willement, the heraldic W window. – By *Kempe,* in the N aisle, 1884, in the s

---

*The recessed lead spire noted in the first edition of this guide was removed in 1975.

aisle, stylistically hard to tell apart, by his student *H. W. Bryans*, 1914. – MEMORIALS. Some good C19 tablets and a brass to Rev. G. Gardner Harter †1872, by *Hart, Son & Peard*.

The Rev. George Gardner Harter also provided the fine stone SCHOOL opposite in 1862. Domestic Gothic with two wings, and an octagonal tower and spire in the angle of the r. one with octofoils in a band. Nice porch with cusped arches to the school house on the l. The architect was *T. C. Hine*, who built a grandiose mansion, CRANFIELD COURT for Harter at Wood End in 1862–4. It was mostly demolished in the 1930s, the remains adapted for a smaller house, but the LODGE, Lodge Lane, with wilful Gothic details, is to his design.

W of the church on the green, the WAR MEMORIAL, a *Blomfield*-designed Cross of Sacrifice, and a nice cast-iron Gothic PUMP, dated 1866; by *S. Owens & Co.* of London.

In HIGH STREET two good groups of ALMSHOUSES, both provided by James Goodman, who made his fortune as a builder–developer in south London: Nos. 51–55, dated 1885, in a C17 style with lavish stone doorcase and sgraffito-style decoration in the coved eaves, and Nos. 14–22 of 1892, red brick with nicely patterned tile roofs, cut bargeboards and a central tower. Both are by *John Hull* of Bedford. Between these, set back on the N side, the charming HARTWELL ALMSHOUSES of 1834; Neo-Tudor with a thatched roof.

UNIVERSITY OF CRANFIELD, W of the village. Originally the College of Aeronautics established in 1946 at the former RAF Cranfield. The original airbase buildings at the centre are of *c.* 1936–7 and 1939–40. They are the expected Neo-Georgian, the early housing of the Welwyn–Wythenshawe kind, notably e.g. in West Road. Three large hangars remain in use. Expanded after 1969 as the Cranfield Institute of Technology and developed as a University after 1993. The following deserve mention:

SCHOOL OF MANAGEMENT. By *IDC Consultants Ltd*, 1975. Light brick, mostly two-storey with a series of overlapping octagons forming a cluster at one end

NATIONAL SOILS RESEARCH INSTITUTE. By *Chamberlin, Powell, Bon & Woods*, 1989. A one-storey steel-framed square pavilion with pyramid roof over a central hall and broad eaves shading offices on four sides.

LORD KINGS NORTON LIBRARY. By *Foster & Partners*, 1989–92 (project architect *Ken Shuttleworth*). A steel, concrete and glass box under four shallow barrel-vaults that are carried over the front as a canopy on five slender columns as high as the three-storey façade. This treatment derives from the firm's earlier Carré d'Art, Nîmes, and designed to function as a colonnaded 'forum' for a campus hitherto lacking a central meeting place. One hopes, however, for a piazza in front where there is only a car park. Screens of silver louvred shades between the columns along the flanks. Interior of graceful austerity, the concrete frame exposed and staircases with glass treads rising through an atrium to the libraries on first and second floors. Top-lit through spines along the vaults.

STRATEGIC CREATIVITY CENTRE, s of the library. By *Niall McLaughlin Architects, c.* 2011. A single-storey studio made exciting by its fractured roofline of overlapping timber polygons raised on deep cross-beams and forming clerestories in the N lights.

STRINGFELLOW HALL, N of University Way. By *Stanton Williams,* 2010; a nicely composed group of flats in brick and timber.

0060

DEAN

ALL SAINTS. The chancel arch with a little nailhead in the responds and the N doorway prove the existence of a church before 1300. Then most of the present building was done, in the first half of the C14. Dec the W tower with very fine two-light bell-openings, a pretty top trail-frieze with heads etc. (cf. Swineshead), impressive and entertaining gargoyles, and a short recessed spire (with two tiers of lucarnes). The arch towards the nave dies into the imposts. Dec also the unusual s doorway with four orders of very thin shafts and a fourfold roll-moulded and filleted four-centred arch almost like a basket arch. The s arcade of four bays and indeed the N arcade are Dec too. They have standard elements, but the piers have clearly been heightened. But when was that done? Not as late as the erection of the Perp three-light clerestory; for the line of the roof preceding that which includes the clerestory is still clearly visible against the tower and takes the present height of the piers well in. The nave roof, with angels carrying the Instruments of the Passion and musical instruments, and with an openwork frieze, also of angels but also shields, below the wallplate, is specially fine. Elaborately carved tie-beams with foliage spandrels. Perp one-bay N chapel. – FONT. Octagonal, Perp, with the usual quatrefoils, but unusual big single flowers on the base. – PULPIT. Of wood, Perp, with simple arched panels. – By the pulpit, front of a bench with tracery bits of a SCREEN. – The SCREENS altogether are remarkable. The present ROOD SCREEN and the chapel W screens were originally probably all one – with one-bay divisions, but specially elaborate details, e.g. panel-tracery along the top of each light. – The gate of the rood screen is Jacobean. – BENCHES. The usual buttressed type of ends. – PAINTING. In the N chapel a small panel on wood with Christ as the Good Shepherd, kneeling to pick up a chalice. The inscription is in Latin. – STAINED GLASS. Original fragments including a kneeling priest in blue (s aisle w) and two whole little figures (N chapel E). Reset with a new figure, 1966 by *Goddard & Gibbs.* – E window, quatrefoils, signed by *Willement,* 1857 – MONUMENTS. Dec tomb recess in the N aisle. The tomb-chest has six quatrefoils with petals. The recess is high, and cusped and subcusped. On the tomb-chest a slab with inscription in Lombardic lettering, for Walter de

Ireland, rector, †1311. Some of the original letters survive, preserved *ex situ*. – Brass to Thomas Parker †1501, rector and Prebendary of the Collegiate Church of St Mary, Shrewsbury. He is shown in vestments, with a scroll. 20½-in. (52 cm) figure. The brass belongs to a plain tomb-chest in the s chapel. – John Neale †1680. Black and white marble with an open segmental pediment and lavish painted arms. Scrolled volutes at the sides. Unquestionably by *Edward Stanton* (GF).

UNITED REFORMED CHURCH. Originally an Independent chapel, 1863, built by the local squire, William Ackroyd, hence 'A' on capitals of pillars. Otherwise wholly Italianate, yellow brick striped with red. Corinthian pilasters to the sides and corbel table.

150 yds WSW of the parish church, DEAN HOUSE, has a fine early C19 garden wing of three bays, stucco, with the ground-floor windows under consoled brackets and a pediment. Nice veranda to the r. wing. Opposite, FRANCIS HOUSE (formerly Lodge Farm), a restored late C16 timber-framed house with a cross-wing, and two square projections, of special interest for the patterns in their gables of circles and semicircles with cusps.

WINDMILL, ½ m. NW. 1850. A sad sight, with its two switches for sails. Red brick tower with a domed cap.

DRAY'S DITCHES *see* STREATLEY

DUNSTABLE

0020

Dunstable is the site of Roman DUROCOBRIVAE, of which practically nothing is known. It is situated on an important road junction, where the Icknield Way crosses Watling Street, and close by from the C12 was its Priory. It was a centre for straw-plaiting and hatting but the restriction of land available for development in the early C19 stymied its industrialization and allowed Luton to overtake it. Nevertheless by 1900 it too was increasingly devoted to engineering and other large enterprises. Settlement still strayed little beyond the historic cross of roads until large housing estates were developed after 1945. By the 1960s in outer Dunstable industry was growing apace with new factories and factory extensions to E, N and S. By then to the E there was no longer any boundary between Dunstable and Luton. Very soon Dunstable had become a C20 town with one major ancient monument.

CHURCHES

ST PETER. Dunstable Priory is traditionally believed to have been founded by Henry I for Augustinian Canons in 1132 but

Prior Bernard was witness to a deed in 1125. Of the buildings for the canons little is preserved (*see* below), of the church a substantial part. The E parts, probably the first to be built, are all gone, and so are the crossing and the very E end of the nave. But the rest of the nave remains, with the W front. The fact that the nave was not destroyed after the Suppression is due to the town having obtained in 1392 the use of the whole nave for parochial purposes. It was in the Priory church that Henry VIII's marriage to Katherine of Aragon was annulled, heralding the English Reformation.

The interior tells the story of the original building more clearly than the exterior. We have seven bays of arcade and gallery, but nothing of the clerestory. The nave is very wide. The bays are separated by giant wall-shafts of oddly imprecise section: a demi-shaft and two broader quarter-shafts. The latter at the gallery level merge with the gallery arches to form a kind of giant arching, as was more clearly done at Romsey, Jedburgh, and Oxford Cathedral. These giant wall-shafts are cut horizontally only by the sill course of the gallery, a billet course. The arcades on the other hand have chevron hoodmoulds, bold in the two E bays, slighter in the others. To the arch openings there are triple shafts with scallop capitals and some waterleaf, and the arches themselves have thick half-rolls. The date of all this may be *c.* 1150–60, but when the gallery was built the late C12 must have been reached. The arches have finer mouldings, and some capitals crockets, and the shafts towards the (undivided) openings l. and r. of the middle one are elegantly detached. In fact three have detached, the other attached shafts. The core is a Greek cross with quadrants to connect the arms. The shafts are set into these – a Lincoln motif. Several other features bear out this chronology. The S aisle, it must at once be admitted, is doubtful evidence, for it was completely rebuilt in 1852 by *George Somers Clarke*, early on in his restoration of the church, which took place at intervals from 1848 to 1878 and was originally intended to be even more thorough. It has Norman windows, set high enough for the cloister to have been beneath, and it has Norman rib-vaults. The two easternmost ones are in fact original, one with a figured capital in a S wall-shaft.

The W front of Dunstable is both confusing and confused. The principal portal is evidently Norman, and very sumptuous, though it is badly preserved. It has four orders of shafts with lively figure capitals and arches, including foliage medallions of the Malmesbury–Glastonbury kind, i.e. of *c.* 1170–90, and an outer order of chevron. The doorway and the tympanum of course were put in in the C15. To the l. of the portal is a piece of Late Norman intersecting arcading with the familiar bobbin motif and more figure capitals. The arcading can be compared with a piece of arcading at St Albans Abbey and there are other close associations in the motifs of the portals with work at the abbey under Abbot Robert de Gorham up to

about 1170.* It is surmounted by a pointed arch with a Late
Norman chain of lozenges. So this may be *c.* 1170 too, i.e. later
than the arcades but not later than the gallery. The church was
indeed dedicated (by Hugh of Wells, Bishop of Lincoln) in
1213. But then, in 1222, the two w towers collapsed. This
information comes as a surprise, for the arcades make no
visible provision for towers. What happened after that was a
rebuilding which suggests anxiety and no consistent plan.
Immediately s of the portal is a buttress erected in the C15 and
connected by a piece of brickwork with a square sw angle
turret which is Victorian. To the N of the piece of Norman
intersecting arcading is a C13 N portal, as sumptuous as the
older, though smaller. It has five orders and five subsidiary
orders, all capitals moulded and finely moulded arches, three
of their orders with stiff-leaf, one as a normal trail, one in
nailhead-like units, one in square leaves. The nearest parallel
is the s transept portal of Lichfield. Above the portal is diapering of the kind known in Westminster Abbey, and also at
Higham Ferrers, Northants, and above that a small frieze of
pointed arches with brackets for statues, and at the N corner
is a broad buttress with a canted N side and pointed niches.
Higher up the w front is a more sumptuous frieze of open
arches, with thickly decorated capitals and cusps. This leads
straight to the two main w lancet windows. Between them is
another, not so high but also thickly decorated blank arch. The
arcading is not and never was repeated s of the s lancet. This
tier cannot be earlier than, say, 1250–60. More blank arcading
above and Perp battlements. In the C15 a NW tower was put
on the NW bay, and it was for that purpose strengthened inside.
The tower has a higher stair-turret, is faced in the chequerwork
of clunch and flint (cf. Luton) and has two-light belfry openings in pairs. Inside, the w wall has above a Norman billet
moulding a C13 gallery of seven stepped arches, the tips of the
outer arches curving inwards (cf. St Albans, w door). The
shafts again have the Lincoln section (cf. above).

The N side of the church was restored in 1876 and extended
one bay E for a vestry, see the large Perp former E window
inside. It was at this time that the Norman N doorway was
uncovered. It was over-restored, so little is original, except the
four charming capitals, one with a hare, another with a hunter,
stag and hounds, a third with a deer and dragon.† The Perp
aisle windows are entirely the restorer's. Externally at the E end
of the church there is the E part of the Norman pier between
the seventh and the lost eighth N bay and on the s side a pier
related to a big strengthening of the C14, when the transept

---

* For this *see* M. Thurlby, 'The Place of St Albans in Regional Sculpture and Architecture', *British Archaeological Association Conference Transactions*, 24, 2001.
† There were more figured capitals originally, of which casts taken in the C19 are
preserved at the Victoria and Albert Museum, showing fighting men, a man fighting
a dragon as well as foliage (Hazel Gardiner).

and crossing tower were rebuilt or remodelled. The pulpitum became the stone ROOD SCREEN which was retained and built up as the E wall when the church was reduced.* The wall is clunch and has two doorways and niches, visible only inside, which were revealed in 1890–1 during restoration by *Bodley & Garner*; the wall was then given a rood[†] but the present statue niche with soaring pinnacle canopy over Christ in Majesty (and the figures in the Perp niches) are of 1962 by *Felix & Sean Lander*, who rebuilt the E wall behind the screen in red brick with Perp-type windows. The ROOF was replaced in the C15 when the clerestory was taken down and the triforium glazed. Traceried trusses by *Somers Clarke*, 1876. On the rafters and jackposts several carved figures with cloaks and shields, interpreted as members of the Fraternity of St John the Baptist.

FURNISHINGS. – FONT. Large, circular, assembled in the mid C19 from Norman fragments, so the decoration is partly original and partly recut, or entirely C19. It is one of the type known as the Aylesbury Group. – SCREENS. The rood screen is of five wide bays, with cusped and subcusped arches and thickly crocketed ogee gables. Perp panelling in the spandrels. It was reset here in 1890 having been placed under a W gallery. – In the last bay of the N arcade a Victorian screen to the vestry, with mysterious long, decorated balusters. They are typical of certain English work of the mid C17. But some also have the arms of Castile, a double-headed eagle, the emblem of the Virgin, and the Five Wounds. Must it then not be Marian? The fragments were found in a pew in the S aisle in 1852. – PARCLOSE SCREENS (S chapel) by *Bucknall & Comper*, 1901. – PULPIT. 1852. Square, of red marble, with two E.E. stiff-leaf bands and eagle. – PULPIT CLOTH (S aisle). Given in 1732. – GATES (S chapel). Wrought iron, C18; previously in the N aisle as a enclosure. – SCULPTURE. On a nave pier, a witchy bronze, the Madonna of the Magnificat by *Laurence Brodrick*, 1970. – STAINED GLASS. Almost all by *John Hayward*, 1974, 1984 and 1989; consistently good, but the W windows earliest and best with single figures in hotly coloured abstract settings. – E windows by *Christopher Webb*, 1962; very limp. One S aisle window by *A. J. Davies* (*Bromsgrove Guild*), 1926. – MONU-MENTS. BRASSES. In the S aisle. Richard Pynfold †1516 and wife, still *in situ* at the E end. 19½-in. (49.5 cm) figures. Origin-ally adjacent but now remounted on the S aisle wall, replicas of Richard Fynche †1640 and his father and mother. Also on panel in the aisle John Blunte and wife (19-in.; 48 cm), 1502; civilian (14½ in.; 36 cm); and large husband and wife (40½ in.; 102 cm), identified as Laurence Pygot, woolman, 1450. Also replica of the brass for Henry Fayrey †1516 and wife,[‡] and one

---

* From 1722 the wall held an altarpiece of the Last Supper by *James Thornhill*.
[†] Removed to Bodley's church of St John, Tue Brook, Liverpool, and made into the reredos and an altar.
[‡] Their son John commissioned the PALL now in the Victoria and Albert Museum. Red brocade, with all along the borders embroidered figures. They look 1530.

other very similar for Robert Alee and wife, 1518. – Incised slab to Richard Duraunt, late C13. Good, large and with Lombardic inscription (N aisle). – Also a remarkable number of quite ambitious monuments of the first half of the C18. They are to members of the related Marshe, Chew, Aynscombe, Cart and Dickinson families. – Mrs Elizabeth Aynscombe †1711 (S aisle E chapel). Columns l. and r., still-life of death in the 'predella'. Attributed to *William Woodman the elder* (GF). – William Chew †1712 (organ chamber, N aisle). By *Thomas Green* of Camberwell. Large hanging monument of reredos type with two standing putti and a death's head between; more putti below supporting consoles. The centre of the monument is an arch with drapes. At the top an achievement with garlands. No effigy (cf. Bishop Cumberland, Peterborough Cathedral, †1718). – Thomas Chew Cart †1722 (N aisle). Standing monument of a grey obelisk and black sarcophagus carrying a detached bust under a broken curly pediment. Rupert Gunnis attributed this monument to after 1732 by *Samuel Tufnell* who signed a similar Cart family monument in St Mary-le-Bow in London (destroyed in 1940).* – Frances Ashton †1727 (S aisle E). Reredos-type with fluted pilasters and broken pediment. In the tympanum four putto heads. – Mrs Jane Cart †1736 (N aisle). Classical reredos with pilasters, finely detailed pediment and sunk frame for the inscription. – The hanging monument in the S aisle to Daniel and John Marshe *c.* 1712 is attributed to *Robert Taylor sen.* (Richard Garnier). Fluted pilasters, armorial cartouche and gadrooned moulding at the base. – Then three separate monuments all by *Sir Robert Taylor*: – Jane Marshe †1730 (N aisle); quite minor, with a small bulbous urn on a scrolly support; – Marshe family (S aisle), probably shortly after 1741. Heavily draped urn before an obelisk; and Francis Dickinson †1747, with a substantial pedestal carrying an urn against a back panel with garland and arms. Only the last is clearly signed. – The monument for Marshe Dickinson †1765, with good oval portrait medallion, is also attributed to *Taylor*.

Of the PRIORY BUILDINGS hardly anything has escaped destruction. The remains of a GATEHOUSE into the outer court are SW of the church. Carriage and pedestrian entrance. C15. Excavation has however identified the site of the priory and its outbuildings.

ST MARY (or OUR LADY IMMACULATE) (R.C.), West Street. 1961–4 by *Desmond Williams & Associates* of Manchester. Large, of brick, essentially circular but with a rhythm of projecting and recessed bays around the exterior, the recessed bays fully glazed, the projections (some for side chapels) with slots. Wavy canopy, lamella roof and spire. Geometric pattern reredos for

---

*I am grateful to Geoffrey Fisher for drawing my attention to this unpublished attribution among Gunnis's research notes in the Conway Library, Courtauld Institute.

large SCULPTURE of the Crucifixion. The previous church of 1935 is now the hall.

BAPTIST CHAPEL, West Street. 1847–8 by *J. Clarke*. Red brick with yellow brick quoins (now painted). Three bays wide, with one-bay pediment. Arched windows. Large late C20 front extension. Galleries inside on cast-iron columns.

BAPTIST CHURCH, St Mary's Gate. Rebuilt 1849 on the site of the first chapel of 1708. Small, with two large arched windows on each side and the front but the latter spoiled by the recent porch. Galleried interior.

METHODIST CHURCH, The Square. 1909 by *Withers & Meredith*. Large, of brick and stone with a landmark SE tower topped by small flying buttresses to an octagonal stone spire. In a free Gothic but with the sparing of enrichment expected of the C20. Capacious interior, with a horseshoe gallery on quatrefoil columns implying arcades of three bays with broader pointed arches at the 'transepts'. Behind the raised pulpit, choir loft and the mighty organ case fill the w end. – STAINED GLASS. Two lancets (w wall) by the *Glasscraft Guild*, 1931.

CEMETERY, West Street. 1863. Red and black brick double chapel with a middle gateway on red granite shafts. The two façade windows both have geometrical tracery, but the tracery differs – a characteristic High Victorian touch.

PUBLIC BUILDINGS

MUNICIPAL BUILDINGS, High Street North. See Grove House, Perambulation, below.

Former POLICE STATION, No. 16 Icknield Street. Dated 1867. Luton grey brick wth stucco dressings and rusticated door surround. Essentially domestic. Its successor of *c.* 1939 (also now in other use) is in High Street South, one of the pleasant Neo-Georgian designs by the County Surveyor with an archway in the centre (cf. Kempston and Biggleswade).

ASHTON MIDDLE SCHOOL, High Street North. The former Grammar School, founded in the C18 by Frances Ashton, rebuilt in 1887–94 by *E. R. Robson*. Free Tudor. Of plum brick with a fleche. Quite ingeniously composed of two parts, each in itself symmetrical. The richly detailed Gothic entrance with a square tower, set totally asymmetrically, is the link. The hall part is Late Perp, the rest, which served as the boarding house and headmaster's residence, is Jacobean and domestic, with half-timbered gables and red tile-hanging. Nice touches of freedom from historicism, e.g. in the hall parapet and inside an impressive hammerbeam roof. Science Laboratories of 1907 by *F. H. Hargrave* of Ripon, a tall two storeys with shaped gable.

PRIORY ACADEMY, Britain Street. The former Mixed Council School of 1909–11 by *Gotch & Saunders*. Attractively done, in an Early Georgian manner, grey brick with red dressings and modillion cornices, steep pediments and a low range with arched windows in stone bays. The most obvious early C20 trait is the flat chimneys, topped by stone cages.

PERAMBULATION

All the older buildings of interest are in the cross of streets in the centre.

In HIGH STREET NORTH several of the frontages incorporate archways to the yards behind, e.g. next to THE WHITE HORSE a good if extensively restored early C17 gateway. Round arch, columns l. and r., and, above, a gabled upper floor of brick with mullioned windows. On the opposite side the OLD SUGAR LOAF, built as a large coaching inn and dated 1717. Nine bays, two and a half storeys, purple brick with red brick dressings and cornice of volute brackets. The major highlight is the former UNION CINEMA on the W side (now Dunstable Conference Centre) by *Leslie H. Kemp* (*Kemp & Tasker*), 1936–7, grey brick with five tall windows along the upper storey and a relief in the centre. The Art Deco interior is completely preserved. Near the street's N end, GROVE HOUSE (Municipal Offices since 1937). Cream stucco, built in the 1740s as the Duke of Bedford's Arms but soon after made into a private house. Windows in lugged surrounds with floating cornices. Early C19 porch of two pairs of sturdy Doric columns, arched window over; staircase with twisted balusters inside and a screen of fluted Ionic columns. To its r. an extension of *c.* 1773 (later a separate house) with Late Georgian Gothick ogee-headed windows and stucco shafting. At the entrance to GROVE GARDENS, impressive GATES, brought here in 1939 from The Gables, a house of *c.* 1890 which stood at Linslade. Good Italianate house opposite (No. 81) in dark grey brick with stone quoins, a two-storey bow and cast iron cresting. The area E of Grove House on High Street was built over *c.* 1960–7 with the town's civic buildings,[*] but has already been partly redeveloped for GROVE THEATRE, 2005–7 by *Glenn Howells Architects*, a mixed development including shops and restaurants. White vertical columns, dark glazing; the theatre auditorium is expressed as a curved brick wall inside the foyer that continues above the roofline. S is the bland QUADRANT SHOPPING CENTRE by *Willoughby Fletcher & Associates*, 1966. It is T-shaped with a short arm to High Street North, and the long arm parallel with that street and with access from Church Street and Vernon Place. In the centre, where the arms meet, was formerly a public square but canopies have been introduced. These obscure an 85-ft (26-metre) long abstract CONCRETE RELIEF by *William Mitchell*. Whose happiness do such things induce or increase?[†]

---

[*]The Queensway Hall, 1962–4 by *Shingler Risdon Associates*, has been demolished.
[†]A vertical clock by *Robin Don* has been removed.

HIGH STREET SOUTH has the best buildings of the town and on its w side the narrow plots indicate the early origins of building here; behind is MIDDLE ROW, the medieval service street which was found in 1979 to have a long range of jettied fronts above shops towards its s end. Little of obviously early date now remains.* The street then opens as The Square, the former market place, with the Methodist church (*see* Religious buildings above) and, opposite, THE PRIORY (Heritage Centre), which has handsome Early Georgian façades, stuccoed to the High Street with arched windows in moulded surrounds with keystones, a pedimented doorway and quoins of even size. The garden façade is brick, with the typical Early Georgian quoins of uneven length and a pedimented centre with arched window. Inside, a fine staircase with three spiral balusters to the tread. However, incorporated into the ground floor of the front is a long medieval room, rib-vaulted in four bays of quadripartite vaults. The ribs are single-chamfered and die into the piers. It lay outside the priory precinct and appears to have been built as a hostelry. Reset in an upstairs room, panels of WALL PAINTINGS dated to *c.* 1610–30 (Andrea Kirkham) and imitating hangings, with all-over patterns of large leaves and a figure of a man smoking a pipe. They were removed from No. 20 High Street North, which was the White Hart Inn in the early C17. A little further s, raised on a terrace, the CART ALMSHOUSES of *c.* 1723, a plain two-storey row of blue and red brick, and then the CHEW GRAMMAR SCHOOL (Chew's House), of 1715, a fine, steeply pedimented front with a curious bell-turret cupola. Five bays, two storeys. On the doorway, two charity children. Plain closed string stair with turned balusters inside. Jane Cart, who founded the almshouses, was the daughter of Thomas Chew, who founded the school. Next to it the school of 1883 (now the LITTLE THEATRE), with single Dutch gable.

In CHURCH STREET, No. 26 on the s side has an C18 front but a medieval jetty to the side and dragon beam inside (i.e. it was also originally jettied to the street). The N side was lost in the mid 1960s to road widening, the Quadrant Shopping Centre (*see* above) and the egregious PRIORY HEIGHTS, seven storeys of offices above a recessed ground floor with angled pre-cast concrete piers. Further on, opposite the church, OLD PALACE LODGE, partly C18 in plum brick, and the MARSHE ALMSHOUSES of 1743, two storeys with a broad pediment over the centre.

In WEST STREET the character of pre-C20 Dunstable survived until the later C20 reconstruction on the s side.† No buildings of note now, except two gable ends (Nos. 18 and 24) showing timber-framing. N in EDWARD, ICKNIELD and

*A tree-ring date of 1310–20 was obtained from timbers removed from a building at No. 30 Middle Row.
†No. 7 West Street, a timber-framed house with jettied front, was taken to the Chilterns Open Air Museum, Bucks.

REGENT STREETS, some good small C19 houses. Luton 'grey' brick with red dressings and simple classical doorcases.

Former WINDMILL, West Street, W of the Catholic church. Built in 1839. Unusually tall, 98 ft (29.8 metres) high, with a straight-sided base below the tapering tower.

LONDON GLIDING CLUB, 1½ m. SW on a plateau at the base of the Downs. 1935–6 by *Christopher Nicholson*, a club member. One of the icons of early British Modernism but in need of some repair at the time of writing. With its window band, its semicircular bow and its rounded corner, it was the convinced statement of a young architect under the influence of Mendelsohn's English work. The materials are a steel frame clad in brick, the social elements defined by a skin of plaster render painted green, the original colour restored. The dining room and lounge bridge in a single span the entrance to the hangar itself and overlook the apron. At right angles is a single-storey wing for the bar, originally with a roof terrace, linked at first floor with the main part by the plain brick stair-tower. The interior was decorated by *E. G. Nicholson* but nothing of her colour scheme is preserved. Some furnishings survive (but not the original chairs by *Alvar Aalto*). The hangar itself is more functional, with light steel roof trusses and moulded cladding. The workshop at its rear was added in 1937. The club suffered the misfortune of use as a prison camp in the Second World War; some of the alterations date from that time.

CHILTERNS GATEWAY CENTRE, off Dunstable Road on the edge of Dunstable Downs. By *Architype*, 2006, for Bedfordshire County Council and the National Trust. One long monopitch roof, oversailing fully glazed walls along the front and sides for café and shop. An energy-efficient design, in its foreground a WINDCATCHER, an eyecatching twist of Corten steel to direct air via an underground tunnel for natural heating and cooling of the building.

FIVE KNOLLS BARROW CEMETERY, 1 m. WSW where the Dunstable Downs begin. This is the finest barrow group in the county, on a site above the Icknield Way. It consists of seven barrows, comprising two bowl, three bell, and two pond barrows and originally probably more. The largest of the bowl barrows is 60 ft (18.3 metres) in diameter and 5 ft high. It covered a Late Neolithic inhumation burial of a flexed female skeleton accompanied by a polished flint knife. An Early Bronze Age collared urn containing a cremation burial was inserted into the existing mound, and during the late Roman or Saxon period ninety-eight intrusive burials were deposited in it. The three bell barrows are enclosed within a single ditch. The largest mound, 80 ft (24 metres) in diameter, and the smallest, 52 ft (15.8 metres) in diameter, were both opened in the C19. The former produced sherds of Western Neolithic and Beaker pottery. Both the pond barrows are slight structures with diameters of 35 ft (10 metres) and 18 ft (5 metres) and depths of 2 ft and 1½ ft respectively. Neither has been excavated.

5   MAIDEN BOWER HILLFORT, 1½ m. NW. Iron Age. Of univallate
    construction with a V-sectioned ditch 10 ft (3 metres) deep
    and 25 ft (7.6 metres) wide. The 11 acres (4.4 ha) enclosed by
    the rampart are provided with entrances on the SW and N. The
    former has been proved by excavation to be original and was
    revetted with timber uprights. Overlain by the fort may be a
    Neolithic causewayed enclosure. There is also evidence through
    coins and pottery of Roman occupation. Geophysical survey
    has produced evidence of a small building inside the fort to
    the W.

2040   DUNTON

ST MARY MAGDALENE. Stone W tower of the restoration of 1861
by *E. Browning*, but the arch to the nave and the stair-turret
both medieval. Of 1861 also the chancel roof with heavy hammerbeams and big angels. The stone corbels have naturalistic
flower representations. The old church is of brown cobble.
Much of it is Dec, namely the four-bay S arcade (piers quatrefoil with four thin shafts in the diagonals), the S aisle E window
with wilfully composed flowing tracery, one S window (reticulated tracery), the chancel with its arch to the nave, the plain
SEDILIA and PISCINA (chancel and S aisle) with cusped arches,
and the grand E window also reticulated. In this, however, in
the head, the advent of the Perp is noticeable. Late Dec also
the S doorway. The porch was heightened in the Perp style, but
deprived of its gable in the C19, and Perp also is the N aisle,
arcade piers with four polygonal projections and thin shafts in
the diagonals, the arches with hollow chamfers. In the S aisle
two brackets. One, a big bust, is Dec, the other Perp. – FONT.
Octagonal, Perp, with simple tracery patterns. – TILES.
Throughout nave and chancel, 1861 by *Maw & Co.* (designs
of circles and birds by *Lord Alwynne Compton*). – ORGAN. A
pretty Late Georgian instrument with pediments and Ionic
pilasters. – STAINED GLASS. Some medieval bits in the top of
the S aisle E window.

                DUROCOBRIVAE *see* DUNSTABLE

                EASTCOTTS *see* COTTON END

1010   EAST HYDE

ST CHARALAMBOS (Greek Orthodox). Formerly Holy Trinity.
1840–1 by *Benjamin Ferrey*, partly paid for by the Marquess of

Bute. Ferrey was one of the first to take archaeological accuracy seriously. He began to do this just about 1841. Yet here he is still entirely in the Commissioners' vein. Brick, Neo-Norman with slender arched side windows and a small apse. The façade, inspired by the Norman guest house of Canterbury Cathedral, has two large round Norman piers flanking the entrance and open staircases with Norman colonnettes turning l. and r. The l. one leads to the w gallery, the r. one is blind. In addition, there is one asymmetrically placed w turret. It is a distressing display. – FURNISHINGS of *c.* 1866, when reordering of the E end was carried out by *James Fowler* of Louth. – STAINED GLASS. Much by *Thomas Baillie & Co.*, 1857–68, except one of 1870 (S wall), attributed to *Lavers, Barraud & Westlake* (M. Harrison). – MAUSOLEUM to Sir Julius Wernher †1912 and family. Dec-style tomb-chest 'cage' with crocketed gables and inside a rib-vault over a massive lead and porphyry casket. The design is possibly by *W. H. Romaine Walker*; it certainly has his lavishness.

VILLAGE HALL, N of the church. Board School of 1901, pretty with half-timbered gable and veranda.

THE HYDE, ½ m. ENE. Early C18 box, reputedly built by Philadelphia, Lady Cotton, presumably after the death of Sir Thomas Cotton (of Combermere, Shropshire) in 1715. Brick, of five bays, and two storeys, the windows with segmental arches. A Venetian window on the SE side. Doorcase with Doric columns and pediment. The parapet with balustrades is of 1952–3 when an attic storey was removed, along with two-storey wings and stucco. Stables with cupola. – LODGE. Thatched. By *Richardson & Gill*, 1930.

EATON BRAY

ST MARY. Externally the church is not specially memorable, partly owing to its restoration – a protacted business begun in 1890 under *R. W. Edis*. Totternhoe stone, short W tower with spike, clerestory, mostly Perp windows, and one (S transept) of four arched lights with a transom which is dated 1608. The tower was first added *c.* 1320 but was enlarged by Sir Reginald Bray soon after he acquired the manor *c.* 1490, and made from a square into one of oblong plan; this was reversed in the 1870s. The parapet and spike are of the final phase of restoration (i.e. rebuilding) of 1914–16 by *W. A. Forsyth*. He added the abutting N vestry in 1930. But its interior one will hardly forget. It is surprisingly splendid, thanks to the two arcades of *c.* 1220 and *c.* 1235–40, the result of new building attributed to the incoming Norman baron William de Cantilupe (or Cantelow) who built the castle (*see* below). Both arcades are of five bays. The S arcade comes first. Octagonal piers and stiff-leaf capitals with big, full leaves, but only at the top of the bell (cf. Studham).

The arches have two hollow chamfers, and the responds are large, conical brackets with very flat decoration of large summarized leaves. The N arcade is yet richer. Here the piers have eight shafts, and as an additional refinement two of them and the E respond have some of the shafts just slightly detached. The W respond is again a cone but composed of shafts with stiff-leaf at the top. The pier capitals are of the most dramatic stiff-leaf variety. The arches consist of eleven rolls each. Moreover across the aisles was some transverse bracing, and this must have consisted or been meant to consist of a bold single-chamfered arch rising from the outer wall (and in two cases stiff-leaf corbels) to the wall above the arcade. But from the springer of the arcade arches a coeval triple-roll arch starts to rise much more gently towards these big arches and would, if completed, have met them. It is a strange, unnecessarily complicated arrangement, but would have been visually effective in so ornate an aisle. The nave is unusually well supplied with brackets and niches for devotional images. The chancel is basically also E.E., see the ANGLE PISCINA. The interior of the E window looks c. 1300. The nave N chapel is a widening of the E end of the aisle; Perp window with a straight-headed niche, like Kensworth, q.v. – Wonderful late C13 IRONWORK to the S door, three hinges with pairs of scrolls in doubles and triples ending in rosettes and foliage, showing the influence locally of Thomas of Leighton. – FONT. The bowl and the splendid stiff-leaf capitals are original and look exactly contemporary with the N arcade. – REREDOS. A handsome Late Perp stone reredos in the S transept, and integral with it the canopied niche incorporated within the cente light of the window. The chancel REREDOS is of 1951 by *Christopher Webb*. – ORGAN. A very handsome Gothick case, 1991 by *Peter Collins*, filling the W end. – STAINED GLASS. Chancel E (1900) and S aisle E (1936) windows, both by *Heaton, Butler & Bayne*. N chapel, 1996 by *Chapel Studio*. – MONUMENTS. Tomb-chest with an interesting mixture of Gothic and Elizabethan motifs. The brass plate which was behind it (now remounted in the S chapel) is indeed to Lady Bray and children, and she died in 1558. Below it, a brass inscription in black letter to Jane, daughter of Lord Bray, †1539 but palimpsest of a bishop or abbot of c. 1430. – CURIOSUM. Two long thatch hooks (W wall).

E of the church on High Street, the COFFEE TAVERN, built 1901 as the village Reading Room; by *J. T. Sloan* of Linslade. Olde English style. N of the church by the green, CHURCH FARM, a timber-framed house with its gabled l. cross-wing jettied on one side. Panel framing infilled with brick. Second gabled wing to the r.

THE LODGE, N of Church Farm, is dated 1878 and is all that was completed of an ambitious plan by Arthur Macnamara (*see* Billington) to rebuild on the site of EATON BRAY CASTLE, which lies ½ m. W by Park Farm. It was a fortified manor house built in 1221 by William de Cantelow and extensive, according to an account of 1274. The large MOAT is substantially preserved and of interest for it clearly shows that it began as a circle later augmented into a typical rectangle, probably in the C16.

EDWORTH

ST GEORGE (Churches Conservation Trust), on the lawn of Manor Farm. Of brown cobble, some ironstone, gratifyingly not over-attended-to, although restored in 1875–6 by *Raynes & Shum* and repaired under *William Weir*'s supervision in 1908–9. Dec two-bay aisles, the piers quatrefoil with thin shafts in the diagonals, the arches with two sunk quadrants. Dec also the two doorways, the s probably earlier than the N, and Dec the two aisle E windows. Dec finally the w tower, its arch double chamfered on semi-octagonal responds. But the chancel arch, the clerestory, crenellation, and the two porches, leaning against the aisles, are all Perp. Chancel shortened in 1836, the new E wall all brick. – PILLAR PISCINA (N aisle E). Square, early C13. – FONT. Octagonal, Perp. With big flowers and shields against the underside and tracery, quatrefoils etc. against the bowl. – BENCHES. Four ogee-topped ends with poppyheads, one normal, one a lion, one a monkey, and one a dressed-up corn cob. – WALL PAINTING. In the N aisle s wall two kings from the story of the Three Quick and the Three Dead. C14. – ARCHITEC-TURAL FRAGMENTS. Two capitals with crockets. – STAINED GLASS. In the chancel s many fragments, rather restored but including a C14 figure of St Edmund. In the clerestory, St James, C15. – E window 1873, attributed to *Heaton, Butler & Bayne* (M. Kerney), lovely deep colours. – w window, the Annunciation, by *Shrigley & Hunt*, 1892. – s aisle E. 1950 by *G. Maile & Son*.

EGGINGTON

ST MICHAEL. Nave of ironstone, chancel of Totternhoe stone. The chancel arch responds are Dec. Pretty shingled bell-turret, added, like the porch, by *Ewan Christian*, 1882–3. – FONT. Cauldron-like, or rather quatrefoiled with corner shafts, oddly undecided in shape. E.E. – STAINED GLASS. E lancets. 1883. Attributed to *W. F. Dixon* (M. Kerney).

EGGINGTON HOUSE. Commonly dated to 1696 and as built for John Reynal (or Renouille), a Huguenot. If so, it is an uncom-monly fine example of latest C17 domestic architecture, com-pletely up to the moment in features. However Reynal seems to have purchased the manor only *c.* 1710–17, dates that would fit the design more comfortably. Seven-bay front, three storeys, brick. Segment-headed windows, panelled parapet with urns, door-hood on carved brackets. Five bays at the rear. (Open string staircase with twisted balusters and carved ends; doors with panelled supraporte and one room with bolection-moulded panelling and niches with shell-heads.)

ELSTOW

0040

The village is famous not only for the remains of the Abbey but also for John Bunyan who was born in the parish, at Harrowden.

ST MARY AND ST HELEN. Elstow was a Benedictine nunnery. It was founded *c.* 1078 by Countess Judith of Huntingdon, niece of the Conqueror and widow of Waltheof, who was executed by the King in 1076; of its buildings only part of the church and part of the W and S range along the cloister remain. Most of the plan is known, however, from excavation (1965–72). The abbey church had a crossing and transepts, a chancel with apse and a later, probably square-ended, Lady Chapel, extending E of the present churchyard wall. S of the chancel there was another building, also probably a chapel in parallel but not conjoined with it. Only the nave remains and even that is not preserved complete. The first bays from the E are missing. The present E end of the church with the lower windows, so far as they are not of the 1880–2 restoration by *T. J. Jackson* of Bedford, is of 1580, when presumably the rest was demolished. It is interesting to see that the details of the windows of 1580 are still entirely in the Perp tradition. Jackson's work was funded by Samuel Whitbread III, as at Cardington (q.v.), encouraging a too-thorough approach. He rebuilt the S aisle and over-restored the N aisle. The clerestory was also taken down and remade, but the windows are basically right and prepare for the interior. The three E bays each side are Norman, the two wide W bays E.E. The interior indeed, impressively high and austere, falls into two parts. The Norman work consists of high arcades, no gallery or triforium whatever, and (originally) the clerestory windows. The piers are plainly oblong cruciform, the arches plainly single-stepped. The capitals are mere imposts; only the two E and W have the smallest bit of billet decoration and flat lozenges. All of this looks early C12. On the other hand, above the N doorway, which is Jackson's very poor imitation-Norman, is an arched panel of mostly genuine Norman workmanship, and that looks rather 1140 than earlier. It shows, very small, Christ in an almond-shaped glory with St Peter on the l., and St Paul on the r.* The style, with inclined heads to the figures, is most decidedly French,

---

*Pevsner interpreted this figure as St John, but the bearded figure with a book is more likely to be St Paul.

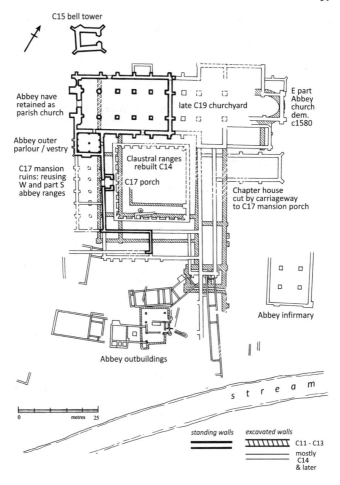

C15 bell tower

Abbey nave
retained as
parish church

late C19 churchyard

E part
Abbey
church
dem.
c1580

Abbey outer
parlour / vestry

C17 mansion
ruins: reusing
W and part S
abbey ranges

Claustral ranges
rebuilt C14

C17 porch

Chapter house
cut by carriageway
to C17 mansion porch

Abbey infirmary

Abbey outbuildings

s t r e a m

0   metres   25

standing walls   excavated walls

C11 - C13

mostly
C14
& later

Elstow Abbey.
Simplified site plan and excavation results

and derived from the stage of Moissac, i.e. *c.* 1120, but it is
also closely related to the figure carving in the s porch of
Malmesbury Abbey, Wilts.★ The panel has an arched frame
with short single-scallop columns and a roll-moulding and a
moulding of pellets.

The E.E. w extension must be of *c.* 1220. It has exceedingly
heavy octagonal piers with characteristic stiff-leaf capitals and
moulded arches, just one of them decorated with dogtooth.

★I am grateful to Ron Baxter for this observation.

The arches are unmoulded to the s aisle. The clerestory lancets
are shafted, the shafts with rings and stiff-leaf. The present w
window is Late Perp (1580?) and not large. It replaces an
enormous window. The w front dates in its start from *c.* 1220
as well. Central doorway with two orders of stiff-leaf colonnettes. The big buttress to the l. with its nook-shafts is of the
same date. The doorway beyond it is in a half-finished state.
What was it for? The lancet above it is original and inside it
too has shafts with stiff-leaf. To the r. of the central doorway
all is in disorder (much as at Dunstable, *see* p. 146) and much
is of the restoration, e.g. the octagonal stair-turret.

The church has a broad and solid, fully detached CAMPA-
NILE, N of the E.E. part, i.e. in the same position as at e.g.
Chichester and other Benedictine foundations. It is of the C15
with massive buttresses and has to each side a pair of transomed two-light bell-openings, a corner turret and on the top
a spike. Presumably it relates to the parochial use of the nave
which ensured its post-Dissolution survival as the parish
church.

FURNISHINGS. The FONT is large, Perp and octagonal. It
has quatrefoils on the bowl and on the foot an animal, two
heads, and a human figure(?). – COMMUNION RAIL (Bunyan
Chapel). Jacobean, turned balusters. – SCULPTURE. E wall. An
excellent bracket of intricate foliage on a bust. Perp. Also a
second bracket in the same wall above the Radclif monument
which cuts into it. It has two angels holding scourges and Arma
Christi. What is the date? It appears to be a C12 capital recut
as an image bracket in the early C16. – STAINED GLASS. E
windows by *Mayer & Co.*, 1887, to *Jackson*'s design. The show-
pieces are the two by *T. W. Camm* of Birmingham (made by
Winfield & Co.), inspired by Bunyan's *Pilgrim's Progress* (s aisle
E, 1883) and *The Holy War* (N aisle E, 1885), showing Mansoul
as an excellently detailed Northern Gothic city. – MONU-
MENTS. Brasses: Margery Argentine †1427 (41 in.; 1 metre)
and Elizabeth Hervey, abbess of Elstow, †1527 (36 in.; 91 cm),
the former very good, the latter a rare survival (cf. Denham,
Bucks.). – Sir Humphrey Radclif †1566 and wife. Alabaster.
Kneeling figures against arches with three slim columns, l., r.,
and between them. Achievement over. The placing in the E wall
is unexpected. – Tablets to Thomas Hillersdon †1656 (helmet
and tabard above) and to John Hillersdon †1684. Both are of
high quality. The first, black and white with shields at the sides
under vertical scrolls, pilasters and a segmental pediment, is
attributed to *Thomas Burman*. The second, in style still rather
1660 than 1680, is attributed to *William Stanton* (GF). – Also
probably by *Stanton* the tablets to Robert Crompton †1681 (N
aisle), oval with a torus wreath, and his son, Lovet Crompton,
†1684/5. – Captain Henry Macan †1898 (s aisle). Unusually
handsome brass with angels surmounting an arch with trophies. By *Gawthorp*.

Excavations exposed the footings of the later medieval
CLOISTER buttresses incorporating two mid-C13 arcade span-

drels, deeply moulded and one of them with fine foliage. Excavation also showed two phases of claustral building. Associated with the first phase is the vestry to the s of the w front, which must have been the cloister's OUTER PARLOUR, its external walls substantially rebuilt in 1880–2. It is a square room, with a central C13 pier of Purbeck marble with eight concave sides and tiny bits of stiff-leaf at the neck. It carries a very curious rib-vault of four bays, but with some ribs transgressing from one bay into the next. The division is in fact rather one oblong E and one oblong W bay. Of wall-shafts there are four in the corners, plus one N and one S, but two W (framing seats) and two E (framing a window). That makes it possible for diagonal ribs to run from mid-shaft S direct to the NW and NE shafts and from mid-shaft N direct to SW and SE. The rib which should divide the NW square from the SW square, and the NE square from the NW square is carried on only till it meets the joining point of the two diagonal ribs, and there are in addition fragmentary diagonal ribs as well. As a pattern it is unique, and moreover each rib starts not from an abacus but from a bracket set on the abacus. Is that C13 as well?

When the outer parlour was built the claustral W range stood immediately to its E, but in the early C14 the cloister was completely rebuilt on a new alignment and the new W range was built in line with the vestry. Then *c.* 1620 this, and part of the S (refectory) range, were made into the HILLERSDON MANSION, a stone and brick house for Thomas Hillersdon, who bought the property in 1616. What survived demolition *c.* 1775 is on a fragmentary E-plan, with the N bar of the E being the church. The S bar is three bays long and one wide. The middle bar, as usual, is the porch. This must have been a handsome job but it is of Totternhoe stone and alas much of the detail has been washed away. It has paired pilasters on two floors, niches between, and a round arch with strapwork under a small pediment. There was originally a third storey. The windows (completely renewed) are mullioned and transomed, in the S bar of two and three lights, in the hall part l. of the porch of three and four. Thoroughly repaired in 2012.

NE of the church on the green stands the MOOT HALL, built *c.* 1500, of timber with diagonal braces and brick infillings. The upper floor overhangs on three sides – dragon beams, rare in Bedfordshire, at the angles – and contains the main room, for the manorial court, with its original tie-beam roof of clasped purlin construction. The fourth side was probably jettied too but an extra bay was added here in the early C16 with rooms heated by fireplaces on each floor. Below, the W part was divided into six shops, each with its doorway and small window which may have been shuttered for dealing in goods. The E part contained the staircase. Restored 1951 for the Festival of Britain (under the direction of *S. V. Goodman*, County Architect) with brick salvaged from the brewery at Ampthill. Inside, the PULPIT from the church. Perp. A fine, complete wooden piece of the wineglass type with tracery panels, buttresses with pinnacles, and some painting. Removed here in 1969. Also part of a late C8 or early C9 CROSS-SHAFT with interlace and beasts. 22 in. (56 cm). Discovered 1967 in the 1580s E wall of the church.

Former BOARD SCHOOL, High Street. *c.* 1873 by *John Usher.* Two large gables, one with the bellcote, and smaller one to the r. for the school house.

JOHN BUNYAN MEMORIAL HALL, next to the school. By *Usher & Anthony,* 1908. Large stained-glass window with fifteen scenes from Pilgrim's Progress, by *J. Egan* of Wardour Street, London.

22 In the High Street E of the church BUNYAN'S MEAD, a long row of timber-framed cottages with overhanging upper floor. Restored, in material terms rather insensitively, in 1977–9 for North Bedfordshire Borough Council (*T. Hinchcliffe,* Borough Architect, with *Chrystal & West*). At least some are likely to have been inns and shops at the gates of the abbey and then altered after the Dissolution, e.g. with stone for fireplaces from the abbey. Especially remarkable displays of ogival bracing in pairs and triplets at the N end (Nos. 2–3) which is of two bays and with a long jetty. The N bay is thought to have contained a shop and has one pointed arch surviving. The bracing and construction technique of the crown-post roof inside indicate a late C13 or early C14 date. More bracing in the gable over a passage from the street. This gave access to a slightly later hall range at the rear, again with crown-post roofs. S of this a corresponding range (No. 8) incorporates the remains of an early C13 base cruck roof of an aisled hall, whose aisles were removed in the C16 and replaced by cross-wings. (Some *c.* 1600 wall painting inside behind early C17 panelling and in the wing fronting the road). No. 15, again, has single ogee braces above the jetty but probably C15. No. 17 has been identified as an altered small Wealden house, one of only seven known in Bedfordshire. The hall was just one bay wide and the wings gable-ended rather than with the more typical hipped roof of the Weald examples. No. 20 – close-studded walls, mid-rail, no jetty – has a Tudor-arched door originally leading into a two-bay open hall and clearly shows the pattern of the two-storey hall window to the r. The l. part contained the chambers above a shop. Behind, some houses with monopitch roofs, 1976 by *Charter Building Design Group.*

ELSTOW LODGE. 1927 by *W. B. Stonebridge* for S. H. Whitbread. Early Georgian style with shallow wings, modillion cornice and central pergola.*

---

*The previous house of this name was taken by M. H. Baillie Scott after his house at Fenlake Manor, Bedford, was burnt down in 1911.

ETONBURY *see* ARLESEY

EVERSHOLT   *9030*

One of the most straggling villages in Bedfordshire with no less than fourteen 'ends'.

ST JOHN THE BAPTIST. An unusually regular Late Perp iron-stone exterior, embattled, with straight-headed three-light windows in the aisles, the clerestory, and even the porch. Earlier Perp w tower. Dec chancel windows, one with a transom and lowside. All very restored by *G. G. Scott*, 1863–4; the medieval E window had already been replaced. The interior, as so often, is much earlier. Three-bay N arcade with octagonal piers and double-hollow-chamfered arches, plus a w bay of *c.* 1300. What is the date of the three bays? The elaborate E respond has a capital of the very latest Norman scallop type combined with a band of dogtooth and a notch corbel of c13 type. The w respond capital has two tiers of stylized leaves. But the rest must be a replacement contemporary with the s arcade of four bays. The chancel, as the windows indicated, is early c14. Pointed chancel arch with dying mouldings. Two-bay N chapel arcade with quatrefoil pier and responds with the familiar diagonal shafts. The PISCINA is original work too of *c.* 1330. – FURNISHINGS by Scott. – ORGAN. Gothic case. Given in 1868 but incorporating parts of a chamber organ by *Snetzler*, 1750, which was in Woburn old church (*see* p. 328) from 1836. – PAINTED DECORATION. An impressive scheme of 1910 by *Edward Aveling Green*, who lived at Berrystead, although in the fag-end of Walter Crane's style, far, far away from anything still alive after 1900. Christ in Majesty over the chancel arch with ranks of angels and archangels; over the tower arch the Expulsion; in the nave, roundels of Elijah, Moses and the Evangelists. In the s aisle, angels with musical instruments. Angel roundels in the choir. The carved REREDOS and STATUE of St John the Baptist (nave w end) are also by *Aveling Green*, as are two of the STAINED-GLASS windows: the E window, 1905, and the s aisle E, 1902. – Most of the other windows by *Clayton & Bell*, *c.* 1860–5. A s window (St Martin) by *Kempe*, 1899. – MONUMENTS. – Part of a mid-c15 BRASS, just the tablet with six sons. – Elizabeth Hyde †1718. Grey marble with gadroon moulded base and segmental pediment broken around an achievement. Attributed to *Edward Stanton* (GF). – Sarah Hogkinson †1788. Sarcophagus with mourning female and draped urn above. – WAR MEMORIAL. Bronze St Michael, again by *E. Aveling Green*, 1920.

s of the church CHURCH FARM, early c18, of blue and red brick with a projecting one-bay centre, segment-headed windows, brick quoins and hipped roof. SCHOOL, sw of the church, by *J. T. Wing*, 1842.

Tyrells End Farm, ¼ m. N. Good timber-framed house of two bays with close studding to the sides and gable end and some original fenestration. Curved brace to the smoke bay. Formerly an open hall. The two bays s of the chimney are later.

Berrystead, Berry End, ¾ m. NNW. Picturesque style with sharp gables, probably built for John Green, a Woburn solicitor who moved here c. 1860. ¼ m. w a curious early C19 Woburn estate LODGE, cruciform with lunette windows under half-hipped roofs. Possibly by *Robert Salmon*, the Duke's surveyor.

EVERTON

St Mary. Dec w tower of ironstone, lowered after a lightning strike in 1974 and given pinnacles in 1999. The rest of the church brown cobbles, essentially Late Norman and unusually complete, see the s doorway with one order of colonnettes with scallop capitals and a round arch already with E.E. mouldings; see also the aisle w windows and the chancel N and S windows, but above all the three-bay arcades of round piers with multi-scalloped capitals and square abaci and of unmoulded arches. The s capitals are somewhat heavier, i.e. earlier than the N capitals, and both arcades are older than the s doorway arch. Perp clerestory, on the N side with quatrefoil windows. Perp s porch with pretty base-frieze of lozenges with quatrefoils. The tower's CLOCK is 1720s, from Everton House's stables, installed 1865–6 when the church was restored by *David Brandon*. – PULPIT. 1885, with open traceried sides. It replaced a three-decker of 1729 whose sounding-board is now at Sutton (q.v.). – STAINED GLASS. E window (1865 by *Ward & Hughes*) destroyed by lightning in 1974. A single medallion of the Ascension remains. Several other windows also attributed to Ward & Hughes (MK). s aisle sw (I am the Light of the World) by *J. Powell & Sons*, 1904. – MONUMENTS. Sir Humphrey Winche †1624. Very high, but flat, hanging monument with frontal demi-figure in an arched frame. He is holding a book. Trio of arches below. Cherubs' heads and allegorical figures. – Richard Astell †1777. A very handsome design. Urn before obelisk standing on a fine chest in light-coloured marbles with Greek key decoration and lions' feet. Signed by *W. Tyler*. – William Astell †1841. Grecian tablet. – J. H. Astell †1887. Classical tablet mostly in alabaster with a broken pediment. – Also Mary Pedley of Tetworth Hall (Hunts.) †1827. Signed by *John Soward*. Plain, pedimented tablet with scrolled sides.*

Methodist church, E on the road to Gamlingay. 1883 by *John Usher* (P. C. Edwards). Fine wheel window. Now a house.

*For St Sylvester, a mission church to St Mary, *see* Gamlingay in the *Buildings of England: Cambridgeshire*.

EVERTON HOUSE stood immediately E of St Mary. It was early C18, altered for the Astells, relatives of the Thorntons at Moggerhanger (q.v.), by *Soane* in 1811, but abandoned for Woodbury Hall *c.* 1850 and later dem. Former laundry and service wing converted as a house.

WOODBURY HALL. N of the church on the W edge of the Greensand Ridge. The appearance of the house is Late Georgian. In fact it was built *c.* 1803 for the Rev. John Wilkieson but received divers Victorian additions for the Astells, which *Philip Tilden* partly removed in 1931, and then suffered from a fire in 1945. After that, in 1952–3, it was given its present form by *Sir Basil Spence* – lowered to two storeys, and shortened to seven bays front and back under a hipped roof. On the entrance front an open pediment in the centre and an Ionic prostyle porch, retained from the previous house. On the garden front, a pedimented centre with quoins and garlands above a canted bay. The N loggia between short wings is Tilden's, as are the principal Neo-Georgian interiors. Some fittings from Everton House (*see* above).

The park was landscaped by *Nathaniel Richmond* in 1764 for Col. The Hon. George Parker. His house was OLD WOODBURY HOUSE, ½ m. NE. Probably C17 but extended for Parker and in 1836–8 transformed for the Rev. William Wilkieson; the Tudor Gothic E porch is of that time. Contemporary W stable court, with battlements. Some windows have painted glass (C18 or early C19) with figures of Julius Caesar, Tiberius and heraldry. On the Everton Road, some ESTATE COTTAGES of a total of sixty built on Gamlingay Heath by Wilkieson in 1833: Gothic windows with distinctive rusticated arches and cast-iron frames.

STOREY'S FARM, at the park's S entrance, is dated 1884, very picturesque, with crowstepped gables, a bellcote and moulded brick panel over the porch.

HAZELLS HALL* (The Hasells), 1⅛ m. SW. The S and E façades are red brick and rubbed brick with a stone balustrade and of 1788–90 for Francis Pym, the work directed by *Martin Cole*, a London surveyor, who may have been the architect. Eleven-bay S front with a three-bay pediment; fine coat of arms and fine detailing of the middle windows. The centre, however, must incorporate the house of *c.* 1698 with two bays added l. and r. after it was sold in 1721 to Heylock Kingsley, whose daughter married William Pym. Round the corner the entrance side is of seven bays, the keystones to the windows vermiculated. Porch of Doric columns added after 1814, when the house was also stuccoed. N wing with archway and clock cupola. Restored and converted to apartments by *Kit Martin* with *Malcolm Leverington*, 1981–5, the interiors of 1790 thankfully unaffected by previous military and hospital use.

GARDENS. Three walled gardens to the W, early C18, and S of these a remarkable tree-lined TERRACE along the edge of

---

*Strictly speaking, the house is in Sandy parish.

the ridge with views across the Bedford plain. Its ends are closed by pavilion shelters, the s one with a front of Tuscan columns but a back, looking into the park, of rustic Gothic aspect, a remodelling by *Humphry Repton*, 1790–1. Payments for making improvements and plantings in the PARK were made to *Mr Richmond* (most likely *Nathaniel Richmond*) 1765–6. Repton removed the Everton road to the E; built to his plans is the rustic STONE LODGE, its chimney dated 1793. Dressed ironstone with a thatched roof and rustic porch. Small room attached to its corner, also thatched. – CRIMEAN LODGE (at the former E entrance). A prefabricated army hut, supplied to Thomas de la Rue, playing-card manufacturer, while tenant of the hall in 1860–6.

EVERTON PARK, ¼ m. NE of Hazells Hall, is the house of 1968–9 for Francis Pym M.P. by *Rodney Tatchell* of *Sydney Tatchell, Son & Partner*. Mildest Neo-Georgian. GARDENS by *Geoffrey Jellicoe*, 1974–5: a 'Long Walk' (a reminder of the terrace at Hazells Hall) runs in front from a gate in the park to a small enclosure with an urn.

EYEWORTH

ALL SAINTS. Brown cobble. The w tower has a Dec w window. It lost its recessed Perp spire in 1967 and now has a saddleback roof with a pepperpot turret. s arcade of standard elements, small quatrefoil Dec s aisle w window, three-light (reticulated) s aisle E window. Dec tower arch and Dec chancel arch. The chancel mostly clunch, extensively patched in red brick (C17?). Perp N windows to aisle and clerestory.[*] – COMMUNION RAIL. C17. – STAINED GLASS. Medieval fragments in several windows. The E window is of 1901, a memorial to the daughter of Viscount Peel, who held the manor. Three Maries, attributed to *Lavers, Barraud & Westlake* (Michael Kerney). – MONUMENTS. Chancel s. Sir Edmund Anderson †1605, Lord Chief Justice of the Court of Common Pleas (cf. Monks Hardwick House, Hunts.). An ambitious piece. Alabaster. Two recumbent effigies. Kneeling children in relief against the base. Columns l. and r. and a flat back arch with coffering. Tall achievement and heraldic shields to the pilasters. Attributed to *Maximilian Colt* (Adam White). – Sir Francis Anderson, his son, †1616. Also alabaster but smaller, the composition no doubt originally similar but now fragmentary. The three principal figures now kneel frontally. Children also against the base. – Sir Richard Gadburye †1624, with wife and (originally) daughter. Brasses, the parents 3 ft 3 in. (99 cm) long. He wears a hat. – Edmond Anderson †1638, with wife and daughter. A very good piece, attributed to *Edward Marshall*. The composition is compli-

---

[*]The PULPIT, its stair with twisted balusters, *c.* 1700, has been removed.

cated. The parents are demi-figures. They hold a heart inscribed
'To God'. Top with broken segmental pediment with allegorical figures on it. Below, the child is seen in a round recess.
Hers is a bust with arms, and she holds a little book. To l. and
r. of her another, rather incongruous, broken segmental pediment with allegorical figures, one of whom also holds a heart.
The widow married Sir Thomas Cotton of Conington in 1640
– part of the inscription relating to her devotion to her first
husband's memory is scratched out – and her daughter wed
Sir John Cotton in 1644.

No trace remains of the mansion of the Andersons, which lay E
of the church.

FAIRFIELD HALL and FAIRFIELD PARK
see STOTFOLD

FARLEY HILL *see* LUTON

FARNDISH   *9060*

ST MICHAEL (Churches Conservation Trust). A small church
with a short W tower. The only remarkable feature is the S
doorway, which must date from *c.* 1210. It has three orders of
shafts, of which two are detached and only the middle one is
attached. The capitals are early stiff-leaf. Three orders of plain
arches alternately brown and beige in colour, i.e. from
Northamptonshire. Dec S nave windows. The W window is Dec
too, and was the nave W window before the tower was built
into the nave in the C15. The N doorway is blocked and very
plain, but could be of the same date as the S doorway. Perp E
window. – BOX PEWS with Victorian Gothic panelling. Installed
in 1846, paid for by a local farmer, W. H. S. Adcock. So the
style is both late and early. – Other furniture of the same time,
with some earlier medieval bits. – ROYAL ARMS. Victorian.
Unusually painted onto a tiled panel. – STAINED GLASS. E
window of *c.* 1846, given by Adcock. A Crucifixion, clearly
displaying German influence. Two other windows by *C. A.
Gibbs*, 1863–4.

GRANGE FARM. Late C17, L-plan, limestone, the front of three
widely spaced bays with three-light mullioned windows and
straight hoodmoulds over in brown ironstone. The composition is symmetrical, which suggests the proposed date.

GREYWALLS, opposite. The vicarage built new in 1859 by *Flock-
ton & Son* of Sheffield. Outbuildings etc. of 1875–6 by *John
Day*.

FELMERSHAM

ST MARY. What can the reason have been for Felmersham
receiving the noblest parish church in the county during the
noblest age of medieval churches, and moreover a church in
spiritual scale, even if not in size, vying with any abbey or
priory church? From the C12 the church came under Lenton
Priory, Notts., a Cluniac order, who relinquished the advowson to the Crown in 1283. It was exceptionally wealthy, but
that alone explains nothing. The church was built at one go
between about 1220 and 1230 or 1240, and it has a classicity
and harmony which – rare indeed in the English C13 – includes
even the W front, which rises high on a terrace immediately
above the village street. So often E.E. W fronts, even Salisbury,
even Peterborough, have elements and motifs which jar. Here
there is nothing to disturb one's quiet admiration. The nave is
represented by a doorway of many orders of slim shafts and
fine filleted mouldings, and this is flanked by one blank arch
l. and one r. with trefoil-headed sub-arches and a plate tracery
quatrefoil. Above that is an arcade of seven arches with dogtooth alternating with other intricate patterns (admittedly
much restored in 1823–6). The supports are composite, of four
detached shafts each, three in a row and a fourth in front.
Above that a high tripartite composition of ring-shafted
windows, with richly moulded pointed arches l. and r. and a
segmental arch in the centre. This contains a C15 window
where perhaps there were once three lancets. Among all the
capitals there is not one displaying stiff-leaf; all are moulded,
but inside two capitals l. and r. show traces of crockets. The
aisles have simply one shafted W lancet each. The doorway to
the S aisle is of the same kind as the W portal and above it is
a trefoil-headed niche. So the church is aisled, but it is a cruciform church, and the crossing tower is nobly E.E. too, below
its Perp top stage. Each face of the belfry has two lancets and
a blank arch on either side, the lancets on the E and W faces
under a round arch. Below is a curiously low stage containing
just two tiny lancets, and the steeper pitch of the original nave
roof shows on the W face. So to the transepts. That to the N
has three widely spaced lancets. The shallow S transept has
plate tracery of two high lancets and an almond shape over
and is furthermore different from the N transept in having its
E and W walls in line with the tower buttresses and inside half-
arches spanning between its S wall and the tower. The transept's E wall has a lancet and drip moulding that ties it in date
to the construction of the chancel, which has three very far-
separated lancets along its sides, with continuous mouldings.
On the S side their hoodmoulds are decorated with dogtooth,
as is that of the small priest's doorway. On the N side there is
no dogtooth. All this seems perfect E.E. but the S lancets are
restorations of 1853 by *Wing & Jackson* following the design
of the S central one and the priest's doorway. The reticulated

E window is also original C14 only in its jambs. It was square-headed until the 1850s but Wing discovered remnants of the Dec tracery as well as traces of the original three lancets. Straight-headed Dec windows to the S aisle, the present tracery again of the 1850s.* Those of N aisle and clerestory are Perp.

The climax inside is the crossing, of cathedral seriousness. The mighty crossing piers are of grouped shafts with round and keeled shafts alternating. The middle shaft of the NE and SE piers is a single broad chamfer. In the arches the innermost order is left as a big plain chamfer but the treatment of the outer mouldings is varied; all have some fine rolls with fillets but the richest are to the W faces of the nave and chancel arches. To the crossing the arches have chamfers and double chamfers above the mouldings.

In the chancel the lancets have a continuous thin roll. There is a DOUBLE PISCINA with a segmental arch and two almost straight-sided sub-arches and a middle shaft with crocketed capital. Now the nave and the aisles. Even here, instead of the usual unevenness, there is perfect poise. Arcades of four bays with alternating round and octagonal piers, alternating also across. It is a beautiful and perfectly logical scheme. The arches have one chamfer and two thin filleted rolls. The nave N, S and W doorways to the inside have a very depressed two-centred arch starting on short vertical pieces, another late C13 motif (cf. a window at Bushmead Priory) and the S door has iron-work strap hinges with zigzag and a handle plate with stamped leaves – that is dated to *c.* 1300. Perp ROOF (renewed) on massive stone corbels associated with the earlier roof including the Evangelists' symbols at the corners. – SCREEN. High and exceptionally beautiful too. Four-light divisions, rich tracery above the doorway, coving on two sides, and a cresting frieze. The crockets of the doorway gable develop into little angels. The screen was given by Richard Kyng and his wife; see the *orate* inscription. Loft removed in 1853, the painted decoration also Victorian. – PULPIT. By *George Highton*, 1895. E.E. style but crude when compared to its surroundings.[†] – WALL PAINT-ING. Part of a (C15?) Doom above the chancel arch (now above the ringing floor). – STAINED GLASS. E window 1949 by *Francis Spear*, in his woodcut style. A Wells family war memorial with the patron saints of the three services for each of their sons. S transept E, 2001 by *Goddard & Gibbs* (*John N. Lawson*).

TITHE BARN, S of the church, originally part of College Farm. Dated to 1428 by the surviving building accounts, for King's Hall Cambridge, who held the advowson. Stone, eight bays long, buttresses, with tie-beams and more closely set collar-beams. One original two-light window. C18 S transepts. Housing since *c.* 1980.

---

*The Perp chancel E window was taken to the garden of The Rectory, Keysoe.
[†]A REREDOS of 1890 by *W. M. Fawcett* has been removed. Fawcett was often employed by Trinity College, Cambridge, the advowson holders.

FELMERSHAM GRANGE, Hunts Lane, w of the church. Rebuilt
c. 1836 by Thomas Abbott Green, who subsequently inherited
The Bury, Pavenham (q.v.). Extended E, doubling its size, in
1886 for his son. The style of both phases is Neo-Elizabethan.
Partly demolished in the late 1960s; now two houses.

FELMERSHAM BRIDGE, NW of the church, over the Ouse. 1818
by *John & Samuel Bell*, masons of Radwell. Five arches, triangular cutwaters.

RADWELL BRIDGE, 1 m. SE. 1766 by *Thomas Morris* of Pavenham. Three plus two arches, the smaller arches at each end
added 1806 and 1832.

0030

FLITTON

ST JOHN THE BAPTIST. Of ironstone. All probably built by a de
Grey, Earl of Kent, whose badge and related heraldry decorated the big Perp s doorway until 1911. A single shield remains
to the l. The first Grey to be created Earl of Kent was in 1465
and the church was complete in 1489. w tower with higher
stair-turret. Short embattled nave and aisles. Rood stair-turret.
Perp arcades of three bays. The slender piers have standard
mouldings. The chancel arch corresponds. The whole E end is
taken up by the cruciform de Grey Mausoleum or Mausolea,
a whole series of rooms, oddly un-religious in character, which
begins on the N side of the chancel. The earliest part was 'lately
erected' by 1614 and extended in the early C18, although the
latest room to be filled, taking the original E portion of the
chancel, is all C19. It was originally of chequered red brick with
Dutch gables but since the C19 has been rendered and crenellated. The present E window of the chancel was inserted in
1924. It is the former E window of Silsoe (q.v.). – BENCHES.
Perp in parts, the ends buttressed. – STAINED GLASS. s aisle
E, pretty designs of local wildlife by *Christine Boyce*, 1976. –
BRASSES (N wall). Alianora Conquest †1434, a good 29-in.
(74 cm) figure, headless. – Mrs Warren, a 17-in. (43 cm) figure;
the figure of her husband Thomas (†1544) in armour is lost.
It comes from the *Fermer* workshop in London. – MONU-
MENTS. – Thomas White †1755, small tablet with yellow marble
obelisk. By *Cox* of Northampton. – George Hadley †1768.
Signed by *Bayliss*, probably *Nathaniel Bayliss* whose workshop
was at Ampthill. – Henry Sharp †1791, by *Charles Drew* of
Bedford. Pedimented tablet, nicely lettered.

The DE GREY MAUSOLEUM is one of the greatest store-
houses of monuments in England. A pity that it somehow has
the storehouse feeling. Few of the many tombs are of the very
best quality but the ensemble effect is excellent. The de Greys'
mansion was Wrest Park (q.v.) at Silsoe but the village had only
a chapel of ease to Flitton until 1831. At the entrance are
GATES, large, wrought iron, C18. The earliest monument is the

1. Marston Vale from the Greensand Ridge at Houghton House (p. 1)
2. Shillington, from the NE (p. 285)

11	13
12	14

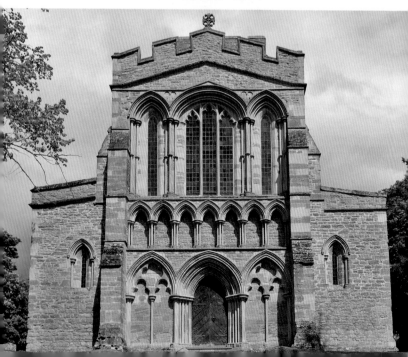

SCS: SEBALDVS   SCS: DVNSTANVS

SCS: SWIBERTVS   SCS: OSWALDVS

22. Elstow, High Street, Bunyan's Mead, C14–C16 (p. 162)
23. Leighton Buzzard, Market Cross, C15, restored 1853 and 1900 (p. 204)
24. Willington, dovecote, 1543–4 (p. 326)
25. Old Warden, Warden Abbey, c. 1552 (p. 262)

<table>
<tr><td>38</td><td>40</td></tr>
<tr><td>39</td><td>41</td></tr>
</table>

42. Stevington, windmill, *c.* 1770, C19 base, restored 1921, 1951 and 2004 (p. 298)
43. Southill Park, Drawing Room, by Henry Holland, redecorated 1808, furniture by C.H. Tatham (p. 292)
44. Moggerhanger Park, N front, by John Soane, 1791–1812 (p. 253)
45. Chicksands Priory, entrance hall, by James Wyatt, 1814 (p. 133)

42 | 43
   | 44
   | 45

51. Turvey, All Saints, chancel interior, by George Gilbert Scott, 1852–4 (p. 315)
52. Milton Ernest, Milton Ernest Hall, by William Butterfield, 1853–8 (p. 252)
53. Woburn, St Mary, interior, by Henry Clutton, 1856 (p. 327)
54. Sharnbrook, St Peter, Magniac monument, by William Burges, 1870 (p. 280)

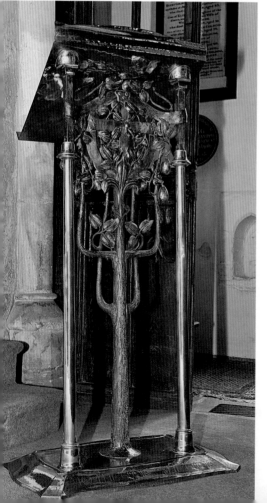

64. Cranfield University, Lord Kings Norton Library, by Foster & Partners, 1989–92 (p. 143)
65. Luton, Vicarage Street, UK Centre for Carnival Arts, by Ash Sakula Architects, 2009 (p. 227)

brass to Henry Grey †1545, son of the 4th earl and father of the 5th, 6th and 7th earls. A 27-in. (68.5 cm) figure, from the *Fermer* workshop (cf. the Warren brass above). – Then follows the monument for which the first room was built: Henry Grey, 6th Earl of Kent, †1614, and wife Mary, one of the Cottons of Combermere, Shropshire. Painted alabaster. Two recumbent effigies. Tomb-chest and back panel. – Next to this, and far more noteworthy, Henry, 10th Earl, erected 1658 by his widow Amabella, who lived another forty-five years. Attributed to *Thomas Burman* (GF). White and grey back wall with two allegorical female figures of Fortitude and Temperance still entirely in the Maximilian Colt or Nicholas Stone Mannerism. These appear early C17 (GF) and must come from elsewhere. Two recumbent white marble effigies. Hers is clearly by a different and less-skilled hand than his, so despite the style of dress perhaps added only *c.* 1710 along with the inscription by her grandson, the 12th Earl (1st Duke) of Kent. She barely fits on the tomb-chest. – Elizabeth Talbot (†1651), Countess Dowager of Kent, widow of the 8th Earl. Erected 1653 (w wall). Large, very fine reredos-type monument in black, white and grey without figures and with a concave face. Segmental pediment, broken and scrolled around the achievement. Ionic columns, and garlands hanging parallel with them. In the plinth, half basins. Attributed to *Edward Marshall* (GF). – Lady Jane Hart, dated 1673, mother of Amabella, Dowager Countess (*see* above). Attributed to *Abraham Storey* (GF). White semi-reclining figure in drapery. Black and white monument with garlands l. and r. Inscription with drapes. Broken pediment with shield and garlands against an arched background. The rest of the mausoleum has a centre, a N, E and S room, with tall round arches between each. In the E room the arch and the window are framed by pilasters and an entablature. Paved stone floor. Over the w arch, WALL PAINTINGS of the date of the mausoleum's extension in 1705 by the 12th Earl of Kent, executing his grandmother's instructions. This relates to the centre and N room, the E room according to the dating of the roof timbers is of after 1726, the S room as has been said is C19. The majority of early C18 monuments are to the 12th Earl's children who died before him. In the N room Anthony de Grey, Earl of Harrold, the Duke's eldest son. 1726 by *John Dowyer*. Semi-reclining white figure in Roman dress on a big black sarcophagus. Not very good. – Also Lady Henrietta de Grey †1716 and Lord Henry de Grey †1717. Identical monuments with steep obelisk background, stiffly garlanded, flaming urns and semi-reclining effigies. Both white marble, both very young, both attributed to *Richard Crutcher* (GF). – Lady Mary Gregory †1761. Simple. With urn on pedestal. – Flanking the arch to the E room, two similar memorials: Lady Amabell de Grey †1727 and her sister, Lady Anne de Grey, †1733. Both without figures, both with pedimented tablets and pyramid above. The former monument at least is designed by *Edward Shepherd*, erected 1739. – In the E room the grandest monument: Henry de Grey, 12th Earl, and 1st Duke, of Kent, and two wives. Designed (and signed) by *Edward Shepherd*, Archt, and commissioned, as the inscription shows, after the death of his first wife, Jemima, in 1728. Very architectural, triptych form with a broken pediment over the projecting centre and inscription panels with lugged frame and egg-and-dart surround. White and grey veined marble. The effigy of the Duke (†1740) in Roman armour reclines on a mat atop a black sarcophagus and to his r. a little lower is the first wife, also reclining. Attributed to *Rysbrack*, who received unspecified payments from 1727 to 1731, but the Duke's figure clearly derived from the monument to the Duke of Buckingham at Westminster of 1720–1 by Scheemakers. No effigy of the second wife, †1748. – Opposite, Philip, 3rd Earl of Hardwicke, †1790. By *Banks*. Mourning woman seated on the ground by an urn. Flanking this, Baroness Grantham †1830 and Amabel, Countess de Grey, †1833, both signed by *W. T. Kelsey* and in a Rococo style unusual for the date; is the design therefore by the 2nd Earl de Grey who commissioned them? – In the s room, Henrietta Frances, Countess de Grey, †1848. 1853, by the Dublin sculptor *Terence Farrell*, who also worked for the 2nd Earl at Wrest (de Grey was Lord Lieutenant of Ireland 1841–4). Very large, with an obelisk back. Relief of the covered coffin and the mourning family. The upright husband, the 2nd Earl, weeps. In the background, in the shallowest relief, tragic, fate-like figures. Up against the obelisk an angel carrying her soul to heaven. – Thomas Philip, 2nd Earl de Grey, †1859, the architect of Wrest Park. By *Matthew Noble*. Effigy, white and asleep on a Gothic tomb-chest. The roof of this room with its lantern and the arch against which he is set must be of the same time. – F. W. Grantham †1831. Tablet by *M. W. Johnson*.

FLITWICK

The tiny village grew a little in the C19 because of the railway station. By 1901 the population was already over 1,000 and it now stretches from the church in the s to the edge of Ampthill in the N.

ST PETER AND ST PAUL. Perp w tower with a turret. Nave and s aisle embattled. Ironstone. A mighty moulding from a Norman doorway is reset in the N wall. Fat roll with beakheads and beakhead-like faces and outer arch of billet. The s doorway with its continuous mouldings must be E.E. Low three-bay s arcade of quatrefoil piers with thin shafts in the diagonals. Double-chamfered arches. Also original the chancel arch, half a quatrefoil, and the transomed lowside window of the chancel. Trefoil-headed piscina in the aisle s wall. The slender N arcade is a copy of 1857–8, when the aisle was added by *Butterfield*.

All features more or less date from then or his further restoration of 1867; his s organ recess was remodelled in 1888 by *W. O. Milne*, who had already lowered the chancel roof and added the parapet and cross over the nave E end. Butterfield's vestry was remodelled in 1907. – FONT. Fluted basin, probably late C12. C19 base. – PULPIT. Made up with linenfold panels and Jacobean framing. – One BENCH (s aisle) with linenfold panelling. – Most of the unfussy woodwork is Butterfield's. – STAINED GLASS. One coat of arms for Richard of Flitwick (mid-C13 to early C14). Chancel window, 1848 by *O'Connor*, Butterfield's preferred maker. Three others by *J. Powell & Sons*, 1880 (chancel s), 1900 (s aisle E) and 1907 (E window). – CHAPTER HOUSE, 1982–4. – LYCHGATE, 1901 by *F. W. Tarte*.

FLITWICK MANOR (Hotel), s of the church. Partly later C17, partly 1736, partly mid-Georgian, and partly 1936 by *Albert Richardson* for Colonel R. A. Lyall. The oldest visible part is the early C18 plain two-storey E front, of six bays but originally nine. Brick with parapet. Panelled room inside. Large wing with gambrel roof behind. The gabled drawing-room wing is of 1872. The pleasure grounds and garden were created in the late C18 and early C19 by George Brooks and John Thomas Brooks, who also planted the arboretum. In the garden a GROTTO-cum-BRIDGE in brick, clinker and stone. One façade is classical, the other Gothic. It linked the garden to a plantation called The Grove (now separate). The younger Brooks created a considerable area of picturesque walks and views. THE MOUNT, 200 yds NW of the church, and now surrounded by housing, is the remains of a small motte-and-bailey castle which was incorporated within Brooks's park.

FLITWICK MILL, Greenfield Road, on the Flit. Brick and weatherboarding, typical of the early C19, and nicely un-restored.

GALLEY HILL *see* SANDY *and* STREATLEY

GIRTFORD *see* SANDY

GOLDINGTON   *0050*
Bedford

A village engulfed by Bedford's E outgrowth but with a clear identity around its substantial green.

ST MARY. Perp W tower and nave. Perp chancel with ANGLE PISCINA. Earlier is the entry arch to a former s chapel. This must be late C13 (semicircular responds). A new nave was built on the site of the N aisle in 1955–6 to the extremely conventional, pre-modern, design of *Felix J. Lander* with large uncusped Perp E window and tall clerestory windows in Tudor style. – FONT. Early C14, round, with ballflower on the underside. – REREDOS. 1956. Classical with Renaissance motifs. STAINED GLASS. E window, 1894 by *Heaton, Butler & Bayne*. S chapel window by *D. Marion Grant*, 1950. – MONUMENTS. Early C14 effigy of a lady, placed upright in the porch. BRASSES. Robert Hatley, †1585, in armour (9 in.; 24 cm). – Benjamin Haselden †1676. Tablet with extremely pretty detailing, black and white marble. The top is a broken scrolly pediment with an urn set in. John Pemberton †1687/8, very similar. Both are attributed to *William Stanton* (GF).

HOLY CROSS (R.C.), Goldington Green. 1956–7 by *Max Lock & Partners*. Nave with transverse glulam arches forming a low pointed roof. Brick-faced aisles added 1966. Spiky cross finial in front.

S of St Mary, GOLDINGTON BURY, a tower block of flats, twelve-storeyed, by *F. W. Dawkes*, Bedford Borough Engineer, *c.* 1960, on the site of an C18 house. Unneighbourly but quite effective in the sylvan setting. Also on Goldington Green there is a seven-storey block, called HERON HEIGHTS, and this one is to a design raised out of the run-of-the-mill. Exposed concrete frame, infill of grey brick and steel windows and recessed balconies. By *Marshman, Warren & Taylor*, 1963–4. Around its base, more routine terraced housing by *Max Lock & Partners*. Of the earlier village, the SCHOOL of 1866 by *James Horsford* has a lively Gothic clocktower. N of the Green also GOLDINGTON HALL, dated 1650 on an ornate downpipe. Symmetrical front of two storeys with attic gables and groups of octagonal chimneys, although much of this is due to the extension in Jacobean style in 1884. Restored *c.* 2012.*

CREMATORIUM, Norse Road. *See* p. 90.

RISINGHOE CASTLE, ¾ m. E on the N bank of the Ouse. Of the motte-and-bailey type. The motte is *c.* 20 ft (6.1 metres) high and looks much like a barrow. Nearby a house of 1954 by *Ian Warwick*.

GRAVENHURST *see* LOWER GRAVENHURST *and* UPPER GRAVENHURST

1050

GREAT BARFORD

ALL SAINTS. By the Great Ouse. Perp W tower of limestone, the rest of the church of brown cobbles. W door with quatrefoils in the spandrels and square stops, the W window with an ogee moulding and statue niche above. The tower bell-openings, with uncusped tracery and a transom, look early C19, although they are recorded by 1820, big pinnacles and a spike. The nave

---

*The POWER STATION of 1951–*c.* 1960 has been demolished.

E quoins have some long stones but whether this is Anglo-Saxon is uncertain, and a Norman chancel arch was removed when the church received its N aisle, by *W. G. Habershon*, in 1848–9; the chancel was then rebuilt and the vestry added. Its E wall has the arms of the Franklin family who moved here from Bolnhurst (q.v.) in the C18. S aisle of 1860 by *J. Horsford* but the details the same. Sensitive N addition *c.* 2000. – SCREEN. The glazed tower screen with large geometrical tracery must be early C19, and is the most effective feature of the church. It related to a gallery erected in 1798. – STAINED GLASS. E window, 1868 by *Hardman & Co.* – Chancel S by *H. W. Bryans*, 1904. – MONUMENTS. Brasses to husband and wife, *c.* 1525 (chancel S), 18-in. (45-cm) figures. – Thomas Anscell †1591 and family. Alabaster tablet with three columns and kneeling figures.

BRIDGE, across the Ouse. Seventeen irregular arches, cutwaters only upstream. The bridge is partly of the C15, for which Sir Gerald Braybrooke left money in 1429, and stone. Five of the S arches are C18 (1704 datestone). Unfortunately it has brick parapets and a brick refacing on the W side of 1874. Great Barford was the head of the Ouse Navigation in the mid to late C17 and prospered as an inland port.

COLLEGE FARMHOUSE in the High Street, ¼ m. NW of the church, is C17 but with a mid-C18 red brick front, of two and a half storeys and a brick cornice, the half-storey of blind openings just a façade. Pedimented doorway.

BARFORD HOUSE, on the hill E of the village. Of 1843, made odd-looking by the extension in 1855–6 for John Arnold by *John Usher*. Prodigiously tall tower over the entrance, and many eclectic details so typical of this architect, e.g. the rusticated entrance and the tower windows with arched tops and bottoms. The tower top was pedimented with a finial but castellated *c.* 1920. – The GATE is a good design too.

S of the house below the road, LOWLANDS, formerly Great Barford Villa, with, to the road, a wall with patterns of ornamental brick arches, quoins and a pediment. Gateways also with brick rustication. Is this *Usher* too? (R. Wildman).

HARLINGTON

0030

In large part a later C20 village but the older part lies beside a green of considerable size, scene in the earlier C19 of the Great St Albans Steeplechase horse race from here to Wrest and back, which inspired the establishment of the Grand National steeplechase at Aintree.

ST MARY. Perp ironstone tower with sandstone dressings and higher stair-turret. A N vestry also ironstone and *c.* 1500. The rest is rendered but clunch and ironstone beneath. Aisles heightened and embattled in the early C16; the Perp roofs remain. However the church is essentially late C13 to early C14 (evidence has been found of a buttress at the E end of the chancel which may be of the C12 church) and the interior better than the exterior. Spacious nave, the four-bay arcades are still C13 but very tall like Ampthill and Houghton Conquest. Quatrefoil piers and double-chamfered arches. The chancel arch is of the same details but behind the arch are thin buttresses and a keeled moulding. Dec the chancel windows and the N aisle E (reticulated tracery) and W windows (tracery broken out). Above the chancel piscina, a damaged head. Also three Perp stone corbels for the nave roof. Elaborate niches l. and r. of the E window, different in the details. – FONT. Octagonal, on eight shafts. On the bowl eight shields and below an unusual crenellation frieze. It is probably Dec too. – BENCHES. Perp, just with little buttresses against the ends. – ALTAR (Lady Chapel). By *Albert Richardson*, 1929; Angels and the Virgin in shallow relief. Vine trail surround. Chancel reordered in 1974. – ALTAR. 1988 by *Tim Jarvis*, incorporating a branch of the so-called 'Bunyan oak'. – STAINED GLASS. E window and N aisle E by *J. Powell & Sons*, 1876 and 1885, the latter designed by *Henry Holiday*.

MANOR HOUSE, by the main cross-roads. Timber-framed with a brick wing to the street. The main front is late C17, with two shallow projecting gabled wings. The plastering is done rustication-fashion. Wooden cross-windows with expressed keystones and projecting hoods above the former doors. Ironstone chimneys. It then belonged to the Wingate family and it was Francis Wingate who sent Bunyan to trial at Bedford for field preaching. The very sympathetic N wing with little bows is of 1937 by *Albert Richardson* for Captain Tabor. (C17 fireplaces and panelling inside and a stone overmantel with royal arms.)

HARROLD

A large village, which grew in the C19 on the back of its leather and bootmaking industries, a reminder of the nearness of the manufacturing towns in Northamptonshire, but of which now no obvious trace remains.

ST PETER. The original church was shared between the village and the Augustinian priory founded alongside it *c.* 1140–50. The nave N wall may be partly Saxon but everything else comes much later. The church received its raw N arcade in the early C13. Parts of the wall were made into pillars and given stiff-leaf capitals; some have chamfers and one has a roll and leaves as chamfer-stops. The arches were left unmoulded. Of the same time the chancel, with an equally rough arch with a single chamfer. Of the chancel windows one S lancet survives, showing by its position that the chancel must have been longer. Its shortening was probably done in the late C16, for the E end had a window of that date until the C19. The S aisle was also cut back, see its plain straight-headed window and the half arch (former tomb recess?) inside the S wall. The aisle itself is late C13, its arcade of two bays only and with semicircular responds, but an octagonal pier. The walls of the aisles are late C13 N, with intersected tracery and three stepped lancet lights, and Dec S, with reticulation. Dec N chapel with one very tall arch, its semicircular respond with a fillet. Inside the chapel an image niche. Dec W tower, built into the nave with Perp recessed spire. The tower pinnacles are connected with the spire by thin flying buttresses (restored). Three tiers of lucarnes. Perp clerestory to nave and chancel. – PULPIT. With Perp panels from the rood screen. – SCREEN. With a nice Jacobean dado topped by short balusters (cf. Wymington). – The woodwork around is also Jacobean. – LECTERN and READING DESK. Also with reused Perp bits. All the woodwork is as altered by *Mallows & Grocock* in 1904. Also by them the CHOIR STALLS and probably the sensitive widening of the COMMUNION RAIL of *c.* 1675, with its characteristic strong turned balusters. (– PAINTING. Saint, very bad, in the N aisle. From a screen dado.) – BENCHES. The usual Perp type with buttressed ends, but also some panelled Gothick box pews of 1845 with pointed ends. – STAINED GLASS. E window, designed by *Francis Stephens*, painted by *John Hayward* and *Francis Spear*, 1952. One other by *J. N. Lawson*, 1967, St Crispin and St Crispinian, recalling the village's leather and bootmaking trades. – MONUMENTS. Tomb-chest of Oliver Boteler †1657. Plain with marble top. – Large hanging tablet to Dame Anne Jolliffe †1732. White marble bust on a fine black sarcophagus. Veined marble frame of Ionic pilasters and open pediment on the top. Volutes at the sides.

Of the PRIORY nothing is left. The Bucks in 1730 and Fisher in 1814 still show quite substantial remains, including the refectory with hammerbeam roof (dem. 1840). Nor is anything to be seen of HARROLD HALL, an E-plan house built on the Priory site in 1608–10 for Francis Farrar, enlarged in 1816 and demolished in 1961 (its staircase is in St John House, Bedford; see p. 102).

UNITED REFORMED CHURCH, High Street. Originally Congregational, erected 1836 and enlarged in 1863 by *John Usher*. His must be the brick front with quoins, a pediment overall and bright red dressings to the two storeys of arched openings. Galleries of the earlier date, the rest ruthlessly reordered in 1998. – SUNDAY SCHOOLS. 1863 but enlarged 1899, with a scooped and curved parapet over the entrance. Foundation stones with excellent Arts and Crafts lettering.

THE OLD MANOR, between High Street and Church Walk. Built *c.* 1600–30, probably for Henry Grey on whom lands were settled by his uncle the Earl of Kent in 1601. Fisher illustrates it in the early C19 as a fine stone U-plan house with crowsteps and carved kneelers to the front gables of the wings. Alas, only the s wing survives, along with the lower central link. Mullioned and transomed windows in each of the gabled ends and on the long sides at the ends. Large chimney on the E front. (Inside, a wooden overmantel with blank arches and strapwork. Also a panelled screen separating the stair hall from the s room. NHLE.)

HARROLD HOUSE, w in High Street, is tall, symmetrical Victorian-Jacobean, with two-storey canted bays topped by strapwork and three gables. Tall, mullioned and transomed staircase window on the side. By *John Day*, 1886, for Charles Pettit, one of the village's leather manufacturers.

Further down, on the green, a stone LOCK-UP of 1824, circular, with conical roof, and larger than most. Also the charming, early C18, open, octagonal, wooden MARKET CROSS with a cupola. It is a handsome, tree-planted green, not too large and fringed on its N side by stone cottages with C18 hooded doorcases and on the s by the former SCHOOL of 1847. Round the turn in the road the attractive VILLAGE INSTITUTE in the gentle domestic style of 1901, by the local builder/architects *Clayson & Son*. Provided by Charles Pettit, whose initials it bears. Orangey brick and stone with tall chimneys and a cupola. Matching hall of 1911. In ORCHARD LANE, No. 6 is the rare survival of a Wealden house, the timber-framing of the wings with downward curving braces exposed but the recessed centre now infilled.

After a run of more good stone houses, THE MANSION, NW of the United Reformed Church (*see* above). Dated 1619 but remodelled in the C19. Early C19 cast-iron GATES by *H. Hobbs* of Northampton, mixing classical and Gothic styles. They came from Harrold Hall (*see* above).

PRIORY FARM, ¼ m. w. The back part is stone, clearly probably *c*. 1600, but the front part quite a powerful C19 rebuilding with two-storey jettied porch.

BRIDGE, over the Ouse. Predominantly medieval but much repaired and widened in 1857. Six major arches between cutwaters, one s arch pointed with two orders. The continuing CAUSEWAY over the meadow is of eleven arches in all, five pointed and eight round.

HAYNES

ST MARY. The church was held by Chicksands Priory from 1150 until the Dissolution. Of ironstone, its C14–C15 w tower with higher stair-turret. Nearly all the rest externally restored or added by *Woodyer*, 1850–1, for the Rev. Lord John Thynne. His grandfather, the 1st Marquess of Bath, had a Carteret as his mother, and Thynne inherited the estate from the 3rd Baron Carteret of Haynes in 1849. Woodyer's most personal contribution is the rose window of the Carteret Chapel (s aisle e) with a six-cornered star. Inside, the s arcade (of four bays) is original work of *c.* 1300 – quatrefoil piers, double-chamfered arches – copied for the arcades of the new n aisle and Thynne Chapel by Woodyer. The chancel and tower arch also Dec. A puzzling feature is the chancel ceiling, which, with its thin rib-patterns, looks decidedly early C19. The colours of the PAINTED DECOR-ATION of the chancel is much muted by dirt but originally vivid blues, reds and golds, in unity with the tiled FLOOR and REREDOS by *Minton & Co.* – The Thynne (n) Chapel was refurbished in 1868 by *G. G. Scott*, as the setting for the monu-ment (*see* below). Pitched roof with angels. It is an outstanding ensemble, the decoration by *Clayton & Bell*, who may have revised the chancel decoration at this time. To Scott's design both the very attractive wrought-iron SCREEN and GATES by *Potter & Son* and the superb Cosmati-style FLOOR by *Poole & Son*, with central panel of Lazarus. – The light metal SCREEN with heraldic shields to the Carteret Chapel is *c.* 1850s; also the Caen stone FONT. – (ALTAR CLOTH. The gold cloth on which Queen Victoria knelt at the Coronation.) – Servery etc. neatly inserted at the w end of the aisles by *Bruce Deacon*, 2001. – STAINED GLASS. The e window of 1851 by *O'Connor*. Cru-cifixion. Small figures, still in strong, simple colours. – All the other glass by *Clayton & Bell*: *c.* 1868 (Thynne Chapel); 1867 (rose window, Carteret Chapel) and 1876 (w tower), 1889 (s aisle). – MONUMENTS. Anthony Newdegate †1568. Kneeling brass figure, from the *Fermer Workshop*, in a broad, very well detailed Purbeck marble surround which must be about fifty years earlier. But the inscription of *c.* 1568 is also still in black-letter. – In the Carteret Chapel, which has a light metal screen. 1st Lord Carteret †1826. By *Sir Richard Westmacott*, with a telling portrait head in an oval recess. White marble. – 2nd Lord Carteret †1838. Grecian tablet. – 3rd Lord Carteret †1849. Black marble floor slab with inlaid cross, enamelled shields and inscription in the border. By *J. G. & L. A. B. Waller*. The tiles surrounding are by *Minton*. – In the Thynne Chapel. Lady Anna Constantia Thynne. 1868, by *H. H. Arm-stead*, who later carved Lord John's monument in Westminster Abbey. Recumbent white effigy of the young woman, praying. The rich Dec alabaster canopy was designed by *Scott*.

WAR MEMORIAL. Portland stone cross by *Basil C. Deacon*, *c.* 1920 (cf. Westoning).

On the main street, the former SCHOOL is dated 1850 and has the same rose window as the church. So it is obviously also by *Woodyer*. Downhill to the e, PUMP, of 1867, erected by Lord John Thynne; it too may be Woodyer's design.

HAYNES PARK, also known as Hawnes.* The house makes a memorable sight across its park from the church. The seat of the Carterets from its purchase in 1667 by Sir George Carteret,

---

* Permission to visit the house was refused so it has not been possible to adequately check or revise this entry.

who became the 1st Lord Carteret, until 1914. A school from 1929 to 1975 and now the headquarters of Radha Soami Satsang Beas, a philosophical organization. A large, square mansion, built partly *c.* 1720, partly in 1794, when Lord Torrington describes the 'august old front – just pull'd down'. The earlier work was done for John, 2nd Lord Carteret (Earl Granville from 1744). The later work, which is attributed to *James Lewis,* was for Henry, 1st Lord Carteret of the second creation. This earliest part is the w range, thirteen bays long and very characteristic of its date. Red brick with broad giant pilasters to mark the slightly projecting angle pairs of bays and the three-bay centre. Segment-headed windows. At that time the house still had a front with mullion and transom windows and shaped gables over the centre and wings. The s and e fronts are of stone, the e front plain except for a Greek Doric porch. This front is of 1849–50 by *Cubitt*'s. The s front, of 1794, is distinguished by two bows l. and r. and a giant Corinthian order of pilasters for the centre. The capitals are excellently carved. The windows have raised stone surrounds. Top balustrade. The spacious staircase of *c.* 1725 has fluted columns as balusters, a swagger newel post as its start and parquetry to the half-landing. Of the furnishings of the 1790s the best are the entrance hall with its discreet stucco decoration and the room behind it with two apses, charmingly decorated with foliage trails. STABLES also *c.* 1720s.

Additions were made *c.* 1949–70, when the house was a school, by *Richardson & Houfe.* – LODGE. 1873. Very Picturesque with inscriptions in French and cast-iron sunflower finials.

HAYNES GRANGE, ½ m. SE, on the edge of the Chicksands estate, to which it belonged. The house is C16, H-plan, but with an uncommonly tall w wing, which contained until the early C20 the late C16 panelled room that is now at the Victoria and Albert Museum and which Mark Girouard believes to have been designed by the amateur architect *John Osborn* for the N range of Chicksands Priory (q.v.). The wing here appears to have been built to accommodate it, perhaps *c.* 1720 for a later John Osborn who resided here after his marriage. However, Manolo Guerci (*Burlington Magazine,* 148, January 2006) also notes that the panelling might have been designed for the Vicarage (dem.), built by John Osborn *c.* 1590.

HAZELLS HALL *see* EVERTON

HEATH AND REACH

ST LEONARD. Originally a private chapel for Heath Manor House opposite (*see* below), only later succeeding the chapel of ease to Leighton Buzzard. A poor specimen. 1828–9 by *R. F.*

Nixon of Woburn, with pointed windows, except for a short C16 W tower and an apse of 1866 by *Joseph P. Neale* of Bristol, yellow brick with red bands, polygonal. The S porch is similar and of 1876. Inside not much more of interest. Some FURNISHINGS of 1949 by *Albert Richardson*. – STAINED GLASS. Apse windows 1866–7, Evangelists, attributed to *Lavers, Barraud & Westlake*.

HEATH MANOR. Properly Heath House. The five-bay brick front of the early C18, with stone quoins and a doorcase of rusticated pilasters and ill-informed triglyph frieze, does not prepare one for the earlier events of the house. On the N side C16 timber-framing and brick infilling to a gable, a C17 five-light window in the adjoining part and on the S side a stately C17 doorway with round arch, columns and small pediment set below a Dutch gable. In line with this, the chimneystack (i.e. the house is a lobby entry plan). Set into the base of the stack two panels, one with a scene of Adam and Eve, the other a rose and crown. (Inside, several Elizabethan or Jacobean chimneypieces and Jacobean carved woodwork, notably the huge timber lintel of the kitchen fireplace with a scrolled leaf motif that also appears on a beam of the corresponding room to the W. But the *clou* of the house is the sumptuous, almost oversized staircase, also Jacobean. Vertically symmetrical balusters, sturdy posts. Panelling with fluted pilasters in the C18 addition.)

WELLINGTON HOUSE, N of the church. The former vicarage. Ironstone. The part with three small gables is by *E. C. Hakewill*, 1852, the rest 1869 by *F. Gotto* of Leighton Buzzard. N, at the head of the hill, a sloping triangular green with the former Wesleyan Schools and Chapel of 1877 presiding at its head. On the green a WELL HOUSE AND CLOCKTOWER of 1873.

THE GRANGE, Woburn Road, ¼ m. N of the green. A fine large house of 1906 by *T. H. Bishop* of Leighton Buzzard around the core of a house of 1799. Arts and Crafts, the motifs drawn from the late C16 and C17. Charming entrance vestibule with vaulted plaster ceiling and snug recess for the fireplace. More good plasterwork in the dining room. In the gardens, laid out in the 1920s, two ponds with a waterfall over sandstone boulders and a grotto.

At RUSHMERE PARK, ¾ m. WSW, GATES and LODGES for Stockgrove Park, Bucks. (by *W. Curtis Green*, 1929–39). Red brick and stone, in Neo-Georgian style; fine stone and ironwork screen. See also *Buildings of England: Buckinghamshire*.

HENLOW

1030

ST MARY. Clunch and brown cobble Perp W tower and N aisle, the rest mostly ironstone. The tower has a higher stair-turret and battlements, the aisles also battlemented. Perp chancel. Its battlements, with knapped flint in the parapet, date from the restorations of 1886–7 by *A. W. Blomfield* and 1889 by *William Watson* (*see* Wren Park, Clifton). Watson himself designed and paid for the N vestry/organ chamber in 1895. Reset in its N wall, a small Norman window from the original aisleless church. Of this building the nave NE quoin can also still be seen inside the organ chamber. The N arcade is of *c.* 1300. Three bays, but formerly four – see the place where the tower buttress touches the pier. Octagonal piers, double-chamfered arches. The S arcade is also of three bays, but the W bay is separated from the others by the place where the original W wall of the building ran. The E bays are early C14, the W bay is Perp. Where the arcades and the tower meet, pointed openings high up made for the C18 gallery. Broad, four-centred, chancel arch. Perp clerestory, now enclosed by the raising of the aisle roofs. The Perp E window of the N aisle also preserved. In the N aisle two attractive three-light windows, remade in 1893 with crocketed pinnacles against reticulation. – PILLAR PISCINA (S aisle E). With a Norman capital, but set in a trefoil-headed recess. – Of the Perp REREDOS in the N aisle E, just one band of quatrefoils and blind tracery remain. The similar REREDOS in the S aisle E is of 1906. – PEWS. S aisle. By *Albert Richardson*, *c.* 1945, as a memorial to the Lennox-Boyd brothers of Henlow Grange. – PAINTING. S aisle. The Preparation for the Passover. By *Frederic Shields*, after an unfinished watercolour of 1856 by Rossetti, commissioned by Ruskin and now in Tate Britain. This painting, which is mentioned in a letter in 1889, and was then probably recent,* used to belong to the Rev. A. Gurney of St Barnabas, Pimlico. Cyril Gurney bought Henlow Grange in 1909. It is iconographically very interesting. St John as a child buckling the sandal of the Child Jesus. Jesus holds the bowl of blood for the Passover. St Joseph in the distance carries the lamb, the Virgin gathers bitter herbs, and Zacharias paints the door with blood. – STAINED GLASS. E window by *J. Powell & Sons*, 1893. Three other windows (chancel S and S aisle E) by *Heaton, Butler & Bayne*, 1909–10. Other routine mid-C20 designs by *A. L. Wilkinson*. – MONUMENTS. Very many tablets, from 1675 into the C19. The quality is high. The best perhaps Christopher Halley †1688, a convex scrolly cartouche set against the curve of the E arch of the N arcade. Attributed to *William Woodman Sen.* (GF). Of the larger tablets: Sarah Edwards (vestry) †1700, with scrolled pediment, heavy garlands and gadroon moulding; George Edwards †1712, in the chancel, and the corresponding tablet for his daughter, Ann Buckby, †1714, both with fluted pilasters, triglyph friezes, and achievements. – George Edwards †1750 and family. A two-tier classical tablet with Grecian pediment, white and yellow marbles. Signed by *John Wing*, Bedford, probably *c.* 1809.

In the churchyard, S of the church, a CROSS in memory of Cyril Gurney †1926. By *Clough Williams Ellis*, 1927. Octagonal

---

* Shields had been commissioned to adapt Rossetti's painting for his memorial window to Rossetti at All Saints, Birchington, Kent, in 1882.

arms and a glory on the face. Elegant plinth. – At the w end, Florence Lennox-Boyd †1949 and her sons. Fine Portland stone urn on a plinth with coat of arms in a roundel. By *Albert Richardson*, *c.* 1950.

w of the church a former PUMP HOUSE, of 1897, with a hexagonal tile roof on columns.

WAR MEMORIAL, High Street. 1920 by *Joseph Whitehead & Sons*. A Portland stone column with Tower of Winds capital and flaming orb finial.

HENLOW GRANGE (Champneys Spa), SE of St Mary. A fine three-storey brick house of five bays with originally single-storey three-bay wings. The date is probably *c.* 1700. Chequer brick, broad giant angle pilasters, finely moulded brick cornice, parapet and chimneys at the corners. The N wing is now two-storey. Garden doorway with carved brackets. The entrance porch perhaps later. Ionic columns and a pediment. Staircase with twisted balusters and a string to hide the treads. That looks late C17 rather than early C18. The room r. of the entrance hall is divided by a screen of Ionic columns *in antis* and has C19 hand-painted scenic wallpaper in a Chinese style. The lavish s loggia with stone arches dates from *c.* 1930. Front garden with piers, and iron fence and gates added in 1911. Former stables etc. with clock turret and cupola. It first became a health farm in 1961, and was repaired at that time. There was a fire in 2002; the extensive additions postdate this. – LODGES, near the church. Red brick with modillion cornices and recessed arches on the façades.

RAF HENLOW, 2 m. s. Established in 1917 as a depot for the repair of aircraft; the RAF's engineering school from the late 1920s. (There are five original GENERAL SERVICE SHEDS, four of 1917 with timber Belfast trusses of 80–100-ft (24–30-metre) spans. In the fifth shed of 1918, the 100-ft (30 metre) Belfast trusses are metal, to cope with the wider span of new aircraft. The principal buildings date from 1933–5, including the interesting group of Garden City-style housing for married personnel, Neo-Georgian barracks and Officers' Mess, with pediment and Doric porch. The building of the church of St Andrew is actually to a large part the Gymnasium.)

HIGHAM GOBION

1030

ST MARGARET. Much of the exterior is of 1879–80 by *Benton & Wood*: the w tower (except for the arch to the nave), the N aisle, and the chancel E wall entirely. This was in spite of efforts by William Morris and the S.P.A.B. to encourage the rector to repair and preserve only. The N aisle is no more than a passage, but inside, on the other hand, the N arcade is good work of *c.* 1300. Three bays, quatrefoil piers with thin shafts in the diagonals, double-chamfered arches. The chancel arch is of the

same type, but has two sunk quadrants in the arch itself.
SEDILIA and PISCINA again are largely Victorian. – MONU-
MENT. – Katherine Browne †1602 and Jane Cason †1603, good
brasses, with the shields above. They were both of the Butler
family who held the manor from the C14. – Dr Edmund Castell
†1684/5, Professor of Arabic at Cambridge and Rector from
1674. The last line of the inscription is in Arabic and reads:
'He elected to be buried in this spot in hopes of a better'. Tablet
with prettily carved emblems of death on the frame.

Immediately E of the church the OLD RECTORY, largely rebuilt
c. 1965 when the timber-framed W wing with narrowly spaced
uprights was exposed. MANOR FARM, behind the church, is a
hall house with cross-wings. Inside, a wooden Elizabethan
chimneypiece with a pedimented centre and inlaid decoration
including coats of arms belonging to the various branches of
the Butler family. In the middle the arms of Sir Henry Butler
and his two wives. That means a date after the first wife's death
in 1572 and his in 1608. Recently uncovered is the associated
fine clunch fireplace, a Tudor arch with the arms of Butler and
his wives in the spandrels.

THE CAMP, ⅜ m. NE. The earthwork of a medieval fishery with
ponds surrounding a mound, probably a nesting island at the
centre of the flooded area.

HINWICK

36 HINWICK HOUSE. Built in 1708–14 for Richard Orlebar, whose
descendants were resident until the 1990s. The building events
of the house are exceptionally fully documented but only the
name of the mason, *Richard Knight*, is known. E front of seven
bays, scanned by giant pilasters into 2–3–2. The pilasters are
Corinthian. The house is of two and a half storeys with a top
balustrade. Brown stone almost as small as bricks and buff
Ketton stone dressings. The windows have moulded surrounds,
the elegantly slender doorway a foliage frieze and an open
scrolly pediment around a cartouche. Round the corner to the
S there are five bays with former doorways in the second and
fourth bays. The scanning is by two tiers of niches thus: 2 –
niches – 1 – niches – 2. Above the centre and awkwardly placed
against the attic storey is a steep pediment of Diana and her
cortege, the subject in honour of Richard Orlebar's wife,
Diana, whose portion paid for the new work. This is carved,
and signed, by *John Hunt* of Northampton. The carving of the
pediment is robust, not delicate. Hunt no doubt also carved
the doorcase and the capitals. The top half-storey differs in
material from the rest, and so the pediment may have been
commissioned before it was decided to have the full attic
storey. The original intention might have been something
closer to Cottesbrooke Hall, Northants (*Francis Smith* of
Warwick, c. 1700–2). To the W are two projecting wings of

unequal size and a doorway with an apsed hood on nicely carved brackets. The wings must be an afterthought, perhaps contemporary with the attic, whose materials they share, as proved by the way in which they cut into the window surrounds of the recessed centre. The bays of this centre are also oddly asymmetrical, the r. windows larger than the two to the l. and reflecting the internal division between the private (r.) and service (l.) parts of the c18 house. The beautiful rainwater head marking the division on this side is dated 1710, made in all probability by the same craftsman as the contemporary ones at Kimbolton Castle in Hunts. Spacious entrance hall with four of the niches so typical of the Queen Anne style, two in the N, two in the S wall, with lugged surrounds. Plain fireplaces between them. Plans, and the 1766 Inventory, show the three principal rooms behind the E and S show fronts and the kitchen, servants hall etc. in the N end. This seems distinctly old-fashioned, and another retardataire feature (but cf. Melchbourne Park) was a long gallery at the attic level.

Apart from the hall, the interior was completely revised in 1859–66 by *F. C. Penrose* for Richard Longuet Orlebar. The original staircase was removed from the SW wing, now the library. E and W of the entrance hall Penrose created two large rooms out of smaller c18 ones. The drawing room (S) has niches with semi-domes, presumably reset, and curiously contrived niches in the N wall. The staircase hall now lies behind the entrance hall, where there was a 'dining parlour' and 'back pantry' (the central door from the hall to these rooms has been blocked); it is generously large, opening to a spacious landing at first floor. The choice for the staircase of the Georgian style for reasons of conformity is remarkable, but the triplets of exceptionally thin balusters and the unmoulded ends of the treads show their true date. The pine dado panelling with fluted pilasters and raised panels may be the original, by *Thomas Wayman*, reused. Several of the bedrooms retain c18 fittings. The N wing of the house, containing the kitchen and offices, is also clearly Georgian in part, probably c. 1774, the date of surviving plans and for which there is correspondence between Richard Orlebar II and *Henry Keene*. Part of the garden elevation was preserved, along with the brewhouse and laundry, but the rest was substantially remodelled into its present form by *Penrose*. He did his job very self-effacingly. The interior was converted for a restaurant in the 1980s, but is no longer so used.

The W side of the house faces the walls of the pre-Reformation manor house, which was converted into STABLES. Its bell-turret with cupola again has the date 1710 on its bell and clock face. The base of the turret is open with double stairs to a charming gallery with seats. What was its purpose? Adjacent to this a PRIVY, octagonal plan interior with four seats. Probably c18.

GATE AND SCREENS. Wrought-iron. By *Thomas Warren* of Castle Ashby. Stone GATEPIERS. They may have been part of the screen shown in a painting of 1715, but later moved to the N gate. Large WALLED GARDEN.

HINWICK HALL. Hinwick Hall is much older than Hinwick House. The W side is essentially C16, where several windows have arched uncusped lights. This front also has a number of gables, large and small, and was probably a typical L-plan with projecting S wing. The best-preserved element is the big chimneybreast with diagonal shafts on the S side of the wing, very probably for the former kitchen. About 1710, the date on a rainwater head, Major-General John Livesay turned the house round and gave it a new E front. This has some of the same motifs as Hinwick House, but they are handled more naively and conservatively. Nine bays, two storeys, angle Corinthian pilasters, and a square porch tower flanked tightly by pilasters too, but here by two tiers with entablatures, a 1660 rather than 1700 motif. On top of the porch tower, an awkward square wooden cupola within a balustrade. Its bell is dated 1709. The doorway has a similar open curly pediment to that of Hinwick House, and the windows have moulded surrounds. The garden porch on the S side and the large mullion-and-transom windows and the corresponding N wing are of 1907 by *Maxwell Maberly Smith* for Gilbert Robinson. The service wing adjoining the E front ends in the former coal store, very Arts and Crafts-style with attractive sloping buttresses. The interior does not have much to single out. There are no C16 features except for a Tudor-arched fireplace on the first floor of the main range. C17 staircase in the S wing, with slender turned balusters and ogee finials. Otherwise the best element is the C18 main staircase, with twisted balusters and carved tread-ends and one room with Kentian-style fireplace and modillion cornice. The other rooms are mostly of 1907. Drawing room in the S end with a large panelled inglenook. A former loggia to the garden, with two Tuscan stone columns, is now enclosed. Billiard room on the E front behind a Venetian window. Fireplace inside with bright green tiling.

A fine wrought-iron SCREEN of *c.* 1710 in axis with the front. It may be by *Thomas Warren*, who worked at Hinwick House, and the screen might indeed have come from there in the early to mid C19 during the Hall's ownership by W. A. Orlebar, for it is not shown in Fisher's engraving of 1823. Good entrance GATEPIERS, also *c.* 1700. A straight avenue leads to the house. It is accompanied by two canal-like sheets of water. In 1943 the Hall was purchased by the Shaftesbury Society as a residential college for the severely disabled. Several additions for this use. The STABLES have been converted.

HOCKLIFFE

ST NICHOLAS. Rendered W tower. The rest Totternhoe and ironstone, and much restored in 1860–1 by *W. G. Habershon*. Mostly Perp, see the C16 porch entrance. Aisleless nave with an upper window w of the porch, perhaps for a priest's room. In the chancel, C14 PISCINA and EASTER SEPULCHRE, and also two niches in the E wall. N transept and vestry by *Habershon*, the FURNISHINGS too, e.g. the robust pulpit. – STAINED GLASS. Two small windows of 1879 by *Lavers, Barraud & Westlake*; the E window of 1870 is also attributed to them. – MONUMENTS. Set into the E wall outside, a fine inscribed Rococo tablet of 1740 marking the Gilpin vault.

HOCKLIFFE GRANGE, ¼ m. NNE. Partly C18, rebuilt by Thomas Gilpin, a London goldsmith who inherited *c.* 1740. Blue vitreous header bond and red dressings. Venetian window under a gable on the entrance front. Substantially added to, probably by Sir Richard Gilpin in the 1840s, in a Neo-Jacobean style with shaped gables and crenellated bays, all cement rendered.

OLD WHITE HORSE, Watling Street. A former inn, with a classic long façade between gabled wings, though of more than one build. Main part and l. wing early to mid-C18, grey brick with red lacing, but the rear wings with half-hipped roofs probably late C17. Set into the front, carvings said to have come from Toddington Manor (q.v.) in the C18, e.g. Jacobean strapwork panels over the carriage arch.

HOCKLIFFE HOUSE, Watling Street, ⅜ m. S. It has a datestone of 1818 at the back, but the house had achieved its present appearance before 1815, as it is illustrated by Thomas Fisher. Garden front of three bays with a doorway with Doric columns: Fisher shows it with a hood on consoles and three cross-windows in the first floor and one sash. Red brick chequered with blue. The rear parts, including the door to the road, are of a different brick. The kitchen exit has a finely moulded Perp arch, of clunch, from the former Hospital of St John which occupied the site from *c.* 1200 and became an inn after the Dissolution.

HOLCOT *see* HULCOTE

HOLME *see* BIGGLESWADE

HOUGHTON CONQUEST   0040

ALL SAINTS. Perp w tower. Remarkably, the contract of 1 November 1392 exists for it, with *William Farele*, a mason of Dunstable, and *Philip Lessy*, a mason of Totternhoe, the cost to be 10s. a foot for foundations and 13s. 4d. plus six quarts of frumenty for work above ground. The work was to be completed in three years. This and the nave and aisles are of ironstone, but both aisles have been heightened when the Perp battlements and clerestory were added. The embattled chancel is also Perp but of stone and brown cobbles and has a two-storey vestry. However, the s doorway with two orders of thin shafts carrying intricate foliage capitals looks Dec. The N aisle has windows with Dec tracery, one design being specially interesting which consists of an arch head on three-light inter-secting lights. One of the same pattern occurs in the w end of the s aisle. Dec also the exceptionally tall four-bay arcades. The piers are quatrefoil with four thin shafts in the diagonals (cf. Ampthill). Hoodmoulds on small headstops. Double-chamfered arches. The chancel arch is like the arcade piers. The nave and aisle roofs are Perp, with carved bosses and in the nave a painted ceilure with stars. The painted trails repeat in the E bays of the aisle roofs. The chancel also has Perp niches l. and r. of the E window and DOUBLE PISCINA. But the tracery was much renewed by *G. G. Scott*, reinstating the E window which had been partially blocked (probably during C17 changes), and his is the rather alien hammerbeam roof with windbraces, superseding a Late Georgian re-roofing. Scott's too the rebuilt s porch with its charmingly carved angels at the corners. All this was done in 1869–70, with good furnishings to match, especially the COMMUNION RAIL and PULPIT. – The mighty ORGAN is by *Hill & Son*. – FONT. Dec, hexagonal, with cusped and crocketed ogee arch heads in the panels. – SCREEN. Nicely painted by *Burlison & Grylls* during Scott's restoration. Not much of the woodwork is old. – STALLS. With good poppyheads: men with dragon's bodies, a grotesque with two dogs, one with two deacons and two heads and one more (C19?) with two angels and two heads. – BENCHES. Some are Perp. – PAINTING. Over the chancel arch a large C14 Doom, Christ in the almond-shaped glory with angels l. and r. – Also a 16-ft (4.8-metre) high St Christopher over the N doorway. This is C15 and very faint. – (In the s aisle traces of a St George with the Dragon.) – BANNER. A remarkable survival, restored *c.* 2000 by *Sally Wigglesworth*. Of the Conquest family, com-missioned after the death of Sir Richard Conquest †1607. White and black quarters overlaid by a sword and beribboned wreath. – STAINED GLASS. Original bits in many windows. E window by *Clayton & Bell*, 1880. – MONUMENTS. Outside the chancel a plain recess with four-centred arch for Thomas Awdley(?) †1531. – In the chancel, tomb-chest with brasses of Isabel Conquest †1493 and her husband and her son. It is worth thinking about the fact that nobody can have cared for the two men to be seen in brass as they had really looked. Instead of that they are identical even in the features. The figures are 28 in. (71 cm) long. Evangelists' symbols at the corners. – In the chancel floor, brasses to Richard Conquest †1500 and wife (13-in. (33 cm) figures). – Monument to Dr Thomas Archer, put up in 1629 during his lifetime. The device is Sustine et Abstine, and the Latin inscription is worth reading. Alabaster. Frontal demi-figure, preaching, i.e. with a cushion lying in front of him and a book held in his hand.

OLD RECTORY, ⅜ m. s. Early to mid-C18, probably for Dr Zachary Grey, who became rector in 1725. A fine full-stop to its lime avenue. Tall, of five bays to front and back, with long sashes in two storeys. Modillion cornice. Doorway with broken pediment and especially fine carved consoles. (Geometrical staircase around an oval well. NHLE.) E addition of 1874 by *John Day* of Bedford.

HOUGHTON HOUSE *see* AMPTHILL

HOUGHTON REGIS   0020

A village engulfed by the development of Luton and Dunstable from the 1960s and finally acknowledged as a town in 1980.*

ALL SAINTS. A stately church. The general impression from outside is Perp. Much flint and clunch stone chequer, except for the W tower, which is all clunch and badly weathered where it has not been replaced. The church is embattled; the tower has two two-light bell-openings to each side and a stair-turret (cf. Dunstable). In the tower W wall are two niches l. and r. of the main W window. S porch rebuilt in 1856–7 by *Henry Clutton*, followed by more thorough restoration of nave and aisles in 1867–9 by *George Somers Clarke*, who then rebuilt the chancel in 1879–80. Most of the windows are largely accurate restorations, including the fine circular W window of the S aisle with cusped surround. The arcades are of five bays with octagonal piers and arches with sunk quadrant mouldings and notch stops above the capital. That points to the early C14 and goes with the internal shafting of the aisle windows. – FONT. Of tub shape; Norman and one of the so-called Aylesbury Group (see Introduction, p. 19). The base is in the form of a flat single-scallop capital with carved lunettes. The bowl is fluted; two bands of decoration. – SCREEN. Little original Perp work. One-bay divisions. C20 ROOD figures. – PULPIT. 1879. Stone, with characteristically High Victorian quatrefoil panels carved in 1892. – COMMUNION RAIL. Twisted balusters; *c.* 1700. – STAINED GLASS. Three in the aisles by *Thomas Baillie*, 1864. – Tower W window by *T. S. Underhill*, 1891. – MONUMENTS. In the S aisle, late C14 knight, his feet originally against a big lion. In an ogee-gabled recess. Tomb-chest front with four quatrefoils and shields. It is identified by the heraldry as Sir John Sewell. – In the chancel floor, brasses to John Waleys, priest, †1410 (demi-figure 12 in. (30 cm) long), and to Sir William Walley, priest, †1506; remounted (the demi-figure was stolen and is now replaced in fibreglass). – Sir William Milard †1710. Hanging tablet with scroll pediment by *Edward Stanton*,

---

*The BAPTIST CHAPEL of 1863–4 described in the first edition of this guide as 'A gruesome Victorian piece with a debased tower and vaguely Gothic, oddly arranged façade windows' – was demolished in 1972–3. It was by *Joseph P. Neale* of Bristol (P. C. Edwards).

erected 1730 by Dame Alice Milard, also in memory of her parents, Henry and Alice Brandreth. The chancel is floored almost wall to wall by ledger slabs for the Brandreths.

HOUGHTON HALL, s of the large green at the centre of the old village, SE of the church. Built *c.* 1700–10 for Sir William and Dame Alice Milard; she was the daughter of Henry Brandreth who bought the manor house (dem. C20) in the 1650s. Originally a fine five-by-eight-bay chequer-brick house with a pediment and raised red brick quoins but altered by *Henry Clutton* in 1847–51 for Humphrey Gibbs Brandreth. He probably added the hipped roof with pedimented attic dormers and the pedimented porch is clearly Victorian. What may have been the pediment of the original doorway to the garden (open and scrolly) is now above the window of a two-storey canted bay which forms part of a later C18 two-bay extension of the s front. Good raised panelling and bolection-moulded fireplaces in most rooms, one room also with a shell niche, but when the house was refurbished in the 1990s it was discovered that much of this had been introduced or moved around in the C19; in the extension, for example, is a room with giant fluted pilasters flanking the fireplace and lugged frame with pediment and bolection moulding. The staircase has three twisted balusters to the tread and carved tread-ends, and is lit by a Venetian window. – Pretty outhouse of *c.* 1700 with a pyramid roof and bellcote. The dovecote with pagoda roof is clearly by Clutton (cf. Sandy Lodge and Old Warden school).

HOUGHTON COURT, E of the house, is one long stable range with diamond stacks in pairs and gabled dormers. C17 but remodelled in the mid C19 and now converted to cottages.

Most of Houghton Regis is a not very interesting postwar story, but the large green is still an asset. It is near enough to Dunstable to have taken part in that town's renewal in the 1960s. Of that period, E of the church, is BEDFORD SQUARE, the shopping precinct by *Willoughby Fletcher & Associates*. It is L-shaped and lies immediately SE of a circular LIBRARY, YOUTH HALL etc., originally by the *Bedfordshire County Architect's Department*, 1963–4, recently remodelled. External staircase to maisonettes above the shops.

(OAKWELL PARK, Thorn, 1 m. NW. Early C20 Neo-Elizabethan country house on an older moated site. Brick, with some timber-framing. Crowstepping on the gables in the Suffolk style. Built for the chemist F. W. Crossley-Holland. Inside, a great hall open to the roof, with minstrels' gallery.)

HOWBURY HALL *see* RENHOLD

HULCOTE

ST NICHOLAS. In general outline medieval, but 're-edified' *c.* 1590 by Richard Chernocke, as his monument says. The moulded plinth, buttresses and s porch are of this time and the DOOR with stud decoration has Chernocke's initials, R.C. The windows are all mullioned and transomed, in the Elizabethan way, mostly of two lights. The E window alone still has the arched lights of Henry VIII's tradition; a N window cuts through a former door. The chancel s door has good scrolling ironwork strap hinges, early C14.* The tower had a spire, and taller pinnacles, until 1867. Inside, its arch is specially Perp. The ceiling on the other hand is white plaster and tunnel-vaulted. The church was restored in 1838: the FONT of that date is an undersized marble piece with a column as support, and in the choir stalls and on the nave walls WOODWORK panels of the C16 and C17, linenfold, Early Renaissance and Jacobean, probably that known to have been collected by the rector during the restoration. – COMMUNION RAIL. With thin twisted balusters; early C18. – MONUMENT. – Richard Chernocke †1615. It is a family monument in three tiers. In the large middle one his father Robert with two wives are seen kneeling. Above, a narrow strip with himself and his wife also kneeling and fourteen small kneeling children in arches with marble columns. In the bottom strip ten kneeling children of Robert. Erected by John Chernocke in 1616. – Edward Hervey †1796. Erected by his daughter's will in 1809. By *Robert Blore Sen.* With the usual woman by an urn.

Opposite, HULCOT MANOR, the former rectory, with an odd portico of four attached giant columns, three blocked arches and a steep pediment. By *Joshua Harrison* of Leicester, 1821.

HUSBORNE CRAWLEY

ST MARY. Has any other church such green greensand as the W tower of Husborne Crawley, where it appears mixed with the usual brownish sandstone? The W tower is Perp with two two-light bell-openings on each side and a higher stair-turret. Next to the s doorway a large stoup. Much of the church is restoration of 1911 by *C. G. Hare*, for the Duke of Bedford, after many years of minor repairs. N aisle and chancel rebuilt entirely, the vestry and organ chamber added. Three-bay arcades of standard elements, s low and C13 (or at least its capitals), N higher and Perp. The tower arch has nicely decorated capitals. In the s aisle E wall a pretty niche. The interior was redone in the 1820s but all of it refurnished in 1911. – TOWER SCREEN. 1957. – STAINED GLASS. E window, centre by *H. W. Bryans*, 1911; the flanking lights by *H. & J. Bryans*, 1927; weakly in the Kempe tradition. – s aisle by *Hardman*, 1950 – MONUMENTS. John Thompson †1597, 'one of the auditors of the Council of the Treasury of her Royal Majesty'. Large standing alabaster monument with badly carved effigies and much better strapwork

---

*I am grateful to Jane Geddes for dating this.

cartouches on the base. Five columns, two back, three front, carry a studded ceiling. Achievement at the top. Children in the back panel. It is a pair to the Snagge Monument at Marston Moretaine (q.v.). – Talbot Williamson †1765, of coloured marbles, with urn before an obelisk.

MANOR HOUSE, by the church. Late C16, T-plan farmhouse, timber-framed with brick infilling. Handsome cluster of octagonal chimneys to the hall range. To the N, THE LODGE, c. 1820–40, red brick with yellow pilasters and geometric glazing patterns.

HENRY VI COTTAGE, Bedford Road. A substantial cruck-framed house of four bays on a plinth of ironstone and brick. Two-bay hall inside. The hall cruck has a low tie-beam, an odd feature of local carpentry (cf. Moretyne Manor, Marston Moretaine). Massive inserted C17 brick chimneystack.

The BEDFORD ESTATE buildings include the former vicarage, 1851, SE towards Woburn, the brick and half-timbered SCHOOL and SCHOOL HOUSE by *Clutton*, 1866–7, and the VILLAGE HALL by *A. J. Pilkington*, 1894.

CRAWLEY PARK. Built in 1777–8 for the Rev. Daniel Shipton, whose wife had inherited the property. Five-bay front, red brick, with three-bay pediment containing a lunette. Pretty doorway with columns, a pediment and Adamish fanlight. Three-bay rear with Venetian windows and an arch for the staircase in the centre. In 1806 the two canted bay windows were added but the two complete bays to the l. with another canted bay window are late C19. The Drawing Room has excellent and rare Egyptian Regency wallpaper, with border of sphinx and sarcophagi, probably that supplied by *Robson & Hale* in 1806. Good white marble chimneypiece too.

ICKWELL
Northill

A very spacious GREEN. Most of the houses are low, the best being on the w side. At the N end, a more formal C18 five-bay house (ICKWELL GRANGE), a nice effect. Venetian window at first-floor level on the w side. Near this the Northill WAR MEMORIAL, *Reginald Blomfield*'s Cross of Sacrifice, 1920. Also standing on the green, the former SMITHY. In Caldecote Road, TOMPION'S COTTAGE, birthplace in 1639 of Thomas Tompion, the clockmaker. The timber frame is indeed C17 but reworked in the C19.

THE OLD HOUSE, SE of the green. A mixture of dates, not least the C19, but the N–S range is the remains of the crown-post roof of an aisled hall – the aisles later removed – which John Bailey dated to the late C13 or early C14. Four bays of the roof survive, the central hall truss with moulded crown-post. The roof is hipped at the s end. The gardens were redesigned by *Gertrude Jekyll* in 1926–31, one of her last commissions, for Col. G. H. Wells, of the Bedford brewers. They have been lost.

ICKWELL BURY. The house built or remodelled in the 1680s for John Harvey, and further altered in the C18, was destroyed in 1937. Its replacement is by *A. S. G. Butler*, 1938–40, in free Neo-Georgian for Col. G. H. Wells (*see* The Old House, above). On two fronts the centres have brick quoins, parapets and ball finials, one with a circular window, the other with a balustraded loggia at first floor. Deep roof with dormers, echoing the adjoining STABLES of 1683 (dated clock, attributed to *Thomas Tompion*). Ten-bay front, cross-windows and a cupola with a square base. Short s return joined to a funny Victorian gate to the court with a tower. The octagonal brick DOVECOTE is also C17. (Also in the grounds a BEE HOUSE, weatherboarded with thatched roof and wooden shelves inside for the hives. A rare survival. Alan Cox.) The remains of extensive Victorian land-scaped grounds are being gradually rescued.

KEMPSTON (RURAL)

0040

ALL SAINTS. Short Perp w tower, short Perp nave with clerestory, lower chancel. Impressive, two-storey Perp s porch with stair-turret and, curiously, also an external stair to the E. Inside, a tierceron-star vault with filleted ribs, Symbols of the Evangelists and little figures on the bosses. s door of the same time. But in the s wall of the tower one Norman window, and in the chancel blocked s and n windows which are Norman, if not Anglo-Saxon. The w door is also Norman and upon entering one sees that the church has a Norman tower arch as well as a Norman chancel arch, the former larger than the latter. One impost of the chancel arch has saltire crosses. The three-bay arcades are both E.E., the n arcade earlier than the s. On the n side, round piers with very simply moulded capitals and only slightly double-chamfered arches, on the s side octagonal piers and normally double-chamfered arches. Yet the arches are unequal; the middle one is lower and has a moulding ending in notch stops. The Perp phase has made it impressively lofty and spacious. There was a restoration by *J. Horsford*, 1864 (nave roof etc.) and another by *Temple Moore*, 1899–1901, including the restoration of the rood loft. MAUSOLEUM (NE). 'Built by Sir William Long, 1823'. VESTRY. 1840s. – DOUBLE PISCINA. In the chancel, C13, with continuous mouldings around the arches. Strangely low to the floor. s aisle PISCINA of same style. – FONT. Square, with chamfered corners, Dec. Low, broad, crocketed ogee arches with single figures in them.* – STAINED

---

*Pevsner described a 'PAINTING. Two panels . . . with Creation of Eve, Temptation, Discovery, and Expulsion. Rustic C15, and no reason not to call it English.' It is no longer displayed.

GLASS. The E window, plain bright colours and pressed clear glass, is characteristic of its date and maker: 1852 by *J. Powell & Sons*. N aisle and S aisle E windows by *Hardman*, distinctive silvery canopies and saints, 1913 and 1923. – S aisle SE by *Christopher Webb*, 1938. – MONUMENT. N aisle. Large coffin lid with a cross with curious small ornamental motifs in places on it. C13 no doubt. Discovered 1840. – William Carter †1705. Tablet with swags and fine death's head. Attributed to *James Hardy* (GF).

S of the churchyard a long row of COTTAGES (Nos. 1–4), originally jettied on two sides and originally a single range, eight bays long, with one upper and one lower chamber, presumably for communal church or guild use. (Late medieval roof of clasped purlins with windbraces.)

THE BURY, ⅜ m. S, is a routine Neo-Jacobean house of *c.* 1851 replacing a fine C17 brick manor house of the Cater family but standing within the original red brick-walled enclosure, with a pair of fine early C18 GATEPIERS topped by volutes and eagles. Picturesque mid-C19 estate COTTAGES on the main road with prettily intricate bargeboards.

BOX END HOUSE, ½ m. NNW. Late C16, probably H-plan originally but its W cross-wing lost. Stone with close studding in the upper floor and a two-storey porch. Taller Neo-Jacobean garden range of 1847. (Inside, early C17 grisaille wall painting showing bull baiting.)

CLOCK HOUSE, ⅞ m. NNW. Dated 1723. Front of three bays, red brick, under a deep continuous modillion cornice, with the centre set forward under a pediment. Built out below in 1884.

CROSSLAND FOSSE, ⅞ m. NNE. Red brick with shaped and Dutch gables. By *Percy G. Stone* for Captain Lindesay Beaumont, 1889. Lodge and stable buildings in matching style.

KEMPSTON (TOWN)

Much of the S end of Kempston parish became a suburb of Bedford in the mid to late C19. Only along High Street are some remnants of the timber-framed rural scene. Bedford Road is the centre now and along this are some major late C20 developments, e.g. the Saxon Centre.

TRANSFIGURATION, Bedford Road. 1938–40 by *J. Harold Gibbons*. Simplified Arts and Crafts Gothic, brown brick with tile-creasing along the eaves and tile roofs. Tall Perp-style W window. Above the porch, a flat section campanile of an arch with buttresses and shaped top and, at the NE corner, a quarter-circle chapel carried on star-shaped brick piers. Fine stark white interior, spatially inventive, with nave and chancel under an acid yellow trussed barrel-vault and a chapel over the (liturgical) E end beyond the high altar. Rood above the high altar.

Wide N aisle under a ribbed half-barrel vault and its arcade of
three broad and unmoulded pointed arches on chamfered
piers contrasting with the narrower s passage aisle behind
round arches and shouldered arches; this motif recurs for
smaller openings, e.g. along the N wall with a bench passing
through arches. – FONT. 1868; from St John's church.* –
STAINED GLASS. E window, fine abstract, highly coloured
design by *Alfred R. Fisher*, 1972.

KEMPSTON EAST METHODIST CHURCH, Bedford Road. 1904
by *Gunton & Gunton*. Rugged stone exterior, Perp, with angle
turrets. Good roof inside, four-centre arch profile with ribs and
hammerbeams.

POLICE STATION, Bedford Road. One of the pleasing Neo-Georgian designs by the County Surveyor *c.* 1938: a central block,
two pavilions and an arch to a rear courtyard.

LOWER SCHOOL, Bedford Road. 1889, probably by *Henry Young*.
Symmetrical front of two wings, nicely cut brickwork for the
dates in their gables, and a bellcote. Nearby, the much larger
ROBERT BRUCE SCHOOL, originally Secondary Modern, of
1960 by *Ken Darby* and *Dennis Sharp* of the *Bedfordshire County
Architect's Dept.* A spacious site whose sloping gradient allows
for a more dynamic and interesting arrangement of its curtain-
walled components. Much good use of coloured panels.

ST JOHN'S HOMES, Bedford Road. Almshouses of 1881 paid for
by Anne Charles Williamson, built by *Samuel Foster*. A very
attractive Old English group, with elaborate datestone.

Nearby to the NW, KEMPSTON MANOR, a compact house of
three bays square, stucco lined out as ashlar with a doorcase
of vermiculated rustication. Rebuilt by *John Wing*, 1815. The
mansard roof is later.

BEDFORD MASONIC CENTRE, Bedford Road. The former Keep
– armoury etc. and lock-up – which fronted the depot built in
1874–6 under the Cardwell programme for building barracks
in the major towns for the local regiments. By *Major H. C.
Seddon, R. E.* About half its original size following demolitions
in the 1980s but still with a formidable gatehouse with towers
at the corners, overall crenellation and machicolation. Long
wings l. and r. are two-storey. Brick banded thinly with stone.
Caernarvon arches to the windows. Opposite, a distinguished
WAR MEMORIAL (Beds & Herts Regiment) of 1921 by *G. P.
Allen*, a domed Neoclassical temple with an open semicircular
Ionic colonnade. Portland stone. Flanking exedra wall with
seats and obelisks in front; the second obelisk added 1950.
Behind this, ADDISON HOWARD PARK, created from the
grounds of THE GRANGE, a house of *c.* 1830–50. Yellow brick
with a veranda. The estate was given to Kempston in 1916.

In the suburban area s of Bedford Road, No. 136 SPRING ROAD
is a house of 1934 by *Frank E. Saunders* with *Edwin J. Smith*.
White walled with streamlined corners and steel windows but
with a pitched tile roof.

*ST JOHN, by *Robert Palgrave*, 1867–8, was closed in 1940 and dem. 1966.

KENSWORTH

ST MARY, ½ m. distant from the village, with only a few houses for company. Nave and chancel were given their steep roofs in 1856, the nave with diaper patterns in the slate. Perp w tower with angle buttresses and a higher stair-turret with a brick top. Perp w door like Caddington (q.v.); both churches were held by the Canons of St Paul's, Bedford. The rest of the aisleless church, except for an E extension of the chancel, is Norman, and quite early if not indeed Saxo-Norman. The chancel has its herringbone flint courses exposed. On the N side are small Norman windows in chancel and nave but they have been completely restored. The S doorway is original, however. One order of shafts, in one capital the fox and crane from Aesop on the S face and to the E face another bird on the back of a beast with a tail, possibly the Kite and Serpent. In the other capital, saltire crosses and close knotwork. The arch face also has rows of small saltires but following no consistent pattern. Also one big roll. There was a w doorway as well, still high and narrow, but it now of course leads into the tower. The decoration of its outer face is very similar to that of the S doorway but yet more varied and the capitals now just geometric patterns. The nave was quite spacious. The chancel arch has scalloped capitals, and there are only two scallops to the main capitals. That also is early. The arch has an inner and outer roll. The chancel E window is Perp, and l. and r. of it are two niches. – COMMUNION RAIL. The dismantled part must be of *c.* 1630–40. – STAINED GLASS. Some grisaille fragments in the tower W window. A large collection of C19 and C20 glass, beginning with S chancel windows of *c.* 1878 by *Baillie & Co.*, but the later in date they are, the more routine. The exception is the chancel SW of 1921 by *Leonard Walker*, St Christopher and St Cecilia, technically superior for the use of thick coloured fragments and a minimum of drawing.

LYNCH HOUSE, I m. SE. Late C18, brick, of seven bays with a three-bay pediment with oculus over a slight projection. Moulded modillion cornice. Porch with thin Roman Doric columns.

OLD VICARAGE, Spratts Lane, ⅜ m. SSE. 1869 by *S. S. Teulon*, but not roguish.

KEYSOE

ST MARY. W tower of the C14 and after. Pairs of transomed two-light bell-openings, four crocketed pinnacles, recessed spire with three tiers of lucarnes in alternating directions, very much in the Huntingdonshire style. Dec N arcade of three bays with standard elements, Dec N aisle windows (restored), two-bay N chapel with Dec arcade but Perp windows. Dec chancel with the appropriate windows (intersecting tracery with ogee) and a PISCINA with sweet small-scale tracery. Only the s doorway and the s chancel doorway and perhaps the s chancel window are much earlier, i.e. late C12 Transitional. – FONT. Of what date is that strange powerful base? It has thick, heavy spurs and eight gables with a ball finial. It has an inscription in old French translated as:

> Trestui qui par ici passerez
> Pour l'ame de Warel priez
> Que dieu par sa grace
> Vraie merci li fasse. Amen.*

Can it be early C13? – BENCHES. Panels with a broad flat ogee arch and a small cresting above. Not the Beds. run-of-the-mill. – STAINED GLASS. Three windows by *J. Powell & Sons*, 1851 (N chapel E); 1868 (N aisle W) and, much better, the E window designed by *H. E. Wooldridge*, 1883. – COFFIN LID. N chapel. 6 ft (1.8 metres). A cross with double-omega pattern, of the C13 type sometimes found in N Bedfordshire. – MONUMENTS. William Dickins †1759, in the external w wall of the tower. The inscription records his preservation after he fell in 1718 while 'pointing the steepol'. Opposite the church a mid-C19 red brick BIER HOUSE.

Former NATIONAL SCHOOL, Mill Hill, ¼ m. ENE. 1850. Tiny brick room, with a gabled front, angle buttresses and a moulded chimney.

BAPTIST CHAPEL, Keysoe Row. Converted from a small barn in 1808. Thatched roof with a half-hip and brick N extension. Sliding sashes. Fine plain interior of benches and rostrum pulpit.

Former BAPTIST CHAPEL, Brook End. Dated 1741, red brick with arched windows. Now a house.

KNOTTING

ST MARGARET OF ANTIOCH (Churches Conservation Trust). One of the most atmospheric church interiors in Bedfordshire. The unbuttressed W tower is dated 1615 on the solid parapet. The bell-openings are plain two-light mullioned windows, part filled by boards dated 1716. But the nave is Norman, see one small s window, and also the flat buttresses at the W end, the remains of a Norman W window, earlier than the tower, and the chancel arch with chevron. A little chevron also survives in the s door. The VCH points out that the W window is set in

---

* Rest; you who pass here / To pray for the soul of Warel / May God by his Grace / Truly thank you. Amen.

such thick masonry that it probably carried a bellcote. The tower arch below is narrow, parabolic and barbaric and quite undatable but may have been the Norman w door, altered to its present form at the same date on the tower. The chancel was rebuilt, the s transept built, and alterations made in the nave at the end of the C13, see the pointed-trefoiled lancets and the window with three stepped lancet lights. Roof tie-beam dated 1669. There was some limited restoration by *Clutton* for the Duke of Bedford in 1876, and by *Albert Richardson* in the 1920s, detectable only in the repairs in brick and tile and the tile chimney. Much more was done in 2009–11 by *Ptolemy Dean* to restore the roof, return the walls to their original subtle pink hue and pave the transept in biscuit-coloured clay tiles. – PULPIT. Jacobean with fluted decoration and square sounding-board; a two-decker although the simple reading desk looks later. – BENCHES. Of the C16 and the C17, both dates of the same straight-topped simple type. Two have backing of rush matting introduced by Richardson, a reminder of the local industry (*see* Pavenham). – CHANCEL GATES. 1637. Set up at the instruction of Archbishop Laud after cock-fighting had been indulged in in the chancel on Shrove Tuesday in the presence of rector and churchwardens. Tall, spiked on the top and with locks. – COMMUNION RAIL. Slender turned balusters. Around the walls, rustic COAT PEGS. – COFFIN SLAB. Chancel floor. C13 cross type, the head elaborated with C curves. – CHURCHYARD CROSS. The base has a quatrefoil frieze. The lantern top was added as the war memorial in 1921 by *Talbot Brown & Fisher*.

LANGFORD

1040

A very strung-out village, and much built up in the second half of the C20.

ST ANDREW. Of brown cobbles, buttressed in ironstone. An uncommonly uniform Dec church, but much of the detail over-restored in 1872–4 by *W. Maynard Shaw*. Nave and aisles and short but broad s porch tower with diagonal buttresses, its crenellated top restored in 1912–14. Before 1874 the church also had an impressively low profile with one roof over nave and aisles, but the pitch of the nave is now higher. The s aisle has flowing, reticulated, and also still geometrical tracery, the two windows of the E end with three spherical triangles in the head. The N aisle tracery is flowing and partly restored. The nave w window has reticulated tracery again (four lights), the aisle w windows again flowing patterns. s porch door with the familiar Dec half-quatrefoil responds with shafts. The s door with an ogee arch. The arcades have standard octagonal piers with moulded capitals and double-chamfered arches. The chancel arch is of the same type, with chevron painting to one chamfer, but the chancel Perp. N vestry and organ chamber 1884–5, probably by *A. W. Blomfield*. – PULPIT. Plain, but nice, with sunk panels; C18. – BENCHES. The nave front rows Perp with standard Bedfordshire buttressed ends. – STAINED GLASS. Old fragments in several windows. Heraldic glass reset in the vestry window. E window, 1949 by *G. Maile & Son*. Lacklustre. – BRASS to Thomas Hundon, vicar, †1520 (18 in.; 45 cm).

Former VICARAGE, at the far N end of Church Street. By *John Norton*, 1854. An eccentric design with terracotta Tudorish chimneys and, over a canted bay, a steep roof with Gothic lucarnes and brattishing.

WAR MEMORIAL, High Street, ¼ m. S, in a raised garden. A square Portland stone clocktower with a pagoda roof, Arts and Crafts-style. By *Charles Wright*, 1921.

LEAGRAVE *see* LUTON

LEIGHTON BUZZARD
Leighton Linslade

9020

The river Ouzel divides Leighton Buzzard from Linslade, which is historically part of Buckinghamshire. It was only in 1965 that the two were made one town and brought entirely into Bedfordshire as Leighton Linslade. For Linslade, *see* p. 208.

Excavated Saxon cemeteries are evidence of an early importance and the town had a market as early as the late C11. Leighton Buzzard was also a royal manor, granted in 1164 to GROVE PRIORY (a.k.a. La Grava), which was founded as a Benedictine cell of Fontevrault. The priory developed the manorial buildings, which lay S of the present centre near Grovebury Farm, into a high-status complex fit for the residence of the Procurator of the Order in England and some fifty royal visits in the late C13 and early C14, but it had been reduced to a farmhouse by the C16. Only the fishponds remain after sand quarrying but comprehensive rescue excavations were made from 1973 to 1985.

The parish church was a prebendary of Lincoln and is among the most impressive in the county. There was a fire in the town in the 1680s, which may account for both the lack of timber-framed buildings and the frequent occurrence of vitreous blue and red brick façades of *c*. 1700. On the Linslade side runs the Grand Junction Canal connecting the town with London and the North after 1805, and from 1838 there was the railway, which thrust into existence New Linslade around the station (*see* p. 208) and made Leighton Buzzard a commuter town by the middle years of the C19. It had its own industries too and, typical of the southern part of the county, was a centre for straw-plaiting for a while, although the extraction of the local fine white sand, much sought after for casting in engineering and for glassmaking, was and remains an important industry. Other sands have been used for bricks and tiles (e.g. Marley tiles were made here from 1928 and Redland roofing tiles still are produced here). The narrow-gauge railway of 1919 which transported the sand from the pits to the Dunstable branch line was reopened in 1983 as a tourist attraction. Of all the market towns in Bedfordshire, Leighton Buzzard has the most to offer in interest.

CHURCHES*

ALL SAINTS. A large ironstone church. Its pride is its crossing steeple, E.E., with single lancet bell-openings flanked by blank

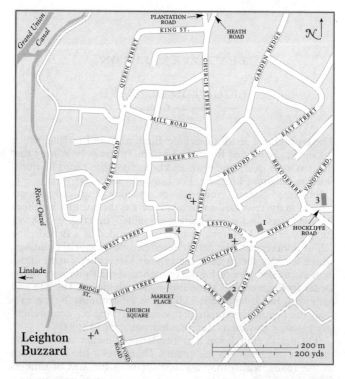

A	All Saints	1	Town Council Offices
B	Baptist Church	2	Library Theatre
C	Friends' Meeting House	3	Police Station
		4	Royal British Legion

* The following churches have been demolished since 1968: ST ANDREW, Church Street, 1866–7 by *Joseph P. Neale* of Bristol; the BAPTIST CHAPEL, Lake Street, 1864, also by Neale; and the METHODIST CHAPEL, Hockliffe Street, 1864 by *Bellamy & Hardy*.

lancets and a high stone ashlar spire with big broaches, three tiers of lucarnes in the same four directions, and small pinnacles on the broaches that were added during a restoration in 1841–3 by *John Livock*. The former E.E. rooflines are visible against the tower. The rest of the exterior is nearly all Perp, in the fenestration of the transepts and aisles, a chancel only 2 ft 6 in. (76 cm) shorter than the nave, and a two-storey N vestry. The nave clerestory is especially impressive, with pairs of tall three-light windows. This work may be dated to the period 1467–75 and is attributed to the patronage of Alice de la Pole, Duchess of Suffolk (i.e. Alice Chaucer), who held the manor. Inside the S transept, the E windows appear to have been designed for altars below. The only earlier feature is the Dec W doorway. Inside it is different, negatively and positively. The crossing arches are not E.E., or at least so ill-treated as not to be recognizably E.E. now, but in the clunch piers are a number of interesting GRAFFITI and carvings that show that the piers are C13. The one really exquisite one is the master-mason's precise drawing of a four-light window with geometrical tracery: a cinquefoiled circle above the quatrefoiled ones (SE pier to the SW). More entertaining is the so-called Simon and Nellie story about first boiling and then baking a cake. She is threatening him with a spoon (SW pier). In both transepts the E wall has a niche with a pointed-trefoiled head, and that too is probably late C13, and there is furthermore a continuous sill band from transepts into the chancel of a recognizably C13 kind of a roll moulding with a fillet. The church was indeed consecrated in 1288, and from the same year dates a bequest by Nicholas de Heigham for its completion. Of this time also are probably the four-bay arcades of standard elements and the W door with its excellent IRONWORK, mostly scrolls with foliage terminals in four pairs to each of the two hinges. A hand grips the door ring. It is convincingly attributed to *Thomas of Leighton*, who was paid in 1292–3 for the iron grille for Queen Eleanor's tomb in Westminster Abbey. It is likely that Thomas came to the attention of Bishop Oliver of Lincoln, who officiated at the Queen's funeral. Similar hinges from the chancel S door have been remounted on the vestry door inside.

The church was severely damaged by fire in 1985 and restored by *Paul Reynolds* and *James Honour* of *H. A. Rolls & Partners*, completed 1989. They added the two-storey link between the vestry and N transept (being restored in 2013), with good stairs from within the sanctuary. The chancel ROOF needed to be entirely replaced; more remained of the nave and aisle roofs, which are of the East Anglian kind with castellated tie-beams, open trusses, large angels to the intermediate principals and spread-winged angel heads to the wall-plate, figures on the jackposts and stone angel corbels.

FURNISHINGS. – FONT. E.E. Of cauldron shape, on five round supports. Astonishingly, the timber chancel furnishings survived the fire. – SCREEN. Tall, of broad single-light openings, cusped. – STALLS. A large set of twenty-eight, evidently introduced from elsewhere; but where? It cannot be St Albans, as has often been claimed, because the stalls there were early C14 and those here are dated to *c.* 1430 by the heraldry of Henry Frowick, alderman of the City of London 1424–57.* Twenty-eight seats, with complete MISERICORDS. They have mostly heads and foliage but where the stalls turn against the screen also fine heads of kings of the type of the late C14 stalls at Lincoln. – Traceried BENCHES with poppyheads. – PULPIT. Given in 1638 by Edward Wilkes (*see* the almshouses, North Street, below). Cedarwood, panels typical of the mid C17. Also carved back panel. – LECTERN. A beautiful wooden eagle on a shaft, assigned to the late C14. – REREDOS by *Bodley*, who restored the interior in 1885–6: triptych with a crucifixion and in the wings angels in low relief. A choir organ, also by Bodley, was destroyed in the fire. In the N transept arch a mighty ORGAN CASE of 1906. – CHARITY BOARD. S transept. An unusually grand triptych case with an angel in a pediment and the shield of Sir Edward Wilkes (†1646). Black with gold lettering, recording donors up to 1715. – STAINED GLASS. Much by *C. E. Kempe* and as an ensemble highly impressive, although the E window was destroyed in the fire. It ranges from 1887 (W and one in the S aisle), 1888 (two S transept), and 1889 (one N aisle) to 1896 (clerestory) and 1905 (also N aisle). The S aisle central window is by *Kempe & Co.*, 1928. The remainder, again all Kempe or his firm after his time, have been introduced since the fire: N aisle (Crucifixion, 1899) from St Michael, Appleby, Cumberland; four large saints, 1909, in the S transept S window, which had been in the possession of *Goddard & Gibbs*, and another in the N aisle from St Edmund, Forest Gate, London, 1904, reset in 2000 with new upper lights. The N transept N window is of 1865 and alone represents the pre-Kempe era. – MONUMENTS. A very good collection in the chancel. – William Jackman †1597. Brass with kneeling figures. – Francis Welles & wife, 1636. Also brass, with their kneeling figures facing each other. – Robert Wyngate †1603 and wife. Alabaster tablet with touch columns and the usual kneelers in an arched recess. – John Welles †1645. Painted alabaster tablet with frontal demi-figure, one hand on a book, the other on his heart. Quite small. Attributed to *Edward Marshall* (GF). – Edward Wilkes †1646/7 and wife †1657, a large wreathed oval with the inscription, attributed to *Thomas Burman* (GF). Next to it, Luke Wilkes †1673. Attributed to *Jasper Latham* (GF). Scrolly pediment and fat fruiting garlands dropping down the sides. – Leigh family. Hanging Corinthian aedicule, with black columns, a white pediment, arms and armorial cartouches. Side scrolls. Also attributed to *Latham* (GF), *c.* 1670. The later inscription to Anne Leigh †1697, first wife of the Hon. Charles Leigh (†1704) is on an open book as large as the tablets of the Law. – Alicia Annesley †1684 and Anne Leigh †1680, daughters

---

* See C. Tracy, 'Medieval Choir-stalls at Leighton Buzzard Church, Bedfordshire', *Bedfordshire Archaeology*, vol. 19, 1991.

of the Hon. Charles Leigh. White marble cartouches with finely cut drapery surrounds, matching if not identical. Also attributed to *Latham* (GF). – Anthony, Christopher and William Sclater, erected *c.* 1690 after the death of the last-named, incumbent at St James, Clerkenwell, London. White marble tablet on a fat moulded base and two finely carved cherubs' heads at the top. Attributed to *Grinling Gibbons* (GF).

VICARAGE, E of the churchyard. 1850 by *Raphael Brandon*.

BAPTIST CHAPEL, Hockliffe Street. 1891 by *Hampden W. Pratt*. Large but routine Italianate with four arched windows under a pedimental gable. W window STAINED GLASS by *Arthur Inns*, 1894.

FRIENDS' MEETING HOUSE, North Street. Tucked slightly back from the street. Of two phases, each of two bays, 1789 (l.) and *c.* 1800 (r.), but seamlessly done in grey vitreous brick in header bond and red brick. Hipped roof. The earlier part with wooden cross-windows. Happily simple interior with the usual seating and moveable screen. Facing North Street a pretty terrace of Early Victorian COTTAGES built for elderly Friends.

CEMETERY, Vandyke Road. Gateway and chapel by *Capon & Littlewood*, 1881.

PUBLIC BUILDINGS

Former TOWN HALL, Market Place. *See* Perambulation below.

TOWN COUNCIL OFFICES, Hockliffe Street. The White House, a large Italianate brick and stuccoed house of *c.* 1850 with a three-storey tower over the porch and elaborate iron cresting.

LIBRARY AND THEATRE, Lake Street. 1979. Undemonstrative but practical modernism, brown brick. In the stairwell, large pendulum CLOCK from St Andrew's School (dem. 1970s).

POLICE STATION, Hockliffe Road. 1939 by *S. C. Jury*, Bedfordshire County Surveyor. An impressive, small classical design, brick and stone, with columned porch and a taller range behind with hipped roof and cupola. It must have included the court house.

Former WORKHOUSE, Grovebury Road. Now offices (Ridgeway Court). 1836 by *W. P. Roote*. Courtyard plan of two-storey ranges. Taller administration tower in the centre of the SW range, with chamfered corners and round-arched windows.

ROYAL BRITISH LEGION, West Street. (Inside, the Beaudesert School WAR MEMORIAL, alabaster hanging tablet with St George in a niche under a pediment. By *Paul Waterhouse*, *c.* 1920.)

PERAMBULATION

Outside the church gate, the WAR MEMORIAL, a powerful 25-ft (7.6 metre)-high Shap granite monolith, lettered by *Farmer & Brindley* and erected 1920. The W side of CHURCH SQUARE is oddly Londonish Early Victorian. One tall terrace of six yellow brick and stucco houses by *W. C. Reed*, 1855 (GS), a speculative venture for John Dollin Bassett, of the town's banking family, intended to capitalize on access to the railway for London businessmen. At the corner of Bridge Street is Bassett's own house, THE CEDARS (now Leighton Middle School), detached, of five bays. Also by *Reed* and also 1855. It succeeded the Prebendal Manor House, which was rebuilt by the Leigh family and demolished in the early C19. The garden TEMPLE remains and is almost certainly by *James Gibbs*, who is credited in his papers with 'the House of the Honble Charles Leigh at Leighton'. The date must be *c.* 1720. Blue brick with red dressings, including red lacing and stone quoins. Portico of four Roman Doric columns with pediment lower than the wall. Hipped roof. The interior has a boldly coved ceiling and stucco decoration. Now used as a library (fittings of 1920s). It is neatly incorporated with the SCHOOL BUILDINGS of 1928–9 by *Oswald P. Milne*, Neo-Georgian with arcaded cloisters around a quad. Gym etc. 1938–9, also by Milne. On the other side of Church Square, the POST OFFICE, which, as Pulford's School, was built in 1790, as the three-bay pediment and the vitreous blue brick header facing laced with red shows, but remodelled in Jacobean style 1884, with cross-windows, and two little shaped gables l. and r. The successor SCHOOL, of 1883, is just to the NE, ironstone with brick dressings and roofed in two-tone bands of fishscale slates.

From the corner of the Square the HIGH STREET rises slightly and widens a little towards the Market Place. It is a good if uneventful street, with a number of shopfronts still well preserved. On the S side, the UNIONIST CLUB of 1913 by the local architect *T. H. Bishop*. Queen Anne-style, with two storeys of canted bays in the centre but nicely non-aligned, cupola on the roof. The BLACK LION is the first of a number of good early C18 façades, blue and red brick, a symmetrical pair of two and a half bays each with rusticated doorcases. Across the street, No. 21, late C18, again blue and red, and with a nice doorcase. Also on the N side the NATWEST BANK, formerly the London & County Bank, built in 1856 by *C. Parnell*. Grey brick originally, with arched ground-floor windows, all foolishly now rendered. Further up on the other side, the SWAN HOTEL, perhaps of *c.* 1840, but still classical. White and cream stucco, with a porch, a rinceau frieze and a parapet rising into an open arch over a swan. Next to it, HSBC, of 1922 for the London, City & Midland Bank, classical, very probably by their usual architects *Gotch & Saunders*. So to the MARKET PLACE and the MARKET CROSS. This is an uncommonly fine C15 piece, stone, pentagonal, with the lower stage vaulted and the recessed upper stage with quite well preserved statues of Christ, St John, the Virgin, a bishop and king. Small buttresses with top pinnacles and one taller pinnacle in the centre. Restored in 1853 by *William Cox* of Leighton, who had been Scott's chief carver on his Martyrs Memorial in Oxford, and again in 1900 by *Bodley*, who designed the crenellated parapet and returned the medieval statues that in 1853 had

been taken to adorn the MARKET HALL behind. This is of
1851, red brick, Gothic touches and a clock turret. Its ground
floor was of course originally open, with the Town Hall above.
It became the fire station in 1919. Wholly undistinguished,
wholly delightful. The Baroque-style former CROSS KEYS INN
(now Lloyds Bank) was rebuilt in 1899 after a fire. To the N
and S the MARKET PLACE has more good, quite early, C18
houses, blue and red brick as before, notably on the S side
above Boots, which has segmental-headed windows, cut frills
to the heads and a parapet. The date must be *c.* 1700. Also the

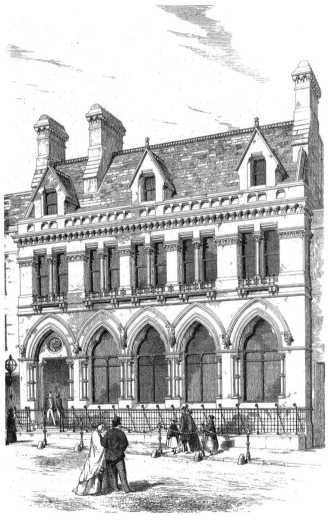

Leighton Buzzard, Barclays Bank.
By Alfred Waterhouse, 1865–7

former EAGLE & CHILD INN, which is a symmetrical pair each of four bays with Gibbsian stone surrounds with flared keystones to the windows. The ground floor was originally treated the same. On the other side of the Market Place, BAR-CLAYS BANK, built by *Waterhouse* for Bassett, Son & Harris in 1865–7, and very similar to his design for Backhouse's Bank, Darlington, of the previous year.* Ancaster stone, Gothic, two-storeyed, with dormers, large pointed arches with cusps encompassing the ground floor, the columns with crockets and gargoyles carved by *Thomas Earp*. The entrance now appears in the centre, rather than to the l. Inside, arcading round the banking hall.

p. 205

In the tight little pattern of streets behind the Market Hall, THE PEACOCK, one of the few exposed C16 timber-frames in the town, with a single gable and jetty. Turn s into LAKE STREET, where, on the s side, a good Early Victorian former draper's shop (now nightclub) has giant fluted Corinthian pilasters and a pediment; but otherwise the street has been badly deprived of almost all its interest by demolitions in the 1960s. The set-piece was the Corn Exchange (of 1862 by *Bellamy & Hardy*), demolished in 1965. Pevsner called it 'Victorian at its most irresponsible . . . The style is a kind of dissolute Renaissance. What has come in its place is as timid as it was gay and vulgar.'

Opposite, THE LANCER (formerly the Unicorn Hotel), a late C17 brick front, with raised brick quoins and platbands, nine bays long with a recessed five-bay centre. Horribly rendered over now. Three storeys; in the top one, three round windows, all now blocked. Otherwise only HODDESDON VILLAS, a reduced version of the Church Square terrace, and LECTON HOUSE, a former temperance hall/institute, built in 1845 by the Bassetts, yet still purely Grecian. Small and very pleasant, with four attached unfluted Ionic columns and a pediment. Now a gym.

N from the Market Place runs NORTH STREET.† A little further N, past the Friends' Meeting House (*see* above), the WILKES ALMSHOUSES, established in 1630, rebuilt 1857. Yellow brick with small gables; modest Jacobean. Extended l. 1873, this part in coursed and dressed bands of ironstone with a kneelered gable and jetty. 300 yds N, in CHURCH STREET, the PAGE ALMSHOUSES of 1903, a sweet design in brick and ironstone with a veranda along the front between two wings. By *J. T. Lawrence*.

N of North Street, and N of Church Street, in HEATH ROAD, HEATH LODGE, a fine small stucco villa, presumably dating from immediately after the enclosure of the Heath in 1841–4;

*The Bassetts and Backhouses were among the small group of Quaker banking families whom *Waterhouse* knew from his schooldays. At Leighton Buzzard he also designed The Heath, a house for Francis Bassett, in 1864–7 (dem.).

†HOLLY LODGE, North Street, has been demolished. Pevsner noted it as 'the most impressive house of Leighton Buzzard and hence, as so often, derelict. Blue and red brick. Centre and two cross gables; later C17.'

three bays with pediments l. and r. of a recessed centre. Doric porch. w of here, along Plantation Road to THE PLANTATION, an enviable wood of pines and specimen trees, created in the mid C19. The planter was the banker J. D. Bassett, and his landscape gardener *Robert Marnock*. In it THE KNOLLS, built by *Norman Shaw* in 1880 for Frederick Bassett. Plenty of tile-hanging, but run-of-the-mill Shaw. The oversailing floor of the service wing on the garden front and hinged casements of the mullion-and-transom windows in the two-storey square bays is a nice touch. Now a nursing home. ('Disappointing interior', says Andrew Saint.) In the grounds to the S, but now incorporated within the housing estates that have invaded the woods, are the 'knolls', two ROUND BARROWS. The lodge for the house is about ¼ m. S on PLANTATION ROAD. There are other minor Arts and Crafts villas in this neighbourhood, e.g. SANDYMOUNT, No. 132 Plantation Road, of 1907, with a brick and half-timbered façade and an M-shaped roof whose gables project over a balcony at first floor. It was built for Joseph Arnold, head of the largest firm of sand quarries in the town.

Off BILLINGTON ROAD, S of the centre, STONHILL, an Arts and Crafts house by *E. Turner Powell*, 1902, for Miss M. A. Bassett; roughcast walls, hipped and half-hipped tiled roofs and slender chimneys. (Inglenook fireplaces inside.)

REDLAND (Van Dyke Plant), Mile Tree Road. Tile factory by *Pollard Thomas Edwards*, 1978. Brown brick and profiled metal sheeting. The long plan is dictated by the internal layout of conveyor belts for tile production.

LEIGHTON LINSLADE *see* LEIGHTON BUZZARD *and* LINSLADE

LEWSEY *see* LUTON

LIDLINGTON   *9030*

ST MARGARET. 1886, a Bedford estate church, by *Alexander Macpherson* of Derby. To be converted to housing in 2013. Ironstone, spacious, E.E., with transepts and a bellcote on the nave E gable. Lancet windows, but the crossing details taken rather from *c.* 1300. (– STAINED GLASS. 1901 by *A. L. Moore* (chancel S) and 1927 by *Christopher Webb* (S transept)).* The ruins of the old church survived until the 1960s.

THE GRANGE, S of the church at the top of the steeply climbing High Street. Charming red-and-white Queen Anne house of *c.* 1900, with tile-hanging, shallow bows on the front and a

*The brass to William Goldyngton, *c.* 1505, is now at Marston Moretaine (q.v.).

canted loggia under a veranda in the centre. Door at the side under a big curved hood.

Former MARSTON VALLEY BRICK COMPANY OFFICES, Marston Road. The Lidlington brickworks opened in 1929 producing Flettons. Neo-Georgian, red brick trimmed with blue, and Spanish tile roof. Stylish stone doorcase. The works closed in 1977.

LIMBURY see LUTON

9020

LINSLADE*
Leighton Linslade

Historically on the Buckinghamshire side of the River Ouzel but since 1965 part of Bedfordshire. A small but flourishing medieval town of Linslade, which lay 1 m. NW of the present centre, had all but disappeared by the early C19, and New Linslade only developed after the coming of the canal in 1805 and more especially the railway in 1838. There are a few unexceptional early C19 buildings that mark New Linslade's early development; otherwise, unlike its neighbour Leighton Buzzard, it has little to recommend it.

ST MARY, Old Linslade, E of Old Linslade Road, N of the town. A survival from the medieval town. The fabric of the nave and chancel, built of dark ironstone rubble, is of indeterminate date but may contain some masonry contemporary with the early C12 unmoulded chancel arch. Late Perp details in the chancel windows and roof timbers of the same date. C15 W tower. Embattled, unaisled nave. Restoration 1877 by *J. T. Lawrence*, including much renewal of window tracery, a new porch and a new nave roof. Further restoration 1897. N of the chancel arch, a Perp recess. To the S of the chancel arch and on its E side a recessed early C13 SEAT, with round arch and two stone arms – a very unusual piece. – FONT. Aylesbury type (*see* Introduction, p. 19) of *c.* 1200, circular, with a band of scrolls and beasts. – SCREEN. Remains of a C15 screen. – STAINED GLASS. E window by *Cakebread Robey*, 1897. – BRASS to a civilian with three wives. 14-in. (35.5 cm) figures (W wall). – MONUMENT. Two unusual wooden boards of 1810 commemorating members of the Corbet family (chancel).

ST BARNABAS, Church Road. By *B. Ferrey*, 1848–9, built to serve New Linslade. So added to that only the wide nave with its typical hammerbeam roof is recognizable as of the 1840s. S aisle and SW tower also by Ferrey, 1868–9; the original turret

---

*This entry is reprinted, with minor amendments, from the *Buildings of England*: *Buckinghamshire* (2nd edn, 1994, revised by Elizabeth Williamson).

is now at Billington (q.v.). *J. T. Lawrence* added the Lady Chapel (N) and began the N aisle in 1905. N aisle finished in 1912–13, along with the N and W porches and the alterations to the W window. Chancel extended by *G. H. Fellowes Prynne*, 1914. The C20 work carefully followed what preceded it, giving a surprising unity despite the long building history. – LECTERN. A fussy piece by *Fellowes Prynne*. – STAINED GLASS. Several by *Percy Bacon & Bros* (e.g. W and Lady Chapel). – The single-light figure of St Barnabas in the vestry is an early work by *Morris, Marshall Faulkner & Co.*, 1865. The figure design was reused at Bradford Cathedral and elsewhere. – E by *Heaton, Butler & Bayne*, 1873. – By *Kempe*, N aisle windows of 1878, 1882 and 1885 and S aisle windows of 1882.

SCHOOL, S of St Barnabas. By *Ferrey*, 1842, extended in 1866 by *E. O. Williams* of Luton, 1866. Plain.

MANOR FARMHOUSE, E of St Mary. A fine early C18 house, built by the Corbets, whose monument is in the church. Of five bays and two storeys, with one-bay additions. Vitreous and red brick with stone dressings. The centre bay is flanked by two sturdy giant pilasters. Doorway with pediment on rusticated Doric pilasters.

LINSLADE TUNNEL, N of Leighton Buzzard Station. 1838 by *Robert Stephenson* for the London and Birmingham Railway. Castellated N portals. Central tunnel original and double-track; E tunnel 1859, W tunnel 1879.

LITTLE BARFORD

ST DENYS (Churches Conservation Trust). Norman S doorway, in the arch very elongated lozenges fitted to make a continuous chain similar to chevron. Hoodmould with dogtooth. Also a reset Norman window in the nave on the S side and, genuinely, in the N aisle W wall. Dec N arcade, clunch, of standard elements and no special interest, and chancel arch also Dec. Perp clerestory. Chancel rebuilt in 1869–71 by *A. W. Blomfield*; its S organ chamber and vestry have an arcade of two bays, the pier of quatrefoil type, and its E bay is filled with a screen wall with a very large, bald quatrefoil. Reset in the vestry, an oddly boxed-out PISCINA. – Chancel CEILING with painted decoration of angels by *Heaton, Butler & Bayne*. – Electrifyingly bright TILES and MOSAIC on the E wall by *W. B. Simpson*. – FONT. Probably later C13. The panels of the bowl have just a plain beading. The supports are square with moulded bases and capitals. – SCREEN. Reset in the vestry. One-light divisions. On the dado painted (repainted) big roses. – STAINED GLASS. E window by *Clayton & Bell*, 1869. The tower W window by *Kempe*, 1887. – BRASS (nave floor) to Thomas Perys †1535 and wife (12 in.; 30 cm).

MANOR HOUSE, SW of the church. Mid-C19. Rambling, with mullioned windows and gables, and decayed. Attributed to *John Usher* (R. Wildman) for the Allington family, their arms above the castellated porch.

POWER STATION, ¾ m. N. A gas-fired station of 1994–6, an early example of the combined cycle type in England. Two tall hip-roofed housings for the gas turbines, each with a central flue. Its predecessor was the coal-fired station by *Farmer & Dark* (1945–7; closed 1981).

LITTLE STAUGHTON

ALL SAINTS. The church lies away from the village on the ridge and makes a dramatic picture seen from the N. Limestone and brown cobbles, W tower with recessed spire. Two tiers of lucarnes in alternating directions. The spire, shortened after a lightning strike in 1900, was not rebuilt until 1910 by *W. B. Stonebridge*. He added the N organ chamber in 1924–5. Embattled S side, S aisle, clerestory, porch and chancel all Perp. But the three-bay S arcade is of *c.* 1300, see the quatrefoil piers and their capitals. The E bay is strange, especially the trefoil pier. Double-chamfered arches. Raw Perp nave roof, repaired in 1900 by *Mallows & Grocock* during their restoration of the W end. Good stone corbels, e.g. a bagpiper. In the chancel an angle piscina with a shield and a C14 recess with crocketed gables and buttress shafts, also raw. The tomb-chest has quatrefoils. The coved chancel ceiling looks late C18 (cf. Melchbourne). – PULPIT. C18 with raised panels. – BENCHES. C15? Of the plain panelled type. – SOUTH DOOR. Traceried; C15. – STAINED GLASS. Medieval bits in several windows.

LOWER GRAVENHURST

OUR LADY (Churches Conservation Trust). Of ironstone, W tower with pyramid roof. No aisles. In the chancel is a brass inscription to Sir Robert de Bilhemore 'qe fiet faire cette eglise de nouele'. He died *c.* 1360, and yet the church is still entirely Dec, see especially the S side with cusped Y-tracery and simple flowing tracery. In the chancel SEDILIA and PISCINA and an embattled CRESSET STONE. A second PISCINA in the nave S wall, but a very odd feature is the absence of any chancel arch. Roof with thin tie-beams and kingposts. Altogether a pleasantly unimproved interior, due to the invisible hand of *Albert Richardson* in 1935. – ALTAR. Substantial stone slab with consecration crosses. Recovered from the floor in 1935. – PULPIT. Jacobean, with sounding-board. Originally double-decker, the rest of its woodwork made into a CUPBOARD in 1935. – SCREEN. One-light divisions. Dado with remains of floral painting. HOURGLASS STAND attached. – BENCHES. The majority are original. Ends with plain buttressing. The others are by *A. W. Blomfield*, who made repairs in 1901 (cf. Upper Gravenhurst). – STAINED GLASS. Fragments in one N window, including a head of Christ. – MONUMENT. Benjamin Pigott †1606 and family. The open scrolly pediment cannot be so early. Back wall with kneeling brass figures. They were kept when the monument was remodelled; either *c.* 1650 or perhaps after the death of the youngest son in 1662.

LUTON

0020

INTRODUCTION

Luton, with over 200,000 inhabitants, is by far the largest town in Bedfordshire, but it is a town of very little architectural interest. Not that the reason is its relatively recent growth – there were only about 3000 inhabitants in 1820 and only 36,000 in 1901. There is not merely, except for the parish church, a lack of worthwhile old buildings, but the C19 and early C20 are weak too, though that is almost entirely due to the destruction visited on the town after the mid 1960s which robbed it of many buildings that paid eloquent testament to the town's bumper periods: the mid to later C19 and the interwar years when first straw-plaiting and hatmaking and then engineering dominated. The former trade was well established in the area by the 1680s, but in Luton it became the chief source of wealth around 1820–40, and hatmaking hit its peak finally in the period *c.* 1880–1930.

By this time the town had spread out to engulf several of the rural hamlets. Indeed, the interwar years were a boom time for the town, for although straw hats and felt hats went out, engineering works had taken their place in the economy of Luton, and by 1963 Vauxhall Motors alone employed 25,000. Nevertheless, although Luton prospered in the middle of the last century, it not only demolished its finest Georgian mansion, Stockwood, but also totally neglected its one and only medieval manor house, Moat House (*see* p. 237). It told of the same lack of visual

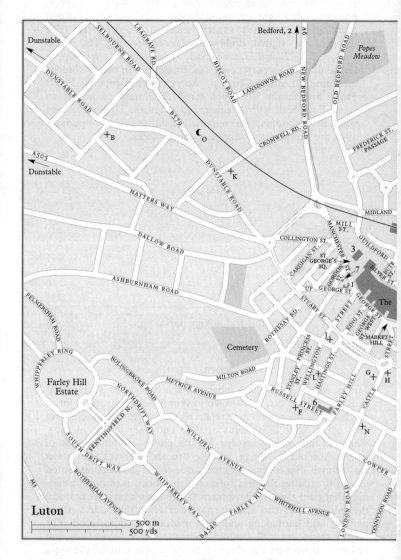

Luton

500 m
500 yds

A St Mary
B All Saints
C St Anne
D St Matthew
E St Paul
F St Saviour
G Our Lady Help
   of Christians (R.C.)
H Union Chapel (former)

J Baptist Church (former)
K Bury Park United Reformed
   Church
L Ebenezer Strict Baptist
   Chapel
M High Town Methodist Church
N Mount Tabor Primitive Methodist
   Church
O Luton Central Masjid

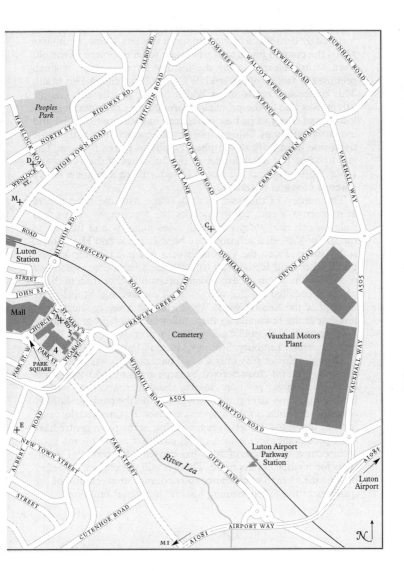

1 Town Hall
2 Art Gallery & Museum
3 Public Library & Theatre
4 University of Bedfordshire
5 UK Centre for Carnival Arts
6 Chapel Street School (former)
7 Tokko Youth Centre

responsibility fifty years ago that the parish church was set against immediately adjoining cooling towers of a power station, now fortunately demolished. Then, to make matters worse, in the late 1960s the council undertook wholesale redevelopment of the old town centre, clearing away the historic street pattern of small premises in favour of an Arndale Centre (now called The Mall). This erased one entire street, Waller Street, which, with George Street, was one of the principal thoroughfares of Luton and the location of many of its best civic, ecclesiastical, commercial and industrial buildings. Other important streets were lost at the same time; one must look to old photographs to gauge the loss. The late C20 was not much kinder to the buildings of the 1920s and 1930s. So throughout the Luton of today there remains a severe absence of visual character.

The pattern of the town is a fan-shape with the town centre at its narrow s end, constrained by the topography of the Lea valley which rises steeply on both sides E and W and funnels to the N. The Victorian suburbs were New Town, S, and High Town, N. By the mid C20 the Vauxhall works (*see* p. 238), airport and parkland around Luton Hoo (q.v.) to the SE and Stockwood (*see* p. 228) to the SW made expansion impossible other than to the N, where it engulfed smaller villages like Leagrave and Stopsley. By the end of the Second World War there was a severe shortage of housing in the town and so there followed major programmes of development, both public and private, with new estates at Farley Hill, Leagrave, Limbury, Stopsley, Vauxhall Park and elsewhere.

Though vehicles play only a small part in the town's industrial life now, it is still characterized by large areas of industrial parks well served by its position close to the M1, the railway and an increasingly busy airport that thrived first on the package-holiday business and then on the low-cost airlines. Business parks came in from the 1980s. Efforts at regeneration in the town centre have been predictably focused on retail, and that rarely means good architecture; the Crash of 2008 has caused a stuttering of intentions for further development. There is still the chance for refurbishment rather than clearance to encourage appreciation of the qualities of the few remaining historic industrial buildings.

RELIGIOUS BUILDINGS

Anglican

ST MARY. The large church of a wealthy town and sizeable parish, indeed the largest medieval church in the Bedford archdeaconry. It is *c.* 182 ft (55 metres) long, externally predominantly Perp. W tower with higher stair-turret and corner turrets, nave and aisles of five bays with two-storey porches, transepts, E of them two prominent chapels, the Hoo Chapel S and Someries (or Wenlock) N, chancel not projecting far beyond them, and two-storey N vestry. But it is also much restored: by *G. E. Street*, principally in 1864–8, but his work continued until 1881 and a multiplicity of other repairs by the early C20 included work by *J. Oldrid Scott*, 1899–1901, and especially *J. Arthur Reeve* in 1904–14. The surfaces are largely knapped flint and stone chequer-work, of clunch in the earlier parts. Flint alone is used in the N and W walls of the N aisle, the adjoining wall of the N transept and in the corresponding part of the S transept. This probably indicates early work, the heightening in stone of the walls of the transepts a particularly obvious revision in the Perp phase. Some of this corresponds with the evidence inside, although the chronology of the church is complex. Even the Perp work in its details suggests more than one phase. A church was built here in 1121–37, with a central tower. The oldest features are inside: the pointed arch from S aisle to S transept, simply and only slightly chamfered, with small moulded stop chamfers to the S respond, say of *c.* 1180, and the arch from N aisle to N transept with three orders of shafts and lush, mature stiff-leaf capitals, i.e. of *c.* 1230. So the church already then had transepts and substantial aisles, as the flint walling outside suggested. Of the C13 chancel part of one shaft with capital of some wall arcading has been exposed on the N side, E of the door to the later chapel. Of the same period perhaps, the remains of a string course around the chancel's E end.

Much was done in the early C14, which must have been occasioned by the collapse of the central tower in 1336. The present crossing piers may incorporate earlier masonry, but the tower was not replaced and instead the W tower was begun. It is indeed in its lower parts Dec, see the fine W doorway with fleurons in the arch mouldings and the W window with cusped intersecting tracery. Dec also the small aisle W windows and the tall arch to the nave with multiple mouldings, its responds have a chamfer with an ogee chamfer-stop, and close leaf in the capitals: on the S capital organized symmetrical patterns but to the N capital naturalistic oak leaves. The same foliage is found on the hoodmould stops of the N transept window, though the window tracery itself is clearly Perp. The heightening of the transepts must date from the same period as the tower arch for it is determined by the remaking of the whole crossing with its trefoil piers; the ogee chamfer-stop appears again on the flat buttresses on the inner faces of the W piers, which also have a broach at the base. Of the same time are the two bays between N transept and Wenlock (Someries) Chapel – double-chamfered arches, quatrefoil pier and trefoil responds – though they must relate to the medieval chapel dedicated to St Catherine. A little later the two bays between S transept and Hoo Chapel with octagonal pier and arches with sunk quadrant mouldings and hollow chamfers. The semi-octagonal responds also have filleted shafts in their jambs. Inside, in the N and S walls are piscina, indicating a division into two chapels. It is just one bay deep, with its own entrance from the churchyard. Dec again the pretty S aisle PISCINA with trail of ballflower, and the EASTER SEPULCHRE in the chancel with fleurons in a moulding; and Dec finally the N vestry, a room

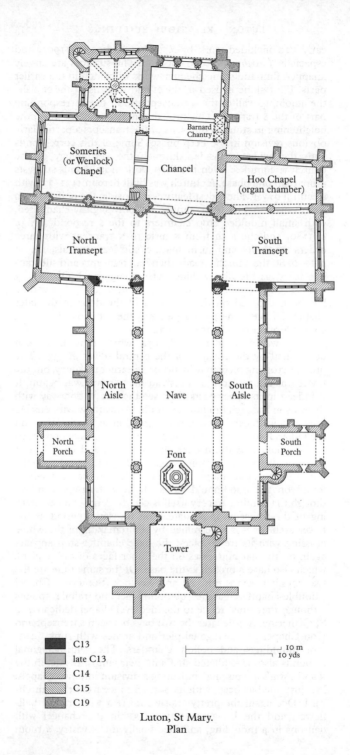

Vestry

Barnard Chantry

Someries (or Wenlock) Chapel

Chancel

Hoo Chapel (organ chamber)

North Transept

South Transept

North Aisle

Nave

South Aisle

North Porch

South Porch

Font

Tower

C13
late C13
C14
C15
C19

10 m
10 yds

Luton, St Mary.
Plan

with a round pier in the middle and each bay vaulted with diagonal and ridge-ribs. The ribs have one long chamfer. But this was formerly in the position where the Wenlock Chapel stands and must therefore have been reconstructed here in the C15. It blocks the chancel N window. Inside it now has a fireplace with a very French Gothic hood. Is it *Street*?

The arcades between nave and aisles are a problem. The trefoil W responds with their ogee chamfer-stops on both sides belong to the tower, i.e. the early C14. But then, on the N side, three piers were erected with the side to the nave and aisle in a continuous chamfer. Springing from their N side, with a typically early C14 dying moulding, also transverse arches with single chamfers. The rest here and the whole S side have normal octagonal piers and normal double-chamfered arches. Over the S aisle again transverse arches. The NW parts come, so it seems, after the responds, but before the rest, the rest being Perp in character and therefore consistent with the fenestration of aisles and clerestory. The roofs of the church are also Perp, that over the nave and crossing reconstructed but contemporary with the addition of the clerestory. In the gable over the chancel arch, behind the roof truss, is the very surprising feature of a window, reopened in 1906, whose lights correspond with the tracery of the truss. The Perp has also contributed more to the interior than has so far been noted. The major contribution is the splendid WENLOCK SCREEN, the two-bay opening between chancel and Someries Chapel (on the monuments, *see* below). It is very high and two tiers in depth, of a super arch divided into two arches over the tomb-chests with open tracery in the spandrel between. The reveals and the arches all panelled and with quite elaborate, though not refined, details above the arches and a cresting. On the chapel side a fine feathered headdress above Wenlock's arms and those of his wife Elizabeth, heir of Sir John Drayton. The date given is *c.* 1460, for Sir John (later Lord) Wenlock, who died at Tewkesbury in 1471. Opposite, inserted below a chancel S window, is the small sunk CHANTRY CHAPEL of Richard Barnard, vicar from 1477 to 1492, a charming piece with three arches, joined by castellated capitals without shafts, under a shallow gable containing his rebus in the spandrels, and inside an ornate vault on angel corbels and a separate entrance from outside through a lobby. In the C18 it is recorded as containing an effigy. Inside it a two-light window and piscina. E of the Barnard Chapel are the SEDILIA, with four ogee arches and shields including the arms of Abbot Wheathampstead of St Albans, who held the advowson, below the crested top. That would date the sedilia to *c.* 1420–40. Four seats is unusual; perhaps the E one was over a piscina originally. The narrow arch from chancel to the Hoo Chapel is also Perp.

Finally the principal contributions of the C19 and C20. By *Street* is the E wall of the chancel in the E.E. style, of three stepped lancets with dogtooth. It replaced a late C18 round-arched window (in the C18 the Hoo Chapel seems to have

19

provided a private passage for the Marquess of Bute to arrive at his pew, which filled the chancel arch). Chancel roof redone in 1912, the corbels carved by *J. E. Taylorson*. He also made the statues in the niches of the tower, introduced in 1911–12. The SOMERIES CHAPEL was completely overhauled in 1913–14 as a memorial to Sir Julius Wernher, after the organ, here since the 1860s, had been moved into the Hoo Chapel. The architect was *W. H. Romaine Walker*, who was also then engaged at Luton Hoo. His is the handsome Dec stone REREDOS, STALLS and ROOF.

FURNISHINGS. Those of the Someries Chapel have been mentioned. – FONT. Octagonal, of Purbeck marble, *c.* 1330–40, with blind arcaded sides and faces in the spandrels. Of about the same date, the majestic stone FONT ENCLOSURE, also octagonal, with thin pinnacled buttresses, eight richly crocketed steep gables, battlemented openings around the sides above a dado of blind gabled arches and fleurons. It once had a door on the E face to complete the enclosure.* Inside, a vault with eight radial ribs and eight ridge-ribs. Big figural boss of a dragon and lion. In total it stands nearly 20 ft (7 metres) high. It is still in its original position (although in the early C19 it was taken to the S aisle). – SCREENS. Between S transept and Hoo Chapel, erected in 1867 by J. Shaw Leigh of Luton Hoo. Two light openings, doors l. and r., painted dado from the rood screen which had been taken down in 1855. – Between N transept and Someries Chapel, a richer screen, but made up of various parts and also over-restored. In the dado, linenfold panels, at the top broad cornice and cresting with birds and beasts. It must be early C16 and is said to have first been taken to the chapel at Luton Hoo in the C17 but returned by the 1st Marquess of Bute for the Hoo Chapel and placed in its present position in 1867. – STALLS. In the chancel, with heads carved on the upper armrests. The other stalls are of 1867–8 with poppyheads. – The chancel was lavishly refitted in 1881–4; the alabaster E wall survives, and the REREDOS (Last Supper, after da Vinci, by *Salviati*) and rich alabaster and mosaic PULPIT, both by *Jones & Willis*. In the blocked N window a MOSAIC of the Three Maries by *Capello* of Chelsea, but the rest of the mosaic and stencilled wall decoration was swept away in 1959 during reordering by *G. G. Pace*; his are the spiky LIGHT FITTINGS and the GATES to the Barnard Chapel. – DOORS. Original SOUTH DOOR. With splendid tracery, including a mouchette wheel; probably C14. The inner NORTH AND SOUTH DOORS are of etched glass by *Tracey Sheppard*, 2002. – EAGLE LECTERN. Handsome brass-type in C13 style, of 1883. – STAINED GLASS. Original fragments in the Wenlock Chapel E window, including four full figures. C15? – Much C19 glass too and the lion's share by *Alexander Gibbs*, 1874–86. The earliest

___
*Professor Achim Timmermann points to the details as evidence of the mason's familiarity with the work of William Ramsey, the king's master mason 1336–49 (cf. e.g. the gables of Archbishop Stratford's monument, Canterbury).

is the chancel E window, in a convincingly C13 style of medallions depicting the life of Christ (the later chancel and Hoo
Chapel windows show His miracles). In the S aisle, Old Testament prophets, in the N aisle the Apostles. – One large N
transept window by *J. Powell & Sons*, 1897. – The three in the
Someries Chapel are of 1914, all by *Carl Almquist* for *Shrigley
& Hunt*, with large Old Testament figures and depictions of
their attributes below. – The tower window and the clerestory
windows are by *Horace Rambart*, 1893, the latter of the coats
of arms of the Anglican dioceses, though the S windows clearly
altered by *Pace*. – In the S transept, the Magnificat window, of
outstanding quality by *Alan Younger*, 1979, with the same tense
structural geometry of black hatching as Pace's designs overlaid with abstract flowing colours.

MONUMENTS. There are so many that they are to be regis-
tered by position. – In the chancel, reset in the arches of the
Wenlock Screen, William Wenlock, Master of the Farley Hospital at Luton, †1392. Large effigy on a big clunch tomb-chest
with inscription and two tiers of quatrefoil panels. It is worth
looking for the abstract pattern of his robe, seen from the E.
– Brass of a widow, probably Alice Rotherham wife of John
Rotherham of Someries (†1492) *c.* 1490. Purbeck marble
tomb-chest with cusped lozenges, inlaid effigy, 3 ft (91 cm)
long under elaborate but fragmentary canopy. – In the Someries Chapel, two late C15 or early C16 tomb recesses, one with
the chest with lozenges and brasses formerly against the back
wall, the other of the familiar Purbeck type with a recess with
flat panelled top and panelled sides. Other floor brasses are
remounted on the walls. – Brass of Hugo atte Spettyl †1416,
his son and (originally) wife. The figure is 13½ in. (34 cm)
long. – A husband with two wives (20-in.; 50 cm) figures,
c. 1525 (E wall). – A priest (18 in.; 45 cm), a layman (20 in.;
50 cm) (N wall). By the rood stair, a civilian (18 in.; 45 cm)
and a lady (24 in.; 61 cm).* – Lt Alex Pigott Wernher †1916.
Marble and brass with a wreath. – In the N transept (W wall),
lively brasses of John Acworth †1513 and wives. The figures are
24½ in. (62 cm) long. Enormous helm with cresting behind his
head. Along with Thomas Rotheram bishop of Lincoln, he was
a founder member of the Luton Guild, or Fraternity of Holy
Trinity, who formed in 1474 and paid for two chantry priests.
Below are members of the Guild. – In the N aisle W wall,
Thomas Waller †1845. Signed: *Pietro Costa* Florentine sculpl,
1847. Urn on a high pedestal, a genius on the l., a mourning
woman on the r. – In the S aisle two C14 tomb recesses, one
very low, containing a CROSS SLAB, with double omega pattern
on the shaft, the other with a four-centred arch and in it the
effigy of a priest, very badly preserved. – In the S transept on
the floor, brasses to John Sylam †1513 and wives (29 in.;
73 cm). – Brass to Edward Sheffield, priest, †1525–6 (24 in.;
61 cm). – Rev. James O'Neill by *F. W. Pomeroy*, 1898. A fine

*Two HELMS formerly in the Wenlock Chapel have been removed.

piece with his portrait bust in a roundel. Classical surround.
O'Neill instigated the major C19 restorations of the church.

In the churchyard, E side, a slate HEADSTONE with characteristically fine lettering, for James Pickard, 'a native of Leicester' who died 1787 while working on the dome of Luton Hoo.

E of the church, the CHURCH HALL etc. by *Pace*, 1969, one
of his last works and quite a forceful but sympathetic composition, with a long monopitch roofline and walls of dark local
brick, knapped flint and grids of concrete slots for windows.

ALL SAINTS, Shaftesbury Road, Bury Park. 1922–3 by *W. D.
Caröe*. More conventional than Caröe was earlier in life, and
intentionally so, for his original plans of 1916 were considered
too expensive. Only the big triple bellcote remains in one's
memory. Light plum brick, with tile creasing. The fenestration
Dec, Perp and even Elizabethan. The nave and aisles are of
nearly equal height. Damaged by a fire 1961 and partly rebuilt
at the E end. Spacious arcades of tile arches dying into piers
clad in panelling with tracery. The S chapel recalls the younger
Caröe: low, under a ceiled timber roof with curved braces and
pegged joints. – Contemporary FITTINGS by Caröe, again
simplified Gothic. – STAINED GLASS. – E window, 1954 by *John
E. Crawford*. – S chapel E window, 1934 by *C. E. Moore*.

Attached to the S, the mission HALL of 1907 by *J. R. Brown
& Son*.

Former CHRIST CHURCH, Upper George Street. Originally of
1856–60 by *H. Elliott*, but nothing of his church survived a
disastrous fire in the 1980s. What has been incorporated into
new offices by *Covell Matthews Wheatley*, 1988, is the clumsy
tower, S aisle and S transept of 1864–6 by *George Halton*, and
the S chapel added in 1881 by *G. Vialls* (whose chancel of this
date was also destroyed). All brick, the details in the style of
1300.

CHRIST CHURCH, Hancock Drive, Bushmead. 2002–3 by *SDA
Architects*. For the new housing area. A brick octagon with
curved outer wall in lighter brick embracing the approach to
the entrance. Internally divided by curved wall into meeting
rooms etc. and auditorium-type worship space.

HOLY TRINITY, Trinity Road, Biscot. 1867–8 by *T. Nicholson* of
Hereford. The first new Anglican church for Luton's rural
hamlets (cf. St Thomas, Stopsley, below). Yellow brick, red
brick and stone. Dec details. Bellcote. (– STAINED GLASS. By
H. Blanchford of Exeter, 1918–20.)

ST ANDREW, Blenheim Crescent, Biscot. 1931–2 by *Giles Gilbert
Scott*. A powerful, mute presence in the interwar suburbs. Built
of very narrow (1⅝ in. thick) bricks, light purple-grey (probably local), and Spanish tile roof. With a tall, plain, square and
massive W tower, implicitly Gothic, with angle-buttressed and
battlemented top, its face recessed under a giant chamfered
arch. Beautiful ironwork to the door. Big solid sloping buttresses through nave and aisle without set-offs but with tumbled
brickwork, narrow aisle passages, and clerestory windows in
groups of eight arched lights. Inside, prominent transverse

pointed concrete arches and narrow passage aisles behind plain round arches, the dark render of the walls creating an exceptionally sombre effect. Green and black geometric pattern floor. The w end has been subdivided by glass screens and rooms inserted into the aisles. – STAINED GLASS. In the tower baptistery and transept chapel. By *J. N. Lawson* of *Goddard & Gibbs*, 1969, 1970 and 1973.

ST ANNE, Crawley Green Road, Hart Hill/St Anne's Hill. 1937–8 by *Franklin & Briars* of Luton. Grey brick, Gothic only in its essentials. Externally a traditional plan of buttressed nave and chancel with bellcote at the division. Inside, however, the chancel can be separated from the nave/hall to the w. The pointed chancel arch rises directly from the floor. Peculiar ORGAN CASE framing the sanctuary of *c.* 1950.

ST AUGUSTINE OF CANTERBURY, Icknield Way, Limbury. 1964–5 by *Caroe & Partners*. Still very traditional, the chapels with tall vertical windows splayed from the sides. (The chancel arch is simply two columns. – STAINED GLASS. N chapel. 2006 by *Michael Stokes*.)

ST CHRISTOPHER, Stockingstone Road, Round Green. Successor to a mission church in an expanding area of Stopsley parish. By *Albert Richardson*, planned in 1931* but only partly built in 1936–7. Chancel added 1958–9 by *Richardson & Houfe*, but the intended transepts and a tower with spire were never realized. Pleasant, though very reactionary by the date of completion. Chancel, nave and aisles under one roof, of slightly cranked profile, with dormers, and the porch in a tall projection. Fine, thin local grey bricks are used throughout, including the windows; the side windows are divided by a thick stone mullion under deep segmental arches. Brick chimney with gabled top at the side and a bellcote below the chancel gable. Internally, a roof supported on pairs of wooden crucks, not on the walls. This is the same delight in timber roof construction one finds in e.g. Richardson's Holy Cross, Greenford, West London. The brick chancel arch rises directly from the floor. – Nice light oak FURNISHINGS in Georgian style. There were always chairs instead of pews. – STAINED GLASS. E window, 1996 by *Peter Archer* (*Chapel Studio*).

CHURCH HALL, adjacent. 1935, also by *Richardson*. Weatherboarded with a Venetian window, and another good structure for the gambrel roof. Slightly spoiled by a recent brick extension.

ST FRANCIS, Hollybush Road/Carteret Road, Vauxhall Park. 1959–60 by *P. Dunham, Widdup & Harrison*. A-frame, of concrete portal frames encompassing nave and aisles. The MURAL behind the altar is 'To the End of Time' by *Mary Adshead*, 1962. Expressionist but of a distinctly post-postwar kind, not least in the colouring and the tormented Crucifixion overlaid by the symbols of the Evangelists and, *inter alia*, astronauts.

*A first sketch design envisaged a church of distinctly Scandinavian character with a flat w front stepping up to a tower with triple bellcote.

– FONT. A copper bowl set in slate on triangular concrete supports.

ST HUGH, High Street, Lewsey. 1966–7 by *Black, Bayes, Gibson & Partners*. E end under a monopitch roof with STAINED GLASS clerestory. – FONT. From Maulden, q.v.

ST JOHN THE BAPTIST, Rotheram Avenue, Farley Hill. 1968–9 by *David Sutcliffe* of Hatfield. FITTINGS of the same date. – STAINED GLASS. Dalle-de-verre by *Joseph Nuttgens*, 1969.

ST LUKE, High Street, Leagrave. A design made impressive by the use of a sloping site. By *Seely & Paget*, 1955–6, and 'in its architectural style startlingly out of touch with the age' was Pevsner's view. But what is the style? Certainly it has a strangely secular-looking façade, closer to the manner of a C17 or C18 Northern European guild hall, with a deep tiled roof topped by a stone cross of Baroque style and two storeys of round arches in the centre, at ground floor forming an open arcade, between splayed wings with pedimented ends. The upper cross-windows light the choir gallery along the N side of the nave. The wings contain meeting rooms, vestry and the Lady Chapel. Inside, plain brick walls, windows in arches along the S wall only, and subtle C18-style decoration. – PAINTING. Behind the altar, filling the wall. 1955 by *Norman Blamey*, commissioned by the architects. An impressive Christ enthroned and holding the Cross, attended by kneeling figures of bishops, priests and deacons. The influence of Stanley Spencer is very clear. – STAINED GLASS. Lady Chapel. 1960 by *M. C. Farrar Bell* (*Clayton & Bell*).

ST MATTHEW, Wenlock Street. 1875–6 by *G. Vialls* and *J. R. Brown*. A very large plantation from St Mary for High Town. Dignified, though dull. The scale is precisely what one expects in Victorian towns. All brick, without a tower, but a double bellcote instead over the W end. Small lancets, aisles, transepts and polygonal apse. Cavernous interior, again almost entirely bare brick but with richly crocketed stone capitals to the circular arcade piers. Odd feature of ringed shafts to the chancel arch. Raised sanctuary. – PULPIT. A handsome stone piece with good wrought-iron stair. E.E. style, signed by *W. C. Haselgrove*, 1884. – REREDOS. Caen stone with cusped gables, Sicilian marble cross and terracotta vines and wheat, 1885. – STAINED GLASS. E windows, three figurative by *John N. Lawson* (*Faithcraft*), 1963–4. S aisle, abstract by *Keith New*, 1963.

ST PAUL, New Town Street. 1990–1, succeeding the church in Hibbert Street of 1890 by *T. N. Laslett* (dem. 1990). Some furnishings from the old church include STAINED GLASS by the *Glasscraft Guild*, 1927.

ST SAVIOUR, Russell Street. Built in two phases by *J. T. Micklethwaite & Somers Clarke*, in 1897–8 (N aisle and Lady Chapel), producing the good view along the street with even windows high up, and 1905 (nave, chancel and part of a raised S aisle which remains incomplete). Brick, without a tower, but originally a W bellcote. Big, as Anglican mission churches to poor districts tended to be. Dec tracery. Wide, low nave, piers and arches typical of *c.* 1900. – COMMUNION RAIL, Arts and Crafts Gothic, and the secular mid-C17-style STALLS both of 1906. – REREDOS. *c.* 1916. Lavish Gothic panelling, painted, and canopied centre. Carved Adoration and top tier of the Apostles. Four larger saints added *c.* 1930. – SCREEN (Chancel), 1916. Perp-style with a sumptuously carved frieze and cresting. The N chapel SCREEN, with wreaths and ribbon patterns, is *c.* 1918 (war memorial). – STAINED GLASS. E window by *Terence D. Randall (Faithcraft)*, 1948. – The original mission room of 1877 is now the CHURCH HALL. It was given a chancel and organ chamber in 1889–92 by *J. R. Brown & Son* of Luton.

ST THOMAS, High Street, Stopsley. 1860–1 by *H. J. Pearson* of Luton. The setting is still a reminder of its rural origins. E.E. style with a shallow chancel, aisleless nave with a bellcote, transeptal organ chamber. Brick with some flint, the bellcote stone. – ALTAR with a front of wreaths in roundels. (TILES by *Maw & Co.*) – STAINED GLASS. E window, 1919, by *H. Blanchford* (cf. Holy Trinity above); the Crucifixion with St Nicholas and St Alban. The small upper lights are unusually blocked with knapped flint. N window (St Luke) by *W. Lawson (Faithcraft)*, 1939. Extended (Church Room etc.) in 2010.

Roman Catholic

OUR LADY HELP OF CHRISTIANS (R.C.), Castle Street. 1910, replacing an iron church of 1886. Simplified Gothic. Tall nave. Restored in 2006 by *Greenhalgh & Williams*. Excellent redecoration, especially the ROOD SCREEN behind the altar, with doors l. and r., gilded and painted with angels and diaper patterns by *Howard & Bellion* with *Anthony Delarue*.

ST JOSEPH (R.C.), Gardenia Avenue. By *J. E. Sterrett*, 1958–60. In the brick Early Christian style which was popular and conservative twenty years earlier. 'For 1960 it is almost beyond belief', thought Pevsner, but it is seriously done and inside has a fine unornamented interior of round arches to the arcades, and semi-dome over the apse pierced by round arch openings.

Nonconformist chapels*

Wesley first preached at Luton in 1772 and within twenty years of the Toleration Act Nonconformity was strong. The Primitive Methodists made a particularly strong showing. A large number

---

*The following Nonconformist chapels and churches have been demolished since the first edition of this guide: CONGREGATIONAL CHURCH, Stuart Street, 1865–6 by *J. Tarring*, and the former WESLEYAN CHAPEL, Chapel Street, 1851–2 by *W. W. Pocock*.

of chapels remain, though still only a minority of the C19 representation, and sadly none of the largest examples survives in the town centre. Of the rest a selection is merited.

Former UNION CHAPEL, Castle Street. Opened in 1837. One of the best buildings of Luton. Three bays with three-bay pediment and an entrance at *piano nobile* level with giant Greek Doric columns *in antis*. Egyptianizing front windows and door. All stuccoed. The interior was already remodelled by 1844 to accommodate large numbers and redone in 1878. It is now flats. – Large former SUNDAY SCHOOLS and lecture hall of 1892 behind, with an Italianate pedimented front, spoiled by the overbearing attic storey added on conversion

Former BAPTIST CHAPEL, Wellington Street. Converted to flats, called The Spires though it has none. Founded 1847. Tripartite façade with pinnacles to the buttresses and originally lancets but remodelled with Perp windows in 1888–9 by *J. R. Brown & Son*. Much more impressive SCHOOL AND INSTITUTE behind by *G. & R. P. Baines*, 1908, in their customarily extravagant Free Perp with Art Nouveau inflections.

BURY PARK UNITED REFORMED CHURCH, Waldeck Road. Originally Congregational. Founded 1895 in the part now used as the school (enlarged 1916), but the principal part is a lavish Free Gothic by *G. & R. Baines*, 1903, red brick and terracotta.

EBENEZER STRICT BAPTIST CHAPEL, Hastings Street. 1853. Stuccoed front with a three-bay pediment over three round arches. Doors with console heads l. and r. Unaltered, even the gates and railings by *Brown & Green*, ironfounders of Luton.

HIGH TOWN METHODIST CHURCH, High Town Road. Two chapels, side by side, the first of 1852 by *Henry Holyoak*, after the first Primitive Methodist chapel was demolished for the Midland Railway. Built of Beart's patent yellow gault brick and red brick with a small pediment. Next to it the much larger successor of 1897 by *J. D. & S. D. Mould* of Manchester (Kelly). It is the best late C19 chapel in Luton. Italian Renaissance with nicely contrasting Luton grey brick, stone and rubbed red dressings. Large arched window under a pediment and towers flanking with aedicules on the pilasters and arched windows with Lombardic tracery. The l. tower ends in a handsome cupola with a dome roof. Paired entrances in arches carried on short square columns. The flanks curve in at the w end to meet the flat projection containing the organ inside. Nice circular stair-tower to the gallery. (Fine interior, with a horseshoe gallery, curved benches and a rostrum pulpit before the organ.)

MOUNT TABOR PRIMITIVE METHODIST CHURCH (now Luton Christian Union), Hibbert Street/Castle Street. 1897–8 by *J. Kerridge & Sons* of Wisbech. Large Geometric Gothic window in the front, buttresses with ribbed spirelets. SUNDAY SCHOOLS of 1905 by *Moulds & Porrit*.

ST MARGARET METHODIST, St Margaret's Avenue/Montrose Avenue. 1935–7 by *Franklin & Briars*. Church and hall in parallel with covered way between. Purple brick chequered with grey, sparely detailed. Sharp gables to front and transepts. (STAINED GLASS. W window 1969 by *H. Warren Wilson* for *Lowndes & Drury*.)

CALVARY CHURCH OF GOD IN CHRIST, Dunstable Road, Bury Park. *See* p. 236.

SIKH TEMPLE, Cardigan Street. Formerly Primitive Methodist. 1880–1. Brick with pressed terracotta tympanum over the entrance. Arched windows. Pediment overall.

LUTON CENTRAL MASJID, Westbourne Road. 1981–2 by the *John Manning Partnership*. Large, and certainly a landmark in Bury Park, it is among the earliest purpose-built mosques in England. All brick, with tall chamfered arches, and a dome.

CHURCH CEMETERY (Anglican), Crawley Green Road. Successor to St Mary's churchyard. 1860. Lodge and chapel, minimal Gothic, some polychromy. GATES by *Brown & Green* of Luton.

CEMETERY (Nonconformist), Rothesay Road. Founded by the General Cemetery Co., 1854. LODGE and GATES by *John Cumberland* of Luton. Chapel rebuilt 1897 by *Albert E. Smith*.

PUBLIC BUILDINGS

TOWN HALL, George Street. 1934–6 by *Bradshaw, Gass & Hope* of Bolton, who won the design in competition in 1930 for a long-overdue successor to the hall of 1847, burnt down by rioters in 1919. 'Proud, but lifeless. Portland stone, the fag-end of the Classical Re-Revival' was Pevsner's opinion. But it is the one really successful building in the town centre. The plan is a truncated wedge, the main front subtly curved inward to a two-storey pedimented portico of fluted Ionic columns *in antis*, beneath the symmetrically placed clocktower, 144 ft

Luton, Town Hall, 1934–6.
Perspective

(43 metres) high, topped by a belfry under a squashed dome. The elevations are gradually stepped back up the low attic, the proportions only slightly spoiled by a later mansard. Minimal decoration. The interior is in the same impressive but restrained manner. Entrance hall with double staircase and bronze balustrade of rose and thistle. In the Committee Room along the front, a fine circular ceiling with emblems of the trades involved in the hall's construction. The adjoining rooms have good Art Deco clocks. The U-plan Council Chamber has a circular top light and square piers carrying the public gallery round the bow. There was originally a small concert hall beneath the chamber, part of an intention to build a much larger complex for entertainments on the site now occupied by the OFFICES of c. 1980.

CROWN COURT, Market Hill. See Perambulation 1 below.

ART GALLERY AND MUSEUM, Wardown Park. This is WARDOWN, a wealthy, but uninspired, gabled brick house of 1875–7 for Frank Scargill, a solicitor in the town. The architect was T. C. Sorby, who is otherwise known primarily as a designer of court houses in England. The tender was £10,070 (GS). The materials are dark brick, dressings of Mansfield stone and mouldings of a bright red including the sculpture of the porte cochère with small heads of Disraeli, Dickens etc. Tall roofs and vertiginous Neo-Tudor chimneys. Some rooms inside with florid plaster ceilings. Remarkable timber-framed WELL HOUSE and pretty thatched SUMMERHOUSE. At the entrance from New Bedford Road, a LODGE of the same date as the house. The park, through which the River Lee runs, was purchased for the town in 1904. Sweet BOWLING CLUB HOUSE of about that time, a single storey with short columns along the front and arched pediment. In the park, the LAKE is crossed by a SUSPENSION BRIDGE.

PUBLIC LIBRARY AND THEATRE, St George's Square. By the Borough Architect, M. H. G. Blackman. Planned in 1958, built 1960–2, still somewhat in the abstractly composed Scandinavian style (Sweden's libraries were visited by the designers in 1959). White stone with grids of windows, recessed ground floor, brown brick upper storeys and a curved roof expressing the theatre. Remarkably large, and pleasant externally and internally, where the reading room is made double height above the first floor with a gallery. Along one side of this a SCREEN of Swedish glass, provided by SKF (see Britannia House p. 239), engraved on the theme of the development of writing and printing. In the foyer a didactic contemporary SCULPTURE: 'He that Loves Reading Has Everything within His Reach' by Uli Nimptsch.

UNIVERSITY OF BEDFORDSHIRE, Park Square. Originally the College of Technology (by Norman & Dawbarn, 1957–9); 'not a memorable building, though reasonable and not marred by gimmicks' was Pevsner's view. An informal plan of two blocks with a bridging link, steel-framed and brick-clad with large panels of glazing and concrete elevations. A number of supplements since 1993 when this became the University of Luton and since 2006 as part of the University of Bedfordshire. Facing the W tower of St Mary's church, the LEARNING RESOURCE CENTRE, 1997 by the *Charter Partnership*, a two-storey curve of glass curtain walling behind full-height columns. S of this, the five-storey CAMPUS CENTRE, for the students' union, lecture theatre etc., by *RMJM*, 2008–10, of dark grey engineering brick contrasting with yellow and here and there cladding of golden mesh. Inside, a lobby/atrium with rooms on the upper floors and stair projecting into the space within curved shells of timber-cladding. Belonging to a second phase, the POSTGRADUATE CENTRE of 2011–13, the top storeys restlessly angled. A commendable attempt to create some sense of place and enclosure around the churchyard's E side. Beyond is the STUDENT VILLAGE (FITZROY COURT) by *O'Connell East Architects*, 2009. Mostly slab blocks but also a drum of flats, with the familiar preference of the date for highly patterned façades composed of varied materials, here brick, render and silvery metallic cladding.

UK CENTRE FOR CARNIVAL ARTS, Vicarage Street, adjoining   65
the university campus. By *Ash Sakula Architects*, 2009, an appropriately free-wheeling design around a courtyard for varied uses: workshops, performance, offices, café etc. The external elevations mix grey brick patterned with white around the windows and corners but to the courtyard a much more varied palette of profiled metal cladding, timber, polycarbonate sheeting, bamboo, foil and even astroturf, all consistent with a DIY carnival aesthetic.

SCHOOLS. The majority lie in the suburban areas. Few are of special note. The Luton School Board architect was *J. R. Brown*. The earliest survivor is CHAPEL STREET SCHOOL, 1880. A long single storey with lancet windows in pairs under rubbed red arches, i.e. churchier in style than schools would become later. In the main projections the windows are stepped above a stone transom and set against a super arch of terracotta diapering. The former SCHOOL in Dallow Street (now Sikh Gurdwara), *c.* 1900, and BEECH HILL SCHOOL, Dunstable Road, of 1910 are good later examples with shaped gables.

BEECHWOOD PRIMARY SCHOOL, Linden Road, Leagrave. 1937–8 by *J. W. Tomlinson*, Borough Engineer, and *W. E. Humphrey*, Architectural Assistant. Quad plan of a courtyard surrounded by covered walks, but at the W end a nursery section with two wings ending in streamlined bows. Their windows could be opened fully to a garden.

DENBIGH HIGH SCHOOL, Alexandra Road. 1930 by *Brown & Parrot* as the Girls' High School. Serious Baroque in red brick with an implied stone portico, eleven-bay wings and pavilions at the ends. E-plan front to the rear with the hall at the centre and wings with arcaded cloisters. Later additions.

BARNFIELD SOUTH ACADEMY, Rotheram Avenue, Farley Hill. A very large secondary school of *c.* 2010 by *Perkins Ogden Architects*. Front block of cubic elements in differently coloured renders within a controlling frame of white. These project above a glazed ground floor. Three lower blocks behind in red brick facing shared gardens. The BARNFIELD WEST ACADEMY, Lewsey, by *architecturePLB*, 2011, explores rather similar ideas of planning with a large top-lit atrium as the core.

SIXTH FORM COLLEGE, Bradgers Hill Road. By *KSS*, 2008–10. Yellow brick with brises-soleil. Central block for administration forming a core surrounded by 'streets' serving four wings for teaching.[*]

STOCKWOOD PARK. The house built by the Crawleys *c.* 1740 was sold postwar and pulled down by Luton Council in 1965. The WALLED GARDEN remains, along with the mid-C18 STABLES, red brick with a pediment over the central arch, converted as part of the DISCOVERY CENTRE by *Buttress Fuller Alsop Williams*, 2006. Pleasant, self-effacing shop and café, light brick. Larger exhibition hall on a cranked plan with cupola. The IMPROVEMENT GARDEN is by *Ian Hamilton Finlay*, *c.* 1992, an informal landscape of plantings and sculpture with complex meanings largely derived from Ovid's *Metamorphoses*. Other features include a humorous 'flock' of recumbent stones, like sheep that have escaped across the park's ha-ha.

TOKKO YOUTH CENTRE, Gordon Street. By *Astudio*, 2012–13. An elevation of two distinct elements, partly adhering to the street line at ground floor, but the upper storeys twisted at an angle. External cladding of vertical strips. A series of small studios inside.

CENTRE FOR CARNIVAL ARTS. *See* University of Bedfordshire, above.

GENERAL POST OFFICE, Dunstable Road. 1957–8 by *T. W. Winterburn* of the *Ministry of Works*. A sensible modern job for the date. Curtain walling, pilotis and an elongated drum on the top.

LUTON & DUNSTABLE HOSPITAL, Dunstable Road. The original part, by *Parrot & Dunham*, 1936–9, was textbook hygienic interwar design, of two flat-roofed ward blocks with sun balconies, linked by an administration wing. This is hardly recognizable now owing to remodelling and many incoherent later additions.

ST MARY'S NURSING HOME, Dunstable Road. The former workhouse, or part of it, of 1836 by *John Williams*. Hip-roofed centre, lower wings. Gibbs surround to the door. The rear wings (dem.) originally formed a cross-in-square plan. Adjoining this, the former BUTE HOSPITAL, 1882.

STATION, Midland Road. 1937–40 by *W. H. Hamlyn*, Chief Architect to the London, Midland & Scottish Railway. One of

---

[*]Its predecessor, built as the Boys' Grammar School, is worth recalling. It was of 1936 by G. L. *Turok*, the Hungarian-born and Viennese-trained assistant of *Marshall & Tweedy*, and a progressive design in brick with thin concrete cornices and flat roofs. One long classroom wing terminated in a clocktower at an acute angle to a splay-fronted hall with curved ends (W. G. Newton was the assessor for the competition and it was not unlike his own school designs).

the relatively few stations of between the wars which were designed in the international style of the 1930s. The brick and the block grouping here derive probably from Holland. The clarity of composition is marred by a later C20 bridge. LUTON AIRPORT PARKWAY STATION, 1999 by *Devereux Architects*, is much less interesting.

AIRPORT. Opened 1938 by the Borough Council and expanded in the early 1960s as charter airlines made foreign package holidays affordable (the headquarters of Thomson, Monarch and easyJet are at Luton). The TERMINAL BUILDING of this period (1964–6 by *Yorke, Rosenberg & Mardall*) was a sound, simple and logical design, all one-storeyed and under one big, flat roof. An international terminal was added in 1985 but shows only in a small way following complete replacement in 1998–9, the original concept by *Foster & Partners* but carried out as a design-and-build scheme by *Bechtel*. This has all functions of the two-storey terminal contained under one big curved aerofoil roof with an angled façade to the airfield, glazed for the departure lounge on the upper floor. Additions in 2004–5 by *McAlister, Armstrong & Partners*, who propose further expansion in 2013.

WATER TOWERS. Built in 1898 after Luton and Stopsley suffered a severe drought. The tower on WEST HILL ROAD, by *Henry T. Hare*, is one of the most enjoyable buildings of Luton (now converted as a house). Decidedly Arts and Crafts and resourcefully handled, roughly square, with curved buttresses, brick walls striped with stone and especially at the top where balconies with water spouts are set under segmental arches. The eaves of the pagoda roof are carried on gigantic griffins at the angles. So it is beyond belief that a large and banal block of flats has been permitted directly behind it, thoroughly spoiling the view of the tower from Luton Hoo Memorial Park. The second tower, on HART LANE, by *W. R. Philips*, engineer, and *W. Philips Jun.*, architect, is a more typical expression of the engineer's art but still worthwhile, with steep octagonal roof. Grey brick dressed with moulded red brick and terracotta. The sides are recessed beneath segmental corbel arches and there is a top storey of round arches.

57

PERAMBULATIONS

1. Town centre

On the general character or lack of character of Luton enough has been said in the introduction to the town. In the centre a continuous walk can be made between the parish church and the Town Hall, and then a second foray towards the station, but it is no good pretending that a very rewarding perambulation is possible. In 1336 there was a major fire in the town, resulting in the destruction of 200 houses. This accounts for the peculiar meandering course of the main street running roughly E–W from Dunstable Road to Park Street.

Beginning at the church one comes into CHURCH STREET, mostly altered for the 1970s shopping centre (*see* below). There is, however, the former MASONIC HALL (now Pizza Express) of 1923 by *Franklin & Deacon*. Neo-Georgian with curved front. Originally single-storey; upper floor added 1934. Inside, fluted columns and a jazzy tiled dome over the centre.

At the top of the street is PARK SQUARE, just a road junction, and on this the BREWERY TAP pub, the oldest building in the town, with (renewed) weatherboarding. Just off in PARK STREET WEST (Nos. 21, 23, 25) are still very minor late c18 or early c19 houses, two (Nos. 21 and 23) with doorways with fluted pilasters of semi-elliptical section; it is commendable that they have not been allowed to disappear. There are other c19 houses here, in the classic Luton livery of purple (a.k.a. grey) brick and rubbed red dressings; some were clearly designed for industrial use behind, see e.g. the blocked central arch to Nos. 11–15. That is a common discovery in the town, where terraces often conceal extensive rear wings for hatmaking or related activities. Turning N from Park Square, Park Street arrives in the triangle that was once MARKET HILL and until the mid c20 had the c19 Corn Exchange at its centre. It is now relandscaped on two levels, for no definable reason, and its backdrop is the CROWN COURT of 1992 by the *Property Services Agency*, yellow brick with a round tower to the r. Turning the corner into CASTLE STREET is the RED LION HOTEL, 1860s, stuccoed, with windows in basket arches with raised voussoirs and two storeys of pilasters. Opposite, a former wine merchants, the shopfront with large arched windows and grapes in the keystones. The CASTLE itself was a motte-and-bailey first built in 1139 by Robert de Waudari and lasted until 1154; a second castle erected by Fulke de Breaute was built in 1221 to the S of the church.

Now down into GEORGE STREET, the main thoroughfare E–W, which has the *clou* of the 1930s Town Hall closing its view. The streetscape is predominantly c20, with just Nos. 35–39 (S side) as evidence of anything earlier. They are red brick, presumably c17 or c18 but so altered by the later shopfronts as to be indecipherable. The rebuildings of the 1960s have left nothing of worth. Of the earlier c20, however, a large and impressive former BOOTS Chemists on the S side; 1915 by *J. R. Brown & Son*, in Carolean style with gabled attics, Ipswich windows and decorative strapwork. On the other side of the street, at the corner with Bute Street and extending down it, a very large single block of later c19 commercial premises, in an Italianate style, pilasters with crocket capitals along the front. All brick and mostly yellow but with a small amount of black, red and blue for polychromatic contrast. Very tall windows at ground floor. Adapted at ground floor for the Capital & Counties Bank (now LLOYDS BANK) in 1898. This is all that remains along the street's N side to hint at the scale and quality of the Victorian town. What one must look for instead are the remnants of the 1930s, when Luton enjoyed a wave of prosperity, although much of this period is neglected. First, a landmark, the former SAVOY CINEMA by *W. R. Glen* of 1938, disused since 2000, with a stern corner elevation of a stone drum colliding with a fin, the rest brick. The streamlined style continues with the former NATIONAL PROVINCIAL BANK of 1936 by their regular architect *W. F. C. Holden*, but in a more *moderne* manner than usual for him, with a subtly bowed elevation in the centre. Double-height opening to the tall former banking hall (now a shop), flanked by two blocks of offices with bands of steel windows curved around the corners.* Also of this time, along the N side of the street at the far end, the former GAS COMPANY SHOWROOMS, by *Whinney, Son & Austen Hall*, 1936, all dark grey brick with red dressings, some Expressionistic jagged patterns of brickwork to the window mullions and thin concrete bands. Asymmetrical, with stair-tower to the r. and the top floor set back with flat roofs. Sculpture by *Dennis Dunlop*. Finally, at the head of George Street in front of the Town Hall, a second triangular space to answer that of Market Hill, with the handsome WAR MEMORIAL of 1922, a Portland stone cenotaph by *Sir Reginald Blomfield* carrying a bronze figure of peace by *Sir Hamo Thornycroft*.

Now some diversions up the side streets climbing s of George Street. In CHAPEL STREET, No. 9, w side, the town's best late C18 building, built as a pub. In grey vitrified brick, in Flemish bond, but with two of its three bays in giant arches of red. Parallel to the w in GEORGE STREET WEST, a small number of painted and stuccoed early to mid-C19 houses, e.g. No. 2 with classical guilloche bands, rusticated quoins and window surrounds and pretty Gothic railings in a pattern very popular *c.* 1830. No. 9 has pilasters and No. 9a is a single storey (probably built as solicitors' offices, for easy access to the County Court which stood nearby) with a fine front of bands of purple and red brick, the windows in stone surrounds with shield keystones. Next, in KING STREET, stepping uphill, some decent examples of the town's commercial buildings of *c.* 1860, notably Nos. 29–33 and 35–37 on the s side, two three-storey ranges in Italianate style with vermiculated rustication to the ground floors and two floors above, their windows in stuccoed surrounds. Also No. 27, its ground floor altered but the windows Florentine-style with double arches and square mullions, the spandrels ornamented. Across the street, the former Stevens & Gee's Straw Hat Factory of 1903 (now *Luton & Dunstable Express* offices), a reminder of the saturation of the town centre by that date by premises for the hatting industry. Large windows for the ground-floor showroom, a central doorway and a gabled top with decorative moulded brick tympanum. Opposite is another premises with a large showroom

---

*The bank had bronze doors decorated with coins, made by the *Birmingham Guild of Craftsmen* (T. P. Smith, *Notes for British Brick Society*, 2000).

window (No. 39). Like a number of such buildings in the town, the workshop was in the separate annex at the rear (now a café).

The final side street here is WELLINGTON STREET, beginning at George Street with one of the only substantial *c.* 1830 commercial premises remaining in the town centre – a stuccoed front with pedimented windows and characteristically Late Georgian quadrant corner. The frontages step up the hill bay by bay, just two storeys above the altered shopfronts. Nos. 8–10, opposite, are small millinery warehouses of *c.* 1880, which have nice Dutch gables and Baroque windows. Another interloper halfway up is a very tall front for a hat WAREHOUSE of 1906 with a shaped gable over two floors of plate-glass showroom windows filling the façade between pilaster buttresses. Associated factories occupied much of the backlands of this street. After this, again a few precious but degraded early survivals of Late Georgian houses at Nos. 35–49, their stuccoed upper storeys with console cornices to the windows and a few Gothick basket balconies. By the end of the C19 they too were in industrial use.

Along the w side of the Town Hall, UPPER GEORGE STREET, with the former POST OFFICE (now Aldwyck House) of 1921 by *R. J. Smith* of *H. M. Office of Works*. Round the back of the Town Hall, in GORDON STREET, the former UNION CINEMA (now nightclub) of 1935–7 by *Leslie H. Kemp*. Brown brick with fins and a very good sculpture above the entrance by *John Alexander*.

N of the Town Hall, the remains of MANCHESTER STREET, whose N side is now open to the large public space of ST GEORGE'S SQUARE in front of the Public Library (*see* above), bounded by the weakly Postmodern LEISURE CENTRE of *c.* 2000 and the entrance to The Mall (*see* below). What remains of Manchester Street on the s is the former LIBERAL CLUB of 1895 by *J. R. Brown & Son*, quite handsome, with Jacobean oriels in the upper floor and a Frenchy roof in the centre. Mercifully unaltered shopfronts under big arches with gauged keystones. MANCHESTER BUILDINGS, 1915, w of Gordon Street, is also good, with carved pediments and Gibbsian details. Round the corner, CHARTER HOUSE, a horrible brown brick tower of offices of *c.* 1970.

St George's Square was conceived along with THE MALL, originally the Arndale Centre, which was built in five phases 1969–77 by *Leonard Vincent, Raymond Gobing & Partners* (succeeded in the last two phases by *Tripe & Wakeham Partnership*), with *Ian Fraser, John Roberts & Partners*, consultant architects. It stretches, with its attendant car parks, over 17 acres from the Square to the church and erased the whole of Waller Street, which ran parallel with George Street, and the side streets N and s.

What remains N of the Mall, and blighted by it, is the area which extends N to the station. It retains a small number of buildings associated with the hatting industry, some restored for other uses, but their circumstances and immediate environs are for the time being uninviting.

GUILDFORD STREET around the junction with Bute Street has most to offer. Indeed here is the earliest hatting factory in the town at No. 47, probably of *c*. 1840, three storeys, in header bond, much like a house with stucco quoins and blocking around the windows, a band to the first floor and a curved corner. Wing behind. The elevation to Barber's Lane is the same. Diagonally opposite, another factory (No. 61, now an hotel) of 1860s date, again essentially domestic in appearance with stuccoed and rusticated ground floor. Its early C20 extension is remarkably in keeping with the earlier part. Then a large example of 1905 for Messrs Durler, five storeys in all and five bays wide, above a deep plinth for the basement, showing the effect on the scale of hatting premises made by the employment of cast-iron frames behind brick façades. The two lower storeys (showrooms and offices) are contained by giant arches, the factory floors above fully glazed between pilaster buttresses and under lintels with exaggerated voussoirs. Netherlandish gable at the top and pinnacles. Durlers' earlier building is further W at No. 50 and better preserved. It seems to have begun as a plait warehouse, the date probably 1880s. Three storeys and five narrow bays above a deep ground floor of three depressed arches for entrance and showroom windows above the basement lights, which rise well above the street level. The materials are glazed brick, stone and moulded terracotta, rather appropriately Dutch in style for the narrow elevation. Adjoining this a terrace of workers' housing, evidently of the same time.

E of Bute Street one can appreciate, in the contrast between No. 32 and its neighbour, the refinements in architectural appearance of the factories built after the First World War. So No. 32, which must be *c*. 1880, has a façade of pier and panel type with three storeys in four bays of giant arches and a wavy parapet, while STIRLING HOUSE of 1919, by *Basil Deacon*, is *p. 234* entirely classical, with large areas of glazing in light steel frames within a framework of pilasters, the outer ones channelled, and top storey above a cornice – *the* style of interwar commercial building before the advent of Modernism. Its ground floor is well preserved, with a bowed section between columns fronting the showroom (now restaurant) with an ornate interior. The rear ranges have continuous bands of windows. Another good example of the 1920s type, very probably also by *Deacon*, is Nos. 57–61, on the S side of the street, which has pairs of curve-sided shop windows. Further E on the street, Nos. 37–39, built for Austin & Co. in 1912 by *Franklin & Deacon*. Tripartite window in the first floor behind Ionic columns and big pedimented dormers over the outer bays. Nos. 23–25, another good earlier C20 building, here by 1920, has two premises making a single symmetrical façade of rusticated brick in the centre and ends. Especially good the ground floor with stone and grey brick in bands around the entrances paired in the centre.

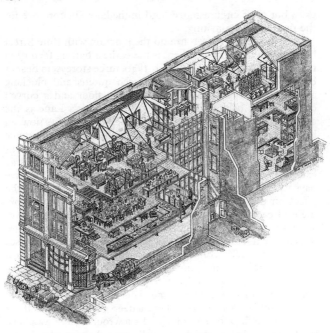

Luton, Guildford Street, Stirling House.
Cut-away drawing

Opposite, Nos. 22a–b, very small commercial premises of
1931–2 by *B. B. Franklin*, appearing as two Neo-Georgian
premises but containing a single room on the upper floor for
the display of imported straw plait. Round the corner in JOHN
STREET, No. 55, a former corn warehouse for Tomson & Son,
c. 1912–13 by *Max Zimmerman*, one of the most original of the
commercial architects of early C20 Luton, though all his other
buildings have been lost. Arts and Crafts Gothic, with two large
superimposed pointed arches in red brick, tile and terracotta
encompassing three storeys. Nos. 35–37 is a good small design
for a hat factory of 1933, probably designed by its builders,
H. C. Janes, the façade now almost entirely reduced to grids
of glazing (recently renewed). Nearby in CHEAPSIDE, a Queen
Anne-style pub (originally the Cowper Arms, a temperance
establishment), 1882 by *Charles Bell* for the Bedfordshire
Coffee Tavern Co., with oriel windows and a jettied top storey
under three gables. Still quite delightful in spite of neglect.

BUTE STREET itself, on its E side, has another good representative of the medium-sized Late Victorian type, C. H.
Osborne's STRAW HAT FACTORY, its gable dated 1889, three
bays with plaster decoration under the brick and stone arches
of the first floor. Ground-floor showroom, partly faced in red
granite. The HAT FACTORY opposite shows the scale of the

largest mid-C20 factories, brick-faced steel frame and concrete floor slabs, with vertical strips of windows over four storeys above a stone-faced showroom floor. Converted by *Fletcher Priest Architects*, *c*. 1996–9. Café and studios in the principal part, with additions for TV studios etc. Courtyard in between. S of Guildford Street, VYSE'S HAT FACTORY, rebuilt in 1930 and also steel-framed, is in a more obviously Deco-cum-Georgian style. Finally the part of Bute Street facing the site (now car park) of the Great Northern Railway's STATION, the first in the town in 1858. The former BUTE MILLS, early C20 for Brown Bros., are built on the site of a large C19 engineering works. Red brick with a modillion cornice and aedicule in the prominent water tower. Good rear elevation, symmetrical with projecting ends. Next to this fragments of the GREAT NORTH-ERN STEAM MILLS, *c*. 1870. Part of the line of the old railway from here to Dunstable is now used by the Luton–Dunstable guided BUSWAY, completed in 2013.

2. Around the centre

There is too little to make up a continuous perambulation in any direction, so a broad survey is called for.

The area N across the railway is HIGH TOWN, largely built up in the mid C19 during the first period of the town's expansion. In MIDLAND ROAD, at the corner with Dudley Street, is another impressive former hat factory, built for Paul Walser & Co., 1930. Stone-faced with a brick top-storey set back. Deep ground floor. Windows in two storeys in each bay. It now has the most ludicrously ill-proportioned upper storeys added for flats. HIGH TOWN ROAD is the shopping street of the district and, excepting the major highlight of the Methodist church (*see* Religious Buildings above), the scale is low. At the corner with Havelock Road, THE PAINTER'S ARMS of 1913 for Pryor, Reid & Co. of Hatfield, faced in green tiles and with more patterned tiles inside the still compartmented interior. St Matthew's church (*see* Religious Buildings above) stands high above the terraced houses in this neighbourhood, though there was much rebuilding at lower densities in the C20. In the streets NW of High Town Road, industry existed cheek-by-jowl with housing, e.g. the former DYEWORKS in North Street, and in several places one can still see the two uses combined in, e.g., the terraced houses which have long rear wings for hat-making in FREDERICK STREET. This street also has an interesting former PRINTWORKS (for Marshall, Brookes & Chalkley) of *c*. 1900 with a frontage of arched windows in muscular Gibbsian surrounds.

W of this, facing NEW BEDFORD ROAD, the LEASIDE HOTEL (No. 72) is a grandiose Italianate villa, dated 1878, for Asher Hucklesby, one of the leading 'hat barons', who had large premises in George Street. In two parts, the original part with its centre recessed and a nice tiled frieze below the eaves of its low-pitched roof. There are other such prominent houses here but mostly in poor condition. ¼ m. further N is Wardown Park (*see* Art Gallery and Museum above) and, as one would expect, a great concentration of better late C19 and early C20 houses is found around the fringes. The best examples of this type are in LANSDOWNE ROAD, e.g. No. 22, with a big slate roof of Dutch barn form containing the upper storey and fronted by a gable with elaborately carved bargeboards. More rich woodcarving along the front. Is it reused? The most remarkable villa, however, is No. 278 OLD BEDFORD ROAD (formerly BLUE RAILS) by *Evelyn Simmons*, 1935, for the Dill-inghams, who owned the largest of the town's hat factories. White walls, a two-storey bow at the front and stair-tower rising to an attic opening to the rooftop solarium. Original pergola shade and nautical tubular railings. The original windows have alas been replaced (in plastic) in 2012 and other inappropriate alterations made.

SW of the railway line, the area called BURY PARK, which has its shopping street along DUNSTABLE ROAD. The land-mark here is the former ODEON CINEMA (now Calvary Church of God in Christ), 1937–8 by *Keith P. Roberts* of *Andrew Mather*'s practice. Sincerely Modernist, not at all Art Deco in its motifs, with a flat tower and few windows. Interior pre-served by its present use. Behind this, in HAZLEBURY CRES-CENT, Nos. 1–19 are houses purpose-built *c.* 1900 with industrial premises behind. Their fronts are indistinguishable from contemporary two-storey suburban terraces but each has an archway to a rear yard and a long workshop wing.

The S of the town is similarly patchy except for a few early C19 houses in the continuation of WELLINGTON STREET and in DUMFRIES STREET crossing it (e.g. Nos. 47–55, W of the Ebenezer Chapel) and a particularly dense concentration of two-storey houses connected with the hatting industry in STANLEY STREET and PRINCESS STREET. Much of this area, the C19 NEW TOWN is a grid of very mean mid- to late C19 terraces, climbing uphill and in character more redolent of northern mill towns than southern England. The generally meagre standard is shown up by the Arts and Crafts-style HIBBERT ALMSHOUSES, Hibbert Street, E of Castle Street, dated 1884. They are by *Alfred Williams*. LONDON ROAD, where the ground rises steeply uphill towards Stockwood Park, has some large individual houses but nothing of obvious dis-tinction except WHITEHILL, a rather dour Gothic house of 1870 by *T. C. Sorby* (cf. Wardown; *see* Art Gallery and Museum above) for Richard Brown. Sharp gables and tall chimneys. Now surrounded by housing of *c.* 1970 in Durler Gardens.

There was a severe shortage of housing in the town by the end of the Second World War, leading the town council to embark on the FARLEY HILL ESTATE, NW of Stockwood Park. It was begun in 1946 and planned for about 10,000 people. Altogether more exciting in plan than in elevation, for the centrepiece is a half-mile long spine (Whipperley Way) that

turns into a double avenue planted with trees along the centre
and has two shorter double avenues forming cross-axes. The
houses are unfortunately too meek to respond effectively to the
challenge of such formal planning. At the N end is the SHOP-
PING PRECINCT, and this is quite prettily handled in the style
of the Festival of Britain; two storeys of flats above a three-
sided colonnade of shops.

The second area of significant early postwar housing is NE
of the centre, begun in 1947, e.g. in BURNHAM ROAD, DOVE-
HOUSE HILL etc., with the then very popular type of semi-
detached cottages prefabricated by the *British Iron & Steel
Federation* (BISF) to a prototype design by *Frederick Gibberd*.
A few retain their brightly coloured upper storeys and light
steel porches.

OUTER LUTON

The sprawling housing areas beyond the centre are very extensive. Apart from the churches (*see* above) only a few buildings or
sites require mention.*

MOAT HOUSE, Moat Lane, Biscot. The one remaining medieval
house of Luton, now a pub. Built, it is assumed, in the late
C14; the E wall is a mix of brick, flint and Totternhoe stone.
Rescued from dereliction in the late 1960s and restored. Fine
roof of *c.* 1500. Collar-beams and arched braces. Some of the
collars are embattled, the purlins moulded. The roof was the
former hall roof but the house is now floored, with central
chimney. In the N wall of the house two original two-light
windows with segmental arches.

STONEWAYS CLOSE, off Toddington Road, Leagrave. An interesting three-storey terrace group by *Farrell & Grimshaw* for the
Maunsel Housing Society, *c.* 1980. Maisonettes over flats, with
stairs to paired entrances and at the back, gardens for the flats,
below patio gardens and shallow balconies for the maisonettes.
The structure is timber-framed, the cladding purple tiles, hung
over the façades. Maroon painted balconies etc. There is similar
housing in a larger block in CRAWLEY GREEN ROAD (No.
50), E of the Vauxhall plant, and in several other schemes in
London. It was conceived as an adaptable type suitable for
mass production.

In LEAGRAVE PARK, ½ m. N of Leagrave railway station, is
WAULUD'S BANK. This is an earthwork inside a bank and
broad, flat-bottomed ditch up to 65 ft (20 metres) wide and
8 ft (2 metres) deep which is now mostly now infilled. The
ditch encloses a D-shaped area of 18 acres (7 ha.). On the
straight W side it abuts on the River Lea and also encloses its
source. This may be of some ritual significance. Excavation

---

*A pair of C18 thatched and weatherboarded cottages which stood in Compton
Avenue, Leagrave, were dismantled in 1983–4 and have been re-erected at the
Chilterns Open Air Museum, Bucks.

revealed traces of what is interpreted as a timber-built hut on the outer N edge of the ditch, and sherds of Late Neolithic grooved ware and Windmill Hill ware pottery and flintwork were found on the floor of the ditch. Further investigations in the S ditch produced more Later Neolithic pottery but also much Iron Age and Roman material.

For DRAY'S DITCHES, *see* Streatley.

INDUSTRIAL, BUSINESS AND TECHNOLOGY PARKS

VAUXHALL (GENERAL MOTORS), Kimpton Road. The Vauxhall Motor Company came to Luton from Lambeth in 1905. It turned to motor cars in 1907 and was taken over by General Motors in 1925. The payroll in 1935 was *c.* 7000, in 1963 *c.* 25,000, but is now only *c.* 1,500. Car production moved to Ellesmere Port in 2002 but vans are still produced here.* The former OFFICES (now Luton Chamber of Commerce) in Kimpton Road are of 1907 by *H. B. Cresswell*, an old boy of Bedford School. Neo-William-and-Mary, of local brick with red brick quoins and dressings. Doorway with a big semicircular pediment containing the company's Griffin emblem under a window with volute surround. Inside, an excellent double-height hall (for the display of a car) with a double staircase to a gallery around it. Original glass and timber screens to the surrounding office. Upstairs, the boardroom, with fittings from *J. P.White*'s Pyghtle Works at Bedford. Bolection-moulded fireplace and glazed bookcases, and director's office with beamed ceiling and panelling. Extensions of 1915 and 1919 in the same style. The early factories, which extended S to the railway, have gone but opposite is a former assembly building of 1935, with channelled red brick facings and between the windows pilasters, two and a half storeys high, within a stone frame. Reinforced concrete structure, probably using the Kahn system. Next to this, the former SHOWROOM (now Wyvern House) of similar date, two-storey with large panels of glazing between brick pilasters. The sloping ground behind made it possible to display vans on the upper floor, with cars below. E of this group, set back, is the former ENGINE PRO-DUCTION PLANT (Building AA; now van production) of 1949–51 by *Howard, Souster & Partners*. Very plain Modernist front, long and horizontal with windows in two storeys of continuous gridded bands; the ground floor behind pilotis. It employed a steel frame brought from the USA which had been fabricated for an unrealized wartime factory. Originally brick-faced; recently reclad.† The HEADQUARTERS OFFICE (Griffin House) is a refacing by *Fairbairn & Partners*, 1991, of their

---

*Vauxhall was not the only vehicle manufacturer in Luton. Commercial Cars Ltd were in Biscot Road from 1907, but nothing survives of their buildings.
†The main car production building (Building AC) by *Howard, Fairbairn & Partners*, 1957–8, has been demolished.

STYLING CENTRE of 1962–4.* The rear part of this is now in other use and only partly preserved.

BRITANNIA HOUSE, Leagrave Road. The former offices of SKF (or SKEFCO), makers of ball bearings, who established their factory here in 1911. They moved to Sundon Park in Luton's N suburbs after the Second World War. Very grand Beaux Arts style of 1916–17 by *P. C. Blow* of St Albans, with shallow portico of fluted giant Ionic columns *in antis* and again at the ends. Seven-bay wings, the arches of the windows with curved extrados. The attic storey was added in 1930. Later additions in brick and steel and concrete. Excellent circular entrance hall with grand double staircase curving around to a gallery on Greek Doric columns.

BUTTERFIELD GREEN BUSINESS PARK, off Hitchin Road, Stopsley. The BUSINESS & INNOVATION CENTRE by *Hopkins Architects*, 2007–8, is a very appealing design, a four-finger plan of two storeys of small office units extending from a spine with continuous colonnades beneath the upper storeys; between the wings, gardens and a square pond. Cedar facings and strips of windows. Drum stair-towers at the corners of the spine, and open spirals from the wings.

CAPABILITY GREEN, off Airport Way, SE of the centre. Originally developed by the Luton Hoo Estate from 1985, masterplanned by *Bruce Gilbreth Architects*, and, by contemporary standards, ambitious. Very formal grid, with a wide central boulevard on the downward slope of the site, divided by an avenue of planting and at the junctions with the cross streets, circuses with fountains etc. The landscapers were *Clouston & Partners*. The best offices are the earliest, notably two designs by Bruce Gilbreth Architects themselves: BUILDING 200 (ANRITSU offices), 1987, is clad in light metal, with porthole windows and curved glazed towers containing yellow and blue spiral stairs; also BUILDING 400 of 1988, in yellow brick, with three blocks facing a garden, the largest (Ernst & Young) a crescent with stepped elevation along the rear. BUILDING 500 (AB Inbev) by *SOM* also shares the classical instinct of the landscaping. Long three-storey wings of brick above a stone basement flanking a recessed centre with an entrance under an elongated Serlian arch. Atrium inside. The failure to secure a major building to terminate the central axis at its N end, where the hill descends towards the town, is a disappointment, and the most recent additions to the park are singularly weak. – SCULPTURE. Fighting Hares by *Barry Flanagan*, 1987.

---

* Pevsner described it as '. . . irritatingly overstyled. A long, four-storeyed façade, all forward and backward in saw-tooth fashion, with restless pre-cast concrete members. The porch is big enough for Gog and Magog to call.' The RECREATION CLUB of 1964 has also gone.

LUTON HOO

The splendour of Luton Hoo is its park by *Capability Brown* of 1500 acres (600 ha) with two lakes. He began this grandiose job in 1764, one year after *Robert Adam* had started drawings for the house. It belonged to the Earl of Bute, then prime minister. He had bought it in 1762 with a brick house built in the early years of the C17. But the thrill of the house as it now stands is not Robert Adam, nor *Sir Robert Smirke*, who remodelled what was there 1826–30, but *Mewès & Davis*, who remodelled it once again in 1903–7 for Sir Julius Wernher, diamond magnate in the heroic years of the diamond and gold discoveries in South Africa. Mewès & Davis were the architects of the Ritz, the RAC, the former Carlton and the Waldorf. To say that is not a slight on Luton Hoo, but a compliment to the Ritz. At Luton Hoo, as in the design of the Château de Rochefort-en-Yvelines for Wernher's fellow diamond magnate Jules Porges, Mewès & Davis worked in partnership with *Georges Hoentschel*, the premier Parisian decorator and collector whose firm, Maison Leys, specialized in the scholarly reproduction of decoration and furnishing in the style of the French Baroque and C18. The combination of Edwardian riches with an exacting French training brought about interiors – at Luton Hoo as at the Ritz – which are of the very highest quality in their own terms. (That they were not the terms of Pevsner's 'Pioneers', i.e. those that led into the new century and its new style, is neither here nor there.) At Luton Hoo display was demanded, and it was provided with a panache of which no one after the First World War would have been capable. Sir Julius and Lady Alice furnished two houses with their celebrated collections and when Bath House in London was given up after 1945 much was brought to Luton Hoo by Sir Harold and Lady Zia and supplemented by their own furniture and pictures. To that end the house was repaired after wartime occupation and reorganized in 1948 so that a home might also become a museum. So it remained from 1950 until the great sale of 1997. Part of the collection is now on display at Ranger's House, London, the rest was dispersed. The house was restored 1999–2007 as a luxury hotel; this suits it well.

The architectural history of the house is complicated. *Adam* made numerous plans from 1764–7, first intending to transform the existing house into a quadrangle around a court before Bute settled on the elongated H-plan still visible today. He began work, but the old house remained, and, though there was a fire in 1771, Mrs Delaney in 1774 still went through principal rooms of the old house to reach the new and especially Adam's sensational Library, 144 ft (43.9 metres) long and facing s. By then work had halted and a drawing by Bray of 1790 shows the old house and its gate house existing cheek-by-jowl with the new s and e fronts. It was not fully completed till Smirke came fifty years later. Moreover, there was a fire in 1843 which gutted all except the Library and it was then sold by the 2nd Marquess of Bute; the shell was partly rebuilt in 1848 for J. Shaw Leigh, a Liverpool solicitor, on this occasion by *Sydney Smirke*, but even so the N wing, which had contained the chapel, was not refitted for another thirty years. Redecorating was done, but was almost entirely replaced by the Wernhers.

The house is of ashlar stone throughout. The W, i.e. the entrance, side is essentially by *Smirke*, although it tallies in some major features with what *Adam* designed and probably built. It has a far-projecting centre with a giant hexastyle Ionic portico of fluted columns and a pediment. Recessed parts of four bays l. and r. and then two wings terminating in bows. The bows and the portico are as in Adam's drawings and inside the portico the centre projects to create a vestibule and is decorated with three large stone laurel wreaths above the entrance. In place of sash windows *Mewès & Davis* introduced French casements and oval openings piercing the walls. In the middle of the recessed parts are two odd set-pieces, Grecian-Mewès & Davis, and they repeated them on the S and E fronts as well. They are of browner stone than the rest and consist of four Doric pilasters only one storey in height and crowned by a frieze with wreaths. To l. and r. in the recessed parts are also doors created in the 1940s. The S side has preserved from Adam the two slender Greek Doric columns *in antis* and entablature in the middle between square projections and the balustrade at attic level. Originally there was a giant arch. The house has always been three-storeyed here, but Adam's attic storeys to the wings were removed after the fire and now have elegant mansards by Mewès & Davis, who otherwise remodelled the façade into a perfect symmetrical conception of a French C18 villa (cf. the illustration of 1819 in Neale's *Seats*). The W side and also the E, i.e. the lake, side were always of two storeys, but for Wernher the gently pitched attic roof and mansards were added. The N side has giant Ionic attached columns *in antis* between square bays, like the S front but of two storeys only above the basement. This may be by *Sydney Smirke* after the fire of 1843. Towards the E Adam built a middle bow and wrapped a hexastyle portico round it. Thus the front was at the time of the fire. After that it was reduced to the bow with attached Ionic columns as we now see it. The view to the distant lake is not easily forgotten.

The interior is, to say it again, neither Smirke's nor Adam's; nor indeed is it entirely Mewès & Davis's or Hoentschel's, for *Philip Tilden* made changes in 1948. Of Mewès & Davis's remodelling the *clou* is the oval STAIRCASE HALL, French Beaux Arts 58 at its most convincing and indeed its most splendid. White walls, and the staircase rising in a dashing sweep, its balustrade of massive wrought iron to contrast against the whiteness of the rest. Sculptured groups high up in niches with shell-heads, corresponding to doors of matching design to the corridor on the first floor. 'L'Amore degli Angeli' by *F. Borganzoli* at the foot (a cast of the original which was the only object purchased along with the house by the Wernhers). Discreet decoration of the walls and the door surrounds, a type of plaster rather than stone. Oval

skylight. There are more rooms on this scale and of this sump-
tuousness of decoration. The top-lit Louis XIV-style ENTRANCE
HALL has a screen to the portico vestibule of two columns and
again a skylight, and mirrored doors with gilt framing. The
DINING ROOM is on the same axis as the hall, beyond double
doors, and has the central E bow, marble walls in two colours,
red for the panels, white and grey for the framing (originally
containing Beauvais tapestries of the Story of the King of China)
and the sideboards, gilded mouldings and mirrors. The DRAWING
ROOM (a.k.a. Pillared Hall) has early C18-style *boiseries*, grained
by Tilden but originally covered with red damask, and four
marble (overpainted) columns around the central skylight.
Finally, the BALLROOM, all white and gold, instead of Adam's
Library, whose form only it preserves. Here the existing panelling
was enhanced with plaster decorations and allegorical paintings
copied from late C18 French originals. The centre room has two
apses behind arches contained within the two square projections
outside, between which are the Doric columns. The rooms E and
W ending in the bows are separated by sliding doors with mirror
glass and gilt fittings. In the E room a fireplace with billy goat
frieze. In the room adjoining the dining room on the E front,
originally the 'Salle des Billards' but refitted as a Dining Room
by Tilden in C18 English style, are wood-carved garlands, birds,
etc. by *Grinling Gibbons*, brought from Cassiobury, the house
begun in 1674 by Hugh May and demolished in 1926. On the
upper floor, a splendid oval BOUDOIR in the E bow of the S wing,
the chimneypiece with pretty Pompeiian decoration. The room
behind the central bow of the E front (Queen Elizabeth Suite)
has an Adam-style ceiling with an oval border of guilloche, central
octagon and painted roundel and semi-roundels. It is the only
one of its kind in the house. The fireplace also also looks C18,
with frieze of billy goats. On the W front, Queen Mary's Suite is
the Ritziest in style, with good pilasters, plaster wall decoration,
painted ceiling in French Rococo style, and extravagant, earlier,
marble chimneypiece.

The former CHAPEL is the one main room older than 1900.
Smirke's chapel of *c.* 1830 stood here but it was destroyed by the
fire.* Its replacement was done for John Gerard Leigh in a kind
of Byzantine style by *G. E. Street* in 1875 and has a barrel-vaulted
and panelled ante-chapel at the N end of the main axis through
the house, below the family gallery. Inside, round-arched windows
with Lombardic tracery, which show incongruously behind the
Ionic screen of the N front. The chapel was dismantled in 1939
and after 1948 a picture gallery was created within it. Restored
1991, when it was given a screen with gates from the garden.
These have been removed (and an inappropriate balustrade

---

* Of medieval woodwork in the chapel, part was given to St Mary, Luton, by the
1st Marquess of Bute and is now incorporated in the screen of the Wenlock Chapel
(*see* p. 218). The rest, which is depicted in the *Illustrated London News* (18 November
1843), was destroyed in the fire. It is claimed that this woodwork was made for Sir
Thomas Pope's chapel at Tyttenhanger House, Herts., and removed from there to
Luton Hoo in the C17 by the Napiers.

introduced) but Street's blank arcading along the walls remains, along with the alabaster-faced apse with its semi-dome of Christ in Majesty and the panelled ceiling, both painted by *Daniel Bell*. *Clayton & Bell* supplied the stained glass.

The GARDENS immediately S of the house are a set of formal terraces, laid out *c.* 1912 by *W. H. Romaine-Walker & Besant*. It is divided into three descending levels, the largest part with apsidal ends and two domed pavilions of strongly Roman character, and a central fountain of mermen supporting a basin. In the PARK, the LAKES created by *Capability Brown*, 1764–74, by damming the Lea. Wernher paid for it to be entirely drained and cleaned. At the S end of the lake, over the river Lea, HYDE BRIDGE of 1830–1 by *Barwell & Haggar* of Northampton. Single span of 45 ft (13.7 metres).

Below the terraced gardens in a dell, the ROCK GARDEN of 1900–10 laid out by *James Pulham & Son* (they may have supplied the fountain in the terraced garden too), with much use of their patent stone for grotto, cascade etc.

The STABLES, also now converted for hotel use, are by *Adam* but altered *c.* 1830. A quiet front with three pediments, the middle one on two pairs of Doric pilasters. Diocletian windows.

The Luton Hoo Estate retains the estate buildings. WALLED GARDEN, S of the house, is a red brick octagon of stupendous scale (5 acres; 2 ha.) with shallow buttresses, apparently designed by *Brown* and completed in 1770 for the 3rd Earl of Bute, whose botanical collection is famous. The builder was *William Ireland*. Later buildings around the N side, the remaining glasshouses including a palatial example for a fernery by *Mackenzie & Moncur*, *c.* 1908. Walls heightened in the C20 in blue brick. Partly restored since 2001. Nearby a charming ORNAMENTAL DAIRY and TEA HOUSE of 1890 by *John Birch* in a picturesque style with rustic veranda and brick and flint walls. Tiled interior to the dairy. It was designed for Madame de Falbe, widow of John Gerard Leigh. Nearby, THE GABLES, a large, half-timbered house of the 1930s, for the Estate Steward.

LADY BUTE'S LODGE, near the E end of the Lime Avenue, 1 m. S of the house, must, with its mullioned windows and gable, date from 1850 or perhaps a little later, but incorporates a genuine if heavily weathered Late Norman doorway with colonnettes and a moulded arch. It probably comes from a church demolished or drastically restored at the time and may have been a priest's doorway. It is in a dangerous condition.

LODGES, S of the house (now the Estate entrance). Symmetrical, single-storey with consoled heads to the windows. Are these *Smirke*? Similar pair to the N entrance.

MARSTON MORETAINE

9040

Marston Vale was formerly an area of brickmaking on a large scale, extending from Elstow to Brogborough. Now there is no trace other than the distinctively post-industrial landscape of flooded former brick pits and replanted woodland, but see also Stewartby to the N. The village is mostly C20 and disappointing.

ST MARY. The church, like Elstow (q.v.), has a detached bell-tower of limestone and ironstone. This is Dec – see the bell-openings. The buttresses have many set-offs, the ground-stage is vaulted. Quadripartite vault with very strongly chamfered ribs. Dec also the ironstone chancel – see the one N window with transom, cut into by the N aisle – and the contemporary two-storey vestry. This has inside a very handsome sexpartite vault, also with single-chamfered ribs. The Perp contributions dominate, datable by heraldry on the S door (for Reynes, Frowick, Mauleverer and Broughton) to c. 1451–71. Six-bay arcades, slender piers of standard moulded section, moulded two-centred arches. The W bay is shorter than the others, an error in the calculation presumably. The chancel arch matches the arcade arches and the four-centred arch to the S chapel which continues without division from the aisle. Good nave roof with angels and carved bosses. Perp aisles, and a fine high Perp N porch with pinnacles (later than the aisle – see the base moulding of the latter). The N doorway has tracery in the spandrels. The nave W window is of five lights with panel tracery just a little out of the ordinary. Major restoration was in two phases in the C19, beginning with the nave in 1861–4, for which *Butterfield* was architect. His plans for the chancel were not carried forward and so its restoration belongs to 1871–2 by *G. G. Scott*. Roof with castellated tie-beams. – SCREENS. S aisle, E end. Small, with one-light divisions and dainty tracery. Bad modern screens in the aisles of 2002 for kitchen etc. – REREDOS. N aisle chapel. Part of a screen dado with four painted prophets (David, Isaiah, Daniel, Hosea) – the East Anglian type – very similar to the figures on the screen at North Crawley, Bucks. – PANELLING. On the N aisle wall, some tracery and linenfold, taken from the benches when they were replaced by chairs. Butterfield's benches removed at the same time. His PULPIT remains. – STALLS etc. by Scott. – REREDOS. Painted by *E. M. B. Tylcote*, the rector's daughter; she also painted the roof. – WALL PAINTING. Above the chancel arch a Doom, uncovered in 1969; it is dated c. 1505 by reference in a will to monies to be left for its painting. – STAINED GLASS. Bits of ancient glass in the N aisle E window. – In a chancel S window, three large figures, Christ, Mary and St John, by *Morris & Co.*, 1901, i.e. *Burne-Jones* designs. Set against the usual quarries. – Chancel N, by *Burlison & Grylls*. – E window, 1952 by *Hugh Easton*, a typically Nordic Christ ascending. – MONUMENTS. In the chancel, brasses to Walter Papley, rector, †1420, a demi-figure, 12 in. (30 cm) long, and to Thomas Reynes †1451 and his wife, 3 ft 1-in. (94 cm) figures. He began the Perp rebuilding of the church. – Tomb-chest at E end of S aisle. With indent for brasses and heraldry for Sir John Reynes †1500, probably originally placed in the arch between aisle and chancel. Also his HELM. – The brass for William Goldyngton (nave W end) is *c.* 1505, originally at Lidlington (q.v.). The figure of his wife is lost. Length of the plate 31 in. (79 cm). – Thomas Snagge, Speaker of the House of Commons, †1593 and his wife, erected by their son (†1626). Standing alabaster monument with recumbent effigies under a five-column tester with nailhead studs. His feet are set against his gauntlets. The children kneel in relief against the back wall. Essentially identical to that of *c.* 1597 at Husborne Crawley (q.v.), with the late Elizabethan motif of circles linked with squares. The painted coat of arms to the r. of the arch to the chancel is related to it.

Former SCHOOL, by the Green, N of the church. A Picturesque design of 1846 by *J. T. Wing.*

MORETYNE MANOR, ¼ m. NW. Formerly Moat Farmhouse. Timber-framed with two front gables. Much restored and modernized in 1880, the brick infill of that date. Originally the house of the Morteynes, who held the manor until 1428. Hall with cross-passage, and a rare instance in the county of a cruck frame (but cf. Husborne Crawley). Its open truss and spere truss are preserved; the moulding of the open truss suggests it was built *c.* 1400. Jettied wings of *c.* 1500. Large chimneystack of Totternhoe stone to the W wing. Hall floored probably in the late C16.

MARSTON FOREST CENTRE, Millennium Park, off Station Road. Opened 2000. Brick and timber facings, low pitch roof.

THE EXHIBITION pub, Upper Shelton, 1¼ m. N. Of interest purely for its PAINTED SIGN which is the Festival of Britain logo by *Abram Games*, 1951.

MAULDEN

0030

ST MARY. High above the sprawling village. 1858–9 by *Benjamin Ferrey*, except for the W tower (but not its pyramid roof) and the W part of the N wall, with the N doorway. Of ironstone, the tracery of the windows geometrical to Dec. Thin piers inside with excellent naturalistic capitals, e.g. little birds in one capital. Over the arcades much ornamental decoration and scriptures, impressed into the plaster using a technique devised by Ferrey. It formerly covered the aisles and chancel walls. – FONT. E.E. style, 'carved by Mr Jaquet, of Vauxhall Bridge Road, London', i.e. *John Lewis Jaquet*, 1859.* – SCREENS. Tower, 1876; vestry (S aisle W) by *W. D. Caröe*, 1912, in simplified Gothic style. – STAINED GLASS. The E window and one in the S wall by *Clayton & Bell*, 1858, not yet in their usual colouring. The other chancel window by *C. A. Gibbs*, 1860. S aisle E window (St Alban) by *Francis Skeat*, 1981. –

---

*A plain FONT of the late C12 is now at St Hugh, Lewsey, Luton.

MONUMENTS. Brass to Richard Faldo †1576 and wife, and Anne Faldo, his daughter †1596. – Richard & Dorothy Allyn †1720 and 1719. A curtain tablet. Attributed to *Stanton & Horsnaile* (GF). – The interest of the church is the octagonal MAUSOLEUM (or funerary chapel) of the Bruces. It is a Gothic rebuilding of 1859, again by *Ferrey*, but before then it was linked to the church. Beneath is a crypt with a quadripartite rib-vault. The room above has three memorials. In the middle the overpowering MONUMENT to Diana, Countess of Elgin, erected with the building in 1656. Convincingly attributed to *Thomas Burman* by Rupert Gunnis. It is a big, rather stark architectural composition with a gadrooned moulded sarcophagus of dark grey stone and a lighter marble top rising to a gadrooned basin like a wine cooler. Out of this appears the white demi-figure of the countess in her shroud, meant to be floating up at the sound of the last trump. One hand is on her heart, the other points upward. The whole is a typical mid-C17 conceit. No wonder Horace Walpole found it 'the most ridiculous that ever was imagined'. At the bottom, three large cartouches, also of characteristic mid-C17 forms. – In the corners of the room, two busts on pedestals: her husband Thomas Bruce, Earl of Elgin, †1663 and his grandson, Edward Bruce, †1663 too, seventeen years old. They seem to have been conceived as the first of a set to form an admiring circle of Bruce descendants around the countess.* On the Bruces *see* Houghton House, Ampthill. – A second MAUSOLEUM for the Brooks family is below the vestry.

WILLOW END, No. 12 Ampthill Road. Originally a *cottage orné* pair. Bowed ends and a thatched roof. It must be *c.* 1800.

LONG BARN, Limbersley Lane. By and for *Nicolas Tye Architects*, 2009, in the yard of an existing farmhouse. Elegant steel-framed rectangle, fully glazed along one side. Larch cladding. The similar WORKING WOODLANDS CENTRE, Maulden Wood, ¾ m. E by the A6, is by the same architects.

MELCHBOURNE

ST MARY MAGDALENE. A Georgian church with a medieval W tower. But the chancel has medieval masonry, including traces of a door and lowside lancet, and the nave is so wide now that it must have had a S aisle. On the other hand the buttresses l. and r. of the Perp pairs of transomed two-light bell-openings appear too thin to be medieval. The Georgian date is 1779, the new work reputedly paid for by Samuel Whitbread I, guardian (and later father-in-law) of the 13th Baron St John, who was

---

*The effigy, cartouches and the two busts are replicas, the originals having been moved by the Brudenells to Deene Park, Northants, in 1966. The original bust of the Earl is attributed to *Edward Pearce* (Bruce Bailey).

then just twenty-one. Large, even, arched windows. Arcades of timber Tuscan columns, round arches including the chancel arch, and coved ceilings inside (cf. Little Staughton). The N porch is obviously Jacobean, with its Roman Doric columns and frieze, its round entry arch, and its oval side windows. It came from the St Johns's manor house at Woodford, Northants (dem. 1783). – PULPIT with concave angles and discreet inlay, and a full set of BOX PEWS, including the squire's pew in the chancel with fireplace.* – ORGAN. 1858 by *Holdich*. Fine case with fretwork crestings. – STAINED GLASS by *Mayer & Co.* of Munich in the E window, as late as 1902 or later, yet in its gaudy Holbeinesque style utterly out of sympathy with either the church or any style of 1900, thought Pevsner.

THE STREET is the name of the long row of thatched C18 St John estate cottages leading towards the church. They were formerly even more extensive. Their walls are made of cob.

MELCHBOURNE PARK. The manor was conveyed to Oliver St John (later 1st Earl of Bolingbroke) in 1608 and he probably rebuilt the house as his own residence separate from his father's seat at Bletsoe. But it is also suggested that as James I liked to hunt at Bletsoe, Melchbourne may have been built to accommodate a retinue too large for the old house. The 2nd Earl was living here in 1673 but after the death of the 3rd Earl, the Lords St John had their seat at Woodford, Northants. Melchbourne was nevertheless substantially remodelled in 1741 (dated rainwater heads) for the 11th Lord St John. Red brick. Of the first date only the two gables at the back with their mullioned windows and probably the H-plan and the big chimneybreast on one of the short sides. The façade of 1741 has two projecting wings with big canted bay windows, a recessed five-bay centre, and a low parapet. All first-floor windows have alternating triangular and segmental pediments. Flush stone quoins. Porch of two pairs of Doric columns, probably added in the 1780s for the 13th Lord St John following his marriage to Samuel Whitbread's daughter Emma. The large staircase hall is of the same time, lit by an arched window at the back of the house. Its ceiling has dainty plasterwork on four shallow pendentives, and the staircase itself a restrained iron balustrade of scrolls and squares. Delicate late Victorian painted portraits in the pendentives. There was a fine long gallery on the second floor, a remarkably anachronistic feature for the date, which must be 1741. Broken pedimented door-heads and overmantels of Kentian type. The coved ceiling may be 1780s; cf. the church ceilings (*see* above). It has been subdivided. Further additions were made at the back in 1875. The house was given up after occupation by the USAAF in the Second World War and was converted to apartments

---

*There was a fine *Wedgwood* basalt font (cf. Cardington above and Essendon, Herts.) given by Emma St John, daughter of Samuel Whitbread. It was removed in the C19 and is now in the Birmingham Museum of Art, Alabama, USA.

c. 1984. Large park; the LODGE at the Riseley entrance is of 1832 by *Henry Garling*.

MEPPERSHALL

A much expanded village but the C19 and C20 have added nothing to its interest.

ST MARY. Of ironstone. Extensively rebuilt in 1875–6 by *Edward Forster* (father of the novelist) but with a Norman crossing tower – see the one original s window. The top of the tower is Perp. The crossing arches are in different states of preservation, the best being the w arch with one angle roll. The transepts are Norman too – see the blocked E arches. Can they have led to apsidal chapels? Or do they only represent altar recesses? In the southern one, there is indeed now a Perp REREDOS with panels and tracery around the recess, and both transepts have Perp windows. The chancel is early C13, the buttressing outside still of the flat Norman kind, but again with Perp windows. Forster replaced the Perp E window with one of three stepped lancets and inside exposed the shafts of the lancets, five originally, in the N and s walls. There was an aisleless Norman nave, but the present nave and aisles are by Forster. Three wide bays, so wide that four lancets in the clerestory correspond to one bay. The piers are round, and the capitals are not at all strictly E.E. The aisle has an uncommonly steep lean-to roof. – SCREEN. In the N arch of the crossing. The former rood screen, taken down in 1875, reset in 2000. – Fine *opus sectile* and red glass tile REREDOS, 1880, by *J. Powell & Sons*. – STAINED GLASS. E window 1880 and w windows 1895, both by *Hardman*. – MONUMENTS. Brasses to John Meptyshale †1440 and wife (18 in.; 46 cm) and to John Boteler †1441 and wife (18½ in.; 47 cm). – Timothy Archer †1672. Badly done demi-figure, frontal, the usual type for clergymen, and he was vicar here. The top is an open scrolly pediment.

29 MANOR HOUSE, by the church. Two-storey and attics with one of the most impressive timber-framed façades in the county. Symmetrical with two big gables with timber decoration of the familiar concave-sided lozenges, and between them three smaller gables, the middle one over a canted bay. On the front of this just one pargetted thistle and crown. The bays l. and r. of this project further out and the r. one contains the porch. The date is probably early C17. The timber decoration was revealed during restoration *c.* 1930. s wing damaged by fire in 1959 and faithfully reconstructed. Traditional oak timber-framed extension, 2003 by *Bruce Deacon*. Within the gardens to SW, THE HILLS, a motte-and-bailey castle of *c.* 1135–54. The inner bailey is E of the motte. The second bailey followed farther E. The motte is *c.* 82 ft (25 metres) in diameter.

St Thomas' Chapel, Chapel Farm, ¾ m. ene. Formerly held by Chicksands Priory. Nave and chancel. Late Norman n doorway of two orders. The capitals are decorated scallop and decorated waterleaf. In the arch, lozenges, each slightly folded across the middle. Also billet and nutmeg. All that means a date *c.* 1170–80. One Dec two-light n window. The chancel was replaced *c.* 1500.

MILLBROOK

St Michael. Alone on a hill above the village. The church is of ironstone. The s arcade is late c13 or early c14, the n arcade Perp. Both have standard elements. Externally the church looks predominantly Victorian because a thorough restoration was done by *Butterfield* in 1857–8. Part of the s aisle collapsed in 1888; its rebuilding was by *A. W. Blomfield*. Undisturbed are the (blocked) n doorway and the n aisle e window. The s doorway is bigger and, as also a small s aisle lancet, goes with the s arcade. In the n aisle ne corner an image niche; statue of 1933 by *Percy Bentham*, Albert Richardson's usual carver. – reredos. 1939 by *Albert Richardson*, who worshipped here; the altar by him, 1945. – font. By *Blomfield*, 1888, to replace a medieval font destroyed by the aisle's collapse. – benches. Some are Perp, with a knob on the top, a knob on the top of the arm, and a third on top of the back; copied in the c19. – stained glass. One (n clerestory) has the arms of Sir John Cornwall, who probably oversaw the Perp work. e window, a single angel, 1876 by *Clayton & Bell*; the two other chancel windows by them also, 1902. – monuments. William Huett and his wife, both †1602, on the same day. Two defaced recumbent stone effigies. Originally on a tomb-chest. Reset on the wall is the back tablet with a very pretty surround: flowers, a death's head, and emblems of death, all threaded together. Central achievement and two smaller shields. The effigies are much damaged. They were buried in the churchyard in the c19 but dug up in 1919. – Lord and Lady Holland, of Park House, Ampthill, †1840 and 1845, and Georgiana Anne Fox †1819, aged ten. By *Westmacott*. White marble. In the centre, big square plinth with a relief of Christ blessing the children, triglyph frieze and scrolls. The child's bust at the top. L. and r., two busts for her parents on columns with a frieze of wreaths. Read his inscription and you will understand why *The Ecclesiologist* called it 'flagrantly Whig'. – Sir Albert Richardson †1964 is buried in the churchyard.

Old Rectory, below the hill to the w. 1851 by *J. Woodroffe* for the Rev. E. H. Carr, who instigated the church restoration. Red brick, Neo-Tudor. Otherwise the village is almost exclusively standard Bedford estate cottages of *c.* 1849–*c.* 1860.

Former station, 1⅜ m. n. One of the enchanting group on the Bedford–Bletchley line of 1846 (cf. Ridgmont (Brogborough) and Woburn Sands). In a many-gabled Picturesque style insisted upon by the 7th Duke of Bedford.

TEST TRACK, immediately S of the station. Begun in 1968 as a vehicle proving ground for the Vauxhall and Bedford motor companies; the model was the first such ground created at Milford, Michigan, by General Motors in the 1920s. Landscaped with sculpted hills and flat straights, one mighty circuit and a series of serpentine tracks through woodland.

CENTER PARCS (WOBURN FOREST). 2013–14, the village buildings by *Holder Mathias*.

9030

MILTON BRYAN

ST PETER. Norman nave and chancel, but treated far too drastically in early C19 restorations. One W window, one chancel S and one chancel N window, and two nave S windows are Norman. Some Perp details also (N doorway and chancel S door). By *L. N. Cottingham* in 1840–1 the porch and the NW tower with single lancet and pairs for the bell-openings, solid and four-square. Inside there is one very curious feature, a Norman nook-shaft halfway along the chancel. As the chancel arch is Norman too, also with nook-shafts, can the other nook-shaft mean an apse arch? The N and S transept arches are Neo-Norman to match the chancel arch. The N transept is of 1827,* built by the son of Sir Hugh Inglis (*see* below), the S transept no doubt contemporary. BOX PEWS of about that time also (the doors mostly removed) and including two seats in front of the N transept arch and a FAMILY PEW in the transept itself with poppyheads and book rests. – STAINED GLASS. E window by *Willement*, 1841. The N transept window is signed by *George Austin Jun.* of Canterbury, 1857, characteristic of his close study of C13 glass. – W window by *Wailes*, 1867, in memory of Sir Joseph Paxton (†1865), born in this parish. – Large GRAVE COVER, C10–C11, a strangely stylized cross and close interlace. – MONUMENT. Sir Hugh Inglis †1820, chairman of the East India Company, who acquired the Milton Bryan estate through marriage in 1784. In the N transept. By *Chantrey*, 1832. White marble. Recumbent effigy, his head on the half-rolled-up mat favoured in Elizabethan and Jacobean monuments. In his hand a bible. The monument cost £1,000.

S of the church, the former VICARAGE. Its S front of double bows was executed in 1812 by *John Wilson*, surveyor. N of the church, out of sight, a disused RADIO STUDIO, purpose-built in 1942 to broadcast 'black' propaganda to Germany. Brick, austerely Modernist, with central tower and wings stepping down l. and r. Design credited to *Sir Edward Halliday*.

---

*The transept has been attributed to *Sir Robert Smirke*, whose office address also appears on plans for the tower in 1832.

FOUNTAINE'S FARM, ½ m. s. Rebuilt by *Clutton*, 1875–6, for the Duke of Bedford. Red brick with some half-timbered gables. The chamfered stone mullions and blind windows are a Clutton motif (cf. Stevington Manor House). Nearby Nos. 9–12 SOUTH END, a picturesque group of timber-framed, thatched cottages. C17 and C18 with C19 reworking. No. 9 has a carriageway with timber supports.

MILTON ERNEST

ALL SAINTS. The church had an Early Norman chancel – see the small N and S windows with dressed surrounds, reset when *William Butterfield* rebuilt the chancel and restored the church in 1858–65. The bold chancel arch of two sweeping continuous mouldings, however, is C13 and the angle piscina. The W tower is C13 too, still unbuttressed (cf. Bletsoe), with a W lancet and bell-openings with Y-tracery. Dec N aisle windows and, inside, a splendid tomb recess, with crocketing and large cusping and subcusping and big leaves in the cusps. The N windows are straight-headed (rather surprisingly with carved timber lintels combined with stone tracery), the W window has intersecting tracery; both are renewed. Dec also the N as well as the S arcade. They have the standard elements, but differ in details. Perp clerestory and nave roof with bosses, two-storey S porch, its entrance with traceried spandrels, and S aisle wall. At the tops of the buttresses pretty bits of decoration. Chancel decoration by Butterfield, a painted open roof with ceilure over the altar, and his familiar inlaid strips and chevrons of tiles in the E wall. – PULPIT and other woodwork including the BENCHES also by *Butterfield*, again typical of him, and the low painted wrought-iron chancel SCREEN. – FONT. Octagonal bowl on eight buttress supports. The panels have simple Dec tracery. – SCREENS. One C15 screen in the N aisle with a central arch, untraceried openings l. and r. and traceried screen above. It seems too narrow to have been the chancel screen. Was it for a family pew? – ORGAN LOFT of 1969–70 but incorporating panels of wrought-iron work, probably early C18. – BREAD CUPBOARD. 1729. With three tiers of four arched pigeon-holes each and a steep pediment. – CHANDELIER. 1728, donated by Thomas Rolt. Of brass, two tiers of curly arms; rehung by Butterfield. – STAINED GLASS. The characteristic glass in the S aisle W, tower W, chancel E, and chancel side windows of 1865–6 is by *Alexander Gibbs*, whom Butterfield patronized. The clear, watery colours are typical, and the strong, bold leading. – MONUMENTS. In the tomb recess, a COFFIN LID with a cross (cf. Kempston). – Tablet to Christopher Turnor †1675 (S aisle). – Tablet to Susannah Rolt †1726, by *Cox* of Northampton, 1733.

In the churchyard, E of the church, William Butterfield †1866, the architect's father. A foliated cross slab.

SCHOOL, W of the church. 1871 by *Edwin Harrison*. Red brick with blue brick.

VICARAGE, NE. Dated 1694 but extensively remodelled in 1836 by *C. J. Carter* of Louth. Stone, the garden front with a pair of gables over square bays.

52   MILTON ERNEST HALL (Care Home). By *Butterfield*, 1853–8, and extremely characteristic of him. It is his only country house, done for his brother-in-law, Benjamin Starey, who also paid for the church's restoration. No one would call the house engaging, but it is done with a grim determination and an unfaltering conviction. Local limestone and red brick trim. Both main façades are extremely asymmetrical, with each element of the house individually expressed, causing a highly varied roofline and vigorous recession and projection of walls in the entrance side, which has the main two-storey porch to the r. and a subsidiary entrance at the base of a stair-tower to the l. Motifs include bay windows, very steep dormers, flat ribbed chimneys, pairs of windows with shouldered lintels, and of course also large and serious Gothic windows, especially the three tall two-light windows to the staircase hall, its role in the plan further emphasized by the wall decoration. On the garden front, windows are contained in Gothic arcading on two storeys, the motif carried on to the r. in a slender three-storey canted bay under a timber gable. The ground falls steeply W to the river, with the kitchen wing kept low and out of view. It has an addition of *c*. 1910 in more conventional Arts and Crafts style. The interior was never lavish. Some rooms have fireplaces with minimal patterns of quatrefoils. The staircase hall has lost its painted decoration but has two-light inner windows, the lights with ogee heads.

S of the hall's grounds, by the Ouse, the former MILL, also rebuilt by *Butterfield* in 1857. The mill stream runs beneath a Gothic arch. In the village, N of the hall, HOME FARM, partly C18 (datestone and Venetian window to the road), altered by *Butterfield* and again in 1938 by *Albert Richardson*, who extended it N and added the strange stone balcony-cum-terrace at the rear. Nearby, No. 13 RADWELL ROAD, also by *Butterfield*, 1859, a diminutive cottage with half-hipped tile roofs. Diaper pattern brickwork, and good robust door.

TWINWOODS BUSINESS PARK. Formerly RAE BEDFORD, an outstation of RAE Farnborough, established postwar for research on supersonic aircraft. Four WIND TUNNELS for testing at a variety of air speeds.

1040   MOGGERHANGER

ST JOHN THE EVANGELIST. 1859–61 by *W. Slater*, in memory of the Rev. E. H. Dawkins. A serious, bold and austere exterior. Bands of brown and buff stone. Chancel tower with pyramid roof and a high polygonal apse immediately abutting on it.

Nave and aisles, the arcades with their French C12 foliage
capitals less original. Low paired aisle windows. They are
pointed-trefoiled. N ORGAN CHAMBER by *Carpenter & Ingelow*,
1889, the ORGAN CASE 1902. – FONT. Tub, E.E. style, with
crisply carved foliage. – SCREEN. 1912 by *A. Needham Wilson*.
– STAINED GLASS. Apse windows by *Clayton & Bell*, 1860, and
two deeply coloured chancel windows (Thornton memorials)
by *Mayer & Co.* of Munich, 1881 and 1885. – S aisle by *Hardman
& Co.*, 1893–1900. – W window by *J. Powell & Sons*, to the
Dawkins. Two lancets (1909) of excellent twining foliage, the
third (1913) with a figure of Patience.

VICARAGE, N, by *Slater* too, 1860–1. Nearby, the SCHOOL,
a gentle Arts and Crafts design by *Herbert Leete*, the County
Surveyor, 1909–11.

ST JOHN'S (Sue Ryder Hospice), ⅜ m. SSE. 1851 by *J. Horsford*
for Col. William Thornton. Neo-Jacobean. Lodge of 1861;
lattice windows.

MOGGERHANGER PARK. By *John Soane*. Godfrey Thornton, of
the Clapham Sect, was first Deputy Governor and then Governor of the Bank of England for which Soane was surveyor
from 1788. The very modest house Thornton acquired from
his brother in 1784 was extended for him in 1791–2, enlargements were planned in 1797 and again in 1807 (by now for
Stephen Thornton), but it was finally designed in its present
form in 1809–12 and Soane remained involved until the 1830s.
Only Soane's own residences enjoyed such continuous attention over several decades and display so clearly his experiments
in design and planning. The Thorntons sold in 1857. The house
became a hospital from 1920 to 1987 but it was thankfully
unmolested and completely and beautifully restored 1995–
2005 by *Peter Inskip* and *Stephen Gee* of *Inskip & Jenkins*.

The house is rendered, coated with limewash and lined out
as ashlar, with a shallow slate mansard roof behind a low
parapet. The facing was originally 'Parker's Metallic Stucco'.
The house as Soane left it in 1791 was an L-plan, represented
by the whole of the E front and the three E bays of the S side
to the garden. The rest of this side is of 1811–12, of seven bays
with, in the centre, a very shallow Grecian pediment on pilas-
ter-strips with sunk panels, its frieze the modillion cornice of
the eaves. Across this front a veranda of timber, the slim
uprights with panels of cast-iron trellis, matching a two-storey
veranda added round the corner to the centre of the E front.
This was the entrance front created by Soane in 1791, and to
l. and r. and in the centre at first-floor level are broad windows
under typically Soanian segmental arches, the l. one blind. All
the windows of the houses are recessed and darkly painted,
from a distance suggesting voids in the wall face. The entrance
side is more eventful. In the centre it is a tower, one storey
higher than the rest, with a balustrade and concave buttresses
at the sides, in form recalling the style of Baroque houses a
century earlier. This is set back between two-storey wings and
the space filled at ground floor by a low link of three bays

fronted by a semicircular stone porch of Greek Doric columns of the Delos type. The end bays of the façade have on the ground floor arched windows with heavy frames projecting and broad Grecian pediments over.

Behind the porch is a square entrance hall with a very shallow pendentive dome, a reinstatement of the original design, the paterae at its centre recast from one now in the Soane Museum. Shallow arched recesses in each wall and doors at the corners and in the centre where the principal axes of the house intersect. Part of the painted decoration is original. Bronzed fireplace with incised decoration. Behind that rises the staircase, square and high. It is all cantilevered and has the simplest iron balustrade just of reversed Ss, a favourite of Soane. On the E side at first-floor level are open arches; such arches were also designed for the ground floor but these were infilled while building and Soane contrived instead in the space between the stair and the E rooms a narrow passage or 'tribune' (of the type encountered at, e.g. Tyringham, Bucks.). It has groin vaults at the ends and an apsidal-ended void in its ceiling below a roof lantern. This opening, later covered over but reinstated during the restoration, penetrates the floor of the exedra vestibule E of the staircase and has been given a balustrade of the same pattern. From a middle landing on the stair's W flight a fine view is set up through the open arches into the vestibule and climaxes in the E room, Mrs Thornton's dressing room, which has the broad segmental arch of the door into it answered by an arch into a recess that opens to the balcony over the E door. The shape of the room, with two apses, dates to 1791 and was decorated by *John Crace* in 1797; the scheme of that date has now been restored. The bedroom to the SE corner still has mid-C18 panelling and cornices. The Drawing Room directly below this was the Eating Room after 1792. Its fireplace of that date, with scrolls and rosettes, is a design found also at the Bank of England. N of this was Mr Thornton's Dressing Room and the Library, with a recess in its wall answering the arched window. In the centre of the S front, the Breakfast Room of 1812 with rounded corners, a Vitruvian frieze and pellet moulding, and a milder fireplace with incised flanks. Next to this, the new Eating Room, the main room of the house after 1812, has four Ionic pillars, one at each corner of the compartmented ceiling. They are the originals, recovered after removal in the C20. The ceiling has, for Soane, rich decoration, guilloche bands, fan mouldings, waterleaf, paterae, and pellet mouldings both large and small, and the soffits of the ceiling are subtly graded in height towards the central panel over the dining table. Indeed, throughout the house there is an impressively precise hierarchy evident in the richness of mouldings, door panellings and wall surfaces. Even in the attic rooms and the functional spaces of the service wing there is the same control over the fine details.

The KITCHEN WING is a brick pavilion of the type found in other country houses by Soane. Its chimneys are contained in towers with incised pilasters at the first stage and stepped rectangles above. Arched windows send light into the passages below and the kitchen itself has a mighty round-arch window in the s wall. The interior also has semicircular transverse vaults, Soane cleverly deploying light through curved windows (now blocked) under two of these.

w again, the two-storey STABLES of 1792, of brick with five bays of tall arches. One original carriage house at the N end, its correspondent a reconstruction *c.* 2000. Like the kitchen pavilion, it is limewashed for tonal and architectural unity with the house. Interior reconstructed for laundry and brewhouse in 1806, when the second group of stables to the w were built. They are red brick, and were extended N in 1811–12.

Humphry Repton remodelled the PARK in 1792, following on from his work at The Hasells (*see* Hazells Hall, Everton), and offered opinions on the newly remodelled house. NW of the house, a rustic ICE HOUSE, probably early C19.

NORTHILL

1040

St MARY. Of ironstone – dressed for the nave, the chancel rubble – and all too drastically restored, including all the tracery, principally by *Henry Woodyer* in 1862–3. Much, however, is Dec and much is Perp. Dec N and S aisle W windows (reticulated tracery), Dec two-storey S porch with a later two-bay vault with diagonal and ridge-ribs and bosses of the arms of Sir John Trailly, who held the manor until 1401. The upper storey contained a chantry chapel from 1489. Dec S doorway with three orders of thin colonnettes. Dec the high tower arch (three sunk-quadrant mouldings), and Dec also the high four-bay arcades. Piers quatrefoil with four thin diagonal shafts, arches with two sunk quadrants and capitals of contrasting Totternhoe clunch. On the other hand, Perp the aisle windows and the chancel windows. The chancel may have been rebuilt in 1404 when Sir Gerald Braybrooke, one of Sir John Trailly's executors, obtained permission from Henry IV to make the church collegiate. The strange vestry group with the rose window dates from 1862. Of the same date the chancel floor, chancel roof, chancel arch, its style similar to the arcades, the tower's arch and stair-turret. – REREDOS. By Woodyer. Rib-vaulted top and painted foliage, rather grim. – STALLS. For the college. Two with carved armrests and poppyheads. The MISERICORDS are very plainly carved. – SCREEN. By Woodyer? With some old elements in the dado. (– TILES. C14 Dec. In the floor of the vestry, formerly a N chapel, 1.5 metres (4 ft 11 in.) by 3.5 metres (11 ft 5 in.) – PULPIT. 1882 by *A. W. Blomfield* (cf. Caldecote). – FONT. 1858. Modelled on that at Wymington (q.v.), the cover copied from the pinnacles of Peterborough Cathedral. – S chapel furnishings by *Bucknall & Comper*, 1904; fine altar

rail with angels made by *Rattee & Kett*. – STAINED GLASS. This
is what will stay for ever in one's memory. Mounted in the
s aisle, three splendidly large-scaled windows of 1664, signed
by *John Oliver*. They were commissioned by the Grocers'
Company, patrons of the living, for the E window of the
chancel, which they restored in 1663–4. The royal arms were
formerly in the centre flanked by the Grocers' arms and those
of Lady Margaret Slaney (†1619) under whose will the living
had been re-endowed. Below, the arms of the Company's
wardens. It is all bold, rich and very secular. The new E window
of 1885 holds a mighty design by *Clayton & Bell* (designer,
George Daniels) with Christ and crowds of supplicating saints.
Also by *Clayton & Bell*, all three of the w windows (1864–75)
and the s aisle E (1904). – One N aisle and one s chancel
window by *Kempe*, 1897 (musical angels only) and 1906
(Ascension); both good. – MONUMENT. John(?) Harvey †1721.
Marble tablet with a segmental pediment, urn and drapery
hanging from scrolls at the sides. – BIER. 1663, inscribed with
the name of Thomas Tompion, the clockmaker, who was
churchwarden (cf. Ickwell). (Sixteen leather BUCKETS. Given
by the Grocers' Company, probably *c.* 1800. In the porch
room.) – LYCHGATE, 1880 by *Blomfield*.

THE GRANGE, E of the church. A fine house, well kept. The date
must be *c.* 1700. Five bays, with an apsidal door-hood on
carved brackets. Staircase with twisted balusters and still a
string hiding the tread-ends. Wrought-iron gates with
anthemion on the uprights.

On BEDFORD ROAD, Nos. 25 and 27, a pair of highly Picturesque Gothick cottages, *c.*1800, facing each other. Ogee-arched
windows and doors. Formerly lodges to Ickwell Bury (q.v.).

HIGHLAND FARMHOUSE, 1 m. ESE. Described as 'newly
erected' in 1825 at its sale by William Walker, a Houndsditch
sugar refiner. A smart square brick job, well above the local
standards of this date with two storeys above a raised basement, a perron stair and a parapet. Rescued from dereliction
by *John Manning*, 1973–8.

FISHPONDS and WARREN, Homewood, ⅜ m. WSW. A very
remarkable rectangular earthwork about 170 metres (557 ft)
long N–S enclosed and subdivided by ditches into multiple
channels and basins. It is believed that the E part served as a
rabbit warren.

OAKLEY

ST MARY. Late C12 w tower – see the small slit-windows halfway
up. The tower was unbuttressed too. Perp top and w window
(renewed 1904). The arch to the nave has a little nailhead, i.e.
is of before *c.* 1300. The nave was originally one bay shorter
than it is now. Early C13 N arcade of two bays, with round piers

and moulded arches, C13 S arcade, totally redone, except for
the responds. The E respond was reused when the E bay was
added with its double-chamfered arches. The S doorway of two
continuous hollow chamfers is of the C13 too. The rest of the
exterior is Perp. Two-storey S porch, its entrance with traceried
spandrels. Battlements everywhere and a bell gable over the
chancel arch. The chancel has a Late Perp four-light E window
and a S lowside window, but throughout was over-restored in
1913–15 by *C. G. Hare*. – FONT. Octagonal, Perp, with tracery
motifs. – SCREENS. One in front of the chancel arch, made up
in 1915 from two screens previously in the aisles. One-light
divisions, vines in the spandrels, coving and loft, and on the
coving PAINTINGS of stars and Christ seated on the rainbow.
It is emulated by the tower screen of *c.* 1900. The original
chancel screen was removed before 1900 but reinstated in the
S aisle W end in 1915. Four-light divisions (cf. Felmersham),
and remains of the rib-vaulted coving. – BENCHES. A complete
set of the standard buttressed type, quite a rarity in Bedfordshire. – CHOIR STALLS. By *W. H. Randoll Blacking*, 1927. –
ROYAL ARMS. Hanoverian. Painted, with scrolled sides and
pediment. – STAINED GLASS. In the E window, two roundels
with suns. – More fragments in several windows. – MONU-
MENT. Coffin lid with a defaced foliated cross growing out of
an animal (cf. Pavenham). – Effigy of a lady, early C14, also
defaced, in a low, later tomb recess with bold pointed trefoiled
cusping. Arms of the Reynes and Chamberlain families.

OAKLEY HOUSE. Oakley manor belonged to the Duke of
Bedford from 1737, and a hunting lodge was built here for him
c. 1748–50, but in 1786–92 it was remodelled by *Henry Holland*
for the occupation of the newly married John Russell, later the
6th Duke. Highly refined, in finely cut stone, its hipped slate
roof with dormers and skirting the S, E and W sides, stylish
chinoiserie verandas. At the rear, two wings with pedimented
gables create a service courtyard. The entrance was at the side,
to an axial corridor. Inside, originally some restrained Louis
XVI-style interiors and Holland's characteristically plain cornices of pellets and waterleaf. The drawing room retains its
fireplace, white and grey marble, and grisaille sopraporta of
winged sphinxes. Other rooms had Chinese wallpapers (supplied by *Robson & Hale*). Some remodelling, including a bath-
room in Ritzy style for Lord and Lady Ampthill, 1919 by
Landers, Bedells & Crompton. The chinoiserie porch to the
service court must be C20 too. Inside the hall also three good
mid-C18 doors from Fineshade Abbey, Northants (dem. 1956).
At the gates to Oakley House, THE LITTLE HOUSE, 1858, the
best of the Bedford estate cottages. The Duke provided the
SCHOOL (Community Centre) in 1841. In High Street also two
COTTAGES (Nos. 26–28) by *Charles Holden* (of *H. Percy Adams*'s
office) 1905, for ex-servicemen of the Bedfordshire Regiment.
Red brick under a deep roof ending in big tile-hung triangular
gables with the slightest of jetties; that on the front of the split
type so popular with the Arts and Crafts designers.

LOVELL ALMSHOUSES, ¼ m. E of the church. 1926–7 by *Ivan Daughtry* of Bedford. A very fine set of pairs with central gables spread along a large green. Late Arts and Crafts style. Added to *c.* 1934 and after 1945.

ODELL

ALL SAINTS. All Perp, except for the lower part of the W tower (see the doorway with shafts to the arch). The tower is an unusually monumental piece of four stages with clasping buttresses, paired transomed two-light bell-openings, a quatrefoil tracery frieze, and pinnacles. In the S porch, a tierceron-star vault. Spacious interior. Four-bay arcades with slender Perp piers of standard section. The same type for tower arch and chancel arch. There was a careful restoration in 1867 by *W. Slater*. Tower W window restored by *G. Highton*, 1888. – ROOFS. Worked on 1928–31 by *W. Talbot Brown*, the nave roof with traceried trusses. – FONT. Octagonal, Perp, with simple arched panels. – Of the Perp ROOD SCREEN little is old. – BENCHES. Oddly small-scale, otherwise the standard type of buttressed ends. Some incorporate Jacobean panels, and there is more panelling in the N chancel chapel. This probably dates from the bequest by William Alston of Odell Castle in 1637, which provided the excellent TOWER SCREEN, with two tiers of balustrading of thick, vertically symmetrical balusters and a cartouche. – PULPIT, also Jacobean but given to the church in 1654, its HOURGLASS STAND on a nice iron bracket. – STAINED GLASS. In the S aisle E window, earlier C15 figurines of angels. Also fragments in a chancel S window, a bishop, Christ's head, St Matthew, all in the yellow stain on white so distinctive of the period. – E window, 1904 by *Heaton, Butler & Bayne*. – MONUMENTS. To the Alston family, probably of 1678 following the death of Sir Thomas Alston. Large, richly decorated tablet with open pediment. Attributed to *Abraham Storey* (GF), the same hand as the monument of 1678 at Bletsoe (q.v.). – Lt Thomas Alston †1807. By *John Bacon Jun*. Hope with her anchor stands by an urn on a pedestal. Landscape relief representing the assault on Montevideo.

ODELL CASTLE. Neo-Georgian of 1962 by *Gerald Banks* for the 2nd Lord Luke; on the terrace of its predecessor destroyed by fire in 1931. Square wings, recessed centre with a veranda, hipped roof behind a parapet. Originally this was a motte-and-bailey castle. Later stone buildings were put up, and they were in ruins in Leland's time. William Alston purchased the estate in 1633 and the keep was then still used, but new building was done for Sir Thomas Alston in the mid-C17 Thorpe Hall style. Of the outbuildings of this much remains.

OLD WARDEN

St Leonard. Of brown cobbles. Late C12 to early C13 w tower, see also externally the absence of buttressing and the tiny lancets and the quoins of an aisleless church. The nave is partly patched in brick; the chancel is almost entirely Victorian, the N vestry of 1901 by *C. Hodgson Fowler* and the s porch of 1952 by *Albert Richardson*. There is nothing in this exterior to prepare for the shock in store upon entering. One can only just register the high unmoulded Norman tower arch, the early C14 s arcade of standard details and slightly earlier chancel arch before going under in the mass of woodwork indiscriminately got together by Robert Henley Ongley, 3rd Lord Ongley, in 1841–2 when the church was restored. Belgian, it is said, is most of what Lord Ongley assembled. It oppresses you from all sides; it is utterly disjointed, and can only here and there be read consecutively. In trying to take it in, one is all the time up against the Early Victorian connecting pieces, often far more than mere connecting pieces. For instance it can be assumed that the wavy tops of the BENCHES, formed from short pieces of carved foliage, are due to Lord Ongley, and they appear again around the s door. One can compare the wavy timbers forming part of the elaborate and indeed thrilling roof of the nave. The doors of the bench ends, with their Gothic tracery, also look Early Victorian. Similarly the Gothic FONT COVER is no doubt English and of the 1840s. But what is one to make of the long serpents wriggling along the tops of the benches? In the SOUTH GALLERY the blank-arched panels are English and may be genuinely Elizabethan or Jacobean. The BOX PEW beneath the monument by *Mabey* (*see* below) has thin openwork acanthus scrolls, typically Belgian late C17 or early C18. Another of the box pews in the chancel has some ogee-headed panelling, ogee also at the foot, which may be Belgian early C16. The many panels with the letters AC are said to come from the House of Anne of Cleves at Bruges. (What has Anne of Cleves to do with Bruges?) They have indeed some discreet strapwork. Many of them are the frontal of the ALTAR. In the panelling behind the altar, young caryatids of saints, and in front an ALTAR RAIL with angels. Hanging garlands are everywhere, small scenic reliefs everywhere. The total impression is as stuffy as are those houses which Early Victorian squires have crowded similarly with the fruits of their travelling. Indeed, Ongley's successors as lord of the manor, the Shuttleworths, continued the embellishments. The cantilevered PULPIT with biblical scenes and (originally) the Signs of the Evangelists on the corner posts was bought in Edinburgh in the 1880s. It too is probably Belgian but C18. Of other FURNISHINGS, the FONT is large and originally had twelve shafts. It will be of the early C14. – STAINED GLASS. In one nave N window, much-restored figures and surrounds of the C14 from Warden Abbey. This is of special significance, for it preserves intact the figures of the Cistercian Abbot Walter Clifton, dated to 1381–2, and St Martha with her broom and dragon, both under canopies and with W monograms in the sides. It was brought here before 1839. Another N window (chancel) by *Swaine Bourne*, 1891, but the rest by *Clayton & Bell*, beginning with the E window of 1899. – MONUMENTS. Sir Samuel Ongley †1726, signed by Scheemakers and Delvaux, or rather '*P. Chiemaker en L. Delvaux Inventor et Fecit*'. It must be Delvaux's spelling, and whose is the Latin? Sir Samuel stands dressed as a Roman Emperor with two putti l. and r. originally (one stolen). Reredos back. A pity it is crowded out by the woodwork. – Lord Ongley †1814. Tablet with a drape and a coat of arms. Also several HATCHMENTS for the Ongleys. – Caroline Jane Shuttleworth †1899. This monument, signed *C. H. Mabey Sc.*, succeeds in the end in outdoing all the collecting of 1841. In the SE angle of the nave, high up, appears a white Magdalen – no, probably Faith – life-size, in the Baroquest of attitudes. It looks as if it were Belgian and real Baroque too. Alabaster surround. Putto heads at the top. – Col. Frank Shuttleworth †1913. Marble wall memorial by *W. Goscombe John*, 1913.

In the churchyard, the ONGLEY MAUSOLEUM of 1787, designed to receive Robert, 1st Lord Ongley. Gothic porch and quatrefoil windows but classical urns on the angles and, inside, wall arcading on fluted pilasters. The Shuttleworth Monument in white marble with a large cross, *c.* 1887, seems very florid by comparison.

OLD WARDEN PARK (SHUTTLEWORTH COLLEGE). The estate was purchased in the late C17 by Sir Samuel Ongley, a linen draper, but the present MANSION is by *Henry Clutton*, built 1875–8 for Joseph Shuttleworth, a partner in Clayton & Shuttleworth of Lincoln, engineers and ironfounders; the contractors were *William Cubitt & Co.* and the structure makes use of iron construction. The design, Clutton's last for a country house, is inspired by Gawthorpe Hall, Lancs., chosen by his client as having been built for the similarly illustrious, though unrelated, Laurence Shuttleworth in 1600–5. Of yellow stone with lighter dressings, large, compact, three-storeyed, Jacobean, with starkly expressed groups of chimneys and stacks of bay windows but also with an asymmetrically placed staircum-water-tower between the house and its lower, gault-brick service wing. The clock is surrounded by an odd openwork grille of stone, an original motif (the clock frame etc. was produced by the Shuttleworth foundry). In front of this on the entrance side a stair in a bridge to a room in the s wing added in 1895–6 by *R. Weir Schultz* for Col. Frank Shuttleworth. The rooms are arranged around a court. Large, centrally placed ENTRANCE HALL, its marble overmantel an excellent hunting scene carved in high relief. Staircase hall with cantilevered stair under a glazed lantern and the secondary stair of the 1890s passing below it to the s wing; in the bay window at first-floor level STAINED GLASS of various sports. The double-height central SALOON, filling the courtyard, is the most impressive, with white and gold coffered ceiling of foliage and wreaths and skylights. Darkly panelled dado. Other rooms in late C18 taste with enriched plaster ceilings and panelling. In the drawing room/ballroom, two matching white marble fireplaces, richly carved. The BILLIARD ROOM has a overmantel made up with C17 religious subjects in the typical arched frames, e.g. the Sacrifice of Abraham, Slaying of the Innocents etc. They look very much like the fittings of the church.

S of the house the STABLES, a U-plan of yellow brick with a striking gateway under pyramidal tile roofs with finials. Over the main range a lively shaped cupola, a *Clutton* motif.

S of this, at a slightly lower level, the COLLEGE BUILDINGS (the college was founded in 1944, principally for agricultural education), mostly in a sympathetic yellow brick and appropriately undemonstrative Modernism. 1968 by *Charter Building Design Group* of Bedford. – LODGES. Also by *Clutton*, with some of the same Jacobean motifs as the house.

The PARK must have been set out in the early C18, and the house sits at the top of a small valley – a formidable presence. The previous mansion was probably a little S. SW, at the top of an avenue on the hill in the woods of Warden Warren, is QUEEN ANNE'S SUMMERHOUSE, a remarkable eyecatcher in a railed enclosure, first recorded in 1736. A cube, red brick of a delightful hue and exquisitely laid, for a single room over a vaulted basement, with arched windows and doorcase with a segmental pediment, and four circular corner turrets rising around a platform roof, one containing the stair, another the chimney (bolection-moulded fireplace). At the roof, the turrets contain semi-domed shelters. Who can have been its architect? The buff terracotta roof balustrade was added 1878 by *John Usher*. Beautifully repaired for the Landmark Trust, 2009, by *Whitworth Co-Partnership*.

Within the gardens N of the house, a rustic, thatched GARDEN HOUSE stands beside the winding path to the SWISS GARDENS, ¼ m. NE, which were largely set out *c.* 1830 by the 3rd Lord Ongley. It is a captivating and enchanting secret place of paths among ponds to islands linked by bridges and grassy hills, with a two-storey SWISS COTTAGE with Gothick details and a first-floor veranda, and numerous other thatched shelters, including the 'Indian Kiosk' with stained glass. The centrepiece is a cast-iron and glass FERNERY made *c.* 1830–3 by *Barwell & Haggar* (*Eagle Foundry*), Northampton, with a dome over the crossing and the distinctive overlapping small panes so characteristic of early glasshouses.* Embellished in 1876 in the craggy rockwork manufactured by *Pulham & Son*, who also made several of the cascades etc. *Edward Milner* was also paid for work on the gardens at this time. Superbly restored *c.* 1974–84 by *Bedfordshire County Architect's Dept* (*J. C. Barker*,

46

---

*Within this fernery there was originally an exquisite ceramic Peacock, one of a series made by *Minton* in the 1870s. It is now displayed in the house.

County Architect, succeeded by *Norman White*). Further restoration underway in 2013–14.

HOME FARM, E of the house. 1873–4 by *W. Wilkinson* of Oxford. Substantial brick farmhouse with trussed gables to the attics. Model farm buildings behind in an E-plan.

The VILLAGE is almost entirely composed of MODEL COTTAGES, either provided new or remodelled by the 3rd Lord Ongley in the early C19 and much supplemented by the Shuttleworths from the 1870s. The earlier ones are of *cottage orné* type, eminently picturesque and of varied aspect, e.g., at the approach to the church, a very pretty terrace of thatched cottages (No. 9 CHURCH END) with bowed ends roughcast in a cream colour. The best is SWISS COTTAGE, in the High Street, close to the gates of Old Warden Park (*see* Shuttleworth College above), with splayed wings ending in rustic verandas and fishscale tile roofs with eyebrow dormers and terracotta chimneys; but almost every house has details to savour. Even the pub joins in, but next to it are red brick buildings, formerly its stables etc., to which Lord Ongley added the big clock turret in 1844. Also red brick, with plain pilasters, are Nos. 24 and 25 but with a C19 attic with ornamental bargeboards. Opposite, No. 19, with a tiny oriel and Gothic windows; further on, THE THATCHED COTTAGE, with decorative bargeboards, twig ornaments and a substantial spiral-cut chimney in the centre. The old SCHOOL is by *Clutton*, *c.* 1875, yellow brick like the mansion's outbuildings, and has a very spirited cupola ventilator of the same antecedence as his stables there (and those at Sandy Lodge, q.v.). The architect for the cottages of this period, with their recurring motif of lozenge-pattern half-timbering and fishscale tiling, was *John Usher* of Bedford, who designed the KEEPER'S COTTAGE (Landmark Trust) in the Warren in 1878. At the top of the village street, a linked trio of COTTAGES (Nos. 1–3 BEDFORD ROAD), Georgian style, by *Albert Richardson*, dated 1948.

QUINT'S HILL. Just to the N of the church are the much overgrown remains of a bivallate earthwork. Only the NW portion of it survives; the remainder was presumably destroyed in laying out the park to the SE. The site is unexcavated but is probably Early Iron Age in date.

WARDEN ABBEY, 1 m. w. Warden Abbey was founded in 1135 by Walter Espec, who had founded Rievaulx before. Like Rievaulx it was a Cistercian house, and the monks came from Rievaulx. It was a wealthy establishment, and excavations and the rumpled contours of the site show it was quite a large house, but nothing of it is visible. All that remains is one part of the successor mansion of the Gostwicks (cf. Willington), erected *c.* 1552 and perhaps incorporating the abbot's lodging, sw of the abbey, and cloister. The Bucks' view of *c.* 1730 shows the house but it was cut down to its present size *c.* 1790 leaving this remnant of its SE wing. Brick, clearly Early Tudor, small and quite irregular. Two ground-floor s windows set back under deep arches, a four-light canted bay in a recess above, and next to it a chimneybreast with crowstepped gable and a decorated stack with star top; next to this at ground-floor level a stone doorway with crocketed ogee gable. At the back a stair-turret and, at the NW corner, but visible only inside, one substantial medieval buttress from a lost N range. Also inside, in the W wall a wide and tall arch, also of the earlier building, blocked in the C16 for a fireplace. The ceilings on two floors have good, moulded axial beams, and there is a door to the upper room with carved spandrels. In the roof are curved windbraces; it is clear that, as Buck shows, the range continued further E. Repaired from near-dereliction by *John Phillips* for the Landmark Trust, 1974–6, restoring the conical top to the stair-turret and unblocking most of the windows. C14 tile pavements have been uncovered: one just outside the building's NE corner contained mosaic elements of an Adam and Eve pavement matching that at Prior Crauden's Chapel, Ely; the other, more elaborate, derives from the nave of the church. Some are now displayed at The Higgins, Bedford, the rest in the museum's store.

BARN, 100 yds NW at Abbey Farm. Possibly of similar date to the Gostwicks' house. L-plan with a roof of five bays with two tiers of windbraces in the W part and similar construction in the longer E range. The walls are brick and of two types, red and yellow, with some diapering. The W range has angle buttresses.

PAVENHAM

9050

A fine stone village on a large bend in the Ouse. The church sits high above the main part of the village. Rush matting and basket weaving was the principal industry from the C17 to the early C20.

ST PETER. A chapel held by Lenton Priory (Notts) until 1283. That might explain the fine C13 S porch, reset. Good capitals and good arches. In the wall to the l. of the door, however, is part of an arch and a C12 scallop capital. W tower with stone spire. Low broaches. Two tiers of lucarnes. Not much else remarkable outside. Three-bay N arcade of standard late C13 elements – octagonal piers, chamfered arches – with unidentified shields on the labels. Aisle W window with Y tracery. One-bay S transept chapel of comparable date, on the arch the shield of the de Pabenham family, lords of the manor 1200–1414, and inside a PISCINA of c. 1300. Also two Dec niches in the E wall. Perp N chapel – see the two-bay arcade and the E window – but reset in its N wall a fine pair of large crocketed ogee niches. Above the arches, also reset, again the arms of the de Pabenhams. Might it all have come from the chancel? In the N aisle E arch an excellent corbel, and to the NE roof corbel of the aisle a yet

better Green Man corbel. Vestry, W of the N aisle, 1847–8 by
J. T. Wing. – The church is full of WOODWORK, mostly Jacobean and collected from chimneypieces, beds etc. It was all
given to the church in 1838 by T. Abbott Green, owner of The
Bury (*see* below), the principal house of the village, which he
was then rebuilding, and set out in the nave and then the
chancel in 1841. The panels now adorn the pulpit, lectern,
stalls, altar wall, side walls, W gallery etc. but in a more organized manner than at Old Warden (q.v.). Chancel roof and E
window restored in 1868–9, paid for by Trinity College, Cambridge, which held the advowson. Much C19 tracery introduced elsewhere, where by the early C19 there was none.
– STAINED GLASS. One C15 roundel in the N aisle W window.
– MONUMENT. Coffin lid of the C13 in the chancel floor. Foliated cross growing out of a lion (cf. Oakley), the foliation being
asymmetrically arranged.

THE BURY stood by the church. It has been demolished but its
STABLES (now Pavenham Court) and a Picturesque LODGE
survive, the latter dated 1863. In the village street, the SCHOOL
of 1853 with an eyecatching front of a buttressed projection
for the bellcote and clock (1877) riding high on a stepped
gable.

STAFFORD BRIDGE, 1½ m. SE, across the Ouse. Originally of
four arches. The first references are C16 but the bridge was
replaced in 1936. Concrete with a cladding of Weldon
limestone.

PERTENHALL

ST PETER. The earliest evidence is the three-bay N arcade. This
is of *c*. 1190 – see the only slightly chamfered arches, the round
piers with square abaci, and the bits of dogtooth on one arch.
The chancel, rebuilt in the C13, received a N chapel of two bays
(only one survives) in the early C14 – the arch with nailhead
and notch stops – but this was replaced as the vestry *c*. 1820,
when the chancel E window must have been provided with its
round arch and intersecting tracery. Of the same date or a little
earlier in the C19, one N aisle window. Perp W tower with a
broach spire with low broaches and two tiers of lucarnes, and
also Perp the large transomed S windows of the nave and rood
stair. – SCREEN. An uncommonly good piece with one-light
divisions, and panel tracery, little restored, with traces of painting. The inscription above the ogee doorway refers to the
Transfiguration. In the C18 it carried the Georgian ROYAL
ARMS now in the N aisle. Painted on canvas and with a cut-out
profile. Other C18 fittings were removed during the restoration
of 1892–3 by *R. R. Rowe* of Cambridge. – COMMUNION RAIL.
Good, late C17, with bell-bottomed balusters. – BENCHES. The
standard Beds kind. – ORGAN. 1783 by *James Crange Hancock*.

A charming case with a swan-neck pediment. Here from
c. 1839. – WALL PAINTING. On the N aisle E wall, traces of a
seated figure, to its l. a female saint, to its r. a male saint and
an angel. – STAINED GLASS. Fragments in a chancel S window
and a shield (E window). – MONUMENTS. In the N chapel,
damaged C13 effigy of a knight, cross-legged. Made of clunch.
– A number of worthwhile tablets: in the vestry †1685 (columns,
broken pediment; possibly by *Jasper Latham* (GF)), in the
chancel, all four very similar (broken pediments and scrolly
achievements), †1732, 1742, 1747, and – consciously archaic,
no doubt – †1825.

OLD RECTORY, E of the church. A C16 or C17 house refronted
on three sides in 1799 by the Rev. Thomas Martyn. Red
and rubbed brick. Three storeys, five bays, with a three-bay
pediment and parapet concealing the roof. The ground-
floor windows l. and r. of the doorway have blank arches.
Library room added 1955 by *Richardson & Houfe*. Pretty
thatched Gothick LODGE, *c.* 1800; seamlessly extended in the
C20.★

MANOR HOUSE, SW of the church. Large E-plan house, *c.* 1600,
originally with three-storey canted bays in the wings and porch
tower, but extensively revised in 1877 and further modified in
the C20. Interior mostly of 1877, including Elizabethan-style
panelling and an overmantel with two broad blank arches and
figures in the former hall. Some pleasant stained glass, Aesthetic style, with flora medallions, in the staircase hall.

GREEN END FARMHOUSE, ⅜ m. SW. The house is T-plan
but of two phases; the E wing added *c.* 1600. The wing has
a massive chimneystack of limestone with red brick top and
three diagonal shafts. The ground-floor room within contains
remains of a deep plasterwork frieze, with succulent fruit and
strapwork.

PODINGTON

9060

ST MARY. The chancel is Norman – see the blocked S and N
windows. Of the Norman nave nothing is visible except its
angles. It received a S arcade of three bays about 1190 – see
the square abaci of the round piers, the elementary leaves of a
capital, and the pointed arches with just one slight chamfer.
Much was done in the C13. Externally this can be seen in the
W tower with the long (later lengthened) W lancet, the small
(restored) S lancet, plain N doorway, the N aisle E (blocked)
lancet, and the chancel S lancet side by side with a window

★The former MORAVIAN CHAPEL, built in 1827, has been demolished. Pevsner
described it as a 'Two-bay building with a truncated pyramid roof and a lantern.
Low one-bay gabled pavilions with a circular window. A wooden veranda between.'
It was established by the Rev. John King Martyn, the former rector.

with Y-tracery indicating a late C13 date. The interior confirms all this. The N arcade has round abaci with nailhead and hood-moulds with coarse nailhead, and in the chancel the windows are shafted inside and the PISCINA has continuous rolls with keels and a fillet. The unfeeling geometrical tracery of the E window is patently Victorian. The S aisle E and W windows are Dec, the S and N aisle windows straight-headed, the clerestory also. The tower top is Early Perp. The spire is slightly recessed and has low broaches, crockets up the edges, and three tiers of lucarnes. The pinnacles have mostly disappeared. Some quoins of ironstone, nicely lettered and with the date 1622. E window, 1841 by *F. C. Penrose*, whose brother was the curate (cf. Hinwick House). Perp porch, largely rebuilt in 1882–3. – FONT. The font is Norman, of drum-shape, decorated with close, big chevrons, and also with blank arches and lozenges. – SOUTH DOOR. Traceried. – BENCHES. Perp, plainly but-tressed. Mostly C19. – ROYAL ARMS. Unusual, small ceramic tile (S door). – STAINED GLASS. One chancel S window by *C. A. Gibbs* of London, *c.* 1861; the other (St Peter) of 1871, unsigned. – MONUMENTS. In the chancel, exclusively to the Orlebars, accompanied by many HATCHMENTS. In the N wall four blocked arches. The two inner ones, with keeled mould-ings, may be late C13 tomb recesses; the two outer ones must be later copies. They are filled with inscription slabs of very good lettering. The dates commemorated are 1647, 1658, 1666 (all to the Orlebars, of 'Raunce' marble) and there is a slate slab to William Payne 1624, reused 1681. The naive, extremely odd finials of the outer ones must date from the same time. But what is that time? Can the chains of rings in the outer arches and the finials be indeed as late as the mid C17? The ornament looks decidedly Elizabethan. So perhaps there was a preceding appropriation. – Brass to John Howard †1518, 18 in. (46 cm) long (nave floor, opposite the entrance). – Mrs Diana Orlebar †1716. By *John Hunt*. Alabaster tablet with two crying putti. Open scrolly pediment (as over the doorways of Hinwick House and Hinwick Hall, qq.v.). – John Orlebar †1765. By *Whiting* of Northampton in grey, white and coloured marbles. Greek motifs. – Richard Orlebar †1803. By *Lewis* of Cheltenham. A female figure kneels by the sarcophagus, which incidentally has a small Gothic quatrefoil. – Richard Orlebar †1833. By *Humphrey Hopper*. Tablet in a Gothic surround, the sort of thing Hopper repeated time and again. CROSS SLAB. Set into the wall outside. Fine scrolling foliage to the cross head. C13.

Opposite and to the W of the churchyard, Orlebar ESTATE HOUS-ING, with steep middle gables, quoins and platbands of Northamptonshire ironstone. One is the former VICARAGE of 1778, the other a terraced group of 1773, and quite an ambi-tious little composition with two concentric arches in the centre below the gable, the smaller one above a narrow pas-sage to the back, the larger one bracketing this and two adjoin-ing doorways. Two further large arches l. and r. W of the church, the former SCHOOL, 1841. Tudor windows, gable with finial.

Behind Manor Farm, a CASTLE. Motte-and-bailey type, with an outer enclosure, large enough to circumscribe the whole village.

POTSGROVE

St Mary (Churches Conservation Trust). Essentially Dec, except for the Perp E window, but completely restored in 1880 by *J. D. Sedding*. He was mostly active in Cornwall and the restoration was done for the Rev. E. Norman Coles who had been assistant curate at Penzance many years before. Ironstone nave and chancel; stone NW bell-turret. In the N wall, built in, some Norman bits. Statue of the Virgin in a niche in the W gable by *J. W. Seale*. – SCREEN. C14, although restored. Shafts with rings instead of mullions, and typical Dec tracery. Decoration of 1880; the wagon chancel roof is typical Sedding. – Of 1880 the FONT of Cornish Serpentine and REREDOS (N wall) with paintings redolent of the date. – STAINED GLASS. W window. Reassembled by Sedding from a once extensive early to mid-C14 scheme. – BRASSES. Richard Saunders †1535 and wife, 15½-in. (39 cm) figures. – William Saunders †1563 and wife. Incomplete figures. On their reverse, Flemish-type canopywork of *c.* 1350.

The Dukes of Bedford provided the other buildings. So, W of the church, the OLD RECTORY, Queen Anne-style by *Frederic Chancellor*, 1889, and opposite it the ironstone former BOARD SCHOOL, of 1897–8 by *A. J. Pilkington*, the last such school provided by the estate.

POTTON

St Mary. Outside the town. A large church of brown cobbles, W tower, nave and aisles. N transept, chancel, S chapel and two-storey N porch with access from W as well as N. The porch is further E than customary and has doors to the stair to its upper floor outside and inside the church. It is embattled, as is the clerestory, chancel and S chapel. The tower parapet and turret are of 1850 by *Wing & Jackson*. The oldest feature is a lancet in the chancel N wall. Then, late C13, the S arcade of five bays. Square piers with broad semicircular projections. Double-hollow-chamfered arches. The abaci are not all the same. Two are chamfered squares set diagonally. The N arcade is C14. Standard elements. The details of the transept are Perp, and so is – Late Perp no doubt – the S chapel. Note the design of the arches with continuous mouldings to N and S, capitals only to E and W. Good carved bosses in the S aisle roof. – STALLS with plain MISERICORDS incorporated with the ROOD SCREEN by *Charles Nicholson*, 1921. – REREDOS. *J. S. Alder*, 1907. – STAINED GLASS. One S aisle window by *J. Powell & Sons*, 1874; very characteristic. The S aisle E window may be theirs too, but *c.* 1855. – Chancel NW signed by *H. Hughes* (*Ward & Hughes*), 1878. – The E window (1888, Last Supper) and the N window of the transept (Jesus sitting at Jacob's Well and the Woman of Samaria, 1894) by *Heaton, Butler & Bayne*, the latter window particularly good. – MONUMENTS. In the porch a big square tablet which formerly held a brass with a chalice. – Rev. R. Whittingham †1845. By *Tomson* of Cambridge. Sarcophagus with strigillated pilasters and a profile portrait in a medallion.

Many rustically carved mid- to late C18 GRAVESTONES in the churchyard. It is interesting to see how families (e.g. the Rugeleys, E of the chancel) opted for a uniform design over many years.

CEMETERY, Sandy Road. Chapel by *Usher & Anthony*, 1882.

BURGOYNE MIDDLE SCHOOL, Mill Lane. Interesting polygonal classroom addition of 2003 by *Sergison Bates*, of timber-clad walls, flat sedum roofs with tall vertical rooflights and covered external spaces (cf. the variations on this design at Sandy Upper School).

The MARKET PLACE is specially attractive (compared with Biggleswade, for instance). Mostly red brick C18 houses, many pre-dating the destruction of much of the town in a great fire in 1783. In the middle, the forgivably Neo-Georgian LIBRARY (a.k.a. Clock House) of 1956 by *S. V. Goodman*, the County Architect, on the site of an C18 market building of similar design; the clock and dials are those of 1877 and 1901. Otherwise, e.g. on the S side, No. 21 with a nice pedimented doorway and No. 23 of 1697, seven bays long with heavy modillion cornice. At the start of KING STREET, the GEORGE & DRAGON, again C18 red brick; in the same street a few other minor Georgian houses.

In SUN STREET, SUN HOUSE (formerly the Sun Inn) with one cross-wing of exposed timber-framing and curved bracing (crown-post roof inside). The main range, whose close-studding is exposed in the carriage arch to the l., seems to have been built first, with a two-bay hall in its centre, the cross-wing replacing its chamber end in the C16. Pretty sign on the wall. Almost behind this, a very large former CONGREGATIONAL CHURCH, of 1847, in carstone slips with yellow brick trim. Pedimented front and arched window in the upper storey.

Former STATION, Station Road. 1862 for the Beds & Cambs Railway, which took over the Sandy & Potton Railway that Capt. Sir William Peel (*see* Sandy) built at his own expense in 1857 to move the produce of Potton's market gardens to London. ENGINE SHED of that date in Biggleswade Road, also red and yellow brick.

w of Potton, on Sandy Heath, is the conspicuous TELEVISION MAST, lattice-construction with cable stays. 750 ft (228 metres) high. 1966, originally for Anglia Television.

PULLOXHILL

0030

St James. Ironstone, mostly 1845–6 by *J. T. Wing*. By that time the medieval building had been reduced to just the chancel and part of the w tower, the rest of which had collapsed in the 1650s. Windows with geometrical to flowing tracery, w rose window. The medieval crown-post chancel roof remains and niches with ballflower in the E wall. Wing's nave roof is an elaborate Victorian piece and his interior is little altered, with w gallery (now enclosed below). – COMMUNION RAIL. C18-style turned balusters, but apparently designed by the vicar, the *Rev. Peter Burman*, in 1968; with inlay. – FONT. Square, Neo-Norman. – STAINED GLASS. E window by *Thomas Baillie*, 1857. – MONUMENT. Sir William Bryers †1653. Attributed to *Joshua Marshall* (AW). Very characteristic of its date and of high quality. The centre is a bust in an oval recess with garlands. The surround is broad, high and massive, with volutes up the half-pilasters and a kind of broken scrolly pediment at the bottom.

On the N of the church, THE GRANGE, a late C17 house of seven bays, chequer brick, with a platband, hipped roof and a doorway with a hood on carved brackets. w of this, the CHURCH HALL of 1880 by *J. A. Reeve*. Straight-headed Neo-Elizabethan windows. In the same brick, the former VICARAGE of 1847 by *William Watson*, the Wrest Park surveyor, with sharp gables and grouped chimneystacks.

(HIGHAM BURY, ¾ m. SW. 1878 by *William White* for Captain E. J. Jekyll. The gardens were laid out by his sister *Gertrude Jekyll*, *c.* 1900.)

PUTNOE *see* BEDFORD

RAVENSDEN

0050

ALL SAINTS. Over the s doorway inside is a Norman tympanum with chequerboard pattern. Small w tower with small recessed spire. N aisle with two cross-gables, probably of 1807. The chancel s wall and the s porch are of brick, probably renewed in the late C17. One s window is Dec, and Dec also is the N arcade. Three bays, quatrefoil piers, double-chamfered arches. The nave has a kingpost roof and plaster vault. Dec E window, geometrical tracery, but the chancel arch was rebuilt in 1906, the S window tracery of the same time, and vestry and organ chamber, 1909, all by *Mallows & Grocock*. Sympathetic N rooms, 1997 by the *Victor Farrar Partnership*. – STAINED GLASS. E window by *John E. Crawford*, 1955. MOWSBURY HILLFORT. Iron Age. Univallate, enclosing medieval manorial earthworks.

0050

RENHOLD

ALL SAINTS. Perp W tower with small recessed lead spire and cusped ogee niche. Perp S side and chancel; brown cobbled walls. The N aisle has Dec windows and also a Dec arcade. Three bays, quatrefoil piers, arches with sunk wave mouldings. Vestry added *c.* 1725. Bare walls inside, stripped by *J. Horsford*, 1862–3; his must be the chancel arch – FONT. Norman, drum-shaped, with two palmettes being the beginning of an ornamental band, never continued. – PULPIT. Mid-C17, with typically detailed panels. – BENCH FRONTS. Two, with simple arched panels. C15 (?) (N aisle). – CHANCEL FITTINGS by *Rattee & Kett*, 1863, the encaustic TILES by *Minton*. – STAINED GLASS. Piggott family crest (N window); dated to 1386, when J. Pigott endowed a chantry. Two windows by *Goddard & Gibbs* (*John N. Lawson*), 1966 and 1990. Baptistery window by *Petri Anderson* (*Chapel Studio*), 2004. – MONUMENTS. Tomb-chest with richly cusped quatrefoils. Barbaric writing on the rim, no longer black-letter. On the lid, brasses of Edmund Wayte †1518 and wife (14 in.; 35 cm). – Tablets to the Becher family, specially good Sir William †1694, attributed to *William Stanton* (GF), with the usual urn in a swan-neck pediment but also an abundance of floral garlands; the cartouche with scrolly sides to Mrs Elizabeth †1701, attributed to *Edward Stanton* after 1705 (GF); and the larger piece to William erected 1753 with a frame of fluted pilasters and a broken pediment around the cartouche; it follows a pattern used in the 1720s by Stanton & Horsnaile, but is too late for them (GF). – Robert Graham Polhill †1854. By *I. Evan Thomas*. Sarcophagus with the inscription ALMA and standing by it a young genius with an extinguished torch. – CHAPTER HOUSE. 1984 by *Bruce Deacon* of the *Victor Farrar Partnership*.

Close to the church, some large and unrestored BARNS, timber-framed with red brick nogging and black weatherboarding.

HOWBURY HALL, 1 m. SE. Purchased from the Bechers by the Polhills in 1780. Rebuilt in 1849 after a fire, by *J. Horsford*, but still quite pre-Victorian. Rendered five-bay front plus wings with canted angle bay windows. The latter have first-floor cast-iron balconies. Top balustrade with urns. Imitation quoins. Part of the previous house was retained at the E end until *c.* 1960. Central hall with screen of Ionic marble columns and imperial staircase behind lit by an arched window with the

Polhill arms. Inside the E wing, however, evidence of earlier date: a reset staircase with rustic columns as balusters and walls with stucco of apparently *c.* 1730–40. Also a panel with a pediment and round arch, perhaps early C17. Nicely restored early C18 outbuildings, e.g. a DAIRY/LAUNDRY and U-plan STABLES with hipped roof, pedimented doors and C19 clock turret.

At TOP END, ½ m. N, Nos. 14–24 are handsome pairs of mid-C19 Polhill estate cottages, yellow brick with red diaper patterns.

At SALPH END, 1 m. W of the church, is ABBEY FARMHOUSE, a largish house of *c.* 1600, timber-framed, with two slightly projecting gables l. and r. of the central hall.

RIDGMONT

Ridgmont is the typical Bedford estate village, with a school (of 1856 and 1878) and groups of gabled brick houses of many dates.

ALL SAINTS. 1854–5 by *G. G. Scott*. A Bedford estate church, succeeding the old church (*see* below), and brilliantly exploiting its high position with a W tower and broach spire in a landscape where towers only are the norm. Goodhart-Rendel rightly called it 'respectable, solid and handsome'. Limestone, with the local ironstone used only for minor decorative enrichment. Late C13 style, the spire ribbed with ballflower and one tier of prominent lucarnes. Clerestory windows quatrefoil, piers of the arcades quatrefoil in section. Hoodmould stops with a variety of naturalistic foliage; also on the PULPIT. Texts in big black-letter on the aisle walls, and stencilled decoration to the roofs. – STAINED GLASS. E window, chancel S and tower W by *Wailes*, 1850s and 1860s. – N aisle E by *W. Glasby*, 1928.

OLD CHURCH, Segenhoe, ⅜ m. S. Derelict, yet a church of considerable archaeological interest. The chancel is C11 with two small N windows with splayed rere-arches. One of the windows has a lintel stone with the arch cut into and very elementary decoration, three crosses in circles and two saltire crosses. It looks Saxon. Opposite it in the S wall is another such window arch, bricked up, and both these E windows are set in thicker walling from which there appears to be a slight trace of an arch springing, perhaps indicating an apse arch. Plain chancel arch, unmoulded but with just a little flat chevron on the abacus of the responds, i.e. Norman. The (reset) S doorway is Early Norman too, with a tympanum whose bottom is cut segmentally. The N arcade is partly C13, partly early C14. The ironstone E bay represents the former, the rest the latter date. Octagonal pier first, quatrefoil piers with thin shafts in the diagonals later. Oddly triple-chamfered arch first, arches of two sunk quadrants later. Submerged in the S wall at the W end is another quatrefoil pier, so it seems the nave had two aisles in the C14. The W window of that period is partly blocked by the w tower added in 1818–19 by *R. F. Nixon* of Woburn. If the s aisle was built, had it by then been demolished?

SEGENHOE MANOR, ⅛ m. E of the old church. A perfect, pocket early C18 country house. Five bays, evenly spaced on the front with just the middle bay projected but arranged 1–3–1 on the back. Nice garden doorcase with fluted pilasters and carved consoles. The entrance porch is probably late C18, see the fanlight. Sunk basement and a hipped roof on modillions. Double stacks on the flanks. Good interior, especially the staircase with spiral and straight balusters and inlay.

Between the cottages in High Street closest to the gates to Woburn, the former BAPTIST CHAPEL of 1811 with a broad dissolute stucco façade which looks Early Victorian. Minor former METHODIST CHURCH at N end of the street, dated 1853 (now a house). THE FIRS, adjoining, has the type of early C19 doorcase found also in Woburn in which the pilasters curl forward to the hood.

WATER TOWER, S of the church. 1913 by *C. Balfour & Son.* Circular, of reinforced concrete, with full-height pilasters.

For the station *see* Brogborough.

RISELEY

ALL SAINTS. Obscured by the s porch is evidence of the jamb of an Anglo-Saxon or Saxo-Norman window in the s aisle wall. This appears baffling as long as one has not seen one special point about the church's architectural history. Until 1895, when the church was restored by *Gotch & Saunders*, the s aisle was the nave: hence the width of the E.E. arch to the s chapel, then chancel, and hence the lancet in the chapel wall now looking into the chancel and the trefoil-headed double piscina. This original nave, early in the C13, received a N aisle of a width unknown to us. But the arcade is there. Four bays, round piers, base spurs, flat square capitals, one with small-scale stiff-leaf, double-chamfered arches. Early in the C14 the then chancel, i.e. the present s chapel, was given a new E window with reticulated tracery and also a N chapel, i.e. part of the present chancel. It has an E window to match, is of one bay and has typical details. The remodelling of the whole came in the C15, and included the new clerestory, the ashlar s porch, s windows and the upper part of the w tower, which is of ashlar too. Pairs of transomed two-light bell-openings. The lower part of the tower is C14. The aisle's arches and the s windows were raised in 1841–2, when a N gallery was introduced. – BENCHES. The usual buttressed kind. – SCREEN. 1909. The s chapel screens are by *Bruce Deacon*, c. 2000, for conversion to a church room.

OLD VICARAGE, by the church. Inscribed 'Built by the Vicar, 1828'. Brick, red and yellow in the chequered pattern favoured locally, with three gables. Trellis porch. The plans are by *John Farrer* of Riseley.

In the village, a great many small cottages in the local vernacular but too densely built up. No. 135 HIGH STREET is mostly late C20 but incorporates a very important survival of a two-storey but one-roomed medieval cottage, timber-framed with close studding. Door in the upper floor, probably to a garderobe or external stair. The barn is partly of clay lump construction, a feature of the locality. Outbuildings incorporate timber-framing etc. salvaged from buildings at Astwood and Wootton.

THE MALLOWRY, ¾ m. SSW. 1905–6 by *S. Carey Curtis* for Col. Spencer Jackson, who had served in South Africa. The design for the garden front intended curly Dutch gables over two projecting bays – in the Cape style – but they do not seem to have been executed. In fact it is closer to Voysey's style, white roughcast, slender chimneys, steep roofs ending in eaves guttering on wrought-iron stays. Lodge and stables in matching style.

RISINGHOE CASTLE *see* GOLDINGTON

ROXTON   *1050*

ST MARY. Short Perp W tower, nave and chancel. Brown cobble walls except for a massive ironstone NE tower buttress. The S aisle has a doorway and W window with reticulated heads of *c.* 1300 and a three-bay arcade of the same date. Octagonal piers, semicircular responds, double-chamfered arches. The N windows of the nave are irregular, two Dec, one Perp. The tower was built into the existing nave. Chancel also Dec but restored and the chancel arch rebuilt by *W. G. Habershon*, 1848–9. Its two-bay S arcade is Perp, with one open arch originally to a chapel which was rebuilt as the vestry/organ chamber in 1931–2; brick with tile quoins and mullions. – SCREEN. Perp. On the surviving dado, cusped arches with painted saints and a Resurrection, the East Anglian way. Conserved 1975 by *A. Ballatyne*. – HANGING ROOD. Acquired in the 1920s but Greek, painted in 1744, signed by *Nicole Doxora*, the ends of the arms with scroll decoration. – STAINED GLASS. E window by *A. K. Nicholson*, 1926. – MONUMENTS. Lady, probably early C14, in a plain recess in the nave N wall. – Tomb-chest to Roger Hunt †1438, against the blocked arch of the S chapel. On the chest, shields in cusped arches. No effigy.

CONGREGATIONAL CHAPEL. Founded in 1808 by C. J. Metcalfe of Roxton Park. A most unusual and a delightful design, thatched with a tree-trunk veranda, ogee windows and roughcast walls. Adapted from a barn and extended to its present T-plan form *c.* 1825 by the addition of apsidal-ended wings for vestry and schoolroom. The S wing has a recessed porch for the Metcalfes, with twig-lined walls, a vault, pine-cone bosses and a concealed study for the minister. Unaltered inside.

p. 274

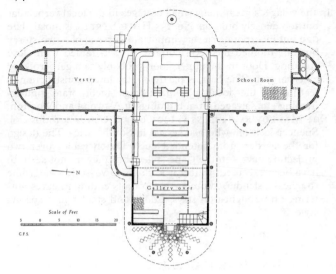

Roxton, Congregational chapel.
Plan

E gallery with box pews and a private S pew behind a row of
ogee arches. Two other such pews open into the wings. –
ORGAN. Introduced 1941. A pretty Early Victorian piece, rose-
wood with ebony. – STAINED GLASS. Two windows by *Goddard
& Gibbs*, 1946 (*A. E. Buss*) and 1997 (*John N. Lawson*).

The style of the chapel is shared by the ROUND LODGE of
1848 at the entrance to ROXTON HOUSE, SW of the chapel
across its park. Its brick front is *c.* 1800, double-pile plan with
a smaller and later third range behind.

CHURCH FARMHOUSE, opposite the chapel, C19 gault brick
over timber-framing. In an upper room, plaster royal arms,
probably James I, flanked by female caryatids with strapwork
and small heads with curly hair (the patterns of the moulds
are identical to Low Farm, Colmworth).

PALACEYARD WOOD, 1⅜ m. W. In the centre, a circular medieval moated enclosure with traces of an earthwork in a solitary
motte or mound, *c.* 40 ft (*c.* 12 metres) in diameter. Surrounding this, a complex of smaller enclosures including cultivation
earthworks.

SALFORD

ST MARY. The most striking features are *William White*'s of 1867:
the bellcote of heavy timbers in curved crossings as if for a
Victorian lychgate. The bellcote is for three bells and carries a

spirelet; it replaced an C18 one that succeeded a brick W tower. The church itself is mainly of *c.* 1300. The reconstructed N porch, open, of heavy timbers with crown-post roof and downward bracing is probably of this date (one beam with dogtooth and some ornament is genuine C13 work). See also the restored W window with bar tracery of three uncusped circles, the NE window, the small S lancet, the S window of three stepped lancet lights, and the S aisle E window, which has cusped intersecting tracery. With this goes the S arcade of quatrefoil piers with moulded capitals. The capitals are perfectly normal, with a little nailhead, except that their bottom member is elongated to meet the pier. Had the masons made a mistake? The chancel arch goes with the S arcade but in the chancel a priest's doorway which, with its unmoulded pointed arch, looks older than the rest, and a Dec E window with reticulated tracery. The other windows are White's. N vestry of 1900 by *William Poole* of Woburn Sands. – BENCHES. A few are pre-Reformation. – PULPIT. 1916. – STAINED GLASS. In the N aisle, one of 1901 by *Hardman & Co.* and another by *T. F. Curtis, Ward & Hughes*, 1921. – MONUMENTS. In the S aisle cross-legged knight, clunch, in all probability he who built the S aisle. The fragmentary canopy is later. The tomb-chest has shields on loops. – Brasses to John Peddar †1505, wife and family, 28-in. (71 cm) figures. COFFIN SLABS. In the chancel and W end, with a sword in relief and moulded sides with freize of fleurons and shields.

MANOR. Next to the church. A good small C18 house of three bays with chequer brick, hipped roof and dormers. The lords of the manor were All Souls College, Oxford. The nice porch with segmental arched hood and one-bay W extension by *E. A. S. Houfe*, 1964 and 1969 for Sir Richard Temple. Further added to at rear.

SALPH END *see* RENHOLD

SANDY   *1040*

Sandy is the site of a small Roman town on the Roman road which formed a route along the Ivel valley parallel to and to the W of Ermine Street between Braughing and Godmanchester (Durovigotum) and is now partly overlain by the A1. Miscellaneous Roman remains have been found in the neighbourhood and the layout of the town is understood but structures are wanting. It was also a centre of significant earlier settlement, attested to by the Iron Age hillforts on the Greensand Ridge which provides the town's eastern backdrop. The ridge also meant that there were stone quarries and brick yards in the C19. The soil of the surrounding land was suited to market gardening on a large scale, even as early as 1600, which was further stimulated by the arrival of the railway in 1850, an event which first led to the discovery of the Roman and earlier remains. The town remained fairly small, with its focus on the market place at the junction of the roads to London, St Neots and Cambridge until the mid C20. It has grown very substantially since, engulfing the formerly separate hamlet of Girtford, which lay along the Great North Road. But to the E all remains rural and unspoiled. Like the expansion of all the towns and villages close to the A1, nearly nothing has been added architecturally.

ST SWITHUN. Essentially by *W. G. Habershon* (of *Habershon & Pite*), 1859–60, but maintaining something of the pattern and character of its predecessor while still a creditable job in its own right. Coursed ironstone, large, with aisles, transepts, chapels and vestry (enlarged 1908), the details mostly Dec. Inside the chancel, the chapel arcades, the chancel arch and the roof corbels all have naturalistic foliage of late C13 inspiration: ivy, oak leaves and here and there small animals crawling. Fine nave roof with castellated trusses, the chancel plainly ceiled. The aisle arcades have arches of dark ironstone. The octagonal S piers are genuine Perp work. The W tower is medieval too. So are the SEDILIA and PISCINA (with credence shelves), both with cusped arches. – FONT. Saxon(?) bowl. – TILES in the chancel (*Maw & Co.*?). – TOWER SCREEN. Lively Tudor Perp by *Horace Richardson*, 1895. – STAINED GLASS. S chancel window by *C. A. Gibbs*, 1862, with medallions of Acts of Mercy. – E window, 1892 by *Belham & Co.*, the design (Faith, Hope and Charity) signed by *Henry G. Murray*. – N transept N by *Camm Bros*, 1881. – S chapel E by *Frederick Drake* of Exeter, 1893. Surprisingly modern treatment of diagonal rays emanating from the resurrected Christ. – S aisle, a superb Annunciation by *Mary Lowndes*, 1902, with her usual blues and greens and fluid drawing. – Tower window, 1902 by *J. Powell & Sons* (St Swithun, St George and St Andrew). – S transept E, the WAR MEMORIAL, powerful figures of Courage and Victory by *Percy Bacon*, 1920, in an alabaster memorial by *Maile & Son.* – S aisle w, over font, by *John Hayward*, 1965. Etiolated Christ and St John the Baptist. – SCULPTURE. In the chancel a small fragment of a C14 or C15 alabaster panel of the frequent Nottingham type. It belongs to a scene of Christ in the Garden of Gethsemane. – MONUMENTS. Several tablets to the Pyms of Hazells Hall (*see* Everton), C18–C20, e.g. two in coloured marble with urns, William Pym †1788 signed by *Tyler & Ashton*, and his son, also William, †1775 signed by *W. Tyler*, with a backdrop of curtains. For earlier conventions, see Elizabeth Pym †1760, with its mourning cherub on top, and that in similar vein to her father (Heylock Kingsley †1749 but also erected 1760). – Two others are by *Benjamin Palmer*: Robert Johnson †1769 (S chapel) and the Rev. Lewis Monoux †1771 (chancel). – By *Thomas Denman*: Francis Pym †1833 and Lt-Col. Francis Buckworth †1845. – Statue of white marble of Capt. Sir William Peel V.C., who died at Cawnpore, India, in 1858. Heroic stance, hand on his sabre. By *W. Theed*, 1861. Now in the S transept but originally in the chancel.

Former BAPTIST CHAPEL, Pleasant Place. 1853–4 by *Henry Usher*. Yellow brick, pedimental gable and round-arched windows.

BAPTIST CHAPEL, Bedford Road. 1887–8 by *Usher & Anthony*. Handsome Quattrocento style with pediment over the centre and terracotta decoration. Two-storey front and flanks.

CHURCH HALL of 1929 also commendable in its own way, with massive volutes at the angles of the gabled front.

PRIMITIVE METHODIST CHURCH, St Neots Road. 1910 by *G. & R. P. Baines* in their unmistakable Tudor Perp. One large window of panel tracery in the face and tower buttresses.

CEMETERY, Potton Road, ⅜ m. SE. Laid out 1890–1 by *John Usher*, over part of the site of Roman settlement. Good cruciform chapel, ironstone with a fleche, of 1892 by *George Highton*.

TOWN HALL, Bedford Road. 1905 by *Usher & Anthony*. A very large building – the town's cinema for many years – with a columned porch, half-timbered upper floor and a bellcote. The gambrel roof added after a fire imposes a slightly ridiculous appearance.

FIRE STATION, Ivel Road. Neat, flat-roofed, in gault brick. By *S. V. Goodman*, County Architect, 1954. The fire station of 1882 survives in Cambridge Road (No. 10; now council offices).

LABURNUM LOWER SCHOOL, Laburnum Road. Originally Girtford School. 1906–7 by *Gotch & Saunders*. The brick tower with a stone belfry and ogee roof is their unmistakable motif.

SANDYE PLACE (ACADEMY), WSW of the church. The house is *c.* 1720–30 for the Monoux family (a plaque in the parapet also records a rebuilding in 1673 for Humphrey Monoux who purchased the manor in 1670). Red brick. Five bays in a 2–1–2 rhythm. Parapet partly balustraded. Horrid 1970s canopy. Round the corner another five-bay façade with a three-bay pediment and a later wide single-storey bow. Arms in the pediment of Sir Richard Edgcumbe, who bought the house in 1897. Round the corner again, five bays once more but with the centre bay as a shallow projection. C19 N addition in ironstone blocks. The earliest SCHOOL buildings are postwar, *c.* 1951 by *S. V. Goodman*, then County Architect, his successor *J. C. Barker*, and *K. P. Roberts*. One or two of the buildings are specially pleasant, notably the pale brick and concrete blocks closest to the house, which include a hall under a gently curving roof.

DOVECOTE, S of the house. Circular, of ironstone, with a conical top. It dates from Edgcumbe's improvements to the gardens, 1897–1904.

SANDY UPPER SCHOOL, Engayne Avenue. Mostly 1970s but with an eyecatching classroom pavilion by *Sergison Bates*, 2003, which has as its signature tall rooflights clad in aluminium and horizontal hardwood cladding to the walls. A similar addition by the same firm at MAPLE TREE LOWER SCHOOL, Hawk Drive, of 2002–3 (cf. Burgoyne Middle School, Potton).

GIRTFORD BRIDGE, crossing the Ivel, W of the town beyond the A1, by *John Wing* the elder, 1781. Ironstone. Three shallow arches.

STATION. By *Henry Goddard,* 1850, for the Great Northern Railway. Typically economical, yellow brick with round-arched windows. Sandy was chosen as the nearest point to Bedford on the GNR line.

SANDY LODGE (RSPB HQ), 1¼ m. SE. 1869–72 by *Henry Clutton* for Arthur Wellesley Peel, on the estate purchased by his brother, Capt. Sir William Peel, from the sale of Sandy Place in 1851. Yellow brick, Tudor, the stables with a fanciful cupola. A porch added by *Alfred Waterhouse* in 1881 has been removed. Much refurbished inside *c.* 1934 for Sir Malcolm Stewart, chairman of the London Brick Co.; possibly by *Murray Adams-Acton* the staircase with its subtle Gothic motifs and crowns on the newels is probably of this date. The former drawing room/library has imported fittings, including C18 marble fireplaces and a fine relief of a bacchanalian scene. Another room is panelled with Rococo ceiling, and in a former bedroom a pair of charming Rococo-style corner cupboards. Office extensions, Neo-neo-Tudor style, by *Fitzroy Robinson,* 1996 and 2005.

Enclosing the garden a balustrade, very similar to that on the roof of Old Warden Park (q.v.). Italianate pond, introduced by Stewart as his swimming pool; pergolas etc. of the same time.

At the entrance is the THE GATEHOUSE, formerly the SWISS COTTAGE, built by 1854 as the seat of Capt. Sir William Peel (†1858). Two storeys with broad-eaved roofs, applied half-timbering and saltire panels, and a balcony over the entrance. Sliding-sash shutters to some of the ground-floor rooms.

The estate also includes the HILLFORT called GALLEY HILL, W of the house on the edge of the Greensand Ridge, and with views N and S along the Ivel valley. It covers an area of 3 acres (1.25 ha) and is of univallate construction with an entrance through the N side. Excavations have also identified a pre-Iron Age fort in its SW corner. It has as its counterpart the so-called 'Caesar's Camp' HILLFORT, NE of the railway station on a spur overlooking the Ivel. It is a contour fort enclosing 7 acres (2.8 ha). The site has been considerably damaged and now presents the appearance of a slight earthwork. Within its site is a house called CAESAR'S CAMP, probably built *c.* 1858 by Captain John Peel who inherited the estate from his brother. Gault brick with some Castellated Gothic features including a square turret.

HAZELLS HALL (The Hasells). *See* Everton, p. 165.

SEGENHOE *see* RIDGMONT

9020

SEWELL

A hamlet of houses strung along a lane NW of Dunstable, below Maiden Bower.

SEWELL MANOR. Substantially enlarged in 1968, but the core is a medieval hall with a superb queen-post roof of two bays, originally clearly longer. Probably late C15, the brackets of the trusses are traceried with quatrefoils, mouchettes etc., and resting on the trusses are pointed arches with pierced spandrels, in turn supporting the queenposts.

SHARNBROOK

9050

A large village with a good mix of stone and brick buildings along its High Street of impressive length, very probably an ancient road with extensive common field behind it. The railway arrived in 1857 (station now closed) but its present extent is mostly due to the period since 1900.

ST PETER. The W tower is Dec below – see the flowing tracery of the W window – but the recessed spire is Perp. Three tiers of lucarnes in the same directions. The thin flying buttresses connected with the corner pinnacles (cf. Harrold) are restorations of the 1930s. The parapet between the pinnacles is of pierced quatrefoils. The rest of the exterior is also Perp, except for the C13 S doorway with two continuous hollow chamfers and the N doorway with many fine mouldings, which is Dec again. Internally the story is different. Both arcades are E.E., i.e. go with the S doorway. Round and octagonal piers and double-hollow-chamfered arches with broaches. The wide chancel arch of the same date, but the N (Tofte) Chapel Dec – see its arch to the chancel and N aisle, also the stepped SEDILIA and PISCINA carved with headstops. The arcades are linked by a Perp bay to the tower, presumably replacing pre-C13 work; the N arch has the shield of the Braybrooks of Colworth who died out by 1429. A visually disconcerting aspect of the church is that the floor of the chancel is lower than the nave, following the nave's restoration by *T. J. Jackson* in 1855–8. – FONT. Octagonal, Perp, with a buttressed shaft and quatrefoiled lozenges broken across the corners. Fleurons on the underside. Charming intricately carved cover with bird finial of *c.* 1910. – SCREENS. The rood screen has one-light divisions, but with a broad ogee-headed entrance with panel tracery over. On the S side, some C17 panelling introduced in the 1850s from the pulpit. – The screen to the N chapel (1908) has kept old tracery bits. Tower screen by *Talbot Brown & Fisher* of Wellingborough, 1931. – STALLS. Late C19, with lockable brass bars added in 1896 by the advowson holder, L. Stileman-Gibbard, after an acrimonious dispute with the vicar over chancel seating rights. – REREDOS. 1901 by *J. Powell & Sons*, Last Supper, with stone inlay, and gold and red glass mosaic – a typical piece. – PULPIT. 1910 by *Jones & Willis*, Gothic with some Art Nouveau-ish motifs in the carving.

– STAINED GLASS. The E window, still pictorial, of *c.* 1855–6, attributed to *Charles Clutterbuck*. – Chancel S, 1873 by *Clayton & Bell*. – MONUMENTS. Brasses to William Cobbe †1522, wife and son, 18-in. (46 cm) figures. – In the N chapel, Boteler family, erected 1618 when the chapel was returned out of use as a schoolroom. Tablet with two columns and strapwork on the entablature. – William Lee Antonie †1815. By *Flaxman*. Portrait in medallion and a landscape with a lion below. – Several standard mid-C19 tablets signed by *Gaffin* to the Gibbards, squarsons of Sharnbrook. – Dr and Mrs Walter Parbury (N aisle). St Luke, the physician, in a round-headed niche, by *Kate Parbury*, 1962. – Hollingworth Magniac †1867 and wife, put up in 1870 for Charles Magniac by *William Burges*. Very different from the run of English monuments, and indeed decidedly Continental. Huge Neo-Baroque tablet with cherubs, and a predella of furled drapery in a surround of much coloured marble inlay. Scrolly iron railings curving out in section, and a matching screen to the aisle arch.★

In the churchyard, under a tile-roofed shelter since *c.* 1900, but alas extensively weathered, is the MAGNIAC MAUSO-LEUM, again by *Burges* and again 1870, equally exotic, and a tomb-chest on a monster scale, with fat cherubs and volutes, cartouches, swags of fruit and a coved cornice. The style is not easily summarized: there are elements of the English style of *c.* 1660 but J. Mordaunt Crook's 'free versions of Sicilian Renaissance' comes closest. – WAR MEMORIAL. Tabernacle finial on a cross-shaft, C14-style. By *Talbot Brown & Fisher*, 1921.

CHURCHYARD GATES. The E gates are wrought iron; early C18. They were made for Sharnbrook House (*see* below). The N gates are fine cast-iron kissing gates of *c.* 1850, stamped by *Williams* of Bedford. The LYCHGATE is by *Gotch & Saunders*, 1910, with a fine lattice of beams in the gable and short columns along the sides. Saunders lived locally.

SHARNBROOK HOUSE, High Street. Early to mid-C18 (rainwater heads dated 1749 are recorded). Red brick, rubbed dressings, stone quoins. Originally seven bays with a centre recessed between shallow wings. Hipped roof. In the centre a pediment. Much extended in a consistent Neo-Georgian style in 1911 by *Clyde Young*, including the whole of the garden side, which has a handsome stone doorcase with Ionic columns below a tall arched window for the staircase. Small oval windows l. and r. Terrible plastic windows.

Further W, the OLD VICARAGE, an even better Neo-Geor-gian design of 1910 by *Gotch & Saunders*. E of Sharnbrook House, many good stone houses, some with thatched roofs, including No. 30 (which has evidence of a cruck frame inside). One (now a shop) has a datestone WB 1671 for *William Bayes*, the mason who held the land behind. Further along the High

★This outstanding monument is sadly blighted by the gross intrusion of the heating system.

Street, the SCHOOL of 1836, again Tudor Gothic windows, and its much larger successor of *c.* 1873 by *Ladds & Powell*; then the former BAPTIST CHAPEL of 1865 by *John Usher*. A typical front – yellow brick with red brick trim. Three bays wide with arched windows with Venetian tracery. Pediment along the whole façade. Inside, galleries with cast-iron fronts by *Macfarlane (Saracen Foundry)* of Glasgow. Almost opposite, the former POLICE STATION and court house (Sharnbrook Court) of 1871–2 by *J. Horsford*.

In TEMPLARS' WAY, ¾ m. NE, TEMPLECROFT is by *M. H. Baillie Scott*, 1910. Nearby, RISDENE, a larger house, also Arts and Crafts, 1911 by *H. Adnitt* of Rushden.

On ODELL ROAD, a group of large 1890s villas (Ailsa Villa etc.) overlooking Felmersham by *Charles Clayson*, the Harrold builder-architect.

TOFTE MANOR, ½ m. NW. Partly of 1613. To this date belong the four gables; the higher castellated part with large mullioned windows and the kitchen wing are additions of 1902 for the Alstons; also the date of the entrance gates. Inside, the drawing room was decorated in 1880 by *J. M. Whistler* for his friends and patrons, Lewis and Ada Jarvis; it was a relative of his scheme for the famous Peacock Room but what remained was sadly destroyed by fire *c.* 2002.

COLWORTH SCIENCE PARK, 1 m. WNW. Developed in the grounds of COLWORTH HOUSE as a research and development centre for Unilever from 1947 and since 2009 as a Science Park in partnership with Goodmans. There was an Elizabethan house of the Montagus; the present house was begun in 1715 after the sale of the estate to their steward Mark Antonie. Originally of Weldon ashlar, supplied by *Richard Knight*, the stonemason earlier employed at Hinwick House. Three-storeys, seven windows wide, with a three-bay pediment over the centre. *John Sumpter* of Higham Ferrers was the 'Stone Cutter & Builder'. The top storey has segment-headed windows. The quoins of even length are characteristically Early Georgian. Work was halted by Antonie's death in 1720 and the family's losses in the South Sea Bubble, resuming only in the 1760s; one rainwater head (S wall) is dated 1762. The two-storey N and S pavilion wings, linked to the centre by low colonnades (now glazed), were completed only in 1772–5 for William Lee by *John Woolfe*. Originally they had giant arches in the centre and hipped roofs behind a parapet but they have been refaced. A grand porte cochère was attached to this front until *c.* 1950. The rear was extensively altered in 1808–12 for William Lee Antonie, with advice from the artist *Samuel Reynolds* and *John Wing* as mason; both men no doubt recommended by Antonie's friend Samuel Whitbread. This includes the N entrance arch. The early C18 rear elevation was identical to the front except for the pediment, but is obscured by the large ashlar-faced wing of 1894–5 for W. C. Watson by *Ernest George & Yeates*, its porch in a recessed centre between gabled wings in simplified *c.* 1700 style. Their interiors, like those of the earlier periods, have gone. The staircase is a slight puzzle, in a rich Rococo style of lyre-pattern balustrade but surely 1890s. Reset here a SCULPTURE in low relief (formerly an overmantel) of Gwen Mond, Lady Melchett, the house's last owner. It is 1930s, by *A. Melnikoff*, Epstein's pupil.

Buildings to the l. were put up in the 1960s. Further numerous laboratories etc. in the grounds, including the MAGNIAC (FOOD SCIENCE) BUILDING, 1994–5 by *Sheppard Robson*, with three laboratories as fingers opening off an atrium office building under a double curved roof, the TONY JAMES BUILDING, conceived as a repeatable modular design of a square block with yellow brick sides, windows in tall square-headed recesses and hipped roof; three blocks in staggered formation completed 2000. Finally, THE EXCHANGE of 2011 by *RMJM*, three conventional blocks in white-render and block stone: two for offices/laboratories, the third for shared conference rooms, café etc. At the former s entrance, classical double LODGES of 1811 by *John Wing* and good Victorian ones at the present entrance.

MILL THEATRE, I m. E of the village. Formerly STOKE MILLS. Four-storey main part, red brick 1892 (and earlier and later) by *Usher & Anthony*. Converted 1979.

SHARPENHOE *see* STREATLEY

SHEFFORD

ST MICHAEL. Originally a chapel of ease to Campton. Of iron-stone. Rebuilt in 1807–8 and given a s aisle of height and width equal to the nave in 1822–3. Windows of early C19 type with Y-tracery and intersecting tracery. E walls rebuilt in brick in 1852–3. The exception is the lower parts of the C14 NW tower, and even there the large window is evidently early C19. The Perp tower arch also remains. Roofs rebuilt by *Mallows & Grocock*, 1907. Cast-iron columns between nave and aisle were replaced by unmoulded pointed brick arches in 1933 by *Albert Richardson*. The nave is now in the s aisle, and the E end of the former nave was divided for kitchen etc. in the 1990s. – STAINED GLASS. Nave s wall. By *Heaton, Butler & Bayne*, 1894. Good, deep colours. E window and N aisle windows by *H. Warren Wilson*, 1930s.

ST FRANCIS (R.C.), a little w on High Street. 1882–4 by *S. J. Nicholl*. Paid for by Mrs Lyne-Stephens of Lynford Hall, Norfolk. Very much better than the parish church, speaking for a Roman Catholic community already strong in Shefford in the C18. The brick façade has an asymmetrically set stone bellcote over the porch and four-light Perp window. Inside, the plan is oblong with two narrow chancel aisles formed by

Shefford, St Francis (R.C.) church and Home
1880

two-bay arcades within the raised (ritually) E parts of the rectangle. Rood beam instead of a chancel arch. – REREDOS. 30 ft
(9.1 metres) high, very lavish and excellently carved. Saints in
the upper tier, angels at the top and little flying buttresses. –
The carving for the PULPIT and LADY ALTAR, with its niche
and window under a vault, is of the same high standard. –
STAINED GLASS. Two by *Lavers & Westlake*, 1884, the W
window with scenes from the life of St Francis, and Mrs Lyne-
Stephens's portrait, the Lady Chapel S and another N of 1920
by *Hardman & Co*.

The church is at the centre of an elegantly composed group
along High Street, also by *Nicholl*, red brick with terracotta
decoration and black-and-white half-timbering. Attached to
the l. is the former ST FRANCIS' HOME for orphans, established in 1869 but rebuilt in 1879–80. Lower l. part. Higher r.
part, as high as the church, with two wooden gables over balconies. To the r. of the church, the PRESBYTERY. In the same
homely style as the rest, but also with a plaque inscribed 'St
George for England', a St George flag over the door and a
small statue of the saint; the first R.C. chapel, of *c.* 1780, was
dedicated to St George.

METHODIST CHURCH, High Street. 1912, by *G. & R. P. Baines*,
in their familiar Art Nouveau-inflected Gothic.

ROBERT BLOOMFIELD ACADEMY, Bloomfield Avenue. Dated
1938, by *S. C. Jury*, Architectural Assistant to the County
Surveyor. Art Deco style, unique among interwar Bedfordshire
schools.

There is little else of note at Shefford. In HIGH STREET,
Nos. 36–38, half-timbered and over-restored, and in NORTH

BRIDGE STREET, the timber-framed house called THE PORCH (now BARCLAYS BANK), externally more picturesque than genuine but dated to *c.* 1499 and formerly the Cock Inn. Carved spandrels to the arch of the carriageway to the l. The very pretty ground floor was altered in 1919, creating a passage of the pavement below the front of the house. The bank interior by *E. A. Beaumont* of Barclays, 1955, is also nicely preserved, with panelling etc. In the same street, the OLD FIRE STATION of 1897 by *James Shilcock* of Hitchin, with a tall brick bellcote.

SHELTON

ST MARY. A rough building, and of a wonderfully unrestored appearance inside, the result of conservation by *Albert Richardson* in 1931. The nave is probably Saxon and originally aisleless, on the evidence of its thin walls and rubble quoins at the SE corner. The principal external features are Dec, though the S doorway, with two slight continuous chamfers, must be early C13, and the chancel arch seems C13 too. Dec especially the two uncommonly enterprising E windows; of the chancel, five lights, and of the N chapel, three lights straight-headed with mouchettes. Inside, the arcades are evidently earlier, the arches wide, pointed and unmoulded, but they are puzzling just because no Victorian do-gooder has tidied them up. The NE respond is Late Norman with a multi-scalloped capital and a square chamfered abacus; the next pier is of the same date, round with a square abacus, but the W pier is Dec with a charming, nodding-ogee upper stop-chamfer. The S arcade is partly probably of the late C12 too, but much pulled about. The N chapel – *see* above for the E window – has indeed a two-bay Dec arcade. Perp S aisle windows and Perp clerestory. The chancel SE window also Perp, with a shuttered lowside window below the transom. – PULPIT. C16. Plain panels. – SCREEN. Perp, of one-bay divisions, buttressed dado. – BENCHES. The usual buttressed type. – ROOD BEAM. Introduced by *Richardson*, the rood carved by *Percy Bentham*, 1932 – WALL PAINTINGS. St Christopher, N wall. – To the E of this two frontal figures, said to represent St Michael with the scales and the Virgin pressing down one scale, weighing souls. Black-letter above the arcades and rosette decoration in the spandrels of the chancel arch. – STAINED GLASS. Many bits, including heads, and the Symbol of the Trinity.

SHELTON HALL. A plain, long front of painted stone, but said to be medieval in origin and one range of a former quadrangle, of which the moated site survives. In its present form probably early C17, see the typical chimneys with cornices, as one finds in Northamptonshire, and fireplaces with four-centred arches at the S end. Interior refitted in the C18.

SHILLINGTON

ALL SAINTS. The church, majestic on the summit of the hill at   2
the centre of the village, is one of the most memorable sights
in Bedfordshire. It was held by Ramsey Abbey, Hunts., from
the CII, and is large, of ironstone, and impressive in its length
with closely set buttresses dressed in grey stone, no division of
chancel from aisles visible externally, and with two square E
turrets (cf. Tingrith, Wymington). The site has also made it
vulnerable. Part of the church fell in 1595 and the W tower
collapsed in 1701 and was only rebuilt in 1750, all the upper
parts in red brick and powerfully plain, with arched bell-openings. The principal restoration took place in 1881–5, by *Vincent
Wing*, who reversed C18 alterations to the chancel, correctly
reinstating its clerestory tracery. Internally, it is the height
which impresses as much as the length. There is a chancel arch,
dividing four-bay nave arcades from three-bay chapel arcades.
Quatrefoil piers with hollows in the diagonals, sunk quadrant
mouldings, i.e. Dec. The details of bases and abaci differ only
slightly. The arches from aisle to chapels have dying mouldings.
The E bay of the chancel chapels has always been blocked by
a screen wall, at least partly perhaps to strengthen the structure
of the E end. The insides of the aisle windows and the E window
also Dec. For the earlier C14 build a date is available: Bishop
Burleigh of Lincoln in 1333 issued a commission to compel
the parishioners to repair the nave. Does that mean that the
chancel had then finished rebuilding? It is suggested that the
church was completed under Matthew Assheton, rector from
1349 to 1400 whose rebus appears in the frieze above the E
window. The window itself was reduced in size as early as the
C15, again perhaps to resist weakness at this end. Is the arch
between the nave and the W tower again C14, though later than
the other C14 work? The S and the smaller N doorway are Perp,
the S porch originally two-storey with a stair entered under an
ogee arch inside the aisle. The nave ROOF is of eight bays with
a painted and gilded ceilure to the E bays, decorated with
bosses of coats of arms, including the Musgrave family, Ely
and Trinity College, Cambridge, which held the church after
the Dissolution. Owing to the position of the church the E end
has a CRYPT under. This looks late C13. Round middle pier,
slim wall-shafts, vault with eight radiating, single-chamfered
ribs. – FONT. With Perp foot. – SCREENS. An exceptional
wealth. The chancel screen is very high, with one-light divisions and crocketed ogee arches. – Several parclose screens,
specially pretty the one between chancel and N chapel, with
alternating tracery patterns. – The corresponding S screen is a
little simpler. – Of the chapel W screens, that of the S chapel is
nearly all new, that of the N chapel has some pretty dado panels.
– BENCHES. Many, with plain buttressed ends. – ARCHITEC-
TURAL FRAGMENTS. The stiff-leaf capitals of a double column
in the crypt. – STAINED GLASS. E window by *Shrigley & Hunt*,

1885 (designers, *Jewitt* and *Almquist*). – In the s chapel, the e window designed by the *Rev. Charles Kerry*, made by *Kempe*'s studio in 1898, and one by *Christopher Webb*, 1937. – Good N aisle window of 1993 by *Jane Campbell* (*Chapel Studio*), no figures, just bell-ringing motifs and peal changes. – MONU-MENTS. Very good brass to Matthew Assheton, priest, †1400, a 4 ft 4 in. (1.3 metre) figure. – Brass to a priest, late C15, an 18½ in. (47 cm) figure. (Both N chapel floor.) – John Briscoe †1766 and members of the Longueville family. Large tablet, of elegant workmanship. Putti at the foot.

Former SCHOOL, s of the church. 1856, gables with cut barge-boards, a fleche and diaper patterns in the brick. The view down Church Street is a good one with a nice mix of brick, timber-framed and rendered fronts to the houses. Along the main road at the bottom, the former WESLEYAN CHAPEL of 1872, quite large, with octagonal turrets topped by castellations and spirelets.

At ASPLEY END, 1¼ m. SW, THE OLD COURT HOUSE is early C17, presumably for the manorial court. Timber-framed with colour-washed brick infill. On the front, applied ogival bracing. Nearby is SHILLINGTON MANOR, with fine early C19 cast-iron Gothick gates. The house is Neo-Georgian of *c.* 1995 by *Robert H. Robertson & Associates.**

ROUND BARROW, in Tingley Wood, Pegsdon. The mound is 20 ft (6 metres) in diameter and 4 ft (1.25 metres) high. No record survives of any excavation carried out on the site, and its over-grown state makes examination difficult.

KNOCKING KNOLL LONG BARROW, Pegsdon, 1 m. SSW of Pirton. The barrow is approximately 100 ft long and 10 ft high at the broader w end. Considerable damage has been done to the mound, which now resembles two round barrows. The site was partially excavated in the C19, but no record survives of the results of this work.

SHORTSTOWN

The site of the Short Brothers' Airship (or Naval Aircraft) Works of 1917–19, subsequently the Royal Airship Works and, from 1936, RAF Cardington. In the midst of new housing (New Cardington), the administration building (SHORTS BUILD-ING), facing The Highway, is Wren style, by *Cackett & Burns Dick* of Newcastle, 1917. They also designed the GARDEN VILLAGE opposite, in 1917–19, all very Unwinian brick cot-tages and for their date an early expression of a style that became universal after the war.

*The previous house, noted by Pevsner, was of 1915 for Capt. R. B. Lucas, partly created from old materials and with a staircase from a house in Droitwich, panelling and a timber-ceiling dated 1581.

SE is the breathtaking sight of the two huge olive-green corrugated steel-clad AIRSHIP HANGARS. One of the two (No. 1) had been built for the Admiralty in 1916–17 (by *A. J. Main & Co.*, Glasgow) and was lengthened and heightened (by the *Cleveland Bridge Co.*, Darlington) to construct the R101 in 1924–6. No. 2 Shed was built to the same length afresh in 1927–9 to hold the R100, but incorporating a shed (again of 1916) brought from Pulham, Norfolk. Their complete dimensions are 812 ft by 275 ft by 180 ft (247 metres by 83 metres by 55 metres) and they have a central 'nave' with aisles for workshops forming the distinctive skirted profile. Vast sliding doors on rails with external framing. Inside, staircases to a series of high gantries for construction of the ships. They were made redundant by the disastrous crash of the R101 and the immediate scrapping of the R100 but were subsequently used for barrage balloon construction and civil purposes after 1945. No. 2 Shed (film studios) was refurbished in 1995; the other shed reclad in 2013–14.

59

SHUTTLEWORTH PARK *see* OLD WARDEN

SILSOE

0030

ST JAMES. An astonishing job for its date: 1829–31. The architect, *Thomas Smith* of Hertford, achieved an antiquarian accuracy here extremely rare ten years before Pugin, i.e. in the years of Commissioners' Gothic. This faithfulness is due to *Earl de Grey* of Wrest Park, who provided the designs and contributed to the cost of rebuilding after an attempt to add a tower to the previous chapel resulted in its destruction. Nave and aisles, w tower with higher stair-turret, long (not short) chancel. All dressed ironstone, all embattled. The two-light windows, it is true, are too monotonous to be genuine, but otherwise, and even in the arcade piers inside, this is the image of the local Perp church. Inside, the w gallery survives. Very faithful addition at W end of N aisle. – PEWS, STALLS etc. by *Ewan Christian*, 1884, in place of the original box pews. – ALTAR and REREDOS, 1920s Perp. – STAINED GLASS. Some heraldic glass by *de Grey*, 1830; three of 1923 by *Arthur Savell*, and one (tower) by *Margaret Chilton*, 1924, in seductively gloomy style.

Silsoe has the pleasant character of a well-tended estate village but with none of the uniformity found in the Woburn villages, for example. The row W of the church (Nos. 15–29), with jettied gable at one end, and entrances up steps, is particularly attractive. In Church Road, by No. 15, a LOCK-UP. Octagonal, with a pointed head to the doorway.

WREST PARK. *See* p. 343.

SOMERIES CASTLE

s of Luton Airport by Someries Farm

John, Lord Wenlock, who fell at Tewkesbury in 1471, built the house whose ruins stand. They date from the middle C15, probably following Wenlock's knighthood in 1447 and appointment as Queen Margaret's chamberlain a year later, and were left incomplete at his death. The building is the earliest in the county to use brick and furthermore makes use of moulded brickwork and elementary diaper patterns. What remains is the gatehouse, to its E the chapel, and to its W some more walling. The gatehouse has bold and broad polygonal projections and to the r. of the carriage entrance a pedestrian doorway which, however, leads into the main gateway, i.e. has no separate exit into the former courtyard. In the extension to the E is a spiral stair with a sunk handrail. The corbel table above the outer archway is a splendid and highly complex piece of brickwork with cinquefoiled archlets, very similar to that on the gatehouse of Rye House, Hoddesdon, Herts.; the same craftsmen, probably immigrants, must have worked on both buildings. The chapel is of different brick and probably built after an interruption caused by Lord Wenlock's attainder for treason in 1459 and his return to favour in 1460. The chapel E window was of four lights and had a segmental arch. There was a vestibule with a gallery and a S chapel or chamber in the E wing, for the squint from it towards the altar remains.

Adjacent to the house are the associated garden EARTHWORKS.

SOULDROP

ALL SAINTS. The unbuttressed W tower is of *c.* 1275 and has a contemporary broach spire which has two tiers of lucarnes, the lower ones with ogee top lights. It is the oldest spire in the county. The rest is by *Henry Clutton*, 1860–1 (replacing a rebuilding of 1800 by *Robert Salmon*, the 5th Duke of Bedford's surveyor); his porch is vaulted, with fat roll-moulded ribs. The chancel side windows are in pairs with, outside, little crockets growing out of chamfers, a motif repeated inside, where the windows have detached mid-shafts. The arrangement for the SEDILIA is especially noteworthy and the interior as a whole is memorable. The chancel is rib-vaulted; so is the adjoining organ chamber, which has a rose window. The capitals are French, not English, Early Gothic (cf. Woburn), and, above the windows, animals in quatrefoils. Weird detailing throughout, all carved by *Thomas Earp*, who executed the PULPIT and FONT. – STALLS and PEWS, all ruggedly Early Gothic. – TILES. By *Maw & Co.* – Marble REREDOS. – CANDELABRA. Dainty brass leaves. – STAINED GLASS. By *O'Connor*, three in the chancel, 1861, and the Te Deum rose window made 1865 and 1869. – BRASS. John Hanger 1608, kneeling at prayer.

WAR MEMORIAL. Slender cross with broaches at the base. By *W. Talbot Brown* of Wellingborough, 1919.

SCHOOL (village hall) and SCHOOL HOUSE, NE of the church. 1867–8, also by *Clutton*.

Further N, a WESLEYAN CHAPEL of 1912 by *Gotch & Saunders* of Kettering.

SOUTHILL

ALL SAINTS. The W tower, the chancel E and SW windows, two N aisle windows, and the N doorway (completely restored) are C15, the tower originally with a spire. Only the N aisle NW window seems to be older. Its tracery looks *c.* 1300 and, like the other aisle windows, has been built up at its base. N of the chancel is the burial vault created *c.* 1732 for Viscount Torrington. But this was remodelled along with the rest of the church in 1813–14 as a vestry (W) and schoolroom (left incomplete). Long nave and long chancel with low parapets. The muddle of medieval stone and C19 brick has been rendered, and should be again. The arcades cut into by the tower must with their quatrefoil piers repeat the Dec arcades that were there. It is unusual to find such painstaking recreation at this date. The clerestory on the other hand looks wholly Late Georgian. Pretty brick flooring. – ORGAN GALLERY AND FAMILY PEW, W end. Gothick, of 1814–16; see the inscription. Lightly detailed front with three arched windows to the comfortable panelled interior for the Whitbreads. – CREED AND COMMANDMENTS TABLETS of 1854, by *Wing & Jackson*, complementing their E window of 1848. – FONT. A fine piece with exquisite lettering around a shallow bowl on a slender baluster, by *Albert Richardson*, 1937. – STAINED GLASS. Chancel windows (Whitbread memorials †1867 and †1871) both probably by *Ward & Hughes*. – In the N aisle a fine evocation of Jacob's Dream, designed by *Charles Hardgrave* for *J. Powell & Sons*, 1894. – Also one by *Hugh Easton*, 1937 in memory of Joscelyne Whitbread. – MONUMENTS. Lots of C18 and C19 tablets, e.g. Nathaniel Fowler †1710 by *Edward Stanton*, a grey marble tablet with broken segmental pediment and gadrooned base; Rev. L. Smyth †1800 by *C. King* of London; Thomas Adkin †1829 by *Theakston* of London, with Grecian scrolled top; and – the handsomest – George Nodes †1777 with a succinct and beautifully designed inscription (chancel S). The signature A . . . s is convincingly connected by George McHardy with *John Atkins*. – In the Torrington Vault, a grand pedimented tablet to George, 1st Viscount Torrington †1732 above an inscription for his son,

the Admiral the Hon. John Byng, court-martialled and executed in 1757 ('a Martyr to Political Persecution'). The
Whitbread monuments are at Cardington (q.v.).

SOUTHILL PARK. Southill is one of the most exquisite English
understatements. That so refined and reticent a house could
be demanded in 1795 by a brewer is a telling illustration of the
rarely admitted cultural possibilities of the Industrial Revolution of the Georgian era. For a brewery surely is an industrial
establishment. It is true on the other hand that the brewers
were ahead of the ironmasters and millowners in matters of
intellectual and social ambition. The Thrales in London, the
Whitbreads here – they have no parallel among the founders
of other enterprises. Samuel Whitbread I of Cardington had
opened the brewery in 1742. He was M.P. for Bedford from
1768 to 1790 and died in 1796, having purchased the Southill
estate from George Byng, 4th Viscount Torrington, one year
before for his son Samuel II, M.P. for Bedford from 1790 to
1815. He immediately engaged *Henry Holland* to remodel the
early C18 house at Southill, which the 1st Viscount Torrington
had begun *c.* 1725. This was of about the same size as now,
brick built with a centre of two and three storeys and single-
storey links to pavilions and with a forecourt on the S front.
Between 1796 and 1801 Samuel spent over £53,000 on its
alteration. Holland had done Brooks's Club in 1777. He had
begun his memorable remodelling of Carlton House for the
Prince Regent in 1783 and had worked at Althorp in Northamptonshire from 1787 till 1791. In 1787 also he had begun the

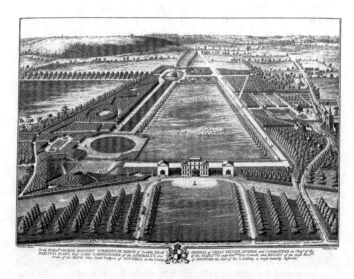

Southill Park, south prospect.
Drawing by T. Badeslade, 1739

alterations and additions at Woburn Abbey (q.v.). So Samuel Whitbread knew exactly what he was going to get, and must indeed have preferred it to the graces and the showy intricacies of the followers of Robert Adam.

Southill is a long house with a moderate-sized core, and two angle pavilions connected by straight links with the core. The house is faced in Totternhoe clunch stone (probably supplied by *John Wing*, who is known to have worked on the estate and may have been Holland's clerk of works; it is now extensively restored with Portland and Bath stone), in smooth ashlar blocks except for the smooth rustication of the ground floor of the centre and the whole of the pedimented pavilions, where rustication was used visually to strengthen the ends of the house. At the basement the rustication is vermiculated, but this only registers at close quarters. In the centre on the N side Holland placed a polygonal bay in the place where anybody would expect the main entrance. This is pushed two bays to the r. and given no emphasis at all. This seems incomprehensible but it placed the entrance hall at the centre of an arrangement of public rooms on three sides. The more private rooms for Mr and Mrs Whitbread were thus removed to the E end of the house, where Lord Torrington's house had its service rooms, including the kitchens in the E pavilion. At basement level Holland created a corridor running from end to end. On the S side, where in the previous house there was the entrance into a great hall, Holland added the portico and to l. and r. the colonnades of the links. He also created the corridors behind these colonnades to secure easier access to the rooms at the far ends of the house. For Holland was a careful planner, as he was a careful detailer in every respect. On the N side the centre is of five bays with a three-bay pediment in which there are two discrete lunette windows. The polygonal bay ends in a pediment too – and that is all. Bareness here was clearly considered a virtue. The garden side is more relaxed, but the pairs of unfluted Ionic columns are of course also far from ornate. There is a balustraded balcony over the centre colonnade and balustrades over the link colonnades. Inside the colonnades, a band of Greek key, arched windows in shallow recesses and simply moulded panels. Beyond that, once more – nothing.

At the W end is a porte cochère, probably *c.* 1880, added in an attempt to create a more impressive entrance, and at the other end of the house a CONSERVATORY.

The interior is not easily described, except in general mood. The restraint in quantity and character of motifs is admirable. Thin friezes, thin cornices, strictly rectangular frames to the wall panels, and no fear of panels left entirely bare. Holland's sources are partly Roman – he used drawings made by Charles Heathcote Tatham in 1794–6 and published in 1799 (it was through Tatham that Holland also found inspiration for the Roman style of much of the furniture, though the details are not the concern of *The Buildings of England*). But the Paris of the Late Louis XVI, especially Neufforge, meant more to him.

The present ENTRANCE HALL is stone-coloured. The bronze-coloured plaster overdoors with horses, bulls, camels, lions and deer are by *George Garrard*, an artist who was extensively patronized by Samuel Whitbread II, and also supplied the posthumous bust of Holland (†1806) with its affecting tribute from his client. E of this is the DINING ROOM, in pale green with French-inspired décor of vertical strips of imitation porphyry overlaid with twining stems of vines matching the colouring of the overdoors of lions and urns. The bay window, polygonal outside, is semicircular inside. Fine grey marble fireplace, again with vines. On the opposite side of the entrance hall, the LIBRARY is the stateliest room. It is divided into an ante-library and the library proper. The connection is a perfectly plain arch. The largely recessed shelves are plain too. Again, the detailing of the tiny frieze along the bookcases and the acanthus cornices of the coved ceiling is exquisite. Fine white marble fireplace with concave jambs containing bronze torcheres. Panels of griffins over the pier glasses, derived by Holland from Tatham's drawings of the Aldobrandini palace in Rome. In the centre of the S front, the DRAWING ROOM has a higher ceiling divided into three parts by flat bands of guilloche. Except for the characteristically spare structural decoration there is a decorative accent only in the frame of the mirror above the fireplace and in the frontal Egyptian termes of the white chimneypiece. However, the walls are crimson silk with green borders and gilded frames and the curtains too, suspended from the claws of eagles on the pelmets. It is a perfect Regency interior of the late phase, redone in 1808 as an enrichment of Holland's original, and has a small ante-room to match. The rooms were superbly restored (by *Alec Cobbe* and *Edward Bulmer*) in 1992.

The drawing room is separated from the dining room by a narrow passage running from the hall to the private rooms at the W end of the house. The main STAIRCASE is simple to the verge of the puritanical – stick balusters and a mahogany rail – but quietly sophisticated, especially at the upper floor, where a double stair leads to a mezzanine of rooms above the drawing room. At the farthest end of the house is MRS WHITBREAD'S ROOM, very probably the earliest of the interiors executed by Holland himself. The end of the room is apsed and leads onto the garden colonnade. Above the doors, lunettes painted with animal subjects by *W. Sawrey Gilpin*, Garrard's father-in-law. Fireplace similar to that in the dining room. The BOUDOIR, an inner room at the end, is even more delightful, in a feminine Louis XVI style, painted by *L. A. Delabriere c. 1796–1800*. Holland designed another like it at Althorp, Northants.

Of the other rooms of Holland's time nothing need be said individually, and the Gainsborough, the Romneys, the other paintings and the furniture and the busts are not the business of *The Buildings of England*. In the W pavilion, Samuel Whitbread III created *c.* 1885 the STAG ROOM, a shrine to an obsession with deer-stalking. Darkly panelled with a staircase to the upper floor. Contemporary with it in the w addition, the top-lit STONE HALL, on two levels with a fantastic black-and-white marble fireplace of Solomonic columns and blue-tiled backs.

E of the house is a long kitchen wing, and the STABLES, both by *Holland*, both yellow brick.

In front of the house a SCULPTURE of Jock, Mrs Whitbread's favourite spaniel, on an oval pedestal with reeded pilasters and arches at the base over a water bowl for his successors. This is again by *Garrard*. – The ironwork GATES of the North Terrace are C18, with the Byng arms – and were brought back *c.* 1900 from a butcher's yard at Shefford. – The lead STATUES here and elsewhere are by the *Cheeres*. They were sold at John Cheere's death and bought en bloc by Samuel Whitbread II in 1812.

The GROUNDS were landscaped by *Capability Brown*, Holland's father-in-law, in 1777, i.e. still for the Byngs. A concealed pathway runs around the E side of the gardens and under a bridge. This bridge and a castellated ironstone GATEWAY to the stable yard existed in 1795. Are they Brown's? The prospect of the N front beyond the terrace is a broad sweep of park down to the edge of a LAKE. On the way to the Fishing Temple is a one-arch BRIDGE with niches in the abutments and a parapet of brick with stone pedestals. It is ascribed without evidence to *John Smeaton*, who worked for the brewery and designed the bridge at Cardington (q.v.). The FISHING TEMPLE itself lies at the head of the present lake but was originally between two lakes. It is of 1807 and has Doric four-column porticoes to front and back, with pediments. The bases of the front columns are inscribed with the names of Samuel II and his family. The back portico, forming a porte cochère, is reached from the sides through two arches and along an arcaded wall.

In the village the VICARAGE, 1858, probably by *John Usher* and many pleasant ESTATE COTTAGES. They carry the dates 1796 (several), 1797, 1800 (the earliest rendered in a honey colour and thatched), 1815, 1855 (lattice windows, picturesque gables), 1874, 1890s (red brick with tile roofs) and right up to 1914.

Also in the main street, SOUTHILL CHAPEL of 1805. Inside, early C19 box pews and gallery. C18 clock by *J. Pepper* of Biggleswade.

Former STATION, Shefford Road. 1857 by *C. H. Driver* for the Midland Railway. Simplified Venetian Gothic. In the middle of nowhere, placed simply for the convenience of W. H. Whitbread, a keen promoter of the railways through the county (as an OBELISK monument of 1864 nearby remembers).

STAGSDEN

ST LEONARD. Much restored in 1848–50 by *T. J. Jackson*. Unbuttressed C13 W tower with a W lancet and an arch to the nave with two continuous chamfers. The upper parts Perp with N stair-tower. Short lead spire. C13 also the S doorway, but the S aisle is early C14, its arcade of five bays, with low quatrefoil piers and double-chamfered arches. The N side has no aisle, but the windows are also Dec, and so perhaps is the low tomb recess inside. The nave's N chapel of two bays is also C14, between Dec and Perp. Double-hollow-chamfered arches. Perp clerestory, Perp niches in the E wall of the S aisle – four of them, rather randomly arranged – and two-storey Perp S porch. Vestry added 1896 by *Henry Young*, further addition *c.* 2000. – Overbearing ORGAN CASE at the W end, 1977. – FONT. Square, with chamfered corners, Dec. In two panels small single figures, recut probably in the C17. On the underside, ballflower and some other decoration. – SCREEN. A good Perp piece, with four-light divisions, the mid-mullion reaching right up into the apex, but much of it looks Victorian. – STAINED GLASS. S aisle windows 1949–50, two (St Leonard and St Michael) by *Maile & Sons*, one by *Francis Spear*. – BRASS. N chapel. John Cocke, a gentleman servant to King James, †1616. Kneeling figures under arches.

Former SCHOOL, ⅛ m. SSW. *c.* 1860. T-plan with cupola over the angle. Gables with shoulder-arched windows in a stepped arrangement. Homely wing for the teacher with a loggia. Extended 2003.

STANBRIDGE

9020

ST JOHN THE BAPTIST. Of ironstone, except for chancel and S aisle (rebuilt by *Ewan Christian* in 1892–3), which are clunch, and a patch of brick in the N aisle. Mostly Perp, especially W tower and clerestory, but Dec the N doorway and probably the tiny quatrefoil N aisle W window. Late C13 chancel – see the arch to the nave with the characteristic notch stops (although rebuilt in the 1890s), the PISCINA and the one-light N window. The arcades are a little later. Four bays, octagonal piers, double-chamfered arches. The piers differ in height. The N side comes first. The arches are indeed very similar to the chancel arch. – FONT. The base of three short shafts is E.E. – PULPIT. Partly Elizabethan; the sounding-board has been made into a table. – STAINED GLASS. E window. 1913 by *Horace Wilkinson*.

VICARAGE, Mill Lane, ¼ m. NNE. By *Ewan Christian*, 1874–5. Yellow brick, quite imposing, with a tall roof and two-storey canted bay on the front under a wider gable carried on braces.

STAPLOE

BASMEAD MANOR. On a moated site that probably pre-dates the late medieval house. The core is a single range E–W,

comprising originally a full-height hall of three bays with a
crown-post roof and at its E end a two-storey chamber block.
In a roof truss, traces of an eight-light traceried window (C15?)
which looked from the upper chamber into the hall. The cross-
wing (gable rebuilt 1973–4 during restoration by *Chrystal &*
West) seems to have been built *c.* 1525–50 at the low end for a
much grander parlour and chamber. In this, much good carved
decoration, including rosettes, leaf spandrels, pilasters. The
stone fireplaces appear to reuse C12 material, perhaps from
Bushmead Priory (q.v.). The N extension of the cross-wing has
a good early C18 fully panelled room. The house was purchased
in 1845 by Peter Squire, the Queen's chemist, to grow herbs
for pharmaceuticals. Farm buildings of about that time and a
pretty LODGE at the gate to a formal avenue of trees.

TITHE FARM, 1¾ m. S at Honeyden, nearer Wyboston. One
of the octagonal-plan farmhouses of *c.* 1800 by *Robert Salmon*,

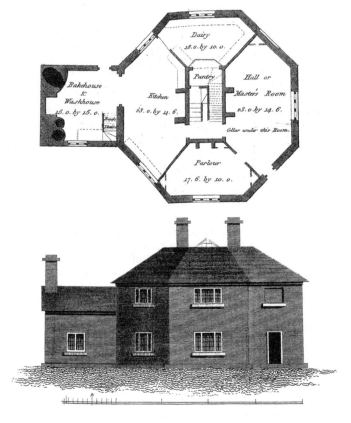

Tithe Farm, Staploe.
Plan and drawing by T. Batchelor, 1808

the 5th Duke of Bedford's surveyor (cf. Cople). Rendered brick.

STEPPINGLEY

A Woburn estate village.

ST LAWRENCE. Rebuilt in coursed small blocks of ironstone in 1858–60 by the 7th Duke of Bedford and the rector, after the C18 chancel collapsed. Like the local medieval churches it has a w tower with higher stair-turret, nave and N aisle, chancel. The architect was *Henry Clutton*. Note his over-pronounced cusping of the round heads of the window lights and their curious combination with panel tracery in the bell-openings. Even odder the small pointed-quatrefoiled N aisle windows and the large rose window in the present organ chamber, which has five circles enclosing such pointed quatrefoils. Just as odd are all the details: the excessive chamfering, the hoodmould stops, the vaulted porch. Disappointing interior, just the BENCH ENDS with odd details. The carving was done by *Thomas Earp*, but alas his PULPIT has been replaced. From the old church the pretty PISCINA in the chancel with Green Man in the ogee arch.

E of the church, the former SCHOOLROOM. Built 1877–8. Also by *Clutton*, also ironstone, small, but unusually monumental and with Clutton's usual unconventional motifs. Embattled Tudor with two doorways, two chimneybreasts up the façade, and, flanking the l., two single-light windows, flanking the r., two four-light windows. The pretty SCHOOL HOUSE of 1879 with the jettied, half-timbered floor above ironstone belongs to the group, and the composition of the two at right angles with a green lawn between is very appealing. Little bridge over a ditch in front. The VILLAGE HALL is the first school provided by the duke in 1851. Lattice-pattern windows.

STEPPINGLEY HOSPITAL, ⅝ m. E. Built as Ampthill's Isolation Hospital, 1903–5 by *H. Percy Adams* (chief designer, *Charles Holden*). Fine Neo-Georgian administration block. Three hip-roofed wards set around a small square behind, more Arts and Crafts in style. Former typhoid ward with verandas l. and r. of a gabled centre.

STEVINGTON

ST MARY. The Holy Well in the wall below the E end is the first clue to the long history of the site. The church itself boasts a late Anglo-Saxon w tower. It is recognizable outside by the

long-and-short quoins, irregularly coursed rubble, and inside
by the extremely narrow and rough arched s opening into a
former *porticus*. Also two double-splayed windows N and S (the
S one above the door with wooden window frame). Nave and
chancel are thinly walled and only slightly wider than the
tower, so may at least in plan be pre-Conquest. The tower-top
is Perp, so too the clerestory. The exterior of the church otherwise is confusing. Both chancel chapels have been unroofed
since *c.* 1665 but left partly standing. Major repair and restoration, with Perp tracery, was undertaken in 1871–2 by *John
Usher*, advised by *Clutton*. The N and E battlements of this date.
Inside, the s arcade is of *c.* 1300, with high quatrefoil piers with
deep continuous hollows in the diagonals and sunk quadrant
arch mouldings. The s doorway is contemporary. The N arcade
is later Dec: filleted quatrefoil piers with thin shafts in the
diagonals. Arches again with sunk quadrants. The same motifs
are used in tower arch and chancel arch. What is left of the
chancel chapels is Dec too. The Perp extension of the s chapel
blocks a shafted chancel window with sedilia and ANGLE
PISCINA of ogee arches below it. The N aisle seems to have
been widened later. Good Perp nave roof and figures holding
shields with the emblems of the Passion and also woolpacks
and the initials of two merchants. Some of this may be due to
the restoration. – SCREEN. Under the tower. High, Perp, of
one-light divisions, C17 arch inserted. The rood screen was cut
down in 1826. – BENCHES. The poppyheads of the front
benches are early C16: two men kneeling and drinking (though
now separate, they were originally one group drinking from the
same cup), two semi-reclining, one seated, one writing, and
three animals. – BRASS. s aisle. Thomas Salle †1422. His head
on a large helmet. The figure is 32 in. (81 cm) long.

SE of the church is the VICARAGE, more than once improved,
principally in 1678, 1833 by *James Woodroffe*, and 1863. Further
work in 2000. s of the church was the medieval hospital, established by Harrold Priory and no doubt associated with the
pilgrims to the Holy Well. It is illustrated by Thomas Fisher in
the early C19, when it had become a farmhouse.* Its site is
covered by FARM BUILDINGS (now housing) erected in 1876
by the Bedford estate in association with MANOR FARM (now
Manor House). This is of 1875–6 by *Clutton*. Surprisingly convincing C17 vernacular, of neatly coursed limestone with mullioned windows and two gables either side of a central hall.
Opposite is the SCHOOL, 1863, another Bedford benefaction,
and nearby the CHURCH ROOM, by *Usher & Anthony*, 1897–8,
in red brick, with Gothic windows and Arts and Crafts porches.

---

*Fisher also records (*Gents Mag*, 1812) 'very near to the church, . . . a long range
of low stone buildings designed for separate inhabitation; each apartment opening
under a small pointed arch to the area in front, and no internal communication
existing between them'. His drawing of them was robbed from him 'upon the
Oxford races'.

VILLAGE CROSS, at the main crossing. Probably C14. In the base, four small pointed-trefoiled niches. Original shaft; the retooled foliage capital and big tabernacle finial with crockets and niches are both mid-C19. E of this, the BARRINGER ALMSHOUSES, a foundation of 1634. Five dwellings, five kneelered dormers. Rebuilt sensitively, reusing much of the original materials, in 1841 by *J. T. Wing*.

W of the centre, the BAPTIST CHAPEL of 1721. Stone, symmetrical front, quite plain. Galleried interior restored 1891 (P. C. Edwards).

42 WINDMILL, ½ m. S. Put up *c.* 1770 (dated timber). A wooden post-mill, board-clad with a gambrel roof, though the post is now within a round stone base, probably late C19. Rebuilt in 1921 and rehabilitated in 1951 for the Festival of Britain by *S. V. Goodman*, the County Architect, with *Clayson & Sons* of Harrold. The present sails are of 2004 (design by *Bruce Deacon*) and all is complete, in full working order.

0040

STEWARTBY

Originally the garden estate on the doorstep of the London Brick Company & Forder's* large brickworks. It was said to be the largest in the world, and could produce *c.* 650 million bricks a year, but was in decline from the 1970s and finally closed in 2008. Two 'Hoffman' KILNS and just four of the thirty-two CHIMNEYS which once dominated the whole of the surrounding landscape have survived and must be preserved from demolition; the disused works is a pitiful sight.

The estate, named after Halley Stewart and his son P. Malcolm Stewart, the company chairman, was begun in 1927. Plans for it are by *F. W. Walker* of Ampthill, 1926. The first phase was complete by 1937. Everything is in the company's pressed Fletton bricks, the semi-detached houses of the Welwyn type with a gable in the centre (non-parlour plan) or over the ends (parlour plan). By the works entrance, the degraded former ADMINISTRATION BUILDING, long and low, with arched niches in the end bays and stone urns. It looks over a semicircle and a rectangular lawn towards the VILLAGE HALL, Neo-Colonial by *E. Vincent Harris*, 1928–30, with a wooden pediment on square pillars and a cupola, and, on the other side, in the style of the housing, the CLUB, with a plainer front with arched windows, also by Harris, 1933–4, and the VILLAGE STORES. The CHAPEL in Park Crescent was added

---

*The London Brick Company was established at Fletton, Peterborough (p. 636). B. J. H. Forder opened the first Fletton brick pits in Bedfordshire in 1897 at Elstow and what is now Stewartby. The Stewarts had a controlling interest in B. J. H. Forder & Son, which merged with the LBC in 1924; its stake eventually covered the whole of Marston Vale from Elstow to Brogborough by absorbing the works of its rival, the Marston Valley Brick Co. Stewartby was the last part to close.

only in 1950. A little further E, the LOWER SCHOOL by *Oswald P. Milne*, 1936–7, also with a cupola on the centre part and lower wings spreading out, conservatively modern. Along a very large crescent, SIR MALCOLM STEWART TRUST HOMES by *Richardson & Houfe*, 1955–6, for 'old servants of the company'. Further blocks arranged to the rear around rose-planted lawns. These are excellent, and are well-kept.* Single-storey with hipped roofs, in long rows like almshouses. Some have square bays with roofs carried over for porches, porthole windows in the ends. The COMMON ROOM for these homes has a veranda all round on slender columns and a roof with concave hips and finial – all rather Swedish of the 1920s type.

61

STOPSLEY *see* LUTON

STOTFOLD

2030

ST MARY. A curious building, externally Perp except for the late C13 S aisle W window (bar tracery with a spherical triangle) and perhaps the round-headed lancet in the W tower belfry. The bell-openings are pairs of two lights. The tower is cement-rendered. Inside one is at first baffled. The N aisle has from W to E two bays, a bit of wall, and a third bay, the S aisle one bay, a bit of wall, and then two bays. The story is presumably this. At first the nave had no aisles. Then, *c.* 1300, a N chapel was built. The responds are half quatrefoil, the arch has two sunk quadrants. Then a S aisle was built, of two bays to the then W wall. This has early C14 quatrefoil piers with thin shafts in the diagonals, ogees to the chamfers, similar arches to the N side, and hoodmoulds with headstops. The decision was then taken to lengthen the nave, and on the N side the chapel was extended to form a N aisle. The clerestory is Perp. The chancel was rebuilt in 1889–90 by *A. W. Soames*; he added the organ chamber, removed a N porch and embattled the nave. The roof is contemporary. – FONT. Octagonal, Perp, with quatrefoils. – SCREEN. W tower. 1930, reset with the new screen to the tower rooms of 2013 by *Michael Dales*. – STAINED GLASS. Old bits in a N window. E window by *A. L. Moore*, 1910; S aisle war memorial, 1920 by *A. L. Moore & Son*.

VICARAGE, N of the church. 1832, the plans by *William Yorke*, surveyor and builder of Cheshunt.

STOTFOLD WATERMILL, Mill Lane, bridging the Ivel. An authentically rural respite from a suffocatingly over-developed village. Working until 1966, the complex is completely pre-served and mostly restored as housing. From l. to r., a granary; the four-storey former roller mill (1902; a house since 2003);

---

*Unlike the earlier housing, where plastic windows now predominate.

the main mill, rebuilt in the early C19 in gault brick with weatherboarded upper parts and a cantilevered lucam; tall tapering square chimney behind; stuccoed C18 mill cottages; former stables. The MILL itself was burnt down to its ground floor in 1992 but the machinery (refitted in 1897, the hurst frame by *Whitmore & Benyon* of Wickham Market) survived and the rest was authentically rebuilt by the efforts of the Stotfold Mill Preservation Trust, 1998–2006.

FAIRFIELD HALL, 1¼ m. SW. The former Three Counties Asylum, erected to supersede Bedford Asylum and to serve Hertfordshire and Huntingdonshire. Later Fairfield Hospital. Closed in 1999 and since converted to housing. A vast group, in well-planted grounds; mostly of Arlesey white bricks, with only the slightest patterns in red. The entire design was by *George Fowler Jones* of York, begun in 1857. The cost in the first four years was £114,831. The result is too much to take in in a single view. In a simplified Elizabethan, E-plan centre on the S front, originally with a clocktower over the entrance. Patients were segregated in the wings that are set back at right angles. Over the angles ogee leaded roofs. The continuation of these wings dates from 1877–81. Open court behind the centre and at the back of this the original chapel (Gothic tracery) set over the kitchens. To l. and r. of this are two impressive apsidal-ended wings with clerestories, added 1868–70 for recreation rooms (one now in use as a spa.) The CHAPEL to the N dates from 1878–9. It has a square and bare SW tower with steep pyramid roof, a wide nave with a big roof, and a polygonal apse. S of this group and associated with the redevelopment, FAIRFIELD PARK, a completely new settlement by a consortium of house builders, completed 2002–6, pleasantly planned around a park and recreation ground with highly traditional but quite varied brick terraces and houses in streets named after C19 writers.

STRATTON PARK *see* BIGGLESWADE

STREATLEY

ST MARGARET. Mostly C14. Four-bay arcades with standard elements. Most of the aisle windows and the N doorway are C14 too. So is the tower arch, though other features of the tower are later. Higher stair-turret. It is a patchwork of materials: flint, Totternhoe stone, grey brick angle clasping buttresses. The aisles are a similar hotch-potch, the tile repairs to the tracery testament to severe neglect in the C19 – the chancel, short, of brick, was rebuilt in 1898–9 – and abandonment during the interwar years before rescue from dereliction in 1937–8 by *Albert Richardson*. Only the brick porch is later, 1957.

Vestry and church room under the tower, 2008 by *Michael Dales*. – FONT. The stem of the font is E.E., and it has vertical strips of dogtooth. The bowl, however, is a mystery. It is octagonal, with foliage motifs largely stiff-leafish. One panel, moreover, has a blank three-light window with geometrical tracery, i.e. typical late C13. But can the other panels be – in spite of their stiff-leaf? The only possible solution seems to be drastic recutting and even remodelling in the C17. – PULPIT. With linenfold panels and a Georgian sounding-board. – BENCHES. With linenfold and also a few Jacobean panels. Others are of the common buttressed type. – ROOD SCREEN. 1937, with some old work; a memorial to Archdeacon Parnell, recording his efforts to secure restorations of twenty-six Bedfordshire churches. – WALL PAINTINGS. Traces on the nave E wall, e.g., above the pulpit, St Catherine.

E of the church, STREATLEY HOUSE, mid-C18, of chequer brick, nine bays long. Original sashes on the upper floor only. Doorcase with pedimented hood.

SHARPENHOE CLAPPERS, I m. N.* An impressive wooded promontory above Sharpenhoe and Barton-Le-Clay. Interpreted, probably correctly, as an Iron Age hillfort. The earthwork across the S neck of the promontory, however, was shown by excavation in 1981 to be medieval and very probably a rabbit warren.

BARROWS, Galley Hill, I¾ m. SE. Two Bronze Age round barrows and two bowl barrows.

DRAY'S DITCHES, I¾ m. S at the edge of Luton. This linear dyke, still the boundary between Luton and the rest of Bedfordshire, was constructed *c.* 500 B.C. It has a length of approximately ½ m. and runs roughly at right angles to the Icknield Way. Its ends have been largely obliterated by ploughing on the W and by the construction of the South Bedfordshire golf course on the S. Originally the double bank and ditches ran from a barrow (destroyed) on Warden Hill in the direction of Great Bramingham, in the area now covered by suburban housing. The only major portion of the bank now visible, which survives to a height of 4 ft (1.25 metres), lies immediately S of the club house. Excavations conducted in this central area revealed two hitherto unrecognized Bronze Age boundary ditches, which contained sherds of Early Bronze Age collared urns, and three main Iron Age ditches. Sherds of Iron Age pottery came from the latter. Between the central and S ditch were located the post-holes of a double palisade with intervening tie-beams. These earthworks probably mark the SW limit of a tribal territorial area.

*The 'timber-framed, aisled barn, probably pre-Reformation' noted in the first edition of this guide at BURY FARM, Sharpenhoe, has been demolished.

STUDHAM

ST MARY. Entirely separate from the village. An unpromising cemented exterior – it has had such an appearance since at least 1774 – W tower with crenellated top, and a spike before the C19, nave and aisles and chancel, the windows Late Perp with straight hoodmoulds. Inside, the story is very different. Four-bay arcades of *c.* 1210–20. The church was indeed consecrated in 1219. There are two puzzling facts. One is that three bays were built at one go and reached as far as the former W wall and a fourth bay was added as an extension to the W, but apparently at once, as there is no stylistic difference at all. The other puzzlement is that the broad and good stiff-leaf capitals of arcades and (rebuilt and widened) chancel arch look just before 1220 indeed (cf. Eaton Bray), but that there are also very big and coarse scalloped varieties which appear 1190–1200 rather. Yet they are not confined to any one place; e.g. the W responds of both arcades are scallops but so is the E respond of the N arcade. There are other inconsistencies, the S arcade for example has a mixture of broach stops and volutes to its arches. One must assume that an old man and a young man worked together. The church was restored in 1892–3 by *J. Sutherland*, of the Ashridge Estate (Herts.); Lord Brownlow was the patron. – FONT. A round Norman bowl with a band of leaf trail and dragons (cf. St Mary, Linslade) on a curving-out base with E.E. stiff-leaf. Is this an inverted capital (cf. Westoning)? – Old TILES by the font. – BENCHES with linenfold panelling. – PULPIT and LECTERN. Mixed marbles, including Cornish Serpentine, by *Doney & Evans* of St Austell, 1893. – SCREEN. Carved by *Noel Rew*, 1916. – LIGHT FITTINGS, WINDOW TRACERY and CHANCEL CEILING decoration all by *G. G. Pace*, 1970. – STAINED GLASS. E window by *Lavers, Barraud & Westlake*, 1904, to the incumbent, and a single light with *Kempe* glass to his son of 1903. – MONUMENTS. The First World War Memorial is unusual, a carved wood cabinet containing photos of the fallen.

MANOR FARM, SE of the church. Originally a small early C17 hall house. Some timber-framing exposed in two gables. (Inside, in an upstairs room, a carved overmantel with raised panels and four allegorical caryatids, two on pedestals with inverted torch and shovel. The style suggests *c.* 1625.)

STUDHAM HALL FARMHOUSE, SW. At the core is a Wealden house, of two bays either side of the hall, transformed first in the C16 into a much longer plan with a continuous jetty. The rest looks *c.* 1900; brick infill to the timber frame.

On Common Road, ½ m. SE a nice asymmetrical row of gabled ASHRIDGE ESTATE COTTAGES, dated 1864, plum brick with red dressings for the mullions windows and dressings. Also ADELAIDE COTTAGE a pleasant mid-C18 house, in blue and red chequered brick.

BARWYTHE HALL, Pedley Hill, ¾ m. SE. Purchased by Earl Brownlow in 1849 and then much extended. Brick, with straight steep gables and stone canted bays to the front. Brick and flint service wing. On the garden side, centre bay under a round gable. This is repeated to the l. as part of the Neo-Georgian addition, dated 1906.

SUNDON

0020

A village only just clear of Luton's N suburbs but surprisingly rural.

ST MARY. Nearly all Dec, and uncommonly impressive inside. Pre-Dec, i.e. C13, the arcades of high quatrefoil piers with diagonal fillets and arches of one chamfer and one sunk chamfer. These arcades embrace the W tower, which is noticeable inside only by the W arches of the arcades being bigger and by a cross-arch. The aisles are also crossed by arches (cf. Luton). The clerestory has round, quatrefoiled windows, a Dec sign. The aisle windows are Dec too, but different N from S and with one curious exception – the N aisle E window, which is again a generation earlier (geometrical tracery) and much more delicate in the mouldings. Dec again the transeptal S chapel. Large reticulated transept S and transept E windows. Crocketed ogee niches to l. and r. of the latter. Dec finally the W tower too, with another large reticulated window. But the doorway is Perp, and so is the tower top of chequer pattern. Higher stair-turret. In the chancel the E window is Perp, but there is a lowside lancet and the niches l. and r. of the E window and the PISCINA (all ogee arches) are Dec once more. Single-framed chancel roof. Along the aisle walls runs a stone bench. – FONT. Octagonal, of Purbeck marble, with two flat, pointed arches to each side (cf. Luton); C13. – SCREEN. Of one-light divisions, Perp, modest. – BENCHES (nave W). Plain, with buttress shafts. – CHEST. Also Dec the front carved with net tracery. – WALL PAINTINGS. N aisle N wall. Devils and a cart carrying a bishop and other figures; mid to late C14. Overlaid by C15 Christ with censing angels. Last Judgement over S door. – STAINED GLASS. Fragments in the N aisle E and S transept S windows. E window, 1966 by *T. D. Randall*.

OLD VICARAGE, ¼ m. ENE of the church. 1848 by *E. F. Law* of Northampton. Neo-Tudor.

SUTTON

2040

ALL SAINTS. The C13 is the first represented in the church. To it belong the S doorway and the S arcade of four bays. The square piers with broad semicircular projections are as characteristic as the hollow-chamfered arches. Next in order of time is the N arcade of quatrefoil piers with plain double-chamfered arches. This is followed by the Dec chancel arch (responds of the type with thin diagonal shafts and the arch with two sunk quadrants). Rich SEDILIA and PISCINA. In the S aisle also a Dec PISCINA. Dec chancel windows, those on the S side with segmental arches. Perp tower largely of ironstone, partly limestone. Tall arch to the nave. The rest of the church brown cobbles. All castellated, except for the chancel. Perp S porch with two-light windows. – SCREEN. C15. – PULPIT. 1628; its sounding-board of 1729 was made for a pulpit at Everton (q.v.) and introduced 1841, when the church was reseated by *Thomas Stevens*; rector's desk probably of the last date. – COMMUNION RAIL. Later C17. – BENCHES. The ends buttressed. – BOX PEWS. C17 and 1841, in the aisles only. – STAINED GLASS. E window by *Lavers & Barraud*, the design by *N. J. Westlake*, 1864. N aisle, Nativity window †1858, but probably by *Heaton, Butler & Bayne*, c. 1870. Possibly by the same firm and of similar period, the N aisle W window, of floral panels with birds and lilies. – MONUMENTS. A good collection for the Burgoynes of Sutton Park. – John Burgoyne †1604. Large standing monument of stone. Recumbent effigy under an arch. Much lively strapwork to the back. Two columns, and, at the top, achievement and two obelisks. – Sir Roger Burgoyne †1677. By *Grinling Gibbons*, one of the earliest documented monuments by the sculptor, ordered by Sir Ralph Verney. Urn on a gadrooned sarcophagus with putti l. and r. All this is high up above a large inscription tablet with garlands. The garlands are the one item that might make one think of Gibbons. The setting is very awkward, partly oversailing the window so that the l. putto leans nonchalantly against the window splay. – Sir John Burgoyne †1709. Reredos-type with two mourning cherubs, fluted pilasters with urns, entablature and an achievement. By *Edward Stanton*.* – William Burgoyne †1835. By *G. Oldfield* of Ashford in Derbyshire. Small tablet with two spiral-carved colonnettes. – CURIOSUM. The church possesses a BARREL ORGAN, of 1820, which is in use.

OLD RECTORY, E of the church. C16 hall house with cross-wings, the S wing with exposed timber frame and jettied front, the jetty on consoles. Inserted C17 red brick chimney. But the character of the main part is now an attractive Tudor Gothic, stuccoed. In the middle of the village is a humped PACKHORSE BRIDGE with two pointed arches, each with two courses of voussoirs and a cutwater on the N side. Restored 1988, when the timber foundations were radiocarbon-dated to the C13.

SUTTON PARK (John of Gaunt Golf Club), ¼ m. NNE. The Burgoynes' house, rebuilt in 1858; the previous house was burned in 1825. Jacobean-style, asymmetrical front with shaped

---

* Stanton also designed a monument for Constance, Lady Burgoyne, †1711 but it is untraced.

gable and an oriel in the centre. Ironstone with limestone quoins and dressings. Canted bays and a deep bow on the garden front. The PARK may have been laid out by *Repton*, who is known to have been consulted *c*. 1792. The avenue at the SE corner relates to the C18 house, which stood to the E, close to JOHN OF GAUNT'S HILL, where a broad and deep ditch around an oval mound marks the site of what is traditionally supposed to have been the manor house. It may have been built by Henry, Earl of Derby, son of John of Gaunt. It measures 91.5 metres (300 ft) by 64 metres (201 ft) by 4.5 metres (14 ft 9 in.) high. The top is now the seventeenth green.

SWINESHEAD   *0060*

ST NICHOLAS. An impressive Dec church. The W tower started Dec, though the bell-stage with pairs of two-light openings and the recessed spire rising behind an openwork quatrefoil frieze is Perp. Two tiers of lucarnes, transparent from a distance. The distinguishing feature of the tower is the shallow W porch with a gable and angle buttress shafts (cf. Keyston, Hunts., a few miles away). Springing of a former vault inside. The door has bold, broad Dec tracery. The tower arch has three chamfers dying into the imposts (cf. Oundle, Raunds, Rushden, all in Northants and all E.E.). The Swineshead tower, however, comes relatively late in the Dec story. It was preceded by a unified plan of nave, aisles, chancel and NW tower. The aisle, even the S porch, and the chancel are all pulled together by the same pretty trail-frieze below the parapet, with heads, ball-flower etc. (cf. Yelden; also the bell-openings of Keyston, and a tomb at Abbotsley, both in Hunts.). In the S aisle the S windows and the S doorway are typically Dec; in the chancel the specially nicely detailed S windows ought to be sampled, though one has been renewed. The flowing E and N chancel windows are Victorian. But the N aisle windows are Dec again. The aisle E window is in two tiers and small and corresponds indeed to a former two-storey vestry which still has a (blocked) fireplace inside. There is also a piscina as evidence of its use as a chapel. The projection of wall in the aisle's W bay represents the thickness needed for a tower. Inside, this projected tower is marked by the thickening of one pier of the N arcade and the springer of an arch across the aisle from that pier. The S arcade has no such break. Both arcades are Dec, with standard elements and the most characteristic Dec bases. Pretty image niche in the S aisle E wall with a nodding ogee canopy, traces of polychromy and either side of this WALL PAINTING recognizable as the outline of two angels censing. The chancel is beautifully fitted up, with shafting of the windows, leaf and flower capitals to the shafts, an ANGLE PISCINA and SEDILIA with stepped seat, but simply a blank lowering of the sill of a s window. In the N wall a sumptuous EASTER SEPULCHRE or tomb recess, cusped and subcusped, with much leaf. This has been blocked and punched through for a tiny stair and passage connecting the chancel with the former vestry. The chancel arch (later reset and widened in the C15 for a rood screen) is on two excellent half-figures. – SCREEN. Partly Perp. – STALLS. With a little carving on arms and MISERICORDS. – BENCHES. The buttressed standard type. – STAINED GLASS. Some bits in a chancel s window. E window 1880 by *James Powell & Sons*.

MOAT FARMHOUSE, W of the church, is a representative design of *c.* 1600, three bays with a cross-wing and two-storey porch in line with the chimney. The hood of the door may be Jacobean. MANOR HOUSE, Green Lane, 250 yds SW, has a comparable plan but also its timber-framing exposed. Only the l. cross-wing and the middle range are genuine *c.* 1600; the rest remarkably is of 1969. Further good traditional timber-framed addition of 2008 by *Bruce Deacon*.

TEBWORTH *see* CHALGRAVE

TEMPSFORD

ST PETER. Not much to interest in the exterior, except for the predominance of horizontal banding of brown ironstone and buff. Much repair was done in 1621; all the banding is of that date. As for features, the W tower is Dec, and the aisle E windows are Dec. Otherwise mostly Perp. Perp also the four-bay arcades of the wide nave. Standard elements, but different N from S. The two niches in the s aisle E wall and the N aisle piscina may be Dec. The nave and chancel roofs are by *Edward Browning*, 1874, but the nave has its wall-plate from the work of 1621. – PULPIT. Perp, of the wineglass type, wood with traceried panels. The door is preserved. – SCREEN. Dado only, with some old parts. – SCULPTURE. Good Virgin by *Lucy E. A. Turner*, 1951, in the smoothly modelled style of Henry Moore. – REREDOS, ALTAR AND RAILS by *Jones & Willis*, 1894. – STAINED GLASS. All by *Percy Bacon*, 1908–29, the E window a Christ in Majesty with figures of King Edward the Elder, in recognition of the significance of the battle of Tempsford in the triumph over the Danes in East Anglia, and St Peter, Alfred the Great and St Swithun. – MONUMENTS. Sir Gillies Payne †1801 and his daughter Elizabeth †1789, both in the W tower. Classical tablets with urns, his with curtains drawn back. The Paynes made their fortune in the sugar plantations of St Kitts and Nevis.

LYCHGATE by *Albert Richardson*, 1931. In the churchyard a TABLE TOMB for Capt. William Stuart †1893. Lion supporters.

Immediately s of the church, GANNOCK HOUSE, a good timber-framed C15 house, with big bracing, ogee members. In its s addition, an arch with carved beam, taken from the Chantry House, a mid-C15 building dem. 1939.

N of the church, a former SCHOOL, 1869, and STUART MEMORIAL HALL, 1924. Portland stone Cenotaph WAR MEMORIAL in front.

ANCHOR INN, on the A1. Built in 1831. Tudor Gothic with a fine cut brick sign in the gable and porch with cusping. Just beyond, the BRIDGE over the Ivel. By *James Savage*, 1815–20. With three round arches of gritstone with ironstone spandrels and parapet.

TEMPSFORD HALL was cut off from the village by the A1 in 1962, but its GATEPIERS and railings, early C19, survive on Church Street. Quite a big gabled red brick house in a joyless Elizabethan style for William Stuart, 1903 by *H. S. East* (*Wimperis & East*), after a fire in 1898 destroyed the previous house (originally of 1769 for Sir Gillies Payne but rebuilt in 1874). Adjoining, OFFICES, brick floor bands and concrete panels, by *Hughes, Lomax & Adutt*, 1968, for French Kier Construction (now Kier).

GIBRALTAR FARM, 2 m. E. An early C19 weatherboarded BARN is preserved as a memorial to the agents of the Special Operations Executive in the Second World War. They were issued with their equipment here before flying to occupied Europe from the airfield at Tempsford; the runways remain.

GANNOCK'S CASTLE, SW of the church. An earth enclosure, 115 ft by 85 ft (35 metres by 26 metres), probably C12. Formerly moated. Some remains of buildings identified in 2003.

THURLEIGH   *0050*

A village with a high concentration of timber-framed and thatched houses. A survey drawn up in 1604 means that several built before that date can be identified.

ST PETER. The crossing tower is *c.* 1150 with quoins and single splayed windows on two storeys. The doorway on its s side must have led into it from outside or from a *porticus* and has a tympanum with Adam and Eve, the tree and the serpent. Its style is a continuation of Saxon sculptural traditions (cf. Covington, Hunts.). The imposts of the arch were originally decorated with chevron. The rest is Perp, except for the early C13 N doorway and the chancel piscina and ogee-headed chancel lowside s window, which seem Dec and the reticulated tracery of the E window. Deep s porch with two two-light windows E and two W. In the chancel, Late Perp ironstone windows. Four-bay arcades of standard elements, also to the tower arches. The whole church was in a bad state by 1956; the chancel E wall was completely rebuilt in 1957–9 and the derelict nave restored to use by *J. V. Gedge* in 1970–1 when the clerestory was removed and nave roof replaced. The beam from the E end is preserved; its inscription relates to a Doom painting formerly over the chancel arch. – FONT. Perp, octagonal, shields on the shaft. – STAINED GLASS. Bits in the S aisle W window. – S aisle E by *S. Evans* of Smethwick, 1902. – BRASS, probably to John Harvey, *c*. 1420, the armoured figure 3 ft 10 in. (1.16 cm) long.

OLD VICARAGE, E of the church. Front of 1750, with two-storey canted bays. Mansard roof.

BAPTIST CHAPEL, ¼ m. E. 1888 by *F. T. Mercer*. The expected pedimented Italianate, with one large Lombardic window to the centre.

BURY HILL. Considerable remains of a motte-and-bailey castle, SSW, S, SE and E of the church. The motte is E of the church and the moat is *c*. 20 ft (6 metres) deep and 25 ft (7 metres) wide but so heavily overgrown as to be almost indecipherable. An outer enclosure circumscribes nearly the whole village.

THE WINDMILL, Mill Hill, ¼ m. SW. Just the tower of 1890, five storeys high, restored *c*. 2000 as a house with a glass belvedere in place of the cap.

(BLACKBURN HALL, 1 m. W. Originally a two-bay aisled hall, possibly C13, from which the aisles were later removed. C16 cross wing. Hall roof of passing brace construction with saltire bracing to the central truss.)

9020

TILSWORTH

ALL SAINTS. Externally the church is a mixture of ironstone and Totternhoe, only the tower predominantly ironstone, and of generally Perp appearance. The S arcade is C13, three bays, with standard elements. But the arcade was longer to the W. The W tower has been built into it and been given its own arch into the aisle, which with the E arch of the tower looks C15. Nave and chancel have single-framed roofs with crown-posts. On the N side one large three-light window with flowing tracery. The N doorway is Dec too. There was a S chapel, its arch with semicircular responds, but it must have been taken down before the C16, for the S aisle has a large Perp E window. This now shows inside the organ chamber/vestry of 1909 by *W. D. Caröe*, who restored the church from 1905. – FONT. Of cauldron-shape, on an E.E. four-shaft foot, its COVER a C17 ogee dome. – PULPIT. Usual Jacobean type with vertical panels quartered around a boss. Splat balusters. – COMMUNION RAIL. Slender turned balusters. – STAINED GLASS. In a N window, fragments including a C15 head. – SCULPTURE (N wall). Discovered in 1905. Three detached statuettes of soldiers and part of a fourth. They are certainly C13. What kind of group did they belong to? – Lower part of a seated figure of the mid C13; beautiful drapery. – Fragmentary Pietà; C15. – Also a stiff-leaf capital. – MONUMENTS. In the nave N wall, Dec recess with a late C13 effigy of a priest; poor quality. – In the chancel big and beautiful, effigyless monument to Gabriel Fowler †1582. Canopy on four slender Corinthian columns, good leaf-trail frieze, extravagant top achievement. This is of Totternhoe stone, but the gadrooned tomb-chest is in different stone. It has typical elements of Elizabethan ornament of linked circles. Was it replaced? – Sir Henry Chester †1666. The same type, but with unfluted columns and (already) an open curly top pediment. In the frieze three elementary cherubs' heads, but nothing like as abysmally elementary as the kneeling effigies. – In the S aisle, W end, a massive table tomb with inscribed black marble top for Thomas Prentis †1707 and his wife Sarah †1729.

27

TILSWORTH MANOR, S of the church. Still surrounded by a large moat on four sides. The GATEHOUSE is C15 and there are accounts recording major repairs here in 1474. Of ironstone, with Totternhoe quoins and dressings. One-light window to the N, a two-light window to the S. The gateway is unvaulted. C17 gableted tile roof. The house is probably partly C17 but extensively added to c. 1955, including the central porch with half-timbered gable over.

WARREN KNOLL, 100 yds N of the church, in the grounds of Orchard Lodge. Simple, poorly preserved motte-and-bailey castle, about 9 ft 10 in. (3 metres) high.

TINGRITH

ST NICHOLAS. Of ironstone, Perp, over-restored in 1845–8 by an unknown hand. W tower, embattled nave and aisles. The chancel E wall with two short polygonal angle turrets. Impressive, large three-light clerestory windows with panel tracery. Better preserved the S doorway with large-leaf spandrels. The arcades, also excessively renewed, have the standard Perp section, here in the details still C14-looking. In the S aisle SE corner, an image niche with fine vaulted canopy and grotesque head as its bracket. A second bracket has an angel corbel. 1840s furnishings, but the REREDOS is by *C. E. Mallows*, 1900. – DECALOGUE etc., of 1848, stone with Gothic frames, nicely lettered and decorated. – STAINED GLASS. Much Early Victorian in the chancel, three of 1848 by *W. J. Bolton*. An important and impressive set, given by the Trevors, especially good the large Italian Renaissance style E window of the Last Supper. Its companions show Christ Carrying the Cross and the Agony in the Garden and continue the cycle begun by the earlier Ascension window in the S wall. The Resurrection of 1850 is signed by Bolton's pupil *W. H. Constable*. Tower window also by Bolton, after Overbeck. – BRASS. Robert Hugeson †1611. Kneeling figure.

Outside, TOMB-CHEST, a Gothic octagon with buttresses, pinnacles and stone tiled roof. For Robert Trevor †1834. Along the church approach, barge-boarded COTTAGES, one dated 1838, another 1841 (formerly the School, with a bell), built for the Misses Trevors, who improved the village after inheriting in 1834; their house was demolished in the 1920s.

TANQUERAY HOUSE, High Street, was the vicarage. Late C18, red brick with white quoins, four bays, pedimented doorcase. E additions of 1859–60.

0020

TODDINGTON

ST GEORGE. Externally a big Perp church with a crossing tower, aisles and transepts. To the N of the chancel is a three-storey vestry, on the upper floors originally the priest's dwelling. Mostly Totternhoe stone – the melted surfaces of the S porch in particular testament to the limits of clunch for building. Mixed in, a good dose of other materials as evidence of several restorations – e.g. early C19 brick in the transepts, and cobbles and tile in the W front, restored in 1892–3 by *R. W. Edis* who had restored the rest in 1879–81. The church is mostly embattled or parapeted, and below these on the N side runs a frieze with lots of beasts and grotesques (some recarved in 1991): an otter, a pair of fishes, a hawk, a fox, a hound, a sow, peacocks, a bull, a horse, a swan, a griffin, a mermaid, a wyvern, and so on. The costume of a human figure (now indistinct but engraved by Fisher in the early C19) allows one to date all this (and most of the exterior of the church) early C16. Chancel windows of three lights N and S, of four E; nave W window of five lights. The tower bell-openings are pairs of two lights on each side (cf. Luton and Houghton Regis). In the N porch, also rebuilt in 1893, an elaborate canopied Perp STOUP. The S porch is again Perp, with an excellent roof of curved windbraces and angels. The only external detail which suggests earlier work is the S doorway, which must date from the late C13, and a lancet in the W end of the S aisle, reopened in the C19. Inside, one can go back yet a little more. The S transept PISCINA, a double piscina, looks mid-C13 at the latest (two pointed arches set in a round arch). The crossing arches are low and narrow and have big semi-octagonal responds and plain two-step (i.e. unmoulded) arches. That also is C13, as is no doubt the plan with the transepts. To the W, above the crossing arch, is a blocked lancet window. The roofline before the Perp clerestory (of three lights) is also visible. Inside the tower, on the first stage, is a room with tall blind arcading on each wall and benches below the arches. The shafts have bell capitals except two with waterleaf, so this too is early C13. Blocked lancets in the next stage, below the belfry. The belfry floor and the tower roof have been tree-ring-dated to 1401–22 but the wall-plate of

the roof to 1336–68. The later date would fit with the style of
the belfry (cf. Houghton Regis and Dunstable). The nave
arcades of four bays may have been added *c.* 1300 or a little
later. High octagonal piers, one on the s side with a little nailhead in the capital. Double-chamfered arches. Perp roofs of
chancel and nave with angels and bosses. Shields refer to
Thomas Peyre †1429. The Perp fenestration makes the whole
church and particularly the chancel very light; the N transept
N window is a restoration of 1880, replacing C17 work. Within
the vestry two separate newel stairs, one entered from within
the chancel, the other from the churchyard. Both rose higher
than now.

– WALL PAINTINGS. Revealed in 1930 and now barely
legible. In the s aisle dim fragments of scenes under arcades,
including the Coronation of the Virgin, also a more clearly
recognizable guilloche band of medallions with leopards' heads
and swans. Formerly visible were scenes of St Michael Weighing Souls and the Seven Acts of Mercy. Also figures of Christ
and two women. – On the N side two trees, one with a bird
and several figures. Band with tools (hammers, nails, pincers
etc.). – PULPIT. Tall, goblet-shaped with a tester. Introduced
c. 1945. REREDOS and ALTAR. 1949 by *W. H. Randoll Blacking.*
English altar, the figure of Christ in Majesty under a thin pinnacle before the E window treated as one composition with the
STAINED GLASS by *Christopher Webb*, 1948. The W window is
his design also (1941), both very recognizably his style in the
use in one of fronds of foliage and in the other branches of
thorns to link the Enid Blyton-ish figure groups against clear
glass. s transept s by *Heaton, Butler & Bayne*, 1892. – MONU-
MENTS. In the s transept, effigy of a knight, early C14, much
damaged. – Two Perp recesses in the s wall, with early C15
effigies of knight and lady, probably Thomas Peyre †1429 (*see*
above) and his wife. – Dame Anne Cheyne †1561. Stone effigy.
– Alabaster effigy of Henry Lord Cheyne †1587. His head is
on a half-rolled-up mat. His legs are lost. – Lady Cheyne
†1614. Alabaster too. Her head is gone. All three on tomb-
chests, the first with medallions and shields, the last awkwardly
built up on a smaller chest with Renaissance motifs. – In the
N transept, which from the C17 was the Wentworth Chapel and
is raised over their vault, Lady Mary Wentworth †1632/3,
attributed to *William Wright* (GF). Frontally seated figure
under a domed baldacchino with two putti drawing back curtains and two mourning figures below l. and r. Of very good
quality. – Opposite, Baroness Henrietta Maria Wentworth
†1686. Grey and black marble. Of reredos type, with an open
segmental pediment. Two allegorical figures and a gruesome
still-life of death. The head, now loose, may have belonged to
a bust. Attributed to *William Woodman Sen.* (GF). The epitaph
is by *Thomas Carew.*

CONGER HILL, s of the church in a field. Motte, 92 ft (28
metres) in diameter at the top. Also remains of earthworks
farther E.

The church lies at the N end of a spacious green of delightfully irregular shape, the location for a substantial market and fair from the medieval period until *c.* 1800 and known as MARKET SQUARE. Agas shows details of the timber-framed buildings in his map of 1581, and no doubt the present frontages conceal earlier fabric. There are no bad houses or cottages around the square, and some very good ones. The best is OLD WENT-WORTH HOUSE of *c.* 1700, chequer brick, of seven bays, with the middle three lying slightly back, and a top parapet. The doorway with fluted pilasters and a pediment must be mid-C18. Also worthwhile, SUNDIAL HOUSE on the N side of the green, with five bays of cross-windows and a pedimented doorcase.

N of the green is PARKFIELDS SCHOOL, 1962–3 by the County Architect, *J. C. Barker.* Curtain-walling, coloured spandrels.*

MANOR HOUSE, set in a low valley below the village to the NE. Toddington Manor, built *c.* 1570–80 by Sir Henry Cheyne and recorded on the Agas map in 1581 and again on a somewhat larger scale by John Thorpe early in the C17, was a quadrangular mansion round a spacious inner court. It had three storeys, mullioned and transomed windows, and round angle towers. Described in a survey of 1642 as 'A goodly faire house . . . wch house coste att leaste 40,000l ye building besides Tymber and brick lying ready there for building or repyring to a great Value.' It came to the Wentworths in 1614 and was mostly demolished by William, Lord Strafford, in 1745 but then taken up after 1806 by the Cooper family and remodelled and extended.† The result has a decidedly curious appearance. All that survives of the early house is its NE corner, comprising a small oblong block of three storeys – in its present form as remodelled with a hipped roof for William Cooper Cooper *c.* 1850 – a brick round tower, and a low extension of old brick and buttresses behind the tower. On the W front, the former kitchen was remodelled as a Dining Room with Perp bay window under a shaped gable and, inside, a broad, rather good, Gothick surround to the original fireplace; there is another in the entrance hall. Separate C18 stables to SE but with a Neo-Georgian linking arch, contemporary with the Billiard Room on the W front of 1913 by *Bromley & Watkins* of Nottingham which has a Neo-William and Mary interior. This now has a late C20 upper storey. The LODGE at the entrance, thatched with Venetian windows in a shallow bow, is also 1913 by *Bromley & Watkins* for W. F. M. Weston-Webb.

---

*Pevsner noted in the first edition of this guide TWO WATERS in Park Road, a house of 1967–8 by and for *Keith Miller* of *Charter Building Design Group.* Its neighbour, WINDSHINE, was designed by and for his colleague, *A. J. Hucklesby.* Both were flat-roofed Miesian boxes, of grey brick and floor-to-ceiling glazing infilling painted steel frames, elevated above open ground floors. Both have been so remodelled, with pitched roofs etc., as to be largely unrecognizable.

†A carved panel of Apollo and the Nine Muses is now in the British Galleries, Victoria and Albert Museum. For other woodwork see also the White Horse Inn, Hockliffe.

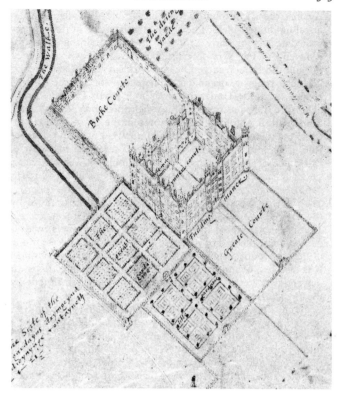

Toddington Manor.
From a survey by Ralph Agas, 1581

TOFTE MANOR *see* SHARNBROOK

TOTTERNHOE

9020

Here were the principal quarries of the neighbourhood in the Middle Ages which were much revived in the late C18 and early C19, e.g. Woburn, Southill, the Swan at Bedford etc. The stone is a clunch and weathers badly, as so many Bedfordshire buildings show, but used internally it is ideal for carved work such as the late C16 monuments at Turvey (q.v.) and elsewhere.

St Giles. Quite big, mostly of clunch, in ashlar blocks. Low w tower. The church is embattled and appears Perp; the battlements of the nave and aisles with crocketed pinnacles, and in the gable of the nave E wall the battlements have flushwork. The chancel E wall has chequerwork. Pretty N vestry. Perp arcades, octagonal piers, triple-hollow-chamfered arches.

Against the NE respond a very handsome demi-figure of an angel holding a shield. The sharp angular folds of the drapery spell late C15 or early C16; the shield contains a rebus for Ashwell (VCH). Very fine original nave roof with moulded purlins and rafters, carved beams with leaf scrolls, and bosses. The aisle roofs are original too. There also appears the Ashwell rebus. – SCREEN. Under the tower arch, partly Perp and probably once the rood screen. Single-light divisions. – BENCHES. Some with linenfold panels, restored in the 1830s. – STAINED GLASS. Fragments in a S aisle window. – E window, Tree of Life, designed by *John Piper*, made by *Patrick Reyntiens*, 1970. Lurid colours, rather harsh. – BRASS. John Warwekhyll, vicar, †1524 (chancel floor; *c.* 6 in.; 15 cm long). – William Mitchell †1621 (29 in.; 74 cm long).

TOTTERNHOE SCHOOL, 250 yds N of the church. 1948–50 by the *Bedfordshire County Architect's Dept* (job architect, *Harold Hartley*), and one of the best early postwar designs, with a curved tower pierced by porthole windows. The concrete frame of the classroom wing is exposed as a series of raking columns. It is also one of the type, quite common in the late 1940s, to use prefabricated aluminium units for the classrooms made by the *Bristol Aeroplane Co*.

LANCOTBURY, ¼ m. N on the main road. A handsome timber-framed manor house with closely set studs infilled with her-ringbone brickwork on the fronts and gable end; early to mid-C16 probably. Long jetty to the front, half-hipped roof at the W end and a stair-tower on the N front in line with the chimneystack. Through passage plan. (Good large fireplaces. C17 stair.)

CASTLE, Totternhoe Knolls, 1 m. NW. In a very impressive posi-tion at the end of a promontory. Small motte about 5 metres (16 ft) tall with a base of about 40 metres (130 ft) surrounded by an almost continuous ditch. There are two inner baileys: an oval one to its W the other to N and E triangular; on the S the land falls away. To the ESE is a further, larger, outer bailey, 150 metres long (490 ft). This was once the strongest of the early castles of Bedfordshire, already here by the 1170s when its lands were given to Dunstable Priory. The medieval QUARRIES were cut into the hillside to the W and NW.

DOOLITTLE MILL, ½ m. SSE. Probably C18 and originally a combined wind- and watermill. The capless tower of the former emerges from the latter, which had an overshot wheel fed from the mill pond. The miller's house abuts it. Such mills are rare and in Bedfordshire unique. Restored since 2001.

TURVEY

A very attractive stone village on the Buckinghamshire border, its appeal largely due to the patronage of two branches of the

Higgins family who acquired the Mordaunt estates in 1786.*
From *c*. 1840 the families initiated much renewal of cottages and
other buildings. The parkland of their houses protects the
approaches from E and W.

ALL SAINTS. A large and very rewarding church, one of the best
in Bedfordshire. The nave is in its masonry still Anglo-Saxon,
as is proved by the remains of double-splayed windows above
the S arcade. The tower is Anglo-Saxon too, and this is visible
in the doorway high up in its E wall, i.e. towards the nave. The
nave no doubt went as far as the pieces of solid masonry in
the present arcades. The lancets in the W tower to N and S on
the other hand are E.E., and so is the arch towards the nave.
Next follows the W part of the S arcade – say late C13. Three
bays, octagonal piers. Two arches have continuous outer
mouldings and chamfers, the middle third continuous mouldings around the arch soffit also. The S aisle doorway, with its
continuous mouldings, and the double door itself with its   14
excellent ironwork hinges of double scrolls with foliate terminals, goes with it. The ironwork is unquestionably by *Thomas
of Leighton*, *c*. 1270–80, and, as Jane Geddes has noted, probably comes before his work at Leighton Buzzard, for the
designs are the same but slightly less refined. The fenestration
too is late C13, i.e. intersecting tracery and three stepped lancet
lights to the S chapel and inside, fitted below it, the fine trefoil-
headed SEDILIA and PISCINA. The aisle's chapel E window
was also of stepped lancets, in two tiers. Then a three-bay N
arcade was built, say *c*. 1320, see the taller octagonal piers and
the unmoulded, chamfered arches and finer tracery. At about
the same time the former Saxon chancel was rebuilt in line
with the S chapel E wall. Finally, the N chancel chapel was
added, probably in the late C15 (Glynne notes 'Tudor arches'
in 1830), corresponding with the two three-light windows of
arched lights under straight heads.

The rest is due to the major Tractarian rebuilding and restoration in 1852–4 by *G. G. Scott* for Charles Longuet Higgins
of Turvey Abbey, representing the summit of his improvements
to the village. Scott took down the C13 chancel arch, added the
two E bays of both nave arcades (which had to be taken down
and rebuilt), with matching octagonal piers and double-
chamfered arches, and placed his chancel arch on the new line
with a much larger chancel behind it, under a pointed timber   51
vault, prickly with cusping and subcusping on the trusses. The
organ chamber and vestry added E of the N chancel chapel goes
with this; the three-arch organ arcade of cusped arches on
polished Purbeck piers is especially lavish and impressive, the
carving here of foliage animated by birds and, on the late C13-
style capitals of the chancel arch, crisp and lively. The tracery
to the ringing chamber in the tower is also of this time. The

*The Mordaunt house was S of the village at Manor Farm. Demolished in the 1650s,
but the site is still evident.

Perp clerestory was extended with the nave, from four to six
windows, and the roof with angels and bosses and figures on
the jackposts also carried on with remarkable felicity. The roofs
over the N aisle and former N chapel also Perp. Two-storey Perp
S porch, originally vaulted. The vestry at the W end of the S
aisle is dated 1589. The tower ends in a Perp belfry and a rather
blunt pyramid roof of 1864 by *J. Horsford*.

FURNISHINGS. – FONT. Is this *c.* 1200? The supports look
E.E., but the four lobes of the bowl have Norman voluted
designs. – WALL PAINTING. In a recess in the S aisle, perhaps
originally an Easter sepulchre, is an exquisite early C14 painting of the Crucifixion. Dark green background with a pattern
of small flowers. The twisted figure of Christ is especially characteristic and moving. Discovered in the 1850s, when further
painting above the arch was destroyed. – The chancel in its
totality is 'the finest mid-Victorian ecclesiastical ensemble in
Bedfordshire' (G. McHardy), with TILES by *Minton* and the
monster ORGAN, encased in lattice-braced panelling, and its
painted pipes within a cage of cast-iron and brass. – PULPIT,
STALLS and LECTERN all by *Scott*, the REREDOS also but
adjusted 1912. – LIGHT FITTINGS. Scott's brass chandeliers
in the chancel replaced by aggressively spiky designs of 1968
by *Bernard West*, surprisingly successful. The thorny aesthetic
is consistent with his COMMUNION RAIL and TOWER SCREEN
of 1972. – STAINED GLASS. In the chancel by *Hardman*. The
date is of course 1854. – MONUMENTS. A most impressive
collection. Brasses in the S chapel to a priest, *c.* 1500 (2-ft;
61 cm figure), a civilian, *c.* 1480 (19-in.; 48 cm figure), and
Alice Bernard †1606 (2 ft 1 in.; 65 cm figure). – In the S aisle,
Sir John Mordaunt †1504 and wife. Tomb-chest of Purbeck
marble with twisted (early Renaissance) angle colonnettes and
highly cusped lozenges. On it the two effigies of alabaster. His
head lies on a helmet with the crest of a screaming man. Or a
biting man, *un homme mordant*? Originally set between chancel
and S chapel, the chantry for which was established by
Mordaunt in 1504. It was moved to the N aisle in 1810, returned
to the S aisle by Scott in 1854, and then taken again to the N
aisle from *c.* 1920 to 1950. – Between chancel and S chapel, i.e.
originally adjacent to Sir John, his son, the 1st Lord Mordaunt,
†1562 and wife, Elizabeth Vere of Drayton. Among very early
Elizabethan monuments, one of the most important in the
county, specified in Lord Mordaunt's will to be built within a
year of his death. It belongs to an interesting group found
within Buckinghamshire and especially Northamptonshire
employing similar materials and motifs, some of which are
associated with the *Thorpe* family of masons of Kingscliffe,
Northants.* Alabaster effigies and sarcophagus in a Totternhoe
stone surround. It is just possible the effigies are 1560s and the

---

* *See* the Introduction to *The Buildings of England: Northamptonshire* (3rd edn, 2013)
for a discussion of work by the Thorpes. For many years this monument was attributed to T. Kirby, a sculptor now regarded as fictitious.

rest a little later for it has coupled Roman Doric columns and an arch decorated with chains of squares and circles, a motif found repeatedly in Northamptonshire houses of the 1570s and 80s. Victories in the spandrels and behind the columns panels of trophies, in character very similar to those of the chimney-piece in the Great Hall at Deene, Northants. The solid upper storey has two caryatids, and the whole is finished by a solemn pediment, again with squares and circles. The tomb-chest has a *bombé* section, with pilasters of buxom grotesques. The monument is the same to chancel and to chapel but the pediment was originally surmounted on the chancel side by three female figures. Moreover, before the erection of Scott's chancel arch, its W face was also exposed and comprised another set of columns and a smaller pediment and little legs, like the Cave monument at Chicheley, Bucks. Reset in the chapel wall is a shield which may have come from this. – 2nd Lord Mordaunt †1571 and his two wives, so presumably erected after the death of the second wife in the 1590s. It is of the type, entirely of alabaster, found also at Bromham, Husborne Crawley and Marston Moretaine (qq.v.), but more elaborate than the others of the group. Eight-poster with plain Doric columns and a frieze with paterae. The three effigies lie side by side, but he, in the middle, is raised higher than his wives. The straw mats on which they lie are rolled up at the feet, and the way his feet balance on the spurs he is wearing is surprising. Ceiling of the tester with more patterns of squares and circles around little pendants. Sarcophagus with winged chimera at the angles and a chained eagle, a motif drawn from Hieronymus Cock's *Pictores, Statuarii, Architecti, Latomi . . .* – 3rd Lord Mordaunt †1601. A rare conceit, originally placed in the N chapel as an altar tomb; moved in 1854. Tomb-chest with a black cloth of stone hanging down like a pall and the inscription plate in white on it. The most similar monument is Maximilian Colt's of Princess Sophia †1606 in Westminster Abbey with the cradle cover of stone hanging down on the ground. – Charles Longuet Higgins †1885, signed by *H. H. Armstead*. Two angels by a sarcophagus, against a blue mosaic background. Chancel N.

In the churchyard, MAUSOLEUM of the Higgins family. Permission was given for it in 1825. With the motif of Jacobean pinnacles borrowed from the early C19 alterations to Turvey Abbey and that of the balustrade with big lettering (Psalm 89) from such houses as Castle Ashby, Northants, though one rarely reads it at such close quarters. Pious inscriptions are a trademark of Higgins buildings, as are salvaged fragments – this incorporates a C16 fireplace! – LYCHGATE. 1856 by *Scott*.

TURVEY ABBEY (Priory of Our Lady of Peace). A Jacobean house, perhaps originally a possession of the Mordaunts, with dates 1603 and 1608. John Higgins inherited in 1792 and took up residence in 1797, making significant additions. Four gables on the front and quite irregular. The garden elevation of this part was originally the same. It is made interesting externally by the balustrades and pinnacles of obelisks on circles, brought from the façade of Easton Maudit Hall, Northants, after its demolition in 1801, and subsequently copied e.g. for the porch (this was added by *c.* 1830, but at that time stood two bays to the r.). Large window on the garden front with a surround of *c.* 1700 and timber Gothic tracery. At that time the room behind it was made – see e.g. the beautiful bolection-moulded chimneypiece (the doors also had pediments, since removed). To the r. of these, two monumental double-transomed windows inserted *c.* 1854 when the ballroom behind was created by C. Longuet Higgins. Dark Gothic ceiling with saltire ribs in panels and figures of saints. Its chimneypiece made up with some of the same chains of plain geometrical ornament as the monument in the church of 1562. The w end of this front originally had three gables corresponding to those of the entrance front but now has a projecting wing, dated 1816, with crenellations and a niche for a statue. In the centre, crenellated additions on two storeys; the gable above is dated 1865. On the w front, now within modern additions, a strikingly robust timber arcade with simplified classical details links a pantry to the kitchen. At the far e end, at an angle, a former billiard room with reused Tudor fireplace.

COACH HOUSE, ashlar with a fine Georgian cupola clock turret, square below and round above; 1800–1 (beam inside signed by *William Dalley*, carpenter, and *John Warren*, mason).* Converted by *Victor Farrar Partnership*, *c.* 1995. Nice skewed passage to the former STABLES (converted *c.* 1980 for the Monastery of Christ the Saviour by the *Charter Partnership*). Beyond a former BARN (C19?), with steep gables and buttresses, also converted by the *Charter Partnership*, *c.* 1995, and late medieval oblong DOVECOTE. – The CHAPEL, between the offices and the house, is of 1990 by *Dennis Bettle*.

At the end of the garden, a Gothick SUMMERHOUSE of 1829. Pious inscription inside. There are several rusticated GATEPIERS, two with urns. These were cut down from taller ones in the entrance wall at Easton Maudit. The stone wall to the road is from the same source.

TURVEY HOUSE. Begun for John Higgins in 1794 (the stable clock is dated 1796). The first house, a small country villa on a new site close to the church and river, is illustrated in the early C19 by Thomas Fisher with two-storey canted bays at the ends and a five-bay centre rising one storey higher. Encompassing it was a chinoiserie veranda. It is now as remodelled *c.* 1840 for T. C. Higgins and in a manner recalling Decimus Burton, although the architect is unknown. The house has an extremely swagger façade, decidedly Empire in flavour. Only seven bays, but widely spaced. The angle bays are flanked by giant Corinthian columns; the recessed centre has giant pilasters instead, with Grecian capitals, and above the door is a

*Warren is one of several estate workers portrayed from the life by John Higgins in his *Turvey Scrapbook*, 1830. He is shown with one of the pinnacles that adorn the house and he evidently constructed all the walls and balustrades.

small Grecian relief. In the angle bays the ground-floor window is set in an aedicule, again with columns; above the upper window another relief. The top of the façade is a rich foliage frieze with tiny cherubs in it and above this a heavy cornice and attic. In the middle this is crowned by an eminence with an acroterion. The undecorated entrance side is less impressive, but has a projecting centre under a pediment and a four-column porch of Greek Doric columns. Inside there is at once an apsed lobby. In the centre of the house is the spacious staircase hall with a spectacular tall coffered dome with circular lantern on four semicircular arches. The staircase leads up to a half-landing with two Corinthian columns *in antis*, and behind this is another coffered-domed room. Passages E and W on each floor are framed by plain, rather Soanian, round arches. The dining room and drawing room along the front are in a consistent late Regency style on the turn of Victorian; the latter has two recesses, one framed by shell niches. The cast-iron spiral attic staircase came from the Crystal Palace. The service wing may be slightly later than the house. A carriage arch with the initials of W. F. Higgins (inherited 1865) topped by an acroterion links it to a plain pedimented brewhouse/laundry with Venetian window.

E of Turvey House on Carlton Road is the former HOME FARM (Priory Farmhouse and Barn), a model mid-C19 design, of three stone ranges with lancets in the gables. The improving hand of that period is immediately apparent in a walk through the VILLAGE from Turvey Abbey to the church, beginning with a large example of the Higgins estate style opposite the Abbey, with steep bargeboards lettered with a pious inscription, Neo-Elizabethan chimneys and red-and-black fishscale tile roof; further down the SCHOOL and VILLAGE HALL (originally the Museum) of 1847 with mullioned windows. Also RICHMOND HOUSE, C18 stone house with Gothick glazing and a Doric porch. On the green before the church, the RECTORY, built in 1839 with a benefaction from Anna Higgins. Highly eccentric details with curly bargeboards, Perp tracery, a gable end with half-timbering and brick-nogging and small graffiti figures of saints, and several reset fragments, including an owl in a niche. Round the bend, by the entrance to the church and Turvey House, THE THREE CRANES, with nice timber porch and Gothic stables. Closer to the bridge, BRIDGE HOUSE, dated 1849 with T. C. Higgins's initials. Opposite the THREE FYSHES, its two-storey porch dated 1624 on a moulded beam. The BRIDGE over the Ouse has eleven arches in all, seven of them pointed, the others round. Cutwaters only upstream. The oldest parts are medieval and there was a chapel by the early C15, but most of what one sees is of 1795 and the 1820s. It was widened in 1930. Close to the bridge on the island midway, two C18 pieces of SCULPTURE, one allegedly Jonah, which was put here in 1844 and came from a fountain at the old house at Ashridge, Herts. (dem. 1802); the other is a man, originally with a three-cornered hat, put up in 1953.

PRIORY FARMHOUSE, 1 m. E. A mid-C19 rebuilding in coursed limestone rubble. With seven buttresses along the road elevation of the house and its barn.

Former STATION, 1¼ m. E. A sweet stone design of 1872 for the Bedford & Northampton Railway (*Charles Liddell*, engineer), a line promoted by W. B. Higgins of Pictshill House.

PICTSHILL HOUSE, 1½ m. E in its own small park. Built *c.* 1830 for W. B. Higgins. Good plain square stone house with a hipped roof and arched doorcase. Diminutive Neoclassical LODGE.

TYRELLS END *see* EVERSHOLT

1030

UPPER GRAVENHURST

ST GILES. Now disused. Ironstone. Norman some of the nave walling and the N doorway with its one-step arch, concealed within a later addition. Perp the W tower. Much of the rest is of 1901–2 by *Arthur W. Blomfield & Sons*. (Inside, they widened the chancel arch with Neo-Norman columns and arched side openings, but the chevron is mostly original. The arch was previously supported by timber columns, probably C17.) Ramsey Abbey held the manor until the Dissolution.

1030

UPPER STONDON

A quiet hilltop setting for the church, old rectory and, E of these, a large pond by Manor Farm.

ALL SAINTS. A substantial rebuilding in 1857 in ironstone (*Ashby & Sons*, builders). Short, with a slightly higher chancel than nave, a S porch tower of three storeys, with pyramid roof, looking distinctly domestic; a form assumed *c.* 1700, when the church was remodelled. The N transept opposite was new in the rebuilding. The one ancient piece is a modest C13 doorway. Reordered in 1971, the altar now at the W end and NE vestry of the same date, enlarged 1994. – STAINED GLASS. Good N transept window of 1886 by *Carl Almquist* (*Shrigley & Hunt*).

WARDEN ABBEY *see* OLD WARDEN

WAULUD'S BANK *see* LUTON

0030

WESTONING

ST MARY MAGDALENE. Perp W tower with later lead spire. The rest mostly early C14 – see the windows (very renewed by

William Slater, 1854–60) and the mouldings of the N doorway. See also the octagonal arcade piers and the chancel arch with notch stops. Among the windows there are some with stepped lancet lights, and two (aisles E) with a cusped and subcusped circle in the top of the tracery. Two-storey S porch. – FONT. Cauldron-shaped, with big bold rolls – obviously C13. The foot may have been made for a pier capital. – ARCHITECTURAL FRAGMENTS. In the S aisle wall. – STAINED GLASS. E window of 1895 by *Heaton, Butler & Bayne* commemorating the Rev. J. W. Coventry Campion. The road to Emmaus; Noli me tangere; Risen Christ with fishermen. The S aisle window of 1903 by the same makers, to J. G. Coventry Campion. – MONUMENT. Bust on a tapered plinth of J. W. Coventry Campion (†1872), signed by *John Adams-Acton*, 1874. It stood originally in the S aisle.

Former VICARAGE, E of the church. Mostly new in 1846 by *James Horsford* but still quite Regency. Yellow brick with bracketed eaves and shallow gables over the ends.

MANOR HOUSE (now apartments). 1842–3 for the Rev. J. W. Coventry Campion, who bought the manor in 1836. Red brick and stone, Jacobean, with shaped porch gable and also shaped gables on the S with a loggia of columns *in antis* and the W front with two-storey canted bays. Flats since 2000. (Inside, much woodwork from the old house at Wrest Park (q.v.; dem. *c.* 1840) and the Palace of Westminster. VCH; the staircase is now at Melford Hall, Suffolk.)* Picturesque LODGE.

The village is large and mostly later C20. On the main road ⅜ m. SE, a CLOCKTOWER like a brick chimney with an ogee cupola top, erected 1897. Nearby, the WAR MEMORIAL, a plain Portland stone cross by *Basil C. Deacon*, 1920.

WHIPSNADE

The village is spread over rolling ground on the Downs, the buildings scattered around a wooded Green so large it resembles parkland.

ST MARY MAGDALENE. It is delightful to find this combination of a C16 brick W tower with a chequer brick nave of 1719. The reused W doorway is of stone, late C15. The nave windows are arched, stone dressed on the N side only and the N door surround rusticated. The angles of the former stone church have been kept. The apsed chancel was added 1860 by *E. C. Hakewill* and is remarkably harmonious with the Georgian nave. Rustic roof. – PULPIT. Jacobean, with back panel and

---

*The house became a residential school for children with severe mental impairment from 1969 to the 1990s. In the grounds were some interesting timber cabins designed by *MacCormac & Jamieson*, 1976, and, behind, workshops and residences by *Edward Cullinan Architects*, 1983.

sounding-board. The usual short blank arches abound. – COM-
MUNION RAIL. Of *c.* 1700, with slim twisted balusters. – Early
C18 painted CREED and COMMANDMENTS. – STAINED GLASS.
Roundels of C18 Flemish glass (chancel).

WHIPSNADE ZOO. Opened in 1931 by the Zoological Society,
which had acquired 100 acres of farmland with the idea, then
novel in Europe, of establishing a park for animals and a
natural habitat in which they might breed rather than be
merely exhibited, developing ideas pioneered by Carl Hagen-
beck in early C20 Germany. In place of caged enclosures, the
animals were to be restricted by pits, ditches and moats, while
others could roam across the park within the main enclosure.
In 1934–5 *B. Lubetkin* & *Tecton*, following their debut success
at London Zoo, built some animal houses and other buildings
which were among the most uncompromisingly modern ones
then put up in England. Four were commissioned, two survive,
and of these the former ELEPHANT HOUSE has aged fairly
well, though now disused and robbed of the original backdrop
of tall evergreens. Like all of the firm's designs it is not in the
straightforward International Style of the 1930s, but with its
four top-lit circular white pavilions for the elephants uncommonly sculptural, dramatic and classically inspired. In plan a
continuous curve tapering at the ends where the thin concrete
canopy forms shelters on slender pilotis and iron stanchions.
In the centre, a solid grid of horizontal glazing, originally set
back from the canopy edge with retractable windows for spectators. The pavilions penetrate through the roof and on the rear
appear as linked silos. Inside, they are open towards the viewing
window, the animals originally dramatized in their pens by the
top lighting. A pond separated the elephants from spectators.
The former restaurant building (now DISCOVERY CENTRE)
was added to the original brick farmhouse. Horizontal grids
of glazing above a plinth and a thin roof oversailing on tapered
piers. One wall entirely of glass blocks with a thin concrete
arch in the centre developing from the plinth and floating in
front of the glass; an anticipation of the façade of Finsbury
Health Centre, London (1935–8).* The main ENTRANCE and

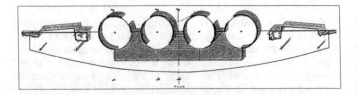

Whipsnade Zoo, Elephant House.
Plan by Berthold Lubetkin, 1935

---

* *Tecton* also designed a Giraffe House and a Shelter with rippling roof. Both have
gone, as have murals by *John Skeaping* in the former restaurant.

OFFICES are of 1963 by *F. A. P. Stengelhofen*, the architect to the Zoological Society. The offices succeeded the original offices/superintendent's houses designed by *Albert Richardson* in 1932, which burnt down.

Of more recent date, the 1970s SEA LION HOUSE (originally Dolphinarium), with swooping, lively roofline and curved brick walls, and on two levels inside to allow underwater viewing.

WHITE LION, below the zoo on the hill. Carved into the chalk in 1933, the design by *R. B. Brooks Greaves*. 483 ft (147 metres) long.

Also in the neighbourhood two excellent BUNGALOWS privately designed by *Lubetkin*, seizing the opportunity for their construction while the builders were still working at the zoo. They face the Ivinghoe Downs and were formerly reached through the zoo. HILLFIELD,* though small, is one of the most important International Modern houses in England. 1933–6, a personal experiment by Lubetkin and his own 'dacha', designed for open-air living. It stands on a platform cut out of the hillside – a horizontal plane on which to set a horizontal composition. It is of *in situ* reinforced concrete, single-storey, and appears to hover over the ground; the long, almost continuously glazed walls (pivot windows within a modular concrete grid) are cantilevered from the foundations. Cruciform plan with a living room to the S, bedrooms etc. to the E (each with a sleeping porch) and a kitchen in the shorter N wing. Between kitchen and living room, the dining area and entrance hall are separated by a curved screen wall which supports a lower ceiling over the hall and is echoed by a similar screen on the flat roof; the rooftop functioned as an outdoor room accessed by a ladder. The loggia wraps right round the N end and is enclosed by a windshield which curves round a pool and circular flowerbed by the entrance; on the W side, an open loggia behind a screen of thin beams and an outdoor fireplace. The curves and the subtle splay of the wings are typical of Lubetkin: the cantilevered 'flashgap' plinth and framed elevations prefigure important themes in his postwar architecture. The original strong colours (not white – a widespread misconception about 1930s Modernism) also became popular post-1950. Parchment walls with white reveals, cobalt blue inside and on the loggia ceiling, Pompeian red for the loggia floor and planting boxes.

HOLLY FRINDLE, uphill to the E, was built for Ida Mann. It   60
is about a third smaller but with the same basic plan and elevations as Hillfield, though the areas for open-air living are reduced, e.g. there is no loggia on the main front. Here the curved screen between the dining area and entrance hall actually penetrates through the roof. Holly Frindle was fully

---

*Hillfield is, strictly speaking, in Dagnall parish, Bucks. The description here is reprinted, with minor revisions, from the *Buildings of England: Buckinghamshire* (1994, revised by Elizabeth Williamson).

restored in 1999–2000 by the *Richard Rogers Partnership* and once more looks pristine.

At the beginning of STUDHAM LANE, S of the green, COTTAGES for Zoo staff. 1930 by *E. Guy Dawber*.

TREE CATHEDRAL, *c.* 150 yds NW of the Green. A plantation of 20 acres with hedges, shrubs and trees of twenty-five different species. It was begun in 1932 by Edmund Kell Blyth as a memorial. Part is laid out as a cathedral, and services are held in it, but the outer walks are in plan closer to a fortification, with bastions at the corners.

0050

WILDEN

ST NICHOLAS. Tall Perp W tower with angle buttresses. In one spandrel of the doorway an owl. Three-light Perp nave windows, but on the S side also one small Dec window. Nave of brown cobbles. Lower Perp chancel. – FONT. Octagonal. Perp, with a flower, a quatrefoil, alternating with shields, on six faces only. – SOUTH DOOR. With charming C15 ironwork, especially a circle handle treated like a rose window. – STAINED GLASS. In the E window two C15 figurines and many fragments of canopy-work and heraldry. – In the upper lights of the E window, more reassembled medieval fragments, the principal lights of the Resurrection by *A. L. Moore*, 1911. – MONUMENT. Large alabaster tablet to Jasper Fisher, rector, †1643. Rinceau frieze and scroll pediment with a cartouche. Attributed to *Thomas Stanton* (GF).

OLD VICARAGE, E. The Tudorish front is of 1836 by *William Railton*.

LION FIELD, Barford Road, East End, ½ m. E. Good C16 house, two storeys with the timber-framing of the first floor exposed.

1040

WILLINGTON

ST LAWRENCE. A historically important church, as it is all Late Perp and on a big scale, probably rebuilt by Sir John Gostwick, Master of the Horse to Cardinal Wolsey and later Treasurer of the Court of First Fruits and Tenths under Henry VIII. He was born at Willington, bought the manor in 1529 and died in 1545. The E end is especially impressive, with the flat expanse of N chapel and chancel wall with their two large windows and their battlements. No roof visible here. It is built of buff stone. W tower; high S side with the porch set symmetrically between two large transomed four-light windows. The lights are cusped below the transom but uncusped above. N aisle windows uncusped. The porch entrance has a basket arch with a lozenge frieze looking Early Gothic Revival rather than Latest Perp. Inside, its roof has spandrels carved with foliage (cf. Dean). Chancel with three-light s windows, the n chapel windows high, of three lights under four-centred arches. The tower was restored and its parapet rebuilt in 1876–7 by *Clutton* for the Duke of Bedford. Inside, the chancel e window (five lights with a castellated transom) has to l. and r. shafts that stand on a head and on two quadrupeds with one head. They must have been intended for a stone vault. The arcades inside deserve attention too. The aisle arcade is high and has the standard moulded type of piers with two-centred arches but capitals of a more refined style, with shields n and s and rosettes on the responds. The chancel arcade has the same type of piers but four-centred arches and no shields. The roofs have elaborately figured corbels of twining branches and figures under canopies. The NE corbel in the chancel is a whole huddle of figures. – BENCHES. 1860s. Some with c16 tracery. – Other FURNISHINGS are by *Clutton*. The impressive scheme of chancel TILES is typical of the moment after the Minton type of the mid c19; they are rather orientally inspired in the Aesthetic style with patterns of circles, squares, triangles, stars and zigzag in strong greens, yellows, reds and blacks. In fact they copy medieval tiles in the n chapel, while others are of similar pattern to c14 tiles uncovered at Warden Abbey (*see* Old Warden). A floret motif compares with some tiles made by *Godwin*'s for Bolton Abbey (West Riding of Yorkshire). – STAINED GLASS. e window by *Heaton, Butler & Bayne*, 1885. – MONUMENTS. First of all Sir John, who died in 1545. A big plain tomb-chest with moulded marble top between chancel and n chapel. The inscription contains the date 1541 and refers to him as having caused 'this work' to be done, meaning probably the chapel, if not the whole church.* – A second completely plain tomb-chest in the NE corner of the chapel with an indent for a brass. – Two HELMETS, one worn by Sir John at the Field of the Cloth of Gold, the other a fighting helmet of a few years later. – Sir William Gostwick †1615. Alabaster tomb-chest and effigy. His head on a half-rolled-up mat. Attributed to *Maximilian Colt* (AW) except for the low wooden tester. – Sir Edward Gostwick †1630 and his wife †1633. Very elaborate alabaster monument with kneeling figures in the usual composition, but note that among the children below the still-born son is also depicted in his shrouded cradle. Two columns, arches with achievements in the tympana, broken pediment over. *Edward Marshall* was paid £58 for it in 1633.

MANOR HOUSE. Of Sir John Gostwick's manor house in which he entertained Henry VIII in 1541 almost nothing survives but the present house (Manor Farm) retains two very large (kitchen?) fireplaces on the ground floor, and barrel ceilings in

---

* On the s side of his tomb-chest a poem, identical to that of the Stanley monument at Tong, Shropshire, traditionally ascribed to Shakespeare. This is noted by Simon Watney in *Church Monuments*, vol. XX (2005).

two chambers one of which has a wooden strip of Renaissance frieze with medallion heads and the initial IG. It was originally carried on to the walls as painted decoration.*

Otherwise two farm buildings of buff stone are all that survives, impressive in their isolation N of the church. One is the magnificent DOVECOTE, its roof timbers tree-ring-dated to 1543–4, an oblong structure with two nesting chambers and stepped gables oddly arranged because of some vertical shuttering halfway up along the roof. That makes the stepped gables start with a coping and above the vertical part continue with a second coping in a rather Netherlandish way. Inside, 1,500 nesting boxes, clunch with brick sills and in one chamber the frame of the potence. The other building, also with stepped gables, was the STABLES, whose roof has been tree-ring-dated to 1539–40. It has always been two-storeyed. It has a large entrance with, l. and r. of it, one five-light window with straight head. Three light windows in the gable ends and on the rear which also has a chimneybreast for the room at the s end of the upper floor (plain chamfered Tudor arch). Fine roof of ten bays with a mixture of open trusses with queenposts, archbraced trusses and a closed truss to the room at the end. A drawing of 1811 shows two other buildings of similar character, dem. c. 1850.

In the village, many mid-C19 yellow brick Bedford ESTATE COTTAGES and SCHOOL HOUSE by *Clutton*, 1868, and many more bungalows and houses since the 1960s.

HILL FARM 1¼ m. SE. One of the curious octagonal (or, as in this case, partly octagonal) farmhouses promoted c. 1800 by the 5th Duke of Bedford and designed by his surveyor, *Robert Salmon*. See also Octagon Farm, Cople, and Tithe Farm, Honeyden, Staploe.

WILSTEAD

A large village, also known as Wilshamstead, owing to much later C20 expansion and sadly the poorer for it.

ALL SAINTS. Ironstone. Early C14 s arcade of four bays. Quatrefoil piers with four thin shafts in the diagonals. Doublechamfered arches. The N arcade uses late C13 piers with abaci chamfered and set diagonally and with double-hollow-chamfered arches. Good nave roof with carved bosses, angels and apostles on the jackposts. Nave and aisles are embattled. The w tower is of 1851 by *Thomas Smith* of Hertford; its Perp predecessor fell in 1742 and was replaced by a simply belfry. The rebuilding of the chancel and porch, the organ chamber and vestry is of 1872–3 by *A. W. Blomfield*. – CURIOSUM. A funeral bier of 1896. – STAINED GLASS. E window, the Ascension, by

---

*I am very grateful to Nicholas Cooper for this information.

Clayton & Bell, given by the Rev. Lord John Thynne of Haynes, who bore much of the cost of rebuilding (there was also a contemporary reredos by *J. Powell & Sons*, now lost). Other early, mid- and late C20 glass in the aisles. – MONUMENTS. Brass to William Carbrok, priest, *c.* 1430, a 14-in. (36 cm) demi-figure. – Alabaster tablet to William Tompson †1596. With a steep pediment and the tiny kneeling figure of the deceased on it. – CHAPTER HOUSE added 1975.

WINGFIELD *see* CHALGRAVE

WOBURN

Woburn is a perfect C18 town, though smaller than many villages in the county, and without peer in Bedfordshire for its unspoiled character.

ST MARY, Park Street. By *Henry Clutton*, 1865–8, for the 8th Duke of Bedford. The typical estate church, even if here conveniently placed in the village and not somewhere in the park. Solidly and expensively built, large and so much all of a piece that atmosphere is hard to come by. The church is in the late C12 style, with some of the details deliberately broad and summary, and others – e.g. the shaft in the middle of the E wall – deliberately wilful. S tower with richly shafted bell-openings. The spire alas proved unsafe in 1890 and was not replaced; instead the parapet and stair-turret were raised by *A. J. Pilkington*. Excellent beasts curling over the parapet. Tall aisle and chancel windows. The interior is amazing. It is not wilful at all, but extremely bold in its handling of French late C12 material. First of all, this is a hall church, and that was unusual in France as well as England. Did Clutton look to Anjou and Poitou? His piers are double columns set in depth, and provided with shaft-rings. The capitals are of the crocket type, and there is throughout solid stone vaulting, with paired wall-shafts. Money was evidently no object. The raised chancel has shafted windows and a flat E wall. Flanking the chancel steps, pretty iron railings, by *Hardman & Co.*, and blind arcading of polished Cornish Serpentine. Below is a large rib-vaulted crypt, intended as the burial place of the Dukes but never used – the Russells are buried at Chenies, Bucks. Its staircase is a mighty spiral under a saucer dome. The vestry is in a two-storey N annex with pyramid roof and sheer battered walls, again strongly French in tone. – FONT. A huge Neo-Norman tub. – REREDOS, STALLS, ORGAN CASE and PULPIT. Very lavish Perp style by *Kempe*, 1902–3, a reminder of his skills as a designer. – COMMUNION RAIL. Of 1868. A robust trellis with a border of carved foliage. – READING DESK (Lady Chapel, N aisle W). Probably that carved by *T. Phyffers*, 1868. – PAINTING

(Lady Chapel). Virgin by *Carlo Maratta*, formerly placed above the early C19 altar of the old church. – STAINED GLASS. One original N aisle window by *Ward & Hughes*. E windows and the rose above, both of 1894 by *Kempe*, complementing his reredos. – S aisle E window, St Francis and the Birds, designed by *A. A. J. Houthuesen*, made by *J. Powell & Sons*, 1938, in memory of the 11th Duchess. Uncomfortably large and rather luridly coloured; the 11th Duke insisted to Albert Richardson 'the window will be so beautiful that nobody will notice any *architecture*!'*

HERITAGE CENTRE. The site of old St Mary,† which was pulled down in 1864 and replaced with a mortuary chapel in a Perp style by *Clutton* in 1865–7. It is surprisingly free of his quirks. Attached to it, the tower of the old church. On it, *Blore* in 1829–30 placed an upper part also of ironstone and then a stone top, a very pretty piece of confectionery, with an open octagonal stage, pinnacles, and a crocketed spirelet. Inside, STAINED GLASS of 1830, of the Evangelists and Bedford arms, reset in Clutton's E window. – MONUMENTS. Sir Francis Staunton and wife †1630, and their family. Two tiers of kneelers, the lower tier without inscription. Alabaster. – Hon. Charlotte Emily Seymour †1824. Signed by *Richard Westmacott*. Matching tablet to her husband †1845. – Robert Salmon †1821, the 6th Duke's agent and surveyor, who designed many buildings for the estate and a series of inventions for improving its agriculture. Fancy honeysuckle cresting.

Woburn is a crossroads and the centre is the MARKET HOUSE, neither perfect nor C18. It is red brick, Gothic, with an oriel, an asymmetrical turret, and narrow dormers. *Blore* is the architect, 1830 the date, but remodelled as the Town Hall by *Clutton* in 1880; see his trademark mullioned windows in the previously open ground floor and extended W with porch in 1912 by *Adams & Holden*. From the Market House northwards runs Market Place and its continuation Bedford Street, with one pleasant brick house after the other, the vast majority with their doorcases intact and the others with good shopfronts. The date for many of these buildings is probably *c.* 1725 after the village had been ravaged by fire.

At the corner of Park Street and continuing along MARKET PLACE, three-storey early C18 fronts, blue brick headers with red dressings and segment-headed windows. Two have aprons, fluted keystones and giant pilasters as well. Between the first and the other two is a late C18 house of four storeys with two shallow canted bay windows that have windows of varied design: arched at the ground floor, Venetian type at first floor and tripartites with chinoiserie centres above that; all the glazing is Gothick. One of the early C18 houses has two charming Late Georgian shopfronts. The first (No. 11) has lunettes

---

* S. Houfe, *Albert Richardson: The Professor* (1980).
† Woburn had only a chapel to a church at Birchmoor until *c.* 1565.

over the top of interlocking circles and Vitruvian frieze, and
also the local motif of pilasters curving forward at the top to
support the hood. Its counterpart also has a lunette but overall
and of solid overlapping discs. Opposite this group is a less
eventful but equally pleasing row, the first house (No. 19) also
with a good double shopfront with diamonds in the upper
lights added *c.* 1820 by *George Maddocks* for a drapers shop.
This row ends in another early C18 front with segmental-
headed windows and a gracious curved end. Set back, now in
BEDFORD STREET, the OLD RECTORY, mid-C18, also brick,
though now whitewashed. It is much statelier than the other
houses, with a centre with pairs of banded columns, and pairs
of columns above. Attic over this centre with pediment. The
side of the house, again with an attic pediment but no columns,
looks over the cemetery. Opposite, next to the chapel (*see*
Heritage Centre above), the SCHOOL, a restoration job really
by *Blore*, *c.* 1830, as the ironstone building is partly original
Elizabethan, with mullioned windows. Two storeys and dormers
and big central chimney on the side. The porch towards the
cemetery is of course by Blore and the small Gothic gabled
building towards the street of the same time. It contained the
village fire engine. Opposite, No. 7 is a bijou front with a
curved balcony on iron posts. No. 12 is a five-bay detached
house with red brick headers, stone quoins and a pedimented
doorway on Doric columns. No. 17, of similar style, has the
doorcase type with curved pilasters. More nice houses follow,
including a pair (Nos. 19–20) with a shared entrance in a
muscular Gibbsian stucco surround with quarter columns and
a segmental pediment. The end along here is of Bedford estate
cottages, indicative of the improving hand of the 7th Duke in
the mid C19, and on the W side two ranges of yellow brick
ALMSHOUSES, dated 1850, with many thin Jacobean stepped
gables, showier than the standard pattern of Bedford estate
building. Both cottage and almshouses have model layouts
with rear ranges containing WCs, sculleries etc. Round the
corner in Crawley Road, the former VICARAGE has the same
essential character.

In the other streets departing from the main crossing less
happens. In GEORGE STREET is the quiet, long white front of
the BEDFORD ARMS HOTEL, repaired by *Holland c.* 1790
(Stroud) and then THE CHESTNUTS, three wide bays with
plenty of Gothick ogee arches, even to Venetian windows, and
a Batty Langleyesque doorcase. Further down, BEDFORD
HOUSE, formerly Crowholt Lodge, extensively remodelled in
stately Neo-Georgian by *Adams & Holden*, 1914, with a covered
way to the street. Two-storey bow on the S front and in the
centre of the garden front a semicircular colonnaded veranda.
The earlier part is incorporated as a wing at right angles.

In LEIGHTON STREET is one good six-bay brick house,
another with a two-bay front and panelled parapet and its
entrance at the side, numerous standard estate cottages from

the 1840s to *c.* 1914. s of here, in BLOOMSBURY CLOSE, on the site of the WORKHOUSE, an especially good Arts and Crafts group by *Charles Holden* (of *H. P. Adams*'s office), 1901–2, with rendered walls and jettied gables. Alone on the village's w edge is MARYLAND, the Cottage Hospital (now apartments) of 1901–3 by the same practice, for the 11th Duchess. Voysey-ish with steep roof, cream roughcast walls, flat chimneys. Three gables in the centre, the middle one half-timbered over the porch. The wings end in bay windows and verandas. In PARK STREET is the church and then LION LODGE at the Park Gate to Woburn Abbey (*see* below).

DRAKELOE LODGE, Crawley Road. Gentle Arts and Crafts-style of 1914, red-tile hanging and brick, by *Adams & Holden*.

BIRCHMOOR FARM, ¾ m. NNW. The C16 H-plan house of the Stauntons, red brick with patterns of vitrified headers. Remodelled by *Henry Holland* for the 5th Duke of Bedford in 1793 and now essentially C19 in appearance. BIRCHMOOR LODGE is by *Charles Holden* of *H. P. Adams*'s office, 1901.

9030

WOBURN ABBEY

37 It is known that houses were open to suitable visitors as early as the C18. Mr Ketton-Cremer long ago drew attention to the case of Holkham Hall in Norfolk, where one party was waiting while another was shown round, and Horace Walpole in 1763 wrote that he had so many visitors at Strawberry Hill that he ought to put up a sign The Gothic Castle. He gave out tickets and hid himself from the sightseers. In cases like Holkham and Strawberry Hill a high tip went to the butler or another servant. A recognition of the fact that visitors can be made a source of substantial income for the maintenance of the house came first at Warwick Castle in the late C19 but otherwise became widespread only after the Second World War. The Marquess of Bath at Longleat was the pioneer of that period. He opened his home in 1949, but when the 13th Duke of Bedford opened* Woburn Abbey fully to the public in 1955, Woburn soon became the case par excellence of mass attraction. It should be said that the duke had been faced with death duties of £4.5 million in 1953, so there was motivation for his entrepreneurial zeal to keep the house rather than see its sale or demolition. In 1965 *c.* 475,000 visitors were counted, and the side-shows included a zoo with e.g. bison and many species of deer, a pets' corner, model soldiers, and sailing. Since 1970 there has been added the Safari Park, and the grounds are home to myriad festivals, concerts, weddings, sales fairs etc. In fact, this manner of attracting the public is now so firmly accepted among the great houses that had Woburn not been there first it would not be worth remarking on. It goes

---

* Or, rather, re-opened, for Woburn, after having been regularly open in the C19, closed its doors to visitors only in 1914.

without saying that the majority of the visitors cared more, then and, probably, now, for the entertainments (including a glimpse of the duke) than for the house, yet Woburn Abbey is among the stately homes of England one of the stateliest. It stands in vast grounds (3,000 acres), it has lakes, woods and plenty of park furnishings, and the house itself is vast, was vaster still till 1950, and has vast adjoining outbuildings.

Woburn was a Cistercian abbey founded in 1145 by Hugh de Bolebec, with monks from Fountains. The cloister was where the courtyard between the three wings now is, with the church to its N, on the line of the N wing, the lay brothers' range to the W, the dorter in the E range and refectory to the S. In 1547 the priory buildings were granted to John Lord Russell of Chenies, an executor of Henry VIII and from 1550 1st Earl of Bedford. However, nothing of the house is older than the time of Francis Russell, the 4th Earl, i.e. c. 1630, and few features are as old as that. Much evidently survived in adapted form when plans were made of the house in 1733 but what we now see is mostly of the C18, principally by *Flitcroft* for the 4th Duke 1747–61,* and *Henry Holland*, one of the most sensitive and discriminating English architects of the late C18, in 1787–90. The 5th Duke was twenty-one when he called in Holland. The stones used at Woburn Abbey are Ketton oolite and Totternhoe clunch; the mason for the late C18 work was *John Wing*, who controlled the Totternhoe quarries and worked in tandem with Holland in Bedford and also at Southill. So Woburn Abbey is not a house of all periods like Drayton or Boughton. But it is not as unified as Houghton or Holkham either.

EXTERIOR. The house is – or was, before the E range was pulled down – oblong, a quadrangle 148 ft by 138 ft (45 metres by 42 metres), with, E of it and uphill, two large square office and stable quadrangles. The visitor can view the whole of the house around the E court from the vantagepoint of the area between these quadrangles where still stands a glorious cedar tree, but which until 1950 were visually linked by a palatial Riding School and Tennis Court range by *Holland*. The demolitions were undertaken by the 12th Duke in 1950, and are very unfortunate. The E range of the house came down together with about a third of the N and S ranges. All this is regrettable, but what remains is enjoyable and admirable enough.

To the court essentially everything one sees is by *Flitcroft*. The W range is the principal range. It cost c. £85,000 to build, but was constrained in its ambition by the Duke's determination to retain much of the plan and footprint of the existing range. To the courtyard it is of eleven bays and two storeys, with a three-bay centre where giant Ionic pilasters carry a pediment

---

* Miss Gladys Scott Thomson, the historian of the house, has recorded that in 1748 a water closet was put up for His Grace in the N garden, that in 1760 there were three more, one of them in the house, that there were then also baths with piped water supply, and that in 1753 and 1756 pottery stoves were imported from France.

with achievement, carved by *James Whittle*, 1754. To the park
the front of this range is the most monumental of the house.
The centre here is raised by a half-storey, and has attached
giant Ionic columns carrying the pediment, with ducal coronet
again by Whittle. The angle pavilions are of two and a half
storeys as well. They have a Venetian window each with a tripartite lunette window over. The lower parts of the front are
balustraded, and the whole ground floor has smooth rustication. It is a dignified façade, faultless, but not moving. The N
range is two-storeyed, with a three-bay pediment, which was
in the centre until the demolitions. The S range towards the
courtyard is three storeys and quite simple, of five bays plus
three in the E angle pavilion. The third storey is a late C18
addition and there must surely have been a pediment like that
of the N range originally. But towards the S this range has a
character quite different from Flitcroft's. Indeed Flitcroft
seems to have left this front in its early C17 appearance. *Holland*
built up the ground in front so it shows just two storeys and
is of thirteen bays divided into 2–9–2, without any emphasis
on the centre. The whole is terminated by a long balustrade,
and the angle pavilions are singled out only by slight projection. The ground-floor windows are all pedimented, and in the
angle pavilions they are set in blank arches. That is all. John
Harris attributes this front to *Sir William Chambers*, who was
called in in 1767 for 'Rebuilding one of the Wings', a commission initially given by the 4th Duke to Stiff Leadbetter, who
died before anything could be done. Chambers claimed that
he built 'a front and parade rooms' to this range. Holland for
his part billed only modestly for 'Alterations of South Front',
so apart from raising the ground level he may only have
inserted the end windows on the projections. The mutilation
of 1950 removed a lower E continuation, which was probably
by Flitcroft but remodelled by Holland contemporary with his
work on the E range. This was built into the rising ground so
that it presented an E face of a single storey but two to the
court. Visitors made their entrance through a grand porte
cochère and passed down steps into the main courtyard. Its
destruction (which incidentally probably removed the last vestiges of fabric of the abbey buildings) was deplored by *Albert
Richardson* and to ameliorate the abrupt curtailment of the N
and S wings he designed new ends as a display of his brand of
C20 classicism, blank ashlar walls of limestone framing giant
Portland stone arches containing Ionic columns *in antis* and
aedicules for statues. This appears rather piled on to the N
range but more comfortably proportioned on the taller S range.
Where the E range stood Richardson introduced the series of
steps from the courtyard to link the C18 curved screen walls
which run out to meet the stables and offices (for which *see*
below). In the courtyard are four STATUES by *J. V. Legterin*, of
c. 1700.

The N front of the N range, where visitors enter the house,
has an odd rhythm, owing to the fact that much of the masonry

of *c.* 1630 is preserved and one can readily see how it formed originally a balanced composition of 3+3+3 bays with a rusticated open loggia at its centre, and in the outer bays windows flanking round-headed niches. The third, fifth and seventh windows on the first floor are also round-arched and have aprons of balusters. They were probably open originally to a gallery, known as the 'Stone Gallery'. This work is now attributed to *Nicholas Stone*, the King's master mason, on the evidence of motifs recorded on the W range (now lost) and their resemblance to Stone's work at Kirby Hall, Northants, 1638–40. In the C17 the attic had three gables but now it has a straight parapet. Its W corner belongs to Flitcroft's angle pavilion, its E bays and corner to Flitcroft and *Richardson*. Sanderson in the 1740s recorded the front of the S range with an arcaded loggia along the whole of the ground floor, shown on a survey of 1661 opening to a garden. Flitcroft certainly retained this and if Chambers did indeed alter the S range then he too accepted these features for they were only obscured by Holland's building up of the ground in front.

INTERIOR. In the 1630s part of the N range on the ground floor are two rooms, W of the visitor entrance, which should be described first although they are now seen last. First, inside the loggia itself, is the GROTTO, the one surviving room of *c.* 1630, beautifully restored. The decoration with bands of shells and of rocky stalactite stuff, a big niche over a central basin and small niches in the other walls, is highly typical of the date and, as Dianne Duggan has shown, may have been devised by *Isaac de Caus*, who was in the Earl's employ in London in the 1630s and almost certainly designed the grotto at the Banqueting House in 1623 in association with Nicholas

Woburn Abbey, north elevation.
Drawing by J. Sanderson, 1733

Stone. It includes masks and garlands and nymphs in rocky mosaic. On the two doorways lie flat-faced putti. The grotto is followed by a room (also known as the Green Parlour) of which the chimneypiece also looks earlier C17, with elaborate scrolled jambs with acanthus decoration, derived from Serlio. This too may be by Stone (cf. a fireplace at Cornbury Park, Oxon), and the Jacobean overmantel with columns carrying projecting pieces of entablature must also be *c.* 1630. But the ceiling is late C17.

Hereafter the rooms will be described as they are seen by visitors, but rooms are included which are not shown. First, the visitor entrance hall itself which also has a good late C17 ceiling with garland decoration. This was known as the 'Grotto Chamber' before 1700 and was hung with Mortlake tapestries of 1661–4. Then the BOOK ROOM in the first bay added by Flitcroft to the 1630s wing. This begins a series of mid-C18 rooms on the two floors of the N range, designed for the family's use away from the state rooms in the W wing. They have Rococo ceilings and in the 4th DUKE'S BEDROOM have been discovered fragments of Chinese wallpaper dated to *c.* 1740. Attributed to Flitcroft is the S corridor, overlooking the court and known as PATERNOSTER ROW, with classical arches at each end.

Up the STAIRCASE, cantilevered with a simple iron railing of curls, to the first floor, and to the attic. *William Yates* was paid for the ironwork in 1759. The position of this stair is interesting: one expects Flitcroft to have created a grand ascent from the entrance hall in his W range but he was constrained by the footprint of the house and so placed his staircases, of rather subdued character, in the angles with the wings. The corridor (Duke's Corridor) is repeated on the first floor too in the N range, and the E room, the CHINESE ROOM, has a wallpaper bought from China in 1753 and another Rococo ceiling but also a Venetian window with fluted Ionic pilasters. Fine marble chimneypiece with rams' heads, and overmantel with broken pediment almost certainly by *Linnell*, who was employed as carver until 1752. The ROOM OF THE FLYING DUCHESS* has a chimneypiece by *John Deval* with young frontal caryatids of Faustina, a plaque by *Rysbrack*, and again a fine overmantel, probably that bought in 1760. The Rococo ceiling of the YELLOW DRAWING ROOM is one of the most gorgeous in the house and in an avowedly French taste, evidently introduced in the late 1760s by the 4th Duke at the end of his term as Ambassador in Paris. The centre has a big face in sun rays and the decoration plays all over the frieze too. The chimneypiece is also different from the preceding rooms and has tapered jambs, yellow marble inserts a concave frieze with acanthus and no overmantel; it is very similar to that in the

---

* In tribute to the daring 11th Duchess, an early female aviator, who set up the cottage hospital at Woburn and the war hospital in the old riding house. She died in a flying accident in 1937.

Chinese Bedroom at Milton, Peterborough (p. 566), where Flitcroft was working in the 1750s. Similar but smaller in its form is the ceiling of the adjoining dressing room (the RACING ROOM), which also has a French late C18 fireplace.

Now we enter Flitcroft's W range and the procession of state apartments. This is a somewhat old-fashioned concept for the mid-C18, but Flitcroft was working for a client keen to maintain the tradition of room arrangements from the earlier house. Nevertheless there is an abrupt change in mood from the Rococo of the family rooms to Palladian of the Kent tradition. So the sequence begins with the STATE BEDROOM (a.k.a. Queen Victoria's Bedroom) in the NW corner, which is known to have occupied this position in the previous house. Stylistically, however, it is right up to date and here the ceiling has a big bold circular centre of Greek key and, surrounding it, heavy octagonal coffering (derived from Wood's *Palmyra*, published in 1753). Overmantel with Apollo's head and eagle, good white chimneypiece by Deval. The QUEEN'S DRESSING ROOM is in the same style, with classical Greek-key bands to ceiling and chimneypiece. The BLUE DRAWING ROOM is also datable to 1756. The fireplace by Deval has yellow marble Ionic columns and a plaque by *Rysbrack*. The overmantel is enriched by an eagle between the scrolly shanks of a pediment. The STATE SALOON in the centre of the range has a broadly coved ceiling with coffering, a frieze of rinceau and ducal lions. The inspiration seems to be Holkham, which the duke visited in 1753, but the proportions of the room are a little too restricted to produce the regal effect enjoyed there. The fashion for such rooms was in any case coming to an end in country houses; Woburn is one of the last. The central doorcase with Corinthian columns is another strongly Kentian motif (cf. the Stone Hall at Houghton, Norfolk). It was supplied along with most of the woodwork in these rooms by *Whittle & Norman* in 1755–6. Two white chimneypieces by *Rysbrack* with frontal and sideways caryatids and a ram's head between cornucopiae. Splendid chandelier of eighteen branches unfurling from an open sphere, by *William Hollinsworth*, 1758. The total cost of the decoration of this room was £1213 18s. The walls were hung with silk but now are painted all over with trompe l'œil capriccio in architectural frames of Rococo inspiration, showing the ducal estates, events from the family's history and even the menagerie of animals in the park. They are by *Roland Pym*, 1971–5, and in the lighthearted theatrical tradition of Rex Whistler. After this, the STATE DINING ROOM has guilloche bands and the caryatids with Diana's head of the chimneypiece (again by Deval) are in profile, the overmantel with Apollo mask again carved by *Whittle & Norman*. Parallel to the E with the state rooms in the W range runs the LONG GALLERY.* It dates from 1754–6, but as elsewhere Flitcroft was working with an existing

38

---

*The visitor route is a reversal of the proper procession from staircase to Long Gallery to Saloon and then to the state apartments.

arrangement, dividing the previous gallery into three parts by pairs of Corinthian columns and with pediments to doorway (to the Saloon) and overmantels. The fireplaces are again by Deval. They cost £120 each. The painted coats of arms in the overmantels were intended to be seen as part of the narrative of C16–C17 family portraits hung here. Below this, and not seen by the visitor, the ENTRANCE HALL in the W range, divided into three by unfluted Ionic columns in pairs, repeated by pilasters on the wall, all of grey Totternhoe stone. Of the same stone the pedimented overdoors and two splendid chimney-pieces beautifully carved in 1755 by *Deval* with flower friezes and acanthus leaves on the jambs. The overmantel reliefs, of sacrifices to Apollo and Diana, are by *Rysbrack*.

The BREAKFAST ROOM adjoining the State Dining Room is a transition between Flitcroft's Palladian decoration and the Neoclassical style of *Henry Holland*, who furnished it with its bookcases. It heralds the suite of his rooms in the S range designed for the family, to succeed the gloomy chambers in the N range. They begin in the SW corner with the celebrated DINING ROOM,* remodelled by *Holland* to contain twenty-two Venetian views by Canaletto – previously at Bedford House in London, which was demolished in 1801. Bronzed overdoors by *George Garrard* (cf. Southill). Holland's hand is clear in the minutely detailed classical motifs of the borders to the panels around the paintings, the tiny frieze of acanthus leaves, the subdued refinement of the whole. Fireplace by *Richard Hayward*, probably from a design by Chambers, 1771. The same exquisite small-scale decoration is yet more evident in the ANTE-LIBRARY in the carving of the pilasters to the book-cases. Over the doors, grisaille paintings by *Biagio Rebecca*. Beyond, at the centre of the S range's S side, the long tripartite LIBRARY, divided by screens of Corinthian columns. The stucco ceiling is ornate, and very different in style from both the earlier Flitcroft and the contemporary Adam, with a central circle of round coffers diminishing towards its centre. The fireplace here has jambs with Egyptian termes (cf. the Drawing Room, Southill), the bookcases with tapered supports. Beyond is the WOOD LIBRARY, with a fireplace of 1818 by *Sir Richard Westmacott*, with a frieze of 'The Progress of Navigation'. The S range contains a corridor all along its N side (early C19 glass). The OFFICES and STABLES are by *Flitcroft*. The centre of the fronts towards the house of both quadrangles has an octagonal dome. The entrances have attached coupled columns or pilas-ters and at the angles is the motif of the tripartite lunette above the Venetian window as we have found it in the W range. The interiors, remodelled in 1903, have been lost. Against the S range of the S courtyard *Holland* created his Orangery in 1790,

---

*This was formerly the Library, part of Chambers' remodelling in 1771; the ceiling was painted by *Cipriani* and *Biagio Rebecca*. The drawing is in the Victoria and Albert Museum. Chambers also created a new dining room, presumably where the present library is.

converted into the SCULPTURE GALLERY in 1816 by *Jeffry Wyatville*. It has arched French windows and in the middle a Venetian French window. Above this a pediment, the tympanum carving by *Garrard*, set against an attic block raised above the rest of the building. Inside, Holland in 1801–3 added at the E end a tetrastyle Ionic temple front, copied from Illisus, with a square top-lit room inside. This was the famous TEMPLE OF LIBERTY, the 5th Duke's shrine to Charles James Fox, whose bust by *Nollekens*, and others of his Whig allies, were showcased within. The mason was *John Wing*. In the frieze a Latin inscription and in the tympanum, Liberty, Peace, Agriculture and Commerce by *Sir Richard Westmacott*, 1818, after the plaster originals by *John Flaxman Jun*. Yellow marble walls inside, and a coffered ceiling. At the other end of the gallery, a screen of Ionic columns under a blind arch containing a massive eagle carrying thunderbolts, by *George Garrard*, 1811. The centre was emphasized by Wyatville to make use of eight antique columns, to which he gave Corinthian capitals. It was also given a shallow dome and a coffered apse in the N wall. As a mirror to the Temple of Liberty, Wyatville added behind the W end the coffered rotunda with a glazed centre to the ceiling and coloured marble floor by *Edward Shepherd* of Plymouth. This was for Canova's Three Graces, installed in 1819 on a rotating plinth, but now contains a copy of the Apollo Belvedere (the gallery is now devoted to weddings).* Good, blocky exterior. Most of the free-standing sculpture had to be removed before the mid 1960s. There were too many hooligans among 475,000 visitors. Apart from Roman statuary there were works by Thorwaldsen, Westmacott, Chantrey and others, of which a few impressive tablets remain *in situ*. Also the massive and famous Lanti Vase, purchased in 1800 and placed here from that time. The CAMELIA HOUSE with its large windows forms a quadrant E of the Sculpture Gallery. It too is by *Wyatville*, 1822. He later built a substantial Botanical House in the area E of the stables court (dem.).

N of the office court, the CHINESE DAIRY, again by *Holland*. Cruciform, with a pagoda roof culminating in an octagonal lantern, a gallery in front; all of wood. Pretty ceiling inside with Chippendale-Chinese trellis motifs, the decoration and furniture similar to the mock-Chinese furniture in the Brighton Pavilion. Painting almost certainly by *John Crace*. A covered way runs around one side of the pond and formerly continued as a link to the riding school and the orangery. In front of the S range a formal GARDEN, *c*. 1840.

In the wider grounds the following items deserve notice, and can be taken in chronological order.

– ICE HOUSE, 500 yds S. Circular and embattled, with a brick dome. – CHINESE TEMPLE, Drakeloe Pond, 1 m. NW. Tent roof and Gothick details. C18, shown on a map of 1738 but now probably as remade by *William Linnell* in 1749. – BASIN BRIDGE, SW of the house across the neck of Basin Pond. By *Chambers*, 1770–2. Of three arches, with rusticated voussoirs, but rebuilt by *Repton*, who removed obelisk pinnacles during his relandscaping of the park and pleasure grounds; he reformed the lake into its present form. Woburn belongs to the climactic years of Repton's career, and in the 6th Duke he found his greatest patron. He was at Woburn first in 1804; the Red Book dates from the following year. Part of his concern was to reverse changes made by Holland, not least by building up the ground in front of his S wing, and by enrichment of the pleasure gardens begun by him. The DORIC TEMPLE, 350 yds E of the house, is shown in Repton's Red Book view of the Chinese Dairy and was built 1804, possibly as a memorial to the 5th Duke. Not all of Repton's plans were carried out but the THORNERY, 1¼ m. NNE on the edge of the park, is to his design, 1808. Square, with four gables. Of stone, with a thatched roof and tree-trunk veranda. (Umbrella ceiling, painted originally by *A. Aglio* but repainted *c.* 1900 and restored *c.* 1980. In the basement a tunnel-vaulted room, tiled white. Probably for preparing food to be consumed inside or outside the upper room.) – In the pinetum, 200 yds E of the Chinese Dairy, a GOTHIC SEAT by *Wyatville*, 1811. Like an open-fronted tent, five-sided, with paper-thin ribs and tracery over the roof. Cusped arch. The 6th Duke made further enhancements in the 1830s, e.g. the CHINESE TEMPLE in the maze, 300 yds SE of the Sculpture Gallery. Octagonal, with a pagoda roof and ogee arches. After a design by *Chambers*, 1757, built 1833. – ROCKERY, 275 yds E of the Chinese Dairy. Proposed by *Repton* but implemented 1838. The Chinese temple is a restoration of 2012. 70 yds NE of the Chinese Dairy is the FOLLY of 1839. Like an igloo. Walls decorated with shells, quartz, geological specimens from Devon and Cornwall. Arched doors, pointed crenellations along the top.

LODGES: LONDON LODGE, 1 m. S. This is the main approach to the house. It is placed in the centre of a sweeping semicircle of walls. *Holland* was the designer; 1804–9 is the date; *John Wing* was the mason, *George Garrard* designed the coat of arms. Triumphal arch with three arches through. Unfluted Ionic columns carrying projecting pieces of entablature. Raised attic over the centre with short pilasters and volutes – all oddly unclassical and more demonstrative than one would expect Holland to be. – PARK STREET GATE, towards Woburn village. Just piers with rocky rustication and *Coade* lions on top. GATES from this road towards the house, with a polygonal middle lodge of *c.* 1810. – IVY LODGE, on London Road, S of the village. Tudor Gothic, perhaps by *Repton*. The PARK WALLS are impressive in themselves. Along the N boundary towards Husborne Crawley, one section has cast-iron buttresses, providing expansion joints, made to look like brickwork.

PARIS HOUSE, ¾ m. S of the house, reached via London Lodge. Designed by *Gilbert Redgrave*, and built by *William Cubitt &*

Co. originally for the Paris Exhibition of 1878 as part of a showcase of international styles of architecture. Large, half-timbered in the Cheshire black-and-white style, with a large gable to the centre carried forward over porch. Acquired by the 9th Duke for use as staff accommodation. A restaurant since *c.* 1980.

PARK FARM, NW of the house. Model farm designed by *Robert Salmon* in 1795–8 for the 5th Duke's agricultural experiments and scene of his annual fair. Salmon began as an assistant to Holland in the design of Carlton House and came with him to Woburn before permanent employment as steward and surveyor. Ironstone, in three ranges. Two-storey centre to the S range with bell-turret. Single-storey sheephouse to E, built for shearing demonstrations in 1801. Its brick front and pedimented portico of correct Tuscan order columns added after Garrard's depiction of 1811. – N of the farm, the DAIRY of 1898 by *A J. Pilkington*, the 11th Duke's architect, with half-timbering and a gable over a veranda. Set in an octagonal enclosure.

WOBURN SANDS*

9030

Development began after the Bedford–Bletchley railway came in 1846 and was given further impetus by the promotion of the elevated neighbourhood as a healthy place of residence and recuperation.

ST MICHAEL, at Aspley Heath, ¼ m. SW. A mission from Aspley Guise, with money for the new building from its late rector, John Vaux Moore. Built 1867–8 by *Clutton* (cf. Woburn), but the chancel was extended and N transept added by *A. W. Blomfield*, 1889. Clutton's work is amazing, the strange and bold single columns to separate nave from aisles, even more the four-light, straight-headed windows with their odd, exclusively German, 'stump' tracery, and yet more the completely free N transept rose window with a cross of two mullions and two transoms; its design derived from the mid-C15 W window of St Lorenz, Nuremberg (Penelope Hunting). The bell-turret with its conical roof is carried up on a central buttress and the waterspouts are dramatically elongated beasts. These things are obviously not Blomfield's; in fact the rose window was Clutton's chancel E window. The N chapel is largely Clutton's but remodelled by Blomfield and with a SCREEN of 1920 for the war memorial chapel. Blomfield's transept is now divided into two storeys. – REREDOS. Reset in the chapel, 1896 by *Blomfield*,

---

*Woburn Sands is really in Buckinghamshire. Historically it has nothing to do with it.

with *C. E. Buckeridge*. – STAINED GLASS. E window and N chapel, both of 1890 by *Burlison & Grylls*.

ST MARY (R.C.), Aspley Hill. 1956 by *J. S. Comper*. Brick with an apse. Lancets with Y-tracery. Brick arches across the nave. Spare fittings. – STAINED GLASS. One (Lady Chapel) of 1956 with *Comper*'s monogram. – Large W window by *Joseph Nuttgens*, 1992.

METHODIST CHURCH, Station Road. 1879. Lancets with plate tracery.

Former FRIENDS' MEETING HOUSE, Hardwick Road. 1901 by *Usher & Anthony*. Domestic Arts and Crafts-style, T-plan, the roof tiles of the wing carried down over a corner porch.

LIBRARY, High Street. Literary and Scientific Institute of 1874, designed by *Thomas Roberts*, the architect/surveyor at Trentham Hall, Staffs. Quatrefoil-patterned half-timbering in the gable.

STATION, on the Bedford–Bletchley line, 1846. Ornate, with bargeboarded gables and cross-bracing (cf. Millbrook and Ridgmont).

Woburn Sands, Aspley Heath, Silverbirches.
1898 by Brewill & Baily

Between the station and the centre, Victorian houses and terraces in a variety of moods. On Aspley Hill, E of Station Road, THE DENE, a big house of *c.* 1890 altered by *G. P. Allen* of Bedford. Half-timbered gables, tiled roofs, a corner spire. The absurdly overscaled porte cochère is a recent addition.

On ASPLEY HEATH, several larger Victorian and Edwardian houses hidden among the pine and oak woods SW of Church Road, though their isolation has been destroyed by intensive late C20 infilling. SILVERBIRCHES, at the end of Silverbirches Lane on the edge of a deep ravine. By *Brewill & Baily* of Nottingham, 1898. Typical of its date. Brick and roughcast, gabled, with mullioned windows and, to the wing, a pretty square tower with a clerestory and finialled dome. The tiled roof descends around this in a catslide. Original fittings. At the far end of Heath Lane, DANESWOOD, founded in 1903 as a Jewish Sanatorium for Consumptives (now flats) by J. L. Bischoffsheim, the financier and art collector; in a revived Georgian style. There were other health institutions planted in this area for the same reasons. Where Church Road disappears into the woods, ASPLEY HEATH LODGE for the Bedford estate by *Charles Holden*, 1907, then of *Percy Adams*'s practice. A perfect square, with a soaring central chimney, the pyramidal roof descending to low windows at the corners and embracing attic windows under their own little roofs. The inspiration is Nesfield's Lodge at Kew (1867).

HENRY VII LODGE, ⅛ m. E of the church, on the Woburn Road (A50). By *Humphry & J. Adey Repton*, 1810–11, for the 6th Duke of Bedford, in an attempt to create the perfect late C15 house. Ironstone and timber. The motifs were taken from 'some curious specimens of Timber houses [communicated] to the Society of Antiquaries in 1810'. 'The hint of the lower storey' was taken from Eltham Palace, the hints for the bricknogging from a house at King's Lynn, for the arches at the top of the narrow panels from a house near Kelvedon, for the bargeboarding from a house at Bury St Edmunds, for the pinnacles from a house at Shrewsbury, for the oriel from Norwich, and for the chimneys from Wolterton Manor House, Barsham, Norfolk (Repton's *Fragments* 1816).

Nearby, FIR TREE COTTAGE (No. 4 Woburn Road), by *Blore*, *c.* 1830, for the Bedford estate. Far more of the same is to be found in Woburn itself (q.v.).

WOODBURY HALL *see* EVERTON

WOODSIDE
Caddington

0010

ST ANDREW. 1888–9 by *J. R. Brown & Son* of Luton. Plum brick, aisleless, with transepts, a bell-turret, and plate tracery.

(Dressed brick interior: cf. St Matthew, Luton. Stone and marble REREDOS. – STAINED GLASS. All to the donors, the Crawleys of Stockwood. E window (1896) and two in the nave (1914, 1925) by *Lavers & Westlake*. One other by *H. Warren Wilson*, 1949.) – Former VICARAGE, immediately w. By *J. R. Brown & Son*, 1905.

At SLIP END, the VILLAGE HALL is by *P. Morley Horder*, 1909.

WOOTTON

ST MARY. Chiefly a Dec church. This is patent first of all in the arcades with quatrefoil piers and double-chamfered arches. The arcades are of a height exceptional for a parish church. The chancel arch with nailhead goes with them. So that will be *c.* 1300. The tower arch is only a little later. The tower w window has cusped intersecting tracery. The N door has keeled shafts, the s door fillets. One door originally had early C14 strapwork hinges (Brandon). Large three- and four-light Perp aisle windows. The w bays of the aisles, embracing the tower, are an addition done in 1857–60 at the behest of, and perhaps designed by, the Rev. Frederick Neale. One might easily think them early C19 when one sees the retardataire plaster rib-vaults and that in the tower, but the heavy mincer-plate tracery of the w windows clearly belongs to the mid C19. The tower has a recessed lead spire. The chancel is Dec too (see the PISCINA inside) but it too was attended to in the 1860s. N vestry also 1860s; extended 1975. – FONT. Perp, octagonal, with panelled stem and traceried bowl. – SCREEN. Perp, but nearly all 1894–6, when the canopy was added. Otherwise furnishings mostly of the 1860s, and more attractive than that might imply. – STAINED GLASS. W (tower) window (1858) and E window (1890), both by *J. Powell & Sons*. – Chancel N window signed by *Lavers & Westlake*, 1905. – MONUMENTS. The chancel is in effect the Monoux burial chapel, with numerous ledger slabs, hatchments and large tablets to Sir Humphrey Monoux, 2nd baronet, †1685, attributed to *William Stanton* (GF), and Philip Monoux †1707, by *Edward Stanton*. They are very similar and both excellent. The tops are open scrolly pediments with an urn set in.

WOOTTON HOUSE, W of the church. Built by Humphrey Monoux, created a baronet in 1660. Late C17, of eight bays by five with a hipped roof. Red brick, now rendered, quite plain. It is quite regular but has a short wing set back on the r. The porch of course is a late addition.

WREST PARK

The manor of Wrest was held by John Grey as early as the C13 and was the family's seat from the C14. At the time of Edward

IV the de Greys were made Earls of Kent, but the 3rd Earl was profligate and sold away much of the estate before his death in the early C16. It was substantially recovered in the mid to late C17 by Amabella, widow of the 10th Earl, whose monument at Flitton (q.v.) records her achievement in restoring the family's fortune. The house preceding the one now standing lay a little to the S and was extensively remodelled by the 11th Earl in 1672, bringing order to a building that was much older. *Leoni* was asked to remodel it for the 12th Earl, who became Duke of Kent in 1710, but nothing was done following in quick succession the death of his heirs, financial losses in the South Sea Bubble and a fire at his London house.* The 12th Earl was also Lord Lucas, a title inherited from his mother. He died in 1740 (cf. Flitton). The estate then went to his grand-daughter, Jemima, Marchioness de Grey and Baroness Lucas in her own right, who married Philip Yorke, the 2nd Earl of Hardwicke. In 1833 her grandson Thomas Philip, 3rd Lord Grantham, succeeded to the title. He became the 2nd *Earl de Grey*, was an amateur architect of some distinction and incidentally first president of the (Royal) Institute of British Architects. He designed every aspect of the house as it now stands, the details of which are set down in a remarkable forty-five-page letter written in the 1840s. To superintend the execution in 1834–9 he engaged the little-known architect *James Clephan* (cf. The Cedars, Ampthill)† on the advice of Lord Barrington for whom Clephan worked at Beckett Park, Berks. Little change occurred after the earl's death in 1859 and up to the death of his grandson, the 7th Earl Cowper, in 1905. Thereafter the house was let to the United States ambassador, then used as military hospital and finally sold, after damage by a fire, in 1917 to Mr Murray, a brewer from Tyneside. He seems to have disposed of some of the fittings and then lost interest in the house. From 1939 it was in institutional use, and after 1948, by then acquired by the Ministry of Works, it was the Institute of Agricultural Engineering (later Silsoe Institute), whose departure in 2006 has finally allowed the house and garden to be restored by English Heritage to their pre-C20 condition.

The HOUSE is absolutely French in style – something unique in   48
England in the 1830s and the product of *de Grey*'s visits to Paris after 1815 as well as his study of French architectural books of the C17 and C18 which he held in his library. There had been odd occasional French *intérieurs* by Benjamin Wyatt in the 1820s, but a French country house with all the rooms in the Louis XV style has no parallel. For interiors one's mind turns to the fifties and the Rothschilds. The house, of Bath stone, has a thirteen-bay front, two-storeyed, with segment-headed windows, their glazing bars originally gilt, and mansard

---

*For the full architectural history of the previous house *see* J. Collett-White, *Inventories of Bedfordshire Country Houses 1714–1830*, BHRS, v. 74, 1995.
†Pevsner erroneously assumed him to be Cléphane, 'an otherwise unknown French architect'.

and pavilion roofs. The centre on the entrance side projects
ovally and has a fancy pavilion roof of a squashed onion dome
and square domes over the projecting angles. On the garden
side the centre is flat, with channelled pilasters and there
are fifteen bays, 1–5–3–5–1, plus single-storey pavilions for
conservatory and dining room. Again the windows are segmental-headed but with enriched keystones and also, over the
centre and ends, carved cherubs. The first floor has iron balconies and in front is a terrace also with a lavish gilded balustrade; made, like all the ironwork, by *Edward Barwell* of
Northampton.

The oval ENTRANCE HALL has boiseries and putto reliefs
all round, high up, of *carton pierre*. It leads into a grand and
elegant STAIRCASE HALL, with the stairs in two arms and with
a painted wooden handrail of scrolls and foliage running up to
a screen of Corinthian columns. Deeply coved ceiling on a
frieze of lush acanthus consoles and a glazed lantern. Pictures
of the earl's ancestors in fixed frames of complementary style;
their design comes from his '60 franc books bought at Paris'
and over the door to the ante-library facing the garden (originally intended as a billiard room) is a stucco allegory of Architecture holding books by Le Pautre, Mansart and Blondel.
Flanking the door, STATUES of Hebe and a nymph bathing by
Richard Wyatt of Rome. The library and its ante-room form the
centre of the principal apartments along the S front. The
ANTE-LIBRARY has, inside, a frieze of motifs appropriate to
scholarship and is the first of the rooms with Rococo ceilings
and Louis XV fireplaces. Inside the LIBRARY itself, ceiling
paintings by *John Wood* of music, poetry, painting, sculpture.
Heraldic decoration to the cornice. Most of the decoration is
white and gold. The DRAWING ROOM similarly decorated,
with an even larger painting by Wood. Originally the walls were
hung with Beauvais tapestries. The DINING ROOM, at the E
end of this suite, is an interesting tribute to the earlier house
at Wrest, the design of the ceiling of C17 type with octagonal
central compartment copied from that of the old library. C18
fireplace from the Back Library of No. 4 St James Square, de
Grey's London house, which he remodelled at about the same
time. The room is tripartite, with ends narrower than the
centre, a refinement of the similar arrangement made by de
Grey at Newby Hall, his mansion in the West Riding of Yorkshire. The N end was adapted in the 1850s to have a moveable
rear wall permitting the formation of a stage. Finally, at the
other end of the house, the countess's SITTING ROOM, a very
enchanting interior with a recess for the fireplace and, in the
ceiling, strange little domes with cherubs suspended inside
(from the library ceiling in the old house). The boiseries here
were unwanted panels intended for Windsor Castle; the fireplace is from the drawing room of the old house. This opens
into the CONSERVATORY, with cast-iron interior and lantern
roof. In upper rooms, remarkable preservation of scenic wallpapers, one Chinese, probably imported in the C18 for the

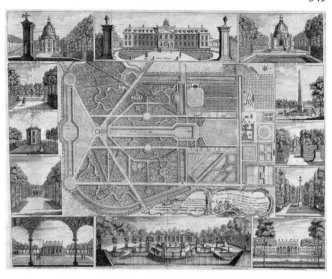

Wrest Park, plan and views.
Drawing by J. Rocque, 1737

previous house and reused, with a little infilling, in the 1830s.
The second, depicting America, Asia, Europe and Africa, is a
gorgeous design ('Eldorado') produced by *Zuber & Cie* of
Paris, *c.* 1848.

The SERVICE WING is of impressive length and also in
French tone but yellow brick and less ostentatious, with the
exception of the STABLES with a short tower, free-English-
Classical. S of this, on the garden side, a pretty DAIRY, also
c. 1830s, with a veranda on three sides, a lantern and clerestory
of Rococo-pattern cast-iron glazing with coloured glass.

What distinguishes the GARDEN more than anything is that it has
remained basically formal, in spite of a compliment paid to
Capability Brown, who worked at Wrest in 1758–60. The gardens
seem to have been begun in the mid C17 by Amabella, wife of
the 10th Earl. They were extended under her influence by the
11th Earl later in the same century, contemporary with the
remodelling of the house. To that period belongs the LONG
WATER extending N–S from the site of the old house. Kip
shows it in *Britannia Illustrata* (1705) along with a characteristic late C17 rigid pattern of enclosed gardens and mazes around
the house. The Long Water is now the spine of the GREAT
GARDEN, the wilderness garden created by the Duke of Kent.
It was begun in 1706 and 'at several times Inlarged and
Adorned to this year 1740', especially during the duke's
second marriage. Early on there was advice from *Thomas
Ackres*, the royal gardener (he is referred to in accounts as Mr

Acres). The main avenues are radially arranged from the parterre and from the celebrated Pavilion by *Thomas Archer*.
Originally they were lined by high hedges. Rocque shows this
garden at its fullest extent in 1735–7, a rectangle enclosed on
three sides by outer canals and, in the insterces of the avenues,
winding paths through the woodland. By then the Long Water
had also received a cross-axis of canals at its widened head,
inspired by Versailles (the arms are separated now as The Leg
o'Mutton Lake, w, and the Ladies' Lake, e). *Brown*, working
for the Marchioness Grey in 1758–60 and again in 1778–9, gave
the wilderness some of its wiggly paths, softened the edges with
tree plantings and gave the canal all round the gardens its
serpentine form, in the process also removing a broad diagonal
canal to the e. The flower gardens, w and s of the new house,
are of the 1830s and its perfect complement. Indeed one may
speculate whether it was deference to the formality of the existing gardens which led Earl de Grey to adopt the French style
of the mansion. w of the house is an ITALIAN GARDEN
(restored since *c.* 2011 to Grey's design) opening from the
Duchess's conservatory. This continues the e–w axis through
the gates of the Walled Garden (*see* below). The principal axis
from the terrace, with SCULPTURE of the Dogs of Alcibiades
brought from Newby Hall, is s across the PARTERRE, with four
lead STATUE groups of *c.* 1730 (by *John Cheere*) and along to
the site of the earlier house, marked by the Round Pond with
a Carrara MARBLE FOUNTAIN, introduced in the 1860s, surrounded by STATUES after the Antique, and along the Long
Water to Archer's Pavilion (*see* below), nearly ½ m. away.

The pavilion is only one of many GARDEN ORNAMENTS. A
number are shown by Rocque in 1737, though a few disappeared in 1809 and more after 1917.[*] The remainder will now
be described in the order of an easy tour.

First, w of the fountain, the ORANGERY,[†] by *de Grey*, also
1830s; a very dissolute design, again in this ahead of its date.
Eleven bays. End bays with square French domes. Strange
pilasters with basket capitals and little mats hanging from
them. Entrance between a caryatid and an atlas. The design
for a trianon is from Blondel, 1737. Inside, a fireplace of
c. 1600, from the old house. Clunch with an overmantel containing the de Grey arms. It was removed from the house after
1917 but recovered *c.* 1957 from Coles Park, Herts., by the
Ministry of Works.

Behind the Orangery, at the mouth of the canal, the BATH
HOUSE, built of ironstone rubble, two rooms, cyclopean, the
first octagonal and thatched, the second domed and half-
ruined-looking, with lower down the cold bath itself. The
building was designed by *Edward Stevens* in 1769–70. s of the
Orangery in the 'American Garden', a large group, called
HAWKING PARTY. A young lady on horseback and two youths.

___

[*] A COLUMN and OBELISK are for example at Trent Park, Herts.
[†] It stands on the site of a Green House by *Batty Langley*, 1735–6.

p. 345

The sculptor working to Grey's design was *Terence Farrell* of Dublin, 1857 (cf. the Countess de Grey's monument at Flitton).

Further s, the BOWLING GREEN HOUSE, a banqueting room, perhaps of *c.* 1720 for which Thomas Archer made drawings, but attributed to *Hawksmoor* and now as altered in 1735 by *Batty Langley*, who added the Doric colonnade of six columns with triglyph frieze and balustrade. At the back towards the canal a plainer arcade with groin vaults. The room inside, now restored, is splendidly decorated in the William Kent taste. Fine doorway with Corinthian columns and pediment, fine chimneypiece opposite with rich, broad volutes and the duke's arms. Wall panels with hanging garlands. To l. and r. of the Bowling Green House, two lead VASES by *Jan van Nost*, 1725.

So to the woodland walks w of the Long Water, populated with numerous ornaments, e.g. in a clearing, the MITHRAIC ALTAR of 1748, faced in flint and inscribed in spoof Greek. Thus, by way of WEST HALFHOUSE in the Duchess' Square, a small pedimented exedra of brick of 1726, to *Archer's*

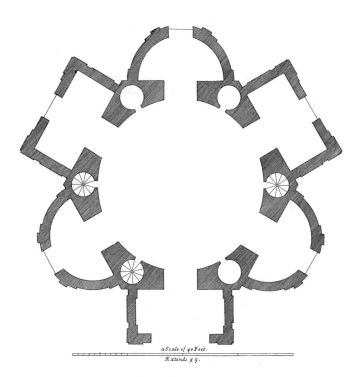

Wrest Park, Pavilion, by Thomas Archer.
Plan, 1717

33,
p. 347

PAVILION.* This is a very curious conceit, in red brick but some of it always apparently colour-washed yellow. It is more Borrominesque than one would expect in England, except from so travelled a gentleman as Archer. The principle of the plan is that of Borromini's S. Ivo, which Archer certainly saw while in Rome *c.* 1691. It is the principle of a star of three identical motifs front and diagonally back and three other identical motifs back and diagonally front. The former motifs in Archer's case are rectangular, the latter semicircular and corresponding originally with the pattern of avenues in the early C18 garden. The whole centre is round and domed above a frieze of consoles, with a lantern. The curved triplet has flat brick pilaster strips, the oblong triplet brick quoins of even length and pediments with modillions. At the junction of the curved parts with the centre are tiny semi-domes. The entrance unit is open. It has Ionic pilasters and, inside, painted rustication. The doorway is most characteristically Archer. It might be described like this. Take two pairs of pilasters, streak them vertically, and turn the outer outward, the inner inward, and continue this in the pediment. It is a device specially favoured in Vienna, Salzburg and Prague at Archer's time, and Archer may well have known any of them. The date of the Pavilion is 1709–11. The surprisingly large circular room inside has painted statues, medallions and cherubs and Corinthian columns below the entablature of a painted coffered ceiling in the dome. These are signed *Hauduroy* (i.e. *Louis Hauduroy*) 1712. There are five windows in the five projections, designed as small rooms for guests to withdraw into – one with a fireplace – and in addition three round windows in the attic. Spiral stairs served kitchen, bath etc. in the basement and servants' rooms in the attic.

In front of the Pavilion stands a lead STATUE of William III. It may be by *Nost c.* 1712 or as late as 1730 but is not shown on Rocque's plan of 1735–7. Other lead statues e.g. of Queen Anne were melted down in 1809. To the NE of the Pavilion is the EAST HALFHOUSE (in the Duke's Square), like its companion (*see* above) but a little larger, i.e. with blank side pieces. From here straight N to the late COLUMN commemorating Capability Brown's contribution 1758–60: an urn on a Tuscan column, weirdly girt by two square rocky blocks. Designed by *Edward Stevens*.

N of this, crossing the canal realigned by *Brown*, is the CHINESE BRIDGE of 1874, not specially Chinese-looking but meant to compose with trees into the Willow Pattern come true. It succeeded a Chinese bridge erected here *c.* 1760. The CHINESE TEMPLE is a mid-C20 reconstruction of a design,

---

*Archer also designed Hill House, on Cain Hill, outside the gardens to the E. It had a Greek cross plan with concave angles. Helen Lawrence has suggested its setting may have been influenced by Archer's knowledge of the gardens at Kleve in the Netherlands. It had gone by the early C19 and on its site was erected a column in memory of Jemima, Marchioness de Grey, also since taken down.

also 1760s, usually attributed to Chambers but probably by *Stevens*. Finally, s e of the house, the P E T I T T R I A N O N, a rustic children's playhouse of 1856.

To the w of the house is the very large WALLED GARDEN (6 acres; 2.4 ha) in six compartments), with gateways so undisciplined that again they look 1850 rather than 1835; big sculptural groups carved by *W. T. Kelsey* and a two-storey gardener's house at the NW angle with oval windows in the mansard. In front of the E gate, STATUES of Bacchus and Flora by *P. Scheemakers*, *c.* 1730. The garden lies on the main approach established by *de Grey* via the WEST LODGES. They too are square and French with their mansard roofs. Remarkably, they were designed by de Grey in 1826, even before he had inherited the estate, and were executed by *Thomas Smith* of Hertford; cf. Silsoe church, 100 yds w. A similar pair, Brabury Lodges to the NE, is now sadly derelict.

WRESTLINGWORTH

2040

ST PETER. Of brown cobbles. In the chancel N wall a small Norman window and a lancet. Short Perp w tower with higher stair-turret and spike. The aisle windows are Dec and straight-topped with reticulation units (cf. Cockayne Hatley). The s arcade and the s doorway are late C13, but the doorway has lost its shafts, and ornamental carving has taken the place of the capitals. The N arcade is a little later. Both have standard elements. Dec chancel – see the arch with responds of half-quatrefoil section with the familiar thin shafts in the diagonals. Arch of two sunk waves. Dec also the transomed lowside windows of the chancel (s side restored), and the PISCINA. Perp clerestory. – PULPIT. Pretty, early C18 stair with twisted balusters. – STAINED GLASS. E window by *Cox, Sons & Buckley*, 1888.

WYMINGTON

9060

ST LAURENCE. Not a large, but an ambitious church, entirely Dec, and mostly built by the munificence of John Curteys, whose family purchased the manor in 1361. It was completed *c.* 1377. The w tower has bell-openings of pairs of two-light transomed windows with ogee arches below the transoms and a flower trail in the surrounds, a quatrefoil top frieze and another flower trail below the decorated battlements, and a crocketed spire whose lowest tier of gabled lucarnes gives the effect of an octagonal stage below the spire proper. The top mini-lucarnes are also gabled. The aisles embrace the tower

18

and have circular W windows. Otherwise aisles and chapels
have straight-headed windows, save one more elaborate to the
N chapel with a depressed arch, and have curvilinear tracery
in the aisles proper and single and halved reticulation units in
the chapels. The E end is a fine sight, with one low embattled
gable above chapels and chancel and higher angle turrets with
battlements (cf. Tingrith; also Shillington). The E window of
five lights with flowing tracery is a facsimile of what was there
before the restoration of *c.* 1843–5, but the flanking lancets are
an invention in place of two-light windows. The S porch is
uncommonly lavish too. It is two-storeyed, with a vault with
diagonal and ridge-ribs and a Green Man boss. The interior is
oddly tight, or, in other words, crowded with motifs. The
arcades inside are identical, of four bays, with standard elements and recognizably Dec details, the arches with alternate
voussoirs of ironstone. The tower arch is unusual. The responds
are one broad splay continuous with the arcade responds,
divided by three niches into four parts. The tops of the niches
are tiny arches like stop-chamfers. In the tower are the remains
of a vault too. Arches from the aisles into the chapels and from
the chancel to the chapels. On the N side it is only one bay
(since 1845), on the S side one plus the Curteys Monument
(*see* below). SEDILIA and PISCINA are obviously Dec, the
piscina with a nodding canopy and traceried bowl like a rose
window. Another such canopy above the S chapel PISCINA. In
the S chapel also, in the angle of the SE window, a clunch niche
with ogee arches but Perp panel tracery over. Next to it, by the
S chapel door, an angel bracket. The chancel roof has traceried
braces, presumably 1840s. The aisle roofs are of 1923 by *Talbot
Brown & Fisher*, who restored the church in the following years.
– FONT. Octagonal, probably Dec. The stem with quatrefoils,
the bowl strongly moulded, and at the top a small frieze of
ogee arches. – PULPIT. Jacobean, with back panel and sounding-board. – SCREEN, in the N chapel (vestry). Jacobean, with
small balusters at the top. – BENCHES. A set of the buttressed
Perp type, some with C17 pull-out auxiliary seats. – REREDOS.
In the S chapel until 1925. Dec. Statues and painting by *Ninian
Comper*, 1938. – WALL PAINTINGS. On the S aisle E wall, high
up, a late C14 Trinity. This is suggested to be the earliest painting in the church. – Of the C15, the large, faint Doom over the
chancel arch and extending into the nave, where, on the S wall,
the damned are consumed by a beast. – Also some ornamental
painting around the arches in the N aisle E wall and in the S
chapel (N wall) with tendril of flowers and the letter M. –
MONUMENTS. Between chancel and S chapel, John Curteys
†1391, Mayor of the Staple of Calais, 'qui istam ecclesiam de
novo construxerat', and wife. Brasses, 34 in. (86 cm) long, the
earliest in Bedfordshire, with an inscribed frame and symbols
of the Evangelists at the corners; on a clunch tomb-chest with
Perp blank tracery, quite plain on the N side and of a more
elaborate cusped pattern on the S. The tomb-chest is placed
under a large ogee arch. The capitals have small foliage strips

and small angels. – Sir Thomas Brunflet †1430 and his wife 1407 (chancel floor). He is 6 ft (1.8 metres) long, she 3 ft (91 cm). Above his head a long inscription in Latin hexameters. – John Stokys, rector, *c.* 1510 (s chapel, floor). The figure is 22 in. (55 cm) long.

SCHOOL, by the church. 1878 by *John Bird*. Good additions by *Oliver Carey* in the idiom of the 1960s: e.g. pale engineering bricks.

POPLARS FARM HOUSE, SE of the church. Originally a lobby entry house, probably *c.* 1680 on the evidence of its staircase, with wavy splat balusters and dodecagonal finials. Extended at both ends and altered in the C18 and C19.

YELDEN

A remote-seeming village, which in views from the E presents the church on high ground with the village houses deferring to it.

ST MARY. Externally mostly Dec, but certain disjointed features are E.E., i.e. the s aisle doorway with one order of shafts, the chancel s doorway, the piece of string course above it inside, a reset PISCINA (trefoil head) in the chancel N wall, the plain blocked nave N doorway, the remains of an E lancet in the s aisle, and the s arcade except for the Perp responds. The s aisle W window looks *c.* 1300, i.e. earlier than the Dec features of the church. To these belongs the W tower, with bell-openings with flowing tracery and a delightful corbel-frieze with a tendril connecting flowers, animals, heads etc. (cf. Swineshead not far away). Short broach spire with two tiers of lucarnes. Dec also the chancel, see the windows, the arch towards the nave, the SEDILIA and PISCINA with their ogee arches in frames, and a N window in the nave. Perp clerestory and s porch. Chancel restored 1892 by *W. Lewis Baker* of Hargrave, Northants. He added the N organ chamber. – FONT COVER. Perp. Conical and crocketed. – PULPIT. Perp, of wood, similar to that at Dean (q.v.), with tracery in the arches. – BENCHES. The usual buttressed type; almost a complete set. – WALL PAINTINGS. On the s wall a St Christopher, his feet resting on fish, and much painted ashlaring with a flower in the middle of each block and tendrils (C14). Also on the aisle E wall, a saint, probably St James; a corresponding figure existed l. of the window. Remarkable C18 DECALOGUE painted onto the N wall, with major and minor arched panels as if on a reredos and with a proper cornice. – CURIOSUM. In the tower, a poem, by Thomas Williamson, hammered into a sheet of roof leading, 1703. – STAINED GLASS. s chancel. 1870 by *Cox & Sons*. Also a window of 1966 by *Goddard & Gibbs*. – MONUMENTS. In the nave N wall simple ogee recess and effigy of a civilian holding his heart. Early C14. The tomb-chest has been cut down but had quatrefoils with shields. This corresponds with the larger and more splendid Dec tomb recess in the s aisle. Cusped and subcusped arch with leaf in the spandrels and crockets on the gable. Buttress shafts l. and r. Two of the cusps are heads of knights. This is the largest and best of the many such tombs in the north Bedfordshire churches. – Brass to J. Heyne, rector, †1433. A 19-in. (48 cm) figure in a surplice. – Also an oblong brass plate with the figure of Christopher Stickland †1628, and a square brass plate with the kneeling figure of Thomas Barker †1617. – Thomas Wylde (s aisle) †1792, by *Sumpter* of Irthlingborough.

OLD RECTORY. Of more than one phase, but principally *c.* 1700 and a little later. Some bolection-moulded panelling inside.

THE MANOR. 1923–4 by *Talbot Brown & Fisher* for T. H. Hawkey, lord of the manor from 1912. Two-storey canted bays with mullions under gables, l. and r. of a door with arched hood.

In SPRING LANE, No. 1 has a timber-framed front with double-curved bracing.

CASTLE. Considerable earthworks remain on the s bank of the River Til, e of the village. The motte is oblong or oval, *c.* 130 ft by 90 ft (39 metres by 27 metres) in size at the top. In addition two large baileys. The principal bailey is w and sw of the motte. During excavations in 1881 stone foundations were discovered, including the bases of two small round towers in the sw corner of the bailey. Further excavation in the 1970s. A little to the w of this, on a small island mound, was another round tower, this one 30 ft (9 metres) in diameter. It may have been a dovecote. Probably begun for Geoffrey de Trailly, tenant of the parish of Yelden which was held by the Bishop of Coutances. The first phase is probably shortly after the Conquest and comprises the motte and w bailey. It then developed into a manorial centre for the barony of Trailly, adding the n bailey and some time later the fishponds.

HUNTINGDONSHIRE AND PETERBOROUGH

INTRODUCTION

First, some explanation of the contents of this guide. Hunting-donshire until 1965 was one of the smallest counties of England – in population it was the last but two, in size the last but four (including London). It had no big town, it was remote and had all the attractions of peace and quiet and intimacy. The 1965 shot in the arm changed all that when it was merged into a new county with the ancient Soke of Peterborough, which lay N across the River Nene and was from 1888 an administratively separate county within Northamptonshire.* To this pairing was appended a small piece of the northern Isle of Ely, containing Thorney. The County of Huntingdon and Peterborough lasted just nine years, long enough to be respected by the previous edition of this guide, before Huntingdonshire disappeared into the enlarged County of Cambridgeshire, while Peterborough was resurrected as one of the new independent unitary authorities under the City Council. Confusing though this is for historians – and indeed for the inhabitants of Huntingdonshire and Peterborough – it has meant mercifully little for the boundaries of these areas. Huntingdon-shire remains a county in all but name, its borders still main-tained as a district within Cambridgeshire, while the urban and rural area governed by Peterborough City Council is only mar-ginally different from the area of the Soke, although it now covers also some places along the s bank of the Nene which were for-merly in Huntingdonshire.† The population of the Peterborough unitary area is now approximately 186,000 inhabitants, a colossal increase since the 1960s and in large part due to the development of the New Town during the 1970s. Huntingdonshire has 169,000, a little over twice its population of fifty years ago.

---

*The Soke of Peterborough was included in the first edition of *Northamptonshire* (1961) in this series.
†Wothorpe, although within the Peterborough City Council area, was not part of the County of Huntingdon and Peterborough and as a result is described in *The Buildings of England: Northamptonshire* (3rd edn, 2013).

In terms of LANDSCAPE, the combined area is divided into three broad zones. The attraction of Huntingdonshire still remains the modest rolling country of the S around the Ouse valley and W in the uplands or Wolds. None of this is easily appreciated if one stays on the A1, but as soon as one diverts from it and takes either a route NE from St Neots to St Ives, or even better W of the A1 from Alconbury to Wansford roughly following the line of the 'Bullock Road' (*see* p. 385), then one sees at once Huntingdonshire's reputation as spire country is amply justified. The total – including three no longer surviving – is over forty if one includes the Peterborough churches, and along the modern A14 it is possible to see four of the best (Easton, Ellington, Spaldwick, Catworth) in a single view. Barnack is one of the earliest spires in England and it stands in the furthest W edge of the former Soke of Peterborough, near the great park of Burghley, where the valleys of the Nene and Welland come close together and the underlying limestone makes its presence felt in highly attractive villages. The Peterborough country is, however, very flat and an occasional change in elevation, e.g. at Ufford, is immediately noticed. The low hills, no more than 30–50 metres (approx. 100–160 ft) above sea level, that form an arc from the Soke villages S through Huntingdonshire contain, like Bedfordshire, several plateaus, very suitable in the mid C20 for airfields. These hills mark the edge of the Fen, the third zone and the most challenging one. The fen country within our areas stretches from the Lincolnshire border at Market Deeping to beyond Fenstanton in the S. This is naturally marshy land within a few metres of sea level and until the mid C17 was substantially flooded. Understanding this helps explain much about the isolated nature of the settlements on the Fen, concentrated at first only where small gravel islands (e.g. Eye, Ramsey, Thorney) provided a suitable place for building. It helps to be reminded too that for centuries places such as Peterborough lay therefore on the edge of the dry land and that travel by water gave them connections further afield than their English hinterland. Once the land had been drained – beginning in the mid C17 and concluding in the mid C19 – the fens assumed their unique landscape of embanked canals or dykes and roads running in rigid lines across the country, besides which the rich peaty soil of the fen has gradually sunk as it dries out – at Holme, the lowest place in England, 9 ft (2.75 metres below sea level), this shrinkage is measured by cast-iron posts driven into the peat up to their head in the mid C19 and now standing high above it. This also occasionally means the odd experience of driving along roads below the waterways. The change from the fen edge to the fen proper is dramatic and an appreciation of skyscape is as important as landscape in this area.

The geology and building materials of Huntingdonshire and Peterborough are described on pp. 3–10. Here it is sufficient to say that excellent stone predominates in the N, timber elsewhere for the earlier buildings and from the C18 and C19 brick. But before considering buildings, now it is necessary to consider the archaeological record.

PREHISTORIC AND ROMAN ARCHAEOLOGY
BY STEPHEN G. UPEX

In recent years aerial photography, continued research and the increase in developer-led excavations have added greatly to the numbers of sites of all periods that have been identified within Peterborough and Huntingdonshire. However, the number of monuments visible from the ground is limited due to the intensive nature of agriculture, quarrying, especially for gravel, and urban expansion.

The earliest PALAEOLITHIC occupation of the region is represented entirely by the finds of flint tools from the gravel deposits of the river valleys, especially the Nene, Welland and Ouse. Such tools indicate roving bands of interglacial hunters following animal herds and living a very nomadic way of life. Acheulean-style hand axes from Woodston were associated with mammoth, cave bear, horse and reindeer bones and indicate the sites of temporary camps or 'kill sites'. Axes from Woodston, Fletton, Orton Waterville and Orton Longueville were collected by George Wyman Abbott in the early years of the C20 and form the core of the collection in Peterborough Museum. The late middle Palaeolithic occupation by Neanderthals is marked by isolated finds from Hemingford Grey and St Ives, whilst the late middle Palaeolithic site at Little Paxton is significant as one of only two known 'open-air' sites in the country and has produced over 200 artefacts, which were associated with finds of woolly mammoth, woolly rhinoceros, horse and reindeer.

During the MESOLITHIC period small populations of hunter-gatherers continued to move across the region, and finds of tools within the fenlands are particularly notable. Most of these finds must represent temporary camps, and the flint working site identified at Godmanchester most probably falls into this category.

Our knowledge of early populations only begins to increase as they develop farming and adopted a more sedentary lifestyle. NEOLITHIC settlements are known from many areas within the region, perhaps the more famous being at Fengate (Peterborough) – which gives its name to a type of Neolithic pottery first found there. At Parnwell, Newark, in the NE suburbs of Peterborough, a site included what is now termed a 'pit settlement', where a series of pits containing pottery, flint artefacts and bone from food debris indicate occupation in the immediate area. Settlement distributions at this period are still poorly understood but may be related to the abilities of early farming communities to clear land from forested areas. Such clearance may have been initially confined to the more fertile and lighter soils of the region, avoiding the heavily wooded clay-lands.

Advances in air photography backed up by excavation, often in advance of development, have seen numerous other Neolithic sites brought to light. Burials from Elton and Ramsey St Mary's can be added to the list of mortuary enclosures and structures from the Fengate area of Peterborough. In addition, LONG

BARROWS at places such as Brampton and those found along the fen edge add to our growing understanding of Neolithic burial rites in this part of Britain.

Air photography has also added considerably to the numbers of known ceremonial monuments within the area. CAUSEWAYED ENCLOSURES are now known from the Welland valley at Etton, Northborough and Upton and at Godmanchester in the Ouse valley. Linked to these sites are a growing number of cursus monuments, known at Godmanchester, Fenstanton, Buckden (where there are three) and in the Welland valley at Maxey, Barnack and Bainton. There is also a series of slightly later henge monuments, some of which have been entirely or partly excavated at Maxey and Elton. Others, like the spectacular group of four HENGES at Chesterton, are known only from the air. The Chesterton group, which lies now by the side of the busy A1 road, is very interesting and consists of two henges, each 120 metres (393 ft 8 in.) in diameter. One of these henges has inner circular features and appears to be partly overlain by a third henge which is 100 metres (328 ft 1 in.) in diameter. A fourth henge lies within the confines of the later Roman town of *Durobrivae* (Water Newton), where it may have been modified during the Roman period – perhaps forming part of a Roman amphitheatre.

All of these henge-type monuments may have continued in use into the Early BRONZE AGE when the burial rites, styles of pottery and improvements in agriculture change noticeably. Finds of flint artefacts from the Bronze Age are numerous across the region and indicate a continued clearance of woodland and an expansion of settlement. The fen edge was particularly attractive to these settlers with its skirt-land of well-drained, fertile and easily worked soils providing good farmland for crops and raising stock. The fenland provided additional resources of summer grazing and also fishing, fowling, reed and peat cutting. Salt extraction from tidal areas of the fen waterways was being carried out throughout the prehistoric and well into the medieval periods.

Changes in the styles of pottery saw the introduction of BEAKERS accompanying burials. The two beakers from Somersham are worthy of comment as one is exceptionally large and is decorated in a style that has parallels with similar vessels from Wiltshire and the Continent – reflecting perhaps the influence of migration into the area. Not only does the type of pottery that accompanies burials change, the form and rites of the burials themselves also appear to undergo considerable modification at this period. Single primary burials in round barrows, often accompanied by later secondary burials, become the norm and a considerable number of such barrows are scattered across the whole of Huntingdonshire, most showing only from the air as cropmarks. The gravels of the Welland, Nene and Ouse valleys form known concentrations of these monuments, often indicating 'cemetery-type' groupings. At Barnack, in the Welland valley, a primary burial (now displayed in the British Museum), dated to around 1800–1700 B.C., was accompanied by a large beaker, a pendant, an archer's wrist-guard and a copper dagger – one of the earliest metal objects from eastern Britain. In addition the fenland areas around Thorney and the fen edge down the eastern side of the county often show the integration of settlements, field systems and barrows within the Bronze Age landscape. Upstanding BARROWS are rare but do occur at Chesterton, Orton Longueville and Ailsworth. Upstanding barrows in the fenland also 'appear' in areas where the overlying peat is shrinking to reveal the underlying and often intact Bronze Age land surface. At Diddington an enigmatic 'ring monument' appears to be linked with cremation rites but not the interment of the actual cremations.

It is into this period that metal tools and weapons are introduced, and there are many isolated finds of early bronze metalwork from Horsey (see p. 654), Whittlesey Mere (Cambs), Pidley and St Neots. In addition, two bronze smiths' hoards were found at Stanground (Peterborough) containing worn and broken artefacts, presumably intended for melting down and re-fabricating. One of the most important excavated sites that has encountered Bronze Age metalwork is that at Flag Fen (Peterborough), which appears to have been a focus for the veneration of water deities and where offerings of swords and other high-class metalwork were thrown into the edge of a mere. As part of this focus for religious rites a series of parallel lines of wooden posts were set out, leading into and across part of the mere. Flag Fen may be typical of other, similar, fen-edge sites either awaiting discovery or destroyed as the overlying protective peat covering dries out.

During the IRON AGE modern archaeology indicates that the landscape was densely populated with farmsteads, linked by track-ways which led through partly planned field systems. Such sites abound within the county area and include typical farmsteads at Haddon and Eaton Socon which contained round houses, set within yarded enclosures. The whole area of the county was within the influence of the Catuvellauni tribe, which was centred on St Albans, but there were other important sub-centres which formed part of the tribal confederacy. At Borough Fen, near Newborough, a 'lowland hillfort' with two encircling ramparts enclosed an area of 9.5 acres (3.8 hectares) and must have formed a tribal sub-centre for the northern arm of the Catuvellauni, whilst at Westwood, within the western suburbs of Peterborough, extensive finds of Iron Age pottery, coins and burials indicate another major concentration of power.

At Orton Waterville (Peterborough) a meander of the River Nene was annexed by the construction of a triple-ditched earthwork within which was yet another major focus of the Iron Age aristocracy. This important site is also associated with finds of Iron Age metalwork, including swords, that have been recovered from the River Nene. These must represent the Iron Age veneration of watery sites – a continuation from the Bronze Age tradition encountered at Flag Fen.

Burials are rarely found from this period, although one from Bluntisham, excavated in 2004, was in a crouched position at the bottom of a pit which was set within an enclosure. Other burials, at Cat's Water (the watercourse running NE from Peterborough towards Eye) and Colne Fen were also laid in a crouched position. Late Iron Age metalwork, including pins and brooches, was excavated in the 1820s by Edmund Artis from a 'tumulus' at Ailsworth, suggesting that the tradition of burial in barrows continued to the end of this period.

The transition from the Iron Age to the ROMAN occupation of the area is seen in sharp focus at Longthorpe (Peterborough) where several burials were interred into the ditches surrounding an Iron Age farmstead. The farmstead was levelled in A.D. 43–44, and its occupants perhaps massacred, to make way for the construction of a 26¼-acre (10.5-hectare) fortress which housed half of the Ninth Legion as they set about the conquest of eastern Britain. The former farmstead area was later used as a 'works depot' for the production of pottery for use within the fortress. A tile stamped with the Ninth Legion's insignia was found at Bainton.

The military occupation in the early years of the conquest of A.D. 43 has left few traces in the county. Early forts are known from Godmanchester, where an area of 6 acres (2.4 hectares) was defended by a pair of ditches, and three gates are known along with an annex towards the river. A similar sized fort is also known from air photographs at Water Newton. This fort has indications of three defensive ditches and gates and some of the internal arrangements can also be seen from the air. Another fort, in Orton Waterville, within the late Iron Age annexed area cut off by the triple-ditch system of earthworks, may be a 'marching' or 'temporary' camp related to a very early phase of the occupation of A.D. 43. Two 'camps' at Upton, previously always thought to be Roman, are now shown by excavation to be Neolithic in date.

It may be that the fortress at Longthorpe and forts at Godmanchester and Great Casterton (Rutland), NW of Stamford, are an early series of installations along the line of an invasion-period Roman road. Troops from Longthorpe appear to have been used in A.D. 60 to head off the rebellious Icenian horde, under the leadership of Boudicca, as it moved towards London, intent on razing the newly founded Roman settlement there. The Roman writer Tacitus tells that this action failed and the Roman troops were cut to pieces and retreated to their base. Tacitus does not mention the site at Longthorpe by name but the indications are that the depleted troops were forced to reduce the size of the defendable area of the fortress – which accounts for its inner and outer lines of defence seen on the air photographs.

It seems likely that in the aftermath of the Boudiccan revolt the troop deployment in the area was revised by the military authorities. The fortress at Longthorpe may have been abandoned in the early to mid 60s A.D. The road system in the area was reorganized, with the road formerly serving Longthorpe now being moved westwards to cross the River Nene at Water Newton. This move may in turn have warranted the foundation of the

Water Newton fort, which could not only have given the new bridgehead protection but also formed part of a general rethinking of the military control of eastern England. This reorganization is also seen at Godmanchester, where the fort size was reduced to 5 acres (2.05 hectares) and the internal arrangements were changed, and at Great Casterton, where a similar situation has been detected by excavation. All of this military planning in the years immediately after the Boudiccan revolt of A.D. 60 may have been an attempt to keep a very watchful eye on the Iceni tribe, and to this end a new road was constructed into the heart of former Icenian territory. This road, the so-called 'Fen Causeway', along with new forts along its route at places like Grandford (Cambs.) and Denver (Norfolk), was meant to give troops quick access into Norfolk should trouble arise again.

Once the road system and its forts were reorganized after c. A.D. 60 the line of what is now termed Ermine Street remained as the main arterial route to the north for the rest of the Roman period. A bridge with stone foundations was constructed at Water Newton and presumably a similar arrangement at Godmanchester carried Ermine Street over the River Ouse.

The abandonment of the Claudian fort with its early extramural settlement at Godmanchester (Roman *Durovigutum*) was followed fairly soon afterwards by the Flavian development of a formally planned settlement laid out in regular units. This development was in a slightly different area from that of the fort and the indications are that wooden buildings (some round and some rectangular) were set along the street frontages, behind which were gardens and croft-like plots for animals. Beyond these garden areas, air photographs show that fields were set out and a spread of Roman finds across this area, recovered from modern field-walking, probably indicates intensive Roman manuring. Shortly after A.D. 120 the western part of the town was cleared for the construction of a *mansio* that must have been linked with the Imperial Post service. This building had ranges of rooms and a bath house to accommodate official travellers. At a similar time a shrine to a native god, '*Abandinus*', was constructed, and other temples of Romano-Celtic form are also known. The settlement seems to have prospered, with major rebuilding after a fire in the middle of the C2. The limits of the settlement are marked at this period by cremation cemeteries at Porch Farm, Green End and along the Cambridge Road, and later inhumation cemeteries are known as far north as Mill Common near Huntingdon. The C3 was marked by the construction of a small basilica and at the end of the C3 by the provision of walls around the town, of which two gates and a smaller postern are known. Later still, bastions appear to have been added to the walls. The town seems to have declined by the end of the C4, rubbish deposits accumulating over the central areas of the town.

Along the line of Ermine Street to the N of Godmanchester a small roadside settlement at Tort Hill, Sawtry, may mark the site of another link with the Official Post system. Large quantities of horse bones from the site could indicate a use linked with changing horses for officials travelling between Godmanchester and the next town to the north at *Durobrivae* (Water Newton).

Durobrivae seems to have developed, like Godmanchester, as a 'garrison settlement' associated with the small fort at Water Newton. First-century traders may have settled at a point just outside the fort where they could trade with the military but also sell their wares to the growing numbers of travellers along Ermine Street. The settlement, which is only known from air photography, seems to have expanded to the SE along Ermine Street in a spontaneous way and with little evidence of any planning. Side roads seem to have been created off Ermine Street as new areas were taken into the urban expansion, and from these side roads there are also a series of alley-ways which must have given access to back-yard areas. At some point, possibly in the late C3, town walls were added, although there may have been earlier defences in the form of a town ditch backed by an earth rampart. Air photographs also show bastions, especially on the western part of the walls' circuit, and these, as at Godmanchester, may have been late additions to the existing walls. Within the walls (which encircle 44½ acres; 17.8 hectares) the town seems to have been crammed with buildings that the air photographs suggest had stone foundations. Gaps in this urban concentration may indicate areas of wooden buildings. Two large rectangular buildings probably represent public buildings of some form, perhaps a *mansio* and a basilica-forum, and adjoining one of these structures there appears to be a formally laid-out precinct with circular and rectangular shrines and temples.

Durobrivae's 'small town' status belies the fact that outside the walled area lay a further 140 hectares (350 acres) of densely packed and planned industrial suburbs where a multitude of trades served the town and its immediate region. Chief amongst these trades were iron working and pottery production. Iron blooms were brought into the suburbs from the Northamptonshire iron stone areas to the W and then fabricated into all manner of tools, utensils and artefacts. Clay for pottery and brushwood for both kiln and furnace fuel were exploited from local sources, and pottery production by the end of the third century marked the area out as one of the chief centres within the province – exports going to London, to the whole of the East Midlands, the fenlands and up to Lincoln, York and Hadrian's Wall.

Around the urban centres of *Durovigutum* and *Durobrivae* wealthy landowners or townspeople built a series of VILLAS. To the N and E of Godmanchester, villas are known at Rectory Farm and Whitehills, and further afield the villa at Great Staughton has evidence for mosaic floors, painted wall plaster, a bath house and heating systems. Around *Durobrivae* an even greater number of major villa sites are known, principally thanks to the pioneering work of Edmund Artis, who, in the 1820s and 30s, excavated and recorded sites at Ailsworth (two villas), Helpston, Water Newton (two villas) and a site at Mill Hill in Castor. Excavations during the mid and late C20 at Orton Longueville added another two

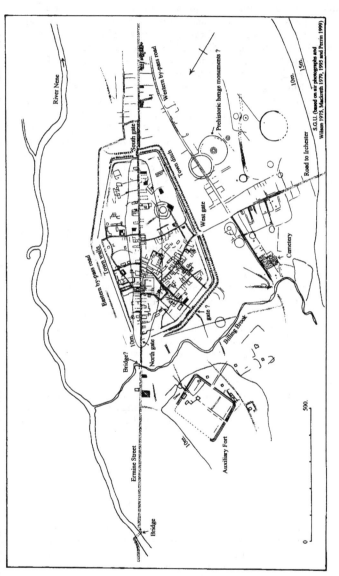

Durobrivae and its western suburbs.
Plan, 2008

substantial sites, while recent fieldwork and geophysical surveys at Upton have added another courtyard villa to the list. The site underneath Castor village, often referred to as a villa, now seems more likely to have been a major, palatial structure, perhaps linked with the administration of a fenland Imperial estate. This was set up after the Boudiccan revolt of A.D. 60 and perhaps reorganized during the Hadrianic period. The Car Dyke (*see* Peakirk), for so long interpreted as either a Roman canal or a 'catchwater' to aid flood control, is probably best seen as a formal boundary dyke for this estate land.

The building at Castor forms one of the largest structures known in Roman Britain and had numbers of mosaic floors, opulent wall plaster and heating systems. This link with the fenland, both administratively and as a conduit for goods, into and out of the fen basin, may also account for *Durobrivae*'s importance. It was recognized as a '*vicus*' by the end of the second century and may even have been elevated to a '*civitas*' later still. The town's importance is reflected in the finds of late Christian objects from the area around and within the town itself, chief of which is the recovery of a late Christian silver hoard of communion plate.

Away from the towns and major villas the countryside appears to have been densely settled with farmsteads, and numbers of new sites, like those recently discovered at Stow Longa and Tilbrook, fall within this category. Many of these farmsteads show that Roman settlement extended onto the clay-land soils, an expansion of what had already begun during the Iron Age.

One of the most enigmatic rural sites was excavated in 2011 at Bretton, a suburb of Peterborough. The general character of the site was that of a typical agricultural farmstead but, in the mid-C3, massive dressed blocks of reused stone were brought to the site and used to line an 8 ft (2.5 metre)-deep cistern. What earlier building was demolished to gain the stone or what the cistern was used for remains entirely unclear. Possible sources for the stone could include major public buildings at *Durobrivae*, the palatial structure at Castor or a major Roman building under the medieval cathedral at Peterborough.

The transition from Roman to the POST-ROMAN or Migration Period occupation of the area is still poorly understood and little archaeological evidence survives from this period. At Orton Longueville a Roman farmstead appears to have had Migration Period halls occupied alongside Roman aisled buildings, and at Haddon part of a late Roman farm was taken over and refurbished to include a small bath house which was re-roofed and occupied in the C5 and C6. The Roman fields associated with this farm simply carried on in use throughout the Migration Period and by the C9 and C10 had become 'fossilized' into what was the embryonic open-field system of the later medieval parish. Other possibly similar sites at Elton and Walton (Peterborough) imply that the transition from Roman into Saxon was smoothly undertaken. Populations appear to have co-existed within an agricultural landscape where farms were either partly worked by both

late Roman and incoming migrant labour or, if land were abandoned due to the reduced demand for both tax and production, by incoming migrants. These migrants often founded new
settlements away from former Roman sites, and excavations at
Maxey in the Welland valley have produced evidence for both
sunken floored buildings and wooden 'halled' structures on a
new site. Air photographs suggest it was set within a landscape of fields and enclosures. Major cemeteries associated with
settlements are known at Woodston (Peterborough), Alwalton,
Gunthorpe (Peterborough) and along the Cambridge Road at
Godmanchester.

Recent work at Orton Waterville, Tilbrook, Stow Longa and
Hilton has shown similar sorts of settlement evidence and suggests that the landscape of the area was scattered with isolated
farms which eventually gave way to increased nucleation by the
later Saxon period. It was these later nucleated settlements,
formed perhaps from the amalgamation and even rationalization
of earlier dispersed farms, that formed the basis for many villages
which were recorded in the Domesday Book.

The situation in the Roman towns at *Durobrivae* and Godmanchester during the C5 and C6 is still very unclear. At Godmanchester stray finds from early Migration Period occupation occur
throughout the town, especially on the site of the *mansio*. An
occupation site of this date was excavated on the eastern side of
the walled area. At *Durobrivae* the situation is less clear because
there has not been any excavation within the walled area of the
town. The whole area of the town was under agriculture by the
medieval period and the development of ridge and furrow caused
by ploughing may have begun as early as the late C9. Stone
robbing at both town sites has been extensive, and stone from
buildings and from the town walls would have been taken to
construct local late Saxon and medieval buildings. At Castor a
nunnery was founded in A.D. 650–675, possibly within the still
standing palatial Roman structure mentioned already, and
Roman walls from this building were observed standing '11 feet
high' in the 1820s. However, much of this structure was robbed
by the C12 and can be seen incorporated into the fabric of the
existing church.

MEDIEVAL CHURCH ARCHITECTURE

Anglo-Saxon and Norman

In the SAXON PERIOD, Peterborough and Huntingdonshire lay
in the SE corner of Mercia on the edge of the East Anglian
kingdom, but the fens was no doubt a disputed border. Peterborough was the settlement called Medehamstede, and Huntingdon
too was a Saxon burh; many of the villages known to us now were
established by the late Saxon period. There is an interesting piece
of evidence for the Christian Saxon period in the rare dedication

of the church at Water Newton to St Remigius, the c5 Bishop of Rheims who is credited with the conversion of Clovis, King of the Franks. Colne has a dedication to St Helen, another early saint in the Roman church.

Among the new RELIGIOUS FOUNDATIONS the Benedictines of course led the way after the foundation of Canterbury. Peterborough Abbey was due to Peada, son of King Penda of Mercia c. 650, and as has been noted above Penda's daughter Kyneburgha is supposed to have founded c. 664 a 'double monastery' at Castor and been its first abbess. Meanwhile Guthlac, a monk at Repton, became a hermit at Crowland on the Fen just across the border in Lincolnshire, and in his memory the Benedictine abbey was founded in the c8. Guthlac's sister Pega (†719) is claimed to have established an anchorite cell at Peakirk.

In the mid c9 the area covered by this volume was overrun by the Danes and incorporated in their territory until they were routed in the early c10. The Benedictine abbey at Peterborough was sacked in 870 but under the supervision of Aethelwold, Bishop of Winchester, was rebuilt and rededicated in 963, like Ely in Cambridgeshire, after new Danish raids. It was given at that time wide transepts and a straight-ended chancel, but of this only a small fragment is to be seen below the floor of the Norman building. Ramsey Abbey was founded afresh just a few years later by Oswald, Bishop of Worcester, and dedicated in 974. It too is said to have had a cruciform plan but with *porticus* on three sides and a w tower. The third of the Anglo-Saxon foundations after Peterborough and Ramsey is Thorney, like Ramsey a gravel island in the watery fenland; the 'ey' of Thorney and Ramsey means island. Like Crowland, Thorney was first home to a community of anchorites that perished in the Danish raid of 870, giving rise to a cult of the 'Thorney Martyrs'. The Benedictine monastery at Thorney was established in 973, again by Aethelwold, with the gift of relics of St Botolph. Again, the Norman rebuilding is all that survives. Foundation of a Benedictine priory at St Neots is also claimed c. 972 but it was rebuilt c. 1081 and of what has been excavated nothing is earlier than the c12. Ramsey from c. 1000 also had a cell at St Ives, then known as Slepe, with the bones of St Ivo, but again there is nothing more than a wall to show for it. Like St Neots and St Ives the other monastic houses were small, and little or nothing of them survives. Hinchingbrooke nunnery (Huntingdon), founded before 1087, of which only traces of the plan and featureless masonry are preserved, was Benedictine. The priory of Huntingdon, possibly a late c10 foundation, was Augustinian by the early c12, as was Stonely. Of the Cistercian Sawtry, founded in 1147, nothing is left above ground, nor is there anything of the only friars' house, the Austin Friars of Huntingdon, which was in the town before 1258. The landholdings of these foundations accounted for the vast proportion of Huntingdonshire and Peterborough. A large estate was held by the Earls of Huntingdon (*see* Conington), lands which descended from Waltheof (†1076) to the Scottish royal family until 1306.

With this discussion, however, we are moving beyond the EARLY ANGLO-SAXON period, which in Peterborough and its villages is best represented by SCULPTURE. At the beginning of the period stands the Hedda Stone in Peterborough Cathedral, dated to the late C8 or early C9. It is carved from a single block of stone with a coped top like a pitched roof, implying a lid over a box but not actually containing a space inside in which to contain bodily remains. The sides are carved with figures of Christ, the Virgin and ten saints, with animals and foliage to the roof. This can be compared with a panel fragment now in the S transept of the Cathedral and also to a panel at Castor carved with a figure probably of St Mark, and the suggestion of a second figure under the same arcading and furthermore with the contemporary pair of saints at Fletton, within the modern city of Peterborough. The technique of the carving, especially the drilling of their eyes and the inward turning stances of the figures who stand on tiptoes, is very characteristic of its date. Also at Fletton are the eminently interesting and in several ways enigmatic bits of a frieze which almost certainly come, along with the figures, from the Saxon abbey at Peterborough. Again, there are the same heads under arcading. What can have been the purpose of the Fletton frieze – and the closely related frieze from the abbey's 'daughter' church at Breedon-on-the-Hill in Leicestershire? The scale is so small that it must have been displayed close to the eye, and the effects also are intimate and miniature. The technique is highly curious, with the scooping out as if into clay and the leaving of thin ridges, a technique in which the negative of flecky space counts almost as much as the positive of tendril, bird and quadruped. There is nothing quite like it, not only in England but also in the Carolingian empire. Altogether it is good evidence for a school or workshop of carvers at Peterborough or one of the other now vanished fenland establishments.

There are a good many CROSSES or fragments of crosses to emphasize the concentration of Anglo-Saxon sculpture within the orbit of Peterborough. Elton and Peakirk have important crosses or cross fragments with interlace and the plant scrolls of the Peakirk cross shows evidence of a response to the new foliage styles well known in Wessex. Castor has a cross-base with interlace, Fletton a cross with some animals, two set in roundels, and Stanground a defaced cross, Maxey also has a cross fragment as well as fragments of late Anglo-Saxon GRAVE COVERS. They reflect the widespread Midland and East Anglian fashion for recumbent covers decorated with panels of simple interlace, and many have also been found at Helpston and Peterborough Cathedral; one now in the crypt below the S transept is a particularly handsome example with a cross and lavish interlace. The date is probably late C10, after the refounding of the abbey by Aethelwold. There is little observable response to Scandinavian art in this period of the Viking occupation from the C9 but at Barnack an Anglo-Scandinavian grave cover has been discovered.

73

LATE ANGLO-SAXON ARCHITECTURE is, compared with the
Continent, backward and provincial rather, and the confidence
that we have that the carvers of Peterborough knew exactly what
they wanted to achieve has no parallel in the buildings, powerful
as their impact may be. One need only remember St Pantaleon
at Cologne, St Michael at Hildesheim, St Mary-in-Capitol at
Cologne, and Jumièges to admit that. The thin pilaster-strip work
of the Barnack tower, with the strips starting without any worry
on the apexes of arches, is a timber-people's misunderstanding
of the properties of stone. The date for the tower may be mid-C10
if the remarkable panels of sculpture set into its walls are to be
our guide. They have stems with curling branches of foliage and,
at the head, birds, whose style is very different from the beasts
encountered in earlier Saxon sculpture. Also at Barnack is one
of the finest pieces of C11 figure carving in England, a seated
Christ. Its softness of modelling and linear style distinguishes it
from C12 work. The demi-figure of Christ blessing at Castor just
might be pre-Conquest but reset in the walls of the Norman
church. The most advanced piece of architecture of that moment
in England is Great Paxton, dated to the mid C11, when it was a
minster church in the possession of Edward the Confessor, for
here the Anglo-Saxon mason built a real crossing such as St
Michael at Hildesheim and Jumièges possessed, i.e. with transepts as wide and as high as nave and chancel, not just *porticus*
or narrower or lower transepts, and moreover he built a nave
separated from aisles by real compound piers, not just chunks of
wall (as at Brixworth, Northants, and Lydd, Kent). They are odd
piers, lacking in logic, but they also possess that sense of mass
which makes the whole church unforgettable. Moreover, the

Barnack, St John the Baptist.
Anglo-Saxon sculpture on tower.

church has always had a raised chancel, with steps that begin with a dais under the crossing. Evidence of the clerestory also remains, but this may be Norman rather than Saxon. Of other pre-Conquest features, all in the Peterborough area, evidence of Anglo-Saxon long-and-short quoins was revealed at Helpston in the C19, Woodston has some little masonry in the tower with a small double-splayed window, Wansford also a single W window, now inside the later tower. Wittering, which must lie on the cusp of or just into the Norman period, represents the two-cell form of C11 churches. It has angles in long-and-short work and the most elementary power of stone is brought out in the massive chancel arch, an informative contrast to the post-Conquest sculpture of the arcade.

So to the NORMAN STYLE and the beginning of a major development in church architecture. Here of course Peterborough Cathedral, or rather the Benedictine abbey of Peterborough, must take precedence over anything else, for it has one of the most complete C12 interiors of all the English cathedrals. The Saxon church was destroyed by fire in 1116, and so the present cathedral has nothing above ground earlier than that date. A rare survival is the choir with its wide apse, accompanied by the side apses of the choir aisles, which ended externally in straight walls. The transepts also have aisles, as at Ely. This was built between 1118 and c. 1150, the nave and aisles in the second half of the C12. The style is therefore High and Late, not Early, Norman. The chevron as a decorative enrichment, for example, appears from the outset. So does the motif of alternating circular and polygonal piers, a motif found also at Ely and accepted widely only in the late C12 and early C13. Especially precocious is the use of chevron at right angles to the wall surface, which begins at Peterborough c. 1130 or 1135 at the latest, although it is as a rule a sign of Late Norman date. The capitals on the other hand still have heavy scallops at first, and the arches heavy roll mouldings. The system of elevation is that almost universally adopted in Anglo-Norman major architecture: arcade, spacious gallery, clerestory with inner wall-passage, flat ceiling. The ensemble is tall, forceful and consistent.

At Thorney all that survives is part of the nave deprived of its aisles. It is somewhat earlier than Peterborough. The church was begun, at the missing E end, no doubt, c. 1085, and the nave must have been started ten years later at the latest. It was completed in 1108, though consecration only took place ten years after Peterborough was begun. The system at Thorney is arcades with alternating supports again, but mast-like shafts, just as at Ely, running up to the ceiling in front of every support. The gallery, as against those of Peterborough and Ely, was unsubdivided. Capitals are mostly scalloped, but there are some also of the primitive volute type characteristic of Early Norman. The W front is preserved too, though much chopped about. The Norman evidence makes it likely that Thorney had three giant niches like Lincoln. At Ramsey nothing remains of before 1180, and what does remain will concern us a little later.

The most important Norman work is at Castor, and that brings us to the subject of NORMAN PARISH CHURCHES. Castor, W of Peterborough along the Nene, was, as has already been mentioned, the site of both a Roman palace and traditionally a major Saxon nunnery. The church has perhaps some Saxon fragments but it is predominantly a grand Norman rebuilding which can be dated by the unique survival of the dedication inscription. Castor is a cruciform with a spectacular crossing tower, including the characteristic Norman style of two-arched openings and of course came at the end of operations. That would be *c.* 1120, as the dedication date appears to be 1124, but readings also suggest 1104 or 1114, and significantly the sculptural detail is very different from that at Peterborough. It is gay, with ornamental fancies and entertaining figural capitals to the arches of the crossing. But no one would call them great art, such as are the capitals, say, of the Moissac cloister. Their detail is thanks probably to a Castor workshop, who probably worked at Maxey too, another large church with tower, again with two-light openings, aisled nave and chancel, and with chevron on the tower arch. Bury evidently had a nave of notable length and in the chancel arch has thick rolls. By their sculpture the chancel arches at Haddon, Morborne, Stibbington and Sutton can be assigned to the early C12, and all exhibit features indicating connections with the Castor workshop. An alternative to the style of chancel arch with carved capitals and fat rolls is the square pier with angle shaft. It appears in Offord Darcy N arcade, Little Paxton and Southoe, three churches within a short distance of each other. The latter has a particularly elaborate S door, crowded with a repertoire of Norman motifs. As regards Norman tympana in Peterborough and Huntingdonshire, where they do not confine themselves to geometric all-over ornament (Bury, Folksworth, Peakirk, Southoe, Stibbington, Wistow) they are outright barbaric. This is less true of the affronted quadrupeds of Covington, as of the incredible mermaid and quadrupeds of Stow Longa and the Christ, the animals and the cross of Little Paxton. Among the most interesting Norman doorway motifs (not at Southoe) is what goes under the name beakhead. It appears just once in the county, in a reset fragment at Little Stukeley. But there and also at Spaldwick and at Toseland is a stylized version of it in which head and beak have become unrecognizable. Another decorative motif, and one of even greater interest, is the lion at Sutton which once carried a colonnette. That is an Italian motif entirely, but it did occur in England originally on the Prior's Door at Ely.

Other sculptural Norman work worth inclusion here is the bronze door knocker at Warboys and the font at Wansford – one of very many of less interest – with the Baptism of Christ, two knights fighting etc. There is no complete Norman tower in Huntingdonshire and Peterborough, and at least three churches, all in the former Soke of Peterborough, have or had bellcotes instead (Werrington, Northborough, Peakirk and – C13 – Sutton). As for arcades, there are plenty of them, all Late Norman, when churches were being expanded from the aisleless Saxon and Early

Norman forms, and often on the verge of E.E. The typical Norman form such as it survives e.g. at Eynesbury has round piers with square multi-scalloped capitals, square abaci and round arches. In several places the abaci have nicks at the angles.

Early English to Perp churches

The various forms the transition to the EARLY ENGLISH STYLE can take have been described in the introduction to Bedfordshire on p. 19. In Huntingdonshire the paradigm of the way into Early English is the church at Ramsey, but this began not as a church but as the hospitium – a hostel for guests – outside the gates of Ramsey Abbey. It is eight bays long plus the chancel. Founded *c.* 1180 and built rapidly till *c.* 1190, it is late C12 architecture at its most monumental. The chancel is heavily rib-vaulted and still fully Norman. The nave arcades demonstrate the precise moment of transition from Norman to E.E. The piers have a glorious variety of shapes, the capitals exhibit waterleaf and again even crockets, and the arches are pointed. It became the parish church only in the C13. The Hospital of St John at Huntingdon, now the Cromwell Museum and formerly the Grammar School, right in the middle of the town, is also Late Norman. The length was also seven bays and a chancel. The details of the two remaining bays, piers and arches, are just like those of a parish church. Among the PARISH CHURCHES in this period of transition, the N arcade at Barnack is much the most rewarding in having round arches with chevron on slender piers but also crockets on the capitals, and in the S arcade appears stiff-leaf. Upton (P) also has not only crockets but on the arcade responds what appears to be a very early form of stiff-leaf, with leaves of thin stems against the bell of the capital. Tilbrook on the border with Bedfordshire ably demonstrates the change to the pointed arch, still very thick with only a slight chamfer. The most characteristic motif of this transition is the waterleaf capital noted above, which at Alwalton, for example, identifies the extension of the late C12 arcade at the time of the building of the C13 tower. Another regularly found motif is dogtooth, which appears in abundance in the W front of Peterborough Cathedral, where conclusion of the whole confused story of the W extension of the Norman building falls into the years between *c.* 1180 and the consecration of 1238. If the layman's vision of the C13 is that of the climax of medieval nobility and harmony, a glance at the Peterborough façade is sufficient to impress him with the degree of discordance which this great Gothic century was ready to accept, at least in England. Perhaps the highest beauty of the façade is the twin portal with the trumeau – to use the French word – and the relief both agitated and nobly carved. It is carved in Alwalton marble, a material also found in small instances of decoration at Castor. At the W end of Peterborough is also the first proper instance of stiff-leaf foliage in the capitals of the shafts, developing in maturity over time from the spindly stems of the foliage inside the W front to the lusher work of the exterior. At Ramsey Abbey, which had about eighty monks in the C12 and C13, there is the remarkable survival of what was most probably the chapter house of the claustral buildings. It must date from *c.* 1240–50 and has pointed-trefoiled, deeply moulded arcading (cf. Westminster Abbey in the same years) and mature stiff-leaf capitals. Before the Black Death the monastery at Peterborough had about sixty to sixty-five monks. Of their quarters much survives, and in particular the refectory, of *c.* 1233–45, with even finer trefoil-headed arcading than Ramsey, and the infirmary, *c.* 1250–63, whose slender piers with a square core and semicircular projections are the classic mid-C13 type found spreading into the church.

The C13 was an increasingly prosperous time for Huntingdonshire and Peterborough and the religious foundations were generous patrons. Of complete Early English churches the best is probably Etton, with a fully developed plan of chancel, aisled nave and W tower. It has an E.E. spire too, and one of the earliest in the county. The earliest of all, and one of the earliest in England, is Barnack, where there is also a porch of the very beginning of the century, with the same blank arcading as found in the Peterborough refectory (Barnack was held by the monastery). The porch is vaulted, and vaulting in England was still an exception at that time, not only in parish churches. It remains noteworthy that even Peterborough Cathedral was satisfied *c.* 1220 with a wooden nave ceiling, however memorable in its lozenge-pattern, though it is clear that vaulting was the first intention. It is one of the most important medieval ceilings in Europe. As for the spires, that at Barnack has low broaches with big pinnacles set on them, that at Etton also low broaches, and so has Warboys, another E.E. spire, but the E.E. Buckworth and Alconbury have high broaches. So the two types developed side by side. A speciality of the county is extremely long lancets in towers. They are to be seen at Bury, Warboys, Chesterton and (bell-openings) Alconbury. Warboys and Alconbury are also predominantly E.E. The chancel at Alconbury remains in one's memory for the noble, close-set shafting up the N and S walls enclosing the windows, a feature that seems to be associated with churches which, like Alconbury, were held by Ramsey Abbey. The same was done with plain giant arches of continuous mouldings at Brampton, Great Gidding and Molesworth. The last-named is mid-C13, the two former late C13. The motif goes on in the Perp churches of Abbots Ripton and Bluntisham. The best all-round E.E. church in Huntingdonshire is Leighton Bromswold, now cruciform, though originally with narrow aisles, beautifully proportioned and puritan in its bare surfaces, even before the C17 started its sympathetic remodelling. One late C13 church is datable with some probability: Yaxley, where an interesting and moving heart-burial monument is likely to record an abbot of Thorney called William de Yaxley who died in 1293. The late C13 windows at Yaxley of stepped lancet lights and stepped lancet lights under one super-arch have a parallel about twenty-five years earlier in the transepts of Peterborough. Another motif appearing at that time is windows or arches which are pointed-trefoiled. You find them at Longthorpe (Peterborough), where the start of building was in 1263–4.

The transition from E.E. to the DECORATED STYLE is fluid. In tracery it lies where the ogee arch comes in. Thus e.g. W towers in the later C13 had here and there in addition to normal windows and bell-openings intermediate windows of a more decorative kind. They are quatrefoil at Orton Longueville, trefoiled-circular at Stanground, quatrefoiled-circular at Alconbury, sexfoiled-circular with the foils enterprisingly cusped at Buckworth, but of lozenge-shape with flowing, i.e. ogee, tracery at Spaldwick and Keyston. The Keyston tower, moreover, has the distinguishing feature of a recessed W porch. Dec windows in the county are unusually often straight-headed, and straight-headed are even three windows of c. 1300 – i.e. pre-Dec – at Hemingford Abbots. Intersecting tracery is a very late C13 or early C14 motif and the more typically Dec reticulated tracery is found at Becket's Chapel, in the close at Peterborough, and not far away at Orton Longueville. At Peterborough Cathedral, the Dec contribution is easily overlooked, but it is there in the E end of the choir, both in the windows with segmental heads and inside in the arches between choir and retrochoir. There are two key motifs in the Dec phase. One is ballflower, and at its most elaborate this is developed into a trail of a long stem linking the ballflower, as found at Offord Darcy and Keyston, and across the border in Bedfordshire at Swineshead. The other is a simple curved moulding which one finds in use as a stop for hoodmoulds, for corbels and for arches etc. This is very regularly used and seems to start c. 1300. To pier shapes applies what has been said in the Bedfordshire Introduction on pp. 20–21. The most usual section is octagonal, the most usual arch-shape double-chamfered. This is what in the gazetteer is termed 'standard elements'. At Northborough a big rebuilding was begun in the mid C14 by the Bishop of Lichfield, and here is found the quatrefoil pier type which one associates with the period, and the S transept S window has fascinating flowing tracery. Another major example of flowing tracery is the E window of Yaxley. Bluntisham is remarkable for its polygonal apse – a great rarity in England. We have no date for it, and dates are indeed rare for the C14. The proud chancel of Fenstanton with its flowing tracery was provided by the man who was rector from 1345 to 1352, the chancel of Wistow was consecrated in 1347, and the N chapel at Maxey was started in 1367. Fenstanton and Wistow are Dec, Maxey is the earliest datable Perp.

The corollary of the richer ornamentation in the C14 is the fine detailed carving given to niches for statues etc., especially good the niches in the transept chapel at Northborough. There are not many C13 and early C14 CHURCH FITTINGS and FURNISHINGS, but they are nearly all worthwhile: the only spectacular piece of equipment is the double piscina with a round arch intersected by two half-arches in such a way that not only the arches but the very mouldings are interwoven. The same motif exists at

Hemingford Grey and St Ives, and also in Jesus College and St John's College, Cambridge, at Histon, and in four other places in Cambridgeshire, and moreover in Herts., Norfolk and Essex. In the cathedral is a type of mid to late C13 double piscina with Y-tracery and trilobes pierced through the spandrels. The same design occurs close by at Stanground. Another at Morborne has simply three recesses over its arch. There are numerous other more conventional piscinas, indicative of an elaboration in the liturgy of the C13 churches, and becoming decoratively more elaborate with the turn into the early C14, often occurring in aisles added as chantry chapels. There are pretty angle piscinas at Offord Darcy and Tilbrook. Other furnishings and fittings of this period include the minor iron scrollwork on doors, e.g. Great Paxton, at Orton Longueville and Wistow (the ironwork at Covington is much earlier, dated to the early C12), the stone seat or throne at Farcet, the Barnack font with pointed-trefoiled arches and leaf decoration, the beautiful stall fragment of c. 1233–45 at Peterborough Cathedral, the two lecterns at Peakirk and Bury, both early C14, and the latter outstanding, the Dec screen at Offord Darcy, the Dec screen and the Dec doors at Brampton (now alas much damaged) and Castor.

Among WALL PAINTINGS the simplest kind is found at Peterborough in the presbytery aisles where there are traces of painting to resemble masonry, quite a familiar C13 technique found also on the W front and on a door at Broughton, where the painters have also attempted to simulate marble. Pictorial cycles occur in several churches; many were discovered in 1848 in the Peterborough churches and unfortunately have faded considerably, but at Castor it is still easy to discern the scenes from the life and martyrdom of St Catherine, who also occurs at Old Weston. The later, much more extensive paintings at Peakirk, with a cycle depicting the Passion, were also uncovered in 1848 but only fully revealed in the 1940s. They are in two tiers like cartoon strips and included among the themes represented is the Three Quick and the Three Dead, which also appeared as part of the late C13 scheme of painting at Yaxley that has sadly all but vanished. There is an interesting fragment at Etton of a Jesse tree, its style clearly influenced by the early C14 Peterborough Psalter, one of the illuminated manuscripts which also supply the source for the painted decoration of the ceiling at Peterborough Cathedral, and see also Longthorpe Tower, below. For C15 wall paintings also see below.

If one wants to understand the development of the FUNERARY EFFIGY from c. 1195 to c. 1225 the abbots' monuments inside the cathedral are a most instructive series. They are of the local Alwalton 'marble', and other effigies of the same materials and the same and the following decades are in Huntingdonshire; an abbot (upper part only) at Great Staughton and the outstanding so-called Aylwin in the abbey gatehouse at Ramsey, both mid-C13. It is still being used in the Franciscan tertiary of c. 1300 at Conington, sensitively characterized and carved. It is also used in the font at Peterborough Cathedral. Of local stone is the priest at Morborne whose feet are supported by two human heads. There are other MONUMENTS of these years – late C13 to early C14 – but they need no individual singling out. The cross-legged knight is a typical late C13 type and there are examples at Barnack and, the best perhaps, at Orton Longueville (Peterborough). What are very much more common are C13 COFFIN LIDS, including some unusual examples, e.g. the priests' monuments at Castor and Southoe and one now in the grounds of Walcot Hall in which the heads show at the top, the feet at the bottom as if under a blanket. More common are those with crosses, especially in the stone areas; though they are rarely noted in the following gazetteer the collection at Barnack is predictably large. One at St Neots has a foliated cross growing out of a dog and has its parallel at Oakley and Pavenham in Bedfordshire. The standard type, however, is a cross adorned with omega or double-omega symbols as found in the Cathedral retrochoir but in many other places besides. With these scrolls one can compare the stone ornament in the tympanum of the mid-C13 chancel window at Haddon, and to this one might append the small incised rose-window-like mass dial in Godmanchester church. In Peterborough Cathedral is the indent of a large brass to an abbot who died in 1321. The uncommonly large indent in the slab to a priest at Great Gransden is of *c.* 1330 and a reminder that brass as a new material had now arrived.

As has been noted already, SPIRES were already a feature of the grandest churches before 1300, and the evident prosperity of the early to mid C14 continues the practice (e.g. the addition of the spire at Castor). The total of over forty has already been referred to. They occur pretty evenly throughout the county, and apart from broach spires (with low or high broaches) there is the type of the spire recessed behind the battlements or parapet of the tower, such as Bluntisham. Of the latter there are nine, one of them with the little flying buttresses connecting it with the tower pinnacles. A few of the broach spires are recessed as well. A specially fine group of early to mid-C14 spires is W of Huntingdon, with Catworth, Easton, Ellington, Spaldwick and Great Gidding all sharing features in common, and a number of them falling within the Bishop of Lincoln's Soke of Spaldwick. The tower of Houghton turns octagonal for a short top bit before starting on the spire, and Grafham and Old Weston have a similar though more compromising arrangement.

The beginning of the PERPENDICULAR STYLE proper in the C15 and early C16 is marked by the preference for the blunt, straight end of a tower, and we may just as well begin the account of this phase with the monumental W towers of St John at Peterborough of 1402–7, with polygonal buttresses and four-light bell-openings, Buckden of *c.* 1430–40, Eaton Socon, Elton, Glatton, Great Staughton, St Mary at Huntingdon, St Ives, and so to St Neots of *c.* 1490–1535 and Conington of *c.* 1500. These towers mostly have decorative quatrefoil friezes, and St Neots, Great Staughton and quite a few others (e.g. Buckden, Eaton Socon) have pairs of transomed two-light bell-openings. St Mary at

Huntingdon is specially ornate, but not high. It seems of before 1400. Conington, like St John at Peterborough, has polygonal buttresses and four-light bell-openings. Several of the others have clasping buttresses. Abbotsley is an unusual tower in having, instead of pinnacles, statues of kings. With these towers most of the leading Perp churches have been named. But a good deal still needs filling in.

90   St Neots is a complete major Perp church. When the tower was begun, the rest of the church was complete. The character is uniform and solid. The piers are of the section with four shafts and four hollows in the diagonals which will, in the gazetteer, be called the 'standard moulded section'. A key change in the parish churches of the Perp phase is the addition of clerestories and, associated with this, the replacement of ROOFS. Grafham has probably the earliest type of roof, with collars to the rafters, but the Perp type by far most frequent in Huntingdonshire and Peterborough is of very low pitch with tie-beams on shallow arched braces and with bosses at the intersection of principals with ridge beam and purlins. There are also often figures of angels against the intermediate principals and other figures against the wall-posts. The best roofs of this type include Conington, Kimbolton and, superior to all, the roof of St Neots. Angel roofs are less common than in East Anglia but there are still a good many examples, of which Castor and Hemingford Abbots are perhaps the best. As for piers, the most interesting ones are those – and there are about ten of them in the county – which have shafts with capitals only to the arch openings but more or less complicated continuous mouldings to nave and

91   aisle. Such was done e.g. at Conington, Godmanchester, Great Gransden, Wistow and Yaxley. VAULTING in parish churches was confined to towers, as remains at St Ives and was intended at Great Stukeley, and to porches (Buckden, for example). Indeed Buckden is one of a number of Hunts. churches with distinguished two-storey porches, e.g. Godmanchester, and one should not forget the exquisite Perp porch slotted between the piers of the central arch of Peterborough Cathedral's W front. So the one

93   major Perp stone vault in the county is the sumptuous retrochoir of Peterborough. The vault is a fan-vault, and it may have been designed by *John Wastell*, who designed the fan-vaults of King's College Chapel at Cambridge.

Finally the NW tower of All Saints at Huntingdon, the W tower and S porch of Diddington, and the NW tower and clerestory of Southoe are of brick, the first C15, the other two of *c.* 1530. At Stilton the tower arch is a short tunnel-vault, Hail Weston has an impressive timber-framed W tower of the type famous in Essex, Bury a mysterious W addition to the W tower, probably a chapel. It had a tunnel-vaulted undercroft.

In some counties it is easy to lay one's finger on the very places where Italian Renaissance forms first appeared. Not so in Huntingdonshire or Peterborough. Take CHURCH FURNISHINGS for the C15 and early C16. The eagle lectern at Little Gidding is of brass, made in East Anglia, and of a type famous on the

Continent. The wooden lectern at Ramsey has a stem of four buttress-like members set crosswise. STAINED GLASS has nothing much to offer: a complete window at Wistow and a window looking more complete than it is at Diddington. Of WALL PAINTINGS the best (or the most easily recognizable) is the St Christopher at Orton Longueville, and there is a St Christopher also at Molesworth, with fish and eels swimming around his feet. He also overlays the earlier work at Peakirk and as everywhere else is placed facing the entrance from the S. The Molesworth painting is doubly interesting for the clues it gives to the style of timber-framing in late medieval houses. There are other paintings at Haddon and Morborne, but by far the most impressive is the scheme at Broughton, of the late C15. This is a largely complete Doom, and here one can appreciate the integrated relationship of carving on the roof to painted decoration. That brings us back to WOODWORK. The best set of STALLS with misericords is unquestionably at Godmanchester, reputedly from Ramsey Abbey but just as likely to have been made for the church in the late C15. The best individual pieces are the three mid-C14 ones at Brampton. The examples at St Neots come from the church at Milton Ernest, Beds. The best set of BENCHES with poppyheads is at Glatton, at Ufford also rather stylized poppyheads, and another good set at Eynesbury, where in addition there is much excellent carving of animals of a style that goes with the carvings of the church roof at neighbouring St Neots. Diddington also has a very good set of c. 1500. ROOD SCREENS are on the whole uneventful and do not survive in any quantity. The best is, again unquestionably, that at Tilbrook with its well-preserved ribbed coving. St Neots has pretty openwork vine scrolls over the entrance. At Great Paxton the screen has been defaced but evidently had a figure of the Virgin with rays carved around her. Kimbolton has PARCLOSE SCREENS in both aisles, and one has painted figures on the dado which, in their mannered elegance, are much above average. At Catworth the rood screen, of three-light divisions, is accompanied by a PULPIT with tracery on the sides. The pulpit at Fenstanton introduces linenfold panels. Linenfold is a motif of the earlier C15 to early C16, and on the Farcet pulpit it appears side by side with Early Renaissance. So there we have arrived, but we do not know at what date.

Among MONUMENTS there is nothing in Huntingdon and Peterborough like the wooden effigies of the late C13 and early C14 in Northamptonshire. The only wooden piece, and a very striking one, is the C15 cadaver at Keyston, part of a monument no doubt such as that of Bishop Fleming at Lincoln. At Marholm is the fine reclining effigy of a knight, carved from clunch, probably c. 1400. The earliest surviving brasses in the county are also of c. 1400 (Tilbrook, Sawtry). The style of monument most common in the late C15 and early C16 has a tomb-chest with a recess under a canopy. Examples are at Barnack and Marholm and at Diddington, the latter also with a fine brass of 1505.

92

MAJOR MEDIEVAL SECULAR BUILDINGS

67   The medieval BRIDGES at Huntingdon and St Ives on the Ouse
66   and Wansford on the Nene all deserve mention as some of the
best of their kind in England, and St Ives possesses one of the
very few surviving bridge chapels in England (the altar was dedicated in 1426). There are a few MOTTES or other earthworks
associated with Norman castles. One survives in the grounds of
the cathedral at Peterborough, thought to have been built by the
Norman abbot Thorold, and another beside Ramsey Abbey.
The castle at Huntingdon was built in 1068 on the orders of the
Conqueror and the burgh repaired. It was the beginning of Huntingdon's medieval pre-eminence. Like other examples, Huntingdon Castle was located close to the Ouse, like the Hillings at
Eaton Socon and a motte at Hartford. Another is at Wood Walton
and one at Helpston too, associated with Torpel manor, one of
the few manors in the Soke of Peterborough that were released
by the Abbot. The earthwork of the first castle of Kimbolton can
still be seen on the low hillside W of the later medieval town,
where in King John's reign was placed the new castle on the site
of the present one. The only truly castle-like building, however,
is late C13 or early C14: the fragment of Woodcroft Castle with
round towers and a moat to defend it. In the woods at Helpston
are also the remains of a hunting lodge associated with the castle
there. Huntingdonshire and Peterborough have large numbers of
moated sites as further evidence of houses that required some
form of protection until a late date. Indeed, Huntingdonshire and
Peterborough have some DOMESTIC BUILDINGS of more than
local interest, foremost the late C12 upper hall of Hemingford
Grey Manor House with its twin windows. At Longthorpe Tower
a hall also exists but attached to a more conventional hall house.
85   It dates from the late C13, and the tower with the frescoes was
added probably for Robert Thorpe, Steward of Peterborough
Abbey 1310–29. It is rib-vaulted on two floors, containing a
chamber on the first floor which could be reached only from
within. The paintings at Longthorpe Tower are perhaps the most
interesting domestic scheme of their date, *c.* 1330, in the country.
They were only discovered after the Second World War and
have therefore been neither over-restored nor neglected. They
give the most vivid impression of civilized life in a manor house
and overlap in their moral themes with much church work but
supplement with others of a strictly secular or decorative
character.

The estate of Peterborough Abbey was already extensive by the
time of the Conquest and gifts of land were confirmed upon it
by the Conqueror. Some of the earliest surviving domestic buildings are connected with it and include of course the Abbot's
House which now forms the core of the Bishop's Palace, containing the C13 rib-vaulted undercroft of its solar and an earlier
chapel. It is protected by the mighty Outer Gate, again C13. In

the outer precinct are other early buildings, including the C13 hall of the Prior's Lodging, though much is concealed behind later remodelling, e.g. the C12 vaulted room in the so-called King's Lodgings on the S side of the outer precinct.

A series of granges were built on the fen edge between Peterborough, Eye and the Lincolnshire border. Oxney was built for the Prior of Peterborough and although remodelled in the mid C19 there are significant remains of rib-vaulting within. Nearby Eyebury was developed as a possession of the Abbot of Bury St Edmunds in the early C13, while Northolm belonged to the Abbot of Crowland. All seem to have doubled as farmhouses-cum-temporary retreats and the same is true of Bodsey House, on the fen near Ramsey, which was a rest house for the monks of Ramsey Abbey. There the C14 chapel survives, and traces of the C13 in the domestic quarters N of the chapel. The chapel has no features of special interest, and much of the house was remodelled after the Dissolution (*see* below). But Northborough Manor House, built for the Bishop of Lichfield *c.* 1320–40 with its gatehouse and its hall is a very significant survival and hardly altered at all. The hall has tall windows with reticulated tracery, and still the three doors inside which led to buttery, kitchen and pantry. Nothing survives of the residence built by the Bishop of Lincoln at Spaldwick, from where was administered the Soke of Spaldwick, W of Huntingdon. Buckden was a possession of the Bishop of Lincoln by the C11 but became his permanent residence by the late C12. It is now predominantly of C15 and C16 date and the finest by far of the late medieval secular buildings. What remains was built *c.* 1475–90. It is the gatehouse, a piece of curtain wall, and the so-called Great Tower, a keep, one is tempted to say, built for living, though a great hall and other domestic quarters are known from excavations to have existed. The Great Tower was apparently built on the pattern of that, some thirty years earlier, of Tattershall in Lincolnshire. The red brick is used with dark blue vitrified bricks in diapers and more elaborately ornamental patterns. But what there is at Buckden is serviceable rather than splendid. One need only compare it with the abbey gatehouse of Ramsey, now partly at Hinchingbrooke, to remember how sumptuous Perp display *c.* 1500 could be. Yet another gatehouse, much simpler and still machicolated, is at Elton, where also the rib-vaulted undercroft of the chapel remains, in the same range, i.e. not the hall-range, of the house. Coming right at the end of the medieval phase is the building called 'Heaven's Gate' at the Bishop's Palace in Peterborough, which is dated by a rebus to the rule of Abbot Kirkton who built the retrochoir. It has two oriels with fine Late Perp panelling. Similarly good Perp decoration to the gate of the Prior's Lodging, again of Kirkton's time. By the 1520s, the castle at Kimbolton where Katherine of Aragon spent her last days seems to have evolved into a large courtyard plan, but the traces of this are minimal following the late C17 and early C18 reworking.

86

94

95

SMALLER HOUSES: MEDIEVAL TO THE LATE SEVENTEENTH CENTURY
BY BETH DAVIS

The three regions of Huntingdonshire and Peterborough, the limestone north, the Ouse valley and the western uplands or wolds are represented by characteristic changes in the vernacular building traditions, brought about by economic conditions and sources of materials. The quality of materials, plans and details reflects the status of the owners from large farms to small cottages. Very few cottages remain from before 1700 but in the C17 Hearth Tax returns there are records of cottages and town houses with one hearth and references to pauper housing. Further evidence of simple medieval buildings has been found through excavation. More would have survived in Huntingdonshire had there not been a policy in the postwar period to demolish, rather than rescue and repair, many cottages and farmhouses, many of which had been divided for labourers' cottages after the C18 enclosures.

The usual domestic PLAN is of an OPEN HALL with service room(s) and parlour in line with the hall and with a cross entry or cross-passage sited at the high or low end of the hall. This was commonplace throughout the medieval period. The details could vary from the simplest single-storey plan to a hall flanked by a two-storey end or with one or two cross-wings. Northborough Manor, referred to in the preceding pages, is the very best representation of this plan type at the highest status, but No. 7 Station Road, Barnack, is also probably C14 and comprises a small hall with parlour and solar above, lit originally by two-light windows.

These buildings belong to the stone area of Peterborough, where the majority of smaller houses are post-medieval. In the cathedral precincts is Table Hall, a timber-framed and jettied building dated to the later C15. Another jettied building survives in Cumbergate but otherwise medieval timber-framing is absent in the domestic buildings of the former Soke. In Huntingdonshire by contrast the majority of surviving medieval buildings at the vernacular level are TIMBER-FRAMED. Good stands of oak for timber grew in Huntingdonshire in the ancient forest areas of the northern and southern wolds but also in the richer parishes of the Ouse valley, and the former fen edge of the NE. In the N and NW of the county, stone predominates, but this may have only been in common use from the mid to late C16, perhaps replacing timber-framed buildings. Timber from the woodlands of Huntingdonshire's great forests was used in Ely Cathedral in the C14 and King's College Chapel, Cambridge, in the C16. The buildings in the former Ramsey Abbey manors show clearly the division between the substantially built timber-framed cottages and farmhouses, the 'rentals' of Ramsey Abbey (*Garsumarum*), and those built after the Dissolution when timber became scarce.

Methods and quality of timber-framing vary across Huntingdonshire. There are no examples of cruck framing known in the area; buildings were instead BOX-FRAMED, i.e. framed in bays using jowled posts and tie-beams of oak with exposed close-studded walls with internal or external tension braces, infilled with panels of wattle and daub. Curved braces to the internal open and display trusses are found from the C14, with wide, curved, tension braces to the closed trusses of the wall frame. Arch-braced trusses are rare, but an example survives in the Old Barn, Upwood. Several good late medieval examples are found in Abbots Ripton and Wennington, both of which villages belonged to Ramsey Abbey.

AISLED HALLS are unknown in Peterborough (but the demolished C12 manor house at Buckden was a high-status example) and rare in Huntingdonshire, only represented by Rectory Farm Cottage, Abbots Ripton, and Weavers (a.k.a. Weepers) Cottage, Wennington. At Moynes Hall, Holywell, there is the enigmatic survival of three late C13/early C14 posts reused in an outbuilding, perhaps taken from the aisled hall of Berenger le Moyne; they were earth-fast posts, a rare survival of the earliest form of aisled hall construction. Priory Cottage, Stonely, is interesting in that it was constructed around the three bays of the Priory's C14 aisled barn. In larger farmhouses and cottages cross-wings were added to the hall range with rooms above the parlour or service rooms, a solar or winter parlour: a good example is The Gables, High Street, Ramsey. The WEALDEN type of open hall is uncommon but was found, much altered, in Nos. 4–8, High Street, Kimbolton. Poet Rowe's House, Glatton, is the one visible example of the type, but it originated in Little Barford in Bedfordshire, where a larger number of Wealden houses are known.

Medieval TOWN HOUSES sited on ancient burgage plots are rare. In some examples the open hall lies behind a gabled street range, which was often jettied to the street; La Côte d'Or in Kimbolton's High Street is an altered example dating from c. 1300. It had a side passage for the entrance, while other town houses set out along the street – which was the usual arrangement in Ramsey – have an additional service cross-passage: Hatton House, Godmanchester, is an example of such a plan continuing into the post-medieval period.

Medieval ROOFS were partly or completely carpentered in bays. They develop from trusses with passing braces in aisled buildings to transitional buildings with crown-post roofs in the C14, an example of which is the late C14 handed pair of open halls at No. 83 High Street, Ramsey. Arch braces and windbraces, with the principal rafters in line with the tie-beam, formed trusses. Collar-rafter roofs in thatched cottages and some farmhouses can also be simple poles of hedgerow timber. Sometimes, as at The Old Manor House, Brington, there is a distinction between the carpentered roof truss and the thatcher's hedgerow-timbered roof. The side-purlin roof with windbraces developed early in the C15 and became the butt-purlin roof of the C17. The timber scantling of roofs for stone slates was considerably heavier, the roof pitches lower than for roofs with clay plain tiles or thatch; they significantly had ridge pieces.

The hierarchy of roofing materials depended on the status of the building. THATCH of reed and longstraw with sedge was an easily available material; clay TILES were produced from the C13; but Collyweston STONE SLATES were reserved for prestigious buildings until the C17.

From the late C16 there is evidence in Huntingdonshire of the 'Great Rebuilding' and many more houses at the vernacular level survive from this period. Accompanying these changes, houses were rebuilt or altered with accommodation for an increasing population. The villages in the limestone areas of north Huntingdonshire and Peterborough favoured a total rebuilding. Elton is a good example. The houses are limestone rubble with freestone quoins, and some have mullioned and occasionally transomed masonry windows, stone slate roofs with swept valleys to dormer windows. A few have 'Stamford' façade dormers, i.e. a gable or dormer on kneelers or topping a canted bay. Examples are commonly found in Stamford (Lincolnshire), and at Littlefield in Barnack there is an example taken from a house in Stamford in the early C20. Two houses in Helpston also have it, and at the Bell Inn in Stilton it is two-storeyed with an attic.

Where adaptation rather than rebuilding was taking place, CHIMNEYS replaced open hearths. Their introduction often coincides with the decision to floor over an existing hall or to build anew to a two-storey plan. While the plans of new cottages and farmhouses in Huntingdonshire of this period remain conservative, repeating the focus on the hall, an internal chimneystack is often inserted into the area previously occupied by the cross-passage and designed to serve both hall and service rooms. The effect is to create the familiar lobby to the main entrance, leaving a recess on the opposite side of the chimney for the staircase. This lobby-entry plan continued well into the C18. Alternatively the chimney might be built against the wall between the hall and parlour, leaving the cross-passage free, or against the cross-passage itself (the so-called hearth-passage plan). Examples of smaller buildings with inserted timber-framed chimneys with a simple masonry fire-back or fire-wall are at Ellington (Crooked Billet) and Upwood (No. 67 High Street), and others have been found in Abbots Ripton and Stow Longa. There is a single-room planned cottage in Great Gransden (Marley's Cottage) too small for an internal stack so the chimney was built externally against the gable wall in the C17. There are dated brick chimneystacks particularly in Wistow and Holywell. In rural areas timber-framed stacks of some sophistication were constructed as back-to-back chimneys: a good example still in use is Highway Farmhouse, Great Staughton. Stone chimneys in the open halls of larger houses are an exception: the mid-C16 Old Manor House, Brington, is a good example. More frequently side stacks were added to the hall and parlour, as seen at Rippington Manor, Great Gransden; the George & Dragon, Houghton, and the Manor House, Tilbrook. There are side stacks also in Elton village, but they are uncommon. Late C17 and early C17 stacks sometimes have brick octagonal or diagonal shafts set independently or co-joined in display, changing style within one building, as at Manor Farm, Alconbury, or The Limes, Spaldwick. At Manor House, Hamerton, the chimneys make a particular fine display with terracotta decoration, and there are similarly fine chimneys at the Old Rectory, Paston (Peterborough). In the villages of the limestone area, the ashlar chimneystacks of the C17 typically have square or rectangular shafts with cornices, a style that continues into the C18 (e.g. Castor House, Castor, and houses at Elton).

Some houses were enlarged during this period by the addition of a kitchen wing or were newly built with one incorporated from the beginning. In such houses the large chimney usually occupied a gable-end position: a good example is London Road Farm, Godmanchester. Smaller buildings had outshuts along the rear wall for service rooms, the dairy, pantry and buttery, e.g. Manor Farmhouse, Spaldwick. At both Tudor House and The Gables, Earning Street, Godmanchester, dated 1601–c. 1630, the former open hall was replaced with two-storey and attic hall ranges where the first-floor rooms were well lit by oriel windows and the attic rooms were formed under multi-gabled roofs. These farmhouses had kitchen wings and two staircases that divided the house and family rooms from the service rooms. A similar arrangement seems to have existed at Town Farmhouse, Old Weston, which is also one of three houses in Huntingdonshire to contain bedchambers with barrel-vaulted ceilings (cf. Bodsey House, Ramsey Forty Foot, and Midloe Grange, Southoe).

STAIR-TURRETS and porches were added to several buildings, e.g. Porch Farmhouse, Godmanchester. Early JETTIES to timber-framed buildings were confined to cross-wings and have exposed bull-nose ends to the floor joists. Long jetties, introduced in the early C16 when chambers were built over the open hall, became commonplace until the late C17. The Old Manor House, Buckden, is probably a very early example, with long jetties to front and back. It is an unusual building altogether in having two halls one above the other, so it may have served some public function, e.g. as a guildhall. There are many examples in Kimbolton and Godmanchester of long-jettied buildings with timber-framed bays for brick chimneys. Another is Pepys House, Brampton, and there are several later examples in Houghton, Wyton and Spaldwick.

WINDOW mullions, whether stone or timber, and soffits of rails and tie-beams in timber-framed houses universally show ovolo- and hollow-chamfer mouldings in the early C17. CARVED DECOR-ATION is fairly unusual, but the motif of a rod with furled leaf carved along the jetty is found at Corner House (No. 51 High Street), Southoe, and in the much-restored house at No. 42 High Street, St Neots. In the early C17 gables, jetties and bargeboards are decorated with finials and egg-and-dart moulding.

The majority of timber-framed houses have plaster panels between the frame but increasingly in the late C16 and early C17 frames were plastered externally and sometimes with pargetted panels. The timbers of some buildings were even painted. Late comes the infilling of panels with brick (e.g. Midloe Grange,

103

Southoe; Old Manor House, Brington) or in some instances were fully encased in brick (e.g. Rippington Manor, Great Gransden). Elsewhere, additions are brick (Manor Farm, Alconbury). So from about this time, as the supply of timber declines, BRICK HOUSES become more common in Huntingdonshire and by 1700 are dominant. About 1670–80 in the villages appear three-bay brick houses with a square porch and either two tiers of brick pilasters (The Limes, Spaldwick; Church Farm House, Yelling) or a framework of broad vertical and horizontal brick bands (Manor House Farmhouse, Sawtry, 1672, with shaped end-gables; Swan and Salmon, Little Stukeley, 1676). The last two named have or had SHAPED GABLES of the Low Countries type, which begin in the aristocratic and gentry houses of the early C17 (*see* below) as frontal gables but carry on especially as end-gables in the smaller brick houses of the Ouse valley and the fen edge. There are still many fine examples of these buildings (but far fewer than was true one hundred years ago), including Bridge Farmhouse, Broughton, late C17, and The Manor House, Fenstanton, Park House, Thorney, and Broom Lodge, Hemingford Grey, which show the tradition going on into the C18. A more typical style of end-gable for the smaller early C18 houses is a straight gable with tumbled brickwork.

It is entertaining to watch how these kinds of house gradually display classical motifs. A doorway of 1684 formerly at Farcet but now at Alwalton has a pediment, but not yet quite a classically correct one. The doorway of Ivy House, Spaldwick, of 1688 has the real thing and also giant angle pilasters, though in the middle still two tiers. Similarly one can watch the longevity of mullioned windows: to *c.* 1680 in Manor House, Alwalton; 1685 in Model Farm House, Upton (P).

Surviving evidence of INTERIOR DECORATION at the vernacular level is sparse. The best is perhaps the ceiling inside the Lion Hotel at Buckden, with moulded beams and a central boss, but that is due to its association with the Palace, and more generally timbers of houses were finished plainly with chamfers and stops. Manor Farm at Orton Waterville (Peterborough) is exceedingly interesting for the survival inside of stone doorcases dated 1571. Quite a lot of C17 STAIRCASES survive in the higher-status houses, not much inferior to the gentry houses. They are usually close-stringed with turned or splat and finally twisted balusters, taking us into the early C18; newels have ball or polygonal finials or ogee shapes (e.g. Hilton Hall) or carved pendants (Church Farm House, Yelling). Domestic WALL PAINTINGS over plastered panels and studs generally have a simple colour range; early C17 work is found in Tudor House, Godmanchester, and Pepys House, Brampton, as well as formerly in The Three Jolly Butchers, Wyton. These are interesting for they share in common a pattern of arcading with pendants. Pepys House in addition has painting in the hall imitating the bottom half of a timber-frame chimneystack. Panelling or textiles are imitated in other houses e.g. Manor House, Tilbrook. The George, Spaldwick, has polychrome early C16 figures, one attired for hunting. The small

Highway Farmhouse, Great Staughton, still has a painted chevron decoration on the ceiling joists in black, white and earth red. Of PLASTERWORK there is almost no survival, but at Ford House, Eaton Ford (Eaton Socon), is one very remarkable panel of *c.* 1630.

AISLED BARNS around the farmsteads date from the C16 and continued to be built into the C19; they were usually timber-framed and weatherboarded or of limestone rubble, with a symmetrically placed porch (midstrey), sometimes more than one, depending on the length. Many barns have been lost but others have been converted for housing. A very impressive early C17 brick barn is at Great Gransden. Mixed farming and particularly dairying needed appropriate buildings similar to those at The Gables, Earning Street, Godmanchester, with barns, granaries, cowsheds and dovecotes; cheese was stored in special cheese rooms in farmhouses, e.g. Brook Cottage, Ellington. There are some good DOVECOTES in Huntingdonshire and Peterborough. That at Hilton Hall is a very good late C17 example with a gabled roof and there is a pleasing circular one at Somersham.

MAJOR ELIZABETHAN AND JACOBEAN ARCHITECTURE

At the time of the Reformation land ownership in Huntingdonshire and Peterborough was heavily concentrated in the hands of the church. At the DISSOLUTION the abbey lands of Peterborough were retained for the Cathedral, granted this status in 1541. The lands of the Huntingdonshire foundations, however, were redistributed. Newcomers reaped significant rewards, notably Sir Richard Williams, nephew of Thomas Cromwell, who took his uncle's name and was appointed as one of the Visitors of the religious houses. For this he was given the property of Ramsey Abbey and its estates, along with the nunnery at Hinchingbrooke (*see* Huntingdon), the abbey and manor at Sawtry, and much other land in Huntingdonshire besides. Sawtry was completely demolished but Ramsey and Hinchingbrooke were remodelled as residences. Ramsey was secondary until the early C17; its buildings were thoroughly cleared and its stone used in the construction of new college buildings at Cambridge. A similar story unfolded at Thorney Abbey, where John Russell, 1st Earl of Bedford, was granted the buildings of the abbey *c.* 1550. Thorney was a rather minor acquisition beside his other gifts at this time – but of great significance to his C19 descendants – and the earl was quick to realize the high value of the stone, comprehensively demolishing the claustral buildings and selling on materials to build Trinity College, Cambridge. Indeed the colleges of Oxford and Cambridge were the other major benefactors of the break up of church estates, so it is common in numerous villages to find houses called College Farmhouse. College Farm, Hilton, is a good example of the higher status of decoration bestowed on their holdings.

The houses produced from the remains of Ramsey and Hinchingbrooke offer limited, not very articulate, evidence of the ELIZABETHAN STYLE in Huntingdonshire. At Ramsey the house followed a standard plan, with the hall in the centre, and in a gable to the former porch above the cross-passage it is dated 1587. Although the building was much worked over in the C19 the surviving windows of the hall bay window and another now inside show that they were mullioned and transomed and without arches at the top of the lights, as one expects for the later C16. That is in contrast to Hinchingbrooke, where the claustral buildings were adapted immediately and never assumed any regularity. There are two-storey canted bay windows originally lighting the hall and solar. These have arched lights and friezes of quatrefoils, which look more convincingly c. 1550; indeed they probably date from the period after 1558. Arched lights occur also at Milton, the house of the Fitzwilliams outside Peterborough, the first of whom bought into the estate in 1502 with money made as a merchant in London. It is uncertain whether he built the house which forms the core of the present mansion. Certainly it had already reached its present, and for its date unusual, length by 1584 at the latest. There are here two sets of canted bay windows with arched lights, and it seems highly probable that these again date from the middle decades of the C16, just as one finds them in Northamptonshire houses of this period.

Arched lights also occur in Castle Farmhouse, Maxey, which seems to have belonged to the Cecils in the C16. Richard Cecil acquired the land of Burghley SW of Stamford in 1520. His son, Sir William Cecil, future Lord Burghley, inherited in 1552 and immediately began to rebuild not once but twice. The first house seems to have been more or less complete by 1564 and introduces to this area the first instance of the great courtyard mansion so familiar for the Tudor and early Elizabethan period. In the late 1560s Cecil concentrated on Theobalds near London rather than on the distant Burghley House, but in the 1570s he returned, and now rebuilt at one go. The W, N and S fronts carry dates 1577, 1585 and 1587. With its turrets and its innumerable chimneystacks, Burghley is the most improbable apparition in the gentle landscaped grounds outside Stamford. In size and in swagger it can compete with any contemporary palace this side of the Alps. When Burghley had finished with it in the 1580s it was, one might well say, the grandest of all Elizabethan mansions. The work includes not only the fantastic frontispiece in the courtyard crowned by spiky obelisks and clocktower and the originally open arcading of the court but also consciously archaic features. So the kitchen still has a soaring Gothic rib-vault, the Great Hall buttresses, arched lights to the large transomed windows and a double-hammerbeam roof, and there is another rib-vault over the western entrance. The motifs of these elements are shared by other parts of the house that are purely classical, notably the fireplace in the Great Hall with its crowning

pediment, based on designs by Serlio, and the Roman Staircase, 98
where the pattern, especially for the tunnel-vaulting, is no doubt
such French staircases as Lescot's in the Louvre. We know indeed
that Burghley was fully aware of what went on in France and
also the Netherlands. In many places the ring and square patterns that are the leitmotif of late C16 Northamptonshire houses
are repeated. That nothing in either Peterborough or Huntingdonshire (and indeed few houses in Northamptonshire) can
compete in scale or splendour with Burghley House goes without
saying.

The JACOBEAN PERIOD is a significant one for the area.
Robert Cotton played a decisive role in the succession of James
VI of Scotland to the English crown, and his property at Conington lay on the route taken by the new monarch from
Edinburgh to London. One of James's first acts was to remove
his mother's body from Peterborough Cathedral to Westminster Abbey. For his services Cotton was knighted by the new king
in 1603 and remained his adviser. The Cotton mansion, Conington Castle, which was demolished in the 1950s, was one
of a number of houses in Huntingdonshire, Peterborough and
Northamptonshire to claim to have been built from the spoil of
Fotheringhay Castle (Northants), which was taken down c. 1635.
Stone from Maxey Castle was also used at Conington.

After the Union with Scotland, Huntingdon was also an
important destination for the drovers bringing cattle along the
Bullock Road from Berwick; this road which runs parallel to the
Great North Road (A1) from the river crossing at Wansford to
Alconbury, where it meets Ermine Street, was already well estab-
lished in the medieval period for fattening cattle on the rich
pastures of Huntingdonshire on the way to London. Another
Bullock Track, now the B660, was created in the C17 from
Ramsey to Kimbolton and Bedfordshire. In the earlier C17
attempts were made to improve the Great North Road but it was
not until 1663 that a system of turnpikes was developed. From
1617, however, work began to make a clear navigation of the
Great Ouse from St Ives to St Neots and eventually to Bedford.
This revitalized the villages and towns in the C17, creating new
commercial areas for malting, brewing, warehousing and milling,
particularly in Earith, St Ives, Huntingdon and St Neots.

Surviving JACOBEAN HOUSES form a good and varied collection and one would do well to start in Peterborough and the N
of Huntingdonshire. Hinchingbrooke (see Huntingdon) evidently
had some remodelling done by Sir Oliver Cromwell. Its generous
bow window is dated 1602 and in its original position had an   100
open ground floor opening off the parlour. The design of this
bow is believed by Mark Girouard to derive from the old house
of Babraham Hall, Cambridgeshire, a house whose remodelling
is attributed to *John Thorpe* (replaced in the 1830s). Thorpe's
family were masons in Kingscliffe, just across the border in
Northamptonshire, and from 1601 he was a surveyor; his drawings (now in the Soane Museum) contain plans for a very large
number of country houses. Some, including Burghley, appear to

be surveys of existing buildings, while others are his own designs. He drew, and probably designed, before 1608, a great courtyard house for Sir Gervase Clifton at Leighton Bromswold. There is good evidence that it was built, although it had been demolished by the early C19 (a story somewhat similar to Toddington Manor in Bedfordshire), but its gatehouse of 1616 is there, with four square, higher angle towers and a frontispiece with columns and odd short pilasters and finials over. Mention of John Thorpe leads to Toseland Hall, which is specially interesting because of its compact plan of three by three bays, a type of plan which Thorpe experimented with in his book of drawings. The house was built *c.* 1600 as a secondary residence for the Lukes of Cople, Bedfordshire, and it is the first example locally of an outward-facing house with regular elevations, attic gables over each of the bays and straight-headed windows with mullion and transoms. Milton, as has been noted, was already a house of uncommon length by the late C16, and by 1626 (on the evidence of a recorded date) it had been given a significant facelift in which all the windows were remodelled into the standard straight-headed type with a transom and mullion and shaped gables set in a row along the attic, in a manner markedly similar to contemporary developments at Apethorpe Hall, Northamptonshire. It retained this appearance until the alterations of the mid C18. The early C17 porch of Milton is of a type well known in the area and in Northamptonshire, with superimposed orders of Doric and Ionic columns and an arch with jewelled keystone. This motif was taken up, probably after 1620, at Chesterton House, which was demolished in 1807 but whose porch the Fitzwilliams re-erected for a gate lodge at Alwalton. The porch at Stibbington Hall, a perfect example of the Jacobean manor house on an E-plan and of moderate size, is dated 1625. Both the Chesterton and the Stibbington porches have big shaped gables, and a rather more bulbous shaped gable was still built at Glinton Manor House *c.* 1630–40. Inside the Glinton Manor House is a fine stone arch, again with a jewelled keystone.

The gables of the Stibbington and Glinton type were soon to be replaced by Dutch, i.e. pedimented, gables, and the earliest of these, of the mid C17, is at Gransden Hall, Great Gransden, of the type found at Kew Palace. The Manor House, Warboys, can be fairly certainly dated to after the death in 1632 of Sir John Leman, who acquired the land at Warboys from Sir Oliver Cromwell in 1622. The gables here are closer in spirit to the bulbous shape of the Glinton house, ending in a bottleneck with curved top, than to Gransden Hall. Shaped gables, especially end-gables, run on locally in smaller houses till after 1700 (*see* p. 382 above).

For CHURCHES there is not a single church in Huntingdon-shire or Peterborough of between the Reformation and 1600. The top of the tower of Wistow church with its straight-headed belfry openings with arched lights is very probably 1550s but still essentially Perp. There are no Elizabethan church furnishings either. After 1600, however, the churches and church furnishings come back into the picture. The chancel at Helpston has some strange

101

96

102

104

windows dated 1609. They are tall, of two lights, straight-headed, and have a pointed quatrefoil at the top of each light. That indicates the intention not to break away from the Perp tradition. The windows of the Dove Chapel at Upton (P) are also still entirely Gothic, although the balustrade inside has vertically symmetrical balusters. Nor is the intention to break new ground noticeable in the early C17 brick tower of Morborne. When Thorney Abbey church was restored in 1638, the tendency was the same, and imitation Gothic forms were used. The roof of Easton church, dated 1630, is an interesting continuation of the low-pitched Perp tradition but the carving now is classical, including egg-and-dart. This may well be an indication of improvements set in hand after the 1st Earl of Manchester acquired the estates around Kimbolton. It is evident that other churches were also improved. The tower of Godmanchester had to be rebuilt from old materials by the borough in 1623 and, except in some small details, it shows little sign of change from what must have been the style of its predecessor. The same is true of St Thomas Ramsey, allegedly rebuilt with stone still available from the ruins of the abbey in 1672. Further evidence of the Gothic Survival may be the date of 1635 on the tower at Brampton. Other churches also have C17 datestones (e.g. Little Stukeley) but there is little justification for believing that they refer to anything other than minor repairs. However, Sir Robert Cotton paid for new building in 1629 at Denton, to which many of the villagers of Conington had been cleared from the park around his house. Here, on the other hand, the 1629 work introduced normal (i.e. domestic) mullioned and mullion-and-transomed cross-windows, i.e. leaving Gothic conventions behind. The same is true on a much more monumental scale of Leighton Bromswold. When the Duke of Lennox rebuilt the tower c. 1637–41, he used, it is true, clasping buttresses and pinnacles, but the pinnacles are obelisks, and the windows and doorway have round arches on pilasters.

Leighton Bromswold and, side by side with it, Little Gidding are among the most interesting C17 churches in the whole of England. This is due to religious and literary reasons as much as artistic. The incumbent (deacon, not priest) at Leighton Bromswold from 1626 till 1630 was George Herbert, the poet, and Little Gidding was the place chosen by Nicholas Ferrar and his mother and then his married brother and married sister for their religious colony. They went there in 1626, and Nicholas was ordained deacon. His inspiration came chiefly from the Cambridge Platonists and Juan de Valdes. The Ferrars restored a small existing church for their purposes. George Herbert restored his large church too, and put a new roof on. A rainwater head gives the date 1632. In his reforms he was responsible for the pulpit with sounding-board and also the reader's desk of the same design and placed as an exact counterpart, for Prayer and Sermon must be given equal right. At the same time new stalls came in, deliberately in no way different from the benches, and a low, deliberately not a high, screen, and also plate. At the same time at Little Gidding the reredos was given with brass plates for the texts, the choir

105

106

panelling, and the seating and the delightful little brass font with its delightful crown-like brass cover.

Of other FURNISHINGS the PULPIT at Orton Waterville is a gorgeous Jacobean piece* but it came from Great St Mary, Cambridge. There are a number of other Jacobean pulpits with familiar patterns of decoration, of which only Yaxley, dated 1631, deserves a place here. William Laud was Archdeacon of Huntingdon from 1615 until 1622. As Archbishop of Canterbury after 1633 his instruction that COMMUNION TABLES should be set altar-wise had a noticeable effect in Huntingdonshire and Peterborough. There is such a table at Leighton Bromswold and at Little Gidding, and at Catworth it is inscribed with the date of its gift in 1634. Other good examples too at Brington, Holme, Buckden, and Upton (P), which is another church of principal interest for its early to mid-C17 furnishings.

The architectural decoration of Elizabethan and Jacobean houses is mostly closely matched in FUNERARY MONUMENTS. One need only think of Lord Burghley's own monument in St Martin's at Stamford (*see The Buildings of England: Lincolnshire*) or his wife's in Westminster Abbey to agree. The best monuments in village churches are often of the four-poster type with recumbent effigies, but in this area it only occurs very late, at Upton for the Dove Monument, which may not have been erected until the 1650s on the evidence of the effigies and the balustrade which creates an enclosure for the monument. A newer type in the early C17 is that with a reclining effigy under an arch (Bridget Lady Carre †1621 at Ufford). The monument at Thornhaugh to William Lord Russell †1613 has obelisks in place of posts on the tomb-chest and no canopy. His effigy is on a rolled-up mat, a familiar conceit in late C16 and early C17 monuments. At his feet and on the sides of the chest are kneeling figures of his children; and another new type of the period has kneeling figures of the commemorated facing one another across a prayer-desk. The Dyer Monument at Great Staughton, probably of *c.* 1605, has two such couples, with three columns and a lot of rather stiff strapwork on top. The Beville Monument at Chesterton, probably of 1611, is similar, but the figures kneel, two facing the other two, and there are only two columns and a pendant in the middle. At Barnack is one of these kneelers' monuments of 1612, and this is signed by *Thomas Greenway* of Derby, a very rare thing still at that time. About 1603 at Conington two Cotton monuments were put up by Sir Robert Cotton facing across the church two memorials of the same date to the Scottish royal family, from whom the Cottons were descended. These are standing monuments with no effigies, just strapwork crestings and heraldry. It is a fascinating example of early C17 antiquarianism and must surely have been intended as a compliment to the new king.

At about this time the desire arose among sculptors to get away from standard types and express new conceits. Thus the monument to George Wauton †1606, at Great Staughton, has the

---

* Or rather it would be if it had not been partly dismantled.

recumbent effigy placed on a slab carried by two atlantes – a Netherlandish motif by origin. Even more original is Elizabeth Talbot †1629 at Orton Longueville; for here the monument itself is a black slab on pink alabaster legs, and the rest is just an inscription tablet behind. About fifteen years later the 1st Earl of Manchester †1642 was commemorated at Kimbolton by a black slab on arches and columns with a white cushion on it carrying the inscription and, behind, two columns and a third high up on a bracket in the middle. For the new types of monument after the mid-century *see* below.

MID-SEVENTEENTH CENTURY TO EARLY EIGHTEENTH CENTURY

The break between King and Parliament in the 1640s merits a pause before an account is given of buildings in the second half of the century. It is to be remembered that Oliver Cromwell was born at Huntingdon in 1599, grandson of Sir Henry Cromwell at Hinchingbrooke; he was elected M.P. for the county of Huntingdon in 1628 and farmed near St Ives for a time in the 1630s before he moved to Ely. It is also worth noting here that Sir Oliver Cromwell sold Hinchingbrooke in 1627 to Sir Sidney Montagu, whose son Sir Edward Montagu was also M.P. for Huntingdon and served the Parliamentary cause before playing a key role in the return of Charles II, by whom he was made the Earl of Sandwich. At about the same time Henry Montagu, of the family at Boughton, Northamptonshire, acquired Kimbolton Castle and was created 1st Earl of Manchester in 1620. He died in 1642 but his son maintained a good position during the years up to the Restoration and after.

A significant new presence in the territory is the Earl of Bedford. The Russells owned land at Thornhaugh, Stibbington, Wansford and Thorney from the C16 and it was the 1st Baron Russell of Thornhaugh who in the 1590s explored the first attempt to drain the peaty fenland around Thorney. His son, Francis Russell, inherited the title of 4th Earl of Bedford and began the great remodelling at Woburn, Bedfordshire while simultaneously embarking on the mammoth DRAINAGE project that created the Bedford Level by cutting a drain through the fen, thereby reclaiming a huge area of land for agriculture and simultaneously bypassing the irregular course of the Great Ouse River to the Wash. The capital was 'adventured' by the earl and a small band of others and *Cornelius Vermuyden* was engaged to engineer the works. At Earith begins the main drain, now called the Old Bedford River, which was cut 1630–6 to take water to Denver (Norfolk). A second drain, the New Bedford River, was cut parallel to the first in 1650–53, and there was also the Forty Foot Drain, which begins near Ramsey and drained much of that area of the Fen into the Old Bedford River. A third, Bevill's Leam (*see* Pondersbridge), was a waterway from Whittlesey Mere, a p. 401

gigantic natural lake between Holme, Yaxley and Ramsey which
would not be drained until the mid C19. Meanwhile Sir Thomas
Cotton started to drain Conington Fen in 1639. Between the Old
and New Bedford Rivers at Earith there is the remarkable sight
of the earthwork of a Cromwellian Bulwark, displaying the latest
– again Dutch-influenced – manner of planning with angle bastions. There is a second Civil War earthwork by the river Nene
at Horsey Hill, Stanground (Peterborough). In the associated
mayhem of the period much damage was done at Peterborough
Cathedral. The high altar was destroyed and the paintings of the
ceiling peppered with shot. Within the same period the Lady
Chapel and cloisters were taken down, the stone partly being
used in the repair of the cathedral.

This discussion of changes in early to mid-C17 Huntingdonshire and Peterborough has a purpose for its impact on DOMES-
TIC ARCHITECTURE. The key buildings of the mid C17 are
connected by style and by patron. Thorpe Hall (Peterborough)
of 1653–6, is by *Peter Mills* for Oliver St John, Lord Chief Justice
of the Common Pleas, who had acquired the property from the
sequestered lands of the Cathedral and used stone taken from
the cathedral cloisters to build it, and Thorney Abbey House of
1660 etc. for the 5th Earl of Bedford by *John Lovin* of Peterborough. It may be to Mills's designs as well. Both are superficially
of the new type established by Inigo Jones and brought to perfection in Roger Pratt's Coleshill (Berkshire), begun c. 1650. They
are square blocks with large hipped roofs and dormer windows.
The windows have (or had) mullion-and-transom crosses, and
some at Thorpe Hall have pediments. That far they are indeed
like Coleshill. But then – even more in the garden piers at Thorpe
and the wooden doorcases inside the same house – odd, Mannerist details come in, and they multiply in the panelling and
chimneypieces: pilasters vertically halved, lugs or ears in unexpected places, volutes, and also fat garlands. The third house in
this group is Wisbech Castle of 1658 in Cambridgeshire, for John
Thurloe, Cromwell's Secretary of State, but only parts of it
survive. The Haycock Hotel at Wansford, an uncommonly large
and architecturally serious inn, of probably c. 1650–80, partakes
of some of these mannerisms; it belonged to the Russells also.
The staircase in Thorpe Hall belongs to the most progressive type
of its time. It has richly carved openwork foliage panels instead
of balusters. The same motif, yet richer, occurred in the staircase
of Hinchingbrooke, which dated from c. 1663 and of which only
single panels survive. In 1665–8 Elton Hall, the medieval house
of the Sapcotes, which had fallen into ruin by the early C17, was
suddenly revived by Sir Thomas Proby, who had married the
second daughter of Sir Thomas Cotton of Conington. The architect there appears to have been the little-known *Isaac Rowe*, who
also worked at Drayton House, Northamptonshire. The 1660s
house was recorded by the Bucks, who show it to have been
entirely up to date. Walcot Hall also dates from this period, and
seems to have been built in 1678 for Sir Hugh Cholmeley, former
Governor of Tangier, and M.P. for Northampton.

p. 401

p. 605

109

110

The classical type of major house, i.e. the type say of Eltham Lodge by May rather than of Coleshill, is accomplished at Walden House, Huntingdon, with its row of giant pilasters and the Dutch garlands below the first-floor windows. It is also accomplished more simply but on a much larger scale in 1690 in the stables of Milton – eleven-bay centre, four-bay wings – and there advice at least was given by *William Talman*, i.e. the man who was second in command during these years under Wren in the Office of Works. It is just possible that Talman directed the late C17 work at Burghley House, but other than the fine doorpiece to the s front and the *Tijou* gates of the w entrance the effort was concentrated on the interior and produced the finest rooms in the 108 whole area, populated with the produce of four separate Grand Tours conducted by the 5th Earl of Exeter. Here *Grinling Gibbons* himself was paid for some carving, but the majority of floral and foliage displays, and of a very high standard, are by the London carvers *Thomas Young* and *Jonathan Maine*, complemented by the richness of the contemporary plasterwork. *Laguerre* also painted there (not so well). The courtyard of Kimbolton Castle on the 111 other hand, probably of *c.* 1690, is provincial, with its schematic leaf decoration above the windows strongly suggesting an attribution to *Henry Bell* of King's Lynn, for the same motifs occur also in his work at Northampton. Most festive is the entrance to the E range from the courtyard. Here there are giant pilasters, and the wide staircase with its wrought-iron railing leads up to a 112 pedimented doorway.

In CHURCHES hardly anything of the mastery of the wood carvers appears. There is just one pretty pulpit at Eynesbury, late C17 in date, and another at Great Gransden of *c.* 1660 given by the Rev. Barnabas Oley, who had been removed from the living in 1644. It has characteristic cartouches on the panels and a dentil cornice. It had a tester with pendant finials before 1873. A chandelier of Dutch type in Catworth church has the – for England early – date 1666; given by Brasenose College in 1675. Brass chandeliers of the Dutch types went on unchanged for a long time. We find them at Somersham with the date 1787 and at Little Gidding of *c.* 1770 (given in 1853).

We have now only to bring the FUNERARY MONUMENTS up to date, and then we shall be ready for the Georgian style. There are few of note, really only about half a dozen. The first is in All Saints Huntingdon and is interesting only because it has the open scrolly pediment typical of *c.* 1700 and after, and yet commemorates a death in 1636. The second is at Marholm and commemorates a boy who died in 1646. He is recorded with a free-standing bust in front of a black needle obelisk. Such busts became fashionable at about that time, and at Conington Sir Robert Cotton, 107 who died in 1631, and Sir Thomas Cotton, who died in 1662, are represented by busts attributed respectively to *Edward Marshall* (who also probably provided the chimneypieces at Thorpe Hall in the 1650s) and *Joshua Marshall*. Both are good also in the surrounds, but the bust of Sir Robert is of a quality not often matched at that early date in the whole of England. At Brampton,

Sir John Bernard Robert †1679 has a monument with a bust of
c. 1690 signed by *William Kidwell.* There are good examples of
work by the *Stanton* workshops at Elton for Probys †1689 and
†1710 and at Ufford †1689 and †1705. At Conington are two
cartouches for Sir John Cotton and wife †1702 attributed to
Grinling Gibbons, who signed the similar one to a Cotton at
Conington in Cambridgeshire. A very fine cartouche in the N
presbytery aisle at Peterborough Cathedral (†1681) is also attributed to Gibbons, and the influence of his style on London workshops may be seen also in a cartouche in the S presbytery aisle
to Joseph Stamford †1683. At Hemingford Abbots a wall monument commemorates a Regius Professor of Greek at Cambridge
†1712 and hence has an inscription partly in Greek. The surround includes a baldacchino and the familiar cherubs' heads.
But this is provincial work.

THE GEORGIAN AGE

The C18 and early C19 has nothing much to contribute to
CHURCHES, except Chesterton where *c.* 1730 the church was
remodelled with arched windows and the porch received its
entrance with a Gibbs surround. Inside there is a reredos with
coupled Ionic pilasters, an altar table on wrought-iron supports,
a very distinguished pulpit with inlay, and a handsome three-
arched screen below the blocked head of the chancel arch. The
work was instigated by Robert Pigott, and he also made alterations to Haddon in 1745 of which the round-arched windows in
the porch might be a trace. Much more interesting is the façade
given to Nicholas Ferrar's church at Little Gidding in 1714,
which by now was simply a chapel of ease. It is eminently suited
to the pervading mood but quite out of the ordinary, stone-faced
with angle pilasters carrying little obelisks, a doorway a little
Archerish in its details, and an odd bellcote with a steep pyramid
on top pierced by three precisely oblong holes.

The lack of new churches does not mean that there were no
changes to the buildings and for much of this period there would
have been the customary additions of galleries, especially in the
expanding towns such as Peterborough, where St John's, already
a sizeable medieval church, was fitted with galleries on three sides
of the nave. There was also some activity in the cathedral in 1780
when *John Carter* designed new choir screens. There are churches
partly rebuilt – e.g. the meagre chancel of Offord Cluny (less
good than the fine communion rail within), the brick E wall of
Diddington *c.* 1700 and much later the replacement of the
chancel at Warboys in 1832 – and one entirely new church, at
Newborough, built by the Crown in 1826–9 once the fen had
been reclaimed. Hemingford Grey and St Ives lost their spires to
a hurricane in 1741 and the former was never replaced, simply
decorated with little ball finials. At Peterborough, St John's was

in a dangerous state by 1819, leading to the removal of the spire from its tower. The remaking of its windows with cusped intersecting tracery is a classic example of the unlearned phase of the early C19 Gothic Revival in church architecture. But nowhere now can be seen the C18 style of church interior with double-decker pulpits etc. Instead one should look for evidence to early NONCONFORMIST CHAPELS, e.g. the Baptist chapel at Great Gransden of after 1734, quite a plain three-by-three-bay house with a hipped roof, or the chapel at Great Gidding of 1790. The latter has sadly lost its fittings. The majority of chapels in Huntingdonshire and Peterborough are of after 1840, e.g. the chapel at Houghton, yellow brick with a pediment.

Georgian CHURCH MONUMENTS of the earlier period begin with Earl Fitzwilliam, who died in 1719 and is portrayed standing, with his wife, on his monument at Marholm. This had become a fashionable way of providing monuments c. 1700 (cf. Sir Samuel Ongley, Old Warden, in Beds.). The Fitzwilliam Monument is by *James Fisher* of Camberwell and until the mid C19 was an even more ambitious item, with figures of Grief and Piety flanking the earl and countess. *Robert Taylor Sen.*'s monument of Thomas Deacon in Peterborough Cathedral, on the other hand, though the death commemorated is 1721, goes on with the reclining effigy, as was much favoured for monuments to the early Georgian Establishment (cf. Bishop Willis, Winchester, 1735). The cathedral has after this no major monument and nor is there much to be found in the parish churches of Peterborough and Huntingdonshire. The largest type of standing monument, of reredos type, is quite rare, but there are good examples at Chesterton (to John Driden), Woodston (Mary Walsham †1745) and Orton Longueville (Sir Charles Cope †1781). But the majority are hanging tablets, including a large classical one of 1729 at Great Staughton, one in the same church of 1731 with an urn in a scalloped niche under a pediment, executed in coloured marbles, one at St Mary, Huntingdon, by *Scheemakers*, with a moulded black frame, and another at Stanground †1752 of the type with a classical bust of the deceased. Many of the later C18 monuments are in the hands of local practitioners, notably *Edward Bingham*, a Peterborough mason, well-represented by the monuments in St John's church. His later tablets introduced Gothic motifs (e.g. Ufford †1790 and Peterborough Cathedral †1787).

That leaves us with the development of secular architecture. Among MAJOR HOUSES, at the beginning all interest is focused on *Vanbrugh*'s Kimbolton Castle, the 4th Earl of Manchester's mansion. This was of course a remodelling job. Parts of the castle and the whole of the courtyard were there. Vanbrugh in 1707–10 provided the rather austere façades, castellated mostly to make it, as he wrote, 'a masculine show', but with the E front partly higher and provided with a two-column giant portico *in antis*. The columns are Tuscan, as Wren and Vanbrugh liked it. But this is dated to 1718–19 and *Alessandro Galilei*, who was consulted in 1714 and in some details was followed by the earl, may well have had a hand in its design. Inside, *G. A. Pellegrini* painted the stair-case, the boudoir and the chapel. They are about the finest decor-ative painting of the whole period in England and show up the rather more routine qualities of *Verrio* at Burghley, where work resumed on the interior in the 1750s after a significant period of consolidation following the excesses of the 5th Earl. It is fascinat-ing in large part for its fidelity to the late C17 work that had been initiated but left incomplete, so the enriched mouldings of the panelling etc. are still palpably Baroque. The painting is more obviously of its time and the effect of entering the Heaven Room from the dark of the corresponding Hell Staircase (painted later) is not easily forgotten. At about the same time Milton received its new S front, the Peterborough companion-piece to the S front of Woburn Abbey in Bedfordshire. Both are by *Flitcroft*, both are strictly Palladian, and both have gorgeous rooms with partly Kentian and partly Rococo decoration. Elton Hall has ample plasterwork and one very grand early to mid-C18 chimneypiece, but the picture of the house is occluded by later C18 and C19 alterations.

What of the growing number of GENTRY HOUSES? Kimbolton has segment-headed windows. Wren had used these at Hampton Court, i.e. in 1689 etc. In Huntingdonshire they appear for the first time at Hemingford Grey House *c.* 1697, and then, together with giant pilasters, panelled parapets, staircases with twisted and then slender and ornamental turned balusters, in several Queen Anne and Early Georgian houses. Of the smaller country houses, Tetworth Hall, on the Greensand Ridge at the border with Bed-fordshire, is the perfect example. Built in 1710 for John Pedley, M.P., it is of brick but with stone dressings and has a handsome stone doorcase under a segmental pediment. Inside is a superb staircase, under a coved ceiling. The finest George II staircase is in Paxton Hall, Little Paxton. It dates, like the beautiful doorway and the plasterwork, from 1738 and was built for Bishop Rey-nolds of Lincoln. Another excellent, if less spectacular, house of those years (1746) is Farm Hall at Godmanchester. Also there, and almost exactly contemporary is Island Hall of 1749. Both are brick houses with pediments and fine interiors. Stamford (Lin-colnshire) at the NW edge of this area was a thriving place in the early C18. One might reasonably expect to see the influence locally of its masons but it seems to be limited to two houses: Ufford Hall, a pocket country house of *c.* 1741–51 for Lord Charles Manners, and a house called Durobrivae at Castor. Both make free use of flared voussoirs to the openings. Ufford Hall has rustication, quoins and a central pediment, the smaller house giant pilasters, a moulded cornice and Gibbsian surrounds to its windows just as one finds in the works of George Portwood in Stamford. Castor House, in the same village, is a grand early C18 house built for the Bishop of Peterborough and quite character-istic of the stone area in having a double-pile plan, stacks on the end-gables, raised long-and-short quoins and raised architraves to the windows. At a level just below the houses described above are some of the manor houses, e.g. Offord Cluny Manor House of *c*. 1704 with short wings, i.e. following an earlier tradition, and several FARMHOUSES. There are two interesting early C18 houses in a remote setting at Willow Hall, near Thorney, where reclamation of the fenland by this time made agricultural a feasible prospect. Part of the interest of these houses is that they are side by side and nearly identical yet separate properties. Indeed across the fen edge as a whole from N to S there are quite a number of good small Early Georgian red brick farmhouses; the places to see these are Fenstanton (Fenstanton Manor), Needingworth, Pidley (Stanley Farmhouse and Fenton Manor), and Woodhurst (Holdich Farmhouse and Manor House).

The changes in the appearance of houses in the village is mirrored (or vice versa) by new developments in the market TOWNS. Many were entering a period of prosperity, partly the consequence of the improvements made to TRANSPORT in the C17 in the navigation of the Ouse. Earith, where the New and Old Bedford Rivers drain off the River Great Ouse, became a thriving little port on the back of this, and St Ives, St Neots, Huntingdon and Godmanchester all show, in the orientation of many buildings towards the river, the benefits of trade in coal and corn etc. See for example Brook House, St Neots, a smart late C17 detached house with a hipped roof. The Nene was also made navigable in the mid C18 with good effect on Peterborough and also on Wansford where, as at Earith, a small inland port was created, perfectly placed at the intersection of the river and the GREAT NORTH ROAD. The road does not in fact run through any of the towns, but passed through Buckden, where the scale of the C18 rebuilding of the George Hotel shows the profit of such business and travel; and N of Conington is the former Crown and Woolpack Inn, a grand late C18 brick U-plan with gabled ends. The Haycock at Wansford itself has already been mentioned (p. 390). A delightful feature of the area around Huntingdon are some MILESTONES (Alconbury, Brampton, St Ives). The Great North Road came close to St Neots at Eaton Socon, but St Neots itself lay at the start of the junction with the road to Cambridge, and so large COACHING ESTABLISHMENTS were needed there too along the road and especially around its colossal market square. Huntingdon is an interesting case in that, having been the pre-eminent medieval town, it was in severe decline from the C16 – a fact made starkly clear by the reduction in the number of its churches – and was then outstripped by Godmanchester to its S, which became the foremost settlement in a large agricultural area, as illustrated by the quality of its C17 farmhouses (*see* p. 381). But from the evidence of its buildings one may clearly see Huntingdon's return to prosperity *c*. 1715 – the major coaching establishment in the High Street is the George Hotel. Cowper House in the High Street has motifs very particular to this period. It is a brick refronting, like so many other houses in the towns, and has brick quoins, a platband at first floor and the eaves of its roof carried on modillions. It furthermore uses rubbed red brick for the dressings of its windows, which have cut brick lintels making frilly patterns. This is a motif very typical of the period *c*. 1710–25, and Dial House, Godmanchester, shows it too. There are also good examples at St Ives (a town badly damaged by fire in 1689), where in the centre of the town on Crown Street and Bridge Street there are a few exquisite small red brick merchants' houses of the most fashionable sort, two bays with segmental-headed sash windows, moulded brick pilasters and parapets hiding the roof. Several of the houses of this date retain fielded panelling and staircases with twisted balusters. A regular motif of the period is the Venetian window, which appears again and again in Huntingdon, oddly not always in the centre of the façade but sometimes at the side lighting a passage. It appears also in the Town Hall, the best Georgian PUBLIC BUILDING in Huntingdonshire. It is of 1745 by *Benjamin Timbrell*, with an extension of 1817 by *S. P. Cockerell*. In the great square of St Neots is without doubt the finest interior of a merchant house (No. 20 Market Square), with Rococo plasterwork. Of Georgian Peterborough the last significant vestiges are confined to a couple of streets.

The earliest appearance of the GOTHIC REVIVAL is probably at Hinchingbrooke *c.* 1759 for the 4th Earl of Sandwich. The house was much visited by Horace Walpole, who was friends with the Earl's son George Montagu, and surviving still is a remarkable series of heraldic stained glass windows by *William Peckitt* of York, whom Walpole then commissioned at Strawberry Hill. They were designed by *Richard Bentley*, one of Walpole's Committee of Taste. Bentley's mother was the daughter of Sir John Bernard of Brampton Park. A second scheme of glass in the 'great chamber' of the house was destroyed in the fire of 1830 at Hinchingbrooke. Just a little later is *Capability Brown*'s Orangery at Burghley. This dates from before 1763 and precedes his interventions in the house, principally remembered for the Gothicization of the window patterns on all the façades, the destruction of one wing to the N front and the insertion of ceilings to the chapel and billiard room (a popular pattern of octagonal coffers taken from Wood's engravings of the ruins of Palmyra). Brown's Neo-Jacobean Banqueting House was not built until after his death, in 1787, and is part of his much greater achievement at Burghley in the transformation of the park. Capability Brown had acquired the manor of Fenstanton in 1767 in lieu of payment by the Earl of Northampton, and there he is buried although he never lived there. His monument – he died in 1783 – is plain, though not small, and also Gothic in detail. He also became Lord of the Manor of Hilton at the same time and is credited with the planting of elms on the expansive green in that village. Some Gothic remodelling took place at Elton Hall *c.* 1790, possibly by *John Carter*. Externally it exhibited a romantic, theatrical character, but the Octagon Room with its Gothic cabinets is a very charming space. *Sir John Soane*'s minor alterations at Ramsey Abbey in 1804–6 use pointed windows too, but his porch is a typically inventive piece of work that makes few concessions to any historic style. The work at Ramsey was done for the Fellowes family. They acquired the property in the 1730s and assiduously built up their estate in other parts of Huntingdonshire, especially around

Abbots Ripton, which became their principal seat in the C20. A remarkable but unattributed late C18 Gothick house was Alwalton Lodge, built for Robert Pigott. It has gone, but is illustrated in Volume III of the VCH volume for Huntingdonshire. In the park at Milton is a charming Gothic lodge of *c.* 1801 by *William Wilkins Sen.*

There is remarkably little to show for late C18 and early C19 NEOCLASSICISM. In Peterborough it is confined to the completion of the interiors at Milton by *Sir William Chambers*, twenty years after Flitcroft (*see* p. 394). The Long Gallery in particular is a design of the first order. The large and monumental gatehouse at Kimbolton dates from *c.* 1764–5 by *Robert Adam*, and it is gratifying to see how this great and agile designer expressed his respect for Vanbrugh. Adam was consulted for the staircase at Burghley but not used. *John Carr* of York was twice engaged for minor additions to Milton. In the second of these the Regency style is reached. *John Nash* worked at Brampton Park in 1806–7 but his work is now represented only by the Neo-Tudor service range. Gaynes Hall, Perry, however, is an elegant house by *George Byfield*, 1800, with Soanian touches.

The GREEK REVIVAL proper is almost entirely unrepresented except for a house at Godmanchester now attributed to the Irish architect *James Gallier*, who also designed the Chinese Chippendale bridge spanning the Ouse in the same town. Otherwise the style is mostly a matter of a handful of CHURCH MONUMENTS. That of the widow of Lancelot Brown Jun. at Fenstanton, dated 1793, was made by *Coade*, i.e. is of Coade stone. The modelling is no doubt by *John Bacon the Elder*, who also did two monuments (†1781 and †1790) at Warboys. The alternative Classical–Gothic in monuments remained throughout the C19. *Sir Richard Westmacott's* monument at Bainton (†1805) is Grecian, *John Flaxman's* at St John, Peterborough, 1804–6, is Grecian too, and *Sir Francis Chantrey's* at Orton Longueville (1827) is at any rate classical (and rather cold); but *Thomas Rickman*, the amateur architect and inventor of the terms 'E.E.', 'Dec' and 'Perp', signed a large Gothic triptych tablet at Buckden with a date of death of 1831. The late Georgian and early Victorian gentry of Huntingdonshire and Peterborough were quite satisfied with standard white and black tablets (see e.g. at Diddington, where in concert with painted hatchments the grouping is rather effective, or the picture-gallery effect of the Heathcotes at Conington).

VICTORIAN AND AFTER

VICTORIAN CHURCH ARCHITECTURE is primarily a story of repair and rebuilding among the parish churches, but the drainage of new tracts of the Fens after *c.* 1840 prompted the Fellowes of Ramsey Abbey to plant barn-like churches on their estate at Pondersbridge and Ramsey St Mary's in 1858–9, for the latter employing *Richard Armstrong*, who had served as Edward Blore's clerk of works in the 1830s. *Blore* himself shows the Neo-Norman fashion of the 1840s in the E end of Thorney in 1839–41, and it continues in the former St John the Evangelist at Huntingdon by *W. G. Habershon* of 1845 and the unattributed rebuilding of the chancel of Folksworth in 1850, the last a case of replacing an early C18 chancel with something more 'correct'. Blore also made alterations to Ramsey (again Neo-Norman) and Conington (Gothic); both retain the distinctive furnishings of the pre-Ecclesiological phase (numbered benches etc.). The small Catholic church of 1841–2 at St Ives is by *Pugin*, but re-erected in 1902 from its original site at Cambridge, and shows an endeavour towards a correct C13 vocabulary. The same may be seen in the few works in the area by *George Gilbert Scott*, who did a successful addition to All Saints at Huntingdon in 1861, restored the chancel of Ellington in 1863, with Geometrical-style windows, inserted the E window of Godmanchester, and added to Upton (Hunts.), in 1870–1, with excellent interior work for such a small building. At Ellington, Scott's involvement is due to Peterhouse, Cambridge, holding the advowson, and University patrons are the explanation for work by national architects elsewhere in the area. *William Butterfield*, for example, was employed in 1861 in the rebuilding of the chancel at Abbotsley, where Balliol College held the living. He had by then already designed the one really distinguished new church in Huntingdonshire: Waresley of 1857. This has one great moment inside, and its chancel exhibits to perfection Butterfield's faith in structural polychromy. *William White* restored Tilbrook in 1865–7 and then largely rebuilt Old Hurst in 1867–9. One of *A. W. Blomfield*'s earliest works is at Eynesbury in 1857–8, the commission secured through family connections; and in the following decades he rebuilt Sawtry, and restored Steeple Gidding among others. *Ewan Christian* was involved wherever the Church Commissioners held the advowson; at Alconbury he carried out a daring restoration of the tower by supporting the spire while rebuilding the masonry beneath.

The 1860s is the period of greatest activity and much of it was in the hands of local practitioners, notably *Robert Hutchinson* in the area around Huntingdon, around Peterborough *Alfred Sykes* (the Milton estate surveyor) and *Edward Browning* (the Diocesan Surveyor), and, along the w edge of Huntingdonshire, *Slater & Carpenter*, who had Northamptonshire connections. *W. G. Habershon* lived at St Ives before establishing his London practice and trained *R. W. Edis*, who was born at Huntingdon and obtained some church work locally (e.g. St Mary, Huntingdon) as well as the new house at Buckden Palace. Another local figure is *S. Inskip Ladds*. His father, *John Ladds*, worked with *Scott* at Ellington, where the Ladds family came from, and on his own account restored some of the churches in the vicinity (e.g. Easton) while also designing the Grammar School at Kimbolton and the rectory at Molesworth. S. Inskip Ladds undertook the lion's share of restorations of Huntingdonshire churches after 1900. He was too keen to scrape plaster from the walls (e.g. Buckden, Great Stukeley) and repoint the rubble below, but in his later works a sensitivity for woodwork shows an Arts and Crafts sensibility emerging.

Scott had been engaged at Peterborough Cathedral in a small way in 1855 to address the precarious state of the building, but the decisive work there was finally undertaken by *J. L. Pearson* from 1883. It was not without controversy, stemming initially from an intention to return the crossing tower to a completely Norman appearance but with a spire added, and then from the plan to take down and reconstruct the W front, which drew the ire of the S.P.A.B. Inside, Pearson gave the choir and presbytery their fittings, the latter including the lavish baldacchino and Cosmati-style pavement. Pearson went on to restore the parish church of St John and also Elton while work was ongoing at the cathedral. His contractor in all three places was *John Thompson* of Peterborough, who emerges first as a mason on the repair of Thorpe Hall in the 1850s in partnership with *Francis Ruddle*, a contractor employed by Blore and others. Thompson was taken up by Scott and enjoyed a distinguished career working for several of the principal Victorian architects. His mark is often the quality of the woodwork in the churches where his firm was involved, including some of the new churches for the expanding town of Peterborough after 1850. They display the evolving Gothic Revival from the Dec of St Mark's by *Edward Ellis* of 1855–6 to the free Perp of *Temple Moore*'s sensitive, quite original design for All Saints in 1886–1905, and *Leonard Stokes*'s less interesting design for St Peter & All Souls (R.C.) in 1896. St Ives has a memorable screen and organ loft by *Ninian Comper*, the best of the High Anglican work.

NONCONFORMIST CHAPELS of the mid to later C19 could be on a very grand scale and many adopted the Gothic as enthusiastically as the Anglicans. That at St Ives, by *John Tarring*, 1863–4, remains one of the landmarks of the town, and his church at Huntingdon (1867–8) was too until its demolition. A less skilled design but impressive nevertheless is the former Congregational Church, St Neots, by *Edward J. Paine*, 1888, which displays the fashion for brick and pressed terracotta decoration. The freer Gothic of the late C19 and early C20 is very well represented by the Baptist Church at Peterborough of 1906.

Among MONUMENTS, an ambitious Early Victorian Gothic one is at Orton Longueville to the Countess of Aboyne by *George H. Smith*, 1841. At the other end of the century, the most ambitious of funerary monuments is to Mr and Mrs Rowley at St Neots. It was designed by *F. A. Walters* and carved by *Thomas Earp* and is as late as 1893. By that time one might expect a deeper understanding of what the Middle Ages meant and no longer a mere imitation of all the details. *William Morris* had preached this from the 1870s and worked in that spirit already much earlier. His stained glass at Peterborough Cathedral is as early as 1862 and yet already far forward on the way out of historicism. It stands alone in its superb quality, but there are other works in STAINED GLASS that deserve mention for their date. First the remarkable E window of Thorney, 1838 by *George Austin Sen.* of Canterbury, copied from the early C13 windows at Canterbury Cathedral and of double significance as one of the only physical records of the Canterbury glass before Austin restored and replaced it. The restoration of Little Gidding by *Henry Clutton* in 1852–5 was accompanied by a programme of glass-making by *William Miller*, to designs by *Charles Winston*, pioneer of the revival of medieval technique. The E window is now in the chapel of the High School, Peterborough. All the key Victorian firms are represented in Huntingdonshire and Peterborough and much of the work is very good. There is an outstanding cycle of windows at St Neots by *Hardman* over five decades, a very fine window by *Heaton, Butler & Bayne* of 1865 at Waresley. Much glass by the principal firms dates from the later C19 decades and will be found in the Index of Artists; Brampton, Godmanchester and St John's, Peterborough, offer some of the best collections. Taking us into the early C20 is the almost unique instance of church glass by *Tiffany* at Kimbolton, 1902, and an exemplary series of Arts and Crafts windows by *Mary Lowndes* at Ufford, 1911–14. Among Victorian and Edwardian monuments, besides the Rowley monument at St Neots (*see* above), the best is the tablet with flag to the 5th Earl of Carysfort at Elton, by *C. R. Ashbee*, 1912.

VICTORIAN COUNTRY HOUSES form a small subject. Remodelling at Burghley was done early and deferentially by *J. P. Gandy-Deering*, but what *Edward Blore* did at Ramsey Abbey and Hinchingbrooke House lacks distinction, and Hemingford Park, Hemingford Abbots by *Decimus Burton*, 1842, is a minor work. Milton had no changes after *John Carr*'s *c.* 1800. Elton Hall, on the other hand, was substantially remade by *Henry Ashton* in 1855–60 and it is a skilful job, returning the house to something of its late C17 appearance. At Kimbolton, *William Burn* was engaged in 1863 and proposed a great porte cochère to go in front of the portico. It is fortunate that this was not acted upon, but inside is a room attractively decorated by Burn in a rather French taste.

Associated with some of the estates are MODEL COTTAGES. The early ones are at Brampton where Lady Olivia Bernard Sparrow built among others the sweet thatched cottages and infirmary for the village. There is another group at Waresley, designed by *Henry Ashton* for the Duncombes of Waresley Hall, a house that has gone. At Ramsey, *Blore*'s cottages and almshouses are rather more appealing than his work on the main house. But the chef d'œuvre is of course the village at Thorney, created from scratch after 1840 by the 7th Duke of Bedford. The history of the development of the Bedford estate cottages is covered on pp. 44–5, but only at Thorney is the effect of a model settlement so total. *S. S. Teulon* was the man appointed to see through the work on the village and to design the public buildings of school, infirmary and estate yard with its magnificent water tower. He also contributed to the design of smaller groups of cottages on the Bedford estate at Wansford *c.*1850.

Victorian PUBLIC BUILDINGS, often a subject of some significance given the tide of legislation for new institutions, offers surprisingly little in Huntingdonshire or Peterborough. The most significant buildings are the Neo-Norman Sessions Court House at Peterborough of 1842 by *W. J. Donthorn,* who was busy in the town at that date, and the still Grecian Commemoration Hall at Huntingdon by *Pocock & Glover,* 1841–2. There are the interesting remains of an early model jail at Huntingdon by *William Wilkins,* 1828–9, and the former hospital there by *Thomas Smith,* 1852–4, and the former workhouse for St Ives at Hemingford Grey of *c.* 1834 but nothing from the High Victorian years.

INDUSTRIAL BUILDINGS also make for a fairly brief summary, especially now that the remnants of the Peterborough brick industry (*see* p. 9) have disappeared. MILLS come first. There is one early C17 post-mill at Great Gransden, and there would have been many windmills on the fen at one time to lift or pump water into the drainage channels, but the majority of windmills are tower-mills and none are now earlier than the early C19. Barnack has a good example of 1840, built of the local stone. WATER-MILLS of considerable size existed on the River Great Ouse and that at Houghton is now a museum, as is the smaller mill at Sacrewell (Thornhaugh), which was built for the Duke of Bedford in 1750. Of the mills along the Welland, Maxey Mill still operates. The large C19 brick-built and steam-powered flour mills at St Ives and St Neots have been converted to housing. There were

Drainage of Whittlesey Mere.
Engraving, 1851

also important PAPER MILLS at Wansford and St Neots, the latter now converted to housing. The wealth produced is indicated by the quality of Paxton Hill House (Great Paxton) above the St Neots mills and Stibbington House for the Wansford miller. Steam-powered PUMPING STATIONS succeeded the C17 and C18 wind pumps on the Fen. A good example of the new buildings survives at Pondersbridge, but most were superseded in the C20.

RAILWAY BUILDINGS are more interesting. The first station at Peterborough was S of the river at the E end of the town (*see* Fletton). Built in 1845 it served the Eastern Counties Railway and the Northampton & Peterborough Railway (built by the London & Birmingham Railway) and from 1846 the Syston and Peterborough Railway built by the Midland Railway. The station, like all those on the N&PR were designed by *John Livock* in a charming Neo-Jacobean style; Wansford Station (at Stibbington), is one of the few remaining. The only section of tunnel on the line is there too, with a handsome Romanesque portal. The 1884 station from Barnwell, Northamptonshire, has been relocated here also. The line closed to passengers in 1957 and to freight in 1972 after which a section was revived for leisure in the New Town era. The Great Northern Railway arrived at Peterborough in 1848, building a new station on the site of the present one, and had stations also at Huntingdon and St Neots. The Italianate station at Huntingdon is a good example of the period. At Peterborough the line is still carried over the Nene by a remarkable cast-iron viaduct by *Sir William Cubitt* and *Joseph Cubitt*, 1849–50, with Greek Doric columns. It is easy to forget that Peterborough is, or rather was, a railway town before it became a centre for engineering; within the vicinity of the station are large GNR wagon sheds and some workshops, in the local yellow brick, as well as remains of the workers' terraced housing built in the area known as New England in the 1850s and 1860s.

The interest of TWENTIETH-CENTURY ARCHITECTURE and the most recent decade in Huntingdonshire and Peterborough is quite limited. *Edwin Lutyens*'s addition to the Bishop's Palace at Peterborough, 1897–8, is good but not by any stretch a major work. The early C20 Arts and Crafts phase in domestic building is represented by some charming but quite amateur work by the vicar of Houghton, the *Rev. F. K. Oliphant*, in Houghton itself and at Hemingford Abbots. At the beginning of the C20 there are some very pleasant schools in the Shaw-inspired line by *Herbert Leete*, Huntingdonshire County Surveyor, at Ramsey and Fletton (Peterborough). The Norris Museum at St Ives, 1932, by *S. Inskip Ladds* is delightful but the only major public building is the Town Hall at Peterborough by *E. Berry Webber*, 1928–33, which shows how strong the classical tradition remained in the years up to the Second World War. Nearby *Palmer & Holden*'s design for the National Provincial Bank in the Cathedral Square, Peterborough, 1928–9, must be one of the best of its date, inspired by Kirby Hall. The road bridge for the A1 at Wansford by *Simpson & Ayrton* with *Sir Owen Williams* is a superb structure of 1925–8, in a simplified medieval but entirely of its date. The radical forms of interwar Modernism are nowhere to be found. Only a little church work is worth noting, especially *Leslie T. Moore*'s superb rood screen at Barnack.

The POSTWAR PERIOD is heavier with new developments in the expansion of Peterborough and Huntingdon, the former as a full-blown New Town from the late 1960s. Peterborough was chosen because up to that time – the mid-1960s – there was concern that the first generation of New Towns – Harlow, Stevenage – were too modest in their ambition to attract new residents. New cities distant enough from London to become their own regional centre promised a better model for a population predicted to grow enormously in England before the end of the C20. A major achievement at Peterborough was the integration of the idea of a vast linear public park running for miles on both sides of the Nene from Peterborough W into the countryside. Whereas C19 and early–mid C20 Peterborough had an industrial base, from the 1970s the revolution came in the growth of services and for this new business parks were created. There is no point pretending that the majority of offices of the period *c.* 1970–1990 are anything more than feeble rehearsals of the more mundane and superficially flashy themes in British architecture of the period but the British sugar offices at Woodston and those at Lynchwood (Orton township) by *Arup* and *Chapman Taylor* deserve praise for the quality of their external and internal environments. Within the city centre itself the shopping centre of 1975–82 is also well-designed – modelled on contemporary American schemes – and the absence of significant alteration to its interior after more than three decades is at the very least an indication that the *Development Corporation Architects* succeeded in their intentions here. The housing is much less interesting but the 1980s work of *Mathew Robotham Associates* is always worth looking out for. The planning of a series of neighbourhoods around the historic centre and incorporating older villages was novel and overall quite successful if not very exciting. The virtue lies partly in the avoidance of sprawl, so that even forty years on the distinction between the rural and urban areas of Peterborough is very well defined, even in the age of the large trading and distribution sheds which lie close to the A1.

What happened at Huntingdon cannot be regarded with such equanimity. There the replanning of the roads has put the heart of the town into a noose and thoroughly spoiled the relationship with the river. It has been compounded by marching the A14 across one of its best open spaces. Meanwhile, however, many places have benefited from bypassing: Buckden and Wansford remain wonderful secrets off the A1 road and St Ives has regained its civility but pity poor Stilton. Kimbolton, well away on its own, must be one of the least-known towns in the Midlands and the conversion of the castle for a school has maintained a good relationship between house and town. In the wider countryside, the decline of agriculture in the C20 and the break-up of estates had a deleterious effect on the stock of vernacular buildings. The Royal Commission surveyed Huntingdon in 1926. It is a sobering fact that many good houses noted in Huntingdonshire had gone or been altered before the first edition of this guide was published in 1968; and others noted by Pevsner have vanished since, partly due to pressures for new housing, which sadly has overwhelmed many of the villages close to the A1. Peterborough was surveyed in advance of work on the New Town with good effect: the losses here have been minimal and since the early 1970s much has been done to record and conserve. While there is very little positive to say about the general quality of postwar architecture in Huntingdonshire and Peterborough there have been some interesting individual developments such as the series of bungalows at Wyton of 1962–4 by *Colin St John Wilson, John Dalton & Anthony Eardley*, and at Hemingford Grey an A-framed house by *Saunders Boston*, 1960, for the designer and artist Elizabeth Vellacott. Of most recent times the Thomas Deacon Academy at Peterborough by *Foster & Partners* is a flagship of the Buildings Schools for the Future programme of the early 2000s and the Creative Exchange at St Neots is a building type suited to a new era requiring small and flexible office spaces. So the towns and villages of Huntingdonshire and Peterborough still have much to entice the architectural traveller.

127

FURTHER READING

The literature for Huntingdonshire and Peterborough is not extensive. The *Victoria County History* (VCH) covered the Soke of Peterborough in vol. II (1906) of the four original volumes for Northamptonshire, with architectural notes by Sir Charles Peers that are models of their date. The VCH has done Huntingdonshire completely (1926–36) in three volumes which pay much attention to the county's buildings, in part because of the contribution of the local architect S. Inskip Ladds as one of the editors. In addition there is the volume of the Royal Commission on Historical Monuments (1926), complete or intended to be complete to 1714 but silent for anything after that. Both sources are on the whole still valid, although some buildings recorded by the RCHM had been lost even before the first edition of this guide. The information contained in the RCHM volumes has of course been greatly supplemented by the statutory National Heritage List for England (available via *www.english-heritage.org. uk*). By the time the RCHM began work on Northamptonshire the 1960s had been reached and the Soke of Peterborough was by then detached from the county and consequently omitted from their surveys. Instead a special volume of restricted focus, *Peterborough New Town, A Survey of the Antiquities in the areas of development*, was published in 1969. It is a pity that Burghley House and Milton were omitted from the RCHM's detailed survey of *The Country Houses of Northamptonshire* by John Heward and Robert Taylor (1996) but this is nevertheless very valuable for comparative study.

Besides the VCH the best sources for general historical information on Peterborough and the former Soke will be found in vol. II of John Bridges's *History and Antiquities of Northamptonshire* (ed. Peter Whalley, 1791) which despite its date of publication was compiled *c.* 1718 (and not updated by its editor). Bridges commissioned drawings of buildings to accompany his text but these were omitted in the eventual publication and will be found instead in *Northamptonshire in the Early Eighteenth Century: The Drawings of Peter Tillemans and others* (ed. Bruce A. Bailey, 1996).

The best general overview of Huntingdonshire has been provided by Peter Bigmore in *The Bedfordshire and Huntingdonshire Landscape* (1979) and for Peterborough in *The Northamptonshire Landscape* by John M. Steane (1974). *The King's England* series covered *Bedfordshire and Huntingdonshire* in a new edition in 1973. Despite the title this also covers Peterborough. The revising author for Huntingdonshire and Peterborough was P. G. M. Dickinson, the Huntingdon County Archivist, and his gazetteer of places remains a perceptive and attractive account. Juliet Smith's *Shell Guide* for Northamptonshire (1968) still includes the Soke in its enjoyable survey. In addition Hunts. matters are dealt with in the *Transactions of the Cambs. and Hunts Archaeological Society* and the *Proceedings of the Cambridge Antiquarian Society*. Buildings of Peterborough and the Soke occasionally feature in *Northamptonshire Past & Present*, the annual journal of the Northamptonshire Record Society.

The standard work to be consulted for pre-Victorian ARCHITECTS is H. M. Colvin, *A Biographical Dictionary of British Architects, 1600–1840* (4th edn, 2008). The *Directory of British Architects 1834–1914* (2 vols, RIBA) assists with superficial biographical information and indicates the sources for lists of work. See also the *Catalogues of the Royal Institute of British Architects Drawings Collection*. SCULPTORS are the subject of A. White's 'A Biographical Dictionary of London Tomb Sculptors *c.* 1560–*c.* 1660' (*Walpole Society*, vol. LXI, 1999, and supplement in vol. LXXI, 2009). M. Craske, *The Silent Rhetoric of the Body* (2008), gives the context for church tomb sculpture of 1720–70. For the ensuing period up to the mid C19 the information previously provided by Rupert Gunnis's biographical dictionary (1953) is now to be found, greatly expanded and supplemented, in I. Roscoe *et al.*, *A Biographical Dictionary of Sculptors in Britain 1660–1851* (2009); also available as a searchable database on the Henry Moore Institute website (*www.henry-moore.org/hmi/library/biographical-dictionary-of-sculptors-in-britain*). The story is taken on in B. Read, *Victorian Sculpture* (1982), and S. Beattie, *The New Sculpture* (1983). The United Kingdom National Inventory of War Memorials includes dates, artists and designers where known (*www.ukniwm.org.uk*).

General works on the PREHISTORIC AND ROMAN ARCHAEOLOGY of the region include A. Taylor, *Prehistoric Cambridgeshire*, 1977. There are four reports by F. M. M. Pryor of the major excavations at Fengate published as Royal Ontario Museum

Arch. Monographs 3 (1974), 5 (1978), 6 (1980) and 7 (1984). By the same author 'Borough Fen' in *Northamptonshire Archaeology* 18 (1983) and *Flag Fen: Life and Death of a Prehistoric Landscape* (2005). For the Roman period the key work is S. G. Upex, *The Romans in the East of England: Settlement and landscape in the lower Nene valley* (2008) which also has an extensive bibliography. Castor's excavations are detailed in *Northamptonshire Archaeology*, 21 (1987) and by S. G. Upex in 'The *Praetorium* of Edmund Artis' in *Britannia*, 42 (2011). The excavations at Godmanchester are covered by H. J. M. Green in *Current Archaeology*, 16 (1969), and by the same author in W. Rodwell and T. Rowleys, eds, *Small Towns of Roman Britain* (1975) and T. Kirby and S. Oosthuizen, eds, *An Atlas of Cambridgeshire and Huntingdonshire History* (2000).

There are very few good written histories for individual TOWNS AND VILLAGES containing more than slight architectural information, but A. G. Clark's *Elton, A History of its Lost and Ancient Buildings* (1992) is useful, as are H. F. Tebbs, *Peterborough* (1979) and A. Akeroyd and C. Clifford, *Huntingdon: Eight Centuries of History* (2004). For Peterborough, the history of the town through the period of the Development Corporation is described in *The Peterborough Effect* by T. Bendixson, 1988. For those interested in the finer points of the planning of the New Town the relevant reports are *Expansion of Peterborough* by Tom Hancock, 1966; the *Greater Peterborough Draft Basic Plan* by Hancock and J. E. Y. Hawkes, 1967; the *Greater Peterborough Master Plan*, by the Peterborough Development Corporation, 1970 and the *Greater Peterborough City Centre Plan*, again by the Development Corporation, 1971. Some of the Peterborough villages are covered magnificently by *Five parishes, their people and places: a history of the villages of Castor, Ailsworth, Marholm with Milton, Upton and Sutton* (CAMUS Project, 2004; also available online at http://thearchive.org.uk/thebook/journal. htm). Also worthwhile are J. M. Goodwin's *The book of Wansford* (2002), *The book of Barnack* (1983) and *The book of Northborough* (2000). Kimbolton has *A Brief History of Kimbolton* by John Stratford (4th edn, 2006) and various aspects of the town's buildings have been covered in the journal published by the Kimbolton Local History Society. C. F. Tebbutt, *St. Neots: A History of a Huntingdonshire Town* (1979), is one of a number of publications by this local historian. St Ives is well served by publications. *St Ives, Slepe by the Ouse*, by N. Hudson, 1989, is the general history with several others on specific periods or themes by Bob Burn Murdoch. In addition, B. Flanagan's *The New Bridges* (2005) discusses the causeway, and, by the same author, *Artists Along the Ouse* (2010) sheds light on a neglected subject. For Godmanchester, the local history website *www.godmanchester.co.uk* is certainly as good as any print publication. Thorney also has an active local history society and museum. They have published Alan E. Teulon's *Victorian Thorney*, covering the development of the model village. S. Wade Martins, *The English Model Farm* (2002) has useful material on the farms built by the Duke of Bedford in the 1850s and 1860s.

For CHURCHES, the essential book is *Cambridgeshire Churches* (ed. C. Hicks, 1997), which covers both Huntingdonshire and Peterborough. The chapters are by period and by theme, e.g. Isabel Henderson on Anglo-Saxon Sculpture and David W. Lloyd's chapter on Huntingdonshire steeples. It also includes a chapter on Nonconformist chapels, a subject covered in more detail by C. Stell, *Nonconformist Chapels in Eastern England* (2002). The context for developments in the C12 churches around Peterborough is described by B. Cherry, 'Romanesque Architecture in Eastern England', *Journal of the British Archaeological Association*, 1978. Robert Walker on Huntingdonshire Bell Frames in *Proceedings of the Cambridgeshire Antiquarian Society*, 95 (2006) has much useful material to consider for the dating of the church towers. It should be said that the claims made for post-Reformation dates for many towers by A. Woodyer in *Archaeological Journal* 141 (1984) were comprehensively challenged by G. W. Barnard in the same journal (149, 1992). There are of course church guides, though they vary widely in quality and often rely entirely on the VCH or the first edition of this guide for their architectural history, but Peterborough and Huntingdonshire are fortunate to have had several of its guides prepared by P. G. M. Dickinson, the Huntingdon County Archivist. For Peterborough, W. D. Sweeting, *Historical and architectural notes on the parish churches in and around Peterborough* (1868), is still vital. It is illustrated with photographs and in several instances details their appearance prior to Victorian restorations. Sweeting was rector of Maxey and published an account of the church in the *Journal of the British Archaeological Association* (New Series) 5, 1899; in the same volume are articles on Barnack and Northborough churches. He also wrote *Bell's Guide to Peterborough Cathedral* (1898).

The CATHEDRAL and its precincts are fully described by Charles Peers in VCH Northampton, vol. IV. Earlier histories are S. Gunton, *History of the church of Peterburgh* (1686; reprinted 1990), *Monasticon Anglicanum* by William Dugdale, new edn, 1817, and R. Willis, *Architectural History of some English Cathedrals* (2 vols, 1972–3), which gives an account of Peterborough in 1861. Lisa Reilly's *An Architectural History of Peterborough Cathedral* (1997) is necessary reading for the medieval period, but her re-dating of the Norman phase is not universally accepted. The most significant recent contributions to the literature on the medieval architecture are M. Thurlby, 'The Romanesque Apse Vault at Peterborough' in *Studies in Medieval Art and Architecture* (1994), and the same author's 'Stone Vault or Painted Wooden Ceiling? The Question of how to cover the nave of Peterborough Abbey Church', in *Ecclesiology Today*, 36 (2006); and P. Binski, 'The Painted Nave Ceiling of Peterborough Abbey', in *The Medieval English Cathedral* (ed. J. Backhouse, 2003). G. Cobb, *English Cathedrals, the Forgotten Centuries, Restoration and Change from 1530 to the Present Day* (1980) fills in the hazier picture of the C17, C18 and C19 history. Also important is 'Architecture at

Peterborough in the 13th century' by Mary Dean, in *Journal of the British Archaeological Association*, 137 (1984). Also articles in *Monasteries and Society in Medieval Britain* (ed. B Thompson, 1999), including D. F. Mackreth, *Peterborough from St Aethelwold to Martin de Bec c. 970–1155*. On the wider estate, *The granges of Peterborough Abbey* by W. T. Mellows, in Peterborough Natural History and Scientific and Archaeological Society 52nd–53rd Annual Report for 1923–24. The most recent interpretation of RAMSEY ABBEY is in *Medieval Archaeology* (vol. 52, no. 1, 2008) and for Thorney see *Medieval Archaeology* (vol. 50, 2006).

For information on CHURCH RESTORATIONS the records of the Incorporated Church Building Society are available online (*www.churchplansonline.org*).

ANGLO-SAXON SCULPTURE in the area still awaits a volume in the *Corpus of Anglo-Saxon Stone Sculpture* but *see* R. Cramp, 'Schools of Mercian Sculpture', in *Mercian Studies* (ed. A. Dornier, 1977), and A. M. Morris, 'A Study in Stone: The "Peterborough Group" of Sculptures', *Friends of Peterborough Cathedral Journal* (2003).

For the succeeding period see the *Corpus of Romanesque Sculpture in Britain and Ireland* (*www.crsbi.ac.uk*).

STAINED GLASS for Huntingdonshire is not yet as fully recorded as for Peterborough, which has been researched by Paul Sharpling and will be published in due course along with his notes on Northamptonshire glass. Brasses have been documented in P. Heseltine, *The Brasses of Huntingdonshire* (1978). The wall paintings at Peakirk are described by E. C. Rouse in the *Archaeological Journal*, 110, 1953.

Huntingdonshire is not rich in COUNTRY HOUSES but Hinchingbrooke, Kimbolton Castle and Elton Hall have all been covered by articles published in *Country Life* and so too Burghley, Milton and Thorpe Hall in Peterborough. G. Worsley, 'Thorpe Hall in context', in the *Georgian Group Journal*, 1993, is also important. Burghley has been the subject of the most serious attention, but the key work of scholarship on the early architectural history is by J. Husselby in 'Patronage, Culture and Power: The Early Cecils 1558–1612' (*Studies in British Art*, 8, ed. P. Croft, 2002), which derives from her unpublished PhD (Warwick University, 1996). Also useful is Eric Till on 'Fact and Conjecture – The Building of Burghley House: 1555–1587' in *Northamptonshire Past and Present*, 52 (1999) and 'The development of the park and gardens at Burghley' in *Garden History*, 19 (2), 1991. For Kimbolton, E. Kieven in *Architectural History*, 51 (2008) discusses the oft-disputed role of Galilei. Several of the more important houses are described in A. Emery, *The Greater Medieval House of England and Wales, 1300–1500* (vol. 2, 2000). Nick Hill, 'Northborough Manor: a re-appraisal', in *Proceedings of the Cambridge Antiquarian Society*, vol. 100 (2011), is an excellent account of this important building. Longthorpe Tower, Peterborough, has a good guidebook by English Heritage, and the wall paintings are described and analysed in G. Casagrande and C. Kleinheuz, 'Literary and philosophical perspectives on the Wheel of Five Senses in Longthorpe Tower', in *Traditio*, 41

(1985), and E. C. Rouse and A. Baker, 'The wall-paintings at Longthorpe Tower', in *Archaeologia*, 96 (1955).

As to VERNACULAR BUILDINGS, the RCHM volumes remain important, but there is no single survey to rely on for either Huntingdonshire or Peterborough and much of the information on individual buildings in this guide comes from unpublished reports by E. M. Davis since 1970. See also her contribution to *Regional Variations in Timber-Framed Building in England and Wales Down to 1550* (ed. D. F. Stenning and D. D. Andrews, 2002). Eric Mercer's *English Vernacular Houses* (1975) draws examples from the territory.

PRIMARY SOURCES. For small local authorities Huntingdonshire and Peterborough are well served by the custodians of their local records and it has been possible to make ample use of them for the revision of this volume. The repositories for records and archives for Huntingdonshire and Peterborough are somewhat spread about, reflecting the administrative history. So, for Huntingdonshire the principal resource is the Library and Archive in Huntingdon itself. However, the Ely Diocesan Archive, which holds material relating to churches in Huntingdonshire, is held at Cambridge University Library, and for the period before 1837 when the Archdeaconry of Huntingdon was part of the Lincoln diocese many of the records are accordingly in Lincoln. For Peterborough, the first port of call is the Peterborough Local Studies and Archives, which have all the relevant records for the City along with much other information on the villages of the area of the former Soke, especially in the indexes of the C19 newspapers (*Peterborough Advertiser*, *Peterborough Sentinel* etc.), which have supplied considerable information on church restorations and stained glass in both Peterborough and Huntingdonshire. However, diocesan records, e.g. church faculties, are held at Northampton Record Office, along with many other records for the Soke prior to 1965, including the estate papers of the Fitzwilliams of Milton. The cathedral records are of course in the Cathedral Library. Archives relating to the Bedford estate holdings (e.g. Thorney, Thornhaugh, Stibbington and Wansford) are part of the Russell Papers at Bedford & Luton Archives and Records centre. Burghley House retains its own archives but these may be consulted by appointment with the curator there. Peterborough Museum has some useful items in its collection but the Norris Museum at St Ives holds the personal papers of Sidney Inskip Ladds, a rich trove of information and analysis of individual buildings as well as his own work on church restorations. The Museum also has an excellent topographical library and collections of prints and drawings. The local libraries in the main towns also as a rule have local studies sections including the publications of the relevant local history societies. Long may they continue.

HUNTINGDONSHIRE AND PETERBOROUGH

(Peterborough entries are denoted [P])

ABBOTS RIPTON

The manor was in the possession of Ramsey Abbey from the C10. Scattered around several large greens are many timber-framed houses. The Fellowes of Ramsey had acquired much of the manor by 1774 and the rest in 1869. That is how the village has retained its well-kept character.

St Andrew. Externally all Perp, of different materials and dates, with windows with two-centred arches and panel tracery to the nave and N aisle, and four-centred arches to the chancel, one-bay N chapel and clerestory, and also – in the tower W – uncusped. E.E. S doorway and, inside the S aisle wall, wide blank arches with chamfered piers rising from a low stone bench, a sign of early C13 date (cf. Alconbury, Great Gidding, Hemingford Abbots). E.E. S arcade piers also. But the spacing of the bays is too wide for E.E. work, and the arches are Perp. So is the W respond. The N arcade is Perp throughout, with capitals to the shafts towards the openings, a moulded continuous order, and the outer order or hoodmould given its own minor shafts with capitals towards nave and aisle. On the aisle side these shafts continue upwards between the arches. The arch to the chapel similarly treated. Fine chancel roof of *c.* 1500 with figures against the principal rafters and the jack-posts; the two at the W end must be the donors. Tracery in the spandrels, one pair with shields. – FONT. Octagonal, Perp, with plain quatrefoils. – ETCHED GLASS. S aisle window by *Laurence Whistler*, to Lady de Ramsey (†1987); tumbling trails of wild flowers and Swallowtail butterflies. – MONUMENTS. – Nicholas Bonfoy, Serjeant at Arms of the House of Commons, †1775. Curvaceous frame with a scrolled pediment. – Rev. John Cranwell †1793, '. . . a lover of polite literature . . .', so piles of books on top. Signed by *Edward Bingham* of Peterborough.

RECTORY FARM COTTAGE, 200 yds N of the church, is the best of the village's numerous thatched houses. The central hall is late medieval and aisled on both sides. Cross-wings of *c.* 1600 projecting under half-hipped roofs. The brick chimney is early C17, when the floor was inserted in the hall. SE of the centre, on a site with the remains of two moated enclosures, MOAT HOUSE has one very fine early C16 timber-framed cross-wing with two rooms and a brick and tile chimney with stone quoins. The room at the opposite end of the house has an inglenook fireplace, with reset *c.* 1600 panels, and also finely carved later C18 Composite pilasters and a frieze of carved swags. Nice pantiled veranda.

ABBOTS RIPTON HALL. Remodelled *c.* 1800 for the Rooper family, this part gault brick with a deep bow porch on the three-bay S front. The rest is brick also but of more than one date. *Salvin* added the N wing in 1856, simultaneously restyling the house in a dubious Jacobean taste, but these frills were stripped, and the Late Georgian appearance restored, by *Ailwyn Fellowes*, 3rd Lord de Ramsey, after the house became his seat in 1931. E porch of this time. On the W front, a loggia by *Peter Foster*; one of several contributions by him since the 1960s that include the Greek Doric SNOOKER ROOM and SWIMMING POOL, the latter top-lit with columns around the pool and shell grotto.

W of the house is the 'Monks' Stewpond' and crossing the S end of this is a brick BRIDGE of 1746, which carried the drive from the St Ives road to the S front. But most of the remarkable GARDEN has been created since 1930, originally to designs by *Humphrey Waterfield* (†1971, commemorated by an urn) and later *Lanning Roper*. Several fine late C20 garden FOLLIES by *Peter Foster*: a thatched Gothick summerhouse, next to a Chippendale Bridge (based on that at Godmanchester, q.v.), a Chinese fishing pavilion by the lake, copied from that formerly at Wivenhoe House, Essex, and, in the rose garden, a sundial of 2000 with quotation from Benjamin Franklin. The principal formal element is a yew-edged walk on axis with the W front of the house; it broadens out at its centre with an elaborate Gothic gazebo, again by Foster, and terminating the walk are GATES whose piers carry urns with ram's heads. The design is based on the famous early C14 incense boat found in Whittlesey Mere in 1850. Two charming little side gates are made of gardener's tools; they are by *George Carter*, *c.* 2000.

WENNINGTON. *See* p. 720.

ABBOTSLEY

ST MARGARET. Of brown cobbles; Dec and Perp except for the C13 chancel arch. Dec the N aisle, according to the two-light windows with reticulation units, and the four-bay arcade with quatrefoil piers and thin shafts in the diagonals. Dec, though much restored, the S aisle too. The doorway anyway, with its

large blocks of sandstone, is reliable, and the s arcade with
standard motifs looks in its detail even earlier than the n
arcade. In the aisle is an ogee-headed tomb recess with crockets and buttress shafts and shields of the Tilly family, who held
the manor from 1312. The long tendril with flowers in one
moulding is reminiscent of the w window at Keyston (q.v.) but
also Swineshead and Yelden in Bedfordshire. Both aisles have
piscina; the n aisle also brackets for statues. Late c14 Perp w
tower, the figures of kings on the pinnacles, supposedly Elizabethan and claimed as Macbeth, Malcolm, Harold and William.
Two were replaced in 1884 by *J. P. St Aubyn*. The chancel is
by *Butterfield*, 1861, with the n vestry and n porch, but there
is nothing that could reveal him at once, other than the
unmoulded tracery. The patrons from 1341 were Balliol
College, which explains Butterfield's involvement. In the vestry
w wall outside, a reset niche of very pretty details, presumably
formerly with a pinnacle. It was formerly in the n wall of the
previous vestry. The FITTINGS are also Butterfield and typically good, especially the pulpit. – SCREEN. In the chancel arch.
Partly (dado) Perp. Removed from the tower arch and supplemented and glazed *c.* 1975 to separate the chancel, which is
now the parish church, from the redundant nave, which is
cared for by the Churches Conservation Trust. – PAINTING.
An interesting Flemish late c15 Adoration of the Magi. The
scene is in demi-figures, which is rare, and derives from an
original by Hugo van der Goes. Incorporated by Butterfield as
the altarpiece and probably given its Gothic frame at that time.
– STAINED GLASS. In the n aisle e window, old bits. – The e
window and the one n and two s windows in the chancel are
by *A. Gibbs*. – MONUMENT. Splendid c18 artisan classical
tomb-chest in the churchyard with emblems of mortality.

RECTORY FARM at the e edge is of *c.* 1840, built by Balliol
College; a very rational arrangement of three-by-three-bay
square and hipped-roofed house with a complete set of gault
brick farm buildings behind around an open court.

AILSWORTH [P]　　　*1090*

A strip of a village, running uphill from the Nene, with a medieval
layout of high street and back lanes e and w still clearly discern-
ible. Many small cottages and former farmhouses typical of the
area. It narrowly avoided becoming a township for Peterborough
New Town in 1979 but has grown together with Castor (q.v.)
since.

In Normangate Field, 900 yds s of both villages, was the site of
major industrial activity associated with the Roman town of
Durobrivae (*see* Water Newton), which lay 1,000 yds further SE
across the river. Pottery and metalworking were chief among

the industries operating here. From the footpath which leads across Normangate Field to Water Newton, ERMINE STREET can be seen as an impressive linear bank running NW–SE. The underlying Roman archaeology is only visible from the ground as cropmarks. See also Introduction p. 360.

ROUND BARROW, 1,200 yds S of the village, close to the Nene. A low mound, some 30 metres (98 ft 5 in.) in diameter, with little sign of an outer ditch. The central area has a depression, perhaps caused by earlier excavations. These may have been carried out in the early C19 by Edmund Artis, who mentions the excavation of barrows in the area and illustrates in 1828 what are late Iron Age objects from 'a tumulus' in this area. Bronze Age, but possibly modified several times. It may even be associated with the ROMAN VILLA discovered 300 yds to the W. See also Introduction, pp. 360–62.

₁₀₇₀

ALCONBURY

ST PETER AND ST PAUL. An E.E. church of high quality, certainly in two of its elements, the steeple and the chancel. The steeple has a W lancet, then a circular window with a quatrefoil, long bell-openings of two lights with bar tracery, a rich corbel table of heads and notch stops, and a spire with high broaches that have little heads at the tops (cf. Buckworth). Three tiers of lucarnes. The lowest ones are large and of *c.* 1300. The arch to the nave is small and triple-chamfered. The chancel is late C13 too. The windows are lancets – three very slightly stepped in the E wall – or have Y-tracery, except the SW one with cinquefoiled heads and a lowside window below the transom. The buttresses are slightly chamfered, and the chamfers end charmingly in a little concavity at the top, just as found in C13 buttresses at Ramsey Abbey (q.v.). Inside, the chancel is quite excellent. It not only has rich shafting to the E lancets, which are a trio of shafts with a pendant of foliage inside, but all along the N and S walls close high blank arcading on shafts – six full arches and at the W and E end the baffling half- and two-thirds arches which the E.E. style never minded, though they contradict so much an ideal of purity which we cannot help attributing to it. An oddity is that the shafts block the doors to N (with rounded-trefoiled head) and S (traces only). Below the E window are three recesses, arranged symmetrically – cupboards probably. The chancel arch matches. The nave arcades cannot have been done much after the tower, yet must be later, though not later than the chancel. This dating is based on the fact that the tower in its position presupposes the S arcade where it is, but a N arcade some feet further S. On the other hand, the chancel arch is centred with the nave. So, when the arcades were built, that to the N was set further N than a preceding N arcade or nave N wall had been. The details of the arcades (standard elements) are hardly later than 1300. The clerestory has plain Y-tracery, and that also means late C13. In the S aisle are a W lancet, a late-C13-looking doorway with fine mouldings, and a window with bar tracery. The buttresses are chamfered, as in the chancel. There is also a Dec window, with reticulated tracery, and a low tomb recess. The Perp window here evidently replaced two C13 ones of which traces remain inside. The N aisle has more reticulated windows, and a doorway with continuous mouldings. So that will be *c.* 1330. Also two more Perp windows, which go with the good roofs of chancel and both aisles. In the chancel, angels against the intermediate principals, in the aisle figures against the wall-posts, holding shields and various other things. The nave roof has shields and a few angels to the wall-plate but was otherwise replaced in 1876–7 by *Ewan Christian*, who then had to save the tower by rebuilding it, with some ingenuity holding up the spire with scaffolding throughout the work. – PULPIT. With some original Perp tracery. – STAINED GLASS. E window. A distinguished design of 1876 of Christ's nativity, road to Calvary and Ascension, but who is it by? – S aisle W, †1901, signed by *Jones & Willis*.

In the churchyard, a tall slate HEADSTONE for Elizabeth Sacheverell †1810 with copperplate inscription, signed by *G. Neale* of Grantham.

By the SE corner of the churchyard, MANOR FARM. A large yeoman house, mostly early C17 and of red brick, but incorporating a C16 timber-framed building at its N end. Symmetrical E front to the farmyard, two storeys with kneelered-gabled wings projecting at each end, a door to the r. of the centre and a horizontal mullioned window lighting the ground-floor hall. Moulded platband below the first floor. Massive chimneystack on the S end for the kitchen. At the back, set against the hall chimneystack, is the former stair-tower, also gabled. The stair itself has been reset inside the hall and has turned balusters and shaped finials typical of the date. There seems to have been a single chamber above the hall, its fireplace now blocked and the room subdivided. The N wing has a winder stair and the back half of this wing is late C17, with two half-hipped roofs. In Chapel Street is THE MANOR pub, a late C16 house with jettied front of one large and two small gables. Good carved beams inside. Otherwise altered.

The S part of the village has a good run of small houses and cottages on two sides of a very long green which is bisected by a stream. The BRIDGE across it is C15, with four pointed chamfered arches. There is a similar pattern to the hamlet at ALCONBURY WESTON, ½ m. NNW. The bridge there, on the road to Hamerton, also has stone piers, doubtfully claimed to have come from the ruins of a church at Coppingford (about 2 m. N).

ALCONBURY HOUSE, off Rusts Lane, in wooded parkland ⅝ m. E of Alconbury. A fine late C18 small country house, probably built for the Rusts, who were bankers in Huntingdon. Red brick, T-plan originally with the stair in the centre and the principal front to the W of three bays and two storeys above a basement with an elegant full-height bow in the centre. Augmented without finesse *c.* 1840 for James Rust by *H. B. Hodson,** adding an attic storey running front to back and a canted bay on the N front, both in gault brick.

MILESTONE. On the Old North Road, near the Alconbury Weston turning. Erected *c.* 1770. Square, with a ball finial. Hands point in different directions, and inscriptions tell you how far it is to Huntingdon, Cambridge, Buckden and Sutton, and how far to London via Huntingdon, via Cambridge, and via Buckden.

WEYBRIDGE LODGE FARM. The house, although rebuilt after a fire in the early C20, has an early C17 brick core and was built as hunting lodge by the Cromwells of Hinchingbrooke. There are large fireplaces in the principal rooms (BD).

ALWALTON

1090

At the furthest W edge of Peterborough and back-to-back with Orton township (p. 647) but still with its own identity.

ST ANDREW. Surrounded by lime trees, a church rich in interest externally as well as internally. The oldest feature of the exterior is the S doorway, which has the Norman motif of chevron at right angles to the wall. It was combined with a pointed arch when reset in the S aisle in the early C13. The interior takes us back yet farther. The N arcade is of about 1170. Four bays, low round piers, the capitals with pre-Gothic leaf volutes or crockets, the abaci square with nicked corners. Round arches of two chamfers with broaches and some scrolled chamfer-stops. The abacus of the W pier is octagonal and has a waterleaf capital. This represents a lengthening of the arcade at the time the tower was begun, with the former respond reused, and the S arcade erected. It is three bays, for the same length as the N arcade's four. Slender round piers on waterholding bases, still round arches. The tower arch has keeled main shafts to the responds, the simplest moulded capitals, and double-chamfered arches. Outside, the tower has clasping buttresses, several lancets, twin bell-openings with mid-shaft and plate tracery and a blank arch either side of each twin. Corbel-frieze, battlements, spirelet, partly due to restoration of 1902–6 by *Townsend & Fordham*, who also partly rebuilt the N aisle and scraped the interior. The transepts are later than the tower, but still C13. They each have at their end a large three-light window with three trefoiled circles in bar tracery. To the E they have Y-tracery. That is clearly late C13. The chancel was done at the same time. Y-tracery with cusping and a foiled circle in the fork of the Y and similar motifs. Lowside windows to N and S. But the

---

*Hodson reseated the church in 1842.

E window has reticulated tracery, i.e. is a generation later. In the chancel, simple SEDILIA and recess opposite. The chancel was originally vaulted in two bays. Traces are recognizable here and in the transepts, whose present arches are Perp but look makeshift and have reused vaulting shafts; this alteration coincides with the nave clerestory. The area round the crossing is confused; the nave arch has shafts and semi-octagonal responds of c. 1330 but an arch of 1840 by *Bryan Browning*. The chancel arch is of the same restoration but l. and r. of the arch are quoins. They must represent the extent of the chancel before the late C13. As puzzling is a blank arch above the blank doorway high up in the tower E wall. – PULPIT and LIGHT FITTINGS by *G. G. Pace*, 1962–8. – STAINED GLASS. Bits in one chancel S window. E window, war memorial of 1919 by *Clayton & Bell*. The other windows are clear-glazed with 'endless' patterns by *Pace*. – MONUMENT. Sir Richard Hetley †1807. By *Sparrow* of Stamford. Fluted pilasters and urns to the top.

ALWALTON HALL, NW of the church. Built or remodelled c. 1840 for the 5th Earl Fitzwilliam. Well-cut ashlar limestone with moulded dressings and low, hipped roof. Three-bay entrance front with the centre set forward under a pediment, the symmetry upset by a single-storey addition to the l. bay. Square and bow-ended bay windows to the rear and flank.

No. 4 CHURCH STREET has a GATEWAY inscribed 'APRIL ICM 1684' which was the doorway to April House, Farcet (dem. c. 1975). Pevsner saw it *in situ* and described it as 'on the way to being classical, but has not quite arrived yet. Pilasters against a rusticated background, but instead of a real pediment a hood starting straight and going segmental only in the middle.' Nearby, MULLION COTTAGE is dated 1645 and has mullioned windows, but the doorway-head is straight and no longer four-centred. NE of this (in Water End) is the former village SCHOOL, Gothic of 1867 by *Clark & Holland* of Newmarket. Opposite, the RECTORY of 1833 by *Bryan Browning*. Principal range to the garden, of three bays with giant pilasters.

NE of this, on a little green, LYNCH LODGE, the two-storey former porch of Chesterton House (the Dryden mansion demolished in 1807), rebuilt by the Fitzwilliams as a lodge by a private road to Milton. It must be of c. 1625 and of a characteristic Northamptonshire/Huntingdonshire type, cf. Stibbington Hall (q.v.) and Glendon Hall, Northants. It has Doric columns and the round-arched doorway below, Ionic columns and a three-light window with transom above, and is surmounted by a shaped gable. In the gable and on the pedestals of the upper columns, simple geometrical patterns of an Elizabethan type. Single-storey addition of 1807, consisting of one room. Interior restored and brick rear addition made for the Landmark Trust by *Philip Jebb*, 1983.

NE of the lodge is the MANOR HOUSE. It is L-plan with an E cross-wing and two-storey W porch, but appears to have been reduced to this by a fire c. 1789 and so may have begun as an

E-plan with its porch in the centre. Its motifs are mostly
c. 1680, with a coved cornice along the side of the wing, a
staircase tower at the rear, square stacks, and on the s front a
type of casement of three lights, the side lights transomed, the
timber middle light arched without a transom. It is a popular
variation on the motif of the Venetian window and seen in its
grandest form at Thorpe Hall. But here it is combined with
window surrounds of smooth rustication in alternating sizes
which must be of *c.* 1700 and are of a refronting that includes
the big modillioned eaves cornice and straight gable to the
cross-wing. On the other fronts are stone mullioned and
wooden cross-windows. C19 NW addition and two striking but
sensitive extensions to W and NW by *Bruce Dilks* of *Jefferson
Sheard Architects*, 1995 and 2005. Inside, one large C17 chimney
piece in the hall and a very fine closed-string oak staircase with
turned balusters and ball finials to newel posts. Some other
good C18 fittings, including, in the C19 part, panelling and
chimneypiece rescued from Stilton House, Stilton (1701; dem.
1970s).

LYNCH FARM, ¾ m. NNE of the Manor House. The L-shaped
house incorporates windows and other details said to have
come from Chesterton House (*see* p. 459) in 1807. The windows
are mullioned and mullioned and transomed. The bay windows
may also be imported (cf. Elton Hall), and even the small
gables. But can the round corner turret be, or is this not rather
a piece of Gothic fancy, intended to catch the eye in the landscape around Milton to the N?

BAINTON [P]

ST MARY. The N arcade first. Probably early C13. Three bays,
circular piers, circular capitals and abaci, double-chamfered
round arches. The narrower W bay is later (pointed arch) and
was built as the link with the new W tower. This is Dec. Angle
buttresses. Each side in addition treated as a giant sunk panel,
W window with Y-tracery but ogee details, tall tower arch
towards the nave with filleted piers, bell-openings with Y-
tracery, ballflower frieze. Spire with two tiers of lucarnes.
The belfry has curious panels with pierced openings (trefoil,
diamond, pointed quatrefoil, quatrefoil). Dec also the s doorway, the windows l. and r. of it, the widening of the N aisle and
the N chapel (one bay, s arch with sunk quadrant mouldings;
the W arch has a reset early C13 keeled shaft and octagonal
capitals). The chancel has mid-C15 E and SE windows (sedilia
below) and tall late C15 s window with a segmental arch. Inside
the SE window slender colonnettes with castellated caps. Such
caps are used in the chancel arch also. Two splendid PISCINAS,
late C13, not *in situ*: in the chancel E wall a tall gable with naturalistic oak leaves and acorns; in the N chapel with crocketed
gable and big finial. A third, in the nave, has a cusped head

(cf. Ufford, of which Bainton was a chapelry). In the E wall, two brackets for images, the l. one a niche with nodding ogee top and vault. Vestry rebuilt by *Charles Kirk* of Sleaford, 1878. – FONT. Probably C13. Cylindrical base with four engaged shafts. – MONUMENTS. Robert Henson †1755 (N aisle). Returning Officer for Stamford: '. . . Bribes not able to corrupt, Promises seduce, nor Threats deter him from doing his duty'. Tablet with a flat obelisk and flame finial. – Mary Henson †1805 (N chapel). By *Sir Richard Westmacott*. With a seated mourning Grecian.

Nearby, the enigmatic VILLAGE CROSS, four big square steps, a fragment of the shaft and a ball finial. The date is uncertain, but one step incorporated a stone with chevron and nailhead. Locally the largest of its kind.

(BAINTON HOUSE. Remodelled in the C19 but probably C16 or C17, with shallow wings on the S front. Reset two-light windows with ogee tracery and straight hoodmould.)

BARHAM

1070

ST GILES. Nave, narrow N aisle, and chancel; no tower, but a bellcote of 1850 by *George Allen* of St Ives. The N wall of the aisle was also rebuilt. W wall reconstructed in 1903 by *S. Inskip Ladds* with a central buttress and Dec window to one side. S porch of the same time, the chancel restored 1905. The S doorway and the three-bay arcade are Transitional between Norman and E.E. The doorway has one order of polygonal shafts, scallop capitals, chevron set diagonally, and the arch just pointed (an alteration?). Reset carved stone with scroll and dogtooth. The arcade has round piers with square abaci and round arches with only a slight chamfer. The hoodmould also has a slight chamfer and stops carved with stems and foliage. But one of the capitals is of the Late Norman waterleaf type; the others are of the E.E. crocket variety. The bases have waterleaf spurs. The E bay is wider than the others. The chancel and its arch is late C13 with (restored) Y- and intersecting tracery. – BOX PEWS. Still facing the pulpit. At the rear, C17 BENCHES with book rests and knobs on the ends (cf. Leighton Bromswold).

At WOOLLEY, 1 m. SE, the poignant ruins of ST MARY (hauled down in 1962), with a double ogee-headed W door in the base of the tower, and some chevron ornament and a Norman capital reset in the S wall (rebuilt in 1907 by *S. Inskip Ladds*). S. P. Cockerell was lord of the manor from 1803.

BARNACK [P]

0000

Barnack was known throughout the Middle Ages for its limestone quarries and it was already used from Roman times for both building stone and stone for sculpture, altars, milestones and coffins. Much of the Roman workings were obliterated by the intensive quarrying which produced stone from the Saxon period onwards. Peterborough Cathedral is built of Barnack stone, as were all the Fenland abbeys and the cathedral at Norwich. The quarries were exhausted by the C15 but their site is marked SW of the village by the rumpled contours of the HILLS AND HOLES (Nature Reserve), a series of near-circular depressions which represent the pits from which limestone was extracted. Their undulations lend a memorable character to the gardens of houses in the S of the village.

ST JOHN THE BAPTIST. Without any doubt one of the most rewarding churches in the area, with interesting work of all periods, none more interesting than that of the Saxon W tower. The exterior has irregular long-and-short quoins, the familiar thin, unstructural lesenes or pilaster strips, windows with arched and triangular heads, some filled with stone slabs pierced by interlace patterns, the typical un-moulded block-like abaci, the flat bands placed parallel with jambs and arch of an opening but at some distance from it, and bands dividing the stages with a recessed horizontal section between. In addition, the most curiously moulded tower arch, an example of how unstructural Late Saxon architectural detail was (this was blocked by a C13 wall until restoration in 1853–5). One ought to observe specially how, between capitals and abaci of the responds (if these terms can be used), the moulding recedes and rounds the corner instead of forming an angle. The form is almost streamlined. At least as noteworthy, the decorative slabs outside the tower with scrolls branching off a stem symmetrically to the l. and r. and birds, one a cock, at the top. The style, if the slabs are contemporary rather than reset, would give a date in the mid C10 for the tower (the West Saxons began to colonize the area c. 920). There are more birds to the round-headed opening on the S front, which also has a sundial with leaves above. The original entrance into the tower was from the S. The triangular-headed W recess inside with a seat can never have been more than a recess, as one of the lesenes runs up the wall outside behind it. Similar seats in the other walls were removed in the C19, but rectangular cupboards of the same rough construction remain, all of which suggest this was formerly a W sanctuary with altar in front of the recess. The S doorway is now blocked inside by the work done in the early C13. This consisted of an internal strengthening, e.g. by a rib-vault on corbels (single-chamfered ribs leaving a large bell-hole open), and the erection of a newel stair to the new octagonal upper part of the steeple. Two big bell-openings of two lights with round arches, triple-shafted jambs and a pierced spandrel (i.e. the Y-motif), low broaches and, standing on them, tall, plain, polygonal angle pinnacles, short spire, or perhaps rather steep-pitched octagonal roof. If it is called a spire it must be one of the earliest in England. The corner pinnacles with their shafts are of the restoration of 1935–7 by *Leslie T. Moore*. The angles of the aisleless Saxon nave can also still be seen and at the E end of the N aisle is the remnant of an arch that might have led into a *porticus*. It was a little wider than the nave is now. The Saxon roofline appears on the E wall of the tower. The Norman style is missing, except for a capital and a head, reset in the former rood stair in the S chapel. Next in time come the N aisle and N chapel. The chapel is of one bay. The big waterleaf capitals of the responds indicate a late C12 date. The arch is round but double-chamfered; the aisle arch is pointed on grotesque corbels. The arcade is of three bays and has slender circular piers with bases with spurs and crocket and volute capitals with small heads.* On the capital facing the S door, an entwined serpent. Square abaci with the corners nicked. Round arches, still with chevrons on the wall surface and at right angles to it, except the W arch. There is also a strange transition from rolled to keeled mouldings round the centre and W arches. The N doorway still has a waterleaf capital. So the date of all this is probably the late C12. Only a little later, the S aisle and S porch. The arcades now have fine quatre-foil piers with subsidiary shafts in the diagonals and shaft-rings. The capitals, all except one, have upright stiff-leaf. The arches are still round but have many fine mouldings.

The S porch is a superb piece, tall and gabled with a tall entrance flanked by three orders of columns with stiff-leaf capitals. Pointed arch with many mouldings. The sides inside with tall blank arcading again with stiff-leaf capitals, S doorway with once more three orders, stiff-leaf capitals, and a round arch with many mouldings. The stiff-leaf is all early, i.e. upright with separate single stems (cf. the W end of Peterborough Cathedral). So the date will be within the first twenty years of the century. An odd rib-vault rises right into the gable (single-chamfered ribs). On the NW corbel a little C13 painting. Shortly after the completion of the porch, work must have started on the upper stages of the tower. The chancel dates from *c.* 1300–30. At the same time the S aisle was widened E of the porch, perhaps for a chapel. Pretty windows with segmental arches and ballflower above them. Simpler Dec the windows in the aisle wall W of the porch, in the N aisle and in the chancel. The chancel E window, however, is a true showpiece: five steeply stepped lancet lights and below the arch of each light a cusped arch with a crocketed gable over – a very rare motif (but cf. Milan Cathedral, late C14). Of the same phase the chancel arch, the SEDILIA (hoodmould on demons' heads and also one head with arms held up), the PISCINA (pointed-trefoiled arch leaning forward, as they do above the heads of C13 effigies, and crocketed gable), and also the N aisle windows. Perp vestry of two storeys, the upper part for the sacristy.

---

*This is similar to the arcade of the hall at Oakham Castle, Rutland, and the C12 hall of the demolished manor house at Barnack had similar features.

Perp s chapel built by the Brownes of Walcot (q.v.); Robert Browne †1506. Presumably he was related to the Brownes of Stamford, who built the hospital there and endowed All Saints. Richly decorated parapet and battlements. Quatrefoil frieze at the base. Simple windows, the sw paired together. Very wide arch to the chancel in Ketton stone; the aisle arch is of 1854. In the e wall brackets and very tall crocketed canopies, richly panelled with quatrefoils, for images. The n one has an Immaculate Conception. The Virgin sits under a canopy, her chest pierced by rays emanating from the Trinity. Above her an inscription: MARIA IHESU IN CONTEMPLACIONE SUA (Mary in her contemplation of Jesus). Reset below the bracket on the s side, a bird of the kind seen on the tower.

– FONT. Early c13. Octagonal. Leaf decoration in segmental lunettes at the foot of the bowl and also as a top band. In between, single flowers. The supports are pointed-trefoiled arches of openwork with continuous mouldings. Trumpet-shaped cover with crockets and angel finials, perhaps 1850s, cf. Ufford. – PEWS and PULPIT, contemporary with restoration of 1853–5. The chancel was embellished by the Rev. Marsham Argles, rector and later Dean of Peterborough: REREDOS marble with mosaic angels by *Salviati* after Fra Angelico, probably 1860s, and painted ROOF of 1879. – ROOD SCREEN. c15 woodwork at the base, the rest in Perp style, 1932 by *Leslie T. Moore* and *Mary Temple Moore*, and highly impressive. Loft on little vaults and the rood on a cambered beam. – SCULPTURE. Seated Christ in Majesty, relief, over 3 ft (91 cm) high and of exquisite quality. It was discovered in 1930 face down in the n aisle. It may have formed part of an altarpiece. Its low-relief carving is in the Saxon tradition, but its monumental character associates it with Continental early Romanesque art of the c11. The draperies are managed as competently as never again anywhere for a century or more, and the expression is as human, dignified and gentle as also never again anywhere for a century. – STAINED GLASS. Mostly given by the Rev. Marsham Argles (*see* above). By *Heaton, Butler & Bayne*, the three in the chancel, with canopywork, a rich silvery patternwork of leaves and tracery lights of bright kaleidoscopic colours (1873), the tower (1876, a king and his councillors – it was thought that the tower had served as a manorial court) and the two in the s aisle (1884). Lady Chapel e by *Clayton & Bell* (†1861), good figure-work in convincing Gothic style, and se by *Hugh Easton*, 1931; the Annunciation against clear glazing with swooping figures and curling Renaissance fronds. Medieval fragments in the tracery of the n aisle, clerestory and vestry (three heads, attributed by Richard Marks to *John the Glazier* of Stamford). – MONUMENTS. – GRAVE MARKER. s chapel. Anglo-Scandinavian. 6 ft (2 metres) long with interlace. Discovered in 2011. – n chapel. Two tomb recesses containing effigies: a cross-legged knight, early c14, in mail with a surcoat, defaced, and lady of *c.* 1400 with deeply cut drapery; this must have been of fine quality. – s aisle. Early Tudor, grey Alwalton marble tomb-chest, with recess above and cresting. The recess has a straight lintel on quadrants. In the S chapel, a similar stone tomb-chest, richly quatrefoiled with two brass shields of John Turner of Walcot, who married the widow of Robert Browne; his will (1541) requested his burial in 'Our Lady chappel on the south side of the high quere in a vaulte at the north ende of the Aulter'. The shields were recovered in the 1930s from the thatch of a village cottage. The recess and four-centred arch are of clunch. The arch is panelled inside and the back wall has a shield to another Robert Browne (impaling Bernard, so the date can be no earlier than 1557) and above it diapering. Truncated top cresting. – Francis Whitestones (a.k.a. Whetstone) †1598 and family. Signed (a rare thing at the time) by *Tomas Greenway of Darby* [*sic*]; 1612. Painted alabaster frame, with two groups of small kneelers, some of which are painted. Frieze of memento mori and strapwork details. – BRASS. Rev. Marsham Argles †1892.

In the raised churchyard is a good display of the C18 school of headstones cut from Barnack stone and numerous C13 coffin lids and other fragments N of the tower. – NE of the chancel, George Ayscough Booth, 'Gentleman Cadet R. M. C. Sandhurst', †1868, a virtuoso piece of stone carving of an uprooted palm tree, its leaves of striking realism. – CROSS. 1930 by *Leslie T. Moore*. Shafts at the angles with vertical strip of dogtooth. Gabled top with figures in niches. Medieval base.

METHODIST CHURCH, Main Street. 1898 by *W. W. Pocock*. Cruciform with canted apse.

Many enjoyable houses in all directions, and especially S and SW of the church, where the ensemble is satisfying on account of the predominance of stone walls and Collyweston slate roofs, with curving streets giving into little squares, and houses facing the street or set at right angles. N of the church a large grassy pasture, bumpy where stood the manor house (destroyed by fire in 1903).

KINGSLEY HOUSE, SW of the church, was the rectory. Big, mostly Victorian Gothic of 1861 by *Edward Browning*, with his typical Dec tracery on two fronts and an oriel over the door. N of this the wall of the pre-Reformation hall survives as a screen, with big buttresses but windows altered in the C19. The former N cross-wing has a pretty oriel window. THE CEDARS, just S of the church, is Georgian, of three bays, its ashlar front dated 1814, with rusticated surrounds to the doorway and all windows. Nice cast-iron railings too. Diminutive outbuildings; one has a 1707 datestone but is Victorian with kneelered gable. W of this, set back, the funny TOWER HOUSE, an impudent Victorian riposte to the church tower with faux-Gothic windows. Designed by its owner, *John William Thompson*, builder and railway engineer.

Among the larger farmhouses, CLOSE HOUSE in Jack Daws Lane, W of the church, is a good C18 example and has a nicely unrestored group of two large barns, stable and dovecote. Inserted into its garden wall is a C13 door, which was removed from the tower arch of the church during the 1850s restoration. Nearby is the former school (WILFRID WOOD HALL),

mid-Victorian Tudor by *Edward Browning*. In MILLSTONE
LANE, a charming group of former almshouses, C15, with
ogee-headed lights at the end and a central gable with dovecote. Several other cottages have reset medieval fragments, e.g.
No. 24 MAIN STREET with blocked traceried window. No. 7
STATION ROAD is probably C14 at its core, a small hall with
parlour and solar above to the l.: see, at front and back, the
blocked two-light windows. Odd reset arch below the front
window with five roses. Hall floored *c.* 1600 and cross-passage
created to the r. end. Set back in a field a DOVECOTE, dated
1789. Nearby LITTLEFIELD is a *mixtum compositum* with a
canted bay window from a C17 house at Stamford (Lincs.), a
small arched Saxon window, and a C13 fragment. A little
beyond is the cottage-like former STATION of 1867 on the
GNR branch line to Wansford (closed 1929). Wings embrace
the platform. There is a second STATION on the Uffington
Road, built in 1847 for the Midland Railway. Neo-Tudor.

WINDMILL, ½ m. W. A tower-mill, of Barnack stone, the best-
preserved in the area. Dated to 1840, if not a little earlier,
ceased use 1913. Partially restored in 1961 (cap of that date),
with most of the timber-built machinery *in situ*.

WALCOT HALL. *See* p. 713.

BLUNTISHAM

ST MARY. Rubble and brown cobbles. The amazing thing about
the church is that it has a trigonal apse which is a genuine Dec
piece. That, as everyone knows, is an extreme rarity in England
and may be explained by the advowson, which was held by the
Bishop of Ely. The windows are small and of two lights with
mouchettes, but there is also one with Y-tracery in the chancel
s wall. Dec also, but later, the arches from the tower into the
embracing aisles; they have three wave mouldings that die into
the w wall and are partly of clunch. The tower carries a recessed
spire behind its crenellated parapet. Mid-C15 Perp the high
four-bay arcades with a typical pier section, like St Ives etc.
but with slender shafts to nave and aisles. The chancel arch
matches. The four-centred aisle windows, another unusual trait
(of East Anglian origin), are internally placed within much
broader blank arches which had wall benches at their foot. So
here – which is also not at all usual – the whole of nave and
aisles is one unified design with a moulded plinth running
around it. Only the N porch comes later, the arch with cusped
cinquefoil head. Formerly two-storey, with a stair-tower to the
upper room. In the s aisle a curious set of piscina, and niche
under a cusped ogee-headed recess. Two large niches l. and r.
of the E window too. The nave roof stands on good stone
corbels, mostly of angels with shields or musical instruments.
The chancel roof is of *c.* 1845 with timber rib-vaulting over the
apse, the aisle roofs 1902–4 by *S. Inskip Ladds*. – FONT. Perp,

octagonal. Panelled stem, quatrefoiled bowl, big flowers and also a Green Man and monkey on the underside. – SCREEN. Three divisions of the dado, discarded in the N aisle. Two are painted crudely with St George and the Dragon and St John the Baptist. C16? – STAINED GLASS. In the apse and chancel SE by *Wailes*, 1851. Chancel SW. Signed but undated by *A. L. Moore*. S aisle E, †1900 by *Jones & Willis*. – MONUMENT. Rev. Samuel Knight †1746. Signed by *Thomas Singleton* of Bury St Edmunds. Tablet with scrolly sides.

Facing the main road, BLUNTISHAM HOUSE, the former rectory. A five-bay, three-storey, E front of yellow brick with a parapet, probably of 1848 because it incorporates a splendid late C17 doorway from Slepe Hall, St Ives, which had been recently demolished. The door surround has big lugs and is framed by fluted Corinthian columns carrying a broken straight hood. In the lintel, large crossed palm-leaves and an entwined monogram. The T-plan house behind this is earlier C18, reputedly built by the Rev. Samuel Knight whose monument is in the church. The wings have Venetian windows.

In High Street, the former church SCHOOL by *John Wallen*, 1841–2, very simple, and the BAPTIST CHAPEL. This was rebuilt in 1874 by the local carpenter, *John Wheatley*. Unusual is the best one can say. Two-tone red brick with two gables, like its predecessor of 1787. Lower porch with three gables. The details Gothic. Complete interior, with much carved woodwork to the tie-beams, galleries and pews in elaborate geometric patterns. *Wheatley* erected the HALL in 1887; fittings detailed as before, including a screen with Doric columns. Nicely extended in 2010 by *Whitworth Co-Partnership*. Opposite a Georgian house (No. 18) of five bays, yellow brick with red brick quoins and band and a door-hood on scrolly brackets. Further up, in similar vein, THE WALNUT TREES, supplemented by an early C19 doorcase and shallow bows with a little Gothic detail, and a superb wrought-iron hanging sign of scrolling foliage, made in 1914 by *V. Pittoors*, a Belgian refugee, for the Tebbutts, family of the St Neots historian C. F. Tebbutt.

BODSEY HOUSE *see* RAMSEY FORTY FOOT

BRAMPTON

2070

The village had five separate 'ends' until the mid to later C20 filled up the spaces with housing.

ST MARY. Perp mostly. But the chancel is late C13, with geometrical tracery, Y-tracery, and similar forms in the windows which are framed inside by giant blank arcading (cf. Alconbury). The coarse PISCINA is late C13 too. The W tower is Dec though the date 1635 appears over the door and below the window (the construction of the bellframe is further evidence of C17 rebuilding). It has set-back buttresses, a doorway with continuous mouldings, pairs of transomed two-light bell-openings, a nice frieze over, and no spire. The arch towards the nave has castellated capitals. Dec also the S doorway, with continuous mouldings too. Its DOOR, with bold Dec net tracery, was tragically damaged by fire in 1994; a poignant fragment is remounted above the door in the S aisle. The arcades of five bays are Perp, with piers of the standard moulded section and two sunk waves in the arches. Also Perp the four-light aisle windows with uniform panel tracery, the clerestory windows, and the ornate S porch with niches l. and r. of the entrance and a small third niche above the entrance arch. The latter contains the lily-pot of the Annunciation. Good nave and aisle roofs with traceried spandrels, large bosses and stone corbels, two in the N aisle with arms of Ely and Canterbury. S aisle roof restored after the fire by *Julian Limentani*. – FONT. Octagonal, with pointed quatrefoils etc. – ROOD SCREEN. Dec, of one-light divisions, the doors each with two ogee arches carrying a circle with flowing tracery. The other ogee arches are combined with round arches. – The mid-C14 STALLS have MISERICORDS, the best in the county. They represent (a) a man writing – a knight and lady with a shield – an animal; (b) a carpenter – a man and a woman haymaking (wool-combing?) – a sheep shearer; (c) a woman gleaning – a man reaping and a woman with a sickle – sheaves of corn. They are what remains of a larger set that was removed in 1878, when the church was being restored by *Ewan Christian*, and only reinstated in 1929. – COMMUNION RAIL. Jacobean. Imported during refurbishment of the chancel by *J. N. Comper*, 1918. – The chancel PAVEMENT follows the pattern 'of Ypres Cathedral'. – PARCLOSE SCREENS (S aisle). 1919–20, also by *Comper*, with heraldic shields recording the descent of the Montagus of Hinchingbrooke from the C12 to C20. – PEWS. Also by *Comper*, 1947. – HANGING ROOD. 1945 by *Edmund Ware*. – STAINED GLASS. Several to the Montagus of Hinchingbrooke and much of *Kempe & Co.*, 1917–21. Their Jesse Window (E), in memory of the 8th Earl of Sandwich †1916, is something of a magnum opus. The windows of the N aisle make a series, with large figures in each light and scenes in Renaissance roundels below, including the First World War Memorial window showing Allenby marching into Jerusalem. – Chancel N, 1888 by *Lavers, Barraud & Westlake*. – S aisle from E to W. First, a very distinctive and darkly coloured window (also probably of the 1880s but to Mary, Countess of Sandwich, †1859) by *Fouracre & Watson*, a rare example of their work outside Devon and Cornwall, and a fine indication of their Morris-influenced style. The others are to the Hon. Sydney Montagu †1860 by *Hardman* with backgrounds of dense silvery foliage, like the firm's tower window; and one by *Lavers & Westlake*, 1894. – MONUMENTS. Sir John Bernard Robert †1679 (s chapel). Signed by *William Kidwell*; his earliest recorded work, of c. 1690. White marble tablet, with lugged surround and hanging swags. It has a remarkably good bust in a black niche on top and skulls with laurel crowns. – In the tower, John and Thomas Miller †1681 and 1683. Cartouche tablet. – Mrs Jackson †1689. Slab in the s aisle. She was Pepys's sister, the last of his family in the parish, and Samuel erected her monument. – Brig. Gen. Robert Bernard Sparrow †1805 returning from Barbados; classical aedicule. Tablet below by *E. Richardson* of London for his son, daughter and widow, Lady Olivia Bernard Sparrow (†1863). – WAR MEMORIAL (under the tower). The former reredos by *A. W. Blomfield*, 1884, mosaic work by *J. Powell & Sons*. Adapted in 1918.

Directly w from the church is the OLD RECTORY, of 1853 by *Henry Roberts*. Constructed of large buff bricks. Later extensions. To its s, THE MANOR HOUSE, an unpleasing replacement of 1875 for the medieval house, which belonged to the Crown and then to the Cromwells and Montagus.

w in the gently curving HIGH STREET, the overbearing INSTITUTE, by *John Bird*, builder of Brampton, 1896. Porch under a recessed balcony in the centre. The gables have pressed terracotta decoration. It was provided by John Newbery, who lived in the adjoining house, No. 16, of 1891. Domestic Revival, with two bargeboarded gables that have half-timbering infilled with carstone slips, some bright tiles to the smaller centre gable and panels of terracotta angels. Porch in the centre with coloured glass.

Further up on this side, THE OLD HOUSE, c18 brick front in English bond of five bays with segmental sashes. Pilasters at the angles. The rear is earlier, c17, including the brick stack and staircase in the angle with the rear wing. Opposite, VINE COTTAGE has inside a Jacobean overmantel. Between here and the Green, a few charming products of the philanthropy of Lady Olivia Bernard Sparrow (*see* Brampton Park) in the early to mid c19, with two pairs of Picturesque Gothic-style COTTAGES flanking a former infirmary (now THE ROUND HOUSE). This last is octagonal, has a tiled roof with a cluster of four chimneys in the centre and an encircling veranda. The architect was *W. G. Habershon* in 1845. His father, *Matthew Habershon*, designed the three pairs of model COTTAGES facing the Green. They are dated 1837, and arranged in a semicircle with the gabled centre one (the former village Reading Room) set back. Less endearing examples of the estate style are of the 1860s, again with Lady Olivia's initials. On the far side of the Green is the mid-c19 SCHOOL, originally the boys' school provided by Lady Olivia. Neo-Tudor red brick schoolroom with buttresses, straight gables and stepped window in the centre. Additions of 1964. Just N of this is the former MODEL LODGING HOUSE, also *c.* 1840.

BRAMPTON CAMP (RAF Wyton). The camp is spread all over the grounds of BRAMPTON PARK. The great house is now the officers' mess. The park was royal hunting ground but nothing seems to be known of the architectural history before the early c19. *John Nash* built offices and made alterations to the house in 1806–7 for Lady Olivia Bernard Sparrow, after the death of her husband. This work must account for the w end of the present house, which is gault brick, castellated, and has steep gables and decorated Tudor chimneys. There was then an alteration to the main (E) part of the house in 1821–2 by *T. S. Whitwell*, with some interior decoration by *J. B. Papworth* in 1823–5, but all of that was destroyed by a fire in 1907, after which the E end was rebuilt on a smaller scale and in unsympathetic red brick for Viscount Mandeville. One room of the early C19 service wing has a shallow saucer dome on squinches. *Papworth* also offered a picturesque design for the grounds. Thatched LODGE, probably by *W.G. Habershon*.

N of the church in HUNTINGDON ROAD, a triangular obelisk MILESTONE of C18 date with hands pointing on one side to Huntingdon and Thrapston, on another to London. E is PEPYS HOUSE. This is the farmhouse that belonged to Samuel Pepys's uncle, where he lodged while at Huntingdon Grammar School. The house he knew is just the front range, of three bays and timber-framed, built *c.* 1600, with a long jetty (underbuilt in the C18) and gabled ends. Pepys made improvements to it after he inherited it in 1680, which may have included part of the back range, although this is now as rebuilt or extended in the early C18; its E gable has the typical tumbled brickwork. Inside it is a cellar/dairy below a fine parlour. It was extended at its w end after the house was acquired by the Pepys Club and restored for it by *W. A. Forsyth* in 1926. Of this date most of the windows and roughcast covering. Inside, some early to mid-C17 decorative painting, imitating in grey the timber frame of a chimneystack over the hall fireplace and in the upstairs corridor remains of a scheme of arcading with drop pendants (cf. Tudor House, Godmanchester). Of the 1920s much good Arts and Crafts woodwork, including the staircase. Forsyth's builder was *M. J. Allen* of Huntingdon, who built the neighbouring Tudorbethan house at the same time. It is well done, incorporating as its wing the C17 timber frame and brick BARN of Pepys House.

Further E by the Ouse, NENE AND OUSE WATER BOARD (Anglian Water). 1962–5 by *H. J. Smith* of *Pick, Everard, Keay & Gimson*; good. S of this, on the river, BRAMPTON MILL. Mostly C18 and C19, with a working undershot cast-iron water wheel. The Miller's House has a Gothic window with intersecting tracery.

BRETTON *see* PETERBOROUGH

BRINGTON

ALL SAINTS. Slender Dec w tower with low broach spire. Foliage above the broaches. Three tiers of lucarnes. The bell-openings are of two lights with a transom. There is a frieze above them, which on the w face is a mix of lancets, quatrefoils and saltires. No parapet, although the spire is slightly set back. The steep roof of the chancel, which was largely rebuilt in 1868–9 by *W. Slater*, is higher than the embattled aisleless nave (cf. Molesworth). The nave has some square-headed ogee windows and on the s side an attractive Dec window of uncommon details and continuously moulded arch to the s door with nicely moulded stops. The s door is also early C14. – DOUBLE AUMBRY. C13 work but heavily restored. The nave roof is of 1674, sensitively repaired by *S. Inskip Ladds*, 1938. Two sculpted corbels at the w angles represent an earlier roof. – ALTAR TABLE. Early C17 with turned legs. – FONT COVER. Also Jacobean. Simple, conical, with a ball finial. – STAINED GLASS. Bits in one s window. MONUMENT. John Kippax, Archdeacon of the Isle of Man, †1760. Limestone ledger slab with fine inlaid lettering.

RECTORY (THE OLD MEAD), SE. 1858 by *W. Slater*. Gothic with polychromy of red and black. Two big stone bay windows. E by the main road, OLD MANOR HOUSE. The principal part, mid-C16, of three bays w–e, has an excellent gabled end, jettied at first floor and attic. Double curved footbraces to the upper storey, here and on the side walls. Inside, the centre and E bay appear to have been an open hall, indicated by the mighty stone chimneystack with its fireplace only at ground floor. The bay E of this has different framing with brick infill, either a replacement or an addition of the C17, when the floor was inserted. The s wing seems to have begun as a separately framed structure that has been incorporated and later extended s in brick. Opposite, YEW TREE COTTAGE is contemporary, with the same curved bracing and one original window. Slightly later medieval addition at the E end.

BROUGHTON

2070

ALL SAINTS. Stone w tower with broach spire. Two tiers of lucarnes. Mostly Perp. Contributions to the building are mentioned in 1528. Exceptions are the E.E. chancel (see the priest's door, the remains of the lowside s lancet and the DOUBLE PISCINA with trefoil head), the nave s doorway of *c.* 1300, and the Dec four-bay arcades of standard elements, but the arches starting with broaches. The advowson was held by Ramsey Abbey from at least the mid C13. – FONT. Square, Norman, with blank arcading and volutes at the corners. – BENCHES. Some Perp ends reused in the seating of 1888 by *W. O. Milne*. – COMMUNION RAIL. C18. – ROOD BEAM. 1915 by *W. A. Lea*. The figures were ordered from Oberammergau but the First World War broke out and so they were carved by Belgian refugees. In a niche adjoining, the WAR MEMORIAL, a limewood figure of St George also by *Lea*, sculpted by *Armitage Bros*, 1920.[*] – WALL PAINTING. Doom; above the chancel arch; late C15. Uncovered in 1892. Conserved in 1988, so all that survives is clearly visible, e.g. the rising of the dead and the elect before St Peter on the l., and on the r., the damned pursued into Hell by avenging angels. Among the suffering, a woman goes to Hell in a wheel barrow: identified as the 'ale wife who gave short measure'. At the apex of the painting, the figure of Christ has gone but his head is carved in wood and is part of the roof. The figures of the Apostles on the E wall-posts of the Perp roof play their part too. Also, round the S corner, Expulsion above Adam delving and Eve spinning. On the chancel door jambs, remains of C13 fictive masonry with scroll patterns alternating with marbling; red joints and voussoirs.

LOCK-UP. E of the church. 1845. Of brick, oblong, with two small barred windows. Of not much interest.

OLD RECTORY, SW of the church, is at least partly timber-framed, as the C17 E cross-wing with its oriel, jetty and eaves with pendants shows, but the hall wing largely rebuilt in brick (probably 1676, the date which was recorded on the central chimney by the RCHM). Pretty veranda along its front. There was formerly also an E cross-wing. Muscular Neo-Jacobean stair inside, made for the Rev. George Johnston (rector 1887–1900, whose rebus decorates the hall fireplace). The late C19 OLD LIBRARY, W, was formerly attached. Steep gable with virtuoso carving to the bargeboard.

BRIDGE FARMHOUSE, SW of the church, is the best house. Mid to late C17, with a square porch under a hipped roof and shaped gables with round tops to the ends, rear wings and stair-turret. Over the doorway a frill cut into the bricks; that is usually an early C18 motif. Elegant stone piers with moulded tops and curved steps to the street.

BUCKDEN

The church with its stone steeple and the dark brick of the Bishop of Lincoln's palace form an unforgettable picture. The church is only a few feet away from the Great Tower of the palace, just like Lambeth parish church and Lambeth Palace.

ST MARY. The W tower, indeed the entire church, is Perp. It has set-back buttresses, pairs of two-light bell-openings and a recessed spire with three tiers of lucarnes. The tower's set-back buttresses are built into the church. So the tower's lower stages came before the nave. As for this and most of the rest, it can be dated by known benefactions of Bishop Gray (1431–6) and the arms of his successor, Bishop Alnwick (1436–9), on a

---

[*] Of the BRASS to Laurence Marton and wife *c*. 1490 there is only part of its inscription fixed to a pew.

corbel of the nave roof. Moreover, an inscription in the E window, now lost, commemorated alterations to the chancel instigated by John Deeping, Prebendary of Buckden in those years. Externally the embattled aisles and clerestory belong to them, and the large transomed windows on the S and E sides. The ornate two-storey S porch is attributed to Bishop Russell (1480–94) on the evidence of a double Tudor rose. It also has a quatrefoil base frieze, a niche over the entrance, and battlements and pinnacles. Below the battlements a frieze of genre-scenes of animals and on the battlements wavy tracery. Inside the porch is a tierceron-star vault with five bosses, the middle one showing the Assumption, i.e. the Virgin surrounded by rays. Chamber above.

The interior is spacious and high, but harsh to the eye since the walls were mercilessly scraped and repointed in 1909 by *S. Inskip Ladds.* The nave is divided from the aisles by five-bay arcades, their piers of standard moulded section. The chancel arch matches the arcades. To l. and r. of the arch, in the aisles, are ogee-headed niches with crocketed mouldings; that to the N aisle has remains of a pillar piscina and an aumbry. The other niche is integral with the door to the roof loft. The chancel roof has angels at the feet of the intermediate principals and stone corbel-angels. One boss is inscribed RW 1665, presumably the date of a repair. The nave roof is supported on the same type of corbels but it is inscribed II. C.P. 1649; perhaps of this date are panels on the rafters with strapwork and other patterns as well as a larger central truss on fluted pilasters. The aisle roofs are Perp and similar too, the details partly restored in 1937 by *Albert Richardson.* However, a few features are earlier, i.e. the S doorway with two orders of shafts (the slenderer ones keeled), carrying stiff-leaf capitals, and fine arch mouldings, the priest's doorway in the chancel, the SEDILIA and the very wide PISCINA, and the small chancel N doorway. All this is E.E. and may date from *c.* 1225, when Bishop Wells was given permission to rebuild the church at the same time as new work on his palace. Later than everything else, the N organ chamber and vestry of the C19. – FONT. Octagonal, Perp, with pointed quatrefoils containing shields. – PULPIT. With good Jacobean tiers of the usual broad blank arches and lozenges in them. Remade in 1909, with new work by *Thompson & Son* of Peterborough, who also made the PEWS. – READERS' DESKS. With eight later C16 Flemish reliefs of scenes from the Passion, acquired in 1842. – ALTAR TABLE. S aisle. Formerly in the chancel. *c.* 1660, with spiral legs and curved stretchers. – STAINED GLASS. In the heads of the S aisle W and E windows, original late C15 figures identified as the Coronation of the Virgin (E) and Annunciation (W) and corn ears typical of the Norwich glass painters. There was formerly much more, including several with the shield of Bishop William Grey (1431–6). – MONUMENTS. In the chancel, Bishop Thomas Barlow †1691. Big, black marble inscription plate with a stone surround with garlands and two sets of cherubs' heads and bishops' mitres at the top. The slightly archaic appearance is due to the reuse of fragments from the monument to Bishop William Barlow †1613, which was destroyed in 1642. The epitaph is to both. – Bishop Green †1779. With crosier and mitre at the top and a very fine roundel at the foot, showing a female figure reading by a funerary altar. – Bishop Pelham †1827. By *E. H. Baily*. White marble, large kneeling woman with a bible on the ground; a composition popular with this sculptor (cf. Harriet Middleton's monument in Bristol Cathedral). Rather cold. It was erected by Pelham's widow although he never visited Buckden. – Robert Stuart Hurst Whitworth †1831. Large white Gothic triptych with shields but without figures. Signed *T. Rickman*, architect. Whitworth is called in the inscription 'of St John's College, Cambridge', and that may explain the presence of Rickman. It is complemented by smaller later C19 Gothic tablets to Hursts by *Gaffin & Co*. – George Maltby †1832 and Mary Maltby †1825; they make a pair, by *Thomas Tomson* of Cambridge. – In the churchyard large obelisk on square base to William Whitworth, C18.

BUCKDEN PALACE. What remains of Buckden Palace is the fragment of something very much larger. The estate was the bishops' of Lincoln already in Domesday, and had been chosen for permanent episcopal residence by the late C12, when it was used by Hugh of Avalon †1220; and that palace was in existence certainly in the middle of the C13, for Bishop Grosseteste died at Buckden. It is said that Bishop Wells erected a stone house *c.* 1225 to which Grosseteste added the hall but both were damaged in 1291 by fire and what survives now is all of the C15 or later. That comprises the outer gateway and walling near it, the inner gatehouse, and the so-called Great Tower. They are of red brick with diapers of dark blue vitrified bricks and were built by Bishops Rotherham (1472–80) and Russell (1480–94). The fishponds to the E of the palace were probably the brick pits (the timber came from Weybridge Forest, near Alconbury). In addition excavations have shown, NE of the Great Tower, the Great Chamber, NE of that the chapel (rebuilt *c.* 1500), and SW of that the great hall, probably about 90 ft (27 metres) long. The latter was taken down in the mid C17. Although there was refurbishment after the Restoration and in the C18, the Bishops gave up Buckden in 1838, Huntingdonshire having transferred to the See of Ely, and a great deal was then taken down. More was destroyed by Arthur Marshall, the owner of the Huntingdon Brewery, for whom the property was purchased in 1870 by his father (founder of the London drapers, Marshall & Snelgrove), initially with the intention of repairing it as a home. A new house was built instead. The Marshalls sold before the First World War and *c.* 1920 the palace and house came into the care of the antiquary Dr R. H. Edleston, who made some excavations and some eccentric additions. Since 1956 it has belonged to the Claretian Missionaries, serving first as a junior seminary and now as a retreat.

The principal building is the GREAT TOWER, also known as 94
the King's Lodgings. It is oblong, three storeys high, with
polygonal angle turrets of yet another storey. Is it a keep then?
The question is not easily answered. The best way to decide is
to look to the solar tower of Lord Treasurer Cromwell's Tattershall in Lincolnshire, built some forty years earlier and no
doubt the pattern on which the Great Tower was modelled. At
Tattershall one can prove that the tower was meant to be
defensible but at the same time had large and well-equipped
living apartments and windows too large for a real keep. Also
brick would in any case not be the safest material. So it might
have been the same at Buckden – the tower was intended
apotropaically as much as for its military potential – but the
details and planning emphasize that here the balance was
tipped towards domestic use, as at the Bishop of Winchester's
castle at Farnham, Surrey (1470–7), and his residence at Esher,
which was being rebuilt at about the same time and also had
a great brick tower within a walled enclosure. The tower has
to the N a small basement entrance and a ground-floor entrance
with a stone four-centred arch. The windows are all of stone
and have cusped lights and straight tops. They are of one, two,
and three lights. On the ground floor to the W is a window of
two plus two lights. There is an elaborate design of blue bricks
on the N side, lozenges and a cross, repeated twice. In the W
wall is a large cross in blue bricks. A large chimneybreast projects from the S wall. The largest chimneypiece is on the ground
floor too (four-centred arch), but there is nothing to match the
elaboration of plan and detail at Tattershall, for the interior of
the tower was taken out in 1842. Refloored and reroofed in the
1950s, there is now on each floor a single room, with stone
door to the NE stair. Although the fireplace is in the centre of
each floor, it is possible that each floor was divided into at least
two rooms. The only surviving staircase is in the NE turret, with
sunk stone handrail, which ascends from basement to roof. A
second stair existed in the NW turret. The garderobes are
placed in the SE turret. There was a closet on each floor of the
SW turret, each with a fireplace whose chimney is integrated
with the top of the turret. It is interesting that there are also
rooms in each of the turrets at roof level. Vaulting from the
basement was stripped out in 1871. The entrance must have
been reached by steps.

W of the Great Tower is a piece of CURTAIN WALL, rather
low to be of much use and thus to be regarded as an ornamental feature from which the bishops could enjoy the view of the
gardens around their residence. The wall-walk behind the
battlements stands on shallow segmental arches. The wall connects the tower with a short brick range which in its turn
connects directly with the inner gatehouse. The range ends to
the S in a stepped gable, and below this is an oriel under a big,
decorative ogee arch with Bishop Russell's arms. The windows
of this range are of brick, two lights and straight-headed. The
room behind the oriel has panelled partitions.

The INNER GATEHOUSE (now converted to residential use) is three-storeyed, with diagonal buttresses. The archway has a four-centred head, and there are rooms l. and r. The windows are of two lights, except for one of three. They are again of stone, and the lights are cusped. The top has battlements. On the inner side is a square stair-tower containing the stair with solid oak treads and two rooms over the archway, one with an C18 fireplace. A timber newel stair continues to the roof. To the N, in place of a wing pulled down in 1842, is a curious extension of 1928, assembled for Edleston (by *Hardwick & Burrows*, contractors) from old stone and medieval and later architectural fragments taken from Stanwick Hall, Yorkshire (dem. 1923), and Sedbury Hall, Yorkshire (dem. 1927), among others. It ends in a pavilion dedicated to Napoleon III. The idea was to start here a museum to the Emperor.* The OUTER GATEWAY is plain, with a four-centred head and battlements. A good deal of the OUTER WALL is preserved too, also embattled. Between the outer and inner courts is part of the original MOAT (re-excavated in 1993), which was crossed by a bridge in the C15. N and E of the palace there remains a section of the 'Little Park', and S of the outer court is a WALLED GARDEN, both restored since *c.* 1990.

On the site of the garth, NE of the Great Tower, is the CHURCH (R.C.) of 1958–9 by *Burles & Newton*, with a cloister in front picking up the motif of the curtain-wall arches. The LADY CHAPEL is on the site of the medieval chapel, and behind this is the CLARET CHAPEL, built up after 1921 by Edleston with old masonry, including a pediment on top of the E wall. The chapels have abstract STAINED GLASS of 1985 (Resurrection) and 1990 (Mysteries of the Rosary) by *Paul Quail*. In the church, reset windows depicting the Life of the Virgin 'from a church in London'.

Finally, to the N of the church is BUCKDEN TOWERS, the house built for Arthur Marshall in 1872 by *R. W. Edis*, after plans to restore and augment the old remains had been abandoned. Of red brick, with a porch tower and mullioned and transomed windows. Inside, an impressive top-lit stair hall with carving to the stair in Aesthetic Movement style and screens inset with stained glass. In several rooms are fireplaces with tiles by *G. E. Cook* of Gower Street; especially good is one set with women's heads – representing the Senses – which are signed also by Cook's designer, *F. V. Hart*, who worked also for William Morris. STAINED GLASS roundels of the same design in the next room. By the outer gatehouse, a LODGE of same date and to the S a COACH HOUSE.

The palace walls define much of the E side of the HIGH STREET, which was until the 1960s on the Great North Road and one of the principal coaching stops, like Stilton and Stamford.

---

*Edleston published *Napoleon III and Italy* in 1922. By 1928 he had already assembled a few objects for the museum, including a bust and panelling from Farnborough Hill, Hampshire, home of the widowed Empress.

Bypassing has guaranteed its character. Opposite the gates, CONEYGARTH was a property of the bishops. It is C17 in its present form, timber-framed but plastered and with C18 windows including an oval window in the gable of the l. cross-wing. Consoled and pediment doorcase. N of this, a number of pleasant brick houses, the best being JESSAMINE HOUSE, late C18 of five bays, the very similar SHERWOOD HOUSE of four, and YORK HOUSE of three, all in Flemish bond with brick bands, gauged brick headers to the windows and dentilled eaves cornice. York House has a doorcase with a frieze of roundels (a date of 1785 is given for it. NHLE).

S of the palace and SW of the church at the main crossing, the LION HOTEL, timber-framed, of c. 1500, with, in the entrance lounge, a wide fireplace with moulded four-centred arch and a ceiling of moulded beams and a big boss with the Agnus Dei. Extended S in the C19 with a gabled tower over a carriage arch (now blocked). Opposite, the GEORGE HOTEL, a three-storey early C18 brick range with a top parapet, of eight windows with the carriage arch to the r. Its present appearance was 'new' in 1722. The C17 S wing, with a gallery (infilled), was pleasantly refronted on its S side some time in the 1920s with a colonnade to its terrace. The Late Georgian buildings along-side, which have early C19 shopfronts below, are of the same scale and plain appearance, totalling fifteen bays. Around the corner, forming the N range of the hotel courtyard, is the Old Tap, late C17. There was also formerly a W range to the courtyard.

In CHURCH STREET, the OLD VICARAGE, its front part of 1795, of yellow brick with two canted bay windows and a steeply pitched roof behind the parapet. Odd composition of large and small windows to first floor. The back is mid-C18 and like the houses in High Street. Then the OLD MANOR HOUSE (now divided), timber-framed and plastered. The range to the street is late C15 and had a long jetty to front and back. It is unusual in having two large rooms on each floor – the upper one with crown-post roof – and therefore unlikely to have been in domestic use. Beth Davis suggests it might have been a courtroom or guildhall. The chimney, inserted c. 1600, has a single octagonal stack. The E extension is a C17 barn, contemporary with the SW wing, which has two gabled stair-turrets on the back. Inside, good panelling and chimneypieces, two with arcaded overmantels, and pilasters either fluted or with arabesques. Further on is BRIDGE HOUSE, a small open hall house dated by its timbers to 1458 and diligently restored c. 2010 with a coating of rust-coloured render and ornamental plasterwork. Then BUCKDEN HOUSE of five bays, Georgian with segmental-headed windows, and another IVY HOUSE, of four bays and again like the houses in High Street. The door-case is the same as that of York House (see above). Opposite, the modest yellow brick ALMSHOUSES of 1840, Tudor-style, with the inscription 'Industry rewarded, Age protected'. Their anonymous benefactor †1834 and has a monument in the N aisle of the church. Then the METHODIST CHAPEL of 1876 with two storeys of round-arched windows. Finally, N into SILVER STREET for FIELD HOUSE, again brick, five bays, but with a parapet and a good late C18 doorway that is pedimented above a triglyph frieze and fluted pilasters.

STIRTLOE HOUSE, Stirtloe, 1 m. S. The house is described in a lease of 1780 as 'lately in part rebuilt' for George Alexander. That accounts for the centre of five bays but the semicircular stone porch of columns with fluted capitals decorated with honeysuckle and the ends and rear wing are c. 1815 when the house was purchased by the Lintons. (Interior also mostly C19.) The Coach House and barn are early C18, with the typical band between the floors. The grounds, originally part of the Bishop of Lincoln's deer park, were redone in the 1760s.

BUCKWORTH

88   ALL SAINTS. The nave E angles are the oldest thing in the church. They are Norman. But it is the splendid late C13 W steeple that one remembers. Set-back buttresses, a doorway with three orders of columns and a handsome moulded arch, a sexfoiled, cusped rose window, bell-openings of two lights with Y-tracery, and to their l. and r. one blank cinquefoiled arch. In the heads of these arches are carvings of three radially placed heads and foliated cusps. The spire has high broaches, with scrolls at the points, and three tiers of lucarnes. The first tier is very high, transomed and with Y-tracery. Quadruple-chamfered arch towards the nave. The S arcade is late C13 too. Three bays, round piers, double-chamfered arches, half-octagonal responds. The N arcade with octagonal piers is a little later; the N doorway goes with it. The two W arches have hollow chamfers and the W respond is in the form of a knot (cf. Diddington and Little Paxton), which suggests an adjustment of the same time as the Perp aisle N windows and clerestory. Whether the chancel is still C13 or just after the turn of the century must remain open. It has, to the s, intersecting tracery in one window and a corresponding priest's doorway. The vestry doorway from the chancel is obviously Dec (ogee arch). So is the tracery of the N aisle W (intersecting) and E window (reticulated) and the S doorway. Nave and aisle roofs of 1862, dated with the arms and crests of Ely, Archdeaconry of Huntingdon and Duncombe Shafto family (the Rev. J. Duncombe Shafto held the advowson), combining hammerbeam with scissor trusses, but with large Perp bosses, heads on the tie-beams and wall-plate of oak leaves. Nicely carved angel corbels and, in the angles of the aisles, the emblems of the Evangelists.
– STAINED GLASS. E window by *Wailes*, 1866. One other ('Be of good cheer, It is I, be not afraid') by *Clayton & Bell*, undated but probably c. 1900.

THE OLD VICARAGE, SW of the church. 1832 by *J. W. Pocock* of Huntingdon, added to in 1856 by *Salvin* who also reseated the church.

BURGHLEY HOUSE [P]   *0000*

Burghley is one of the largest of the Elizabethan mansions, presenting itself in supreme self-confidence on the wide lawns of its c18 garden, and is the foremost expression of the c16 great house as the centre of political and dynastic power. William Cecil was born in 1520. In 1535 he entered St John's College, Cambridge, in 1541 Gray's Inn. His first wife had been a sister of John Cheke of St John's College, the Greek scholar, his second was Mildred Cooke, sister of Edward VI's governor, as Cheke was his tutor. Another sister became the mother of Francis Bacon. When Edward VI ascended the throne and Somerset became Protector, William Cecil was made Somerset's secretary, and, after two months in the Tower in 1550, became a Secretary of State. He was knighted at the age of thirty-one, in 1551, became Chancellor of the Garter in 1552, and, after an eclipse in the years of Mary Tudor, Chief Secretary of State in 1558 and Lord Burghley in 1571.

Burghley's father, Richard Cecil, had bought the manor of Burghley at about the time when William was born. His mother lived there, and if any parts of the house still represent the state it was in before William started enlarging and remodelling it immediately after inheriting in 1552, they would be only walls of rooms in the E range facing the E cloister and the courtyard. The history of the buildings, as far as published dates help,* begins in 1555 with letters from Cecil's mason and clerk of the works mentioning dormer (or 'French') windows, an inner court, bay windows, the hall, its future screen, and the pantry and a gallery, both under construction. The kitchen roof also is referred to as a major piece of work yet to be done. By 1564 it seems that Cecil had created a substantial courtyard house, not dissimilar in its form from the house of today. Gardens were also well advanced and work may well have gone on until 1566, when a visit from the Queen was expected. By then Cecil had purchased Theobalds near London and began the building of the prodigious house there. He seems to have finished for a time with Burghley, which now became the residence of his son Thomas, but he returned his attentions to it in the next decade, now as Lord Burghley, a Knight of the Garter and Lord Treasurer. With more money, renewed vigour and the assistance of men from the Royal Works,

---

*Discussion of the c16 house is revised according to the interpretation of Dr Jill Husselby for her PhD thesis (Warwick University, 1996) and summarized in 'Patronage, Culture and Power: The Early Cecils 1558–1612' (*Studies in British Art*, 8, ed. P. Croft).

he proceeded to direct the expansion and further enrichment of Burghley as the family seat. It amounted to little less than a complete reconstruction.

The plan and appearance of the house as Cecil left it in the 1560s can only be a matter of speculation, but Dr Husselby has found enough evidence in the present building and documents to indicate that its form – an irregular courtyard plan in which no two sides are precisely parallel nor the axes straight – dictated much of what one sees now. The entrance was from the W and proceeded through the courtyard into the screens passage of a great hall in the E range. The S range, overlooking the gardens, was already reserved for a suite of apartments suitable for royalty at first floor and contained an open loggia across the ground floor, while the W range provided fine guest lodgings and a gallery in the attic floor. Sir William's private apartments were almost certainly in the N range and, perhaps the most unusual feature for a country house of this date, there seems to have been a private suite for his wife, with its own gallery, in the E range. In the expansion of the house all of these aspects of planning were retained and improved upon. The likely sequence for this phase is as follows: c. 1573 the addition of a new E range, containing the present kitchen, buttery and great hall; the complete reconstruction of the W range, set slightly further W than its predecessor and of a broader width, which was complete by 1577 (the date on the vault of the W gateway); then the reworking of the S range, and finally the N range with its great frontispiece which is dated 1587.

Theobalds as well as Burghley show William Cecil as a disciple of Protector Somerset, whose Somerset House of c. 1548–52 is the watershed in English C16 architecture. Sir William Sharington, also a protégé of Somerset, followed his example at Lacock in about 1550, Sir John Thynne, again a protégé, at Longleat. Thynne's brother-in-law was Sir Thomas Gresham, and in his Exchange in London ties with Somerset's architectural tastes are also traceable. Correspondence exists between Cecil and Gresham, who was then English Resident at Antwerp. From this it is clear that Flemings were involved in the work for him, whether at Theobalds or at Burghley. Of William Cecil's personal interest in architecture there can be no doubt. From later correspondence with Sir Henry Norris it is also apparent that he knew French architectural books. He refers once to Delorme and to an unnamed book he had seen in the library of Sir Thomas Smith of Hill Hall, Essex, yet another protégé of Somerset. Smith owned e.g. four editions of Vitruvius and Philander's commentary on Vitruvius. Cecil's brother-in-law, Sir Thomas Hoby, built Bisham Abbey, Berkshire, so William may also have been acquainted with the French-inspired work there. He was also closely involved in directing works at Whitehall and Windsor, among others, and to implement the designs at Burghley, largely undertaken in his absence, he seems to have engaged men associated with the Works, principally *Henry Hawthorne* up to c. 1576 and later *John Symonds*, but how much of the final design can be attributed to their contribution and how much to the genius of Lord Burghley, or indeed his son Thomas, is impossible to say.

William Cecil died in 1598. Thomas Cecil was created Earl of Exeter in 1605. *John Thorpe*'s survey of the ground and first floor of the house is inscribed for him and is our only evidence for the planning of the interior before the great changes of the 1680s and 1690s made by John, the 5th Earl, who married Lady Anne Cavendish and required apartments appropriate to the collections acquired by the couple on four separate Grand Tours. The Earl was first cousin to the Duke of Montagu, who remodelled Boughton (Northants) at the same time, and brother-in-law of the Duke of Devonshire, who rebuilt Chatsworth again at the same time. At least some of the work at Burghley may have been directed by *William Talman* who visited in 1688–90. But much remained undone at the Earl's death in 1700. The 9th Earl, another collector, completed the decoration after an interval of over fifty years, and at the same time commissioned a great plan for work to the house and park from *Capability Brown*, undertaken 1755–79. Some important changes were also made in 1828–33 for the 2nd Marquess of Exeter, but the debts of his successors ensured that little else could be done in the later C19 and C20. Exemplary conservation and repair began in the late C20. The house has been open to tourists since at least the 1770s (the earliest recognizable guidebook is of 1797) and by the 1890s it was receiving over 4,000 paying visitors each year.

The building is mostly of Kingscliffe limestone, quarried at Cliffe Park, of which Cecil was Keeper, and Barnack rag. In its final form the house is an oblong, 240 by 125 ft (73 by 38 metres), with originally two wings projecting N by another 115 ft (35 metres); and, apart from the forecourt between them, a large oblong centre courtyard. The house was in this respect of the type of Longleat. Theobalds, like Somerset House, Holdenby (Northants) and the later Audley End (Essex), had two courtyards; Wollaton, Hardwick, and Hatfield, none. Each of the ranges is of three storeys with the angles stressed by taller towers. The elevations are characterized by a continuous classic entablature at each floor and even, large, unadorned, mullioned and transomed windows, although these are mostly C18 alterations. They are the *continuo* which sets off the other motifs. The style of the whole is uniform in spite of the variety of elements and motifs, except for the E range, which although of the same date as the rest is clearly intended to be architecturally distinct. Burghley also has the exciting skyline of Henry VIII's Hampton Court or the Richmond and Greenwich of the earlier Tudor period. Its short square towers, ogee-capped turrets, frilled balustrade, and countless tall chimneyshafts in the form of Tuscan columns are unforgettable, even if they will not easily be remembered in detail. The motifs are those of the Somerset circle, but their combination in this profusion remains unique at Burghley.

We shall look at the façades first, the courtyard second, the interiors third, the surroundings last. Chronologically one begins with the EAST RANGE. This overlaid the existing E range of the courtyard, so at this end the house is a double-pile. In this part are also the most significant survivals of William Cecil's house: the hall and the kitchen at the NE corner. In style it is clearly distinguished from the other ranges, for it has a steeply pitched Collyweston slate roof over the hall and also arched lights at the top of its three- and four-transomed windows. There is a six-light S window with intersecting tracery and a very large bay window to the E, and to the N of this three more large windows. They are blind but John Thorpe's survey shows only the l. one as a dummy. The reason is the fireplace inside, whose flue had to be taken up diagonally to reach a chimneybreast that stands awkwardly at the top of the bay window. S of the bay window there is the outline of a fourth window, also as shown on Thorpe's survey, and what appears to be a blocked door below. Documents show that Brown unblocked the other windows but threat of collapse of the wall required hasty filling in again. The r. blocked opening and a door below it (now obscured by a covered service passage of 1830) is in line with the screens passage inside. Thorpe shows a square projecting bay in this position but this has been superseded by the present projection in the next bay to the r. Its window rises the full height and has taller lights than those of the hall. In style this also goes with the next two bays to the r. and all this must be another later C17 alteration, perhaps determined by changes inside to the chapel on the first floor which lies behind these windows. The penultimate bay on this side lights the kitchen and it too seems to have been altered but before Thorpe's survey to provide a secondary kitchen at the NW corner (now the visitors' entrance). The angle buttresses with ogee turrets also appear to be additions of the C17 and the same may be true of the buttresses against the E wall of the hall.

The covered passage running between the E range and the NE service courtyard is of 1830 by *J. P. Gandy-Deering*. It terminates at its N end in a tall arch in a porch. Inset into the parapet, William Cecil's coat of arms, dated 1576, which Gandy-Deering noted had come 'from the courtyard'. Plausibly, then, it came from the WEST RANGE since this was much altered on its courtyard side in 1830 (*see* below). If so the date stone might give us the year of commencement for the range, which also carries the date 1577 inside its gateway. This was the principal access to the house in the C16, from the entrance to the park on the Great North Road, and stands in the same relation to the hall range as e.g. at Kirby and indeed the standard medieval English manor house. It is also the relation between the two parts of St John's College. This range is more conventionally Tudor in style than the S and N fronts, again perhaps as a conscious desire to express tradition within a façade of otherwise advanced sensibility. The motif of the gatehouse, higher than the rest, and with four yet higher polygonal turrets, is familiar from Hampton Court, St James's Palace, Layer Marney and so on. The square angle projections occur

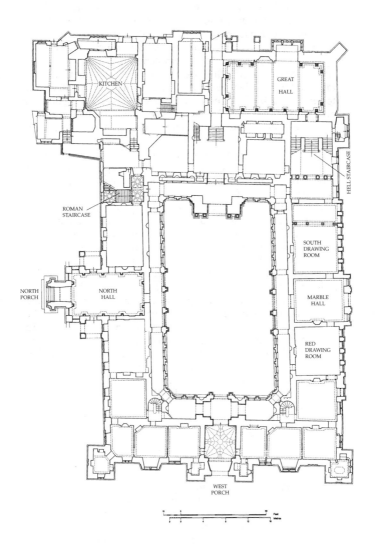

Burghley House.
Ground floor plan

e.g. at Syon House and Osterley Park *c.* 1550–75 but are ultimately of French derivation also. The entrance itself is in the
form of a classical triumphal arch with socles in the spandrels.
The even fenestration to which reference has already been
made, and the bay windows in the recessed portions of wall
between the angle projections and the gatehouse, connect
these fronts of Burghley with the slightly earlier Longleat. The
openwork cresting with Cecil's emblems also can be compared
with Longleat motifs. But here again there is another interesting development beyond such houses in the way in which the
tower concludes in a room above the roof level designed for
prospects of the park. The archway is closed by a pair of exquisitely beautiful wrought-iron and gilded GATES. These were
seen by Celia Fiennes in 1697 and are by *Tijou*.

The SOUTH FRONT is quieter in its rhythm. It has a middle
of five bays with a two-bay projection. The ground floor is
shown by Thorpe as a nine-bay loggia open to the formal
gardens, which could be accessed from the state rooms on the
first floor. This was a novel feature of the 1560s house, and has
no parallels in English house design of that period. Although
the design is different from that shown by Thorpe – with arches
in five bays l. and r. of the centre – the motifs accord with the
late C16 work elsewhere of socles in the spandrels of the arches
and square and ring motifs in the soffits of the arches, which
suggests alteration soon after 1605. The centre, however, is
provided with a segmental open and broken pediment, dated
1683. In the pediment, a shield with thick garlands. The
London mason *John Thompson* received payments for this work
in 1682–7 and it is possible that this included the filling in of
the arches as windows for the new apartments behind, which
were then under construction. The parapet of the centre part
was originally slightly lower than the outer bays but it was
raised to form an even roofline by *Capability Brown c.* 1765; it
had already lost its fantastical Elizabethan cresting of the type
still seen on the N front. To Brown are due also the four-light
mullioned and transomed windows with Gothic heads; replacing C17 openings. The effect is orderly, certainly not exciting.

The NORTH FAÇADE was completed last. It has a date 1587.
Its centre is the unique motif of a triple projection. The first
step is square on the ground floor and treated as a loggia with
open arches to N, W and E, but a quarter-circle above; the
second is a normal step; the third rectangular on the ground
floor and a semicircular bow above. The portal has Tuscan
columns. And whereas the N façade (like the S side) has a plain
balustrade at its top (cf. Somerset House and Longleat), the
bow and the quarter-circle have a varied, more fanciful cresting
with little obelisks. By its grandeur this entrance became the
state approach. The doorway has an arched soffit decorated
with bands of circles and squares, a hallmark of the work at
Burghley after 1570 and the same as those that occur in
Northamptonshire houses of about that year. The gates are
again in the Tijou style. To the l. of the N façade is a low

projecting service wing ending in a four-storeyed tower with an octagonal fifth storey and a cap. The corresponding wing to the r. was pulled down in the late C18 at Brown's instruction, to improve views of the house from the park. The forecourt is enclosed by a fine semicircle of C18 iron railings.

In the COURTYARD (which regrettably is rarely seen by the visitor) the dependence on Somerset House is once again obvious. The centre is a 'frontispiece' in the E range of three storeys crowned by a fabulous top storey supported by lions and an obelisk – all this a later addition dated 1585. The fantastic obelisk spire, the two supporting lions in the openwork, and the smaller obelisks behind them make a splendid if somewhat gross final flourish. The main obelisk may well be a reminiscence of Delorme at the chapel of Anet. Two smaller obelisks stand at the corners behind the lions. This finds a parallel in Lord Burghley's monument in St Martin's, Stamford (attributed to *Cornelius Cure*, who might have undertaken other work for Burghley). If all this is of 1585, the storeys below seem to date from *c.* 1564, and they repeat the 'triumphal arch' motif which Alberti and Bramante had used in Italy and which had then migrated to Fontainebleau and Anet. Another source is Ecouen, which Cecil knew from first-hand accounts. It is the most characteristic and advanced motif of Somerset House, and appears there, as at Burghley, with pairs of columns separated by niches and with the Orders correctly superimposed (Doric, Ionic, Corinthian). The archway in the centre is repeated on the first floor by a deep, coffered giant niche (of Fontainebleau derivation). On the second floor, however, there

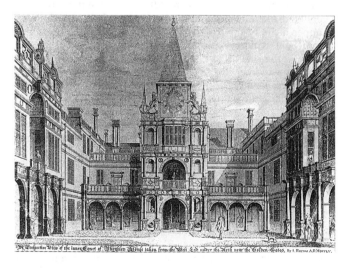

Burghley House, Inner Court.
Drawing by John Haynes, 1755

is a canted bay window instead, marking a turn from the Franco-Somerset style to the more indigenous mature Elizabethan, which may have been introduced along with the clock-tower. The iconography of this frontispiece is interesting, for in the spandrels of the arches are profile medallion portraits of Aeneas and Paris to the entrance and Charles V and Suleiman above, no doubt intended to flatter the visiting monarch when framed in the entrance to the house or standing in the loggia arch (which now frames the bust of Charles II in antique dress by *Honoré Pellé*). To l. and r. of the frontispiece there was originally arcading of three bays, with Tuscan columns. This motif of the open colonnade, a continuation really of the medieval cloister, had of course been a universal feature of the Italian Renaissance courtyards. It also was the motif of Gresham's Exchange of the 1560s. At Burghley it may have been the work of the Antwerp mason, *Hendrik van Paesschen*, whom Gresham had introduced to Cecil in 1563. At Burghley it existed only at the E and W ends, and now, in any case, what one sees is the work of *J. P. Gandy-Deering*, who in 1828–30 carefully reproduced the form of the arcading for enclosed two-storey corridors running round the court. At a stroke the spaciousness of the courtyard was destroyed. In the spandrels, roundels with heads of English kings and queens that complement the scheme of armorial glass in the corridor windows by *Willement*, showing descent from Edward I through the Neville family. A few of the heads are clearly older and may have been rescued from the destroyed arcading, which was decorated with Greek and Trojan heroes.

The N and S ranges have a centre motif as spectacular as, but subordinate to, the frontispiece, even before it received its crown of 1585. Tall triple arches flanked and separated by Tuscan columns. Above the middle bay on the first floor a big coffered niche corresponding to, but much higher than, the upper niche of the frontispiece. To its l. and r. big transomed four-light windows (two plus two lights), much taller than those of the wall l. and r. of the centre, i.e. appearing somewhat like bay windows. These less stressed walls are now flush with the centre as a result of the insertion of the two-storey corridors. Filling the N arch, a birdcage, also of *c.* 1830. The W side, like the E side, originally had three bays of arcading either side of the open archway through the base of the gatehouse. Originally there seems to have been a shallow oriel above the arch. Most likely it was removed in the 1680s, when the rooms at first floor were made redundant by alterations inside. The entire façade is now overlaid, however, by an exciting piece of Elizabethan-style scenery by *Gandy-Deering* that balances, or rather calls for, the frontispiece opposite. The portal has Tuscan columns, and the same arcading l. and r. Above the portal bay a curious motif, also frontispiece-like but less classical. Columns above the columns below, but in the middle a transomed window of five lights of which the centre three come forward as a narrow bow in the tradition of Windsor, Henry VII's Chapel, and Thornbury. Big attic with simple geometrical decoration. To the l. and r. lower and simpler first floor with balustrade. Polygonal stair-turrets with caps in the NW and SW angles, adding yet more excitement. Only on the second floor, which recedes as it does on the N and S sides, can one see the original windows.

INTERIORS. Inside the original GATEHOUSE (part of the private quarters), the entrance hall across the centre of the W range has a wide four-centred arch and a tierceron vault, a little incorrect in its details but essentially Gothic, with Cecil's achievement and the heraldry of related families. It is dated 1577. In the part added in 1828, it is continued by a second vaulted room, forming the centre towards the courtyard, and from this radiate tunnel-vaulted and coffered arches. All the motifs are copied from the late C16 Roman Staircase (see below).

The KITCHEN, in the NE corner of the house, also has a stone rib-vault with mouldings similar to those of the porch, but it is extremely lofty and has a central octagonal louvre towards which the ridge-ribs and the three pairs of tiercerons in each pair of cells run, and mighty fireplaces. Its Gothic character would fit a large and utilitarian piece of work of the 1550s and, as in the entrance hall, it was no doubt a conscious archaism. The roof covers a square space with large arches framing bays opening off to the E and W. N of the W bay is the original window, converted as the door to a store-cum-passage which must therefore be an addition though it is shown on Thorpe's survey; it must go with the N addition to the kitchen (now the visitors' entrance).

The GREAT HALL to the S, lying twelve steps higher up, partly due to the contours, partly because of the vaulted basement beneath, corresponds stylistically. The steep double-hammerbeam roof of the hall, though it has Gothic tracery in the spandrels, has Renaissance pendants with volutes decorated with bands of circles and squares as found in the N entrance arch and Roman Stair (see below). In the heads of the gables were formerly also windows lighting the roof frame (cf. Hampton Court, and Deene Park, Northants). The huge and noble fireplace on the other hand, with its big fluted volute corbels, its broad, bulging frieze with leaf and geometrical ornament, and its tall concave-sided chimneybreast ending in a pediment, is purely classical and adapted from Serlio. The circle round the coat of arms with the four bars connecting it with the four sides of the chimneybreast is the same motif as the clocktower and thus occurs right at the last stages of work at Burghley and is derived (once more) from Somerset House. The Hall was refurbished in c. 1835–6 for the 2nd Marquess of Exeter, when the bookcases were introduced and a minstrels' gallery created above the screens passage. The twisted columns are Belgian, from Tongerloo, and Baroque. In the great S window and the bay, heraldic stained glass by *Willement*, executed in 1838. In the upper parts he reset some medieval glass from Tattershall Castle and church (Lincs.), which had

99

been removed from there in 1757 and given to the Earl of Exeter. More of it is in St Martin's Stamford. The two coffered archways in the w wall are puzzling. They are blocked at their ends with mirrors. John Thorpe's plan of the house clearly shows windows in these positions between the hall and rooms in the inner E range but these arches are so like those in the w entrance hall and others in the screens passage that they might be *c.* 1830 also.

From here description can follow the route prescribed for visitors, in which the kitchen is seen first, the Great Hall at the end.

98   The ROMAN STAIRCASE, at the E end of the N range, was the more private of the two great stairs in the C16 house and primarily for the use of the family, although it also served a role in the processional route, transporting visitors from the first floor to the roof. It is as purely French and Renaissance as the courtyard frontispiece, and the initial source of it is the typical Florentine and Roman Renaissance staircase; but the more immediate source is probably either the staircase of Henri II in the Louvre, begun in 1546, or the upper flights of the staircase of the Hôtel de Ville, Paris, begun *c.* 1550, both of which Thomas Cecil may well have seen on visits to Paris in the 1560s. In English building it is something new. It has solid walls, with the handrail moulded and partly recessed into them and tunnel-vaults again with geometrical patterns made up of circles and squares connected by bands. The pattern is pierced by tiny holes, a motif which has been traced to the engravings of Vredeman de Vries. Here again is Cecil family heraldry, including the crescent moon emblem of the Chekes, the family of Cecil's first wife and mother of Thomas. The landings, however, are still rib-vaulted, with pendants that are of similar design to those of the great hall's roof. It will be noticed that the stair is a slightly awkward fit for the space and the decorative motifs of the vaults have been ingeniously distorted by the masons. The windows in the N wall do not seem to relate at all and in 1755 they are shown as continuous sheets of glazing for the full height of the stair, which must have created a remarkably luminous space inside, rather different from the chiaroscuro interior now. The remodelling of this feature into the regular mullions must be *Brown's* doing.

The rest of the interiors are mostly by the 5th Earl, executed during the 1680s and 1690s. Starting from the Roman Staircase and turning first E, then w, one sees first the CHAPEL and its ante-room. The chapel was here from at least the late C17. Thorpe's plan shows a series of small rooms here, and a plan of *c.* 1680 appears to be for remodelling it into its present shape. This must have involved extending the E wall further out from the line shown on Thorpe's plan; evidence of these changes was noted outside (*see* above). But it was described by Walpole in 1763 as 'too low and as yet unrestored'. So the ribbed Elizabethan plaster ceiling and diaper pattern of the

upper walls is by *Brown*, but the dark Elizabethan-style panelling looks 1830s. Remounted on the upper walls are some
swags of lively and daring woodcarving in the style of Gibbons;
they are probably by *Thomas Young* and *Jonathan Maine*, who
received large remunerations in the 1680s. Altar painting by
Veronese, from San Jacopo, Murano, purchased by the 9th Earl
in 1769. Pretty fitments also of *c.* 1770, Chippendale designs
made by *Mayhew & Ince*, including a communion rail, pulpits
and chairs and benches with openwork Gothick backs. Sumptuous scagliola fireplace, set up in 1846, brought from the
monastery of Passo de Arcos near Lisbon (bought by the 2nd
Marquess from Lord Howard de Walden) and ten lampholding
Virgins of bronzed plaster, 1801.

To the w of the Roman Staircase along the N range the first
three rooms must originally have been one impressive saloon
opening into the bow on the N front. Now they are as divided
by the 5th Earl. First, the BILLIARD ROOM with a stucco
ceiling based on an engraving from Wood's *Ruins of Palmyra*
(1754), again probably by *Brown*, but with earlier panelling
hung with portraits, including members of the 'Little Bedlam
Club' that include Kneller and Verrio; next, the BOW ROOM
lying in the centre, at right angles to the front and projecting
N into the curve of the centre bow, whose quarter-circle returns
are cut off, however, and serve as closets to the adjoining
rooms. Its ceiling and walls were painted by *Laguerre* in 1698.
The pictures represent Anthony and Cleopatra, the Conti-
nence of Scipio, and the Battle of Cannae. The way in which
painting runs without any caesura from ceiling into walls is
typical of English painting of the late c17, and it is never
satisfactory.

After the Bow Room, the BROWN DRAWING ROOM and
the BLACK AND YELLOW BEDROOM, both with stucco ceilings by *Edward Martens*, one of twenty in the house done
c. 1680–2, and more woodcarving in the Gibbons style of
splendidly free garlands and fruit, birds, etc. In the second
room also early c18 Soho tapestries in Grotesque style by *John
Vanderbank*.

The w range, also on the first floor, was originally filled
entirely by the long gallery. It was divided in 1679–82 into a
symmetrical arrangement of bedrooms and dressing rooms.
The two at the ends have corner chimneypieces with recreated
stepped tops for the display of china. The ceilings now have a
coved shape above cornices with scallop shells. At the centre
is the PAGODA ROOM with closets in the projection over the
w gates. These recesses are original to the 1570s gallery and
retain geometric panelling of that date with blind arches and
classical pilasters. The base is concealed by the floors, which
were raised in the 1670s. The most remarkable room is the
BLUE SILK BEDROOM, with tapestries and a fine bed by
Mayhew & Ince, but the so-called QUEEN ELIZABETH I'S
BEDROOM also has Gobelin tapestries and the mid-c17 state
bed.

The room in the sw corner begins the sequence of STATE ROOMS along the s front, signalled by a sudden enrichment of surfaces. Their evolution is a little complicated but appears to begin with the state apartments of Lord Burghley's house. By the late C17 they were known, as now, as the GEORGE ROOMS* and had been rearranged *en enfilade*. The height of their ceilings must have been raised, because the second-floor rooms in this range are redundant (behind the coving of the Heaven Room are remnants of Elizabethan wall decoration). They are distinguished by much painting, unfortunately not of a distinguished quality. *Verrio* did most of the work, 1686–97. Much, however, was unfinished at the death of the 5th Earl in 1700 and made habitable only by the 9th Earl, who commissioned new wainscoting in a Baroque style from the London cabinetmakers *Fell & Newton*; they were occupied with these rooms until the end of the 1780s. The fireplace interiors are especially magnificent, setting C17 silverwork in C18 steel surrounds.

In the First George Room (or DRESSING ROOM),[†] the ceiling represents Morning chasing Night; the marble chimneypiece is by *J. A. Richter*, *c.* 1780, the woodcarving of the sopraporta is accepted as the work of *Grinling Gibbons*. It is known that he was paid for work in 1683–5; this might be the one piece of work by him. Opening off this at the corner is the JEWEL CLOSET, again with a Gibbons-style overmantel. The ceiling shows Fortune blindfolded and tied to a wheel. Then the Second George Room on the s front proper (a.k.a. the STATE BEDROOM). Its ceiling depicts the Rewards of Virtue. The fireplace was made in Rome in the 1760s to a design by *Piranesi* and has red marble inserts, including pilasters with masks and elephants' heads. More tapestries by *Vanderbank*; these include, in the borders, vignettes of Burghley and the Cecils' house at Wothorpe, Northants. The bed was made in 1795 by *Fell & Newton*, but reduced in scale and given regal motifs for Queen Victoria in 1844. Next the DRAWING ROOM (Third George; ceiling of 1691: Reunion of Cupid and Psyche, late C18 fireplace, again by *Richter*), the DINING ROOM (Fourth George) with Feast of the Gods ceiling, 1692, and a fireplace in the Adam style, and the awesome HEAVEN ROOM (ceiling an Assembly of Gods, painted walls with giant Composite colonnading, E wall Cyclops' Forge with Verrio's own portrait). Finally the HELL STAIRCASE. Its ceiling dates from 1696–7, and is the climax of Verrio's contribution to Burghley, but the present staircase was not built into it until 1786, and the wall paintings of War were done by *Thomas Stothard* in 1801–2 in a remarkably Rubensian vein. His portrait is included

* One explanation for this is that the great staircase which served the E end of the apartment suite was decorated in the late C16 with the badges of members of the Order of the Garter, to which William Cecil was appointed in 1571. St George is the patron saint of the Order.

[†] The order is of course the reverse of the proper sequence through the state apartments, which begins with the staircase at the E, concluding with the private closet in the sw tower.

on the s wall. The painted architectural setting of darkly
marbled columns and a deep entablature originates in a design
for the stair by *Robert Adam*, supplied in 1779, but the executed
staircase is different and attributed to *Thomas Lumby* of
Lincoln. The stair rail, made by *William Johnson* of London, is
no more than a simple, graceful trellis. The landing rests on
Tuscan columns and the plaster walls are rusticated. The
Gibbons garlands over the hall door are not *in situ*. The C16
stair was also in this position and there survives one indication:
the fragment of a ceiling with pendants in the se corner bay
at first floor.

The rooms on the GROUND FLOOR, not open to the public,
are no less splendid. They retain the private function designed
for them in the late C17 and in terms of chronology and style
go with the rooms on the first floor of the w range rather than
the grand state rooms. But in decoration they are yet richer.
The climax here is the MARBLE HALL in the centre of the s　108
front, where new apartments were created from a series of
small rooms and the former s loggia. The hall has a prodigious
plaster ceiling, like the others by *Martens*, and an overmantel
lively with animals, shells and carved game birds. Two rooms
adjoin it to the e and w: the South Drawing Room (formerly
Dining Room) with a screen of four Corinthian columns
across; and the Red Drawing Room with a sumptuous stucco
ceiling and also a gorgeous gilt Rococo overmantel of *c.* 1750.
Along the w front are suites for the Earl and Countess, separated by the w porch. Even the small room in the NW corner
turret has a stucco ceiling of coronets. There are also Gibbons-
style chimney friezes and overmantels in several of these rooms.
Other rooms on the N side were redecorated some time after
1760, including the central NORTH HALL, which was enlarged
by extending into the N frontispiece and given Ionic columns
of deep yellow scagliola along the walls, made by *Richter*. The
ceiling is adapted from Adam's design of 1767 and in the
Library is another ceiling inspired by Woods's *Ruins of Palmyra*.
While one is thus amply compensated for the loss of William
Cecil's original interiors, one yet remains intrigued as to what
they might have looked like.

Finally, the ROOF. This functioned almost as a garden in
stone, with the elaborate crestings of the parapets controlling
views into the parkland and gardens below. At close quarters
the details can be appreciated, notably the recurrent motif of
a little castle and stone spheres with copper flames. The effect,
as Dr Husselby suggests, is of walking among ruins and there
are in all the turrets a fascinating number of small chambers
that originally had windows permitting outlooks in every direction. Over the w gatehouse is the Prospect Room, originally
looking into the courtyard as well as w across the park. Spiral
stairs gave private access from the rooms in the w range.

The KITCHEN COURT, e of the house, is mostly C17 and includes
a reservoir that has a frieze of little barrels between triglyphs.
But the principal OUTBUILDINGS are by *Capability Brown*,

1755–79. The ORANGERY lies to the E of the E front. It is Gothick, and was seen by Horace Walpole in 1763. Eleven bays, four angle turrets, Perp panelling, battlements. Plaster ceiling with pendants inside. The STABLES run along three sides of a courtyard, each with a tall, pointed arch in the centre. They have nine bays, the windows are mullioned with arched lights, and there is a hipped roof. W of the stables, and of the same build, the BREWHOUSE. Now the entrance to the house, with a fine, undemonstrative steel and glass addition by *Richard Griffiths Architects*, 2001.

PARK AND LANDSCAPE. In common with other Northamptonshire houses, the GARDENS known to Lord Burghley were composed of terraces and mounts and a large pond to the S of the house. As in the mansion, the 5th Earl made great changes between 1678 and 1700, creating a landscape of formal avenues radiating from the house and immediately around it walled compartments with terraces and a parterre. A long double avenue of trees, QUEEN ANNE'S AVENUE, apparently planted by *George London c.* 1702, extends S from the house for a mile. Another avenue extends to the N. *Capability Brown*'s presence at Burghley was of course more concerned with the remodelling of the grounds than with the design of the buildings, but he did not concentrate on it fully until after the outbuildings were complete and his contract was suddenly ended in 1779. Nevertheless, work continued to his intentions and by the time it was finished, there had been created one of the most perfect landscape settings in England. The LAKE, a relic of the C16 garden, was expanded into a serpentine form and is crossed at its W end by a fine BRIDGE of three arches, erected 1773–8. The lions on the bridge are by *Henry Gilbert* of Stamford, 1844, to replace the smaller originals supplied by *Coade*.

Towards the other end of the water, on the N bank, the BANQUETING HOUSE (built to Brown's design in 1787), overlooking the lake and framed by splendid cedar trees. This is Neo-Jacobean, which is a rarity at so early a date, small, with a pierced strapwork cresting and spiral-moulded finials. Brown's model was the pair of *c.* 1620 pavilions at Campden House, Chipping Camden, Glos. The BOATHOUSE on the opposite side of the lake is Neo-Jacobean too, but its date is 1871, of terracotta, by *J. M. Blashfield*, who had his works at Stamford. The WEST GATES, with the well-named 'Bottle Lodges' from the old Great North Road, are again Neo-Jacobean. They are, however, a much grander affair, with three archways, designed by *W. D. Legg* of Stamford in 1801 to celebrate the 10th Earl's accession to the Marquessate.

DAIRY FARM, SW of the house on the hill above the lake. Picturesque Gothic of *c.* 1800 in stone and thatch. A model establishment with cowshed to the fore and a smaller pair behind; one contains the former milk room with splendid plaster rib-vaulting inside. HOUSE behind, dated 1848. Neo-Jacobean. Brick range of 1875–6 to the E.

BURY

Now essentially a suburb of Ramsey.

HOLY CROSS. A large church on steep ground S of the Bury   87
brook, which divides the village. Formerly a chapel to Wistow
but the relationship had been reversed by 1178. Puzzling in one
or two ways. It has an excellent C13 W tower with very long
paired lancet bell-openings and yet longer single lancets on the
stage below. It also had a fine W doorway with mature stiff-leaf
on the responds. To N and S, sharing a continuous moulding
with the W arch, are also arches that have circular responds.
They are now blocked but originally must have been open and
would have allowed passage under the tower. There are traces
of roofs having existed higher up. There was also a W annex,
and that is completely mysterious. It was evidently Perp, see
the niches in its E (i.e. the tower W) wall with their little vaults
and brackets on shafts and the E jambs of the side windows.
That is a reminder of the S porch at Godmanchester. Also this
annex has a tunnel-vaulted undercroft of which the springing
courses remain. So the tower doorway was then blocked and
plastered over until the late C19. Above the door is a bracket
for a statue. What was the purpose of this annex? One possibil-
ity is a chapel holding an image of the Virgin, which is known
to have existed at Bury. When the W tower was begun, i.e.
before 1240, the church wall was made the tower E wall. This
was Norman and still has its Norman W portal of *c.* 1100, with
two orders of colonnettes carrying decorated scallop capitals
with incised patterns of concentric semicircles, an arch with
rolls and a double row of saltire patterns and a tympanum with
the plainest trellis pattern formed by the joints of the stones
(cf. the restored door at Stibbington, but otherwise uncommon
in Hunts.). The Norman chancel arch also remains, and shows
that the Norman nave was quite long, with double responds
and nook-shafts on the W side, crudely decorated capitals, and
two thick rolls in the arch (cf. Warboys and Morborne). The N
arcade dates from the years when the tower was begun, or
perhaps just a little earlier. Three bays, octagonal piers, big
stiff-leaf capitals in which, however, the individual leaves are
still static. The arches were redone *c.* 1500. Perp S side of the
church, the windows with panel tracery and stilted pointed
arches. The S doorway is again C13. The chancel (*c.* 1400?) has
been shortened, see the blocked N and S windows inside. The
N and S lowside windows have medieval SHUTTERS, something
rarely found *in situ.* – SCREEN. Perp, of not too narrow one-
light divisions. It was in the chancel arch until the late C19. –
LECTERN. Of wood. An outstanding piece of the early C14; the
oldest in Huntingdonshire (and Cambridgeshire, for that
matter) and superior to the lectern at Ramsey. Ogee-trefoiled
arcading on one outer side, oak leaves and acorns on the other;
on the side covered by the book, a symmetrical middle panel

of big leaves and a border of small foliage with a Green Man
in the centre. The foot of the lectern is a C13 stone with leaf
decoration on top and on all four sides. What was it? –
BENCHES. Plain, straight-topped, Perp. – STAINED GLASS.
Ancient fragments in a chancel N window and some N aisle
windows.

BYTHORN

0070

ST LAWRENCE. An unhappy sight. The early to mid-C14 tower
lost most of its spire c. 1960, and what remains looks like a
tower-mill with its cap and without sails. It is splay-footed,
rather than the broached form usual locally, and one tier of
lucarnes of an original three. The bell-openings are of two lights
with a transom and sub-tracery, and there is a quatrefoil frieze
over. The W window is Dec; so is the spherical triangle window
above it (cf. Great Gidding and Catworth). The chancel with
its steep roof is higher than the embattled nave, and that does
not make things better. The plain N and S doorways are of
c. 1200, the N and S arcades of the years either side of c. 1300.
They are of four bays. N has alternating round and octagonal
piers, S all quatrefoil. Both have double-chamfered arches. N
probably precedes S by a little and the S aisle also extends a
little E of the corner of the chancel. Its E window is c. 1340 and
the chancel has details probably of that time, although its
windows are 1874. The two-bay N chapel arcade is elementary
Perp, the arch to the aisle C19. Perp clerestory and roof. –
MONUMENT. Francis Parris †1725. Pedimented wall tablet of
white, grey and coloured marbles. Escutcheon at the base.
Village green with a pleasant mix of cottages and Gothic former
SCHOOL by *W. Slater*, 1860s, with stone bellcote.
BYTHORN HOUSE, SW of the church. Big, stuccoed Late Georgian farmhouse. Three-bay front with tripartite sash windows,
stone Doric porch but a Gothic arch doorway with nicely pat-
terned glazing.

CALDECOTE

1080

CHURCH HOUSE. Formerly St Mary Magdalene; converted
1988. Nave and chancel. Restored (i.e. rebuilt) 1874 by *Edward
J. Tarver*, who erected the double-bellcote in place of a diminutive bell-tower. The chancel lancets and the shafts of the
chancel E window are C13. So is the handsome DOUBLE
PISCINA with a fleur-de-lis in the spandrel and the bracket
opposite. The chancel arch responds are made up of twin-
scalloped Norman capitals. The W window has a late C13
quatrefoil in the spandrel.* S door with C13 iron straps and

---

*The PULPIT is now at Hilton (q.v.).

scrolls. Nicely carved timber porch of the restoration. Two-light windows l. and r.

CASTOR [P]

A large village, on rising ground above the N side of the Nene valley. Although somewhat built up in the later C20 it has a prosperous rural air, dominated by the church with its mighty tower and spire. A good mixture of houses, large and small, and numerous former farmsteads.

The early history is of exceptional interest, evidenced by the ROMAN REMAINS excavated by E. T. Artis, Lord Fitzwilliam's agent, before 1828. N of the church he found the foundations of a palatial structure, which appears to have developed in two major phases, initially constructed in the Hadrianic period as a group of buildings with mosaic floors, heating systems and a large bath house situated below the present site of the church. Excavation suggests that these were demolished and replaced *c*. A.D. 240 by a massive single structure some 190 by 90 metres (623 by 295 ft) which may have been two or three storeys high. This structure also had mosaic floors and heating systems and was partly terraced into the rising ground. Little can be seen of it now other than two sections of Roman herringbone masonry which protrude from the garden wall of the Old Rectory along Stocks Hill E of the church and other wall lines protruding onto Church Hill near the W gate into the churchyard. Extensive stone robbing from the Post-Roman period onwards has removed all other traces, but some of the stonework, also including tile and

Castor, Roman remains.
Drawing by E. T. Artis, 1828

column sections, can be seen in the walls of St Kyneburgha (*see* below). Artis recorded walls, with painted plaster, standing 11 ft (3.3 metres) high, and one of the mosaic floors discovered by him is preserved in the dairy at Milton (q.v.). His headstone is in the graveyard.

ST KYNEBURGHA. The dedication is unique in England. St Kyneburgha was the daughter of Penda, King of Mercia, and wife of Alhfrith, King of Northumbria. He died in 664 and she is supposed to have founded soon after a 'double monastery' at Castor, possibly occupying upstanding remains of the palatial Roman building. She was succeeded as abbess by her sister Kyneswitha and their bodies are said to have been removed to Peterborough in 1012, after the church had been ruined in raids by the Danes.

The church is the most important Norman parish church in the area and from the evidence of its decoration must have been underway *c.* 1100–10. It appears to incorporate some Saxon masonry, see the massive quoins and some long and short work, and much reused Roman red tile and brick scattered about its walls. The original parts extend from the spectacular crossing tower to W, N, S and E. To the W it includes the W end, where there is a shafted Norman window, and the fine S doorway (reset?), which has two orders of shafts with the capitals of the inner order decorated by beaded interlace, masks and beasts' heads, an arch with roll mouldings, and an outer billet frieze (the nailhead border is a C13 addition). It also includes: the N transept, where part of a N window remains (with billet decoration); the S transept, which has a fragment of a Norman W window (visible inside above the S aisle's E arch, with roll and a billet frieze); and of the chancel at least the famous inscription above the priest's door which records the rededication of the church on 17 April 1124, although the year is untidily inscribed; some read it as 1114, and it might even be 1104, when 17 April was Easter Sunday. Such an early date is supported by what one finds inside.* The stone is tympanum-shaped, but its bottom line rises in the middle in a smaller semicircle over a blocked opening. Another tympanum, not *in situ*, is in the S porch gable and just might be Anglo-Saxon. This has a demi-figure of Christ blessing; scrolls around the curve of the arch and a base of billet moulding. But the glory of the church is its tower and its sculptural decoration by a local workshop. To the outside it rises in four stages, each divided by a corbel table and with nook-shafts at the upper stages. First a plain storey up to the ridge of the roofs. Then a stage with large two-light windows, the lights having chevron arches (the only chevron proper at Castor) and the windows billet surrounds. The windows are framed by narrower, two-light blind arcading, also with billet. Over the heads of the arches, lozenge-pattern diapering laid to produce a lively

*I am grateful to Dr David Parsons for this suggestion.

texture (cf. the choir arcades at Peterborough Cathedral). The next stage has the bell-openings, three tall, slim two-light openings, framed by one blocked arch l. and one r. of identical pattern and fishscale diaperwork over. Finally the Norman top corbel table with band of nutmeg. Inside, it rests on four sturdy Norman arches with demi-shafts and roll mouldings. The steep bases have, mostly, a very flat chevron decoration (cf. Thorney) and the capitals rope-mouldings and beaded interlace decoration in addition to stalks, leaves and a wonderful variety of birds, beasts, monsters and small figures, including a combat, a hunting scene and a woman pursued by two soldiers (possibly the legend of St Kyneburgha), both of whom have the distinctive type of Early Norman, kite-shaped shields. The capitals of the w arch are more elaborate, with volutes. Only the NE capitals appear to have been restored (1851). The arches have a moulding including two rolls and a small hollow.

Next in order of time comes the C13. It did much. The chancel, possibly originally apsidal, was rebuilt early on: priest's (s) doorway still with a round arch (segmental rere-arch) and bell capitals, its SEDILIA still round-arched, the DOUBLE PISCINA with much dogtooth decoration and shafts of Alwalton marble, and lancet windows. In the N wall are some circular stones; they appear to be sections of columns, probably Roman spolia, and the walls also contain Roman stonework and tile. The s aisle must be of about the same time as the chancel. It has three bays, with round piers and round abaci, a little nail-head decoration, and round double-chamfered arches. The w window is a lancet, but the rere-arch is round. The s transept was then rebuilt with an E aisle c. 1280. The windows have bar tracery with circles (originally foiled, as Tillemans' early C18 illustration shows), except for those to the E, which have Y-tracery. A small tomb recess outside the s wall. The arches are double-chamfered and slightly pointed. Dec N arcade (octagonal piers but with concave joins to circular capitals, double-chamfered fully pointed arches and two expressive heads); Dec window in the s aisle (reticulated tracery), and Dec probably also the tomb recess below it on the outside of the aisle. Of the same period or a little later, i.e. mid C14, the tower's parapet of openwork tracery and short spire with two tiers of lucarnes (both probably slightly reconstructed after a lightning strike in 1795). At the same time the tower was strengthened inside by a plain rib-vault with ridge-ribs. The Perp contributions of interest are the big five-light E window, which replaced a group of three lancets, with panel tracery in three tiers and trefoils and ogee daggers in the head of the arch.

Inside, a fine ROOF over the nave with gilded angels and corbel figures carrying musical instruments in the East Anglian tradition. It is a rare example in this area and wonderfully complete, with over fifty figures including those in the aisles.
– FONT. C12. Restored on a new base, 1928. – Lady Chapel.

ALTAR. A large mensa, probably C14, uncovered in 2000 close to the priest's door and restored in 2003 with a base of octagonal columns. Incised with crosses. – REREDOS. St Kyneswitha's Chapel (N aisle). Five blank ogee arches, reset into the aisle E arch; below, a screen of reticulated tracery. – The S DOOR is C14 and has a foliate border with an inscription 'Ricardus Beby Rector Ecclesie de Castre Fec', probably for Richard of Leicester, rector in 1372. – BREAD SHELF. S aisle. C18. Provided by Robert Wright for the poor of Castor and Ailsworth. – WALL PAINTINGS. N aisle. Of the first half of the C14 (uncovered during restoration in 1843) and even in their faded state with all the vigour characteristic of the date. Three scenes of the Life of St Catherine, one below the other: Maxim's Entry into Alexandria, the Execution of the Philosophers and St Catherine and the Wheel. Keyser in 1888 described a much more extensive cycle including a Deposition and Entombment. – SCULPTURE. N aisle E. Small Saxon stone panel with a man, probably St Mark, holding a book, and the fragment of a second figure to his r., both under arcading. Only 19 in. (48 cm) tall. The classicizing style is connected with that of the Hedda Stone at Peterborough Cathedral and the figures at Fletton (see p. 637), but somewhat harder and more linear. The suggested date is late C8 or early C9 and the fragment is assumed to have come from the shrine of St Kyneburgha. It was discovered in 1928, beneath the chancel floor. – N aisle N. Traditionally identified as a Saxon CROSS-BASE with interlace and also two dragons (cf. the Hedda Stone), but with a bulging top that might suggest another use. Originally probably a Roman altar. – MONUMENTS. Coped coffin lid with, at the head end, bust of a priest, his head surrounded by a rounded-trefoiled canopy; early C13 (chancel). Several C18 and early C19 wall tablets: Rev. Stephen White †1824. Quite metropolitan with a draped urn and grey marble back. – *Robert Wright* †1736 built the stables at Milton and Blatherwycke Hall, Northants, and is very probably the same man who was Peterborough Cathedral's surveyor.

The VILLAGE has several large houses along the Peterborough Road. CASTOR HOUSE, at the E end, is the grandest and appears to have been a residence of the Bishop of Peterborough from at least the late C18. He was also the rector. Double-pile. To the street it is Early Georgian. Two storeys and five bays with quoins and sash windows in moulded stone surrounds with keystones. The walls, uncommonly for the neighbourhood, are rendered. Nice early C18 staircase inside with moulded risers. But the gatepiers with niches seem mid-C17, and that is perhaps the true date. The rear range is set so closely at right angles to HOME FARMHOUSE, which has a central chimneystack and dovecote in its adjoining range, that both houses might have originally been a 'double-unit', i.e. for different members of the same household. SE, in the former farmyard, a BARN (now converted), dated to c. 1600, of impressive scale with rows of triangular openings in the flanks. E of the house, climbing uphill, woodland garden with picturesque walks laid out in the mid C19.

Back towards the centre, the VILLAGE HALL, the school of 1829 with later C19 wing and round-arched windows. Near this, THE OLD SMITHY (No. 47), a good example of the C17 former farmsteads, its wing dated 1676. Opposite, set well back in grounds, is THE CEDARS, also originally a farm. To the fore, square block with a hipped roof, stuccoed front and a Greek Doric porch without pediment (interiors including a curved stair of the same period). The date is probably 1799, as inscribed on the gable of the stone rear wing, which also includes a coachhouse, barn and what must be the original, C17, farmhouse. A little further w, beyond the Fitzwilliam Arms, THE ELMS, mainly C18, with front and rear ranges in parallel, the s one ashlar-faced and slightly asymmetrical, no doubt concealing something older. Its E gable is dated 1769 and initialled WWF, probably for William Fitzwilliam. Next w, entered from The Green, is DUROBRIVAE, a complete house of c. 1730 with a splendid ashlar façade of four bays, with giant pilasters and windows with Gibbsian surrounds and flared keystones; the style suggests it must be by one of the Stamford masons. Furthest w, VILLAGE FARMHOUSE has an H-shaped plan with gabled wings, one with kneelers, the other with a carved stone at its apex. But the house also has one single-light window with a pointed trefoil above the side entrance and an ogee-headed archway inside. To the N, THE GROVE, an unexpectedly urbane Regency refronting of an earlier house. Three bays with a shallow pediment supported by volutes, niches in the outer bays and casements with wreaths in the upper lights.

GUNWADE BRIDGE, ½ m. E, crossing the Nene. Three arches with fluted keystones. Triangular cutwaters. A very attractive design, dated 1716, erected 'at the sole cost and charge of the Right Hoble. William Earl Fitzwilliam'. The N end incorporates two chambers below the road, lit by portholes. 400 yds w, by the river, are two stones (ROBIN HOOD AND LITTLE JOHN), 1 ft 6 in. (46 cm) high, which may have served as markers on the droveway along which stone from the quarries at Barnack was carted down to the River Nene and onto barges for shipment.

BELSIZE FARM. *See* Marholm.

CATWORTH

ST LEONARD. A mid- to late C14 church,* except for the half-destroyed E.E. DOUBLE PISCINA in the chancel and the lavish

---

* Some needlework cushion covers, made from parts of a cope (dated to *c.* 1329–54), were sold to the Victoria and Albert Museum in 1902. The cope was perhaps contemporary with the rebuilding and if so might indicate a rich patron.

E.E. s doorway, with three orders of shafts carrying mature stiff-leaf capitals and an arch of three hollow chamfers, the N door with its double-chamfered arch, and a stiff-leaf bracket in the N aisle. The W tower is slender, of five stages, ashlar-faced and well detailed. A W opening which is a spherical triangle with six spokes as tracery (cf. Great Gidding) is still essentially Dec, and so are the two-light bell-openings with transom. But the top frieze of the usual quatrefoils, the battlements, and the recessed spire (with two tiers of lucarnes) are Perp. The stair-turret rises in a buttress at the SE corner to the very top stage. The gargoyle on the N side is reused and marks the outlet of a flue from a recess inside, probably for baking the communion wafers. The arcades of four bays inside are quite typical of the late C14, i.e. the standard Perp moulded pier-section but still rounded bases and capitals and still sunk-quadrant mouldings in the arches. The chancel arch matches, but the chancel itself is late C15 (rebuilt in 1876 when the N vestry was added) and contemporary with the battlemented clerestory and nave roof (almost entirely renewed in 1939 by *S. Inskip Ladds*) with traceried spandrels to the braces and carved bosses. Bosses also on the S aisle roof of an unusual form, with the carving continued onto the beams. – PULPIT. Of wood; Perp, with traceried sides and an embattled base. It goes with the Perp SCREEN, of three-light divisions, a sensitively handled reconstruction of 1939 by *Ladds*. – ALTAR TABLE. A very good piece, with plump gadrooned and fluted legs. Inscribed 'the gift of Thomas Ekins in the year 1634'. – CHANDELIER. Of brass, one large ball and a double-headed eagle. It is inscribed by Brasenose College, which purchased the advowson in 1675, but also with the arms of John Morris of London, who gave it to the college in 1666. – PAINTING. 'The Lamentation' after Van Dyck. It appears to be signed *Farasyn* (possibly Louis Farasyn of Antwerp, 1822–99). Given by Sir Felix Booth. – ROYAL ARMS. Oil on canvas. C17. At the base the words of Isaiah 49:23 (And Kings Shall be Thy Nursing Fathers . . .) as they appear in the King James Bible. – STAINED GLASS. Fragments in the chancel S windows and the N aisle E (part of an angel and a head). Chancel E, †1876, possibly by *W. H. Constable* (Rodney Hubbuck) and N and S, 1912 by *J. Powell & Sons*. – MONUMENTS. – Elizabeth Brudenell †1656. Small bust with shield above. – Matthew Maddock †1788. Signed by *Cox* of Daventry. Dark pyramid with scrolled sides and an urn. – Sir Felix Booth, F.R.S., †1850 by *S. Manning Jun*. Large HATCHMENT above.

The CHURCHYARD GATES, robustly crafted, are by *John Ladds*, 1864.

Of the houses close to the church, THE GLEBE HOUSE was built in 1706. Pretty red brick, in Flemish bond, of six bays with segmental-headed sashes to the ground floor and a platband. Porch with segmental pediment and Ionic columns. Later C18 addition at the rear with big canted bay. The S end is of 1875 by *John Day* of Bedford.

Brook House, away from the village to the w, is another palimpsest, the principal part early C17 and a typical three-bay farmhouse with the chimney between the second and third bays (stone Tudor-arched fireplace with fluted frieze). Sashes of *c.* 1800 and additions of this date and *c.* 1840, when Sir Felix Booth, the London distiller, was the owner. A veranda runs round two sides.

CHESTERTON*

St Michael. A fine E.E. w tower with a small blocked C18 doorway, chamfered buttresses with stop-chamfers, two extremely long lancets to w and s, twin bell-openings under one pointed arch, fully shafted. Of the same time the s doorway, with early stiff-leaf of not very high quality (including one small head) and an arch of many mouldings. This doorway was provided at the same time as the s aisle and four-bay s arcade. The piers alternate between round and octagonal and three capitals have early stiff-leaf, vivid waterleaf, and real stiff-leaf crockets. The N arcade is later C13, of standard elements. The clerestory is Dec and the spire with a corbel-frieze of small heads, low broaches and two tiers of lucarnes of the same build. In 1736–7 the chancel was rebuilt by Sir Robert Pigott who held the advowson (cf. Haddon).† It is of ashlar with round-arched windows, raised quoins and a doorway of flat rustication of alternating sizes. The s porch was also built, its entrance with a Gibbs surround, and some new aisle windows put in. Internally the Georgian work in the chancel is very complete, with black and white paving, a SCREEN of three arched openings across the blocked chancel arch, a broad REREDOS with coupled Ionic pilasters and a wide broken pediment, a COMMUNION RAIL, and also the PULPIT on a broad base, with a little inlay, and the baluster FONT. – MONUMENTS. Plain tomb-chest to William Beville, 1483–4 (anno regis Richard tertii 1°). – Large standing stone monument to Robert Beville †1602 and wife and Sir Robert †1634 and wife. The date is probably that of the death of Sir Robert's wife, i.e. 1611. Two kneeling couples, husband and wife, facing one another, the children small below. The couples kneel under pendant arches, and there are Corinthian columns l. and r. Big top achievement. – John Driden, cousin of the poet, †1707. A

---

*Chesterton House, the early C17 Beville mansion, was held by the Drydens from the 1640s and demolished in 1807 by the Earl of Aboyne. J. Carter's sketch of 1798 shows it as a large house with wings, canted bays in two storeys and straight gables. Reused parts are at Elton Hall and at Lynch Lodge and Lynch Farm, Alwalton (qq.v.).

†Pigott owned Chesterton House but also built Alwalton Lodge in 1777 as his new home. This remarkable Gothick house is illustrated in the *Victoria County History* but the date of its demolition is uncertain.

fine piece of reredos type with a flat-topped ogee pediment
framing his arms. White and veined marble. Fluted pilasters,
hanging garlands and urns along the top. No figures. The base
is inscribed with lines from Dryden's 'To My Honour'd
Kinsman', written for his cousin in 1699. Original iron
railings.

THE PRIORY. The old rectory, so-called because the advowson
of the church was held by Royston Priory. C18 wing but the
rest of 1852 by *Edward Browning*, for the Rev. Lord George
Gordon, son of the Marquis of Huntly. Standard Neo-Tudor.

KATE'S CABIN, Great North Road (A1). An C18 house of two
gabled ranges of equal size, but with a datestone of 1819 and
the initials of John Watts, who ran it as an inn.

ROUND BARROW, 800 yds S of the church on a track to Hill
Farm. 5 ft 6 in. (1.7-metre)-high mound, 65 ft 7 in. (20 metres)
in diameter, surrounded by a ditch. Variously described as a
barrow and a Roman signal station. The site might also suggest
its later use as a windmill mound.

DUROBRIVAE. *See* Water Newton.

COLNE

ST HELEN. 1899–1900 by *W. M. Fawcett* of Cambridge (cf.
Pidley), with materials of the old church which collapsed in
1896, e.g. the piers and arches of the arcade, the PISCINAE, a
tower lancet etc. Two brackets have knotted tails. The tower is
at the SW end and has a lead spike. Crown-post roof, painted.
– ORGAN CASE. A pretty, early C19 piece. It is thought to have
belonged to Lady Olivia Bernard Sparrow (*see* Brampton) and
was also in the previous church (*Hunts Post*, 2.5.1896). –
SCREEN. Formerly in the chancel, *c.* 1900. – MONUMENT.
Charles Wandisford †1693. Small cartouche, very delicately
carved with drapery. Attributed to *James Hardy* (GF).

OLD CHURCH, 600 yds WNW along a lane. All that survives is
the S porch. The entrance has a basket arch.

CONINGTON

A possession of the Scottish royal family, who were also Earls of
Huntingdon, from *c.* 1190 until 1237 and then the de Brus family
(i.e. the ancestors of Robert Bruce). A moated site 1 m. S of the
village is still called Bruce's Castle. The Cottons inherited by
descent in 1460 but their mansion, CONINGTON CASTLE, was
built mostly late in the C16 and early in the C17, reputedly with
material from Fotheringhay Castle, although stone from Maxey
Castle (q.v.) was bought in 1630 and 1632 (VCH). In 1639 Sir
Thomas Cotton, one of the Duke of Bedford's Co-Adventurers,

started draining the Conington Fen. The house was acquired by the Heathcotes in 1752, enlarged and then totally demolished in 1956. The present CONINGTON HOUSE is the C18 stables. The GATEPIERS by the entrance to the church with their shaped finials look *c.* 1625 (cf. Stibbington Hall). Mid-C19 LODGE to the w on the Great North Road.

ALL SAINTS (Churches Conservation Trust). By the site of Con-ington Castle and to all appearances an estate church. It is a large and important work, all, it would appear, of *c.* 1500 but with a w tower truly monumental. It is ashlar-faced and of four stages and has panelled polygonal buttresses, a base frieze and a panelled top frieze, a surprising recessed doorway with a small pointed tunnel-vault, a transomed (over-restored) w window of five lights, then, above small two-light windows, round windows, looking C17 in their details, four-light bell-openings under four-centred arches, and big pinnacles. These are known to have been redone in 1638 by Sir Thomas Cotton. Quite possibly the whole tower was completed at that date and may have been begun by Sir Robert Cotton (†1631) at the same time as he was working on the house; Robert Walker has shown that the bell frame exhibits innovative bracing found only in the early C17. The rest of the church is rubble and cobble. Embattled nave and aisles, four-light aisle windows, three-light windows in the unusually tall clerestory (the much wider w bay has five-light windows), a higher rood-stair turret with an external door, and a chancel only projecting by one bay beyond the chapels.

Internally, the greatest surprise is due to the restoration by 91 *Blore* in 1841. The tower was originally open to the nave by a high arch, and at that height there was a vault. Now there is a low w entrance hall with a tierceron-star vault and, as high up as the original vault, a plaster vault. The head of the tower arch has outer and inner chamfered arches. The arcades are of four bays with a very complex Perp section to the piers and capitals only towards the arch openings, and mast-like wall-shafts car-rying the nave roof. This is dated 1615: can it possibly be that late? The aisle roofs stand on the wall side on shafts carried up from the floor. Over the chancel arch, three brackets for the missing rood (cf. Glatton). The chancel chapels are of only one bay.

In the chancel very handsome SEDILIA, straight-topped with three little hanging vaults. The seat front has a frieze of reticu-lation units. The PISCINA has a shelf, like the (later?) piscinas in the chapels. – FONT. Octagonal, probably C13, but Late Norman style with intersecting pointed arches on restored colonnettes (cf. All Saints, St Ives). – SCREENS. To the s chapel, of broad one-light divisions with ogee arches and ogees under round arches to the doors (cf. Brampton). – To the n chapel simpler. – CHAIR. High-backed Gothic armchair, prob-ably late C14. The back has a blank panel with a cusped and subcusped arch and the Annunciation in the spandrels. Seated figures on the top. Heavily restored, perhaps at the same time as the PEWS. They are by *Blore*, 1841, and characteristic of the date, with tall ends and poppyheads.

MONUMENTS. Conington is uncommonly rich. The series starts in the S chapel with the memorable Purbeck marble EFFIGY of a knight, possibly one of the de Brus family, in the robes of a Franciscan tertiary, a young face, perhaps someone who joined, as was not unusual, shortly before he died to be buried a religious. It is a noble, very sensitive piece, about three-quarters preserved. The date, judging by the style of the helmet, must be about *c.* 1330 and it is very probably the product of a London workshop (Claude Blair). – Then a remarkable set of four monuments, all of about 1603. They were raised by Sir Robert Cotton, the famous antiquary whose collection of manuscripts is now in the British Library, as a celebration of the Scottish royal descent of his manor and a flattery to the new king, James I, by whom he was knighted. In the N aisle, Prince Henry of Scotland (1115–52), a blank recess framed by Corinthian columns with a top crest of his arms, and a much larger one to his son David, 4th Earl of Huntingdon (†1219), in two tiers with columns. Blank recesses but in the upper part lies just a crown in the arch between the two columns. Supporting unicorns to l. and r. Along the base, the badges of kings from whom David was believed to descend. In the same positions in the S aisle, and corresponding in design, a memorial tablet between two columns to Thomas (inscribed XIII) Cotton †1519 and his wife and one much larger double one to Thomas (XV, †1547) and Thomas (XVI, †1592) Cotton and their wives with two arches and columns and an upper display of strapwork and heraldry. At the base, Roman Catholic symbols, an indication of Sir Robert's recusancy. – In the S chapel, Sir Robert Cotton †1631, and Sir Thomas †1662, the first erected 1655, the other by Sir John Cotton *c.* 1675 or thereabouts. The composition and details of the two tablets are identical except that Sir Robert's bust is in an oval recess and the garland below is of laurel, whereas Sir Thomas's is in a circular recess, and the garland is of bay. In spite of the identity in so many ways, the sculptural quality differs. The bust of Sir Thomas is good, that of Sir Robert outstanding. Who was capable at the time of characterizing so strikingly and modelling so perfectly? The answer is very probably *Edward Marshall* for Sir Robert and *Joshua Marshall* for Sir Thomas. – Sir John Cotton †1702 (N chapel) and his second wife, Elizabeth, also †1702 (N aisle W). Two identical tablets, with portraits at the top framed by palm fronds, cherubs' heads below and long inscriptions. Attributed to *Grinling Gibbons*, they are very similar to the Cotton monument at Conington, Cambridgeshire, dated 1697, which is signed by Gibbons. – Also in the S chapel, several to the Victorian Heathcotes, with Gothic frames, those on the S wall artfully arranged *c.* 1860. – BRASS. Nave W end. Rev. George Heathcote †1895. By *Hart, Son, Peard & Co.*

Enclosure in the early C17 and creation of the park was the cause of the village's displacement to its present position NW of house and church. Close to its entrance from the Great North Road is YEW TREE FARM, the large former rectory, *c.* 1830. Brick with raised stucco quoins and windows in moulded frames.

Former CROWN AND WOOLPACK INN, ¾ m. NW by the Great North Road. Lord Torrington in 1791 calls it 'just built'. Two storeys with an attic and arranged in a U with the open side to the road. Red brick, in Flemish bond, with *œil-de-bœuf* windows in the gables; but the whole thing is made lop-sided by the coating of the N wing in render. Later C19 alterations include the two-storey brick S porch. Later a farmhouse. Outbuildings to the rear, with pyramid roofed granaries.

ROUND HILL. *See* Glatton.

COVINGTON

0070

ALL SAINTS. A grey stone, aisleless church of small size, much of the character of its E end established by a restoration of 1882–3 by *W. Lewis Baker*, who added the N vestry and organ chamber. The earliest part, however, is the tympanum of the N doorway. This is Norman, with its two affronted quadrupeds: a lion and a wingless griffin(?). The ironwork C and strap hinges are early C12, along with part of the door. More evidence of the Norman church is to be found built into the S wall of the vestry, e.g. some chevron and the fragment of a colonnette. Then follows the priest's doorway, which must be *c.* 1200. Very good early C13 S doorway with one order of shafts with shaft-rings and leaf capitals. Arch with many mouldings, including rolls with fillets. Also good late C13 chancel S windows. The chancel arch corresponds to them, though it is completely restored. Above it two deep arched recesses in the nave E wall and one in the chancel W wall, not aligned. Two similar C19 openings in the tower wall. An arch to a lost S chapel (blocked with late C15 window) has Dec details. The small W tower is Dec too – see the arch towards the nave with broaches in the arch,* and the W window. The tower originally carried a spire. – FONT. Octagonal, Norman, with scalloped and quirked base and underside. – BENCHES. Three Perp ones, of the type with buttressed ends, the rest C19 copies.

THE OLD HALL, Keyston Road, has a stone front range with gabled ends on carved scroll kneelers and inside a typical lobby-entry plan. The date inscribed inside on the chimneystack is 1659. Early C18 fielded panelling in the parlour, probably of similar date to the projecting brick range at the rear, which has segmental headed windows. Opposite, THE OLD RECTORY is gault brick, dated 1849 and still quite

---

*The VCH and RCHM call it *c.* 1500 with reused stones from *c.* 1330.

classical, with shallow gabled wings and a recessed stucco porch. By *J. Horsford* of Bedford.

DEEPING GATE [P]

An expanded hamlet by the Welland.

BRIDGE to Deeping St James (Lincolnshire) of 1651. Three nearly semicircular arches with two slight chamfers. Cutwaters with pedestrian refuges.

DENTON

ALL SAINTS. In ruins since it was unroofed in 1962 and thoroughly overgrown. It was essentially a C17 church. Nave and chancel, and a small, short SW tower. Certain minor old parts were reused (e.g. the C13 chancel arch), but the windows – three lights with transom in the nave, two lights in the chancel – are of 1629, and the mouldings of the chancel arch responds too. The N porch was dated 1665, the W tower of unknown date. Its offset position might mean that it too is medieval. The E window tracery looks *c.* 1800. The work of 1629 was paid for by Sir Robert Cotton (*see* Conington), who was born at Denton, the work of 1665 by his grandson Sir John. Sir Robert rehoused at Denton some of the villagers removed from Conington by his enclosures in the early C17.

DIDDINGTON

ST LAWRENCE. A brick W tower and a brick S porch, both Henry VIII and rare in the county, although early C16 brick is a feature in the locality (cf. Southoe and Buckden, of course). E.E. cobble-walled chancel, cut short and finished off in small yellow bricks *c.* 1700. It has S and N lancets and a two-light lowside window which is Dec. The reset E window also Dec. On the S side only a two-bay chapel. This is Perp and probably of *c.* 1505 (*see* below), its E window blocked. The porch is in line with it, as at Grafham (q.v.). The three-bay N arcade is also E.E. Round piers and double-chamfered arches, a fourth arch removed and the W rebuilt in red brick at the same time as the tower. Perp windows. The chapel has an octagonal pier, the responds corbels in the form of a knot (cf. Buckworth and Little Paxton). – BENCHES. Perp. Many, with buttressed and traceried ends and backs, better than most in the county, with some lively carving in the spandrels. More tracery used for the screen to the s chapel. – PULPIT AND READING DESK. *c.* 1858, the latter with more tracery. – FONT. C13. Elaborate dome COVER of 1900. – STAINED GLASS. The collection of glass in the s chapel seems to have been assembled in the early C19 but restored (i.e. rearranged) in 1949 by *G. King & Son* of Norwich. The sw window looks more complete than it is. It contains fine C15 figures of St Catherine (her head of 1948, copying the original head of the figure of St Margaret), surrounded by made-up parts from a Resurrection etc. Also a kneeling donatrix and St Matthew, both from Boyland Hall, Norfolk (dem. 1947). – In the neighbouring window, Netherlandish C16 and C17 roundels of the Prodigal Son and the Virgin. – MONUMENTS. In the s chapel, tomb-chest with tracery, shields and fleurons and, against the back wall, kneeling brass figures of William Taylard †1505 and wife (11 in.;28 cm). The brass must once have been very handsome, and even in its partial state it is still one of best in the county. There was a Trinity above, and the figures of their children. There still are framing strips l. and r., each with three saints. In the floor, by the tomb-chest, Alice Taylard †1513. Kneeling figure, 12 in. (30 cm) long, with her three sons. In the s chapel, numerous hatchments and tablets to the Thornhills, who took this part of the s aisle as their 'dormitory' in 1814.

The setting is the large former park of DIDDINGTON HALL, which was the Thornhills' mansion, demolished by them in 1962. It stood to the SE. The forecourt and garden walls remain, along with the mid-C19 STABLES, small but with a powerful rusticated archway below a pedimented attic. *Salvin* made alterations to the house in 1857. The PLEASURE GROUNDS may have been worked on by *Richard Woods c.* 1768. LODGE by the A1. C19 brick with stone crowsteps.

The village is one street, much of it provided or improved by the Thornhill estate, including the former HOME FARM of 1873 (designed by *Frederick W. Thornhill*), some COTTAGES and a SCHOOL of 1892.

DOGSTHORPE *see* PETERBOROUGH

DULOE HILL *see* EATON SOCON

DUROBRIVAE *see* WATER NEWTON

EARITH 3070

At Earith start both the Old and the New Bedford Rivers, two of the principal enterprises in the draining of the fens by *Cornelius Vermuyden*. The OLD BEDFORD RIVER was begun in

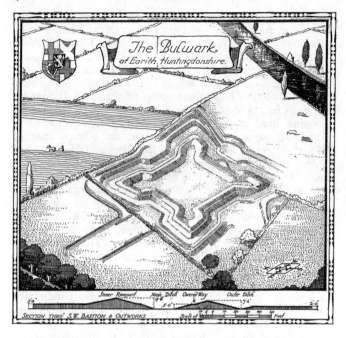

Earith, The Bulwark.
Bird's-eye view.

1631, an enterprise of the 4th Earl of Bedford and thirteen
Co-Adventurers. The NEW BEDFORD RIVER, or Hundred
Foot River, dates from 1651 etc. They run in straight diagonals
20 miles long, to Salter's Lode Sluice and Denver Sluice in
Norfolk, whereas the Ouse meanders on from Earith to the E
to Ely until at the two sluices it receives the drains again and
carries the water N to King's Lynn. The present bridge and
electric sluice is 1950s.

THE BULWARK, 150 yds N of the main road, on the floodplain
between the rivers, is one of the best-preserved Parliamentary
fortifications of the Civil War, erected on the fen edge to
control the road to Huntingdon. The earthwork, on the Dutch
model, is square, with four arrow-shaped angle bastions, an
inner ditch, outer ramparts also with corner bastions, and an
outer ditch but also two longer projections, or 'hornworks', to
SW and NW. It comprises 4½ acres (1.8 ha).

The village thrived as a port until the C19. In the now degraded
HIGH STREET, WOODLANDS (No. 50) has a nice doorway
with Doric pilasters and a pediment. Also No. 73 opposite, late
C18, its doorcase with fluted columns, an open pediment and
delicate fanlight.

THE OLD SCHOOL. A British School of 1839 by *Abbott* of Eynesbury (probably *W. Abbott*, Habershon's partner). Fine, plain

classical design expressive of the confidence of Nonconformity locally. Yellow brick, one-storeyed, of seven bays with a three-bay pediment and a cupola, the ends also pedimented. In Chapel Road, the WESLEYAN CHAPEL, 1828, is like (and now is) a small house.

EAST PERRY see PERRY

EASTON

1070

Easton fell within the Soke of Spaldwick and from the late C12 was a possession of the Bishop of Lincoln, with a road leading directly to Buckden. The layout is unusual with many small plots that suggest that it was a planned settlement. It was one of the largest villages in Huntingdonshire by the C18 but there is no clue of that now.

ST PETER. The late C14 W tower is of especially fine proportions. Setback buttresses, pairs of two-light transomed bell-openings, a top frieze of quatrefoils and pointed quatrefoils, and a spire with low broaches and three tiers of lucarnes on the cardinal faces. The S arcade is of *c.* 1300, four low bays, round piers and double-chamfered arches. The S doorway is contemporary, the door (replaced) has strap hinges with scrolls and a rosette. Perp nave N side with a large three-light and a large two-light window, both transomed. The porch, S aisle windows and W window are of the same phase. Excellent nave roof with the date 1630, the quality no doubt due to the Earl of Manchester, who held the manor. Moulded and carved tie-beams with a crude egg-and-dart moulding and open pendant finials. The clerestory with three-light windows is surely of the same time. Restored first by *John Ladds* in 1869–72 (chancel) and 1876–9 (the rest, adding his distinctive rainwater chutes) and by *S. Inskip Ladds* in 1903 (S aisle rebuilt) and 1905 (chancel again). The walls have been scraped and repointed. In the S wall, C12 fragments built in and in the N wall, also built in, the head of a small Norman window and a C13 coffin slab. – SCREEN (chancel). Perp, of broad one-light divisions with blind traceried panels. Otherwise ruthlessly stripped. The newel stair to the rood loft survives. – SCREENS (S aisle). By *Julian Limentani*, 2010. – BENCHES. Three C16 ones remain with rough fleur-de-lis on the ends. The other PEWS are made up of domestic panelling. – PULPIT. C18, of mahogany and ebony. It came in the late C19 from St Helen, South Shields. Formerly double-decker.

SE of the church is THE GRANGE, no doubt the site of the Bishop's grange, an Early Georgian house of brick and five bays. Tall segment-headed windows, doorway with straight hood on brackets. N of the church, COTTAGES in a row. They are C16 but altered in the early C17 when Easton became part of the Earl of Manchester's estate.

MANOR HOUSE, Church Road. Formerly the village farm. Jettied wing to the E of a former open hall.

WEST FARMHOUSE, The Lane. Retains a jettied gabled wing to a demolished hall range; the stone side chimneystack has a small carved face built into it.

EATON FORD *see* EATON SOCON

EATON SOCON

On the opposite bank of the Ouse from St Neots (and originally in Bedfordshire), but the space between the two is largely built up with late C20 housing.

ST MARY. Gutted by fire in 1930 and restored and partly rebuilt in 1932 by *Albert Richardson*. Only the shell of the Perp chancel, its N and S chapels and the outer walls of the aisles and the S clerestory remained, and of course the high W tower with set-back buttresses and pairs of transomed two-light bell-openings. On its W front, three canopied image niches and a traceried square window. There is much sandstone used in the tower and it continues briefly in the S aisle, so the tower must be contemporary with the S arcade. This is of five bays, and also survived the fire, with octagonal piers and early C14 (reused) arches. The matching N arcade follows its original design. Otherwise it is all Perp, C15. The SEDILIA consist simply of a seat with, as its back wall, blind tracery, the window above having its jambs and sill taken lower down. The reconstruction is a noble work, with ROOFS that have traceried spandrels in the aisles, angel corbels in the nave and cambered tie-beams in the chancel, painted and gilded. The aisle corbels are an excellent set of allegories (gluttony, gossiping etc.) carved by *P. G. Bentham* and including, in the N aisle, the architect and his foreman. Bentham also signs the REREDOS. – FONT. Square, Norman, of Purbeck marble. The decoration is intersecting arches. – All of the WOODWORK is carved by *Bentham* to Richardson's design, principal among it the ROOD SCREEN, of East Anglian Perp type, with rib-vaulting to a loft that is served by a SPIRAL STAIR in a very enjoyable wooden cage in the N chapel.* The Beauchamp Chapel (S) is intimately filled with stalls returned against the parclose screens. Its COMMUNION RAIL, however, is of *c.* 1640, curving forward. Balusters, and between them sharp pendants. – ARCHITECTURAL FRAG-

---

*The medieval rood screen and stair survived until the fire. The church had been restored in 1868 (date on the tower S door) by *Cory & Ferguson* of Carlisle (Kelly).

MENTS. Found after the fire. Large parts of the arch of a main doorway with chevron. – Also E.E. pieces. In a case under the tower, fragments of an alabaster angel, C15. – STAINED GLASS. In the S chapel S window four armorial roundels (St Albans, Ely, Lincoln and Beauchamp) and memorials to glass destroyed in the fire. – N aisle W. Some reassembled medieval fragments, rescued after the fire. Three young men in a barrel. Presumably from a window depicting St Nicholas. – TAPESTRIES. One large scenic Flemish C17 piece (and one smaller foliage piece with a pelican). They were obtained for the church in 1932 by Richardson. – BRASSES to a civilian and his wife, c. 1450. Also scrolls. The figures are 19 in. (48 cm) long. A fragment of another female was found after the fire.

On the green in front of the church, WAR MEMORIAL. Stone obelisk by *Alfred B. Yeates*, 1921. Bronze wreathes around the shaft by *Thomas Elsley* of London. S of the church, a LOCK-UP. 1826. Oblong, of brick, with an arched doorway. There are two cells inside.

In the main street, called GREAT NORTH ROAD,* there is, S of the church, the former METHODIST CHAPEL, dated 1850. Yellow brick Neo-Norman but with a pediment. Terribly businesslike. Just arched openings with bits of brick decoration. Opposite, the WHITE HORSE, timber-framed behind an Early Georgian red brick facing with one range with panelled parapet to the street and a later C18 five-bay range at right angles to it with a very pretty doorcase with consoles supporting a pediment, and the OLD PLOUGH (now a restaurant), low, timber-framed with closely set studs. N of the church some good houses of the early to mid C19 and in gault brick: No. 153 with a fluted Doric porch and traceried fanlight; THE GLEBE HOUSE (former vicarage) of c. 1810, which sits back in a large garden and has a shallow hipped roof and two-storey canted bays on the front flanking a stone Doric porch (enlarged 1875 by *William Jackson* of St Neots); THE LIMES must be closer to 1840, the eaves bracketed and the front asymmetrical with the canted bays placed together and the door to the r. Opposite, probably nearer c. 1800, a tall house of three bays (now divided) with stone cornice and windows recessed under brick arches at ground floor.

The Great North Road, N of the St Neots Road, climbs up to DULOE HILL. On the Duloe Road, a former WINDMILL, a tower-mill of c. 1815 without sails and converted to a house in 1947. Further N, THE CHESTNUTS (No. 401) is the best of the Edwardian villas. Dated 1906, conventional Domestic Revival with half-timbered gables but also a fine central balcony porch with elaborate ironwork.

On the St Neots Road the former ST NEOTS UNION WORKHOUSE, yellow brick, of 1841–2 by *W. Abbott*, with the

*'. . . as anybody will find appropriate who has tried to cross it . . .' wrote Pevsner in 1968, but it is quieter now that the A1 bypasses. 'No. 117, timber-framed and gabled with overhang and (at the time of writing) derelict' has been demolished.

usual octagonal centre to a cruciform plan of wings. It is not strictly classical, but in its utilitarian way certainly not yet anti-classical. Now converted to housing with embellishments in similar style. At the back, the former infirmary wing. Closer to St Neots, FORD HOUSE (Nursing Home), the manor house of the hamlet of Eaton Ford. A *c.* 1500 half-H plan with a symmetrical front of gabled cross-wings, originally jettied, with arched bracing in the heads. Stair with long, turned balusters. It also has some early C16 panelling from Netherstead (a vanished house which stood near Colmworth, Beds), introduced in the 1920s, and two strange C17 plaster reliefs: one is an overmantel with monkeys, birds, a man under a tree and a turtle, embellished with painted vignettes of churches at Eynesbury and St Neots; the other, larger, is probably of *c.* 1630–40 and depicts the Abduction of Proserpine by Pluto as related by Ovid in *Metamorphoses*. From where do they come?

RIVER MILL (Riverview Tavern), on the W bank of the Ouse. Former corn mill, of 1847 (datestone with initials T.G.C.). Three storeys tall, and seven bays broad with the centre one slightly projecting under a lucam in the attic. Outshot on the back. No machinery. N of the mill, also on the W bank of the Ouse, THE HILLINGS (or Castle Hills). A post-Conquest earthwork, on the site of a Saxon, if not earlier, settlement. Excavations in 1949–50 and 1960–2 have shown that the castle was of three periods: the D-shaped enclosure first, then the two others, one C11, the other C12. The S bailey was the innermost defence, as there was no motte.

ELLINGTON

ALL SAINTS. Set on a small hill S of the A14, giving even greater presence to the very fine, slender Early Perp W tower. This has set-back buttresses, pairs of two-light transomed bell-openings, a top frieze of pointed and round quatrefoils, and a broach spire with low broaches and three tiers of lucarnes in alternating directions. The details are all very similar to Easton. Inside, the buttresses are exposed, evidence that the tower was built independent of the church or might have been built for an aisleless nave. The start of a vault in the tower is preserved. The chancel is later C13, i.e. the Victorian geometrical tracery of 1863 (by *G. G. Scott*, paid for by Peterhouse, Cambridge) represents the style correctly. Original are the shafts of the E window, the chancel arch with stiff-leaf capitals, a little of the sill-frieze, and the priest's doorway. Of the same date approximately is the reset N aisle doorway, with three shafts and multiple mouldings. The S door is early C14, but the aisle itself and the N aisle, both embattled, and the embattled clerestory and the N porch (with leaf spandrels to the entrance) are all Perp. The four-bay arcades have piers with the standard

moulded section and arches with two sunk-quadrant mouldings. The outer moulding of the arches is unusual, with the tips
touching the sill of the clerestory (cf. Hamerton). Very good
nave roof (restored) with carved braces, embattled collars,
pendant heads on the ties, angels with spread wings against
the feet of the secondary principals, and figures against the
wall-posts. The N and S aisle roofs are similar, but also have
ornamented bosses. Newel stair to the rood loft. – FONT.
Octagonal, Perp, with quatrefoils and one other simple motif
of a saltire cross and cusped triangles. – STALLS, PULPIT,
COMMUNION RAIL etc. Victorian, and, curiously enough, in
the E.E. style. They are by *John Ladds*, 1863. He lived at Ellington. – TILES (chancel) by *Godwin*. – MONUMENT. N aisle.
Badly defaced effigy of a lady, C14, the effigy carved on a coffin
lid and the coffin preserved too. Discovered in 1915 under the
E end of the S aisle.
  Outside the S porch, a pair of large, heavily weathered, limestone TOMB-CHESTS with sides of big quatrefoils. Early C16?
The decoration is on no more than three sides. Were they
originally inside the church, and placed against the wall? –
TABLE TOMB. By the tower, Thomas Ladds †1805. Some Neo-
classical decoration.
Almost everything of the VILLAGE is post-1950 but close to the
church, where the High Street is broadest, is THE MERMAID
pub, C16 and C17 with a jettied gable, and a few cottages of
C17–C19 date. At the W end of High Street, where it meets the
Thrapston Road, BROOK COTTAGE has a late C16 timber-
framed and jettied part with a half-hipped roof, close studding
and bracing, abutting the remains of an earlier open hall. (The
W room of the attic had a board outside declaring it as a 'cheese
room', exempting it from window tax. BD)
CROOKED BILLET, Ellington Thorpe, ¾ m. S. C17. It has a
complete timber-framed chimney supporting the brick stack.

ELTON

0090

One of the finest in Huntingdonshire, Elton is a village of stone-
built houses and cottages, on the edge of the park of Elton Hall
(*see* below). There are two main streets: Over End and Middle
Street, the former N–S, passing the church, the latter E–W.

ALL SAINTS. Outside, Perp of *c.* 1500 dominates, inside, it is the
decades around 1300. The date for the exterior features might
be provided by bequests for a new screen in 1516, for decoration in 1527 and for bells in 1516–40. Proud ashlar-faced W
tower with clasping buttresses, a base frieze of pointed quatrefoils, a doorway with traceried spandrels, a three-light W
window with a niche over, three-light transomed bell-openings,
a quatrefoil frieze below them and another at the top of the
two patterns intermingled. No spire. High arch to the nave.

Ashlar-faced also the s porch, which has niches with hanging vaults. Late Perp aisle windows. *J. L. Pearson*'s restoration (with *John Thompson* of Peterborough as his builder) in 1886 revealed the Perp clerestory, which had been covered up by the aisle roofs in the C18. The aisles embrace the tower. Only the chancel points to what the interior has to say. Here is a window with bar tracery (quatrefoiled circle), a window with cusped Y-tracery, and one later one with flowing tracery, all with headstops. Lowside window. Inside, the chancel arch is definitely of some time before 1300. Triple shafts and nailhead. The SEDILIA and PISCINA and the AUMBRY opposite have cinquecusped arches. Then the arcades. Four bays. Quatrefoil piers, differing a little in the details. Arches s with one chamfer and one hollow chamfer, except the easternmost, which, like the N aisle, already has two sunk quadrants. – FONT. Octagonal, with simple cusped blank arches, *c.* 1300 too. – BENCHES. Some ends with traceried blank arches and also some linenfold. – ORGAN CASE and other furnishings by *Pearson*. – STAINED GLASS. Mighty E window, heavily populated with figures, by *Hardman*. Erected by the 5th Earl of Carysfort to his father, †1872. Other chancel windows of 1887 and 1888, also by *Hardman & Co.*, and two typical early C20 windows by the same firm in the N aisle. – s aisle E and SE by *Baillie & Meyer*, erected by the 4th Earl of Carysfort in 1870 as a memorial to the 3rd Earl and Countess. – By *Morris & Co.*, the chancel SW (executed 1893), tower W (1895), and s aisle W (1905). An outstanding set, especially the luminescent tower window of St Stephen with angels. All three commissioned by the Newman family. – MONUMENTS. In the s aisle N wall, a small coat of arms and inscription in raised letters to Sir Richard Sapcote (*see* Elton Hall). – Robert Sapcote †1601, a large incised effigy (s aisle floor), his armour described by fluent, flowing lines. – Thomas Proby †1684. Attributed to *Thomas Cartwright I* (GF). – Tablets of black and white marble with voluted sides, columns and crests to Sir Thomas Proby †1689 and his brother, John Proby, †1710; both extremely impressive, the former attributed to *William Stanton*, the latter to *Edward Stanton* (GF). – John Joshua, Lord Proby †1858. Tablet by *Tyley* of Bristol. Georgian-looking seated female figure in front of a grey, summarily indicated, mausoleum with arched entrance. – 5th Earl of Carysfort †1909. Decidedly Neo-Jacobean wall tablet, with gilded lions in the frame and finely carved predella of angels and bay leaf. Sprouting from the top, a scrolly wrought-iron bracket and banner. Designed by *C. R. Ashbee*, who refers to '. . . polishing off my defunct Earl . . .' in February 1912; his favoured sculptor, *Alec Miller*, was paid for the work. – In the chancel, Jane Forster †1764, signed by *E. Bingham* of Peterborough.

CROSSES. N of the w tower, two Anglo-Danish Crosses with wheel-heads and interlace. Discovered in 1885.

ELTON HALL. Huntingdonshire mansions are composite affairs. That applies to Elton Hall as much as to Hinchingbrooke (*see*

Huntingdon, p. 531) and Ramsey Abbey. At Elton Hall, work of the C18 and C19 is overlaid over work of the late C15, and of the important work of 1664 no features have been allowed to remain above ground. The late C15 work was done for Sir Richard Sapcote (†1477) and perhaps his son, Sir John (†1501). It consists of the former gatehouse and, in line with this, but originally separate from it, the former chapel. Nothing is known for certain about the further extent of the house but one might assume that the Sapcotes' hall range lay N of the surviving range, separated from it by a courtyard where the entrance court is still and that other ranges completed the square to E and W. The property was sold in 1617 and was ruinous by the time of the Restoration. Sir Thomas Proby, who married the daughter of Sir Thomas Cotton of Conington, then pulled down most of it and built the W range in 1665–8 (the architect, *Isaac Rowe*), smaller, however, than it is today and of which the vaults, a few quoins and blocked windows at basement level remain. We know from the Bucks' engraving of 1730 that it was to the E of seven bays and two storeys with a hipped roof. They also show that at that time the chapel remained complete (though its E window had been blocked and so it may have already been converted to its present use as the principal drawing room; Bridges, the Northamptonshire historian, writing only a decade before, describes the chapel as still in use). It was attached to the C17 range by a tower of stepped plan. On its W front Proby's new building was very probably a shallow U-plan with the S wing abutting the chapel range, but the centre seems to have been infilled in the earlier C18 to create a double-pile plan. About this time, if not earlier, the chapel was altered to become a drawing room and a wide canted bay was added on its S front.

John Proby was given Elton by his father in 1749 and became 1st Lord Carysfort in the Irish peerage in 1752. Under his son, also John, there began an extended period of transformation into a Gothick castle, for which at least part of the responsibility lies with *John Carter*. Precise dates are missing but work

Elton Hall, north view.
Drawing by S. and N. Buck, *c.* 1730

probably began *c.* 1790, after his marriage to Elizabeth Gren-
ville and creation as 1st Earl of Carysfort. Work was still going
on into the early C19 and was no doubt extended to accommodate the earl's growing collections of pictures and books.
Nevertheless, almost all of these interventions were reversed
or done over again in 1855–60 for the 3rd Earl by *Henry Ashton*
in a manner remarkably tactful to the medieval and later C17
parts.

Description can begin in the entrance court where something of
nearly every phase can be seen. On the s side the GATEHOUSE
has a four-centred arch, and two quadripartite rib-vaults
inside, preceded by a shallow entrance bay with two quadripartite vaults placed across, not along, i.e. rising to a middle
ridge, each with its own apex. There are two tiers of two-light
windows, and the top is embattled and strongly machicolated.
The CHAPEL was in the same range to the w. Of the chapel
itself above the undercroft, some masonry survives, and also
the E end-gable, with hoodmould over the former window. Of
the later C17 w range, what we see now from this side is as
refaced by *Henry Ashton*. The window details are different; a
mansard roof with Frenchy dormers is introduced, and the N
end is a three-storey extension on the site of a late C18 addition.
There is also a porch with two pairs of Doric columns on this
side of the range, the entrance having been moved to the new
w front in the late C18 and then back again. Between the w
range and the gatehouse, Ashton doubled the thickness of the
s range by adding the dining room along the N side of the
chapel, taking up its theme with three large three-light Gothic
windows and undercroft windows lighting a passage to the
former kitchen below. In the angle between this and the main
front is a Gothic tower, also by Ashton, rising higher than the
rest and with a crenellated top. The two-storey link between
the former chapel and the gatehouse was first made after 1790
but it too is overlaid by 1850s extensions. Beyond the gatehouse, a new kitchen wing and billiard room, all of *c.* 1870.

On the garden (s) front, the alterations of the late C18 and
early C19 are altogether more evident. Inside, on the principal
floor, that is easily seen, but outside it is all bits and pieces.
The centre of interest is of course the ashlar-faced part, containing the drawing room, with the canted bay window and the
outer staircase. This stands above the chapel undercroft, i.e.
takes the place of the chapel itself, and the storey below the
canted bay is very probably medieval also. The bay itself seems
to have been created *c.* 1720–30 (dating of the roof timbers)
but the wide pointed windows with their (restored) tracery,
and the whole general character, make a later C18 date probable for the refacing, and this is the one part of the house still
indicative of the aspect given to it by the 1st Earl. To the r. of
this part is the two-storey link between chapel and gatehouse,
created when the canted bay window in its upper floor was
brought over from Chesterton House (dem. 1807; *see* p. 459).
To the l. of the ashlar part is rough late C17 masonry to the

end, and a mullioned window is just round the corner. But the features of this part are not C17: they too belong to the remodelling of the late C18 and early C19, and have as their centre a small embattled gable between buttress shafts ending in pinnacles. Above the gable, a second stepped gable between turrets created in the 1880s when a square tower with embattled top was taken down. The very W end of the whole range is a projection terminating in a pair of round towers. Their construction is dated to 1812–14. Placed against the wall of this range are two small angels. They were brought over from the damaged part of the Houses of Parliament after the Second World War. The W side starts with the pair of round towers just referred to, continues with a mid-C18 stretch of three storeys, undisguised, and then with Ashton's remodelling of the principal range, which is even statelier than on the E side and eradicated all evidence of Carter's design, which built up in the centre into the form of a gatehouse over the entrance between buttress towers.

So to the INTERIOR, beginning with the CHAPEL UNDER-CROFT, which consists of two chambers – one serving as the present chapel – each of two bays of rib-vaulting, the single-chamfered ribs growing out of the wall-shafts without capitals and forming tierceron stars. The bays are separated by four-centred transverse arches. As for the C18, the best-preserved is the OCTAGON ROOM, W of the drawing room. This is a Gothick room, and good evidence of Carter's greater skills as a designer of interiors than as an architect. Here (and formerly in the room below, which has a Rococo chimneypiece) the angles of the octagon are formed into vaulted niches with slender rib-vaults holding glass cabinets with traceried panes – although these cabinets may be extremely faithful mid-C19 insertions. A date of 1783 in the stained glass refers to the creation of the Order of St Patrick, with which the 1st Earl was invested in 1784. Hereafter the interlocking of C18 and C19 is puzzling, especially since Ashton was evidently bent on conforming in decoration with the C18. The adjoining room, the principal DRAWING ROOM of the house, received its decoration earlier than the Octagon Room. From the details of the stucco ceiling one would assign it to c. 1760. However, the wall treatment is Ashton's. The spectacular early to mid-C18 chimneypiece of the drawing room, with its scroll-headed pedimented overmantel, is now in the DINING ROOM, where the rest of the decoration, including that of its ante-room, is also imitation-classical. The LIBRARY between the drawing room and the C15 gatehouse has another ceiling in C18 style with a saucer dome in the centre, but in the coving charming floral painting in the style of c. 1860 gives the game away (the room was widened on its N side at this time to join up to the dining room and fitted with bookcases brought from the drawing room; views of c. 1850 show a Gothick window in the N wall). In the gatehouse itself a further library, with Elizabethan-style panelling of 1894 following a fire. Of Ashton's time is of course

119

the MARBLE HALL and the STAIRCASE with its cast-iron handrail, which continues upwards in the tower. This is strikingly classical, with a gallery on one side supported on thick acanthus consoles. Ashton's detailing in the Georgian manner is remarkably competent throughout. In the range of *c.* 1665, i.e. the one facing E, there is more mid-C18-style work in the YELLOW DRAWING ROOM, with scagliola columns at one end that formed a screen to the adjoining ENTRANCE HALL. This is now darkly panelled with fittings of *c.* 1600 from Antwerp Town Hall, purchased in the 1850s for the family's seat at Glenart Castle, Co. Wicklow, and brought here in 1921. The Probys' other Irish property was Stillorgan House, near Dublin, which has been demolished; a painting of its landscape in the Yellow Drawing Room shows the stupendous early C18 obelisk designed for its park by Edward Lovett Pearce.

w of the house, fine STABLES, a double courtyard and of two periods; that to the W of late C17 and early C18 date, stone-built with Collyweston slated roofs, and the smart E court of *c.* 1870 with characteristic coursed masonry and a pediment over the archway. Fittings all preserved.

The GARDENS were remodelled in the 1890s by *H. E. Milner*, whose father had been Paxton's partner, with fine topiary and yew hedge *allées* etc., but most of this was taken out in the 1960s. The present layout, mostly created since 1983 by the present Lady Proby, has as its structure the design of 1911 by the artist and book designer *A. H. Hallam Murray* for Col. Douglas Proby, whose son had married Murray's daughter. Gothick ORANGERY of 2000 and a SHELL SEAT (based on a Kentian design known to have existed in the gardens in the C18), both by *Christopher Smallwood*.

The PARK is large, and the principal approach to the house is down a superb lime avenue, although this dates only from *c.* 1870; before then the entrance was close to the church. The landscaping is subtle, and Reptonian in character, with a lake to the SW. Terminating a view across the lake from the house is a TEMPLE OF SYLVANUS, primitive Doric à la Athenian Treasury at Delphi. It looks Georgian at first, but is in fact of 1957 by *Hope Bagenal*.

Close to the entrance, on the opposite side of the road, is THE OLD DAIRY (now offices and a restaurant), model buildings of 1901 with parallel ranks of gabled ranges and a nice cupola. The VILLAGE has several centres, including a small green with houses on three sides, close to the gates to the Hall. N from here, in OVER END, several C17 houses with mullioned windows, and two Georgian ones, the BLACK HORSE of five bays, and, on the other side, a battlemented one (No. 15) with two canted bay windows. This was the home in the early C19 of James Hayes, iron founder, whose works are partially preserved to the rear (now the Estate Yard) and consist of brick ranges around a courtyard, several with iron-framed windows. One notices a good deal of quality ironwork in the village. N of the church, in School Lane, the SCHOOL of 1876–8 by *Walter*

E. McCarthy. Stone and low with kneelered gables at the ends
and little bellcote. Extended since but always to the same
formula. In MIDDLE STREET (a.k.a. High Street) again some
mullioned windows at No. 5, which is mid-C17 with cross-wing
and two-storey canted bay. Also ANGEL HOUSE, which is of
three bays, symmetrical, and must be later C17, or just possibly
as late as 1703, the date on its chimney. On the other side is a
stately five-bay house dated 1690 over the door. It has wooden
cross-windows but they are not original. Inside, a good staircase with turned balusters. THE PRIORY may be of similar
vintage but to the street presents a front of *c.* 1860, the windows
with Elizabethan-style arch heads. Weathered niche in the r.
gable. Good iron railings with feathered heads and gates, probably from the Hayes foundry. The changes were made for the
agent of the Elton Hall estate and the house has as its view the
park of the house, through late C19 railings and gates by *Amies
Barford & Co.* of Peterborough. Diagonally opposite is a former
farmhouse (No. 19) adapted in 1878 by *John Day* of Bedford
for the Ven. Richard Kempthorne, rather in the manner of a
gate lodge to the park. At the w end is the METHODIST
CHURCH, dated 1864, but still with arched windows. However,
the Jacobeanish gable would rule out a much earlier date.
Pitch-pine fittings inside, with a gallery at the rear and an
upper room in the other part.

BERRY LEAS, Duck Lane. Built *c.* 1929–31 for Major Sir Richard
Proby by *Sir Guy Dawber*, in his sensitive Neo-Cotswold style
with gables and mullioned windows; some are reused, like the
porch, from the Rectory previously on this site.* Nicely detailed
stair inside and rooms with panelling in *c.* 1700 style. The
gardens run down to the Nene.

ETTON [P]

ST STEPHEN. Memorable as a completely C13 church, although
the base of the w tower is earlier than the rest (see the roofline
inside above the tower arch). It has flat angle buttresses, lancet
windows, and bell-openings of two lights with a circular shaft
between and under a shafted, still round arch. This is remarkably late for a round arch. Frieze with heads, dogtooth, stiff-
leaf, and a horizontal figure, or *sheila na gig*, on the s side.
Shortish, simple broach spire with low, broad broaches and
two tiers of lucarnes in alternating directions. They are just
single-chamfered lancets. The aisle windows are of two lights
with circles over (originally they were foiled, as the chancel
windows show). The blocked N door has a pretty trefoiled head.
The s porch entrance is round-arched with a chamfer and a

---

*From 1842 until his conversion to Roman Catholicism in 1845, the rector was
Frederick William Faber, a leading figure in the Oxford Movement.

hollow chamfer; the door itself is pointed. Chancel E window of five steeply stepped lancets under one arch, and the S windows have two lights and a trefoiled circle. Nice C14 lowside window under an ogee. There are no N windows. A blocked arch and piscina in the N wall shows that there was a chapel here and E of this perhaps a vestry too, indicated by a blocked doorway. Inside the church, the tower arch is pointed and double-chamfered and has semi-octagonal responds with concave mouldings (cf. the N chapel, Maxey). Arcades, not in axis with the tower arch, are of three bays. Circular piers, circular capitals and abaci (different S from N; with some nailhead ornament on the S side (as at Peakirk), but both with pointed double-chamfered arches). The chancel arch has two hollow chamfers, possibly later than the half-round responds. PISCINAS in the chancel (cusped Y-tracery with a pointed quatrefoil, restored) and S aisle (deep basin under a trefoiled head with cusps like the N door). Grander SEDILIA in the chancel, pointed-trefoiled, between shafts. – CREED AND COMMANDMENT BOARDS (N and S aisle); the S one covers a tiny fragment of WALL PAINTING of an early C14 Tree of Jesse, all of which was first revealed in 1848. Its style was close to the illuminated 'Fenland' manuscripts and was probably associated with a side altar to the Virgin.

MANOR HOUSE, E of the church, is probably late C17. A not quite regular H-plan with gabled porch slightly off-centre. Coursed stone walls and mullioned windows except for the N wing, containing the former kitchen and hayloft above, which is blind on the front. Lobby entry plan. The stair at the rear has turned balusters. The Hall has a massive external stack of stepped profile with set-offs. Two rooms in the S wing, one with an inglenook, and in the rooms above fine fireplaces with Tudor arches.

OLD RECTORY, SW of the church. 1853–4 by *Edward Browning* for the Rev. Charles Mossop. The outstanding feature is the staircase window, its design copied from Northborough Manor (q.v.), i.e. two lights, square-headed with a mullion and cusped tracery of a full quatrefoil and two halves.

WOODCROFT CASTLE. *See* p. 724.

EYE [P]

A possession of the abbot of Peterborough and originally a one-street village on an island in the Fen. W of the village is a very well-preserved section of CAR DYKE (cf. Peakirk).

ST MATTHEW. The medieval church was destroyed by fire and replaced in 1846–7 by *F. T. Dollman*, from designs by *G. Basevi* (†1845, falling from the scaffolding at Ely). Cruciform. Lancet windows. Dull. Dollman completed the W tower in 1857–9 with more 'correct' E.E. details. Spire replaced by a saddleback roof *c.* 1982. S vestry by *Townsend & Fordham*, 1914. Interior originally set out for preaching, with only a shallow raised sanctuary. Church room in place of the gallery, 2007. – FONT. C14 octagonal bowl, on eight C19 supports, the spaces between which form recesses and the decoration of the bowl is their ogee gables. – STAINED GLASS. E window 1863 by *A. Gibbs*, vividly coloured scenes from the life of Christ. Three of saints by *J. Powell & Sons*: S transept E, 1889 (*J. W. Brown* & *C. Hardgrave*), S aisle S (E), 1882 (*Holiday*) and N transept E, 1877 (*H. E. Wooldridge*). The rest by *H. A. Hymers*, 1899–1903, quite good, with watery green tones.

In HIGH STREET, a few memories of the C17 and C18 village. Furthest W the attractive BLUE BOAR INN, C17 of rubble stone with nice early C20 arched hoods to the doors, and the METHODIST CHAPEL, 1851. Most of the houses are brick, but STONE HOUSE (No. 14, N side), *c.* 1800, is unusually polite. Ashlar-fronted with windows in raised architraves, arched door and taller central window under a raised parapet.

Former VICARAGE, No. 1 Thorney Road. Solid Late Georgian, three bays square. 1838 by *Francis Ruddle*.

In the neighbourhood are the sites of three monastic granges or occasional residences for the abbots of Peterborough:

EYEBURY HOUSE, Eyebury Road, ⅝ m. S, was a moated site. From the early to mid C13, as the possession of Abbot Walter of St Edmunds, it evolved into a considerable complex of house and farm. The Crown leased it to Sir John Russell in 1541, and Dugdale in 1657 noted the remains of a medieval barn of prodigious size. (The present house is late C17, with a front of four by three bays with hipped roof (now with a lantern) and two chimneys. The windows are symmetrically arranged but have mullions and transoms. The E doorway looks a little more classical. In its cellar an octagonal stone pier. NHLE)

OXNEY GRANGE, ¼ m. S of Eyebury, was held by the sub-sacrist of the abbey and functioned as a retreat for the Prior as well as a dairy. It is now a Neo-Tudor farmhouse of 1839 (rebuilt after a fire in 2003) but incorporates four rooms with rib-vaults. In one the ribs rise straight from the ground and have an uncommonly long chamfer. The other three have corner shafts for the ribs. The house stood in a moat enclosing some 7 acres (2.8 ha).

NORTHOLM FARM, 1 m. N of Eye, was established by Abbot Godfrey of Crowland in 1305–6. It became a dairy to the abbey and remained a possession of the Bishop after the Dissolution. The L-shaped house is now predominantly of 1711 (dated) and has interiors to match that date, although at its W end is one part with traces of mullioned windows. In the garden an arch incorporates some medieval fragments, including a gargoyle and a strip of finely carved foliage.

(TANHOLT FARM, ¾ m. SE. A model farm of 1856 by *Beadel, Son & Chancellor* of Chelmsford.)

EYEBURY HOUSE *see* EYE

EYNESBURY

The village precedes St Neots in date and is separated from it by the Hen Brook, but has become its s suburb, with much late c20 development.

St Mary. Of brown cobbles, except the ashlar s tower. This has the date of 1687, referring to rebuilding with E.E. materials after a lightning strike. The obelisk pinnacles with ball finials are obviously late c17. E.E. also the s doorway. Otherwise mostly Dec and Perp and much redone in 1857–8 by *A. W. Blomfield*. He substantially reconstructed the chancel which had a flat roof by that date and a window above it in the nave e wall. The n porch was paid for by Lt Col. W. Humbley as a thank-offering for his survival of more than twenty battles, from the fall of Copenhagen to Waterloo, 'in which the British were always victorious'. He is buried beneath. But on entering one is at once faced with much more ancient history. The n arcade is clunch, partly Late Norman and partly earliest E.E. Round piers, square abaci, five bays. The Norman part has multi-scalloped capitals. Then follows one capital with flat stylized pointed leaves and then stiff-leaf. The capitals are low, and the stiff-leaf is on a small scale with the arrangements symmetrical. The s arcade is of the late c13, with octagonal piers, arches with two hollow chamfers, and broaches at the start. The aisle is narrow, as the s tower determined its width. The arch from the tower to the aisle is c13 too. Small nailhead in the respond abaci. Ballflower over the w door also. Of the same style the chancel arch with saltires in the moulding, but this is by Blomfield. Its red marble responds are of 1933, when the rood beam was erected by *Albert Richardson*, the heavy angel corbels and the rood figures carved by *P. G. Bentham*. The e window, three stepped lancets with dogtooth surround and marble shafts, was inserted in 1868. Stone vestry of 1929 by *S. Inskip Ladds*, with a brick extension of 1977 by *Marshall Sisson*. – PULPIT. An unusually beautiful late c17 piece, the panels with a little inlay, the angle posts carved with cherubs' heads and garlands. Stem of 1974 by *Sisson*. – BENCH ENDS. An excellent set (n aisle and two in the s aisle). Traceried fronts and ends modestly decorated with palms or an edging of fleu-rons and with bold poppyheads of leaf in plain outlines far from the usual fleur-de-lis type. Also human heads, stags, a sitting hen, a camel, and other animals and birds and monsters, cf. the bestiaries on the roofs of St Neots Church. – STAINED GLASS. w window, 1860 (Joshua, David and Cornelius) by *Clayton & Bell*. The chancel e, 1863, is by *Hardman*, its fine c13-style design superbly complementing the window sur-round of this date. In the porch, four figures (the Virgin, St Mary, St Joseph and St Philip) by *Hardman*, 1873. Other of

the 1860s and 1870s by *Heaton, Butler & Bayne*. – MONU-
MENTS. Baroque oval tablets to John Turner †1705, London
work but dull, and a superior one for his son, Edward, †1714,
attributed to *William Woodman the elder*. The Turners were successive rectors who paid for the tower's late C17 restoration.
– WAR MEMORIAL. Cross by *S. Inskip Ladds*, 1919.

Across the road a SCHOOL of 1868. Its flowing Dec window is
the former E window of the church, by *Blomfield*, which was
removed in 1863. The view N up St Mary's Street, with the
tower of St Neots church rising above the low houses, is a good
one. Out of sight to the W is TUDOR HOUSE, the former
rectory manor house, timber-framed, multi-gabled and plastered. It is probably late C16, a hall with two cross-wings, of
which the N one seems to have been rebuilt in the late C17.
The windows all of the mid to later C18, and some Victorian
additions at the S end also. At the S end of Montagu Street,
MONTAGU HOUSE is late C18 but was completely refaced with
its original brick in the C20. Three widely spaced bays, pedimental gable with an arched window reaching up into it. Neo-
Georgian doorway, pretty but damaged. The house is now flats.

E of the church, in Berkley Street, the METHODIST CHURCH
of 1928 by *H. K. Armitage*, very trad but with a bright extension for a hall of 2005. By the Green, some COUNCIL HOUSING
by *Barry Parker*, probably *c.* 1920–4 (cf. Cromwell Gardens,
St Neots).

FARCET

2090

Precious little in the village from before the late C19, and much
of what was recorded by the RCHM in 1926 has been destroyed
or altered.*

ST MARY. The W tower is Late Norman and E.E. but restored
in 1894–7, the date of the corbel-frieze, small recessed lead
spire and stair-tower. Clasping buttresses. The lower windows
are still round-headed lancets, with wide splays inside, but the
bell-openings have two pointed openings under a round arch.
The low arch towards the nave, however, is already pointed.
The pointed arch was usually adopted structurally before it
became accepted decoratively. The S arcade has octagonal piers
looking fully E.E. but round, if double-chamfered, arches. The
oddest feature is that the W bay of the aisle overlaps the tower,
but is separate from it, and has a complete arch, also pointed.
The chancel arch has one chamfer and one hollow chamfer.
All this is C13 and not late, and so is the arch to the S chapel,
although the chapel was completely rebuilt with the E end of
the chancel in 1852 by *E. G. Paley*. N aisle and clerestory date
from the same time (the N aisle windows reused C15) and the

---

*The doorway of a house noted by Pevsner is now at Alwalton (q.v.).

nave roof no doubt also does, but used in it are some C15 heads and angels. – SEDILIA. A C13 stone throne, partly original. At the top of the arm a flower in a roundel. PISCINA of the same time. – PULPIT. An Early Renaissance piece still with linenfold but also with arabesques including mermaid-like creatures. The remaining fragment of the back panel carries the date 1612, but that cannot apply to the parts described. It must either refer to the addition of a tester, now missing, or the date at which it was made up from earlier bits. – STAINED GLASS. N aisle E window by *Kempe & Co.*, 1917. Annunciation. – Good TABLE TOMBS outside.

FENGATE *see* PETERBOROUGH

3060

FENSTANTON

ST PETER AND ST PAUL. The most interesting part of the church is the chancel. It is higher than the nave, and has a proud seven-light E window and high three-light side windows with reticulated tracery such as also appears prominently in the E window. Headstops and animal stops, original. The priest's doorway is well moulded, and the SEDILIA and PISCINA have an even row of ogee arches. This chancel was built by William of Longthorne, whose brass – now only the indent – is in the middle of the floor, and he was rector from 1345 till 1352. The lettering on the tomb-slab incidentally is still Lombardic. So here is a dated piece of the mature Dec. The W tower cannot have been started much later. The W doorway is also still Dec. To it belong the two fragmentary windows to S and N cancelled when the mason of the Perp church decided upon aisles to embrace the tower. The head corbels of these new S and N arches look C13, but they must be reused. The SE and NE buttresses intrude into the aisles and have half-arches with a roll moulding at the base. The church is of rubble and brown cobbles. The ashlar spire with low broaches is Perp. Two tiers of lucarnes in alternating directions with carved heads to the gables. Perp aisles and clerestory; the early C16 aisle roofs have large carved angels and furled foliage along the wall-plate. Perp arcades of three wide bays, the piers with four polygonal projections and four diagonal hollows. The tall tower arch and chancel arch more or less match, though the bases of the chancel arch are E.E. As early as this is the S porch entrance, reset no doubt. This has dogtooth and an almond-shaped recess above. S door also C13? The porch itself rebuilt. – PULPIT. With linenfold panels, perhaps early C16, reframed in 1860 and given pinnacles from the rood screen. – STAINED GLASS. E window. Scenes from the life of St Peter, 1876, probably by *Henry Hughes* of *Ward & Hughes* (MK); chancel N, Adoration, 1880, and St Gabriel, St Michael and St Raphael,

1907, and a third of Martyr saints of 1884 on the s side, all by *Clayton & Bell* and intended as a scheme of six. – s aisle e. Conversion of St Paul, by *Ian Thompson* and *Nicholas Bechgaard*, 2000. – MONUMENTS. For William of Longthorne, *see* above. – Lancelot Brown †1783, i.e. Capability Brown, the celebrated garden designer, and his family. He acquired the Manor from the Earl of Northampton in 1767 but never lived here. The monument is a flat tomb-chest on steps with a back plate with modest Gothic detail and a crenellated top. The inscription, poorly lettered, reads:

> Ye Sons of Elegance, who truly taste
> The Simple charms that genuine Art supplies,
> Come from the sylvan Scenes His Genius grac'd,
> And offer here your tributory Sigh's.
> But know that more than Genius slumbers here;
> Virtues were his which Arts best powers transcend.
> Come, ye Superior train, who these revere
> And weep the Christian, Husband, Father, Friend.

– Frances Brown, wife of Lancelot II. By *Coade*, 1793, i.e. made of Coade stone. Mourning vestal by an urn on a pedestal. The pretty corbel is of Coade stone too. An oft-repeated design, originally by *John Bacon*, first used in 1788 at Langley Marish, Slough. – Peter Cowling †1786. Obelisk against a dark background. It has been suggested by Jane Brown that Mary Cowling †1846 was Capability's illegitimate daughter and may have been the reason for his acquisition of the manor.

UNITED REFORMED CHURCH, Chequer Street. 1874–5 by *James Tait* for the Congregationalists. In a fanciful Gothic, rock-faced, and looking more like a school than a chapel. An apse, N gable with a rose window and N porch at the w end with a turret like a bold chimney since its spirelet was removed.

The VILLAGE has been heavily built up since the mid C20, but in the area w of the parish church there are plenty of pleasant houses on twisting streets and a number of small greens. In CHURCH LANE, Nos. 1–5, C16?, has a continuous jetty, a gabled cross-wing, four octagonal brick chimneyshafts in the centre and a brick wing projecting at the back ending in a swoopingly shaped gable. The same wavy end-gables appear on THE MANOR HOUSE, w of this in Chequer Street, which is earliest C18, with a square two-storey porch under a hipped roof. Painted brick with quoins.

FEN MANOR, 200 yds sw of the church, is the large former vicarage of *c.* 1810–50 for Thomas Bourdillon (the living was in the gift of Trinity Hall). Five-bay front, gault brick, with a fluted Doric porch under a pediment. Nearby, MATHYNS (No. 9 Bell Lane), a surprising thatched Swiss chalet by a large pond built *c.* 1900 for the Coote family. Walls of carstone slips, brick quoins and tile-hanging. Otherwise the interest is on HIGH STREET, which at its w end has the late C17 LOCK-UP with a bell-turret and a clock (from Conington Hall, Cambs.). GROVE

HOUSE (now flats), in grounds W of the lock-up, is notable Early Georgian, red brick, with segment-headed windows, a segmental pediment for the doorways, and a parapet curving up to the corners, but the life has been restored out of it.

W and N of Huntingdon Road, FENSTANTON MANOR is better preserved, a very fine early C18 red brick L-plan farmhouse with later additions. The front is of seven bays, and has a hipped roof, a modillion cornice, stone platband and keystones and four giant stone pilasters to accentuate the façade. N of this, HALL GREEN FARMHOUSE, also C18, has a Venetian window.

FENTON MANOR FARM see PIDLEY

FLAG FEN see PETERBOROUGH (FENGATE)

FLETTON see PETERBOROUGH

FOLKSWORTH

A large village but scarcely a house of before 1950. The church stands aloof to the N.

ST HELEN. Nave, chancel and s transept. A steep bellcote on the W gable. At first it all seems Victorian, but then one realizes that the masonry and the buttressing are medieval, and one is not surprised to find a Norman N doorway. One order of shafts with scallop capitals. Arch with a roll, tympanum with a pattern of gridiron and pellets. The chancel arch is indeed also Norman, also *c.* 1125–50. It is quite high and has thick chevron in the arch. The capitals are decorated, two with small heads, the others with volutes and leaves with keeled mouldings, a type found at Ely (Ron Baxter). The arch to the s transept has two continuous chamfers and may well be contemporary with the buttressing, *c.* 1300. The Victorian work is of 1850, especially the blatantly Neo-Norman chancel; the medieval chancel had been replaced in 1702–6. – STAINED GLASS. E window. C14 style. By *Wailes*, 1866.

ELM FARM, Elm Road. L-shaped brick façade, rendered. Early C17 N end with two buttresses, deep plinth and square porch, the s end rebuilt in the late C17 with a projecting wing. HALL FARM, ½ m. SW, mid-C19, stands in the park of WASHINGLEY HALL, the C17 mansion of the Apreeces, remodelled in 1861 and pulled down in 1951. In the grounds are EARTHWORKS of a motte-and-bailey and medieval stew ponds. E along the road, a charming brick COTTAGE, of cruciform plan with frilly bargeboards under thickly thatched eaves. Little iron bridge in front.

GAYNES HALL *see* PERRY

GLATTON

St Nicholas. A proud, w tower with an ashlar-faced Perp top stage and buttressed w front. The doorway has traceried spandrels, and the quatrefoil base-frieze runs right round it. Above it a four-light transomed window, then a blank crenellation frieze, to the w with quatrefoils, to the w also a beautifully rich transomed four-light window over, and above that, to the same design, the bell-openings. Top frieze, battlements, pinnacles with animal supporters on them (cf. Yaxley). The body of the church is embattled and the large three-light N and s windows of the tower match those of the clerestory, which are unusually large for Huntingdonshire. The aisles embrace the tower, which must therefore at this level be earlier than the top. The s aisle is of 1290–1300 externally – see the intersecting tracery in the w and e and the Y-tracery in the s windows. The chancel has one lowside window with Y-tracery too, but the rest is Perp, over-restored in 1839–40 and 1857 in rock-faced stone. The N transept windows are again of the date of the s aisle – see the e windows with a quatrefoil placed diagonally above two lights (one blocked by the Perp vestry N of the chancel, which also has a quatrefoil frieze) and beneath it a big bracket with nailhead – i.e., like the window, late c13. Yet the transept and aisle also have a continuous keel-moulding at sill height that might in time go with the arcades, for they are also earlier than anything outside, though much changed. They were built *c.* 1230–40, but were then considerably lower. They are of three bays with round piers. Round bases on the N side but on the s side they have moulded octagonal waterholding bases and all have octagonal capitals – except for one on the s side which is still many-scalloped. That is a Norman motif. The round arches have double chamfers. A puzzling remnant is the base of a c13 clustered shaft in the N wall of the N aisle, close to the junction with the transept. The chancel arch goes with the chancel, but the three brackets above it for the rood are of course Perp (cf. Conington).

The Perp N chapel, formerly a vestry, is interesting. It is two storeys, the upper stage accessed from the rood stair and without windows. The lower stage has an external door, a fireplace inside and is vaulted in two bays of quadripartite ribbing with slender mouldings. – SCREEN. High, Perp, with one-light divisions. Ogee arches and panel tracery – all almost entirely c19; tendrils in the central arches are positively Art Nouveau. – BENCHES. A specially good set of poppyheads on the ends. – WALL PAINTING. On the nave e wall: N, St Mary Magdalene, standing, against a background with ornamental crowns, s, Christ rising from the tomb, a kneeling priest round the corner on the nave s wall. Both are of *c.* 1500 and well drawn. – SCULPTURE. At the w end of the s aisle, a lion-mask (discovered in 1928). Anglo-Saxon. – STAINED GLASS. Only in the s aisle E window, to Lord Sherard of Glatton Hall †1886. – MONUMENT. Large, unidentified hanging monument, probably for a member of the Castel family, whose arms it is reported to have held (VCH). Two arched recesses with shell tops between three columns. On the columns weird short pilasters of bulgy outline with inverted scrolls. The most likely date is c. 1600. – Rev. Castel Sherard †1803 and wife †1810. By *Coles* of Thrapston. Marble obelisk against a grey background. Motto and heraldry at the base.

The village roads make a square around the raised and walled churchyard. N of the church, CHURCH COTTAGE, one of a small number of good timber-framed and thatched houses, the best of which is ALLDAYS (No. 2 Glatton Ways), 100 yds SE of the church. This is nicely irregular with one cross-wing and appears to have lost a further bay at its service end. Central door (tiled floor inside). In High Haden Road, NE of the church, POET ROWE'S HOUSE is a surprise: a Wealden house of c. 1500. Formerly at Little Barford, Bedfordshire, and reputedly the birthplace of Nicholas Rowe, poet laureate (born 1674). Reconstructed here in 1977–8. ADDISON ARMS, S on Sawtry Road. Early to mid-C18 with big shaped gables at either end, a reminder that the villages of the Fen edge belong to East Anglian traditions.

ROUND HILL, S, off the Sawtry road. A five-sided enclosure of 17½ acres (7 ha) with a moat and a tapered projection to the SW. Its original purpose is as uncertain as its date. However, on the map of Glatton manor of 1613 it is shown with a lodge and surrounded by formal pleasure gardens, possibly for the Cottons at Conington (q.v.).

GLINTON [P]

The most inflated of all the villages around Peterborough since suburban building began between the wars but with a pleasingly coherent centre of houses grouped around the church in its square, walled churchyard.

ST BENEDICT. A chapel of ease to Peakirk until the late C19. By the early C14 it had probably achieved its present form of chancel, N chapel, nave and N and S aisles. But the overall appearance is Late Dec and Perp defined by the battlemented clerestory and W tower with a taller spire recessed behind battlements with two tiers of lucarnes and a marked entasis to its silhouette. Inside, the tower arch and arcades have octagonal piers and castellated abaci, and of the former roof (rebuilt 1817) remain the big stone corbels, a mixture of grotesque beasts, female figures and at the E end angels with the shields of St Peter and St George. The porch also has a nice Perp timber roof with bosses and s door of the same date, but the porch entrance, with dogtooth in the arch, is *c.* 1300 and goes with the s aisle windows and some work in the chancel that includes the cone-shaped roof corbels with ballflower and heads. But there is also a Norman w window in the N aisle, and the responds of the chancel chapel arch have late C12 or early C13 capitals with single upright (E) and flat (W) leaves. The pointed arch with one chamfer and one wave moulding is probably C14, when the chapel seems to have been extended E (SEDILIA with traceried, ogee arch under a gable). The chancel arch looks contemporary, but the responds earlier. – C15 chapel E window, the chancel window restored 1878. – FONT. Square, late C12; decoration on two sides of two rows of chevron forming zigzag and a third row of dogtooth and on the other two sides of saltire crosses with carving of scallops and triangles between the arms. – WALL PAINTINGS. Unidentified subjects above the door to the rood (N arcade) and in the s aisle wall. – STAINED GLASS. Chancel E (1911), with a memorial portrait of the churchwarden, Samuel Vergette, and s aisle (1920), both by *A. O. Hemming.* – MONUMENTS. John or Joan Wyldbore †1696, Baroque tablet, with cherubs' heads, drapery and a gilded crest. – James Edings †1767 (N aisle) and his son-in-law, Richard Arnold †1792 (chancel); identical tablets by *Edward Bingham*, with wheatsheaf motifs. – In the porch, stone EFFIGIES of a forester with horn and bow and arrows, and a lady, early C14, very defaced. They were outside from the C18 to the C20. – WAR MEMORIAL. 1920. In an appropriate East Anglian Perp style, the cross-head with cusped spokes. By *Talbot Brown & Fisher.*

ARTHUR MELLOWS VILLAGE COLLEGE, Helpston Road. 1949 by *F. J. Smith*, the Peterborough City Engineer. Austere, rational brick Modernism typical of the date. Much extended.

The immediate surroundings of the church are good, with distinguished stone houses along THE GREEN (N), including GRANVILLE HOUSE, NW of the church, dated 1790 and, set back to the N, BLEACH HOUSE, of 3 + 1 bays with expressed keystones and quoins. At the churchyard's NE corner, BALCONY HOUSE, C17, of three bays with a two-storey porch of ashlar, arched doorway, mullioned window, and top balcony with fine vertically symmetrical balusters. This is probably C18 with some reused bits.

E in the High Street is the MANOR HOUSE. The date is *c.* 1630–40, built probably by the Wyldbore family. Two-storeyed with mullioned windows and ogee gables of different sizes, the smaller ones drawn in at the foot so as to make a bulbous shape (cf. Stanway, Gloucestershire). The porch is at the r. end, but was probably originally in the centre of a symmetrical façade, of which, to the r. of the porch, only a fireplace, a window and some walling survive. The porch has a doorway with a rusticated surround. The doorway is arched and has a keystone with weird curly rustication similar to C18 vermiculated rustication. Rusticated square chimneyshafts. On the N front there is another two-storey-and-attic porch, also with a rusticated round arch, and an ogee-shaped gable. It seems certain that the house also originally extended to the l. of this, where there is now a single-storey C19 range, for inside is a massive stone arch with jewelled keystone. STABLE, small but also with a gable. In the garden, the so-called Malt House. Evidently of domestic origin with blocked windows inside that have shafts. MANOR HOUSE COTTAGES, S of the Manor House, have a fairly symmetrical front with mullioned windows. Only the centre window on the first floor has a transom. It is of four lights and placed under a big gable. Near the top of this an oval window. Is the date *c.* 1660?

PETERBOROUGH CORPORATION WATERWORKS, Waterworks Lane, 1 m. SW. 1906, probably by the *Peterborough City Engineer*. English Baroque-style pump house with vigorous Gibbsian rustication around circular windows. Nicely lettered terracotta frieze and shaped parapet. ½ m. S is the eyecatching GAS COMPRESSOR STATION of 1972 by the *Architects Design Group* of Nottingham, designed for the rapid movement of North Sea gas inland. The three compressor units are cubic and rather sculptural, with fibreglass shells coloured red, white and black.

GODMANCHESTER

2070

One of the pleasantest towns in Huntingdonshire. Godmanchester was, as the last syllables of its name show, a Roman station, of Claudian or Neronian date and possibly that known as *Durovigutum*. Its position is explained by the fact that Ermine Street crossed the Ouse here and was itself crossed by the road between Colchester and Chester. We know something of its plan. The polygonal outline of the town, 24 acres (9.6 ha) in extent, is shown up well by the present-day roads, which encircle the Roman nucleus, but the line of Ermine Street running through the centre has been lost (except for a short section which has been exposed in a private garden). Of the defences there is nothing to be seen. The S gate was, however, examined *c.* 1960 when blocks of flats were built between Piper's Lane and London Street, and found to consist simply of two gate-towers flanking a 30-ft (9 metre) – wide road which is thought to have been spanned by a single arch. The town had a small, central market area with a small basilica nearby – this would have acted as a council hall dealing with urban and local administration. Otherwise the buildings of the town are not well known, and the area within it was much rebuilt in the mid C19 and mid to later C20. A courtyard-plan *mansio* (official guest house) was discovered near Pinfold Lane in 1963. It was built at the beginning of the C2, had black-and-white mosaics in the rooms but was destroyed by fire in the late C3. To its S, and apparently associated with it, was a bath suite, with its rooms arranged linearly in strip form. This continued in use, with modifications, throughout most of the Roman period. See also Introduction, p. 359.

The size of the church proves Godmanchester's importance in the Middle Ages as well – the manor was granted self-governing status in 1212, and in 1604 was incorporated as a free borough. It was by then 'a very great county Toune', a commercial town of merchant farmers, though there is little sign of that now.

ST MARY. The W tower is exceptionally interesting, as it is Perp in appearance and yet of 1623, when it was rebuilt with money levied by the borough, whose arms are over the W door. The use of the materials from the C13 tower is recognizable by the stiff-leaf responds of the arch towards the nave. The Stuart modifications of the Perp style come out in the W doorway with its faceted orders and the arched windows above it. But their tracery and the pairs of two-light transomed bell-openings and the recessed spire with its three tiers of lucarnes are Huntingdonshire Perp obviously. Cresting of Jacobean style, obelisks at the corners and stair-turret with pepperpot top. The tower is ashlar-faced, the rest of the church is of brown cobbles. Perp are the N and S windows, the big two-storey S porch with a broad entry flanked by niches with nodding ogee canopies and more niches flanking the W door, and the not so big N porch; Perp also the original chancel windows. But the chancel is an E.E. piece; this is shown by the buttressing and the exquisite MASS DIAL on one of them, in the form of an incised rose window with trefoiled arches between the spokes. The vestry lancet could be reset from that chancel; the vestry itself and the lancets of the chancel E window are of 1853 by *G. G. Scott* (Kelly's Directory) but *W. G. & E. Habershon* were employed in 1852–4 for reseating etc. The arcades are Perp as well, with a complex continuous moulding to the nave and capitals only to the shafts towards the arch openings (cf. Conington). But the E bay of the arcades stands in place of a crossing tower. The two small lancets above the present chancel arch prove that. They were in the tower E wall and both have traces of painting – dogtooth and foliage – to their reveals. The tower no doubt soon turned out to be unsafe and so was replaced by the W tower. The tower arch is a Perp heightening; the contemporary rood stair is in a round tower outside the S aisle. – FONT. C13 but heavily weathered, having been put outside in 1853. – Splendid gilded REREDOS with canopied niches and ROOD SCREEN, both by *G. F. Bodley*, 1901, carved by *Rattee & Kett*. The figures on the rood are by *R. Bridgeman* of Lichfield. – TOWER SCREEN by *W. D. Caröe*, c. 1919, and a good Perp-style piece with characteristically well-crafted fittings; the LAMP standard by the W door is his also. – STALLS with a good set of MISERICORDS, said to come from Ramsey Abbey but with a WS interpreted as referring to William Stevens, vicar in 1470–81, so they may well have originated here. They have the Borough arms and also show e.g. a fox and goose, a wyvern,

a falcon, a cat, a dog, a rabbit, a monkey, a lion, a horse. –
STAINED GLASS. The E and SE windows of the chancel are by
A. Gibbs, 1858, in strongly coloured C13 style. – One S aisle
window by *Morris & Co.*, 1896; Justice, Courage and Humility.
Nothing special, despite being a *Burne-Jones* design. – Much
by *Kempe* (S aisle S, 1889, a Jesse window; S aisle W, 1894;
N aisle NE, 1896; chancel S, 1901; S aisle SW, 1903; N aisle NW,
c. 1911). – N aisle centre, 1903 by *J. Powell & Sons* with the
figures surrounded by thick twining stems of passion flowers
(it is a memorial to Francis Thomas McDougall, vicar and first
Bishop of Labuan and Sarawak). – S aisle E of 1883 by *Burlison
& Grylls*. – MONUMENTS. Brass to a civilian, early C16, a 14-in.
(35.5 cm) figure, formerly accompanied by his two wives.
Repaired by *Bryan Egan*, 1983. – Tablet, †1696, in the S aisle,
rustic classical but attractive. – Alured Clarke †1744. Marble,
pedimented with finely cut volutes and a crest. – GATES,
Gothick style of 1850, nicely repaired and renewed by *A. J.
Bernasconi*, 2004–5.

PERAMBULATION

The centre of Godmanchester is the small widening W of the
meeting of Cambridge Street with Post Street and Causeway.
Here the Town Hall and Queen Elizabeth's Grammar School
flank the approach to the delightful arched CHINESE BRIDGE,
Chinese meaning Chippendale-Chinese. Its date is surprisingly
as late as 1827, by the Irish architect *James Gallier* (now as
rebuilt in 2010). The bridge leads to the islands in the river
Ouse which make the view W so enchanting, looking to the
backs of houses N of the bridge with their picturesque boathouses. On the larger of the islands was the town mill.

The TOWN HALL is of 1844, by *Abbott & Habershon* of St
Neots, and was then just a small rectangle of yellow brick with
a big shaped gable. A two-storey addition was built in 1899.
QUEEN ELIZABETH'S GRAMMAR SCHOOL (now public hall)
was founded in 1559. The original building is small, of red
brick, with a square porch that has pilasters and moulded
string. Altered in 1851; the back part added 1900, further
extended in 1987.

We move N first. In POST STREET on the E side is HATTON
HOUSE, C17, a pretty timber-framed and plastered house with
vertical sliding sashes and an overhang around which are fitted
two Georgian pediments to the doorways. The placing of the
doors, one to the hall, the other to the cross-passage of the
service end, is typical of an urban frontage where the houses
were closely built. Then, opposite, ISLAND COTTAGE, also
C17, also with overhang, an C18 doorcase and two-storey bay
window with Gothic arches. Its neighbour is ISLAND HALL,
lying back from the street behind railings. It was 'new built' in
1749 for John Jackson, who became Receiver-General for
Huntingdon, and is a large red brick house of three bays and
two and a half storeys with pediment and lower two-bay wings.

The windows have stone architraves on brackets and in the pediment are stone modillions, details which appear to be original.* Tuscan porches. Front and back of the house are identical. Inside, all of the rooms have been handsomely restored and decorated since 1983 by *Christopher Vane Percy*. Large entrance hall filling the centre with a handsome chimneypiece and overmantel with consoles and doorcases with enriched friezes (their pediments possibly a later embellishment). A very fine Doric screen of fluted columns and entablature between the hall and the staircase with its fluted twist balusters and carved string. The screen is repeated to the first-floor passage, which has arches at each end. Above the hall the saloon with fine Kentian doorpiece. The best chimneypiece is in the small drawing room, with console brackets and an overmantel flanked by volutes inset with a lugged frame and topped by a broken pediment. Lovely carved overdoors in the adjoining dining room. Later kitchen wing and behind this an outbuilding with attractive Gothick cupola. Crossing from the garden to the island in the river, a second CHINESE BRIDGE, though in date it comes first and is no doubt contemporary with the house (but reconstructed in 1988). It is placed at a slight angle just so it can be admired. The C18 gateway in front of the house is from the walled garden at Hinchingbrooke (*see* p. 531), brought here in 1970. Further gardens lay across Post Street, where the school is now.

Next to Island Hall is ERMINE HOUSE, double-gabled, of 1887, with moulded terracotta details and THE HOLME, three-storeyed, apparently early C18, of yellow and red brick, with segment-headed windows, though essentially Victorian like its gabled N part, which was added *c.* 1870 and with an Olde English-style back range of *c.* 1890. The domestic character up to the end of Post Street is remarkably consistent. After the WAR MEMORIAL, a cross with fleur-de-lis by *Ernest George & Yeates*, 1921, there is open water meadow as far as the eye can see and the road runs through it along a tree-lined causeway called THE AVENUE. No. 3 has a stuccoed Greek Revival façade with Doric doorcase inset. It is also by *James Gallier*, for a Colonel White, 1827.[†] At the N end of the causeway, which was created 1776–84 by the Royston-Wansford Turnpike Trust, is the brick BRIDGE across a stream of the Great Ouse on eight round arches. It was repaired at the same time by *Richard Holland* (cf. Nuns' Bridge, Hinchingbrooke). Low curved buttresses on the N side, probably originally for a timber bridge. For the mill buildings to the N, *see* Huntingdon (pp. 528–9).

A short move E from the hub to see one timber-framed house in CAMBRIDGE STREET, dated 1611 and 1613. Closely

margin: 116

---

*There is no evidence that they are Victorian, as Pevsner believed, and similar motifs are found at Whitwell House, Huntingdon.

†The plan is in the library at Tulane University, Louisiana. Christopher Vane Percy identified it and kindly drew my attention to it.

set studs and a gable with curved brackets, one of a number like this in the town. Now s, i.e. along THE CAUSEWAY, all the time open to the river basin on the w side. A large watermill dominated the scene until 1967. On the e side pubs and inns come first; the largest, now in other use, is c18 with Venetian windows on two sides. Then more houses. Nos. 10–12 is timber-framed with closely spaced studs, i.e. *c.* 1600, when much rebuilding was going on in the town. Then No. 13, yellow brick, Late Georgian, with a nice doorway. Before turning into West Street, we continue s into OLD COURT HALL, for a smart early to mid-Victorian villa in gault brick with shutters, then a timber-framed house with wonderfully phoney c19 decoration to its jettied and gabled front.

Now into WEST STREET from the s end of the Causeway. The front of No. 44 of red and rubbed brick (one dated 1747), quite narrow, but with two Venetian windows, one above the other. The type is the same as the garden front of Farm Hall (*see* below). The back is rebuilt. After that on the other side, No. 42 (County Council offices), formerly The Chestnuts, yellow brick of 1873 with some Gothic features to the porch; the house belonged to Robert Beart, the local brickmaker and was presumably built by him. Beart subsequently developed the brickworks at Arlesey, Beds.

And so to FARM HALL, the finest house in Godmanchester. Built in 1746 for Charles Clarke, Recorder of Huntingdon and a baron of the Exchequer. The front is of three storeys, red and rubbed brick, of five bays with a pedimented three-bay projection and a parapet. Tuscan porch with pediment. Contemporary cast-iron railings. But this front is only one room deep and seems to be grafted over something older, remodelled at the same time. The garden side has seven bays, asymmetrical, and the centre here has a group of three windows on the first floor, which is a simplified version of a Venetian window. This part looks a little less sophisticated than the front but the windows have good rubbed headers and the keystone of one in the sw wing is a coat of arms. The plan of the house is interesting in that it has a cross corridor. The w end (i.e. the bays w of the projection on the garden front and the short projecting sw wing) appears to be older than the rest. The rooms here, both with characteristically simple panelling and fireplaces of *c.* 1710, one with a shell, appear to have formed a suite. It also has its own staircase, although its upper flights differ from the lower, which is curved and in its details matches the elegant, if oddly inconspicuous, mid-c18 staircase at the e end of the corridor. In the front part, there are some extremely fine timber and marble chimneypieces with acanthus consoles and enriched surrounds. Good doorcases on the first floor. The rooms are higher than those below, i.e. we have here a *piano nobile*. The former service wing, e, is 1860s. A splendid lime avenue runs away from the garden side and in the view is a cottage with Gothick windows. Towards the river, across the road, is another avenue (now of poplars) and a canal. They are separated from the entrance side of the house by a garden wall with two gates also of *c.* 1746.

Now s and e of the centre, via London Street from Old Court Hall to LONDON ROAD. On the e side, LONDON ROAD FARM is early C17, with close studs, but unlike contemporary houses in Godmanchester has no jetty and a central lobby-entry plan. Unusually, its rear service wing was separated originally from the body of the house at ground floor. Just across the road, PORCH FARMHOUSE had the more typical jettied front of earlier timber-framed houses but a very complex evolution that has resulted in its prodigious length. The first part, s of the porch, seems to come first, maybe late C15 (curved braces to two bays of the roof), while the N end is early C16 on the evidence of ceiling beams with double-ogee mouldings and leaf stops. This part now has an inserted brick chimney, contemporary in date with the stair-turret adjoining it (splat balusters) and the large BARN continuing the house to the s. Nice brick DOVECOTE with gableted roof, early C18. Cross-wing at the rear also extended in the C17.

EARNING STREET, which traces the line of the ditch of the Roman defences, has a series of very good houses, beginning with THE GABLES on the e side which has two gables to the street and a jetty. The door to l. is dated 1625, apparently referring to rebuilding of its hall and service end, for the s cross-wing is evidently a separate build, probably *c.* 1600, with bracing under the gable and scalloped edging. Long windows of multiple single lights (blocked). The l. gable has pendants. The cross-passage runs into a corridor behind the hall and between the stair and parlour, an unusual plan which may be a later alteration made when the kitchen wing was rebuilt. Good set of former farm buildings behind. Almost opposite, PLANTAGENET HOUSE has a bargeboarded gable to its cross-wing, again early C17, and an oriel window also with bargeboards, both carved with egg-and-dart mouldings. Cross-passage from the entrance to the stair in the angle between the wing and the main range, which has been truncated at its w end, revealing the large brick chimney. The stacks have excellent diagonal shafts.

Then TUDOR HOUSE, the most ambitious timber-framed house in Godmanchester, restored from a dilapidated state in 1994–5 by *Graham Black*. The composition is very similar to The Gables (*see* above) but more generous. Built in 1600–3 (dates inscribed), with gabled wings l. and r. of the centre, both with oriels, and formerly a third gable in the centre. There is an overhang all along on scrolled brackets, and a second for the gables. At the back, the stair-tower continues above first floor as a gabled oriel, originally lighting a recess off the hall chamber. The long rear wing appears to have been added *c.* 1625. As in the other houses here the cross-passage runs to the staircase but also into an axial corridor. Some painted arcading in the parlour of typical early C17 type (cf. Pepys House, Brampton). Also a most unusual door frame to one of the rooms in the service wing which has a bowed profile halfway down. What was it for? DIAL HOUSE, Cambridge Road. Dated 1714, with a cut brick frill over the centre window (cf. Cowper House, Huntingdon).

1060

GRAFHAM

ALL SAINTS. Not a large church and typical of the locality for the extensive use of brown cobbles in its walls. The w tower turns octagonal at the very top, for the short length above the springing of the arches of the bell-openings, a version of the more ambitious tower of Old Weston (q.v.) and, as there, on the lower part four shafts that have C17(?) obelisk pinnacles. The spire has two tiers of lucarnes in alternating directions. The tower is made to seem larger by disproportionately mighty ashlar angle buttresses at the w corners and an octagonal stair projection to the SE. Late C13 chancel with Y-tracery, and intersecting tracery, the E an adaptation of this tracery made probably in 1803. The DOUBLE PISCINA is late C13, and so is the N arcade of four low bays with round piers and double-chamfered arches. The two-bay s arcade of standard elements is Dec and opens to a former s chapel. The s porch (rebuilt in 1902 by *S. Inskip Ladds*) is a continuation of this chapel. The interior can have hardly changed since the early C19. Coved plaster ceiling concealing all but the C15 tie-beams of the roof. No clerestory but two C18 s dormers. Floor of buff bricks, set down in 1880. – Timber REREDOS with Creed etc. – PEWS. C19, with sloping fronts. – FONT. Octagonal, Dec, with quatre-foils of three varieties and simple blank-arched panels. – ARCHITECTURAL FRAGMENTS. Reset in the s porch along with the upper part of an early C14 effigy of a priest. – MONU-MENTS. Thomas Puckle †1914 and Lt Col. John Puckle, DSO, †1917. Identical alabaster tablets with gilded regimental insignia.

MODEL FARM, 1 m. SE. Fine purpose-built covered yard, dated 1834, of red brick. Projecting from the long spine, five pitched roofs ending in gables over big arches.

GRAFHAM WATER. *See* Perry.

1080

GREAT GIDDING

A long village street running downhill. In the upper part, some C18 and C19 houses, but none of individual note. Improvements and rebuilding of cottages was undertaken in the later C19 at the instigation of the Rev. W. Hopkinson (cf. Little Gidding).

St Michael. Early C13 s doorway, later C13 arcades with round piers, octagonal abaci and double-chamfered arches, and much more interesting late C13 chancel. The chancel has N and S windows of three stepped lancet lights, a lowside lancet by a simple N doorway, and inside giant blank arches, one for each bay, above a low stone bench (cf. Alconbury). Good PISCINA. Another, early C14, in the s aisle. The w tower is Dec, with a spherical triangular opening in the w face that has straight spokes of tracery (as at Catworth and Bythorn). The buttresses and the stair-turret in the SE buttress terminate before the Perp top stages, which have a battlemented transom to the pairs of two-light bell-openings, a quatrefoil frieze and a recessed spire with two tiers of lucarnes, very like Catworth and of course Buckden (q.v.). The rest is also Perp, except for one Dec s aisle window and one Dec chancel s window, both with reticulated tracery. Nave roof, cambered with moulded tie-beams on traceried braces. Church repaired and refitted in 1866–9 by *James Fowler* of Louth: in the chancel, *Minton* tiles, plate tracery E window and REREDOS in E.E. style. – COMMUNION RAIL. Early C17 and one of the best pieces of its date in Huntingdonshire. Two tiers, the lower one short, stubby balusters, the upper arches with pendants (cf. Leighton Bromswold). – On the inner walls of the chancel also are stone-carved SHIELDS. They refer to the Watson family and their relations and must have been erected after 1621, for they show the arms of Sir Lewis Watson and his second wife, Eleanor Manners. The Watsons bought the manor *c.* 1546 and owned the whole of the parish from 1587. – Octagonal wood PANEL (s wall) dated 1614 with the words: SATOR ARIPO TENIT OPERA ROTAS, which is intended to read the same forwards and backwards. – STAINED GLASS. E window of 1869 by *W. Webb*. – MONUMENT. Pilot Officer H. J. H. Jones †1943 (s aisle chapel); St Michael, his wings streamlined and his helmet a flying cap. By *Harold Youngman*, 1947.

E of the main street, set back in a graveyard with a pond and weeping willow, the BAPTIST CHAPEL. Built 1790 for Particular Baptists. A plain oblong house of three-bay frontage with a hipped roof and sash windows. Two arched windows at the rear. Three galleries on wooden columns.*

GREAT GRANSDEN

2050

St Bartholomew. Of brown cobbles, and Perp throughout. Embattled throughout as well, w tower of four stages with pairs of two-light bell-openings and a spike and beast at the angles. Its w door has the arms of Clare Hall, Cambridge, which held the advowson from the mid C14. Three-light windows, with

*The BOX PEWS, PULPIT etc. recorded in the first edition of this guide were removed in 1992.

clunch surrounds, and a rising NE rood turret in the clerestory. Doorways with traceried spandrels, the N porch renewed in 1873 by *G. Vialls*, who added the vestry and organ chamber. Arcade piers (four bays) with capitals only to the shafts towards the openings, not to the moulded projections towards the nave. Handsome roofs with figures; the figures in the aisles defaced. The E end of the N aisle roof is further enriched and in the S aisle is a statue niche with a little vault. Ogee-arched piscina with credence shelf in the chancel. The will of John Grante in 1497 made bequests for the furnishings and decoration, suggesting recent completion of the building. Organ chamber separated from the chancel by a tall round arch that has angels on corbels playing a harp and positive organ. ORGAN of 1888, the case to Vialls' design. – PULPIT. Given to the church by the Rev. Barnabas Oley, probably *c.* 1660, when he was reinstated to the living he had been deprived of in 1644. Characteristic cartouches on the panels and a dentil cornice. It had a tester with pendant finials before 1873. – SCREEN. Partly Perp with some original painted decoration. Removed in 1873 but reinstated in the C20. – TOWER SCREEN with lancets and intersecting tracery to the ringing chamber of 2005. – BENCHES. C16. The simple buttressed type of ends, and fronts with cusped arched panels carved with fish, animals etc. (cf. Diddington). – STAINED GLASS. Old fragments in one chancel window. – Impressive E window of 1901 in memory of T.V. Webb (†1885), probably by *Heaton, Butler & Bayne*, who sign the S aisle E window of Faith, Hope and Charity for his widow (†1911). – S aisle, to the 405 Squadron (RCAF) by *Glenn Carter*, 1989, with maple leaves descending over the figures. – CLOCK. The carillon and chimes mechanism was made in 1682 by *Thomas Powers* of Wellingborough for the Rev. Barnabas Oley. He was rector for a total of fifty-two years. – MONUMENT. Very large indent slab with Lombardic lettering to Thomas de Neusum, priest, *c.* 1330. – LYCHGATE. 1920. Hipped tile roof on traceried sides.

BAPTIST CHAPEL, off Sand Road. Built shortly after 1734. A plain brick house of three by three bays with a hipped roof, whose valley is supported on tall columns. Gallery on two sides with Doric frieze on iron posts.

Round the church an exceptionally satisfying triad of houses:

The VICARAGE, W, is a plain but tall five-bay house with hipped roof above a cornice of cogged bricks. It was originally built by the Rev. Barnabas Oley (†1685) but altered in 1812 by *Charles Humfrey*.

RIPPINGTON MANOR FARMHOUSE, E, is an H-plan with three enormous late C16 sandstone chimneybreasts and a timber frame behind an early C17 brick case. The hall is in the centre, with the parlour to the l. Both rooms have C16 fireplaces. There was originally a large chamber over the hall and separate rooms in the wings. In the W wing, an original three-light mullioned window and another, ovolo-moulded, lighting the stair within the NW angle. The stair has some late C17 twisted balusters mixed with the type that are simply turned. Dining room in the E wing with panelling; the room was extended in the late C20 by *Peter Foster*. One odd feature of the interior is a room between the kitchen and hall which is raised over the cellar and must be a C18 alteration. It is entered by fine semicircular stone steps, possibly reused.

RECTORY FARMHOUSE, S of the church. Built by Clare College, which held the advowson. Brick, with a five-bay front of *c.* 1700 and the gable ends still in a late C17 fashion, i.e. with S-curves up to a raised parapet. Moulded brick band to the front and a fragment of the moulded door cornice.

GRANSDEN HALL, ¼ m. W, has a front of two periods. The two-bay side-pieces have massive Dutch gables carried by giant pilasters and arched windows in the gables. That will be just before the mid C17 and a motif derived ultimately from Kew Palace and London craftsmen, but the centre has a panelled parapet curving up in the middle to a higher centre part, all in finer red brick, and that belongs to a remodelling of 1716. The flanking square piers with ball finials must be contemporary. The centre bay projects in a moulded frame but the doorcase has gone. The back and sides are *c.* 1840 and later. Later still the roof behind the gables has been raised. Between Gransden Hall and the church is a stupendous early C17 brick BARN with tall cart entrance and vertical slots in the sides.

In the rest of the village, Nos. 16–18 MIDDLE STREET, despite its façade, is late C15 on the evidence of a splayed scarf joint in the wall-plate at first floor, a cross-beam in the room to the r. of the entrance which has rosettes on the stops and a finely moulded beam (reset) over the fireplace. Before the C19 it appears to have had a hearth passage. The open truss over the hall is also preserved, with curved braces and hollow chamfers. Further up, MARLEY'S COTTAGE is a diminutive early C16 hall house with N aisle and a brick chimney (dated 1676) detached from its gable. Of the same scale but probably C17 or C18 is No. 48 WEST STREET, which has a timber-framed chimney. Its thatched extension, of *c.* 2000, is well handled, with brick interior to the staircase and a timber-framed link between the two phases. Close by, in Fox Street, the VILLAGE HALL, built as the reading room in 1871, paid for by T. V. Webb. This has two reused pedimented early C18 doorcases of the same design, with Gibbsian blocking and keystones, as is found at AUDLEY HOUSE, in East Street, where Webb lived. The house is solid early to mid-C18, brick with a platband and hipped roof. In CHURCH STREET, a group of Neo-Tudor cottages.

WINDMILL, ½ m. E. A weatherboarded post-mill with a double-pitched top, still on its post and trestle. The timber post is dated *c.* 1612–60 (tree-ring dating) but reused in the main body of *c.* 1803–32 and windshaft renewed 1845–77. Completely restored in 1982–4.

GREAT PAXTON

HOLY TRINITY. There are very few Anglo-Saxon buildings one
can call grandiose. Stow in Lincolnshire is one, Great Paxton
is without doubt another. Yet on approaching the building, no
one can form any idea of what is in store. Here is a church of
grey stone and brown cobbles with a Perp w tower, Perp
windows – faithfully replaced in 1880 – and s doorway, and a
Perp chancel, except for one N window with intersecting
tracery, i.e. of the late C13. The clerestory is Perp too, but there
a hint at the interior is given. Some windows on both sides are
round-arched (in ironstone) and double-splayed. That is
Saxon, and where the w tower commences are more windows
that had to be curtailed. In the N aisle is a door, also round-
arched, which was blocked in 1880. The interior is not only a
surprise, it is also an architectural shock of a high order. This
was a cruciform church with a true crossing, and it was an
aisled church. Both in pre-Conquest times are extreme rarities.
The date of the church is not known, but it is not likely to be
earlier than 1040, and its scale is explained by it having been
a Minster church on an estate held by Edward the Confessor
between 1042 and 1066. The extent of the N transept has been
discovered by excavation and it extended about 13 ft (4 metres)
N of the aisles, which in their present form are Perp reconstruc-
tions. The transepts were almost certainly lower than the nave.
As for the crossing, a true crossing means that it is as wide as
the nave, as the chancel, and as the transepts. This was a matter

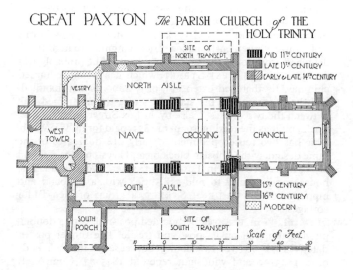

Great Paxton, Holy Trinity.
Plan

of course in Romanesque architecture on the Continent at that date, but it does not even apply to Stow.* It does, however, apply to Great Paxton, as is fully displayed in the N transept arch. Or so it appears. In fact, as Eric Fernie has shown, the crossing in its intact state was longer E–W (20 ft; 6 metres) than it was wide N–S (18 ft; 5.4 metres) and this discrepancy is overcome only by making the responds to the transepts mightier than those to the chancel (and presumably the lost nave) arch. The transept responds are four big demi-shafts with thin shafts between. They carry lumpy, shapeless capitals and a plain abacus, and then the unmoulded arch is thrown across at a height unparalleled in early English architecture. The same arrangement applied to the other arches, even if the responds are not so well preserved, and the arches to the S transept and chancel are triple-chamfered of the late C13. The responds to the chancel arch are a more complex variation on what has already been seen, with five demi-shafts and spurs between, instead of thin shafts. Moreover, as a kind of framing to these groups of shafts side by side, a thin pilaster strip ran up and no doubt continued all round the arch. This is a usual Late Anglo-Danish thing (cf. e.g. St Benet, Cambridge), and it is visible in several instances. The only oddity is the piece of Norman billet moulding on the abacus of the chancel arch respond. The bases of the crossing piers and the responds of the chancel arch also show that the chancel was always raised with a dais for an altar under the crossing and further steps beyond the arch to the chancel.

The nave is just as amazing. The only other Anglo-Saxon aisled naves are Brixworth (Northants) and Lydd (Kent), and the arcade piers of both are just untreated chunks of wall. But at Great Paxton there are proper compound piers, even if they are of a very strange kind, as if Continental compound piers had been misunderstood. Nevertheless there are parallels for such unconventional designs in earlier to mid-C12 churches in Lotharingia. All the piers are quatrefoil in section, placed diagonally, and on the easternmost piers with thin shafts between the foils so that they come out in the cardinal directions and on the westernmost piers spurs instead of the thin shafts. The shafts have square bases, the spurs have round ones and here and there is some carved detail. As the clerestory windows indicated the arcade went on to three (probably four) instead of the present two bays and a bit. On the S side, one W respond was reused in the new place and the truncated third arch remade in pointed form (the opposite arch is blocked with a door to the vestry of 1880). This W respond and the two E responds are much more acceptably detailed than the capitals and abaci of the piers: capitals as bulgy as those of the crossing and one-step abaci. The arches are single-step too. The responds

---

*Nor to Norton-on-Tees (Co. Durham), which has crossing arrangements similar to Stow, but is smaller (transept arches c. 14 ft. wide at Stow, c. 11 ft at Norton, c. 15 ft at Great Paxton).

are built up of long and short stones rather like late Anglo-Saxon quoins. – SEDILIA. Late C14. – SCREEN. Under the tower arch but formerly part of the rood. Perp. It originally had the Virgin of the Assumption above the entrance, but only the rays which surrounded her survive. Above, in the arch, a glazed screen with Y-tracery by *Julian Limentani*, 2010. – ROOD BEAM. Early C20. – REREDOS. An elaborate work, of 1899, and an impressive termination to the view E. Openwork canopies over the nativity and two tall pinnacles with carved angels, flanked by curved screens. – BENCHES. C15, the ends of the plain buttressed type. – SOUTH DOOR. Early C15 but with C13 ironwork, scrolled but not of the elaborate type as in Bedfordshire. – STAINED GLASS. C15 fragments in one chancel N window.

The village was little more than the High Street until the mid to later C20 but is extensive now, and few of the older cottages have escaped alteration. E of the church, PAXTON PLACE, the rectory of 1842 by *J. W. Pocock* of Huntingdon. Gault brick with a low slated roof.

PAXTON HILL HOUSE, 1 m. S. 1820s, very probably built for the Towgoods, the St Neots paper millers whose works lay SW on the Ouse. A regular three-bay square, with two-storey bows on the S front, looking down to St Neots. Minor Victorian additions. The LODGE has openwork bargeboards and Neo-Tudor details.

GREAT STAUGHTON

ST ANDREW. The W tower is Perp and more ambitious than most, with its quatrefoil base frieze and its quatrefoil top frieze and its pinnacles. Set-back buttresses. Pairs of transomed two-light bell-openings. There are bequests for it and its bells between 1480 and 1545 (although one bell is by *William Dawe*, *c.* 1400). Earlier is the chancel, say early C14. One window has cusped Y-tracery, and the lowside window of two lights even a reticulation unit. Definitely Dec is the S aisle. Again reticulated tracery. The S doorway is something special, with its dainty foliage capitals and the many mouldings of the arch. That the tower must be later than the S aisle is obvious from the aisle W window. Inside, the arcades (of five bays) are both older than anything outside. First come three bays on the S side (round piers with broached bases and round abaci), then the rest of the S arcade and the whole N arcade, which have round piers and the abaci chamfered squares set diagonally. All arcade arches are double-chamfered. But the chancel arch and the tower arch are Perp. The Gaynes (N) Chapel has a tomb recess under a panelled vault with heraldic bosses; probably built by Robert Stoneham, who died 1455. Former Perp window to the chancel, later cut down to form an arch. The separate N vestry is dated 1526. Arch from the chapel to the N aisle is by *A. W. Blomfield* who also rebuilt the chancel arch during the restoration in 1866. Roofs and tracery (accurately) replaced. – COMMUNION RAIL. Late C17, of strong, twisted balusters. – Chancel PANELLING with geometric patterns of about the same time. – ALTAR TABLE. 1754 by *Edward Webster* of St Neots (church guide). Completely domestic, with claw feet and acanthus leaves to the legs. – STAINED GLASS. Tower window, life of St Andrew by *Clayton & Bell*, 1890. – E window. Christ, and SS Peter, John, James and Andrew by *Lavers & Westlake*, 1900. – Chancel SW, Dorcas and Anna, signed by *Arthur J. Dix*, 1908. – N chapel. †1870; very late for the style. – S aisle E (†1872) and the two matching windows in the S aisle, undated, are by *Clayton & Bell*. – N aisle NE. C16 and C17 heraldic glass from Gaynes Hall, arranged as a memorial (†1943). N aisle W. †1944, by *A. J. Davies* of Bromsgrove, in his usual Arts and Crafts style and colours. A knight at prayer before the quest for the Holy Grail; a theme oft repeated by this artist. – MONUMENTS. A good collection. – Large stone monument (chancel) to Sir James Dyer †1582, in judge's robes, and his wife, and Sir Richard †1605 and wife. Two kneeling couples, husband facing wife across a prayer-desk (but Sir Richard has put his helmet on it). Three columns and pendant arches. Big strapwork, on the top, and obelisks. – George Wauton †1606 (S aisle). Recumbent effigy, the slab on which he lies supported by two free-standing atlantes with short skirts. Shell-headed niches l. and r. Top panel with arched centre. Erected by Sir Oliver Cromwell of Hinchingbrooke. – Christopher and Mary Conyers, both †1679. Cartouche, good London work, unusually mannered forms. – Sir Baldwin Conyers †1731. A conservative composition for its date, but probably from a City of London workshop. An urn on a small sarcophagus in a shell-headed niche. Roman Doric columns and a pediment broken back in the centre. Two cherubs playing on it and (originally) two cherubs' heads at the foot. – In the Gaynes Chapel, upper part of a C13 monument to an abbot. Alwalton marble. The head in a pointed-cinquefoiled surround (cf. the abbots' monuments at Peterborough Cathedral). The monument used to be at Gaynes Hall (*see* Perry), its provenance unknown. – The rest of the monuments are for the lords of the manor of Gaynes. – Sir James Beverley †1670. Large tomb-chest, with festoons flanking the inscription. – Major-Gen. Thomas Handasyd, governor of Jamaica, †1729. A marble wall monument of prodigious size, the inscription framed by splayed pilasters on scrolled consoles, a top crest and two helms against an armoury of weapons and flags. Attributed to *Francis Bird*. – Others to Duberlys, notably two to Major Grey William Duberly of the Grenadier Guards †1915, one a white marble tablet supporting a bearskin by *Maile & Sons*, from the tenants (N aisle), the other from his wife in the Gaynes Chapel by *S. Inskip Ladds* with swan-neck pediment.

PLACE HOUSE, opposite the church. One red brick range of a formerly larger mansion, built after 1539 by Sir Oliver Leader

(†1557), who acquired the Rectory Manor, previously a property of the Carthusians. It comprises the whole of the s, and part of the w, range of what was probably a typical E-plan or half-H-plan mansion, of which the rest was destroyed in the C17. Evidence of the lost w range is the blocked fireplace in the N wall of the s range and, on its w face, an arcaded loggia of three bays, with chamfered brick arches – a precocious feature for its date. The E end of the s range has some stone mullioned and transomed windows, widely spaced, a substantial chimneystack with stepped sides on the s front, timber-framing inside and a robust newel stair against the s wall, roughly in line with the N door. Other features belong to early C18 remodelling: segmental-headed sashes on the gable end, doorcases inside, and a panelled room at the w end on the first floor with bolection-moulded corner fireplace. The C16 character of the s front was only re-established c. 1920 when render was removed from the walls and C18 sashes replaced by timber mullioned and transomed windows (cement-coated). The gabled SE tower was given its second storey at this time and a small NW wing was also added.

STAUGHTON MANOR has a rainwater head dated 1768, though not *in situ*. The manor was bought in that year by Earl Ludlow, M.P. for Huntingdonshire. Of this date perhaps the stone doorcase with rusticated arch, fluted pilasters and triglyphs, and probably the uncommonly fine EAST GATE-PIERS to the park; also rusticated with paterae, swags and Greek key decoration. The house looks predominantly early C19 – rectangular, stuccoed, two storeys with a panelled parapet – and was probably remodelled for General Denzil Onslow, who occupied it from 1806 to 1838. The staircase has Doric columns at first floor. Early C18 STABLES to the N, with brick pilasters.

Former RECTORY, w of the church in its own park. 1852–3 by *W. G. & E. Habershon*. Brick, shallow hipped roof and symmetrical, i.e. the Georgian tradition carrying on. Four bays to the front, long windows to ground floor.

The VILLAGE proper is about ½ m. E, along Staughton Highway. THE WHITE HART, is early C17, with a two-storey-and-attic gabled and jettied cross-wing to the l. of a tall arch to the inn yard. Also the VILLAGE CROSS, a fluted pillar with a square sundial and a ball finial, erected in 1637 by Edmund Ibbett, whose initials it bears. HIGHWAY FARMHOUSE, Causeway Close, is mid-C16. Two rooms divided by an original back-to-back timber chimney bay and some painted decoration to floor joists (NHLE). The former BAPTIST CHAPEL, 1871, has a spirelet tower and coloured tile trim to the brick.

EARTHWORKS, I m. SW. The large moated enclosure of the principal medieval manor house. Rectangular, about 650 ft (198 metres) long by 430 ft (131 metres) wide. In the centre, a circular moated mound is probably an earlier motte and bailey.

GAYNES HALL. *See* Perry.

GREAT STUKELEY

St Bartholomew. Substantial Perp W tower with clasping buttresses chamfered towards the middles of the four sides of the tower (the SW one has a curiously shaped incised sundial). At the corners are the stumps of pinnacles, the low roof is post-medieval. The openings are a mix of Dec (Y-tracery with cinquefoils to the belfry) and Perp. The arch from tower to nave is Perp, and a vault was begun inside the tower. The ribs rest on figural brackets, one of a frightening frog creature and another of a lady with a typical early to mid-C15 head-dress. Also Perp, but late C15, the windows in the S aisle. On the chancel N side, a pair of E.E. lancets, uncovered and restored by *S. Inskip Ladds* in 1910. He thoroughly scraped and repointed the walls and, as was his custom, reset some C12 fragments (cf. Little Stukeley). Discoveries suggested that the chancel arch may have been Norman, and internally the evidence is indeed earlier. Arcades of four bays. N differs from S in interesting ways, suggesting only a small difference in time. On the S side the piers and abaci are round, and one capital has early stiff-leaf. The arches are pointed, of one step and one slight chamfer – say 1190. But the W bay has two slight chamfers, i.e. is a little later. On the N side the abaci are octagonal, and arches two and three are of the earlier, arches one and four of the later variety and have in addition mouldings around the arches on the aisle side. The N aisle itself is wider than the S, possibly rebuilt in the C14 (see the E window, and the remains of others in the N wall superseded by Perp ones). – STOUP. Square and gabled. It may be part of a pinnacle. – PULPIT. Densely carved panels of grapevines by *P. R. Edwards* of Letchworth, 1933. – In the baptistery (N aisle W end), panelling, seats and font cover by *Peter Foster*, 1967; of the same date the two strong STAINED GLASS windows of Pentecost and the Baptism by *Donald Drury*. – BRASS. Nave aisle. The indent only but impressive nonetheless. A figure in armour of *c.* 1460, identified as Sir Nicholas Styvele, set against an earlier C15 cross.

COLLEGE FARM, Owl End, N of Ermine Street, is early C17. L-plan and of two storeys, the principal part of two rooms divided by the chimneystack and with a lobby entry originally. The stair rises against its opposite side. The wing was originally a single bay for the kitchen, with its own large fireplace and big brick chimney, but extended in the late C17 for a brewhouse etc. This is of two bays and open to the roof. Impressively restored from dereliction since the 1980s.

STUKELEY HALL, E, within a late C20 housing development. Early C19, probably built for James Torkington (†1827). Stuccoed. Curved Doric portico on the front of 1904; of the same date the loggia on the side facing the park. This front is of nine bays, the centre three projecting under an attic storey and with a bow window. Much extended.

HADDON

1090

St Mary. The NE angle of the nave has quoins of long and short work of the church mentioned at Domesday, when it was held by Thorney Abbey. Mighty Norman chancel arch of the early C12. Capitals with interlaced bands (cf. Castor), thick rolls in the arch. Along the hoodmould and down the jambs saltire crosses, like flattened-out dogtooth (cf. Morborne). Then, still Norman, the N aisle W window, and after that, early C13, the S aisle W window and both arcades. They are of three bays and have round, double-chamfered arches. Octagonal piers and odd W responds with shafts, the S with a head, the N with scrolls. N comes before S. Some nailhead on the S side. The pointed arches from the aisles into the transepts are contemporary. The transepts are clearly contemporary too (see the N transept N lancet), as is also the W tower with its lancets below. The curious twin rising arches to the W ending on a long midshaft must indicate that in the C13 a bellcote and not a tower was planned. The top stage is indeed Perp, C16 or even C17, like the clerestory and the N transept roof. The N doorway is like the S doorway but the N porch is a puzzle. Its entrance arch is pointed with slight chamfers and the piers have a keeled main shaft and responds with nailhead. That must be early C13 but the sides have twin openings with round arches. These could be alterations of 1745, when the church was repaired and beautified by Robert Pigott (cf. Chesterton). In the S transept S wall is a three-light window with cusped intersecting tracery, i.e. of *c.* 1300, and the N and S aisle windows of three stepped lancet lights under one segmental arch are most probably of such a date too. The chancel is *c.* 1300 at the latest, but more probably *c.* 1250–75. It has twin lancets under one blank arch to N and S. That on the N side has in the blank tympanum a charming foliated cross, just like those on coffin lids or indeed like the ironwork on C13 doors. Inside, l. and r. of the chancel arch are the recesses for seats. Re-fixed against the nave roof (of 1901 by *J. C. Traylen*) are men and angels from the roof's predecessor. – WALL PAINTINGS. Revealed in 1901. Over the chancel arch C15 figures associated with a Doom painting, hardly recognizable. Decorative patterns of the S transept E wall. – SCULPTURE. S aisle by the S door. A crouching lion, very worn. C12? – STAINED GLASS. E window, St Michael and St George, by *Kempe*, 1901.

Hardly a village, just MANOR HOUSE farm with its Georgian front and rear of 1875 added by the Huntly estate, some contemporary estate cottages and former schoolroom.

1060

HAIL WESTON

St Nicholas. A chapel to Southoe and a sweet building with its cobbled walls, its one big old tiled roof over nave and chancel, and its totally shingled W tower with jettied belfry, whose pyramid roof starts lower than the ridge of the tile-roof. Until 1884, however, the tower roof was gabled and the exterior weatherboarded, rather like a windmill without sails. Architecturally the tower is nevertheless of great interest. It represents a type familiar in Essex but unique in Huntingdonshire. It is entirely timber-framed, with heavy posts along the S and N walls, four tie-beams, two across the space, two against the E and W walls, and scissor-bracing as well as windbraces against the walls. The impression is confusing but powerful. Is the tower of *c.* 1500, or earlier? Dating in Essex has gone earlier. The building itself is E.E. – see the chancel N lancet with continuous outer mouldings and the small DOUBLE PISCINA. The nave N doorway has a finely moulded arch. The roof, largely replaced in 1884, has a late C16 castellated wall-plate and one tie-beam carved with rosettes, stems and other emblems. The ALTAR TABLE has a similarly carved top rail. – SCREEN. Dado only, the upper lights roughly cut off. – BENCHES. Eight with summarily shaped poppyheads, copied for the others in the C19. – STAINED GLASS. Good E window, Christ in Majesty, by *Clayton & Bell* (design by *George Daniels*), 1913.

HAMERTON

ALL SAINTS. It is odd that the S porch windows should be late C13, with bar tracery. Do they come from a porch preceding the present one? The W tower is ashlar-faced and Perp, with the features common to other villages nearby of set-back buttresses, a W doorway with traceried spandrels, bell-openings in pairs of two lights each, a quatrefoil frieze over, battlements, but no spire. Embattled S and N aisle and clerestory, all Perp. But the S doorway seems to be of *c.* 1300 (continuous mouldings) and the chancel and its arch of about the same date, though refaced in 1854–6. Windows with Y-tracery and two lowside windows, that on the S a prolongation below a transom of one light of a two-light window. Early C14 N and S arcades of four bays, tall piers, standard elements. The hoodmoulds with labels touching the clerestory is found also at Ellington (q.v.). The nave roof has figures on the wall-posts and angels against the intermediate principals, the N and S aisle roofs only the former. In the aisles, four of the wall-post figures represent the Evangelists, with heads of eagle, bull etc. – FONT. A big, ambitious Perp piece, designed for its position against the W pier of the S arcade. Panelled stem, bowl with alternating patterns of quatrefoils etc. – MONUMENTS. In the S aisle, two large, uncouth standing monuments, both no more than an inscription tablet in big letters with strapwork around or on top and crestings. Mawde Bedell †1587, dated 1597, of Ketton stone, and Sir John Bedell †1613. – In the vestry, Ferrar Colet, rector, †1679. An excellent small marble tablet with death's head and finely cut drapery. Attributed to *Jasper Latham* (GF). – Rev. Robert Payne †1822. Grecian style, white marble tablet by *L. W. Pocock* of Huntingdon.

The Bedells acquired the manor *c.* 1565; their mansion stood to the SE but was taken down in the mid C19. Sales particulars of 1669 make it clear that it was of impressive scale and there are remains of its GARDENS of late C16 or early C17 date, including terraces and a canal. On part of its site, the former RECTORY of 1860 by *Rohde Hawkins*.

MANOR HOUSE is a fine yeoman farmhouse of *c.* 1600. L-plan, two-storey and attics, all of good red brick with a continuous moulded string course. The three-bay front range has a central gabled porch with moulded arch. Gabled ends on kneelers. The rear kitchen range is attached N to a lower brewhouse and dairy to E. Moulded terracotta chimneys with interlinking lozenge patterns and even some arabesque decoration. Interior restored to its lobby-entry plan with the newel stair rising against the opposite side of the chimneystack. In the former kitchen, part of a screen protecting the back door and a funny seat (C18?) built into the wall.

PARISH ROOM, 350 yds NE of Manor House. Arts and Crafts style. By *S. Inskip Ladds*, 1902. Chimneypiece from Stow Longa Manor House (dem. 1903).

HAMPTON *see* PETERBOROUGH

HARTFORD

Separate from Huntingdon until the late 1960s, when overspill dragged it into the town's E edge. But no harm has been done to the church in its delightful position by the Ouse with a landing place to the E and the trees of Hartford House.

ALL SAINTS. Perp W tower with battlements and pinnacles, the middle merlons on all sides connected by thin ogee arches. The S doorway has traces of E.E. origin; all other external features are the restorer's. But internally there is something of interest. First the restorer's work, *Robert Hutchinson*'s* of 1861, i.e. the imitation-Norman chancel arch with its billet, nutmeg and chevron surround, the strips of nutmeg on the N and S chancel walls and REREDOS in early E.E. style with double pointed arches under a round arch, all with dogtooth and diaper patterns. The inspiration might be the piscina at St Ives (q.v.). Then the four-bay arcades, both late C12, but N in character-

---

* *Hutchinson* had designed the vicarage, W of the church, in 1853.

istic ways just a little earlier. Both sides have round piers and round abaci already, but the N arches are round, of one step and one slight chamfer, the S arches pointed and of two slight chamfers. – FONT. Norman, with stop-chamfered angles. – PULPIT. High Victorian, of 1867 by *Hutchinson*. Caen stone with pink marble colonnettes, dogtooth decoration and nice metal tracery by Messrs *Hart*. – TOWER SCREEN. Arts and Crafts Tudor. In memory of the Hon. Patience Seely †1935 who has a Neo-Georgian table tomb in the churchyard. – STAINED GLASS. Chancel E. An Ascension of the 1860s. Chancel SW. Full-length portrait of the son of the rector, drowned in the Ouse in 1885, aged ten. He stands in the chancel at the lectern. – MONUMENTS. Some C18 and C19 tablets. Also one to J. R. Coleridge, who went down with the *Titanic* in 1912.

HARTFORD HOUSE. Early Georgian refronting, probably to a C17 house, of five bays and two storeys plus parapet; red brick. The lower windows are segment-headed. Excellent fittings also *c.* 1730, especially the curved staircase and the egg-and-dart moulding around its arched window and ceiling. Later C18 extension to the rear wing and sensitive addition of *c.* 2000 by *Julian Limentani*, facing the river. The colossal addition, amounting to a new house, by *Salvin* in 1856 for the Desboroughs, Huntingdon bankers, was taken down in 1924. Red brick garden wall all around it.

MANOR HOUSE, a little NE of Hartford House, in Main Street. The suggested date is *c.* 1500 (1540 on the door). Hall-house type with two gabled wings, the l. gable jutting on brackets. The two-storey gabled porch is, in the traditional way, not in the middle of the hall part but into a lobby against the chimney. The door canopy is Victorian but the doorcase with a pediment early C18 like the windows. Back part also Georgian with a Venetian window (lighting a fine staircase, which inside opens off the hall behind a screen of arches. Much good panelling, some bolection-moulded. BD).

EARTHWORK, 2 m. NNW. With a moat, probably the fragment of a motte-and-bailey CASTLE. The motte is now only 9 ft (2.7 metres) high.

HELPSTON [P]

ST BOTOLPH. Unique in the area on account of the form of its W tower, which turns octagonal at the clerestory level and ends in a very short spire. This was rebuilt entirely in 1865 by *Edward Browning*, but as he found it and reusing the C14 bell-openings (two-light with a quatrefoil) and lucarnes. He discovered Saxon long-and-short work foundations. But the earliest period now seen is the early C12 arch towards the nave with scallop capitals, one with scrolls (cf. Maxey). The pointed arch is a remodelling and the arches to N and S are replacements but with their original thick roll mouldings copied. Of the early C13 the s arcade of two bays with circular pier and circular capitals and abaci. Round arches with two slight chamfers. The s doorway has a pointed arch with one order of colonnettes and one waterleaf capital and one with upright leaves (restored). In spite of this, the doorway could go with the arcade. Mid-C13 N arcade with octagonal pier and responds and double-chamfered arches, the w one pointed. Then *c.* 1300 the chancel and the E bay connecting it with the arcades. The chancel arch has clustered shafts with a fillet. Lowside sw window with hinges for a shutter. Original also the SEDILIA and DOUBLE PISCINA, the AUMBRY on the N side and, on the original lines, the restored E window. A vestry was N of the chancel (blocked door). The porch is early C14 and Dec also the pretty s aisle E window. Inside it has a segmental arch, slender filleted colonnettes with foliage capitals and a frieze of ballflower brought forwards l. and r. as bases for statues. C15 battlemented clerestory of two-light windows with arches on the N side and under square heads on the s; w window of about the same time. Finally, the other chancel windows are strange replacements of 1609 (dated lintel of the SE window). Tall, of two lights, straight-headed, with a pointed quatrefoil at the top of each light. The strange stepped merlons of the aisle may be contemporary.

– BENCH ENDS. Of stone seats formerly along the chancel N and s walls. One carved with a death's head, the other a winged beast (cf. Sutton). Below the chancel step, two reset sections of medieval TILE pavement in geometric patterns, of a type found in Eastern England (cf. Old Warden, Beds.) and with similarities to examples at Ely (Prior Crauden's chapel). The likely date is 1300–25. – SOUTH DOOR. Inscribed W. G. *fecit* 1708. – ROYAL ARMS. James II, painted on canvas. Not a common item. – STAINED GLASS. Chancel E, an impressive Christ in Majesty, 1983 by *Francis Skeat.* – w window 1884 by *Burlison & Grylls.* – MONUMENTS. Rebuilt into the walls of the w tower are fragments of Anglo-Saxon GRAVE COVERS found in 1865 built into the upper stages of the tower. Crosses in relief, similar to the stones at Barnack and Peterborough Cathedral. – BRASS. N aisle. Covered over. Bust of a priest, Roger de Hegham, †1320.

The centre of the VILLAGE is the crossroads sw of the church, marked by the C14 VILLAGE CROSS, raised on circular steps. A thin, tapering shaft on a tall polygonal base with blind crocketed arches and battlements. Opposite is the JOHN CLARE MONUMENT of 1869 by *Alfred Sykes,* in an uninformed Gothic of two stages with quatrefoil panels and a thick shaft under cone roof. Clare's birthplace in 1793 was the low, whitewashed, thatched COTTAGE in Woodgate, s of the crossroad, now restored to its unpretentious C18 state of two rooms l. and r. of the entrance and a kitchen range at the rear. s end C19, when the house was divided in two. VISITOR CENTRE, a robust barn, by *Jefferson Sheard Architects,* 2008–9; a DOVECOTE, stone with brick interior, has been converted for exhibition use.

W of the village cross, the BRADFORD ALMSHOUSES of 1907 by *Clayton & Black* of Brighton. Jacobean-style door with obelisk finials, the ends red brick with half-timbered gables. 50 yds W is HELPSTON HOUSE, dated 1660, an L-shaped gentry house with gables, dormers, and a canted bay window. CROMWELL HOUSE, Maxey Road, E of the church, has a similar gable over its door and is dated 1658, but the rest is a little too pristine.

E of the centre was a station of 1846 on the Midland Railway. It was demolished in 1974 but the Picturesque STATION-MASTER'S HOUSE survives. 250 yds SE, a former GRAIN SHED, a standard design for the Midland Railway, 1846. Brick with arched windows to three floors and a broad roof whose eaves are carried by cast-iron brackets. The Neo-Jacobean house on the other side of the crossing appears to have been built as a hotel, although not by the railway company.

MOTTE AND BAILEY, ¾ m. W of the village centre, by the Bainton road. Remains of a small C12 castle or fortified house. In Lawn Wood, 600 yds SSW, substantial walling of a STONE BUILD-ING, 40 ft (12.1 metres) square inside, with rubble walls 9 ft (2.7 metres) thick and with projections at the corners. It is identified as a medieval hunting lodge to the castle. Both sites are associated with Torpel manor, one of the largest manors in the Soke of Peterborough.

HEMINGFORD ABBOTS   2070

ST MARGARET. Of brown cobbles, Perp W tower with clasping buttresses with chamfers towards the middles of the sides and tabernacles on the angles of the second stage. Spire recessed behind battlements with pinnacles, with two bands and two tiers of lucarnes in alternating directions. S porch rebuilt during the restoration of 1872–6 by *Herbert Green* of London, but the entrance is E.E. and to its E inside the S aisle wall are three pointed arches with slight chamfers, typically C13 (cf. Abbots Ripton, another church held by Ramsey Abbey). Interesting N aisle with windows and doorway of *c.* 1300. All three windows are of two lights and straight-headed, which is remarkable, and the E window with cusped lancets and squashed trefoil is just as remarkable, provided it is not interfered with. The interior has arcades of three bays (standard elements) plus a truncated fourth into which the tower now cuts. The E bay represents a former crossing. This is evident from the thicker octagonal piers, the wave-moulded half-arches, i.e. flying buttresses, across the aisles, and the thickening of the upper nave walls. The S half-arch has a corbel head of a king. Another distur-bance in the clerestory walls is the replacement of two-light by three-light windows, probably of the same time as the panelled nave roof. It has a wall-plate with furled leaf decoration (cf.

Fenstanton) and a finely decorated rood bay with Latin inscriptions on the beams. Decorated bosses of roses and pomegranates in the nave, also in the N aisle roof. The chancel is of C19 yellow brick in two phases, the E window's reticulated tracery of 1912 by *S. Inskip Ladds*, the Tudor-ish S window inserted by him in 1932. – FONT. Early C13, with blank arches. – PULPIT. 1937, a late C17 revival design by *Theodore Fyfe*. – ALTAR. By *Peter Foster*, late C20. – WALL PAINTING. Part of a St Christopher and next to it a version of the same on canvas by *Brian Thomas*, 1974, muscular Brangwynesque style. – STAINED GLASS. In the N aisle E window, good C18 heraldic glass (dates of death 1731–48) formerly in the chancel E window. In its place a Crucifixion by *J. Powell & Sons*, 1913, a rich minuscule design of fruiting vines around the figures. – In a S aisle window, Suffer Little Children, †1873 by *Heaton, Butler & Bayne*. – N aisle window by *Kempe & Co.*, 1928, incredibly reactionary. – In the tower screen and S aisle, beautiful ENGRAVED GLASS by *David Peace* (†2003), who lived in the village. – MONUMENTS. Joshua Barnes †1712. Baldacchino above the inscription; putto-heads and palm-fronds at the bottom, all quite crude. He was Regius Professor of Greek; so the inscription is partly in Greek.

SW of the church, the OLD RECTORY has a front of 1813–14 with Gothic windows and castellated porch, by *George Woolcott*. Many other attractive houses along Common Lane, despite suburban density of building, e.g. No. 24, late C17 with shaped gable ends. Further out, THE GRANGE of 1906 by the *Rev. F. K. Oliphant*, the vicar of Houghton, for Arthur Astley-Cooper. Recessed porch with screen of twisted balusters and at one end the upper floor is jettied over a veranda. (Well-crafted interior fittings and a galleried hall; cf. Diss Cottage, Hemingford Grey.) Nearby, the THATCHED COTTAGE (three times the size of its neighbours!) was by *Oliphant* for Astley-Cooper's brother; see e.g. the motif of wrought-iron ties to the chimneys. Rebuilt anew after a fire in 1996 by *Pitts Architects*.

RIDEAWAY DRIVE. A small scheme of Huntingdonshire Council houses of 1948–52 by *Lea, Milner & Wardley* of Huntingdon, using thatch roofs, something that ought to have been done more widely in the county's public housing.

HEMINGFORD PARK. Built for the squarson, the Rev. J. Linton, by *Decimus Burton*, 1842–3. Italianate without much personality, in yellow brick with stucco trim. Three-bay front with a small pediment above the eaves. Modest emphasis to the centre of the longer E front, which has the principal rooms. Pediment on this side also. Stables with double pediments and a clock turret. NE of the house, its former CRICKET PAVILION, built by the owner Sydney Williams in 1897. Thatched roof descending in hips and half-hips and with verandas to front and wings. The upper floor provided bedrooms for visiting professionals. Neo-Tudor gate LODGE (built of concrete, it has been discovered).

HEMINGFORD GREY 2070

The excellent setting by the Ouse explains the village's fascination in the late C19 and early C20 for artists and weekenders in search of a country retreat. Still perfectly rural until the late 1950s, it then suffered from an invasion of small speculative private houses and bungalows. It is a great pity but has not destroyed its integrity.

ST JAMES. The W tower faces the Ouse only a few feet away. It is a pretty position. The history of the building begins with the N arcade. The middle arch is round, with one step and one slight chamfer. The piers are round and sturdy, the abaci square and nicked at the corners. The capitals have small scallops decorated with beading. That makes it *c.* 1180. E bay and W bay are later, late C13 and late C14 respectively. The meeting of two responds W of the E bay deserves a good look. The S arcade has one arch almost identical with the earliest on the N side, but probably some twenty years later. The piers now have round abaci. The E and W bays are as above. The S doorway is over-restored but matches the S aisle. It is suggested that there was a central tower which was removed in the C13 and the W tower was made *c.* 1400 (cf. Hemingford Abbots above and Soham and Great Wilbraham, Cambs.). The chancel is mid-C13 – see the two N lancets and the lovely DOUBLE PISCINA with its intersecting not only arches but mouldings (of the same type as St Ives, S aisle, but more elaborate, with cusping). The arches stand on Purbeck shafts. Opposite a plain DOUBLE AUMBRY with round arches, possibly C12. Dec S chancel window with segmental head and intersecting curvilinear tracery, but the other windows, including the E window, are all of 1859, when the church was extensively restored and partly rebuilt (e.g. N aisle) by *W. Perkin* of Leeds. Finally the details of the Perp W tower. Clasping buttresses, turning diagonal higher up. Ball finials of the C18 on the buttresses, and a truncated recessed spire also crowned by ball finials. The rest of the spire was blown down in the hurricane of 1741. – STAINED GLASS. E window, 1864, a poor Crucifixion. S aisle E, the Ascension by *Ward & Hughes*, 1892. One window of the S aisle ('Maria. Rabboni') by *Kempe*, 1906. – MONUMENTS. Enjoyable cartouches. Gruffin Lloyde †1682, with foliage twisting around swords and shields. Attributed to *Jasper Latham* (GF). – Also James Johnson †1727, with finely undercut Baroque details, perhaps by a Cambridge mason (cf. 1720s cartouches at Whittlesford and Dullingham, Cambs.). – One outside, Thomas Newman †1715. Scroll sides and a death's head.

MANOR HOUSE, ¼ m. SW of the church. A MOAT surrounds the house on three sides; on the fourth is the river down to which the garden extends. The house is of very special interest, because its whole centre is C12, stone built, and probably represents the solar wing of a hall now lost. It was converted in 76 the late C16 into a farmhouse and further remodelled in the C18 and C19. That one may see so much of the early fabric is due to revelations in 1937–9 by *Hugh Hughes* of Cambridge, who refitted the house for Lucy Boston, author of the *Green Knowe* series which has the building as its setting. The original part had a room on the upper floor, and there was in all probability a chapel wing attached to its E side. Norman two-light windows are preserved in the W, S and E walls; one on the W side converted to a door in the 1930s after removal of additions. The arches are decorated with pellets at the l. and r. starting-points and the apex, almost anticipating cusping. The jambs and the intermediate pier are single-chamfered. The S window has in addition an arch of chevron. The entrance was on the S side, where the doorway remains. This is one of the short sides, which is unusual (but cf. King John's Hunting Box, Romsey, Hants). There must have been wooden steps up to the doorway. On the same side is a narrow, straight-headed window on the ground floor. Also on the ground floor, to the E, is a doorway which was originally an arched window. The N gable end is early C18, oddly askew to the ends of the C12 walls. The finest internal feature is the mighty chimneypiece in the E wall at first floor with two Norman columns with two-scalloped capitals. Segmental arch of one slight chamfer. Are the tiles at the back of the fireplace Norman too? The large central chimneystack is C16, when the attic floor was inserted, but this was partly removed in the 1930s to restore the hall's S end to its full height (the large tie-beam probably held a screen dividing the first floor). Here and there some painted decoration by *Elizabeth Vellacott*, done in the 1940s, and some engraved glass by *David Peace*.

Immediately N of the church is HEMINGFORD GREY HOUSE, the former rectory, possibly of *c.* 1697, when the vicar petitioned for its rebuilding, or only just a little later. Red brick, two storeys, five bays on two fronts, with segment-headed windows, a platband and hipped roof. Apsed door-hood on well-carved brackets to the W front. Neo-Georgian addition to the r. with a curved end, by *Edwin Bradbury*, probably before 1902 for the Whiteaways, whose heraldry is in the staircase window. (Panelled rooms and fireplaces. Staircase with three turned balusters per tread.) By the river one of the largest plane trees in England, planted in 1702; 5 ft (1.5 metres) from the ground the girth is over 20 ft (6 metres).

The HIGH STREET runs towards the E from close to the Manor House. At the start, RIVER HOUSE, C18, of yellow brick. Five bays, and a handsome late C18 pedimented doorway. Good recessed cupboards with shaped shelves in one room. The house belonged *c.* 1900 to the artist Dendy Sadler, who erected the studio and boat shed. At the corner of Braggs Lane another five-bay house, called BROOM LODGE. This, though early C18, still has shaped end-gables. Others of note are HARCOURT, early C19, which belonged to the architect *Peter Foster* in the late C20. He adapted the outbuildings as the offices of Marshall

Sisson Associates; Greek Doric colonnade in front. The garden of the house has follies to his design (one a Grecian Doric temple made up with columns salvaged from a shopfront in St Ives in 1955). Much further E, THE GLEBE, dated 1583, timber-framed with closely set studs, a jettied W cross-wing with original windows (blocked) and thatch. Formerly an open hall house, the floor and stack inserted in the C17. Some pargetting of thistles on the chimney in a first-floor room. Also ROSENTHAL, a proud Early Victorian house, yellow brick with a Doric portico.

DISS COTTAGE, Mill Lane. Charming Arts and Crafts style by *Rev. F. K. Oliphant* of Houghton, *c.* 1910. On a small scale, with a porch recessed below the eaves of the upper storey and inside a snug galleried hall and a sunken sitting room at one end with fitted cupboards, and inglenook etc. Sympathetically extended by *Pitts Architects*, *c.* 2010.

THE STUDIO, No. 4 Langley Way. By *Saunders Boston*, 1960, for the designer and artist Elizabeth Vellacott. A-frame, Scandinavian style, with the shingle roof descending almost to the ground. Full-height room at one end.

LIMES PARK, St Ives Road. The former WORKHOUSE for the St Ives Union by *W. T. Nash*, *c.* 1834. Yellow brick, classical and very fine, with central and outer pavilions with round-arched windows. Wings behind.

HILTON

ST MARY MAGDALENE. C14 W tower, the rest Perp. Brown cobbles. The arcades of four bays have typical Perp piers with capitals only to the arch openings and the same slender section as at St Ives. In the chancel a bracket on a head, in the S aisle a mutilated vaulted niche containing an aumbry, with a C20 brasswork door by *Eve Garnett* (*see* Hilton Hall). Good Perp aisle roofs, both skilfully repaired *c.* 2000. The tower's NW buttress and stair inside were rebuilt in 1904–6 by *S. Inskip Ladds*; he discovered the CROSS-HEAD now in the W wall of the tower reused as a step. In the upper part the Crucifix, in the lower defaced foliage. – PULPIT. From Caldecote (q.v.). Dated 1646, plain panels and small arabesque panels over. Much repaired 1983. – ROYAL ARMS. Charles I. Painted on plaster. From Park Farm (dem. *c.* 1950).* – STAINED GLASS. In a chancel N window, a head of Christ. – E window by *Wailes* of Newcastle, 1861. Bad W window by *W. H. Constable* of Cambridge. – Also

---

*The arms were removed from the ruins of Park Farm in 1946 by David and Angelica Garnett of Hilton Hall. Other wall paintings of the Prince of Wales feathers, dated 1632, and a contemporary allegorical panel of Taste and Sight from a series of the Five Senses, were given to the Victoria and Albert Museum (now in the British Galleries).

two windows by *Kempe*, 1896 and 1898. – MONUMENTS. In the chancel, two alabaster pieces from a tomb-chest, one with two quatrefoils enclosing shields, the other with two kneeling angels holding a shield. – Mary Powell †1736. Grey and coloured marbles with volutes at the sides and an urn against a flat obelisk.

METHODIST CHURCH. 1867 by *Hutchinson*. Brick with lancets. Also by Hutchinson, the VILLAGE HALL (former school) of 1856.

The road to Fenstanton runs through the extensive and much-wooded GREEN, said to have been planted with 160 elms by *Capability Brown* after he acquired the manor in 1767. Here and there the houses must be reached by little bridges spanning a brook. E of the church is a nicely kept circular grass MAZE, first cut in 1660. In the middle a PILLAR with a ball finial to record the death in 1729 of William Sparrow of Park Farm, who had it cut. SE of the maze, THE GRANGE is mostly *c.* 1815 but with two large C16(?) BARNS, now converted. One of seven bays and aisled, the other taller, of six bays with brick infill to the frame. On the Green's N side, THE LIMES is especially attractive, with two Late Georgian bows on the rendered front but earlier C18 behind, unusually with diaper-pattern brickwork. Some earlier timber-framing at the back. W of this, THE MANOR HOUSE, a small, brick box of *c.* 1700 with three bays under a moulded cornice and a hipped roof. Unaltered large brick BARN behind, dated 1683.

Nearby, HILTON HALL has a quirky façade of segmental-arched openings currently arranged 9:5:3 in three storeys. They are in pairs at ground floor and most puzzling now that some have had C18 sash windows inserted. It does not relate easily to the early to mid-C17 red brick house behind, whose staircase, rising inside a gabled wing, has shaped finials and turned balusters. Evidently the end-gables were originally shaped. The Garnetts, associates of the Bloomsbury Group, owned the house from the mid 1920s. Above one chimneypiece is decoration by *Angelica Garnett* in the Charleston style. There is more in the handsome late C17 DOVECOTE, with gabled roof. It was converted into a painter's studio *c.* 1917. The house has significant, but subordinate, timber and brick additions of 2009–10 by *Frazer Stannard*. Incorporated in the walls some (C16?) moulded terracotta tiles with roses and fleur-de-lis and inside reset early C18 panelling, originally salvaged by the Garnetts from Park Farm (*see* above) in 1946.

On the Graveley Road, HILTON HOUSE is two storeys above a shallow basement, with two wings and a parapet, all rendered as ashlar probably *c.* 1800. The centre and the l. wing, which has a Venetian window, are early to mid-C18, the r. wing is the formerly separate coach house, which was incorporated in the 1930s. Inside this, a fireplace whose jambs are moulded shafts brought from the Palace of Westminster.

W is COLLEGE FARM, a C15 open hall house with a jettied two-storey wing. Altered in the C17 and later extended. It belonged to St John's College, Cambridge. Parts of the hall's roof remain, including a braced truss at first floor. Moulded trusses and beams in the wing, indicating its high status. One first-floor room has the former entrance to a garderobe, and at its N end the wing has a garret room reached by a winder stair against the brick chimneystack. Simple foliage trails in pargetting to the cross-wing gable, unusual in Huntingdon (if indeed it is entirely genuine). Two sides of the moat survive.

KINGSWILLOW. Brick, by *Dyson & Hebeler*, 1937–8. In the 'International Modern' of the most progressive English houses of those years. Specially typical the linear plan, the glazed semicircular projection of the staircase and the long window bands. Circular dining room and folding glass screen windows to the garden. Also by *Dyson & Hebeler*, PUNCH'S GROVE of 1939, on the Green 150 yds E of The Limes, but how different. Neo-Georgian of American swagger with a giant Ionic portico. Originally cubic, massively enlarged *c.* 2010.

HINCHINGBROOKE *see* HUNTINGDON

HOLME

1080

A hamlet until the draining of Whittlesey Mere in 1849–53, which was partly funded by William Wells of Holme Wood Hall. The village expanded thereafter as part of his estate.

ST GILES. 1862 by *Edward Browning*, replacing a chapel of ease to Glatton (q.v.). Rock-faced, with a double bellcote. Dec in style, even the round clerestory windows with flowing tracery. The even, straight-headed three-light aisle windows look well from inside. Inside old materials were reused. The E respond and two pier capitals N and S are medieval, S with a scalloped C12 capital and a moulded C13 capital, N with C13 octagonal capitals and three of its arches (double-chamfered). – COMMUNION TABLE. *c.* 1630. – REREDOS. 1901 by *A. H. Skipworth*, a pupil of Bodley & Garner. Bronzed gesso panels with ogee tops and feathery fronds – STAINED GLASS. To William Wells †1889. The Sower. Unidentified maker. Wells's MONUMENT in the churchyard is an open-sided table in C18 style, with gadrooned balusters and moulded top with palm fronds.

HOLME WOOD HALL (now Conference Centre). Rebuilt in 1872–7 for William Wells M.P. around the remains of an earlier house that had been gutted by fire. It is an early work by the Paisley architect *William Young*, who was introduced by his patron, Wells's brother-in-law, Lord Elcho. Rather Waterhouse-ish. Red Chilton brick and red terracotta. Mullioned and transomed windows. Gables. Good big cast-iron garden gates and railings. Characterful gatehouse to the service yard with a steep roof, an oriel with coloured glass, and sgraffito panels. The interiors are Jacobethan, arranged around a large staircase hall. One very long room along the E front, with ribbed plaster ceiling, two-tier fireplace and Aesthetic Style glass by *J. Powell & Sons*, 1875. Impressive stone Gothic arch framing the fireplace in the former billiard room.

FEN POSTS, Holme Lode. Holme Fen is the lowest place in England, now 9 ft (2.75 metres) below sea level, and the posts record the shrinkage of the peat after the draining of Whittlesey Mere. One is of 1851, an 18-ft (5.4-metre) cast-iron fluted Doric column, originally buried up to its head. Over two thirds has reappeared since. The second post was erected in 1957.

HOLYWELL

3070

ST JOHN THE BAPTIST. The W tower is a mystery. Churchwardens' accounts show it was built in 1547–51 (mason *Thomas Roper*) and of stone from Ramsey Abbey, to which the church belonged before the Dissolution. What does that statement involve? The tower is broad and substantial and built of regular stone blocks. Its buttresses start with chamfers, i.e. semi-polygonal, and the W window is indeed Tudor. But the bell-openings are Dec, and the doorway with its broadly rounded-trefoiled head and the big cusped tracery motifs of the spandrels defeats dating. The arch inside towards the nave and the narrower ones in the N and S walls are Dec anyway, with fleurons in the mouldings and moulded responds with foliage. Is it then all reused Ramsey material? The N and S arches are now blank with later windows and appear to fulfil no useful function in their position, but were they originally open, as appears to have been the case at Bury (q.v.)? The holy well lies immediately S. The body of the church is stone and cobbles, and the features over-restored by *Robert Hutchinson* in 1863; porch and vestry of this time. The chancel, however, is a beautiful early C13 piece with paired lancet windows, with a detached middle shaft between them inside and a rib rising from the shaft to the rere-arch, an unexpected personal touch. Big PISCINA with cusped trefoil head. The aisle windows are Early Dec. So are the three-bay arcades with their standard elements. Roofs of 1863, but figures from the old nave roof are displayed in the church. – ROOD SCREEN. 1923 by *S. Inskip Ladds*. – STAINED GLASS. E window. *A. K. Nicholson*, 1931. St Edmund and St Oswald.

A string of pleasant small thatched C16 and C17 COTTAGES along one side of the front lane, some dated. On the back lane, THE PANTILES incorporates in its staircase and mantel beam Jacobean woodwork taken from Conington Castle (q.v.).

MOYNES HALL. C17, within a moated site. An outbuilding, however, has three medieval posts, perhaps taken from the aisled hall of Berenger le Moyne; they were earth-fast posts, a rare survival of the earliest form of aisled hall construction.

HOUGHTON

St Mary. Of brown cobbles. Partly Dec and partly Perp. Late
c13 to early c14 the chancel with windows from the cusped
lancet to reticulation. The DOUBLE PISCINA with shelves
indeed looks no later than *c.* 1300. Early c14 also the N arcade
of standard elements. Late c14 Perp w tower of unusual shape.
The buttresses stop below the bell-openings, and above them
the tower turns octagonal to carry the stone spire (cf. Bythorn
and Old Weston). The spire has two tiers of lucarnes, the
square part of the tower very prominent pinnacles, the top
parts of which unfortunately were blown off in the hurricane
of 1741. The chancel was restored in 1851 by *Wyatt & Brandon*
but little seems to have survived the restoration of 1870–1,
which included the cheap brick refacing of the N aisle and the

Houghton, St Mary, former rood screen,
by Rev. F. K. Oliphant, 1902

refitting of the chancel; the diaper pattern of the REREDOS is a match for Hartford (q.v.) so must be by *R. Hutchinson*. – In the chancel a stone SEAT, with arms like that at Stanground (*see* Peterborough). – Vestry SCREEN (N aisle). Constructed *c.* 1970 from the chancel screen of 1902 by the incumbent, the *Rev. F. K. Oliphant* who had worked in Frederic Chancellor's office; its Art Nouveau rood is discarded by the organ. – STAINED GLASS. Chancel SW (Gilbert Ansley †1860) by *Lavers & Barraud*; the NW window probably by the same. Another in the chancel (Haigh memorial) by *D. Marion Grant*, 1959, of roundels encircled by the Creed. – N aisle. Very traditional St Michael by *Harcourt M. Doyle*, 1959; and Millennium window by *Alfred R. Fisher*. The subjects drawn from Houghton and Wyton's history, including the obligatory – for this area – aircraft.

p. 517

UNION CHAPEL, W of the church. 1840, built by Potto Brown, flour miller of St Ives. He and his business partner Joseph Goodman established Nonconformist preaching in the village. Yellow brick with arched doorway and windows, a pediment across the façade, and a small pediment over the doorway. Vestry 1860, organ chamber 1877. Converted as a retreat centre in 1986.

SCHOOL adjoining of 2010–11 by *Mirijana Corovich* of *Mouchel Parkman Architects*, very attractive with timber-clad exterior and low-pitched tile roofs.

CEMETERY, Houghton Road. WAR MEMORIAL. 1921. By the *Rev. F. K. Oliphant*. In the form of the Victoria Cross (in honour of Leslie Green V.C. †1916).

HOUGHTON MILL, S of the church. The last unspoilt example of the many mills which stood along the Ouse. Rebuilt in the C17 and again after 1822, when it was acquired by Potto Brown and Joseph Goodman (*see* St Ives). Three storeys with an attic and two-storey outshot at the E end. Timber-framed, with walls of brick and weatherboarding in the upper storeys and in the deep attic a dormer in the half-hipped roof. The lucam rises higher still on the quay side. Originally with two water wheels working a total of eight stones; the N wheel and its timber-clad housing restored in 1998–9 by the National Trust, which was given the mill in 1939.

The village centre is the grassless GREEN, with a thatched memorial SHELTER and clock of 1902, designed by the artist *Charles Whymper*, who lived in the village, and a Victorian Gothic PUMP (cast by *Warner & Sons* of Cripplegate). On the N side, surprisingly unrestored, the former GEORGE & DRAGON inn, with a drunken timber-framed cross-wing l. and the unusual feature of a C17 brick stack built against the front.

N of this on the St Ives Road, another fine timber-framed house, MANOR FARMHOUSE, which has a long jetty with dragon beams, close-studding with straight braces, three brick chimneyshafts in a row and a small timber oriel under the jetty of the S gable end. Some pargetting too. The best houses are along THICKET ROAD, notably BUCKLEY HOUSE, a yeoman house with a continuous jetty on carved brackets and a dragon beam at the corner with its gabled cross-wing.

Further on is the THE MANOR, a very charming red brick house of 1905–6 by the *Rev. F. K. Oliphant*. Arts and Crafts with Elizabethan details, including a two-storey brick porch that has recessed quoins and, on the garden side, two-storey canted bays with a veranda between and five small gables along the top. The interior is in Baillie Scott's style, including a galleried hall and rooms with panelled inglenooks; little windows around the chimneybreasts. E again is THE ELMS (now apartments), built for Bateman Brown in 1868. *R. W. Edis* was the architect, the style Italianate with tiled eaves. Good Quattrocento porch with carved capitals to its arches. Conservatory of *c.* 1900. In the grounds to the W, THICKET LODGE of 1911 with two storeys of bay windows under a tiled roof. Built for the artist Arthur Beckingham.

On Houghton Hill are some small country houses in large grounds. First, HOUGHTON HILL HOUSE of *c.* 1840, square and plain in gault brick, built for Gilbert Ansley. Set above terraced gardens. Then HOUGHTON BURY, originally The Dingle, in Surrey-style Arts and Crafts, erected by the Coote family (*see* Houghton Grange below) *c.* 1925. Two principal wings at right angles with bow windows in the ends. The rooms and staircase open off a cosy hall and are nicely detailed, e.g. barrel-vaulted bedroom ceilings with plaster ribs.

HOUGHTON GRANGE, 1 m. E. By *James Ransome*, 1896–7, for C. H. Coote, coal merchant in St Ives. Ransome was an assistant of Ernest George & Peto and the house is Elizabethan in the free latest C19 way, e.g. with a big segmental pediment over the porch and above it a square bay window of altogether eleven lights. Four gables face the garden with canted bays under balustrade balconies. Two nice identical free-Tudor entrance LODGES.

THE HOW, 1¼ m. E, is the final house in this sequence and both closer to St Ives and nearer the Ouse. It was built for G. J. Ansley by *William White*, 1868–70. Ansley was a relative of White's sister. Yellow brick with some crazy patterns in red. Hipped and half-hipped roofs and tile-hung gables.

HUNTINGDON

INTRODUCTION

Huntingdon lies on the N bank of the Great Ouse on Ermine Street, although the Roman settlement was principally across the river at Godmanchester. It was a Saxon burgh. In 1068 William the Conqueror ordered a castle to be built and the burgh repaired. A priory was founded before 1092, perhaps before 973. By 1108 it had become Augustinian. Canons were sent to Hexham in 1113. Its site was where the cemetery now is. The Benedictine nunnery of Hinchingbrooke just outside to the w was also founded before 1100. Before 1258 came the Austin Friars. At that time the town had sixteen parish churches. Deterioration of the Ouse, the growing competition from the market at St Ives, and the Black Death did much damage, and the town declined. Early in the C16 there were only four parish churches left and just two by the early C19. Yet John Evelyn called Huntingdon a fair town, and so did William Cowper, who lived there from 1765 to 1767; to Cobbett it was a 'very clean and nice place'. The town's best

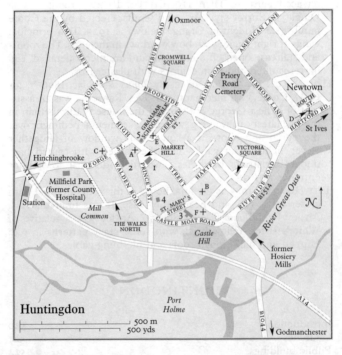

Huntingdon

A	All Saints	1	Town Hall
B	St Mary	2	Law Courts/
C	St John the Evangelist (former)		County Council Offices
D	St Michael (R.C.)	3	District Council Offices
E	Union Chapel (former)	4	Archdeaconry Library
F	Methodist Church	5	Cromwell Museum

domestic buildings are all of the period *c.* 1725, by which time it was an important coaching stop and trading centre and benefited from the agricultural improvements which followed drainage of the surrounding fens. There was some limited change in the later C19, expressive of its role as the county town, but only after 1960 was the picture significantly altered by expansion to receive over-spill population from London. Since Pevsner's visit in the mid-1960s a lot of damage has been done by the bypass, which marches over the W side of the town, and the ring road, which is like a noose around the centre. Together they have caused the destruction of several fine buildings, the disruption of the hith-erto unaltered medieval pattern of the town centre and they have interfered with the historic relationship of the town to the river and its water meadows as well as producing the inevitable exurbia of sheds and trading estates.

CHURCHES

ALL SAINTS. Along the Market Place. The E end is close to the High Street. The church is varied in outline and fits well into its surroundings. The tower is placed at the NW corner. It was set into an existing building, as its S wall stands on the first bay of an E.E. N arcade, the oldest remaining feature (but some N walling is Norman). That it was an arcade and not a tower arch is evident from the fact that the W respond of the arch is a respond indeed – it has stiff-leaf decoration and a shaft – but the E respond is simply a round pier with an octagonal abacus. Some of the buttresses and the upper parts of the tower are of brick, rebuilt after the Civil War, and the very top is Victorian. Otherwise the church is essentially Perp, except for the N aisle windows, which with their crocketed arches and tracery look Dec. The S aisle, with its pinnacled buttresses and saints in niches, is a careful rebuilding of 1861 by *George Gilbert Scott* (builder, *John Bird* of Brampton); he had restored the nave, N aisle and chancel in 1859, adding the organ chamber and vestry. The organ chamber is the prettiest feature of the church, with St Cecilia at the apex playing on a positive organ. The arcades, of four (on the N side of course three) bays, are char-acteristically Early Perp. Piers of standard moulded section, arches of two sunk-quadrant mouldings, the arch tops slightly ogee and with a label up to the clerestory sill. The E window of the S aisle has mullions carried down blank to form a reredos of angels holding shields with instruments of the Passion (restored and gilded in 1932 by *Ninian Comper*). Blank arcad-ing also below the S windows of the aisle. In the SE corner charming niche on a shaft with foliated capital and with a canopy. Good Perp chancel roof with carved bosses and angels, recoloured in 1950. All the roofs have stone angel corbels and carved wooden saints. – CHANCEL FURNISHINGS. Of Scott's restoration, typically high quality. His SCREEN is now in the N aisle. FONT. Stone octagon with traces of blind arcading; base and elaborate crown cover of 1927. – STAINED GLASS. The clerestory windows are of 1862, by *Clayton & Bell*. Trios of Old Testament prophets. – By the same, the former chancel E window, now in the W wall of the S aisle. It shows the Te Deum in the presence of Prophets, Apostles and Saints, and also the Venerable Bede, William of Wykeham, Archbishop Cranmer, Bishop Ridley, George Herbert, Newton, Handel, Queen Victoria and Prince Albert, and the Duke of Wellington. – The W window is by *C. E. Kempe*, 1900 (with his wheatsheaf). – The E window (war memorial) is by *Kempe & Co.*, 1920 (with the tower emblem), a tree of life with the martyr saints. – The other chancel windows are by *Heaton, Butler & Bayne*, 1872 (Sermon on the Mount) and *W. F. Dixon* of London, 1878 (a grim Last Supper). – MONUMENTS. Alice Weaver †1636, wife of a mercer from London. She died travelling through Huntingdon. Tablet with kneeling figures in relief. The top has already – very early – an open scrolly pediment. At the base the 'Mercer's Maiden'. The Mercers were patrons of a preaching lectureship founded in the town by a Mr R. Fishbourn in 1625. – Two plain tablets with crests: Fullwood family, erected 1756, and Sir Lionel and Elizabeth Walden, erected 1749.

Good Victorian CHURCHYARD RAILINGS, and outside the NE corner, the SOUTH AFRICAN WAR MEMORIAL of 1903 by *Edgar W. Davies* and *A. J. S. Scott-Gatty*. Of unusual design, with a tempietto of columns with scalloped capitals and conical roof topped by a lantern. Inside, St George, after Donatello, by *Guglielmo Tosi*.

ST MARY, High Street. The W tower is the most ornate piece of the church, Perp, probably mid- to late C15, with a doorway flanked by niches and decorated with quatrefoils in spandrels, buttresses clasping and at the same time set back and enriched by gablets, and niches for images on brackets with e.g. a Pelican and a Green Man, bell-openings as pairs of two-light openings, two quatrefoil friezes, and battlements and pinnacles. On the ground stage to the N was originally large gabled blank arcading. But the NE part of the tower came down in 1607 and was rebuilt by 1613, the date on the N side. Part of that repair was in brick but it was refaced in stone on the E side in 1913. But the earliest parts of the church are, first, the remains of flat Norman buttresses in the SE corner of the nave and the SW corner of the S aisle – proving the existence of a large, aisled Norman church – and then the chancel, early C13, with a priest's doorway which still has waterleaf capitals and keeled moulding inside. Keeled shafts are reused inside the Perp S windows but on the N side is a complete lancet window, with shafts inside and out. Two more lancets are reset in the vestry and organ chamber (added 1869 by *R. W. Edis*, who was born at Huntingdon and restored the church in 1862); the latter has late C13 Y-tracery. The position of the priest's doorway shows that the chancel was originally longer and there is an odd piece of arcading preserved in the NW buttress. The present E wall is of 1876–7 by *A. W. Blomfield*, with three tall and stepped lancets, replacing one window with intersecting tracery – indicating that the shortening of the chancel took place in the late C13. Blomfield also replaced the chancel and N aisle roofs. Aisles and clerestory appear Perp externally, but the arcades tell a different story. They are both E.E., S perhaps of *c.* 1240, N of *c.* 1260. The S arcade has a variety of supports. The W respond of the S arcade has a stiff-leaf capital on a short triple shaft, two piers are octagonal, one is round, and one consists of four keeled major and four minor shafts. The arches are of many fine mouldings, and the stops of the hoodmould are pretty stiff-leaf balls. The narrow E arch is late C17. The N arcade is simpler, mostly of standard elements, e.g. double-chamfered arches, but much of this side is a rebuilding of 1608–20 after the tower collapse, as the inscriptions in several places show. Tower arch of 1869. FONT. E.E. – ALTAR. By *Ninian Comper*, 1920, with carved figures on riddel posts. – BENEFACTION BOARDS. Late C18. Lugged frames with arched tops. – SCULPTURE. Oak figures of St Stephen, St Bartholomew, St Jude and St Matthew. *c.* 1500. They come originally from All Saints but were previously fixed to the outside of the Archdeaconry Library. – STAINED GLASS. E window 1876, given by Archdeacon Vesey. – Chancel N, St David, by *J. Powell & Sons*, 1900. S *c.* 1884, N aisle 1895, S aisle 1881, 1900 and 1897, makers unknown. – MONUMENTS. Tablets, tidied away into the tower in 1876, the largest to the Carcassonnett family, 1749, assigned to *Peter Scheemakers* (pilasters, moulded black frame and broken pediment), and Sir Nicholas Pedley †1685. Wall tablet with an urn and two cherubs at the base. Attributed to *Grinling Gibbons* (GF). – Also some enjoyable cartouches, especially Elizabeth Sayer †1729 with scrolly carving, fringed drapery and cherubs' heads. – First World War Memorial. The reredos of 1896, by *J. Powell & Sons*, with opus sectile angels; re-erected under the tower in 1920 (cf. Brampton). In the N aisle, George Maule †1812. By *Coles* of Thrapston and Huntingdon. – In the chancel, the Crimean War Memorial (31st Hunts Regiment), 1857. White on grey, with draped flags, sword and a helmet.

ST BARNABAS, Conygear Road, Oxmoor. 1968 by *Donald Gillatt*. The segmental-vaulted worship space at the front intersects with a hyperbolic paraboloid roof over the hall.

Former ST JOHN THE EVANGELIST, George Street. Neo-Norman of 1845 by *W. G. Habershon* of St Neots, paid for by the evangelical Lady Olivia Bernard Sparrow of Brampton Park. Yellow brick but with an ornate portal of Caen stone, with billet and beakhead mouldings. The windows had chevron surrounds too and there was originally an impressive spirelet over the centre. It all looks sad now. It became Anglican after Lady Olivia's death and was slightly altered by *R. Hutchinson*.

ST MICHAEL (R.C.), Hartford Road, Newtown. 1900–1 by *A. J. C. Scoles*. Brick and stone, round-arched, very simple. The entrance is in a gabled projection, now flanked by late C20 additions in matching style. Over the door a rather butch SCULPTURE of St Michael.

Former UNION CHAPEL, Grammar School Walk. 1826, for Baptists and Independents, probably by *Edward Harratt*, brother of the first minister. Three bays at front and sides; two arched windows at the back.

METHODIST CHURCH, High Street. 1878 by *R. Hutchinson*. Rock-faced, geometrical tracery, no tower.

TRINITY FREE CHURCH, Buttsgrove Way, Oxmoor. By *Max Lock & Partners*, 1969. Low-key, brick, with a drum-shaped worship space and flat-roofed halls.*

CEMETERY, Priory Road. CHAPELS by *R. Hutchinson*, 1855, a 'rogue' job, as cemetery chapels often are. L-shaped, of ironstone, with a totally asymmetrically placed angle turret. Lodge also by him, 1856.

PUBLIC BUILDINGS

CASTLE. *See* Perambulation 1 below.

69   TOWN HALL, Market Hill. Red brick, of seven bays and three storeys. The two-storey rear portion with its fine cupola is of 1745 and probably designed by its builder *Benjamin Timbrell*, the London carpenter.† Most of the cost was met by the 4th Earl of Sandwich and Charles Clarke of Farm Hall, Godmanchester. It had short wings whose ground floor was open, in the way usual for market halls. The top storey, containing the Assembly Room, has Venetian windows on the sides and rear. At first floor another Venetian (W) and large tripartite (E), each lighting double-height courtrooms. There were alterations by *Richard Holland*, the London builder, in 1784–6 but the whole of the front, with its strong three-bay projection with arched sashes and a pediment, is an addition of 1817–18 by *S. P. Cockerell*, who was also one of the magistrates. At that time the whole building was stuccoed (foolishly stripped in 1936–7) and had a continuous colonnade which ran round the three sides, infilled in 1865 by *R. Hutchinson*. The former Courts have their original fitments, with minor C19 alterations. The staircase is late C17, retained from the previous Town Hall, with turned balusters. Fielded panelling in the former Grand Jury Room at first floor, and on the second floor, in the front projection, the former Tea Room (Council Chamber) with plaster octagonal ceiling. Adjoining this is the Card Room (Mayor's Parlour) and the splendid Assembly Room which fills the length of the original building and has a balustraded recess on the S side. The dome in the centre is 1817. Full-length C18 and C19 portraits in good frames.

LAW COURTS AND COUNTY COUNCIL OFFICES, George Street/Walden Road. 2004–9 by *CPMG Architects* of Nottingham. The large blocks of FLATS adjoining to the S, the LIBRARY

---

* Successor to the impressive Trinity Church in the High Street (1867–8 by *John Tarring*, dem. 1967).

† I am very grateful to Richard Hewlings for his research on the architects of the Town Hall.

AND ARCHIVES building on Princes Street, and the DISTRICT COUNCIL OFFICES between St Mary's Street and Castle Moat Road are of a piece with it.

ARCHDEACONRY LIBRARY, Princes Street. 1890 by *R. Hutchinson*, his last work for the town. A good piece of Elizabethan revival.

LIBRARY AND ARCHIVES, Princes Street. *See* Perambulation 1 below.

CROMWELL MUSEUM. Originally the W end of the long infirmary hall of the Hospital of St John, founded by David, Earl of Huntingdon (†1219) (cf. Conington). It was owned by the burgesses and so escaped destruction at the Dissolution to be fitted up in 1565 as the Grammar School – the one attended by Cromwell and Pepys. What survives is the two W bays of nave and aisles, but there were seven bays and the premises of the master, the refectory etc., round a courtyard to the N. The remaining fragment is of *c.* 1170–90. The S arcade was built before the N arcade. On the S side are round piers with multi-scalloped capitals and square abaci. The arches are round, and one has chevron at right angles to the wall. Also there is a hoodmould with nutmeg. On the N side the abaci are round, the arches pointed, and one capital has stylized upright leaves. These details can now be seen from outside as well as inside, as the outer aisle walls have disappeared. The façade has the portal not in the centre but to the r., with a small window on its l. However, before the N aisle was built it was central. The portal has two orders of colonnettes and the arches chevron, also at right angles to the wall. Above is a frieze of five large shafted arches containing two windows, but otherwise blank. All this was covered over in brick in the later C16 and given a Dutch gable, but in 1877 the whole building was rebuilt 3 ft higher up by *R. Hutchinson*, who invented the gable with its vesica opening and bellcote. At the back a window with flowing tracery. The expense was met by the Irish playwright Dion Boucicault, whose son had been killed in a train crash at Abbots Ripton. The buildings behind it are the former SCHOOL HOUSE, again by Hutchinson.

HUNTINGDONSHIRE REGIONAL COLLEGE, California Road, Oxmoor. Formerly the Technical College, of 1963–5 by *Twist & Whitley*. Glass, grey brick, and black granite chippings. Nicely grouped and only one to two storeys high. Remodelled entrance in a brighter palette of colours by *Saunders Boston*, 2011.

SCHOOLS. Nothing now of before 1950 except the NATIONAL SCHOOL of 1842, off Walden Road.* ST PETER'S SCHOOL, St Peter's Road, is Anglo-Dudok of as late as 1953–7 (it looks as if it were done in the 1930s) by the County Architect, *S. M.*

---

*Pevsner noted BROOKSIDE SCHOOL, free Tudor with three identical gables, of 1905, and the GRAMMAR SCHOOL of 1939 in the Brampton Road, which was interwar-Tudor with William and Mary hipped roofs but mullioned and mullioned and transomed windows. Both have been demolished.

Holloway. The best of the next decade is the HARTFORD COUNTY JUNIOR SCHOOL in Mayfield Road of 1963–4, yellow brick and very well grouped. This is by *K. G. Sparrow*, County Architect, and *K. G. Dines*.

FIRE STATION, Hartford Road. 1964–5 by *K. G. Sparrow*, the County Architect. A good-looking job for its date. For the Fire Service HQ, *see* Hinchingbrooke below.

COUNTY GAOL (former), St Peter's Road. A model establishment of 1828–9, by *William Wilkins* (his clerk of works was the Irish architect *James Gallier*). Yellow brick, classical. The gatehouse is demolished but the two pavilions l. and r. for the governor and warden remain. Between and behind, the octagon which was the watching-centre at the centre of a radial arrangement of cell blocks. Enlargements of 1850 by *Thomas Smith* were taken down after the prison closed in 1886.

RAILWAY STATION, Brampton Road. Opened 1850 by the Great Northern Railway; probably by *Henry Goddard*. Italianate.

PERAMBULATIONS

1. The town centre

69   MARKET HILL, the market square, is the natural start. The bronze WAR MEMORIAL ('the brooding soldier', essentially Rodin's 'thinker' in tin hat and puttees) is by *Lady Katherine Scott*. The best house no doubt is WALDEN HOUSE behind the church, built for Lionel Walden, the town's M.P. in the late C17. Of red brick, five bays and two storeys, with hipped roof, brackets beneath the eaves, tall panelled chimneys, giant Ionic angle pilasters, raised window surrounds, and Dutch garlands below the first-floor windows – a tradition from the Hugh May generation. Inside, the staircase has heavy turned balusters. It has additions of *c.* 1885–1900 for H. C. Geldart, a partner in the banking firm of Veasey, Desborough & Co. Next to it, WYKEHAM HOUSE, early C19. Yellow brick with a porch of heavy pillars. Beside it is the entrance to the THE FALCON INN with a shallow segmental archway, robust gate, and a nice bow window over it; the inn is set at right angles, running behind Wykeham House (with cellar beneath the house), indicating its C16 origins. On the other side, i.e. at No. 110 HIGH STREET, is an Early Georgian three-bay, three-storey house with giant brick pilasters and both mid-windows round-arched. Parapet with the date 1727 and cipher of John Pasheller, who established the town's first bank here. Next to it, No. 111, the former FOUNTAIN HOTEL, of six bays with a two-bay pediment and a Venetian mid-window, though its façade is a complete reconstruction by *S. Inskip Ladds* in 1912 using the original bricks. Ground floor badly altered.

We continue down PRINCES STREET, s of the Town Hall, which has some early C19 houses on the w side, and then the LIBRARY AND ARCHIVES of 2009 by *CPMG Architects*. Fully glazed façade within yellow brick flanks and oversailing timber-

Huntingdon, Commemoration Hall.
Lithograph, *c.* 1842

clad upper storeys at the rear. Behind this, restored and
extended as part of the same scheme for this part of the town,
is LAWRENCE COURT (registry office), which is a mid- to
late C18 L-plan house with a Venetian window lighting the
stair. The pretty 1880s porch has lively carved Gothic corbels
inside.

Now we go down the pedestrianized HIGH STREET from
the market place to the bridge and not with much pleasure at
first, because the predominantly C20 façades and shops offer
nothing of interest. There are little passages off, reminders of
the medieval pattern, mostly going nowhere. In High Street is
another small square, with blocks of the 1980s, on the site of
the churchyard of St Benet. The church disappeared in 1802.
Next, on the same side, the first memorable front in the form
of the COMMEMORATION HALL, the former Literary and
Scientific Institute of 1841–2. Established by Robert Fox, a
surgeon from Godmanchester. *Pocock & Glover* of Huntingdon
were the architects. Stuccoed, of three bays, with giant Corinthian pilasters, a deep entablature and a *Coade* statue of Pallas
Athene (Minerva) on the top. Surprisingly late for the Grecian
style.

Now High Street rediscovers some architectural consistency.
Nos. 36–38 is a Late Georgian group of two-and-a-half-storey
houses in grey brick, with arched doorways in reeded surrounds. Nos. 28–32 make a long group of red two-storey
houses with modillion frieze. The climax is COWPER HOUSE
(Nos. 29 and 30), where Cowper, the poet, lived from 1765,

when it was the house of the Rev. Morley Unwin. This has a steep three-bay pediment and, on the first floor, window-lintels with brick frills. This front is early C18, and two of the houses have doorcases of similar date. The last house of the group has a touch of Gothick in the windows and a doorway inside. Inside, a fine room with fireplace, doorcase etc., the details suggesting *c.* 1720. But the timber-framed structure is probably C16, and the upper room is open to the roof with arched braces. Hidden by the panelling on the ground floor are fragments of Elizabethan paintings with large flowers and leaves and a dog. Some smaller leaf painting has been discovered in an upper room as well.*

Opposite St Mary's church is CASTLE HILL HOUSE, built in 1787 for Owsley Rowley, a lawyer and adviser to Lord Montagu. It stands back on its own, after houses along the High Street were demolished to make way for it. Of fine yellow brick with a gambrel roof adding presence. Good pedimented doorway and guilloche bands to the first floor at front and back. N additions, for the Veasey family, bankers, who owned the house 1837–1916. Its grounds formerly extended as far as the river, including Castle Hill (*see* below), but now its unsylvan back drop is the District Council Offices (*see* above). In moving on towards the bridge, more Late Georgian yellow-brick houses, No. 151 and Nos. 154–155, with giant pilasters. In the yard behind these the buildings of the former GAOL. (Beneath is the condemned cell with a vault on a brick pillar.) No. 152 between the two has a nice late C18 doorway. Then, back on the S side, across the ring road, the OLD BRIDGE HOTEL, another late C18 house with gambrel roof. A specially good late C18 doorway, reset. Corinthian columns, finely detailed frieze, pediment.

Behind the hotel lie the earthworks of HUNTINGDON CASTLE. It was established in 1068 by William the Conqueror, later held by the Earls of Huntingdon and dismantled after the siege of 1173–4. The inner bailey lay along the Ouse, the motte to its W, now only 12 ft (3.6 metres) high, and an outer bailey followed W of both.

The BRIDGE to Godmanchester is of the early C14. It is called 'lately built' in 1332. It has cutwaters to both sides. Their tops differ W (rounded) from E (pointed), an indication of two authorities building from their sides at the same time. The bridge chapel of St Thomas Becket stood on the E side of the Huntingdon portion and was converted into houses after the Dissolution. Next to the bridge a PEDESTRIAN BRIDGE, 1965–6, by *R. E. C. Darling*, engineer and county surveyor, crossing the river with an elegant sweep, and the A14 ROAD BRIDGE by *Stirling Maynard & Partners*, *c.* 1973.

On the S side of the medieval bridge, the former HUNTINGDON HOSIERY MILLS, now converted to flats. Along the river,

---

*A series of late C16 Flemish 'verdure' tapestries was acquired from the house by the Victoria and Albert Museum in 1894.

two three-storey ranges, the one nearer the bridge bigger and more important. It has round-arched openings at the back. Behind, a later seven-storey range with tiers of giant pilasters. The buildings were probably erected *c.* 1847 but adapted in the 1850s for the Veaseys. They were at first an oil and then flour mill. Opposite a charming little group of 1801, formerly the WOOLPACK INN, ending in a two-storey bow under a steep gambrel roof. That completes the SE walk.

In the area NE of HIGH STREET is a tight little district of Victorian terraces and tiny villas, e.g. in OUSE WALK, leading into VICTORIA SQUARE, which was laid out in 1860 by *R. Hutchinson* for the 7th Earl of Sandwich. It has a small green in the centre surrounded by limes, very civilized.

Now NW, along the other half of the HIGH STREET. The first notable building is the GEORGE HOTEL, a former coaching inn. Its three-storey yellow-brick front of eleven bays is of 1865–8 (by *Hutchinson*). It is vaguely Italianate with a pedimented gable and segment-headed ground-floor and taller round-arched first-floor windows for the ballroom. The yard behind still has some timber-framing in the N range and its late C17 gallery along the W side. The shape of the balusters allows the dating. The back of this range is of brick and looks a little later. C18 stables to the W.

Next, on the other side of High Street, NATWEST (former Westminster Bank), *c.* 1867, three storeys, of yellow brick, with a columnar Gothic ground floor – a townish job and entirely characteristic of its architect, *Frederic Chancellor*. Opposite is ROYAL OAK PASSAGE, the only such passage to preserve its character intact. It passes under No. 58, which was the ROYAL OAK and runs parallel to the passage. Timber-framed inside, with remains of mullioned windows in the N wall. No doubt most of its two-storey neighbours conceal similar secrets. No. 68 is early C18. Red brick and taller than the houses running up to it. Segmental-headed sashes, moulded brick keystones, brick bands and cornice and at the top the remains of cut brick Ionic capitals. Next door stood the FALCON BREWERY, of which the Victorian offices remain (now a restaurant), with classical shopfront, a falcon crest and initials of Jenkins & Jones, the brewing partnership formed in 1884. Then the CHURCHYARD of St John the Baptist (dem. 1650s) with a few C18 table tombs, notably that of Edward Ferrar (†1759; he was of the Little Gidding family), with a fine obelisk with volutes at the sides, abutting the tomb of his daughters. FERRAR HOUSE (Nos. 70 and 70a), which his father built in the early C18, stands alongside the churchyard. Red brick, of seven bays with hipped roof and arched middle window in a smart cut-and-rubbed brick surround, which continued down as the door surround. The door was destroyed in the mid C20 and an archway crudely cut through. The elegant staircase was moved at the same time. It was originally where there is still the characteristic Venetian window at the back. Later C18 wing at the rear.

Twice in the course of this stretch of the High Street, Georgian brick houses stand across the vista, an always welcome townscape effect. The first is WHITWELL HOUSE, dated 1727, of five bays and three storeys with segment-headed windows to first and second floors. It was built for Edward Audley, town alderman, whose initials are on the downpipe. Pretty railings to the front garden and a trellis porch. Arched staircase window at the side. The later back range is intriguing, also brick but with stone dressings. It is narrower than the front, just four bays with the ends projecting and a flat parapet. The side elevation is pedimented and the windows have raised surrounds with console brackets. Inside, an early C18 staircase, arches to the hall on paired columns, some panelling and fireplaces. But also one room with Tudor-style panelling and very good inglenook in best early C20 Arts and Crafts style with copper hood, and in another room one in Queen Anne style, probably for G. E. Brown of the Houghton millers who lived here c. 1912. Along the N side, extensions of c. 1900 for a service range, with half-timbered hall at the end. The second is MONTAGU HOUSE of c. 1720, also of five bays. This has a pretty doorway and a Venetian window over. Two Venetian windows to the back range also. The stair is at the side, with arch windows on two storeys, and a through passage runs across the back to another arched window.

Opposite Whitwell House is CROMWELL HOUSE (No. 82 High Street), on the site of the house where Oliver Cromwell was born. This had been remodelled in the C16 from the remains of the C13 Austin Friary, foundations and fabric of which was identified in the building in the C20. Externally it is now of c. 1810, when it was stuccoed and the N wing added. Pediment on the pilastered front and three segmental arches at ground floor. W of Whitwell House, the former PARISH ROOM for All Saints, chapel-style by *R. Hutchinson*, 1885.

2. *Around the centre*

N of the ring road, the High Street is now called ERMINE STREET, with a terrace of three three-bay houses of yellow brick, early C19, with pedimented doorways. The middle one is distinguished by columns and acanthus leaves; the other two have pilasters only. NE of the centre, on BROOKSIDE, facing the Town Park but now separated from it by the ring road, CROMWELL SQUARE is old people's housing of 1960, incorporating at the rear one range of the former MILITIA BARRACKS (1854 by *R. Hutchinson*), which became the town's first council housing in 1913. Classical, brick pilasters with round arches under pediments.

Towards Hartford (q.v.) is the area called NEWTOWN, laid out in 1860. In PRIMROSE LANE, some Corporation housing of 1920. Very typical of the date, in pairs with roughcast upper storeys and hipped roofs. Most of the area to the N and E was developed in 1962–9 by the town council, in conjunction with the London County Council, as the OXMOOR estate for families and industries moving from London. It is a classic Radburn-type layout with a perimeter road encircling shortish terraces of pitch-roofed brick houses off pedestrian walkways and greens. The centre is on MAYFIELD ROAD, where there are shops for the neighbourhood, a stubby tower of flats and low, cubic groups of housing for the elderly. Also some interesting housing in GREENHART GROVE, by *PRP Architects*, 2008–9, of timber-framed construction with timber-cladding, sedum roofs, photovoltaic panels etc.

The w edge of the town has been seriously blighted by the ring road and bypass. At the SW edge is THE WALKS, a small piece of Georgian planned development on the edge of Mill Common, of two streets at a right angle built up on one side only behind rows of lime trees. By way of The Walks lay the Georgian racecourse and Portholme meadows. Now it is split in two by the road and here is the bus station.

N, on the W part of GEORGE STREET, the former church of St John the Evangelist (*see* above), next to a mid-C19 house, built for Charles Windover, whose carriage works stood next door. Yellow brick but with florid Italianate stucco details. Later extended as the Post Office. Flats occupy the site of Windover's factory, which Pevsner described as also of yellow brick, with giant pilasters. Further out, ALMSHOUSES of 1843–52 by *George Glover*, again yellow brick, successors to an Elizabethan foundation and accordingly Tudor and humble. Opposite, MILLFIELD PARK is the former INFIRMARY of 1852–4 by *Thomas Smith* of Hertford. More yellow brick. Thirteen bays. Latest Classical, going free, i.e. still with a pediment, but with arched as well as segment-headed windows, and with garlands in the pediment, i.e. a touch of the English Classical as against Roman or Greek. Now sheltered housing, converted *c*. 1987. The way in which a stair-tower has been forced against the W bays of the front is a disgrace. The railings and PIERS to the street are of 1889, originally part of the setting for the Sandwich Memorial Fountain by *R. W. Edis*, which was terracotta with a strapwork top like Hobson's Conduit, Cambridge. It was destroyed in the 1960s.

BRIGHT INSTRUMENT COMPANY, St Margaret's Way. 1983 by *Archer Boxer Partners*. Profiled sheet metal cladding, pre-cast window units, and a gridded façade of mirror glass.

HINCHINGBROOKE
¾ m. W

HINCHINGBROOKE HOUSE, Brampton Road. Hinchingbrooke started life as a Benedictine nunnery. It was founded before 1087 and soon moved here from Eltisley in Cambridgeshire. It was never large, and at the time of the suppression had only its prioress and three nuns. In 1538 the site was given to Sir

Richard Williams (alias Cromwell), who one year later also received Ramsey Abbey. He died in 1544, but before then had begun to demolish and adapt. His son built on after 1558 and into the C17. It was sold by Sir Oliver Cromwell in 1627 to Sir Sidney Montagu, who married Paulina, great-aunt of Samuel Pepys. Sir Sidney's son became Viscount Hinchingbrooke and Earl of Sandwich at the Restoration. Pepys records the alterations made to the house in the 1660s, and more was done in the early C18 and a century later after a fire, on that occasion by *Edward Blore*. This was the first of several alterations for the 7th and 8th Earls, which take us into the early C20. The Montagus retained the house until 1962, when it was given to the County Council, which converted it as the Sixth Form Centre for HINCHINGBROOKE SCHOOL, opened 1970. The school buildings, erected to the N on the site of the stables and walled garden, are kept intentionally low and unobtrusive.

The house makes an exceptionally varied picture – 'old, spacious, irregular, yet not vast or forlorn' is how Horace Walpole describes it – but in spite of what the centuries have done, the conventual core is still recognizable. The principal range has an inner hall with skylight. This before the C19 was a courtyard and represents the cloister of the nunnery. Medieval walling exists to its S, where the church lay, and also to the W and E. Two lancet windows with splayed reveals have been uncovered on the first floor of the S range and a chamfered round-arched doorway to the room at the S end of the E range, which may have been the chapter house. Two coffins were also discovered in the SE angle of the cloister and remain *in situ*. Otherwise visible remains begin only with the Cromwells, and as they are scattered, it is more useful to walk round the outside and then the inside and sample them as they come.

95   First the GATEHOUSE, but this is not germane to Hinchingbrooke at all. It was brought over by the Cromwells from Ramsey Abbey, where part of it remains still, after the Dissolution. It dates from *c.* 1500 and has to the outside a carriage way and a pedestrian way. The duplication of the pedestrian archway is not medieval. The main archway has traceried spandrels, two wild men with clubs to the l. and r. and a quatrefoil frieze over. The pattern repeats to the inside, except that pedestrians are here no longer segregated. The battlemented top is late C18 or early C19; before that it had an oriel window over the gateway in a complete upper storey and a roof with gables. Behind the gatehouse is the entrance court to the house, although the visitor now enters at the NW. By this approach is first encountered the former BREWHOUSE and BAKEHOUSE on the l. and the detached LAUNDRY range to its NW. Both are C16, of Tudor brick and stone mixed, the latter possibly with earlier origins as a tithe barn. Its upper storey, largely rebuilt *c.* 1910, has crowstepped gables at the ends and merlons to the sides. The top storey of the brewhouse/bakehouse is C17, a row of small timber-framed gables, cutting off the hefty chimneystacks on the W side. On the E side to the entrance court,

the brick has blue-brick diapers and in the s half five buttresses, set close to each other and connected at the top by shallow arches. At the s end inside is the KITCHEN, with a large N fireplace and a W fireplace arch (visible outside).

The position of the C17 kitchen relates to the NORTH RANGE of the house, facing the entrance court, which was the Elizabethan hall and solar. It has two two-storey canted bay windows, both of the mid C16, but both built with ornamental materials of *c.* 1500. The two differ one from the other. The l. one has altogether nine lights, the r. seven, and the arch heads, all uncusped, are not the same. Between the ground-floor and the first-floor openings is decoration including Cromwell heraldry. But the overall appearance is now of 1833–6 when, after the fire, *Blore* remodelled the house drastically, moving the entrance porch one bay to the l. and adding the battlemented tower with its oriel and ogee window in the upper storey. The l. gable was also remodelled as a conventional straight Tudor type in place of one with swept sides and pedimented top. Chimneys occur in triplets and pairs.

The EAST FRONT in its N part was ashlar-faced and redone by *Blore* but must be C16, since this part contained the Great Chamber on its upper floor, open to the roof; here until the C19 stood the great bow added in 1602 (*see* below). Then C16 brickwork appears again, with the blue, vitrified bricks forming diapers. The gable is old too and seems to have been stepped from the start – the gable end of the roof behind is treated the same. In 1730 there was also a two-storey canted bay window. The canted bay window which remains to the l. is also C16, built after the E end of the nunnery church was curtailed. The pointed windows are of *c.* 1759 for the 4th Earl of Sandwich, who made other improvements to the house about this time.

Round the corner the first feature of the SOUTH FRONT is an ample bow window, and this is dated 1602, i.e. the 100

Hinchingbrooke, north-east view.
Drawing by S. and N. Buck, 1730

contribution of Sir Oliver Cromwell. It belonged originally to the N part of the E front, was deeper than it is now, and the ground floor had open arcading. A crest of strapwork and obelisks flanks the Elizabethan royal coat of arms. Mark Girouard has noted that the design of this window probably derives from John Thorpe's Babraham Hall, Cambridgeshire (*c.* 1590s, dem.), which belonged to Sir Horatio Palavicino. Cromwell married Palavicino's widow in 1602. The S front otherwise is of the 1830s, including the chimney at the W end, which covers traces of a large C16 window. In the late C18 the chimney is shown on the S front and abutted a two-storey projection with a stepped gable. Between this range and the SW tower is reused old ashlar work with a brick parapet and a reset door with pointed arch on shafts (C13?). The SOUTH-WEST TOWER itself, and its lower W projection, is mid-C16, but has windows of the C18 and later. It may be based on the prioress's lodgings.

The WEST SIDE is below all C16, but above 1660s brick with cross-windows and a straight parapet. This includes the short wing to the W – there was formerly here a long wing of the 1890s, which came down in 1947. Where this begins appears part of a medieval chimneybreast, stone with offsets, a reminder of the nunnery. The doorway beside it is also 1660s, with a straight hood on carved brackets.

The main rooms of the house are all by *Blore*, and, as in his work at Ramsey, nothing is specially grand. He was a dull man; Hinchingbrooke confirms it. In the space of the hall and solar in the N range Blore created his ENTRANCE HALL and a drawing room (now ASSEMBLY ROOM) with a Neo-Tudor ribbed ceiling with pendant drops. Of the mid C16 there remains, on the first floor of the S range, which was probably the long gallery, a large Tudor-arched fireplace with carved spandrels and Richard Cromwell's cipher. In the room at the base of the SW tower, a ceiling of moulded beams and, behind the panelling, an impressive fragment of WALL PAINTING depicting a tournament (possibly the Westminster Tournament of 1540 at which Cromwell became the 'King's Diamond'*). There is little more from the 1660s apart from the back staircase with vertically symmetrical balusters and also a doorcase with an open segmental pediment and some carved panels of scrollwork with the 1st Earl's initials made for the original staircase by *Thomas Kinward*, master joiner, *c.* 1660–2. This is reset into the staircase hall as recreated by Blore, although the present STAIRCASE is from Rolls Park, Essex (dem. 1951–3), and was fitted here by *Marshall Sisson*, who made other alterations. It is of *c.* 1660, with lush openwork panels, carving along the strings and baskets on the newels (cf. Thorpe Hall).

The LIBRARY in the S range was created in the 1860s from two rooms and fitted out with much excellent Low Countries woodwork, including a chimneypiece with two caryatids, dated

---

*This suggestion is made by Thomas Wheeley in his guide to the house.

1580, and sumptuous overdoors with medallion portraits. But the best feature of this room is the STAINED GLASS in the E bay window, an heraldic scheme in yellows and greens commemorating the 1st to the 3rd Earls, designed by *Richard Bentley* and executed for the 4th Earl by *William Peckitt* of York in 1759 (when this was the 'best eating room', in Walpole's description). In the centre it includes a scene from the life of the 1st Earl welcoming Charles II at Dover, after *Benjamin West*, and the scene of his death when his ship exploded at the battle of Sole Bay in 1672, after *Willem van de Velde the Younger*.* More late C19 heraldic glass in similar tones but of a more mechanical style at the W end. The INNER HALL, i.e. the former courtyard, was roofed over in 1909 and has an Ionic screen on one side. Some sumptuous C18 doors with swan-neck pediments are reset to the rooms behind. Also one C18 fireplace in the Walkelin Room with painted overmantel and another in the Pedigree Room, of Italian marble, with a top frieze of the birth of Venus amid gambolling mermen. The DINING ROOM in the W range is *c.* 1900, turgid Tudor.

Running along the S front of the garden is the KING'S WALK, a raised terrace with parapet of ball finials, for views down to the Alconbury Brook. Pepys mentions it. SE of this a GATEWAY, tickled up by *Blore* from medieval fragments and sculpture found during the rebuilding. It includes a strip of trailing ballflower of the type found at Offord Darcy.

NUNS' BRIDGE, S of the grounds of Hinchingbrooke, crossing the Alconbury Brook. The three E arches are of the C15 or C16. Cutwaters on the S side. Much rebuilt in the C18, including *c.* 1785 by *Richard Holland*, the London builder.

HINCHINGBROOKE PARK. After 1962 Huntingdon County Council intended to erect new County Buildings in the former park as part of a civic group. E of the house then, the COUNTY FIRE AND RESCUE SERVICE occupies a Tudoresque villa designed as the dower house in 1892 (builder, *Page* of Buckden). Low-key extension by *Cambridgeshire County Architect's Department*, 1985. N of this is the municipal Brutalist COUNTY CONSTABULARY HEADQUARTERS of 1970 by the *Cambridgeshire County Architect's Department* and HINCHINGBROOKE HOSPITAL, mostly a dismal spread of flat-roofed pre-fabricated boxes of 1979–83; one of a number of hospitals (cf. e.g. King's Lynn, Norfolk) following a model developed by the *Regional Hospital Board for East Anglia* for flexibility and further additions. The DIAGNOSTIC & TREATMENT CENTRE by *Frank Shaw Associates* of 2005 is more memorable, with bowed front

---

*Peckitt's Commission Book shows he executed two on the death scene: the one surviving 'and this last represented in a different manner'. Walpole in 1763 notes the second panel with 'The Admiral's arms . . . in a bedchamber'. A letter from George Montagu to Walpole (29.12.1759) informs him that 'Mr Bentley's designs are executed and put up in the great chamber at Hinchingbrooke of the life and death of your admirable Earl of Sandwich.' Richard Bentley's mother was the daughter of Sir John Bernard of Brampton Park. Peckitt of course also executed glass for Strawberry Hill.

and outer skin of metal and terracotta tiles. Inside, top-lit hall under an ETFE (ethylene tetrafluoroethylene) roof.

KEYSTON

At the head of the Ellington valley.

ST JOHN THE BAPTIST. A big church with a richer treatment than is usual in this area. Of grey stone. The W tower is highly unusual and also poses a problem. Its W doorway with continuous filleted mouldings is recessed behind a porch which is, however, flush with the wall. This porch has a high ogee arch beneath a gable with billet, the arch with crockets and cusped and subcusped with carved spandrels (one with the bust of a goat) and buttress shafts that end in pinnacles. Bracket on the reclining figure of a man above the door. Above is a lozenge-shaped window with flowing tracery. All this is clearly Dec. The bell-openings are Early Perp – pairs of two lights with transom and a trail of flowers around the arch as well as flowers on the tips of the cusps – and the blank arcading above is of course Perp too. But the broach spire (with high broaches), while typical of the mid–late C14 locally, has three tiers of lucarnes in alternating directions that are as clearly C13 in style with round shafts, tracery of two lights and quatrefoils in circles at the head. How does one explain this? Was it introduced in 1883–4, when repairs were made to the spire by *H. M. Townsend*? The tower buttresses are of the set-back type, with extra mouldings at the belfry stage, that become strips at the level of the blank arcading. The arch towards the nave has three chamfers and may well be Dec. Vaulting springers with grotesque heads are preserved inside the tower. As for the rest of the church, the chancel is late C13, see the pointed-trefoiled priest's doorway with stiff-leaf capitals and the chancel arch, the window with Y-tracery, and the good SEDILIA and PISCINA. Of the same time the arcades. They have piers alternatingly round and octagonal, and not only along but also across the nave. The S arcade is substantially a Victorian rebuilding or re-tooling. The N doorway with one order of (missing) colonnettes is E.E. too. Dec S porch entrance. The spacious scale of the interior is due to Late Perp transepts and clerestory, the Perp windows of specially nice design in the westernmost windows of the chancel and in the S transept and aisle. The S transept S window has been replaced but was probably like the N transept N window, which has an embattled transom. Inside, the N transept has a good roof (restored 1924), the tie-beams carved all over, e.g. with a Green Man spouting branches of leaves. This must have been a chapel, possibly for the Ferrers family, who held the manor from the late C13 until the mid C15. N aisle and nave roofs of the same time. The S transept roof is cruder and the s aisle roof was replaced, sympathetically, in 1898 by *H. M. Townsend*; the chancel roof by him in 1904. – LECTERN and READING DESK. With Jacobean pieces. – BENCHES. A few are old, and one of them in the s aisle carries the date 1608. – STAINED GLASS. In one N and one s chancel window, including one small figure and the lion of St Mark. C15. More in the N transept. – Chancel N lancets, C13 patterns by *Willement*, 1853. – The lavish E window, and the flowing Dec tracery setting, is by *F. C. Eden*, 1919. Partly a war memorial with St George and Joan of Arc flanking the Crucifixion. Christ in glory above and the Evangelists along the base, especially well done. The silvery architecture is crammed with small figures. – MONUMENTS. N aisle w. Oaken cadaver from a C15 tomb (cf. Bishop Fleming at Lincoln). – N transept. Early C16 indent for a brass, reset in the w wall. Two kneeling figures, a device and D monogram. Is it for one of the Devereux who obtained the manor through marriage to the Ferrers in the mid C15? – LYCHGATE of 1936 by *S. Inskip Ladds*.

w of the church must have stood the manor house, described as 'newly built' in 1589, when it belonged to Robert Devereux, Earl of Essex. The house now called MANOR HOUSE is mid-C18, its wide front of mellow red brick given a good makeover in 1908 by *Martin S. Briggs* in Queen Anne style. Across the road, a sublime rockery garden with mature cedars and sequoia, of the same date and also by *Briggs*.

KIMBOLTON 0060

The little town stretches w–E between the church and the mansion. Geoffrey Fitzpiers, Earl of Essex and Chief Justice to King John, built the first castle and established the market and fair *c.* 1200. The pattern of the streets must have been planned at about that time.

St ANDREW. The w tower is a fine piece, early C14 throughout, including its broach spire – see the details of the three tiers of lucarnes – which has sculpted finials to the broaches (cf. Buckworth etc.). The w portal has thin shafts with deep mouldings between them, and each group of mouldings has ballflower. The w window and the bell-openings have Y-tracery. At the top of the tower itself is a frieze of small heads. Perp s aisle and handsome s porch with, at the entrance, openwork tracery spandrels and on the side walls wide blank arches enclosing the (now blocked) small windows. The s door has a little C14 tracery. The N aisle is Perp too, but the clerestory is still Dec and has handsome figured stone corbels as the roof supports inside. The chancel s wall is of brick, probably of 1748, with a stone arched surround to the door, but inside in the N wall is a blocked late C13 window with formerly intersecting tracery.

The chancel arch matches such a date. The N and S chapels, however, are Perp, like the aisles, and both have their original roofs with carved figures and bosses. The nave roof is original too but only parts of the chancel roof. The oldest feature of the church is the arcades. Four bays. The S arcade has round piers and arches of one chamfer and one slight chamfer, i.e. early C13. The N arcade with alternatingly round and octagonal supports has a little nailhead in the capitals and a big nailhead hoodmould. The arches are of one chamfer, one slight chamfer, and a third chamfer. So that may be later C13. However, the NW respond is earlier than either arcade. With its single fleur-de-lis-like leaf motifs it looks *c.* 1200. The tower arch has three continuous chamfers, which suggests *c.* 1300, and that agrees with the external evidence. The N aisle chapel is on a mezzanine above the Montagus' vault created *c.* 1710 when the E end was remodelled (*William Coleman*, the duke's clerk of works at the castle, was paid for inserting a window, probably that in the E wall of the vault) and outside is a fine C19 stone Neo-Tudor porch, with the Montagu coat of arms and heraldic beasts on its gable. N vestry of 1847. – FONT. Brought in 1918 from the castle but before that at Little Stukeley, where it had been a cattle trough. Support of that time. Very large and very uncouth. Consequently called Saxon, though more probably C12. No decoration at all. Dr Ron Baxter rightly says it looks like an arch springer inverted. – SCREENS. The screen to the S chapel is uncommonly good. It has broad ogee-headed divisions with tracery above. Four of the panels of the dado have PAINTINGS of *c.* 1500 of SS Anne, Michael, Edmund and Edward Confessor against a vivid red ground. Note the mannered elegance of St Edmund. – The screen to the N chapel is a little simpler.* – ROYAL ARMS. Queen Anne, 1712. – STAINED GLASS. In the S chapel one small complete figure of Symon; in the N chapel E window a few bits; C15. The E window. (Adoration of Magi) is by *A. O. Hemming & Co.*, 1887, but less good than the densely populated five-light S chapel E window of 1890 by *J. Powell & Sons* (*C. Hardgrave*) in memory of the 7th Duke of Manchester. S aisle window (Angel appearing to Maries) signed by *Lavers, Barraud & Westlake*, 1868, and Good Samaritan, †1899. N aisle NE, war memorial of 1922 by *Morris & Sons*, Kennington, and rather above their usual standard. But the showpiece is the S chapel SE window by *Tiffany* of New York (designer, *Frederick Wilson*), 1902, commissioned by Duchess Consuelo in memory of her daughters (†1895 and 1900).†They kneel before Christ, whose robe of patterned brocade is the best of the layered effects created by the artist's opalescent technique. – MONUMENTS. – S chapel. 1st Earl of Manchester

---

*The sculpture noted by Pevsner of the Virgin and Child with the Baptist by *P. Romanelli*, 1859, after Raphael's Belle Jardinière in the Louvre, has been stolen.
†After the death of her first daughter the countess commissioned an extravagant tomb from *Waldo Story* which was to have stood in the S chapel (Kimbolton Local History Journal, No. 13, 2009).

†1642. Attributed to *William Wright*. Standing wall monument with the impressive conceit of a marble table with an arched front but angle columns, a black top slab, and on it a white marble cushion with an inscription. Against the back wall, and as though quite a separate monument, the commemorative inscription flanked by two black columns. A third column stands on a bracket above and is crowned by a helmet with crest. Between the columns, the sun and moon. Over the monument is a CEILURE, apparently *ex situ*. – To the l. and r. of this, identical cartouches set on plinths to two (of the five) wives of the 2nd Earl (who has no memorial): Lady Mandeville †1641/2 and the Countess of Manchester †1658. The fleshy, gristly details are characteristic of the later date and both are attributed to *Thomas Burman* (GF). – Many tablets, the best to Walpole's friend George Montagu †1780, signed *J. Wilton*, very sparse and elegant, with an urn on top. Put up by Frederick Montagu. – Consuelo, Dowager Duchess of Manchester; signed and dated by *R. S. Marceaux*, 1912. White marble relief in the *schiacciato* technique, very Paris-Salon in style. She is seen surrounded by clouds and reaches up to angels, her twin daughters, who died before her. – William Ashton (s aisle) †1722. A shield between a swan-neck pediment, fluted pilasters and death's head at the base. Signed by *Samuel Cox* of Northampton.

LYCHGATE, probably by *S. Inskip Ladds*, *c.* 1929; the WAR MEMORIAL cross outside it was designed by him in 1920.

CEMETERY, ½ m. N. MORTUARY CHAPEL, GATES and LODGE of the 1850s, picturesque Gothic, the walls with diaper patterns and roofs of red and blue fishscale tiles.

KIMBOLTON PREP SCHOOL, Thrapston Road. The former GRAMMAR SCHOOL of 1876 by *John Ladds*. Domestic Gothic, in red brick with yellow dressings, and informal, with the master's house at one end and a bellcote cupola above the two-storey school house. Good interwar additions and later.

PERAMBULATION

N of the church, houses open directly onto the grassy churchyard, a very nice effect. HIGH STREET is wide, wide enough for a market place, neat, well-kept, and disappears round a bend at both ends to rejoin the main road, with the N angle pavilion of the castle's gatehouse closing the view to the E so the town at its heart feels intimate and secret. It also has the most attractive streetscape in Huntingdonshire, with an overwhelming Georgian inflection made yet prettier by the painting of the fronts of houses in pastel tones. Several are former inns, with large archways to former yards and there are some nice doorways, notably the late C18 pedimented ones of WHITE HOUSE and COURT HOUSE, and the recessed round arch with fanlight and columns of early C19 CLANCARTY HOUSE. This is three storeys high and of a more urban character than its neighbours. KIMBOLTON HOUSE, which was owned by the Welsteads, the

68

wealthiest gentry family of the town, is also tall and has a door of attached columns and a triglyph frieze, but what catches the eye is the all-over covering of close dark green trellis-work (a replacement of the mid-C19 original), bringing order to a disordered arrangement of windows, the clue to its earlier origins. Older buildings lie behind most of the other fronts too, notably No. 19 (La Côte d'Or), s side, which has a charming Late Georgian bowed shop window almost filling its single bay width. This is the gable end of a medieval house that lies at right angles, dated by its carpentry to *c.* 1300, with entry from the side passage. Several other frontages also retain their side passages, some revealing the timber-framing of the houses, and evidence of jetties, e.g. Nos. 12 and 14 across the street. Nos. 4–8 disguise the remains of a timber-framed Wealden house. That is unique in Huntingdonshire. Next, the NEW SUN INN, whose C18 façade has a pediment containing an ogee window.

The medieval pattern is also traceable in the backs of these properties where there were narrow passages (only Watson's Passage remains open), leading through the crofts to EAST STREET. This runs parallel with High Street and was its service street. More good small houses here too, e.g. DIAL HOUSE, C17 with a large painted sundial and rare examples of pargetting in the cornice. Just before this at the N end, set out of sight, is the former MORAVIAN CHAPEL of 1823, the best of the town's several former chapels, with giant pilasters, pyramid pinnacles and arched windows with intersecting tracery. Extended in matching style, 1836. Further down on the s side, HOTHORPE is of *c.* 1500, with gabled cross-wing and timber-framing crudely exposed. The C18 doorways of No. 7 and No. 5 are the prettiest at Kimbolton, both houses earlier C18; the latter house has some panelled rooms inside.

Set back off the sw end of High Street is the former VICARAGE, in two phases and looking like two houses, one early to mid-Georgian of red brick with a three-bay front and shallow roof, the other of 1820 by *John Quick*, surveyor of Kimbolton, of similar character and of the usual yellow. There is a curious blind oculus in its wall. Good panelled room and open-string stair in the C18 part. Porch of 2010. The garden (now divided) is enclosed on two sides by a moat and on the third by a crinkle-crankle wall. W of the church is the Victorian former VILLAGE SCHOOL, one part with a bellcote on its gable and plate tracery.

KIMBOLTON CASTLE. *Vanbrugh* had turned to architecture with spectacular suddenness in 1699, when he designed Castle Howard, the largest country house of the period up to that date in England. Among the first letters referring to the building is one to Charles Montagu, the 4th Earl of Manchester.* So when the Earl, in 1707, decided to remodel Kimbolton, he invited Vanbrugh to design and supervise the work. The choice was even more understandable if one remembers that mean-

---

*He was created the 1st Duke of Manchester in 1719.

while Vanbrugh had also designed Blenheim and that both men were members of the famous Kit Kat club, which also counted among its number the Duke of Newcastle, Vanbrugh's client later at Claremont. The job at Kimbolton must at first have appeared unpromising. There had been a castle on the site in the Middle Ages, succeeding the MOTTE that lies on the rising ground ½ m. wsw of the present house. The mansion developed into four ranges around a courtyard with an outer court and protected by a double moat. The major remodellings were in the late C15 for Anne Stafford and again shortly after 1521 by Sir Richard Wingfield and again in 1617–20 for Sir Henry Montagu. Of this building remain a single ogee-headed window, a few minor Tudor mullioned windows at ground floor and some Jacobean mullioned attic windows. All are in the former N wall of the s range, which is now an inner wall, standing to the full height of the house, after this range was doubled in depth and pushed into the court in the late C17. Moreover, there are two arched doorways, one in this same wall at its E end and again Tudor, the other in the return wall that is possibly late C15. These opened into the courtyard.

Charles Montagu inherited in 1683; the remodelling of the interior façades of the courtyard was done soon after, probably *c.* 1690 after his marriage to one of the Grevilles, and almost certainly by *Henry Bell* of King's Lynn. The walls are of exposed brick, basement and two storeys except for the five bays of the E range, which has large windows through both floors and projections in the angles l. and r. The contemporary extension of the s range into the court effected symmetry on the E and w sides by bringing the existing w gateway and entrance to the hall in the E range into the centre of their elevations; previously they were off-centre and in this we can still recognize the fact that here was the hall already in the Tudor building. Talman had done something very similar at Drayton (Northants), just a few years earlier. A wide staircase with a splendid wrought-iron handrail leads to a portal with unfluted Corinthian columns and a segmental pediment with recessed centre and some carving. There is a coat of arms above it. This is what must be regarded as the main entrance before the C18. This whole bay is stone-faced, and this side also has giant stone pilasters above the basement. The rest is finely jointed red brick like the s and w sides of the courtyard, and it is an unexplained curiosity that the N wall and the N part of the W wall is of inferior colour and craftsmanship: has it been rebuilt? The windows have lintels decorated with two leaf volutes meeting in the middle around heraldry and the earl's cipher on the E and w walls and carved heads to N and s, decoration that has much in common with *Henry Bell*'s decoration of the Sessions House, Northampton, and buildings in his native King's Lynn. The lead downpipes are among the finest in all England, with acanthus leaves bursting upwards at the heads and other vigorous ornaments. It is the pleasantest contrast to the severity of the outer elevations created by *Vanbrugh*. That work was

prompted, we hear, when the SE corner collapsed in 1707. So
Vanbrugh went in July, at the invitation of the countess while
the earl was ambassador to Venice, taking with him *Hawksmoor*,
who was his chief assistant and collaborator at Castle Howard
and Blenheim and was paid for 'two packets of draughts' in
1710. They and *William Coleman* agreed on the design. Coleman
was a joiner, who had acted on the earlier remodelling and also
submitted plans of his own in 1707, but when these were set
aside he became the resident clerk of works; for Vanbrugh says
that, 'if only they had such a man at Blenheim, it would save
£1,000 a year'. Coleman, in return, said about Vanbrugh: 'If
their is anay Credet Gayned In this Bulden, I beg that he may
have it.' Building went on quickly, as Coleman's account book
in the county archives records. In 1708 the battlements were
reached. In 1709 work went on on the S side and the E side.
In 1710 the W front went up – there are payments in that year
to the mason *John Johnson* of Kingsthorpe, Northampton. By
1719, probably, the E portico was complete.

113   We can start DESCRIPTION with the E front. It is of thirteen bays,
coming forward from the angles in two steps to reach the
PORTICO, the most monumental feature of the house, though
of course nothing like as grand as that at Blenheim or indeed
as dramatic. That is the remarkable thing. Kimbolton is very
severe and of few words. The portico has two giant Doric
columns *in antis* and closed bays l. and r. with giant pilasters
flanking two tiers of niches. There is a triglyph frieze and a
balustrade. A wide staircase leads up to the portico and below
this at an angle are two separate flights of steps. That is all. But
for the portico there are no building accounts left, and this is

Kimbolton Castle, east portico.
Elevation and plans by A. Galilei, *c.* 1719

where a complication comes in. Vanbrugh at the beginning had apparently thought of three giant arches instead of the portico. There is a sketch of this (in the Victoria and Albert Museum), in all probability by Vanbrugh himself. Moreover, in 1714 *Alessandro Galilei* came to England from Rome, and a letter of 1719 exists in which the earl refers to the front towards the town as finished, to 'what you designed over ye gate', to two pairs of stairs to be made in the middle of the colonnade, 'as you first proposed it', and to chimneypieces being made in London 'according to your design'. There is also in the county archives a drawing dated to before 1719 of the great E portico inconspicuously initialled A.G.,* and the declaration of a visitor in 1724 that he '. . . gave the Design for the Castle the main front of which has four windows on each side of a noble Doric Portico to which you ascend 18 steps'. What does all this amount to? Pevsner's opinion was that 'Its significance has . . . been overrated. Galilei, the architect of the famous façade of S. Giovanni in Laterano, of the Corsini Chapel in the same church, and of the façade of S. Giovanni dei Fiorentini was only twenty-three when he reached England and twenty-eight when the letter reached him. The three works in Rome date from 1732 and after. Moreover, Kimbolton by 1714 was finished.' Nevertheless, Elizabeth Kieven has shown that the portico must date to 1718–19, and it is clear from the letters that Galilei was at the very least involved in the design of the flights of steps from the portico. The drawing, however, may just as well represent Galilei's proposals, unfulfilled, for some enriched ornamentation to the plain wall and door behind the colonnade. It has nothing at all of the festive swagger of Galilei's later designs. Yet there is a further complication regarding the portico, for another visitor in 1727 claims it as the work of *Thomas Archer*, 'about ten years'† ago and there is indeed a clear resemblance to the portico of St John, Smith Square, in London.

So, to Vanbrugh. The recessed wings of his front are lower and have a basement and two floors, segment-headed windows with flat raised surrounds, angle quoins of equal length or, if you like, rusticated giant pilaster strips, and top battlements. They are a surprise after the strictly classical portico. But we know that Vanbrugh liked medieval evocation, and in this case we have Vanbrugh's letter to the earl telling him that this 'castle air' would give the building the 'masculine' character which he wanted. He was continuing in the same vein as the S front, where his work began, and here the design is only prevented from uniformity by a projection of the three middle bays and by a big portal with Doric columns, a triglyph frieze, and a straight hood. Tall arched windows on the principal floor, which is approached by steps at right angles to a terrace with

---

* Marshall Sisson drew Pevsner's attention to this. The two initials are hidden l. and r. of the scale of feet.
† This is in an anonymous travel diary in a private collection.

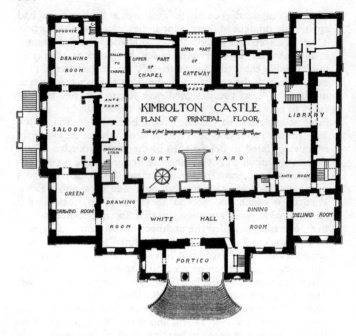

Kimbolton Castle.
Plan of principal floor

fine wrought-iron balustrade, very probably by *Thomas Warren* of Castle Ashby, who made ironwork for Vanbrugh at Blenheim (Bruce Bailey). The lead downpipes are dated 1709 and hardly less impressive than those of the court. To the W there are eleven bays, and the centre is a giant stone archway, although this is almost certainly due to the late C17 remodelling of the court. A cupola which stood over it was taken down in 1709. Over the arch may have been the decoration by Galilei referred to in the duke's letter. This façade has an unexpected rhythm. The two angle bays are three-storeyed and project forward of the rest, which is lower, perhaps another allusion to medieval castles. The N side is less formal, because on this side the angle bays hardly project. Here it appears that Vanbrugh added the centre of five bays to the existing N range on the evidence of a colonnade of five rusticated depressed arches on the ground floor (two blocked in the C19) whose keystones drop down from the aprons of the first-floor windows. At this level were the kitchens etc. The attic storey was put on only in 1869 by *William Burn* (at the end of his career and by then assisted by *J. Macvicar Anderson*). The merlon-style battlements, however, though different from Vanbrugh's, appear already in a print of 1831 and were reused. Fortunately the duke did not act on

Burn's proposals to build a porch for carriages onto the C18 portico.

The 10th Duke of Manchester sold Kimbolton in 1950 (the breaking up of the estate had started in the first half of the C20, and the final parts went in 1975). It became a school almost immediately and with commendable foresight the school acquired some of the paintings when the contents were auctioned. So the interior is still more domestic than institutional. The two entrances into the E range from the courtyard and the giant portico lead into the principal room on this side, the WHITE HALL. It is of Bell's time, not Vanbrugh's – i.e. in the Gibbons tradition. Panelled walls, wood Ionic pilasters with swags between the volutes and garlands hanging down them. These seem oddly old-fashioned for c. 1690, one would expect them c. 1660 (cf. Thorpe Hall, Peterborough), but the wooden leaf cornice and plain coved ceiling are up to date. The entrance is not in the middle of the hall. In this we can still recognize the fact that here was the hall already in the Tudor building. This position is in the medieval tradition; neither Bell nor Vanbrugh would have chosen it; and the position of the chimneypiece does in fact try to neutralize it. Above the chimneypiece is the family of the earl painted by *Giovanni Antonio Pellegrini*, the Venetian painter who had been brought to England by the earl in 1708, started with Castle Howard and began at Kimbolton in 1709. It does not prepare one for the brilliance of his work in other rooms of the house. (Behind this, discovered in 1965, is some Tudor wall painting. Its frieze has in relief a black-letter inscription which is a quotation from the Cranmer Bible. That gives a *terminus post quem* of 1540.) To the N, the DINING ROOM, with the first of a series of marble chimneypieces in the house that are of a straightforward bolection-moulded type – the standard type of the earliest C18. But the ceiling, in a rich French style, is of 1863, to *William Burn*'s design, with painted ovals of the Seasons in gilded oval frames and painted panels of flowers too. Off this room a back staircase, with a mixture of twisted and turned balusters. S of the White Hall is the RED DRAWING ROOM (in which a patch of the Tudor wall is exposed in the SE corner). This was originally coeval with the Hall and probably its dais end. Then, at the SE corner, i.e. beginning the sequence of state apartments along the S front, is the GREEN DRAWING ROOM, followed by Vanbrugh's principal room, the SALOON, Vanbrugh's 'room of Parade' which he introduced as an interval between the Drawing Room and the Earl's Bedchamber. Here is a more splendid chimneypiece, with a big shell and garlands. That may well be to Galilei's design. The N quarter of the room is treated as an alcove with a screen of two Corinthian columns close to the pieces of solid projecting wall and pairs of pilasters against the walls and in the angles. The ceiling is partly Victorian – *Burn* refers to its decoration in a letter in 1864 – with a torus-moulded border of oak leaves and painted roundels of the Arts at the corners. The next room is the former bedchamber, known as the QUEEN'S ROOM in tribute to Katherine of Aragon, who lived here for the last twenty months of her life. The fireplace here is different too, with Ionic columns and dentilled cornice. The SW room, the Great Cabinet (now the BOUDOIR), on the other hand, has the first of the Pellegrini ceilings, and this is a delightful piece, with Venus and Cupid against a light blue sky and vases and garlands in the coving.

As already noted, it was the architect of the courtyard façades who made the S range 'double-pile', and deep enough not only for an inner N corridor, but also for the principal STAIRCASE. This arrangement admittedly did not leave quite enough space for the stair, whose flight runs up E to W. It has a wrought-iron handrail, and it leads through an upper arch to the landing. To the r. of the arch is a second arch with a railing to look down. The two arches are separated by one fluted Corinthian pilaster – a daring solecism. The r. arch stands on another, at main floor level, which contains the access from the W–E corridor and all three arches have palm fronds curving around the spandrels. Below the single pilaster is another with a fat console and a hanging garland very similar to the pilasters of the White Hall. Coleman's account book refers to his making of these arches and it is quite clear that they have been concocted from older pieces, but from where is uncertain. That includes three cartouches in the heads of the arches with the garter arms of the 2nd Earl (†1671). Was the 4th Earl paying tribute to his illustrious ancestor, who had played as important a role in the restoration of Charles II as his grandson had played in the accession of William III in 1688? The latter is the theme of the PAINTED DECORATION, which on the two main walls are Trionfi of *Pellegrini*'s, in the spirit of Mantegna rather than Veronese, and darker and heavier than he usually is (overpainting?). The black-faced king on the E wall is unusual. The ceiling on the other hand has all Pellegrini's sparkle. It was completed by 1710 and is thus pre-Rococo at its most exhilarating. Only Sebastiano Ricci could do likewise at so early a date. The ceiling represents Minerva pointing to a portrait medallion of William III with fame floating and blowing the trumpet. Against the outer wall between the windows are trophies and single figures, and here, close to the eye, one can fully appreciate Pellegrini's *tocco*, i.e. his rapid, sketchy technique. Another enchanting Pellegrini ceiling is above the upper landing of the staircase, where the ceiling had to be lifted to permit the second flight of stairs to reach the upper floor, which had to be raised to accommodate Vanbrugh's saloon below. Putti are playing about with the successive coronets which the Montagus had acquired. Also female figures in niches, a monkey, a parrot, trophies, drapery, and flowers.

Finally the CHAPEL, in the W wing, reaching as far N as the great archway into the courtyard. The room was fitted up by Coleman in the early C18, including the arched W gallery, which hides the curious inward slope of the wall. But some of this may be before Vanbrugh, e.g. the S balcony with heavy drapery surround around the door below it, and also the reredos with its broken pediment of Corinthian pilasters. But *Pellegrini* painted above the altar and on its sides the Transfiguration, and on the two window walls the four Evangelists (only three are by Pellegrini, the other (St Luke) is mid C18). There is, however, no ceiling decoration at all. Fine wrought-iron ALTAR RAIL. The other rooms of the castle are predominantly former bedrooms etc. with simple panelling of the late C17 or early C18 remodelling. In the N range on the principal floor is the T-plan LIBRARY created by *Burn*. One oddity is the room in the NE corner on the principal floor, formerly the Billiard Room, with a quasi-Moorish style of decoration. The date is unknown but could be 1930s.

Of other buildings, the GATEHOUSE was designed by *Robert Adam* and built 1764–5, i.e. early in his career. It is a gatehouse only in the sense that it protects the approach to the back of the house from the town, and its real function must be regarded as a screen to hide the castle. The most interesting thing about it is that it must be meant as a conscious compliment to Vanbrugh. It is square and more solemn than Adam is otherwise. The composition is tripartite. The centre is an archway with one window either side. They have Gibbs surrounds, which is also a backward-looking motif. The archway has coupled Tuscan columns and the surround is rusticated. On the top is a balustrade. Three-bay links connect the centre with pedimented angle pavilions. They are windowless to the outside and have just a niche and angle pilasters. The surrounds of the niches are again rusticated. The composition is more or less the same towards the house. In its N part was the brewhouse, in the other part the laundry. The EAST GATES along the London Road have square rusticated pillars and early C18 wrought-iron gates (crest of the 4th Earl), probably by *Thomas Warren*. Before 1765 these stood at the E end of the axial approach to the E portico, where there is now the splendid avenue of Wellingtonia planted in the C19. *Joseph Spence* deformalized the landscape. *Adam* also supplied drawings for many other buildings in the park and garden. STABLES, N of the gatehouse, are by *Burn* (but executed by *J. Macvicar Anderson*). Very plain indeed. Converted to school dining hall etc. in 1953–9 by *Marshall Sisson*; the classrooms nearby are also by him. Little roundels in the parapet. Of most recent date, SW of the house, QUEEN KATHARINE BUILDING by *RMJM*, 2009–10. Yellow brick with screens of vertical timber louvres, some placed at right angles as shades.

At the W edge of the park, in Pound Lane, a KEEPER'S COTTAGE, mid-C19 Tudor Gothic. SW of the castle on the hill above the site of the earlier castle mound, PARK LODGE, thought to have been erected *c.* 1630 by the 1st Earl as part of the planned landscape around the castle. Two rooms have panelling but the rest is a remodelling in 1870 (builders, *Wildman & Edey* of St Neots). Also intended as an incident within the parkland is

WARREN HOUSE, 250 yds NE of the castle on the hill. It is a C17 timber-framed cottage for a warrener, small and square, with brick and stone walls. The doorway and the main window are round-arched, the latter of Venetian type, and evidently designed to please the eye from the castle. Straight parapet with a gable end behind. A drawing in the Manchester archives, undated, proposes a choice between a shaped gable and crenellated parapet. Restored in 2011 by the Landmark Trust and extended by *Oliver Caroe*.

KINGS RIPTON

2070

ST PETER. A rough building, inside and out. Perp W tower still with putlog holes (probably *c.* 1500; two bells by *William Culverden*, i.e. *c.* 1497–1522, and contemporary bellframe), rubble- and cobble-built nave with N aisle, and chancel. The chancel PISCINA is of the second third of the C13, but the S wall of the chancel is faced with early bricks, mostly headers. Perp N arcade of three bays; standard elements. Chancel arch contemporary, and the tower and the N clerestory with quatrefoil windows. Restored 1851. Bare limewashed interior, a rarity now. – FONT. Square, with tapering sides. Norman stylized leaves on the sides, including, on three sides, colonnettes to separate the leaf motifs.

Opposite the W end of the church, THE LIMES has a good late C16 timber-framed front with continuous jetty and original door with moulded surround with carved spandrels. Close-studded upper floor with some wavy-profile bracing.

LEIGHTON BROMSWOLD

1070

ST MARY. This is a wonderful church, thanks to the E.E. architects, and a highly interesting church, thanks to the patrons of the first half of the C17. What faces the visitor first of all is the C17, a strong W tower, ashlar-faced, cream-coloured. It exhibits no Gothic yearnings, except that from a distance its general shape is traditional. But the W doorway and the W windows are round-arched, and so are the twin bell-openings. There are battlements and pinnacles, but the pinnacles are obelisks with ball finials. The C17 dates, as far as we know them, are as follows. The church was ruinous about 1600. The S aisle was demolished in 1606. The nave was then roofless. In 1626 George Herbert, the poet, was ordained deacon and became prebend. In 1630 he was ordained priest and took over the parish of Bemerton, Wiltshire. In 1633 he died and left his manuscript of *The Temple* to Nicholas Ferrar of Little Gidding. In Herbert's years the N aisle was demolished and the church re-roofed and furnished, under the supervision of John Ferrar

105

of Little Gidding; the date 1632 is stamped on the lavish rain-water head of the chancel, with strapwork and motifs of a lamb and eagles etc. and 1634 on the N transept. The Duke of Lennox was Lord of the Manor and he paid for the W tower, which means a date of after 1637 and before 1641, when the bells were made for it.

Behind the tower, however, there is the C13 at once, in its details and even more in its clear plan of the noblest simplicity: nave, transepts, chancel. In fact, as the roofline against the W walls of the transepts proves, the E.E. church had narrow aisles, and the two doorways must have belonged to them. The N doorway, with a bold, rather blunt semicircular moulding and two orders of colonnettes, may – so the RCHM suggests – even be *in situ*. The S doorway is the more splendid, with four orders and fine arch mouldings, one of them occupied by dogtooth. Leighton was a prebendal manor of Lincoln and held in 1230 by William, archdeacon of Wells and canon of Lincoln. In the transepts no E.E. features remain, except the buttresses and inside the E responds of the arches towards the former crossing, following rebuilding in the mid C14. Their large E windows with reticulated tracery are Dec. The chancel appears to be wholly of the latest C13. The chancel arch stands on triple shafts which start high up, i.e. presuppose a low stone screen. The arch is double-chamfered. In the chancel is the finest of all E.E. DOUBLE PISCINAS, square-headed with a large round arch intersected, even in the individual mouldings, by two half-arches. Opposite is an AUMBRY with a shelf. Two large, clear windows with intersecting tracery in the N and S walls make the room beautifully light. The large E window with panel tracery, almost entirely uncusped, seems Late Perp but has a somewhat inauthentic character. Was it altered in the C17 rebuilding? Genuine Late Perp, however, is one chancel S and one N window. The S window is inserted where traces of a blocked door can be seen, and below the sill of the window outside there is a blocked lowside. The roofs transport us to the C17. They are original in transepts and nave, with tie-beams on short straight braces and arched braces up to the collars, and also windbraces. The tower arch has C17 responds too, though the arch is pointed. The chancel roof is of 1868–70 by *Ewan Christian*. He restored the church, removing a W gallery of *c.* 1840 from in front of the tower and ruthlessly stripped the walls to create an interior of bleak unbroken surfaces.

The C17 FURNISHINGS are these. PULPIT and READER'S DESK. Two identical pieces with sounding-boards, l. and r. of the chancel arch – like Early Christian ambos, giving equal status to preaching and reading. They are five-sided, with turned pendants. The BENCHES in the body of the church are long, with open front and open ends. Balusters for the front with knobs on top. Knobs also for the arms. In the transepts they face inwards to the pulpit and reader's desk but originally might have run along the walls. Several benches are good

106

copies of 1868–70; *Christian* also remade the college-style benches in the chancel, to the same design as the originals, which had been removed to the transepts *c.* 1840. Part of the desks may be C17. – CHANCEL SCREEN. Only 5 ft high, also open, and also with knobs. – ALTAR TABLE, also early C17. – The LECTERN, the LITANY DESK, the VESTRY SCREEN (S transept, probably of 1840) and the TOWER SCREEN all have original C17 parts. Those of the lectern, 1903 by *S. Inskip Ladds* in memory of his great-uncle, the vicar of Leighton, come from Stow Longa Manor House (dem. 1903). – COMMUNION RAIL. By *Ewan Christian*, 1870, keeping faith with the rest. – MONU-MENTS. Sir Robert Tyrwhitt †1572 and wife. Alabaster effigies, defaced, on an alabaster tomb-chest with stiff standing figures of children and in the middle the coat of arms. – Lady Darcy, daughter of Sir Robert, †1567. By the same hand, and also defaced. Both are attributed to *Richard & Gabriel Royley* (Jon Bayliss).

LYCHGATE. 1909 by *S. Inskip Ladds*. The gates evoke the C17 woodwork in the church.

E of the church, formerly with an avenue of trees leading up to it and still partly enclosed by a moat, is CASTLE HOUSE. This was the gatehouse to Leighton Bromswold Castle, originally a prebendal manor house of the late C15, then the seat of Sir Richard Tyrwhitt, of his son-in-law Sir Henry d'Arcy, and then of d'Arcy's son-in-law Sir Gervase Clifton. The Duke of Lennox mentioned above was Clifton's son-in-law. Clifton, before 1608, intended to build an up-to-date mansion. *John Thorpe* either designed it or drew it but whether or not it was built is uncertain. In support of its existence is a detailed eleva-tion on a map of 1680 and its plan shown on a map of 1793, both agreeing with Thorpe. As for the stately gatehouse, this dates from 1616. It is large and oblong, with four square pro-jecting corner towers and of red brick. The centre is a wide and high stone archway, now cruelly hidden in its lower part by an addition of 1904 by *S. Inskip Ladds*, when it was con-verted as the rectory. The arch is flanked by Tuscan columns on pedestals carrying a highly incorrect triglyph frieze, broken in the centre by a later C17 window, and above that short pilasters with a simple geometrical pattern of chains of pyra-midal lozenges. The top is a balustrade of vertically symmetri-cal buttresses. The towers are three storeys high and have cross-windows except at the top storey. The back is not identi-cal, but very similar. However, it lacks the pilasters and balus-trade. On this side the arch is fully revealed but blocked by a shallow bow window, also of 1904, and on the sides between the angle towers are additions of the same time. Inside, two C17 fireplaces, panelling and stair balusters (SW tower), from Stow Longa Manor House (dem. 1903). The manor house stood immediately behind and beyond it was a GARDEN. This was terraced with prospect mounds to two outer corners, the general form still preserved. The medieval village was also in this area.

The long tree-lined AVENUE which leads from the W to the church seems to have been laid out in the C17 but there is little building of before the C19. No. 1, early C19, has been well restored. It has a weatherboarded forge (fittings preserved). Of the other COTTAGES several were built as good but plain pairs of brick dwellings for farm workers by the Church Commissioners, who bought the manor in 1853, creating the tone of a model village. Also the former SCHOOL by *Ewan Christian*, 1872. On the N side, a former CHAPEL, quite a characteristic domestic-style work of *c.* 1900, with tall transomed windows and a porch with scooped parapet and *œil-de-bœuf* windows.

LITTLE GIDDING   *1080*

Nicholas Ferrar was the son of a wealthy merchant. He was born in 1593 and studied medicine. He went abroad, to the universities of Padua and Leipzig, and returned home in 1618. He was a man of a mystic bent, impressed by the Cambridge Platonists, Juan de Valdes, and the Arminians. The idea of forming a religious community came to him in 1624. His mother felt as he did, and they decided to buy a house at Little Gidding. Nicholas Ferrar was ordained deacon in 1626. The community numbered about thirty to forty, and Nicholas's brother John Ferrar with wife and two children and their sister with husband and sixteen children also joined. There was a school with three schoolmasters, and there were alms-people. The discipline was demanding, three services a day and only two meals for the adults, but no vows were prescribed. Nicholas Ferrar worked on Concordances or Harmonies of the Bible, i.e. biblical materials presented as consecutive stories. The books were written and bound by hand. Embroidery was cultivated too. The community was in close touch with George Herbert at Leighton Bromswold and Sir Robert Cotton at Conington. Charles I visited them three times, the last time on his flight. Bishop Williams of Lincoln also paid them a visit (from Buckden). Mrs Ferrar died in 1634, Nicholas Ferrar in 1637, and the nephew whom he had regarded as his successor in 1640. In the mood of the forties the community was decried as popish and John Ferrar, the brother of Nicholas, went to Holland with his family for the period 1642–5. He returned to his estate thereafter, but the end seems to have come with his death in 1657.* The last of the Ferrars died in the late C18. Nothing survives of the Ferrars' house, but next to the church is FERRAR HOUSE, a C19 farmhouse, where a successor Christian community was founded in 1971 and lasted until 1997.

---

*The belief that the church was sacked in 1646 seems to be without foundation and is not mentioned before the late C18. See D. R. Ransome, *John Ferrar of Little Gidding*, in Records of Huntingdonshire, v. 3, No. 8 (2000).

The house remains in use as a retreat. The outbuildings have been converted to housing.

St John the Evangelist. The community did not build a new church: they remodelled a dilapidated old one *c.* 1630. Excavations in 1921 have shown that this old church was larger than the present one, with a N transept and W tower. Anyway the present church is very small. It consists of nave and chancel only. It lies with trees l. and r. looking into spacious fields and towards the gently rolling country. The building is of brick and only its façade is of stone. This façade is dated 1714, when the Ferrars rebuilt and shortened the church. It is a strange façade, not in any Queen Anne tradition. If a big name were to be connected with its style, it would be Archer rather than Hawksmoor. The façade is quite narrow and has two giant angle pilasters with small obelisks on. The doorway has a kind of pilaster strips with sunk panels carrying big corbels for the straight hood instead of capitals. In the middle is a bellcote of rusticated pilasters, and on that a flat obelisk or steep pyramid with a ball finial and three mysterious pierced oblong openings. The S vestry is of about the same date.

122   The interior seems too good to be true, for it was restored by *Henry Clutton* in 1852–5 for the Rev. William Hopkinson, F.S.A., who had purchased the manor. The stipulation was that it should be returned to its C17 condition and Clutton did the job extremely well, inspired perhaps by his own sympathy for the Anglo-Catholic rituals practised by the Ferrars. The roofs, ceiled vaults criss-crossed by ribs, are his own invention, executed, like all the new woodwork, by *Francis Ruddle* of Peterborough. The most interesting feature is the arrangement of the seating in the nave college-wise. This is decidedly a monastic tradition, wholly appropriate to the private devotions of the community, and one may attribute it to Nicholas Ferrar's time, for it is so described in a report of *c.* 1633–4. At that time there was also a pulpit and reading desk flanking the chancel step, as at Leighton Bromswold (q.v.), both now lost. The stalls in the nave have thick balusters and the backs high detached baluster-like columns carrying segmental arches. In their present form they are by Clutton, who added the stalls and lifted the columns to stand on their shoulders. Previously they rose from a low bench, as is still the case in the chancel, where the panelling has long balusters too. The panelling here was also topped by rows of triangular pediments. The black-and-white floor is probably of 1714. – The arched brass tablets with the creed, commandments and lord's prayer were made in London in 1630; originally they were set above the panelling but were moved in 1853 to make way for a large arched E window, itself replaced in 1990 by the present Venetian by *Julian Limentani*. Of the original reredos may be the Jacobean panel, with one of the usual broad blank arches, which was discovered in 1921 and made into the credence table. – The communion rail is original, though it was removed to Caldecote church in the 1850s and from there to

Little Gidding, St John.
Drawing by the Rev. E. Bradley, 1851

Prestwood, Bucks., in 1884. Returned in 1921. – Also of *c.* 1630, the FONT (now kept at Ferrar House, *see* above); a curious but delightful assembly of a brass baluster and a brass bowl on top surrounded by a kind of cut-out crown. It was fixed to the pulpit in the C17. Of the same time and in a similar style the iron HOURGLASS STAND, where the preaching pulpit stood. – The LECTERN is the one medieval piece in the church. It is of brass, of a well-known East Anglian type, of the late C15. The same moulds were used for the lecterns of Peterborough Cathedral but also e.g. Urbino Cathedral and Oxburgh in Norfolk. It was presented by the Ferrars and is a splendid eagle; the moulded stem is splendid too, and the little lions at the base are pretty enough. – CHANDELIER. Of *c.* 1770, and of a familiar Baroque type with two tiers of branches and three globes. Given by Hopkinson in 1853, and matching the description of one removed from Uppingham church at about that time (Robert Sherlock). – The Arts and Crafts CANDLE SCONCES of slender turned balusters, extremely well grouped, are by *W. A. Lea*, 1921. – STAINED GLASS. Executed by *William Miller*, 1853, to the designs of *Charles Winston*. Each of the windows has an armorial in a clear setting of leaded roundels: Charles I, Bishop Williams, Nicholas Ferrar and William Hopkinson. (Miller's Crucifixion, which filled the E window, is now at Peterborough High School; *see* p. 625.) – TABLE TOMB. Outside the w door. Nicholas Ferrar †1637. Paths have been made from the slabs to his family.

LITTLE PAXTON

ST JAMES. Over the s door a barbaric and entertaining Norman tympanum with a Maltese cross in the middle, on the l. Christ and the Lamb (?), on the r. two indefinable animals. The shafts of the door have little scrolls. In the chancel s wall, the head of a Norman window. The chancel arch responds are Norman too, square with an angle shaft, although the arch, like Southoe (q.v.), is later and pointed. So nave and chancel were once Norman. Perp w tower with its buttresses inside the church. Perp s arcade of four bays, very rough. Octagonal piers, but the responds just corbels in the form of a knot (cf. Didding-ton). N door, C14, reset when the wall was rebuilt in 1849. s porch of 1998. – ROYAL ARMS. Georgian, in spite of the inscribed date of 1610. – STAINED GLASS. E window, Crucifix-ion, by *Heaton, Butler & Bayne*, c. 1909. – Chancel s lancets by *Hardman*, c. 1880.

In the churchyard N of the N porch, plain coped stone to John Buonarotti Papworth (†1847), architect to the King of Württemberg, as the inscription tells you, and Fr. Roy. Inst of Br. Arcitects [*sic*]. Paxton Park, which he built and retired to, was demolished in 1959.

PAXTON HALL (care home) is N of the church in the densely over-built-up village. Purchased by Bishop Reynolds of Lincoln in 1730. Finely detailed brick front, dated 1738 on the rain-water heads, of nine bays with slightly projecting two-bay side parts that belong to the cross-wings of the earlier house behind. Two storeys, hipped roof with dormers behind a low parapet. The windows have raised and moulded stone frames, and the doorway a pediment on beautifully carved brackets. A com-pletely inappropriate square porch covers this. The finest interiors must be of 1738 too. The staircase starts in the entrance hall. It is spacious and also beautifully detailed. Bal-usters with turned bulbous foot, carved tread-ends, fluted Corinthian newels, on the top landing Greek-key frieze. Panel-ling with fluted pilasters. Stucco ceiling with guilloche sur-round, Rococo ornament and, in medallions, the Four Seasons. In the former dining room an excellent stone chimneypiece, with lugged surround and above it a broken pediment. In this, formerly, was the profile of a young man, possibly Bishop Reynolds's son, who inherited in 1744. Wing added in 1988–9.

LITTLE RAVELEY

ST JAMES. Originally a chapelry of Wistow and then Bury. A house since *c.* 1985. Nave and chancel, gable bellcote. Chancel probably early C13 (piscina inside: NHLE), but the two-

66. Wansford, High Street, Haycock Hotel and bridge (p. 714)
67. St Ives, view w along the Great Ouse (p. 668)
68. Kimbolton, High Street, view towards Kimbolton Castle (p. 539)

77. Castor, St Kyneburgha, church tower, *c.* 1100–24 (p. 454)
78. Peterborough Cathedral, presbytery and crossing, *c.* 1118–1175 (p. 596)
79. Ramsey, St Thomas a Becket, nave and chancel, *c.* 1180–90; pews and roof by Edward Blore, 1843–4 (p. 663)

80. Peterborough Cathedral, w front, early C13 (p. 593)
81. Peterborough Cathedral, nave ceiling, paintings, *c.* 1230 (p. 603)
82. Alconbury, St Peter and St Paul, chancel, interior, late C13 (p. 414)

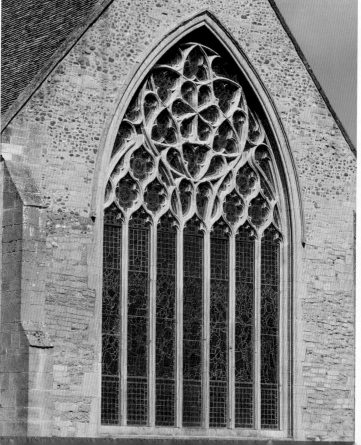

83	85
84	86

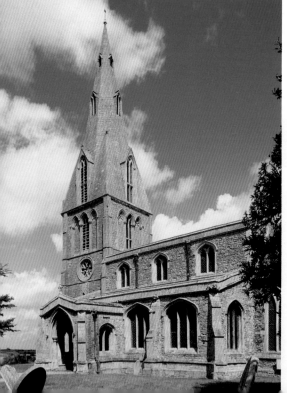

91. Conington, All Saints, nave, *c.* 1500; pews by Edward Blore, 1841
    (p. 461)
92. Tilbrook, All Saints, rood screen, Perp; restored 1867 (p. 706)
93. Peterborough Cathedral, retrochoir, attributed to John Wastell, begun
    c. 1508 (p. 589)

101. Toseland, Toseland Hall, *c.* 1608 (p. 707)
102. Stibbington, Stibbington Hall, 1625 (p. 693)

103. Godmanchester, Earning Street, Tudor House, 1600–3 (p. 493)
104. Warboys, Manor House, E front, mid C17 (p. 717)

109 | 111
110 | 112

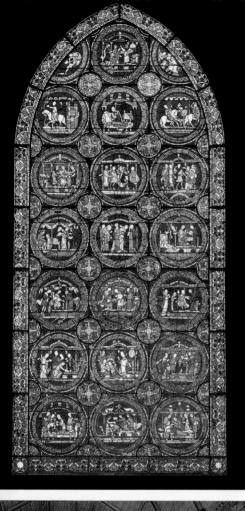

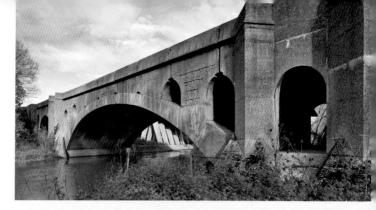

light E window and the chancel arch are Dec. Perp nave S windows.*

LITTLE STUKELEY

The main street runs uphill from Ermine Street, with the church near the top.

ST MARTIN. The most interesting thing about the church is that *S. Inskip Ladds*, who restored the tower in 1933–4, collected Norman remains carefully and displayed them to advantage. Thus in the S wall of the tower outside are Norman column-shafts, and inside the tower whole collections, including an arch with proper beakhead and an arch with beakhead stylized to excess. This is found also at Spaldwick and Toseland; they belonged to the Bishop of Lincoln, and Little Stukeley was a possession of the Archdeacon of Huntingdon who was closely associated with the Bishop. Also two Norman window-heads, lengths of a battlement frieze and billet, and a lion, like that at Sutton [P] (q.v.). Similar discoveries were made in 1910 during work on the N aisle and chancel E wall, again by Ladds, indeed enough to enable his re-creation of the length of Norman corbel table in the N wall. In the N chapel S arch there is a whole order of short Norman rolls or tubes set at right angles to the arch. The arch around which they are reset is early C14, i.e. the date of the chancel itself. Was this the chancel arch of the C12 church? As for the rest, the W tower is short, late C13, but has Perp buttresses and ashlar belfry (repaired in 1659) with a quatrefoil frieze and big pinnacles but no spire. The top of the belfry stage, including the window arches, was much rebuilt in 1887 by *Robert Hutchinson*. Clerestory, S aisle and the chancel chapels are Perp. The S porch is of the same campaign, although it is dated 1652, and the S doorway inside is ornate with a (restored) cusped outer arch, a stoup in a niche on the r. and a bracket on the l. The two-bay arcades of standard elements are Perp also. The SE respond is a monster devouring a man, the deed performed horizontally. A large winged man is attached to the N arcade, and there are plenty of other smaller corbels reused. The chancel arch and the arch to the S chapels are contemporary with the arcades. Inside the nave, there are carved friezes of Early Renaissance foliage reused (when?) to form a vertical strip (N), a cross (S), and a square set in a lozenge (E). – FONT. Octagonal, with quatrefoils. Leaves on the underside. – STAINED GLASS. In the S chapel parts of canopies made up as canopies. – BRASS. S aisle.

---

*The FONT recorded in the first edition of this guide is now in Peterborough Museum. It is Perp. Against the underside an eagle, a tree(?), and two unidentified figures.

William Hall †1618. Full-length bearded figure in a gown and skull cap.

N of the church is the OLD RECTORY, gaunt, lofty and square with a deep basement and an attic above a big cornice on the rendered front. Plans of 1828 are by *William Biggs*, surveyor of Linton, Cambs. But the sides are red brick, so perhaps mid-C18. OLD CHAPEL, Ermine Street, 1871 by *John Bird*.

Downhill, across Ermine Street, is the former SWAN AND SALMON inn. Dated 1676 on the sign* on its gable to the road, which refers to the recasing in brick of a timber-framed house (of which the rear wall is largely preserved, including a diagonal-mullioned window, within the later rear extension). The front is a coarser version of The Limes at Spaldwick (q.v.), i.e. brick, with a square porch, giant pilasters so rustic that they stop being pilasters, and broad raised surrounds to the windows. The pilasters in fact belong to a system of raised verticals and horizontals articulating the front, but the details have been obscured by a thick coat of render. Until the mid C20 the S gable was in the shapely Dutch style with the chimney rising against its centre. Circular attic windows in the gables.

RAF ALCONBURY. Opened in 1938 and used by the USAAF from 1942. The airfield was abandoned in 1993 and is now a distribution centre. From the very last years of the Cold War several impressive concrete and steel 'hardened' AIRCRAFT SHELTERS, the largest built by the *Property Services Agency*, c. 1989, for Lockheed TR-1 tactical reconnaissance aircraft, and an associated communications BUNKER of the same date, the so-called 'Magic Mountain'.

LOLHAM [P]

LOLHAM HALL, ½ m. W of Maxey church. Essentially C18, but see the C16 gabled wing at the rear. (Inside, three medieval stone archways and at first floor a panelled room with Tudor-arched stone fireplace. NHLE) The house belonged to the Claypoles (cf. Northborough). ⅛ m. N by the Welland is LOLHAM MILL, late C18, of three bays and two storeys above a basement. Doorcase with open pediment and Gothic staircase windows at the rear.

S along King Street are the stone LOLHAM BRIDGES, five in line from N to S and of varied spans. Apparently 'built at the general charge of the whole County of Northampton in the year 1652', though evidently repeatedly repaired. The broadest, with five arches, buttresses and pedestrian refuges, passes over the

---

*The sign appears to be a composite. The swan is carved in stone and goes with the date. The salmon is added in metal and may be more correctly identified as a pike. The VCH suggests these as the emblems of the Druell and Pickering families.

MAXEY CUT, a C19 channel designed to supersede the water-courses that the bridges originally spanned. They now cross meadows liable to floods.

LONGTHORPE *see* PETERBOROUGH

LYNCH FARM *see* ALWALTON

MARHOLM [P]   *1000*

Only just outside the built-up area of Peterborough but still rural by virtue of the park around Milton (q.v.). The church is S of the village in a parkland setting, with a ha-ha in front, four cedar trees to the W and three to the E.

ST MARY. The visual memory is the contrast between the ambitious chancel and the rest. Short Early Norman W tower with clasping buttresses and slit windows. Tower arch narrow, single-stepped, with responds carrying late C12 crocket capitals. Earlier C13 nave arcades and chancel arch. The arcades, which have quatrefoil piers and double-chamfered arches, were blocked after a fire destroyed the aisles in the C16; they are now as rebuilt in 1868 by *Kirk & Parry* of Sleaford, with windows copied from a surviving example (two lights with a quatrefoil in the head), reset in the S aisle E wall. Reset PISCINA, N aisle E wall, on a chamfered shaft. The chancel was rebuilt by Sir William Fitzwilliam of Milton, who died in 1534 and wished to be buried in the chancel 'lately edified' by him.* Ashlar-faced to the S. Five-light Perp E and four-light side windows. In the NE window a silver-stained fragment of Abbot Robert Kirkton's rebus. He died in 1528 so the work must have been complete by then. Nave clerestory of about the same time, the roof replicated in 1868. – FONT. Octagonal, probably of the 1660s, with panels each with a leaf and a rose. – REREDOS. Gothic, of Caen stone with cusped arched panels for commandments tablets etc.; it is of 1833 by *Edward Blore*, carved by *Francis Ruddle* of Peterborough, as a memorial to Viscountess Milton (†1830). – STAINED GLASS. Some of the original glass is preserved in the chancel. E window mostly C16 heraldic (Fitzwilliam alliances). The other windows have C15 and C16 pieces rearranged as decorative borders. N aisle window by *Cox & Sons*, 1895, executed by *J. Noble*, plumber and glazier of Cowgate, Peterborough. – SCULPTURE. Above the tower arch a small figure (C12?) with one hand raised, the other across its chest. – MONUMENTS. Under the E arch of the S arcade, a

---

* Fitzwilliam also paid for the rebuilding of the chancel of St Andrew Undershaft in the City of London at about the same time.

Marholm, monument to 1st Earl Fitzwilliam.
Drawing *c.* 1720

recumbent effigy of a knight in ornately trimmed armour, his
head resting on a helmet draped in a jester's hat with bearded
face. He is cut from clunch. The effigy is of *c.* 1400, traditionally John Whittlebury, but the tomb-chest of 1868, before
which he was set into a recess in the S wall. In the S aisle a
COAT OF ARMS, apparently of Sir William Fitzwilliam, 1st Earl
of Southampton and Knight of the Garter,* †1542. He was not
related to the Fitzwilliams at Milton. Why is it here? – Sir
William Fitzwilliam †1534. Canopy tomb with Alwalton marble
tomb-chest with ornate quatrefoils. Kneeling brasses (15½ in.;
39 cm high) against the back wall. Repaired 'and beautified' in
1674 by the 3rd Lord Fitzwilliam, including replacement of the
top half of the Sir William brass.† The architectural parts of

---

*Tillemans's drawing of *c.* 1720 shows the effigy built into the blocked aisle arcade
with this coat of arms above it; it is there described as the 'Earl of Southampton's
tomb'.
†The original part is now in the British Museum.

painted plaster may have been attended to by the restorers. Colonnettes with raised lozenge pattern and canopy of four small ogee arches with blind tracery on the soffit. – Sir William Fitzwilliam, Lord Lieutenant of Ireland, †1599. Two recumbent effigies in black and gold costume, with hands held, on a Renaissance-style chest. Nice scrolled inscription panel. – Edward Hunter alias Perry †1646 aged nine. Bust of a boy in front of a black needle obelisk with panelled sides (cf. the Buckingham Monument at Westminster Abbey, 1634). Attributed to *Henry Boughton* (AW). Below a cartouche with weeping putti and an unusual inscription 'To the courteous soldier' ('grassante bello civili'), 'Noe crucifixe you see, noe Frightfull Brand Of supstitions here, Pray let mee stand' – evidently addressed to Cromwellian marauders. – William, 1st Earl Fitzwilliam, †1719 and wife. By *James Fisher* of Camberwell; he was contracted in 1718, the cost £900. Standing white marble figures on a plinth. Her dress has unusual, restless draperies. Grey marble architectural surround with detached Corinthian columns and a broken, open, segmental pediment and feathers sprouting from an urn. The *magnum opus* of this little-known sculptor and originally with attendant figures of Grief and Piety which, as Sweeting noted in 1844, blocked out the chancel windows. They must have been removed in the restoration of the 1860s. There were also originally railings by *Montigny* (cf. Milton).* Good groups of TABLE TOMBS in ranks outside the S porch, some with balusters, volutes and bow-ended chests. Several for the Bull family, headstones also in the local style.

MARHOLM FARM, NE on Woodcroft Road. In spite of the datestone 1633 (with ENGROS in a cipher) this must be essentially late C17. H-shaped, with mullioned windows, some straightheaded, others with pediments, triangular as well as segmental in the wings. At the rear of the S wing, one reset small medieval ogee-headed window and tucked across the re-entrant angle an oriel, with a two-light mullioned opening and oval window above. These lit a newel staircase, now removed. Set into the SW and SE corners, cube sundials. Single-storey hall inside, its fireplace remodelled in the mid C20 with reused early C17 panels. Two rooms at the service (N) end, with a winder staircase in a compartment between them.

BELSIZE FARM, ¾ m. SW of the church. On the site of a grange of Peterborough Abbey, founded by Abbot Robert de Lindsey in 1214. The remains of carp ponds and cobbled paths have been discovered. The buildings include one impressively large rubble-built BARN, about 155 ft (47.2 metres) long, with stepped buttresses to the entrance, a Collyweston slated roof

---

*Bridges describes them in his *History of Northamptonshire*, which was being prepared in the 1720s, and Sweeting notes the way in which they blocked the chancel windows. The drawing at the British Library (Add. MS 32467, fols 57V–58R), which shows its more elaborate form, is, however, attributed to *William Palmer* (GF). No doubt James Fisher undercut Palmer on price.

with queenposts and windbraces. Later cart openings under brick arches.

MAXEY [P]

Maxey was settled in the Iron Age and between the church and the present village to its E is a Saxon site of some importance, which gave its name to the style of pottery found there. It had timber-framed long houses (the first of the period to be found in this area), hearths and rubbish pits. Of the six houses discovered so far, the largest measured 51 by 23 ft (15.5 by 7 metres).

ST PETER. Raised on a slight eminence. Grey stone, broad and of irregular blocks of varying age and shape. Broad Early Norman W tower with flat thin buttresses (strengthened at the NW in the C14, when a pretty ogee-headed stair doorway was inserted inside). String course of diamond patterns and billet to the corbel table with its row of beasts' heads. Above this, narrow two-light bell-openings flanked by blank arches in pairs (W) and singles (E, N and S). Blank arcading inside this stage (VCH). All this is a reminder in a modest way of Castor (q.v.). The battlemented top is Perp. The tower arch to the nave makes an early C12 date certain. Shafted responds with demi-column. Steep bases with a flat chevron, like Castor. Decorated capitals with volutes like those of Helpston, but also the masks spewing foliage seen at Castor and Sutton. The arch was remodelled later. The original church was aisleless, see the W angles. Norman also and not much later than the tower the N arcade of two bays. Big circular piers with many-scalloped capitals and heavy square abaci. Arches with thick rolls. The S arcade is Norman too, but later, say *c.* 1175–95 (cf. Peterborough). Circular piers and square abaci, less heavy. More busily scalloped and angular capitals, nicked at the corners. Arches with two chamfers and a big outer nailhead. The Norman church had a clerestory. Its small windows can be seen from inside the aisles. Aisles rebuilt in the C14, straight-headed Dec windows in the N aisle and its W window with reticulation (restored). Of the C13 the chancel and the responds of the chancel arch but the arch itself made taller in the C15 to accommodate a rood loft, of which two newel stairs and an associated aumbry or piscina are preserved. Clerestory of the same date, with two-light openings. The chancel S windows seem later C13 but not identical – one of *c.* 1290 of two lights with a foiled circle over, the other early C14 Y-tracery cusped and with a segmental arch inside on filleted shafts with nice Dec capitals (cf. Helpston S aisle). SEDILIA and PISCINA with ogee arches and crocketed gables. Blocked lowside window. Perp E window. Attached to the chancel on the S side, a treasury of the late C13 or a somewhat later date. It is a small chamber with lancet windows, some of them still with iron grilles, and has a vault. This has diagonal and ridge-ribs (sunk wave moulding). Finally the ambitious, battlemented, N chancel chapel (founded as a chantry in 1367 for Sir Robert de Thorpe). Two bays, four-light E and three-light N windows, with transoms (tower W window of similar date, with shields of Thorpe and Ros as hoodmould stops). Arch to the chancel with two sunk quadrant mouldings. An octagonal S respond in the chapel with coved moulding (cf. Etton) shows that a C13 chapel had existed before. Tall late C14 arch to the aisle, splendidly cusped and subcusped with cinquefoils in pierced work. In the chancel a Perp EASTER SEPULCHRE, ogee-arched, with much quatrefoiling etc. It is made of clunch (Sweeting relates it to a recorded inscription of 1402). S door of *c.* 1500, quite handsome, with blind arcading in the surround. S aisle extended W in 1720 as a vestry and remodelled during restoration in 1864 by *Alfred Sykes* of Milton (see the arch with corbel heads and screen). Of this date also the S aisle tracery and FURNISHINGS. – Chancel TILES are by *Maw & Co.* – Under the tower, a number of Anglo-Saxon and other FRAGMENTS gathered together by the Rev. W. D. Sweeting, the antiquary and historian. He was vicar of Maxey 1881–1901. – STAINED GLASS. Decayed C15 Virgin and St Peter and grisaille fragments in N chapel E and S aisle E. Chancel S, SS Michael and Gabriel, 1916 by *A. L. & C. E. Moore.*

MAXEY CASTLE, the manor house, stood at the far NE corner of the village. Licence to crenellate was granted to Sir William de Thorpe in 1374. The castle has disappeared but three sides of its MOAT still exist to the N of CASTLE FARMHOUSE. The house itself is a single range with gabled ends, probably C16, when it belonged to the Cecils. In the N gable-end, i.e. facing the site of the castle, are two pairs of two-light windows in two storeys. They are straight-headed, with arched lights, and there are several other mullioned openings (some blocked) with straight chamfers and ovolo mouldings on the E front, where in addition there is a stair-tower with slit windows (the original stair has been removed but inside are pointed arches to the chambers at first floor). The linear plan of parlour, hall and service end is preserved and appears to have had a lobby entry from the E against the massive stack between hall and kitchen. At the service end some beams have moulded chamfers. W front remodelled in the C18. Sashes in stone surrounds and inside a passage containing the staircase inserted at this date.

Several other houses incorporate medieval fragments, e.g. THE FRIARY to the S, with a C15 doorway and an angle fireplace in the former parlour, and CHAPEL COTTAGE to the E in Mill Road, which has a blocked two-light window in its N wall.

MAXEY MILL, 600 yds N of the church on the Welland. Built by John Molesey, 1779 (datestone with initials) and still operating. Three tall storeys with an attic, rag stone with contrasting limestone bands and quoins. Timber breastshot wheel in a rear outshot and much of the original workings. Restored in the 1960s and again 1979, by *Peter Wright.* Later C19 mill house.

MIDLOE *see* SOUTHOE

MILTON [P]

William Fitzwilliam, of an old Yorkshire family, bought Milton in 1502 from John Wittlebury, Lord of the Manor of Marholm, Milton and Longthorpe. It was Fitzwilliam's grandfather, Sir John Fitzwilliam of Sprotborough, who had established relations with this region by marrying Eleanor Greene of Drayton (Northants). William, who was a merchant of London and kept a seat at Gaynes Park in Essex, became High Chamberlain to Cardinal Wolsey, Alderman of the City, and Master of the Merchant Taylors' Company. He was knighted in 1522 and died in 1534. The house had reached its present extent by 1582* at the latest, with a moat enclosing three sides, the entrance side (N) closed by the road. The earliest work surviving at Milton is very likely of the first Sir William's time; we know that he was a builder in that before his death he rebuilt the chancel of the church at Marholm (q.v.) and also St Andrew Undershaft in the City of London. He had a son, Sir William (†1576). His grandson, Sir William, who died in 1599, was twice Lord Deputy of Ireland till 1594, and lived mostly over there, except for the years 1575–88, which he spent at home, during which time he was Governor of Fotheringhay Castle and custodian of Mary, Queen of Scots. The next identifiable period of work on the house is therefore likely to be of about 1600 for his son, Sir William IV, who married the daughter of Sir Walter Mildmay of Apethorpe, or after 1618 for their son who was made the 1st Lord Fitzwilliam (in the Irish Peerage) in 1620. After the sale of the Essex estate in the 1630s Milton became the principal seat. An estate map of 1643 records the layout of the house shortly before the 1st Lord's death. It appears only a little different from 1582, its long E–W range just one room deep with the usual linear arrangement of a hall separated by a screens passage from the E service end and to the W a parlour, drawing room, and chapel at the W end. There was a large well staircase on the S side and kitchens and lodgings also projected from the rear of the E end in a range enclosing the E side of the garden. In front was a large forecourt with lodgings and stables along the outer side.

The 3rd Lord was created Earl Fitzwilliam (also in the Irish Peerage) in 1716 and his grandson, the 3rd Earl, married in 1744 the daughter of Thomas Wentworth, Marquess of Rockingham, and then began work on a major remodelling of Milton. An entirely new house had already been considered by his father, to whom *James Gibbs* and *Roger Morris* supplied proposals in 1726. But the 2nd Earl died in 1728 and the son's ambitions were restricted to a reworking of the S façade, so the house now wears two faces. *Matthew Brettingham* was consulted in 1747 and in the

---

*This is the date of an estate plan in the Fitzwilliam papers. It should be noted however that the plan bears a second inscription giving the date as 1532.

same year also *Flitcroft* who was successful. No doubt he was recommended by the Marquess of Rockingham, for whom *c.* 1735 he had begun remodelling the E front of Wentworth Woodhouse in the West Riding. The new work, begun 1750–1, is therefore Palladian in style and executed in such a way that the visitor never sees both periods at once. The interiors were only partly complete by the earl's death in 1756 and not resumed fully by his son until 1769, now under the direction of *Sir William Chambers*, who was also then at work on Fitzwilliam's house in Piccadilly, London (dem.). In 1782 Wentworth Woodhouse was inherited from the 2nd Marquess of Rockingham and that became the Fitzwilliams' principal seat, with Milton as a resort for hunting. The two estates were divided once more in the mid-C19, then reunited about a century later until the sale of Wentworth Woodhouse after the death of the 10th and final Earl in 1979.

The earliest work is the NORTH FRONT. Its present appearance dates from *c.* 1600 or a little later, with windows of the normal mullioned and transomed kind. It is a curious composition, long, two-storeyed, with eight projections (the bays divided 2:1:5) of which the third contains the porch, the others being bays with windows. To the r. of the porch all is symmetrical, with the middle bay coming forward more than the others and the l. and r. (i.e. the fourth and eighth) being treated as one-storeyed with three transoms and the rows of four lights arched. The l. of these tall one-storey windows corresponds to the hall, a room which is at a very slight angle to the rest of the house and seems certainly to belong to the early C16. The far r. bay window lit the chapel at the W end. Neither is shown on the C16 sketch plan of the house but they most probably date from the time of William Fitzwilliam II after 1534 – inside the corners of the hall bay is a moulding like thin columns that is found also on a bay window of *c.* 1530 at Deene Park, Northants, erected for Sir Thomas Brudenell, whose wife was the sister of the second Sir William. It has, however, also an odd heavy transom below the lowest row of lights, which inside has a moulded profile not shared by the upper lights. So the lowest

96

Milton, north front.
Drawing by P. Tillemans, 1721

tier may be an insertion, perhaps prompted by later removal of the dais inside. In the bay to its l. there was also originally a tall square-headed window of three lights and a transom with arches to the upper lights. Tillemans shows it in 1719 but now there are two windows (the upper blind) to conform with the rest as remodelled *c.* 1600. Typical of Northamptonshire houses of that date is the porch with Doric columns below, Ionic above and an arch with jewelled keystone. This front is embattled and originally had shaped attic gables over each projecting bay. An undated pencil sketch in the Fitzwilliam papers shows one of these gables clearly dated 1626 and they are markedly similar to those added in the 1620s by Sir Francis Fane to Apethorpe Hall, Northants. Within the battlements a taller attic was contrived in 1773 by *Chambers*. Behind the four main accents, i.e. bays one, four, six and eight, he placed tripartite lunette windows, but chose to give them Gothic details of quatrefoils in the spandrels and crestings (since removed) of the same motif.

E of the N front is the OFFICES AND STABLING RANGE. This occupies three sides of a quadrangle and although no taller than the house is more monumental. It is dated 1690 but completed 1693. *William Talman* provided advice on its siting to Lord Fitzwilliam in 1688 but no more than that; Talman refers in a letter to '. . . Mr Sturges his draughts . . .', so the design is credited to *John Sturges*, but *Robert Wright* of Castor was in charge of building and may have had a hand in its final appearance. The recessed centre has eleven bays, the projecting wings four, plus, on the r., i.e. connecting with the house, two more. Two storeys, cross-windows, quoins, hipped roof. The centre has its own quoins, a pediment, and a clock turret. Doorway with a pediment with a three-centred top, i.e. the form the French call *anse de panier*. Staircase with turned balusters. It incorporated coach houses in the N wing with stabling restricted to the main range. Two rooms have William and Mary panelling, one of them in the link to the house, which must therefore be contemporary with the work of 1690. In the wall between the work of *c.* 1600 and the link of *c.* 1690, a former external window survives.

Now to *Flitcroft*'s SOUTH FRONT. This is of nine bays, two and a half storeys, ashlar-facing of Ketton stone. The first and last bays project and are canted. The centre bay projects slightly, has a Kentian doorway, a Venetian window above this, a tripartite lunette window in the half-storey, and a pediment with shield and cornucopia. Venetian windows also in the canted bays. The W front is of three bays, also with a canted bay. To the E of the S front two more bays by Flitcroft, or remodelled by him, and at the furthest end, offices of the same time. Between house and offices, however, is an ample bow window which is associated with work of 1803–5 by *John Carr*. The room behind the bow he had designed as the library in 1792 and before that it had been a courtyard, and a Venetian window which looked into this from the N has been found.

The INTERIOR is mostly Georgian, of the Flitcroft, Chambers and Carr periods, i.e. of *c.* 1750, *c.* 1770 and *c.* 1800, with the first dominant on the ground floor, the middle period on the first. The ENTRANCE HALL on the N front is a fine example of the style of *c.* 1750. Double-height with coved ceiling, chaste stucco work by *Thomas Clark*, whose bills survive. Sumptuous fireplace, if restrained in its motifs, with acanthus and flower and fruit garlands almost certainly by *John Deval* (cf. the entrance hall at Woburn) who received payments for chimneypieces. Open curly pediment and a wind-clock with a map of England (cf. Kent's Long Gallery at Kensington Palace).* To the W, the DINING ROOM with sunk panelling and a Rococo ceiling divided into panels with a central oval and roundels at the corners. Buffet recess at one end with a bacchus keystone head. Then the SMALL DINING ROOM with a specially lovely ceiling of a rectangle with lozenge-shape sections at the angles and delicately figured decoration including dragons and at the corners roundels with portrait heads (Homer etc.). Was this perhaps the Library in the mid C18? Next, the GUN ROOM with a pretty cornice of decorative, almost Gothic, arcading. This room also has reset *c.* 1600 panelling. In the BILLIARD ROOM (former chapel) more stucco decoration of *c.* 1750, and fireplace with swags of fruit tumbling from volutes at the sides. The same mode of decoration continues along the W front.

The centre of the S front is the stone-coloured PILLARED HALL, tripartite with Doric columns as division, doorcases with torus mouldings and one with a broken pediment and two chaste stone fireplaces with consoles and cushion mouldings at their most rustic. This room is in axis with the symmetrical part of the Elizabethan front. Accessible from here and from the entrance hall is the STAIRCASE HALL. Cantilevered stair, its wrought-iron handrail with S-motifs decorated with leaf. The motif is the same as was used by Kent at No. 44 Berkeley Square and Holkham. Sumptuous stucco coved ceiling and panels to the upper landing with drops containing plaster portraits in medallions. Glazed lantern. Vitruvian frieze at mid-height. The style continues through to the Study. The DINING ROOM is the former Library, made by Carr in 1792 out of Flitcroft's yard. It has beautiful Adamish decoration and in addition a fine marble fireplace, supplied by *John Fisher* of York, with rams' heads and a swagged frieze, that is identical to one ordered for Wentworth Woodhouse. The SMALL LIBRARY next to it belongs to Carr's work of 1803–5 (there was a pantry formerly in this position) and it is nearer the Regency in its motifs, including a fireplace with tapered grey marble supports, reeded doorcases and a fasces moulded dado rail. Behind the Small Library and of the same time, a connecting LOBBY. It has an oval opening to an upper miniature

---

* Other chimneypieces (unidentified) were also supplied by *Thomas Carter* and *Edward Bingham* in the 1750s.

colonnade and an oval lantern. The porch-bay of the hall can be reached from here.

118   On the upper floor the LONG GALLERY lies above the Pillared Hall. It was finished by Chambers and is the finest room in the house. It is five bays long and tripartite, with delightful segmental vaults and a shallow dome over the middle, all with banded plaster surrounds and elaborate decorated pendentives (plasterer, *Thomas Collins*), springing from Corinthian pilasters that at the angles are halved and squeezed in in a most unacademic way (and show the architect disregarding, as John Harris has noted, rules set down in his own *Treatise* of 1759). The main doorway has Ionic columns and a pediment. Two chaste fireplaces. The style is instructively different from Flitcroft's before and Carr's after.

The adjoining rooms along the N front were also redone by Chambers. The PETERBOROUGH DINING ROOM is the most interesting of these. Its ceiling has an oblong panel and a broad frame with a diagonal trellis and guilloche surround. Guttae cornice. Arched recess at one end. The fireplace here is white with yellow Siena marble, almost certainly one of those supplied by *Edward Bingham*. It is followed by a smaller ANTE-ROOM (or Tea Room), leading directly into the Long Gallery and then the (present) LIBRARY, whose Savonnerie carpet repeats the pattern of the ceiling with a circle and surrounding frame of squares and octagons with lattice patterns.

At the E end of the house on the first floor (i.e. partly above the service range) are some other fine mid-C18 rooms, including the BLUE BEDROOM of Flitcroft's time, in a strongly Kentian manner with broken pedimented overmantel and arched recess for a bed (the present bed, an outstanding early C18 piece with contemporary *chinoiserie* hangings, is of *c.* 1720 and came from Wentworth Woodhouse). On the S front another room (formerly BOUDOIR) with a Chinese wallpaper dated in Chinese 1748. Such rooms were popular at this date, but Milton's is very early indeed for the use of genuine, imported papers. It comprises sets of individual pictures with figures interspersed with objects set in perspectival frames, like windows, tied together by a grid of trelliswork. Larger panels for the overdoors may have been painted specially. Very prettily decorated wooden chimneypiece, very like one in the Yellow Drawing Room at Woburn Abbey and therefore attributable to *Deval*, and doorcase with an open scrolly pediment. Next to this another room with a more usual kind of Chinese wallpaper, perhaps *c.* 1770, held in place by bamboo-style fillets. Its doorcase and fireplaces are clearly mid-C18 but look reset. A third room contains a bed with Chinese-style cornice and contemporary cotton hangings, also probably *c.* 1750.

Behind the main stabling is a separate STABLES, dated 1720, evidently designed for the hunters. Like the late C17 range (*see* above) it also consists of three ranges, centre and wings, but lower. In the courtyard thus created stands an octagonal harness-house. The architect may have been *Robert Wright* of

Castor, who remained active on the estate and also contributed his own plans to the 2nd Earl for rebuilding the house. In addition, E of the S front, the LAUNDRY of *c*. 1690, with cross-windows and hipped roof.

The GARDEN had been altered from its early C17 state before remodelling by *Repton* in 1791,[*] with flat lawn to the S, deer park to the N, and informal plantings of trees and a LAKE to the SE. Also preceding Repton is the large WALLED GARDEN, which has a gate in its S wall with fine C18 ironwork, which may be attributed to *Jean Montigny*, who supplied a weather-vane and railings (now removed) for the earl's monument in Marholm church. There is a second, smaller gate, of similar design. Abutting the garden's N wall a tiny late C18 DAIRY. This has a segmental rusticated arch with cow's head keystone and a perky cresting of pine cone finials. Pretty, tiled interior. – Is it *Repton*? A S addition, with coloured glass roundels and niches for milk dishes, contains a C3 Roman MOSAIC found at Castor (q.v.) in the early C19 by E. T. Artis. He was the earl's steward, having begun as a confectioner in London. The mosaic has a diamond-shaped border with guilloche; the central part was probably remade when resited. Divers garden furnishings, notably the ORANGERY, SE of the walled garden, of seven bays with Doric columns, the outer ones coupled. Lord Torrington in 1789 refers to 'an ugly Green-House . . . now building', and the *Coade* stone urns and figures along the parapet are dated 1791. Is it by *Carr*? Outside the house is also *Coade* stone sphinx, dated 1789. SW of the house is a circular TEMPLE, reconstructed with Corinthian columns from the remains of a temple (the design attributed to *Chambers*, and built originally by *Edward Bingham*, 1774–6) which had a tetrastyle front.

In the wider PARK, some other items of interest: furthest E of the house are the picturesque KENNELS, possibly of 1767, when the Fitzwilliam Hunt was established, but first shown on maps in 1790. It takes the form of a ruined medieval gatehouse or castle, with conical-roofed turrets for the hounds' quarters and pointed arches opening to their yards. The architect is unknown.

GOTHIC LODGE, near the E entrance,[†] has a polygonal front, spiky pinnacles flanking a rose window and a gable with the peculiar Norman scallop frieze seen at Peterborough Cathedral. It must have been conceived by *Repton* but it was designed by his frequent collaborator *William Wilkins Sen.*, *c*. 1801. At the S end of the park, above the A47, is a second LODGE, larger, also Gothic, but lower-key Strawberry Hill-style with big quatrefoil window, ogee windows on the sides and corner turrets. It stood on the approach from Gunwade

---

[*]i.e. contemporary with his work on the grounds of Wentworth Woodhouse.
[†]This was not designed as an entrance lodge, for the late C18 entrance was even further to the E than it is now. The present entrance was created in the 1970s when part of the park was purchased to build the Bretton township of Peterborough New Town.

Ferry (*see* Gunwade Bridge, Castor) but was moved for road-widening and rebuilt in 1992–6. Nearby, FERRY HOUSE, formerly an inn on the old road. It is of the C17, with later additions, but gutted by fire in 2003 and restored.

MOLESWORTH

ST PETER. Short W tower without spire, unusual in the locality, and an aisleless nave. The steep chancel roof is higher than the nave. The chancel, though it looks all Victorian because it was demolished and rebuilt in 1884–5, is in fact a genuine and fine design of the C13. This is evident from the chancel arch and the beautiful blank giant arches enclosing the windows, single lancets and triplets of lancets as at Great Gidding (q.v.). Externally the buttresses are original too; on the N and S of the nave they continue upwards as a framing pilaster. The nave S doorway is C13 as well. It has one stiff-leaf capital, and the arch starting with broaches. The rest is Perp, except the porch of 1890 with a figure of St Peter. Chancel roof, Victorian, with carved angels against the arched braces. – PULPIT. Early C18; plain. – ARCHITECTURAL FRAGMENTS. In a niche in the N wall, a spiral-fluted Norman column-shaft and a piece of Norman abacus, and elements of tracery and other pieces cobbled together to form a cross. – WALL PAINTINGS. Late C15. Large St Christopher (N wall). It includes a coat of arms in the r. corner, identified (by Roger Rosewall) as the arms of Sir Stephen Forster, Lord Mayor of London in 1454. His widow held the manor and advowson from 1465. Note the timber-framed house in the middle distance on the l. from which a hermit emerges. It has the kind of braced panels typical of vernacular buildings of the mid C15. The pattern of the brocade drapery to the l. of the figure is taken from Flemish sources. Around the saint's feet swim fish and an eel. – St Anthony and the pig (S wall); unrecognizable but with well-drawn foliage on the trees. This painting is late C15. – STAINED GLASS. E window by *M.E. Aldrich Rope*, 1937. Christ in majesty. Good but rather typical insipid colouring of the interwar years.

Immediately S, the OLD RECTORY of 1874 by *John Ladds*, a very good example of the scale and style of such buildings by that time, compete with coach house. Partly of coursed limestone, reused from the previous house on the site, with the rest in pressed red Leicestershire brick and moulded terracotta details.

MONKS HARDWICK HOUSE
2 m. NE of St Neots

Elegant front range of *c.* 1840, gault brick with a stone pedimented Doric porch. The back wing is much older, evidently part of a large house which was built by Sir Edmund Anderson, Chief Justice of the Common Pleas (1582–1605; cf. Eyeworth, Beds). Timber-framed and red brick chimneybreast on the E side. House and farm yard surrounded by a MOAT, about 660 ft by 300 ft (200 metres by 91 metres), entirely complete except behind the farm buildings.

MORBORNE

1090

ALL SAINTS. The most prominent part is the early C17 brick tower with its crenellated top. The W window has a pediment. Of the same time also probably the low mullioned windows with uncusped lights to the N aisle and the porch entrance with four-centred head. The oldest feature dates from c. 1140, when the church was held by Crowland Abbey, namely the chancel arch with big scalloped capitals, rope-moulding, fat rolls, and abaci and bases with a flat chevron decoration as at Castor (q.v.). That the arch is pointed must be a late improvement, but carefully done, so that the rolls continue as before. Around the arch, flattened saltire patterns (cf. Haddon). After that several parts of c. 1190, i.e. the priest's doorway and the N and S doorways, with waterleaf capitals and arches of one step and one chamfer. Of c. 1240 is the N arcade. Three bays, round piers with base-spurs, double-chamfered arches, some with nice scrolly stop-chamfers. Of c. 1260 the S arcade, similar but with a little nailhead. The bases of both arcades are of the waterholding variety. The chancel N window, on the evidence of its wall painting (*see* below) is mid-C13, and the SE window too, but it is of two lights with plate tracery and inside an attached mid-shaft that ends in foliage (cf. the chancel window at Haddon). The DOUBLE PISCINA belongs to this, with the three curious recesses in the tympanum. Can they have been for relics? The S transept S window of three lancet lights, very slightly stepped, looks late C13 too and this end of the transept appears extended. Nothing medieval is later. Restorations in 1864 (E window) and 1901–2 (roof etc.). Lovely C19 hanging OIL LAMPS. – WALL PAINTING. In the reveal of the N chancel window. Part of a St Christopher. Dated to the mid C13 by the early Gothic style of his dress. That is rare. – MONUMENT. Almost totally defaced effigy of a priest, first half C13, his feet placed against two human heads.

MANOR HOUSE, S of the church. Stone front with a datestone of 1692 over the door and the arms of Sir Anthony Forrest. C19 brick wing to the rear. Also some brick COTTAGES built by the Milton estate; by their surveyor *Alfred Sykes*, c. 1872–6.

PETERBOROUGH TRANSMITTING STATION, Morborne Hill. One long, slender, cable-stayed, latticework RADIO MAST, 505 ft (153 metres) high, of 2006, replacing the original of 1959 destroyed by a fire. Shorter TELECOMMUNICATIONS TOWER, a reinforced concrete column ringed by circular platforms.

ROUND BARROW, 1¼ m. E of the church. The mound is 50 ft (15 metres) in diameter and 6 ft (1.8 metres) high. Traces of the surrounding quarry ditch are still visible.

NEEDINGWORTH

THE CHESTNUTS. Red brick farmhouse, dated 1710 inside on the staircase. Of that date convincingly the l. wing with hipped roof and modillion cornice. The r. part has a moulded cornice, its doorway and windows remodelled later.

LOCK-UP, Church Street. Brick, dated 1838.

NETHERTON *see* PETERBOROUGH

NEWBOROUGH [P]

Borough Fen was drained and enclosed by Acts of 1812 and 1819, which also created the parish and provided for the church.

ST BARTHOLOMEW. 1826–9 by *William Custance*, the cost met by the Crown. Yellow brick with a thinly detailed, crenellated, W tower, plain pointed windows with timber tracery and shallow sanctuary. – ROYAL ARMS and marble COMMANDMENTS AND CREED TABLETS. – STAINED GLASS. 1938 by *A. K. Nicholson Studios* (*G. E. R. Smith*).

DUCK DECOY, 1¼ m. N in a wood. One of the oldest in the Fens, first referred to in 1670 and operated by the Williams family from then until 1958. Radiating from the central pond are eight tapering 'pipes', for the netting of wildfowl.

HILLFORT, 1 m. NW, bisected by Decoy Road. Two concentric lines of ditched and banked earthworks can be seen W of the road. Outer one very poorly preserved. All traces of the remaining earthwork circuit E of the road have been obliterated. The site appears to have formed a defended lowland settlement during the Iron Age and may have been the seat of a petty local chief.

NORMAN CROSS

A stop on the Great North Road until the A1 became a motorway. PREMIER INN, on the E side, is the former Norman Cross Hotel, of 1962–5 by *Messrs Charrington's Architects' Department* and one of an early generation of motels, with a distinctive circular bedroom wing, two storeys around a central court.*

---

*I am grateful to John Minnis for drawing my attention to the significance of this design. The ENGLISH GARDEN HOTEL, noted by Pevsner on the W side of the A1, has been demolished.

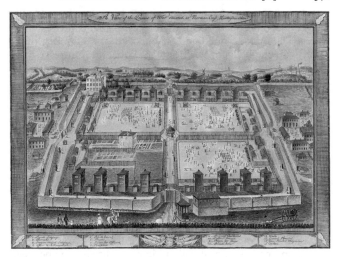

Norman Cross Depot, bird's-eye view.
c. 1810

The large open field to its E is the site of the DEPOT built for
French and Dutch prisoners of war by the Transport Office of
the Admiralty, under the direction of *William Adams*, Master
Carpenter to the Board of Ordnance, 1796–7. It was the first
of its kind, with a grid-plan layout of block houses etc. whose
timber frames were prefabricated in London. The Entente
Cordiale Society erected a MONUMENT in 1914, by *H. P. Cart
de Lafontaine*. It is a bronze eagle on a Doric column, the
original eagle by *J. A. Stevenson* stolen but replaced by *John
Doubleday*, 2004–5. NORMAN HOUSE was the Barrack-Mas-
ter's residence. It is a three-storey, five-bay box with later walls
l. and r. screening additions of *c.* 1900 behind curved parapets.
The house is timber-framed but brick-cased soon after 1816,
when it was purchased by Major Kelly, the last Brigade Major
of the military barracks. Inside it has an interesting plan of a
transverse corridor with staircases at each end. The walls are
simply boarded with planks, just as the block houses must have
been. Fielded panelling in one room is a later improvement.
Behind the house, a section of the camp WALL with round
arch. E is the former Superintendent's House (now called OLD
GOVERNOR'S HOUSE), also timber-framed but cased in brick
in 1816. Three storeys of large sashes on the entrance front,
two bays of arched windows to the garden and one at the rear.

NORTHBOROUGH [P]

1000

ST ANDREW. The general impression is more curious than beautiful – a small church like many others in the neighbourhood

and the fragment of an enlargement so bold that it would have given Northborough one of the biggest parish churches in the area. The original building is late C12 to C13. Late C12 the w end with the bellcote (cf. Peakirk). Four thin buttresses, two open bell arches with continuous roll mouldings, a gable, and inside the line of the former roof. s porch c. 1500 but C13 the s doorway (orders of colonnettes, moulded arch with very wilful details, a little stiff-leaf, two headstops and volutes surviving from a gable that contained a statue). Of the same date the s aisle windows (the N aisle renewed in the C17), the arcades inside (typical E.E., three bays, circular piers, circular capitals and abaci, double-chamfered arches), the double SEDILIA and PISCINA in the s aisle, and the clerestory with dogtooth.

Then comes the start of a great Dec renewal, beginning with the chancel – see the chancel arch with fillets on the responds and knobbly leaves on one capital and the N and s windows. The transeptal s chapel follows, probably c. 1350, on the cusp of Late Dec and Perp. It is taller than the rest, two big bays long, and ends in a wall with a big five-light window between two polygonal turrets with pointed roofs. The window has flowing tracery of original design under a four-centred arch. The E and w windows are equally interesting. They have segmental arches, and the tracery beneath them is of arch heads standing on the apexes of the arches of the lights. The arch heads are filled with minor tracery motifs. The transept is embattled and below the parapet has a frieze of ballflower that is repeated inside. The w wall is obviously not in its final form. To the N of the window it recedes, and there is an arch there rising only partly above the roof of the old aisle. This arch must have been intended to be the connection between the new work and a new, much higher aisle i.e. a completely new w arm. In the interior, the incompleteness is even more noticeable where the aisle roof cuts across the arch head. Here one can also appreciate that the arch is one of a fine pair with continuous mouldings of two waves – as also in the broad arch to the chancel – sharing a slender, detached pier that has a square core with four demi-shafts (i.e. quadrilobed section) and moulded capitals. This is an East Anglian fashion in the early to mid C14 among the more ambitious churches. A narrow passage is formed between this arcade and the w wall but the transverse arch between the pier and the aisle s wall is abruptly terminated (its E pier cutting through the piscina in the aisle). The respond of the s arch stands on a small horizontal human figure.

The s window of the transept chapel is shafted inside, the other windows have headstops. In the E wall between the two windows, and originally no doubt above the altar, a long bracket with defaced foliage for statues and two rich canopies with intricate tracery and mini-vaults (Christopher Wilson has suggested that the work might have been executed by the author of the early C14 High Altar screen at Peterborough Cathedral). Piscina in the angle with the end wall, where two large tomb recesses are provided. Beneath the w side of the aisle is a barrel-vaulted ossuary (still with some bones). Vice stair in the SE turret. The work is lavish throughout and done in excellent masonry. But who paid for it? Like the manor house, with which it shares so many details, it surely must have been instigated by Roger Northburgh, Bishop of Lichfield and Coventry (see the mitred head corbel on the arch to the chancel). – ORGAN. By *John Avery*, 1784. Made for Apethorpe Hall (Northants). A charming piece. – WALL PAINTINGS. Uncovered in 1894. Patterns over the N arcade (C13?) and on the S aisle wall cartouches (C18?). – MONUMENT. In the S chapel. James Claypole, the tomb dated 1594. Big, rather bare standing monument with a plain arch and strapwork tomb-chest. No effigy. Claypole arms above, probably added in the C17.

NORTHBOROUGH MANOR HOUSE. A remarkable survival of 86 hall and gatehouse of a major manor house of *c.* 1320–40, saved from dereliction in 1972–4. It was almost certainly built for Roger Northburgh, Bishop of Lichfield and Coventry, but much altered in the earlier C17 for the Claypoles. James Claypole, whose monument is in the church, bought the manor in 1563. Oliver Cromwell's daughter married John Claypole in 1646 and Cromwell's widow also lived at Northborough. She was buried in the church in 1665.

The early C14 GATEWAY has a mystifyingly skewed plan. Broad N and S arches with one chamfer and one wavy chamfer (cf. the S chapel of the church). From the N there is inside first a very narrow bay, formerly rib-vaulted, then an acutely set cross-wall with entrances for carriages and pedestrians (cf. Abbot's Gate, Peterborough), then a wider bay, also formerly rib-vaulted. The entrances in the cross-wall have a simple rounded moulding. Integral with the gate is the two-storey lodging to the l., with vice stair showing that it formerly had a full upper storey. The roof is now as altered in the early C17 when the range to its r. was rebuilt, or added, for STABLES AND LODGINGS above (converted as a house 1972–4). On the outer front this has a row of circular openings and three-light mullions to first floor and attic, and on the inner front three storeys of the same windows and doors with round arches and four-centred heads. Cube sundial on the middle dormer. The attic has fireplaces at each end.

The HOUSE is set at an angle from the gatehouse. The hall of the C14 can easily be picked out from the C17 surroundings. It has to the N two tall two-light windows with straight heads and reticulated tracery of a quatrefoil between two half quatre-foils (unblocked in 1972–4 following the removal of an early C17 floor – see the dormers of that date), ballflower frieze (cf. the church) and a thick buttress. To the r. is the doorway behind the Jacobean porch. The doorway has a filleted roll moulding to a two-centred arch, and originally led into the screens passage. The back doorway is also preserved, and there are two hall windows to the back as well, though one of them is not in line with the front window again to accommodate the buttress. Especially rare is the survival of the W gable of the hall range with bold leaf crockets and the chimneyshaft at its apex. The W cross-wing was the service end with a fine chamber on the first floor, although its roof has been rebuilt. Fleuron on the gable and a quatrefoil. The two-light window is the head of the window for the medieval chamber (rere-arch visible inside). The W door to this wing, a pointed and chamfered surround, is another C14 survival. At the SE (rear) corner of this range are traces of slit windows which lit a vice stair to the room above (removed). Corresponding with the porch to the E is a projection that seems to have contained a staircase (slit windows and fine blocked moulded arch in the E wall at first floor). It must have connected with an E solar wing (the E wall of the hall was completely rebuilt in the 1970s), for which foundations have been discovered.

Inside, the hall windows have segmental heads and caps of shafts, again of similar character to the church's S chapel. Fine smoke-blackened roof, revealed in the 1970s, of coupled rafters with braced double collars. Most likely the buttresses seen outside anticipated construction of a yet grander roof. W of the former screens passage one can still see the three low doorways which, according to the standard arrangement of the English manor house, must have led into buttery, kitchen passage to the W door, and pantry. They have crocketed ogee heads below taller ogee gables and this profusion of fleuron and ballflower is very exciting, although defaced.* In the first-floor room of the cross-wing, a fireplace of *c.* 1600.

Between church and manor house the architectural interest of the village is almost exhausted. 100 yds E of the church, the PRIMITIVE METHODIST CHAPEL of 1869, also brick. The cottages nearby are typical for the locality. CLARE COTTAGE, E of the chapel, was given to the poet John Clare in 1823 by Lord Fitzwilliam. He lived here for ten years (see also Helpston) and his wife and children are buried in the churchyard.

NORTHOLM see EYE

2060

OFFORD CLUNY

The village is so called because it lies by a crossing on the Ouse and because the famous Cluny Abbey in Burgundy was lord of the manor from the C11 to the early C15.

ALL SAINTS. Primitive C13 S arcade with octagonal piers and single-chamfered arches. N arcade of three bays with round

---

*The tops of the arches have been cut off. Very probably this was caused by insertion of a gallery or similar feature at this end of the hall, level with the blocked opening at the S end of this wall.

piers, octagonal abaci, and double-hollow-chamfered arches with broaches. That must be late C13. The chancel arch matches. In the S aisle a C14 piscina with cusped arch in a square frame and reset windows of similar date in the S porch. Otherwise a Perp church, built of cobbles, with a W tower whose spire was removed in 1851, a clerestory and a nave roof (much replaced) with six well-detailed carved figures, including two angels with furled wings. The minimum red brick chancel is dated 1726, with Gothic windows of the early C20 (strange roof inside, the trusses edged in fretwork lending an alpine character). – PULPIT. Jacobean, with two tiers of the familiar broad blank arches. – LECTERN. Also with minor Jacobean panels. – COMMUNION RAIL. 1752. Given by the rector, Dr Newcombe, Master of St John's College, Cambridge. – COMMANDMENTS BOARDS. 1788, 'the gift of John Parker' M. D. At the base of one, a hand clutching an unfurling scroll. – STAINED GLASS. E window, 1850, and typical of that date in the vivid colours, trellis patterns and Evangelists' symbols in roundels. Equally typical of its time the S aisle window (35/635 Squadron Memorial) by *George Monaghan*, 1998. – MONUMENTS. E of the S aisle. Rev. George Deane †1782. Chest tomb with full and half balusters of square section on dainty bases.

MANOR HOUSE, E of the church, was built *c.* 1704 for the Deane family, on the site of an earlier house to which the extensive demesne belonged, and later owned by the Sismeys. A stately nine-bay front, hard to the street, with somewhat projecting two-bay wings in line with the garden walls extending N and S. Red brick, Flemish bond with a platband, two storeys, modillion cornice, hipped roof. The doorway is reset in a later porch. Half-hipped NE wing and half-hipped dormer to a projecting bay at the rear which contains the door. SE wing in matching style added 1902. Fine gatepiers to the street and to the garden across the road.

S of this, the MANOR FARMHOUSE. Its earliest part, at right angles to the street, is C16 and timber-framed with a gabled oriel at the back. Twice added to, first for a jettied projection on the S front and stair-turret to the N side, then comes the much larger two-storey range to the street, either late C17 or early C18. Further S on the opposite side, IVY COTTAGE has a good mid- to late C17 plastered front of three gables and another gable to the S end. The middle bay projects forward and has the entrance and, inside, a stair of flat section balusters and faceted newels.

OFFORD MILLS (former), by the Ouse. Flour mills, built *c.* 1880. Biscuit-coloured brick. By the river lock, and associated with the navigation, a TOLL HOUSE of 1851. Neo-Tudor details. Nearby, a red brick GRANARY, *c.* 1800.

OFFORD HILL HOUSE, 1½ m. N. 1908 by *S. Inskip Ladds* for J. P. L. D. Stables. Domestic Revival in red brick with stone dressings and gables half-timbered. At one end a tower with a wavy parapet.

OFFORD DARCY

St Peter (Churches Conservation Trust). Externally the church is of cobbles. The N arcade is Norman, with square piers with angle shafts (cf. Southoe and Little Paxton chancel arches). E of the arcade was an arched recess in the N aisle which was converted into an opening in the C19. The chancel is C13, with a S and a smaller N lancet (heavily restored in the C19), although traces of yet earlier windows were uncovered in 1985. The E window is Perp. Then follows the S aisle, which is of *c.* 1300 and has curvilinear tracery and a fine trail of ballflower around it. Inside, the S arcade with quatrefoil piers with fillets and double-chamfered arches. Handsome ANGLE PISCINA with a vault and a boss and stepped sedilia. The W tower seems of about the same time or just a little later. It has clasping buttresses and a recessed stone ribbed spire (the top rebuilt in 1870), with roll-moulded ribs to the bell-openings and lucarnes. These look early. Perp N aisle and clerestory. C19 roofs on stone corbel heads in the nave and S aisle. – SCREEN. Fixed to the chancel arch, the former top rail of a parclose screen from the N aisle. Dec – which is rare; with ogee arches and foiled circles. – ORGAN SCREEN, filling the tower arch. 1925. – STAINED GLASS. Bits in a chancel S window. – S aisle (war memorial); by *W. Glasby*, 1920, hot-hued figures of archangels. – BRASSES. Reset in the nave floor, Sir Laurence Pabenham †1400 and two wives. Demi-figures, *c.* 22 in. (55 cm) long. He is in armour. According to Mill Stephenson, *c.* 1430. The backs of the wives had been engraved already with canopywork (casts are displayed on the wall). – Brass to Dr William Taylard, priest, †1532, son of William Taylard whose brass is at Diddington. Kneeling figure, 23 in. (58 cm) long. – MONUMENTS. Civilian and wife, sunk stone effigies, her draperies very confused. The suggested date is late C14 (N aisle). – Richard Nailour †1616 and family. Kneeling parents above, children below. Alabaster (S aisle) with a curved top and skulls.

Manor House, to the SW, was built between 1606 and 1608 by Richard Nailour as a conventional brick house with wings and hipped roof but it was overlaid in the early C18 with a stage-set thin façade of three storeys. This is irregular in its fenestration, and in the middle it has a curious giant arched recess, revealing the depth between the old and new fronts, with a balustraded loggia and gigantic shell-head. (Early C17 fireplace in the entrance hall with Nailour's arms, an overmantel in the chamber above with the usual Jacobean blind arcading and staircase with heavy turned balusters. NHLE.)

The Limes, E of the church, is the former rectory of 1859 by *Edward Habershon* for the Rev. William Thornhill, who was also the patron. Yellow brick with red brick diapering and some tile decoration. (Stables etc. of 1874 by *John Day* of Bedford.) In the village, No. 79 High Street, NE, is a good early C18 red brick farmhouse with segmental-arched windows. Also the Horseshoe Inn, its jettied cross-wing dated 1626.

OLD HURST*

ST PETER. Nave and chancel in one. The building is E.E., see
the s doorway with a pointed-trefoiled head and strap hinges,
the lancets and pairs of lancets as windows, and the Y-tracery
of the E and W windows. Restored and refitted for the Rev.
Charles Dashwood Goldie by *William White* (cf. Woodhurst) in
1867–9, when the space was made for two bells in the gable
and the tie-beam roof with crown-posts made. Vestry added
1925 over the N door; C13 ironwork recorded by the RCHM
may have been lost at that time. – FONT. Octagonal. Probably
of *c.* 1300. Blank windows with intersecting tracery on all eight
sides. – PILLAR PISCINA (SE corner). Norman stem decorated
with diamond patterns. – SCULPTURE. In the chancel. From
a very odd rood erected on the roof by White. Roughly human
shapes of the Virgin and St John carved with flowers. – STAINED
GLASS. E window, *c.* 1870 and probably by *N. J. Westlake* (MK).
– s window, *Kempe & Co.*, 1922.

OLD WESTON

ST SWITHIN. Completely separate from the village. The square
W tower has an odd octagonal top. It starts with broaches at
the angles that continue as pinnacles, but then there is another
string course before the spire begins properly. Two tiers of
lucarnes, the lower three-light Dec. Also unusual is the way
that the heads of the bell-openings rise into the octagon. They
are Perp, of two lights with transoms and show the concurrence
of Dec and Perp in the mid to later C14. The earliest part of
the church is the plain N doorway, which must belong to
c. 1200. The chancel follows. Its Y-traceried windows indicate
the late C13. A little later are the four-bay arcades. Octagonal
piers and double-chamfered arches. One (s) has a little nailhead, and so has the one pier with round abacus. The s arches
have scrolled stops. The s doorway with continuous filleted
mouldings belongs to the arcades, as does the chancel arch.
The chancel SE window continues down as a sedilia, with
piscina alongside. Straight-headed Dec N aisle and clerestory
windows. In the s aisle is a specially pretty three-light Perp
window with traceried spandrels to connect a four-centred
arch with a straight top. Roofs of, or repaired in, 1657 (nave),
1638 (N aisle) and 1785 (s aisle). Restored in 1847 by *George
Allen* of St Ives. His are the BOX PEWS, PULPIT, STALLS AND
TOWER SCREEN. – WALL PAINTINGS. Revealed during a
restoration in 1895 and at that time more extensive. In the s
aisle, C14 scenes: the enthronement of one bishop by two others,
the beheading of St John(?), part of a wheel of fortune with
figure behind, and, in the jambs of the E window, St Margaret

---

*MANOR FARM with its fine Jacobean staircase, noted in the first edition of this
guide, was demolished in 1984.

and St Catherine. – PISCINA (s aisle) and FONT. Both C14. –
CROSS SLABS (chancel). Two good large examples of *c*. 1300,
one with double omega symbols, the other with a cusped cross.
– ROYAL ARMS. Above the chancel arch; tiled. Presumably
of 1847.

In the village, TOWN FARMHOUSE is especially interesting and
well restored. It must be *c*. 1600, has a smart uniform timber-
framed façade of five, rather than the usual three, bays with a
central doorway and gabled wings at either end. Impressive
brick stack at the S end. The usual lobby entry against the
centre chimneystack but no obvious distinction between a
domestic and service end, so that each of the rooms to l. and
r. of the entrance appear to be the hall, with further rooms in
the wings. Can it have been designed for two families living
in the adjoining parts? Some minor C19 additions at the rear.
On the upper floor, the chambers over the S end have plaster
barrel-vaulted ceilings, and one has its closet over the entrance.

ORTON LONGUEVILLE *see* PETERBOROUGH

ORTON SOUTHGATE *see* PETERBOROUGH

ORTON WATERVILLE *see* PETERBOROUGH

OXMOOR *see* HUNTINGDON

OXNEY *see* EYE

PASTON *see* PETERBOROUGH

PAXTON HALL *see* LITTLE PAXTON

PEAKIRK [P]

ST PEGA. A unique dedication but not its original one, which
was to the Holy Trinity, the Virgin Mary and All Saints. St Pega
was the sister of St Guthlac of Crowland (Lincs.), 5 m. E. She
became an anchoress, founded a cell here and died in 719,
returning from pilgrimage to Rome. In spite of this early
history there is only a little long-and-short work to be seen at
the SE corner of the nave.* The W wall belonged to an aisleless
Norman building (earlier roofline visible inside) and the bellcote is Norman too (cf. Werrington and Northborough). It has

---

*An impressive fragment of a Saxon CROSS-SHAFT with interlace, foliage and
Mercian beasts, was discovered under the church floor in 1879–80. It was moved
to The Hermitage and is now in private ownership.

Peakirk, wall paintings.
Drawing by E. C. Rouse, 1953

two plain arches on plain imposts and one above them. Gable
with one set-off to allow for the two lower arches. Norman also
the ornate s doorway, the best in the area. One order of slim
colonnettes. Tympanum with three fan-motifs, two horizontal
from the bottom corners spreading to the centre, the third
vertically rising in the middle. Arch with chevron on the surface
as well as at right angles to it and with other motifs. The outer
porch entrance is Dec (cf. Werrington), the roofline of the
former porch may still be seen. The N doorway is plain, round-
arched, and single-chamfered. Of the c13 the w lancets. The
straight-headed aisle windows are Dec, the s aisle s with ballflower. Internally the mid c12 is represented by the N arcade
of three bays. Circular piers with many-scalloped capitals of
mixed design and square abaci with nicked angles. Round
arches with roll mouldings. A little later the N chancel chapel.
One respond still has many-scalloped capitals, the other with
crude vertical leaves, and the arch still has rolls, but it is
pointed. The capitals of the responds have late c12 leaves, the
s ones like waterleaf but the N ones developing into crockets
and both with strings of beading. The chancel arch is pointed,
without the roll and of the same form as the s arcade. This is
fully E.E. Circular piers, circular moulded capitals, and abaci
with a little nailhead decoration. Double-chamfered pointed
arches. The chancel is largely Perp, with big three-light windows
and a great E window of five, filling the gable. Sweeting says it
was rebuilt in 1477 by the Abbot of Crowland. In the E wall
an odd quatrefoil. c19 roof but head corbels are preserved,
repeated in the E wall of the N aisle.

Chancel reordered by *E. M. Barry*, 1878–9; TILES by *Maw
& Co*. Chapel restored by *Leslie T. Moore*, 1944–8. – LECTERN.
The wooden stem is of the early c14 – a rarity. It has slender
attached shafts. – WALL PAINTINGS. An outstanding, mostly

C14, scheme, uncovered and restored in the 1940s by E. Clive Rouse, but still less extensive than when it was first revealed in 1848. Cycle of the Passion above the N arcade in two tiers (top l. the utensils on the table of the Last Supper, below, Scourging of Christ; then a St Christopher interrupting the cycle; then Christ washing St Peter's feet and Crucifixion and Deposition below, followed by Entombment and Resurrection; at the E end, Mocking of Christ and the Noli me Tangere below). Below both tiers a zigzag band painted in perspective. The Crucifixion scene includes the Miracle (Conversion) of Longinus, the figure very similar to that of Reason at Longthorpe Tower (*see* p. 640). In addition, in the N aisle, E of the N door, the Three Quick and the Three Dead of very sophisticated details, again like Longthorpe. Also, over the N door, a scene representing a Warning to Gossips. Two women sit whispering to one another. A devil presses their heads together. Two further paintings in the S aisle SE and N aisle NE are unidentified. – STAINED GLASS. E window by *Kempe & Co.*, 1914. Crucifixion with flanking figures of St Pega and St Peter. Instruments of the Passion in the top lights. – Chancel S 1860s and S aisle E, 1856, by *J. Powell & Sons*, the former with gold leaf patterns. – Chancel SW by *Percy Bacon*, 1917. Masculine figures and a dark palette. – Four by *M. & A. O'Connor*, 1839–50 (S aisle SE, S aisle W, W and N aisle W). – N aisle, 1952 by *Francis Skeat*. – N chapel N, 1995 by *Norman Attwood*. – MONUMENTS – William Whitsed †1796 and Sarah Whitsed †1810, signed by *Edward Sharman* of Peterborough. – Richard Cumberland, rector, †1737. Very simple, by comparison with his father's monument in Peterborough Cathedral; palm fronds and crest. By *John Hunt* of Northampton.

E of the church is a GREEN with houses around one side and, set back to the N (No. 7 Chestnut Close), a perfect Regency villa, three bays to front and sides under a platform roof and a lovely cast-iron Gothick porch. E, on Northborough Road, THE HERMITAGE is a house of 1936 (in use as a convent until 2001), attached to a small CHAPEL. This was the C13 successor to St Pega's cell and is now as restored in 1879–80 by *E. M. Barry*. Nave perhaps C15, the chancel *c.* 1300, see the three-light window with trefoiled lights and small trefoils between them. – STAINED GLASS, abstract, by *Robert Maguire* (with *Julia Sheridan Read*), 1999.

Down St Pega's Road is GREYSTONES, the best individual house, set back behind railings and a fine cedar tree in front. Mid-C18 ashlar façade of five bays, with windows in moulded surrounds and in the centre a pedimented doorcase with Venetian window above it. C19 rear addition with ornate cast-iron porch.

Slightly further S on the opposite side, the former RAILWAY STATION of 1848 by *John Taylor* for the GNR. Italianate, with low single-storey wings either side of a short tower for the stationmaster's house, rather altered.

CAR DYKE. A well-preserved section of the Dyke lies 400 yds W of Peakirk village centre. It is 9–16 ft (3–5 metres) wide at this point, and consists of a shallow ditched feature with banks on either side. Formerly interpreted as a canal and a drainage 'catchwater' it is best understood as a boundary dyke marking the edge of a Roman Imperial estate set up in the Fenland from land confiscated from the Iron Age Icenian tribe in the aftermath of the Boudiccan revolt of A.D. 60. Other sections of the Dyke, with recent modifications to its profile, can be seen to the S, running along the Paston Parkway around Peterborough.

PERRY

1060

Originally two hamlets of Grafham (East Perry) and Great Staughton (West Perry). Now they are one, with not much that is of before the mid 1960s when the reservoir was created to the N.

GAYNES HALL, ⅜ m. S. By *George Byfield*, the design exhibited at the RA in 1800. For Sir James Duberly, who bought the manor in 1797. *Repton* produced a Red Book in 1798. Of the medieval manor house of the Engaines, parts of moats survive. Yellow brick, of seven bays and two and a half storeys. Semicircular porch of unfluted, not at all elegant Ionic columns with *Coade* stone capitals. The ground-floor windows are set in blank arches, and the pedimented middle window and the attic window above it are included in one blank arch. Nice broad door under a segmental arch fanlight. On the middle of the eaves a raised parapet with Soanian incised decoration (there was also formerly an urn, also by *Coade*). Oval entrance hall with arched recesses and staircase hall with a circular skylight. NE are STABLES of *c.* 1870. An enclosed court with central carriageway and pedimented ends (now used as a training centre by H.M. Prison Littlehey, opened in 1988). The approach to the house is THE DRIVE. At the top, a charming mid-C19 LODGE, yellow brick with trimming of red around the gables and windows. Tile cresting and ball finials. Timber porch in the angle.

GRAFHAM WATER. A reservoir, begun 1961 and completed 1966 by flooding the valley between Grafham and Perry (*Binnie & Partners*, engineers) with water pumped from the Great Ouse. The water surface created is at the highest level 1,570 acres (628 ha); the deepest depth at that level is 70 ft (21 metres). The dam, at the E end, has a length of 5,600 ft (1,706 metres), but is quite low. Attached to it is a VALVE TOWER, a circular glass pavilion with a saucer-shape domed roof on slender concrete fins. The SAILING CLUB is by *S. Johnson-Marshall* and *Kenneth Buffery* of *Sir Robert Matthew, Johnson-Marshall & Partners*, 1965–6. A nice, nautical-looking job – in its style carrying on from the 1930s rather than succumbing to the Brutalist fashion of the 1960s despite cladding of rough aggregate panels. Circular drum to the roof, flying staircases with tubular steel balustrades and a bridge to the racing box dramatically perched on a tall, slender column.

PETERBOROUGH

The entry for Peterborough covers the city centre and the whole of the built-up area N and S of the Nene which has developed since the New Town was created after 1968. This includes several formerly separate villages.

INTRODUCTION

Peterborough grew up outside the gates of the monastery. The monastery is now a cathedral, and the small town is no longer so small. Celia Fiennes in 1698 after visiting Ely drove on to Peterborough and found the town neat and the cathedral 'a magnificent building standing in the midst on advanced ground'. In 1801 the town still had only 4,075 inhabitants, but in 1874 it was granted city status. When Pevsner visited in 1967 it had grown to nearly 80,000 and it is now over 160,000. The initial growth was due to the railway, several large engineering works and the numerous brick manufactories, whose tall chimneys at Fletton and Woodston were a formidable presence along the S fringe of Peterborough into the later C20 (the last brickworks, at Orton, closed in 1998).

From 1929 the outlying villages of Walton, Werrington, Paston, Gunthorpe and Longthorpe were brought within the city boundaries, and in these areas the council built new housing estates after the war. The government commissioned a special study on the expansion of Peterborough (the *Wells Plan*, published in 1964); a double-decker city centre, with cars on freeways above pedestrian streets, was the vision (to which *Chamberlin, Powell & Bon* contributed). Another followed in 1965 by the relatively unknown *Tom Hancock* (from 1967 in partnership with *John Hawkes* in preparing the more detailed plan for the city), after the decision to make Peterborough one of the third (and as it turned out final) generation of New Towns, along with Milton Keynes and Northampton.

The final scenario closely following Ebenezer Howard's original idea of the 'social city' was for four new townships to N and W of the city centre: Milton (renamed Bretton), Castor (unrealized), Orton, and Paston (later Werrington), all but the first surrounding existing villages. Suburbs S of the Nene – Woodston, Fletton and Stanground – were also drawn within the city, and a large industrial zone expanded to the E on the fenland edge. New industrial areas were also planned close to the A1. The Development Corporation was established in 1968, and after initial co-operation with *Hancock Hawkes*, took the lead in producing and delivering the *Greater Peterborough Master Plan* (1970), with its own architects (Chief Architects *John Cresswell*, 1968–72, and *Keith Maplestone*, 1972–88) designing most of the buildings.

The first housing was underway from 1970, mostly intended for skilled workers drawn from inner London, but with a change in government policy the original target population figure of about 185,000 by 1985 was reduced. Accordingly the plan for Castor township was ditched, and by the end of the Development Corporation in 1988 the population stood at just under 135,000. The emphasis at Peterborough was upon an efficient and brisk implementation of housing targets and the attraction of businesses, especially service industries. The architectural results are mixed and in the main unexceptional for their date. The flat landscape is an obvious disadvantage and great efforts were made to offset this by planting thick belts of trees throughout the outer areas of the city and along the roads (dubbed Parkways), and by creating Nene Park, which runs W from the city centre for several miles along the river with additional lakes and ponds created from the gravel pits left by construction. The extent to which this leafy character has been maintained and the edges between the city and the villages are still clearly defined must be regarded a success, whatever one thinks of the buildings. In the centre, much decrepit building was swept away for the shopping centre, and its multi-storey car parks etc., but the decision to drive Bourges Boulevard across Bridge Street catastrophically destroyed the centre's historic relationship with the river (cf. Huntingdon). Trying to reach the market square on foot from the station is a discouraging experience. Instead, the motorist is rewarded on the sweeping curve of the elevated parkway around the E edge where the cathedral's pre-eminence on the skyline has been respected.

Peterborough.
Engraving by S. and N. Buck, 1731

CATHEDRAL CHURCH OF ST PETER, ST PAUL
AND ST ANDREW

INTRODUCTION

Henry VIII raised Peterborough to cathedral rank in 1541, perhaps encouraged by the fact that his late queen, Katherine of Aragon, had been buried here in 1536. It had been originally the abbey of Medehamstede, founded *c.* 655–6 by a monk, Saxulf, with the patronage of Peada, the first Christian king of Mercia, but was under Benedictine rule by 673. The monastery was sacked by the Danes in 870 at the time of their raids on fenland establishments, but was recolonized and rebuilt in 963 by Aethelwold, Bishop of Winchester, contemporary with his reconstruction of the Benedictine establishments at Ely and Thorney. But the monastery was sacked again by Hereward the Wake in 1070. The church, whose w steeple had been consecrated as recently as 1059, was spared but burnt in the great fire of 1116. The remarkable Chronicle of Hugh Candidus (compiled *c.* 1155–75) relates the beginning of new work. Rebuilding of the monastic quarters was already underway by the time of the conflagration, but the reconstruction of the church was not started until 8 March 1118,* under Abbot John de Séez. He died in 1125. The monks, led by Abbot Martin de Bec, held their first services in the presbytery in 1140; the transepts and tower followed, along with part of the nave, by *c.* 1175. By the mid C12, if not earlier,

---

*This account observes the dates given in the majority of published descriptions of the Cathedral, although Lisa Reilly in her *Architectural History of Peterborough Cathedral* (1997) has advanced the idea that rebuilding began as early as 1107 and only resumed in 1118.

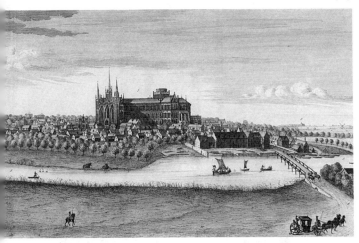

the arm of St Swithun had been brought from Winchester,* and the abbey also possessed the even more precious relic of St Oswald's arm. The W end of the nave cannot have been reached before 1177, for the continuation of the Chronicle, by Robert of Swaffham, tells us that Abbot Benedict built (i.e. probably completed) the whole nave 'usque ad frontem', and he ruled the monastery from 1177 to 1194. He was formerly prior at Canterbury, and in charge there of the cult of Becket; on his removal to Peterborough he brought with him stones from the site of the archbishop's murder, and developed Peterborough as regional centre for the cult with the establishment of a chapel adjacent to the outer gate of the monastery.

It is during Benedict's rule, or in the first years of his successor, that the first flowerings of the Gothic style emerge, with the addition of the W transept. Finally, after many changes of mind, the present W front with its mighty porch was complete. The abbey was dedicated in 1238, although work on the interior was undoubtedly still in hand by that year and in particular the majestic nave ceiling. After that there was a good deal of activity in the cloister and precincts, including the rebuilding of the refectory and infirmary c. 1230–65. A Lady Chapel was built E of the N transept in 1272, apparently by Prior Parys (†1286), and consecrated in 1290 (in type and position probably influencing Ely's a generation later), roughly contemporary with several other embellishments to the cathedral, especially the completion of the NW bell-tower, heightening of the galleries and much refenestration, and major improvements to the precinct

---

*It is of course possible that the relic had been brought to Peterborough much earlier. St Swithun was interred in the Old Minster at Winchester in 973 and his skull was taken to Canterbury in 1005. His remains were translated to the high altar of the new cathedral at Winchester in 1097, but some bones may have been redistributed c. 1150 when the apse was reorganized by Bishop Henry of Blois.

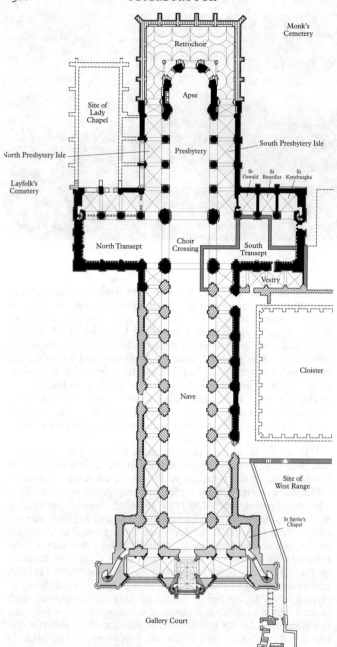

Monk's Cemetery

Retrochoir

Apse

Site of Lady Chapel

North Presbytery Isle

Presbytery

South Presbytery Isle

Layfolk's Cemetery

St Oswald St Benedict St Kyneburgha

North Transept

Choir Crossing

South Transept

Vestry

Cloister

Nave

Site of West Range

St Sprite's Chapel

Gallery Court

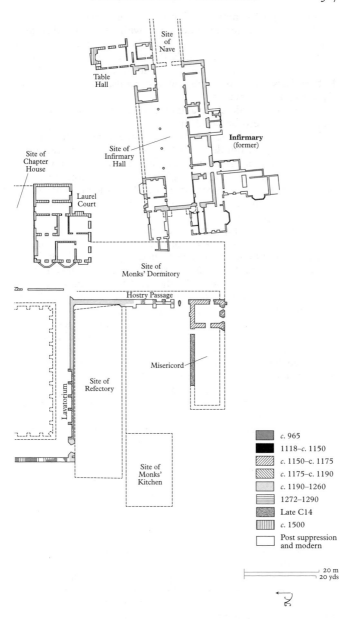

Site
of
Nave

Table
Hall

Site of
Infirmary
Hall

Infirmary
(former)

Site of
Chapter
House

Laurel
Court

Site of
Monks' Dormitory

Hostry Passage

Misericord

Lavatorium

Site of
Refectory

Site of
Monks'
Kitchen

c. 965
1118–*c.* 1150
c. 1150–*c.* 1175
c. 1175–*c.* 1190
c. 1190–1260
1272–1290
Late C14
c. 1500
Post suppression
and modern

20 m
20 yds

Peterborough Cathedral. Plan.

buildings. The Norman crossing tower was replaced in the late
C14 by a lower and less ambitious one, with an octagonal lantern.
A porch was inserted in the W front at about the same time, much
tracery was renewed, and finally the retrochoir, or 'New Building', was erected E of the Norman E end during the rule of Abbot
Robert Kirkton (1496–1528), whose rebus, initials and other
signets appear all over it.

There was considerable vandalism of fittings in the Civil War,
including the destruction of the C15 reredos and high altar. The
cloisters and Lady Chapel were taken down from the early 1640s,
the sale of stone from the chapel enabling the town to repair the
rest of the church. At around this time the retrochoir was converted into the cathedral library. Repairs and restorations were
made from the 1730s, especially in the domestic buildings of the
precincts, and we know that in 1780 new choir screens were
designed by *John Carter*. These were replaced in 1827–32 by
Edward Blore, contemporary with some restoration.

The mid C19 saw another programme of rebuilding in the
precincts but little seems to have been done to the cathedral until
1855, when *George Gilbert Scott* was appointed to make repairs:
'My works here have been slight, and having mainly safety as
their object – much should be done but there are no friends and
little zeal' (*Recollections*, vol. III), preventing him from attending
to the unstable crossing tower in 1874, which was left to *J. L.
Pearson*'s restoration of 1883–97. This was the principal C19 work,
undertaken by *John Thompson & Sons* of Peterborough, twice
bedevilled by public controversy and conflict with the youthful
S.P.A.B. Uproar was first provoked by Pearson's proposal to
restore the Norman design of the crossing tower all round and
build a taller tower with C13-type spire. What Pearson actually
did was rebuild the crossing and its tower in replica, at the
instruction of Archbishop Benson, and design new fittings. At the
same time, his assistant, *J. T. Irvine*, made the first excavations
of the pre-Conquest church beneath the S transept and part of
the crossing. It had wide transepts and, Irvine believed, a straight-
ended chancel. Its nave must have been where the N walk of the
cloister is now. The size of the church shows that this was the
C10 church, rather than anything earlier. Some fragmentary
Roman inscribed slabs of Barnack rag were also found. As the
site of Durobrivae (*c.* 4 m. SW; *see* p. 720) belonged to the medieval monastery, that may have been their source. Next, after a
gale blew down a pinnacle in 1895 and the gables proved unstable,
Pearson took down the entire upper W front and rebuilt using
the old stones. Work on the W front was completed in 1902. A
brief pause, then, from 1920, yet further programmes of sensitive
repair and replacement by *Leslie T. Moore*, which engaged him
until his death. *G. G. Pace* continued the work, with some minor
contributions of his own. Major repairs proceeded in 1994 under
the direction of *Julian Limentani* and were nearly complete when
a calamitous fire in 2001 required extensive cleaning of the paintings of the nave roof.

EXTERIOR

The cathedral is built of limestone, which is assumed to have come from a quarry near Barnack (q.v.), where the abbey owned manors. This has ensured a unity and consistency of appearance over several centuries. It is 481 ft (146 metres) long and 81 ft (24.6 metres) high inside, and its PLAN consists of nave and aisles, a W transept and W porch with towers, a crossing with tower rising to a height of 143 ft (43.5 metres), transepts with E aisles for chapels, a presbytery with aisles, and retrochoir, also known as the 'New Building'. Despite the fact that medieval Peterborough was never more than an abbey, its plan and elevations show ambition well above its station.

A tour should begin with the EAST END of the Norman church. This largely remains, though partly obscured by later alterations. It had one wide apse, a rare survival among major Norman buildings in England, which still forms the E end of the presbytery, and two smaller side apses (both removed) which were contained within the square ends of the aisles, as existed at Ely. The main APSE is embraced by the Perp retrochoir, so that the exterior of its ground floor is only visible inside (*see* below). But above the ground floor there are windows in two tiers (comparable to the elevation of the apse at Cerisy-la-Forêt in Normandy) with a frieze of intersecting blank arcading between the two tiers. Intersecting arches are found at Durham as early as 1093, though at Norwich they appear first in work of *c.* 1120 (ambulatory wall under throne, upper N transept front). The bays are separated by demi-shafts, rising to a corbel course. In the top tier, in the straight bay on each side before the curve of the apse, the round-arched form of the original windows is preserved complete. The other windows must have been the same, with a principal arch flanked by narrower blind arches, but the central openings are taller replacements, with segmental heads and sills cutting into the frieze. All the windows have flowing Dec tracery. The parapet has medallions with busts in trefoils. These belong to the C13 (and stem of course from much older, Roman tradition).

The RETROCHOIR or 'New Building', erected by Abbot Kirkton (1496–1528), abuts the E end of the C12 presbytery aisles and is as wide as the church nave and aisles. John Harvey suggested that *John Wastell*, before he began at King's College, Cambridge, may have been the designer. It is four bays deep on the sides, arranged 1+1+2 and separated by buttresses. The set-offs of these are decorated with fleurons. Four-light and three-light windows with cusp-headed panel tracery and central upper lights divided into four, a design that is indeed related both to windows at King's College and also to Wastell's work at St James, Bury St Edmunds. The work is crowned by an openwork parapet with triangular merlons, again very similar to that of King's, and including a string of bosses below the parapet with Kirkton's rebus. Seated figures on the tops of the buttresses, probably the Apostles, which must have been of good quality when they were newly made and still have a fine architectonic effect (cf. similar figures at Norwich).

Now, to return to the Norman work W of the apse, with the PRESBYTERY and the TRANSEPTS. One can begin on the S side, although the details are essentially the same to the N also. The junction with the presbytery is stressed by spirelets to the turrets containing stairs above gallery level. This is an unusual survival in England but has precedent in Normandy and is also a feature of the choir at Canterbury. The presbytery is four bays long and has the same continuous corbel course as the apse, as well as preserving the original tripartite clerestory windows, whose side pieces are blank arches. The bays are, as before, separated by demi-shafts. The tracery of the clerestory is Perp and there is in addition a Perp parapet with blank quatrefoils. The aisles are of only three bays. They have courses of chevron above and below their windows, and this frieze evidently continued around the ends of the aisles and the apse (traces can still be seen inside where the ground floor of the main apse is exposed). It is always said that such chevron decoration, which became the main stand-by of the Anglo-Norman style when it came to enrichments, was introduced c. 1110 at Durham. At Peterborough it occurs, as this course shows, from the very beginning, i.e. from 1118. The lower course of chevron denotes the sill level of the original windows although nothing on this side indicates their form other than a tiny strip of billet at the E end which was part of the hood-mould. The plinth is moulded and continues, almost without interruption, throughout the whole of the church from E to W. The bays are separated by broad Norman buttresses with shafts at the angles that terminate about halfway up the gallery and show that the gallery wall was raised c. 1300 to accommodate taller windows that have flowing tracery of three stepped ogee arches and elongated mouchettes in the heads. The aisle windows are also typical work of the same date, with five stepped lancet lights with traceried heads under a wide segmental arch. The E wall of the S transept is similarly affected. Again, chevron ran at sill-level to the aisle but on the gallery this is reduced to a plain moulding. All the windows have been replaced: at gallery level the centre one is of the same type as the presbytery gallery, the other two with pointed arches and fancier tracery. The aisle chapels have taller late C13 Geometric ones with three stepped lights and three foiled circles over; the pattern derives perhaps from Lincoln's Angel Choir (1256–80). At the clerestory level the design of the Norman clerestory remains, again with demi-shafts and Perp tracery in the Norman surrounds.

The transept end wall has on the ground floor windows with chevron and billet surrounds and the same chevron sill course continued as before. The S doorway also has chevron in the arch. It has three orders of colonnettes. But in the upper storeys the undecorated sill course of the transept's E wall is carried on and simpler roll mouldings of the kind used for all the other Norman windows are substituted. Much blank arcading of small arched friezes (not intersecting) above the first and the second upper windows are another subtle change from the treatment of the presbytery and apse. The wall ends in a gable flanked by polygonal turrets. Very oddly the angle shafts of the centre buttresses die into the face of the gable, and since the gable has crockets running up it this too must be a later alteration. Within the Norman surrounds the windows are all Perp of the type already seen.

The character of the Norman elevations of the presbytery and transept E walls can be appreciated more easily on the N side, where the presbytery aisle E window has its original shape preserved, with a chevron and a billet surround continuing as a string to l. and r. Traces of such details survive also above the later arch of the W window. There is also fragmentary arcading at the gallery level and it survives complete with its windows and blank lower coupled arches l. and r. in the N bays of the transept gallery below a corbel course. The reason for this survival is the construction in the late C13 of the Lady Chapel, which stood against these two bays and parallel with the presbytery aisle. It was demolished either c. 1652 (Gunton) or c. 1661 (Britton), but the outline of its gable building is preserved and at its head has slender colonnettes framing former window openings. The other gallery windows to the transept and presbytery are, accordingly, late C13 and clearly done in one campaign with the windows at this level on the S side. Also associated with the Lady Chapel are the other ground-floor windows, of which the l. window in the transept aisle wall is of the same type as those seen in this position on the S transept. Although restored it appears to be of a pattern adopted for the Lady Chapel itself. The two other transept windows and the middle one of the presbytery aisle have chamfered arches and circular filleted shafts characteristic of c. 1280. Evidently the transept windows were originally full-height arches open to the chapel. Their Perp tracery and door is an insertion, perhaps c. 1669, when *John Lovin* buttressed the transept following the chapel's demolition. In the angle with the N buttress of the transept (i.e. the former NW corner of the Lady Chapel) is the beginning of wall arcading, our only clue to the interior elevations of the chapel. The middle window in the presbytery aisle must have been an open arch which provided an entrance to the chapel of St Thomas, which was erected shortly before 1298 by the abbey's cellarer, Godfrey of Crowland, in the space between the aisle and the Lady Chapel. Its position, under the Norman aisle window, is marked by two blank arches, a blocked piscina (?) and the springers of a vault. The arch of the W window in the presbytery aisle is later again, Perp, with chamfered shafts and polygonal moulded caps. It too was full-length but blocked and given tracery at the same time as the others. The transept buttresses are probably those erected in the mid C19 by *Scott*, but the presbytery buttress with a flying arch is 1923 by *Leslie T. Moore*.

The N wall of the N transept repeats the programme of the S transept except that there is chevron and billet moulding only in the window of the E aisle. In the W wall there is again much blank arcading of the same system as on the S and N sides, and on this side, where one can see N wall and W wall together, the full power of the Norman elevational composition of the transepts can be appreciated.

The CROSSING TOWER is *Pearson*'s of 1884–6. It was originally work of *c.* 1155–75, probably as high as now but altered *c.* 1371–2 (according to the dendrochronology) and crowned by a wooden octagon somewhat like the lantern at Ely (though at Peterborough only the lantern was octagonal) with corner turrets. The octagon was removed in 1813 and the turrets heightened. Pearson's tower is a careful rebuilding in replica, omitting only the early C19 turrets, and has polygonal panelled buttresses, two three-light bell-openings with transom, and, flanking them, blank two-light and four-light windows. Some of the tracery designs match that of the aisle galleries. The parapet is panelled.

The N side of the NAVE continues the Norman system of the E part for one and a half bays at clerestory level before a new pattern of windows with single lower arches l. and r. is established. Of details the following ought to be noted also. The corbel table carries on the system of the E parts, although with some odd changes, e.g. the carving of the corbels at the W end. There are certain other changes in various points. Such changes are that the chevron frieze at the sill level of the aisle windows goes on for three bays before it is discontinued; indeed it actually reappears in the gallery sill course from which it had been omitted for the transepts. Also the buttresses abandon their shafts at the level of the arcading of the gallery. Near the middle of the N aisle is a doorway with three orders of colonnettes and capitals with decorated scallops. The arches have exceptionally much chevron, both on the front and at right angles to it. The details look mid-C12 but it is much restored. That the Norman nave was originally intended to be nine bays long with W towers over the ninth aisle bays (i.e. producing a W front with two towers, like, e.g., the Benedictine abbey of St Etienne, Caen) appears in a thickened buttress between the eight and ninth bays. Rather surprisingly the moulded plinth continues beyond this and around the late C12 W transept without any sign of change. It is broken only where the W front begins (*see* below). The ground-floor windows of the aisles, with their five stepped lancet lights under depressed arches, go with the windows seen in the presbytery S aisle. The pointed gallery windows are of the Dec heightening – three lights with cusped arches under a pointed head – but preserving the bases of the coupled Norman arches to each side. The clerestory windows are Perp and the parapet now has cusped wavy decoration instead of quatrefoils.

Turning to the s side of the nave, visible only from within the former cloister, one finds the same changes but with some important differences. In the clerestory the rhythm of the bays of the s transept w wall continues for only one bay and there is no use of chevron at all. Instead the plain sill course of the s transept is continued, all of which suggests that work on the upper storeys of the nave began on the N side. The buttresses halt at the level of the sills of the ground-floor windows, where the roof of the claustral N range would have abutted, so it seems likely that the lowest storey of the s wall might have been carried up very early. Since the cloister seems to have been begun before the fire (*see* below) a gap may have been left between it and the new s transept, filled in the second half of the C12 by the vestry, once the remains of the pre-Conquest church had been removed. The top storey of the vestry appears to have had gables. There are two doorways which originally led from the nave into the cloister. The Canons' Door is in the first bay from the E and extensively renewed. It has four orders with block capitals. In the inner arch moulding fleur-de-lis foliage is set in the triangles of a beaded chevron – the only occurrence of Norman foliage at Peterborough (cf. Ely). The Bishop's Door to the w walk of the former cloister is a C13 insertion, contemporary with other improvements in the cloister (for which *see* below). Four orders of colonnettes, big dogtooth between. Finely moulded arch. To its l. is the same wider buttress as seen on the N side, indicating the planned extent of the nave in the mid C12 was in line with the w cloister walk. The aisle windows are a repeat of the N side, but the gallery windows, while Dec again, have segmental heads and curvilinear tracery; they must be of the same date as the upper windows of the apse and their insertion is much more neatly crafted on this side, where they would be seen from the cloister.

The WEST END of the church is an area of many changes 80 and problems, whose history is complicated. Sir Charles Peers tried to elucidate it in the VCH (1906), and the account here still follows many of his explanations. He distinguished four stages in the development of the w end as a whole. The first and second stages have been discussed already, concluding in the late C12 with the extension of the nave and the building of the w transept with towers. The third stage, Peers believed, was the addition of a porch as wide and as high as the transept and one bay deep. It was to have had three openings in giant arches just like Norman Lincoln, where three deep niches, the central one wider and taller than the others, receive the faithful, and the three or possibly five niches at the abbey of Bury St Edmunds of about half a century after Lincoln's and about a century before Peterborough's. At Peterborough, Peers judged that this motif was developed into arches of equal height endowed with quadripartite vaults in seven bays, of which the outer corresponded to the transept projections, three of the others to the portals, and the remaining two to the spaces between the portals. The last stage, when the w front received its present form, was complete by the dedication in 1238. If Peers' assumption about the character of the third stage is correct, and there is some cause to doubt it, then this final stage represents a revision in the design, altering the porch to five vaulted bays in width instead of seven, with the outer arched openings consequently made wider than the middle one, and with two angle stair-turrets to project beyond the line of the transept and give the effect of a wider screen, comparable e.g. to Salisbury. Finally, in the later C14, probably in the 1360s, a little Perp porch containing the Trinity Chapel was tucked into the middle opening, filling it in width but not in height.

In relating what one sees in detail to the ideas about the evolution of the WEST FRONT, description should begin with the exterior of the façade wall of the W transept, since it seems certain that this was at first conceived as a screen front in itself but altered once construction had begun. Peers perceived a change from horizontal to vertical tooling in the masonry, something one might expect *c.* 1215–20. The middle portal has a trumeau or middle post of the local Alwalton marble with a beautifully carved relief round the circular base, which is also of such marble. This represents a man upside-down and tormented by devils. He has been interpreted as Simon Magus and it seems possible therefore that the top of the shaft originally carried a statue of St Peter vanquishing him, but this has been cut off by the insertion of the Perp porch. As Paul Binski has noted, the spiritual triumph represented by this sculpture finds its echo in the placing of St Peter within a circle of vices on the nave ceiling; the two may be seen in their proper relationship when the W doors are open. The portal had five or six orders of colonnettes; the side portals have five orders with stiff-leaf capitals. The lower parts of the wall are thinly decorated, the mouldings unpronounced and shafts rarely multiplied. Large expanses of wall are left plain and there are odd details, e.g. moulded string courses with pendant capitals too shallow to have carried statuary. At ground floor the wall has tall blank arcading with sub-arches sharing their outer mouldings with the super-arch, then a frieze of small trefoil-headed blind arcading, and then again tall arcading broken by the windows over each of the portals and the transeptal bays. Here the rhythm goes restless, apparently owing to the requirements of the vaulting of the porch and the designer choosing to give the quadripartite vaults an additional W–E rib running against the façade wall of the church. This plays havoc with the blank arcading and fenestration at that stage, which is forced into a curious asymmetry of three large arches and two subsidiary ones of different widths squeezed between.

The system of blank arcading and frieze of trefoil-headed arches in the lower storeys is also continued on to the inner sides of the N and S walls of the stair-turrets, but on the outer elevations of the turrets where each one joins the W transept there is a visible sign of an interruption to work where immediately W of the start of the W buttresses the wall projects a little and has a shaft at the angle just like those of the transept buttresses. The projection reaches up only a few feet and is then discontinued. It seems then that the provision of the stair-turrets was not settled on until the W wall was already partly built and that they belong with the design of the great PORCH with its three tall arches. In the C18 this impressed Horace Walpole as 'noble & in great taste' but to Pevsner sixty years ago was 'an unhappy addition . . . The details must be seen to judge of the truth of this indictment . . . The most painful thing is the way in which the wide side openings lead to side portals appearing out of axis.' The wide–narrow–wide composition is unusual, perhaps essential to avoid blocking existing openings in the wall behind, but not necessarily an accident, and it has been explained by Geoffrey Webb as the consequence of experimenting with ratios based on Antique theories of proportion. In detail the three truly monumental giant portals have six orders of detached shafts each with three shaft-rings and subsidiary keeled orders between them; in the centre arch these have tufts of foliage (a Lincoln motif). The arches are decorated with a stiff-leaf, a bobbin motif, foliage and dogtooth.

The upper storey and gables above the portals have the most varied but symmetrically disposed assembly of motifs, quatrefoil in circles, trefoil pointed arch heads, niches with statues (many replaced from 1949 on by *Alan Durst*), foiled circles with heads, more trefoiled pointed arcading again with statues and in the head of each gable wheels with six (N and S) or eight (centre) spokes etc. This richer character is consistent with the second quarter of the C13 in England (e.g. Beverly Minster E end and Wells W front). Above the string course which runs around the whole of the W end, i.e. at the level of the gables, there is another apparent discordance in the composition. In particular, the strong bundled shafts which are set between the three portals are suddenly halted and gargoyles at the angles with the stair-turret seem redundant (in fact they were still used until the C19 rebuilding). Slightly set back from the tops of the shafts and to one side are spired turrets. This has been identified as another change of mind, and J. T. Irvine produced a design contemplating a more comfortably proportioned arrangement of higher gables between taller pinnacles. But the placing of these pinnacles also adds breadth to the vertical emphasis of the central bay, an effect negated by the insertion of the Perp porch, and may have been intended also to relate to the towers of the W transept behind (*see* below). The N and S gables of the W transept are similarly, but more plainly, treated. Each has a many-foiled circular window and, up the slope of the gable, a frieze of lunettes. The gables are flanked by polygonal turrets. On their top storey dogtooth occurs.

The square STAIR-TURRETS are in line with the porch and continue the system of the W façade wall on their outer faces but at third stage have an interesting motif of blank intersection with dogtooth decoration set in front of blind arcading, a motif which may well be inspired by the angle turrets of the façade of Ely Cathedral. Then more conventional patterns of blind arcading. The tops of the turrets were completed only in the C14. The top of the S turret is the more elaborate of the two. The angle shafts turn into square pinnacles set diagonally, and behind these rises an octagonal spire with one set of lucarnes and four triangular spirelets accompanying it and linking it to the angle pinnacles. These spirelets have an open bottom stage and are crocketed. The N turret is simpler. The angle shafts here end with taller hexagonal pinnacles, and the spirelets are omitted. This embellishment was not to the benefit of the former conception of the whole W end, for they compete with and obliquely upstage the W transept's NORTH TOWER (of the S one there is no more than a stump) diagonally behind them. The tower can only be seen and appreciated in its original meaning if one stands far enough away from the cathedral, where the general effect is one of profusion – it is true – but also of confusion. The tower has lancet windows on two storeys and blank arches to their l. and r. The pinnacles are polygonal. As a bell-tower it was emphasized from at least the early C17 by a curious, waisted spire, removed c. 1812. If the W transept's S tower had been completed, the originality of the whole composition would have been even more striking.

Finally the late C14 PORCH. It is like a little house, two bays deep and two storeys high. It has tierceron vaults with ridge-ribs (star-vaults) on the ground floor (the Coronation of the Virgin and the Trinity on the two main bosses), and an upper floor, for the Holy Trinity Chapel, with a large Perp window. The upper floor is reached by two spiral staircases which project in front of the C13 jambs. (On one of these a fireplace with flue has been built in.) The doorway has a depressed arch. The spandrels have blank tracery decoration. The gable above the Perp window is of low pitch and embattled. Excellent roof, inside, with big pendant bosses. Converted for the cathedral library in the C19, restored after 1944 by *Leslie T. Moore* as a memorial to the son of the historian W. T. Mellows.

INTERIOR

78   The impression, as one enters from the W, is strong and consistent, thanks to the survival of Norman work all the way from W to E and the absence of any obstacle to the eye in trying to penetrate to the apse. The architecture is robust and determined, reiterating its simple statement with conviction.

Description, as outside, should begin at the E end with the APSE. In detail its bays are separated on the outer face, the lowest storey of which shows within the retrochoir, by demi-shafts (as we have seen outside) and inside by triple shafts. At first floor is a wall-passage round the apse, which has, against the back wall, blank intersecting arcading, at the same height as the same motif occurs outside. Also following the exterior pattern are the upper storeys of the straight bay between the former apse arch and the apse proper, which again has two-thirds of the tripartite arrangement in the presbytery – 'It is remarkable how little C12 and C13 masons worried about such incongruities', thought Pevsner. The former arch between apse and presbytery has triple responds too. The arch itself has disappeared, and the verticals of the piers are continued instead by ogee-headed niches. There are many small discrepancies on the top level of the apse to indicate that in the C12 there was a semi-dome behind the arch, emphasizing the sanctuary itself. The date of the alteration to a flat ceiling is not certain but since the wall-shafts of the apse have chalice capitals this may have been in the early C13, contemporary with the introduction of flat timber ceilings elsewhere. The ground-floor bays of the apse have no trace of their Norman form (except some capitals of former blank arcading in the SE corner) and instead have very fine Dec frames of cusped arches of a fascinatingly varied and lively design, some of ogee form, some with bosses, carried on colonnettes with foliage and with straight-headed hood-moulds of ballflower. The NE bay is the most lavish and has square shafts with pinnacles. On the outer face, i.e. towards the later retrochoir, are panels of enjoyable tracery and in the soffits of the arches are delicate flying ribs. The windows of the apse chord have window tracery of elegant flowing forms and below these (shown in C18 drawings) were sedilia and aumbries with canopies. It is neither clear what occasioned this enrichment, nor is it obvious whether these were full-length openings before the retrochoir was built, but it goes with the insertion of flowing tracery in the upper storeys and the other decorative changes of *c*. 1300 encountered outside. From the C15 the apse was cut off from the rest of the presbytery by the high altar, 'a stately skreen . . . , painted and gilt, which rose up as high almost as the roof of the church in a row of three lofty spires, with other lesser spires, growing out of each of them'.

The PRESBYTERY is four bays long and has a three-storey elevation including a large gallery, like Ely and Norwich. The piers are octagonal, circular and dodecagonal. The apparently planned but unique variety of pier-forms at Peterborough, at ground and gallery level and with intentional, not random, placing of angles and attached shafts, was unprecedented in 1118, forming a series not of changes of mind but of deliberate experiments improving on the octagon-circle alternation already existing at Canterbury. The responds are triple groups like the shafts of the apse and the arches have heavy roll mould-ings and billet frieze round the outer edge. The GALLERY has large arched openings subdivided by a tall shaft helping to carry two sub-arches. The piers alternate between a compound shape and a circular one with demi-shafts on rectangular pro-jections, with the disconcerting result that polygonal arcade piers correspond with circular gallery piers and circular arcade piers with the clustered form. The capitals are slightly busier than below. As if to emphasize the visual eccentricity, the tympana have different fillings, starting on the N side with a pierced circle and a group of four pierced circles, on the s side with one plain tympanum. The others have diapering in the flat and in relief and no piercing. A frieze at the floor-level of the gallery has chevron coming forward at right angles to the wall plane. The outer moulding of the arch has the same motif. Chevron mouldings are known from the late C11 and were first used on an extensive scale at Durham c. 1110, but horizontal chevron or chevron at right angles to the wall plane is usually regarded as a Late Norman motif. Here it can hardly be later than c. 1135. At the floor-level of the CLERESTORY chevron was begun at the E end on the s and the w end on the N side but was soon discontinued and replaced by an undecorated course. The clerestory has a wall-passage with the tripartite stepped arcading familiar in English Norman buildings (e.g. Winchester, Ely, Durham transepts).

Between the bays shafts rise in front of the piers to the CEILING. There is no indication that a rib-vault was ever intended and in all probability the original ceiling was flat. It was replaced c. 1500 (the felling date of the roof timbers) by the present complicated wooden ceiling-cum-vault, i.e. a panelled ceiling, four square cross-ribbed panels wide, on a deep coving with tierceron ribs. The ceiling has many bosses. Among them are the Crucifixion, the Assumption, Christ in Majesty, the Annunciation. The flat ceiling over the apse, renewed in 1856 by *Scott*, has a Christ in Majesty at the centre of a vine with the Apostles as branches, painted by *Charles Castell*. This is inspired by the medieval design described by Gunton which had been shot at by Cromwell's soldiers, but which is still evident in Tillemans's drawing of 1719, with borders of lozenge patterns like those of the transepts and nave roofs and only later painted over. The painted decoration of the presbytery ceiling, with angels in roundels, is also 1850s.

The presbytery AISLES are rib-vaulted, an early occurrence for England and indeed Europe. The earliest rib-vaults in existence are at Durham of c. 1095–1100. In France they appear c. 1100–20 and elsewhere in England at Winchester in the reconstruction of the transept aisles following the collapse of the tower in 1107. The date of the design at Peterborough is, as we have seen, 1118 and it is alone among the East Anglian churches to make extensive use of such a feature. The transverse arches have a rectangular section with rolls along the angles, the ribs have a demi-roll on a rectangle. The mouldings are big and bold. The capitals are of the block type, or varieties of heavy scallops. They are all big and bold, as far as the piers are concerned, but more playful in the wall-shafts of the aisles (where of course they might well be the result of recarving). The outer walls have large intersecting arcading, complete on the s side but preserved only in one bay of the N aisle, beneath the Norman rere-arch of the window seen outside, which also has above the arcading a small frieze which seems

chevron at first, but is in fact nutmeg. This frieze was presumably continuous in each of the bays of the aisles, before the
alterations to the windows, and is preserved in the W bay of
the S aisle above a low arched recess on short Norman columns;
and it is found throughout the transepts at this level. At the E
end of the S aisle the line of the Norman side apse is marked
out. This apse, and that to the N aisle, must have been removed
in the late C13 – see the elegant quadripartite rib-vaults (the S
one with fictive masonry) and the handsome double piscina in
each bay N and S with Y-tracery and trilobes in the spandrels,
and delightful scalloped drains.

Then in the early C15 the end walls of the aisles were broken
through to the new RETROCHOIR and broad arches inserted
with big, heavy fleurons in the deep main moulding both to
the W and E. The windows have dados of blank panelling with
cusped tracery and stone benches. The vault is a very handsome fan-vault carried on slender shafts, the fans each with
eleven ribs and panelled tracery with brattishing in three tiers,
meeting along the axes where bosses form the centre of lozenges and divided into panels so the fans are cut off by each
other rather than forming a continuous flowing pattern. Once
more, all this is a very close relative of the roof at King's
College Chapel. The bosses have an emblem of the Passion
(centre), and symbols of St Edmund, St Peter etc. The new
building is internally slightly higher than the presbytery aisles,
and the closely panelled vaulting at that height gives it a sense
of comfortable as well as rich enclosure. The curve of the
Norman apse is enclosed by the straight-side enclosure, with
three tall arches to the E and one to N and S, all with continuous mouldings of hollow chamfers, fillets etc. of a kind characteristic of *John Wastell* (cf. for example, St Mary, Saffron
Walden, Essex, of 1485). The NE and SW arches have free-
standing lozenge-shaped piers, and thus a slightly awkward
junction is created with the apse. But this is concealed by
plenty of enjoyable tracery, including cusped four-centred
arches over the apse openings and strainer arches spanning the
triangular spaces between the apse and the piers. The precise
date of the building is uncertain. In the frieze of the second
bay from the N are faces of a King and Queen: might that mean
that the work was completed after Henry's marriage to Katherine in 1509? If *Wastell* was the designer before he began the
vaults at King's (the contract for which was signed in 1512)
then one may see Peterborough as an intermediate stage
between his vaults in the Bell Harry Tower at Canterbury
(completed *c.* 1504–9) and the final innovations of the roof of
King's. But it is also the case that the vaulting here is of a more
ambitious form of construction, with interlocking masonry
allowing the fans to flow in an uninterrupted sequence over
the space and without the transverse arches of King's College.
In these ways it seems related to the vaulting of the Henry
VII chapel (1503–*c.* 1510) at Westminster (e.g. the rising and
falling profile of the ridge-ribs) and so may be therefore a

development informed by the design of King's but entrusted to another mason.

The CROSSING was entirely rebuilt by *Pearson* from 1883 but as he found it: the N and S crossing arches Norman with chevron at right angles to the wall plane, the other two pointed and dating from the C14. The piers also differ; those to the E and W arches have responds with three shafts in a line, those to the N and S triple responds as we have found them in other places. The tower has a late C14 lierne vault of timber, painted by *Clayton & Bell*. The central boss shows Christ in Majesty, the other bosses the Signs of the four Evangelists and the Instruments of the Passion.

The E sides of the TRANSEPTS are aisled and continue the design of the presbytery, though with significant changes. The alternation of round and octagonal piers is simpler, and the shafts up to the ceiling are no longer in front of the piers, but start above them from the abaci, a form of articulation which was increasingly in vogue after 1125 (cf. St Botolph's Priory, Colchester, Essex). The impression is above all of a gradual paring away of the presence of the walls, in spite of their thickness, in favour of spacious voids. The arcade responds are segments of circular piers, containing stairs – the placing of these stairs in line with the arcades is a feature shared with Ely and Bury St Edmunds – and the doorway to the N stair has fishscale decoration in its tympanum. Although this decoration is encountered nowhere else in the cathedral, such ornament is, of course, found at Castor church (q.v.). The tympanum has also a cable-moulded surround and bobbles around the outer edge. The billets of the arcade arches are slightly coarser. Just as in the chancel a course with horizontal chevron runs above the arcade, and the gallery piers also alternate, but, unlike the presbytery, now following the pattern set by the arcade piers and ensuring a vertical formal consistency. The gallery tympana have on the S side the same relief diapering as in the presbytery (except that the southernmost tympanum is left plain). On the N side the first bay has diapering in the flat, the second in relief, the others again in the flat. Below the clerestory the string course has a very little chevron in the N transept and none in the S. In the clerestory there is no change from the presbytery. Between the aisle bays of the S transept low separating walls are inserted to divide them into chapels (the N transept aisle is undivided except for the relatively modest screen to the N and this is much later). In the middle chapel (St Benedict) is flat intersecting arcading. The S chapel (St Kyneburgha) has normal blank arcading like the rest of the transepts. The N chapel (St Oswald) has an extraordinary turret inside, apparently built as a watchtower for guarding the relic of St Oswald's arm. The other walls of the transepts have tall blank arcading on the ground floor, shafted windows in two tiers, and the familiar tripartite stepped arcading of the wall-passage on the clerestory level. The bays are divided by tall demi-shafts. In the blank arcading of the S transept s wall one capital is a big monster head. The string course above the blank arcading again has nutmeg instead of chevron decoration. This applies to the end and w walls of both transepts. The s transept has a doorway in its s wall. The transepts both have boarded CEILINGS of C19 date. They are flat, of wood, and have bold lozenge patterns, some with traces of decorative painting.

Adjoining the w wall of the s transept is the VESTRY (sacristy). This dates from the late C12 but has a Dec doorway with an ogee arch, the DOOR itself with mid-C14 strapwork hinges and ring and plate of *c.* 1400. The vestry is of three bays, with low cinquepartite rib-vaults (quadripartite plus a spare rib towards the main wall where the Norman buttresses show). The ribs have a slight chamfer, the transverse arches a rectangular projection and keeled rolls at the angles. The arches and ribs rest on short piers with scalloped capitals.

The NAVE goes on without change of system, though changes of detail are as noticeable inside as they are outside. It achieves a consistency of design hitherto absent. The arch mouldings change at once w of the crossing. They contain one more roll moulding to the nave. The arcade piers resume the shafts towards the nave but in shape the piers differ from those in eastern arm and transepts. They begin from the crossing with a respond (with the same triple shafts as in the presbytery and transepts, but with pairs of shafts to the aisle); then follows a circular form with attached shafts on flat projections in all four directions – a compound form developed from the piers of the gallery in the eastern arm and transepts in which a shaft is added to support the inner arch – then a more complex pier of stepped plan with the same attached shafts but with slimmer shafts in the angles. In these first two bays the gallery tympana have relief diapering. The treatment of the piers and bays may denote the original position of the C12 choir and pulpitum, for after that the next five piers and the respond of the sixth (i.e. up to and including the eighth bay on each side) are like the second, i.e. they are circular with projections on all four sides consisting of a rectangle with a demi-roll, and the gallery tympana are plain. Each bay also becomes entirely uniform vertically in the use of the compound piers at arcade and gallery, and the spacing of the bays, tighter than in the E arm, builds a more urgent rhythm from w to E. The capitals of the arcade are busier and have a number of small variations, including concave scalloping, and there are many small changes in the details of the bases within the nave. The blank wall arcading in the aisles resumes the intersecting of the eastern arm. The capitals on the s side are as simple as those of the E arm and transepts, which again indicates that the s aisle wall was carried up very early. On the N side the capitals are more decorated and clearly later. They play on forms of scalloping, of little volutes etc., and beasts' heads with wide open mouths. The aisle vaults occasionally have very small bosses at the intersection of the ribs. From these details one can detect that there was a change in the construction of the N side of the nave once the builders had reached the fifth bay of the arcade, the third bay of the gallery and the second bay of the clerestory. It is most likely that this coincides with the arrival of Abbot Benedict from Canterbury in 1177, indicated by the sudden appearance of crocket capitals at the third gallery pier on this side. At about this time it was decided to extend the nave by one more bay plus W transepts, on the lines of Ely and Bury St Edmunds. Just as, outside, the previous plan for W towers is indicated by thicker buttresses between the eighth and ninth bays, so inside the piers are of greater width and this is specially noticeable on the gallery level, and the transverse arch over the S aisle is doubled. On the S gallery one can also see that a transverse arch ran across, of which the N respond survives and a lump of stone where the S respond was. Close to this there is a spiral staircase whose W wall was clearly butted originally against a cross wall. In spite of the change of plan the system was still not changed. So bay ten and the openings from the aisles into the new W transept keep to the elements already described, and the windows behind the N and S gables of the W transepts follow the tripartite system of the Norman clerestory. The wall-arcading on the S side now at last takes up the lively forms of capitals which had been used on the N side from the E end of the nave onwards; on the N side the tenth bay has for the first time waterleaf capitals. Only in the bays of the transepts has the wall-arcading been hacked away.

The first major change of the late C12 is the fact that the arches across the WEST TRANSEPTS are pointed. Their details are typical Latest Norman, with big, rich chevron and similar more complicated and even bigger motifs set at an angle. The vaults are quadripartite, with the much finer details and more delicate members of the E.E. style. In the aisle bays below the towers, bell-holes are left, that under the N tower being surrounded by playful ribs. The centre bay has a boss with stiff-leaf foliage. The W wall is purely E.E. in its motifs, except that the three doorways are still round-headed. But they have finely moulded arches and stiff-leaf capitals (the leaves at the centre arch semi-naturalistic), and there is pointed blank arcading at the ground-level, and the upper storey tall E.E. arches in front of the wall-passage (for singing?) beneath the W windows (altered Perp tracery). In the shallow projecting bays of the transept the change is also made to E.E. forms and proportions from E–W so that the windows in the terminal wall have cushion capitals for responds on one side but bell capitals on the other. One must assume that the E, N and S walls of the transept were completed first, and that the W wall and the vaulting followed. The cusped intersected tracery of the N and S windows are of course a late C13 alteration of former windows which must have been lancets. Inside the S arm is a double piscina of that date, identical to those in the presbytery aisles.

Angled shafts and springers for vaulting can be seen in the first nave bay from the W, proving that in the late years of the

C12 the intention existed of roofing the nave in the new style (Benedict would have known the high vault introduced at Canterbury in 1175, but the stone vault at Lincoln also provides a precedent). That provision needed to be made for such a vault shortly after work had already begun is shown in the first bays from the E by an obvious disjunction between the clerestory openings and the pointed wall arch which frames them (and which suggests the outline of the intended vaults). Presumably the first intention was an open roof or flat ceiling, as in the transepts and presbytery, and this form was adopted in the early to mid C13 with the construction of the present NAVE CEILING. This is a very precious survival, the largest of its kind in a major medieval English church, and more precious because it was so nearly destroyed by the fire of 2001. Its oak timbers were imported from eastern Europe, at a time well before the trade with the Hansa, and a reminder that the lowlying waterlogged fenland made medieval Peterborough an inland port. From E–W the timbers have been dated to after 1238, so the work was probably commenced by Abbot Walter of Bury St Edmunds (1233–45; see also the Refectory), who also provided new choir stalls (which had painted scenes from the Old and New Testaments). The style of decoration, however, suggests earlier instigation, perhaps under Abbot Robert de Lindsey (1214–22), who is credited with other decorative embellishments of the cathedral, and the conception may indeed have its roots in the time of Benedict, who knew the painted ceiling in the choir at Canterbury that was destroyed shortly before his move to Peterborough. The ceiling is canted, decorated with lozenge patterns, divided into smaller diamonds (originally with borders of crocketing) like those of the transept ceilings, and retains much of its original colouring, in spite of C18 and C19 repainting. In the central spine of diamonds, from the W to the centre, are figures of kings, bishops and archbishops, perhaps representing the early founders and Anglo-Saxon benefactors of the abbey. In the flanking diamonds is a unique representation of the liberal Arts (Rhetoric, Grammar, Logic, Music, Arithmetic, Geometry – an architect with L-square and dividers – and Astronomy). Then from the centre to the E, Saints Paul and Peter divided by a monkey on a goat, the Agnus Dei and also a Janus head. The sacred figures are thus framed by images of sin and vice, further represented in the flanking panels by comic and demonic figures with musical instruments – including an ass playing the harp – as well as a monster feeding on the bleeding limbs of a man etc. The designs are closely related to medieval manuscripts and illuminated books, notably two psalters made for Peterborough *c.* 1220. In the groupings Paul Binski identifies three themes – Power, Knowledge and Morality – and suggests the iconography might be evidence for the placing of the pulpitum, rood screen and choir in the C13, with the Agnus Dei (over the second piers from the E) marking the entrance to the choir and the Janus over the entrance to the pulpitum.

81

CEILING

East End
Lions and Fish

Green Man   Green Man
Janus
Devil

Fox and ?   Anthropophagus
Agnus Dei
St Peter

Ass and Harp   Fiddle
Goat riding an ape
St Paul

Symphonie   Dulcimer
King with torch
Archbishop

Fiddle   Cornetto
King
Archbishop

Rhetoric   Grammar
King
Bishop

Logic   Music
King
Bishop

Arithmetic   Geometry
King
Bishop

Sun   Astronomy
King
Eagle

Unidentified   Lion
Moon
West End

FURNISHINGS, STAINED GLASS AND MONUMENTS

A scanty collection for such an ancient site, thanks to the ruthless destruction of the 1640s. Description is from E to W.

RETROCHOIR. In the central opening of the apse, the so-called 'HEDDA STONE', an extremely important piece of Anglo-Saxon funerary sculpture to be dated to the late C8 by comparison with illuminated manuscripts and High Crosses. It is a single block of grey stone with a pitched roof, like the Mercian stone boxes found at Lichfield and Derby. Against the long sides, standing figures of Christ, the Virgin, flanked by St Peter and St Paul and eight other saints, perhaps Apostles. They stand in close-fitting arcading; the central figures stand frontally, the others turn inward in characteristic pose. They have the fluffy carving and the deeply drilled eyes characteristic

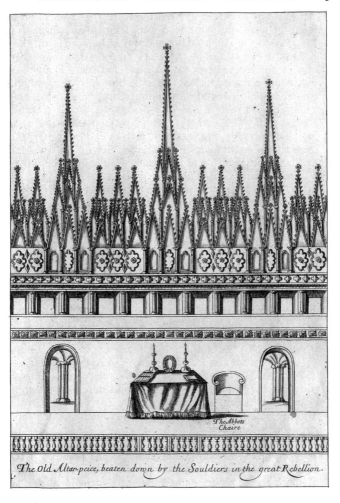

The Old Altar-peice, beaten down by the Souldiers in the great Rebellion.

Peterborough Cathedral, high altar, by S. Gunton, 1686

of their date. The short sides are defaced and the details worn away. The roof is pitched like that of a metal shrine (cf. e.g. the Gandersheim Casket) and has scrollwork with interlace, affronted pairs of animals, and also what has been called an 'inhabited scroll', i.e. a vine scroll with an animal inside. Comparable work is also to be found at Castor, Fletton (qq.v.) and also at Breedon-on-the-Hill in Leicestershire, a monastic foundation established from Medehamstede. The stone's original purpose and setting is uncertain but carefully drilled into the faces are circular recesses which have been used as reliquaries. The stone is claimed to have been set up at Peterborough by Abbot Godric of Crowland in memory of Abbot Hedda, who was killed by Danes in 870 but the name may refer to an C8 figure of the same name who went from Medehamstede to Breedon-on-the-Hill as abbot and was bishop of Lichfield.

– ARCHITECTURAL FRAGMENTS. In the N aisle, three bays of a stone screen, Perp, with a quatrefoil frieze at the foot, panels and canopied niches, and a cresting with a frieze of little beasts. Possibly assembled from diverse fragments. – STAINED GLASS. N wall E: by *J. Powell & Sons*, 1914; E wall centre by *Heaton, Butler & Bayne*, 1875, and s by *Clayton & Bell*, 1861, in C13 style. s aisle, two windows: 1910 by *Burlison & Grylls* in memory of Canon Alderson †1907, with views of the cathedral, St Mary Lutterworth and All Saints, Holdenby; and 1904 by *Lavers, Barraud & Westlake*. – MONUMENTS. – s aisle. C13 COFFIN LID with cross carrying the familiar double omega motif. – Abbot, either Robert Kirkton †1528 or John Chambers †1556. Recumbent effigy of stone; defaced. Two angels by the pillow. – Orme family. Hanging monument, erected 1627 by Sir Humphrey Orme, ferociously attacked by Cromwellian soldiery in 1643, while Orme still lived. Of the figures only one small group survives. – Thomas Deacon †1721. Signed by *Robert Taylor Sen*. Standing monument, the best in the cathedral. White and greyish marble. Semi-reclining, well-carved effigy with wig. Reredos background with Corinthian pilasters and a broken segmental pediment. – Dean William Ingram †1901. Recumbent effigy of white marble on a fine Purbeck stone casket. By his brother, *W. R. Ingram*, 1903; his last work. – N aisle. – Bishop Cumberland †1718. Signed by *Thomas Green* of Camberwell. Hanging monument with open segmental pediment above the inscription plate and standing putti to its l. and r. – Canon Clayton †1917. By *F. J. Wilcoxson*, 1919. Another recumbent effigy, rather stern. Numerous other small but good wall tablets.

PRESBYTERY. – BALDACCHINO (or ciborium), presented 1893, designed by *Pearson* in richest Italian Gothic. Made by *Robert Davison* of Derbyshire alabaster (of the same hue as the surrounding Barnack stone of the building), enriched with mosaic. A most architectural yet transparent altar canopy, it is as successful an addition to its setting as the very different one now in St Paul's. Davison also supplied the fine inlaid Italian marble PAVEMENTS with geometric patterns from apse to choir, also designed by Pearson (cf. e.g. Bristol, Truro), Cosmati style. – In the apse, two TAPESTRIES, late C16, probably Flemish, and WALL PAINTINGS of shields and crescent emblems discovered in 1887. Probably mid- to late C13 (the Dec apse openings overlay it) but the heraldry unidentified. – Wrought-iron PAR-CLOSE SCREENS, to the aisles by *Pearson* (made by *White & Son*); the lower APSE SCREENS by *Leslie T. Moore*, replacing Dec-style stone screens and a reredos erected by *Blore* in 1832. – STAINED GLASS. In the upper windows of the apse, Perp fragments assembled in the later C18 by Dean Tarrant from glass destroyed by the Puritans. They appear to have included a narrative of the life of St Peter. – MONUMENTS. The graves of Katherine of Aragon †1536 (under the iron screen of the N arcade E bay) and Mary Queen of Scots †1587 (opposite in the S aisle till translated to Westminster Abbey by James I) are marked by banners and monuments of 1895. The fine incised marble slab for Katherine of Aragon is by *Alec Peever*, 1986.

SOUTH PRESBYTERY AISLE. – FRAGMENTS (N wall). Perp. Possibly from the great screen formerly in the apse. – RADIATORS (in all of the aisles). Mighty Victorian cast-iron pieces with a coronet, by the *London Warming & Ventilation Co.* – MONUMENTS. Four abbots, all of local Alwalton marble varying in hue from light tan to nearly black. All made within the thirty years from *c.* 1195 to *c.* 1225. They were arranged into their present positions in the early C18, several having formerly resided in the chapter house. The first from the E and in date the latest (supposed to be Alexander of Holderness †1226) has a tomb-chest. It has short columns and quatrefoil panels (cf. the Marshall Monument in Exeter Cathedral). The effigy is flanked by shafts carrying a projecting pointed trefoiled canopy. Stiff-leaf ornament. The third of the series alone has a rounded-trefoiled canopy over his head, also carried on shafts. It is much defaced. The second has a rounded cinque-cusped canopy which is very depressed and carries bits of buildings. The curly hair and beard are a sign of an early date. The fourth, within the arched recess close to the junction with the crossing, is in higher relief. It has no flanking shafts. Two angels at his head, a dragon at his feet. – Joseph Stamford †1683. Pretty cartouche with cherubs' heads and death's head below and trails of fruit and flowers in the manner of Grinling Gibbons. First-rate London work. – Archbishop Magee of York, former Bishop of Peterborough, †1891. By *J. Forsyth*, 1893. White recumbent effigy on a Renaissance chest of Sicilian marble designed by *Pearson*. – Bishop Mandell Creighton †1901. Substantial floor slab, marble and opus sectile.

NORTH PRESBYTERY AISLE. – CHEST. C15, with elaborate tracery. – CLOCK. 1450 and after. – STAINED GLASS. One window by *Wailes*, 1859. – MONUMENTS. Another early abbot of the same material and date as those in the S aisle. Beardless head under a rounded-trefoiled arch. Shafts by his sides with capitals clearly still of the C12. A dragon at his feet. – Abbot Godfrey †1321. Slab rebated for a full-length brass under a canopy. – Dean Duport †1679. Very classical, with broken pediment with curly ends and garlands and cherubs at the sides. Attributed to *Jasper Latham* (GF). – Constance Workman †1681. Cartouche with exceptionally fine flower carving and folded drapery, attributed to *Grinling Gibbons* and *Arnold Quellin* (GF). – Richard Tryce, steward to the Dean and Chapter, †1767. Hanging monument by *Edward Bingham*, highly coloured marbles with a weeping cherub against the top. – William Gery †1787, also by *Bingham*; essentially classical but with Gothic pilasters.

CROSSING. – THRONE AND PULPIT, 1892 by *Pearson*; the latter superseding *Edward Barry*'s gross Neo-Norman huge stone pulpit of 1873. Soaring Perp spire, in keeping with Pearson's choir stalls. The pulpit is especially handsome, a goblet shape with an elegant curved stair. Early abbots and saints are carved in niches.

SOUTH TRANSEPT. Chapel SCREENS. Late C15 or early C16 with some polychromy on the inner face. – REREDOS (St Oswald's Chapel). Stone. By *Leslie Moore*, painted later by *G. G. Pace*. – AUMBRY (St Benedict's Chapel) with reset panel with a relief containing the rebus of Thomas Dove, dated 1601, when he was appointed Bishop of Peterborough. – SCULPTURE. In the W wall, a small Saxon panel with two figures under arches (cf. the Hedda Stone, above); in the crossing pier also a panel of interlace ornament (other Saxon stones are displayed in the crypt, where the Saxon S transept is revealed). – STAINED GLASS. S wall, lowest tier, easternmost. By *Morris, Marshall & Faulkner*, 1862, i.e. a very early work of the firm, in memory of Sir Chapman Marshall, an alderman of the City of London who was born in Peterborough. Two scenes, predominantly red and brown, by *D. G. Rossetti* (who only designed glass 1861–4): Sacrifice of Abraham and Joseph Lifted from the Pit, with four small figures above by *William Morris* and shields below by *Philip Webb*. – The centre and W windows are by *A. Gibbs*, 1861, and *Heaton, Butler & Bayne*, 1864, with the strong colours of the 1860s but unavoidably emphasizing the advanced style of the Morris workshop. St Oswald's Chapel, by *Burlison & Grylls*, c. 1900. St Benedict's Chapel, 1958 by *W. T. Carter Shepland*. W wall, one window by *T. Baillie & Co.*, 1878 – MONUMENT: St Kyneburgha (E) chapel. Clare Durst †1968. A miniature Annunciation, by *Alan Durst*.

NORTH TRANSEPT. – SCREENS. Perp with much tracery, three doors and spaces for two altars. This appears to be the remains of a screen thought to have been erected in the late C15 or early C16 by Abbot Kirkton in the nave W of the pulpitum but cut to fit when moved here in 1734. – In front are two STALLS assembled from a fragment of the canopied choir stalls provided by Abbot Walter some time between 1233 and 1245 but also removed in 1734. Slender double shafts and stiff-leaf capitals are supplemented with panelling of late C16 or early C17 date.* – ALTAR. Formerly in the nave, Neo-Georgian, mid-C20 by *Leslie T. Moore*. – STAINED GLASS. N wall, lowest tier, first from E: *Clayton & Bell*, 1862, second by Gibbs, 1863, to the Prince Consort, and third by *Hardman & Co.*, 1859, a strongly coloured sea of Galilee; tier above this from E to W: *T. Cox & Son*, 1864; *M. & A. O'Connor*, 1865; the Betrayal, prettily coloured in the background, *Heaton, Butler & Bayne*, 1864; top tier 1865 by *A. Gibbs*. NE window by *Wailes*, 1863; and E window by *Clayton & Bell*, undated.

NAVE AND CHOIR. – The original CHOIR STALLS were removed c. 1780 when new screens and stalls were designed by *John Carter*, incorporating the organ. These were replaced 1827–32

*They are as shown in the early C18 drawing of the choir by Tillemans.

by *Edward Blore*★ but in turn removed by *Pearson* and superseded by his stalls, 1890–2, which evoke the medieval arrangement of stalls extending into the two E bays of the nave,
although not under the crossing. Prickly row of canopies over
the Canons' stalls. Some of the desks appear to be reused
medieval survivors, their traceried fronts dictating the design
of the rest. Originally with stalls returned at the W end but
realigned by *Leslie T. Moore* in 1923, for an uninterrupted view
along the nave and chancel; cancelli at the W end of this date.
– LECTERN. Brass eagle. Late C15, English, given by Abbot
Ramsey and Prior Malden, as an inscription formerly recorded.
The same pattern as at Little Gidding but also St Nicholas,
King's Lynn, Christ's College, Cambridge, St Mark's, Venice,
etc. – ORGAN CASE. By the organ-builder and antiquary *Dr
Arthur Hill*, 1904. It acts as a screen to the instrument (by the
Hill firm 1868 etc.; rebuilt by *Harrison*, 1980), which stands in
the gallery, and so it is rather less architecturally successful
than Hill's earlier Chichester case (which completely contains
the instrument), while forming an excellent composition (Gill-
ingham). – PULPIT. A fine piece with a tester and big foliate
brackets supporting in late C17 style. Also a READING DESK in
Neo-Baroque. Both by *Leslie T. Moore*. – Large hanging ROOD,
1975, by *G. G. Pace*, with aluminium figure by *Frank Roper*, gold
against red. Amazingly effective in this austere Norman place.
– FONT. C13 bowl, of Alwalton marble. The bowl has twelve
shallow projections or undulations decorated with stiff-leaf;
until the 1820s it was used as a flower-pot in a prebendal
garden. C21 supports. – WALL PAINTINGS, above the W doors.
Old Scarlett the gravedigger (†1594) who buried two queens
(*see* presbytery above) in 1537 and 1587: N of the central door
painted on the wall and found under the copy of 1747 on panel
now hanging S of the door; Celia Fiennes saw the original in
1698. – Three WEST DOORS, possibly C12 strengthened by
C13 saltire-ledging. – MONUMENT. Edith Cavell †1915. Irish
marble wall tablet (S arcade pier) with her portrait. By *Temple
Moore*, 1916.

WEST TRANSEPT. – St Sprite's Chapel (S). Beautiful ironwork
SCREEN AND GATES with riddel posts etc. by *Moore*, 1923.
Reordered by *Pace*, 1963–7, who oddly affixed three C14 miseri-
cords to stall-backs, a very unpleasant effect.

TRIBUNE. – A variety of FRAGMENTS. One of these is a large
mid- to late C10 GRAVE-SLAB, discovered with its foot stone
in the wall of the N transept in 1888. With four-fold cross and
cable work as well as interlace.

PORCH. Fine and elaborate iron GATES, probably by Pearson.

CHURCHYARD. Surprisingly little of interest. There are lots of
the C18 limestone headstones typical of the area tidied away
into the E end and a few chest tombs of conventional character.
Outside the S transept, a large collection of the familiar C13

★ Parts of Blore's stalls are now at St Dominic's Priory, Newcastle.

COFFINS AND CROSS SLABS, their design inspiring many of the monuments to C19 Bishops, e.g. Magee †1891, also with Celtic cross. – S of the retrochoir GRAVE MARKERS to Canon John Stocks †1926, with canted top and head and foot stones, and Emily Stocks †1938; both by *Eric Gill*.

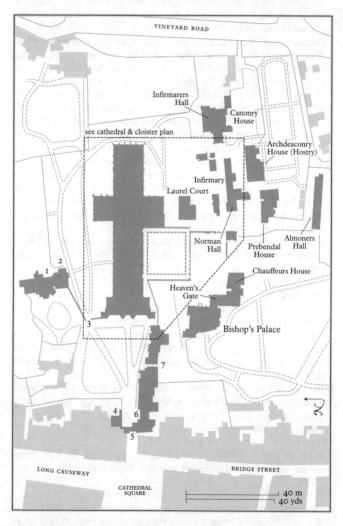

VINEYARD ROAD

Infirmarers Hall

Canonry House

see cathedral & cloister plan

Archdeaconry House (Hostry)

Infirmary

Laurel Court

Norman Hall

Prebendal House

Almoners Hall

Chauffeurs House

Heaven's Gate

Bishop's Palace

LONG CAUSEWAY

BRIDGE STREET

CATHEDRAL SQUARE

40 m
40 yds

Peterborough Cathedral Precincts

1 Deanery
2 Prior's Gate
3 Priory Gate
4 Becket's Chapel
5 Outer Gate
6 King's Lodging & Abbot's Prison
7 Abbot's Gate

THE PRECINCTS

Cloister and buildings to the south

The CLOISTER can be reached from inside the cathedral by the W door in the nave S aisle. The cloister walks survive nowhere, and against the church there are not even any traces of the bays and their vaults remaining. Only the two portals in the nave already noted indicate the line of the E and W walks. Abbot Ernulf (1107–14), formerly prior at Canterbury, is credited with having begun the rebuilding of the monastic buildings before the great fire. Although the refectory, chapter house and dormitory were complete and survived the conflagration, little of the early C12 can be seen except two blocked doorways in the wall of the WEST RANGE, the S one of which includes rare disc moulding in its arch, a sign of an early date, and at its N end the much larger and well-preserved arch with one order of columns and one continuous roll moulding. The arch has a big outer billet moulding, similar to those of the transepts, but the character is altogether earlier in style than the church. There is also a small C14 doorway with flowing tracery, one Perp doorway with a four-centred arch, and one doorway with Late Norman arch fragments (crenellation, frieze of lobes – cf. the gables of the cathedral). The remains of the arcading are superimposed on all this. They are Perp and date from the rebuilding of the cloister in the C15, see also the arcades on the vestry wall, opposite. The W range contained the cellarer's range with Abbot's Lodgings (or Abbot's Hall and chapel) above. It eventually extended S to include what is now the Bishop's Palace (*see* below) but was taken down in 1643.

The S range contained the REFECTORY etc. and was built, or rather rebuilt, by Abbot Walter of Bury St Edmunds (1233–45), to accommodate the growing body of monks; it has remains partly E.E., partly Perp. E.E. the blank arcading with sub-arches, whose outer mouldings are those of the super-arch as well, and also two doorways, at the E and W ends. The W doorway, the entrance to the Refectory, has four orders of colonnettes and pointed moulded arches, except for the inner order, which has a beautiful round arch with extremely fine, deeply cut stiff-leaf frieze and tympanum with a quatrefoil and two dragons. The E doorway, to the Hostry Passage (*see* below), is simpler, with a segmental arch and a quatrefoil above this. Fine mouldings; stiff-leaf detail, cf. the W door of the nave S aisle (*see* above). Towards the interior, i.e. the S, the wall has blank arcading with very varied paterae in and above the spandrels, although this is only visible from the bishop's garden. They contain much stiff-leaf. Of the Refectory E wall the N springer of some taller blank arcading is the only sign of decoration. The C13 arcading in the five bays next to the Refectory doorway on the cloister side was overlaid during the C15 by a renewed LAVATORIUM, originally comprising three basins and two cupboards under four-centred arches. Above the arches and in the back of these bays very rich Perp panelling.

The E range exists no longer. The CHAPTER HOUSE was pulled down in the mid C17. N of this may have been a room or passage; the springers for an early C13 vault may still be seen. The MONKS' DORMITORY, which lay over the top, extended S of the cloister and was apparently enlarged and improved by Abbot Robert de Lindsey (1214–22). The HOSTRY PASSAGE ran S, beneath the dormitory wing, and was vaulted in fourteen bays. The N bays are contemporary with the Refectory, with chamfered columns. The bays to the S were probably open to a courtyard behind and have round shafts and capitals with traces of foliage; where this has survived (notably where there was a doorway towards the S end of the wall, which led into a vaulted C14 passage behind) the naturalism suggests a late C13 or early C14 date. Yet these arches also have Dec tracery, now blocked, whose details point to c. 1330–40. S of the blocked door, two more bays, associated with a square vaulted building behind (now within the garden of the Bishop's Palace). This is of the later C12 (two oblong quadripartite rib-vaults, chamfered ribs) and may have formed part of the undercroft of a W attachment to the S end of the dormitory. Indeed it seems very likely that extended W by at least one bay.

On the site of the dormitory building is LAUREL COURT, the smartest house in the precinct, with an entrance off the cloister. Probably Early Georgian, with a three-bay entrance front and S front, both ashlar-faced, of three storeys with windows in raised surrounds. Straight parapet. Later enlarged by two bays to the N and altered in the C19 with the addition of two bay windows with crenellated tops. Doorway with pediment on Doric columns. Excellent staircase, probably c. 1720, with twisted and straight balusters, good raised panelling in the principal room on the first floor, and some nice late C18 details in other rooms.

From the S end of the Passage one has to turn E to visit the impressive remains of the INFIRMARY. It was built by Abbot John de Caux, a former prior of Winchester who ruled from 1250 to 1263, and comprised a large hall with a nave and aisles, seven bays long, and at its E end a chapel (St Laurence) with nave and chancel. The nave of the hall was unroofed c. 1650 and now provides a street between houses built into the former aisles. By the early C18 both arcades are shown continuously built up (i.e. blocked) with such dwellings, although this is no longer the case. The arcades have tall, slender, but strong piers with a square core and four semicircular shafts with fillets giving the impression of a quatrefoil section. The arches have many deep mouldings, and there is excellent stiff-leaf enrichment. In the spandrels of the arches are triple shafts rising from head corbels to moulded capitals. The W responds stand on corbels, and these are carried by a human figure and a grotesque. There is also blank arcading to the W wall, and this may have originally been open, for on the outside are traces of voussoirs. The outer aisle windows were tall and shafted with shaft-rings, moulded caps and bases, and probably had two-light plate tracery with a circle over (see the restored window in the N wall of No. 16). Other evidence has to be pieced together from the interior of the houses: Nos. 16–19 all preserve elements of the arcading and rere-arches of the aisle windows. In addition No. 18, S side, preserves inside on the first floor some blank arcading from the W wall of the S aisle, remains of a spiral staircase at the junction of S aisle and hall (a corresponding stair survives in No. 19, N side), and the original round-headed S doorway from the aisle. But the house itself is predominantly Georgian, with some early to mid-C18 features (fireplaces etc.) and a brick SW extension dated 1772. Mid- to late C18 changes are also evident at No. 16 (extended or refronted 1762) and No. 17. These houses also provide the clearest evidence that their evolution began with the insertion of floors during the late medieval period. No. 16 inside also has the remains of a close-studded wall, incorporating an internal window, which appears to have belonged to a room above the first floor.

Adjoining this house at right angles, i.e. attached to the NE corner of the N aisle, is TABLE HALL. Its original function is unknown but it is later C15; the splendid roof with collar-beams on braces and windbraces is dated to c. 1461 (dendrochronology). Much of the structure is timber-framed, of two storeys, with a jetty along the W side, and was evidently jettied on the E side also where it has been underbuilt with a thin stone wall. The N wall, however, is very thick masonry and appears original. At first floor is a (C16?) fireplace. The ground floor was originally one room (subdivided in the C20) with a ceiling of carved beams, now only partly exposed, and a moulded wallplate with frieze of carved emblems (repeated in stone at the NE corner). The gable of the roof breaks above No. 16 in a highly picturesque manner.

The chancel of the Infirmary chapel was converted into yet another house (CANONRY HOUSE) but the nave was demolished, so the house stands separate from the rest. The blocked chancel arch, preserved in its W wall, has slender blank arches l. and r. of the beautifully moulded arch, a gabled top and traces of a window jamb to the S. Eight banded detached jamb shafts, stiff-leaf capitals and deep moulding. Colonnettes in two orders, best seen from within. Fine double piscina inside (revealed in the 1970s) with moulded arches, Alwalton marble shaft and foliage capitals. Of the chancel itself remains are partly C13 (buttresses, reused mask-corbels) and partly C14 alterations. E window also partly preserved. The house itself is C17 (mullion windows), C18 (staircase) and C19, and since at least the C16 has been linked with the building to its N, which is supposed to have been the INFIRMARER'S HALL. It too is C13, probably c. 1220, i.e. earlier than the main Infirmary, and has windows consisting of two pointed-trefoiled lights with a circle, trefoil, quatrefoil and cinquefoil in plate tracery. The lights are separated by a polygonal shaft, not a mullion. Chamber block at the W end, separated by a cross-passage (now part of the Precentor's Lodging, which extends S on the E side of Canonry House).

S of the Infirmary is ARCHDEACONRY HOUSE, originally, it is suggested, the hostry or guest house. The building is largely Victorian, probably *c.* 1875–80; its principal part is of two storeys and an attic in the straight gables, but has medieval buttresses incorporated on the S front and late C13 N windows that are tall, shafted, with shaft-rings, and have two lights with a plain circle over. They appear original and *in situ*. Nice row of quatrefoil openings above, designed to light a gallery along this side. The lower W range (now NORMAN HALL) has a hall open to the roof with a splendid wide (late C12?) arch on the S side, blocked during remodelling by *G. G. Pace*, 1971. This rests on shafts with waterleaf capitals. The large N fireplace looks C19 Romanesque. Further evidence of the C12 to C17 in the building is scanty and confused.

SW is PREBENDAL HOUSE, of C14–C15 origin but much remodelled and extended, for the final time in the 1850s. Between this building and Norman Hall is a fragment of a tall arch incorporated within an outbuilding. To what did it belong?

Finally, close to the entrance to the precincts from the SE, is the ALMONERS HALL. It consisted (E–W) of a two-storey chamber block (stair with tiny window inside), hall (with tall transomed one-light windows of *c.* 1300), service area and bakehouse with an added room to the W. The chamber block and hall were converted to a dwelling in the C16, but the hall was made into stables in the C19 with a coach house at the W end. All a little over-restored 1992.

S, outside the precinct, BISHOPS GARDENS, with Gothic FOUNTAIN by *James Ruddle*, 1898, originally set up in the market place in memory of H. P. Gates, the first mayor. Octagonal open lantern and spire with crocketed finials and cross.

Minster Yard, a circular tour

The MINSTER YARD (or Galilee) is entered from the Market Place by the OUTER GATE. This was built by Abbot Benedict. His work consists of the two archways (columns with scalloped capitals, arches with roll mouldings), the blank wall arcading raised above the doorways to N and S, and the rib-vault of the same elementary moulding as in the Norman work in the church. The C14 placed a higher arch in front of the Norman W arch; the gates, hung from a rare type of rotating hinge, are dated by their timbers to after 1356. The upper parts are also C14. Panel-motifs and two turrets. It was originally of two storeys above the arch but the top storey removed before 1800 and now as restored in 1952 by *Leslie T. Moore* with mullion windows. Adjoining N, the former Porter's Lodge, with, inside, remains of a substantial stone arch; the rest much remodelled in 1924–5 by *Traylen & Lenton*.

The large SOUTH RANGE contains much medieval fabric but its original purpose is uncertain and obscured by remodelling in the mid C19 as houses and C20 conversion to offices. The w end, that part known as the ABBOT'S JAIL or KING'S LODGING, adjoining the Outer Gate, was largely rebuilt in 1929–30 by *Caröe & Passmore*. Its face to Cathedral Square is nicely cut stone, with a chimneybreast protruding, battlements and mullioned window in keeping with the gate. But its basement is a late C12 vaulted room, in two bays with a short circular pier and slightly chamfered arches and ribs. The slit window with deep splay was reopened during the rebuilding. A longer range also existed to the s, the foundations for which were revealed in 1927 during construction of the bank adjoining. The range continues E along the s side of the Minster Yard. No. 28 also has the remains of two vaulted rooms, probably late C12 or C13, the ribs with chamfers and moulded responds. Then Nos. 26–27, 1840s, by *W. J. Donthorn*, with canted bays through two floors and shaped attic gables; apparently emulating its mid-C17 predecessor. Donthorn also recast the range E of Abbot's Gate (*see* below), especially No. 25, with mullioned windows, a buttressed porch tower and a projecting oriel to the l. This part appears to have contained a series of medieval lodgings, as an C18 drawing shows, and originally incorporated a gateway to the Bishop's Palace at its w end. Its E end has a buttress tower containing a stair, some Dec-style two-light windows (C19 tracery) and, inside, the enigmatic remains of two bays of quadripartite vaulting with ribs that have very deep chamfers. Perhaps C13? Oddly the vaulting is truncated by the N and s walls (i.e. they are later medieval). The room to its w has a good ceiling of carved beams.

In the centre of the s range is the ABBOT'S GATE, attributed to Abbot Robert de Lindsey, 1214–22. It projects squarely to the N, and has square turrets. Two-centred archways to N and s; four orders of colonnettes with moulded capitals. To the N as well as the s are original figures, deserving to be better known than they are. They may be later C13, for there is evidence that the upper parts of the gate were rebuilt at that time (as two storeys above the arch, including the so-called 'Knight's Chamber'). The upper windows altered in the Jacobean style; narrow staircase of same period with flat, pierced balusters. Inside the gateway from N to s, first one bay with slender blank arcading very similar to that of the w wall of the church and a quadripartite rib-vault, then a cross-wall dividing the traffic into pedestrians (two-centred double-chamfered arch) and carriages and horsemen (depressed double-chamfered arch). Then two more bays much as the N bay.

Through the Abbot's Gate one reaches the BISHOP'S PALACE. This was the Abbot's House of the monastery and lay within a separate court, although adjoining the Great Hall in the w claustral range. It was much abused in 1644 but seems to have been made habitable again *c.* 1661 by *John Lovin* for Bishop Laney, who had attended the King in exile. It is now mostly Victorian. In it, however, survive two undercrofts, usually interpreted as having had the solar of the lodging above. The larger, now the entrance hall, is earlier C13, probably built by Abbot Alexander, 1222–6, of two bays wide and four bays long, divided by circular piers with moulded capitals. Arches and ribs are chamfered. Medieval work, however, is restricted to the two N bays, the rest much restored in 1864–5 by *Waring & Blake* of Westminster, who also added a dining room and built the present staircase. *Minton* tiled floor. The smaller room at the N, now the CHAPEL, is also rib-vaulted but probably later C12 with a transverse arch that has the roll on a flat section as found in the cathedral. The E window is an original slit lancet within a shallow full-height recess. Original also the splendid buttress, with very long set-offs. To the N stood a chapel erected by Bishop Magee in 1869–70 (by *Edward Browning*). The former door to it has been made into a window with Expressionist STAINED GLASS by *Patrick Reyntiens*, 1958.

At right angles to the undercroft's S end, an addition known as 'HEAVEN'S GATE' (now Diocesan offices), perhaps designed as a set of superior chambers for guests. Two Late Perp oriel windows facing N. One of them has on its underside a church, very nicely portrayed, and standing on a tun – the rebus of Abbot Kirkton (1496–1528) who built the retrochoir. The ground floor was of course originally open – see the two blocked four-centred arches. On the S (garden) front there is another very fine polygonal oriel window at the same level as those on the entrance front, with panelled sides, fan-vaulted corbel and inside an exquisite panelled roof. The gatehouse is continued S by a range, probably mid-C17, of three bays long, with, on its W front gables, over each of the bays and mullioned windows at first floor. Ground floor originally arcaded along its W side, the arches (now blocked with big quatrefoil windows) have keystones with carved shields. At right angles to this is a taller range, perhaps of the same date, with stair-tower on its S side. Early C18 prints show that the S and W fronts of the palace had the same crenellated parapet but they have been subject to numerous changes and two additions, including the Tudor Gothic N (service) wing, possibly by *W. J. Donthorn*, who designed the stables (dem.). The SERVICE WING, extending E, is a minor early work by *Lutyens*, 1897–8, very attractively handled with his usual asymmetry. Ketton stone and local brick, with roofs of Collyweston slates, triple-gabled on the side elevation. The two-storey gabled section with battered sides framing the entrance is a presentiment of the mannerism of Lutyens's maturity. In the bishop's garden (and only visible from there) one can also see the interior of the Refectory (*see* above).

From close to the NW angle of the church façade is the PRIOR'S GATE, built under Abbot Kirkton, i.e. early in the C16. It is very richly decorated with a frieze of quatrefoils, heraldic and saints' badges (St Oswald, St Edmund and St Edward) and heraldic emblems, including that of the Prince of Wales (cf. the retrochoir roof), crenellations with blank tracery etc. Around the four-centred arch are bosses of similar type to the arches between the aisles and retrochoir in the cathedral. It has a separate opening for pedestrians, above which appears the abbot's rebus. Another gateway, at right angles to this, formerly led into the monastic graveyard, which was originally separated from the minster yard by a wall. The gate leads to the former Prior's Lodging, later DEANERY (now divided into the Dean's house, N, and cathedral offices, S). It contains little that is medieval but at its core is a late C13 hall (now entrance hall), of which the E wall, with a former spiral staircase, exists. The house was altered in the early C18 with the addition of a S wing (Little Prior's Gate) which has panelling, staircase and windows of this date. It is now Tudor Gothic, the remodelling perhaps by W. J. Donthorn, 1842. Edward Browning then rebuilt the N end beyond the hall in 1853 in his usual Gothic style. The hall windows, front and back, are of two pointed-trefoiled lights with a circle over, possibly reproducing the original tracery. They have original depressed rere-arches. Browning added the bay window on the W front and everything to its N along with the garden front. He did more in the early 1870s, heightening the W wing, extending the service range, adding the fanciful turret at the SE corner and the unsatisfactorily skewed porch. Inside, the DRAWING ROOM of 1853 has a ceiling copied from the early C16 presence chamber at the Bede House, Lyddington (Rutland), with coving of tracery-like fan vaults. STABLES also mid-C19, probably of the same date as the former ALMSHOUSES (No. 10) facing the Minster Yard.

In the garden of Prior's Gate to the E, TOUT HILL, a large circular mound, 120 ft (36.5 metres) in diameter and 20 ft (6 metres) high, with a flat circular top 35 ft (10.6 metres) across. Traces of a surrounding ditch survive only on the NW where there is a slight hollow 20 ft (6 metres) wide and 2 ft (0.6 metres) deep. By tradition the motte was heaped up by the unpopular, Norman, Abbot Thorold in the 1070s. There are no signs that it ever carried more than wooden fortifications. To its SW a picturesque ARCH with chevron made up in 1906 by Dean Barlow of fragments from the cathedral.

Finally the buildings of the Minster Yard's W side, which begins N of the Outer Gate with BECKET'S CHAPEL, the chancel only of St Thomas's church of c. 1330. It replaced a chapel begun by Abbot William of Waterville in 1170–5 and completed after 1177 by Abbot Benedict, who brought relics from Canterbury to Peterborough. Its nave was pulled down in the early C15 for the building of St John's church (see Religious Buildings, below). Five-light E window with reticulated tracery, three-light side windows with Dec tracery. It was the King's School from the Dissolution until 1885. To the N, at right angles, stood the 'Sister House', a hospital founded by Benedict, part of its site now occupied by the former headmaster's house (No. 2), built or rebuilt in 1842 by *Bryan Browning*, with a tall gabled wing. Next comes a large Early Georgian terrace of three, also for the school. The date given is 1727–8 (rainwater heads), built for Earl Fitzwilliam. Three storeys, yellow and red brick an early use in the town, segment-headed windows, doorways with open segmental pediments on pilasters and top parapet. The oddest feature is the terrace in front, built up over vaults and creating an area in front of the basements. This would only make sense if the vaults and basements were beneath street level but as executed looks very peculiar. The planning inside is also unusual and might have been divided into lodgings at each floor with lobbies off the staircase.

CITY CENTRE

RELIGIOUS BUILDINGS

St John the Baptist, Cathedral Square. Built on its present site in 1402–7, reputedly reusing material from old St John, which stood E of the cathedral at Boongate, and the nave of St Thomas W of the cathedral (*see* Becket's Chapel, p. 617). A big Perp town church, largely of one piece but much detail due to restorations begun by *J. L. Pearson* in 1882–3 and continued by *A. W. Blomfield & Sons* from the early 1890s to 1909; the builder on both occasions *John Thompson*. Nave with a clerestory, embattled chancel of equal height and continuous N and S aisles which embrace the tower. The S porch is of two storeys and two bays deep, the outer bay open to the W and E as well as to the S. The lower storey has tierceron vaults with ridge-ribs and bosses with Annunciation and Crucifixion; the upper part is gabled with corner pinnacles and a creature, the antelope emblem of Henry IV. Later stair-turret. A date of 1473 is given for the N porch. Rubble walls, stripped of plaster in 1916, but ashlar for the buttresses and upper parts of the tower, which has large bell-openings of four lights with transom and a frieze of the same flowing pattern as the cathedral nave parapet. The tracery of the W window, of late C13 type, appears to date from the restoration in 1909. The tower buttresses are polygonal. Decorated parapets; pinnacles. A spire was removed and extensive repairs made in 1819 by *Bryan Browning* of Stamford, who rebuilt the clerestory and added a steep roof (returned by Pearson to a more appropriate low pitch). Of about the same date are the five windows with intersecting Gothic tracery of inauthentic design. From 1885 all the others of this type were gradually replaced by large Perp four-light windows with panel tracery, inspired by the surviving E window (which Pearson moved to a higher position between two image niches). They are variations on a theme.

Impressive interior of seven bays, the tall early C15 arcades with slender piers of the usual section with four shafts and four hollows. The chancel arch of the same type, the E chapel arches too. The tower arches are a puzzle. Their bases are consonant

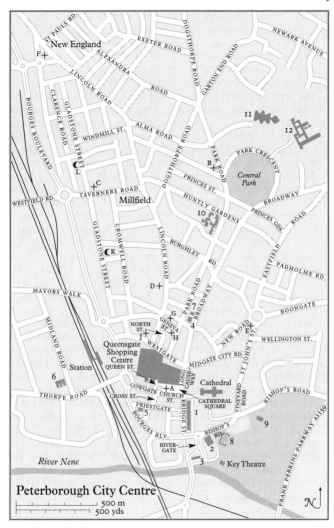

Peterborough City Centre

500 m
500 yds

A	St John the Baptist	I	Town Hall
B	All Saints	2	Crown Courts
C	St Barnabas (former)	3	Police Station
D	St Mark	4	Library
E	St Mary the Virgin		(and John Clare Theatre)
F	St Paul	5	Museum
G	St Peter & All Souls (R.C.)	6	Peterborough District
H	Baptist Church		Hospital (site of former)
J	Westgate Church	7	Broadway Theatre
K	Central Mosque	8	Lido
L	Jamia Ghousia Mosque	9	Leisure Centre
		10	Kings School
		11	Thomas Deacon Academy
		12	Peterborough Regional
			College

with the arcade piers yet in their complex mouldings and responds seem earlier than the work of 1402, if probably not earlier than the C14. They were blocked from the C18 until 1907–9, when they were restored by *Blomfield & Sons* (head-stops of George V and Queen Mary). Can the mouldings be of that date? – Excellent ROOFS by Pearson in an appropriate and very fine Perp, the nave roof low-pitched with wall-posts carved with saints and panelling with cuspwork at the angles.

FURNISHINGS. – FONT. Big, Perp, octagonal, with quatre-foil panels. – PULPIT. Late C19. Given by John Thompson, with saints in canopied niches at the angles. Fine set of woodwork in the chancel and S chapel, the CHOIR STALLS of 1900 by *Blomfield & Sons*, but the rest by *Bodley & Hare*, 1915–19, in lavish Perp style: ALTAR, REREDOS, PANELLING, SEDILIA and SCREENS (rood added 1938 to the original design). The aisles' W screens, erected 1909, are of the same design. – STAINED GLASS. E windows (chancel and aisles, Ascension, Resurrec-tion, Pentecost) of 1885 by *Heaton, Butler & Bayne*, the aisle tracery designed by *Pearson*; by the same firm, given in 1902, the second window from the E in the N aisle, Christ in the storm on the Sea of Galilee, dramatically rendered. – In the N and S aisles several windows by *Clayton & Bell*, installed 1883–1919 but to a consistent composition of principal figures in each of the main lights under canopies. – Following the same scheme the N aisle sixth from E by *Kempe*, 1896, with Old Testa-ment prophets, and fifth from E of 1968 by *Brian Thomas* of *J. Powell & Sons*, depicting C19 and C20 luminaries (Florence Nightingale etc.), both good. – Tower W by *A. K. Nicholson*, 1922, Christ in Majesty with St John and St Luke; quite atmo-spheric and well coloured. – In the porch, John the Baptist by *Hardman & Co.*, 1891. – MONUMENTS. A good Georgian collection. William Wyldbore (SE chapel) †1781, by *Richard Hayward*. Standing monument. Obelisk with urn in relief on lion's paws, two female classical allegories in relief to the l. and r. – Several monuments signed by *Edward Bingham* in S chapel and S aisle: Charles Balguy †1767, with classical and Gothic motifs; Thomas Warriner †1767; William †1782 and Frances Bowker †1783, with flaming urns; John Image †1786, with a female figure by an urn; and the Sambrook family, *c.* 1795. – Agnes and Agnes Squire (N aisle), wife and daughter of William; he mourns in Grecian robes by a tall pedestal with medallion showing their portraits in profile. By *Flaxman*, 1804–6. – WAR MEMORIAL, W end of the nave in the angle with the tower, by *Bodley & Hare*, *c.* 1918. St George under a Dec canopy.

ALL SAINTS, Park Road. The church for the suburb around Central Park (*see* p. 631) and largely funded by Canon Ball, its first vicar, formerly of St Paul (*see* below). Won in competition in 1886 by *Temple Moore* (J. Oldrid Scott was the judge) but built to a modified design and in phases: 1886–7 (chancel and nave), 1894 (S aisle) and 1905 (tower). In a Dec style, much simplified from the original design. The tower, built last, stands at the E end of the S aisle. This is uncommonly wide, almost equal to the nave. Spacious interior, all the details restrained, with the mouldings of the windows and the tall arcade flush to the painted brick walls; the arches die into the lozenge piers. Inventive flamboyant tracery to the E window, flanked inside by blank arches. Pointed tunnel-vault over the nave. – The best FURNISHINGS are the PULPIT, ORGAN CASE and CHANCEL SCREEN by Moore, 1887–94, and REREDOS of 1898, quite an elaborate piece with shallow relief panels and two canopied tabernacles flanking. Other furnishings and painted decoration by *Leslie T. Moore*, 1921–36 (s chapel screens, rood) and 1945 (chancel and aisle chapel gates and kneeling desks). – STAINED GLASS. Three by *H. Victor Milner*, the E window, five lights with the Virgin and saints, 1919; the N aisle (a gloomy St Pega and St Guthlac), 1907, and s chapel E, undated.

CHURCH ROOMS, N, by *John Beardshaw*, 1985–6. In the churchyard, the WAR MEMORIAL, also by *Temple Moore*, 1920. Wooden calvary. – Across Park Road, the VICARAGE, 1902.

ST BARNABAS (former), Taverners Road/Gladstone Road. Now a nursery. 1899–1900 by *William Boyer* of Peterborough as a chapel of ease to St Mark for the artisan district of Millfield. Brick; quite plain throughout except at the E end. A lavishly finished w front with tower was intended. – STAINED GLASS. By *Morris & Co.* of Westminster, 1906 (E window, Te Deum) and 1908 (s and N transepts). In the vestry a single figure of *c.* 1875–80 by *James Bell*, Street's protégé.

ST MARK, Lincoln Road. 1855–6 by *Edward Ellis*; the first of the Victorian churches, built for the developing suburb N of the centre. The builder was *John Thompson* of Peterborough, who was also churchwarden. Quite an original and picturesque design. Early Dec style with a NE tower and spire. Nave with stone dormers with fanciful circular windows. Also two half-timbered dormers, dated 1906, attractive but not in keeping. Narthex at the w end, 1889 by *H. M. Townsend*. Lofty interior with pointed arcades on octagonal piers and scissors brace roof; some nice carving on the corbels of the trusses. Chancel refurnished 1867; fancy marble REREDOS by *Ellis* and encaustic TILES by *Maw & Co.*; the SEDILIA, with crocketed canopies, is the old reredos. – Lady Chapel REREDOS by *Bodley & Hare*, *c.* 1918 – STAINED GLASS. E window, 1869, Good Shepherd and the Evangelists by *A. O. Hemming*; given by Thompson. Five windows by *J. Powell & Sons*: in the s aisle, two of 1892, in matching style with canopies, and a larger window of 1895, designed by *Holiday*; in the N aisle, fourth from w, 1898; and second from E, 1914.

ST MARY THE VIRGIN, Boongate. 1989–91 by *Covell Matthews*. On the site of the church of 1859–60 by *Ewan Christian*, and incorporating its w door. Substantial, of white blockwork striped with coloured stone, with a bell-tower. Inside, a fan-shaped worship space, the raised sanctuary set against a backdrop of banded Purbeck marble with concealed top lighting. – SCULPTURE. Christ Rising, of abstracted forms carved in oak, by *Lee Grandjean*. – STAINED GLASS. Reset in lightboxes.

One of 1926 by *A. K. Nicholson*, two more of 1960 by *A. E. Buss* (*Goddard & Gibbs*).

ST PAUL, Bourges Boulevard/Lincoln Road. The church for the Great Northern Railway workers' suburb of New England. First proposed in 1854 but turned down by the company's shareholders; finally built in 1867–9. The architect was *James Teale* of Doncaster, assisted by *Edmund Beckett Denison* (later Lord Grimthorpe, of notorious reputation), who with his brother, Edward Denison, former chairman of the Great Northern Railway, met most of the cost.* Quite an impressive design in the E.E. style, built of neatly coursed limestone: cruciform, with aisles, an apse and big central tower, with a pyramid roof, open to the inside. Lancets, Geometrical E and W windows and quatrefoils and sexfoils in circles. W porch added 1887, the vestry 1902. Austere interior, relying for effect on the lighting through the tower. Four-bay nave arcades rising from octagonal piers, wider arches at the crossing on shafted responds. – FONT. E.E. style with spiral carving to the base. – ROOD SCREEN, 1907, in East Anglian Perp style with ribs supporting the loft. – ALTAR by *Leslie T. Moore*, 1950 – STAINED GLASS. By *Cakebread, Robey & Co.*, several signed, 1888–1912, the best in the apse lancets, with censing angels above. – CHURCH HALL, 1905 by *J. G. Stallebrass*. Free Style with a big shaped gable.

ST PETER AND ALL SOULS (R.C.), Geneva Street. 1895–6 by *Leonard Stokes*, succeeding a chapel of 1856 in Queen Street (by *W. W. Wardell*). E end completed 1904. In Stokes's characteristic stripped Dec style, sparsely detailed. Of small squared rubble with courses of dressed stone in bands. Short transepts and small polygonal bellcote at the W end, where the Priest's House is attached. Interior with aisle of no more than passage width. Tall aisle windows. The arcade arches are so tall as to embrace them. Sanctuary reordered on several occasions, the last in 2006. – The BALDACCHINO and REREDOS are copies of the originals (removed in 1971) but incorporate carvings of 1913 of the Crucifixion, St Peter and Judas Maccabeus. The scale is all wrong without the High Altar. Lady Chapel ALTAR, highly coloured Sienese marble, by Stokes, 1913; it has a C14 icon of the Virgin, by *Ugolino*. – ALTAR (N chapel), 1912 by *Stufflesser* of St Ulrich, Tyrol. Relief of the Last Supper, and Crucifixion in the reredos. – Impressively large STATIONS OF THE CROSS, 1903 by *Feuerstein*. – SCULPTURE. In the sacristy, a fine small alabaster relief of the Annunciation, 1585, with the Virgin under a canopy. – STAINED GLASS. Lady Chapel, 1914 by *Hardman & Co.*

Former ALL SOULS SCHOOLS, Manor House Street. Now St Theresa's House. 1893 by *Messrs Hart* of Corby and Grantham.

---

*Most of Teale's works were associated with E. B. Denison, by whom he was allegedly bullied.

BAPTIST CHURCH, Park Road. 1906 by *S. S. Dottridge* with *Walford & Thompson*, all of Leadenhall Street, London. Quite large, red brick, with tracery in the free Gothic usual for this date. Cruciform plan. Church now at the level of the former galleries. Ceiled vaults spring from luscious Art Nouveau foliage capitals.

WESTGATE CHURCH, Westgate. Congregationalist chapel by *R. Moffat Smith* of Manchester, 1859. Gothic, brick with twin stone spirelets flanking the entrance, six-light traceried window. Five sharp gables along the flanks. Gutted by fire in 1891 and 1991; the interior rebuilt the first time (by *Alfred Sykes* of Milton and *John Thompson*, builder) with twisted cast-iron columns supporting a handsome timber roof with Gothic spandrels. – Art Nouveau brass LIGHT FITTINGS, 1901. – STAINED GLASS. Good s window by *J. W. Knowles* of York, 1891; the others by *A. L. & C. E. Moore*, also 1891.

FAIZAN-E-MADINA (CENTRAL MOSQUE), Gladstone Street/ Cobden Street. 2006, 'designed and donated by *M. Arif*, building contractors'. On a grand scale; its minaret and dome form a landmark among the two-storey terraces of the neighbourhood. Brick, polygonal plan with storeys of windows in each bay and decorative mosaic panels.

JAMIA GHOUSIA MOSQUE, Gladstone Street. *c.* 2008. Buff brick with red trim, flatly detailed. Two minarets at the corners and central dome.

CEMETERY, Eastfield Road. Opened 1858. Gateway and chapels by *Bellamy & Hardy* were demolished before *c.* 1960. (Monument to Canon Moser by *Leonard Stokes*, 1912.)

PUBLIC BUILDINGS

OLD GUILDHALL, Cathedral Square. *See* Perambulation 1 below.

TOWN HALL, Bridge Street. Designed in 1928, built 1929–33, as combined offices for the Soke and Borough councils. By *E. Berry Webber*, who won the design in competition. English Baroque, brick with stone dressings. 'The choice of the style at so late a date may be deplorable,' wrote Pevsner, 'but the building is tactfully fitted into the street architecture of Peterborough. The architect has resisted the temptation to set his work up as a monument to compete with the cathedral.' Thirteen-bay centre with a narrow portico of four tall giant Corinthian columns. Turret with detached, diagonally set columns and cupola. The parts to the l. and r. of the portico have widely spaced tall arched windows. In addition long, lower, two-storey wings ending in giant arches and fitting the building into the street frontages to the l. and r. and opposite; they contain shops and an arcade on the ground floor. The rear elevation, in fact a separate office range, is more self-effacing, compositionally similar but with only a minor accent at the centre of a pediment. Darker brick with closely set sash windows. The addition of a mansard in 1984, although anticipated in the original design, is regrettable. Spacious STAIRCASE HALL of a kind of Quattrocento character, with outlandish blue marbled columns and groin-vaulted passages. MAYOR'S PARLOUR behind the portico, panelled. Adjoining COUNCIL CHAMBER (N) in a most unusual Italian Renaissance style with a beamed roof, painted with symbols of the municipality, and a public gallery on Solomonic columns. Fitted out by *Frederick Sage & Co.* of Walton. RECEPTION HALL to the S. Much quieter but with some jazzy bronze and crystal light fittings.

CROWN COURTS, Rivergate. *c.* 1987–8 by *Cambridge Design Architects*; a Postmodern interpretation of a Roman villa with shallow pantiled roofs carried on broad eaves over a tubular streel structure. Gabled attic storey.

H.M. PRISON PETERBOROUGH. *See* Westwood, p. 656.

POLICE STATION, Rivergate. In a bad position, but nicely designed, by *L. H. Robjohn*, City Engineer, 1957, with minimal decoration in the form of projecting brick headers, a motif of the period.

LIBRARY (and JOHN CLARE THEATRE). 1988–90, by the *Peterborough Design Group*; the last public work commissioned by the Development Corporation. Light brown brick and smoked glass, dully composed with bowed projections for the stairs. Undemonstrative interior.

MUSEUM, Priestgate. 1816, built as a house for Thomas Alderson Cooke. Fine, plain, three-storey ashlar front, with a one-storey portico of pairs of Greek Doric columns. Big projection at the rear ending in a bow – when built the house would have had good views to the Nene. It was used as the infirmary from 1856, partly rebuilt after a fire in 1884 (by *H. M. Townsend*) and wings added 1897 (W) and 1902 (E). The museum since 1931.

Former PETERBOROUGH DISTRICT HOSPITAL, Thorpe Road. Begun as the town's war memorial, opened 1928. Neo-Georgian by *Wallace Marchment*. Closed in 2010; the postwar additions due for demolition and housing to be built 2015–18.

BROADWAY THEATRE, Broadway. The former Odeon cinema of 1935–7 by the *Harry Weedon Partnership* (to a design by *Roland Satchwell*), a minor work for the chain but beautifully revived and expanded as a multi-purpose performance space in 2001–2 by *Tim Foster Architects*. From the centre of the upper floor thrusts a striking glass box. The auditorium, with subdued Art Deco fittings, is a faultless evocation of a 'picture palace'.

KEY THEATRE, Embankment Road, by the river. 1971 by *Mathew Robotham Associates*, in pale yellow brick. Low profile without a flytower. Slickly remodelled with a sheer glass front and canopy by *Spacelab*, 2006.

LIDO, Bishops Road. 1935–6. The city's principal private architects decided to work together and for free: *Dodson & Dodson*; *A. W. Ruddle*; *W. P. Hack*; *Wilson & Wilson*; and *Traylen, Lenton & Warwick*. Hacienda-style with a clocktower. Open colonnade below sun decks around the pool.

LEISURE CENTRE, Bishops Road. The Regional Pool of 1974 by *Scott, Brownrigg & Turner*. A big, brutal job, faced in pale bricks with a brindled surface. The novel feature was the placing of the swimming pool above ground, expressed as a solid volume between piers. The upper storeys are cantilevered from the frame.

Schools and colleges

The town's growth in the later C19 is represented by a handful of surviving, though altered, single-storey Board Schools, and the postwar expansion by their Modernist equivalent. Few merit individual attention.

KINGS SCHOOL, Park Road. Founded in the cathedral precincts in the C16. Present buildings of 1885 by *Reginald Naylor* of Derby; collegiate Neo-Tudor in the characteristic Late Victorian arrangement of master's house (l.), hall (r., with Perp window; now library) and central castellated tower porch. Bland 1960s additions to the N by *S. Dodson*. Several additions at the rear, the latest of 2004–9 by *Saunders Boston* of Cambridge.

PETERBOROUGH HIGH SCHOOL, Thorpe Road. The school occupies WESTWOOD HOUSE, one of the largest villas off Thorpe Road, set within its own grounds. Built in 1858–9 for Henry H. English by *Edward Browning*, it is of limestone ashlar and still in a Georgian manner rather than the coming Italianate, with a balustraded parapet and two-storey canted bay windows on the front. Beautifully preserved panelled entrance hall, of more distinctively Victorian character, with tiled floor in geometric patterns, a screen of grey scagliola columns and a plaster frieze of birds and fruiting vines. The CHAPEL is the former stables. Converted in 1971 and extended in 2006, well designed with a lean-to roof punctuated by square dormers. – STAINED GLASS. An important, large window of 1853 by *William Miller*, made for the church at Little Gidding (q.v.). C16 style; the Crucifixion in a blasted landscape. The design was supervised by *Charles Wilson*, using the new glass available from *J. Powell & Sons*.

THOMAS DEACON ACADEMY, off Queen's Garden. By *Foster & Partners*, 2004–7. One of the first and best of a new generation of secondary schools for England. Designed for 2,200 pupils and accordingly monumental, of three storeys covering 18,000 square metres. Its plan is symmetrical but organic, with a sinuous outline of three projecting lobes on the N and S elevations. Windows are in continuous bands and the glass roof describes a shallow curve with a web of triangular glazing (cf. the British Museum's Great Court). Inside, each of the six projections represents zones of classrooms and study areas, grouped vertically, which function as 'colleges' within the larger school. In each a feature is made of a glazed classroom for each specialism (Arts, Science, Maths etc.). The planning, as this suggests, is non-traditional and this is also expressed in an emphasis on teaching in seminars and lectures and shared

p. 626

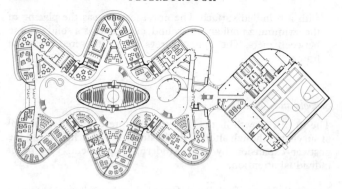

Peterborough, Thomas Deacon Academy, by Foster & Partners.
Plan

study spaces for various ages. On the main axis of the central hall is an elliptical plan LECTURE THEATRE (in fact two theatres which can be joined together) with RESOURCE CENTRE (library) on top. Also a curious circular tower with an open top storey for an art gallery. A separate pod at the E end contains the SPORTS HALL.

PETERBOROUGH REGIONAL COLLEGE, Park Crescent. The former Technical College built in stages: 1949–52 by *David Jenkin*; and 1957–8 and 1961–5 by *Portess & Richardson*. On the same campus the UNIVERSITY CENTRE (H.E. College), 2009, by *Dyer Associates*, who also have a scheme for reconstruction of the main college.

Railway buildings

The STATION of 1850, built for the Great Northern Railway, was demolished in 1976. The present building of 1980 is of no distinction and is due to be replaced. It makes a poor neighbour for the GREAT NORTHERN HOTEL, a large, simple, Latest Georgian building with eleven bays to its former garden. Only the rocky rustication of the ground floor betrays the real date: 1851–2 by *Henry Goddard*; extended 1859, 1971–2 and restored 1993 and 2009. The GNR's engine works and other buildings to the N have been largely cleared except for a former DISTRICT ENGINEER'S DEPOT and CARPENTERS' SHOP of *c.* 1865–70 between Mayors Walk and Bourges Boulevard. Ten bays long with two storeys of workshops. S of the station, CRESCENT BRIDGE, a steel bow string with the roadway on jack arches. 1911–13 by *Alexander Ross*, the GNR's Chief Mechanical Engineer, and the *Cleveland Bridge and Engineering Co.* of Darlington. To its W, at the corner of Thorpe Road and Midland Road, is a WAGON REPAIR SHOP, a remarkably unaltered building of 1883–4 for the Midland Railway. Timber-framed and timber-clad (the roofs on wide-span kingpost trusses supplemented by crown-posts on iron collars).

The most important survival, and visible from a footbridge behind the feebly detailed Rivergate Shopping Centre, is the NENE VIADUCT of 1849–50 by *Sir William Cubitt* and *Joseph Cubitt*. Spanning the water, three cast-iron segmental arches with latticework spandrels, springing from coupled Greek Doric columns, also of cast-iron and in groups of twelve to each pier. Uniquely of its generation it still carries trains, though at speeds four times as fast as the locomotives of its own time. Between the viaduct and station, in the Bourges Retail Park, are two big SHEDS in yellow brick, with double gables, pilasters and cast-iron columns inside, built *c.* 1894 as tarpaulin stores for the GNR.

PERAMBULATIONS

1. City centre

There is surprisingly little of interest in the city centre, in spite of its age. The medieval street pattern can still be understood, a basic grid w of the cathedral precinct.

The natural start is CATHEDRAL SQUARE, formerly the Market Place, which lies just outside the w gate to the precinct. Here is the OLD GUILDHALL (or market house), and the way in which it and cathedral gatehouse face one another is telling. Dated 1671 and built in the warm local limestone by *John Lovin*, the master mason. Three by two bays with an open ground floor on plain columns and arches. Upper windows of cross type, some later converted to doors on the w side. Coved eaves, a steep hipped roof and steep gable towards the square, with painted royal arms, between dormers, and shields with arms of Bishop Henshaw, Dean Duport, Sir Humphrey Orme and the Montagu family. Behind, although not in line with it, is St John's (*see* Religious Buildings above). To the r. of the cathedral gate, NATWEST (formerly National Provincial Bank) of 1928–9 by *Palmer & Holden*, an expensive-looking job, in the style of Kirby Hall (Northants), with a mighty porch, big fluted pilasters and an extravagant gable; inside, a compartmented plaster ceiling of strapwork and ribs with fruiting vines. Balancing it to the l. of the gate, the former LLOYDS BANK, of 1913 by *A. W. Ruddle*, in a more restrained Neo-Tudor and apparently of Portland stone above a polished black granite plinth, with some nice quirks of detail, e.g. twisty chimneys. Completing the trio, at the corner with Bridge Street, is HSBC, pedestrian Baroque, in warm sandstone, of 1902 by *T. B. Whinney* for the London, City & Midland Bank. After this, there is little to choose other than a few oddities, such as the former BOOTS store (w side, now a restaurant), an Olde English confection of 1911 with historical figures in shell-headed niches and a corner turret (cf. Bury St Edmunds). The setting of St John, which lies below the level of the square surrounded by railings, has been greatly improved by the relandscaping of the square in 2009–11 by *LDA Design*.* Partly preserved, facing the N side of the church, are Neo-Tudor ALMSHOUSES (now café) built by the town Feoffees in 1835, probably by *Francis Ruddle*, and extended in 1903 by *J. G. Stallebrass*. Set back round the corner, i.e. facing CUMBERGATE, are some of the former dwellings; they have alas lost their front gardens and now abut the Queensgate Shopping Centre in a very crude way. It could have all been done so much better. Facing these is one of the only timber-framed houses left in the city, the E range of an earlier group of almshouses, with rubble ground floor and oversailing close-studded upper floor.

QUEEN STREET, W, has another rarity, a brick Georgian town house (No. 10), of five bays, with a stumpy Venetian window in the centre and urns to the parapet. S, in COWGATE, one can still appreciate the medieval pattern of long burgage plots. The best Georgian houses of Peterborough are, or were, S again in PRIESTGATE, although much is now mid-C20 pastiche. One is of five bays with a handsome stone façade with quoins. But its memorable feature, framed in the view down Cross Street, is the centre bay with its tower and low spire of somewhat Vanbrughian proportions and detail, dating from 1864, when the house was extended as the Trinity Presbyterian Church by *Habershon & Pite*. The largest house is the Museum (*see* Public buildings above) at the W end of the street. Otherwise only No. 45, which was the vicarage from 1836, needs singling out. C17 rear but a mid-C19 front with Gothic fittings and a Chinese Chippendale style staircase. Further E, YORKSHIRE HOUSE (S side, now a restaurant) is probably C16, built for the Hakes, a merchant family, but altered 1663 (dated sundial at the rear with loyal inscription). L-shaped, and partly of stone, partly timber-framed. Mullioned windows; much renewed. Central gable with a quatrefoil. Long cross-wing at the rear.

The 1930s Town Hall (*see* Public buildings above) occupies almost the entire E side of BRIDGE STREET, which was widened at the same time, bringing the new buildings into line with the cathedral gate. Nothing may now be seen of the C18 houses and hotels which used to line the street. In the middle the WAR MEMORIAL, a stone obelisk of 2012 by *Architects Design Consortium*. The street's S end is cut off by the inner ring road, which is a shame, for here are a few buildings of interest, including the so-called CUSTOMS HOUSE (Sea Cadets) on the river. Built after 1731 (i.e. after the Bucks' view of that date), probably as a granary and later in use as a bonded warehouse. Its front is of rubble with quoins, three widely

---

*Vital to its success has been the demolition of the former NORWICH UNION BUILDING (by *Feilden & Mawson*, 1964–6, on the site of the C19 Corn Exchange) which, as Pevsner wrote, clashed 'most painfully' with the church tower.

spaced windows, hipped roof, and cupola. s wall of brick, the others all of stone. Loading windows to the river. The medieval bridge was taken down in 1870 and replaced in iron, then superseded in 1931 by TOWN BRIDGE, which continues as a viaduct across the railway to the s.* By *Gotch & Saunders* in reinforced concrete (*Major E. M. Stirling*, engineer).†

Now for the area N of the Cathedral Square, beginning with LONG CAUSEWAY. Like Bridge Street, this is planted with trees, an enhancement proposed by *Gordon Cullen* in the early 1970s. Of the same period, on the N side, is the public face of the QUEENSGATE SHOPPING CENTRE of 1975–82 by *Keith Maplestone*, the Development Corporation Architect. This is quite successfully integrated into the streetscape, with a light stone façade, comprising an open arcaded ground floor, partly set forward to the r., and an upper storey of projecting bays with chamfered corners and slit windows – traditional without being too explicit about it. Inside, covered malls maintain the lines of the medieval streets and lead into a central two-storey top-lit area; such use of natural lighting was a first in England. Restaurant in a bridge.

At the junction with MIDGATE, evidence of the thoughtless planning of the postwar years in the form of HEREWARD HOUSE of 1963–6 by *Douglas Stephen & Partners*, a high slab of offices on a two-storey podium for a shopping centre, with a ramp to the rooftop car park, all very characteristic of the date. s of it on CITY ROAD, the former COUNTY COURT, Italian Romanesque of 1873 in yellow and red brick. Facing this is PETERSCOURT, formerly St Peter's Training College for Anglican schoolmasters, 1856–8 by *G. G. Scott*. Red brick, Gothic, quite tame, with rows of gablets and paired diamond stacks. At the w end is a very attractive C18 doorcase, with Corinthian pilasters and a full entablature with frieze carved with fauna (allegedly from the Guildhall in London, brought here in 1953, when this was the office of Perkins Engines, and reset in 1985). The surrounding area was the Development Corporation's office quarter. Much mirror glass combined with brick, of course. e in ST JOHN'S STREET, council flats (St Mary's Court) by *Ruddle & Wilkinson*, 1964, comprising a twelve-storey tower and lower blocks, quite nicely grouped.

Cattle Market Road leads back to BROADWAY, which was mostly built up in the first half of the C20 for a mixture of civic buildings and places of entertainment. At the corner, the former EMBASSY THEATRE (now a pub) of 1937 by the cinema architect *David Evelyn Nye*, and an overwhelmingly plain brick job, without ornamental relief except thin stone bands and the typical concrete fins on the curved elevation.

---

*The footings of the medieval bridge have been excavated (Ben Robinson).
†Between the two parts of the bridge was BRIDGE HOUSE, former offices of the Mitchell Engineering Co., of 1955–6 by *Howard V. Lobb & Partners*. Demolished in 2012, but an impressive bas-relief by *A. J. Ayres*, 'Every Addition to True Knowledge is an Addition to Human Power', has been preserved for re-setting.

Opposite, the former TECHNICAL COLLEGE (College Arms pub), mildest Jacobean, of 1902–3 by *J. W. Walshaw*, City Engineer, and the more confidently Wrenaissance-style CARNEGIE LIBRARY (now a restaurant) of 1904–6 by *Hall & Phillips* of London; both horribly converted to their present use. Also BAYARD PLACE (E side), big 1980s Postmodern offices now occupied by the City Council.

Finally along WESTGATE past THE BULL HOTEL, which has a low, two-storey front of nine bays, probably *c.* 1700, of good quality. Finely cut limestone blocks and bracketed cornice. Opposite, DARCY'S JEWELLERS with a nicely preserved shopfront by *Frederick Sage & Co.* of Walton, *c.* 1920, and then the entrance to the WESTGATE ARCADE, of 1927–8 by *A. W. Ruddle*. Inside, it is two-storeyed and top-lit, in the C19 manner, with an open colonnade above the shops and transverse arches. Further W, a unique, and handsome, Georgian house of five bays, of ashlar with moulded window surrounds, and then WORTLEY'S ALMSHOUSES (now a pub), remodelled in 1837 in the Tudor style, probably by *Francis Ruddle*; the building was the N range of a larger group erected in 1744 by Edward Wortley, M.P. for Peterborough, see the cartouche above the entrance. The rest was demolished for the Queensgate Centre.

Running down PARK ROAD, the WESTGATE DEPARTMENT STORE incorporates Westgate House Buildings, competent English Baroque of 1911–12 for the Unionist Club, and the Northern Renaissance-style former Peterborough Equitable & Industrial Co-op Society premises of 1888–99, by *Thomas Hind* of Leicester, extended by *G. H. Hind* and completed by *Townsend & Fordham*.

2. Inner Peterborough

Brief description is needed of part of the area immediately around the centre, although a true perambulation is not required. Constrained by the railway on the W, the river to the S and the fenland to the E, the town's suburban expansion from the mid C19 was northwards. The best place to see the effect is along LINCOLN ROAD in the vicinity of St Mark (*see* Religious Buildings above). The earliest houses are its vicarage (No. 84), N of the church, also designed by *Edward Ellis* in a nice asymmetrical Gothic and built 1858 of coursed limestone. Also, THE LINDENS, built *c.* 1865 by *John Thompson*, the contractor, for himself. The garden front is almost certainly of this date, in a Picturesque Gothic with black-and-white half-timbered cross-wings; the front elevation is similar but must be later, more Arts and Crafts-style with projecting stone porch. Flush dressings to the windows in the Voysey manner. Sombre panelled interiors, especially the staircase hall, with minstrels' gallery (stained-glass portraits of Mozart, Bach etc.) and former dining room with Renaissance style carving.

s of the church, THURSTON HOUSE, formerly Gayhurst, of *c.* 1873; red brick with mullioned windows and diamond stacks. Opposite, four large semi-detached brick villas (Nos. 79–93), developed by the Rev. E. Davys, vicar of St John, in 1864–6. The best, Nos. 91–93, has a mildly Butterfieldian character with polychromed window heads, fishscale tile hanging in the gable and nice timberwork pentices, latticework and bargeboards. The architect was *William Young.* s of this group on Lincoln Road's E side, ROTHESAY VILLAS, a tall ashlar terrace of quite plain houses with canted bays and dormers in a steep mansard, with towered ends. Built 1892 for J. M. Craig, partly on the site of the medieval tithe barn of the abbot's manor of Boroughbury.

The PARK ESTATE, E of Lincoln Road, was set out from 1876 by the Peterborough Land Co., who envisaged a spacious suburb of over 500 houses along parallel tree-lined avenues (PARK ROAD and BROADWAY) extending from the town centre for ¾ m. to CENTRAL PARK, which was intended for private use. Around the N side of this curves PARK CRESCENT, where the best houses were to have been built (indeed a double crescent was the original ambition). The scheme foundered, the park was acquired by the city in 1908, and there was much infilling of the large plots between the wars, and some destruction in the later C20. One or two larger houses deserve attention, e.g. N of King's School, No. 195 PARK ROAD, by *H. M. Townsend*, 1880, textbook Queen Anne revival; also by *Townsend*, but in duller Arts and Crafts style, No. 201 (Madeley House), of 1885 for the Rev. C. R. Ball, the wealthy incumbent of All Saints (*see* Religious Buildings above). Of similar character, No. 1 PRINCES GARDENS, off Broadway, built for T. L. Barrett, draper and mayor of Peterborough, by *J. W. Gibson*, *c.* 1909. There is also one likeable oddity in this area: No. 10 BURGHLEY ROAD, gimcrack Arts and Crafts with gnomic features, of 1920 by *Thomas Ellington*, builder, for himself.

MILLFIELD, a densely developed area of late C19 two-storey artisan terraces, lies w of Lincoln Road and N of Bright Street. It was originally served by St Barnabas (*see* Religious Buildings above) but the city's mosques are now the landmarks. Furthest out, about 1½ m. from the centre, is NEW ENGLAND, the workers' suburb built in 1854–66 by the Great Northern Railway. 226 cottages were laid out in a primitive grid of streets, known colloquially as 'The Barracks', close to the engine works. A few survive at Nos. 620–736 Lincoln Road, just N of St Paul's church (*see* Religious Buildings above). They are in two long plain terraces behind front gardens and – plastic windows and doors aside – are impressive. The rest of the cottages to the w were swept away in the early days of the New Town. Also the WESLEYAN CHAPEL of 1866 by *Alfred Sykes* of Milton, which provoked the building of St Paul. Close to the Anglican church is a FOUNTAIN, in the form of a Dec spire, erected 1886 by the first vicar, the Rev. C. R. Ball.

Finally, the town W of the railway along THORPE ROAD, which is carried over the railway by the CRESCENT BRIDGE (*see* Railway Buildings, above). S of the bridge is a unique suburban survivor, ORCHARD HOUSE (No. 15), very plain Late Georgian in gault brick with pilasters and solid Grecian porch. The open fields N of Thorpe Road provided the space for the town's early Victorian institutions, including the SESSIONS COURT HOUSE (now a restaurant) of 1842 by *W. J. Donthorn*. Neo-Norman, symmetrical, with tall battlemented circular towers in the centre and at the corners. Inside, the former courtroom, with open timber roof. There was a gaol block to the rear contained within an octagonal wall (dem. 1962). As the only road with a view in the flat town, both sides were colonized from the 1890s by large villas in the mixed styles of the period, see e.g. Nos. 61–63 Thorpe Road, of *c.* 1911 by *Herbert Sutton* – William and Mary revival with pedimented gables, nicely detailed bay windows and side porches and walls of roughly cut stone. Also one interesting later C20 development: ASH-FIELDS of 1978–80 by *Mathew Robotham & Quinn* for the Nene Housing Society. Three blocks, up to four storeys, the one facing Thorpe Road with a front composed of small arched windows in pairs and projecting stair-towers. Some patterning of brickwork in the gable ends. Stepped rear elevations.

Further W, set back from the N side of the road, is THE GABLES, a large Neo-Elizabethan house of 1896 by *Gotch & Saunders* for J. H. Beeby, coal merchant, who had his offices by the railway. A maternity hospital after 1945, subsequently offices. Now being restored after long institutional use. For WESTWOOD HOUSE *see* Peterborough High School (Public Buildings above). Part of its estate was laid out after 1905 for speculative development of villas along Thorpe Road and WESTWOOD PARK ROAD. The largest houses, at the S end, are mostly by local architects: especially good Nos. 18 and 20 (W side), Arts and Crafts/English Domestic of 1905 by *A. W. Ruddle*. He designed others here, including No. 19, a big house with half-timbered gables of 1912 (his own house was No. 22, 1911). The others of note are No. 15, for W. G. Barford of Barford & Perkins, 1921, and No. 28 of 1924 for a director of the Itter Brick Co., good Early Georgian style with a smart hood to the door on consoles: both are by *Traylen, Lenton & Warwick*. The largest house, but not the finest, is THE LEIN-STERS (No. 29), stuccoed Neo-Georgian by *Kenneth Broad* of London for J. S. Baker of Baker Perkins, engineers.

OUTER PETERBOROUGH

BRETTON

The first of the New Townships created from scratch and conforming to the linear pattern advocated in *Hancock & Hawkes*'s plan (but departed from at Orton and Werrington). Hancock's team initially produced a pilot study for the housing arranged in closes in winding culs-de-sac off the heavily wooded N–S spine of Bretton Way, with wide-fronted houses and space for cars in front and gardens and play areas behind. This was a rejection of the Radburn layouts of the first housing at Ravensthorpe (q.v.) but in practice the Development Corporation carried on as before and so the housing, built 1970–5, is at high densities and in short terraces with front doors off pedestrian paths and still has courtyards for cars (but fewer garages). Much of the housing is in short terraces and some of it designed at surprisingly high densities, but there is no architectural novelty or experimentation. The district centre is BRETTON CENTRE, a large shopping centre for the wider area, and THE CRESSET, designed by *Roger Kirkwood*, 1976–8, as a multi-functional centre for library, theatre, YMCA, workshops, sports, offices, church, day centre etc. Buff brick, with two parallel ranges with split gable roofs. The C21 riposte to the ahistoric tone of the township is a shameless pretend village, THE DEANERY, King Henry Chase, S of the Bretton Centre, with phoney chapel and duckpond.

DOGSTHORPE

The City Council's principal postwar housing estate, planned in 1945 by the *City Engineer's Dept* and begun in 1951. By 1957 it had overtaken the old hamlet of Dogsthorpe, the chief relic of which is the stone-built BLUEBELL INN on Welland Road, C17 to the r. with a carefully matched 1920s addition to the l. Curved hooded doorcase, big bracketed cornice and gabled dormers. The estate extends as far E as Newark, 1,600 houses in all.

CHRIST THE CARPENTER, Central Avenue. 1957–8 by *S. Dodson* of Peterborough. Pale Fletton brick. Nave and chancel in one, with vertical strip windows angled along the sides and a prow-like w front. Slim, square tower. – ETCHED GLASS. W window. With carpenter's emblems. – STAINED GLASS. Four abstract panels by *M.C. Farrar Bell* (*Clayton & Bell*), 1970.

OUR LADY OF LOURDES (R.C.), Welland Road. 1965. Postwar traditional, with nave, chancel and transepts.

METHODIST CHURCH, Birchtree Avenue. Begun 1967. An odd design; square with chamfered, fully glazed corners, and a pitched roof topped by a tapering fleche. Low brick halls etc. to the S.

DOGSTHORPE JUNIOR AND INFANT SCHOOL, Central Avenue. 1950 by the *City Engineer's Dept*. Good early postwar Modernism but still with vestiges of the mood of the 1930s. Long, low, red brick range to the street, flat-roofed, incorporating the entrance. Pre-cast concrete framing is expressed as mullions along the front. Parallel N range, courtyard gardens between.

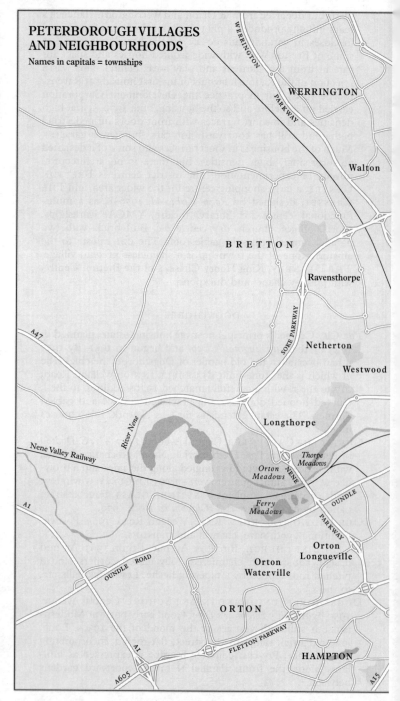

PETERBOROUGH VILLAGES AND NEIGHBOURHOODS

Names in capitals = townships

WERRINGTON

WERRINGTON PARKWAY

Walton

BRETTON

Ravensthorpe

SOKE PARKWAY

Netherton

Westwood

A47

River Nene

Nene Valley Railway

Longthorpe

Thorpe Meadows

Orton Meadows

NENE

Ferry Meadows

OUNDLE PARKWAY

A1

Orton Longueville

OUNDLE ROAD

Orton Waterville

ORTON

A1

A605

FLETTON PARKWAY

HAMPTON

A15

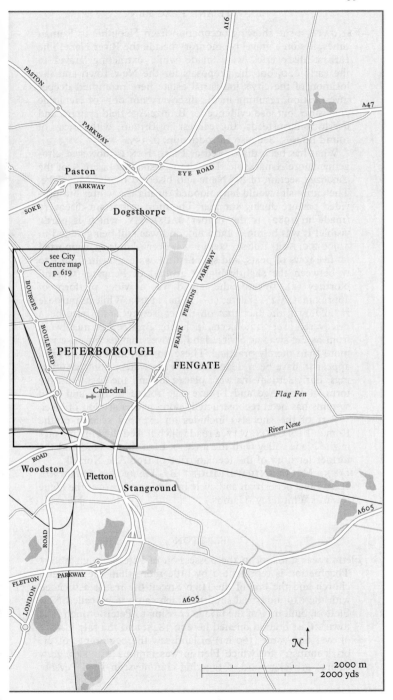

PASTON PARKWAY

A16

A47

Paston

PARKWAY

EYE ROAD

SOKE

Dogsthorpe

see City
Centre map
p. 619

BOURGES

BOULEVARD

PETERBOROUGH

FRANK PERKINS PARKWAY

FENGATE

Cathedral

Flag Fen

River Nene

ROAD

Woodston

Fletton

Stanground

A605

FLETTON

PARKWAY

LONDON ROAD

A605

N

2000 m
2000 yds

FENGATE AND FLAG FEN

FENGATE, a site showing occupation from Neolithic to Roman times, lies on a gravel promontory beside the River Nene. The earliest discoveries were made while extracting gravel in the early C20, but the proposals for the New Town and the location of the city's industrial estate here prompted deeper investigation, resulting in the discovery not only of Neolithic enclosures but also evidence for Bronze Age field systems and livestock farmsteads, the earliest in Britain, with traces of round houses. See also Introduction, p. 355.

What has been discovered at FLAG FEN is, however, altogether more remarkable. The site is a shallow basin, N of the canalized section of the Nene and bisected by the Mustdyke. The entire site would have flooded during the winter but provided pasture during summer. The most important discovery (made in 1982) is the timber CAUSEWAY, which is partly visible. It was begun c. 1300 B.C. and was still being added to c. 900 B.C. At its fullest extent it was over 1 km long, supported on five rows of posts, and spanned the watery basin from E to W between the slightly higher ground of Fengate (W) and Northey (E). Towards the E end was a wider platform of approximately 2½–3 acres (1–1.25 ha) in area. While its purpose is unknown, the fact that on the causeway alone have been discovered over 300 objects, including Bronze Age metalwork from as far away as Switzerland, proves that its purpose was more than merely practical. These objects, including swords, appear to have been deposited into the watery pools as offerings. Early settlements were placed around the basin and the form of Iron Age and Bronze Age round houses and field systems has been reconstructed, along with a section of lake.

Part of the site also includes an exposed section of the Roman FEN CAUSEWAY, a road which linked the military sites in the Nene valley with the areas of both the fenland and the former territory of the Icenian tribe of Iron Age Norfolk.

SHANKS MILLENNIUM BRIDGE.* By *Whitby Bird & Partners*, 2001. Steel pedestrian and cycle bridge, curving over the Nene towards Whittlesey (Cambs.).

FLETTON

Fletton was a manor in the possession of Peterborough Abbey. That period is represented by little more than the medieval church and the line of the High Street; the rest is associated with the C19 industrial suburb, which came to be called New Fletton, built up S of the bridge crossing to Peterborough. The town's East Station opened here in 1845, and the sale in 1877 of over 400 acres (160 ha) of land saw the beginnings of the brick industry for which Fletton was famous. Housing grew against a background of tapering chimneys; in 1968 Pevsner

---

*Strictly speaking this in Cambridgeshire (Whittlesey).

could describe them as 'almost a palisade along the s fringe of Peterborough' but not one remains. The vacant land, stretching as far s as Farcet (q.v.), is mostly taken for distribution centres (notably the gargantuan early C21 Ikea warehouse) or a country park with the brick pits flooded for lakes.

St Margaret, Church Lane. Still in its large wooded graveyard. Extensively reconstructed *c.* 1300 with a w tower with Y-traceried bell-openings, a band of ballflower ornament and broach spire with high broaches and two tiers of lucarnes (top rebuilt 1917). The chancel was Norman, shown by the corbel table, one blocked s window and the buttressing. The present windows are Dec, with a lowside window. Inside, the N chapel arcade, chancel arch and N arcade are of *c.* 1175. The piers are sound and sturdy, with square abaci nicked at the corners and round arches with two very slight chamfers. All capitals are multi-scalloped and the chancel arch in addition has nook-shafts with waterleaf capitals; the pointed form of the arch must be later. The N arcade either originally had four bays, from which one pier was removed and then a wide arch introduced, or it was always of three bays and the third bay was widened. This might have been done *c.* 1300, the date of the tower and the s arcade. Its thin octagonal piers carry capitals with polygonal projections, like Stanground and Orton Longueville (qq.v. below). Of the same date the s aisle w and E and the N aisle w window, all with three lancet-lights under one arch. Other s aisle and clerestory windows are straight-headed and must be C17. Chancel and nave roofs and s porch of 1872 by *Alfred Sykes* of Milton. N aisle, chapel and vestry widened 1901–2 by *William Boyer* of Peterborough.

Now the reason why Fletton has not only a national but also an international claim to be visited: Anglo-Saxon sculpture. Assembled under the E window are fragments of a frieze or friezes. Until 1981 they were set into the buttresses of the E wall, where they suffered from the sulphurous smoke of the brickworks. They are small in scale – minute, one might well say – and their original position and purpose remain a mystery. They are startling in style and have no parallel in earlier or late Anglo-Saxon art, and none in contemporary Continental art. Thanks to the close link of some of them with the 'Hedda Stone' in Peterborough Cathedral (*see* p. 604) and others with Breedon-on-the-Hill (Leicestershire), their date is certain between the late C8 and early C9, i.e. the time of Charlemagne and his immediate successors. As they are discoloured pink by fire, it is quite likely that they come from Anglo-Saxon Peterborough Abbey, which had a conflagration in 1116. At the very least they must come from the Peterborough workshops. One fragment has human figures – three heads with halos under arches, just like the figures on the Hedda Stone. But here the whole fragment is a mere 18 in. (45 cm) wide. Two others have busts of angels. The others, as at Breedon, are ornamented with interlace, weird little birds and quadrupeds, and they are scooped out in a peculiar technique so that just the ridges remain. The best has a figure grasping the entwined tails of birds. The style is lively, even humorous, and not really primitive at all. They are not great sculpture, like the Ruthwell and Bewcastle Crosses well over a hundred years earlier, but they are done by someone who knew exactly what he wanted to do and found his means to achieve it. Set into the chancel s wall are two panels with saints carved in round-headed niches. The l. figure is an archangel with a halo and staff, identified as St Michael, his hand raised in blessing; the other has a scroll. They are precise in their carving, whereas the other artist modelled softly, as though in clay. Although not identically treated, they share the characteristic tip-toe contrapposto pose and folded drapery of the early c9, somewhat stiffly realized. The r. figure in particular recalls the contemporary figure at Castor (q.v.), with some classicized details, while the l. figure is in several respects a close relation of the remarkable angel discovered at Lichfield, although the figure carving is less self-assured. – FONT. Probably of c. 1661–2. Octagonal, of plain panels, four of them just vertically fluted. – STAINED GLASS. E window †1888, and s aisle E c. 1919, the British Saints. The makers are unknown.

CROSS. In front of the w tower, an Anglo-Saxon Cross. The shaft has been cut down, so that only the upper two sections are preserved, divided by a raised band. The cross-head was of the wheel type but now has a finial, from elsewhere. On the back, roundels with beasts and a quadruped, on the front also a larger animal in roundel. The sides have foliage in panels and between this a continuous band of interlace. It has been reset on a later base inscribed Radulph Filius Wilielmi, copying the inscription, now illegible, cut into the cross-shaft. Maybe the cross was appropriated to his memory. By the porch, a second cross-shaft with chamfered sides.

OLD RECTORY, NW of the church. Quite handsome Late Georgian double-pile of 1835 by *Bryan Browning*. Nothing else villagey remains. S is the HIGH STREET. It hardly needs saying that almost all the houses are brick, and very modest too. The only item for attention is the reset achievement stone at Nos. 98–100 with the arms of Whitbrooke of Water Newton. That dates it to before 1633. On FLETTON AVENUE, N of the church, the former UNITED METHODIST FREE CHURCH by *A. W. Ruddle*, 1900, with gabled front and a pediment.

OLD FLETTON PRIMARY SCHOOL, London Road/High Street. 1908–9 (extended 1912 and 1914) by *Herbert Leete*, Huntingdonshire County Surveyor. A nice job, with half-timbered gables to the front. Late C20 rear extensions with a curved drum in the middle.

FLETTON TOWER, Queens Walk. An unexpected survival of a handsome Tudor-style Victorian house in large grounds, including a walled garden. It was built, or rebuilt, by *W. J. Donthorn* (his drawings are dated to 1850 for William Lawrance, Clerk of the Peace for the Liberty of Peterborough). Symmetrical front, wide mullioned windows and a big central porch tower with battlemented top and oriel. Fine Gothic staircase and doors with linenfold panelling. Painted ceiling dated 1869 with the initials of Thomas Mills, a Bradford cabinetmaker* who retired here; see his initials on the oriel. Louis Quinze-style fireplace in the drawing room. E wing added by *Traylen, Lenton & Warwick*, 1939, for the Hartley family: L. P. Hartley wrote *The Go-Between* here; his father had interests in the Whittlesey Brick Co. Coach house (former) at the W end, and later outbuildings. A gatehouse, on Oundle Road, was recorded by the RCHM in 1969 but was demolished shortly after.

RAILWAY BUILDINGS, East Station Road. Peterborough's EAST STATION (Tudor style, 1845 by *John Livock* for the Peterborough & Northampton Railway) was demolished *c.* 1972. Close to its site is an ENGINE SHED of 1848, comprising two parallel ranges, one for the Eastern Counties Railway, the other for the Midland. The openings for the engines at the E end are now blocked. Across the W end a former carpenters' shop under a water tank. NW, the Great Eastern Railway's half of a shared GOODS SHED, the other part dem. Also stables.

HAMPTON

A vast area of former brickworks, and the first new township since the demise of the Development Corporation, first identified for development in 1984 after the plan for Castor township had been abandoned. Currently over 4,200 homes but very little character to it.

HAMPTON COLLEGE. By *Lyster, Grillet & Harding*, 2006. Animated roofline of butterfly roofs and monopitches.

LONGTHORPE

A village-cum-suburb, densely built up but still with a clear identity.

ST BOTOLPH. A chapel of ease to Peterborough until 1850. Permission for rebuilding the chapel on a site closer to the village was given by the Abbot of Peterborough to Sir William de Thorpe in 1263–4. Nave and aisles and originally a W bellcote; the bell-openings now incorporated within the gable. The present bellcote is of 1892, contemporary with the handsome roof, by *Alfred Sykes* of Milton. No structural division between nave and chancel. The windows have pointed-trefoiled lights; the W window has a quatrefoiled circle over its two lights. Two lowside lancets to the chancel, piscina in the S aisle. Wide nave of three bays. Slender circular piers with circular capitals and abaci. Single-chamfered arches with hoodmoulds. SE vestry of 1927, extended 1981. Enclosed cloister along the S front and

---

*Mills supplied the furniture for the board room of Titus Salt's mill at Saltaire (Yorks. West Riding).

neat infill between vestry and chancel, of 1999 and 2005 by
A. J. Robertson of *Caress Robertson*. – FURNISHINGS mostly of
1869 by *Sykes*. – ROOD SCREEN, REREDOS and PANELLING.
1914–19. – STAINED GLASS. Five windows by *A. L. Moore*,
1899–1907. – MONUMENTS. Frances St John †1794. Finely cut
with an urn against an obelisk.

TOWER HOUSE, 100 yds W of the church. The late C13 manor
house, begun by Sir William de Thorpe, probably contemporary with the church. N window, lighting the chamber end, of
two lights divided by a shaft and a quatrefoil in plate tracery
(traces of contemporary wall painting inside). The hall was
floored in the C17; of the same date the W wing. The house was
given a fortified appearance in the early C14 by the addition at
its NE corner of a solar tower (now LONGTHORPE TOWER),
probably built for Robert Thorpe; he was Steward of Peterborough Abbey 1310–29. The tower had access to the ground floor
as well as the upper floor only from the house, not from the
outside. The tower is square, and has walls 6–7 ft (1.8–2.1
metres) thick and square turrets on the corners. The windows
are small, of single lights, with trefoiled heads or shouldered
lintels. Some early C17 alterations. The ground-floor room, a
store, has a quadripartite rib-vault. So has the room on the
principal floor, which would have served as the withdrawing
chamber. It has an aumbry, a fireplace, one unaltered single-
light W window (the corresponding window removed in the
C17 when a door was inserted) and a large N recess. The ribs
are single-chamfered and stand on corbels. The second-floor
room has no vault. It is reached by a straight staircase in the
thickness of the S wall and at this level the window-recesses
are retained intact with their benches. Both of the upper rooms
also have garderobes. The roof has a parapet walk.

85   The outstanding interest of Longthorpe Tower is the WALL
PAINTINGS in the principal room, which were discovered only
after the Second World War. They date from *c.* 1330 and are
more extensive than any of so early a date in any house in
England. Covering every surface are subjects taken from the
Bible, including the Nativity and a complete group of the
Apostles, as well as moralities such as the Three Quick and
the Three Dead (E wall recess) and didactic and secular subjects: on the W wall, a philosopher teaching a boy (the inscription here is in French); a praying figure (interpreted as St
Anthony) facing a youth making baskets and another figure
behind, both believed to be angels in secular dress; the Labours
of the Months, including the slaughter of a hog for December;
Wheel of the Seven Ages of Man (N wall), and at the margins
plenty of birds and flowers, including curlew and bittern, taken
from the locality and many others copied from bestiaries. In
the vault, figures of musicians (notably King David playing the
harp) and the Signs of the four Evangelists,* and on the S wall

*A detailed description by E. Clive Rouse is given in the booklet published by
English Heritage and in *Archaeologia* XCVI, 1955, 1–57.

geometric patterns imitating wall hangings with heraldry, incorporating the Thorpe arms, and two seated figures with shields, thought to be Edward II and Prince Edmund of Woodstock (the composition closely related to a manuscript at Christ Church, Oxford, dated to *c.* 1326). Over the entrance from the hall defecates the mythical Bonnacon. The picture of greatest significance, and unique in England, is the Wheel of the Five Senses (E wall), figured as animals – Boar (Hearing or Smell), Cock (Sight or Hearing), Monkey (Taste), Vulture or Eagle (Smell or Sight), Spider's Web (Touch). Behind the wheel, steadying it, stands a king, depicting Reason, pointing to an inscription now lost. His position closest to the sense of touch has been interpreted as a reminder that it was this sense which was believed to place Man higher than the beasts. As for the style, it has been compared with such somewhat earlier C14 illuminated manuscripts as Queen Mary's Psalter, Chronicles and Bestiary but also several manuscripts associated with Peterborough such as the Peterborough Bestiary.

CROSS-SHAFT. 7 ft (2.1 metres) tall. At the E end of the village street by the green. Pre-Conquest. Latticework on the sides.

THORPE MEADOWS (Nene Park), SE of the village by the Nene. The centrepiece is a broad rectangular ROWING LAKE. Also over a dozen SCULPTURES, commissioned 1984–8. They are mostly between the lake and river, notably works by *Sokari Douglas Camp* (Festival Boat) and *Miles Davies* (Untitled).* N, on the higher ground by the road, two pieces designed to be seen in longer views: *Miles Davies* (also Untitled) and *Lee Grandjean* (Peterborough Gate). Crossing the Nene and the railway to the W, NENE PARKWAY BRIDGE (chief engineer, *Ken Hutton*), 1974.

THORPE HALL. By *Peter Mills* for Oliver St John, Lord Chief Justice of the Common Pleas during the Commonwealth, who purchased the manor in 1653 from the sale of sequestered lands of the Dean and Chapter. His family came from Bletsoe in Bedfordshire and already owned lands in Longthorpe. In 1638 he had married Elizabeth Cromwell, cousin of the Lord Protector. The contract with the stonemasons, *John Ashley* and *Sampson Frisbey* of Ketton, is dated 1654; a rainwater head has the date 1656 but work no doubt continued into the 1660s. Mills had leased land from St John to build in Holborn in 1642, was Bricklayer to the City of London from 1643, Master of the Tyler's and Bricklayers' Company, and a man of considerable competence and reputation. His connections with the Parliamentary cause were no impediment and after the Fire of London he was appointed with May, Pratt and Wren, all three younger men, to supervise the rebuilding. He also designed the Selden end of the Bodleian Library at Oxford, Hitcham's Building at Pembroke College, Cambridge, and Wisbech

109,
p. 642

*The most important sculpture in the park was Lagoon by *Anthony Caro*, 1976–7, which was acquired in 1984 but augmented for its new setting. It was disowned by the sculptor when it was put on sale by the Peterborough Sculpture Trust in 2011.

Castle (after 1654, dem.), one of a group of houses, including Thorney Abbey (q.v.), in the area between Peterborough and Cambridge which have the same characteristics as Thorpe Hall. In their employment of a lively, mannered, somewhat fantastical style, they place Mills in the tradition of the London artisans, which Sir John Summerson christened Artisan Mannerism. But this does not mean that Mills did not possess a close understanding of the architecture of Inigo Jones and John Webb, and both the energetic and scholarly aspects of his manner are evident at Thorpe in the apparent discrepancy between unorthodox, decorative motifs and the controlled and sophisticated handling of the astylar principal elevations (unique among Mills's works) and the plan, both of which show a debt to, and advance beyond, progressive country house designs of the Jonesian circle (e.g. Chevening, Kent, begun before 1630, and Forty Hall, Enfield, 1639–42).

Oliver St John left England in 1662 and died abroad in 1673. His son Francis inherited and it is very possible that the interior was completed by him. Some improvements certainly appear to have been made *c.* 1769 for Sir Robert Bernard, who married Francis's daughter Mary, but Thorpe then passed out of the family's possession and from 1791 it was in the hands of the Fitzwilliams. By 1850 it was in a perilous state, from which it was rescued by the Rev. William Strong, who moved from Stanground Manor (q.v. below). He employed the Peterborough surveyor *Francis Ruddle* (the contractor was *John Thompson*) to make many alterations, detailed in a journal of work done in 1850–5, and undertook works in the gardens. The house has been in institutional use since the Second World War but has been well restored since 1986 by the Sue Ryder Foundation.

Thorpe Hall stands foursquare and solid, with walled entrance court and gardens to the N, S and E and kitchens and offices to the W. The walled court and gardens have GATES with Man-

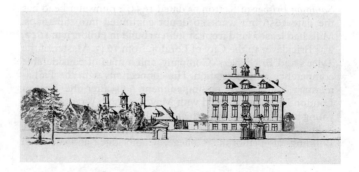

Peterborough, Longthorpe, Thorpe Hall.
Drawing by P. Tillemans, 1721

nerist details, especially those to the N and S, which provided carriage entrances, where tall slender niches have seats in the outer faces and on the inner face are partly filled by pedestals in relief carrying vases in relief which end in Ionic capitals. The E gate, to give another example, has a pilaster against the rusticated pier which stands on a volute. All have lovely lions' heads and three have lead falcons. Avenues were originally planted in line with them. Secondary gateways with rusticated surrounds and pediments lead into each of the separate walled gardens. The gate from the service court to the garden introduce one of Mills's favourite motifs, which occurs inside on several occasions, a pilaster halved vertically and placed l. and r. of the big, heavy, eared door frame. In this particular case the pilasters again start out of volutes, but here volutes in profile. The top has a pediment. The KITCHENS and OFFICES, an L-plan range, also have similar motifs, the centre of the S front, e.g., a big pedimented dormer with volutes l. and r., and the small window below it small volutes and ears.

Now for the HOUSE itself. Its N and S fronts are identical. Seven bays, two and a half storeys, quoins and a hipped roof. In the roof dormers with alternatingly triangular and segmental pediments. The house is slightly elevated on a half basement, although only on the N side does this contain cellars (with vaults on square piers) and on the E side it is concealed by a balustraded terrace. On the roof originally a balustrade and lantern or belvedere (see the staircase inside), just as at Coleshill (Berks.) by Pratt, and at Wisbech, Tyttenhanger, and many other houses of the second third of the C17. Also on the roof square groups of rusticated chimneyshafts. Porch on Doric columns and with an iron balcony of flat scrolly patterns and turned columns at the corners, a rare survival of 1650s ironwork. The window above the porch on both fronts has a segmental pediment and a broad eared frame, again with halved pilasters on volutes in profile. To the l. and r. of this central window the other central windows, i.e. those of bays two and six, are stressed by triangular pediments. The windows probably had mullion and transom crosses and in the half-storey mullions only. This can be guessed from the state of the W side, for the glazing elsewhere was replaced in the mid C19. The E side is the most remarkable side of the house and, in its departure from the conventions of classicism of the other fronts, the one to which the term Mannerist might be applied. There is a terrace here with a balustrade of dumb-bell balusters, and the wall has three instead of the expected five bays. These three bays are treated on both main floors in a tripartite rhythm, bays one and three as bay windows, the middle bay flat but wider than the others, as was the case at Forty Hall and, as recent research has shown, also at Bertie House, Kent, a house of the 1650s now demolished. The centre has a segmental pediment, the centres of the bay windows triangular pediments. The Venetian (or Serlian) motif is of the normal kind (first introduced into England by Inigo Jones) in the middle bay, but in the bay windows there is a variation which was to become specially popular in the 1660s and 1670s and of which a version appears in Hitcham's Building at Pembroke College, Cambridge, in 1659. The spaces above the lower side lights are opened, so that the side lights can be called transomed, the transom being discontinued under the middle light because of the higher arched opening. All pilasters of these tripartite openings have sunk panels. The windows were lengthened behind their open guilloche bands in 1851.

The PLAN of Thorpe Hall is very clear and simple. Like other advanced designs of the earlier C17, such as Forty Hall, the house is a 'triple pile', i.e. has rooms in three rows, one facing N, the other S and another in between, expressed externally by the placing of the two groups of chimneystacks. A passage runs through between them from front (N) to back (S) at ground floor, dividing it into superior rooms for entertaining (E) and private and service rooms (W). In the upper floors the axis is reversed and the passages run E–W. So in the E half is a large room behind each of the bay windows (Hall, NE, and Great Parlour, SE) and the principal staircase between them behind the broader centre bay. The W half is similarly divided with smaller rooms and a broad central passage for a secondary staircase. Of the medieval and Elizabethan principles there remains the arrangement of the hall, placed to one side of the cross-passage and originally entered through a screen of Composite columns (as A. W. Hakewill's 'General Plan . . .' of 1852 appears to show, representing 'Thorpe Hall as the structure of the 17th century'). The columns were moved in the 1850s to mark the crossing of the N–S and the E–W axes, where also small lobbies between the main passage and staircases are. The principal staircase, an open well newel, originally served (as at Forty Hall, Tyttenhanger etc.) only the two large rooms at the SE and NE corners, both of which begin a suite of chambers along the N and S fronts. The grandest rooms are those of the 'state apartment' on the N front – great chamber, withdrawing room, bedchamber – on the S side was a corresponding set of five rooms for Sir Oliver and Lady St John (bedchamber, closet, withdrawing room, closet, bedchamber). In the centre of the first floor is a landing and from here rises the fine subsidiary staircase to the second and attic floors, which have transverse passages running E–W. At attic level the passage is vaulted and it surely must have functioned as a long gallery with, right in the middle, the spiral staircase going up to the former belvedere. As one ascends the house a view of the W front of the Cathedral is gradually revealed through the E windows, and this must have been intended as the visual coup in the landscape when seen from the belvedere. There is in addition a service stair rising from the ground floor W passage to the second floor. Hakewill shows this in a different position and it may be that Strong relocated it so that servants could reach the attic bedrooms without using either of the main stairs (the top flights have now been removed).

As to DECORATION, many of the motifs in the house are those typical of Peter Mills and find their source in C16 and early C17 prints (e.g. Dietterlin and others): swags on panelling, frames on volutes in profile turned inward as well as outward, pilasters and consoles with garlands hanging down them, pilasters with a volute or small scroll replacing the base, and especially the half-pilasters noted outside. The style was best represented by the GREAT PARLOUR (SE), with its curiously carved panels, stuck one into another, which also had a fine chimneypiece attributed to *Edward Marshall* (GF),* but alas all of this was sold to Leeds Castle in 1926 (the ceiling, however, was lost before the mid C19). A hint of its character, though more restrained, is the LITTLE PARLOUR (SW), which not only retains its panelling (originally painted) but also its plaster ceiling with fat wreath framed by guilloche and in the outer sides festoons linked by classical masks emerging from scrolls. All this has a strongly Jonesian character and is directly modelled on a design for the Countess of Caernarvon's bedroom at Wilton (1649).† The adjoining ANTE-ROOM also shares this Courtly style, with a coved cornice with shells, swags, grotesques and cartouches at the corners. Its bolection-moulded panelling, however, looks *c.* 1700. All the principal rooms have heavily and richly decorated fireplaces, typically combinations of stone, marble and alabaster in black, white, grey and green. The largest, though not the most elaborate, is in the HALL, with sumptuous plaster overmantel with a torus-moulded frame and big cherubs holding a cartouche with St John's arms.

The principal STAIRCASE has a broad balustrade with heavily and richly carved openwork panels of acanthus leaves, a little more advanced in style than those of Lamport Hall (Northants) and an early example of the type, but with fruiting baskets on the newels like those at Ham House (1637–9). It has been attributed to *Edward Pearce*‡ but if this is correct it is either among his earliest works or the interior was completed in the 1670s or 1680s after Oliver St John's death. The stair rises on its inner side against a stone screen, with openings at half-landing to the ground-floor passage and taller arches above, emulating the style of the bays of the E front but with the narrow opening in the centre, which reveal the landing at the centre of the house. The lower openings had circular and oval frames inserted above the stair panels, again echoing the circular opening on the E front. Through the arch on the r. a short flight connects the main stair with the principal landing, but this arrangement dates only from the 1850s (when Strong also seems to have had panels of carved elm inserted into the

110

---

* In its place, an extraordinary and inappropriate medieval fireplace, with vast hood, moulded frieze and twisted jambs. It is thought to be Belgian or German.
† It is not certain that the design for Wilton was ever used, so it is possible that the plasterer at Thorpe Hall was using the drawing for the first time (Dr Claire Gapper).
‡ A. V. Grimstone, *Building Pembroke Chapel: Wren, Pearce and Scott* (2009).

screen at this level, imitating the C17 work). The secondary stair, behind a timber screen with two arched openings, is an open well with Vitruvian scroll to the closed strings. The turned balusters make use of the motif of leaves growing up the bulbous bottom part of the baluster. The service stair has an even further simplification of this motif, and the spiral stair to the roof repeats the Vitruvian scroll.

The extravagance of the main stair is continued in the design of the doorcases of the STAIR HALL to the rooms N and S – broken pediments at ground floor with brackets for busts (as Stukeley noted in 1724); flat consoled cornices at first – and in the larger Ionic doorcases from the central landing to the rooms N and S. Both these rooms, i.e. in the centre of each suite, have plaster ceilings with geometric patterns, guilloche borders, wreaths and garlands. In their cluttered and unsophisticated design they are poor relations of those on the ground floor and might well have been the work of another group of craftsmen at a slightly later date. The GREAT CHAMBER, the principal room at the NE corner, is the most richly treated and for its date (if it is contemporary with the rest) precocious. Panelling to dado only, a cornice of acanthus modillions, doorcases and window frames with enriched surrounds and consoles with lions crawling over them, round niches over doors for busts etc. It is true that the lion consoles are close relations of the lions carved on the gatepiers but much of the detail is very credible for 1769, when it is known that alterations were made for Sir Robert Bernard. The chimneypiece is the best in the house and is attributed to *Edward Marshall* (GF). It has not only the motif of a festoon dropping from a scroll but again a half-pilaster turned sideways. The geometric ceiling is mid C19.

In the NW former BEDCHAMBER, the overmantel of the fireplace has pilasters with baskets of acanthus integral with a frieze of original painted decoration, with scrolls, lions' heads and squirrels, which may derive from prints published *c.* 1640 by *Edward Pierce Sen.* In the entrance passage two stone tables on piers with consoles at the sides. One puzzle is the doors to the rooms off the central passage, which have identical surrounds of an interwoven pattern continued up as frames for overdoors. It has been suggested that these originated in the central rooms of the first floor. Their advanced character would certainly go with the work in the Great Chamber but not with the plasterwork of those rooms. Might they instead belong to improvements made *c.* 1769? The staircase halls to E and W have black-and-white paving, originally in the Hall.

GARDENS. The layout is still largely as it would have been in the 1650s, a series of compartments around the house. Formal garden on the E front, originally quartered into platts with statuary in typical mid-C17 fashion but now with mid-C19 raised beds, the urns probably of the same date. Along the S side a formal terraced walk and on the N side a raised shrubbery.

Set into the wall at the NE corner some medieval ARCHI-
TECTURAL FRAGMENTS, including tracery. They were revealed
during rebuilding of the wall in the C19 and must derive from
the cathedral cloisters, stone from which was brought to
Thorpe in 1651–2. Much more must still be concealed.

At the garden's SE corner a small mid- to late C18 GARDEN
HOUSE, with a pediment, half-columns, and walls of channelled rustication. It terminates the end of a long E–W axis
running across the S garden and through a free-standing tripartite ARCHWAY. The arch is based in its design on the motif
of the Venetian window. The side parts and the big voluted and
pedimented attic have oval openings. It belonged to a demolished W range, probably stables, illustrated by Hakewill. Nearby
an octagonal SUMMERHOUSE, brought from Stanground
Manor (q.v. below) by Strong. In the outer walls of the gardens
are pairs of niches with seats, further evidence of the C17
fashion for surveying the wider landscape.

HALLWELL PONDS, ¾ m. S of the house. These are the
remains of C18 landscaping, with GROTTO, probably built by
Francis St John, who inherited in 1673.

ORTON

The second of the townships created after 1970 and encapsulat-
ing *Hancock Hawkes'* planning concept of a township with
several neighbourhoods, each with its own primary school and
neighbourhood centre. Two existing villages, Orton Waterville
and Orton Longueville, are built around rather than incorporated. Unlike the linear arrangement at Bretton, the road runs
around the perimeter of the entire township but the clustering
of housing within culs-de-sac is otherwise the same. Between
1976 and the late 1980s, more than 23,000 flats and houses
had been built, over half for the private sector and for sale, at
Orton Brimbles, Orton Goldhay, Orton Malborne and Orton
Wistow. The township is served by the large ORTON CENTRE,
off Orton Parkway, of 1979–80 by the *Development Corporation
Architects*. This has supermarket, flats, a public square, library,
health centre, community college etc. in the era's familiar, and
unattractive, brown brick and tile, hardly improved by additions in white blockwork of 2008–9 by *Haskoll*.

Little can be picked out for individual attention among the
HOUSING but the following are significant deviations from the
norm: COLLINGHAM and BECKINGHAM at Orton Goldhay.
Long terraces of bungalows with vertical accents in the form
of three-storey houses with monopitch roofs. Nearby, S of the
Orton Centre, HINCHCLIFFE, a sheltered housing scheme of
1987 with a U-shaped plan of dwellings around a central
garden (each with its own private garden within this communal
space). The buildings have gables split by a glazed rooflight
over an internal street, are timber-clad and painted blue.
There are two later developments aimed at higher earners:

SVENSKABY, Orton Wistow, is a curious 'village' of Swedish timber houses, chalets and bungalows. Some have double mansards, others steeply pitched roofs incorporating balconies. Some of the houses even had saunas. The plantings are pines, silver birches etc. Also SUNNINGDALE, Orton Brimbles, on rising ground S of Oundle Road, a dense private development of quite large houses in a Postmodern Surrey vernacular, some with little towers rising from the angles. 1987 by *Trevor Denton Wayland Tunley*.

The township's industrial estate is to the W at ORTON SOUTH-GATE, placed here by the Development Corporation for proximity to the A1. Some factory units were built in advance of demand, e.g. in MANASTY ROAD and MILNYARD SQUARE, the latter with cheery pyramidal roofs. Later, office uses were permitted, and typical of that period is PEGASUS HOUSE, by *Aukett*, 1980s, for flexible office space. Heavy striped brick walls framing glazed atria under pitch roofs. N of this, the EAST OF ENGLAND SHOWGROUND, where the PETERBOROUGH ARENA by *BRP Architects*, 2008, has a floor area of 6,000 square metres and a roof structure hung from masts to permit an unimpeded space within.

At LYNCH WOOD BUSINESS PARK, N of Oundle Road, the following office buildings are of interest – LYNCH WOOD PARK. 1990–2 by *Chapman Taylor Partners*, originally for Pearl Assurance. A quasi-Roman-style group under low-pitched, red pantile roofs, with pale brick walls and stone dressings and a series of square service towers with pitched roofs. To the front the offices are placed around a square and elevated above a basement car park. In the centre of the square a star-shaped FOUNTAIN with a sculpture. The main entrance is a big round arch with gross roll-moulded orders; inside is an arcade and vaulted passage across a bridge to the rear offices: three square pavilions linked at the angles and with atria in the centre of each. They have rather attractive jettied upper storeys behind a Japanese-style timber grid inset with primary-coloured glass. Formal gardens on the NE side. – Outside, the WAR MEMORIAL, from the Pearl Assurance offices in High Holborn, London. By *George Frampton*, 1919, a victorious St George.

126   W of this LYNCHWOOD HOUSE, a similarly impressive job by *Arup Associates*, 1989–91, originally as headquarters for Royal Insurance. Gently curving brick block to the fore and offices to the rear, facing a wooded landscape, enclosed by an undulating glass screen wall behind a tightly gridded steel frame. Linking the two, a full-height open street under a mono-pitch roof. At the W end, a lake and waterfall; excellent land-scaping by *Derek Lovejoy Associates*.

N of the township is FERRY MEADOWS COUNTRY PARK (NENE PARK). 500 acres (220 ha) with lakes created S of a bend in the Nene. – In the park some exposed ROMAN REMAINS of a farmstead and barn, one of a large number of villa sites etc. found here.

Orton Longueville

HOLY TRINITY. There was a church here by 1247, but of this
date there are only the bases, with spurs, of the nave arcades.
The rest was rebuilt after *c.* 1275, beginning with the N chapel
(enlarged 1861) and chancel, see the chancel N window, which
has bar tracery with a quatrefoil, and inside the arch with two
hollow chamfers, also the niches l. and r. of the chapel E
window and a piscina. The W tower is only a little later. It has
an arch to the nave of one chamfer and two continuous chamfers, in its mid-stage walls quatrefoil windows. Upper parts
apparently rebuilt C15 (one BELL has the stamps of *John Wal-
grave*, i.e. *c.* 1420–40) but no spire. But most of the church is
Dec, i.e. the fenestration with a large E window with elongated
reticulated tracery, an ogee-headed chancel S doorway with
good original iron scrollwork to the door, dated *c.* 1330–50,
and two big odd niches in the S wall. The SW window also
incorporates a lowside window. The N aisle windows have
cusped Y-tracery. The S aisle was widened in 1675 (date on the
S porch) after the parish church nearby at Botolphbridge was
demolished, but it has two early C14 E windows, both with
three lights under one arch, with the middle one slightly ogee-
headed. The reconstructed S windows have basket arches,
almost semicircular. The three-bay arcades are Dec too. Octagonal piers with capitals with polygonal projections or brackets,
the brackets displaying some ballflower and carrying the outer
of the two chamfered orders of the arch (cf. Fletton and Stanground). A length of ballflower in the chancel S wall also, and
in the W wall, l. and r. of the arch, also two flat niches. They
contain seats. ROOFS all renewed, the N aisle and N chapel in
1889–90 by *J. C. Traylen* of Stamford, the nave and S aisle in
1908–9 by *Townsend & Fordham.*

   WALL PAINTING. St Christopher, mid-C15? Only the upper
part is preserved. Uncovered in 1848. – STAINED GLASS. Fragments in the N aisle W and N and the tower W window. In the
N aisle W window some C13 foliage scrolls. N chapel E window
to 10th Marquis of Huntly †1863 by *F. Smith* of London, 1866;
in the chancel S wall, the Ascension, 1907 by *Morris & Co.* of
Westminster. – Many HATCHMENTS and early C17 FUNERAL
HELM in the N chapel, grouped with the principal MONU-
MENTS. – Effigy of a cross-legged knight, possibly John de
Longueville. Late C13; damaged. – Elizabeth Talbot, daughter
of Sir William Rayner, †1629. Attributed to *William Wright*
(GF). Purbeck marble table-top on five alabaster legs with
columns, the back panel with arched head and inscription. No
figures, but many armorial shields linked by dainty little hands.
– Lady Mary Seymour, wife of the 9th Marquis of Huntly.
Signed by *Chantrey*, 1827. Rather cold compared with other
monuments of his. Seated young woman against Grecian background. All white marble. – Elizabeth, Countess of Aboyne
†1839. Large standing Gothic monument, an extremely rich
Dec tomb-chest with canopy. The inscription will be read with

profit. The design is by *George H. Smith*, 1841, and for its date surprisingly accurate in its use of the Dec style. Facing this, under the E window, the 10th Marquis of Huntly †1863. Massive granite tomb-chest with Gothic inscription and memorial shields around the sides for his sons Lords Randolph, Bertrand and Lewis Gordon †1859, 1869 and 1870. – Monuments not in the N chapel: Sir Charles Cope †1781 (S aisle). A charming large standing monument of coloured marbles, with flaming urns. Formerly at the E end of the N aisle (his grave slab is in the chapel). – Lord Douglas William Cope Gordon †1888 (N aisle). By *H. H. Armstead*. Portrait in a roundel set in a Quattrocento surround. – Marie Antoinette, Marchioness of Huntly, †1893. Alabaster, in an interesting Neo-1630. With two angels flanking the inscription. – WAR MEMORIAL. Wheel-head cross with a sword on the shaft, 1920, in grey Rubislaw granite, presumably sent from the Huntlys' Aberdeenshire estates.

ORTON HALL (Hotel), NW of the church. Owned in the C18 by the Cope family. Catherine Cope married George Gordon, later 5th Earl of Aboyne, in 1791, and the house was extensively remodelled in 1831–6 for their son, Lord Strathavon, initially by *T. F. Hunt* but completed after his death by his pupil, *George H. Smith* of London.* Picturesque Tudor Gothic with mullioned and transomed windows, two-storey square bays on the S front and ornate parapet details. Conservatory with an iron hammerbeam roof, heraldic frieze and coloured glass in lattice patterns. Lord Strathavon became the 6th Earl in 1836 and 10th Marquis of Huntly in 1853. W wing of 1861, brick Jacobethan with stone turret on the (N) entrance front and strapwork cresting on the S bay (initials of the Marquis and his wife). In the dining room much reset woodwork, C16–C17 and English as well as foreign, and stained glass of similar date (other panels are reset in windows of the E front); *Willement* records that he did the heraldic glass on the staircase in 1831. Great Hall in the 1861 wing, rather grim with a stone fireplace.

A reset DOORWAY between the house and an outbuilding (dated 1654) has the Talbot and Rayner coat of arms in a florid strapwork setting; this dates it to the later C16. It was brought from Fotheringhay Castle (Northants), probably by Elizabeth Talbot (née Rayner), who inherited the estate at Orton in 1606. Early C18 STABLES with cupola, now converted and unfortunately overlaid by additions for the hotel. N of the house, remains of the C18 WALLED GARDEN. Brick with two doorways with ashlar Gibbsian surrounds.

THE OLD SCHOOL, S of the church. Delightful domestic Gothic with mullion windows and gable, the schoolroom to the rear with its own porch and bellcote (dated 1853) over a rose window. By *Denton & Drake* of London.

---

* Smith also inherited from Hunt the design for Bifrons, Patrixbourne (Kent; dem.), for Lord Strathavon's father-in-law, the 1st Marquess of Conyngham.

Orton Waterville

ST MARY. Unbuttressed, i.e. early, W tower with a battered middle stage and a small arch to the nave. The Perp top with quatrefoil frieze and blank cusped arches in the battlements, formerly with pinnacles, is contemporary with the clerestory. E.E. S porch with fillets on the principal respond shafts and two hollow chamfers in the arch and stiff-leaf capitals. This belongs with the four-bay S arcade, which has standard elements except for one capital with good stiff-leaf and headstops. The N arcade is Perp and poorer. Dec N and S aisle walls with flowing tracery in the windows. Chancel rebuilt in the C17; its roof cuts across the chancel arch. The nave roof was rebuilt in 1752, again at a lower pitch. Plain medieval FONT with short hexagonal columns. – PULPIT. An exceptionally sumptuous Jacobean piece with dogtooth (an interesting touch) in the usual blank arches, full-bosomed caryatids, and arabesque decoration of pilasters and panels. It came from Great St Mary at Cambridge in 1736, Pembroke College being the patrons. The sounding-board has been removed and the other such panels reused in the N aisle reredos, noted by Pevsner, are gone. – ROYAL ARMS. Over the N door. Stuart; of wood, small and exceptionally fine.

The village street is lined with small cottages, several of them thatched and many with dates. MANOR FARM, W of the church, is an H-plan hall house, built of stone with three-light mullions. Dated 1571 on the S front, with the initials RM (probably Robert Milsent). Perched on the N gable a crouching lion. Inside, in the former hall, is a remarkable reused stone doorway. Also dated 1571, and with the same initials, it has two steep pediments above the inscription and, l. and r., two shapes like goblets with domed lids. A somewhat barbaric but not unimpressive design.

PASTON AND WALTON

Paston village was engulfed by interwar suburban housing and then by the Paston Ridings council estate built *c.* 1959–60. It was to have lent its name to the northern township of the New Town, but Werrington was chosen instead and Paston was expanded as one of its neighbourhoods. For Walton, *see* below.

ALL SAINTS, Fulbridge Road. W tower of *c.* 1260 with lancets, a big quatrefoil window, bell-openings of two lights with encircled motifs in bar tracery. Angle buttresses rise higher than the later top stage with its broach spire with two tiers of lucarnes above a string course of ballflower. The finest piece in the church is the triple-chamfered tower arch towards the nave. It rests on two splendid horizontal figures. But the earliest part of the church is the N chancel chapel. Two bays, semicircular responds, octagonal pier, single-chamfered arches. One stiff-leaf label stop. The date may be *c.* 1225. Of the late C13 the

SEDILIA in the chancel, the PISCINA slightly later. Sweeting described the E window as 'a wreck', of *c.* 1320. The straight-headed chancel S windows look as if they were Perp, but in spite of the Perp principle of panel tracery the details are mid-C14 – and extremely pretty at that. Perp arcades of four bays with octagonal piers and double-chamfered arches. Perp chancel arch, aisle windows, clerestory and tall SCREEN with one-light divisions (upper parts restored 1896). – ROOFS. Probably of the restoration, 1880–1 by *H. M. Townsend.* – SCULPTURE. Inside the E bay of the S aisle, fragments of very small blank arcading. – STAINED GLASS. E (1889) and W (1888) windows by *Heaton, Butler & Bayne.* – MONUMENTS. C15 CROSS SLAB for Roger Hawville, rector. – Edmund Mount-steven †1635. Aedicule tablet with kneeling figure between black columns, attributed to *William Wright.* – PORCH GATES of 1973 by *Peter Brotherhood Ltd.* – Nice SUNDIAL on the porch gable, dated 1756.

ST OSWALD KING & MARTYR (R.C.), Lincoln Road/Paston Lane. 1959 by *Portess & Richardson.* Later porch by *Marshall Sisson.* Very modest.

VOYAGER SCHOOL, Mountsteven Avenue. 2006–7 by *Aedeas.* Like Thomas Deacon Academy in the city centre (*see* p. 625), an ambitiously large secondary school (for 1,175 pupils) with a distinctive architectural identity, here created by abstract sea-blue tiling in patterns on the main elevation. Radial plan form with two large blocks to the fore flanking the entrance (assembly hall, library etc. to the l., sports facilities r.) and covered street running E–W across the school with gallery along the N side. This serves the teaching areas, contained in finger blocks with courtyards between. The finishes are economical but bright, e.g. the roof of corrugated steel with triangular rooflights.

S of the church, within a housing development of *c.* 2000, the OLD RECTORY. Of two storeys with cross-wings, gables with finials and mullioned windows to front and back. A row of four decorated brick chimneys above the S wing proves that the house dates from the time of Henry VIII and was progressively developed, by *c.* 1600, into an H-plan with a hall in the centre range. In the face of the N wing a doorway (blocked) with moulded arch, reset from the porch, which was destroyed when the space between the wings was infilled by a mid-C19 addition with crenellated top. On the rear of the S wing, a bay window of 1697. The N range was extensively rebuilt on the garden side in the late C19, Arts and Crafts style. In the front ground-floor room of the S wing, a chimneypiece with panelled overmantel in a classical style. A fire in 1996 destroyed the roof and with it the evidence (recorded by the RCHM in 1968) that it concealed an 'earlier roof of narrow span and steeper pitch' rising from plates inside the E and W walls.*

---

*The phasing of the house was analysed by Donald Mackreth in an unpublished report in Peterborough Local Studies Library.

SE of the vicarage, off PASTON RIDINGS, is the first phase of Development Corporation housing (*K. Maplestone*, Chief Architect). More interesting architecturally is the terrace of housing in STOWEHILL ROAD of 1985 by *Mathew Robotham Associates* for Nene Housing Society. Designed for single people, with communal living rooms etc. Deep tile roofs sweep low to the front punctuated by dormers, containing bathrooms, with pitched roofs and porthole windows. Colourful doors. As part of the same scheme, a community hall with triangular gable inset with a big square window, vertically set. The hamlet of WALTON has vanished: WALTON HOUSE, No. 1103 Lincoln Road, on the corner with Kelso Court, is dated 1668 but much altered and no longer has all the traditional Jacobean features noted by Pevsner.* w of Lincoln Road, by the railway, is a handsome brick WATER TOWER, with pyramid roof, built to serve a factory begun in 1911 for Frederick Sage & Co., shopfitters, but expanded during the First World War for the manufacture of aircraft, notably seaplanes. Some of the workshops demolished in 2010 had lightweight Belfast trusses (30-ft (9-metre) span). On their site is now housing.

STANGROUND

On the edge of the fenland s of the Nene. The medieval manor and the advowson were in the possession of Thorney Abbey. Heavily expanded after 1945 for council estates and finally absorbed into suburban Peterborough in the later C20. The setting of the church has been utterly spoiled by the elevated Frank Perkins Parkway of the 1970s.

St JOHN THE BAPTIST. Almost entirely of the early C14. The w tower starts with such a motif as circular trefoiled windows and ends with a ballflower frieze. Diagonal buttresses with gables. Octagonal broach spire with high broaches and two tiers of lucarnes, grander than that of nearby Fletton (*see* above); top rebuilt 1895. The chancel has high windows with Y-tracery. The five-light E window with intersecting tracery is over-restored (1948). Below the sw window is a lowside window of three uncusped lights, rebated for a shutter. Very pretty DOUBLE PISCINA, identical in design to those in the Cathedral presbytery aisles, with Y-tracery and pierced trilobes. SEDILIA under one long segmental arch. The arch is hollow-chamfered and has a moulding with headstops. The chancel arch has two hollow chamfers, the tower arch even three. The aisle windows are characteristic too, i.e. they have intersecting tracery and three lancet lights under one arch. In the N vestry is even a slightly earlier-looking window, bar tracery with a foiled circle. The thin octagonal piers of the

---

*Also, demolished since the first edition of this guide, No. 1066 Lincoln Road. It had a big straight hood on excessively voluted brackets apparently of the time and style of Thorpe Hall and the date 1600 on a beam inside.

arcades have the curious capitals with polygonal projections carrying the outer chamfer (seen also at Fletton and Orton Longueville, qq.v. above), and some characterful headstops. The three leaf capitals on the N side with their nobbly leaves, the E respond with a Green Man, are typical too of the date. But there is evidence of some reused material; the base of the NW respond is an inverted Norman capital (is it from Fletton, which appears to have lost one of its Norman piers at this time?) and the E bays of the taller S arcade appear to have reused C13 bases, cut from a different stone. C15 staircase within the N pier of the chancel arch, apparently serving the pulpit via a door (now blocked) and the lost rood; a turret projects into the chancel and is lit by a cross-slit (the same motif also seen between the chancel N aisle and vestry at Fletton). – FONT. Early C14, octagonal on shafts, with some intersecting arcading. SEAT. In the chancel on the N side a stone seat with low arms (cf. Houghton). – BENCHES. The ends with poppyheads, including human heads, remade in 1886. – ROOFS. Of the 1872 restoration by *Edward Browning* of Stamford. – ALTAR (war memorial). Clipsham stone. By *Sir Charles Nicholson*, 1918; he seems to have intended a wider restoration (see his watercolour in the N aisle dated 1916). – STAINED GLASS. E window by *A. Gibbs*, 1863. – N aisle by *Wailes*, 1857. – S aisle E, 1920 by *A. K. Nicholson* with reset early C14 glass – shield of the arms of England – above St Etheldreda, the Virgin and St John the Baptist. – MONUMENTS. There is a recess in the S aisle, holding a coped slab with a cross and double-omega ornament. C13 – John Forster †1752. Hanging tablet with a lively bust on top in classical attire, perhaps the work of a London mason?

In the churchyard a Saxon CROSS of Barnack stone, probably of the first half of the C11. The shaft is 5 ft 4 in. (1.6 metres) tall and much defaced. The wheel-head is incomplete. But the two shoulders are preserved. Of carving one can recognize small round arcading and a simple geometrical pattern: a circle and a larger saltire cross across it. It was found near Farcet in 1865 and reset here in 1927.

100 yds S of the church is the former VICARAGE (now Polish Club). Square two-storey Late Georgian brick house with low stone-built N wing and columned porch. Further S on the E side of the street is MANOR FARMHOUSE. Early C18. Five bays. Mullioned windows at the back. Originally of through-passage plan. N of the church are the remains of the grounds which surrounded the Manor House (destroyed by fire in 1899). The Rev. William Strong commissioned drawings for its rebuilding from *W. J. Donthorn c.* 1840, but after the arrival of the railway he moved to Thorpe Hall (*see* p. 641).

HORSEY HILL FORT, Toll Road, 1¼ m. SE of the church between the Nene and Kings Dyke. Remains of the pentagonal Cromwellian fort, one of the best-preserved in England. Probably built 1643–4.

THORPE HALL *see* LONGTHORPE

WALTON *see* PASTON

WERRINGTON

The village was first suburbanized after the war with two council estates, but in the 1970s its expansion accelerated as part of the northern township to which it gave its name (population now 15,000).

St John the Baptist, Church Street. A chapel of ease to Paston until 1877. Primarily a Norman church, see the double bellcote with continuous roll mouldings around the arched openings and a gable, the s doorway with one order of colonnettes carrying decorated scallop capitals and an arch with an outer chevron at right angles to the wall plane; see also the handsome chancel arch, which is narrow and has responds of two shafts and a half-roll with decorated scallop capitals with beading; and see finally the s aisle w window with its deep splay. The arcades of three bays are early C13. That on the s side has piers with four shafts and in the diagonals four rectangular projections. The moulded capitals are simple but have a little nailhead. The bases have angle spurs. The arches are round, double-chamfered, and have stiff-leaf label stops. The n arcade is much simpler: round piers, round capitals and abaci, round double-chamfered arches. Also of the early C13 the chancel chapel. It has to the chancel one wide, round, double-chamfered arch on semicircular responds with fine stiff-leaf details. To the aisle its arch has a chamfered moulding dying into the wall and half-octagonal respond, i.e. early C14. The outer entrance of the s porch (cf. Peakirk) is of the same date. Nave and aisles restored by *J. C. Traylen* of Stamford in 1884, replacing the roof and tracery; in 1901–2 he also rebuilt the wide Dec chancel using some of the old materials, i.e. the reticulated tracery of the e window (the s windows restored in matching style), the beautiful head corbels inside to its l. and r. and trefoil-headed piscina. Good roof with castellated trusses and foliage bosses. Sweeting (1869) also describes a blocked Norman arch to a former chantry chapel, replaced by the vestry. – FONT. Plain C13 bowl, octagonal, on restored shafts with moulded capitals. – STAINED GLASS. Three windows by *Kempe*, the aisle w windows, 1896, and the n aisle ne, 1918.

The VILLAGE is one long street. Opposite the church, a well-preserved late C17 house in coursed rubble with ashlar platband and segmental door head (staircase with wavy, flat balusters. RCHM). Further e on the n side is WERRINGTON HOUSE, refronted *c.* 1820 in fine ashlar, with a nice doorcase with Gothic details to the jambs. Its staircase is in a tower at the rear. WERRINGTON HALL, Hall Lane, is the best house; dated *c.* 1779, with a modillion eaves cornice, blocked rustication and Gothic glazing; to its r. is its former wing, probably early C18.

The 1970s TOWNSHIP to the N is planned with a grid of avenues (i.e. a much more formal layout than Bretton or Orton, qq.v. above) contained by a perimeter road which also serves the usual culs-de-sac of housing. At the heart is the WERRINGTON CENTRE, Staniland Way, a low cluster of pub, supermarket, health centre, offices etc. by the *Development Corporation Architects*, in Neo-Vernacular style. W is KEN STIMPSON COMMUNITY COLLEGE, in similar style but with some more distinctive additions of 2004–7 by *Avanti Architects* (cf. Jack Hunt School, Westwood, below) finished in brick and glazed tiles. E of the centre, two-storey housing (CROWHURST and PLOVERLY) with half-timbered upper storeys, formally arranged with their fronts to a shared green space and access for cars at the rears.

WESTWOOD, RAVENSTHORPE AND NETHERTON

The suburban district between the railway and Soke Parkway.

ST JUDE, Cranford Drive. Externally mostly of 1982–4 by *Mathew Robotham Associates*, red brick with an expressive roofline, sweeping in a curve up to a tall circular tower with small staggered bell-openings. This was added to the buff brick hall of 1969, at the N end, which was first extended (including the S chapel) in 1977–8 by *Terrence Hodgkins*. Inside, an interesting collection of ARCHITECTURAL FRAGMENTS and SCULPTURE from redundant and demolished churches, e.g. the DOOR into the nave and the FONT (both of 1850 by *Teulon* from Benwick, Cambridgeshire), coloured C18 window glass from Normanton (Rutland), ROOD from St Peter and St Paul, Teddington (London) and delightful open tracery reset as a squinch to the Lady Chapel, from Higham Ferrers (Northants).

H.M. PRISON PETERBOROUGH, Savile Road. 2005, by *John Seifert Architects*. Built on the site of the Baker Perkins Engineering Works. The only prison in England for male and female prisoners on one site. The two cell blocks (N and S) are strongly reminiscent of C19 planning, with wings radiating from a central core. Separating these a large block containing *inter alia* gyms, health centre etc.

CITY HOSPITAL, Bretton Gate. 2008–10 by *Nightingale Associates*. Large but not specially interesting. Exterior of gridded façades with coloured panels.

JACK HUNT SCHOOL AND SPORTS COLLEGE, Ledbury Road. Comprehensive school, erected in several phases, 1969–75. Following the community model advocated for the New Town it also incorporates a public swimming pool. Refurbished and extended 2004–7 by *Avanti Architects*, introducing much-needed coherence to the disparate elements. Walls of brightly coloured render and tile. Nice *sans serif* signage of 1930s type.

WESTWOOD, W of Bourges Boulevard and the railway, was mostly allotments until the mid C20. WESTFIELD ROAD was the only street, serving the massive WESTWOOD ENGINEERING WORKS of Baker Perkins (established 1904).

NETHERTON, to the W and SW, was a private housing scheme begun *c.* 1956–7 by *Ruddle & Wilkinson*. The earlier part, laid out around Atherstone Avenue and Ledbury Road, is mostly of conventional appearance but incorporates some experimental Radburn-type planning of houses facing pedestrian-access paths with garages at the foot of their rear gardens; the second phase to the SW, developing these principles on a larger scale, was to be a neighbourhood of 1,500 dwellings but construction of Soke Parkway left the rump of 182 houses in tight, staggered patterns enclosed by Bradwell and Elmore Roads. It is a rare British example of a Radburn layout designed, like the orginal in New Jersey, with detached housing.

The more typical type of estate with traffic and pedestrians rigorously segregated is at RAVENSTHORPE. Here the first Development Corporation housing was built from 1970 on the site of RAF PETERBOROUGH (opened 1932); in Cottesmore Close is the former Officers' Mess, Neo-Georgian, dated 1931.

WOODSTON

A former village on the S bank of the Nene. It had a wharf for unloading goods, which was in the possession of the Abbot of Thorney and allowed him to avoid taxes payable at Peterborough. From the later C19 it became an industrial suburb; it was dominated by brickworks (like Fletton, q.v. above) and, from 1926 to 1990, a large sugar-beet factory.

ST AUGUSTINE, Oundle Road. Partly rebuilt 1844–5 by *Stephen Fry* of Leicester and 1883–4 by *A. W. Blomfield*, who widened the aisles, added the vestry, organ chamber etc. Chancel extended in 1896. The W tower, which is embraced by the aisles, has a recess on the W side, where Anglo-Saxon masonry is exposed, and a small double-splayed window. It also has Norman twin bell-openings with a thick roll on the Peterborough example and nutmeg frieze below. Perp top with a quatrefoil frieze. Also original is the S transept S window of three stepped lancet lights, i.e. *c.* 1300. and that would go with the S arcade with its octagonal piers. Chancel arch a little older. The hefty tower buttressing inside and N arcade are of 1844, E.E. style with crocket and volute capitals. – FONT. Late C13. Five supports, the four outer ones acting as knobs or spurs to the plain octagonal bowl. – Nice encaustic TILES in the chancel, one dated 1832. – SCREENS. Perp style, presumably 1884. – STAINED GLASS. Mostly 1885–93: two at least by *Lavers, Barraud & Westlake* (chancel S, 1890 and S transept). The aisle windows make a set. – MONUMENTS. N aisle. Mary Walsham †1745, local benefactor. Large standing monument of coloured marbles with a pediment, fluted Ionic pilasters and flaming urns. In the former N chapel, matching tablets by *John Fellows* of King's Lynn for her sons, Vokes Walsham †1714 and John Dickenson †1730/1, recording his gifts to St John the Baptist in Peterborough. Between these, Major J. D. Brighurst †1815 at 'the ever memorable battle of Waterloo'. – LYCHGATE, 1920 by *H. F. Traylen.*

BAPTIST CHURCH, Oundle Road. 1935–8 by *W. E. Norman Webster* of Spalding. Churchy but with Art Deco overtones, e.g. streamlined buttresses of the type seen on cinemas, and stepped parapets to the aisles and transepts. Apse.

E of St Augustine, the former RECTORY, of two phases, *c.* 1700 and the mid C19, with some Neo-Tudor details. Opposite, GUILD HOUSE, the former head offices of the Mitchell Construction Company, by *H. V. Lobb & Partners,* 1961–2. The block has curtain walling with slate infill. Subsidiary blocks at right angles at the rear. Now an annex of Anglia Ruskin University, refurbished 2010, the original zigzag canopy over the entrance removed.

BRITISH SUGAR HEADQUARTERS, Oundle Road/Sugar Way. Interesting two-storey OFFICE pavilion of 1972–3 by *Arup Associates.* It has a double skin, i.e. the sheer full-height smoked glazing is independent of the internal structure, allowing natural ventilation through the space between the two and sound insulation (originally) against the beet lorries. Octagonal entrance tower, in dark engineering brick like the refaced range to the E. The factory site (opened 1926) has been redeveloped for housing and a shopping centre.

PIDLEY

3070

ALL SAINTS. 1864–5 by *W. M. Fawcett* of Cambridge (cf. Colne, which was also a chapel of Somersham). Nave and chancel, w tower with tiled splayfoot spire. Small lancet windows. Inside, exposed brick and odd painted roof. – PULPIT. 1915 by *C. M. O. Scott,* with tracery of twining organic forms. – STAINED GLASS. Chancel windows all by *W. Glasby,* 1921–30. Excellent colouring in the angels of the E window.

STANLEY FARMHOUSE, at the start of the road to Old Hurst. Early C18. Five bays, red brick, with segment-headed windows and a hipped roof. Doorway with hood on carved scrolly brackets.

FENTON MANOR FARM, ¼ m. NNW. Early C18, H-shaped, which is unusual, and with the principal façade along one of the arms of the H. Modillion cornice and steep one-bay pediment. Doorway with scrolls brackets for the hood, a guilloche frieze and a segmental arch in a lugged surround.

PONDERSBRIDGE

2090

A plantation in the Fen after the draining of Ramsey Mere *c.* 1840.

ST THOMAS. 1869–71, largely paid for by Edward Fellowes of Ramsey Abbey (q.v.), who provided a parsonage (dem.). Yellow brick, lancet-shaped windows, with a double S transept and a polygonal NW turret to add the High Victorian touch. Polygonal apse with quatrefoils in plate tracery. Stark, lofty brick interior. – Late C19 STOVE by *Musgrave & Co.* – STAINED GLASS. C13-style by *Wailes*.

Former PUMPING STATION, Glassmoor Bank, 1 m. NE by Bevill's Leam (constructed *c.* 1630–40). 1857–9. Red and yellow brick, fine chimney with corbelled top. Steam engines were introduced to pump water from the drains to the rivers, a task previously undertaken by wind-powered water scoops.

RAMSEY

2080

Like Ely and Thorney, an island in the fens. Access from the nearest dry land to the W was from Bury via a causeway or by a navigable channel from the Nene to the N.

RAMSEY ABBEY was founded *c.* 969 by Aylwin and Bishop Oswald of Worcester and dedicated in 974, i.e. just a few years after the older Benedictine establishments at Ely and Peterborough were rededicated after the Danish troubles. It developed into one of the important English monastic houses and seems to have had about eighty monks in the C12 and C13. The Anglo-Saxon church is described as having a cruciform plan with porticus on three sides and a W tower. From the early to mid C12 it seems to have been much rebuilt and in 1143 it was occupied and damaged by Geoffrey de Mandeville. There were still thirty-four monks at the time of the Dissolution. The premises then, together with those of Hinchingbrooke nunnery (*see* p. 531), were given to Sir Richard Williams, nephew of Thomas Cromwell, whose name he adopted. In the Elizabethan decades stone from Ramsey Abbey was used for Caius, King's and Trinity Colleges, Cambridge, and in the C17 for the towers of Ramsey, Godmanchester, and Holywell churches. The quarrying was thorough and there has been surprisingly little investigation to establish the position of abbey church and monastic buildings.

So, little can be said of the medieval buildings except of the part that is incorporated into RAMSEY ABBEY HOUSE. This was built as a summerhouse for the Cromwells and it became their principal residence after the sale of Hinchingbrooke in 1627. The Fellowes family took over in 1737 and became Lords de Ramsey in 1887. The architects acting for them in remodelling were *Soane* in 1804–6, for W. H. Fellowes (whose uncle had engaged Soane at Shotesham, Norfolk), and *Blore* in 1838–9 for Edward Fellowes. To the unwary the whole building appears to belong to the early C19. In 1937 Lady Fairhaven presented it to the town as its grammar school (now Abbey College). The

120

surviving medieval work appears of the first half of the C13 and is interpreted as the Lady Chapel, an independent building to the N of the chancel, just as at Ely and Peterborough. But without knowing the location of the abbey church this remains speculative. What seems just as, if not more, likely is that it was the chapter house on the E side of the cloister. Externally what can be seen are the five buttresses along the S side with chamfers and stop-chamfers. For some one must specially look. They strongly suggest that the building was two-storey. There is also part of the arch of the S doorway, at basement level. In line with this on the N side is another door, but this and the N buttresses are inside the house, following the early C19 changes. The E buttresses appear in all their monumentality, and a pinnacle marks the NW corner. Inside, i.e. at the basement level, the wall is surrounded by a continuous dado of blank pointed-trefoiled arcading of the highest quality above stone benches. Some of the colonnettes have been robbed or broken, but stiff-leaf capitals remain. The arches are richly moulded. The S doorway has, to the inside, a segmental arch on short vertical pieces, although how this corresponds with the pointed arch outside is unclear. There is also a N door but this has a Tudor arch head and was a back door to the house. At the E end the arcading is interrupted so that in the centre two bays the arcading and seats (one turned into a door in the C19) are independent of the rest.

The activity of the Cromwells is not dated but the medieval building was floored and turned into a house around 1587 (the date given on the S gable) and before 1620 (the date scratched in the wine cellar). This was of typical plan of parlour, hall, cross-passage and service end. It had a two-storey S porch (in the same position as now, though altered by both Soane and Blore). Of this era are also the two-light basement windows and the big rectangular bay window. This has windows in two tiers and a gabled attic storey, which originally projected higher than the eaves of the roof. The Cromwell hall was probably only one-storeyed then, with a chamber above and the bay window corresponding to the dais end. It means an oddly short hall. One of the hall's N windows is exposed. It is of four lights with a transom, and to its E is part of a large chimneybreast (standing on Tudor arches in the basement that connect two pairs of the N buttresses already mentioned). The fireplace itself was discovered c. 1967 behind C19 panelling (it has stone jambs and a brick arch) directly opposite the big S bay window. The principal staircase was in the tower attached to the NE corner, i.e. serving the rooms in the solar. The height of this tower is original, as is proved by the mullioned windows on four floors in the E face. There was it seems also a lesser newel staircase in a tower on the N side of the house, in line with the passage from the S porch.

Before his changes, *Soane* shows that the gabled W wall had four tiers of windows, those of the two main stages having transoms. He then extended the whole house W and moved

the entrance to the NORTH FRONT, creating the present symmetrical façade in a Gothick style with a new tower to the W
corresponding with the old one to the E. The two towers have
diagonal buttresses with the same chamfered stops as Soane's
compliment to the medieval work, and their windows have
mullions and transoms but also unmistakable Soanian incised
surrounds and floating cornices. The late C16 middle projection went on to the full height of the house, as a small gable
still shows. But this no longer appears as a projection, because
Soane put in front of it an odd truncated circular porch or
lobby and infilled the space between it and the E and W towers
with corridors at each level. These have pointed windows,
again with incised heads, but round rere-arches. Cast-iron
Gothic tracery with coloured glass. The lobby is stylistically
something else again, has apsidal ends, idiosyncratic angle buttresses with ball finials and some pleasant tricks in the geometry of the steps, which begin convex outside, turn concave
inside and convex again.

The openwork balustrade here and elsewhere is by *Blore*,
and on the SOUTH FRONT the final result is even more preva-
lently his, accounting for the whole present top storey with
angles stressed by ogee-roofed turrets and the grander porch
with its flying stair. Soane built the large square W tower of
three bays and three storeys above its basement but Blore
added the projecting full-height bay, and on the E front his is
the big canted bay window and steps. He also took out the last
of the C13 lancets.

Inside, Soane's corridors, with their barrel vaults interchang-
ing with domes, and his plain apsed subsidiary staircase are
preserved, but otherwise the style is the mechanical Jacobean
of Blore's time, including the main STAIRCASE (a replacement
of Soane's) and the former drawing room (now library) and
dining room (common room). The service wing added by
Soane was a single storey and is now as remodelled entirely by
Blore in 1839. To the N are the former STABLES of about the
same time.

The other significant medieval remain is the GATEHOUSE of
c. 1475–1500 (given to the National Trust in 1937). This is an
uncommonly ornate piece and would have served the abbey's
inner precinct. Its arch was removed for the gatehouse at
Hinchingbrooke (q.v.) but some of the shafting survives to
show its impressive scale. What remains otherwise is E of the
original carriageway for the porter's lodge, which has a door
on the side to the road. It had identical inner and outer fronts
of windows with a two-light oriel window over, all with fleuron
and quatrefoil friezes. The buttresses are panelled. The present
arch to the grounds of Ramsey Abbey House was formed by
Soane in 1804, from old bits, including a bellcote. In the gatehouse are heated rooms on both floors, a garderobe in the
surviving buttress and remains of a stair in the other. The door
is reused Elizabethan woodwork. Also on the ground floor is
the MONUMENT to Aylwin, who founded the abbey. It is of

unpolished Alwalton marble and dates from *c.* 1230; it resembles the abbots' monuments of Peterborough Cathedral. The head is in a cinquefoiled pointed arch. The face has a short beard. Stiff-leaf crockets run up the edges. At his foot a lion and an eagle. – Also a stone with blank arcading and some bosses found in the churchyard wall. They may be C14 work.

sw of the abbey site, by the road is BOOTH HILL, an overgrown small C12 motte-and-bailey castle.

CHURCHES AND PUBLIC BUILDINGS

ST THOMAS A BECKET. This is not the original dedication; there was none, and with this is connected the sensational impact of the building. It was not built as a church at all, for at the time to which most of its details point, the laymen had parochial rights in the abbey church. It was built as a HOSPITIUM, i.e. a guesthouse or maybe a hospital. Such a hospital was founded *c.* 1180 and seems to have been dissolved before 1291. A dedication date 1237 for the parish church appears in the literature but seems unconfirmed. As a guesthouse-hospital its position outside the abbey walls is not unusual (cf. Sawtry Abbey). Its size appears spectacularly large, but it is not larger than other hospitals, e.g. the former Hospital of St John at Huntingdon (*see* Cromwell Museum, p. 525) of a few years earlier. The details of the building point to dates between *c.* 1180 and *c.* 1190. Work proceeded from E to W. The chancel (or rather the chapel of the hospital as it would have been) is pure Norman, and it is distinguished by a heavy rib-vault with broad, unmoulded ribs. The chancel arch has triple responds, the main shaft keeled, and scallop capitals. There were S and N two-bay chapels as

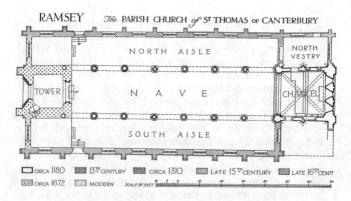

Ramsey, St Thomas a Becket.
Plan

well. That is recognizable from outside (i.e. for the N, from the vestry). The supports have keeling again, and apart from scallop capitals one has some kind of waterleaf. The E wall has three lancets, still round-headed and inside with a continuous roll, but an almond-shaped window above and a small round-headed one in the gable. But the chancel arch is again pointed.

The Late Norman or rather Transitional story goes on in the nave with seven bays of large, spacious arcading, and there were formerly eight. The arches are all of one step and one slight chamfer and pointed, and the bases are uniform, square with an attic base of nicked corners, but the piers are a most instructive assortment of late C12 possibilities. They ought to be looked at one by one. The sections from E to W go as follows: triple respond with keeling (i.e. part of the design for the chancel arch and sharing its large circular base), quatrefoil with rather indistinct keeling, quatrefoil with subsidiary diagonal shafts, round, quatrefoil with foils all keeled with fillets between, octagonal, eight keeled shafts. The capitals are as varied. They still comprise many scallops (E responds, but also pretty far W), waterleaf of several varieties, and crockets of several varieties but none of French purity. The W doorway ends this story but it is probably reset and may come from the remains of the abbey, for it shares few of the motifs inside. There is waterleaf, and some more conservative Late Norman capital types. The arch here, with several rolls, is still round. There are three orders of shafts, with shaft-rings. The doorway is built into a W tower, which in its present form, ashlar-faced and big, is of 1672. But the bell-openings and other places, e.g. the arch to the nave, show clearly the reuse of C13 materials. If then a W tower was built into the hospitium, by that time the use must have changed and the building become a church. The PISCINA and SEDILIA on the chancel are also C13. The aisle walls have mostly Late Perp windows, except three in the N aisle which seem late Dec. In the Perp clerestory, above the second piers of the nave arcades are blocked openings for the rood loft; the screen itself was removed as part of the restoration in 1843–4 by *Blore*. Open, trussed roof of the same date. – FONT. Hexagonal, absolutely plain, and of some species of dark, probably Alwalton, marble. Probably C13 too. The existence of a font would also point to parochial use in the C13 – i.e. if the font is in its original habitat. – LECTERN. The stem is C15, with diagonally set, openwork, traceried supports and small figures of the Evangelists (stolen in 1934, replaced in 1972). The rotating top is mostly of 1885. – PAINTING. Dim remains of a man and an angel in the nave above the N arcade. – PEWS. A rare survival. Numbered, with poppyheads. Of 1843–4, made for Blore by *Francis Ruddle* of Peterborough. – Painted ORGAN CASE of 1903. – STAINED GLASS. Much of *Morris & Co.*, but all of after the deaths of Morris and Burne-Jones. The dates recorded here and in the Morris accounts are 1915–27. – There is also the W window, 1912, and completely indifferent glass in

79

the s aisle of 1917, both by *Morris & Sons*, but there is no risk of confounding the one with the other. – Also two by *J. Powell & Sons*, a war memorial window of 1918, with a scene of stretcher-bearers against a shattered town, and, in the N aisle, St Thomas flanked by St Etheldreda and St Felix with their foundations of Ely and Soham, 1919. – MONUMENTS. W. H. Fellowes †1837. Large, ornate standing monument in the Gothic style with two small allegorical figures. By *Hopper*. Emma Fellowes †1862; she has a more prosaic Gothic tablet by *T. Gaffin*. – In the s aisle a memorial to the contribution made by Edward Fellowes to the restoration of 1843–4. Cartouche with garlands à la Gibbons. This and the leaf decoration look very improbable for 1844. – In the churchyard, many good C18 and early C19 headstones of the local carving traditions. Also the shaft and base of a churchyard CROSS with broaches to the base. Monuments to the Fellowes including fine C18-style table tomb to Lord and Lady de Ramsey (†1993 and †1987). By *Peter Foster*.

SALEM BAPTIST CHURCH, High Street. 1857. Of four bays, with arched windows and a big pediment. Two recessed entrances. Note the giant pilasters and the naughty way they are given two eaves brackets each to carry instead of capitals. Largely preserved inside, tight with box pews and with a horse-shoe gallery whose balustrade is finely twirled tendrils of cast-iron.

BAPTIST CHAPEL, Great Whyte. 1894, yet still in a mid-Victorian mixed Italianate. Two pedimented entrances. A group of narrow round-headed windows and a pedimental gable with a kind of Lombard top-frieze.

METHODIST CHAPEL, High Street. 1898–9. Only four years later than the Baptist chapel, but now with the pretty free-Gothic details of the Arts and Crafts generation. Yellow brick with a square SW turret and spire. Coloured glass. The earlier chapel (1830s, later Drill Hall) lies behind.

CEMETERY, Wood Lane. Laid out 1858 (*J. Ellis & Son* of Peterborough, builders). Dec-style chapels with an archway between them and a spire to the rear.

POLICE STATION. Blenheim Way. Of 1910 by *Herbert Leete*, Huntingdonshire County Surveyor. In a suburban street and much like a suburban villa: white roughcast walls, brick quoins and a porch with big arch of tile creasing. Nice globe lamp. Wing to the r. for courtroom. Big semicircular window in the gable.

RAMSEY SPINNING INFANTS SCHOOL, High Street. 1905–7 by *Herbert Leete*, Huntingdonshire County Surveyor. Built as the Grammar School. Arts and Crafts style, in red brick with tall canted bays under linked half-timbered gables in the centre and a ventilator on the roof. Subtle low wing to the r. with a hipped roof and entrance under a segmental hood. Similar rear elevation with full-height windows. The previous schoolroom was incorporated at the E end as a laboratory. Deferential additions of 1950–1 by the *Huntingdon County Architect*.

PERAMBULATION

The town has two rather different aspects. N of the abbey gate-house is ABBEY GREEN, N of the church CHURCH GREEN. Both must have been part of the abbey's outer precinct, containing the Hospitium (*see* St Thomas, above), and with an outer gate to the W where the High Street now begins. Abbey Green has on its N side two similar symmetrical groups, r. the former SCHOOL of 1848, yellow brick, gabled, l. the ALMS-HOUSES of 1839, stone, but again gabled with two little wings. They share good cast-iron railings. Both were provided by Edward Fellowes; was *Blore* the architect? On its W side a symmetrical group of gabled yellow-brick estate housing dated 1863, and a similar group to its S (now the GOLF CLUB, and altered).

Church Green is narrow and has a pond at its E end. It is very probable that there was a dock here in the medieval period, served by a channel that branched off the brook that ran into the town from the River Nene. On the Green, the WAR MEMORIAL of 1921 by *F. W. Pomeroy*, a Portland-stone column with bronze St George enthusiastically slaying the Dragon. On the Green's N side, one five-bay Georgian house, ABBEY HOUSE, and next to it the former ESTATES OFFICE (now town council), which is probably of after 1873, one-storeyed, of nine very closely set bays with red brick round arches. Next to this, more mid-C19 gabled estate housing. Two are in yellow brick with wavy bargeboards, dated 1866 and 1877, a third is red brick with lattice-pane Gothic glazing. Round the corner, attached to the walled garden of Ramsey Abbey, is another house (ABBEY GARDEN) of the same date and style. In the wall itself, a fragment of medieval tracery.

After this piece of planned perfection, the HIGH STREET has nothing of such note but is typical of the fenland towns in being one long narrow two-storey run of small houses and several former inns (cf. Eye), a few well-concealing medieval origins (e.g. phony half-timbering at No. 83 but the real thing inside, with a crown-post roof; others on the N side at Nos. 84–86, where timbers survive along with medieval roof ridge tiles and a smoke louvre). To begin with the street was open on the N side as a large market place, the N side of which is represented by Little Whyte (earlier still Little Whyte may have been a water channel up to the gates of the abbey precinct). First on the S side is ABBEY ROOMS, another Fellowes benefaction, of 1877. It looks like a chapel, i.e. yellow brick with red dressings, and arched windows. Then, midway, NATWEST (former National Provincial Bank) by *Palmer & Holden*, 1923, cute English Baroque. Next to this, the GEORGE HOTEL, now barely recognizable as C17 but inside there is a staircase of *c.* 1630 with heavy balusters and faceted newel finials.

GREAT WHYTE meets the High Street at a T. It is wide, market-like, but the scale is explained by the Bury Brook, which ran down the centre until the mid C19. It is now in a culvert below. The CLOCK on its cast-iron column, with lamps and typical leaf decoration of its date: 1888. It is signed by its makers, *Walter MacFarlane & Co.* of Glasgow (Saracen Foundry) and commemorates the 1st Lord de Ramsey. The street has no greater surface interest than the High Street but goes on and on. Of houses there is Nos. 1–5, early C19, yellow brick, with giant pilasters, and a former house at No. 13 which is brick, early C18, with an arched window in the centre. Two diminutive buildings at No. 63 and No. 113 are evidently medieval, each an example of a tiny open hall house, probably C14. But almost everything else has been improved out of recognition or demolished, like Nos. 66–68, which Pevsner noted as 'one of the only two at Ramsey given grade II by the MHLG and hence (at the time of writing) derelict'. Furthest N is a converted MILL by the dock basin which was formed in the mid C19 after the brook was culverted. It gave access to the Middle Level Navigations.

w of the junction with Great Whyte, HIGH STREET goes on, with the Salem and Methodist chapels (*see* above) and, opposite the school, THE GABLES, a neglected house of outwardly mid-C19 appearance, brick-faced and sporting curly bargeboards. But its general form, two-storey with cross-wings, suggests its earlier origin. The hall is C15 but the E wing even earlier, perhaps early C14, and the w wing late C16. The rear part is also early to mid-C19 and has a charming garden porch with fishscale tiles. Like a number of Huntingdonshire houses the kitchen was detached.

RAMSEY FORTY FOOT

2 m. N of Ramsey

So named from the FORTY FOOT DRAIN (a.k.a. Vermuyden's Drain), which begins here and was cut in 1651 between the Nene and Old Bedford River, 10½ m. E. BRIDGE HOUSE is mid-C18 with the tumbled brick gables typical of the fen edge. The church (St Felix, 1902, provided by the Fellowes) has been demolished.

BODSEY HOUSE, ½ m. W, was built on the site of an island hermitage which then became a place of resort for the monks of Ramsey. As such it was provided with a chapel (S) and a dwelling (N) that form the stone spine of the present house. In the dwelling part is a corbel with dogtooth decoration, and next to it a lancet window. So that is C13, and the corbel may suggest that this was originally single-storey (upper storey now C19 brick). The chapel seems a hundred years later. It has its SW buttresses and two blocked S windows. In the N wall the entrance arch, with an ogee moulding on the S side, i.e. inside

the chapel. Also the original wooden bar was fastened on the
N side. This means that the doorway was seen as the entrance
to the house, not to the chapel, which was probably open to
laymen. The chapel's E end was demolished, the gable
rebuilt in brick and a floor inserted *c.* 1540 when Sir Richard
(Williams) Cromwell acquired the property (see also Ramsey
Abbey). There were four other doors in the dwelling part and
they seem C14 also; remains of an early C14 roof truss have
been discovered. The door now opens into later additions to
E and W. Also two E windows, probably of the mid C16,
when the interior was subdivided and a passage formed
between the rooms; all with close-studded walls. Projecting W
from the S end is a hall range, also *c.* 1540; its W end, containing a parlour, was removed in the mid C19 for the cutting of
the road onto the fens. Big chimney, the base ashlar-faced but
the stack and three diamond shafts of Tudor bricks. There is
another, even mightier, for the kitchen at the N end. Above the
hall, a chamber with a timber wagon roof and a very large
limestone chimneypiece, with a four-centred arch. The other
projection on the W front is also timber-framed but covered
over. The rear additions are C19 and C20. The staircase is
constructed with turned balusters salvaged from Priory House,
St Neots.

RAMSEY ST MARY'S *2080*

A parish carved out of Ramsey after the drainage of the mere.*

ST MARY. Built in 1858–9 by *Richard Armstrong,*[†] at the expense
of Emma Fellowes, widow of W. H. Fellowes of Ramsey Abbey.
It is a strikingly large church for its situation in the sparsely
populated fenland. But churches were specially urgently
needed after the draining of the land (cf. Pondersbridge or
Newborough). Yellow brick with a NW tower (spire removed
1929), nave, aisles and chancel. Tracery of before and after
1300 and good head corbels. The chancel arch rests on demi-
figures of angels with a positive organ and a lute. CREED and
COMMANDMENTS on painted tin. The STAINED GLASS is
original. Trefoil-shape E windows of Christ above two angels
and the Evangelists in lancets l. and r. To the foundress (†1862).
ASHBEACH SCHOOL. 1993. In the grounds a quirky CLASS-
ROOM (The Hazel House) built by the children in 2007 from
straw bales and topped with a curvy roof. The style is Tolkien
Gothic.

---

*Formerly part of the County of Huntingdon, Ramsey St Mary's is now within the
District of Fenland in the present county of Cambridgeshire.
[†]Armstrong had been Edward Blore's clerk of works in the 1830s and no doubt
worked with him for the Fellowes at Ramsey Abbey (q.v.).

RAVENSTHORPE *see* PETERBOROUGH

ROUND HILL *see* GLATTON

3070

ST IVES

67 St Ives was a cell of the Benedictine Priory of Ramsey, known as
Slepe until a cult developed around the priory's shrine of relics
identified by the Abbot of Ramsey as the bones of St Ivo. The
buildings, demolished after 1539, lay at the E end of the market
place and at the other end of the town was built the parish
church; it was in existence at Domesday. The prosperity of the
town in the Middle Ages was founded on the Easter Fair,
granted in 1110. It was one of the four busiest fairs of England
(with Winchester, Northampton and Boston) but declined
after the Black Death and in the face of competition from
Stourbridge fair at Cambridge. Like Huntingdon the town
benefited in the early C17 from improvements to the navigation

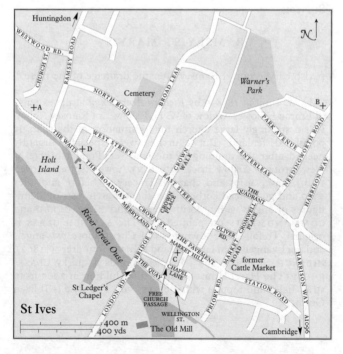

A All Saints
B Sacred Heart (R.C.)
C Free Church
D Methodist Church

I Norris Museum

of the Ouse between here and King's Lynn, and it became a major market for cattle in the C19 (continuing a market that was already important in the medieval period), assisted by the opening of a station in 1847 (closed in 1970) on the line from Wisbech to Cambridge. A major fire in 1689 did away with many of the town's buildings, so the overwhelming character of the streets of the centre is principally C18 and C19 and the atmosphere is pleasantly quiet, now that traffic is discouraged. There has been substantial growth in the outer area of town, especially postwar for public and private housing and some industries, and again in most recent times as a dormitory serving the expansion of Cambridge, but none of this detracts.

CHURCHES AND PUBLIC BUILDINGS

ALL SAINTS. In an enviable position by the Ouse and normally reached by a footpath from The Waits. The advowson was held by Ramsey Abbey and there was a church here by 1086. It is now a large church as rebuilt mostly between *c.* 1450 and *c.* 1470, and its steeple is exceptionally fine in its proportions. The bell-openings are pairs of slender two-light openings, Perp, and the spire is recessed but has low broaches behind the battlements and pinnacles. Two bands run across it and contain the lucarnes, the upper ones being just quatrefoils. The spire has been rebuilt more than once: in 1748 after it was blown down in a gale, again in 1822, once more in 1879–80 by *A. W. Blomfield* (who restored the pinnacles) and for the final time after an aeroplane toppled it into the N aisle in 1918 (replaced, along with the roofs, in 1924 by *Ninian Comper*). The W door is very elaborate, with traceried spandrels and a frieze of pointed quatrefoils and two figure niches l. and r. under ogee canopies with brackets on shafts (this is the pattern of Godmanchester S porch and the W front of Bury). There is another tiny niche over the door. The buttresses start out with canted faces on each side, then clasping and finally angled. The aisles and the chancel are also all Perp, except for the C13 N doorway with a hoodmould on headstops and the latest C13 S aisle E window of five lights with intersecting tracery broken at the top to allow for an encircled quatrefoil. Inside the S aisle is a splendid DOUBLE PISCINA with a surround of big dogtooth in high relief. Each half has a pointed arch, but they are taken together by a round arch. The date could be as late as that of the E window, but is more likely to be earlier in the C13. The interior is as obviously Perp as the exterior. Arcades of high and exceptionally thin piers and thin arches with the shafts towards the arch openings with capitals (cf. Godmanchester) and a continuous roll moulding to the nave and aisles; four bays. Against the piers a whole series of brackets for images, all decorated, some with foliage, one with a dog, another with a bull baited by a dog. Very high tower arch, as at St Neots (q.v.), and tierceron-star vault in the tower with bosses of a pelican in its piety and shields decorated with instruments of the Passion. Embracing aisles. Two niches in the s aisle e wall. Perp ROOFS, in the chancel with carved figures to the wall-posts and bosses, stars and fleurons to the two e bays. – The N organ chamber and vestry is probably by *Robert Hutchinson*, c. 1885.

– FONT. Octagonal, Norman, with blank intersecting arches (cf. All Saints, Conington). – PULPIT. Elizabethan or Jacobean, with a trumpet shaft, very elongated blank arches and panels with elementary geometrical motifs. Scrolled brackets for the book rest and (later) stairs with miniature turned balusters and finials. – PEWS. Undoubtedly by *G. G. Scott*, who made repairs and oversaw the reseating in 1854–6. – The vast, painted, ORGAN SCREEN is by *Ninian Comper*, 1893–4, i.e. very early in his long career and in the tradition of his master, Bodley. It doubles as the rood screen, with Crucifixion and angels l. and r. on the upper part, an open oriel in the centre of the loft and the screen itself with rib-vaulting and frilly tracery. This was Comper's first act in a major restoration and Anglo-Catholic refurnishing initiated by the Rev. Arthur Stapylton Barnes and continued by his successor Dr Salisbury Price, for whom Comper designed the comparably lavish screen at St Peter, Ely. Work carried on until 1936 and included the STATUES on the brackets (later described by Comper as 'the worst examples of bad copies of bad German figures . . .') and the fine brass LECTERN. – REREDOS of 1899 with statues and tabernacle. Comper's Gothic reredos of 1893 lies behind and the ALTAR associated with it is now in the s aisle, with riddel posts with angels. Embellished later by *Sebastian Comper*. – STAINED GLASS. Much by *Wailes* of the 1850s (e and w windows) and the 1860s (chancel and aisles), also one window by *Kempe*, 1903 (chancel s), and two by *Comper* – 1896 (s aisle, St Gregory, St William and St Richard) and 1924 (N aisle with Thomas More and St Alban) – showing a remarkable adjustment in his style. – MONUMENTS. Many C18 and C19 tablets, e.g. a curtain tablet for Dingley and Frances Askham, both †1728, attributed to *William Palmer* (GF). – Elizabeth Ingle †1857, a large tablet which has a kneeling Hope by a Bible and an urn (also late for its type). Signed by *Bingham*, Brompton, London. – Taylor White R.N. †1827. White marble tablet with Grecian motifs and a crisply cut arms. By *Tomson* of Cambridge.

In the churchyard, some good naïve C18 HEADSTONES, e.g. Margaret Hunt †17(86?) facing the w door, with an angel lifting the lid on an urn of her remains. – N of the chancel, John Ashton †1833, an obelisk on a Gothic plinth, and a ledger slab to the Rev. C. J. Baines †1839 with fine cast-iron arms in an oval. – Fine Gothic cast-iron GATES at the entrance from the town, mid-C19, probably by the Ulphs' foundry in St Ives (cf. Cemetery below).

ST LEDGER (bridge chapel). *See* p. 674.

SACRED HEART (R.C.), Needingworth Road. By *A. W. N. Pugin*, 1841–2, as St Andrew, Union Street, Cambridge, and transferred here in 1902. The re-erection was by *J. Morley* of Cambridge and *Edward W. Robb* of St Ives. Brick with stone dressings and not large. Nave and aisles and flat (liturgical) E end; W bellcote over a mid-buttress with a lancet. The windows are small lancets or have low-pitched triangular heads and often appear in pairs. Three E lancets, stepped. The clerestory was added at the rebuilding. Inside, round and octagonal piers, i.e. an endeavour towards a correct vocabulary. Vestry annex and two-storey Presbytery of 1906. – ALTAR. By *Pugin*. Painted Caen stone, Evangelists' symbols in three quatrefoils. – FONT. C13 style with a base of short columns. – STAINED GLASS. The E lancets are original, by *Wailes* to Pugin's designs. Some other later C19 glass in the aisles and more of C20 and C21.

FREE CHURCH, Market Hill. By *John Tarring*, 1863–4, for the Congregationalists and with money from Potto Brown, the local miller.* A fussy façade with not enough space l. and r. It is simply one of a terrace of buildings. Dec detail, embracing aisles with swirling mouchettes in the tracery, and a steeple of 156 ft (47.5 metres), as impressive in the market place as Tarring's Trinity Church was to the High Street of Huntingdon. The interior, originally just one unified room with no galleries but an apse for the organ, was subdivided in 1980. The worship space is now on the first floor with thin twisted iron columns carrying the roof trusses, which have spandrels pierced by quatrefoils. Organ now at the W end with a singers' gallery, reusing some original ironwork. – STAINED GLASS. Over the entrance, by *Ward & Hughes*, 1864.

METHODIST CHURCH, The Waits. 1905 by *F. Sidney Webber*, succeeding a chapel of 1815 (the congregation was formed in 1784). In a heavy-handed fancy Gothic, but not bad for all that. Façade of dark chunks of Snettisham carstone, the dressings in Portland stone including the Tudorish cupola on the gable ends. One large Perp window. Interior damaged by fire in 1997.

PARTICULAR BAPTIST CHAPEL, East Street. *See* Perambulation below.

CEMETERY, Broad Leas. Opened in 1848. Tudor Gothic LODGE and good cast-iron GATES with castellated Gothic piers and spear railings, probably made by the Ulphs, ironfounders in St Ives. Thomas Birt Ulph †1856, the cemetery's principal promoter, is remembered by a maiden on a circular plinth. – CHAPEL attached to the lodge, 1902 in ironstone.

TOWN HALL, Market Hill. *See* Perambulation below.

NORRIS MUSEUM, The Waits. By *S. Inskip Ladds*, 1932, for the collections accumulated by the town's historian, Herbert Norris. The museum is one-storeyed Tudor with an entrance from The Waits that is guarded college-style by the keeper's house, and with a garden open to the river. The fittings are, as usual for the architect, beautifully made in the Arts and Crafts tradition.

*Tarring's son, F. W. Tarring, married Eliza Brown.

PERAMBULATION

St Ives has put its river, the Ouse, to good use visually. The river
is indeed good enough to be made a feature of. It is in view
along The Waits and again along The Quay. Starting the walk
from the church, there is an attractive ensemble to its W and
NW giving the air of a close around the churchyard. BARNES
HOUSE is to the NW; it must be early C18, for it has tumbled
brick gables (the iron ties with the initials IB) and a lugged
fireplace inside but also two two-storey canted bay windows
which may be later. Very pretty doorway with Gothick quatrefoils in the spandrels, but Doric pilasters and a pediment. The
stair is in a hip-roofed projection at the rear with an arched
window. The garden behind has been taken for housing but in
the wall overlooking the river is a two-storey GAZEBO with
steps to the first floor and a pyramid roof with chimney. The
adjoining house may have been part of Barnes House originally. It has the same modillion cornice.

A little to the N in WESTWOOD ROAD, THE CHESTNUTS
is again Early Georgian, but with a Venetian window in the
centre, with intersecting tracery, and single-storey canted bays
l. and r. that may be embellishments of *c.* 1800. Beyond it some
brick cottages of *c.* 1700 made picturesque in the later C19 by
oriel windows and gabled porches. The road curves around the
extensive gardens of WESTWOOD HOUSE, in which there are
soaring Wellingtonia and cypresses. The house is an odd
muddle, partly mid-C19 brick but with a creditable Arts and
Crafts addition in red brick with half-timbered gables.

E of here on RAMSEY ROAD, the pleasant CLARE COURT,
housing by *E. Fawcett,* 1965, in the tile-hung SPAN style with
a low block of flats on piloti and a green in the centre. This
was the site of the vicarage (rebuilt by *Joseph Gwilt* in 1804 and
enlarged by *William White,* 1867–8). Further up, SLEPE HALL
is a gault brick villa with Doric porch (now an hotel), built
c. 1848 by the Rev. John Rugeley and large enough to accommodate the girls' school he had established at the old Slepe
Hall (*see* Cromwell Place below). At the S end of the street,
some Late Georgian-style houses in terraces, of 2003–4, quite
convincingly done and right for the setting. Facing these, at
the corner with the churchyard path, No. 1 is a handsome late
C18 house with a broad doorcase, its pediment on consoles,
beneath a Venetian window. Behind this, another C18 house
and its little coach house with a window in a blind arch at the
end.

Now the main walk, all straight, through the town from W
to E. THE WAITS is an agreeable street, with one side open to
the river from the beginning up to the Norris Museum, and,
on the N side, pleasant but undemonstrative frontages of small
houses, concluding with the set-piece of the Methodist church.
No. 12 has a former butchers' shopfront, tiled with pictorial
panel. The only notable house comes after that, set back in its
garden: BURLEIGH HOUSE, a merchant's house built *c.* 1730;
its first owner was Edward Smith, a maltster and grazier. The

front is late C18: five bays, white, with a Doric porch, a Venetian window above it and a low pediment in the parapet. (The rear wing has a half-cellar with storeroom or office above. BD) Screen wall to one side with a pedimented opening. Just beyond is the CONSTITUTIONAL CLUB of 1891.

The continuation is THE BROADWAY, a widening where the Bullock Market was held from the medieval period until the 1880s. The C18 and early C19 predominate in the aspects to the street on both sides. The repetitive appearance of large arched gateways to yards behind suggests that the S side was largely the preserve of merchants with business on the river, while the N side was dominated by inns. On the S side, FLOOD'S TAVERN probably comes first in date, perhaps c. 1700, with its bracketed eaves. No. 11 is the most impressive of the early C19 façades, probably built for the Osbornes, whose brewery lay behind. Three storey, gault brick, its ambitious doorway with Ionic columns recessed in a round arch. The odd fenestration in the centre bays is a later C19 alteration. No. 18, opposite, has another good doorcase of Corinthian columns with an entablature. This was the Globe Inn from c. 1732 to c. 1795, when it became domestic. It belonged to the Day family, the town's leading solicitors, and very probably they remodelled the whole of the front, which also incorporates No. 16. The cement-render façade with rustication and consoled cornices to the windows is c. 1840. The former carriage arch, r. of the main door, has been filled in (the room inside has panelling and classical decoration of c. 1800) and a passage made to No. 16. At the back is a corridor lit by a charming octagonal lantern on a coved ceiling, added in the C19 for access to the large reception room at the rear. This wing has its own staircase and a top storey of rooms. There is another house (No. 20) facing the yard, with a smart early C19 front and lantern over the arched door. The room at its N end was designed as a solicitor's office and has enriched plaster cornices and arched niches.

At the E end of The Broadway, the MONUMENT to Queen Victoria's 1897 Jubilee, though not erected until Edward VII's coronation, 1902. A Gothic column with a lamp, looking like G. G. Scott about 1860; in fact it is by *J. Newman* and is a copy, commissioned by the St Ives brewer Eliot Odams, of Newman's Victoria monument (now dem.) at Sandown, Isle of Wight. Then the walk splits around a building. The streets either side are Merryland on the r. (*see* below), CROWN STREET on the l. In Crown Street, No. 5 is Early Georgian, an unaltered house of three storeys, red brick and rubbed brick trim, segment-headed windows, a door-hood on carved brackets and a passage through it to the back. Off to the N in CROWN YARD, the former PUBLIC INSTITUTION, 1848, one-storeyed, stuccoed, with giant pilasters and pedimented doors at the ends. In the next part of Crown Street a nice Victorian shopfront, cast-iron with Gothic tracery, c. 1885.

In MERRYLAND, more small C18 and C19 frontages, e.g. THE NELSON'S HEAD, 'new erected' in 1802 and so named from a few years later. Off it, with its front to the river, and in character like the smarter houses round the church, ELWYN HOUSE, which is dated by its deeds to 1736. Like Barnes House (*see* above) it combines yellow brick with red dressings.

Then turn s along BRIDGE STREET, where all the interest is down the w side, beginning with two more Early Georgian houses, like that in Crown Street, both of only three bays but three storeys, both with segment-headed windows and panelled parapets. The first (No. 10, Oxfam) is dated 1728. It has a doorway with fluted pilasters and strips of rustication. The second house has giant moulded brick pilasters. Further down, Nos. 24–26 is possibly from soon after the rebuilding after the fire in 1689. Five bays with the arch to the yard (now The Mews) in the centre and a low hipped roof above eaves with console brackets. Two of the windows are shallow bows of early C19 date. (Room on the upper floor with bolection-moulded panelling.) The back range has C17 timber-framing. The so-called MANOR HOUSE by the river, with three gables that side and four to the street, is too much restored to be enjoyable. It has ornamental bargeboards and moulded jetties. It may be late C16, and Norris, in his history of the town, recorded dates of 1616 and 1619 inscribed and a completely panelled room inside but its eccentric restoration *c*. 1910 destroyed all this. The ground floor now has diamond rustication in concrete. Inside the archway is a late C18 doorcase.

The BRIDGE is the most memorable monument of St Ives. Pevsner's wish that '. . . the temptation be resisted to sacrifice it to a through-traffic which should not at all rush along here' has been fulfilled. The bridge is still narrow and has preserved its cutwaters on both sides and pointed arches with ribs in the soffit. It dates from the 1420s and was paid for by the Benedictines. Midway along it is still a bridge chapel, one of only three surviving in England, the others being at Wakefield and Rotherham, or four if you include Bradford-on-Avon. The chapel is dedicated to St Ledger (though later thought to have been St Lawrence), and its altar was consecrated in 1426. It has an E apse and below the main room a lower one, thought to be for the monks serving the chantry. It became a residence for the dispossessed prior after the Dissolution and remained in such use until 1927, having been extended by two storeys in the C18. Restoration to its medieval state, the plain parapet excepted, was made in 1929–30 following advice from *William Weir*. The s end of the bridge was partly reconstructed in 1716 (two round arches) and on BRIDGE END are two houses of about the same date, one with a fancy cast-iron veranda. A third early C18 house on the w side, where the 1980s Dolphin Hotel stands, was lost in the late 1960s.*

*Pevsner described it as '. . . of five by five bays, with to the street a doorway with a big segmental pediment, to the river a round-arched middle window. All other windows are segment-headed.'

Here the remarkable CAUSEWAY begins. This was thrown across the water meadows to take the turnpike road to Potton (Beds.) in 1822, and has fifty-five low brick arches (the dark engineering brick of its mid-section shows where the railway to Huntingdon crossed it in the C19). The architect is believed to have been *Thomas Gwyn Elger* of Bedford (Bridget Flanagan), the surveyor *William Biggs* of Linton. John Margetts, a local businessman, not only advanced the loan of £5,000 but sold the builders the 1,200,000 bricks needed for its construction. Thomas Telford admired it in 1826 and it is still the best way to approach St Ives rather than the bypass to the E of 1980.

Just off to one side, powerful in its presence on the S side of the river, is THE OLD MILL. Built *c.* 1854 by Potto Brown for flour milling. It was steam-powered and automated, following Continental models. Converted as a printworks in 1901 and now flats. Six storeys plus attics in the pitched roof projecting on bracketed eaves and forming pedimental gables. Yellow brick with minimal classical patterns of decoration of pilasters. The lucams have been removed, along with the engine house and chimney.

Now back across the river and along THE QUAY, the old wharf which was widened to its present proportions in 1724 by the Duke of Manchester. The houses make a fine and varied ensemble, including one, C19, with a Dutch gable. The continuation is WELLINGTON STREET (called Fish Street until the victory of 1815), part of a charmingly intimate district between river and market place with cottages and working premises tightly built up on both sides of narrow lanes. THE OLIVER CROMWELL, an early C18 house, has a fancy wrought-iron bracket for its sign (formerly of the Ship Inn). In CHAPEL LANE to the N is the former FRIENDS' MEETING HOUSE (now Gateway House) of 1691. In FREE CHURCH PASSAGE, some timber-framed cottages but also the former LITERARY INSTITUTE and the former INDEPENDENT CHAPEL of 1811, predecessor of the Free Church on Market Hill, and its hall from 1864. Both of these in gault brick and severe.

And so to the Market Place, called MARKET HILL, but the houses along the N side are called THE PAVEMENT. In the middle, bronze STATUE of Cromwell, who farmed at St Ives before coming into his inheritance. By *F. W. Pomeroy*, 1901. In front of him the WAR MEMORIAL, *R. Blomfield*'s Cross of Sacrifice. No houses of great interest but over the door to the shop at No. 7 The Pavement (M & Co.) is a reset early C16 beam with the arms of Ramsey Abbey flanked by an ox and sheep and a crown, a rose, and the name W. Wesbyche. Above the shop this is Early Georgian, the former Bell Inn of 1719, in purplish brick with red dressings and gauged headers to the windows and the inn sign also of moulded brick in the centre. Opposite, a complete five-bay Later Georgian house of three storeys in red brick. Doorway with Doric pilasters. The TOWN HALL was built in 1850 by the local architect *George Allen* as a house for the Warners, who were leather curriers. Italianate stucco trim to the windows and doors, balconies at first floor for the piano nobile of principal rooms. Top-lit staircase inside with cast-iron lyre-shaped balusters. (Plasterwork in the former drawing room, now Council Chamber.) It was converted in 1924. Next to this the GOLDEN LION HOTEL, C18 with big plaster lion. The former ROBIN HOOD pub has an early C19 stucco front but at the back of the r. part, formerly the Swan Inn, there remains the splat-balustered gallery of c. 1680. The former CORN EXCHANGE on the N side, with an Italian Renaissance front in yellow and red brick, is of 1864 by *Robert Hutchinson*, who was born in St Ives but made his career in Huntingdon. Big doorcase with consoles and a little pediment over the centre. The early C20 has offered more interest, notably the stone Baroque of LLOYDS BANK of 1924–5 by *H. Munro Cautley*, with long arched windows between pilasters and some lavish sculpture by *Gilbert Seale & Son*, and a top-lit banking hall inside with late C17-style plasterwork. Next to it, NATWEST (originally London, County & Westminster Bank) in more conventional Bankers' Georgian by *Cheston & Perkins*, 1910–12.

From the end of the Market Place, to the NE is the site of the CATTLE MARKET (bus station and car park) still with its gate lodges and railings of 1886 by the local architect *Edward W. Robb*. The former market toll house lies just to the SW by Priory Road. E of here STATION ROAD runs out into the GUIDED BUSWAY, opened 2011, two concrete troughs following the old line of the railway to Cambridge. At the corner with Priory Lane is the former NATIONAL SCHOOL, originally Neo-Tudor of 1844–5 by *J. D. Hopkins*, a pupil of J. B. Papworth. It has a centre with two shaped gables, for the master's house, and sharply gabled classrooms flanking, all converted to shops in 1890. Behind in PRIORY ROAD is the former POLICE STATION, also 1840s, Neo-Tudor, with an extension for a courtroom of 1884 by *Robert Hutchinson*. Opposite, the house called THE PRIORY is of 1870, also by *Hutchinson*. It is intensely Gothic and rather grim. Yellow brick and stone dressings with some fleshy sculpture to the capitals of the projecting porch. All that is left of ST IVES PRIORY is two lengths of wall and buttresses of a BARN, which was taken down in 1859. It was 90 ft (27.4 metres) long with aisles.

N of where the Market Place is was the site of SLEPE HALL, the manor house, whose estate was sold off after the death of Lt Col. Taylor White in the late 1840s; its doorcase is now at Bluntisham, p. 425. In its place, CROMWELL PLACE, dated 1848, a yellow brick terrace of urban sophistication, the houses each of two bays with arched doorways. The S end is expressed as a pediment by the bracketed eaves of the roof. At right angles to it and overlooking gardens is the grander CROMWELL TERRACE, built in 1849. The houses are three-storey, with the largest one facing Cromwell Place with a pedimental gable. The garden front is asymmetrical with an open pediment to the r. above an arched window. The developers may have been the Ulph family; if so the especially lovely cast-iron veranda must have come from their iron foundry. But the architect is unknown. The terrace continues E in a different style. Behind this a DENTAL SURGERY, good hard modern style of the 1960s in dark engineering brick.

In EAST STREET, at the corner with Crown Place, the PARTICULAR BAPTIST CHAPEL of 1839 (extended 1862), gault brick with a severe pedimented front and arched windows, the side openings also arched. Schools behind of 1887 with red brick dressings. Facing the chapel, a delightful group of ALMSHOUSES ('The Pilgrims Rest') erected for James Piggott, one of the brethren, in 1885 by *James Johnson* of London. Picturesque Gothic with bargeboarded gables.

MILESTONE, Needingworth Road/Somersham Road. Erected *c.* 1790. It is of the obelisk type with dainty pointing fingers in relief, as found at Brampton.

ST NEOTS

1060

St Neots was the site of a Benedictine PRIORY, founded according to tradition *c.* 972–5 and containing the relics of the Cornish St Neot. It was refounded as a dependency of Bec in Normandy *c.* 1081. It lay along the river, N of the bridge. Excavations *c.* 1960 showed that the church lay S of Priory Lane, partly where the back premises of the former Cross Keys hotel are, that the cloister was N of the church and of Priory Lane, and was of C15 timberwork, that the dormitory undercroft was two-naved and dated from *c.* 1250, that the refectory was in the N range and had a two-naved undercroft and a pulpitum, as usual (the substructure was found), and that the kitchen stood W of the refectory and was 68 ft (20.7 metres) by 22 ft (6.7 metres) in size, with three massive piers along its middle axis. They dated from the C12. N of the claustral parts was apparently the infirmary (not in axis). Nothing of all this is visible and even some windows discovered in the cellar of houses along the N side of the market place have been covered up.

The town developed outside the priory gates with a weekly market being held by 1150, though its parish church was at Eynesbury (q.v.) until the late C12. The key to the later importance of St Neots was making the Ouse navigable, completed by *c.* 1630. By the late C17 'great quantities' of grain and other commodities were being imported to the town and on the back of this trade developed large numbers of merchants' houses and warehouses close to the river banks. The high period was in the C18 and early C19, by when there were also larger enterprises in the form of flour and paper mills and breweries, and business to be had from the coaching trade coming from the

Great North Road and between Bedford and Cambridge. The opening of the railway in 1850 maintained its importance and from *c.* 1960 it grew, like Huntingdon, to absorb large numbers of Londoners and new industries. It is this which has largely erased the division between the town and the once separate villages of Eynesbury and Eaton Socon. Yet more new housing neighbourhoods are nearing completion in the NE corner of the town.

CHURCHES

90   ST MARY. One of the largest, most uniform late medieval churches in the county. Apart from one (blocked) early C13 lancet window in the N wall of the chancel, better visible from the late C19 vestry, and a pretty niche with a nodding ogee arch in the N aisle by the door, all is Perp. The body of the church was apparently complete by 1486, the porches were added in 1489, and the W tower begun at about the same time. The tower is the most impressive element of the church, 130 ft (39.6

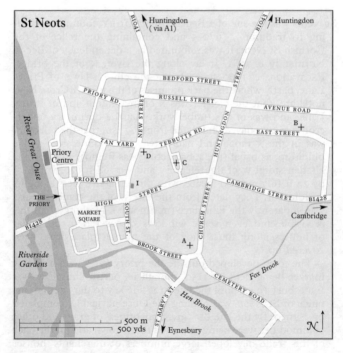

A	St Mary	I	Museum
B	St Joseph (R.C.)		
C	United Reformed Church		
D	Baptist Church		

metres) high and broad, with uncommonly high and substantial pinnacles. Wills refer to work on the top pinnacles in 1526–35. There are intermediate pinnacles on merlons as well, decorated with the signs of the Evangelists. The parapet has faces and paterae. The buttresses are of the set-back type and have gablets applied to them. They end in their own pinnacles, detached from the body of the tower – a Somerset trait. Doorway with tracery spandrels and little double-X motifs in one moulding. They repeat in the moulding of the broad middle mullion of the large four-light w window, which has a castellated transom. Large blank three-light N and s windows. The bell-stage has pairs of two-light openings, again with a castellated transom. There are decorative quatrefoil friezes as well at base, top, and in between. It is all entirely of a piece and done without faltering. The rest of the church is embattled. All the windows are large with hexagonal label stops, the buttresses have gablets, the s porch is two-storeyed with pairs of windows to the E and W, and the s doorway has traceried spandrels. The N porch is similar but a C19 rebuilding, with much original material reused. Both it and the N doorway have traceried spandrels. Three-light clerestory windows with steep four-centred arches. Long chancel, flanked by chapels for half its length, that on the N side erected as the Jesus Guild Chapel; IHS symbols adorn it. Its walls are ashlar. The chancel E wall is also ashlar but as remade in 1855–6 with the window to the same pattern as before.

The arch from the tower to the nave is extremely high. The nave is separated from the aisles by high five-bay arches with piers of the standard moulded section. The arches still have the two sunk quadrants of the Dec style. Shafts between the arches to the roof. At the E end of the s arcade an arch starts into the chancel arch. How did that come about? It is probably the one-bay s chapel which interferes. To the N its W arch dies into the impost, to the s there is a respond, so it may be that the chapel was there earlier and a plan existed to do away with it. However, if so, it was given up; for the chapel's arch to the chancel is Perp like the arcades, and also like the corresponding chancel arch and the W and s arch of the N chapel. Original, exceptionally ornately decorated roofs in the nave, the N and s aisles, and both chapels. They have crested cornices and ornaments, plenty of angels with shields to the principals and the tie-beams, and in addition in all sorts of places angels, monsters, a mermaid, camels, dogs, lions, fishes, an eagle, an elephant, fox and goose, hare and hound, and so on. The gilded chancel roof, remade in 1901–2 (supervised by *F. A. Walters*), has original figures of the Apostles. – PEWS of 1846–8 by *J. T. Wing* of Bedford. – Of 1860, by *Rattee & Kett*, the PULPIT, a fine piece with the Evangelists under nodding ogee canopies and the eagle lectern perched above St Mark. CHOIR STALLS, by the same firm. – A few STALLS are of the C15 or early C16, from Milton Ernest (Beds.), introduced in the 1840s. Carved arms, misericords with shields and inscriptions. –

COMMUNION RAIL, C18, of wrought iron. – ALTAR. Painted and gilded traceried front. Angels on riddel posts. Early C20. – SCREENS. Several Perp screens, the most attractive the W screen of the N chapel, with lovely transparent vine scrolls over the entrance. – The others have broad ogee-arched one-light divisions. – In the N aisle, moreover, a few fragments from painted panels of a screen dado. – TOWER SCREEN. 1918 by *S. Inskip Ladds*. – STAINED GLASS. Reassembled C15 panels of St Stephen and St Lawrence (vestry E window), originally in the room above the S porch. The rest was mostly provided by the Rowley family, 1850s to *c.* 1900, twelve alone by *J. H. Powell* (*John Hardman & Co.*) on the Life of Christ, beginning with the Annunciation in the S chapel and concluding with the Crucifixion and Ascension in the E window of 1865. Notably good the Woman of Samaria with exquisite twining vines (S aisle, exhibited at the Paris Exhibition in 1878), the Widow of Nain, undated, and the House at Bethany (N aisle, exhibited at the Centennial Exhibition, Philadelphia, in 1867, and, as Michael Fisher has noted, the only one of the scheme unconfined in design by the tracery, as was the American preference). The exceptions are N aisle NW (Miraculous Draught of Fishes) by *Heaton, Butler & Bayne*, and N chapel NE (Christ before Pilate) by *Kempe*, 1900. Also W windows (tower and aisles) and clerestory by *Clayton & Bell* (*c.* 1868–70 and *c.* 1879). – MONUMENTS. The monument to G. W. Rowley and his wife is a fabulous piece of display in the medieval tradition. The recumbent effigy of Mrs Rowley †1886 by *Thomas Earp* (his last work) is hardly visible behind a grille of the closest, most ornate decoration, and the canopy rises, with statuary and canopies and pinnacles, to the roof. It was designed by *F. A. Walters* and put up in 1893. (In the N chapel on the floor a defaced C13 slab with a foliated cross supported by a dog; cf. e.g. Pavenham, Beds.)

ST JOSEPH (R.C.), East Street. Built for General Baptists, 1873; converted by *A. S. G. Butler*, 1931. Large window of intersecting timber tracery. W gallery. – ALTAR AND REREDOS. Grand Italian Baroque, containing a painting of the Nativity, signed *J. G.*

UNITED REFORMED CHURCH, High Street. Formerly Congregational. 1888 by *Edward J. Paine*, whose father was the town's brewer and a deacon of the church. The town's principal Victorian monument owing to the Free Perp W steeple that stands slightly forward of the church over the porch but linked to it by the gallery stairs. Angle buttresses ending in double pinnacles and pinnacles at the angles of the spire. Red Suffolk brick with stone dressings and terracotta decoration. Moulded chimneys flank the gables of the church. Reordered 2011, but still with some of the original fittings by *Harry Hems*. Especially nice wrought-iron lamp fittings by *Starkie, Gardner & Co.*

BAPTIST CHURCH, New Street. 1816. Domestic appearance, in gault brick. Horseshoe gallery with decorative iron balustrading of 1897.

PUBLIC BUILDINGS

PRIORY CENTRE AND LIBRARY. *See* Perambulation below.

MUSEUM, New Street. The former police station. 1860. Yellow and red brick with a pediment in the centre. Cell block added 1907, still complete with its fittings and covered exercise yard.

WINHILLS PRIMARY SCHOOL, Duck Lane. 1969. Low, yellow brick but with pitched roofs raised on clerestories over hall etc. Brightly painted window frames.

LONGSANDS COMMUNITY COLLEGE, Longsands Road. Built *c.* 1966–7. With the usual low-profile flat-roofed components and spreading layout typical of 1960s secondary schools. Close to the entrance, the CREATIVE EXCHANGE by *5ᵗʰ Studio* of Cambridge, 2007–8, is an exciting design, a low tower, with restless elevations of overlapping, projecting and receding planes, the upper storeys faced in timber over a glass envelope around a two-storey foyer. On the back, a sheer wall of opaque glass planks, sweeping around the corner following the line of the staircase. Functional interior, divided into a mixture of shared and private studios for small companies. The concrete frame is left bare, the walls clad with timber boards. The setting is PRIORY HILL PARK, the former parkland of the late C18 mansion of the Rowleys (dem.). 127

PERAMBULATION

The centre is the Market Square, long, spacious, and not too rigid in its alignments. Along its N side runs the main traffic to the BRIDGE and into Bedfordshire. The bridge was replaced in 1963–5 (architectural consultant *F. Gibberd*) by a long concrete structure, part bridge, part causeway. It is of no special interest, like so much of the same date in the town. At the corner of the bridge and market place is the BRIDGE HOTEL, predominantly a rebuilding of 1912–14 to capitalize on the motor trade along the road between Bedford and Cambridge. Reset in the wall, a C17 decorative panel rescued from a building that stood opposite. The pub belonged to the Days, whose Priory Brewery lay immediately N in the street called THE PRIORY and was established *c.* 1780 by William Fowler. The house called THE PRIORY is late C18, three bays with a pedimented doorway. The architect W. G. Habershon lived here in the mid C19. Across the end of the street is four-bay PRIORY HOUSE, which may have been built by the Fowlers and extended for the Days. Of the brewery itself there is part of the malthouse and its excellent tapering barley-drying KILN, supplemented by extensions for the PRIORY CENTRE AND LIBRARY, 1980, in an appropriately agricultural style, the main building with a long hipped roof with gableted ends.

In the centre of the MARKET SQUARE is a LAMP on a tapering fluted pillar, with four thick scrolly arms in the main directions. It was given to the town in 1822 by John Day. There are no houses of great merit around, but nothing has gone wrong either, except on the N side, where there is some bland late C20 rebuilding. Almost all of the properties here were shops and inns, their narrow frontages separated by yards. Hardly any of that is obvious now, except at the former CROSS KEYS inn, which is low and has a brick front with two canted bay windows. The front is of before the mid C18, although the bays were evidently rebuilt (and not very well) in recent times. But behind the l. bay and the part of the frontage W of the archway is a C17 timber-framed building of the usual H-plan, probably built as an investment by the 1st Earl of Sandwich, who owned much of the property along the N side of the square.

Opposite, a row of uniformly acceptable frontages, several with shopfronts and almost all with archways leading to the yards that ran down to wharves on the Hen Brook between warehousing. Most, if not all, combined working premises with shops and residences for the town's merchants and testify to the wealth of trade along the river, especially in corn, during the C18 and C19. To the SW corner, a timber-framed later C17 house with four gables; a unique survival of an urban type that must have been commonplace before refronting and rebuilding in the Georgian years. The centre of attraction, however, is Nos. 32–36, a mid-C18 house, yellow brick, of seven bays and three storeys with a broad archway, a Venetian window over and a pediment with an arch rising into its base, also originally containing a Venetian window. Its r. half fronted the former Bull Inn, which faced the yard. The house was taken over in 1831 as the entrance to Paine's Brewery; the buildings flanking the narrow courts were mostly adapted and added to from that time and include the former brewhouse in yellow brick with polychrome patterns, almost certainly by *Edward J. Paine* (cf. the former Paine's Flour Mill in Bedford Street, below), who made additions in 1906 after a major fire. Now redeveloped as housing (Chandlers Wharf). James Paine lived in the house to its l., which is also mid-C18, but red brick with raised stone window surrounds and a stone cornice. No. 32 has a fine early to mid-C19 shopfront with Ionic columns. There is a grander one with Corinthian columns at No. 28. No. 24, a five-bay red brick merchant's house, double-fronted with a panelled parapet, is Early Georgian probably. Nos. 18 and 20 have an early C19 front and their entrances to the sides. The interior of No. 20 is an exceptional survival, its mid-C18 staircase with Rococo carved ends and enriched balusters and handsome plasterwork to the walls and ceiling – roses, urns, swags, cherubs, musical instruments and quiver of arrows – and a Venetian and circular window. Equally good ceilings also in the rooms on ground and first floors overlooking the square. There is nothing else like it in the county.

On the square's W side, the OLD FALCON (presently disused) contains C17 parts but is mostly a refronting of the mid to late C18. Its neighbour – also C17, also refronted – has some charming Gothick windows to the river-facing rear. On the E side of the market place, a sober frontage of *c.* 1828. Paired Ionic pilasters on the first floor between long sash windows. This replaced a multi-gabled frontage, probably C17, of which a single gable survives at the s end.

Turn into SOUTH STREET for the KING'S HEAD, an old inn but remodelled in the mid C18. Pevsner noted 'the curious brackets for the door-hood growing straight out of demi-columns, the type occurring here and there at Ampthill, Bedford'; they have been removed and should be reinstated. Then round the corner, BROOK STREET, with small premises facing the Hen Brook. No. 1 is especially diminutive and was probably a chandler's shop, with warehouse behind. BROOK HOUSE, w of the church, is red brick, seven bays to the front, three storeys, with a hipped roof: c. 1700. The Reynolds family had it by 1748. On the e side at ground floor there are blind arches instead of windows. One room has bolection-moulded panelling, but its staircase with slim twisted balusters and carved tread-ends was replaced in the late C20. How was that allowed? Opposite, CHURCH HOUSE, one of a nice group with their backs to the brook. It retains its Regency fittings. There are still some large former warehouses on the wharf and in the adjoining yard a stout brick CHIMNEYSHAFT. Again round the corner and up CHURCH STREET for the VICARAGE (now AISLING LODGE nursing home) of 1849, but with gabled Tudor enlargements of c. 1855–60. Strange facing of rubble and brick, not attractive. To its l. C18 walls and GATEPIERS with a very fine set of wrought-iron GATES that served Hall Place, a large house erected by the Pulleyn family c. 1712, see below. To the n more gatepiers, presumably for their stable yard and opposite yet more C18 gatepiers to a house called THE SHRUBBERY, which also belonged to the Reynolds, though its appearance is predominantly of the early C19, when it belonged to John Day, the brewer. Its large stables survive to the n.

This takes us to the HIGH STREET, which is rather disappointing because of some very poor rebuilding in the last decades of the C20. Facing down Church Street, however, the WESTGATE CO-OP department store is a seven-bay front of painted brick. This was built as the George Inn c. 1750 by Joseph Eayre, the town's bellfounder, and at the second floor, where the Venetian window cuts into the pediment, was the Assembly Room, which had a domed ceiling and musicians' gallery (removed in 1983). Opposite, the former ROYAL OAK is good Domestic Revival of c. 1885 and has a free classical doorcase of some ambition. After that No. 42 (A. Freeman), a low C16 half-timbered house with closely spaced studs, extensively restored in 1958, when C18 mathematical tiles were removed. It probably extended further w originally. Nice moulded bressumer with a motif of a furled leaf, found also at Corner House, Southoe (q.v.). Reset window in the e wall, from No. 9 South Street. Behind this, towards the church, the former BOYS' SCHOOL (now day centre) by S. S. Teulon, 1858–60. After this, further up High Street, a red brick building of two bays, free Jacobean with a big gable and a bow at first floor. Finally, to the corner of South Street, an egregious red brick rebuilding of 1970 on the site of the Corn Exchange of 1863 (by *Bellamy & Hardy* of Lincoln).

NEW STREET was new in the early C19 and still has something of that character, e.g. the former MUNICIPAL OFFICES on the W side, with recessed arched windows at first floor, and the little terrace of three cottages further up on the opposite side with their pretty timber porches.

E from the centre, in HUNTINGDON STREET, CRESSENER HOUSE is C17, a timber-framed farmhouse with gables but cased in C19 brick. The same is true of HALL PLACE in CAMBRIDGE STREET, which also has gabled wings. Its good Late Georgian doorcase and sash windows in the centre suggest a refacing by *c.* 1800. Two-storey canted bays at the rear. The structure is undoubtedly older, for this was the original Hall Place, before it was superseded in the early C18 by the mansion off Church Street (*see* above). The E end is a mid-C19 rebuilding.

Some Garden Suburb type of yellow brick houses in CROMWELL GARDENS, designed for the council by *Barry Parker*, *c.* 1920–1. They are the customary regular pairs with hipped roofs but some (Nos. 30 etc.) are designed with projecting wings ending in kneelered gables. Before this, set back from Cambridge Road, FRANCIS HOUSE (formerly Longsands) is early C19 with Greek Doric portico and cantilevered stair inside, but otherwise spoiled.

Former PAINE'S FLOUR MILL, Bedford Street. By *Edward J. Paine*, 1890. A compact but soaring cluster, working up to a mighty NE tower with a corbelled top capped by a steep red tile roof behind a parapet; a chimneyshaft provided a riposte to this at the SW corner but has been cut down. Walls of yellow brick with Gothic windows and polychrome decoration in blue and red like needlework patterns. Converted to housing *c.* 2000.

SAWTRY

Originally a polyfocal village, with three churches in 1086 and separate settlements on both sides of the Great North Road, but coalesced into one from the end of the medieval period. At that time it stood at the end of one of the great droving roads from the N. Intensively built up since *c.* 1970.

ALL SAINTS. 1880 by *A. W. Blomfield*, following the demolition of the earlier church on this site and the church of St Andrew (*see* below). With a very steep bellcote of tricky details. Old materials were much used and improved, e.g. the two-bay arcade of the N chapel, the late C13 N aisle W window with bar tracery, and one straight-headed N window with ogee-headed tracery. Heaped outside the S aisle W end, a number of C13 ARCHITECTURAL FRAGMENTS from Sawtry Abbey (*see* below). Inside, from the same source, some TILES, C13 and C14. – STAINED GLASS. In two chancel windows, English and Continental fragments from the Manor House of Sawtry Beaumes. C15, C16 and C17, including ten heads and Stuart royal arms, the setting devised in 1905 by *S. Inskip Ladds*. – N chapel E window by *W. Webb*, 1864. – MONUMENTS. Four C13 coffin lids with foliated crosses are displayed at the W end. – Brass to Sir William le Moyne, who owned one of Sawtry's three manors, †1404 and wife (chancel). Outstandingly good, in line-work as well as interpretation. The figures are 4 ft 6 in. (1.4 metres) long and his head rests on his helm, a half-length figure of a monk with a scourge. At her feet a perky lapdog. The setting is Alwalton marble.

Sawtry, All Saints, brass to Sir William le Moyne †1404 and wife.

St Andrew's Cemetery, 400 yds e of All Saints by the Old North Road. The overgrown and unkempt site of St Andrew. Some large mid- to later c18 headstones, artisan Rococo, including one special one to Mary Andrews †1756, with the deceased on a bed and two flanking cherubs with torches standing on pedestals with memento mori.

In the fields between All Saints and the cemetery are earthworks of the medieval village, including a moated site. nw of the church at the junction of Church Lane and Tinker's Lane, a couple of timber-framed cottages indicate the shift of settlement by the late c17, possibly retreating from the fen edge. The heart of the present village is 100 yds further nw around a triangular green. Most of the few notable buildings are here. Best is The Manor House, n of the green in High Street, set back in a large garden. It is L-plan, the front range of three wide bays under a tall, mansard roof. Pedimented doorcase of refined Neoclassical details with Ionic half-pilasters. Good plasterwork in Adam style to the drawing room and a little more in same taste to the (altered) staircase. Complete range of contemporary outbuildings at rear. A little later but in the same gault brick, in Tinker's Lane, e of the green, is a seductive five-bay house, also called The Manor. Open pedimented door, and behind it a staircase with stick balusters and curved rail. Its former tack room, in the outbuildings, has some medieval fragments reset, including two heads.

Sawtry Community College, Fen Lane. 1961–3 by *S. M. Holloway*, Huntingdon County Architect. Originally Sawtry Village College, the conception taken over from Henry Morris's Cambridgeshire colleges (cf. Glinton) with buildings for shared use between pupils and the villagers. It was led by a warden rather than headteacher. Extended in the mid-1970s to include the Public Library and new teaching facilities.

Manor House Farmhouse, Judith Lane, at the s edge. A funny composition of a low, L-plan thatched cottage with a byre in the e wing and a compact two-storey and attic red brick house adjoining with a curious flat framework of pilaster strips and horizontal bands and big shaped end-gables to the pantiled roof, a rarity now on the fen edge. This has a date 1672 and the initials R^{A}S. Front of three bays, two to the side, and a stair-tower and chimney at the rear. The windows have been altered. The dog-leg stair has slender turned balusters and ascends to the very top of the house.

Sawtry Abbey, 2½ m. sse of the village, close to Abbey Farm. Founded in 1147 for Cistercians by Simon de St Liz, Earl of Northampton and Huntingdon. It was colonized from Warden in Bedfordshire (*see* p. 262). Nothing remains above ground, but the site has been excavated. The church was of the standard Cistercian type with a square-ended chancel and two square-ended chapels e of either transept. The nave had aisles. The refectory was placed in the s range, running n–s, as was also Cistercian standard. An aisled guesthouse stood ssw of the claustral precinct, not in axis with it. St Mary's church, for the parish of Sawtry St Judith, seems to have stood close to the abbey gate and was demolished at the Dissolution. NW of the site is MONK'S LODE, a navigable channel cut from here to Whittlesey Mere (Cambs) in the later C12.

SIBBERTON *see* THORNHAUGH

SIBSON *see* STIBBINGTON

SOMERSHAM 3070

St JOHN. An almost completely E.E. church, perhaps so sweepingly done because at Somersham was a palace of the Bishops of Ely. Externally the chancel has single widely spaced lancets along its sides above a moulded sill and a group of over-restored lancets in the E wall. The priest's door and the S and the N aisle doorways have mature stiff-leaf (N badly preserved) and arches of many mouldings. Inside, above the N door is also the remains of C13 painted decoration of jointed masonry and part of a floral border. The windows of the aisles are Perp, as is the clerestory, although the E bay of the S aisle (organ chamber) is Perp of 1885 (covering a genuine Perp chancel window). Only the W tower with its spike is later. One W window looks *c.* 1300, and the bell-openings are Dec. The weathervane on the tower spike and the cube-and-ball sundial on the S porch are both C17. Internally the four-bay arcades have piers of four shafts and four thin polygonal shafts in the diagonals and typically E.E. moulded capitals. The crenellation is of course a Perp recutting. The bases, except those of the responds, are also recut. Double-hollow-chamfered arches with a step between the chamfers. Moreover E.E. tower arch with keeling, chancel arch with keeling, and PISCINAS in the chancel, S aisle (both double), and N aisle with trefoil arches. In the chancel the SEDILIA have responds in the form of stiff-leaf corbels. The chancel side lancets are surrounded by a continuous thin roll, but the E lancets are fully shafted with rings to the shafts. The nave roof is Perp, late C14, and has a large number of bosses carved with foliage, beasts and faces, including a king and queen. The structure consists of tie-beams on arched braces, the braces sweeping up in the same curvature to the ridge-piece, a very fine effect. It was restored in 1931 by *William Weir*. – FONT. Given in the 1840s. Overblown C13 style. – PEWS. By *J. Oldrid Scott & Son*, 1915. – STALLS. 1927. Late Arts and Crafts, with linenfold and a foliage frieze. – CHANDELIER. Of brass. 1787. Two tiers of arms. The centre is of a very Baroque, baluster-like shape. – BRASS. The indent only of a Priest, early C16, 2 ft (0.6 metres) long (chancel floor). – STAINED GLASS. E window. Christ in Majesty flanked by

Warriors of the Old and New Dispensation. 1922 by *T. F. Curtis, Ward & Hughes*; the N aisle W is an individual memorial by the same firm, 1916. – MONUMENTS. Anthony Hammond †1680. Big black-and-white tablet with Ionic columns, volutes to the sides and his achievement supported by cherubs. Undoubtedly by *William Stanton*. – Fleet Surgeon Percival Kent Nix †1914. In the style of a century earlier, his bicorne hat and dress sword rest atop the tablet.

In the churchyard, a circular DOVECOTE with conical roof, originally associated with the parsonage which stood here until the early C19.

N of this on the High Street is the former TITHE BARN, impressive in scale but rather ruthlessly converted to housing. The bishop's palace lay S of the church. The MOAT remains but the buildings seem to have been pulled down entirely by the late C18. The early C19 is architecturally most apparent in the village as a whole, the consequence of major fires in 1815 and 1824, see e.g. MULBERRY HOUSE in the High Street, dated 1825, which has very fine cast-iron gates with crescent-moon finials. In Parkhall Road, the former WESLEYAN CHAPEL of 1845. Entirely gault brick with moulded pilasters and a pediment.

SOMERSHAM HOUSE, Rectory Lane. The former rectory of 1819–21 (by *Daniel Blacklee*, surveyor and builder of Cambridge), in gault brick with a low slate roof and broad door under an arched fanlight. The living of Somersham was held by the Regius Professor of Divinity at Cambridge University; the house was occupied by a paid curate.

SOUTHOE

ST LEONARD. Essentially Perp outside, the nave, aisles and chancel all with battlements. The nave is as broad as it is long. Much of the walling is brown cobbles but the N aisle, of *c.* 1460, is a little more ornate than the rest and of stone; its E end was a chapel for the Rous family. The Late Perp clerestory and the tower are both brick, the latter with ashlar buttresses, quoins and pinnacles. There were bequests for the tower in 1505 and 1518. The odd thing is its position, built into the W bay of the N aisle. The nave has a Perp W window and door with the initials of John Baldwin, who held the advowson in the late C16. But the S doorway is Norman, *c.* 1100, with about as many motifs as could be accommodated. One order of shafts with trellis decoration. In the l. lozenges one pellet each, in the r. a cross of pellets. One capital with a kind of stylized upright shrub, the other with the same trellis with pellets. Abacus with a lozenge-chain, roll moulding covered with saltire crosses or lozenges, extrados with saltire crosses, hoodmould with billet, tympanum with chequer and inside with chevron for good measure. There is another fragment of sawtooth carved string course on the aisle w wall. The deep chancel arch is Norman too. Responds with angle shafts, small, coarse scroll capitals, which derive from Ely. Pointed arch with a step and two slight chamfers, perhaps a little later. Of the late C13 the chancel, which has not only a lancet but also Y-tracery. The lancet has a rere-arch with continuous keeled moulding. Of the same time the (much restored) s arcade: three bays, round piers, double-chamfered arches. The N arcade is Perp, of standard elements, the w arch is preserved despite the insertion of the tower. Tomb recess in the N wall with ogee arch. – MONUMENT. Coffin lid with a foliated cross and the bust of a priest. It has initials, identifying it as the rector, John of Clipston, †1334.

CORNER HOUSE, No. 51 High Street, facing the E end of the church, is much restored but has a C16 gabled cross-wing with jetty beam carved with leaf motifs. ¼ m. w, overlooking its small park, the OLD RECTORY has a handsome gault brick E front of seven bays and two storeys with a stucco sill band, cornice, panelled parapet and Doric porch. The date must be c. 1800. Big, plain staircase inserted within the earlier back range, which faced w and has mid- to late C18 sashes, a sweetly detailed doorcase and little bow.

MIDLOE GRANGE, 1 m. further w in a solitary moated setting, is the former manor house of Midloe. Probably built c. 1590, when Robert Payne of St Neots acquired the manor. Hall and two gabled cross-wings, originally jettied; the timber frame with brick nogging is revealed inside. Slightly remodelled in the C18, when the N wing was extended. Gabled stair-turret, probably of the same time. Former parlour in the s wing, with a large fireplace with limestone jambs. Later, the two-tier oven. Above this, a chamber with impressive barrel-vaulted ceiling, one collar truss exposed; cf. Bodsey House, Ramsey Forty Foot, and Town Farmhouse, Old Weston. Late C16 stone fireplace, with recut ornament.

SOUTHORPE see WALCOT HALL

SPALDWICK

1070

Granted to the Bishop of Lincoln in 1109 and from that time the centre of his Soke of Spaldwick. An episcopal residence and manorial complex probably occupied the open fields now surrounding the church and were enclosed by a ditch. The pattern of the village, which is a single straight street dividing at a green by the entrance to the churchyard, may indicate a planned settlement (cf. Somersham).

ST JAMES. The connection with the Bishop of Lincoln would explain the fascinating w tower of the C14, 152 ft (46.3 metres) high. The doorway has continuous mouldings, and on the stage above are lozenge-shaped windows to N, S and W with flowing tracery, a typically Dec conceit. Above, two-light transomed bell-openings and a broach spire with three tiers of lucarnes. On the broach tips are little beasts. The stair terminates at the second stage under a stone vault with chamfered ribs and a boss. A second stair to the belfry in the NW corner is a later insertion. The oldest part of the church is the Norman N doorway with continuous mouldings, including one of stylized beakhead (cf. Stow Longa, also in the Soke of Spaldwick, and Little Stukeley and Toseland, both of which also have Lincoln connections). Hoodmould with billets. The masonry on this side (brown cobbles) is Norman too but tidied up. The chancel is latest C13 – or is the chancel arch with its cone-shaped responds a little earlier? The windows have excellent tracery, of the stage just before ogees appeared, i.e. pointed-trefoiled lights, pointed trefoils but also a large circle and rounded trefoils. Good headstops inside. The S arcade is no later. Four bays, round piers with round or octagonal abaci, bits of nailhead, double-chamfered arches, and coarse nailhead in the hoodmoulds. Wide Late Perp S aisle and S chapel. One-bay arches to the aisle and chancel. The clerestory is also Perp, fine small two-light transomed windows, but the parapet brick (C17?), and the unduly cumbersome nave roof of 1846 by *W. G. Habershon*. – FONT. C12. Octagonal with step-chamfered angles. – SCREEN. To the S aisle, Perp, only bits original and apparently partly assembled from the former chancel screen. Cresting of two crowns and frieze of fruiting vines. – STAINED GLASS. Medieval fragments in the S aisle E window. In the nave windows *J. Powell & Sons* quarries of various designs, dating from the restoration by *R. W. Edis*, 1862–3. Heraldic glass in the clerestory, 1918, by *Heaton, Butler & Bayne*.

At the W end of the village is a small C15 BRIDGE of three arches, the middle one with chamfered ribs. Nearby, CHURCH HOUSE, the rectory of the 1840s, rather picturesque despite its size and of good red brick with moulded details. Big roofs with fishscale tiling, tall chimneys and curly bargeboards. Along the main street, E of the church and green, first the village SMITHY, C19, brick-built with a curved corner and chimney. Then THE GEORGE INN, jettied and gabled, with, on the upper floor, paintings of single figures about 31 in. (80 cm) high. The best-preserved figure carries a long bow and a long arrow. The date must be temp. Henry VIII and shows the E end to come first, including the cross-wing, then extended W in the C17. Separate barn to the W, now incorporated. Just beyond this a C19 brick forge. Next E, of similar date but remarkably decayed, bent, and unloved at the time of writing, is MANOR FARMHOUSE, a house of two phases: to the r. a C16 part of five bays with a jetty (now propped by posts) and a central stone chimney between kitchen and parlour and a lobby entry in line with it. At back an outshot for service rooms contained under a cat-slide roof. To the l. two bays added in the C17, also jettied, for a tiny additional dwelling with its own entrance and in the end bay a granary and cheese room above it.

Then THE LIMES, a late C17 farmhouse, red brick, with hipped roof and a square porch that has a gable. This porch and the angles of the house have brick pilasters in two tiers (cf. the Swan and Salmon, Little Stukeley, of 1676). Inside, the staircase is placed behind an entrance lobby and has wavy splat balusters. The windows are late C18 sashes and no doubt there were originally casements in raised surrounds, as one finds across the road, and a little further on, at IVY HOUSE. This is more advanced, i.e. it has a hipped roof and flat five-bay front and giant angle pilasters. Also its doorway carries a pediment. But the middle bay is still flanked by two tiers of pilasters, and the windows have broad raised brick surrounds. Platband across the middle and continuing down the sides of the rear wings. The kitchen was originally separate from the wing. The front is dated 1688 but inside a fireplace has been found with Tudor arch and the date 1582 (now covered up). Good late C17 staircase from ground floor to attic, with turned balusters and ball finials. Finally, the former BAPTIST CHAPEL of 1844, set back from the street with its former manse at the entrance. Quite big, with a pediment across the front, and beneath it a group of three arched windows. Projecting eaves to the sides. Converted to a house c. 2000.

STANGROUND see PETERBOROUGH

STEEPLE GIDDING

1080

Just the church and former rectory (of 1858) on their own at the end of the track that leads to Little Gidding church. In the fields descending s are the remains of the former settlement, including the probable moated site of the house of the Cottons, lords of the manor.

ST ANDREW (Churches Conservation Trust). The steeple is rather underfed. The narrow arch towards the nave is of three chamfers and dies against the imposts. This, and the whole tower, is Dec. Recessed Perp spire; shortish and with two tiers of lucarnes (restored 1899). Dec also the s arcade of four bays (standard elements) which embraces the tower, and the chancel, the s aisle, the clerestory, and the straight-headed N nave windows. The s aisle E window still has intersecting tracery and the chancel SW window has a salamander carved on the hoodmould. Only the s doorway is much earlier, though perhaps reassembled at the same time as the rest. It is partly late C12 and partly C13. Outer arch with chevron at right angles to the wall. Inner arch pointed. The capitals of the colonnettes have one normal stiff-leaf, the other oddly stylized and interlocked stiff-leaf. At that time the advowson was held by Ramsey Abbey. Porch 1872–3 by *A. W. Blomfield*; his restoration makes a clear impression inside. The E window is of the same date by *W. H. Constable.** – MONUMENTS. C13 COFFIN SLAB. A large example of the genre. – Mrs Mary Kinyon (née Cotton) †1714. Attributed to the *Chevalier Claude David*, which would explain the 'eccentricities of form and composition' (GF) that make it look wrongly assembled, with a grey sarcophagus supporting a stack of panels with volutes and a bust on top. – Sir John Cotton †1752. Large, but mostly an inscription plate. He was the last of his line and it records his descent from the Scottish kings (cf. Conington).

<!-- 0090 -->

STIBBINGTON

The parish is Sibson-cum-Sibbington, of which the Sibson part lies on the A1, and the picture is further muddled historically by the fact that the NW part, by the Nene crossing, is in every respect part of Wansford (q.v.).

ST JOHN THE BAPTIST. The church as a whole represents 1848–9, the work of *S. S. Teulon* for the Duke of Bedford and the Rev. William Wing, uncle of the Duke's agent and surveyor at Thorney (q.v.). To Teulon belongs the idea of the broad three-gabled front, where previously there was a C15 tower, and the lancet fenestration of the sides and also the N transept which inside has a spiral stair in a turret to the organ loft. Medieval are the chancel (Dec windows) and a very little of the Norman W doorway with two orders of columns, rolls, billet and rough diaper work. But the chancel arch is a real, serious early C12 piece. The responds have big, heavy two-scallop capitals and the arch one step and one big half-roll. As for the chancel, the E wall has two long lancets and a large quatrefoil over. Rere-arches inside. But inside more is medieval, namely the later C12 N arcade and the late C13 S arcade. The former has two, the latter three bays, but the Norman arches cannot originally have been as wide as they are now. The piers are round, the abaci square with nicked corners, the arches single-stepped. The S arcade has standard elements. – FONT. Octagonal, with arched panels, the arches standing on thin colonnettes sunk into the angles. The date may be the late C12. – CREED AND COMMANDMENT BOARDS. Mid-C19. – STAINED GLASS. S chancel E, 'Faith & Hope', by *Jones & Willis*, 1899. – S window by *J. Powell & Sons* (the design by *E. Penwarden*), 1923. – MONUMENT. In the chancel, the defaced effigy of a priest, probably

*The 'ALTAR CLOTHS. One large mid-C16 piece, Flemish, with the Virgin and angels, and one small, early C17 one, also Flemish, with a hunting scene', mentioned in the first edition of this guide, were removed before the church passed to the Churches Conservation Trust.

C14. Fragments of cross-heads. – Capt. John Wright R.N.
†1785. Tablet with Adamesque and Gothick elements and
martial emblems in the pediment.

STIBBINGTON HALL. The former manor house, with the finest
Jacobean façade in Huntingdonshire. It is dated 1625 on the
porch, and the inscription 'Deo trin-uni sit Gloria' is added.
It was begun for Peter Edwards (†1619), whose shield is over
the door; he bought the manor from the Bevilles of Chesterton.
The façade is on the E-plan with gables, canted bay windows
in the wings, dormers in the recessed parts, and a shaped gable
on the square porch. The porch is a relation of that formerly
at Chesterton House (*see* Lynch Lodge, Alwalton). All windows
are mullioned and transomed. The house is altered and
enlarged on all other sides (one rainwater head dated 1835)
and has inside just some panelling, some stone fireplaces and
a staircase with slender turned balusters and finials on the
newels.* A very handsome gateway led into the front garden.
It has strapwork bordered by truncated ogee curves on the top
enclosing a circle. The Neo-Jacobean STABLES are by *Teulon*
(whose sketch is in the British Architectural Library, although
not as executed).

The OLD RECTORY, s of the church, and STIBBINGTON
MANOR, w of the church, have flat fronts with mullioned and
mullioned and transomed windows, typical of the early C17
and with the entrances placed off-centre.

STIBBINGTON CENTRE, at the entrance to the village, is the
former school, the gift of the 8th Duke of Bedford in 1871–2
and therefore very probably by *Henry Clutton*. Two large chimneys on the front.

WANSFORD STATION, ½ m. SSE. A fine Ketton stone job by
John Livock, 1845, for the Peterborough & Northampton
Railway. Jacobean gables and arches to the ground floor.
Closed in 1957, but the platforms and railway yard have been
resurrected for the Nene Valley Railway. On the opposite platform the former station building from Barnwell (Northants)
of 1884. w of the station, a TUNNEL, 616 yds (⅓ m.) long, with
stone portal in Romanesque style and a brick-lined vault. The
line's engineer was *Robert Stephenson*. By the level crossing, on
the old Great North Road, railway COTTAGES of similar date
and SIGNAL BOX of 1912.

SIBSON MANOR HOUSE, ¾ m. SSE, by the A1. Like Stibbington
Manor, a flat front with mullioned and mullioned and transomed
windows and the doorway placed off-centre. The fenestration
here, however, is perfectly even. Stack of four chimneys in a
line to the w end. The house must be of the early to mid C17
but was rebuilt after a fire in 1847, the date of the rear wing.†

---

*The 'domestic panels of *c.* 1535 with heads in medallions and a Jacobean overmantel with caryatids and some inlay' noted in the first edition of this guide have
been removed.
†The RCHM reported medieval stonework in a summerhouse, thought to come
from the demolished church for Sibson.

SIBSON INN, on the w side of the A1, was formerly the Wheat-sheaf Alehouse, rebuilt in 1762–4 for the 4th Duke of Bedford (stone mason *Thomas Thompson*, carpenter *William Bradshaw*) but looking rather earlier. Extended N and at the back in the early C19.

STIBBINGTON HOUSE. *See* Wansford.

STILTON

ST MARY. Tall Perp w tower. The thick arch to the nave has ribs rising from two pairs of responds whose capitals are castellated. The ashlar chancel is of 1808 by *John Johnson*, but in all its details is of 1857, when the church was restored by *Edward Browning*. It was then also that most of the other external features, including the whole of the N aisle, received their present appearance. Inside it is different. Both the three-bay arcades are of the early C13, N a little before s, for N has single-step arches, s double-chamfered ones. But both are still round. The piers are also round on both sides, except an octagonal one in the w bay on the N side, and the w arches are later, in order to connect with the tower, but it should be noted that the SW respond has nailhead, i.e. cannot be later than *c.* 1300. At the E end of the N aisle a blocked arch, showing there was a chapel. It was curtailed in 1808 and rebuilt in 1993 as the Church Room. Chancel arch of 1887–8. – STAINED GLASS. E window by *Clayton & Bell*, 1867. – N aisle, by *William B. Simpson & Sons*, 1897. – MONUMENTS. In the churchyard, a table tomb of *c.* 1800, with outstanding rustic Neoclassical motifs and carved reliefs, one of Time emptying his hourglass over the head of the commemorated, the other of a disconsolate cherub; the sculptor has signed it: *Andrews* of Wisbech. By him also the big square tomb alongside, for Lockhart Thornton †1810, with fluted pilasters at the corners and slate panels in the sides.

Stilton stood on the Great North Road but was bypassed by the A1 in 1958. Bypassing has done a lot of good to places like Wansford and Stamford, but at Stilton the street is perfunctorily cut off at its s end and when Pevsner visited it seemed to have left Stilton 'in a sad state of dereliction and dispiritedness'. Within a few years the BELL INN, its finest building, was given up. The date on the wide gable at the s end is 1642 and it is of an earlier tradition than the Haycock at Wansford, i.e. mullioned, two-storey canted bay windows. One s of the central carriage arch rises into a dormer and no doubt all three others were the same, but these have had sash windows since the C18. The N bay is brick and may be of 1736, the date of plans for rebuilding at this end which are attributed to *Charles Bridgeman*, the royal gardener, who owned the inn. This part is now as carefully restored in 1989, when the entire NE wing was replaced for hotel use, by *Saunders Boston*. Gracing the front a lovely and exceedingly large early C18 curly wrought-iron bracket for the sign. Distances to London, Buckden, Huntingdon and Stamford are inscribed inside the arch. Inside the bar (s of the arch), a C17 winder staircase against the chimneystack and a C18 stair also. From *c.* 1730 Stilton cheese was distributed from the inn by its enterprising owner, Cooper Thornhill, whose grave is in the churchyard; when the trade outstripped local production it was superseded by makers in Leicestershire and Nottinghamshire. The C18 plans show a grocer's shop in the property to the s.

Opposite is the former ANGEL INN, originally another fine coaching stop but badly restored after a fire in the 1970s when it was reduced from three storeys to two, and now further disfigured by inappropriate porches. Venetian window over the carriage arch and above this originally a lunette window, which has been reset in the end bay. In this bay also a carved stone sign dated 1741. Its neighbour is a stately five-bay brick house, also with a Venetian window in the centre, but later. The best domestic building is STONELEIGH, N of The Bell, a well-kept Georgian ashlar-faced house, also of five bays with round-arched doorway with fanlight. It is one room deep with a brick kitchen wing at rear (big fireplace and axial beam inside with hooks). One room has early C18 panelling and cupboards with painted shell-heads. Down Fen Lane, MRS WORTHINGTON'S ALMHOUSES, Gothic of 1868 by *Robert Hutchinson* for the landlady of the Angel.

STIRTLOE *see* BUCKDEN

STONELY

1060

A hamlet 1 m. SE of Kimbolton. On Ford's Lane, THE COTTAGE which Lt Frederick Welstead, one of Nelson's officers, built for himself before 1815. It is thatched, with a bargeboarded gable, a perky oriel below that, a tree-trunk veranda and porch and diamond-shaped stacks.

1 m. N of the main road is the site of the small Augustinian PRIORY of Stonely. All that is visible now is PRIORY COTTAGE, made in the C17 from original masonry. Single-chamfered doorway. The arch is four-centred. The roof, however, is three bays of an original five reused and with the remains of arcade posts showing it comes from an monastic aisled barn. Beth Davis dates it to the C14. On the NW front the wall has been raised into a crenellated parapet of C19 yellow brick, suggesting it was remade as an eyecatcher in views from Kimbolton (cf. Warren House, Kimbolton).

STONELY GRANGE, Easton Road. By *George Devey*, 1870–4, for Col. Montresor. Domestic Revival, red brick with a huddle of plastered gables on the asymmetrical elevations, some with curly bargeboards, and tall panelled chimneys. Now flats.

STOW LONGA

ST BOTOLPH. The church is outside the village. It is quite large, expressive of its role as the ecclesiastical centre of the Bishop of Lincoln's Soke of Spaldwick. The church may well have been important before that. The Norman tympanum of the priest's doorway is more barbaric than almost any other. The centre is a mermaid, and l. and r. are quadrupeds of uncertain identity (cf. Little Paxton). This may be CII, reset in an early CI2 arch of coarse chevron surround. Wildly detailed capitals of the octagonal nook-shafts below. The rest seems no earlier than the CI3. E.E. S doorway with three orders of colonnettes with very damaged stiff-leaf capitals. Arch with hollow chamfers. The arcades are E.E. too, N being a little earlier than S. Four bays, round piers, double-chamfered arches, those of the S arcade with broaches. The N aisle was never widened. The aisle windows partly straight-headed Dec (S), partly Perp (N). E.E. again the chancel arch, probably of the same time as the N arcade. The respond shafts start high up; there was probably a stone screen here. W tower with pairs of transomed two-light bell-openings. No spire. The tower can be dated c. 1500 from an inscription to Robert Becke (S wall) and the arms of Bishop Smith of Lincoln (1496–1514; W wall). The chancel was restored in squared stone in 1880, the nave clerestory and roof rebuilt in 1900–1 by J. Ladds & Son. – FONT. Octagonal, but the round support made up of two E.E. capitals. – SCREEN. Perp, with wide one-light divisions, and tracery to the dado. Re-erected in 1880. Its E side incorporates a bench and a STALL END with a poppyhead. – REREDOS. This incorporates one panel with reticulated tracery brought in from an Oxfordshire church. – SOUTH DOOR. With a little tracery. – STAINED GLASS. Small bits in two N aisle windows. – MONUMENT. On the chancel floor, a slab with an indent for a floriated cross. A large example of the genre. Tablet to Sir Thomas Maples †1634. Classical stone surround and brass inscription in the frieze. Indent for a missing brass. The coat of arms on top is not his. On the village green, the VILLAGE CROSS. Moulded base and part of the shaft, CI5? Odd ball top (S. Inskip Ladds gave it a taller shaft with a cross-head in 1902; since removed).

SUTTON [P]

A charming small village between the A47 and the Nene.

ST MICHAEL. Built as a chapel of ease to Castor. The principal item of interest is the fine Norman chancel arch, by the Castor workshop, with two strong shafts (cf. Upton(P)) and capitals with beaded interlace and masks. The date probably c. 1120. The arches with fat rolls, however, are of 1865–8, when the arch was unblocked and the chancel restored by *Alfred Sykes* of Milton (the roof typical of his style). S arcade of *c.* 1200. Two bays, circular pier, simple moulded capital, square abacus with nicks, double-chamfered round arches. A little later the S chapel with pairs of tall lancets and ballflower outside. One bay, semi-octagonal responds, pointed double-chamfered arch. By the S door large C12 BENCH END of a crouching lion, very well carved. It carried a creature on its back. The bench is recorded in the *Archaeological Journal*, 1861. Perp roof, and clerestory. Less interest externally. Bellcote originally of the double type, perhaps C13, but rebuilt by *John Thompson & Sons*, 1914. The vestry and S door have shouldered arches with lintels of reused chevron work. Along the S side of the nave, reset C12 corbel heads. – STAINED GLASS. E window (Good Samaritan), *c.* 1870, and S chapel E by *T. Cox & Sons*. – W window, 1869 by *Frederick Preedy*. – NE, small St Michael, by *Kempe & Co.*, 1918. – MONUMENTS. W. H. Hopkinson †1851. Tablet with laurel, cross and open Bible. By *S. Manning*.

In the churchyard, Rev. J. H. Clarke †1846. TABLE TOMB with Gothic details. S of the churchyard is a DOVECOTE (dated 1803, associated with The Grange, *see* below). Rebuilt into its wall, a CROSS-SHAFT with typical Anglo-Saxon interlace. E of the church is tiny CHURCH COTTAGE, C17, but with a reused chevron strip above the fireplace. Outdoor privy.

The largest house is THE GRANGE, or manor house, W of the church in large gardens. Neo-Tudor style in rough-faced stone, the three-bay centre with gablets and shallow wings projecting l. and r., the latter blind, both with central stacks; 'recently . . . erected . . . by William Hopkinson FSA'* (*Archaeological Journal*, 1861), who reset the two-light C13 window with dog-tooth moulding in the bay r. of centre, but remodelled in 1880 for his son the Rev. William Hopkinson (terracotta datestone with his initials). Earlier outbuildings including a granary, dated 1786 and extensive farmyard, now a separate dwelling.

At the opposite end of the village is MANOR FARM, a handsome hip-roofed job of 1700, restored in 1900. Five bays, mullion windows and shallow projections at the ends.

TETWORTH HALL

Waresley-cum-Tetworth

2050

Built in 1710 for John Pedley, M.P. (†1722), on the edge of the Greensand Ridge. Red brick, five bays, two storeys over a basement, with a parapet, giant angle pilasters of stone and a central stone doorway flanked by Corinthian demi-columns

---

* It was Hopkinson who purchased the manor of Little Gidding (q.v.) in 1848 and paid for Clutton's restoration of the chapel. See VCH v. 3 and *Notes & Queries*, 22 June 1883.

supporting a segmental pediment with a cartouche containing the arms of Pedley and his wife. The windows are later c18, as is most of the lower E kitchen wing and the two-storey bow on the w side. w loggia by *Marshall Sisson*, 1961. Double-pile plan inside. Much original panelling in every room, bolection-moulded in the former dining room and raised-and-fielded in the hall. The fireplaces also bolection-moulded with keystones. Good staircase with twisted balusters and a Corinthian newel, divided from the hall by two Corinthian columns. At first floor a fine doorcase to the room on the s front with a swan-neck pediment, and a semi-domed lobby to the rooms on the N front.

THORNEY [P]

Like Eye (q.v.), a gravel island in the fens. It is two things: the remnant of one of the five great Fenland abbeys, dissolved in 1539, and the model village instigated by the reformer 7th Duke of Bedford, to whose ancestor, the 1st Earl of Bedford, Thorney had been granted in 1550. It was the 4th and 5th Earls who drained the land to which the much enlarged parish subsequently owed its prosperity.

St Mary and St Botolph.* Thorney was reputedly settled by hermits or anchorites, from which its ancient name 'Ancarig' ('island of anchorites') derives. The community was destroyed in the Danish raid of 870, giving rise to a cult of the 'Thorney Martyrs'. In 973 a monastery was founded for Benedictine monks by Aethelwold, Bishop of Winchester, and granted relics of the body of St Botolph. After the Conquest, Abbot Guenther of Le Mans rebuilt the church. He must have begun immediately after he had been elected in 1085, for in 1089 the monks could move in. By 1098 the chancel and crossing tower were ready. The church was completed in 1110, though consecrated only in 1128. That puts the building phase concurrent with the transepts at Ely. All that remains of it is part of the nave, shorn of its aisles and of its E end. The total original length is estimated to have been nearly 300 ft (91 metres). The crossing, with crossing tower, the transepts and chancel were taken down by the 1st Earl of Bedford and the materials reputedly used in the building of Trinity College and Corpus Christi Chapel, Cambridge, *c.* 1580. The present E end, of chancel flanked by short transepts, is by *Edward Blore*, in the Norman style, 1839–41. The original fragment, inadequate as it may be, is yet very impressive, owing chiefly to its tall w front. This is a composite structure to which the c12, the c15 and the c17

---

*The revision of this entry is indebted to Justin Ayton's MA Thesis, Courtauld Institute, London (1998), and to his other observations on the post-Reformation building.

have contributed. Norman are the angle turrets, starting as broad buttresses and continued octagonal. These have stepped angles and originally separated the w end of the nave from that of the lower aisles and may originally have had spirelets like the e end of Peterborough Cathedral, which was begun just a few years later. Blocked doors from the spiral stairs inside the buttresses served galleries, roughly corresponding with the gallery, clerestory and roof, and indicate that the windows of the w front were originally in tiers, perhaps like the transepts at Norwich. The buttresses now end in Perp battlements and between the battlements are ogee-headed niches with local saints. With this goes the full-height blocked opening for the w window. Probably Perp also the doorway with panelled soffits and, l. and r. of this, blank arcades carved with ogee heads and a frieze above decorated with heads like fleurons. But at least some of the details, the blocking of the w window and the insertion of the present one and the entrance door with its ogee-headed arch, must be of 1638, the date inscribed when the ruin was restored as the parish church. All this is in a typical imitation-Perp of which a contemporary example is Peterhouse Chapel at Cambridge.

Along the n and s sides the design of the Norman arcades can be studied, as the arcade openings were blocked in 1638, when the aisles were pulled down. One bay of the Norman clerestory also survives, a plain arched window (blocked) on the s side, but decorated by billet friezes on the n. The interior elevation is quite evident when one enters the church. The arcades, which may have gone on for three extra bays up to the crossing, are remarkably tall and narrow, so that although the nave is not spacious the original effect would have been one of impressive loftiness. They are designed with alternating supports, but the principal motif, the shaft rising without interruption from floor to ceiling, is the same everywhere. The design towards the arch openings, however, differs between segments of fat circular projection and three stepped shafts – just as at Ely. The arches are single-stepped, but the capitals are scalloped. The gallery openings are not subdivided (cf. e.g. Colchester St Botolph and Norwich). They are now filled with C15 tracery, perhaps from the former clerestory. The piers have two shafts towards the openings, and the arches two roll mouldings. The capitals have early examples of the primitive volute type, notably in the e bays on both sides, where they might denote the position of the pulpitum; one (SE) has a criss-cross pattern of Normandy derivation. But others are also scalloped and others simply cushions. w gallery removed in 1880 during restoration by *Henry Clutton*. – ORGAN LOFT (s transept), inserted 1888 (organ by *William Hill & Son*). – Handsome brass eagle LECTERN of 1904, with spiral supports and gemstones – STAINED GLASS. The e window is a very remarkable work by *George Austin Sen.*, 1838. Its details derive directly from the windows of *c.* 1220 in the Trinity Chapel at Canterbury Cathedral, which Austin repaired and extended

121

c. 1819–40, so this is a valuable record of their original appearance. Nineteen roundels showing miracles at Becket's tomb. Commissioned by the 6th Duke; reset by Blore. – C15 German panels reset in the nave windows, probably from Cologne (one inscribed with the name of Goddart Hauyser); including a Pietà, the denial of St Peter, supper at Emmaus etc. Possibly acquired in the mid C17 by the 4th Earl of Bedford.

In the CHURCHYARD a good many fine late C18 and early C19 headstones. Ann Burrow (née Wallis) †1820, NE of the chancel, has a relief of the sacrifice of Abraham.

The extensive monastic buildings, much developed during the course of the C13 and early C14, have gone. The cloister of the abbey extended to where now lies the pretty turfed square to the S of the church, which was also formerly the market place. On the E side of the square, two stately houses, CHERITON HOUSE (formerly the vicarage), stone, of 1728, double-pile of three bays and attic, ashlar-faced with later bay windows on the front. The house S of it (No. 2 The Green), looking late C17 but with an C18 facelift, is taller and more impressive with two projecting gabled wings.

On the W side of The Green is the most important house in the village, the site of which, in a survey of 1574, already contained 'a dwelling house of stone in length 60 feet . . .'.* That very probably refers to the part facing the village street (ABBEY HOUSE, now divided), which seems to have been a hall (l.) with cross-passage and kitchen (r.). Despite C18 refronting with sashes, this is later C16 with gables and mullioned windows (two blocked windows and a fireplace inside). It was doubled in size in 1660 to provide a kitchen wing for the house that stands to the W; on the S front the C17 addition has a two-storey shallow canted bay window, originally one of a pair with the earlier part. For the house of 1660 (THORNEY ABBEY HOUSE), the contract exists between *John Lovin*, mason of Peterborough and the 5th Earl of Bedford, who made Thorney his residence while engaged in the drainage of the Great Level *c.* 1663–85. The house is a square, stone-built, with two storeys, a hipped roof, dormer windows, and one central chimney. The quoins are hewn stone, and so are the windows, with mullion-and-transom crosses and broad frames. They are quite small in proportion to the whole, except on the S and W fronts, where they have been lengthened, and the architraves of the upper windows are contiguous with a platband. The eaves cornice is of a characteristic shape, deep and coved. There are central doorways on three sides, two now blocked, which have odd broad corbels carrying flat pediments. On the E front, two windows are obscured by a short, two-storey, link to the service range. This had a passage running behind an arcaded loggia of three bays with round piers (partly infilled).

*The description of Abbey House is indebted to research by Justin Ayton.

Inside, the house is divided into four rooms on each floor around the central chimney, with the staircase at the NE corner, and entrance vestibules in the centre of the W and S sides. There is clear evidence of a secondary stair having existed between the Hall (NW) and the 'Great Closet' (SW). The plan is quite advanced for its date, even if the exclusion of the kitchen in a separate wing seems archaic. The 'Great Parlour' (SE) has its original panelling incorporating a big fireplace surround with odd and wilful volutes and eared panels, all of a quite remarkable closeness to the panelled rooms at Thorpe Hall (*see* pp. 641–2). Similar fireplace in the corresponding room, the Parlour Chamber, on the first floor (SE), which has volutes to the window architraves. A repetitive motif is a tulip flower in conjunction with the scrolls. The staircase, from ground floor to attic, has sturdy balusters with leaves growing up their lower moulding, a Vitruvian scroll to the string, and heavy square newel posts decorated by hanging-down garlands and ball finials that are repeated as silhouettes on the wall panelling. It is the twin of the subsidiary stair at Thorpe Hall. The doorcases are again in the style of the fireplaces, a style characteristic of East Anglia at that particular moment and matched not only by Peter Mills at Thorpe Hall for Oliver St John but also at Wisbech Castle in Cambridgeshire, the house of *c.* 1658 for John Thurloe, Cromwell's Secretary of State, for which Mills was almost certainly responsible too. Howard Colvin noted that Lovin's contract of 1654 for Thorney only relates to the masonry; the designs for the joinery could thus very easily have been supplied by Mills.

The entrance to the main house is now via a C19 covered passage. But in axis with its former N entrance are sturdy square rusticated GATEPOSTS (cf. Wisbech Castle, Cambs.), with inverted volutes. Equally impressive gatepiers towards the village. Pedimented GATEWAY of similar character in the garden wall to the NW. Former STABLES, N of the house, probably also 1660s but so altered that only the carriage arch and the coping of the gables can be trusted.*

Next to the stables, the buildings of the mid C19 erected by the 7th Duke of Bedford are heralded by the small but ornate former Post Office (formerly incorporating the parish relief office at the N end, and a house for the constable). This is by S. S. *Teulon*,† whom the duke engaged in 1847 to set out plans for his estate village. It is like a plate from Pugin's *Contrasts*. Its counterpart is the former SCHOOL (now Library and Nursery), N of the church, erected by *Teulon* in 1848–51 in the same enchanting Gothic. Schoolrooms for girls and infants (l.) and boys (r.) of the teacher's house, each with open roofs of horseshoe trusses.

---

*Excavations in Abbey Fields S of the gardens have identified a medieval aisled hall.
†Teulon was then at work on Stibbington church for the Rev. William Wing, uncle of Tycho Wing, the duke's agent at Thorney.

Lining the N side of Wisbech Road are terraces of over sixty Bedford estate COTTAGES, made of the yellow bricks produced in the estate brickworks (closed *c.* 1870). Nos. 42–52 comprise three sets of pairs with hipped roofs and charming shaped parapets as links between them. They are probably *c.* 1838 and like Late Georgian improved housing. The rest were set up from 1849 to 1865, and are picturesque but unextravagant Neo-Jacobean, Teulon following the model evolved in the late 1840s for Woburn (Beds., q.v.) and the other estate villages. The largest terrace (W) has shops at each end, one with an attractive veranda. Behind each cottage row is a yard and a continuous range of outhouses (originally with WC and copper) and behind that individual ⅓-acre plots for each tenant to cultivate. Gas lighting and purified water were supplied from the TANK YARD to the N, a remarkably distinguished group that provides the most conspicuous accent of Thorney, in spite of the church, in its WATER TOWER of 1855 by *Teulon*, with *J. Hodgson Jones*, engineer. This is Jacobean-style, with a higher polygonal stair-turret. At its base the former keeper's house, carpenter's shop, smithy etc. with mullion windows, gables and bellcote (now converted to Bedford Hall). Also by Teulon is the detached former 'Tap Room' of the ROSE & CROWN, the pub itself rebuilt 1899 as a model establishment for the People's Refreshment House Association (run on Gothenburg principles, investing profits locally). Domestic Revival-style, the strong red brick clearly from elsewhere.

s of the Wisbech Road, lying back somewhat, PARK HOUSE, C18, with a big shaped and pedimented gable to its roof, originally one of a pair. Further E, the DUKE OF BEDFORD SCHOOL of 1938–40 by the *Isle of Ely County Architect's Department* (*R. D. Robson*, County Architect),[*] with two projections l. and r. of the hall, also with Dutch gables.

WINDMILL, Causeway Road. Tower-mill, now converted for a house, with datestone 1787. It had seven storeys, and the diameter at the base is 26 ft (7.9 metres).

In WILLOW HALL LANE, 3 m. SW, are two good early C18 houses, which may have been built at the instigation of Thomas Deacon (†1721), who endowed his school at Peterborough with 225 acres (90 ha) of land in Priors Fen, Whittlesey. WILLOW HALL has a five-bay front with stone-framed window frames terminating in keystones and a pedimented doorway, and PRIOR'S FARM, further S, boasts a near identical front in brick and with two good panelled rooms inside. A curious feature is that one house faces E, the other W. Both were tenanted in the C18 by the Bayley family, Huguenots, whose monuments are in the church.[†]

---

[*]The project architect may have been *Stirrat Johnson-Marshall*, who was the county's Assistant Architect.
[†]BAR PASTURE FARM, brick, stone-slated, L-shaped, noted in the first edition of this guide, has been replaced.

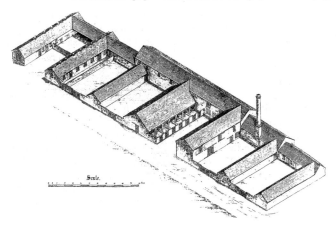

Thorney, Bedford estate farm, *c.* 1863.

Many FARMS were built anew in the 1850s and 1860s to model standards, e.g. WHITE HART FARM of 1859, on English Drove N of the village, with a house in the estate style and farmstead in a characteristic four-finger plan (now converted to housing) with open yards between. The designs were provided for the 7th Duke by his agent *Robert Mein* (although the design of the farmhouse itself follows the pattern established for the estate in the late 1840s). Many model labourers' cottages in the wider area.

TONEHAM FARMHOUSE, ¾ m. SSW. Good Early Victorian, three bays with a Doric porch.

CANARY COTTAGE, Thorney Toll, 3¼ m. E behind the Dalmark grain silo. Rare survival of a tiny thatched fenland cottage.

ST VINCENT'S CROSS, 2½ m. NW by Vincent's Cross Farm, another Bedford model farm. Originally the boundary marker with Lincolnshire. C15(?), tapered octagonal shaft splayed out at base to form four feet. A shield in recessed panels on each side has symbols of St Guthlac. A cross-base at Singlesole Farm marks the site of a medieval chapelry of Thorney.

THORNHAUGH [P]

The manor, including Wansford (q.v.), belonged to the St Medards after the Conquest and from the mid C16 to John Russell, 1st Earl of Bedford, who inherited it through marriage. The Bedford estate held the manor until 1931.

ST ANDREW. The interior, as often, older than the exterior. N arcade of *c.* 1200, although the aisle was rebuilt, with vestry, in 1889 by *J. T. Micklethwaite & Somers Clarke*. Four bays with circular piers, square abaci with nicked angles, and simple double-chamfered arches. The S arcade was the same, but was destroyed when the spire fell *c*. 1500. All that remains of it is the present S wall of the S porch and the arch to the S chapel. The fall of the spire also destroyed a former S porch into the tower. The tower itself of the C13 but as faithfully rebuilt in 1889. Of the C13 also the chancel arch, the piscina with dog-tooth decoration, and the E window – and the clerestory with encircled trefoil windows. Much of the external appearance Perp, including the fine four-light nave windows and the crenellated S chapel. The chapel had a separate door (blocked). – SCREEN. Only the base survives. – FONT. Round, on a round stem. – Some FURNISHINGS of 1889, well crafted. – WALL PAINTING. Traces over the chapel arch, possibly arms of the St Medard family; also chevrons on the N arcade. – STAINED GLASS. Clerestory. Heraldic badges, 1889. – MONUMENT. William Lord Russell †1613. Free-standing in the S chapel. Recumbent stone effigy on a partly rolled-up mat. Kneeling at his feet is his son, later the 4th Earl of Bedford and Inigo Jones's patron at Covent Garden. Against the tomb-chest are kneeling figures of Lord Russell's brothers and his daughters. On the corners of the tomb-chest stand four obelisks. HELM on the S wall.

The buildings of the village amount to a handful of houses on Russell Hill. E of the church is the OLD RECTORY, late C17, formerly of five bays with a hipped roof. Cross-windows. To this in 1878 *T. G. Jackson**★** added a new r. half with a powerful two-storey porch and one large room inside. Reset into its wall, a few medieval fragments. At its rear an earlier addition, dated 1703. Good original staircase with turned balusters from ground floor to attic. Uphill, opposite the church, a thatched cottage that was enlarged and refronted in the mid C19 for the Bedford estate as the SCHOOL (now a house again). Ashlar stone front with porches. Further uphill, some Bedford ESTATE HOUSING (e.g. Nos. 10–12, dated 1850) in the usual Jacobean. Here also THE MANOR, an L-shaped farmhouse, again late C17, again five bays, of two storeys, with mullioned windows below, replacement cross-windows above. The doorway is going classical. Rusticated gatepiers. N of the house is the outline of a garden feature, possibly fishponds, associated with the medieval manor house.

(THORNHAUGH HALL, ¼ m. W. 1913–14 by *George Crawley* for his brother-in-law, Stanley Brotherhood, whose engineering firm had moved to Peterborough from London in 1908. Formerly three storeys, in a gabled Neo-Jacobean style, faced in rock-faced coursed limestone, but lowered after a fire in 1937 and given a hipped roof. E of the house a LAKE with an island and arched timber bridge, created 1993–4 by *LDA Design*.)

★ Jackson's family lived at Duddington, Northants, just a few miles away.

HOME FARM HOUSE, ½ m. SW of Thornhaugh Hall by the A47.
The site of the medieval manor house. Tillemans in 1721 shows
it as adapted by the Russells. The early C18 W wing is stone,
of five bays with the typical raised surrounds. Two storeys with
attic and at the rear a basement also. Porch of 1863. The three-
bay E wing (now a separate house) was built in matching style
1911. C18 farm buildings at rear (stables, barns, granary and
dairy), mostly converted.

E of the A1, SACREWELL MILL, at Sacrewell Farm. Built in 1750
for the 4th Duke of Bedford. Picturesque stone group of mill,
in two parts, with the weighing room etc. in the lower part, the
mill itself adjoining, and, at right angles to this, the miller's
house. The Victorian breastshot wheel and the machinery
survive inside, in full working order.

½ m. SW of Thornhaugh was the medieval village of SIBBERTON.
Immediately S of its site is SIBBERTON LODGE. Dated 1659,
a single straight range of two storeys with ovolo-moulded
mullion windows and staircase tower on its E front. At its N
end and projecting W also a short two-storey wing that has a
rib-vaulted undercroft of two oblong bays with quadripartite
vaults, single-chamfered ribs, chamfered tapered corbels and
a central round pier. Of the chamber above, a blocked window
remains in the W wall. Two lights and a trefoiled head. The
date probably *c.* 1300. Two large barns with steeply pitched
roofs, C18, and other outbuildings. Gardens by *Bunny Guin-
ness*, since *c.* 2005, nicely formal on the E front with a straight
pond between beech hedges.

THORPE HALL *see* PETERBOROUGH
(LONGTHORPE)

TILBROOK   *0060*

ALL SAINTS. A good Dec church. Externally it is the W tower
that dominates. It has two-light bell-openings with transom
and a recessed broach spire with low broaches and two tiers
of lucarnes. Gargoyles spring at the angles and masks in the
frieze. Buttresses with blocks of dark sandstone. The nave S
windows are also Dec, reticulated tracery, but by *William White*,
1865–7. The chancel and N vestry appear Perp, but the eaves-
frieze includes ballflower; so that is Dec too, and Dec is indeed
the ANGLE PISCINA in the chancel. The most telling exception
to the Dec is the N aisle. Externally the N doorway seems early
C13, and the N aisle W lancet and the NW window of two separate lancets with a tiny blank quatrefoil belong to the late C13.
The arcade inside is hard to understand. It was first a matter
of three bays added to a Norman nave. The Norman piers are
round, the abaci square but chamfered, the arches pointed with

just a slight chamfer. That makes the work *c.* 1190, but the capitals are odd, one with a multi-cusped form of scalloping, the other with this on only half of it, the rest made up with what looks like the notched heads of the Dec style. The w bay was later cut into by the tower, but the w respond was found in 1930. Then, in the late C13, the arcade was extended E with circular piers whose abaci are alternatingly octagonal and round, double-chamfered arches, and a little nailhead enrichment. The w wall of the chancel (whose arch is Dec) cuts into this lengthening, so that the easternmost of the late C13 arches now rests on the octagonal pier for the one-bay N chapel, which is Dec (squinch with an ogee arch), but later than the chancel and vestry, for the plinth of the vestry wall appears inside. Late Perp the clerestory, Late Perp a head corbel and the brackets l. and r. of the chancel E window, and Late Perp the N aisle roof with angels against the intermediate principals, one in the N chapel with its wings. The nave roof replaced by White has large corbels of angels with musical instruments. – FONT. Perp bowl with quatrefoils. – SCREEN. Perp, of three-light divisions and without doubt the best in Huntingdonshire, restored in 1867 by the Bedford Archaeological Society. It still has its ribbed coving with three patterns of ribbing and much original blue and gold. On the dado, painted Saints no longer clearly recognizable. The screen formerly extended across the N chapel but that part is now in the Victoria and Albert Museum. – STALLS. 1860s. Two have old poppyheads incoporated. – SCULPTURE. In the s porch a C12 cross-shaft, probably not from Tilbrook. On one narrow side, a bishop standing on a colonnette rendered in relief. On one broad side, fluting but with two big flowers. – Above the s porch entrance, a man with a pig; C12? It might be of the same workshop as the tympana at Stow Longa and Little Paxton. – STAINED GLASS. Fragments in a chancel s window, including the Georgian (i.e. 1714–1800) royal arms. – In the E window two early C16 roundels. – s chancel. 1864 by *Wailes*. – BRASSES. Under the organ, brasses of a civilian and wife, *c.* 1400. The sizes of the figures are 3 ft 3 in. (99 cm).

VICARAGE, E of the church. By *R. C. Hussey*, 1855.

MANOR HOUSE, 200 yds N. A substantial early C17 farmhouse. (Painted decoration in upper rooms of imitation panelling with arcading and in a second room imitation textiles, all *c.* 1625. More at BROOK FARM. Andrea Kirkham.)

TOSELAND

ST MICHAEL. A chapel to Great Paxton until the late C20. Rebuilt by *A. W. Blomfield*, 1875. Neo-Norman, of nave and chancel with w bellcote and impressively bare interior with a raised sanctuary. But the masonry is mostly original Norman

work, and there are a Norman s window and an elaborate
Norman s doorway, evidently late. Two orders of shafts, single-
and double-scallop capitals, undecorated (or rather, replaced)
tympanum but a band of rosettes round it, chevron arch, the
chevron also placed at right angles to the wall. The single-step
chancel arch is C19 but mostly Norman below, where the capitals have Corinthianesque leaves, volutes and also inturned
volutes, for which the source must be Ely. In one abacus a little
decoration of lozenges and chip-carving (cf. Southoe), a motif
found also in some fragments of string course. Vestry added
1897. – Outside the s wall lies a large Sarsen stone. – STAINED
GLASS. E window by *J. Powell & Sons*, 1899.

The medieval village was N of the church, where there is a single
house. Everything else is along the road cutting through the
original green.

TOSELAND HALL. An exceptionally compact, outward-facing
and symmetrical red brick-clad house of *c.* 1600, probably built
by Sir Nicholas Luke, who died in 1613. His ancestor, a justice
of the King's Bench, had purchased the manor in 1540 but the
principal seat was always at Cople (Beds.), so Toseland may
have been erected as a pleasure house. It is two storeys high
with moulded strings plus an attic storey in the gables which
have moulded copings. Along the spine are four pairs of octagonal chimneystacks and one group of six (originally of nine*)
in the centre, all with moulded lozenge patterns and castellated
tops that make a major display in such flat country. The front
has two tiers of pilasters and three gables, and to them correspond two canted bay windows and a middle porch. The
windows are transomed except in the gables. The fenestration,
which is brick and has always been rendered, is perfectly symmetrical, except that on the l. of the porch is an extra two-light
window, lighting a vestibule between the two principal rooms.
If this is the original arrangement it is novel for its date. The
sides also have three bays, but only two gables. The position
of the middle window on one side demonstrates where the
staircase is. The windows on the sides have no transoms, but
that may be a later alteration. The kitchen is at the back in the
centre, again with a bay window, and inside is separated by
timber screens with pairs of doorways from rooms E and W.
The plan is interesting, for it has a lateral corridor dividing
these front and rear piles with the main staircase at its W end.
This has typical early C17 symmetrical turned balusters, shaped
finials to the newels, with an especially tall one at the attic level.
The service stair may have been at the opposing end, against
the central chimneystack, but replaced in a new position in the
C19. The attic floor may have been intended as a prospect room
or gallery.† Moated site to the N.

---

*This information came from the late Andor Gomme and was discovered during
re-roofing in 1991. The missing chimneys were dummies.
†A barn noted by Pevsner was destroyed by fire.

A long and thin village with the rare advantage in this area of an elevated setting. The main street runs downhill from the church.

St Andrew. There was a church at Ufford in 1191. Two strips of nutmeg are reset in the chancel N window and in the N aisle W wall. Otherwise, the chancel comes first. Probably late C13 or *c.* 1300: N and S windows with a variety of Y-tracery, two E windows (their tracery restored in 1883 by *J. C. Traylen*), and, inside, the chancel arch and the damaged sedilia and piscina (uncovered at the restoration). Two S windows are Dec with segmental arches. Dec also the aisle windows. The porch and the arcades (three bays) are Early Perp. The slender piers are typical, still with a square core and four demi-shafts, but Perp-looking octagonal capitals and headstops. Arches with sunk mouldings. W tower just a little later (the bells are assigned to *Richard Hill*, who †1440). Arch piers with castellated capitals and concave bases. Lion headstops. On the clasping buttresses concave-sided gables in relief. Tall two-light bell-openings with transom. Battlements. Rood screen removed in 1860, its stair reused, however, in a turret added in 1883. – FONT. Tall, octagonal, Perp, with shields etc. Cover with crockets and figures (cf. Barnack). – PEWS. C16 bench ends in the N aisle with unconventional poppyheads, diamond-shaped, carved with leaves and faces. Nicely copied in the late C19 pews. – DECALOGUE. Signed by *John Everard*, painter, Stamford, 1790. Ionic pilasters with Gothic arches as frames. – STAINED GLASS. A complete and very good scheme of six in the chancel by *Mary Lowndes*, 1911–14, scenes of Christ's ministry framed by dense foliage and fruiting vines. – Lowside window, signed by *T. F. Curtis, Ward & Hughes*, 1910. – MONUMENTS. Bridget Lady Carre †1621; Gentlewoman of Queen Elizabeth's Privy Bedchamber. Semi-reclining on her side. Back arch with well-carved gristly cartouche. Columns l. and r. and crest with her arms. – Three good tablets in the S aisle: the Bourne family, erected 1689, attributed to *William Stanton* (GF); Richard Bourne of Clements Inn, London, †1705, by *Edward Stanton*, with excellent ornament and three cherubs' heads at the top; and Lord James Manners, youngest son of the 2nd Duke of Rutland, †1790, by *Edward Bingham*. Classical but with just a trace of Gothic (cf. the Gery Monument at Peterborough Cathedral, p. 607). – In the churchyard, close to the S porch, a striking double headstone for Thomas Porter †1808, still in a vigorous Rococo style.

OLD RECTORY, immediately SE of the church and making with it an excellent group. The position, and the survival of remarkable C14 roof timbers belonging to a hall house, in three equal bays with cusped windbraces and chamfered trusses, suggest this must have been the manor house.* There may have been cross-wings but in their present form they are C17 (blocked mullions and corner fireplaces in the W wing) and C18. The most prominent external motif is two tall imitation church windows in the centre in the style of *c.* 1300, due to an early C19 remodelling. That to the l., with a quatrefoil in a circle, may be partly genuine but reset; a plan prior to remodelling notes 'an old Gothic window' centrally placed where the porch is now. Close by, THE ROOST (formerly Newport Farmhouse), plain mid- to later C18, with moulded window surrounds and arched doorcase. The former STABLES adjoining, dated 1770, are the largest of three outbuildings, all with a distinctive motif of lunettes infilled with stone chequerwork to the lofts. It spans a pond with two arched openings.

Downhill, set back behind a walled court, is UFFORD HALL.† It was begun by Lord Charles Manners, son of the 2nd Duke of Rutland. He acquired the estate from his mother in 1741, the completion date might be 1751 (rainwater heads), but the architect is unknown. At that time it seems to have been a square box of just two storeys above a basement. Then, perhaps *c.* 1778 (dated sundial on the W front), it received a half-storey above the cornice and wings of two bays and two storeys. At the same time, on the E front, was added a deep, canted bay in which lies the entrance and a geometric staircase. This composition is made even more disjointed by the canted projections to either side of it, added *c.* 1900. The garden side is the show front and very handsome, with a pediment (apparently reused when the attic was added) and five-bay centre rusticated in the central three bays below the cornice. The window architraves have flared voussoirs and keystones characteristic of the early to mid-C18 'Stamford style'. The basement was originally exposed and there is evidence that further wings projected N and S. Inside, some mid-C18 decoration in the central block but the most noteworthy rooms are the former dining room and drawing room, which fill the two side wings completely. Both have marble chimneypieces with coloured inserts and carved reliefs. Later C18 service wing on the S side of the courtyard and opposite, the U-plan STABLES with good GATEPIERS with late C18 fan decoration. The grounds to the N have been built upon; on both sides of Walcot Road are former GATES which provided a private route to the church. They are perhaps early C19. The style is a mixture of Gothic and Jacobean, with old bits.

*Ufford was a possession of Torpel manor, one of the largest estates in this area and including lands at Bainton, Maxey and Northborough.
†The interpretation of the house's evolution is taken from a report by John Heward, 1998.

UPTON [P]

The church, built as a chapel of ease to Castor, stands by the former manor house in open fields. Earthworks suggest the medieval village was here too.

ST JOHN THE BAPTIST. Very odd but very engaging. Intensely domestic front. Nave and N aisle of the same width and height and with the same gables and domestic windows. The windows are straight-headed, of arched lights. A third smaller gable in the middle for the bellcote with a buttress up its centre. The other windows also all straight-headed. Chancel and all the roofs rebuilt 1842. The rest looks C17 Gothic – and such it is indeed. All the more surprising is the interior. For now we are transported into a much earlier time. The chancel arch has early C12 shafts with scalloped capitals, with an angle shaft and decoration on the N side. N aisle arcade of two bays, late C12. Shortish circular pier, square abacus with the usual nicks at the angles. Capitals with upright leaves and crockets, the W responds with tendrils forming into leaves. The chancel and arcade arches are C17, this work connected with the rebuilding of the N aisle over a burial vault. The aisle floor is raised by four steps, and separated from the nave by a big classical balustrade with vertically symmetrical balusters and newels with spheres. – ALTAR TABLE. *c.* 1620 with characteristic bulbous legs; the COMMUNION RAIL also Jacobean but probably earlier, with flat openwork balusters. – CHAIRS. Rustic pieces assembled from bits; one dated 1700 and inscribed 'Joane Browne A Want Not'; the other with a figure in the centre. – PULPIT. Jacobean, elaborate and impressive in this small space, with arcaded panels and tester, uncommonly well preserved. – FONT. C17. – MONUMENTS. In the N aisle. Sir William Dove, son of Bishop Dove, †1633 and his wives (Frances Downhall †1622 and Dorothy Neville †1665). A four-poster with Ionic columns. Three recumbent effigies. One would like to date it from the aisle balustrade and the big open segmental pediments with mannerist scrolls as *c.* 1650–60, rather than *c.* 1633, and this seems likely because Sir William and Lady Dorothy are made of terracotta but the first wife of stone, i.e. probably earlier (she was buried in Peterborough Cathedral). Her effigy is in the manner of Nicholas Stone.* – William Games †1731. Aedicular frame with fluted pilasters and escutcheon, signed by *William Palmer*.

MANOR HOUSE, s of the church. Built by Robert Wingfield in the mid to late C16, acquired by Sir William Dove in 1625 but sold *c.* 1750 to the Fitzwilliams, who reduced it to a farmhouse. Three bays, two storeys. Doorway with four-centred arch. The

---

*Bruce Bailey compares her head with that of Lady Spencer at Great Brington, Northants, carved for Stone by *Richard White*.

ground-floor windows with arched lights. Among the outbuildings a square DOVECOTE. C18.

W of the house, a remarkable mid-C17 astronomical
SUNDIAL, nearly 6 ft (1.8 metres) high. The sides have divided
rectangular concavities diagonally set and concave hemi-
spheres. The front has a deep heart-shaped concavity. The
front face of the top is inclined forward and has a divided
rectangular concavity with semicircular ends. Evidently it did
more than show the hours of the day.

At the entrance to the hamlet is GLEBE HOUSE, the former
vicarage of 1912 by *H. F. Traylen*. In it two stone fireplaces from
The Grange at Sutton (q.v.), both with Tudor arches. Immediately SW is MODEL FARM. The farmhouse is dated 1685.
The hipped roof with oblong moulded chimneyshafts goes well
with that date, but the windows are still mullioned, though now
symmetrically placed. Cross-passage plan. S of the house, the
remarkably well-preserved model FARM BUILDINGS of 1881.
Four parallel brick ranges, symmetrically arranged, incorporating an older stone barn in the E range. Large arches at the S
end into the cowshed, which extends the full length. Roof of
big queenpost trusses. Many of the original fittings are *in situ*.

UPTON

ST MARGARET. Not a large church. The W tower has a short
broach spire with ballflower at the points of the broaches and
two tiers of lucarnes. This is C15 but in the style of the previous
century. The tower W wall was once the nave W wall and has
two ogee-headed lancets, flanking a big mid-buttress. That is
odd, but fully justified by the fact of a tower being raised on
the former W wall of the nave. The S doorway is the oldest
feature. With its thin angle shafts it is undoubtedly Late
Norman (there was a church at Upton in 1086). Then follow
the arcades. They are mid-C13, with round piers, round abaci,
and double-chamfered arches. There were originally three bays
until the tower was built into the nave. The chancel is E.E. too,
see the lancet giving into the vestry, the priest's doorway with
its rounded-trefoiled head, and the tomb recess, but it has a
C14 E window of intersecting tracery and the chancel arch is
Perp. Straight-headed Dec S aisle and clerestory windows. The
N aisle, vestry, the S porch and W bay of the S aisle are by *George
Gilbert Scott*, 1870–1. Of his work also the ROOFS, especially
impressive the chancel's pointed wagon roof with trusses
springing from mighty kneeling angels, and FITTINGS, notably
the SCREEN of five lights. – TILES by *Godwin*. – FONT. A tre-
mendous Norman piece like a two-scalloped capital. It stands
on nine E.E. supports, renewed by Scott.

The village has been much built up since *c.* 1970. NW of the
church, CHRIST'S COLLEGE FARM stands on a moated site,

but the thatched house is C17 of two phases; the taller S end comes first and has a flat brick ridge stack. Big, ugly, former RECTORY to the S, dated 1885. Facing the N side of the church, two appealing Dutch-style brick houses of 1996–7 by *Julian Limentani*.

COPPINGFORD HALL, 2 m. N by the A1. 1860s, gault brick and a little orange trim, with full-height canted bays and tall chimneys. Later extensions. Grounds of mature specimen trees.

UPWOOD

ST PETER. The tower (restored in the 1890s) is late C13, see the bell-openings with two sub-arches on a polygonal shaft. But it also has Dec pinnacles and a tiny spire. To the W a small Dec niche and a kneeling figure and a soul in a napkin. The W window is a five-pointed star in a circle with cusping; Victorian. The nave has a Norman N arcade, but above it appear the traces of two Norman windows from the time before the arcade was built. The arcade is later C12. Round piers, cruciform multi-scalloped capitals, one-step arches with two tiny chamfers. The W bay was rebuilt when the tower was built, but the Norman pier shows that such a bay had existed already in the C12. Norman also the chancel arch, depressed rounded and slightly drunken. In the chancel N and S walls a long round-headed lancet, i.e. late C12. The S arcade is ambiguous. The arches are C13, but the capitals Perp. – FONT. Square, undecorated Norman, with Jacobean COVER, a pyramid with nicely decorated ribs and bobbin handle. – SCREENS. Modest screens of one-light divisions to chancel and N chapel. – STAINED GLASS. In two S aisle windows good C15 canopies. – MONUMENTS. Tablet to Peter Phesaunt, Justice of the King's Bench, †1649, still Elizabethan in style. Latin inscription and some of the original colouring. – WAR MEMORIAL (S aisle reredos); Crucifixion with two angels. Mosaic and opus sectile by *W. Glasby*, 1920.

UPWOOD HOUSE, W of the church, is the former manor house, now divided into three. It was a property of the Cromwells until 1649, when it was purchased by Peter Phesaunt II. Externally of the later C17. Front with two projecting wings under half-hipped roofs. It is brick-faced with modillions under the eaves and, as the E side still shows, had windows in raised brick frames. On the front, where everything is covered with thick white render, the wings have giant angle pilasters. Giant pilasters also to emphasize the middle bay of the recessed centre. They carry a steep gable with an oval window in it. Is this original? To the flanks and rear, big flat stone chimneybreasts, probably older than the façades (fireplace of *c.* 1600 inside), with later brick tops. At the S flank the chimney is obscured by a two-storey early C19 addition, whose interior was remodelled for himself by *Terry Farrell, c.* 1985, in eclectic style, e.g. Egyptian columns in one room and the sky painted over the ceiling.

Immediately N is THE OLD BARN, with, inside its rear wing, a remarkable preservation of the roof timbers of a two-bay C14 open hall (one truss with a strip of flower carving is now reused as the lintel of a large fireplace in the two-storey C17 front range) and its two-bay C16 additions. In the High Street, TOWNEND FARMHOUSE is upscale late C18, its doorcase with lugged surround and pulvinated cornice. No. 67 High Street is a small medieval cottage that has been added to in the C18. Inside survives the timber-framed chimney inserted in the C17.

WALCOT HALL [P]
Southorpe

oooo

Reputedly built for Sir Hugh Cholmeley, former governor of Tangier, who acquired Walcot in 1671. He was M.P. for Northampton in 1679. The architect is unknown. Nine by five bays, of limestone ashlar, two-storeyed over a full basement that is sunk on the principal (W) front but exposed at the rear and buttressed in a manner that looks oddly unfinished. Quoins of even length, hipped roof with a platform and four square rusticated chimneys. Windows on the show fronts with pulvinated cornices and alternating triangular and segmental pediments, straight-headed on the rear. That far the house goes well with the date 1678 on two rainwater heads. But there are others of 1767, when the house was owned by Thomas Noel, and they may refer to the addition of the three-bay pediment on the W side, the present shape of the dormer windows and the tall sashes – Tillemans in 1721 shows that the windows were then of the cross type. Inside, originally, there must have been a large central room on both floors of the N front. Doors and windows have lugged heads. But now the entrance hall is open to the roof with a Victorian staircase climbing impressively, if rather clumsily, round four sides. Where was the late C17 stair? The basement kitchen has three remarkable arches over the former ranges, with rustication of sunk panels. Rooms *en enfilade* on the E front. Interiors of mixed dates. Two late C18 fireplaces and C19 plasterwork in a Rococo style. Fine W and S terraces; the N porch is C19, possibly of 1843 (the late Eric Till claimed that the house was reconstructed and extended E in that year for the Nevile family, who acquired the estate in 1837).

GARDENS, mostly laid out by the Dearden family after their purchase in 1891, with many fine specimen trees. Only the straight canal SE of the house and the impressive W avenue look earlier. At the canal's S end a domed ROTUNDA, with fluted Corinthian columns and Grecian details. Dated 1925. Similar COLONNADE and circular pool in the former walled garden to the SE, which also has a gate with Jacobean-style cresting. One curious FOLLY (C19?), with walls of knobbly reconstituted stone inside and some medieval bits, including a fine double effigy with only the heads and feet showing beneath a blanket. Early C14? (cf. Stoke Rochford, Lincs.). Also a delightful water garden (now swimming pool) with two pools, a bridge and classical balustrade, below a LOGGIA with Ionic columns (dated 1931). NW of the house a TEMPLE with Serliana and two nice marble reliefs inside. OUTBUILDINGS E of the house, partly C17 but altered, especially the STABLES, dated 1860 on the Italianate clocktower. Good C17 GATEPIERS.

WALTON *see* PETERBOROUGH
(PASTON AND WALTON)

0090

WANSFORD

66   The village is of the one-street type, because it was on the Great North Road, and lay in both Peterborough and Huntingdon with the Nene as the boundary. The early village began N of the river where the church stands, and was on the Bullock Road taken by drovers travelling S across the Nene to Glatton and Alconbury. It spread S, partly to serve the coaching trade but also on the back of increasingly busy traffic along the river as Wansford became an entrepot for goods transported from the Wash to the Great North Road. Wansford was also, like Thornhaugh and Stibbington, part of the Bedford estate. Bypassed since the 1920s, very much to its benefit.

St MARY. Originally a chapel of ease to Thornhaugh. In the W wall a Saxon window which now looks into the C13 tower. This has lancet windows, bell-openings of two lights with a separating shaft, a dogtooth frieze, and a not too tall broach spire with two tiers of lucarnes in alternating directions with cross-heads. The spire seems early C14. The S wall of the nave (straight-headed windows) and the porch redone in 1663 and hence very domestic-looking. But the coarse S doorway is of *c.* 1200: two orders of shafts and a round arch. A little later the N arcade of two bays. Short quatrefoil pier and responds, a little nailhead decoration, round double-chamfered arches. Chancel (with organ chamber and vestry) added in 1902 by *J. C. Traylen* of Stamford, C14 style with reticulated E window. Of the earlier chancel are the reused bases of the arch responds. PULPIT and SEDILIA have Jacobean panels. – FONT. Reputedly found at Sibberton (*see* Thornhaugh) and set up on the base of a font discovered here in 1902. Circular, Norman and a quite exceptional piece of carving. Figures under arches. A border of leaf-trail above. The figures include a Baptism, two knights fighting (cf. SE capital of the tower arch at Castor), and two Evangelists. *c.* 1120 is the likely date.

The position of the village explains the amazing spaciousness of the HAYCOCK HOTEL. Its date must be *c.* 1650–80, although a datestone of 1632 is preserved inside. The building has a five-bay centre and shallow two-bay wings. Coved eaves cornice and scrolled kneelers to the gables. The fenestration was originally no doubt cross-windows; one survives on the N side, although the rear SE wing also has moulded mullion windows. The carriage arch was in the centre (now replaced by a porch). The window above it has a pediment and details with those curious mid-C17 mannerisms seen at Thorpe Hall (p. 641), e.g. the square blocks in the middle of the pilasters. And what on the pilasters is capital, what abacus? Symmetrical plan inside with closed string staircases to N and S from ground floor to attic. Both have those fully fashioned balusters which again characterizes 1650 to 1680. The RCHM in 1926 found evidence of a gallery on the rear elevation to the courtyard.

WANSFORD BRIDGE is a splendid specimen, in spite of the irregularity of its arches. On the S side there is after a small round arch a very wide one with rusticated voussoirs, dated 1795, over the river itself and then the cutwaters begin on both sides that are carried up as refuges for pedestrians. The next three arches are of 1672–4, the following seven of 1577 (dated on the E side with initials PM). These latter have stepped arches and cutwaters on one side only. Downstream E is the NEW BRIDGE of 1925–8 by *Simpson & Ayrton*, with *Sir Owen Williams* as consultant engineer. A very fine work in bush-hammered mass concrete, with a single segmental arch over the river, 109 ft (33.2 metres) wide, smaller sub-arches N and S and arched voids in the spandrels. Sans-serif lettering for the county names N and S. The motifs of its predecessor – triangular cutwaters and refuges – are alluded to. The third BRIDGE is for the A1 south-bound, 1975. Flat deck on stanchions of inverted scissor profile.

125

In the main street, opposite the Haycock, some nice (restored) C18 houses and further S good Bedford estate housing, especially Nos. 3–11 Elton Road, dated 1856, with gables and lattice windows, and Gothic House (W side), dated 1858. Further N the METHODIST CHAPEL of 1900 by *W. Hinson* of Stamford. Simple cruciform with timber plate tracery.

N of the river, some agreeable C18 houses and further up in Old North Road No. 19, dated 1850, is by *S. S. Teulon* for the Bedford estate. Very picturesque Elizabethan. Designed for the village cooper, George Eayers, to replace the 'wretched cabin' where he formerly lived; barrel motif over the door. No. 23 has GATEPIERS of reused piers of clustered shafts with deep hollows between. They are claimed to come from *J. L. Pearson*'s choir screen at the Cathedral,* taken out *c.* 1920.

---

* *Friends of Peterborough Cathedral Journal*, 1993.

STIBBINGTON HOUSE, ¼ m. S, set back in its grounds. The former miller's house for Wansford Paper Mill (dem.). Rebuilt c. 1805–10 after a fire. Three-bay front, square plan, a clock belvedere on the roof (added 1844) and a charming iron veranda. Doorcase with fluted Ionic pilasters. Single-storey wing of c. 1825. By the river is a building formerly used for storing rags. Fantastical mid-C19 LODGE, probably built after the mill had been demolished, with lacy bargeboards and a turret with a spire carried on little heads.

WANSFORD STATION. See Stibbington.

3070

WARBOYS

ST MARY MAGDALENE. On the edge of the former village green. A stately church of brown cobble, but how could *Henry Harrison*, in 1832, rebuild the chancel in yellow brick, even if he chose lancets to match the superb C13 W steeple – C13 to the top of the broach spire? The tower is high and has broad flat buttresses with shallow set-offs and a lancet window, once, it seems, not divided across but of its whole astounding length in one (cf. Bury). The next stage has a cusped W lancet, shafted. Then the bell-openings, pairs of the lights each with Y-tracery with a foiled spandrel and much shafting. The lowest of the three tiers of lucarnes is in exactly the same style. At the top, a crenellated band. After this most impressive piece one must look at the oldest piece: the Norman chancel arch, with scalloped capitals to the triple responds, a tiny tree motif on one of the capitals, and an arch with two rolls, a step and hollow chamfer and chevron (cf. Bury). Then, still chronologically before the tower, both arcades. They are of four bays and quite different one from the other; yet both date from the early C13. N has round and octagonal piers and arches with one chamfer and one more complex moulding, including keeling, S has round piers, round capitals, and round abaci and double-chamfered arches, i.e. a more conventional *parti*. Very good bases. Then, to continue chronologically, the tower. What has not yet been said is that the arch to the nave goes with all the rest, and so do the lower N and S arches. So embracing aisles were provided for, although they (see the E arches) and most of the fenestration of the church are Perp. Nice N doorway of c. 1300. Plaster stripped from the walls in 1926, when galleries of 1832 were removed from the aisles and tower. – FONT. The font was obtained at the time when the enlargement by aisles took place. It is of table-top form and has stiff-leaf of the mature kind to the N. All the other sides are recut out of recognition. – DOOR KNOCKER. Chancel N. A small C12 bronze piece with a lion's head, and the ring made into two dragons fighting. – STAINED GLASS. Bad C19 in the chancel. – S aisle. 156 Pathfinder Force Memorial, 1991. Large wreath around a

scene of a bombing raid. – MONUMENTS. John Leman †1781.
By *John Bacon the elder*. Hope pointing to an urn. – Elizabeth
Strode, his relict, †1790. Also by *Bacon the elder*. Mourning
woman by an urn. On the pedestal a fine small relief of the
Good Samaritan.

WARBOYS GRACE BAPTIST CHURCH, High Street. 1831,
heavily concealed by Gothic reworking in 1898–9.

MANOR HOUSE, N of the church. Of two periods, the three-bay 104
E front of the mid C17, probably for William Leman, whose
uncle, Sir John Leman, a merchant and former Lord Mayor of
London, had bought the manor from Sir Oliver Cromwell in
1622. Red brick, with two large shaped gables with rounded
tops on the front and a straight parapet between them. The
brick is laid in Flemish bond already. But there is a clear
change in the colour and bonding of the brickwork in the
centre and r. of the door (a good *c.* 1800 piece), which indicates
that the part facing N is earlier and had straight gables. This
side has two substantial chimneys with diamond stacks. In the
centre, the Jacobean staircase with long, turned balusters and
shaped finials and pendants to the newels. C19 W additions.

THE MOAT HOUSE, E of the church. The large former rectory,
substantially rebuilt in yellow brick by *Henry Harrison* in 1829.
Five bays with the centre slightly recessed. Windows and door
surrounds have upright consoles. But at the back is an early
C18 broken scrolly door pediment on scrolled brackets.

In the centre of the village, the Jubilee CLOCKTOWER of 1887,
and of no merit despite its prominence. Red brick trimmed
with the local white is not a pretty combination. Gothic below,
square above, with a pyramid roof. N of this, in Ramsey Road,
THE CHESTNUTS has an early C19 front to earlier rear wings
(one brick inscribed 1675 and traces of vertical pilasters usual
for then but also a 1785 datestone on the back wing and late
C18 stair inside). In the garden a fine red brick square dovecote.
Datestone of 17[3 or 8]5. Handsome cast-iron Grecian gates
made by *E. & T. B. Ulph* of St Ives. Good gatepiers in this style
also at THE ALMONDS, another house refronted in the early
C19 and with an Ionic doorcase.

WARESLEY   2050

ST JAMES. By *Butterfield*, 1857, superseding the chapel of 1728 123
which stood opposite the vicarage to the S.* Built together with
the Duncombe Mausoleum, which connects with the interior
of the church by a wall with a window of three stepped lancet
lights with foiled circles over. The E wall of the mausoleum has
two strange blank arches with blank sexfoiled almond-shapes

---

*The chapel was itself a rebuilding, by *Andrews Jelfe*, of the church brought down
by the 'Tempest' of 1724. It is described as a small version of Pembroke College
Chapel, Cambridge.

hanging from their apex. This is the only oddity of the church. Otherwise it is all normal late C13 detail, and the N porch tower (which is unexpected) is slender and noble, with its sheer, steep shingled spire (rebuilt in 1987 by *Levitt Architects*) with just a suspicion of broaches. Gothic PUMP HOUSE by the street, also by *Butterfield*.

Inside, the chancel is one of the most perfect examples of Butterfield's structural polychromy: stone, red tiles, green tiles, and a little yellow – all in elementary geometrical patterns and including the reredos with inlaid cross. Texts in quatrefoils on two walls. – The FONT COVER, with reticulation spreading up the steep sides, and the BENCHES are excellent and typical. *John Thompson* of Peterborough was the contractor, and probably did the carving. – STAINED GLASS. The E and S windows of the chancel, judging by their style, must be by *O'Connor* (Michael Kerney), but the N transept window is by *Heaton, Butler & Bayne*, 1865. The background of broad patches of ruby, lilac and dark mauve is entirely out of the ordinary. Large W window of 1879 by *Clayton & Bell*. – MONUMENTS. A few from the old church in the N transept. S wall. Lady E. Caroline Duncombe †1911. Her portrait is revealed by an angel seated against a Late Norman arch. Signed by *F. J. Williamson*. – WAR MEMORIAL. Cross of 1920, by *A. E. Cogswell*.

Much of Waresley's appeal is as the model estate village created by the Duncombes after they purchased Waresley Hall (*see* below) in 1834. Facing the church is a group of thatched brick COTTAGES, all to a similar picturesque pattern with tall chimneys but with nicely varied details between them. The architect was *Henry Ashton*, 1864. Opposite, a nice LAMP in front of the DUNCOMBE ARMS, which has a two-storey porch under a shaped gable. Former READING ROOM of 1906 at its E end. The same Dutch gables appear in VICARAGE ROAD on cottages dated 1846. The houses here are even more varied, including a half-timbered pair with jettied and gabled bays. At the bottom of the road, by the site of the old churchyard, the OLD VICARAGE is a rather engaging red brick C18 house with a two-storey pedimented projection in the centre that is flanked by single-storey pedimented pavilions in gault brick joined by a porch, additions made by *W. Abbott* of St Neots in 1817.

WARESLEY HALL, NW of the church, is the converted office wing of the original mansion which stood to the W and was demolished after the estate was divided in 1932. The wing has a pedimented centre with urns on the S front and a reset doorcase with columns and triglyph frieze on the N side. It existed by 1826 and it was probably about this time that the old house was 'repaired and improved at great expence' for Lord Kilmorey. The Duncombes enlarged it *c.* 1840. Immediately E, the fine red brick U-plan STABLES (now Waresley Grange), which have a pediment and cupola over the central archway (now blocked) and arches to the bays l. and r. Erected before 1792, the stables are shown in *Repton*'s Red Book for the park.

In the park's w half, looking down to a lake, is WARESLEY PARK. 1934 by *Guthrie* of *Wimperis, Simpson & Guthrie* for A. J. Redman, chairman of Wells & Winch Brewery at Biggleswade. It has been altered but is a large painted brick villa with a round tower in the centre and wings at an angle, i.e. the sun-trap plan that was in vogue between the wars.

WASHINGLEY *see* FOLKSWORTH

WATER NEWTON

'Water' here means the Nene, on whose bank the church lies.

ST REMIGIUS. An uncommon dedication outside East Anglia and usually clear evidence of an Early Christian site. That is supported by the discovery in 1975 of a hoard of C4 Roman liturgical silver, the so-called Water Newton Treasure. Ashlar-faced early C14 w tower with an inserted niche on the w side in which stands a small praying figure in a gown. The inscription beneath reads: *Vous ke par issi passez pur le alme Thomas Purdew priez.* Long twin bell-openings with shaft and reset Norman chevron on the super-arch. Continuous roll mouldings. Do they come from an earlier church here? Broach spire with two tiers of lucarnes. The arch towards the nave is small, no more than a door, and the blocked triangular head above it remains a mystery. E.E. the s arcade. Three bays, the first pier octagonal, the second quatrefoil. Round single-chamfered arches. The same in the N arcade of octagonal piers, which is E.E. too but much replaced in 1886–7 by *J. C. Traylen* along with the rebuilding of the aisle and the chancel. Very curiously the aisle's w arch has its respond inside a separate chamber at the aisle's w end; the date of this chamber is probably late C14 (slit windows and a little trefoil high up in its w wall) but its purpose is unclear. To the s arcade belong in style the s porch entrance, but the s doorway with its filleted roll mouldings must be late C13. The clerestory has Y-tracery, and so it too is no earlier than the end of the C13 but probably of the same time as the tower. But most of the windows of the church are later, with square heads and chamfered mullions. This applies to the chancel throughout, except the Dec E window, yet the SEDILIA and PISCINA are E.E., and there are traces of the E.E. windows also. – FONT. Perp, octagonal. – SCREEN. Perp, of high and narrow one-light divisions. – DESK. The two ends have poppyheads, each with two little human heads; copied for the late C19 choir stalls etc. – STAINED GLASS. Mostly of after the 1880s restoration, the E window (Crucifixion, Resurrection and Ascension) by *Clayton & Bell*, the excellent composition typical of its designer, *George Daniels.* – MONUMENT. Defaced effigy of a civilian, late C13 (s aisle).

In the foreground of the church, the early C18 RECTORY makes a pretty picture. On the village road, which was the Great North Road, are two former inns, of which the larger is WATER NEWTON HOUSE, also with a regular C18 front, but mullioned windows at the back and a staircase inside of *c.* 1680. Opposite is the site of Water Newton Hall, which was ruinous and mostly demolished by 1742, when it was sold. A straight row of COTTAGES is adapted from its outbuildings. E of the church a large former WATERMILL of 1791.

The site of the former Roman town of DUROBRIVAE lies NE of the A1 road between Water Newton and Chesterton. The line of the TOWN WALL, enclosing an area of 44 acres (17.6 ha), is marked by a substantial bank with, on the western side of the town, a broad and now shallow depression which formed the town ditch. Across the middle of the enclosed area the impressive bank of ERMINE STREET can be seen, but nothing else is visible. The road continued NE across the Nene through the town's industrial suburbs; *see* Ailsworth. See also Introduction, p. 360.

WENNINGTON

2070

A hamlet of Abbots Ripton (q.v.), almost exclusively of timber-framed houses, with a pond in the centre. The most interesting is WEAVERS (or WEEPERS) COTTAGE, most likely late C15 or early C16. Hall and parlour separated by a cross-passage (into which a late C17 brick chimney is inserted) and with an aisle along the N side. Some small diamond-mullioned windows. At the E end a small attached byre, converted in the C17 into two rooms with a staircase to chambers above.

WERRINGTON *see* PETERBOROUGH

WEST PERRY *see* PERRY

WESTWOOD *see* PETERBOROUGH

WILLOW HALL *see* THORNEY

2060

WINTRINGHAM HALL
2 m. E of St Neots

Built for Thomas Day in 1868–71 by *John Usher* of Bedford. Dated on its weathervane. Gables and clusters of tall Tudorish chimneys with spokes. The staircase window has the Rowleys' coat of arms, dated 1899, for Charles Percival Rowley. s is the farmyard, including a brick GRANARY with arcaded lower storey. Surrounding the garden, three sides of a MOAT, one of three associated with the vanished hamlet of Wintringham.

WINWICK

1080

ALL SAINTS. Perp w tower with broach spire for which money was left for bells in 1496 and its 'edification' in 1502. Angle buttresses with ashlar dressings and set-offs. Two tiers of lucarnes. The aisles embrace it. The s aisle is *c.* 1300 – see one window with intersecting and one (w) with reticulated tracery – but the s doorway is a late C12 reuse of Late Norman chevron set at right angles to the wall. The s transept has a Dec PISCINA, but a large Perp window with a transom. The chancel is a good C13 piece, although restored by *Slater & Carpenter*, 1864–5. Chamfered buttresses similar to those at Leighton Bromswold (q.v.), and two N lancets. The chancel arch responds are C13 too; the arch has two hollow chamfers. Dec s window. The large geometrical E window dates from 1864–5, along with the round, octofoiled clerestory windows. The arcades are late C13 and early C14. Four bays, low, on the s alternating round and octagonal piers with a little nailhead, on the N octagonal piers. The N aisle E window of about the same time, with intersecting tracery of elongated quatrefoils, but the other window straight-headed and C16, to go with the roof of the aisle and transept which have straight ties with carved bosses, some in the N aisle with names carved on scrolls. – SCREEN (s transept). Wide one-light divisions with ogee arches and busy details. Mostly C19. – ALTAR TABLE. Early C17, tapered and fluted baluster legs. – EAGLE LECTERN. Mid-C19, carved by *W. Pepper* of Brighton.

Grim PARSONAGE by the church of 1864, provided by the Duke of Buccleuch; also by *Slater & Carpenter*.

Former CONGREGATIONAL CHAPEL of 1865 with a pedimented front and channelled brick pilasters.

WESTWARD HOUSE. Outwardly uninteresting but concealing a substantial roof structure and traces of decorative wall painting on the roof plaster, suggesting it was in the C16 a larger house of some importance.*

WISTOW

2080

ST JOHN THE BAPTIST. Of cobbles, but the Late Perp w tower of stone, with straight-headed door and round-headed windows.

---

*I am grateful to Louise Brown for drawing this to my attention.

The top part at least must be mid-C16: bequests for bells were made in 1537, 1545 and 1557. Perp also the high and wide two-bay arcades. Piers of continuous mouldings to the nave, shafts with capitals to the arch openings and fleurons in their mouldings. To each bay corresponds a pair of two-light clerestory windows which have the unusual feature of cusped and subcusped rere-arches. Indeed, despite the small scale of the nave, the detail is rather richer than is usual locally for Perp. The mouldings of the arcades and the hoodmouldings of the clerestory windows have crawling beasts as stops. A higher rood-stair turret at the E end of the clerestory. The chancel arch corresponds to the arcades, the tower arch is plainer and very oddly the capitals of its shafts carry nothing. Was there a screen? The nave roof has figures against the wall-posts and against the sub-principals. The N aisle roof has figures on the wall-posts only; they also carry the dates 1668 and 1845. In the chancel ogee-headed SEDILIA and a lowside window of two lights with a transom. The lights are ogee-headed too, and the chancel was indeed consecrated in 1347. Close to the S doorway is evidence of the church preceding this, thought to have been rebuilt by Abbot Robert Trianel (1180–1200) of Ramsey: a fragmentary Norman tympanum with diapering of four-petalled flowers and a bit of chevron, discovered in the restoration of 1931–2 by *W. A. Lea*. C19 chancel roof with tracery in the tie-beams and big standing angels on the corbels. – SCREENS. In the S chapel of three-light divisions with single ogee-headed arches to the centre doors. – Under the tower arch, the former rood screen is plainer, of one-light divisions. – SOUTH DOOR. Symmetrical sparse iron scroll-work of the mid C14; also the ghost of a C strap and fleur-de-lis of *c.* 1200. – ROYAL ARMS. Victorian. Painted and carved wood. – STAINED GLASS. The S aisle W window is complete, with figures of the Virgin of the Annunciation and the Resurrection and small angels below and in the tracery head. It is all early C15 and was originally in the chancel E window. How is it no one smashed it up? Reassembled in 1872 to make way for the present four-light E window (Calvary, Crucifixion, Resurrection, Ascension) by *Clayton & Bell*, 1873; by the same firm, the S aisle E window, the Adoration, *c.* 1883. In the chancel N and S windows, glass by *Wailes* of *c.* 1860; the N aisle E and W windows of *c.* 1867 and 1869 to the same family must be his too. – MONUMENTS. Virginia Mary Thatcher †1895. A brass plaque with an angel and scroll. By *Jones & Willis*.

ROOKS GROVE FARMHOUSE, 350 yds SW. Timber-framed, early C16 hall and cross-wings behind C19 yellow brick. In the hall a moulded beam and in the W wing a ground-floor room with good early C18 panelling, including a shell-headed niche and fluted pilasters to the fireplace.

MANOR FARM, 175 yds E of the church. Dated 1662 on the chimney. Plastered timber frame with some attractive decoration of swags and scrolls.

WITTERING [P]

A flat broad heath by the Great North Road, just s of Stamford. There must have been little of a village before the RFC airfield (now RAF Wittering) was established in 1916. Both have grown sizeably since the Second World War. Until 2010 the scream of Harrier jets provided the soundtrack for most of the surrounding villages.

ALL SAINTS. At the E edge of the village. People who visit come to gaze at the chancel arch, which, in its cyclopean crudity, is without equal. It is probably mid- to late C11, perhaps of the earlier date given its proximity to Barnack, from where the stone was quarried,* although no church is recorded in 1086. A half-roll in the respond, a half-roll just outside the angle, a rectangular projection further out. Combined capital and abacus block 18 in. (45.7 cm) tall and three times that wide, tapering out towards the top but without any moulding whatever. The three mouldings or bands are carried on round the arch. On the W face there are pilaster strips. It all makes even Barnack (q.v.) look refined. Yet of its rude force there can be no question. Perfect long-and-short work is preserved at the angles of the chancel and the nave (the NE angle to be seen inside). Mid-C12 N arcade of two bays with big circular pier and square abacus. Many-scalloped capital. Similar triple-shafted responds but with the nicks so common in the area. The odd feature is that the arches have one big roll much like the chancel arch but outer bands of well-cut point-to-point lozenges (E) and chevron at right angles (W), which collide rather awkwardly above the centre pier. Late C13 W tower, see the pointed-trefoiled windows and the bell-openings of two lights with a quatrefoiled circle. Short spire with two tiers of lucarnes in alternating directions. Of about the same time the N aisle, chancel S window and the S doorway of the nave. Early C14 N chapel, opening to the chancel in one arch of one chamfer and one hollow. The inner arch is carried on head corbels. Early C14 also the tomb recess in the chapel. Reroofed in 1874–5. – FONT. Norman tub. – STAINED GLASS. – E window by *Kempe*, 1903. – N aisle, 1920s by *A. L. & C. E. Moore*. – Chapel E (RAF Memorial), by *W. H. Harvey* of York, 1968. Typically vivid, with air crew and an aerial St Michael slaying Satan.

RAF WITTERING. The base was a 'V', i.e. nuclear, bomber station from 1954 until 1968. Associated with this period of the Cold War, a HANGAR for storage and service of Blue Steel missiles and FISSILE CORE STORE, with wavy concrete roof.

---

*It could be even earlier, since estates at Wittering were purchased for the abbey of Peterborough from Thorney in the late C10.

WOOD WALTON

St ANDREW. All alone, a familiar sight from the railway line. Redundant from 1967, but cared for by the Friends of Friendless Churches from 1979 and since 2000 partially restored. Dec w tower with pyramid roof, given battlements and heightened in 1859–60 by *Edward Browning*. More carefully reconstructed Dec chancel with straight-headed windows, including a lowside window. The s arcade is E.E., of four bays with two round piers and arches of one step and one chamfer. The w pier and w respond and the E respond are Perp. Perp also the N arcade. The piers are double-chamfered, the outer chamfers continuous, the inner with capitals, two with shields, two with crenellation. – TILES. In the chancel, of 1874, laid over earlier encaustic tiles. Mosaic work to the reredos and painted Creed and Commandments. – STAINED GLASS. Mostly lost.* – MONUMENTS. Lt Gen. Vere Warner Hussey †1823, signed by *S. Manning*. Plain white marble on grey. Vice Admiral Sir Richard Hussey Hussey †1842, signed by *Hopper*. A little Neo-Grec detail and a crest.

Above the church, by the road, the old RECTORY. Gothic, 1856 by *Fulljames & Waller* of Gloucester. Spired roof over the staircase.

CASTLE HILL, *c.* 700 yds NNE. A motte and bailey, the motte being *c.* 135 ft (41 metres) in diameter. The date is most probably early to mid C12. The position of the church may be explained by having to serve one settlement around the castle and the present village to the s.

WOODCROFT CASTLE [P]
1¼ m. s of Etton

A fragment of a late C13 or early C14 fortified house, surrounded by a moat on three sides, with later alterations and additions. Almost nothing is known of its history. The present front has a stout circular tower on the l. and had an identical one on the r. Gatehouse in the middle of three storeys, the rest of two and a half. There was originally probably a courtyard and perhaps two more towers, on the pattern of Barnwell (Northants) and also Harlech. The windows with shouldered lintels and transom in the gateway and tower are in fact characteristic of the Welsh Edwardian castles ('Caernarvon arches'). The ranges between towers and gateway have a cornice above the upper floor, and this is taken up to include the second upper floor of the gatehouse. The entire attic storey of these ranges above the cornice is late C19 with straight parapet where formerly there was a

---

*Two complete C14 figures of St Catherine and St Lawrence are now at the Stained Glass Museum, Ely.

Woodcroft Castle.
Drawing by P. Tillemans, 1721

pitched roof, and the traceried windows of two and three lights
are of the same date. Gateway with segmental double-chamfered arches. (Inside the gateway are cross walls that are built
at an oblique angle (cf. Northborough Manor). Above the
gateway a former chapel, with piscina (C15). It had a balcony
to the S wall, lit by a window which shows that the S range was
originally much lower. A three-bay chamber inside with one
big medieval fireplace. In the tower a chamber with garderobe.
Behind the remaining tower a projection, probably the former
stair-tower, and an Early Tudor range. Windows with arched
lights and hoodmoulds, also late C19.)*

WOODHURST

St John the Baptist. A chapelry of St Ives. Chancel, nave, S
aisle, and shingled bell-turret supported inside on a braced
post. Restored in 1871–2 by *William White* (cf. Old Hurst). The
N wall was rebuilt but the N doorway is basically Norman. S
arcade E.E. Four bays, round piers, double-chamfered arches.
The S windows are Perp, the SE window with a piscina in the
sill, the roof and clerestory post-medieval, possibly of 1624, the
date on the bell (by *William Haulsey* of St Ives). Chancel of
1848, unfortunately yellow brick, its E window redone by
White. – STALLS. By White, returned against the screen. –
BENCH ENDS. Four, with elementary poppyheads, provide the
model for the C19 ones.
At the E end of SOUTH STREET is a late C17 or very early C18
brick T-plan house (HOLDICH FARMHOUSE) of seven bays
with hipped roof, modillion cornice, platband and raised keystones. N of this, at the E end of CHURCH STREET, the MANOR

---

*It was not possible to obtain access to the castle so the description is revised
according to the account given in A. Emery, *Greater Medieval Houses of England and
Wales*, vol. II (2000).

HOUSE, also brick, but a little later. Five bays, deep hipped roof, windows now with segmental heads. Narrow windows, mostly blocked, on the flanks. The doorcase with segmental pediment is 1950s. The rear wing is C17. Both houses have good staircases with turned balusters climbing to the attics.

WOODSTON *see* PETERBOROUGH

WOOLLEY *see* BARHAM

WYTON

ST MARGARET AND ALL SAINTS. Now a house. Brown cobbles and externally mostly Perp, with chancel and nave of almost

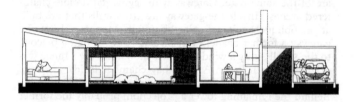

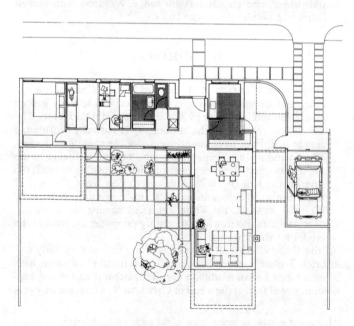

Wyton, Victoria Crescent, housing.
Elevation and plan, 1960–4

equal length. The label stops of the s doorway and s window are specially pretty. However, the following are not Perp. First the sw steeple (rather starved), the s porch and the rebuilt N aisle,* all by *R. Hutchinson*, 1865–6. A tower of 1846 preceded the present one and replaced an 'unpretending bellcot' (*Ecclesiologist*, 1845). Then the priest's doorway, with a little dogtooth, and the paired lancets in the chancel. They are early C13. A very little later is the N doorway, with stiff-leaf capitals looking *c*. 1230–40 and a keeled roll moulding. The doorway goes perfectly with the N arcade, which is a beautiful design. Four bays and two different pier shapes: octagonal, and four keeled shafts and four minor shafts. Deeply moulded arches, including keeled rolls. Very bold and animated stiff-leaf capitals, all different. The Perp roof-corbels of the nave deserve notice: foliage, grapes, a rose-sprig, heads. – N vestry etc. 1912. N DOOR. Ironwork *c*. 1300–50, with hinge scrolls emanating from animals. It is reset from a larger door. – STAINED GLASS. E window, 1917.[†]

THREE JOLLY BUTCHERS. Timber-framed and plastered. Dated 1622. A good example of the yeoman class of house, with a long jetty and gabled cross-wing. Inside, the l. room has a beam with scroll ornament. Wall paintings with arcades whose arches support pendants (cf. Pepys House, Brampton) are no longer visible. W of this and in a similar class, MAGDALENE HOUSE (originally Magdalene College Farm), again with a long-jetty and a lobby entry, and STUART HOUSE, dated 1648 on its central stack.

In VICTORIA CRESCENT some interesting single-storey courtyard houses with monopitch roofs and exteriors of white brick and black weatherboard, a private development of 1962–4 designed by *Colin St John Wilson, John Dalton & Anthony Eardley*. Each is L-plan with the nice feature of a curved screen wall meeting the garage. Some have an additional bedroom forming the house into a U.

RAF WYTON. Established 1918 but much expanded in 1936–7 for bombers, including the Pathfinder force in the Second World War. Four large HANGARS of that date and the CONTROL TOWER. A rare survival is the concrete DOME, designed for training gunners. Much redevelopment *c*. 2010 for the RAF Logistics HQ.

YAXLEY

1090

A prosperous place in the medieval period, as the church indicates, with good trading connections along the Nene. It enjoyed

---

*Pevsner noted 'three incongruously placed gargoyles in the outer wall of the N aisle' from the tower of 1846. They have been removed.

[†]A N window with *Kempe & Co.* glass of 1906, noted in the first edition of this guide, has been removed.

a revival from the late C18, when the Yaxley Fen was drained. It is now of two parts, with the earlier settlement on the low ground at the base of a long ridge above the fen but considerable late C19 and C20 development on the crest of the hill. The church lies between the two in a surprisingly rural setting.

89 ST PETER. One of the most rewarding churches in Huntingdonshire. It is large, and it represents all medieval styles after the Norman and yet does not lose its unity. One niche in the E wall of the S transept with a round head and a continuous roll moulding might even be accepted as Late Norman, but it is most probably reset. By the C13 it was cruciform, for the transepts themselves are E.E., see the E lancets and, in the N transept, a W lancet too. Then comes the ambitious late C13 work. Yaxley was held by Thorney Abbey and Abbot William de Yaxley founded a chantry here in 1291, which may help to date the remodelling of the E end with N and S chapels. In the N chapel are three-light windows of stepped lancet lights with trefoils in the tracery, and the same type also occurs not only in the N transept N wall but also in the S chapel, where the lancet lights are under one arch. The two E windows of the N aisle are also of three stepped lancet lights under one arch but without tracery, and in the W bay of the S aisle, which now embraces the later tower, the windows are again of three stepped lancet lights without tracery. It is incidentally worth noticing how wide this S aisle already was. Such wide aisles only came in in the later C13 (cf. e.g. Grantham, Lincs.). The S doorway has three orders of thin shafts with rings and three orders of thin roll mouldings, two with fillets. It appears also to have had cusping around the inner frame, now lost. The S transept had its S window replaced early in the C14 by a large window with elongated reticulated tracery, and the dominating E and SE windows of the S chapel have lively flowing tracery of, say, c. 1330–40. Also flowing tracery, but much more exuberant, in the chancel E wall (and much more restored) in 1868 by E. L. Blackburn who rebuilt the chancel and recreated the nave. Five lights, a delightfully sinuous pattern.

There now only remains the Perp contribution of the late C15, and it is considerable: not only the S porch with the three niches above the entrance and three supporter beasts on the gable, and the remaining aisle and chapel windows, but also the clerestory, and of course the grand W tower, which is a descendant of the tower of Whittlesey (Cambs.) and for which money was left in wills of 1486 and 1506. This is high, ashlar-faced, and kept together by clasping buttresses with many shallow set-offs (cf. Elton), and it has large three-light bell-openings of a typically elaborated kind, and a recessed crocketed spire with two tiers of lucarnes. The spire is steadied – so the eye feels – by the delicate flying buttresses with openwork quatrefoils which connect it with the pinnacles in the four corners of the tower. The design is unique in Huntingdonshire but to be found also in Northamptonshire. The arches towards nave and aisle W bays

are all Perp too and the four-bay arcades. The piers have characteristic mouldings, capitals only on the shafts towards the
arch openings and wall-shafts to the nave carrying the roof
trusses, which make the interior seem so impressively open and
lofty. Over the aisles the roofs have traceried spandrels. Between
the aisles and transepts the arches are equally tall but with
four-centred heads. They are accompanied by earlier arches
which have lost their jambs on one side, presumably the
remains of the late C13 openings into the transept chapels.
Tower arches glazed for parish rooms etc. in the late 1990s.

The rest of the interior confirms the late C13 exterior.
Chancel arch, two-bay N chapel arcade with quatrefoil piers
and double-chamfered arches, three-bay S chapel arcade with
quatrefoil piers with fillets. Double-chamfered arches again. In
the N chapel also a good late C13 SEDILIA and PISCINA
(pointed-trefoiled arches under gables). Flanking the early C14
chancel E window two high niches with ogee canopies and in
the S chapel brackets for images also of the same date as the
windows; one wide and one narrow, which is interpreted as the
setting for a kneeling angel and standing Virgin, indicating this
as the Lady Chapel. The S chapel has two sets of aumbries and
piscinae, suggesting it was lengthened by one bay in the early
C14. – FONT. Octagonal, the panels simply bordered by a thin
roll moulding. This probably represents the late C13. – PULPIT.
Dated 1631. With back panel and sounding-board that has
pendants. The patterns are mostly stylized leaf. – STALLS. The
kneeling-desks are Perp, with arched panels in front and poppyheads on the ends. They are returned against the SCREEN,
also Perp, tall, of one-light divisions. Above it rises, in the
manner of a rood loft (the original taken down in 1868), the
large ORGAN LOFT and CASE of 1910 by *Temple Moore*.
The transition from old to new is handled superbly with tracery
in the heads of the lights and mini-vaulting to the loft. Stair in
a stone tower, its door with reused linenfold panels. Moore
restored the chancel well in 1902–5 (paid for by Lord Carysfort) and the rest in 1907–10, reusing much plain WOODWORK
in benches, the chancel screens etc. – REREDOS to Moore's
altar by *J. N. Comper*, 1946; of one mind with the E window.
– WALL PAINTINGS. Rediscovered in 1848 when the church
was restored. Still extensive but sadly nothing any longer that
would be enjoyable. Above the arcade on the S side of the N
chapel are early C14 post-Resurrection scenes. More above the
E bays of the nave arcades, indistinguishable. The early C16
Doom over the chancel arch is obscured. On the W wall of the
nave, early C17 texts, a gravedigger, a skeleton, a man in Roman
armour, as well as the ROYAL ARMS of Charles, Prince of Wales,
c. 1611. Uncommon style, with angel supporters. Also Queen
Anne's arms, 1702. – STAINED GLASS. In the S chapel E
window humble but characteristic glass of 1849. The E window,
alas just as characteristic of 1949 (in its refusal to accept the
C20 at all), is by *Geoffrey Webb*, to Comper's design. Christ
Pantrokrator, the faces all youthful and clean-cut, as was the

preference in the mid C20. – MONUMENTS. In the N transept one arched panel with sunk carving of two arms holding a heart. This represents a heart burial, and the small tubular box found behind it contained the heart. The burial is convincingly attributed to William de Yaxley, Abbot of Thorney, †1293. – Many tablets in the S chapel. Thomas Squire †1789, a merchant who 'paid to make Nene navigable from Peterborough to Islip'. Captain William Papp †1797 at the Norman Cross barracks and Martha Smith †1801, both signed by *Samuel Andrews* of Wisbech and in his artisan classical style. – Elizabeth Hopkins †1870. A Dec niche by *Thompson*, Peterborough.

In the churchyard, by the S porch, Robert Nicholes †1733. Table tomb with slate panels of exquisite copperplate inscription and patterns. (Cross by *Comper*, 1936.)

E of the church, the former VICARAGE of 1870 by *James Shilcock* of Hitchin; he added the stables etc. in 1877. The MAIN STREET is SE of the church and runs NE – far from straight. Nos. 215–17, at the start, has the kind of flat framework of vertical and horizontal raised brick bands typical of *c.* 1675. There are also two blank ovals placed vertically, and they were just as popular about 1675. However, the broad doorway with its Doric pilasters and triglyph frieze looks 1700 and evidently stands r. of the door's original position. Inside, panelling of *c.* 1700 in one room with a shell-headed niche. In the rest of the street, several houses have the distinctive early C18 feature of tumbled brick gables. Of individual note, No. 183 (S side), with its charming early C19 shopfront, and No. 159, a rather too keenly restored late C18 house with brick front and sides, two canted bay windows on the ground floor, tripartite windows above them, an arched window in the centre and a stone doorcase with columns and an open pediment. Lovely cast-iron railings and gates. Furthest E is the former SCHOOL, dated 1848. It is of yellow brick and Gothic and has, to one's surprise, a triangular porch under a bellcote. School house of 1892. Opposite, the former METHODIST CHAPEL is dated 1812. It is also of yellow brick. Three-bay width, pyramid roof.

YELLING

HOLY CROSS. Of brown cobbles. The three-bay N arcade is of *c.* 1190, i.e. the piers are round, but the abaci square and the capitals still of the multi-fluted and multi-scalloped kind, but the arches, though unmoulded, are pointed. Their form and the simple responds remind one of the chancel arch at Little Paxton (q.v.). The S arcade of four bays with standard elements (but broaches at the start of the arches) looks *c.* 1300. So do the S aisle windows (Y-tracery, still geometrical tracery with a quatrefoil and a trefoil in a circle) and S doorway (two continuous chamfers). A plain, low tomb recess in the aisle wall inside, with coffin slab of a foliate cross and circle head. Again, the chancel is of *c.* 1300 or has work of that date. The SEDILIA and PISCINA with filleted shafts fit it, but the wide chancel arch with its trilobe piers looks a little later. Late C14 W tower, but still with Dec bell-openings. The tower had a spire up to the C19. Most of the rest is Perp, e.g. the large E window of five lights with two tiers above it and a battlemented transom. N aisle rebuilt in 1868–9 by *Frederick Preedy*, the window details in Geometrical style. – STAINED GLASS. E window. C19. Five saints in clear settings. Two in the N aisle, St Paul and the Sermon on the Mount of *c.* 1870 by *Preedy*. – Good Perp-style LYCHGATE, *c.* 1900, with cusped bargeboards and four-centred arches.

BAPTIST CHAPEL. 1850. Yellow brick, three by three bays. Segment-headed windows (a solecism in 1850) with plastic frames (a solecism today), pilaster strips, a triglyph frieze of brick, very incorrect, and a big pediment across the façade. Restored 1883; pulpit of that date.

CHURCH FARM HOUSE, opposite the church. An interesting mid- to later C17 brick job, five by three bays. Angle pilasters and pilasters flanking the middle, all in two tiers with a moulded string between and dentilled and sawtooth eaves cornice above. On the W front a reset pediment from a former window or doorway. Two flat brick stacks across the middle. Behind the skin a stout timber frame and a splendid staircase which is placed between an entrance lobby (cf. The Limes, Spaldwick) and the central passage. Splat balusters, angled to the ascent, and shaped finials on the newels. At the base and first floor are arches with pendants. Good stone fireplaces and in two rooms C18 panelling, one imported from Albury Hall, Herts. (dem. *c.* 1950).

OLD RECTORY, W of the church, is Early Georgian, soft red brick of five by three bays, a stucco band, box cornice and a hipped roof but also a taller addition of 1851 by *George Allen* of St Ives, still very Georgian in fine gault brick, which almost amounts to a house in itself.

GLOSSARY

Numbers and letters refer to the illustrations (by John Sambrook) on pp. 742–749.

ABACUS: flat slab forming the top of a capital (3a).

ACANTHUS: classical formalized leaf ornament (4b).

ACCUMULATOR TOWER: *see* Hydraulic power.

ACHIEVEMENT: a complete display of armorial bearings.

ACROTERION: plinth for a statue or ornament on the apex or ends of a pediment; more usually, both the plinth and what stands on it (4a).

AEDICULE (*lit.* little building): architectural surround, consisting usually of two columns or pilasters supporting a pediment.

AGGREGATE: *see* Concrete.

AISLE: subsidiary space alongside the body of a building, separated from it by columns, piers, or posts.

ALMONRY: a building from which alms are dispensed to the poor.

AMBULATORY (*lit.* walkway): aisle around the sanctuary (q.v.).

ANGLE ROLL: roll moulding in the angle between two planes (1a).

ANSE DE PANIER: *see* Arch.

ANTAE: simplified pilasters (4a), usually applied to the ends of the enclosing walls of a portico *in antis* (q.v.).

ANTEFIXAE: ornaments projecting at regular intervals above a Greek cornice, originally to conceal the ends of roof tiles (4a).

ANTHEMION: classical ornament like a honeysuckle flower (4b).

APRON: raised panel below a window or wall monument or tablet.

APSE: semicircular or polygonal end of an apartment, especially of a chancel or chapel. In classical architecture sometimes called an *exedra*.

ARABESQUE: non-figurative surface decoration consisting of flowing lines, foliage scrolls etc., based on geometrical patterns. Cf. Grotesque.

ARCADE: series of arches supported by piers or columns. *Blind arcade* or *arcading*: the same applied to the wall surface. *Wall arcade*: in medieval churches, a blind arcade forming a dado below windows. Also a covered shopping street.

ARCH: Shapes *see* 5c. *Basket arch* or *anse de panier* (basket handle): three-centred and depressed, or with a flat centre. *Nodding*: ogee arch curving forward from the wall face. *Parabolic*: shaped like a chain suspended from two level points, but inverted. Special purposes. *Chancel*: dividing chancel from nave or crossing. *Crossing*: spanning piers at a crossing (q.v.). *Relieving or discharging*: incorporated in a wall to relieve superimposed weight (5c). *Skew*: spanning responds not diametrically opposed. *Strainer*: inserted in an opening to resist inward pressure. *Transverse*: spanning a main axis (e.g. of a vaulted space). *See also* Jack arch, Triumphal arch.

ARCHITRAVE: formalized lintel, the lowest member of the classical entablature (3a). Also the moulded frame of a door or window (often borrowing the profile of a classical architrave). For *lugged* and *shouldered* architraves *see* 4b.

ARCUATED: dependent structurally on the arch principle. Cf. Trabeated.

ARK: chest or cupboard housing the

tables of Jewish law in a syn-
agogue.

ARRIS: sharp edge where two
surfaces meet at an angle (3a).

ASHLAR: masonry of large blocks
wrought to even faces and square
edges (6d).

ASTRAGAL: classical moulding of
semicircular section (3f).

ASTYLAR: with no columns or
similar vertical features.

ATLANTES: *see* Caryatids.

ATRIUM (plural: atria): inner court
of a Roman or C20 house; in a
multi-storey building, a toplit
covered court rising through all
storeys. Also an open court in
front of a church.

ATTACHED COLUMN: *see* Engaged
column.

ATTIC: small top storey within
a roof. Also the storey above the
main entablature of a classical
façade.

AUMBRY: recess or cupboard to
hold sacred vessels for the Mass.

BAILEY: *see* Motte-and-bailey.

BALANCE BEAM: *see* Canals.

BALDACCHINO: free-standing canopy, originally fabric, over an
altar. Cf. Ciborium.

BALLFLOWER: globular flower of
three petals enclosing a ball (1a).
Typical of the Decorated style.

BALUSTER: pillar or pedestal of
bellied form. *Balusters*: vertical
supports of this or any other form,
for a handrail or coping, the whole
being called a *balustrade* (6c).
Blind balustrade: the same applied
to the wall surface.

BARBICAN: outwork defending the
entrance to a castle.

BARGEBOARDS (corruption of
'vergeboards'): boards, often
carved or fretted, fixed beneath
the eaves of a gable to cover and
protect the rafters.

BAROQUE: style originating in Rome
c.1600 and current in England
c.1680–1720, characterized by
dramatic massing and silhouette
and the use of the giant order.

BARROW: burial mound.

BARTIZAN: corbelled turret, square
or round, frequently at an angle.

BASCULE: hinged part of a lifting (or
bascule) bridge.

BASE: moulded foot of a column or
pilaster. For *Attic* base *see* 3b.

BASEMENT: lowest, subordinate
storey; hence the lowest part of a
classical elevation, below the *piano
nobile* (q.v.).

BASILICA: a Roman public hall;
hence an aisled building with a
clerestory.

BASTION: one of a series of defensive semicircular or polygonal projections from the main wall of a
fortress or city.

BATTER: intentional inward inclina-
tion of a wall face.

BATTLEMENT: defensive parapet,
composed of *merlons* (solid) and
crenels (embrasures) through
which archers could shoot; sometimes called *crenellation*. Also used
decoratively.

BAY: division of an elevation or
interior space as defined by regular
vertical features such as arches,
columns, windows etc.

BAY LEAF: classical ornament of
overlapping bay leaves (3f).

BAY WINDOW: window of one or
more storeys projecting from the
face of a building. *Canted*: with
a straight front and angled sides.
Bow window: curved. *Oriel*: rests
on corbels or brackets and starts
above ground level; also the bay
window at the dais end of a medieval great hall.

BEAD-AND-REEL: *see* Enrichments.

BEAKHEAD: Norman ornament
with a row of beaked bird or beast
heads usually biting into a roll
moulding (1a).

BELFRY: chamber or stage in a
tower where bells are hung.

BELL CAPITAL: *see* 1b.

BELLCOTE: small gabled or roofed
housing for the bell(s).

BERM: level area separating a ditch
from a bank on a hill-fort or
barrow.

BILLET: Norman ornament of small
half-cylindrical or rectangular
blocks (1a).

BLIND: *see* Arcade, Baluster, Portico.

BLOCK CAPITAL: *see* 1a.

BLOCKED: columns, etc. interrupted by regular projecting

blocks (*blocking*), as on a Gibbs surround (4b).

BLOCKING COURSE: course of stones, or equivalent, on top of a cornice and crowning the wall.

BOLECTION MOULDING: covering the joint between two different planes (6b).

BOND: the pattern of long sides (*stretchers*) and short ends (*headers*) produced on the face of a wall by laying bricks in a particular way (6e).

BOSS: knob or projection, e.g. at the intersection of ribs in a vault (2c).

BOWTELL: a term in use by the C15 for a form of roll moulding, usually three-quarters of a circle in section (also called *edge roll*).

BOW WINDOW: *see* Bay window.

BOX FRAME: timber-framed construction in which vertical and horizontal wall members support the roof (7). Also concrete construction where the loads are taken on cross walls; also called *cross-wall construction*.

BRACE: subsidiary member of a structural frame, curved or straight. *Bracing* is often arranged decoratively e.g. quatrefoil, herringbone (7). *See also* Roofs.

BRATTISHING: ornamental crest, usually formed of leaves, Tudor flowers or miniature battlements.

BRESSUMER (*lit.* breast-beam): big horizontal beam supporting the wall above, especially in a jettied building (7).

BRICK: *see* Bond, Cogging, Engineering, Gauged, Tumbling.

BRIDGE: *Bowstring*: with arches rising above the roadway which is suspended from them. *Clapper*: one long stone forms the roadway. *Roving*: *see* Canal. *Suspension*: roadway suspended from cables or chains slung between towers or pylons. *Stay-suspension* or *stay-cantilever*: supported by diagonal stays from towers or pylons. *See also* Bascule.

BRISES-SOLEIL: projecting fins or canopies which deflect direct sunlight from windows.

BROACH: *see* Spire and 1c.

BUCRANIUM: ox skull used decoratively in classical friezes.

BULL-NOSED SILL: sill displaying a pronounced convex upper moulding.

BULLSEYE WINDOW: small oval window, set horizontally (cf. Oculus). Also called *œil de bœuf*.

BUTTRESS: vertical member projecting from a wall to stabilize it or to resist the lateral thrust of an arch, roof, or vault (1c, 2c). A *flying buttress* transmits the thrust to a heavy abutment by means of an arch or half-arch (1c).

CABLE OR ROPE MOULDING: originally Norman, like twisted strands of a rope.

CAMES: *see* Quarries.

CAMPANILE: free-standing bell-tower.

CANALS: *Flash lock*: removable weir or similar device through which boats pass on a flush of water. Predecessor of the *pound lock*: chamber with gates at each end allowing boats to float from one level to another. *Tidal gates*: single pair of lock gates allowing vessels to pass when the tide makes a level. *Balance beam*: beam projecting horizontally for opening and closing lock gates. *Roving bridge*: carrying a towing path from one bank to the other.

CANTILEVER: horizontal projection (e.g. step, canopy) supported by a downward force behind the fulcrum.

CAPITAL: head or crowning feature of a column or pilaster; for classical types *see* 3; for medieval types *see* 1b.

CARREL: compartment designed for individual work or study.

CARTOUCHE: classical tablet with ornate frame (4b).

CARYATIDS: female figures supporting an entablature; their male counterparts are *Atlantes* (*lit.* Atlas figures).

CASEMATE: vaulted chamber, with embrasures for defence, within a castle wall or projecting from it.

CASEMENT: side-hinged window.

CASTELLATED: with battlements (q.v.).

CAST IRON: hard and brittle, cast in a mould to the required shape.

Wrought iron is ductile, strong in tension, forged into decorative patterns or forged and rolled into e.g. bars, joists, boiler plates; *mild steel* is its modern equivalent, similar but stronger.

CATSLIDE: *See* 8a.

CAVETTO: concave classical moulding of quarter-round section (3f).

CELURE OR CEILURE: enriched area of roof above rood or altar.

CEMENT: *see* Concrete.

CENOTAPH (*lit.* empty tomb): funerary monument which is not a burying place.

CENTRING: wooden support for the building of an arch or vault, removed after completion.

CHAMFER (*lit.* corner-break): surface formed by cutting off a square edge or corner. For types of chamfers and *chamfer stops see* 6a. *See also* Double chamfer.

CHANCEL: part of the E end of a church set apart for the use of the officiating clergy.

CHANTRY CHAPEL: often attached to or within a church, endowed for the celebration of Masses principally for the soul of the founder.

CHEVET (*lit.* head): French term for chancel with ambulatory and radiating chapels.

CHEVRON: V-shape used in series or double series (later) on a Norman moulding (1a). Also (especially when on a single plane) called *zigzag*.

CHOIR: the part of a cathedral, monastic or collegiate church where services are sung.

CIBORIUM: a fixed canopy over an altar, usually vaulted and supported on four columns; cf. Baldacchino. Also a canopied shrine for the reserved sacrament.

CINQUEFOIL: *see* Foil.

CIST: stone-lined or slab-built grave.

CLADDING: external covering or skin applied to a structure, especially a framed one.

CLERESTORY: uppermost storey of the nave of a church, pierced by windows. Also high-level windows in secular buildings.

CLOSER: a brick cut to complete a bond (6e).

CLUSTER BLOCK: *see* Multi-storey.

COADE STONE: ceramic artificial stone made in Lambeth 1769–*c.*1840 by Eleanor Coade (†1821) and her associates.

COB: walling material of clay mixed with straw. Also called *pisé*.

COFFERING: arrangement of sunken panels (coffers), square or polygonal, decorating a ceiling, vault, or arch.

COGGING: a decorative course of bricks laid diagonally (6e). Cf. Dentilation.

COLLAR: *see* Roofs and 7.

COLLEGIATE CHURCH: endowed for the support of a college of priests.

COLONNADE: range of columns supporting an entablature. Cf. Arcade.

COLONNETTE: small medieval column or shaft.

COLOSSAL ORDER: *see* Giant order.

COLUMBARIUM: shelved, niched structure to house multiple burials.

COLUMN: a classical, upright structural member of round section with a shaft, a capital, and usually a base (3a, 4a).

COLUMN FIGURE: carved figure attached to a medieval column or shaft, usually flanking a doorway.

COMMUNION TABLE: unconsecrated table used in Protestant churches for the celebration of Holy Communion.

COMPOSITE: *see* Orders.

COMPOUND PIER: grouped shafts (q.v.), or a solid core surrounded by shafts.

CONCRETE: composition of *cement* (calcined lime and clay), *aggregate* (small stones or rock chippings), sand and water. It can be poured into *formwork* or *shuttering* (temporary frame of timber or metal) on site (*in-situ* concrete), or *pre-cast* as components before construction. *Reinforced*: incorporating steel rods to take the tensile force. *Pre-stressed*: with tensioned steel rods. Finishes include the impression of boards left by formwork (*board-marked* or *shuttered*), and texturing with steel brushes (*brushed*) or hammers (*hammer-dressed*). *See also* Shell.

CONSOLE: bracket of curved outline (4b).

COPING: protective course of masonry or brickwork capping a wall (6d).

CORBEL: projecting block supporting something above. *Corbel course*: continuous course of projecting stones or bricks fulfilling the same function. *Corbel table*: series of corbels to carry a parapet or a wall-plate or wall-post (7). *Corbelling*: brick or masonry courses built out beyond one another to support a chimney-stack, window, etc.

CORINTHIAN: *see* Orders and 3d.

CORNICE: flat-topped ledge with moulded underside, projecting along the top of a building or feature, especially as the highest member of the classical entablature (3a). Also the decorative moulding in the angle between wall and ceiling.

CORPS-DE-LOGIS: the main building(s) as distinct from the wings or pavilions.

COTTAGE ORNÉ: an artfully rustic small house associated with the Picturesque movement.

COUNTERCHANGING: of joists on a ceiling divided by beams into compartments, when placed in opposite directions in alternate squares.

COUR D'HONNEUR: formal entrance court before a house in the French manner, usually with flanking wings and a screen wall or gates.

COURSE: continuous layer of stones, etc. in a wall (6e).

COVE: a broad concave moulding, e.g. to mask the eaves of a roof. *Coved ceiling*: with a pronounced cove joining the walls to a flat central panel smaller than the whole area of the ceiling.

CRADLE ROOF: *see* Wagon roof.

CREDENCE: a shelf within or beside a piscina (q.v.), or a table for the sacramental elements and vessels.

CRENELLATION: parapet with crenels (*see* Battlement).

CRINKLE-CRANKLE WALL: garden wall undulating in a series of serpentine curves.

CROCKETS: leafy hooks. *Crocketing* decorates the edges of Gothic features, such as pinnacles, canopies, etc. *Crocket capital*: *see* 1b.

CROSSING: central space at the junction of the nave, chancel, and transepts. *Crossing tower*: above a crossing.

CROSS-WINDOW: with one mullion and one transom (qq.v.).

CROWN-POST: *see* Roofs and 7.

CROWSTEPS: squared stones set like steps, e.g. on a gable (8a).

CRUCKS (*lit.* crooked): pairs of inclined timbers (*blades*), usually curved, set at bay-lengths; they support the roof timbers and, in timber buildings, also support the walls (8b). *Base*: blades rise from ground level to a tie- or collar-beam which supports the roof timbers. *Full*: blades rise from ground level to the apex of the roof, serving as the main members of a roof truss. *Jointed*: blades formed from more than one timber; the lower member may act as a wall-post; it is usually elbowed at wall-plate level and jointed just above. *Middle*: blades rise from half-way up the walls to a tie- or collar-beam. *Raised*: blades rise from half-way up the walls to the apex. *Upper*: blades supported on a tie-beam and rising to the apex.

CRYPT: underground or half-underground area, usually below the E end of a church. *Ring crypt*: corridor crypt surrounding the apse of an early medieval church, often associated with chambers for relics. Cf. Undercroft.

CUPOLA (*lit.* dome): especially a small dome on a circular or polygonal base crowning a larger dome, roof, or turret.

CURSUS: a long avenue defined by two parallel earthen banks with ditches outside.

CURTAIN WALL: a connecting wall between the towers of a castle. Also a non-load-bearing external wall applied to a C20 framed structure.

CUSP: *see* Tracery and 2b.

CYCLOPEAN MASONRY: large irregular polygonal stones, smooth and finely jointed.

CYMA RECTA and CYMA REVERSA: classical mouldings with double curves (3f). Cf. Ogee.

DADO: the finishing (often with panelling) of the lower part of a wall in a classical interior; in origin a formalized continuous pedestal. *Dado rail*: the moulding along the top of the dado.

DAGGER: *see* Tracery and 2b.

DALLE-DE-VERRE (*lit.* glass-slab): a late C20 stained-glass technique, setting large, thick pieces of cast glass into a frame of reinforced concrete or epoxy resin.

DEC (DECORATED): English Gothic architecture *c.* 1290 to *c.* 1350. The name is derived from the type of window tracery (q.v.) used during the period.

DEMI- or HALF-COLUMNS: engaged columns (q.v.) half of whose circumference projects from the wall.

DENTIL: small square block used in series in classical cornices (3c). *Dentilation* is produced by the projection of alternating headers along cornices or stringcourses.

DIAPER: repetitive surface decoration of lozenges or squares flat or in relief. Achieved in brickwork with bricks of two colours.

DIOCLETIAN OR THERMAL WINDOW: semicircular with two mullions, as used in the Baths of Diocletian, Rome (4b).

DISTYLE: having two columns (4a).

DOGTOOTH: E.E. ornament, consisting of a series of small pyramids formed by four stylized canine teeth meeting at a point (1a).

DORIC: *see* Orders and 3a, 3b.

DORMER: window projecting from the slope of a roof (8a).

DOUBLE CHAMFER: a chamfer applied to each of two recessed arches (1a).

DOUBLE PILE: *see* Pile.

DRAGON BEAM: *see* Jetty.

DRESSINGS: the stone or brickwork worked to a finished face about an angle, opening, or other feature.

DRIPSTONE: moulded stone projecting from a wall to protect the lower parts from water. Cf. Hoodmould, Weathering.

DRUM: circular or polygonal stage supporting a dome or cupola. Also one of the stones forming the shaft of a column (3a).

DUTCH or FLEMISH GABLE: *see* 8a.

EASTER SEPULCHRE: tomb-chest used for Easter ceremonial, within or against the N wall of a chancel.

EAVES: overhanging edge of a roof; hence *eaves cornice* in this position.

ECHINUS: ovolo moulding (q.v.) below the abacus of a Greek Doric capital (3a).

EDGE RAIL: *see* Railways.

E.E. (EARLY ENGLISH): English Gothic architecture *c.* 1190–1250.

EGG-AND-DART: *see* Enrichments and 3f.

ELEVATION: any face of a building or side of a room. In a drawing, the same or any part of it, represented in two dimensions.

EMBATTLED: with battlements.

EMBRASURE: small splayed opening in a wall or battlement (q.v.).

ENCAUSTIC TILES: earthenware tiles fired with a pattern and glaze.

EN DELIT: stone cut against the bed.

ENFILADE: reception rooms in a formal series, usually with all doorways on axis.

ENGAGED or ATTACHED COLUMN: one that partly merges into a wall or pier.

ENGINEERING BRICKS: dense bricks, originally used mostly for railway viaducts etc.

ENRICHMENTS: the carved decoration of certain classical mouldings, e.g. the ovolo (qq.v.) with *egg-and-dart*, the cyma reversa with *waterleaf*, the astragal with *bead-and-reel* (3f).

ENTABLATURE: in classical architecture, collective name for the three horizontal members (architrave, frieze, and cornice) carried by a wall or a column (3a).

ENTASIS: very slight convex deviation from a straight line, used to prevent an optical illusion of concavity.

EPITAPH: inscription on a tomb.

EXEDRA: *see* Apse.

EXTRADOS: outer curved face of an arch or vault.

EYECATCHER: decorative building terminating a vista.

FASCIA: plain horizontal band, e.g. in an architrave (3c, 3d) or on a shopfront.

FENESTRATION: the arrangement of windows in a façade.

FERETORY: site of the chief shrine of a church, behind the high altar.

FESTOON: ornamental garland, suspended from both ends. Cf. Swag.

FIBREGLASS, or glass-reinforced polyester (GRP): synthetic resin reinforced with glass fibre. GRC: glass-reinforced concrete.

FIELD: see Panelling and 6b.

FILLET: a narrow flat band running down a medieval shaft or along a roll moulding (1a). It separates larger curved mouldings in classical cornices, fluting or bases (3c).

FLAMBOYANT: the latest phase of French Gothic architecture, with flowing tracery.

FLASH LOCK: see Canals.

FLÈCHE or SPIRELET (lit. arrow): slender spire on the centre of a roof.

FLEURON: medieval carved flower or leaf, often rectilinear (1a).

FLUSHWORK: knapped flint used with dressed stone to form patterns.

FLUTING: series of concave grooves (flutes), their common edges sharp (arris) or blunt (fillet) (3).

FOIL (lit. leaf): lobe formed by the cusping of a circular or other shape in tracery (2b). Trefoil (three), quatrefoil (four), cinquefoil (five), and multifoil express the number of lobes in a shape.

FOLIATE: decorated with leaves.

FORMWORK: see Concrete.

FRAMED BUILDING: where the structure is carried by a framework – e.g. of steel, reinforced concrete, timber – instead of by load-bearing walls.

FREESTONE: stone that is cut, or can be cut, in all directions.

FRESCO: al fresco: painting on wet plaster. Fresco secco: painting on dry plaster.

FRIEZE: the middle member of the classical entablature, sometimes ornamented (3a). Pulvinated frieze (lit. cushioned): of bold convex profile (3c). Also a horizontal band of ornament.

FRONTISPIECE: in C16 and C17 buildings the central feature of doorway and windows above linked in one composition.

GABLE: For types see 8a. Gablet: small gable. Pedimental gable: treated like a pediment.

GADROONING: classical ribbed ornament like inverted fluting that flows into a lobed edge.

GALILEE: chapel or vestibule usually at the W end of a church enclosing the main portal(s).

GALLERY: a long room or passage; an upper storey above the aisle of a church, looking through arches to the nave; a balcony or mezzanine overlooking the main interior space of a building; or an external walkway.

GALLETING: small stones set in a mortar course.

GAMBREL ROOF: see 8a.

GARDEROBE: medieval privy.

GARGOYLE: projecting water spout often carved into human or animal shape.

GAUGED or RUBBED BRICKWORK: soft brick sawn roughly, then rubbed to a precise (gauged) surface. Mostly used for door or window openings (5c).

GAZEBO (jocular Latin, 'I shall gaze'): ornamental lookout tower or raised summer house.

GEOMETRIC: English Gothic architecture c. 1250–1310. See also Tracery. For another meaning, see Stairs.

GIANT or COLOSSAL ORDER: classical order (q.v.) whose height is that of two or more storeys of the building to which it is applied.

GIBBS SURROUND: C18 treatment of an opening (4b), seen particularly in the work of James Gibbs (1682–1754).

GIRDER: a large beam. Box: of hollow-box section. Bowed: with its top rising in a curve. Plate: of I-section, made from iron or steel plates. *Lattice*: with braced framework.

GLAZING BARS: wooden or sometimes metal bars separating and supporting window panes.

GRAFFITI: *see* Sgraffito.

GRANGE: farm owned and run by a religious order.

GRC: *see* Fibreglass.

GRISAILLE: monochrome painting on walls or glass.

GROIN: sharp edge at the meeting of two cells of a cross-vault; *see* Vault and 2c.

GROTESQUE (*lit.* grotto-esque): wall decoration adopted from Roman examples in the Renaissance. Its foliage scrolls incorporate figurative elements. Cf. Arabesque.

GROTTO: artificial cavern.

GRP: *see* Fibreglass.

GUILLOCHE: classical ornament of interlaced bands (4b).

GUNLOOP: opening for a firearm.

GUTTAE: stylized drops (3b).

HALF-TIMBERING: archaic term for timber-framing (q.v.). Sometimes used for non-structural decorative timberwork.

HALL CHURCH: medieval church with nave and aisles of approximately equal height.

HAMMERBEAM: *see* Roofs and 7.

HAMPER: in C20 architecture, a visually distinct topmost storey or storeys.

HEADER: *see* Bond and 6e.

HEADSTOP: stop (q.v.) carved with a head (5b).

HELM ROOF: *see* IC.

HENGE: ritual earthwork.

HERM (*lit.* the god Hermes): male head or bust on a pedestal.

HERRINGBONE WORK: *see* 7ii. Cf. Pitched masonry.

HEXASTYLE: *see* Portico.

HILL-FORT: Iron Age earthwork enclosed by a ditch and bank system.

HIPPED ROOF: *see* 8a.

HOODMOULD: projecting moulding above an arch or lintel to throw off water (2b, 5b). When horizontal often called a *label*. For label stop *see* Stop.

HUSK GARLAND: festoon of stylized nutshells (4b).

HYDRAULIC POWER: use of water under high pressure to work machinery. *Accumulator tower*: houses a hydraulic accumulator which accommodates fluctuations in the flow through hydraulic mains.

HYPOCAUST (*lit.* underburning): Roman underfloor heating system.

IMPOST: horizontal moulding at the springing of an arch (5c).

IMPOST BLOCK: block between abacus and capital (1b).

IN ANTIS: *see* Antae, Portico and 4a.

INDENT: shape chiselled out of a stone to receive a brass.

INDUSTRIALIZED or SYSTEM BUILDING: system of manufactured units assembled on site.

INGLENOOK (*lit.* fire-corner): recess for a hearth with provision for seating.

INTERCOLUMNATION: interval between columns.

INTERLACE: decoration in relief simulating woven or entwined stems or bands.

INTRADOS: *see* Soffit.

IONIC: *see* Orders and 3c.

JACK ARCH: shallow segmental vault springing from beams, used for fireproof floors, bridge decks, etc.

JAMB (*lit.* leg): one of the vertical sides of an opening.

JETTY: in a timber-framed building, the projection of an upper storey beyond the storey below, made by the beams and joists of the lower storey oversailing the wall; on their outer ends is placed the sill of the walling for the storey above (7). Buildings can be jettied on several sides, in which case a *dragon beam* is set diagonally at the corner to carry the joists to either side.

JOGGLE: the joining of two stones to prevent them slipping by a notch in one and a projection in the other.

KEEL MOULDING: moulding used from the late C12, in section like the keel of a ship (1a).

KEEP: principal tower of a castle.

KENTISH CUSP: *see* Tracery and 2b.

KEY PATTERN: *see* 4b.

KEYSTONE: central stone in an arch or vault (4b, 5c).

KINGPOST: *see* Roofs and 7.

KNEELER: horizontal projecting stone at the base of each side of a gable to support the inclined coping stones (8a).

LABEL: *see* Hoodmould and 5b.

LABEL STOP: *see* Stop and 5b.

LACED BRICKWORK: vertical strips of brickwork, often in a contrasting colour, linking openings on different floors.

LACING COURSE: horizontal reinforcement in timber or brick to walls of flint, cobble, etc.

LADY CHAPEL: dedicated to the Virgin Mary (Our Lady).

LANCET: slender single-light, pointed-arched window (2a).

LANTERN: circular or polygonal windowed turret crowning a roof or a dome. Also the windowed stage of a crossing tower lighting the church interior.

LANTERN CROSS: churchyard cross with lantern-shaped top.

LAVATORIUM: in a religious house, a washing place adjacent to the refectory.

LEAN-TO: *see* Roofs.

LESENE (*lit.* a mean thing): pilaster without base or capital. Also called *pilaster strip*.

LIERNE: *see* Vault and 2c.

LIGHT: compartment of a window defined by the mullions.

LINENFOLD: Tudor panelling carved with simulations of folded linen. *See also* Parchemin.

LINTEL: horizontal beam or stone bridging an opening.

LOGGIA: gallery, usually arcaded or colonnaded; sometimes free-standing.

LONG-AND-SHORT WORK: quoins consisting of stones placed with the long side alternately upright and horizontal, especially in Saxon building.

LONGHOUSE: house and byre in the same range with internal access between them.

LOUVRE: roof opening, often protected by a raised timber structure, to allow the smoke from a central hearth to escape.

LOWSIDE WINDOW: set lower than the others in a chancel side wall, usually towards its w end.

LUCAM: projecting housing for hoist pulley on upper storey of warehouses, mills, etc., for raising goods to loading doors.

LUCARNE (*lit.* dormer): small gabled opening in a roof or spire.

LUGGED ARCHITRAVE: *see* 4b.

LUNETTE: semicircular window or blind panel.

LYCHGATE (*lit.* corpse-gate): roofed gateway entrance to a churchyard for the reception of a coffin.

LYNCHET: long terraced strip of soil on the downward side of prehistoric and medieval fields, accumulated because of continual ploughing along the contours.

MACHICOLATIONS (*lit.* mashing devices): series of openings between the corbels that support a projecting parapet through which missiles can be dropped. Used decoratively in post-medieval buildings.

MANOMETER or STANDPIPE TOWER: containing a column of water to regulate pressure in water mains.

MANSARD: *see* 8a.

MATHEMATICAL TILES: facing tiles with the appearance of brick, most often applied to timber-framed walls.

MAUSOLEUM: monumental building or chamber usually intended for the burial of members of one family.

MEGALITHIC TOMB: massive stone-built Neolithic burial chamber covered by an earth or stone mound.

MERLON: *see* Battlement.

METOPES: spaces between the triglyphs in a Doric frieze (3b).

MEZZANINE: low storey between two higher ones.

MILD STEEL: *see* Cast iron.

MISERICORD (*lit.* mercy): shelf on a carved bracket placed on the underside of a hinged choir stall seat to support an occupant when standing.

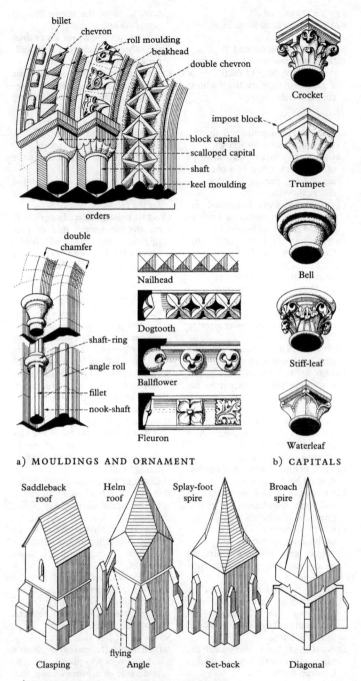

a) MOULDINGS AND ORNAMENT

b) CAPITALS

c) BUTTRESSES, ROOFS AND SPIRES

FIGURE 1: MEDIEVAL

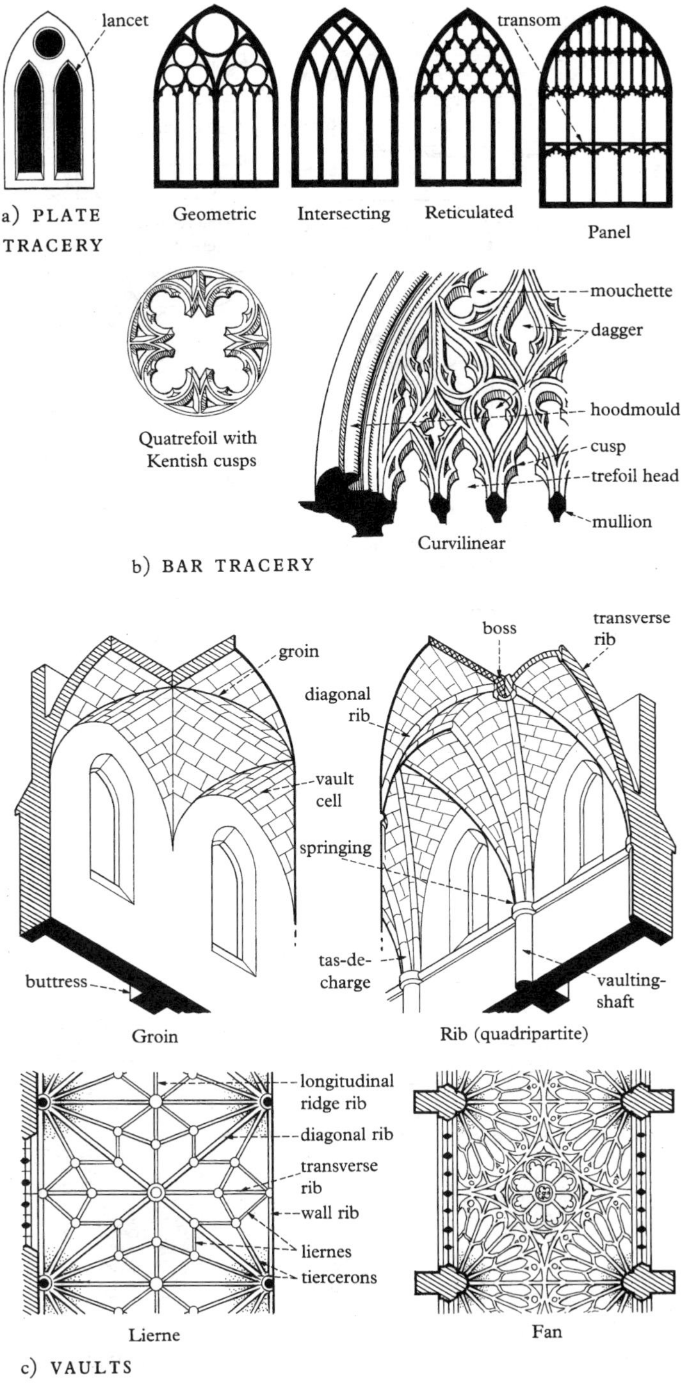

a) PLATE TRACERY

Geometric   Intersecting   Reticulated

Panel

lancet

transom

Quatrefoil with
Kentish cusps

mouchette

dagger

hoodmould

cusp

trefoil head

mullion

Curvilinear

b) BAR TRACERY

groin

diagonal rib

vault cell

springing

buttress

Groin

boss

transverse rib

tas-de-charge

vaulting-shaft

Rib (quadripartite)

longitudinal ridge rib

diagonal rib

transverse rib

wall rib

liernes

tiercerons

Lierne

Fan

c) VAULTS

FIGURE 2: MEDIEVAL

ORDERS

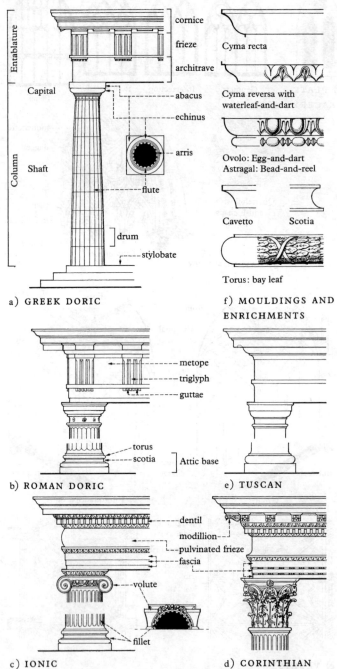

a) GREEK DORIC

- cornice
- frieze
- architrave
- abacus
- echinus
- arris
- flute
- drum
- stylobate

Entablature

Capital

Column

Shaft

f) MOULDINGS AND ENRICHMENTS

Cyma recta

Cyma reversa with waterleaf-and-dart

Ovolo: Egg-and-dart
Astragal: Bead-and-reel

Cavetto   Scotia

Torus: bay leaf

b) ROMAN DORIC

- metope
- triglyph
- guttae
- torus
- scotia

Attic base

e) TUSCAN

c) IONIC

- dentil
- modillion
- pulvinated frieze
- fascia
- volute
- fillet

d) CORINTHIAN

FIGURE 3: CLASSICAL

a) PORTICO

Distyle in antis   Prostyle

Anthemion & Palmette   Guilloche   Key pattern

Rinceau   Husk garland   Vitruvian scroll

Console   Diocletian window   Acanthus

Broken pediment   Lugged architrave

Segmental pediment   Shouldered architrave

Venetian window

Open pediment   Swan-neck pediment   Gibbs surround

b) ORNAMENTS AND FEATURES

FIGURE 4: CLASSICAL

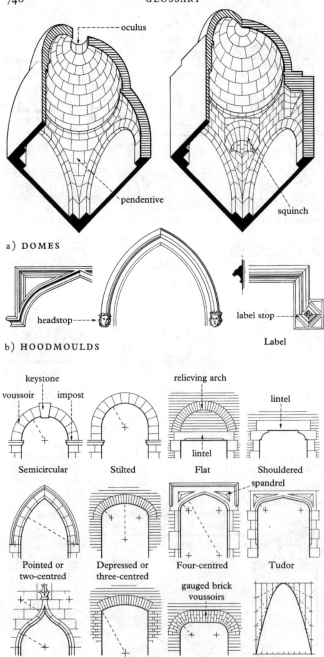

a) DOMES

b) HOODMOULDS

Label

c) ARCHES

FIGURE 5: CONSTRUCTION

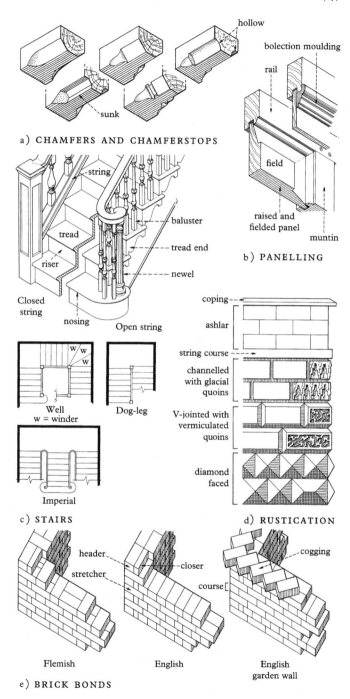

a) CHAMFERS AND CHAMFERSTOPS

hollow

sunk

bolection moulding

rail

field

raised and
fielded panel

muntin

b) PANELLING

string

baluster

tread

tread end

riser

newel

Closed
string

nosing

Open string

Well
w = winder

Dog-leg

Imperial

c) STAIRS

coping

ashlar

string course

channelled
with glacial
quoins

V-jointed with
vermiculated
quoins

diamond
faced

d) RUSTICATION

header

closer

stretcher

course

cogging

Flemish

English

English
garden wall

e) BRICK BONDS

FIGURE 6: CONSTRUCTION

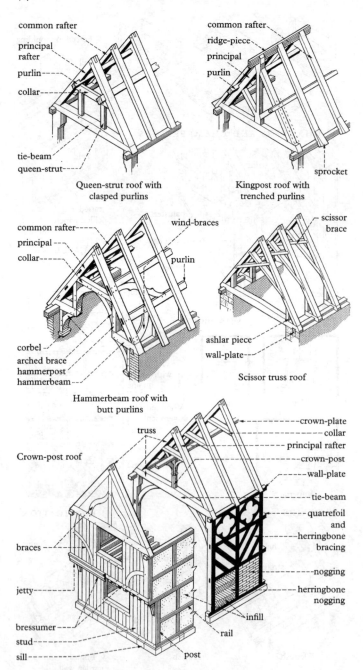

Queen-strut roof with clasped purlins

common rafter
principal rafter
purlin
collar
tie-beam
queen-strut

Kingpost roof with trenched purlins

common rafter
ridge-piece
principal
purlin
sprocket

Hammerbeam roof with butt purlins

common rafter
principal
collar
wind-braces
purlin
corbel
arched brace
hammerpost
hammerbeam

Scissor truss roof

scissor brace
ashlar piece
wall-plate

Crown-post roof

truss
crown-plate
collar
principal rafter
crown-post
wall-plate
tie-beam
quatrefoil and herringbone bracing
nogging
herringbone nogging
braces
jetty
bressumer
stud
sill
post
rail
infill

Box frame: i) Close studding   ii) Square panel

FIGURE 7: ROOFS AND TIMBER-FRAMING

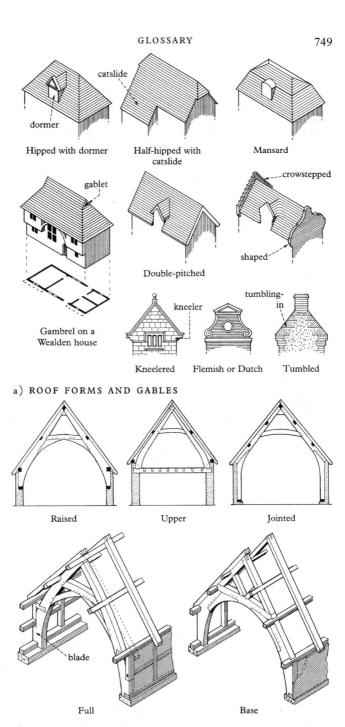

a) ROOF FORMS AND GABLES

b) CRUCK FRAMES

FIGURE 8: ROOFS AND TIMBER-FRAMING

MIXER-COURTS: forecourts to groups of houses shared by vehicles and pedestrians.

MODILLIONS: small consoles (q.v.) along the underside of a Corinthian or Composite cornice (3d). Often used along an eaves cornice.

MODULE: a predetermined standard size for co-ordinating the dimensions of components of a building.

MOTTE-AND-BAILEY: post-Roman and Norman defence consisting of an earthen mound (motte) topped by a wooden tower within a bailey, an enclosure defended by a ditch and palisade, and also, sometimes, by an internal bank.

MOUCHETTE: see Tracery and 2b.

MOULDING: shaped ornamental strip of continuous section; see e.g. Cavetto, Cyma, Ovolo, Roll.

MULLION: vertical member between window lights (2b).

MULTI-STOREY: five or more storeys. Multi-storey flats may form a *cluster block*, with individual blocks of flats grouped round a service core; a *point block*, with flats fanning out from a service core; or a *slab block*, with flats approached by corridors or galleries from service cores at intervals or towers at the ends (plan also used for offices, hotels etc.). *Tower block* is a generic term for any very high multi-storey building.

MUNTIN: see Panelling and 6b.

NAILHEAD: E.E. ornament consisting of small pyramids regularly repeated (1a).

NARTHEX: enclosed vestibule or covered porch at the main entrance to a church.

NAVE: the body of a church W of the crossing or chancel often flanked by aisles (q.v.).

NEWEL: central or corner post of a staircase (6c). Newel stair: see Stairs.

NIGHT STAIR: stair by which religious entered the transept of their church from their dormitory to celebrate night services.

NOGGING: see Timber-framing (7).

NOOK-SHAFT: shaft set in the angle of a wall or opening (1a).

NORMAN: see Romanesque.

NOSING: projection of the tread of a step (6c).

NUTMEG: medieval ornament with a chain of tiny triangles placed obliquely.

OCULUS: circular opening.

ŒIL DE BŒUF: see Bullseye window.

OGEE: double curve, bending first one way and then the other, as in an *ogee* or *ogival arch* (5c). Cf. Cyma recta and Cyma reversa.

OPUS SECTILE: decorative mosaic-like facing.

OPUS SIGNINUM: composition flooring of Roman origin.

ORATORY: a private chapel in a church or a house. Also a church of the Oratorian Order.

ORDER: one of a series of recessed arches and jambs forming a splayed medieval opening, e.g. a doorway or arcade arch (1a).

ORDERS: the formalized versions of the post-and-lintel system in classical architecture. The main orders are *Doric*, *Ionic*, and *Corinthian*. They are Greek in origin but occur in Roman versions. Tuscan is a simple version of Roman Doric. Though each order has its own conventions (3), there are many minor variations. The *Composite* capital combines Ionic volutes with Corinthian foliage. *Superimposed orders*: orders on successive levels, usually in the upward sequence of Tuscan, Doric, Ionic, Corinthian, Composite.

ORIEL: see Bay window.

OVERDOOR: painting or relief above an internal door. Also called a *sopraporta*.

OVERTHROW: decorative fixed arch between two gatepiers or above a wrought-iron gate.

OVOLO: wide convex moulding (3f).

PALIMPSEST: of a brass: where a metal plate has been reused by turning over the engraving on the back; of a wall painting: where one overlaps and partly obscures an earlier one.

PALLADIAN: following the examples and principles of Andrea Palladio (1508–80).

PALMETTE: classical ornament like a palm shoot (4b).

PANELLING: wooden lining to interior walls, made up of vertical members (*muntins*) and horizontals (*rails*) framing panels: also called *wainscot*. *Raised and fielded*: with the central area of the panel (*field*) raised up (6b).

PANTILE: roof tile of S section.

PARAPET: wall for protection at any sudden drop, e.g. at the wall-head of a castle where it protects the *parapet walk* or wall-walk. Also used to conceal a roof.

PARCLOSE: *see* Screen.

PARGETTING (*lit.* plastering): exterior plaster decoration, either in relief or incised.

PARLOUR: in a religious house, a room where the religious could talk to visitors; in a medieval house, the semi-private living room below the solar (q.v.).

PARTERRE: level space in a garden laid out with low, formal beds.

PATERA (*lit.* plate): round or oval ornament in shallow relief.

PAVILION: ornamental building for occasional use; or projecting subdivision of a larger building, often at an angle or terminating a wing.

PEBBLEDASHING: *see* Rendering.

PEDESTAL: a tall block carrying a classical order, statue, vase, etc.

PEDIMENT: a formalized gable derived from that of a classical temple; also used over doors, windows, etc. For variations *see* 4b.

PENDENTIVE: spandrel between adjacent arches, supporting a drum, dome or vault and consequently formed as part of a hemisphere (5a).

PENTHOUSE: subsidiary structure with a lean-to roof. Also a

separately roofed structure on top of a C20 multi-storey block.

PERIPTERAL: *see* Peristyle.

PERISTYLE: a colonnade all round the exterior of a classical building, as in a temple which is then said to be *peripteral*.

PERP (PERPENDICULAR): English Gothic architecture *c.* 1335–50 to *c.* 1530. The name is derived from the upright tracery panels then used (*see* Tracery and 2a).

PERRON: external stair to a doorway, usually of double-curved plan.

PEW: loosely, seating for the laity outside the chancel; strictly, an enclosed seat. *Box pew*: with equal high sides and a door.

PIANO NOBILE: principal floor of a classical building above a ground floor or basement and with a lesser storey overhead.

PIAZZA: formal urban open space surrounded by buildings.

PIER: large masonry or brick support, often for an arch. *See also* Compound pier.

PILASTER: flat representation of a classical column in shallow relief. *Pilaster strip*: *see* Lesene.

PILE: row of rooms. *Double pile*: two rows thick.

PILLAR: free-standing upright member of any section, not conforming to one of the orders (q.v.).

PILLAR PISCINA: *see* Piscina.

PILOTIS: C20 French term for pillars or stilts that support a building above an open ground floor.

PISCINA: basin for washing Mass vessels, provided with a drain; set in or against the wall to the S of an altar or free-standing (*pillar piscina*).

PISÉ: *see* Cob.

PITCHED MASONRY: laid on the diagonal, often alternately with opposing courses (*pitched and counterpitched* or *herringbone*).

PLATBAND: flat horizontal moulding between storeys. Cf. stringcourse.

PLATE RAIL: *see* Railways.

PLATEWAY: *see* Railways.

PLINTH: projecting courses at the

foot of a wall or column, generally chamfered or moulded at the top.

PODIUM: a continuous raised platform supporting a building; or a large block of two or three storeys beneath a multi-storey block of smaller area.

POINT BLOCK: *see* Multi-storey.

POINTING: exposed mortar jointing of masonry or brickwork. Types include *flush*, *recessed* and *tuck* (with a narrow channel filled with finer, whiter mortar).

POPPYHEAD: carved ornament of leaves and flowers as a finial for a bench end or stall.

PORTAL FRAME: C20 frame comprising two uprights rigidly connected to a beam or pair of rafters.

PORTCULLIS: gate constructed to rise and fall in vertical grooves at the entry to a castle.

PORTICO: a porch with the roof and frequently a pediment supported by a row of columns (4a). A portico *in antis* has columns on the same plane as the front of the building. A *prostyle* porch has columns standing free. Porticoes are described by the number of front columns, e.g. tetrastyle (four), hexastyle (six). The space within the temple is the *naos*, that within the portico the *pronaos*. *Blind portico*: the front features of a portico applied to a wall.

PORTICUS (plural: porticūs): subsidiary cell opening from the main body of a pre-Conquest church.

POST: upright support in a structure (7).

POSTERN: small gateway at the back of a building or to the side of a larger entrance door or gate.

POUND LOCK: *see* Canals.

PRESBYTERY: the part of a church lying E of the choir where the main altar is placed; or a priest's residence.

PRINCIPAL: *see* Roofs and 7.

PRONAOS: *see* Portico and 4a.

PROSTYLE: *see* Portico and 4a.

PULPIT: raised and enclosed platform for the preaching of sermons. *Three-decker*: with reading desk below and clerk's desk below that. *Two-decker*: as above, minus the clerk's desk.

PULPITUM: stone screen in a major church dividing choir from nave.

PULVINATED: *see* Frieze and 3c.

PURLIN: *see* Roofs and 7.

PUTHOLES or PUTLOG HOLES: in the wall to receive putlogs, the horizontal timbers which support scaffolding boards; sometimes not filled after construction is complete.

PUTTO (plural: putti): small naked boy.

QUARRIES: square (or diamond) panes of glass supported by lead strips (*cames*); square floor slabs or tiles.

QUATREFOIL: *see* Foil and 2b.

QUEEN-STRUT: *see* Roofs and 7.

QUIRK: sharp groove to one side of a convex medieval moulding.

QUOINS: dressed stones at the angles of a building (6d).

RADBURN SYSTEM: vehicle and pedestrian segregation in residential developments, based on that used at Radburn, New Jersey, USA, by Wright and Stein, 1928–30.

RADIATING CHAPELS: projecting radially from an ambulatory or an apse (*see* Chevet).

RAFTER: *see* Roofs and 7.

RAGGLE: groove cut in masonry, especially to receive the edge of a roof-covering.

RAGULY: ragged (in heraldry). Also applied to funerary sculpture, e.g. *cross raguly*: with a notched outline.

RAIL: *see* Panelling and 6b; also 7.

RAILWAYS: *Edge rail*: on which flanged wheels can run. *Plate rail*: L-section rail for plain unflanged wheels. *Plateway*: early railway using plate rails.

RAISED AND FIELDED: *see* Panelling and 6b.

RAKE: slope or pitch.

RAMPART: defensive outer wall of stone or earth. *Rampart walk*: path along the inner face.

REBATE: rectangular section cut out of a masonry edge to receive a shutter, door, window, etc.

REBUS: a heraldic pun, e.g. a fiery cock for Cockburn.

REEDING: series of convex mouldings, the reverse of fluting (q.v.). Cf. Gadrooning.

RENDERING: the covering of outside walls with a uniform surface or skin for protection from the weather. *Limewashing*: thin layer of lime plaster. *Pebbledashing*: where aggregate is thrown at the wet plastered wall for a textured effect. *Roughcast*: plaster mixed with a coarse aggregate such as gravel. *Stucco*: fine lime plaster worked to a smooth surface. *Cement rendering*: a cheaper substitute for stucco, usually with a grainy texture.

REPOUSSÉ: relief designs in metalwork, formed by beating it from the back.

REREDORTER (*lit.* behind the dormitory): latrines in a medieval religious house.

REREDOS: painted and/or sculptured screen behind and above an altar. Cf. Retable.

RESPOND: half-pier or half-column bonded into a wall and carrying one end of an arch. It usually terminates an arcade.

RETABLE: painted or carved panel standing on or at the back of an altar, usually attached to it.

RETROCHOIR: in a major church, the area between the high altar and E chapel.

REVEAL: the plane of a jamb, between the wall and the frame of a door or window.

RIB-VAULT: *see* Vault and 2c.

RINCEAU: classical ornament of leafy scrolls (4b).

RISER: vertical face of a step (6c).

ROACH: a rough-textured form of Portland stone, with small cavities and fossil shells.

ROCK-FACED: masonry cleft to produce a rugged appearance.

ROCOCO: style current *c.* 1720 and *c.* 1760, characterized by a serpentine line and playful, scrolled decoration.

ROLL MOULDING: medieval moulding of part-circular section (1a).

ROMANESQUE: style current in the C11 and C12. In England often called Norman. *See also* Saxo-Norman.

ROOD: crucifix flanked by the Virgin and St John, usually over the entry into the chancel, on a beam (*rood beam*) or painted on the wall. The *rood screen* below often had a walkway (*rood loft*) along the top, reached by a *rood stair* in the side wall.

ROOFS: Shape. For the main external shapes (hipped, mansard, etc.) *see* 8a. *Helm* and *Saddleback*: *see* 1c. *Lean-to*: single sloping roof built against a vertical wall; lean-to is also applied to the part of the building beneath.
Construction. *See* 7.
Single-framed roof: with no main trusses. The rafters may be fixed to the wall-plate or ridge, or longitudinal timber may be absent altogether.
Double-framed roof: with longitudinal members, such as purlins, and usually divided into bays by principals and principal rafters. Other types are named after their main structural components, e.g. *hammerbeam*, *crown-post* (*see* Elements below and 7).
Elements. *See* 7.
Ashlar piece: a short vertical timber connecting inner wall-plate or timber pad to a rafter.
Braces: subsidiary timbers set diagonally to strengthen the frame. *Arched braces*: curved pair forming an arch, connecting wall or post below with tie- or collar-beam above. *Passing braces*: long straight braces passing across other members of the truss. *Scissor braces*: pair crossing diagonally between pairs of rafters or principals. *Wind-braces*: short, usually curved braces connecting side purlins with principals; sometimes decorated with cusping.
Collar or *collar-beam*: horizontal transverse timber connecting a pair of rafter or cruck blades (q.v.), set between apex and the wall-plate.
Crown-post: a vertical timber set centrally on a tie-beam and supporting a collar purlin braced to it longitudinally. In an open truss

lateral braces may rise to the
collar-beam; in a closed truss they
may descend to the tie-beam.

Hammerbeams: horizontal brackets
projecting at wall-plate level like
an interrupted tie-beam; the inner
ends carry *hammerposts*, vertical
timbers which support a purlin
and are braced to a collar-beam
above.

Kingpost: vertical timber set centrally on a tie- or collar-beam,
rising to the apex of the roof to
support a ridge-piece (cf. Strut).

Plate: longitudinal timber set
square to the ground. *Wall-plate*:
plate along the top of a wall which
receives the ends of the rafters; cf.
Purlin.

Principals: pair of inclined lateral
timbers of a truss. Usually they
support side purlins and mark the
main bay divisions.

Purlin: horizontal longitudinal
timber. *Collar purlin* or *crown plate*:
central timber which carries
collar-beams and is supported by
crown-posts. *Side purlins*: pairs of
timbers placed some way up the
slope of the roof, which carry
common rafters. *Butt* or *tenoned
purlins* are tenoned into either side
of the principals. *Through purlins*
pass through or past the principal;
they include *clasped purlins*, which
rest on queenposts or are carried
in the angle between principals and
collar, and *trenched purlins* trenched
into the backs of principals.

Queen-strut: paired vertical, or
near-vertical, timbers placed symmetrically on a tie-beam to
support side purlins.

Rafters: inclined lateral timbers
supporting the roof covering.
Common rafters: regularly spaced
uniform rafters placed along the
length of a roof or between principals. *Principal rafters*: rafters
which also act as principals.

Ridge, ridge-piece: horizontal longitudinal timber at the apex supporting the ends of the rafters.

Sprocket: short timber placed on
the back and at the foot of a rafter
to form projecting eaves.

Strut: vertical or oblique timber
between two members of a truss,
not directly supporting longitudinal timbers.

Tie-beam: main horizontal transverse timber which carries the feet
of the principals at wall level.

Truss: rigid framework of timbers
at bay intervals, carrying the
longitudinal roof timbers which
support the common rafters.

Closed truss: with the spaces between the timbers filled, to form
an internal partition.

See also Cruck, Wagon roof.

ROPE MOULDING: *see* Cable
moulding.

ROSE WINDOW: circular window
with tracery radiating from the
centre. Cf. Wheel window.

ROTUNDA: building or room circular in plan.

ROUGHCAST: *see* Rendering.

ROVING BRIDGE: *see* Canals.

RUBBED BRICKWORK: *see* Gauged
brickwork.

RUBBLE: masonry whose stones are
wholly or partly in a rough state.
Coursed: coursed stones with
rough faces. *Random*: uncoursed
stones in a random pattern.
Snecked: with courses broken by
smaller stones (snecks).

RUSTICATION: *see* 6d. Exaggerated
treatment of masonry to give an
effect of strength. The joints are
usually recessed by V-section
chamfering or square-section
channelling (*channelled rustication*). *Banded rustication* has only
the horizontal joints emphasized.
The faces may be flat, but can be
diamond-faced, like shallow pyramids, *vermiculated*, with a stylized
texture like worm-casts, and
glacial (frost-work), like icicles or
stalactites.

SACRISTY: room in a church for
sacred vessels and vestments.

SADDLEBACK ROOF: *see* IC.

SALTIRE CROSS: with diagonal limbs.

SANCTUARY: area around the main
altar of a church. Cf. Presbytery.

SANGHA: residence of Buddhist
monks or nuns.

SARCOPHAGUS: coffin of stone or
other durable material.

SAXO-NORMAN: transitional Romanesque style combining Anglo-Saxon and Norman features, current *c.* 1060–1100.

SCAGLIOLA: composition imitating marble.

SCALLOPED CAPITAL: *see* 1a.

SCOTIA: a hollow classical moulding, especially between tori (q.v.) on a column base (3b, 3f).

SCREEN: in a medieval church, usually at the entry to the chancel; *see* Rood (screen) and Pulpitum. A *parclose screen* separates a chapel from the rest of the church.

SCREENS or SCREENS PASSAGE: screened-off entrance passage between great hall and service rooms.

SECTION: two-dimensional representation of a building, moulding, etc., revealed by cutting across it.

SEDILIA (singular: sedile): seats for the priests (usually three) on the S side of the chancel.

SET-OFF: *see* Weathering.

SETTS: squared stones, usually of granite, used for paving or flooring.

SGRAFFITO: decoration scratched, often in plaster, to reveal a pattern in another colour beneath. *Graffiti*: scratched drawing or writing.

SHAFT: vertical member of round or polygonal section (1a, 3a). *Shaft-ring*: at the junction of shafts set *en délit* (q.v.) or attached to a pier or wall (1a).

SHEILA-NA-GIG: female fertility figure, usually with legs apart.

SHELL: thin, self-supporting roofing membrane of timber or concrete.

SHOULDERED ARCHITRAVE: *see* 4b.

SHUTTERING: *see* Concrete.

SILL: horizontal member at the bottom of a window or door frame; or at the base of a timber-framed wall into which posts and studs are tenoned (7).

SLAB BLOCK: *see* Multi-storey.

SLATE-HANGING: covering of overlapping slates on a wall. *Tile-hanging* is similar.

SLYPE: covered way or passage leading E from the cloisters between transept and chapter house.

SNECKED: *see* Rubble.

SOFFIT (*lit.* ceiling): underside of an arch (also called *intrados*), lintel, etc. *Soffit roll*: medieval roll moulding on a soffit.

SOLAR: private upper chamber in a medieval house, accessible from the high end of the great hall.

SOPRAPORTA: *see* Overdoor.

SOUNDING-BOARD: *see* Tester.

SPANDRELS: roughly triangular spaces between an arch and its containing rectangle, or between adjacent arches (5c). Also nonstructural panels under the windows in a curtain-walled building.

SPERE: a fixed structure screening the lower end of the great hall from the screens passage. *Spere-truss*: roof truss incorporated in the spere.

SPIRE: tall pyramidal or conical feature crowning a tower or turret. *Broach*: starting from a square base, then carried into an octagonal section by means of triangular faces; and *splayed-foot*: variation of the broach form, found principally in the southeast, in which the four cardinal faces are splayed out near their base, to cover the corners, while oblique (or intermediate) faces taper away to a point (1c). *Needle spire*: thin spire rising from the centre of a tower roof, well inside the parapet: when of timber and lead often called a *spike*.

SPIRELET: *see* Flèche.

SPLAY: of an opening when it is wider on one face of a wall than the other.

SPRING or SPRINGING: level at which an arch or vault rises from its supports. *Springers*: the first stones of an arch or vaulting rib above the spring (2c).

SQUINCH: arch or series of arches thrown across an interior angle of a square or rectangular structure to support a circular or polygonal superstructure, especially a dome or spire (5a).

SQUINT: an aperture in a wall or through a pier usually to allow a view of an altar.

STAIRS: *see* 6c. *Dog-leg stair*: parallel flights rising alternately in opposite directions, without an open well. *Flying stair*: cantilevered from the walls of a stairwell, without newels; sometimes called a *Geometric* stair when the inner edge describes a curve. *Newel stair*: ascending round a central supporting newel (q.v.); called a *spiral stair* or *vice* when in a circular shaft, a *winder* when in a rectangular compartment. (Winder also applies to the steps on the turn.) *Well stair*: with flights round a square open well framed by newel posts. *See also* Perron.

STALL: fixed seat in the choir or chancel for the clergy or choir (cf. Pew). Usually with arm rests, and often framed together.

STANCHION: upright structural member, of iron, steel or reinforced concrete.

STANDPIPE TOWER: *see* Manometer.

STEAM ENGINES: *Atmospheric*: worked by the vacuum created when low-pressure steam is condensed in the cylinder, as developed by Thomas Newcomen. *Beam engine*: with a large pivoted beam moved in an oscillating fashion by the piston. It may drive a flywheel or be *non-rotative*. *Watt* and *Cornish*: single-cylinder; *compound*: two cylinders; *triple expansion*: three cylinders.

STEEPLE: tower together with a spire, lantern, or belfry.

STIFF-LEAF: type of E.E. foliage decoration. *Stiff-leaf capital see* 1b.

STOP: plain or decorated terminal to mouldings or chamfers, or at the end of hoodmoulds and labels (*label stop*), or stringcourses (5b, 6a); *see also* Headstop.

STOUP: vessel for holy water, usually near a door.

STRAINER: *see* Arch.

STRAPWORK: late C16 and C17 decoration, like interlaced leather straps.

STRETCHER: *see* Bond and 6e.

STRING: *see* 6c. Sloping member holding the ends of the treads and risers of a staircase. *Closed string*: a broad string covering the ends of the treads and risers. *Open string*: cut into the shape of the treads and risers.

STRINGCOURSE: horizontal course or moulding projecting from the surface of a wall (6d).

STUCCO: *see* Rendering.

STUDS: subsidiary vertical timbers of a timber-framed wall or partition (7).

STUPA: Buddhist shrine, circular in plan.

STYLOBATE: top of the solid platform on which a colonnade stands (3a).

SUSPENSION BRIDGE: *see* Bridge.

SWAG: like a festoon (q.v.), but representing cloth.

SYSTEM BUILDING: *see* Industrialized building.

TABERNACLE: canopied structure to contain the reserved sacrament or a relic; or architectural frame for an image or statue.

TABLE TOMB: memorial slab raised on free-standing legs.

TAS-DE-CHARGE: the lower courses of a vault or arch which are laid horizontally (2c).

TERM: pedestal or pilaster tapering downward, usually with the upper part of a human figure growing out of it.

TERRACOTTA: moulded and fired clay ornament or cladding.

TESSELLATED PAVEMENT: mosaic flooring, particularly Roman, made of *tesserae*, i.e. cubes of glass, stone, or brick.

TESTER: flat canopy over a tomb or pulpit, where it is also called a *sounding-board*.

TESTER TOMB: tomb-chest with effigies beneath a tester, either free-standing (tester with four or more columns), or attached to a wall (*half-tester*) with columns on one side only.

TETRASTYLE: *see* Portico.

THERMAL WINDOW: *see* Diocletian window.

THREE-DECKER PULPIT: *see* Pulpit.

TIDAL GATES: *see* Canals.

TIE-BEAM: *see* Roofs and 7.

TIERCERON: *see* Vault and 2c.

TILE-HANGING: *see* Slate-hanging.

TIMBER-FRAMING: *see* 7. Method of construction where the structural frame is built of interlocking timbers. The spaces are filled with non-structural material, e.g. *infill* of wattle and daub, lath and plaster, brickwork (known as *nogging*), etc. and may be covered by plaster, weatherboarding (q.v.), or tiles.

TOMB-CHEST: chest-shaped tomb, usually of stone. Cf. Table tomb, Tester tomb.

TORUS (plural: tori): large convex moulding usually used on a column base (3b, 3f).

TOUCH: soft black marble quarried near Tournai.

TOURELLE: turret corbelled out from the wall.

TOWER BLOCK: *see* Multi-storey.

TRABEATED: depends structurally on the use of the post and lintel. Cf. Arcuated.

TRACERY: openwork pattern of masonry or timber in the upper part of an opening. *Blind tracery* is tracery applied to a solid wall.
Plate tracery, introduced *c.* 1200, is the earliest form, in which shapes are cut through solid masonry (2a).
Bar tracery was introduced into England *c.* 1250. The pattern is formed by intersecting moulded ribwork continued from the mullions. It was especially elaborate during the Decorated period (q.v.). Tracery shapes can include circles, *daggers* (elongated ogee-ended lozenges), *mouchettes* (like daggers but with curved sides) and upright rectangular *panels*. They often have *cusps*, projecting points defining lobes or *foils* (q.v.) within the main shape: *Kentish* or *split-cusps* are forked (2b).
Types of bar tracery (*see* 2b) include *geometric(al)*: *c.* 1250–1310, chiefly circles, often foiled; *Y-tracery*: *c.* 1300, with mullions branching into a Y-shape; *intersecting*: *c.* 1300, formed by interlocking mullions; *reticulated*: early C14, net-like pattern of ogee-ended lozenges; *curvilinear*: C14, with uninterrupted flowing curves; *panel*: Perp, with straight-sided panels, often cusped at the top and bottom.

TRANSEPT: transverse portion of a church.

TRANSITIONAL: generally used for the phase between Romanesque and Early English (*c.* 1175–*c.* 1200).

TRANSOM: horizontal member separating window lights (2b).

TREAD: horizontal part of a step. The *tread end* may be carved on a staircase (6c).

TREFOIL: *see* Foil.

TRIFORIUM: middle storey of a church treated as an arcaded wall passage or blind arcade, its height corresponding to that of the aisle roof.

TRIGLYPHS (*lit.* three-grooved tablets): stylized beam-ends in the Doric frieze, with metopes between (3b).

TRIUMPHAL ARCH: influential type of Imperial Roman monument.

TROPHY: sculptured or painted group of arms or armour.

TRUMEAU: central stone mullion supporting the tympanum of a wide doorway. *Trumeau figure*: carved figure attached to it (cf. Column figure).

TRUMPET CAPITAL: *see* 1b.

TRUSS: braced framework, spanning between supports. *See also* Roofs and 7.

TUMBLING or TUMBLING-IN: courses of brickwork laid at right-angles to a slope, e.g. of a gable, forming triangles by tapering into horizontal courses (8a).

TUSCAN: *see* Orders and 3e.

TWO-DECKER PULPIT: *see* Pulpit.

TYMPANUM: the surface between a lintel and the arch above it or within a pediment (4a).

UNDERCROFT: usually describes the vaulted room(s), beneath the main room(s) of a medieval house. Cf. Crypt.

VAULT: arched stone roof (sometimes imitated in timber or plaster). For types see 2c.
Tunnel or *barrel vault*: continuous semicircular or pointed arch, often of rubble masonry.

Groin-vault: tunnel vaults intersecting at right angles. *Groins* are the curved lines of the intersections.

Rib-vault: masonry framework of intersecting arches (ribs) supporting *vault cells*, used in Gothic architecture. *Wall rib* or *wall arch*: between wall and vault cell. *Transverse rib*: spans between two walls to divide a vault into bays. *Quadripartite* rib-vault: each bay has two pairs of diagonal ribs dividing the vault into four triangular cells. *Sexpartite* rib-vault: most often used over paired bays, has an extra pair of ribs springing from between the bays. More elaborate vaults may include *ridge ribs* along the crown of a vault or bisecting the bays; *tiercerons*: extra decorative ribs springing from the corners of a bay; and *liernes*: short decorative ribs in the crown of a vault, not linked to any springing point. A *stellar* or *star* vault has liernes in star formation.

Fan-vault: form of barrel vault used in the Perp period, made up of halved concave masonry cones decorated with blind tracery.

VAULTING SHAFT: shaft leading up to the spring or springing (q.v.) of a vault (2c).

VENETIAN or SERLIAN WINDOW: derived from Serlio (4b). The motif is used for other openings.

VERMICULATION: *see* Rustication and 6d.

VESICA: oval with pointed ends.

VICE: *see* Stair.

VILLA: originally a Roman country house or farm. The term was revived in England in the C18 under the influence of Palladio and used especially for smaller, compact country houses. In the later C19 it was debased to describe any suburban house.

VITRIFIED: bricks or tiles fired to a darkened glassy surface.

VITRUVIAN SCROLL: classical running ornament of curly waves (4b).

VOLUTES: spiral scrolls. They occur on Ionic capitals (3c). *Angle volute*: pair of volutes, turned outwards to meet at the corner of a capital.

VOUSSOIRS: wedge-shaped stones forming an arch (5c).

WAGON ROOF: with the appearance of the inside of a wagon tilt; often ceiled. Also called *cradle roof*.

WAINSCOT: *see* Panelling.

WALL MONUMENT: attached to the wall and often standing on the floor. *Wall tablets* are smaller with the inscription as the major element.

WALL-PLATE: *see* Roofs and 7.

WALL-WALK: *see* Parapet.

WARMING ROOM: room in a religious house where a fire burned for comfort.

WATERHOLDING BASE: early Gothic base with upper and lower mouldings separated by a deep hollow.

WATERLEAF: *see* Enrichments and 3f.

WATERLEAF CAPITAL: Late Romanesque and Transitional type of capital (1b).

WATER WHEELS: described by the way water is fed on to the wheel. *Breastshot*: mid-height, falling and passing beneath. *Overshot*: over the top. *Pitchback*: on the top but falling backwards. *Undershot*: turned by the momentum of the water passing beneath. In a *water turbine*, water is fed under pressure through a vaned wheel within a casing.

WEALDEN HOUSE: type of medieval timber-framed house with a central open hall flanked by bays of two storeys, roofed in line; the end bays are jettied to the front, but the eaves are continuous (8a).

WEATHERBOARDING: wall cladding of overlapping horizontal boards.

WEATHERING or SET-OFF: inclined, projecting surface to keep water away from the wall below.

WEEPERS: figures in niches along the sides of some medieval tombs. Also called mourners.

WHEEL WINDOW: circular, with radiating shafts like spokes. Cf. Rose window.

WROUGHT IRON: *see* Cast iron.

INDEX OF ARCHITECTS, ARTISTS, PATRONS AND RESIDENTS

Names of architects and artists working in all the areas covered by this volume are given in *italic*. Entries for partnerships and group practices are listed after entries for a single name.

Also indexed here are names/titles of families and individuals (not of bodies or commercial firms) recorded in this volume as having commissioned architectural work or owned, lived in, or visited properties in the area. The index includes monuments to members of such families and other individuals where they are of particular interest.

INDEX OF PLACES: BEDFORDSHIRE

Principal references are in **bold** type; demolished buildings are shown in *italic*.

INDEX OF PLACES:
HUNTINGDONSHIRE AND PETERBOROUGH

Principal references are in **bold** type; demolished buildings are shown in *italic*.
P = Peterborough